MW01599697

———— SIXTH EDITION ————

# UNITED STATES HISTORY

## bju press®

Greenville, South Carolina

Note: The fact that materials produced by other publishers may be referred to in this volume does not constitute an endorsement of the content or theological position of materials produced by such publishers. Any references and ancillary materials are listed as an aid to the student or the teacher and in an attempt to maintain the accepted academic standards of the publishing industry.

## UNITED STATES HISTORY Student Edition
### Sixth Edition

**Writer**
David Lattner, MA

**Contributing Writer**
Michelle Johnson, MA

**Writer Consultants**
Kirsten Alexander, MEd
Elizabeth Olsen, MEd

**Biblical Worldview**
Brian Collins, PhD
Bryan Smith, PhD

**Academic Integrity**
Jeff Heath, EdD

**Instructional Design**
Rachel Santopietro, EdD
Michael Winningham, MA

**Editor**
Joanna Lynch, MA

**Book and Concept Design**
Garison Plourde

**Cover and Lead Designer**
Garison Plourde

**Designer**
Dan VanLeeuwen

**Design Assistant**
Erika Brunson

**Illustrators**
John Cunningham
Jullianna Eckardt
Alex Green
Carlo Molinari, Advocate-Art Inc.
Priscilla Smith
Dan VanLeeuwen
Tina Zellmer

**Production Designer**
Sarah Centers

**DesignOps Coordinator**
Kaitlyn Quevedo

**Permissions**
Maria Andersen
Jessica Every
Stacy Stone

**Project Coordinator**
Darren Shaffer

**Postproduction Liaison**
Peggy Hargis

**Indexer**
Shannon Li

Photo credits begin on page 740.
Text acknowledgments appear on-page with text selections.
The text for this book is set in Adobe Minion Pro, Adobe Myriad Pro, Arial, Battery Park by Rian Hughes, Bookmania by Mark Simonson, Calibri by Monotype, CC Meanwhile by John Roshell, CC Sign Language by John Roshell and Richard Starkings, Council by John Downer, Free 3 of 9 by Matthew Welch, Montserrat by Julieta Ulanovsky, Proxima Nova by Mark Simonson, Times New Roman PSMT, Video by Patrick Griffin, and Wingdings 3.

© 2025 BJU Press
Greenville, South Carolina 29609
Fifth Edition © 2018 BJU Press
First Edition © 1982 BJU Press

ISBN: 978-1-64626-455-1

15 14 13 12 11 10 9 8 7 6 5 4 3 2 1

# CONTENTS

**Welcome to** *UNITED STATES HISTORY*! . . . . . . . . . . . . . . . . . . . . . . . . . . . . . . . . x

**Using Your Book** . . . . . . . . . . . . . . . . . . . . . . . . . . . . . . . . . . . . . . . . . . . . xi

## 1 America, Europe, and Africa before 1620 . . . . . . . . . . . . . . . . 2

    Introduction: Who Decides What History We Learn? . . . . . . . . . . . . . . . 3

        **Analyzing Sources:** Robert Tracy McKenzie . . . . . . . . . . . . . . . . . . . 4

    1.1 Pre-Columbian America . . . . . . . . . . . . . . . . . . . . . . . . . . . . . . . 6

    1.2 Age of Exploration . . . . . . . . . . . . . . . . . . . . . . . . . . . . . . . . . . 10

    1.3 English Exploration and Colonization . . . . . . . . . . . . . . . . . . . . . . 16

    1.4 Early African Trade . . . . . . . . . . . . . . . . . . . . . . . . . . . . . . . . . 21

## 2 The Thirteen Colonies . . . . . . . . . . . . . . . . . . . . . . . . . . . . . . . 26

    2.1 The New England Colonies . . . . . . . . . . . . . . . . . . . . . . . . . . . . . 27

        **Analyzing Sources:** William Bradford . . . . . . . . . . . . . . . . . . . . . . 28

        **Analyzing Sources:** John Winthrop . . . . . . . . . . . . . . . . . . . . . . . 29

    2.2 The Middle Colonies . . . . . . . . . . . . . . . . . . . . . . . . . . . . . . . . . 32

    2.3 The Southern Colonies . . . . . . . . . . . . . . . . . . . . . . . . . . . . . . . 34

    2.4 Colonial Life . . . . . . . . . . . . . . . . . . . . . . . . . . . . . . . . . . . . . . 38

    2.5 Colonial Religion . . . . . . . . . . . . . . . . . . . . . . . . . . . . . . . . . . . 46

## 3 The Struggle for Independence . . . . . . . . . . . . . . . . . . . . . . . 56

    3.1 The French and Indian War . . . . . . . . . . . . . . . . . . . . . . . . . . . . . 57

    3.2 The Growing Divide . . . . . . . . . . . . . . . . . . . . . . . . . . . . . . . . . 61

    3.3 The Road to Independence . . . . . . . . . . . . . . . . . . . . . . . . . . . . . 68

        **Analyzing Sources:** Patrick Henry . . . . . . . . . . . . . . . . . . . . . . . . 68

        **Analyzing Sources:** Thomas Paine . . . . . . . . . . . . . . . . . . . . . . . 73

    3.4 Fighting the War for Independence . . . . . . . . . . . . . . . . . . . . . . . . 77

    3.5 Winning the War for Independence . . . . . . . . . . . . . . . . . . . . . . . . 82

## 4   Confederation and Constitution ..................................... 90

    4.1 Government by Confederation ....................................... 91

        **Analyzing Sources:** George Washington ........................ 95

    4.2 Writing the Constitution ............................................. 98

        **Analyzing Sources:** James Madison ...........................102

    4.3 Ratifying the Constitution........................................107

        **Analyzing Sources:** Alexander Hamilton ......................108

        **Analyzing Sources:** Patrick Henry ..............................109

## 5   Federalists and Democratic-Republicans ...................114

    5.1 The New Government under Washington ........................115

        **Analyzing Sources:** Thomas Jefferson ........................121

        **Analyzing Sources:** Alexander Hamilton ......................122

    5.2 The Presidency of John Adams ...................................125

    5.3 Jeffersonian America ...............................................130

    5.4 Challenges for Madison............................................136

    5.5 The Era of Good Feelings .........................................142

## 6   The Age of Jackson ................................................. 152

    6.1 John Quincy Adams and Nationalism ...........................153

    6.2 Jacksonian America ................................................156

        **Analyzing Sources:** John Marshall..............................161

    6.3 Domestic Controversies............................................163

        **Analyzing Sources:** John C. Calhoun ..........................163

        **Analyzing Sources:** Robert Hayne..............................164

        **Analyzing Sources:** Daniel Webster ...........................165

        **Analyzing Sources:** Andrew Jackson ..........................167

    6.4 Party Politics........................................................170

## 7   The Growth of American Society ...............................176

    7.1 Advances in Transportation .......................................177

    7.2 Advances in Technology ...........................................182

    7.3 Religion and Reform ...............................................188

        **Analyzing Sources:** William Lloyd Garrison ....................193

# 8  Manifest Destiny ...................................................... 200

8.1 Texas ................................................................ 201

   **Analyzing Sources:** John Louis O'Sullivan ........................ 201

8.2 The Mexican War ..................................................... 207

   **Analyzing Sources:** John C. Calhoun ............................. 208

   **Analyzing Sources:** Ralph Waldo Emerson ........................ 213

8.3 Westward Expansion ................................................. 214

# 9  A House Dividing ..................................................... 222

9.1 Sectional Differences ............................................... 223

9.2 American Slavery ................................................... 226

   **Analyzing Sources:** Solomon Northup ............................ 226

9.3 Sectional Conflict .................................................. 231

9.4 Secession .......................................................... 242

   **Analyzing Sources:** Abraham Lincoln ............................ 243

9.5 Fort Sumter ........................................................ 244

# 10  The Civil War ...................................................... 250

10.1 Preparing for War ................................................. 251

10.2 The War in the East ............................................... 259

   **Analyzing Sources:** Abraham Lincoln ............................ 265

10.3 The War in the West .............................................. 266

10.4 The Road to Appomattox ......................................... 269

   **Analyzing Sources:** Abraham Lincoln ............................ 269

   **Analyzing Sources:** Charles Hodge ............................. 271

# 11  Reconstruction ..................................................... 282

11.1 Presidential Reconstruction ....................................... 283

   **Analyzing Sources:** Black Codes of Opelousas, Louisiana .......... 286

11.2 Congressional Reconstruction ..................................... 288

11.3 The End of Reconstruction ........................................ 297

   **Analyzing Sources:** Group of Kentucky Freedmen ................. 298

11.4 A Reconstructed Nation ........................................... 300

   **Analyzing Sources:** Frederick Douglass .......................... 301

## 12 The Gilded Age ........................................ 306

12.1 Change and Challenge ................................. 307

12.2 Industry and Invention ............................... 315

12.3 Big Business........................................... 318

12.4 Labor Issues.......................................... 326

## 13 Westward Expansion ................................ 334

13.1 Rails, Miners, Cowboys, and Lawmen ................. 335

    **Analyzing Sources:** English Observer..................... 336

13.2 Settlers and Sodbusters.............................. 346

13.4 Conflicts with Native Americans...................... 350

    **Analyzing Sources:** Sitting Bull......................... 352

## 14 Age of Imperialism ................................. 360

14.1 Populism.............................................. 361

14.2 International Expansion ............................... 365

14.3 The Spanish-American War............................ 371

    **Analyzing Sources:** George F. Hoar .................... 375

14.4 The Turn of the Century.............................. 377

## 15 The Progressive Era ................................ 386

15.1 Society of the Progressive Era ....................... 387

    **Analyzing Sources:** Booker T. Washington.............. 393

15.2 Goals of the Progressive Era......................... 398

15.3 Presidents of the Progressive Era ................... 403

## 16 World War I ......................................... 414

16.1 The Powder Keg of Europe ........................... 415

16.2 American Neutrality .................................. 420

    **Analyzing Sources:** Woodrow Wilson .................. 420

    **Analyzing Sources:** Woodrow Wilson .................. 426

16.3 The War to End All Wars.............................. 427

16.4 Aftermath of World War I ............................ 433

## 17 The Twenties .................................................. 440

17.1 Postwar Difficulties ........................................ 441

17.2 The Growth of Consumer Society ........................... 445

17.3 The Roaring Twenties ...................................... 449

17.4 Harding and Coolidge ...................................... 459

## 18 Depression and New Deal ................................. 464

18.1 The Great Depression ...................................... 465

18.2 Hoover Responds .......................................... 474

18.3 Roosevelt and the New Deal ................................ 477

18.4 Responses to the New Deal ................................ 483

## 19 World War II .................................................. 490

19.1 The Coming of War ......................................... 491

   **Analyzing Sources:** Winston Churchill ...................... 496

19.2 Isolation and Infamy ....................................... 498

19.3 The European Theater ...................................... 504

19.4 The Pacific Theater ........................................ 513

## 20 The Postwar Era ............................................ 522

20.1 The Postwar Era ........................................... 523

20.2 The Cold War Begins ...................................... 528

   **Analyzing Sources:** Winston Churchill ...................... 529

20.3 Life in Postwar America .................................... 537

## 21 Struggles of the Sixties ................................... 548

21.1 The Kennedy Years ......................................... 549

   **Analyzing Sources:** John F. Kennedy ....................... 553

21.2 The Johnson Administration ................................ 556

21.3 The Vietnam War Era ...................................... 560

## 22 The Civil Rights Movement ............................... 574

22.1 Early Civil Rights Movement ............................... 575

   **Analyzing Sources:** Martin Luther King Jr. .................. 582

22.2 Advances In Civil Rights ................................... 586

   **Analyzing Sources:** Martin Luther King Jr. .................. 588

22.3 Civil Rights Struggles ..................................... 591

   **Analyzing Sources:** Martin Luther King Jr. .................. 595

## 23   Challenges of the Seventies .................................. 600

23.1 The Nixon Administration ................................. 601

23.2 The Ford Administration ................................. 608

23.3 The Carter Administration ................................ 610

23.4 Issues of the Seventies ................................. 617

## 24   The Turn of the Century .................................. 626

24.1 The Reagan Era ....................................... 627

24.2 George H. W. Bush and the End of the Cold War ............... 635

24.3 The Clinton Administration .............................. 641

24.4 George W. Bush and the World ........................... 646

Analyzing Sources: George W. Bush ......................... 650

## 25   America and the Modern World ........................... 660

25.1 The Obama Years ..................................... 661

25.2 The Trump Presidency ................................. 665

25.3 The Biden Administration ............................... 674

25.4 Contemporary America ................................. 678

### Analyzing Sources

Robert Tracy McKenzie ...................................... 4

William Bradford .......................................... 28

John Winthrop ............................................ 29

Patrick Henry ............................................. 68

Thomas Paine ............................................ 73

George Washington ........................................ 95

James Madison ........................................... 102

Alexander Hamilton ....................................... 108

Patrick Henry ............................................ 109

Thomas Jefferson ......................................... 121

Alexander Hamilton ....................................... 122

John Marshall ............................................ 161

John C. Calhoun .......................................... 163

Robert Hayne ............................................ 164

Daniel Webster ........................................... 165

Andrew Jackson .......................................... 167

William Lloyd Garrison . . . . . . . . . . . . . . . . . . . . . . . . . . . . . . . . . . . . . . . . . . . . . 193

John Louis O'Sullivan . . . . . . . . . . . . . . . . . . . . . . . . . . . . . . . . . . . . . . . . . . . . . 201

John C. Calhoun . . . . . . . . . . . . . . . . . . . . . . . . . . . . . . . . . . . . . . . . . . . . . . . . . . 208

Ralph Waldo Emerson . . . . . . . . . . . . . . . . . . . . . . . . . . . . . . . . . . . . . . . . . . . . . 213

Solomon Northup . . . . . . . . . . . . . . . . . . . . . . . . . . . . . . . . . . . . . . . . . . . . . . . . . 226

Abraham Lincoln . . . . . . . . . . . . . . . . . . . . . . . . . . . . . . . . . . . . . . . . . . . . . . . . . . 243

Abraham Lincoln . . . . . . . . . . . . . . . . . . . . . . . . . . . . . . . . . . . . . . . . . . . . . . . . . . 265

Abraham Lincoln . . . . . . . . . . . . . . . . . . . . . . . . . . . . . . . . . . . . . . . . . . . . . . . . . . 269

Charles Hodge . . . . . . . . . . . . . . . . . . . . . . . . . . . . . . . . . . . . . . . . . . . . . . . . . . . 271

Black Codes of Opelousas, Louisiana . . . . . . . . . . . . . . . . . . . . . . . . . . . . . . . . 286

Group of Kentucky Freedmen . . . . . . . . . . . . . . . . . . . . . . . . . . . . . . . . . . . . . . 298

Frederick Douglass . . . . . . . . . . . . . . . . . . . . . . . . . . . . . . . . . . . . . . . . . . . . . . . 301

English Observer . . . . . . . . . . . . . . . . . . . . . . . . . . . . . . . . . . . . . . . . . . . . . . . . . 336

Sitting Bull . . . . . . . . . . . . . . . . . . . . . . . . . . . . . . . . . . . . . . . . . . . . . . . . . . . . . . 352

George F. Hoar . . . . . . . . . . . . . . . . . . . . . . . . . . . . . . . . . . . . . . . . . . . . . . . . . . . 375

Booker T. Washington . . . . . . . . . . . . . . . . . . . . . . . . . . . . . . . . . . . . . . . . . . . . . 393

Woodrow Wilson . . . . . . . . . . . . . . . . . . . . . . . . . . . . . . . . . . . . . . . . . . . . . . . . . 420

Woodrow Wilson . . . . . . . . . . . . . . . . . . . . . . . . . . . . . . . . . . . . . . . . . . . . . . . . . 426

Winston Churchill . . . . . . . . . . . . . . . . . . . . . . . . . . . . . . . . . . . . . . . . . . . . . . . . 496

Winston Churchill . . . . . . . . . . . . . . . . . . . . . . . . . . . . . . . . . . . . . . . . . . . . . . . . 529

John F. Kennedy . . . . . . . . . . . . . . . . . . . . . . . . . . . . . . . . . . . . . . . . . . . . . . . . . . 553

Martin Luther King Jr. . . . . . . . . . . . . . . . . . . . . . . . . . . . . . . . . . . . . . . . . . . . . . 582

Martin Luther King Jr. . . . . . . . . . . . . . . . . . . . . . . . . . . . . . . . . . . . . . . . . . . . . . 588

Martin Luther King Jr. . . . . . . . . . . . . . . . . . . . . . . . . . . . . . . . . . . . . . . . . . . . . . 595

George W. Bush . . . . . . . . . . . . . . . . . . . . . . . . . . . . . . . . . . . . . . . . . . . . . . . . . . 650

**Appendixes** . . . . . . . . . . . . . . . . . . . . . . . . . . . . . . . . . . . . . . . . . . . . . . . . . . . . 688

   A. Map of the United States . . . . . . . . . . . . . . . . . . . . . . . . . . . . . . . . . . . . . . . 688

   B. Declaration of Independence . . . . . . . . . . . . . . . . . . . . . . . . . . . . . . . . . . . . 690

   C. The Constitution of the United States . . . . . . . . . . . . . . . . . . . . . . . . . . . . . 692

   D. States of the Union . . . . . . . . . . . . . . . . . . . . . . . . . . . . . . . . . . . . . . . . . . . 702

   E. Presidents of the United States . . . . . . . . . . . . . . . . . . . . . . . . . . . . . . . . . . 703

**Glossary** . . . . . . . . . . . . . . . . . . . . . . . . . . . . . . . . . . . . . . . . . . . . . . . . . . . . . . . 704

**Index** . . . . . . . . . . . . . . . . . . . . . . . . . . . . . . . . . . . . . . . . . . . . . . . . . . . . . . . . . . 722

# WELCOME TO *UNITED STATES HISTORY!*

Is it best to study history by examining the writings of people who lived during historical events and periods? Or is it best to study by reading information from a wide range of sources with the advantage of hindsight? Should a history course focus on biographies of important individuals? Or should it present the major trends in a nation's culture and explain how those trends have changed over time? In *UNITED STATES HISTORY*, Sixth Edition, all of these approaches are presented to give you a broad understanding of key figures, events, periods, and trends in the history of the United States from pre-Columbian times to the present-day. Important quotations from key historical figures have been included with analysis questions for you to interact with primary sources. Feature boxes allow you to explore more about a topic or person. Interesting historical facts you may not have known before are sprinkled throughout the book in Did You Know? boxes.

To assist your preparation for assessment, Comprehension Checks follow each section to ensure you have understood important people, places, events, and concepts. Each chapter also concludes with a Chapter Summary reviewing key ideas, as well as a Chapter Review of bold terms and both comprehension and application questions to help you prepare for a test. Hopefully, however, you enjoy the study of history and will read for comprehension and understanding that go beyond any immediate assessment your teacher provides. The study of United States history enables you to appreciate and evaluate the contributions of human beings throughout the country's existence. Additionally, this course guides you to approach any evaluation from a biblical worldview, reflecting the themes of Creation, Fall, and Redemption and noting the wisdom and providence by which God governs all affairs in human history (Isa. 46:8–10; Dan. 4:17, 35).

The Electrical Building at the World's Columbian Exposition, Chicago, 1893

# USING YOUR BOOK

An **essential question** in each section focuses students on the central idea.

**Guiding questions** in each section prepare students to engage the material for comprehension.

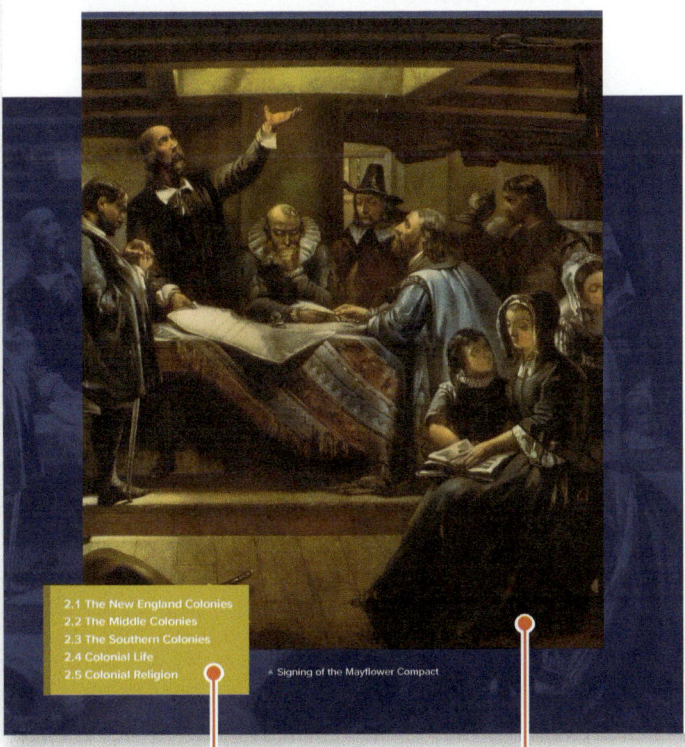

## 2  The Thirteen Colonies

2.1 The New England Colonies
2.2 The Middle Colonies
2.3 The Southern Colonies
2.4 Colonial Life
2.5 Colonial Religion

▲ Signing of the Mayflower Compact

By 1700 the eastern coast of North America was dotted with many thriving English settlements. The English colonies can best be studied by arranging them geographically. The four northernmost colonies were known as New England. The four colonies below New England were the middle colonies. The remaining five were the southern colonies.

There were three types of English colonies: charter, proprietary, and royal. A **charter colony** was one governed by a trade company (such as the Virginia Company) that received authorization from the king. In a **proprietary colony**, such as Pennsylvania, the king gave control of the colony to one or more proprietors. A **royal colony** was controlled directly by the king, who appointed a governor. Most charter and proprietary colonies became royal colonies during the 1700s.

### 2.1  The New England Colonies

How were the New England colonies founded?

#### Massachusetts

To study the settling of Massachusetts by the Pilgrims and then a decade later by the Puritans, one must understand the religious situation in England at that time. The official church was the Church of England, or the Anglican Church. Although technically Protestant, many traces of Roman Catholicism remained in its rituals. Two groups, the Puritans and the Separatists, emerged in opposition to those problems. The **Puritans** wanted to purify the Anglican church from within. They pushed for reforms that would rid England of Roman Catholic influences and bring greater spiritual vitality to the nation.

The **Separatists** believed that Christians needed to separate from the Anglican Church. They thought each congregation should be independent of other churches, free to worship and serve God without interference. Because the Separatists refused to attend Anglican churches or recognize the authority of the official state church, they were harassed, and many were jailed.

##### Plymouth

In 1607 one congregation of Separatists from England migrated to the Netherlands because of the religious tolerance there. After a decade in Holland, however, they noticed that the worldly atmosphere and hardships of life in Holland threatened the spiritual and physical well-being of their children and their congregation, and that few other English families were willing to join them. Because of these concerns, the Separatists obtained a land grant from the Virginia Company to settle in America. Under the terms of the agreement, they would receive land and the right to worship freely.

In September 1620 these Separatists, known as "Pilgrims," boarded the *Mayflower* and left Plymouth, England, bound for America with a charter to settle in Virginia. Aboard were 102 passengers, about half of whom were Separatists. The Pilgrims referred to the other travelers as "strangers." The ocean passage was stormy, and the little *Mayflower* was blown far north of the Virginia colony to Cape Cod, Massachusetts. Another attempt to reach Virginia was also beaten back by a storm. By then it was November, and scant provisions remained. Consequently, the Pilgrims decided to settle in Massachusetts.

**GUIDING QUESTIONS**

- Why did the Separatists and Puritans come to New England?
- How were the Separatists and Puritans different?
- Why were the colonies of Rhode Island, Connecticut, and New Hampshire founded separately from Massachusetts?
- How did the colonists make a living in New England?

**The New England Colonies**

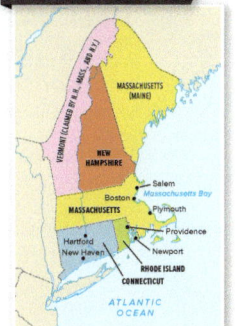

The Thirteen Colonies    **27**

The **chapter outline** introduces the main topics that will be covered.

**Photographs, illustrations, and artwork** assist with comprehension and provide opportunities for visual analysis.

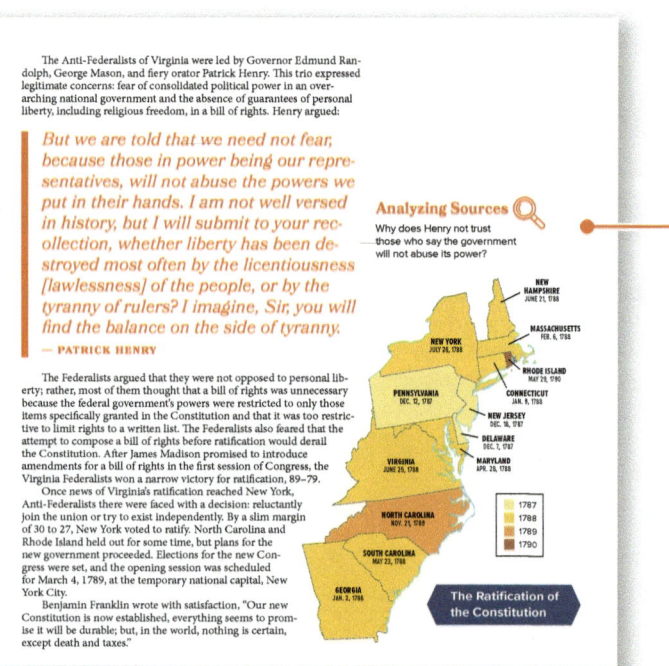

The Anti-Federalists of Virginia were led by Governor Edmund Randolph, George Mason, and fiery orator Patrick Henry. This trio expressed legitimate concerns: fear of consolidated political power in an overarching national government and the absence of guarantees of personal liberty, including religious freedom, in a bill of rights. Henry argued:

> *But we are told that we need not fear; because those in power being our representatives, will not abuse the powers we put in their hands. I am not well versed in history, but I will submit to your recollection, whether liberty has been destroyed most often by the licentiousness [lawlessness] of the people, or by the tyranny of rulers? I imagine, Sir, you will find the balance on the side of tyranny.*
> — PATRICK HENRY

**Analyzing Sources**

Why does Henry not trust those who say the government will not abuse its power?

The Federalists argued that they were not opposed to personal liberty; rather, most of them thought that a bill of rights was unnecessary because the federal government's powers were restricted to only those items specifically granted in the Constitution and that it was too restrictive to limit rights to a written list. The Federalists also feared that the attempt to compose a bill of rights before ratification would derail the Constitution. After James Madison promised to introduce amendments for a bill of rights in the first session of Congress, the Virginia Federalists won a narrow victory for ratification, 89–79.

Once news of Virginia's ratification reached New York, Anti-Federalists there were faced with a decision: reluctantly join the union or try to exist independently. By a slim margin of 30 to 27, New York voted to ratify. North Carolina and Rhode Island held out for some time, but plans for the new government proceeded. Elections for the new Congress were set, and the opening session was scheduled for March 4, 1789, at the temporary national capital, New York City.

Benjamin Franklin wrote with satisfaction, "Our new Constitution is now established, everything seems to promise it will be durable; but, in the world, nothing is certain, except death and taxes."

**NEW HAMPSHIRE** JUNE 21, 1788
**MASSACHUSETTS** FEB. 6, 1788
**NEW YORK** JULY 26, 1788
**RHODE ISLAND** MAY 29, 1790
**CONNECTICUT** JAN. 9, 1788
**NEW JERSEY** DEC. 18, 1787
**PENNSYLVANIA** DEC. 12, 1787
**DELAWARE** DEC. 7, 1787
**MARYLAND** APR. 28, 1788
**VIRGINIA** JUNE 25, 1788
**NORTH CAROLINA** NOV. 21, 1789
**SOUTH CAROLINA** MAY 23, 1788
**GEORGIA** JAN. 2, 1788

1787
1788
1789
1790

**The Ratification of the Constitution**

**Baptists** *and the* **Bill** *of* **Rights**

Many Protestants, including Baptists, had supported the War for Independence. One reason for their support was the anticipation of religious freedom that would result. However, when the text of the Constitution became known, Baptist leaders, including Pastor John Leland, expressed serious concerns because the document contained no guarantees of religious freedom. James Madison and others argued that these guarantees were unnecessary because the federal government's powers could likely not attain a level of power that would threaten freedom of religion. However, Pastor Leland and many others insisted that their support for the Constitution was contingent on the addition of a bill of rights. When Pastor Leland convinced Madison to offer the suggested amendments, Leland and other Baptists supported the ratification of the Constitution and helped to ensure its passage.

Confederation and Constitution **109**

**Analyzing Sources** provide opportunities for students to interact with primary sources.

**Feature boxes** provide brief biographical sketches, additional information, or insight into a particular topic.

**Maps, charts, and diagrams** help students visualize locations and concepts.

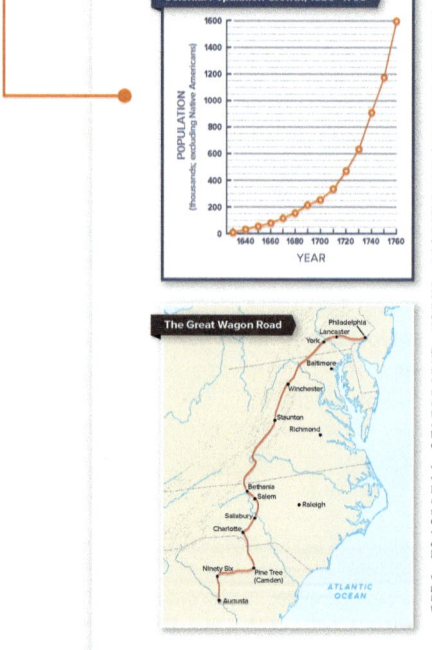

**Colonial Population Growth, 1630–1760**

POPULATION (thousands, excluding Native Americans)
1600
1400
1200
1000
800
600
400
200
0
1630 1640 1660 1680 1700 1720 1740 1760
YEAR

**The Great Wagon Road**

Philadelphia
Lancaster
York
Baltimore
Winchester
Staunton
Richmond
Bethabara
Salem
Salisbury
Raleigh
Charlotte
Ninety Six
Pine Tree (Camden)
Augusta
ATLANTIC OCEAN

**Colonial Growth**

The American colonies te...
young, single men who lacked...
advancement in England. Beca...
outnumbered females in the co...
and Maryland. The New Engla...
other hand, attracted whole fa...
between men and women was...

Growth in the New Engla...
naturally through the birth of...
in the southern colonies grow...
through the arrival of new col...
and slaves from Africa. Unfort...
mothers, difficult deliveries se...
an early grave, and their babie...
Yet the infant death rate was...
than in Europe at the time. Th...
settlements and America's pr...
land restrained the disease and...
prevalent in Europe's crowded...
pectancies in New England we...
longer than those in the south...
slaves, however, harsh working...
climate, and disease led to hig...
new slaves were imported con...
with demand.

Large families provided an...
source for the home, and child...
helping hands to put food on...
market. Families with six to ei...
common, and it was not unus...
have a dozen or more children...

Despite the spread of dise...
growth of cities, the colonies g...
In 1700 the population was ro...
it increased ten times by the o...
tionary War. Hungry for land,...
migrated inland from the big c...
an old Iroquois trail which wa...
frontier settlements from Virg...
of thousands of settlers travel...
by foot or in wagons, and it be...
**Great Wagon Road.**

The two largest groups of...
were Scots-Irish and German...
were from Protestant northern Ireland. Economic hard times and religious intolerance sent as many as a quarter-million to the colonies. Most other German settlers were Protestants from southwestern Germany. Thousands of them arrived in Pennsylvania, attracted by the religious freedom of Penn's commonwealth and the rich farm country so much like their homeland.

The American colonies included a diversity of ethnicities and religions. Blending these diverse groups into one culture that could be called "American" was a process that would take many decades to complete.

The Thirteen Colonies **41**

In the early years of the Carolinas, raising cattle and harvesting timber were the primary economic activities. Lumber and pitch (used to make tar for waterproofing ropes and caulking ships) were valuable exports. North Carolina developed small tobacco farms. In the 1690s rice became the primary cash crop for export. Rice was familiar to slaves who had grown it in West Africa. Slaves were brought to the Carolinas to teach planters how to cultivate rice and to engineer the tidewater marshes and swamps for growing it. Annual rice exports from South Carolina grew to 43 million pounds by 1740. Indigo, a plant that produced a blue dye that was in high demand in the clothing industry, became a second important cash crop in the Carolinas.

Growing and harvesting rice was labor intensive. As the amount of cultivated rice increased, the number of slaves increased. By 1730 enslaved peoples in the Carolinas outnumbered free people two to one.

Because Georgia had been established to encourage its settlers to work for themselves, slavery was originally prohibited, and settlers were limited to 500-acre plots of land. As the colony struggled to succeed, settlers blamed their lack of success on these restrictions and demanded their removal. Eventually Georgia became a royal colony, and slavery was allowed. Georgia quickly developed rice and indigo plantations like South Carolina, and the enslaved population soon nearly equaled the free population.

Not all southern colonists were wealthy plantation owners. Most lived on small farms and grew just enough to feed their families and to barter for other needed items. This was especially true of those who lived further inland and along the frontier.

**Comprehension Check 2.3**

1. The primary crop of Virginia was _____.
   A wheat
   B tobacco
   C indigo

2. The _____ system gave fifty acres of land to any person who paid for another person's passage to Virginia.
   A mercantile
   B triangular trade
   C headright

3. The colony of _____ was established as a refuge for Roman Catholics.
   A Maryland
   B North Carolina
   C Georgia

4. Each of the following was a reason for the founding of Georgia except _____.
   A to be a place where debtors could start a new life
   B to develop large plantations for growing rice for export
   C to be a military buffer against Spanish Florida

**MAKING CONNECTIONS**

5. How was the economy of the southern colonies different from that of the other colonies?

The Thirteen Colonies **37**

**Comprehension Check questions** give students an opportunity to assess their understanding of each section.

## Results of the Awakening

The Great Awakening had several effects on life in colonial America.

 **Church Growth**

First, church growth was the most visible result. Because of the many conversions and the spiritual renewal of many Christians, the number of churches and church members increased significantly. Presbyterians and Baptists experienced the greatest growth. The Half-Way Covenant began to vanish; increasingly, churches in America required personal salvation for membership. This growth also promoted unity among the churches. Different congregations and even different denominations overlooked their minor doctrinal differences in the interest of evangelism. This tendency toward unity helped pave the way for a political uniting of the colonies in the coming break with England.

 **Religious Division**

Second, the Great Awakening also brought division to America's churches. Nearly every denomination had those who favored the revival (often called New Lights or New Side) and those who opposed it (Old Lights or Old Side). Not all Old Lights were against revival itself; some were simply offended by, in their view, the fanatical extremes of some people. Many of the opponents, though, were theologically opposed to the revival. They disliked the emphasis on personal experience, criticism of unsaved pastors, and the general upsetting of "good church order."

 **Religious Training**

Third, the number of colleges founded as ministry training centers increased. Princeton, Brown, Rutgers, and Dartmouth were established. Yale experienced a renewed spiritual emphasis. Harvard, however, continued its move away from its Puritan spiritual roots.

 **Separation of Church and State**

Fourth, the Great Awakening increased the separation between church and state. The revival showed that the church could exist without government support and that established state churches were not necessary or even desired. This anti-establishment movement, especially where the Anglican church was strong, may have contributed to the increased tension between Britain and the colonies when Britain began to tighten its control in America.

 **Political Unity**

Fifth, the Great Awakening had political effects on the colonies. It was the first truly national movement in American history. The revival cut across regional lines and touched every colony and nearly every class of people. The Great Awakening was not southern or northern, Presbyterian or Congregationalist, upper class or lower class; it was American. It caused colonists to begin to think in terms of liberty and rights in both spiritual and political affairs and caused some to think more about their status in the British Empire.

 **Democratization**

Sixth, the Awakening advanced the idea of the equality of all men by reaffirming the equality of all before God. A democratic influence swept into the churches; people's wealth or status did not determine their spiritual condition. However, not all effects of this greater democracy proved positive. As democracy and individualism became stronger, some Americans began to doubt fundamental Christian doctrines. Before the Great Awakening, people usually respected the expertise of their pastors in understanding the Scripture. Now, many thought their own unstudied opinions were just as valid.

Many movements that were unleashed in the Great Awakening saw their full development in the American Revolution. Foremost was an awakening of both the spirit of democracy and the spirit of religious liberty.

**Graphic organizers** allow students to readily analyze characteristics, causes, or effects.

**Bold terms** highlight key people, events, and concepts.

---

▲ Death of Metacomet in King Philip's War

▼ Nathaniel Bacon

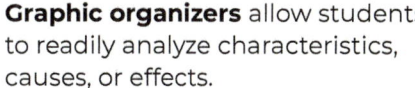

Did You
**Know?**

Nathaniel Bacon and Governor William Berkeley were cousins, and Bacon served on the Council of Virginia.

### Colonial Interactions

#### Conflicts with Native Americans

As colonists continued to push further inland and claim more land for themselves, clashes with Native Americans increased. One of these conflicts was the **Pequot War** from 1636 to 1638. The Pequots were a powerful group in the Connecticut River Valley who controlled the fur trade there. Rivalry between the Dutch, English, and Native American tribes led to bloodshed. After some Englishmen were murdered, Massachusetts Bay responded by attacking and burning some Pequot villages and farms. The Pequots responded by attacking an English fort. The colonists then ambushed a Pequot fort and set it on fire. Many of the Pequots who survived the attack were captured and sold as slaves in the West Indies or in New England.

After the Pequot War, there was relative peace in New England for about forty years. However, conflict erupted again in 1675. Metacomet, called King Philip by the colonists, was the son of Massasoit (who had helped the original English settlers at Plymouth) and was the leader of the Wampanoag. When three Wampanoag men were tried, convicted, and executed for murder by the Plymouth colony, the Wampanoag and other area tribes responded by attacking the colonists. The resulting conflict from 1675 to 1678 was called **King Philip's War** and resulted in the deaths of at least six hundred colonists and more than two thousand Native Americans. Metacomet was killed in 1676, and his head was mounted on a pole and displayed in Plymouth for the next twenty years.

In Virginia, bad weather, declining tobacco prices, and increasing competition from other colonies caused economic problems. Frustrated colonists, particularly frontier farmers, blamed the Native American population for their misfortune. When Indians raided the farm of a Virginian for failing to pay for some items, colonists retaliated against the wrong tribe. This resulted in further attacks by the Native Americans. Governor William Berkeley attempted to preserve peace, but Nathaniel Bacon accused Berkeley of failing to protect Virginia from the Indians and of levying unjust taxes. In **Bacon's Rebellion**, Bacon and his followers ignored Berkeley's desire to pursue peace and began attacking Indians throughout Virginia. Berkeley declared Bacon a rebel, and Bacon and his men laid siege to Jamestown in September 1676. Berkeley fled, and Bacon's men burned the city. Bacon died in October 1676, and the rebellion ended. Many of Bacon's followers were hanged by Berkeley.

Additional wars were fought on the frontier. Three wars—King William's War, from 1689 to 1697; Queen Anne's War, from 1702 to 1713; and King George's War, from 1744 to 1748—were primarily between France and England and had spilled into North America. Native American tribes allied themselves with one side or the other and attacked French or English settlements. These wars were the prelude to the more decisive French and Indian War.

#### Missions to Native Americans

Throughout the colonial era, many devout Christians attempted to reach Native Americans with the gospel. Sometimes personal contact resulted in a conversion, such as with Pocahontas. Ministers often preached to the Indians in addition to their other duties. Roger Williams and Jonathan Edwards were among the first in New England to preach to the Indians.

**Did You Know? boxes** present interesting facts to spark curiosity about people or events.

Each **chapter summary** reviews bold terms and provides a brief overview of the important concepts of each section.

# CHAPTER 2 REVIEW

## 2.5 Colonial Religion

- Puritan New England adopted a congregational form of church government. The Half-Way Covenant allowed the children of members who had not made a profession of faith to be baptized into membership.
- The middle colonies were the most religiously diverse with religious groups such as the Quakers, Anabaptists, and Moravians.
- The Anglican Church was the established church in the southern colonies, but other groups were allowed to settle as long as they paid taxes to the state church. Maryland was a haven for Roman Catholics.

- The Great Awakening was a period of religious revival in the colonies. Preachers such as Jonathan Edwards, George Whitefield, and Samuel Davies traveled the colonies preaching the need for salvation. The Great Awakening had several significant effects on American society, including the growth of churches, the separation of church and state, and growing democratization.

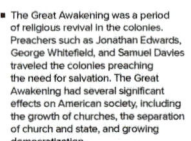

### TERMS

Half-Way Covenant
Quakers
Baptists
Anabaptists
Moravians
Great Awakening
Jonathan Edwards
George Whitefield
Samuel Davies

## Chapter Review Questions

### RECALL

1. What was the first document of self-government in America by which the Pilgrims bound themselves to submit to the colony's laws and duly elected leadership?
2. Who helped the Pilgrims in Plymouth Colony by teaching them about crops and fishing and working to establish peace between the settlers and the Wampanoags?
3. What was the first written constitution in America?
4. What were the main economic activities in New England?
5. What religious group did William Penn belong to?
6. What was the main cash crop of Virginia?
7. Why was the colony of Maryland founded?
8. For what reasons was the colony of Georgia founded?
9. What were the main cash crops for the Carolina colony?
10. What were three ways that people in colonial America spent their leisure time?
11. What were the two largest non-English groups to settle in the colonies?

12. Where could the most direct form of democracy be found in the colonies?
13. What two wars were fought between the New England colonists and the Native Americans in the 1600s?
14. Who translated the Bible into the Algonquian language?
15. Which colonies were the most religiously diverse?
16. What was the established church in the southern colonies?
17. What was the great religious revival in the American colonies called?

### UNDERSTAND

18. What was the difference between charter colonies, proprietary colonies, and royal colonies?
19. What role did religion play in the founding of Plymouth Colony and the Massachusetts Bay Colony?
20. What was the difference between the Puritans and the Separatists?
21. What beliefs of Roger Williams's caused him to be banished from Massachusetts?

22. Why was Anne Hutchinson banished from Massachusetts?
23. How did Massachusetts Bay Colony influence the founding of Connecticut, Rhode Island, and New Hampshire?
24. What was triangular trade, and what were some goods shipped on each leg?
25. Why were Peter Stuyvesant's reforms in New York rejected?
26. Why were the middle colonies known as the "bread colonies"?
27. What was the composition of the upper, middle, and lower classes in New England, the middle colonies, and the southern colonies?
28. What were the three main divisions of government in the colonies, and what powers did each have?
29. Why was there more population growth in the New England colonies than in the southern colonies?
30. What were Nathaniel Bacon's reasons for his rebellion against the government of Virginia?

31. Describe the beliefs and worship of the Quakers.
32. How did the Half-Way Covenant affect religion in New England?
33. What caused the Salem witch trials, and how did the trials affect the reputation of the Puritans?

### THINK ABOUT IT

34. How did colonial growth relate to colonial interactions with Native Americans?
35. Contrast education in New England with education in the middle and southern colonies.
36. How did the idea of religious freedom in Massachusetts Bay differ from the idea of religious freedom in Pennsylvania or Maryland?
37. Identify and explain six effects of the Great Awakening on American society.
38. Analyze the New England town map below and answer the following question:
   *What are four things that can be learned about New England society from this map?*

▲ Layout of a New England town

Each **chapter review** helps students prepare for the assessment by asking them to recall important people, events, and concepts; connect events and people to deepen understanding; and think critically about people, actions, and ideas.

SIXTH EDITION

# UNITED STATES HISTORY

# 1 America, Europe, and Africa before 1620

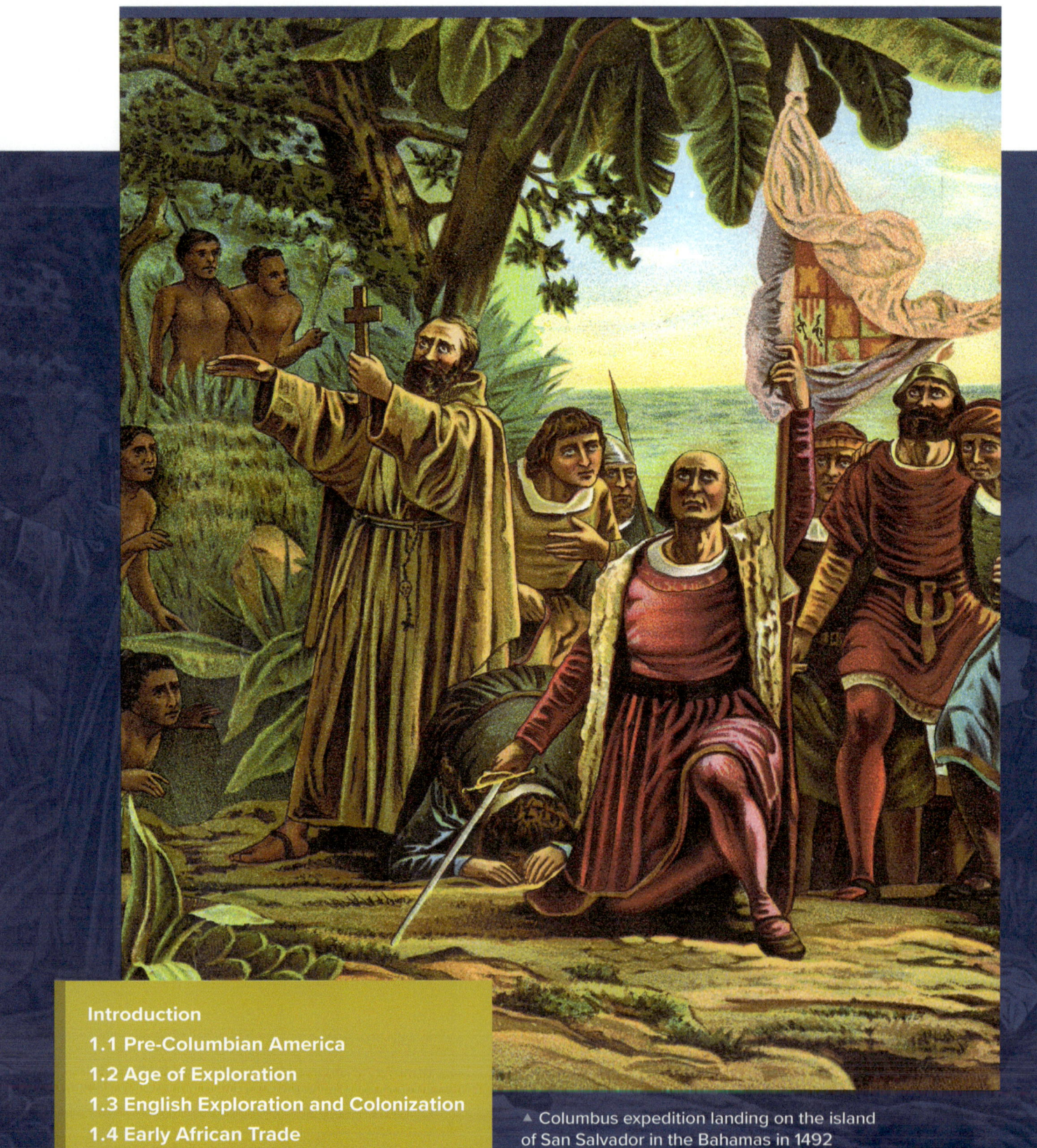

**Introduction**
**1.1 Pre-Columbian America**
**1.2 Age of Exploration**
**1.3 English Exploration and Colonization**
**1.4 Early African Trade**

▲ Columbus expedition landing on the island of San Salvador in the Bahamas in 1492

# Who Decides What History We Learn?

**M**any people believe that history is simply a list of facts woven together into a story and therefore not subject to bias. "History is history, it's just the facts, right?" But of all academic disciplines, history has perhaps been the most controversial when it comes to deciding what should be taught. In fact, in the early 1990s the US Department of Education together with the National Endowment for the Humanities funded an effort to create a set of national history standards for K–12 schools. Upon completion of the standards, the US Senate, in a rare show of near unanimity, rejected them in a 99–1 vote.

Why has it been so difficult to decide which parts of history are important for students to learn? To answer that question, let's look at an example:

**Columbus set sail in 1492.**

This seems like an indisputable fact of history. Every history book that discusses Columbus will include this fact. But good historians will not just give a list of facts. They will try to explain those facts, give meaning to them, and even evaluate them. Why did Columbus sail in 1492? Where did he come from? Where was he going? What events led up to his voyage? What happened when he got there? Were the results of his voy-

age positive, negative, or a bit of both? What did his voyage mean to the bigger picture of the history of civilization? Was Columbus good or bad?

This is where history gets messy. Historians may agree on the facts (although not always!), but they may disagree on what those facts mean and how to evaluate the events. Every historian begins with a set of presuppositions (ideas or assumptions already held) about what is true, what is good, and what is important. These presuppositions are part of what makes up his or her worldview. This worldview will shape how the historian writes history. It will determine the selection, interpretation, and evaluation of the facts.

## Selection

Because history is all-encompassing, no history book can include everything that has ever happened. Historians must make choices about what to include and what to leave out of the story. Those decisions are influenced by worldview and historical perspective. What role did religion, the arts, science and technology, or economics play in the story of American history? Which primary and secondary sources will be used? Which people and events are essential to the story the historian is telling?

## Interpretation

The historian's worldview and perspective also influence how the facts are interpreted. What do the facts mean? **Historiography** is the study of the writing of history. As long as people have been writing history, there have been differing perspectives on how history should be written. Some historians emphasize the importance of political events or great people in history, while others focus on military conflicts. Some use an economic interpretation of events, while others focus on social history and the lives of ordinary people. One current interpretation of American history says that slavery and racism were at the center of the founding of the nation, while another says that although slavery existed, it was a deviation from the ideals upon which America was founded. It is important to recognize the historian's perspective as you read. While it is true that every historian has a bias, that does not mean that every interpretation is equally valid. As historian Robert Tracy McKenzie says,

> *This means that no interpretation is ever wholly objective. And yet—this is a crucial qualifier—the range of valid interpretations is not limitless. The historical evidence that survives constitutes the boundary that the historian can't cross without leaving the domain of history for the realm of historical fiction. Unlike the fiction writer, the historian is constrained by the historical record.*

— **ROBERT TRACY MCKENZIE,** *The First Thanksgiving,* (Downers Grove, IL: IVP Academic, 2013) p. 27.

 **Analyzing Sources**

What is the difference between history and historical fiction? What would make an interpretation invalid?

▼ When you read an author's interpretation, ask yourself several questions.

DOES THE PRESENTED EVIDENCE SUPPORT THE AUTHOR'S INTERPRETATION?

IS THE AUTHOR IGNORING EVIDENCE THAT CONTRADICTS HIS OR HER INTERPRETATION?

DO I AGREE WITH THIS INTERPRETATION?

▲ Historians will select, interpret, and evaluate historical evidence differently based on their worldviews.

## Evaluation

Every historian who makes an evaluation uses some basis to make a judgment about what is right or wrong, good or bad. Ultimately, the historian's worldview will determine how a person, event, or idea is evaluated. In this book, when we make an evaluation, our basis will be what God has revealed in His Word. God has given us clear standards for making moral judgments in certain areas. While Christians often disagree on how to apply those standards (or even which standards to apply) to a given situation, any moral evaluations we make should be rooted in God's Word.

One goal of this course is to help you understand the basic structure of American history—the important people, events, and ideas that have shaped America. A second goal is to spark an interest in history so that you might be motivated to dig more deeply into historical events and personalities on your own. A third goal of this course is to help you begin to think like a historian. Learning facts about American history is important, but equally important is the ability to analyze and evaluate sources and evidence, distinguish fact from opinion, recognize and evaluate varying interpretations and points of view, interpret significance, and make sense of complicated issues. This will help you become a more critical thinker, recognize the author's perspective, and learn to evaluate what you read. By achieving these goals, we hope to achieve the larger goal of this course, which is to help you develop wisdom for life as a Christian citizen.

## Discussion Questions

1. What types of evidence do historians use?

2. What are some strengths and weaknesses of each of the types of evidence listed in Question 1?

3. What factors might help you determine whether to accept an author's historical interpretation?

4. Why are all historical interpretations not equally valid?

5. On what basis do historians make evaluations, and on what basis should Christian historians make evaluations?

6. What is historiography?

## GUIDING QUESTIONS

- What were the major cultures in the Americas before Europeans came?

- What was Native American religion like?

## 1.1 Pre-Columbian America

How did people originally get to North and South America?

Long before Europeans discovered the Americas, people lived in developed civilizations in South, Central, and North America. Where had they come from? There are many theories. Some believe that these indigenous Americans entered near the Arctic Circle where Asia and America almost touch. They may have crossed the Bering Strait by boat, or over an ice bridge when it was frozen, or over a land bridge when the sea level receded. Others believe that these ancient peoples sailed across the oceans.

However they came, these groups moved slowly southward and eventually settled the entire Western Hemisphere. When European explorers arrived, they found millions of Native Americans already living in developed societies.

### The People of the Americas

Native Americans are usually grouped into tribes (several families sharing common customs) and culture areas (several tribes with similar customs living near each other). These societies shared certain common characteristics, yet each group differed from the others.

ARCTIC

SUBARCTIC

NORTHWEST COAST

PLATEAU

GREAT BASIN

GREAT PLAINS

EASTERN WOODLANDS

Mississippi River

SOUTHEAST

SOUTHWEST

OLMEC

AZTEC

MAYA

INCA

INCA

## Central and South American Peoples

Much of the west coast of South America was home to the grand Incan civilization. Mesoamerica (Central America and Mexico) was home to the Maya and the Aztecs.

Great creativity is evident in what remains of the intricate pyramids, canals, and temples of both the Mesoamerican and South American cultures. A high level of intelligence would have been necessary to produce the mathematical calculations, architecture, and calendars that archaeologists have found. But worship of the true God had long been abandoned. Many instead worshiped other gods, including the sun god. Some practiced horrific human sacrifices.

▼ Aztec calendar depicting the sun god Huitzilopochtli

*Handwritten note:*
- West coast South america → grand incan civilization
- mesoamerica → maya + aztecs
- high level of intelligence
- many worshiped sun god

## Northwest Coast

The Pacific Northwest was home to many who used the water supply (oceans and rivers) to find food. They often built **totem poles** to represent what was important to them, with the lowest carvings having the most importance.

◀ Totem Pole, Ketchikan, Alaska

## Great Basin and Plateau

The Shoshone, Ute, Nez Perce, and others lived between the major western mountain ranges and hunted, fished, and gathered berries for food. They are famous for basket-making and for creating **petroglyphs** (rock drawings).

▶ Native American petroglyph, Nine-Mile Canyon, Utah

## Southwest

▲ Ancestral Puebloan cliff dwellings, Mesa Verde, Colorado

In the American Southwest lived pueblo dwellers such as the Zuni, Hopi, and Taos. The Pueblo lived in small villages made of family groups or clans. Some lived in caves along the rims or under ledges of canyons and became known as cliff dwellers. These people were farmers, growing maize (corn), squash, and beans. They also made baskets and pottery. The Pueblo reached their "golden age" around AD 1000, but lack of water, frequent raids by neighboring tribes, and severe drought led to the decline of the civilization.

### Did You Know?

The "three sisters"—corn, beans, and squash—were often grown together. Beans climbed the cornstalks, while the low-growing squash reduced weeds. The three sisters provided most of the essential nutrients needed in the Native American diet.

## ▶ Arctic and Subarctic

In the frigid climate of Canada, Alaska, and Greenland, near the Arctic, the Inuit settled. These groups lived in igloos and used small boats to hunt for whales and other animals for food, clothing, and lamp oil.

◀ An Inuit boy climbing out of an igloo

## ▶ Eastern Woodlands and Southeast

Major Eastern Woodlands tribes included the Mohawk, Oneida, Seneca, Cayuga, Onondaga, and Tuscarora in the north and Cherokee, Chickasaw, Choctaw, Creek, and Seminole in the south. Five of the northern tribes formed an alliance during the 1500s called the Iroquois League of Five Nations, later called the Iroquois Confederacy. One main type of housing in the northern Eastern Woodlands was the longhouse, built to house multiple generations of the same family. They grew maize, squash, and tobacco, among other crops.

The Adena culture developed in what is now the Midwest between 1000 BC and AD 200. After them, the Hopewell culture flourished until around AD 500. The Mississippian period lasted from around AD 1000 to AD 1540. These people are referred to as the **Mound Builders** for their construction of mounds used to bury the dead along with artifacts. Most of the artifacts, except for pottery and stone or iron tools, have rotted in the damp soil. The most famous mound is the Great Serpent Mound in southern Ohio. It portrays a slithering snake more than 1,300 feet long. The snake's mouth is open, apparently swallowing a small round mound. The largest group of mounds was located at Cahokia (near East St. Louis, Illinois), whose population may have been as high as 20,000 in AD 1200, which would have been larger than London at that time.

▶ Ancient burial mound, Cahokia, Illinois.

▼ Seminole chickee dwellings in the Florida Everglades

## ▶ Great Plains

The Sioux, Cheyenne, and Blackfoot were the powerful tribes of the Great Plains. Living on the vast grasslands of the prairies, these groups hunted bison and often lived in tepees. These dwellings were easy to pack and transport when necessary to new food-supply areas.

◀ Plains Indian tepee, Montana

# Native American Religions

As image-bearers of God, the native peoples of the Americas before Columbus's arrival were artistic, skillful, and cultural. In many ways they unknowingly fulfilled God's command to replenish and steward the earth. But like every culture, in other ways they demonstrated the fallen nature of mankind.

Most North American tribes believed in the Great Spirit. The idea of **animism**, in which all things (living or nonliving) have souls, pervaded the cultures. The spiritual leaders of villages and towns, known as shamans, claimed to be in contact with the spirits. Many traditional Native American ceremonies come from these beliefs. The people did not want the spirits to be angry and worked to appease them in many ways.

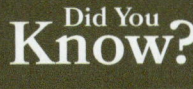

*Handwritten notes:*
- animism = all things living/nonliving have souls
- spiritual leaders of village could be in contact w/ the spirits
- ceremonies to not anger the spirits

## Did You Know?

According to the Smithsonian's National Museum of the American Indian, the terms "American Indian" and "Native American" are both considered acceptable. It is preferable to refer to the specific tribal name.

## Comprehension Check 1.1

1. Theories of how Native Americans first came to North America include the possibility that they crossed the ____ on a land bridge or ice bridge.
   A Strait of Magellan
   B Bering Strait
   C Atlantic Ocean

2. The Native American cultures of ____ featured pyramids, advances in mathematics, and the practice of human sacrifice.
   A Central and South America
   B the Southwest
   C the Eastern Woodlands and Southeast

3. Native American groups from the ____ region often built totem poles to represent what was important to them.
   A Eastern Woodlands and Southeast
   B Arctic and Subarctic
   C Northwest Coast (Pacific Northwest)

4. Native Americans from the ____ hunted whales for food.
   A Eastern Woodlands and Southeast
   B Arctic and Subarctic
   C Southwest

5. Cultures known as Mound Builders were found primarily in the ____.
   A Eastern Woodlands and Southeast
   B Arctic and Subarctic
   C Pacific Northwest

### MAKING CONNECTIONS

6. How did Native American cultures adapt to the areas where they settled?

7. Did Native American cultures align with biblical teaching? Explain your answer.

GUIDING QUESTIONS

- What factors led to exploration?
- Who were the early European explorers of the Americas?

▼ Marco Polo

# Age of Exploration

What led to the early exploration of the Americas?

## Factors Leading to Exploration

The period from the late 1400s to the early 1500s became known as the Age of Exploration. Several factors in Europe made voyages of exploration desirable and possible.

### Crusades

One factor leading to exploration was the Crusades. The Crusades marked the beginning of the Reconquista, or reconquest, in which Christians sought to retake the Holy Land and parts of Europe which had been conquered by the Muslims. While in the Middle East, European crusaders encountered luxury goods such as spices and silk from the Far East. As the knights returned to Europe with these products, demand increased significantly. Marco Polo's account of China in the 1200s fired the imaginations of Europe's merchants and adventurers. The Silk Road, the land route by which trade goods flowed between the Far East and the West, stretched from Asia to Europe. But this overland route to China was costly and dangerous. The closure of the Silk Road to European traders in 1453 by the Muslims motivated European nations to search for another route to the Far East.

### Renaissance

A second factor leading to the Age of Exploration was the Renaissance, the period marking the end of the Middle Ages and the beginning of the modern age. The Renaissance was a rebirth of interest in the learning of classical Greece and Rome which led to advances in art, architecture, politics, literature, and science. The renewed interest in scientific discovery led to many technological advances. Some of these greatly increased sailing capabilities. The **compass** enabled sailors to know which direction they were heading in. The **astrolabe** allowed them to determine the ship's latitude on the ocean. Another important innovation was the **caravel**, a small, light ship with two or three triangular sails. The caravel's swiftness, combined with its overwhelming cannon power, enabled the expansion of European trade with China and the East Indies as well as the discovery of the Americas.

In the fifteenth century, Portugal's Prince Henry (the Navigator) desired to bypass the Muslims and trade directly with West Africa and the Far East. He sponsored voyages exploring the coast of Africa. In 1488 Bartolomeu Dias sailed southward and rounded Africa's southern cape, which he named Good Hope. A decade later, Vasco da Gama extended Dias's path by sailing to India. Da Gama returned to Portugal with a cargo of spices worth sixty times the cost of his expedition. Such fantastic profits signaled the end of the Muslim monopoly on the spice trade and the beginning of the European scramble for wealth. Ships laden with cinnamon, gold, ivory, and sugar revolutionized Europe.

▼ An explorer on a caravel using an astrolabe to guide the way

◄ Portuguese bronze astrolabe, circa 1608

## Reformation

A third factor contributing to the Age of Exploration was the Protestant Reformation. For centuries Roman Catholicism had dominated every aspect of European society. But by the late Middle Ages, Martin Luther, a German monk, began to take a stand against the corruptions of the Roman Catholic Church which taught that God's grace flowed to sinners only through the Church. However, after much Bible study, Luther realized that salvation was a work of God's grace received only by faith in Jesus Christ.

Eventually, Luther and others separated from the Roman Catholic Church. They emphasized that all Christians should be able to read the Scriptures for themselves in order to apply God's Word to their lives. The invention of the movable-type printing press by Johannes Gutenberg in 1440 made the Bible and other theological works much more accessible to the common people and enabled the ideas of the Reformation to spread rapidly.

As the Reformation spread, the religious rivalry between Protestantism and Roman Catholicism motivated explorers from each side. Each saw the new lands as an opportunity to spread their influence. As wars of religion occurred throughout Europe, persecution of the losing group was common, causing many to flee to places where they could practice their chosen religion in peace.

# Early Explorers

## Vikings

No one is quite certain which ancient and medieval explorers may have visited North America first. There are legends of visitors from such places as Phoenicia and the British Isles. Artifacts and foundations found in Newfoundland, Canada, show evidence that Scandinavian Vikings came to North America around AD 1000. These Norsemen had established colonies in Iceland and Greenland. From there, they sailed west to Canada. **Leif Ericson** called the new land Vinland. This settlement did not last, and word of this discovery did not find its way back to Europe.

## Spanish

While Portugal explored the African coast, Spain, led by King Ferdinand and Queen Isabella, could finally focus on developing western trade routes, having ousted the rest of the Muslim Moors from its realm in January 1492. Having driven the Muslims from Spain, the monarchs saw exploration and colonization as a way to continue the religious conquests by retaking the Holy Land and converting unbelievers, thus securing Christian dominance of the globe.

Like most educated Europeans of the time, the Italian-born **Christopher Columbus** believed that the world was round, but he was incorrect about its size. He estimated that by sailing west three thousand miles he could reach the fabled riches of Japan. In reality, Japan was more than twelve thousand miles away. When the king of Portugal refused to support such a voyage, Columbus turned to Spain and, having suggested that the profits of his voyage be used for the reconquest of Jerusalem, was granted permission. Columbus departed in August 1492 with three ships and a letter of greeting from Spain to the king of Cipango (Japan).

◄ (top) Martin Luther nailing his Ninety-Five Theses to the door of the All Saints' Church in Wittenberg, Germany, in 1517; (middle) Leif Ericson's voyage to Newfoundland; (bottom) Columbus landing on San Salvador in 1492

In the early hours of October 12, land was discovered. Without realizing it, Columbus had stumbled onto the Bahamas. He named the island San Salvador (Holy Savior) in gratitude for the merciful journey God had given. Curious natives gathered about the strange band of pale visitors and offered gifts of parrots and raw cotton. Columbus was certain that he was on an island of the Indies off the coast of Asia; thus he called the people *los indios*—Indians. Many more misunderstandings between the two cultures would occur in the centuries to follow.

Columbus made three more voyages to the region in a vain search for China and Japan and at the time of his death in 1506 apparently still believed he had reached Asia. Others, however, came to realize what Columbus had not—that this was a new world. In 1507 a German mapmaker named this area not for Columbus, but rather in honor of **Amerigo Vespucci**, who had made exploratory trips to the Caribbean and South America between 1499 and 1502.

Two continents were added to the world map. Explorers set about finding a way to bypass them, believing riches lay just beyond. Ferdinand Magellan determined to reach the Spice Islands of the Far East by sailing south around the Americas. Taking five ships and a crew of about 270 men in 1519, he had to overcome a mutiny, the sinking of one of his ships in a storm, and the abandonment of the expedition by the crew of another. Unfortunately, Magellan was killed by poison arrows in a tribal squabble in the Philippines. Three years after the fleet left Spain, one ship, the *Victoria*, returned with only eighteen of the original fleet's crew, but they had circumnavigated the globe! The voyage made it painfully clear that Asia did not lie just beyond the Americas and that a western route to Asia was impractical. Increasingly, the focus would be on the Americas.

In 1519 **Hernando Cortés** reached Mexico and became the first great conquistador (conqueror). Disobeying orders to proceed no farther than exploring the coast, Cortés marched inland. He discovered that the Aztecs were the strongest tribe in the region. He enlisted support from many tribes who were being required to pay tribute to the Aztecs and to provide the best of their young warriors as human sacrifices for the bloody religious rituals of the Aztecs. Many welcomed the Spaniards as deliverers.

The great Aztec king, Montezuma, sent representatives to Cortés with gifts. He may have thought Cortés was an Aztec god. The enticing gleam of turquoise masks, intricate gold figurines, and massive golden disks made Cortés greedy. He marched to Tenochtitlán, the capital of the Aztec empire located at modern-day Mexico City. Despite the advanced cultures of the Aztecs and other tribes in Central and South America, they were no match for the military strength of the Europeans and were soon conquered.

Far more devastating to the native population than European guns and horses were European diseases (smallpox, chicken pox, measles, mumps, whooping cough, cholera, and influenza) to which the native population had little or no immunity. Over the next two centuries, the indigenous population would diminish by an estimated 90 percent due to disease, war, enslavement, and intermarriage. In some places such as the West Indies, the loss of entire native populations created a labor shortage that the Spanish would remedy with African slaves.

In the Spanish **encomienda system**, conquistadors were given land and the right to the labor and tribute of the native people. In return, the conquistadors were to care for, pay, protect, and Christianize the native people. But in reality the native peoples were treated like slaves and forced to work in mines or fields. When reports of abuse and cruelty reached Spain, King Ferdinand pressed for reforms that would protect the Native Americans from the worst abuses. However, the colonists resisted these reforms and Spain had a difficult time enforcing them.

▼ Spanish encomienda system on a sugar plantation

Spain also explored parts of North America, hoping to find more wealth. In 1513 **Juan Ponce de León** sailed from Puerto Rico up the east coast of Florida in search of rumored wealth. He claimed the area for Spain. He may have been searching for the legendary Fountain of Youth, although this claim is disputed.

In 1540 **Francisco de Coronado** left Mexico on what would become a four-thousand-mile trek. Believing legends about the mythical Seven Cities of Gold, Coronado explored present-day Arizona, New Mexico, Texas, and Kansas. His expedition did not find gold but did discover the Grand Canyon. In 1541 **Hernando de Soto** discovered the Mississippi River. In 1565 the Spanish established **St. Augustine**, the oldest permanent city settled by Europeans in the United States.

Through their exploration and settlement efforts, the Spanish claimed much of what is now the United States. But to Spain, the New World was more of a treasure chest than a resource to be cultivated. The Spanish and Portuguese introduced slavery—a practice which would create long-lasting problems—to the New World. Not only did the Spanish enslave conquered Native Americans, but both the Spanish and the Portuguese purchased captured African slaves to bring to Caribbean island settlements. Eventually, slaves were also sold to North American mainland colonists. The effects of the slave trade would be felt for centuries.

The Spanish colonization of the New World led to a flow of new goods between Europe and the Americas called the **Columbian Exchange**. In addition to slaves and diseases, Europeans brought a variety of animals and plants to the Americas. In turn, they brought different animals and plants and other goods back to Europe from the Americas.

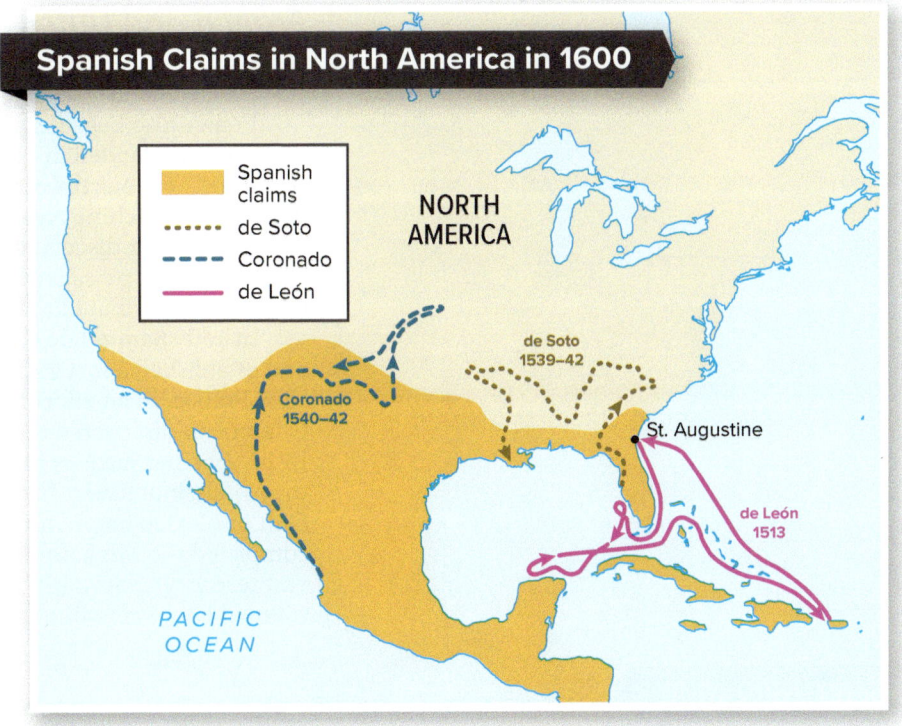

▼ Goods introduced from Europe and Africa to the Americas and from the Americas to Europe in the Columbian Exchange

America, Europe, and Africa before 1620  **13**

## French and Dutch

### FRANCE

France also began exploring North America. In 1524 Giovanni da Verrazano landed in present-day North Carolina and began searching for a Northwest Passage to Asia, sailing up the east coast until finally reaching Newfoundland. Between 1534 and 1536 **Jacques Cartier** discovered and explored the St. Lawrence River in his search for a passageway to Asia. His inland exploration of the continent contributed to the later establishment of New France.

In 1603 **Samuel de Champlain** explored the St. Lawrence River and established a fort at Quebec, which would become the capital of New France. In an effort to find a water route across the continent, Champlain discovered the Great Lakes and its network of rivers. In 1673 Father Jacques Marquette and Louis Joliet set out down the Mississippi River. They came within three hundred miles of the Gulf of Mexico before turning back. In 1682 **Robert de La Salle** completed the Mississippi River journey to the Gulf and named the vast territory "Louisiana" in honor of King Louis XIV. France now claimed land stretching from Quebec to the Gulf of Mexico.

**French Exploration**

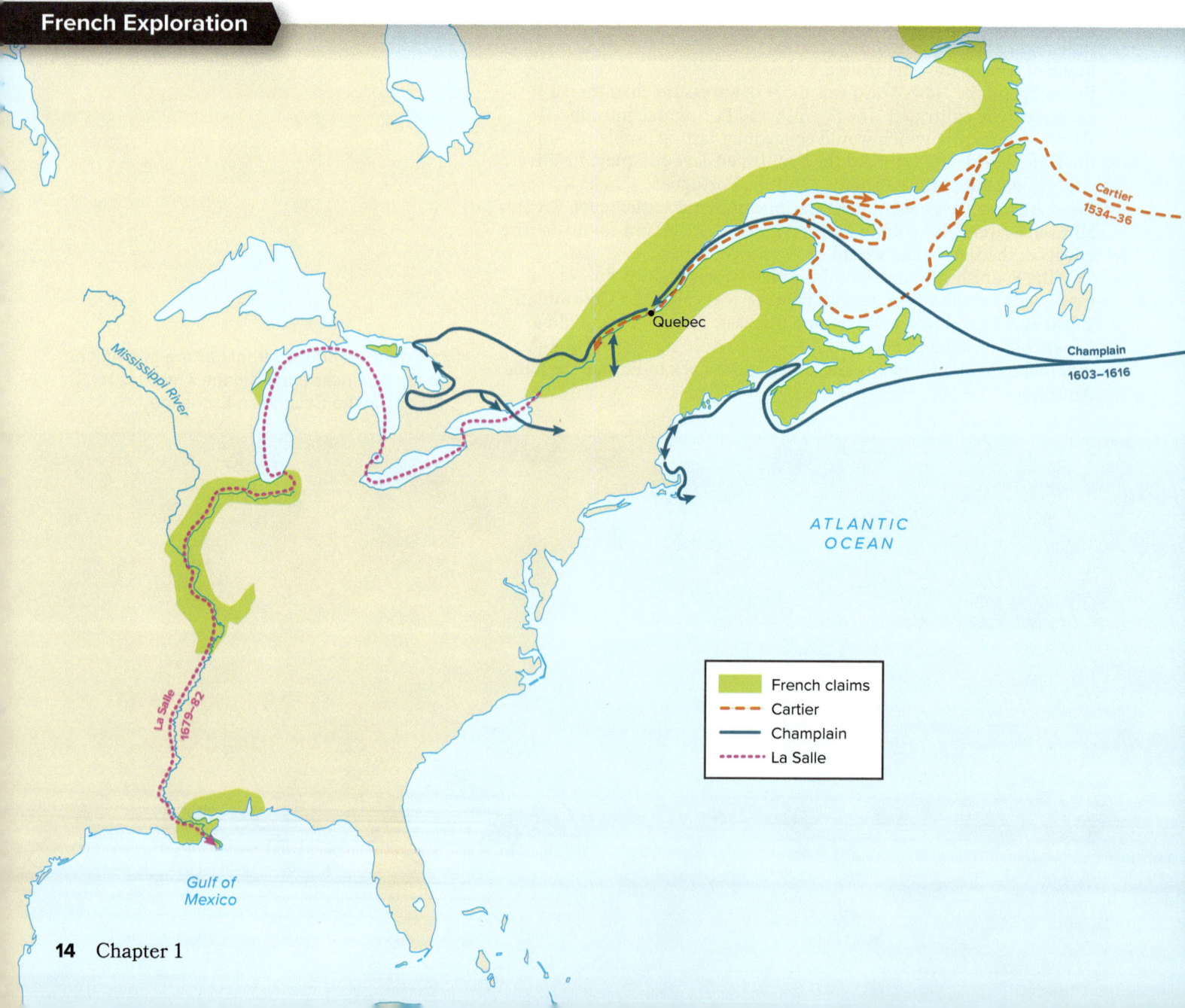

Cartier
1534–36

Champlain
1603–1616

Quebec

Mississippi River

La Salle
1679–82

ATLANTIC
OCEAN

Gulf of
Mexico

French claims
Cartier
Champlain
La Salle

The French set up trading posts along these waterways and established profitable enterprises in fur trading and fishing. Because of their focus on trade, the French developed cooperative relationships with the Native Americans. But New France had difficulty attracting settlers. French settlements were largely dependent on the mother country (the country from which the settlers came) for their success, and the king exercised complete control over the colonies. The long Canadian winters left few farm goods to export, and fishing and fur trading were more suited for frontiersmen than for farmers and merchants. In addition, dissenters from Roman Catholicism were not allowed to settle in New France. Because of this, the Huguenots, a skilled, hardworking group of French Protestants, were banned from the colony. Many would eventually settle in the English colonies to Canada's south to flee French persecution.

## THE NETHERLANDS

The Netherlands, long known for its vibrant commercial trade, joined the competition. In 1609 the Dutch East India Company hired English navigator **Henry Hudson** to search for a Northwest Passage to Asia. He entered New York Harbor and sailed up the river that now bears his name. He claimed the land for Holland, and the colony of New Netherlands was established. Like the French, the Dutch in New Netherlands sought to establish trade with the Native Americans for goods that could be sent back to Europe.

**Did You Know?**

The Netherlands is also known as Holland. The people are Dutch and speak Dutch. The country has two capital cities—Amsterdam (the official capital) and The Hague (the seat of government).

---

## Comprehension Check 1.2

1. The nation of ____ was the first to find a sea route to the Far East by sailing around Africa.

   **A** Spain

   **B** France

   **C** Portugal

2. The first Europeans thought to set foot in the Americas were ____.

   **A** Vikings

   **B** Spanish

   **C** English

3. Columbus differed from most educated Europeans of his time by believing that the world was round.

   True

   False

4. The Spanish explorer who first saw the Grand Canyon was ____.

   **A** Juan Ponce de León

   **B** Hernando de Soto

   **C** Francisco de Coronado

5. French settlement in North America was concentrated along the ____.

   **A** Atlantic Coast

   **B** St. Lawrence River, Great Lakes, and Mississippi River

   **C** Appalachian Mountains

### MAKING CONNECTIONS

6. How did the Crusades, the Renaissance, and the Reformation each contribute to the Age of Exploration?

GUIDING QUESTIONS

- Who were the early English explorers of North America?
- Why did the English colonize North America?
- How did Jamestown develop?

▼ Sir Francis Drake

## 1.3 English Exploration and Colonization

**Why did the English explore and colonize North America?**

## Early English Explorers

England was not idle during the race to Asia. In 1497 the Italian explorer Giovanni Caboto—known to the English for whom he sailed as **John Cabot**—reached Newfoundland, Canada, in his search for a passage to China. His discovery changed the course of history, for it provided the basis for England's claim to North America.

By the late sixteenth century, the Spanish shiploads of gold and silver coming from the New World heightened French, English, and Dutch envy of Spain. Additionally, Spain's Roman Catholic king, Philip II, was bent on crushing Protestantism in western Europe. His army, funded by gold from Mexico and silver from Peru, was the largest, best-equipped in Europe. Envy over Spain's wealth and bitterness over Spain's military threat made Spanish New World outposts a tempting target for Protestant sea captains like England's **Sir Francis Drake**.

Drake was the most famous admiral during Queen Elizabeth I's rule. He and other commanders targeted, attacked, and often plundered Spanish ships in the New World. They called themselves Sea Dogs. The Spanish viewed them as pirates. In 1577 Drake followed the course around South America taken by Magellan a half century earlier. Drake looted Spanish outposts in the Pacific and, failing to find a northern sea route back to the Atlantic, sailed from California westward to England. The circumnavigator reached England again in 1580, his ship laden with Spanish treasure.

The rights to exploring and claiming lands in the Western Hemisphere were determined by a ruling of Pope Alexander VI and later settled by the Treaty of Tordesillas. Its "**line of demarcation**," giving Portugal rights to lands east of the line and Spain rights to lands west of the line, would have shut the English out of the Americas. Sailing for the honor of England, Drake was determined to challenge this ruling that gave Spain a monopoly on the Americas. However, Drake's attention quickly turned back to his homeland when, in 1586, King Philip II began amassing a huge fleet to conquer Protestant England. The outcome of this conflict would determine not only the fate of the island kingdom but also who would colonize most of North America—Catholic Spain or Protestant England.

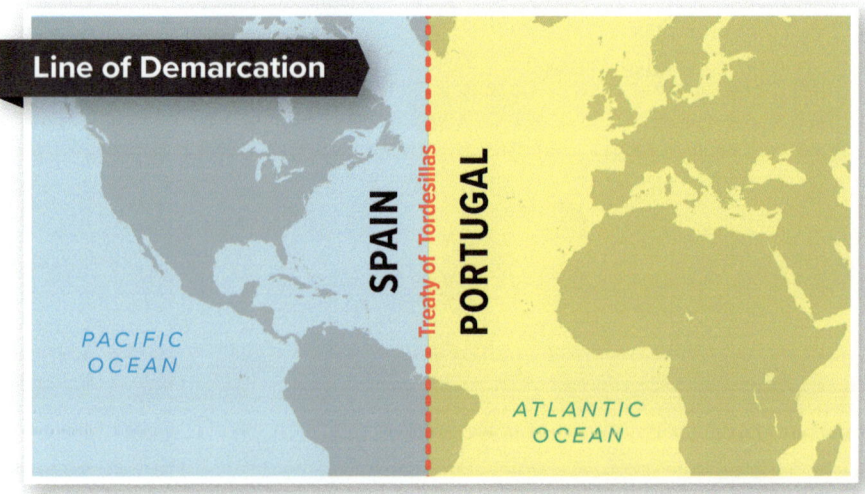

Line of Demarcation

In 1588 the huge **Spanish Armada** entered the English Channel. Drake's use of fire ships (ships filled with pitch and gunpowder which were set on fire and sailed into the Spanish fleet) caused much of the armada to scatter. The Spanish attempted to outrun English guns by sailing around Ireland but were devastated when a fierce storm, which the relieved English later called the "Protestant Wind," destroyed much of Spain's fleet. Philip's dream of conquering Protestant England lay amid the wreckage of the armada.

The defeat of the Spanish Armada was dramatic and decisive. It secured the future for Protestants in England. It also brought about the end of the Spanish century and the beginning of English dominance on the seas and eventually in North America.

Queen Elizabeth I gave **Sir Walter Raleigh** permission to plant a colony in the land he called Virginia in honor of Queen Elizabeth, the "virgin queen." Although Raleigh himself never came to North America, he sponsored an expedition of colonists that settled on Roanoke Island along North Carolina's Outer Banks. The colony was short-lived. After wintering on the island, the colonists encountered rough treatment from neighboring Native Americans and threats of a Spanish attack. The English abandoned Roanoke in 1586.

The determined Raleigh financed a second group to Roanoke Island in 1587 under the command of John White. Unfortunately, the colonists arrived too late in the summer to plant crops. With the prospect of a lean winter, they urged White to return to England for supplies. Once he reached England, however, the war with Spain delayed his return until 1590. When White returned, the little colony had disappeared. All he found was a single word carved on a tree where the village had once stood— "Croatoan." The Croatans were a tribe of Native Americans in the area. The fate of the "Lost Colony" has never been determined. Perhaps they were killed or captured by Native Americans. Perhaps they joined a nearby tribe. When Elizabeth I died in 1603, no trace of her colonizing efforts remained in the hostile wilderness that bore her name.

▲ The Spanish Armada being driven from Calais by fire

◄ Watercolor by John White, commander of the second group of settlers at Roanoke Island, of a Native American man, entitled *The manner of their attire and painting themselves*, from sometime between 1585 and 1593. White made these watercolors on voyages to Virginia (now North Carolina) in the 1580s.

# Why the English Came

## Personal Wealth

The English came to America for many reasons. First, many of them were fortune seekers drawn by dreams of quick riches. When the gold and silver did not appear, the settlers took advantage of the many resources found in America. Tobacco, rice, lumber, pine tar, indigo, and furs became valuable exports, enriching individuals, England, and the colonies.

## Land

Second, some traveled to the colonies for the opportunity to own land. In England, wealthy families owned much of the land. Families did not sell their land to anyone else, and only the firstborn inherited land. Younger family members and most other Englishmen had little hope of owning property. However, the English saw America as a source of abundant available land.

## Political Freedom

Third was the desire for political freedom. The Magna Carta, signed by King John in 1215, had limited the power of the English monarch. It also guaranteed certain basic rights to the nobility, but most people remained unprotected from government abuse. For example, James I and Charles I tried to strengthen royal power at the expense of personal liberty. As a result, many settlers went to America to escape oppressive leaders.

## Adventure

A fourth reason settlers came to America was a longing for adventure. However, most found that this adventure included great hardships and difficulty. The costs were often high for the first colonists.

## Mercantilism

A fifth motivation for establishing colonies was to increase the wealth and power of the mother country. An economic system known as **mercantilism** guided most European nations during the 1600s and 1700s. Mercantilism believed that a nation's wealth consisted of precious metals, especially gold. This economic philosophy said that a country should increase its wealth by increasing its gold surplus. The desire for gold led to numerous conflicts between nations, seen especially in the efforts of France and England to separate Spain from its treasures. Mercantilism led to the desire to build colonial empires that would serve as sources of riches and raw materials used to manufacture goods. The colonies would serve as markets for those goods. By exporting more than they imported, mercantilist nations could greatly increase their wealth.

## Religious Freedom

Lastly, religious freedom became a powerful force in attracting settlers to America. Most who immigrated for religious liberty wanted the freedom to structure their own societies as they saw fit. As a result, these settlers viewed America as a haven where they could establish communities and worship as they felt the Bible commanded. This reason for settlement distinguished the colonial heritage of the United States from that of new colonies established in other regions of the New World.

# Jamestown

Sir Walter Raleigh's Roanoke expedition was the last individual effort by an Englishman to establish a colony. Later attempts were made by **joint-stock companies**. These companies raised large amounts of money to fund colonies by selling stock to investors in return for a share of any profits. In 1606 King James I granted a charter to the London Company, permitting it to colonize Virginia.

The London Company (later renamed the Virginia Company) sent 104 men and boys to America. After a rough ocean passage, they reached the Chesapeake Bay in May 1607. They named the river the James River and their fort Jamestown. It became the first permanent English settlement in America.

The first years were bitter ones for the colony. Disease took a devastating toll. By the end of the first winter, over half of the colonists had died in the hostile land.

At first, relations between the English and the Powhatan Confederacy were friendly enough, but as the colonists began to clear more land, the Powhatans sent war parties to attack. A shaky peace came to the area in 1614 with the marriage of Pocahontas, the daughter of the Powhatan chief, to Englishman John Rolfe. The Native American princess converted to Christianity and made a celebrated tour of England. The trip ended tragically when she died from disease right before she was to return to Virginia.

▼ The wedding of Pocahontas and John Rolfe

▼ Recreation of the fort at Jamestown, Virginia

▲ Captain John Smith

Fever from disease was not the only fever present in the colonies—gold fever consumed much of the settlers' time and resources. As a result, they neglected and even scorned planting and hunting. This attitude threatened the colony with starvation. Captain **John Smith** worked to enforce the kind of discipline necessary for the survival of Jamestown, drawing from the biblical principle that, regardless of social class or status, only those who work should eat. Smith also improved the settlers' relations with Powhatan's men, who taught the settlers how to grow maize and melons.

In 1609 hundreds of new colonists arrived in Jamestown. Unfortunately, that same year a gunpowder explosion forced the severely injured John Smith to return to England. The winter of 1609–10 was known as the "starving time" because death due to hunger became common. Settlers ate horses, dogs, cats, mice, and snakes. Some even ate the bodies of the dead settlers. Roughly 90 percent of the colony died during that terrible winter. Survivors were ready to abandon Jamestown by the spring. However, when three supply ships arrived, they decided to remain. Although many more hardships awaited the settlement, the starving time was over.

In 1618 the Virginia Company granted colonists the right to elect a law-making body. The **House of Burgesses** became the first self-governing assembly of colonists in America. By 1619, women and families began to arrive in the colony. Over the next three years Virginia's population grew to about 4,500.

As the population of Jamestown grew and spread inland, the Powhatans grew increasingly concerned. On Good Friday morning in 1622, warriors attacked and killed more than three hundred colonists. The Virginians gathered their forces and exacted heavy revenge. Another attack on the settlers resulted in a treaty restricting where the English could settle, but the treaty was soon violated. For these reasons and others, King James I dismantled the company, and Virginia became a royal colony in 1624.

## Comprehension Check 1.3

1. The English "Sea Dog" who raided Spanish ports in South America and who circumnavigated the globe was ____.
   A Sir Francis Drake
   B Sir Walter Raleigh
   C Captain John Smith

2. Mercantilism says that ____.
   A a nation's wealth is measured in the amount of gold and other precious metals that it has
   B a nation gains gold either by taking it from someone else or by trading goods for gold
   C colonies are important for providing raw materials and markets for manufactured goods
   D all of the above

3. For what purpose was Jamestown primarily founded?
   A religious freedom
   B political freedom
   C economic gain

4. Captain John Smith brought much-needed discipline to Jamestown and required men to work.
   True
   False

5. Each of the following is true about the Jamestown colony except that ____.
   A John Rolfe's marriage to Pocahontas improved relations with the Powhatans for a time
   B colonists faced disease and starvation in its early years
   C Powhatan attacks decreased as Jamestown's population grew and moved inland
   D the Virginia House of Burgesses was the first self-governing assembly in America

### MAKING CONNECTIONS

6. What was the significance of the English defeat of the Spanish Armada?

7. What factors led the English to come to America?

## GUIDING QUESTIONS

- How did exploration lead to the arrival of Africans in the Americas?
- What was the trip to the Americas like for captured Africans?

## Western Africa

From about 600 to 1600, a succession of empires flourished in West Africa—first Ghana, then Mali, and later the Songhai. Each was larger than the previous one. West Africa was a land of thriving trade, diverse societies, and many wealthy states.

The empire of Ghana was located between the Sahara to the north and the African rainforests to the south. Ghana amassed great wealth through trading and taxing copper, gold, salt, and ivory as well as slaves. The discovery of new gold mines, trade routes that bypassed Ghana, wars, and soil depletion led to the empire's collapse by the early 1200s.

The Mali Empire conquered Ghana in 1240. Mali reached its height under Mansa Musa who increased its wealth by expanding the salt, gold, and ivory trade. On a pilgrimage to Mecca in 1324, Musa's traveling party included thousands of people and dozens of camels, each carrying three hundred pounds of gold. He spent so much gold in Egypt that its value there declined for years. Musa turned the city of **Timbuktu** into a center of Islamic learning and culture.

As the Mali Empire began to decline in the mid-1400s, the Songhai Empire along the Niger River grew in power. King Sunni Ali seized Timbuktu in 1468 and conquered the remainder of the Mali Empire. Using his armored cavalry and northern Africa's only navy, he then pushed north and south, extending his empire farther than Ghana or Mali. With wealth from the trade routes, rulers conquered new territory. The Songhai became the largest West African empire in history. But in 1591 the spear-throwing Songhai army was defeated by the Moroccan army and its Portuguese-supplied muskets.

Slavery existed in African society, as it did in other parts of the world, even before the Europeans established trade with the continent. Often prisoners of war were held for ransom or became slaves of the conquering people. Debtor slavery and military slavery were also common. Slave labor was often used in salt and gold mines. West African slavery changed with the arrival of Muslim traders who exchanged horses, cotton, and other goods for enslaved people. Soon Islam became the dominant religion in North and West Africa.

West Africans knew little about Europeans before the 1400s when Portuguese traders established outposts on Africa's coast. In addition to trading goods, the Portuguese began purchasing slaves. At first, such transactions were limited to a small number of people bought from village chiefs, usually captives from rival groups. But soon the transatlantic slave trade exploded, and new slaves were captured by Africans to meet the demand.

Of the eight to ten million slaves who reached the American continents, more than three million went to Portuguese Brazil, about a million and a half went to the Spanish colonies, and over three million were imported to the British, French, and Dutch plantations in the Caribbean. Approximately half a million Africans were transported to the thirteen British colonies.

▼ Mosque in Timbuktu, Mali, West Africa, built in 1327

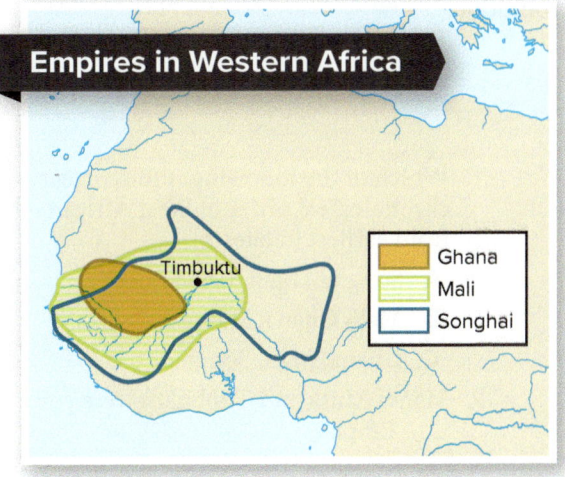

**Empires in Western Africa**

Timbuktu

| | |
|---|---|
| ▨ | Ghana |
| ▥ | Mali |
| ▢ | Songhai |

# The Middle Passage

In 1619 a Dutch ship arrived at Jamestown. No one could have foreseen its significance. John Rolfe simply recorded in his journal that "about the last of August . . . twenty [Africans]" arrived. The first Africans in British North America were treated like indentured servants, working for a time and then receiving their freedom. Gradually, though, racial distinctions were made among indentured servants, and blacks were placed in permanent bondage. Though the cost of a slave was about five times more than the cost of bringing an indentured servant to America, the slave's bondage was for life, and any children born to a slave became the property of the master.

The slaves' trip to the Americas typically began with a forced march, often led by traders who were also Africans, to the West African coast. This was the First Passage. The **Middle Passage** was the sea voyage that brought the slaves across the Atlantic to the Americas. As they boarded ships, they were crammed as closely as the captains thought possible, often stacked on top of one another or chained side by side. For weeks or even months they endured dirty, stifling, and wretched conditions. They were given little food and drink. Sometimes contagious diseases, such as smallpox, spread throughout the ship. The death toll was often enormous, and those who died or became ill were thrown overboard. While revolts on the slave ships were not common, slaves rebelled in other ways. Some committed suicide, and others refused to eat in the hope that they would die, thus spoiling the ship's "cargo" and profit. Roughly two million slaves died at sea during the Middle Passage.

The Final Passage referred to the sale of the slave to the slave owner. When the ships arrived at port in the Americas, slaves were fed and cleaned with oil to improve their appearance before being sold. Some were held longer for fear that they carried disease, and others were rejected because of their poor condition.

▲ Cutaway model of a typical slave ship

---

## Comprehension Check 1.4

1. Which of the following is the correct chronological order of West African empires from earliest to latest?

   **A** Songhai, Mali, Ghana

   **B** Mali, Ghana, Songhai

   **C** Ghana, Mali, Songhai

2. Mansa Musa and Timbuktu were parts of the _____ Empire.

   **A** Ghana

   **B** Mali

   **C** Songhai

3. The transatlantic slave trade resulted in eight to ten million Africans being transported and sold in the American continents.

   True

   False

4. The first Africans arrived in Jamestown in _____.

   **A** 1607

   **B** 1619

   **C** 1630

5. Acts of rebellion by slaves, such as refusing to eat or committing suicide, were uncommon during the Middle Passage.

   True

   False

### MAKING CONNECTIONS

6. How did trade influence West African cultures?

## Chapter Summary

### Introduction

- The worldview of historians affects their selection, interpretation, and evaluation of historical events and people.

- While every historian has a bias, valid interpretations must be based on historical evidence.

**TERMS**

historiography

**TERMS**

totem poles

petroglyphs

Mound Builders

animism

### 1.1 Pre-Columbian America

- Theories on how Native Americans came to the Americas include crossing the Bering Sea by boat, over an ice bridge, across a land bridge, or by sailing across the ocean.

- Native American groups from different regions developed different cultures and had different food sources, but all were able to demonstrate their God-given abilities and exercise a degree of dominion over Creation.

- Native American religions were contrary to biblical religion in many ways.

### 1.2 Age of Exploration

- The Crusades exposed Europeans to luxury goods from the Far East, and demand for these goods in Europe increased. The closure of the Silk Road caused European nations to begin searching for a sea route to the Far East.

- Renewed interest in scientific discovery during the Renaissance led to technological advances which enabled European nations to explore eastern and western sea routes to the Far East.

- The Reformation challenged the teaching of the Roman Catholic Church. Rivalry between Roman Catholic and Protestant nations and wars of religion motivated exploration and migration.

- While the Vikings were the first Europeans to land in America, the Spanish explorers established permanent settlements in North and South America. Disease, war, and enslavement nearly destroyed Native American groups.

- French exploration and settlement in North America was concentrated along waterways, including the St. Lawrence River, the Great Lakes, and the Mississippi River, and the fur trade was the primary economic activity. France's territory stretched from Quebec to the Gulf of Mexico, but New France had difficulty attracting settlers.

**TERMS**

compass

astrolabe

caravel

Leif Ericson

Christopher Columbus

Amerigo Vespucci

Hernando Cortés

Juan Ponce de León

Francisco de Coronado

Hernando de Soto

Columbian Exchange

encomienda system

St. Augustine

Jacques Cartier

Samuel de Champlain

Robert de La Salle

Henry Hudson

# CHAPTER **1** REVIEW

## Chapter Summary

**TERMS**

John Cabot

Sir Francis Drake

line of demarcation

Spanish Armada

Sir Walter Raleigh

mercantilism

joint-stock companies

John Smith

House of Burgesses

### 1.3 English Exploration and Colonization

- Sir Francis Drake challenged Spain's dominance of the seas and the Americas by attacking and robbing Spanish ships and looting Spanish outposts. Failing to find a sea route back to the Atlantic, he sailed westward to England, eventually circumnavigating the globe.

- King Philip II of Spain raised the Spanish Armada to conquer Protestant England, but the Armada was defeated, thus preserving Protestantism in England, ending a century of Spanish domination, and beginning the period of English domination of the seas and North America.

- Sir Walter Raleigh's attempt to form an English colony on Roanoke Island failed when its inhabitants mysteriously disappeared.

- Reasons the English came to America included seeking fortune, the opportunity to own land, political freedom, religious freedom, increasing the wealth and power of England, and adventure.

- Jamestown, England's first permanent colony in North America, was established in 1607 by a joint-stock company. Settlers faced many difficulties, including disease, starvation, and Powhatan attacks.

### 1.4 Early African Trade

- The Ghana Empire amassed great wealth through trading gold, copper, salt, ivory, and slaves, and by taxing goods that passed through its territory.

- During the Mali Empire, Mansa Musa developed Timbuktu into a leading center of Islamic learning and culture.

- The Songhai Empire conquered the Mali Empire and expanded, using its navy and armored cavalry. It was defeated by the Moroccan army.

- Slavery existed in West Africa before the arrival of the Europeans, but the arrival of Portuguese traders led to a vast transatlantic slave trade.

- The first Africans arrived in Jamestown in 1619 and may have been indentured servants rather than slaves. Eventually a distinction was made between servants and slaves, and blacks were placed in permanent bondage.

- Enslaved Africans faced brutal conditions on the Middle Passage from Africa to the Americas.

**TERMS**

Timbuktu

Middle Passage

## Chapter Review Questions

### RECALL

1. What is the study of the writing of history?

2. The crew of what explorer was the first to circumnavigate the globe?

3. What nation's North American territory extended from Quebec to the Gulf of Mexico?

4. What was the name of the Dutch settlement in North America? Along what river was this settlement?

5. What Englishman looted Spanish ports in the Pacific and circumnavigated the globe?

6. What Englishman established Roanoke Colony, which became known as the Lost Colony?

7. What was the first self-governing assembly of colonists in America called?

8. When did the first Africans arrive in Jamestown, and what was their status?

### UNDERSTAND

9. What are three ways worldview affects the way historians write history?

10. What determines whether a historical interpretation is valid?

11. What theories exist about how Native Americans got to the Americas?

12. Why did some Native American groups build mounds?

13. What impact did the arrival of Spanish explorers have on the Native American populations of the Americas?

14. What were three factors that helped make the Age of Exploration possible? How did each factor lead to greater exploration?

15. What things flowed from the Americas to Europe and Africa and from Europe and Africa to the Americas as a result of the Columbian Exchange?

16. Why did New France have difficulty attracting settlers?

17. What was the significance of the defeat of the Spanish Armada?

18. What were six reasons why the English came to America?

19. How did mercantilism lead to the creation of colonies?

20. What challenges did the early Jamestown settlers face?

21. How had the relationship between the Virginians and the Powhatans changed by 1622?

22. How did the empire of Ghana gain its wealth?

23. Describe Timbuktu during the rule of Mansa Musa.

24. How was the Songhai Empire able to expand, and how was it defeated?

25. What was the Middle Passage?

26. How did the Age of Exploration lead to the arrival of slaves in the Americas?

### THINK ABOUT IT

27. In what ways did Native American cultures demonstrate their God-given creativity and dominion over the earth?

28. In what ways were Native American religions contrary to biblical religion?

29. How did the Middle Passage in particular violate the dignity of enslaved Africans as image bearers of God?

▲ Hernando de Soto discovering the Mississippi River on May 21, 1541

# 2 The Thirteen Colonies

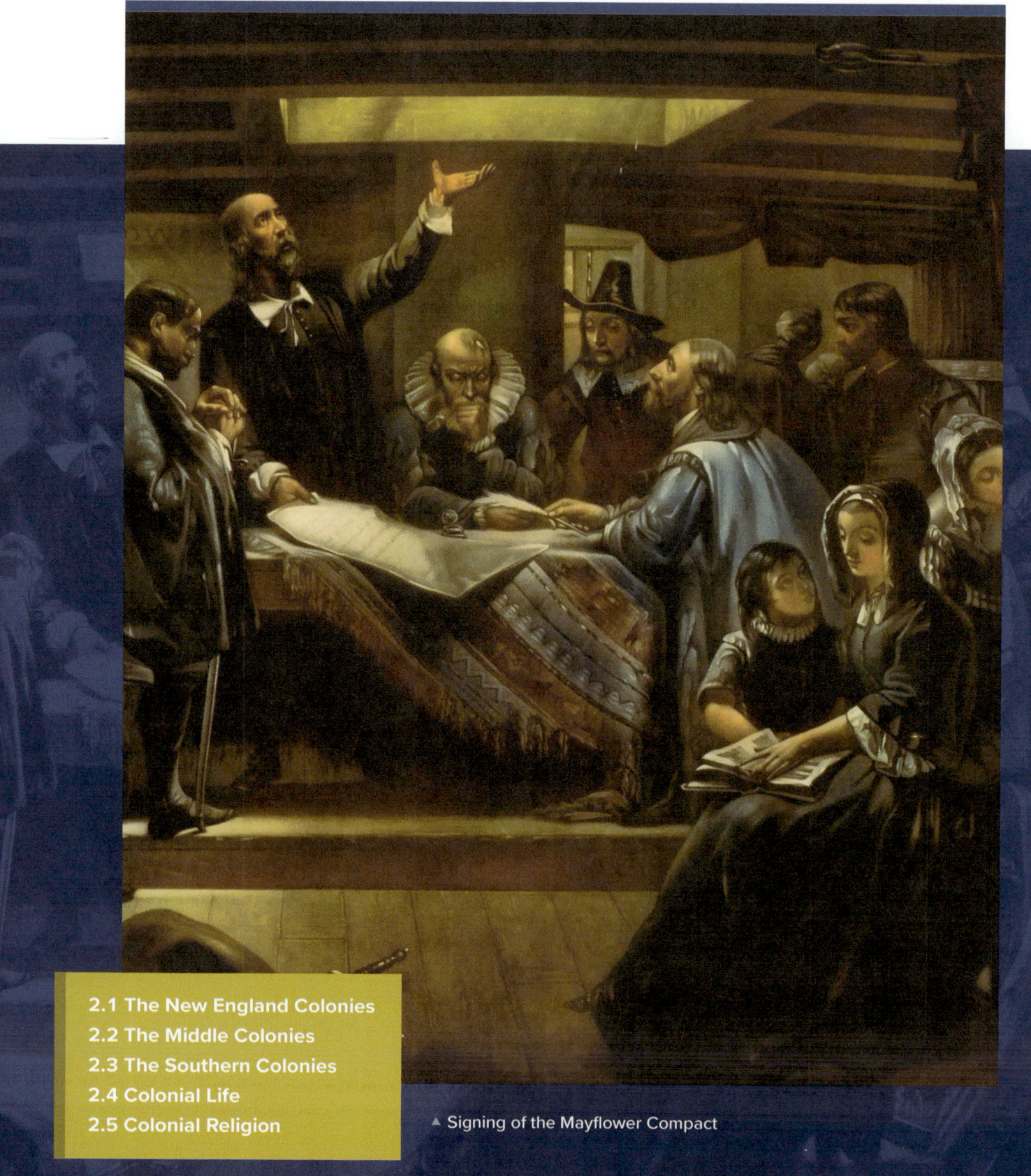

2.1 The New England Colonies
2.2 The Middle Colonies
2.3 The Southern Colonies
2.4 Colonial Life
2.5 Colonial Religion

▲ Signing of the Mayflower Compact

By 1700 the eastern coast of North America was dotted with many thriving English settlements. The English colonies can best be studied by arranging them geographically. The four northernmost colonies were known as New England. The four colonies below New England were the middle colonies. The remaining five were the southern colonies.

There were three types of English colonies: charter, proprietary, and royal. A **charter colony** was one governed by a trade company (such as the Virginia Company) that received authorization from the king. In a **proprietary colony**, such as Pennsylvania, the king gave control of the colony to one or more proprietors. A **royal colony** was controlled directly by the king, who appointed a governor. Most charter and proprietary colonies became royal colonies during the 1700s.

## 2.1 The New England Colonies

How were the New England colonies founded?

## Massachusetts

To study the settling of Massachusetts by the Pilgrims and then a decade later by the Puritans, one must understand the religious situation in England at that time. The official church was the Church of England, or the Anglican Church. Although technically Protestant, many traces of Roman Catholicism remained in its rituals. Two groups, the Puritans and the Separatists, emerged in opposition to those problems. The **Puritans** wanted to purify the Anglican church from within. They pushed for reforms that would rid England of Roman Catholic influences and bring greater spiritual vitality to the nation.

The **Separatists** believed that Christians needed to separate from the Anglican Church. They thought each congregation should be independent of other churches, free to worship and serve God without interference. Because the Separatists refused to attend Anglican churches or recognize the authority of the official state church, they were harassed, and many were jailed.

### Plymouth

In 1607 one congregation of Separatists from England migrated to the Netherlands because of the religious tolerance there. After a decade in Holland, however, they noticed that the worldly atmosphere and hardships of life in Holland threatened the spiritual and physical well-being of their children and their congregation, and that few other English families were willing to join them. Because of these concerns, the Separatists obtained a land grant from the Virginia Company to settle in America. Under the terms of the agreement, they would receive land and the right to worship freely.

In September 1620 these Separatists, known as "Pilgrims," boarded the *Mayflower* and left Plymouth, England, bound for America with a charter to settle in Virginia. Aboard were 102 passengers, about half of whom were Separatists. The Pilgrims referred to the other travelers as "strangers." The ocean passage was stormy, and the little *Mayflower* was blown far north of the Virginia colony to Cape Cod, Massachusetts. Another attempt to reach Virginia was also beaten back by a storm. By then it was November, and scant provisions remained. Consequently, the Pilgrims decided to settle in Massachusetts.

GUIDING QUESTIONS

- Why did the Separatists and Puritans come to New England?

- How were the Separatists and Puritans different?

- Why were the colonies of Rhode Island, Connecticut, and New Hampshire founded separately from Massachusetts?

- How did the colonists make a living in New England?

**The New England Colonies**

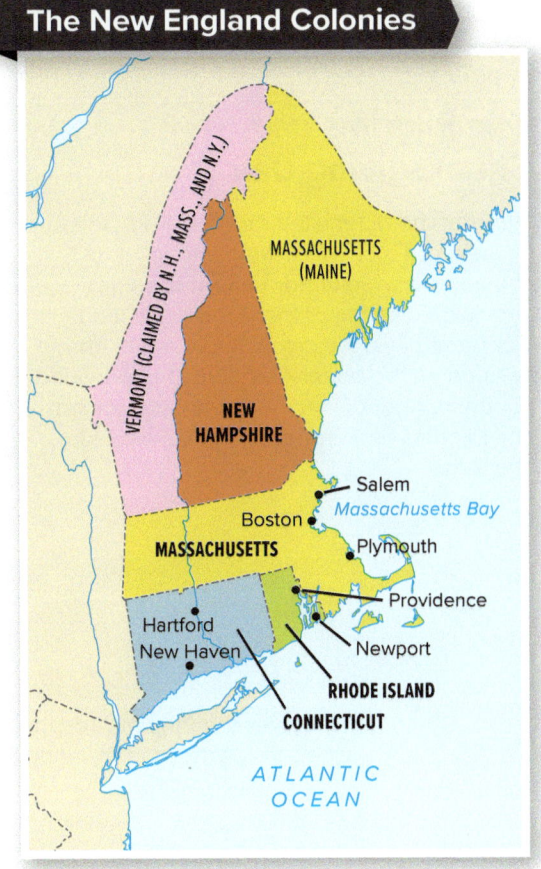

The Pilgrims arriving in Plymouth, Massachusetts

## The Pilgrims *and* Thanksgiving Day

After the bitter winter of 1620–21, the harvest of 1621 was a welcome relief to the colonists. Governor William Bradford proclaimed a time of thanksgiving to God. For three days, the colony celebrated. They feasted on the bounty that God had provided for them. About ninety Wampanoags joined the Pilgrims and brought fresh venison for the feast.

 **Analyzing Sources**

What was the Pilgrims' response when they arrived in Plymouth?

A scouting party went ashore and chose a site that Captain John Smith had named "Plymouth" during his New England trip six years earlier. Because they were outside the area claimed by the Virginia Company, the leaders devised a contract of government to guide themselves. This agreement, known as the **Mayflower Compact**, bound the settlers to submit to the colony's laws and duly elected leadership. It was the first document of self-government in America. The Pilgrims were later granted a charter giving them the right to live and establish a government of their own in Plymouth.

**William Bradford**, who became governor of Plymouth in 1621, later wrote the history of the colony. In *Of Plymouth Plantation* he recorded the spirit, courage, and faith of the Pilgrim families:

> *Being thus arrived in a good harbor, and brought safe to land, they fell upon their knees and blessed the God of heaven, who had brought them over the vast and furious ocean, and delivered them from all the perils and miseries thereof, again to set their feet on the firm and stable earth, their proper element.* — **WILLIAM BRADFORD**

The first months at Plymouth were devastating. Half of the little group died before spring. Following that first winter, however, the colony began to prosper. Friendly Indians helped the colony raise native crops of maize (corn), pumpkins, and squash. Under the leadership of Governor Bradford, Plymouth gained a firm foothold.

Plymouth Colony grew steadily, though after 1630 it would be surpassed in size and influence by the Puritan Massachusetts Bay settlement in Boston. In 1691 Plymouth would merge with the rest of Massachusetts.

## Massachusetts Bay

In 1630 a fleet of about a dozen ships carrying a thousand Puritans arrived in America to establish the Massachusetts Bay Colony. The Puritans set out to apply biblical principles to every aspect of their society. The group brought their charter to settle the colony with them, making it possible to establish a self-governing commonwealth. Over the next decade, thousands of settlers sailed from England to various American colonies. With the flood of new arrivals, towns quickly emerged.

**John Winthrop**, the governor of the Puritan colony, preached "A Model of Christian Charity" aboard the ship before going ashore. Winthrop declared that the colony had been given an opportunity and responsibility to represent God and that every member should contribute to its success:

> *We shall be as a city upon a hill. The eyes of all people are upon us.*
> — **JOHN WINTHROP**

As many as twenty thousand settlers arrived in Massachusetts in the 1630s, and Boston soon became the largest city on the continent. Those colonists did not all stay in Massachusetts, however. Two factors—disagreement and expansion—led them to settle other colonies throughout New England.

# Rhode Island, Connecticut, and New Hampshire

Disagreement with the Puritan leadership of Massachusetts contributed to the formation of Rhode Island. In 1631 **Roger Williams** arrived in Massachusetts and soon gained a reputation as a troublemaker for his unusual ideas. He denounced his fellow Puritans for not severing all ties with the Anglican Church. Williams preached about a "pure church." According to Williams, preaching and praying were worship activities reserved only for true Christians. He therefore claimed that the unregenerate should not be allowed to attend church services and that family prayers were wrong because at least one family member was likely not a true believer.

## Squanto and Samoset

In March 1621 the settlers in Plymouth received a surprise visit from Samoset, an Abenaki chief. He greeted them in broken English he had learned from contact with English fishermen. A few days later, Samoset returned with **Squanto**, a Pawtuxet man. Squanto had been captured by an Englishman in 1614 and sold as a slave in Spain but had escaped and made his way to England. In 1619 he had returned to his homeland to discover that his and neighboring tribes had been wiped out by a plague.

Squanto helped the settlers learn about crop fertilization. He also led them to areas where they could catch fish and eels to supplement their diet. Squanto worked to establish peace between the settlers and the neighboring Wampanoag tribe, leading to a peace that endured for nearly fifty years.

## Analyzing Sources

What do you think Winthrop meant when he said Massachusetts Bay would be a "city upon a hill"?

▶ Roger Williams

Though Williams did believe that government should enforce laws that prohibited theft, murder, adultery, and other immoral acts, he advocated complete separation of church and state. Williams did not want the state to support a specific church or doctrinal system. He also argued that a person's religious views should not affect his influence in society and that it did not matter whether those who governed were Christian or not, but rather that they fulfilled their government responsibilities to protect people from physical harm or theft. Williams also declared that it was a "national sin" for England to take Native American land without paying for it. Williams's ideas angered Puritan leaders. As a result, in 1635 the Massachusetts General Court ordered his arrest and return to England. Williams fled the colony and wintered with the Narragansetts. In the spring, he and his followers established Providence, a settlement on land he purchased from the Narragansetts. This town later became the capital of Rhode Island.

**Anne Hutchinson**, another leading dissenter, arrived in Massachusetts in 1634. She hosted regular gatherings at her home to discuss Sunday sermons. Later, Hutchinson went far beyond simply reviewing sermons. She taught what Puritan leaders considered heresy (religious beliefs contrary to Christian teachings). For example, she proclaimed that outward obedience to the Scriptures was unnecessary to demonstrate an inward relationship with God. Furthermore, she taught that God had given her direct revelation that was more important than the Bible. When the Puritan leaders attempted to counsel her, she was uncooperative. A year later, the General Court voted to banish her from the colony. A few supporters went with her to Rhode Island, where they established a small settlement in 1638.

In 1636 the Puritan minister **Thomas Hooker** disagreed with the practice in Massachusetts Bay of limiting voting rights to male church members with property. He supported a more universal suffrage that would be independent of church membership, so he moved his congregation into the Connecticut River Valley and established the colony of Connecticut. The fertile land and boundless forest drew additional settlers west from Massachusetts. Eventually, the settlements there united politically under the **Fundamental Orders of Connecticut** (1639). This document has been called the first written constitution in America and established a framework for representative self-government.

In 1638 the first significant settlement in New Hampshire, still controlled by Massachusetts, was established. New Hampshire would become a separate royal colony in 1679.

▶ (top) Anne Hutchinson; (bottom) Thomas Hooker and Puritan group arriving in Connecticut

# The Economy of the New England Colonies

Because of its rocky soil and short growing season, New England did not develop a cash crop or plantation economy. Instead, New England farmers planted wheat, rye, corn, potatoes, and beans and raised a small number of livestock such as oxen, sheep, and pigs. They used what they produced to provide for their own families, and any surplus was usually sold locally rather than exported. Because farming was done on a small scale, there was little demand for indentured servants or slaves. Family members were the source of labor for the typical New England subsistence farm.

Fishing off the coast of Maine, New Hampshire, Massachusetts, and Newfoundland was another important economic activity in New England. Between 1641 and 1675 the number of fish caught and sold multiplied ten times. Whaling also became a prosperous trade, and whale oil and products made from whale bones were valuable exports. New England also became the shipbuilding center of North America. An abundance of timber meant that a ship could be produced in Boston for half the cost of one built in London.

New England merchants and shippers developed trade with the West Indies as part of the **triangular trade** routes (trade between Africa, the Americas, and Europe). Products produced in New England were traded for rum, sugar, tobacco, cloth, and tools. New England shippers also made large profits trading goods that were neither produced nor consumed in New England. Thus, even though slavery was not common in New England, New England shippers profited from trade between Africa (which supplied slaves), America, and Europe.

▲ Whaling off the coast of New Bedford, Massachusetts

## Triangular Trade

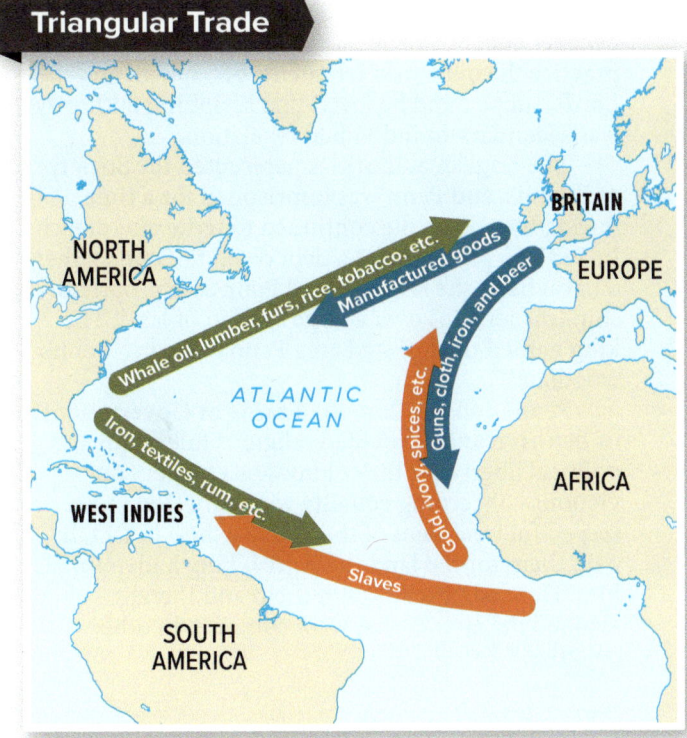

NORTH AMERICA

Whale oil, lumber, furs, rice, tobacco, etc.

Manufactured goods

BRITAIN

EUROPE

Guns, cloth, iron, and beer

ATLANTIC OCEAN

Gold, ivory, spices, etc.

Iron, textiles, rum, etc.

WEST INDIES

Slaves

AFRICA

SOUTH AMERICA

┌ **Comprehension Check 2.1**

1. Before coming to America, the Pilgrims had migrated to ____ because of that nation's religious toleration.

   A the Netherlands

   B France

   C Scotland

2. Massachusetts Bay Colony was described as a "city upon a hill" by Governor ____.

   A Thomas Hooker

   B William Bradford

   C John Winthrop

3. The Fundamental Orders of Connecticut was the first written constitution in America.

   True

   False

4. Roger Williams and Anne Hutchinson are associated with the founding of ____.

   A New Hampshire

   B Rhode Island

   C Connecticut

**Making Connections**

5. How did the Separatists and Puritans differ from one another?

6. What goods were shipped on each leg of the triangular trade routes?

- How did New York and New Jersey become colonies?
- How did the founding of Pennsylvania reflect changing ideas about religious freedom?
- What was the economy of the middle colonies like?

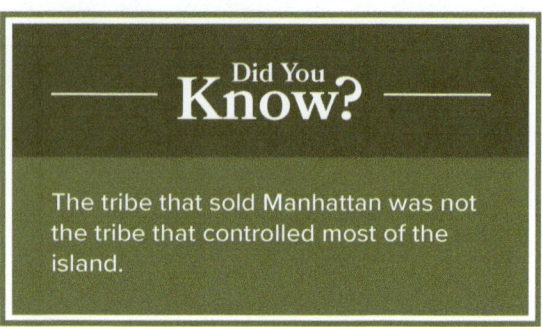

### Did You Know?

The tribe that sold Manhattan was not the tribe that controlled most of the island.

## 2.2 The Middle Colonies

**How were the middle colonies founded?**

No other region of the colonies reflected such cultural diversity as the middle colonies. English, Dutch, Germans, French, Finns, Scots, and Swedes all found a home in the stretch of land between the New England and the southern colonies.

## New York and New Jersey

New York began in 1609 when Henry Hudson claimed the land for the Dutch. It became known as New Netherland. In 1626 Peter Minuit purchased Manhattan Island from a group of Native Americans with a small amount of cloth and trinkets, and New Amsterdam (now New York City) was born. People from many different cultures and religions settled in the colony. When Peter Stuyvesant arrived as governor in 1647, he attempted to pass laws to curtail immorality and ban Jews and non-Reformed Protestants from the colony. However, the Dutch West India Company insisted that general toleration was best for business and reminded Stuyvesant that Jews had invested much money in the company.

The English were not content to have the Dutch as neighbors in the New World. Consequently, they invaded New Netherland in 1664. The Dutch chose to surrender rather than resist. The area was renamed New York to honor the Duke of York, brother of King Charles II. The duke gave the southern portion of his new territory to two friends. Eventually, the area became a royal colony and was named New Jersey.

## Pennsylvania and Delaware

Pennsylvania was the product of **William Penn**'s vision and labor. He was a member of the Society of Friends, or Quakers. Like the Puritans, Quakers objected to certain teachings of the Church of England. Unlike the Puritans, the Quakers abandoned many biblical teachings. For example, they held that a believer could achieve perfection in this life, did not practice the outward sacraments of baptism and the Lord's Supper, and believed that scriptural authority was secondary to individual revelation.

The English authorities persecuted the Society of Friends, and Penn was imprisoned for a time. Following his release, he continued to write and preach. In 1681, as payment for a debt owed to Penn's father, a naval hero, the king granted Penn sole proprietorship (ownership) over a large section of land. The king named the forested area Pennsylvania ("Penn's woodland").

Penn's constitution, the **Frame of Government of Pennsylvania**, provided religious toleration and political liberty for the colony. His Quaker convictions concerning equality were reflected in his respectful treatment of the native tribes. In fact, he paid them for the land the British king had granted him. He made friends with them and thereby avoided the attacks that were common in other colonies.

### The Middle Colonies

Lake Ontario

Connecticut River

Albany

**NEW YORK**

**PENNSYLVANIA**

New York City

Philadelphia

Wilmington

**NEW JERSEY**

*Delaware Bay*

**DELAWARE**

*Chesapeake Bay*

▼ William Penn

The open political and religious environment, the fertile land, and Penn's advertising in England and Germany attracted thousands to the colony. Philadelphia—the "city of brotherly love"—rapidly became an important trading center. As more and more non-Quakers moved into the colony, Quaker values became less evident.

William Penn's land also included what is now Delaware. The Swedish settlers there resisted being ruled by Quakers in Philadelphia. The area was eventually granted the right to form its own legislature and became a separate colony in 1704. However, it continued to have the same governor as Pennsylvania until 1776.

## The Economy of the Middle Colonies

Unlike New England, the middle colonies possessed vast amounts of fertile soil, a landscape of gently rolling hills, and a relatively long growing season. These conditions were ideally suited for growing grains and raising livestock. The middle colonies were known as the "bread colonies" because they produced most of the grain for the colonies and for export. Families typically worked their own farms, and indentured servants were common.

Because of its larger farms, longer growing season, better soil, and network of navigable inland rivers, farmers from the middle colonies could produce larger crops and herds for a lower cost than New England farmers. Trade with the West Indies grew tremendously. The ports of New York and Philadelphia grew into major shipping centers, and Philadelphia soon became the largest city in the colonies.

Abundant forests provided timber for shipbuilding, furniture, barrels, and other wood products. Flowing rivers powered sawmills. In western Pennsylvania and upper New York, frontier settlers continued to trap furs and trade with the Native Americans.

◄ 1799 engraving of Second Street in Philadelphia, Pennsylvania

---

### Comprehension Check 2.2

1. Before the English took control, the colony of New York belonged to _____.

   A the Netherlands

   B France

   C Sweden

2. Each of the following is true about Pennsylvania except that _____.

   A its founder was determined to treat the Native Americans with respect and to pay them for their land

   B it was open to settlement only by Quakers and no other religious groups

   C the land was given to William Penn by the king as payment for a debt owed to Penn's father

3. The colony of _____ split from Pennsylvania and created its own legislature.

   A New Jersey

   B New York

   C Delaware

4. The primary agricultural crop of the middle colonies was _____.

   A grain

   B tobacco

   C rice

**MAKING CONNECTIONS**

5. How did the economy of the middle colonies differ from the economy of New England?

▲ Dried tobacco leaves

## GUIDING QUESTIONS

- What was the culture of colonial Virginia like?
- What was unique about the founding of Maryland?
- How were the Carolinas settled?
- What was unique about the establishment of Georgia?
- What was the economy of the southern colonies like?

### The Southern Colonies

MARYLAND
— Baltimore

VIRGINIA
Williamsburg
— St. Mary's

Jamestown
*Chesapeake Bay*

*Roanoke Island*

NORTH CAROLINA

SOUTH CAROLINA

GEORGIA • Charleston

Savannah

• St. Augustine (owned by Spain)

## 2.3 The Southern Colonies

How were the southern colonies founded?

The third geographical division of the English colonies was the southern colonies. These were Virginia, Maryland, the Carolinas, and Georgia. Virginia's founding has already been covered in Chapter 1.

# Virginia

Only sixty settlers had survived the "Starving Time" of Jamestown in 1609–10. However, new settlers arrived in 1610 and 1611, bolstering the spirits of the colonists. The one thing that saved the colony economically was tobacco, which King James I referred to as a "noxious [harmful, unpleasant] weed." John Rolfe brought tobacco seeds from the West Indies and after much trial and error was able to find the right combination of seed and soil to produce the product. He shipped four barrels of tobacco to England in 1614. Despite the king's disapproval, tobacco began selling in England for three shillings per pound. By 1628 the colony was exporting more than one million pounds of tobacco annually. It became a means of currency, and the price of goods was measured not in shillings but in pounds of tobacco. Attempts to diversify the economy by introducing silk worms or other products were not successful. In Virginia, tobacco was king.

Growing tobacco was labor intensive and a year-round job requiring a large labor force. Indentured servants, who gained their freedom after their indenture, were not a reliable source of labor, so planters began to rely on slaves to work the fields. Slavery was lifelong and any offspring became the property of the owner. By 1750, slaves made up over forty percent of Virginia's population.

The opportunity to own land was a major reason for settlers to come to Virginia. Indentured servants were often given land once they completed their time of service (usually four to seven years). To attract additional settlers, a **headright system** was established in 1618 that awarded fifty acres of land to any person who paid for another's passage to America. For example, anyone who paid to bring ten people to Virginia would have the right to 500 acres of land.

As previously mentioned, the Virginia House of Burgesses became the first self-governing assembly in the colonies. The House of Burgesses passed laws for the colony. When King James I took control of the colony from the Virginia Company in 1624 and made it a royal colony, he appointed a royal governor and council but allowed the House of Burgesses to continue meeting.

In 1698 the Virginia statehouse in Jamestown was destroyed by fire, and the next year the capital was moved about ten miles away to Williamsburg. The population of Virginia was over 60,000 by then and was spreading inland from the Chesapeake Bay to the Blue Ridge Mountains.

## Maryland

**Cecilius Calvert**, also called Lord Baltimore, inherited a large land grant given to his father, a Roman Catholic, by King Charles I. Roman Catholics were another group that faced religious persecution in England during the 1600s. Calvert wanted to provide a refuge for English Catholics and became the proprietor of the first group of settlers who arrived in 1634. In order to assure liberty to the Catholics yet still attract Protestant settlers, the colony established religious toleration through the **Maryland Toleration Act** of 1649 which stated that anyone professing belief in the Trinity would have religious freedom. In reality, Protestant settlers outnumbered Catholics from the beginning of the colony's settlement.

## The Carolinas

In 1663 Charles II gave the land between Virginia and Spanish Florida to eight noblemen. The region these proprietors controlled was named Carolina (from the Latin *Carolus*, or Charles) in honor of the king's father, Charles I.

Two areas of settlement emerged: Albemarle to the north, and Charles Town (later called Charleston), a harbor settlement, to the south. The northern part of Carolina attracted settlers from other colonies such as Virginia and Pennsylvania, as well as a large group of Scots-Irish (see Section 4) who settled in the backcountry. Charleston attracted English planters from the Caribbean islands, (particularly Barbados), as well as French Huguenots and Scots-Irish, and the city became an important commercial center. The two regions grew separately from one another. In 1712 the Albemarle settlement was granted its own governor and named North Carolina. In 1719 South Carolina became a royal colony. Proprietors continued to rule North Carolina until 1729 when it, too, became a royal colony. Both colonies retained their colonial legislatures.

### Skull *and* Crossbones

"Blackbeard," whose real name was Edward Teach, was the most notorious pirate who plagued the settlements along the Carolina Outer Banks. He twisted his long, black beard together into little "tails" which he tied with ribbons. He wore a belt with six guns draped from one shoulder across his chest in a fight. He would also wear a fur hat and place a lighted match on each side to make himself look more frightful.

▼ The Huguenot Church in Charleston, South Carolina

## Georgia

The settlement of the southernmost British colony of Georgia did not begin until 1733, making it the last of England's thirteen colonies. The British established Georgia to create a military buffer against Spanish Florida and to provide a colony where debtors, who often languished in English jails, could start a new life.

Georgia's founder, **James Oglethorpe**, wanted to reform prisoners rather than punish them. He wanted to build a colony that would provide rehabilitation through opportunity and hard work. The first settlers in Georgia established Savannah, and a variety of settlers quickly followed the initial migration. The trustees took applications to determine which settlers to send to Georgia "on charity," and thirty-five families were selected, although not a single debtor prisoner was chosen. Those "charity" colonists were each given fifty acres of land in the colony, along with weapons, tools, and seed in return for their labor to clear land, plant crops, and construct public buildings in the colony.

## The Economy of the Southern Colonies

Because of the long growing seasons, fertile soil, and many rivers which connected the interior of the colonies to the sea, the southern colonies were primarily agricultural. The Chesapeake colonies of Virginia and Maryland were heavily dependent on tobacco. Plantations (large farms) were often widely scattered, which meant that few towns developed. Planters invested their profits into more land and slaves, so few industries developed in the southern colonies.

In the early years of the Carolinas, raising cattle and harvesting timber were the primary economic activities. Lumber and pitch (used to make tar for waterproofing ropes and caulking ships) were valuable exports. North Carolina developed small tobacco farms. In the 1690s rice became the primary cash crop for export. Rice was familiar to slaves who had grown it in West Africa. Slaves were brought to the Carolinas to teach planters how to cultivate rice and to engineer the tidewater marshes and swamps for growing it. Annual rice exports from South Carolina grew to 43 million pounds by 1740. Indigo, a plant that produced a blue dye that was in high demand in the clothing industry, became a second important cash crop in the Carolinas.

Growing and harvesting rice was labor intensive. As the amount of cultivated rice increased, the number of slaves increased. By 1730 enslaved peoples in the Carolinas outnumbered free people two to one.

Because Georgia had been established to encourage its settlers to work for themselves, slavery was originally prohibited, and settlers were limited to 500-acre plots of land. As the colony struggled to succeed, settlers blamed their lack of success on these restrictions and demanded their removal. Eventually Georgia became a royal colony, and slavery was allowed. Georgia quickly developed rice and indigo plantations like South Carolina, and the enslaved population soon nearly equaled the free population.

Not all southern colonists were wealthy plantation owners. Most lived on small farms and grew just enough to feed their families and to barter for other needed items. This was especially true of those who lived further inland and along the frontier.

## Comprehension Check 2.3

1. The primary crop of Virginia was ____.
   A wheat
   B tobacco
   C indigo

2. The ____ system gave fifty acres of land to any person who paid for another person's passage to Virginia.
   A mercantile
   B triangular trade
   C headright

3. The colony of ____ was established as a refuge for Roman Catholics.
   A Maryland
   B North Carolina
   C Georgia

4. Each of the following was a reason for the founding of Georgia except ____.
   A to be a place where debtors could start a new life
   B to develop large plantations for growing rice for export
   C to be a military buffer against Spanish Florida

### MAKING CONNECTIONS

5. How was the economy of the southern colonies different from that of the other colonies?

- What were the characteristics of colonial culture?

- What different people groups came to America?

- How was education in New England different from education in the middle and southern colonies?

- How did government in the colonies develop?

- What were the challenges of frontier living?

## 2.4 Colonial Life

**What was life like in the colonies?**

## Colonial Culture

As the colonies grew and developed, they began to develop their own cultural characteristics. In England, wealth and power were concentrated in the hands of a small group of aristocrats who comprised less than five percent of the population but owned most of the land and passed their wealth and titles down to their children. The American colonies rejected titles of nobility; yet, an upper class developed in the colonies through a combination of ambition, talent, wealth, family background, and political skill. Many from the upper class became America's political leaders. Another difference between English and American culture was the ability of people from the lower classes in the colonies to improve their position and rise on the social ladder. The exception to this was slaves, who had little chance of changing their condition.

### New England

In New England, the poor soil and short growing season encouraged settlement in towns rather than in widely dispersed farms. Towns were also desirable because they enabled consistent church attendance, allowed for the support of public schools, and provided a gathered population for the defense of the colony.

The lack of a plantation class meant that wealth in New England was more evenly distributed than in the other colonies. Settlers were originally awarded farms of ten to fifty acres, although some were able to expand their holdings. While some New Englanders grew wealthy through farming, the upper class was generally composed of lawyers and merchant shippers.

Cities such as Boston developed a large middle class consisting of carpenters, shipbuilders, shopkeepers, fishermen and whalers, and skilled craftsmen. Most small farmers also belonged to the middle class. There was a relatively small lower class in New England. Since most immigrants could afford to pay their own way to the New England colonies, indentured servants amounted to less than five percent of New England's population in 1700. Slaves were typically household servants or skilled tradesmen such as blacksmiths, bakers, weavers, tailors, or sailmakers. There was also a population of free blacks who earned or purchased their freedom or were freed by their master.

◄ Iron foundry

## Middle Colonies

William Penn's view of religious freedom led to rapid growth and a diverse population in Pennsylvania. Philadelphia was established in 1682 on a grid with broad streets and spacious parks. Within two years it had 2,500 residents.

The upper class in the middle colonies was made up of a few large landholders as well as a small group of wealthy merchants who controlled trade. These merchants copied the British aristocracy by wearing fancy imported clothing and building fine mansions. Skilled craftsmen and shop owners made up the large middle class.

▲ Colonial farm

Many **indentured servants** worked in the fields or in the cities with the promise of receiving land once their time of service came to an end. These servants would have been unable to afford to pay their passage to the colonies, so they would have entered contracts to work for a period of five to seven years for the person who paid for their passage. These servants were not enslaved, but they also were not truly free. For example, servants could not marry without the contract-holder's consent. But the reward was that, when the contract was fulfilled, indentured servants would receive "freedom dues" that typically included several bushels of corn, a sum of money, and a musket besides the promised land. Many former indentured servants were able to rise to the middle class and beyond. Slaves also worked alongside whites in fields or in cities as dockhands, household servants, or craftsmen.

## Southern Colonies

Wealth was unevenly distributed in the southern colonies. Wealthy plantation owners comprised the upper class. In Virginia they sought to replicate English aristocratic life by building grand homes, wearing wigs and the latest fashions, and importing the finest goods from Europe. The planting class exercised tremendous power in the southern colonies.

A tiny middle class, made up of a few merchants, craftsmen, and some small farmers existed in the colonial south. Most landowners in the south were poor small farmers, many of whom had been indentured servants, who lived in small homes and worked their fields themselves. The southern colonies had the greatest number of indentured servants.

At the bottom of the social ladder was a growing population of slaves. In the later 1600s it became harder to recruit indentured servants to come to North America. In addition, slavery was lifelong, and the children of slaves became the property of the master. Slaves were not able to change their condition and rise on the social ladder. Even free blacks were limited in their ability to own property, carry a weapon, vote, or receive an education.

▼ Virginia planter family visiting the slave quarters

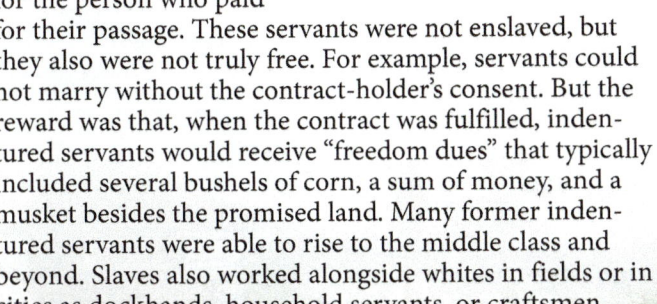

◀ Benjamin Franklin

## Poor Richard's Almanack

Benjamin Franklin's *Poor Richard's Almanack* was published from 1733 to 1758. In addition to the usual astronomical and weather predictions, it was filled with sayings emphasizing thrift, honesty, and diligence. Here are a few examples:

- Fish and visitors stink in three days.

- Well done is better than well said.

- Little strokes fell great oaks.

- Beware of little expenses; a small leak will sink a great ship.

- Lost time is never found again.

- Haste makes waste.

- Early to bed and early to rise, makes a man healthy, wealthy, and wise.

- Keep your eyes wide open before marriage, half shut afterwards.

- Glass, china, and reputation are easily crack'd, and never well mended.

- If Jack's in love, he's no judge of Jill's beauty.

## *Leisure*

The modern view of the colonists (particularly of the Puritans) as sour, gloomy people with dark clothes and dreary looks is inaccurate. Colonial Americans did enjoy life. Puritans had colorful wardrobes, listened to music, and enjoyed literature and wholesome games. Naturally, in the early years of settlement along the coast, survival was the priority; church was generally the only contact among pioneers in a nonwork setting. When life became more settled, more leisure time was possible.

Leisure activities in the cities and those in the country differed. Those who lived in the country were scattered and isolated by long distances, rivers, and dense forests. Yet they still found ways to combine work and play. Barn raisings, corn huskings, and quiltings gave opportunities for frontier families to gather and socialize while sharing the workload. At such events, adults exchanged news and children played with one another.

Since those living in cities were closer together, they had more opportunities to socialize. In large eastern cities wealthy planters and merchants kept a full social calendar through countless clubs, balls, and parties. Other city dwellers enjoyed bowling games on the village green, picnics, or trips to the tavern where they could hear the news either through story swapping or from a patron reading a newspaper aloud.

Colonial newspapers were published in all major cities and featured colonial happenings, advertisements, obituaries, and humor, as well as the "latest" news (usually several months old) from London. The papers eventually filtered to frontier communities.

The toys and games of colonial children included marbles, hoops, dolls, puzzles, hopscotch, shuffleboard, shuttlecock (badminton), and whoop-and-hide (hide-and-seek). Toys were few and generally homemade and simple. For example, a girl might have only one doll during her childhood, often carved from a stick or made from a corncob. Swimming and fishing were popular in the summer, as were ice skating and sleigh rides in the winter.

▶ Hoop and stick at Colonial Williamsburg

▼ Corn husking

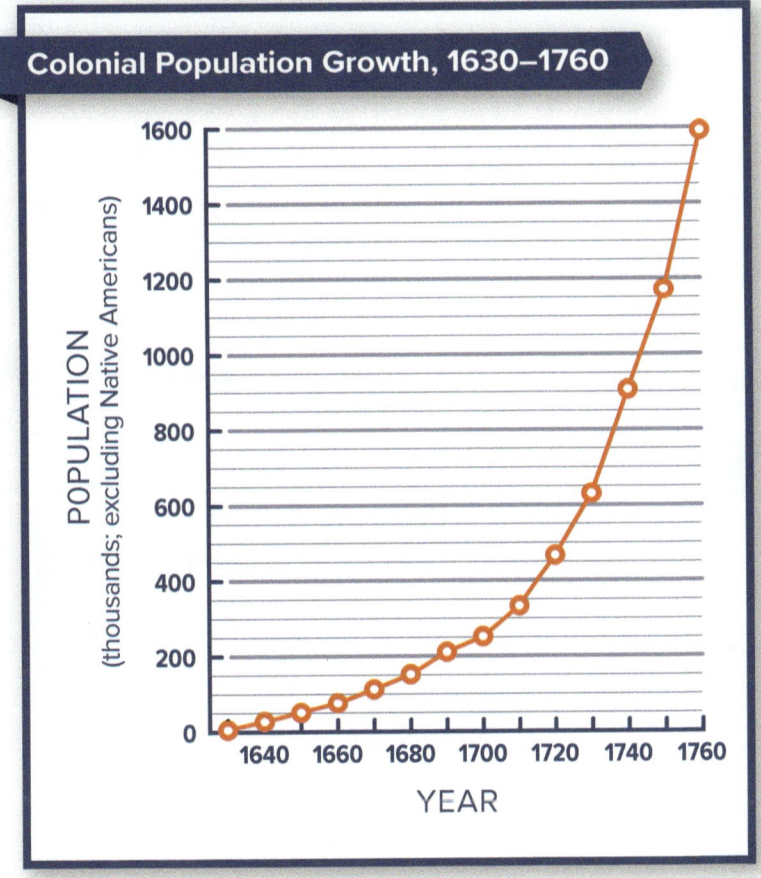

**Colonial Population Growth, 1630–1760**

POPULATION (thousands; excluding Native Americans)

YEAR

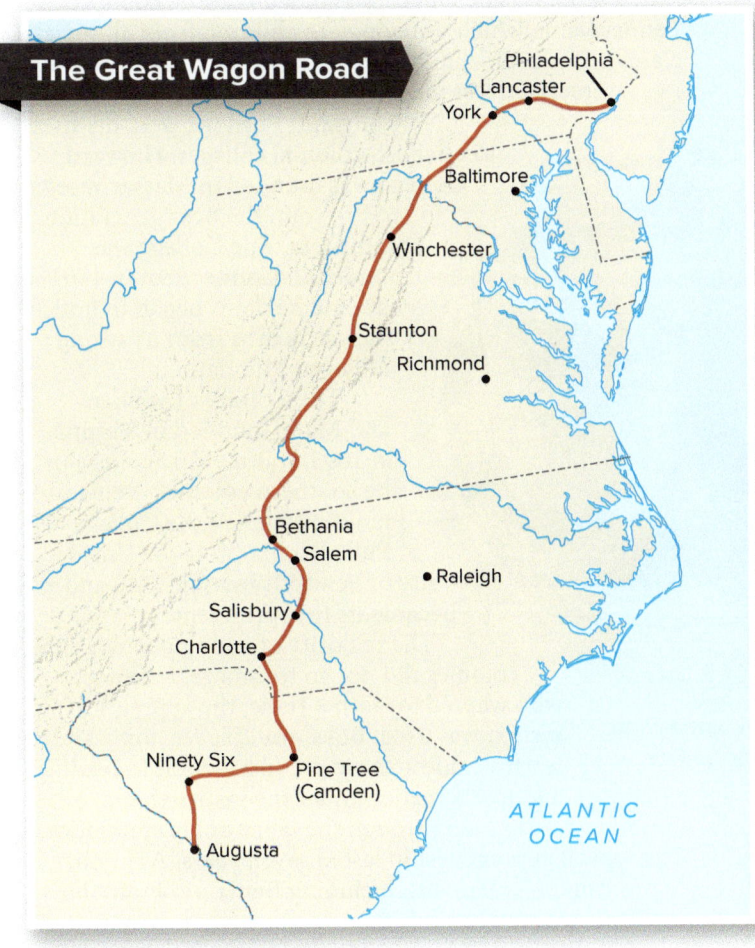

**The Great Wagon Road**

Philadelphia
Lancaster
York
Baltimore
Winchester
Staunton
Richmond
Bethania
Salem
Raleigh
Salisbury
Charlotte
Ninety Six
Pine Tree (Camden)
Augusta

*ATLANTIC OCEAN*

# Colonial Growth

The American colonies tended to attract poor, young, single men who lacked the opportunity for advancement in England. Because of this, males outnumbered females in the colonies of Virginia and Maryland. The New England colonies, on the other hand, attracted whole families, so the balance between men and women was nearly even.

Growth in the New England colonies came naturally through the birth of children, whereas in the southern colonies growth came primarily through the arrival of new colonists from Europe and slaves from Africa. Unfortunately for colonial mothers, difficult deliveries sent many women to an early grave, and their babies often followed. Yet the infant death rate was dramatically lower than in Europe at the time. The scattered colonial settlements and America's productive and plentiful land restrained the disease and famine that were prevalent in Europe's crowded conditions. Life expectancies in New England were also considerably longer than those in the southern colonies. Among slaves, however, harsh working conditions, a brutal climate, and disease led to high death rates, and new slaves were imported continuously to keep up with demand.

Large families provided an important labor source for the home, and children provided helping hands to put food on the table and in the market. Families with six to eight children were common, and it was not unusual for families to have a dozen or more children.

Despite the spread of disease due to the growth of cities, the colonies generally flourished. In 1700 the population was roughly 250,000, and it increased ten times by the outset of the Revolutionary War. Hungry for land, many newcomers migrated inland from the big cities. Their path was an old Iroquois trail which was the chief access to frontier settlements from Virginia to Georgia. Tens of thousands of settlers traveled the rutted pass by foot or in wagons, and it became known as the **Great Wagon Road**.

The two largest groups of non-English settlers were Scots-Irish and Germans. The Scots-Irish were from Protestant northern Ireland. Economic hard times and religious intolerance sent as many as a quarter-million to the colonies. Most German settlers were Protestants from southwestern Germany. Thousands of them arrived in Pennsylvania, attracted by the religious freedom of Penn's commonwealth and the rich farm country so much like their homeland.

The American colonies included a diversity of ethnicities and religions. Blending these diverse groups into one culture that could be called "American" was a process that would take many decades to complete.

# Colonial Education

The purpose of education in New England was primarily religious. Puritans believed that it was essential that all Christians be able to read the Bible. The Massachusetts General Court passed a law in 1642 requiring parents to teach their children about religion and the laws of the colony. In New England, the concentrated pattern of village settlements contributed to the development of the village school. Such schools were often called dame schools since they were generally taught by women. Grammar schools, usually open only to boys, continued the education and included subjects such as Latin, Greek, math, rhetoric, and philosophy.

In 1647 the leaders of Massachusetts passed a law requiring every village of fifty or more families to hire a schoolmaster, and towns of one hundred or more families to establish a grammar school. This law, known as the **Old Deluder Satan Act**, said that Satan (the deluder, or deceiver) wanted to keep people from the knowledge of the Scriptures. The Puritans and other Protestants viewed a basic education as essential to an informed and Christian-influenced society.

In the middle and southern colonies, those who could afford it hired private tutors for their children or sent

▲ A bookbinder and his apprentice

them to boarding schools. Some religious groups established schools. The Quakers founded many schools in Pennsylvania which were open to children from all social classes. However, children from the lower classes generally received less formal education.

New England Puritans were the first to establish colonial colleges. **Harvard College** was founded in Massachusetts in 1636 to train the next generation of ministers. Yale College was founded in Connecticut in 1701 as some Puritans began to notice Harvard's drift from its strong religious foundation.

The College of William and Mary, founded in Virginia in 1693, was the first college in the southern colonies. Benjamin Franklin founded the College of Philadelphia (now the University of Pennsylvania) in 1740 and became its first president.

The majority of young people in the colonies did not go to college. For those who wanted to learn a trade, the apprentice system was used. Boys would leave home and learn a trade and receive instruction in reading and mathematics under the instruction of a master, who was paid through the labor of his apprentice. The typical apprenticeship lasted seven years. A number of prominent Americans, including Benjamin Franklin, began as apprentices.

## Colonial Governments

When the king revoked the Virginia Company's charter in 1624, Virginia became the first royal colony. Gradually, other proprietary and charter colonies lost or surrendered their charters and became royal colonies as well.

In a royal colony the king appointed the governor, who represented the king's interests. In proprietary colonies, the proprietor appointed the governor. The governor could veto legislation, summon or dissolve the colonial legislature, and command the militia. A governor could reward his supporters with positions such as sheriff or surveyor or with grants of land.

Most royal colonies had an advisory council to the governor. Members of the council were appointed by the king and usually represented the upper class in the colony. The council acted as the upper house of colonial legislatures and could introduce bills, pass resolutions, and act as the final court of appeals in the colony.

Each colony had an assembly, or lower house of the legislature. Its name varied by colony—in Virginia it was the House of Burgesses, in Massachusetts it was the General Court, and in South Carolina it was the Commons House of Assembly. Members were elected annually by **freeeholders**, (free adult white males who owned property). In addition to passing laws related to the colony, the assembly controlled issues related to taxes and budgets, holding the "power of the purse." Colonial legislatures often used this power to restrain the power of the royal governors.

Yet full equality as it is defined today did not exist. Neither black males nor Native Americans could participate. Indentured servants did not own property, so they could not take part. Neither could women. Nonetheless, political freedom and power in the colonies were open to more common people than in any previous time. Up to sixty percent of white males could vote in the colonies, compared to only twenty percent in England.

Locally, most colonies were divided into counties. In New England, the primary unit of government was the township. All freeholders were able to attend town meetings and could vote directly on issues. This was the most direct form of democracy in the colonies.

▲ The Governor's Palace, Colonial Williamsburg

▼ Old South Meeting House, Boston, Massachusetts

▲ Death of Metacomet in King Philip's War

▼ Nathaniel Bacon

# Colonial Interactions

## Conflicts with Native Americans

As colonists continued to push further inland and claim more land for themselves, clashes with Native Americans increased. One of these conflicts was the **Pequot War** from 1636 to 1638. The Pequots were a powerful group in the Connecticut River Valley who controlled the fur trade there. Rivalry between the Dutch, English, and Native American tribes led to bloodshed. After some Englishmen were murdered, Massachusetts Bay responded by attacking and burning some Pequot villages and farms. The Pequots responded by attacking an English fort. The colonists then ambushed a Pequot fort and set it on fire. Many of the Pequots who survived the attack were captured and sold as slaves in the West Indies or in New England.

After the Pequot War, there was relative peace in New England for about forty years. However, conflict erupted again in 1675. Metacomet, called King Philip by the colonists, was the son of Massasoit (who had helped the original English settlers at Plymouth) and was the leader of the Wampanoag. When three Wampanoag men were tried, convicted, and executed for murder by the Plymouth colony, the Wampanoag and other area tribes responded by attacking the colonists. The resulting conflict from 1675 to 1678 was called **King Philip's War** and resulted in the deaths of at least six hundred colonists and more than two thousand Native Americans. Metacomet was killed in 1676, and his head was mounted on a pole and displayed in Plymouth for the next twenty years.

In Virginia, bad weather, declining tobacco prices, and increasing competition from other colonies caused economic problems. Frustrated colonists, particularly frontier farmers, blamed the Native American population for their misfortune. When Indians raided the farm of a Virginian for failing to pay for some items, colonists retaliated against the wrong tribe. This resulted in further attacks by the Native Americans. Governor William Berkeley attempted to preserve peace, but Nathaniel Bacon accused Berkeley of failing to protect Virginia from the Indians and of levying unjust taxes. In **Bacon's Rebellion**, Bacon and his followers ignored Berkeley's desire to pursue peace and began attacking Indians throughout Virginia. Berkeley declared Bacon a rebel, and Bacon and his men laid siege to Jamestown in September 1676. Berkeley fled, and Bacon's men burned the city. Bacon died in October 1676, and the rebellion ended. Many of Bacon's followers were hanged by Berkeley.

Additional wars were fought on the frontier. Three wars—King William's War, from 1689 to 1697; Queen Anne's War, from 1702 to 1713; and King George's War, from 1744 to to 1748—were primarily between France and England and had spilled into North America. Native American tribes allied themselves with one side or the other and attacked French or English settlements. These wars were the prelude to the more decisive French and Indian War.

## Missions to Native Americans

Throughout the colonial era, many devout Christians attempted to reach Native Americans with the gospel. Sometimes personal contact resulted in a conversion, such as with Pocahontas. Ministers often preached to the Indians in addition to their other duties. Roger Williams and Jonathan Edwards were among the first in New England to preach to the Indians.

▲ John Eliot, missionary to the Native Americans

Puritan **John Eliot** (1604–90) became concerned about the Native Americans in Massachusetts. With the help of one of them who knew English, Eliot learned their language and began to preach to them. He translated various devotional works and finally the entire Bible into the Native Americans tongue. His success was remarkable; it appears that some four thousand Native Americans were converted under Eliot's ministry. Those converts, called "praying Indians," formed communities called "praying villages," with Native Americans often serving as pastors. That ministry came to an end, however, during King Philip's War. The praying Indians sided with the English, which caused other Native Americans to hate them. Unfortunately, the colonists also distrusted them and even disbanded some of their villages.

**David Brainerd** (1718–47), a close friend of Jonathan Edwards, conducted a brief work among the Native Americans in New York, New Jersey, and Pennsylvania, until his death from tuberculosis at age twenty-nine. Although Brainerd's ministry was not long enough to succeed in numerical terms, his *Journal*, published after his death, inspired many other young men to enter successful mission work.

**Samson Occom**, a member of the Mohegan nation in Connecticut, was converted to Christianity as a result of the preaching of the Great Awakening. He became the first student in a school established for Native American youth by Eleazar Wheelock, who ministered to the Iroquois and the Mohegan. Wheelock sent Occom to England to raise money for the American Indian education. Occom was later disappointed when Dartmouth College, founded with the money Occom raised, educated mostly whites and only a few Native Americans.

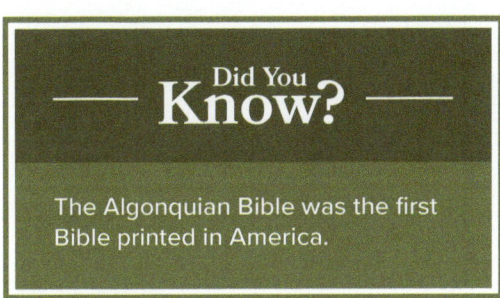

**Did You Know?**

The Algonquian Bible was the first Bible printed in America.

## Comprehension Check 2.4

1. The upper class in New England was made up of ____.

   A plantation owners

   B clergy

   C lawyers and shipping merchants

2. People were most likely to live in towns in the ____ colonies.

   A southern

   B middle

   C New England

3. Those who entered contracts to work for a period of time for the person who paid their passage to the colonies were ____.

   A indentured servants

   B slaves

   C freeholders

4. Because colonists came primarily as families rather than as individuals in the ____ colonies, growth came mainly through the birth of children.

   A southern

   B middle

   C New England

5. The power of the purse in colonial governments was given to the ____.

   A governor

   B assembly

   C council

6. The conflict in Virginia between the governor and frontier farmers over protection from Native Americans was ____.

   A Bacon's Rebellion

   B King Philip's War

   C the Pequot War

7. The Puritan missionary to the Native Americans who translated the Bible into their language was ____.

   A David Brainerd

   B Samson Occom

   C John Eliot

### MAKING CONNECTIONS

8. Compare and contrast education in the New England, middle, and southern colonies.

- What was religion like in the colonies?
- What happened during the Great Awakening?
- What impact did the Great Awakening have on America?

## 2.5 Colonial Religion

What role did religion play in the colonies?

## Religion in the Colonies

### New England

The Puritans believed that their community should be a model society ruled by God's laws. They hoped to demonstrate to England how such a godly society should operate.

The Puritans adopted a congregational form of church government. Each congregation elected its own officers, and each church remained independent of other churches. Other groups, notably the Baptists, also adopted this system. Because of this system, most Puritans in America came to be called Congregationalists.

Later generations were prosperous and usually outwardly moral, but most lacked the passionate faith of the original generation of settlers. This decline created a serious problem in the Congregationalist churches.

Children of church members were baptized as infants. These children were considered members of the church but could not become full members and take the Lord's Supper until they declared their personal faith in Christ. As the years passed, fewer members made such a profession. The presence of church members who had been baptized but who had not made a profession of faith led to another issue: could the children of these members be baptized into church membership? Eventually, the ministers of New England devised what became known as the **Half-Way Covenant**. Church members who lived moral lives could present their children for baptism. Despite its purpose of keeping people in the church and in the presence of sound preaching, the Half-Way Covenant increased the number of unconverted church members.

## The Salem Witch Trials

The low point in Puritan history came in 1692 when several young girls in Salem Village, Massachusetts, claimed that witches were afflicting them. The authorities took the charges seriously and began to place those accused on trial. Before the hysteria was over, nineteen people were hanged, one man was pressed to death with heavy weights, and several people died in prison.

Ironically, only those who maintained their innocence were executed; those who confessed were imprisoned. Realizing this, some of the accused confessed in order to save themselves. Authorities hoped those in jail would identify other witches.

The clergy of Massachusetts counseled caution and restraint. It was their opposition that helped end the witch trials. Boston pastor Increase Mather said:

> It were better that ten suspected witches should escape than that one innocent person should be condemned.
> — . . .Cases of Conscience (1692)

Within five years the citizens of Massachusetts held a day of prayer and fasting to implore God's pardon for their actions.

Ann Putnam, one of the hysterical girls, apologized for being "an instrument for the accusing of several persons of a grievous crime, whereby their lives were taken away from them, whom now I have just grounds and good reason to believe they were innocent persons."

What exactly happened in Salem Village? No one can be quite sure. It is certain, however, that innocent people died because of fear and hysteria, and the reputation of the Puritans suffered permanent damage. Regrettably, the worthy contributions of early American Puritanism have been largely obscured by the wild fanaticism of a few.

## *Middle Colonies*

The middle colonies were the most ethnically and religiously diverse. Jews, Lutherans from Germany and Scandinavia, Anglicans and Puritans from other colonies, Scottish Presbyterians, French Huguenots, and others enjoyed broad toleration in New York.

Pennsylvania, founded by William Penn, had no established church and promised religious freedom to **Quakers**, or the Society of Friends, and other persecuted people. Most Quakers opposed participating in war, taking oaths, or holding political office. Those opposed to them assigned them the name Quaker from the practice of some who shook while worshiping. They preferred to be called Friends. The Quakers practiced a plain method of worship. Believers sat in silence, often in a circle, and waited for the "inner light" (what they believed to be a spark of divinity in each person) to move a member to give a word of testimony or exhortation. The Quakers did not have regular ministers and did not practice baptism or the Lord's Supper.

When Roger Williams fled from Massachusetts and founded Rhode Island, he founded what is considered the first **Baptist** church in America. This group grew slowly at first and suffered persecution from colonial authorities. Nonetheless, the Baptists succeeded in founding churches throughout the colonies, especially in religiously tolerant Pennsylvania. As their name suggests, Baptists differ from other groups regarding the practice of baptism. Unlike other groups that baptize infants, Baptists baptize only professing believers by immersion in water.

An Amish family in Lancaster County, Pennsylvania

Several Anabaptist groups, persecuted by governments in Europe, fled to America and established farms and towns in Pennsylvania. Like the Baptists, **Anabaptists** believed in believers' baptism rather than infant baptism. Unlike Baptists, most Anabaptists were pacifists who refused to serve in the military, vote, or hold office. They stressed the importance of a simple, holy life. The Anabaptists split into Mennonites and Amish when the Amish determined to become even more conservative.

**Moravians**, a German Reformed group from southern Germany, migrated to Pennsylvania in the 1740s. Persecution in Europe led many Moravians to flee to America. They emphasized the importance of conversion, the need for personal piety (devoutness), and the necessity of living a holy life. Evangelism was also a primary concern; thus, they conducted mission work among the slaves in the Caribbean and the colonies and among Native Americans.

## Southern Colonies

The Church of England, or the Anglican Church, was the established (official, state-supported) church in most southern colonies. Because settlements in the southern colonies were spread far apart, access to religious services was difficult. Another problem was a general lack of Anglican ministers. The College of William & Mary was founded in Williamsburg, Virginia, in 1693, partly to train Anglican ministers.

Other religious groups were allowed in the southern colonies as long as they paid taxes to the state church. Baptists and Scots-Irish Presbyterians moved into the frontier. French Huguenots settled in Charleston and other coastal areas. Other German groups, including Moravians, settled in the southern colonies, and some Jews established themselves in Charleston and Savannah.

As mentioned previously, Maryland was established as a haven for Roman Catholics and allowed religious toleration. This opened the door for many Protestant groups, too, and Roman Catholics became a minority in their own colony.

## The Wesleys in Georgia

In 1736 John and Charles Wesley, two of nineteen children in the Wesley family, traveled to the new Georgia colony at James Oglethorpe's request. On the voyage, John Wesley was impressed by the faith of the Moravians aboard the ship. At one point, a violent storm nearly sank the ship. While the English panicked, the Moravians calmly sang psalms.

John pastored for the Anglican Church in Savannah but returned to England after a little less than two years. On his voyage home, he wrote in his journal, "I went to America, to convert the Indians; but oh! who shall convert me?"

In May 1738, a few months after returning to England, he placed his faith in Christ. Three days later Charles also became a Christian. John founded the Methodist denomination, and Charles wrote thousands of hymns.

▶ John Wesley preaching to Native Americans

# The Great Awakening

Religious life in the North American colonies had begun to wither by the early 1700s. Although some religious groups experienced growth, most were in a spiritual lull. The colonies needed a spiritual awakening. In New England, the Half-Way Covenant was slowly filling the Congregationalist churches with unsaved members. Some areas, such as the frontier regions of the Carolinas, had almost no religious life. Many who attended church did so because of tradition, but they lacked spiritual zeal. It appears that even some colonial ministers were not converted.

Beginning in the 1720s, a great religious revival known as the **Great Awakening** began across denominational lines. Dutch Reformed pastor Theodore J. Frelinghuysen and Presbyterian minister Gilbert Tennent were early lights in the Great Awakening. They emphasized personal conversion and the holiness of life that an awareness of God's holiness brings. Both Frelinghuysen and Tennent saw fruit for their labor in converted souls and rededicated saints. New England Congregationalist churches were inspired to follow this method of revival, which Tennent reported to them by letters.

**Jonathan Edwards** was minister of the Congregational parish in Northampton, Massachusetts, and led the most influential revival of the Great Awakening during 1734–35. Edwards began preaching a series of sermons on justification by faith, which sparked a series of awakenings in the church that surprised even Edwards. He wrote glowingly of the revival's results, but he also cautioned against overemphasized emotion. He warned against excessive shouting in services, working oneself into a trance, or claiming to receive visions from God. Edwards documented the impact of the Great Awakening in his book, *A Faithful Narrative of the Surprising Work of God*. He preached his most famous sermon, "Sinners in the Hands of an Angry God," in 1741.

The Northampton revival declined in 1735, but in 1738 the Awakening continued under **George Whitefield**. Born in England, Whitefield became a friend of John and Charles Wesley while studying at Oxford. He was later converted and became a powerful preacher. But the doors of England's churches were often closed to him by ministers who did not share his zeal, so Whitefield began to preach outdoors wherever he could gather a crowd.

After seeing remarkable results from his preaching in Britain, the twenty-four-year-old Whitefield came to America in 1738. Over the next thirty years, he made seven preaching tours of the colonies. He preached in large cities, villages, and crossroads, carrying the revival throughout the colonies. Whitefield was a gifted preacher with a powerful voice. By 1740 Whitefield preached to thousands daily, with many conversions. Whitefield also became a close friend of Jonathan Edwards, preaching at his Northampton church.

Presbyterian minister **Samuel Davies** was a leader of the Great Awakening in the South. A gifted speaker, he led services in a large portion of Virginia from 1748 to 1759. Patrick Henry attended many of Davies' sermons as a child and credited the pastor as an influence on his own speaking skills. Davies preached to slaves and insisted they be taught to read so that they could have access to God's Word. He baptized many slaves, allowing them to take communion alongside white church members and to preach in his congregations. Davies pushed for greater religious toleration in Virginia for dissenters from the established Anglican church. He spent the last two years of his life as president of the College of New Jersey (Princeton).

▲ George Whitefield

# Results of the Awakening

The Great Awakening had several effects on life in colonial America.

 ## Church Growth

First, church growth was the most visible result. Because of the many conversions and the spiritual renewal of many Christians, the number of churches and church members increased significantly. Presbyterians and Baptists experienced the greatest growth. The Half-Way Covenant began to vanish; increasingly, churches in America required personal salvation for membership. This growth also promoted unity among the churches. Different congregations and even different denominations overlooked their minor doctrinal differences in the interest of evangelism. This tendency toward unity helped pave the way for a political uniting of the colonies in the coming break with England.

 ## Religious Division

Second, the Great Awakening also brought division to America's churches. Nearly every denomination had those who favored the revival (often called New Lights or New Side) and those who opposed it (Old Lights or Old Side). Not all Old Lights were against revival itself; some were simply offended by, in their view, the fanatical extremes of some people. Many of the opponents, though, were theologically opposed to the revival. They disliked the emphasis on personal experience, criticism of unsaved pastors, and the general upsetting of "good church order."

 ## Religious Training

Third, the number of colleges founded as ministry training centers increased. Princeton, Brown, Rutgers, and Dartmouth were established. Yale experienced a renewed spiritual emphasis. Harvard, however, continued its move away from its Puritan spiritual roots.

 ## Separation of Church and State

Fourth, the Great Awakening increased the separation between church and state. The revival showed that the church could exist without government support and that established state churches were not necessary or even desired. This anti-establishment movement, especially where the Anglican church was strong, may have contributed to the increased tension between Britain and the colonies when Britain began to tighten its control in America.

 ## Political Unity

Fifth, the Great Awakening had political effects on the colonies. It was the first truly national movement in American history. The revival cut across regional lines and touched every colony and nearly every class of people. The Great Awakening was not southern or northern, Presbyterian or Congregationalist, upper class or lower class; it was American. It caused colonists to begin to think in terms of liberty and rights in both spiritual and political affairs and caused some to think more about their status in the British Empire.

 ## Democratization

Sixth, the Awakening advanced the idea of the equality of all men by reaffirming the equality of all before God. A democratic influence swept into the churches; people's wealth or status did not determine their spiritual condition. However, not all effects of this greater democracy proved positive. As democracy and individualism became stronger, some Americans began to doubt fundamental Christian doctrines. Before the Great Awakening, people usually respected the expertise of their pastors in understanding the Scripture. Now, many thought their own unstudied opinions were just as valid.

Many movements that were unleashed in the Great Awakening saw their full development in the American Revolution. Foremost was an awakening of both the spirit of democracy and the spirit of religious liberty.

▲ Worship service led by Samuel Davies in which white and black congregants celebrated communion together, demonstrating the Great Awakening's democratizing principle of the equality of all people before God

## Comprehension Check 2.5

1. The ____ allowed Puritan church members who had not made a profession of faith to have their children baptized.

   A  Great Compromise

   B  Great Awakening

   C  Half-Way Covenant

2. The ____ colonies were the most ethnically and religiously diverse.

   A  New England

   B  middle

   C  southern

3. Each of the following is true about Quakers except that they ____.

   A  had ministers and celebrated the Lord's Supper

   B  opposed participating in wars

   C  would not take oaths or hold public office

4. The official church in the southern colonies was the ____ church.

   A  Baptist

   B  Anglican

   C  Presbyterian

5. Jonathan Edwards, George Whitefield, and Samuel Davies were all ____.

   A  preachers of the Great Awakening

   B  missionaries to the Native Americans

   C  presidents of universities

### MAKING CONNECTIONS

6. What were the six results of the Great Awakening on American society?

## Chapter Summary

### 2.1  The New England Colonies

- Plymouth Colony was founded by Separatists who broke away from the Anglican Church. Because they were not free in England to worship according to their beliefs, these Pilgrims moved to the Netherlands and then to America. Under the leadership of William Bradford and with the help of friendly Native Americans such as Squanto, the Pilgrims survived a difficult beginning and the colony grew.

- Massachusetts Bay was founded by Puritans who wanted to purify the Anglican Church from within. This group, led by John Winthrop, attempted to establish a godly Christian community that would serve as a model for others.

- Roger Williams and Anne Hutchinson were banished from Massachusetts Bay because of beliefs that were not in line with the colony's leaders. Their new settlements became parts of the colony of Rhode Island.

- The economy of New England was made up of small farmers, fishermen, whalers, shipbuilders, shopkeepers, and craftsmen. The upper class were primarily lawyers and shipping merchants, who profited from trade between Africa, Europe, and America.

**TERMS**

charter colony

proprietary colony

royal colony

Puritans

Separatists

Mayflower Compact

William Bradford

Squanto

John Winthrop

Roger Williams

Anne Hutchinson

Thomas Hooker

Fundamental Orders of Connecticut

triangular trade

**TERMS**

William Penn

Frame of Government of Pennsylvania

### 2.2  The Middle Colonies

- New York began as the Dutch settlement of New Netherland. Manhattan Island was purchased from the Native Americans. The Dutch surrendered the colony to the English. The Duke of York gave the southern portion of the colony to two friends, and the area became New Jersey.

- Pennsylvania was founded by Quaker William Penn, and the colony promoted religious toleration and political liberty. It attracted a diverse group of settlers.

- The middle colonies were called the "bread colonies" because they had fertile soil, a long growing season, and a gentle landscape that were ideal for growing wheat and other grains. Furs and products made from the abundant timber of the colonies were other important parts of the economy.

## 2.3 / The Southern Colonies

- Tobacco became the primary cash crop in Virginia. It required a large labor force, which consisted primarily of indentured servants and slaves. The colony used the headright system to attract new settlers by giving people fifty acres of land for every person whose passage was paid to come to Virginia.

- Maryland was established to provide a refuge for English Roman Catholics. The Maryland Toleration Act gave religious freedom to anyone who believed in the Trinity. This attracted a large number of Protestant groups, who soon outnumbered Catholics in the colony.

- Carolina was a proprietary colony which eventually split into the separate colonies of North and South Carolina.

- Georgia was established to be a military buffer against Spanish Florida and to provide debtors a new start in life.

- The southern colonies had a plantation economy with large tobacco farms in Virginia, Maryland, and North Carolina, and rice and indigo in South Carolina and Georgia. The economy depended on slave labor. The majority of southerners lived on small farms that grew just enough food to provide for their families.

TERMS

indentured servants

Great Wagon Road

Old Deluder Satan Act

Harvard College

freeholders

Pequot War

King Philip's War

Bacon's Rebellion

John Eliot

David Brainerd

Samson Occom

## 2.4 / Colonial Life

- Culture in the colonies varied by region. The upper class attempted to model the lifestyle of the wealthy in England, while the lower classes lived relatively simple lives.

- The colonies grew rapidly both through the birth of children and through immigration. More settlers began moving further inland toward the Appalachian Mountains.

- Colonial education varied by region. In New England the establishment of schools was required so that children could be taught to read the Bible, and colleges were established to train ministers. In the middle colonies religious groups established some schools. In the southern colonies the wealthy were able to hire tutors or send their children to boarding schools and the lower classes had little access to education. The apprentice system was used to train young people for skilled trades.

- Colonial governments included the governor, a council, and a representative assembly. Members of the assembly were elected by the freeholders, and the assembly controlled issues related to money for the colony.

- As the colonies grew and moved further inland, conflicts with the Native Americans increased. A number of colonial ministers attempted to evangelize the Native Americans, with varying results.

## 2.5  Colonial Religion

- Puritan New England adopted a congregational form of church government. The Half-Way Covenant allowed the children of members who had not made a profession of faith to be baptized into membership.

- The middle colonies were the most religiously diverse with religious groups such as the Quakers, Anabaptists, and Moravians.

- The Anglican Church was the established church in the southern colonies, but other groups were allowed to settle as long as they paid taxes to the state church. Maryland was a haven for Roman Catholics.

- The Great Awakening was a period of religious revival in the colonies. Preachers such as Jonathan Edwards, George Whitefield, and Samuel Davies traveled the colonies preaching the need for salvation. The Great Awakening had several significant effects on American society, including the growth of churches, the separation of church and state, and growing democratization.

### TERMS

Half-Way Covenant

Quakers

Baptists

Anabaptists

Moravians

Great Awakening

Jonathan Edwards

George Whitefield

Samuel Davies

## Chapter Review Questions

### RECALL

1. What was the first document of self-government in America by which the Pilgrims bound themselves to submit to the colony's laws and duly elected leadership?

2. Who helped the Pilgrims in Plymouth Colony by teaching them about crops and fishing and working to establish peace between the settlers and the Wampanoags?

3. What was the first written constitution in America?

4. What were the main economic activities in New England?

5. What religious group did William Penn belong to?

6. What was the main cash crop of Virginia?

7. Why was the colony of Maryland founded?

8. For what reasons was the colony of Georgia founded?

9. What were the main cash crops for the Carolina colony?

10. What were three ways that people in colonial America spent their leisure time?

11. What were the two largest non-English groups to settle in the colonies?

12. Where could the most direct form of democracy be found in the colonies?

13. What two wars were fought between the New England colonists and the Native Americans in the 1600s?

14. Who translated the Bible into the Algonquian language?

15. Which colonies were the most religiously diverse?

16. What was the established church in the southern colonies?

17. What was the great religious revival in the American colonies called?

### UNDERSTAND

18. What was the difference between charter colonies, proprietary colonies, and royal colonies?

19. What role did religion play in the founding of Plymouth Colony and the Massachusetts Bay Colony?

20. What was the difference between the Puritans and the Separatists?

21. What beliefs of Roger Williams's caused him to be banished from Massachusetts?

22. Why was Anne Hutchinson banished from Massachusetts?

23. How did Massachusetts Bay Colony influence the founding of Connecticut, Rhode Island, and New Hampshire?

24. What was triangular trade, and what were some goods shipped on each leg?

25. Why were Peter Stuyvesant's reforms in New York rejected?

26. Why were the middle colonies known as the "bread colonies"?

27. What was the composition of the upper, middle, and lower classes in New England, the middle colonies, and the southern colonies?

28. What were the three main divisions of government in the colonies, and what powers did each have?

29. Why was there more population growth in the New England colonies than in the southern colonies?

30. What were Nathaniel Bacon's reasons for his rebellion against the government of Virginia?

31. Describe the beliefs and worship of the Quakers.

32. How did the Half-Way Covenant affect religion in New England?

33. What caused the Salem witch trials, and how did the trials affect the reputation of the Puritans?

## THINK ABOUT IT

34. How did colonial growth relate to colonial interactions with Native Americans?

35. Contrast education in New England with education in the middle and southern colonies.

36. How did the idea of religious freedom in Massachusetts Bay differ from the idea of religious freedom in Pennsylvania or Maryland?

37. Identify and explain six effects of the Great Awakening on American society.

38. Analyze the New England town map below and answer the following question:

*What are four things that can be learned about New England society from this map?*

▲ Layout of a New England town

# 3 The Struggle for Independence

3.1 The French and Indian War

3.2 The Growing Divide

3.3 The Road to Independence

3.4 Fighting the War for Independence

3.5 Winning the War for Independence

▲ Benjamin Franklin, John Adams, and Thomas Jefferson (left to right) reviewing a draft of the Declaration of Independence

# The French and Indian War

- What were the causes of the French and Indian War?
- What were the major events of the French and Indian War?
- What were the results of the French and Indian War?

From the 1680s to the 1760s, recurring wars raged on the American frontier. Two colonial empires—the English and the French—fought from Florida to Canada. Though France's claims in North America stretched from Quebec to New Orleans, New France amounted to little more than a scattered string of outposts and was never heavily populated with French settlers. In 1750 the population of New France was about eighty thousand compared to more than one million people who lived in British America.

As the French expanded their claims in Canada, the Great Lakes region, and the Mississippi River basin, and as the English moved farther west, friction was inevitable. Furthermore, when France and England were at war in Europe, their colonists fought in America as well. Between 1689 and 1763, these rival nations were involved in four wars. In America, the last of these wars was called the **French and Indian War**, while in Europe it was known as the Seven Years' War.

## The Outbreak

In 1752 the French governor of Canada ordered the construction of a chain of forts extending from Lake Erie to the Ohio River, designed to keep the English from crossing into territory claimed by France. In the spring of 1754, Virginia's governor Dinwiddie ordered Lieutenant Colonel **George Washington** to clear the territory of the French, who the English believed had illegally entered the area. On the way north, Washington and his troops surprised a small group of French soldiers. In the ensuing skirmish, ten Frenchmen were killed, and the remainder were captured.

However, a much larger force of French soldiers and Indian warriors was waiting at the newly constructed **Fort Duquesne**. Realizing that he was outnumbered, Washington retreated and hastily built defenses. Fort Necessity, the main defense, showed Washington's inexperience. Located in a low area, the fort allowed the French to fire directly into it from nearby heights. Washington was forced to surrender. The French allowed the Virginians to march home after Washington signed a note of surrender placing the blame on the British. The British government repudiated Washington's note, and Britain and France went to war.

Over the years the French had forged alliances with numerous Native American tribes but could not win the powerful Iroquois because the French were already aligned with the Algonquins, enemies of the Iroquois. The Iroquois were allies of the British-American forces. The French had an advantage in using guerrilla warfare (sudden surprise attacks), borrowed from the American Indians, against the British. Another factor assisting the French was the frontier. The vaguely defined western boundary of isolated farms and villages was difficult to defend.

**French and British Claims in North America, ca. 1750**

Quebec

Boston

Providence

New York City

Williamsburg

ATLANTIC OCEAN

Charles Town

Savannah

St. Lawrence River

Mississippi River

British
French
Spanish
Disputed

▲ Political cartoon used for supporting the Albany Plan

Yet the British also possessed certain advantages. First, British colonists established deep roots in America that included land, businesses, and families. By contrast, many of the French were isolated traders and trappers who removed products, such as furs, from America but brought little to it. Second, British colonists in America outnumbered French colonists by more than twenty to one. Third, the British navy controlled the waterways and thereby hindered the arrival of French reinforcements and supplies.

The chief British disadvantage was a lack of unity among the colonies, who often competed with one another for trade and the allegiance of Native American tribes. In June 1754 delegates from most colonies north of Virginia met in Albany, New York, to discuss this issue. Benjamin Franklin proposed his **Albany Plan** calling for a Crown-appointed president and a congress. The plan was rejected, however, because the colonists feared a strong central government even more than they feared France.

## The Course

The early years of the war were disastrous for the British. General **Edward Braddock** and over one thousand seasoned British troops were sent to capture Fort Duquesne. Braddock was joined by Colonel Washington's colonial forces, but his failed attempts to recruit the Cherokee or other tribes to join him proved costly. As Braddock's men painstakingly cut a road through the wooded wilderness to the French fort, Washington tried in vain to warn Braddock that the enemy would not fight in the open, organized fashion that the general was accustomed to in Europe.

On July 9, 1755, the French, along with Canadian militia and over six hundred Native American allies, attacked. They hid in the trees and thick brush and poured deadly fire into the British ranks. Without a Native American force of his own to fight in a similar manner, Braddock ordered his men to form firing lines, which only made them easier targets. Braddock was shot, and the remaining officers led by Washington organized a retreat. Over half of the British force was killed or wounded, and Braddock died of his wounds a few days later.

▼ General Braddock fatally wounded at Fort Duquesne

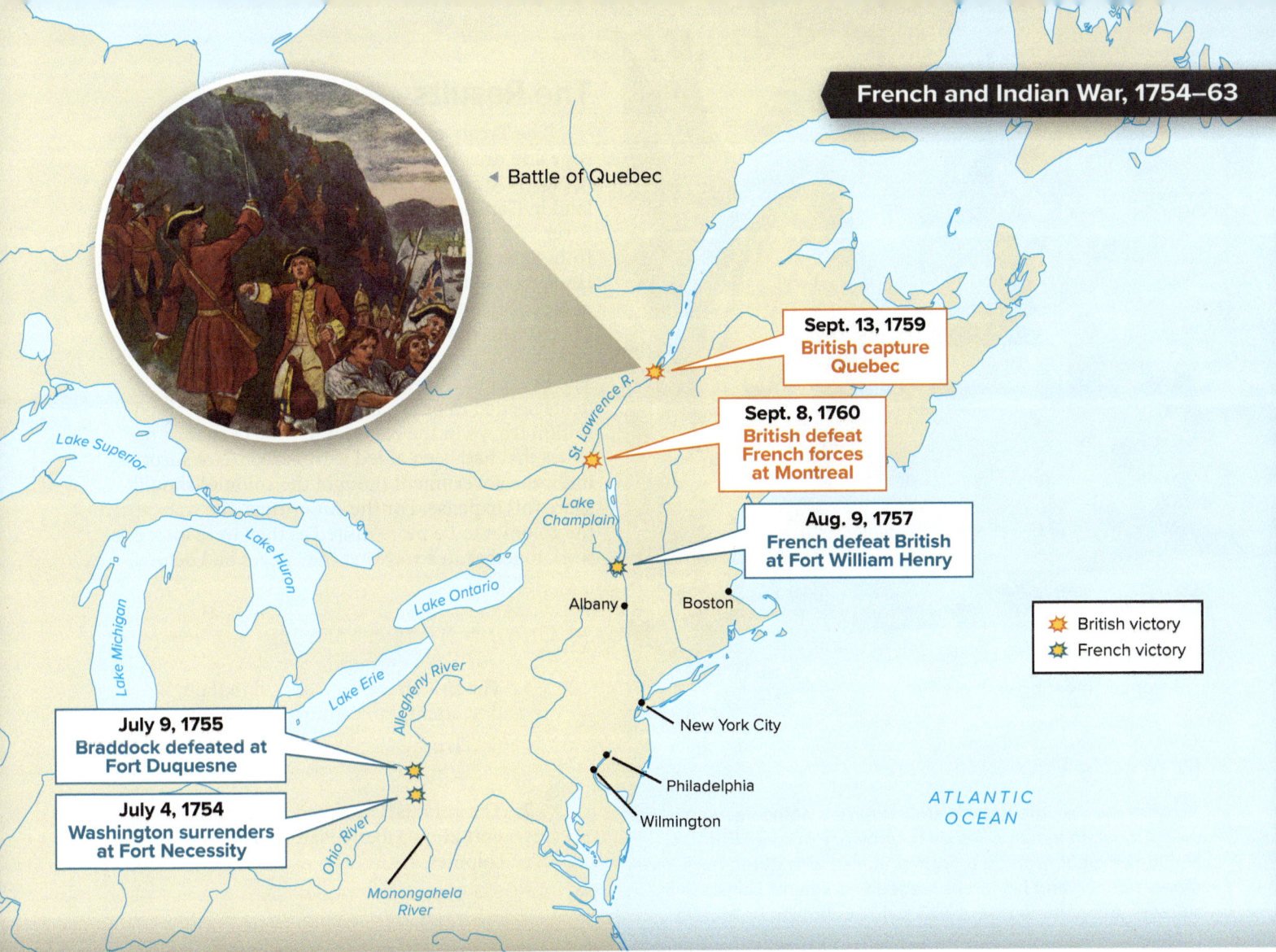

◄ Battle of Quebec

**Sept. 13, 1759**
**British capture Quebec**

**Sept. 8, 1760**
**British defeat French forces at Montreal**

**Aug. 9, 1757**
**French defeat British at Fort William Henry**

St. Lawrence R.

Lake Superior

Lake Huron

Lake Michigan

Lake Ontario

Lake Erie

Lake Champlain

Allegheny River

Albany

Boston

New York City

Philadelphia

Wilmington

ATLANTIC OCEAN

⭐ British victory
⭐ French victory

**July 9, 1755**
**Braddock defeated at Fort Duquesne**

**July 4, 1754**
**Washington surrenders at Fort Necessity**

Ohio River

Monongahela River

After the British formally declared war in 1756, the French forces in America, commanded by the **Marquis de Montcalm**, won a series of victories over the British from 1756 to 1758. In addition, French-allied Native Americans raided the frontier, terrorizing the British colonists.

The situation improved for the British in 1757 when William Pitt, the British secretary of state (who later became prime minister), took control of military operations. Pitt quickly adopted a plan to win the war, devoting more resources, troops, and naval assets to the cause and replacing old, incompetent commanders with those younger and more energetic. British troops captured Fort Duquesne and renamed it Fort Pitt (now Pittsburgh) in Pitt's honor.

Among these new commanders was General **James Wolfe** who was entrusted with a key attack on Quebec, the capital of New France. Montcalm knew that Quebec, high on cliffs above the St. Lawrence River, was a natural fortress. A determined Wolfe, however, devised a plan to capture the city. In 1759 under cover of darkness, British soldiers scaled the cliffs and swarmed the Plains of Abraham, a field just outside Quebec. In the brief but deadly battle, the British won a great victory. However, Wolfe did not live to savor the victory; both he and Montcalm were fatally wounded. The British triumph at Quebec and another in Montreal ended the war in North America.

▲ Pontiac meeting with the British

## Pontiac's War

After the war, the French army returned home, leaving their American Indian allies on their own. However, **Pontiac**, an Ottawa chief, worked to form alliances with other tribes. Pontiac and his forces waged war against British soldiers and settlers from 1763 to 1766, hoping to protect Native American land by driving settlers back across the Appalachian Mountains. Hundreds of people, both soldiers and civilians, were killed. But Pontiac was unable to hold his alliance together and eventually made peace with the British. Pontiac's successful attacks on British territory had raised a serious question in the minds of the colonists: why should they help pay for the costly British army if it could not offer protection?

## The Results

The **Treaty of Paris of 1763** ended the war in Europe and drastically changed the political boundaries of North America. France surrendered nearly all its land in Canada and its claims east of the Mississippi River to Britain. The British also acquired Florida from Spain, a French ally. Spain gained the French lands west of the Mississippi River, including the city of New Orleans.

For the victorious British, the costs of the war and of governing the new possessions were high. The British had borrowed heavily, and now the debts needed to be repaid. Parliament also wanted to station troops in the colonies to protect against the tribes that had been allied with France. Not surprisingly, the government thought the colonies should share this expense. For the Americans, the war caused the colonies to be more united as they were forced to work together in a way that they never had before.

---

### Comprehension Check 3.1

1. The British were successful in their first attempt to capture Fort Duquesne.

   True

   False

2. The colonists accepted Benjamin Franklin's Albany Plan to unite the colonies.

   True

   False

3. British General Wolfe and French General Montcalm were both fatally wounded in the British victory at the Battle of _____.

   A  Fort Duquesne

   B  Quebec

   C  Albany

4. Each of the following was a result of the French and Indian War except that _____.

   A  France gained control of Florida from Spain

   B  Britain gained Canada and France's land east of the Mississippi River

   C  Britain was in debt from the war

**MAKING CONNECTIONS**

5. What advantages and disadvantages did the British and French have during the French and Indian War?

---

## 3.2 The Growing Divide

Why was there a growing divide between Britain and the American colonies?

### GUIDING QUESTIONS

- How did the French and Indian War lead to changes in British policies toward the colonies?

- How did the Americans react to changes in British policies?

## Taxes and Tensions

After the French and Indian War, the relationship between Britain and the colonies changed significantly. The British government believed it was reasonable to ask the colonists to help pay for their defense. After over a century of "salutary neglect," in which England had avoided strict enforcement of parliamentary laws in the colonies and allowed the colonies a large degree of autonomy, the British government resolved to exercise greater control over its American subjects.

King George III, who had come to the throne in 1760, issued the **Proclamation of 1763** which restricted the colonists from settling beyond the Appalachian Mountains. The British viewed this as a way to diminish conflicts with the Native Americans. American colonists, however, viewed these restrictions as a violation of colonial charters that granted the colonies land from the Atlantic to the Pacific. They had fought to open the frontier to expansion, and they were angry that the British government was restricting where they could settle.

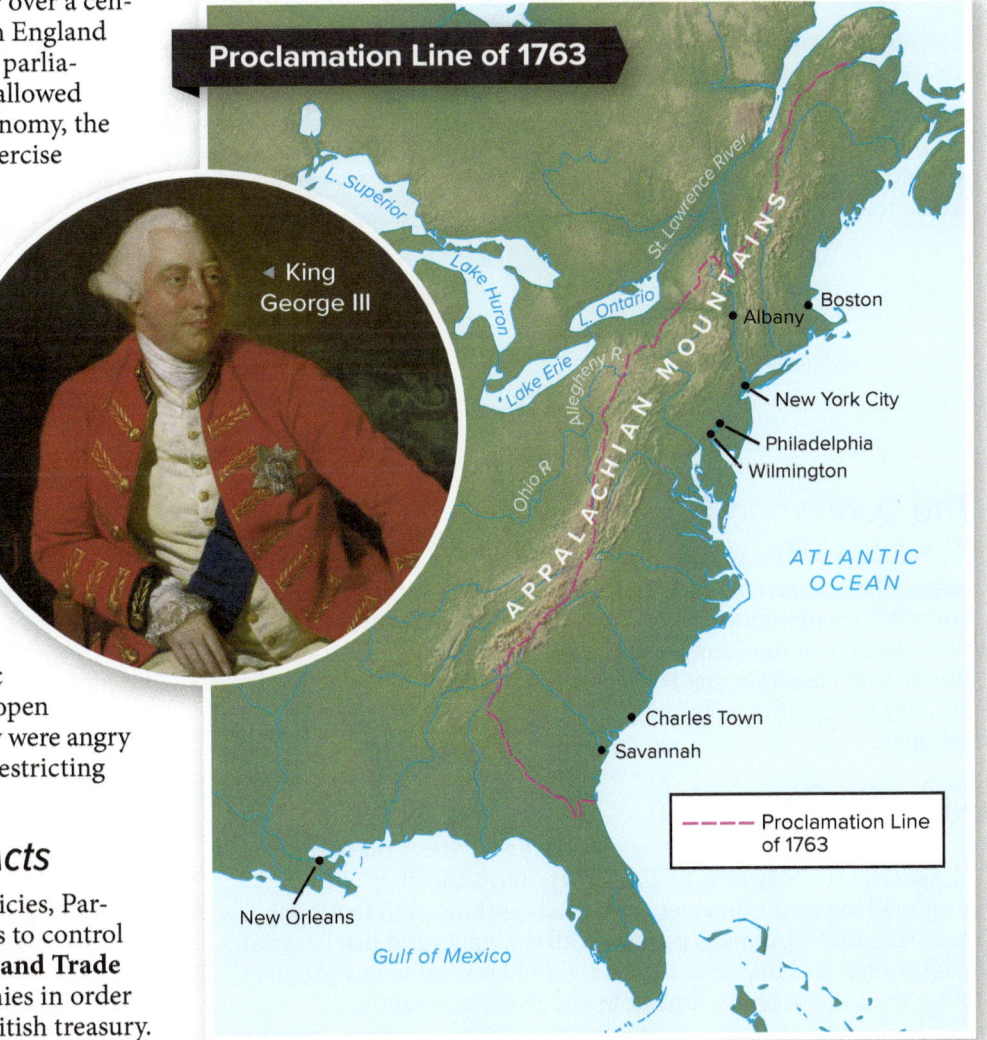

Proclamation Line of 1763

◄ King George III

### Navigation and Trade Acts

As part of its mercantilist policies, Parliament had passed a series of acts to control colonial trade. These **Navigation and Trade Acts** restricted trade for the colonies in order to bring greater revenue to the British treasury. But for the most part these rules had not been enforced. After the French and Indian War, British officials began to enforce the trade laws more strictly to put an end to illegal trade and smuggling which had deprived the British of revenue. Customs officials were given **writs of assistance**, or general search warrants, to search for smuggled goods anywhere, including private homes. Colonial leaders protested that this was a violation of their rights as Englishmen.

### The Sugar Act

In 1764 the British Parliament passed the **Sugar Act**, which taxed certain goods including sugar, molasses, and coffee that were imported into the colonies. The stated purpose of the Sugar Act was to raise revenue "for defraying the expenses of defending, protecting, and securing" the colonies.

▲ Deck of cards
featuring the stamp

## The Stamp Act

In 1765 Parliament levied a stamp tax for newspapers, playing cards, printed sermons, and a variety of legal and commercial documents. Stamps or special stamped paper had to be purchased and attached to each item. The **Stamp Act** levied the first direct tax (on items produced and used entirely within the colonies) on the colonies.

▼ Burning an effigy of a stamp collector in Virginia

## The Quartering Act

Two days after the passage of the Stamp Act, Parliament passed the **Quartering Act**, which created a peacetime standing army and required food and housing from the colonists. The close passage of the Stamp Act and the Quartering Act led some colonists to conclude that Parliament's purpose was an unlawful military occupation to enforce parliamentary taxation of the colonies.

## Colonial Opposition

These parliamentary decisions sparked a firestorm of protest in America. In May of 1765 **Patrick Henry**, a member of the Virginia House of Burgesses, presented resolutions to that body declaring that Virginians possessed all the rights and privileges of Englishmen and that to grant the right of taxation to any group other than the Virginia Assembly was an act of tyranny.

In October delegates from nine colonies met in New York for the **Stamp Act Congress**. They formally denounced the Stamp Act and its seizure of colonial rights, particularly the right that only representatives elected by the colonists could levy taxes. Matters became violent in some places. In Boston, the **Sons of Liberty**, led by **Samuel Adams**, hanged an effigy (crude likeness of a hated person or group) of the royal stamp distributor, and some ransacked his home, smashing windows and furniture. Although Samuel Adams distanced himself from the vandalism, he was generally pleased with the success of the protest since the tax official resigned.

In March 1766 Parliament repealed the Stamp Act. However, at the same time, it passed the **Declaratory Act**, which stated that Parliament had the right to pass any law that it desired regarding the colonies.

▼ Patrick Henry denouncing the Stamp Act

## Patrick Henry, "Voice of the Revolution"

Among the voices raised in defense of American liberty, few were as eloquent as that of Patrick Henry of Virginia's House of Burgesses. In 1765 he fiercely denounced the Stamp Act. He gave a blunt warning to King George III about the consequences of tyranny. Henry told the Assembly, "[Julius] Caesar had his Brutus, [King] Charles the First his [Oliver] Cromwell, and George the Third. . . . " He was interrupted midsentence by the Speaker of the House of Burgesses, who is said to have cried, "Treason!" Indeed, many present thought Henry was implying that the king should be assassinated. Though he later apologized for his remarks and assured his fellow legislators that he was loyal to the king, the tension evident that day was spreading throughout the colonies.

## The Townshend Acts

An uneasy calm followed the repeal of the Stamp Act, but the quiet was soon shattered by a new revenue plan in Parliament. In 1767 Charles Townshend, the head of the British Treasury, proposed a series of taxes and enforcement measures. These **Townshend Acts** placed taxes on glass, paint, paper, lead, and tea, and also strengthened the writs of assistance.

As opposition to the Townshend Acts grew, colonists organized boycotts (refusals to buy British goods). In 1768 a riot broke out in Boston when customs officials seized a ship belonging to one of the city's leading businessmen, John Hancock. British troops and artillery arrived to police Boston and to quash the growing unrest.

The colonists' outrage over the new taxes did not center primarily on the cost of the taxes but rather on the fact that they had no voice in the approval of them. "No taxation without representation" became a rallying cry for many colonists. They complained that there were no colonial representatives in Parliament; but Parliament insisted that the colonists, as well as all other citizens of the British Empire who could not vote, were "virtually" represented. Britain, faced with huge debts from the recent wars and large costs for maintaining an army to protect the expanding empire, thought it reasonable for the colonists to share the expense. In addition, people in Britain were paying substantially higher taxes than those in the colonies. Colonial leaders argued that the colonists were being deprived of their freedoms and their long-practiced rights of self-government.

# The Eve of War

## *The Boston Massacre*

British troops arrived in Boston in 1768. The sight of the British force and its fleet of warships overseeing a city at peace irritated Bostonians. On March 5, 1770, a band of Patriots gathered in the square outside the British barracks to demand the departure of the unwelcome soldiers. The angry crowd hurled sticks and snowballs at several soldiers. One of the soldiers was struck and fell on the ice. While it is unclear who issued the command, British troops fired into the mob, killing five and wounding others. Among those killed was Crispus Attucks, a former slave. As news of the shooting spread, many in Boston were wild with anger. Soon the event was being called a "massacre."

Nine British soldiers were placed on trial for murder. One of the defense attorneys was John Adams, Samuel Adams's cousin. Though John had been critical of Parliament's actions and considered himself a Patriot, he also believed that everyone was entitled to a fair trial. All the soldiers except two were acquitted. The others were found guilty of manslaughter rather than murder. Their thumbs were branded, and they were released.

After the Boston Massacre, tensions eased in the colonies. The calm, however, was not to last. In 1772 an armed British customs ship, the *Gaspee*, ran aground near Providence, Rhode Island. The ship's captain, who had previously searched ships without a warrant and had sent his crew ashore to seize food without paying for it, was not welcome in Rhode Island. On the night of June 9, citizens boarded the *Gaspee*, captured and removed the crew, and burned the ship.

This attack on one of His Majesty's ships prompted the British to investigate and make arrests, actions that had previously been handled by colonial courts. At the same time, the Massachusetts governor announced that his salary would now come from the king rather than the colony. No longer would the legislature be able to limit the governor by using the "power of the purse." More and more, the colonists came to believe that their rights were being stripped away.

In November 1772, the Boston Town Meeting authorized the formation of a **Committee of Correspondence**. Led by Samuel Adams, the committee provided information to other areas of the colony about British threats. In March 1773 the Virginia legislature voted to establish its own Committee of Correspondence, and other colonies quickly followed. The committees provided information and intercolonial cooperation that would be an important step toward a united political and military response to British actions.

◀ Paul Revere's engraving of the Boston Massacre

■ No snow or ice is shown, though some in the crowd had hurled snowballs at the soldiers.

■ The building on the right is labeled as "Butcher's Hall"; however, it was really the Customs House.

■ A sniper (circled) is erroneously shown from a window on the right.

■ British soldiers are shown in a line of attack, but the scene was chaotic, and the soldiers were separated from each other by the crowd. Captain Preston appears to order the soldiers to fire by waving his sword, but he denied ordering them to fire.

■ See Student Activities for a guided analysis of this engraving and other sources related to the Boston Massacre.

## The Boston Tea Party

By 1770 all the Townshend duties were repealed except for a small tax on tea. The profitable British East India Company faced a challenge: because of colonial boycotts and because the colonists were buying cheaper, smuggled Dutch tea, its British warehouses were stuffed with millions of pounds of tea. The company turned to its powerful friends in Parliament for help. At the urging of Lord North, the prime minister, Parliament passed the **Tea Act** of 1773, which reduced the tax on tea and granted the East India Company a monopoly on the shipment and sale of English tea in America. British tea was now cheaper to buy than the Dutch tea; however, colonists were enraged. If Parliament could grant a monopoly on tea, what next? In port cities from Boston to Charleston, opposition to the tea shipments was intense. In several colonies, protestors successfully forced tea ships to return to England.

When three tea ships arrived in Boston Harbor in November 1773, Patriots made every effort to have them returned to England without unloading their tea. However, Governor Hutchinson refused to allow the ships to return without paying the duty. British law required that the ships be unloaded and the duty paid within twenty days.

On the evening of December 16, 1773, the deadline for the duty to be paid, thousands gathered around the Old South Church, not far from the waterfront. Many belonged to the Sons of Liberty. When word reached the crowd that Governor Hutchinson had again refused to let the ships return their cargo, approximately 150 men and boys, some disguised as Mohawk warriors, boarded the tea ships.

In the **Boston Tea Party**, the group dumped huge amounts of tea into the harbor. After the tea was emptied, the participants cleaned the ships and released their crews. The Patriots then lined up at attention on deck, emptied any loose tea from their boots, swept it into the harbor, and marched away singing. John Adams was both shocked and impressed at the action, recognizing that it would bring important and lasting consequences for the colonies' relationship with Britain. He wrote in his diary, "There is a dignity, a majesty, a sublimity, in this last effort of the Patriots, that I greatly admire." However, not all Patriots approved of this act. Benjamin Franklin wrote in a letter to Adams and Hancock "I am truly concerned . . . that there should seem to any a necessity for carrying matters to such an extremity, as . . . to destroy private property" and encouraged repayment for the destroyed tea.

### More Tea Parties

Boston was not the only colonial port that protested the tea tax. The "tea party" was copied in New York. Charleston stored its tea until the war broke out and then sold it at auction to help pay for colonial forces. Philadelphia let its tea rot in warehouses.

Another protest to the Tea Act occurred in Edenton, North Carolina, on October 25, 1774. A group of fifty-one women pledged not to drink any more tea (or buy British-made cloth and other British imports). Their action was one of the earliest-known instances of political activity on the part of American women in the colonies.

### The Coercive ("Intolerable") Acts

Across the Atlantic the Boston Tea Party was not regarded lightly. A law had been disregarded and property had been destroyed. King George III instructed Lord North that it was time for strong measures against the colonies. The colonies "must either submit or triumph," the king declared. On this, at least, the Patriots and the king agreed.

# The Coercive Acts

In 1774 Parliament passed four acts, known collectively as the **Coercive Acts**, intended to punish troublesome Massachusetts. In America these measures were called the "Intolerable Acts" by Patriots who refused to be coerced. General Thomas Gage was appointed as the governor of Massachusetts, which signified to the colonists that they were now under military occupation.

▼ Closing of Boston Harbor

**1 Boston Port Act**

The first act closed Boston Harbor until the cost of the destroyed tea was repaid.

**2 Massachusetts Government Act**

The second act revoked the Massachusetts colonial charter. Officials would be appointed by the royal governor, and town meetings would be allowed only with the governor's approval.

**3 Administration of Justice Act**

The third act dictated that British officials accused of committing crimes would be tried in England.

**4 Quartering Act**

The fourth act was a new Quartering Act that required increased housing and feeding of British soldiers.

Another act that angered Americans was the **Quebec Act**, passed by Parliament in 1774. The act established a government for Quebec that included a Crown-appointed governor but not an elected legislative assembly, guaranteed free practice of the Catholic faith, restored the Roman Catholic Church's ability to impose tithes, and extended the boundaries of Quebec southward to the Ohio River. American colonists were angered by what they saw as the establishment of Roman Catholicism and the giving away of land belonging to the colonies according to their charters.

## *First Continental Congress (1774)*

Sympathy for Boston spread throughout the colonies, and some sent food and other aid to the beleaguered city. A growing sense of colonial unity was evident: in the Virginia House of Burgesses, a young Virginian named Thomas Jefferson called for a day of fasting and prayer as a show of support for the Boston Patriots. Virginia's royal governor dissolved the House, so the legislators reconvened in a nearby tavern, adopting a resolution for the meeting of a Continental Congress. Similar calls came from other colonies until the Massachusetts House of Representatives invited all the Colonial Committees of Correspondence to meet in Philadelphia in September.

On September 5, representatives from all colonies except Georgia gathered in Philadelphia for the **First Continental Congress**. The fifty-five delegates included distinguished men such as Virginia's George Washington and Patrick Henry and Massachusetts's John Adams and Samuel Adams.

The delegates were united in their opposition to the Intolerable Acts, but they did not all agree on how to respond to Britain's actions. After seven weeks, they adopted a **Declaration of Rights and Grievances** that voiced their objections to the recent acts of Parliament and stated that the colonies must be self-governing in nearly every respect. Although they maintained their allegiance to the king, they asserted that his actions had to be consistent with their rights as British citizens. As self-governing states, the colonies had the right to raise militias to defend themselves.

Congress also approved the formation of the **Continental Association**, which called for the thirteen colonies to boycott all imported British goods as well as the export of any goods to Britain. Local committees of association enforced the boycott by intimidating, harassing, and even tarring-and-feathering those who violated it.

The delegates sent the king their petitions, hoping he would address their grievances. But Britain was determined to maintain control over the colonies. Congress agreed to reconvene in May 1775 if the crisis with Britain had not been resolved.

### Comprehension Check 3.2

**MATCH THE DESCRIPTIONS WITH THE TERMS.**

1. prevented colonists from settling west of the Appalachian Mountains
2. gave customs officials search warrants to find smuggled items
3. taxed printed documents
4. stated that Parliament had the right to pass any law it desired for the American colonies
5. taxed glass, paint, paper, and tea
6. punished Massachusetts after the Boston Tea Party

**A** Coercive Acts
**B** Declaratory Act
**C** Proclamation of 1763
**D** Stamp Act
**E** Townshend Acts
**F** writs of assistance

**MAKING CONNECTIONS**

7. What was the primary objection of the colonists to British actions after the French and Indian War?

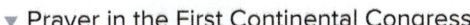

▾ Prayer in the First Continental Congress

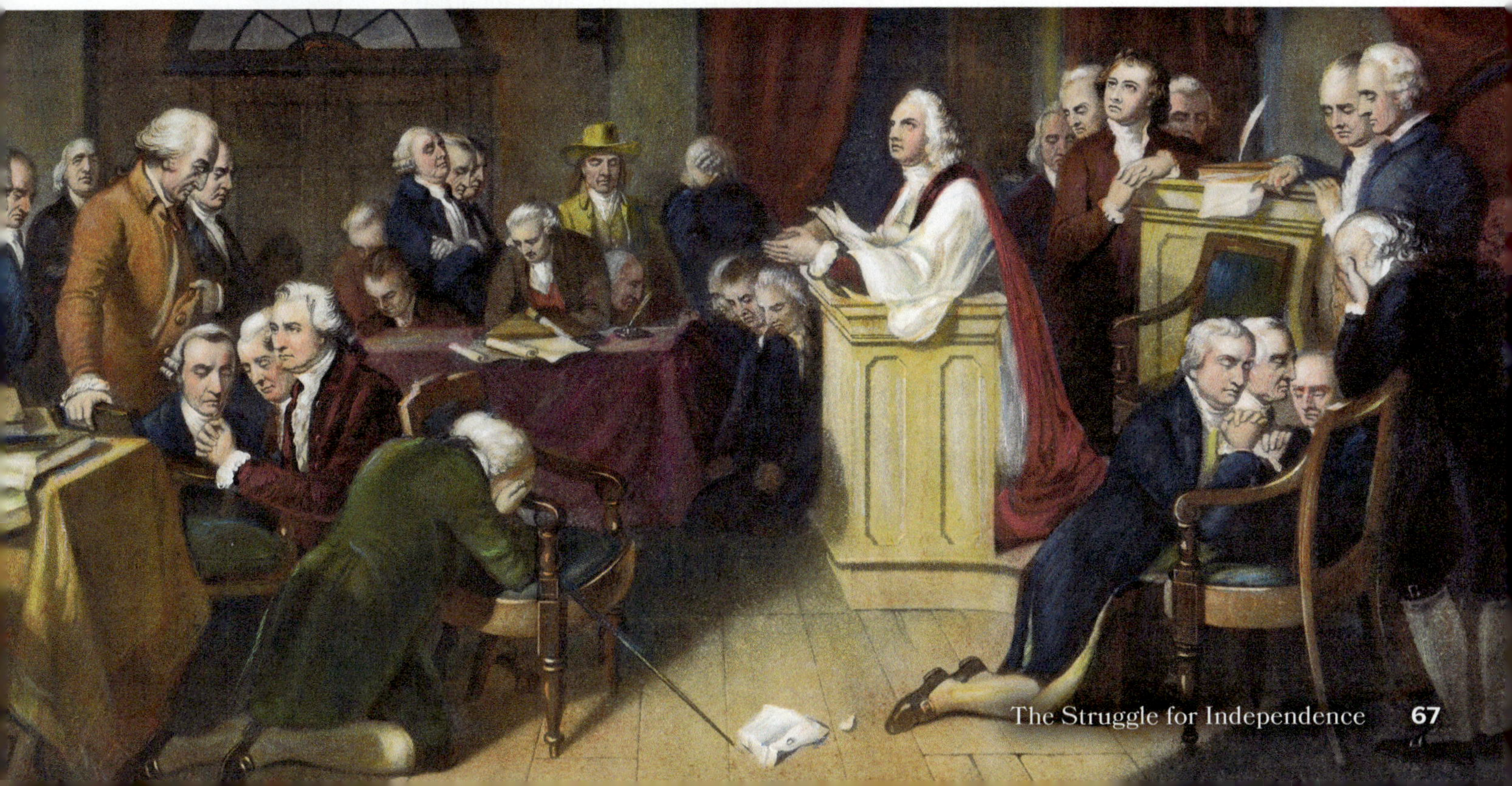

- What was the significance of Lexington and Concord?
- What did the Second Continental Congress do?
- What battles were fought during the early War for Independence?
- Why were colonists for or against independence?
- How was the Declaration of Independence developed?

 **Analyzing Sources**

To Henry, what was more valuable than life and peace? How might a Loyalist have responded to Henry's speech?

### 3.3 The Road to Independence

What events and arguments led to the Declaration of Independence?

## The Shot Heard 'Round the World

In October 1774 Massachusetts established a Provincial Congress elected by the people. They authorized the organizing, drilling, and supplying of Patriot militias.

When representatives of Virginia met for a second time in March 1775, they discussed organizing volunteer militias. Patrick Henry rose to address his fellow legislators with powerful words:

> *Gentlemen may cry, Peace, Peace—but there is no peace. The war is actually begun! Our brethren are already in the field! Why stand we here idle? . . . Is life so dear, or peace so sweet, as to be purchased at the price of chains and slavery? Forbid it, Almighty God! I know not what course others may take, but as for me, give me liberty or give me death!*

— **PATRICK HENRY**

In April 1775 British General Gage learned that a large stock of Patriot munitions was stored in **Concord**, sixteen miles west of Boston. He ordered 700 soldiers to quietly seize the stockpile.

On the night of April 18, the British rowed across the bay and assembled for the march to Concord. They planned to stop along the way in **Lexington** to arrest Patriot leaders John Hancock and Samuel Adams. Learning of the plot, Paul Revere and William Dawes rode separately to Lexington to warn colonists. Dr. Samuel Prescott joined them as they rode to Concord. Each was stopped by the British, but Prescott managed to reach Concord.

▶ Paul Revere warning colonists in his midnight ride

### Did You Know?

Apollos Rivoire, a French Huguenot, made many sacrifices for his new country. Altering his name he became known as Paul Revere. His son, Paul Jr., became the famous midnight rider.

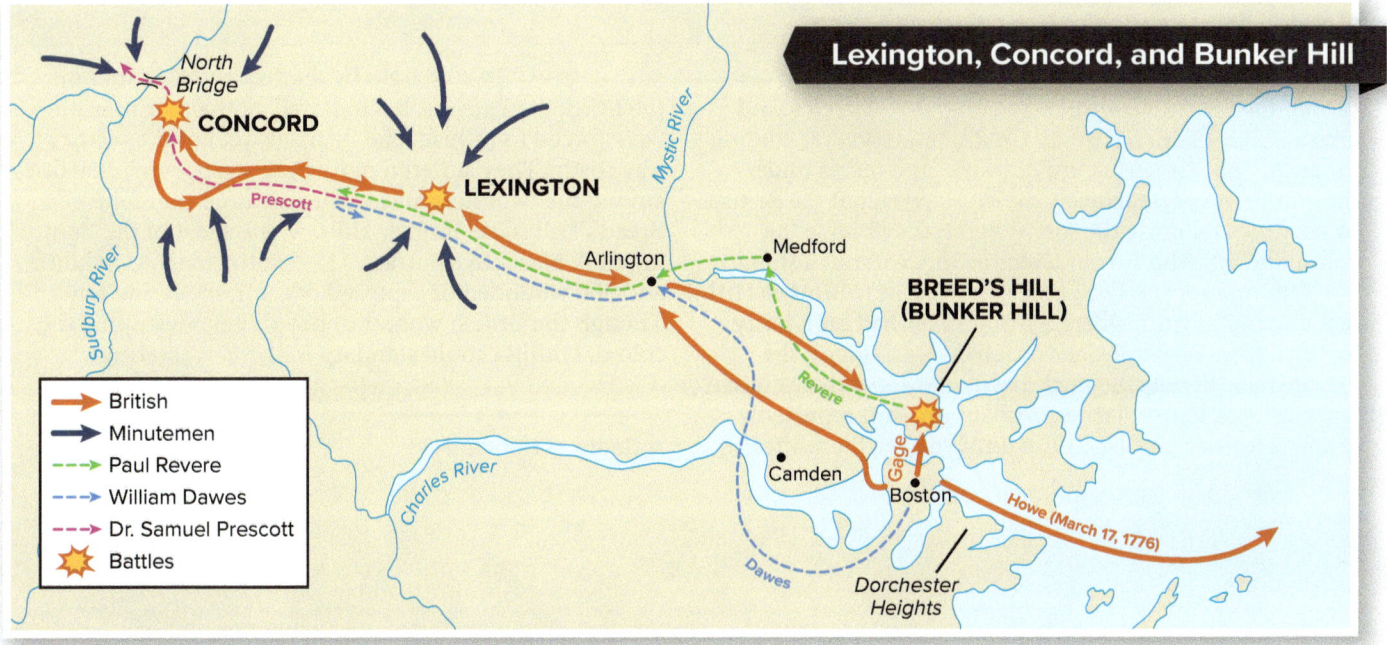

About seventy Lexington minutemen were waiting when the British arrived in the early morning of April 19. The British commander spotted the thin line of Patriot militia and ordered the troops to hold their fire as he ordered the Americans to disarm and disband. The minutemen's commander had also ordered not to open fire. Having proven their opposition, the militia began to disperse. At that point, a shot rang out—no one knows by whom—but the British regulars shot into the soldier-farmers, killing eight and wounding ten. The British proceeded to Concord.

Alerted to the British advance, hundreds of minutemen converged on the outskirts of Concord. The Patriots met the British at the North Bridge that led into town. Fatal shots were exchanged, and the British were pushed back. For the British, the march back to Boston was difficult as minutemen circled the city and pinned them down by firing from the cover of stone walls, trees, and barns. The Americans had clearly won the day, and the war had begun.

## The Second Continental Congress

When the delegates gathered in Philadelphia on May 10, 1775, for the **Second Continental Congress**, they found themselves in a difficult situation. The original purpose of the Continental Congress was to debate and deliver cooperative resolutions concerning British colonial policies, not to make laws and supply armies. Yet war had erupted three weeks earlier, and the New England militia had the British army pinned in Boston.

The assembly's first priority was to deal with Boston's military situation. The delegates appointed George Washington, who had arrived in Philadelphia to offer to command Virginia's militia forces, as commander in chief. He was being asked to take charge of a shabby collection of farmers and shopkeepers facing the best-trained, best-equipped army in the world. Washington was a natural choice. Washington had emerged from the French and Indian War as a hero. As a Virginian, he could help link the Patriot cause in New England to the southern colonies. His commanding presence, coolness under fire, and keen ability to lead and inspire became essential to the seemingly impossible task to which the Continental Congress had unanimously elected him.

### The Shot Heard 'Round *the* World

Poet Ralph Waldo Emerson later commemorated the event in "Concord Hymn":

> By the rude bridge that arched the flood,
> Their flag to April's breeze unfurled,
> Here once the embattled farmers stood,
> And fired the shot heard round the world.

### Militia v. Regulars

The militia was made up of those who were prepared to leave their farms and businesses to fight in military emergencies. The famous "minutemen" (citizens ready to fight on a minute's notice) were an example of American militia. Militia units might serve for months or even years, but only as long as the emergency lasted.

Regulars, on the other hand, were professional, full-time soldiers, such as the British army or the American Continentals during the War for Independence.

## Early Military Action

On May 10, 1775—the same day as the opening session of the Second Continental Congress—**Fort Ticonderoga** in New York fell to the Continental forces including Ethan Allen's "Green Mountain Boys" and forces under the command of Benedict Arnold. They caught the British by surprise. Entering the fort at night, they awoke the commandant, who surrendered the fort without a shot.

On June 16, a major battle occurred near **Bunker Hill** just north of Boston where Patriot forces had built hasty fortifications. General Gage ordered an assault on the entrenched Patriots the next day. To conserve their limited ammunition, Patriot leader William Prescott reportedly ordered the troops, "Don't fire until you see the whites of their eyes." Two charges by the British failed; but on the third, the Patriots, having used all their ammunition, were forced to retreat. The British won, but the victory was costly. They suffered more than a thousand casualties among the two thousand soldiers sent up the slope of Breed's Hill (near Bunker Hill), where most of the fighting took place. By contrast, 115 Continentals were killed and 300 wounded or captured of the 1,500 in the army. Though the British won, the encounter showed that the colonial militia could stand up to the British army.

▼ Battle of Bunker Hill

When Washington arrived to take command, the siege of Boston was in a deadlock. He sent Colonel Henry Knox to Fort Ticonderoga to retrieve the captured British cannons. Knox and his men used oxen, sleds, and rafts to transport many pieces of heavy artillery on a wintry, mountainous, three-hundred-mile trek.

On the evening of March 4, 1776, Washington placed the cannons on Dorchester Heights, overlooking Boston and its harbor. When the British awoke, they found themselves in an indefensible position and were forced to evacuate Boston. Many colonists loyal to Britain went with them.

## Debating Independence

The war deeply divided the colonists. Many became **Patriots**, supporting or fighting for the cause of American independence. Others were **Loyalists**, or Tories (named after the political party in Parliament that supported the king), because they continued to acknowledge the king's authority. The division cut across regions and social classes. It tore communities and even families apart. In some areas (such as South Carolina), the War for Independence was fought almost entirely between American Patriots and American Loyalists.

▲ Knox bringing cannons from Fort Ticonderoga to Boston

### Loyalists (Tories)

Some colonists were loyal to England for political, religious, and economic reasons. Many believed that they were fairly represented by Parliament and that taxes to fund the defense of the colonies were just. Others disagreed with Parliament's various acts but did not think that those mistakes justified war. Furthermore, many Loyalists feared that independence would lead to mob rule and tyranny.

Some Tories thought it was wrong to rebel because they saw the king as God's authority over them. They believed that Romans 13:2 and 1 Peter 2:13–17 were clear that God placed rulers in authority and that Christians were called to submit and honor even unjust leaders. Some Tories also feared that cutting ties with Britain would remove the colonies from profitable trade relations in the British Empire. Others remained loyal to Britain because of family connections.

Many Loyalists fled to England, Canada, or the British West Indies. But most Loyalists stayed in the American colonies, probably because they did not want to risk losing their property. To avoid trouble, some kept their opinions to themselves. Other Tories fought for the British or aided them by selling them food and supplies.

Some historians believe that Loyalists comprised about 20 percent of the population. Others estimate that allegiances were divided almost equally among the colonists: one-third Loyalists, one-third Patriots, and one-third neutral.

## Patriots

The Patriots had political, religious, and economic reasons for their cause, too. They believed that their political right to a representative government was at stake. The colonists were used to representing themselves locally by creating many of their own laws and taxes. When a distant Parliament began to tax the colonies, many Americans saw this as a loss of their liberty. Those who were influenced by the ideas of John Locke and other writers believed a government that had become oppressive was no longer legitimate and Americans were justified to cast off this illegitimate government.

Religious beliefs also greatly influenced the Patriots. In fact, the war might not have been as popular without the influence of preachers, many of whom called for independence. Religious colonists wrestled to decide to which authority they should submit. For more than a century, the colonists had followed their own local governments as their founding charters stipulated. Patriots did not want to defy these authorities. Some Patriots believed they should submit to local governments, or "lesser magistrates," rather than to the British government. They also believed that their responsibility to submit to governing authorities (Romans 13 and 1 Peter 2) ended when those authorities acted contrary to the general good and destroyed the God-given liberties of the people.

Some became Patriots for economic reasons. Parliament's new policies hurt many wealthy American merchants, and colonists resented Parliament's interference with trade.

## Neutral Colonists

The remaining colonists joined neither side. Some lived in remote areas and were not greatly concerned about the political conflict unless it came near their homes. Others, such as the Quakers and Moravians, rejected all participation in war. Others were neutral for business reasons, fearing that they would suffer financial loss if they chose sides.

## Taking Sides

| | Loyalists | Patriots | Neutral Colonists |
|---|---|---|---|
| **Political** | Sided with England<br><br>Willing to put up with England | Wanted to retain representative self-government<br><br>Saw England as abusing authority | Lived in remote areas mostly unaffected by policies |
| **Religious** | Viewed loyalty to the king as loyalty to God-given authority<br><br>Feared mob rule | Viewed loyalty to local rulers as loyalty to God-given authority<br><br>Saw England as forfeiting authority | Practiced pacifism |
| **Economic** | Maintained business and family ties | Protected local trade<br><br>Resisted trade interference | Feared loss from offending either side |

## Thomas Paine

Even after sending Washington to Boston to take command of the army, delegates of the Second Continental Congress still hoped to reconcile with Great Britain without sacrificing American rights.

On July 5, 1775, the delegates adopted the **Olive Branch Petition**, which pledged loyalty to the king and requested his intervention concerning Parliament's actions. The next day the Continental Congress issued a "Declaration of the Causes for Taking Up Arms," in which they stated that British actions had left the American people with two choices—"unconditional submission to the tyranny of irritated ministers, or resistance by force." They had chosen resistance, but they emphasized their purpose as gaining recognition of the colonies' rights, not yet as seeking separation from Great Britain.

The Olive Branch Petition was an attempt to settle matters peacefully, but King George III refused to even read it. Instead, in August 1775 he issued a **Proclamation of Rebellion**, which declared that parts of the American colonies were "open and avowed enemies" and instructed his Boston army and British subjects to "suppress such rebellion, and to bring the traitors to justice." Parliament followed this up in December 1775 with the **Prohibitory Act**, which ordered that all trade with the American colonies be stopped and all ships involved in colonial trade be seized. Parliament sent more troops and authorized hiring thousands of mercenaries (professional soldiers who are paid to fight). These mercenaries were Hessians, named for their German province of Hesse-Cassel.

To some Patriots, including John Adams, these acts in essence severed the relationship between the colonies and Britain. Public opinion was further influenced by the 1776 publication of ***Common Sense***, a pamphlet by **Thomas Paine**. Paine, an Englishman who lived in America, argued that the king, not just Parliament, was the enemy. He asserted that while government is a necessary evil in a sinful world, monarchy was a foolish form of government that contradicted God's will and whose path through history was strewn with human wreckage. Paine concluded that separation from Britain was the only common-sense option, stating "the blood of the slain, the weeping voice of nature cries, 'TIS TIME TO PART."

Within three months, over 150,000 copies of *Common Sense* were circulating in the colonies, and during the war over a half-million copies were printed. This document more than any other moved the colonists toward declaring independence.

In December 1776, Paine wrote *The American Crisis*. In these papers, he argued the Patriot cause:

> *These are the times that try men's souls. The summer soldier and the sunshine patriot will, in this crisis, shrink from the service of their country; but he that stands by it now, deserves the love and thanks of man and woman. Tyranny, like hell, is not easily conquered; yet we have this consolation with us, that the harder the conflict, the more glorious the triumph. What we obtain too cheap, we esteem too lightly; it is dearness only that gives every thing its value. Heaven knows how to put a proper price upon its goods; and it would be strange indeed if so celestial an article as FREEDOM should not be highly rated.* — **THOMAS PAINE**

 **Analyzing Sources**

What is Paine's criticism of the "summer soldier" and the "sunshine patriot"? What is Paine's point about the cost of freedom?

Washington had *The American Crisis* read to his men before the Battle of Trenton and later at Valley Forge to strengthen their resolve to persevere.

Despite his use of biblical allusions in his writings, Paine opposed Christianity and advocated an unrestrained form of democracy thought dangerous by some. After the Revolutionary War, Paine wrote a stirring defense of the French Revolution (see Chapter 5) called *Rights of Man*. He moved to France in 1792, where he was imprisoned for a time for his political views. After his release, he wrote his last great essay, *Age of Reason*, which critiqued organized religion and Christian theology in favor of reason and scientific inquiry.

## Declaring Independence

Many colonies began to change their constitutions to include the republican idea of rule by representatives chosen by the people. In June 1776 Richard Henry Lee of Virginia presented a resolution to the Second Continental Congress calling for complete independence from Britain:

> *These United Colonies are, and of right ought to be, free and independent States.*

Such a final and potentially fatal resolution required serious consideration, and debate continued. In the meantime, a committee of five—John Adams of Massachusetts, Benjamin Franklin of Pennsylvania, Roger Sherman of Connecticut, Robert Livingstone of New York, and Thomas Jefferson of Virginia—were appointed to draft a declaration in support of Lee's resolution. Most of the work on the draft was done by the eloquent Jefferson.

On July 2, Congress approved the resolution. Two days later on July 4, 1776, Congress approved the final draft of the Declaration of Independence. It not only listed the grievances that Americans had against the king but also stated universal principles that would shape the character and direction of the emerging nation.

> *We hold these truths to be self-evident, that all men are created equal; that they are endowed by their Creator with certain unalienable rights, that among these are life, liberty and the pursuit of happiness. That to secure these rights, governments are instituted among men, deriving their just powers from the consent of the governed.*

Fifty-six delegates from thirteen colonies inscribed their names on the document. Each man knew the British government would view this document as treason. If the cause failed, he could face execution. These courageous leaders found the cause worth the risk. As Jefferson's closing words of the document state,

> *We mutually pledge to each other our lives, our fortunes, and our sacred honor.*

◄ *Declaration of Independence* by John Trumbull. (Left to right) John Adams, Roger Sherman, Robert Livingstone, Thomas Jefferson, and Benjamin Franklin present the final draft to the Second Continental Congress.

## John Locke and the Social Contract Theory

Ideas such as life, liberty, pursuit of happiness, and natural rights reflected the philosophy of the day. **John Locke**, whose ideas were used extensively in the Declaration of Independence, taught that citizens have the right to overthrow tyrants, although he also recognized the danger of frequent rebellions. Locke said that a tyrant violates the contract between himself and those he rules, and therefore is not a lawful ruler. John Locke believed that a ruler who makes a mistake is not a tyrant, but rather that tyrants are those who commit a series of abuses. Many Americans believed this to be true of King George III. A list of his abuses was recorded in the Declaration of Independence.

Americans were also influenced by the political thoughts of John Calvin and other reformers. Though these reformers emphasized obedience to rulers, they noted that some political systems (such as Rome's) had governmental officials whose job it was to protect the people from tyranny. Later theologians believed that rulers and people were bound in a covenant. A ruler who violated the covenant lost the right to rule, and governmental officials should ensure that he left office. By the 1770s many Americans believed they could justify their separation from England.

## Comprehension Check 3.3

1. The British wanted to seize a stockpile of militia weapons located in ____.

   **A** Concord

   **B** Philadelphia

   **C** New York

2. The Second Continental Congress chose Washington to be the commander in chief because ____.

   **A** he was a hero of the French and Indian War

   **B** he was from New England

   **C** he was the main writer of the Declaration of Independence

3. The captured British cannons from Fort Ticonderoga were brought by ____ to Boston to end the siege.

   **A** Ethan Allen

   **B** Thomas Gage

   **C** Henry Knox

4. King George III refused to read the Olive Branch Petition sent by the Second Continental Congress.

   True

   False

5. Thomas Paine's *Common Sense* urged the colonists to remain loyal to Britain.

   True

   False

6. The Declaration of Independence was greatly influenced by the philosophy of ____.

   **A** Ralph Waldo Emerson

   **B** John Locke

   **C** Apollos Rivoire

**MAKING CONNECTIONS**

7. How did the religious reasons for the Loyalist cause differ from the religious reasons for the Patriot cause?

# Fighting the War for Independence

How did the War for Independence proceed?

**GUIDING QUESTIONS**

- What were the important battles in the north during the War for Independence?

- What challenges did the Continental Army face during the winter of 1777–78?

- What was the War for Independence like in the west and at sea?

## The War in the North

### Challenges in New York

After the British army left Boston, it turned its attention to New York City. Washington marched his army there to defend the city, but it was not easily defensible. The Americans had no navy, and the British could land troops at numerous points on the surrounding rivers or in the large harbor and march against the American forces. The Americans could not give up one of their most important cities without a fight. The American people, still divided about the war, would see such an act as a sign of defeat.

General William Howe, Gage's replacement, arrived in July 1776. The British won a series of easy victories from summer to late fall. The inexperience of the American troops and the superiority of the British navy combined to contribute to the defeat of American forces. Washington retreated across the East River. By November, New York City was in British hands, and the Continental army was in New Jersey.

### Successes at Trenton and Princeton

The onset of winter in late 1776 found the Continental army in great despair. They had been driven from New York, and many troops appeared unwilling to re-enlist at the end of the year. Faced with this disheartening situation, Washington decided to attack.

On Christmas night Washington led some 2,400 men across the Delaware River during a storm. The weather hid their movements. The Hessians did not expect an attack in such weather and were comfortably sleeping after their Christmas merry-making. Washington attacked **Trenton** near dawn and caught the Hessians completely unprepared. Nearly one thousand were killed or captured, and Washington did not lose a single man in the fighting.

Washington followed with an attack on Princeton on January 3, 1777. The British forces fled. The victories at Trenton and Princeton had a dramatic effect on American morale, and many soldiers re-enlisted.

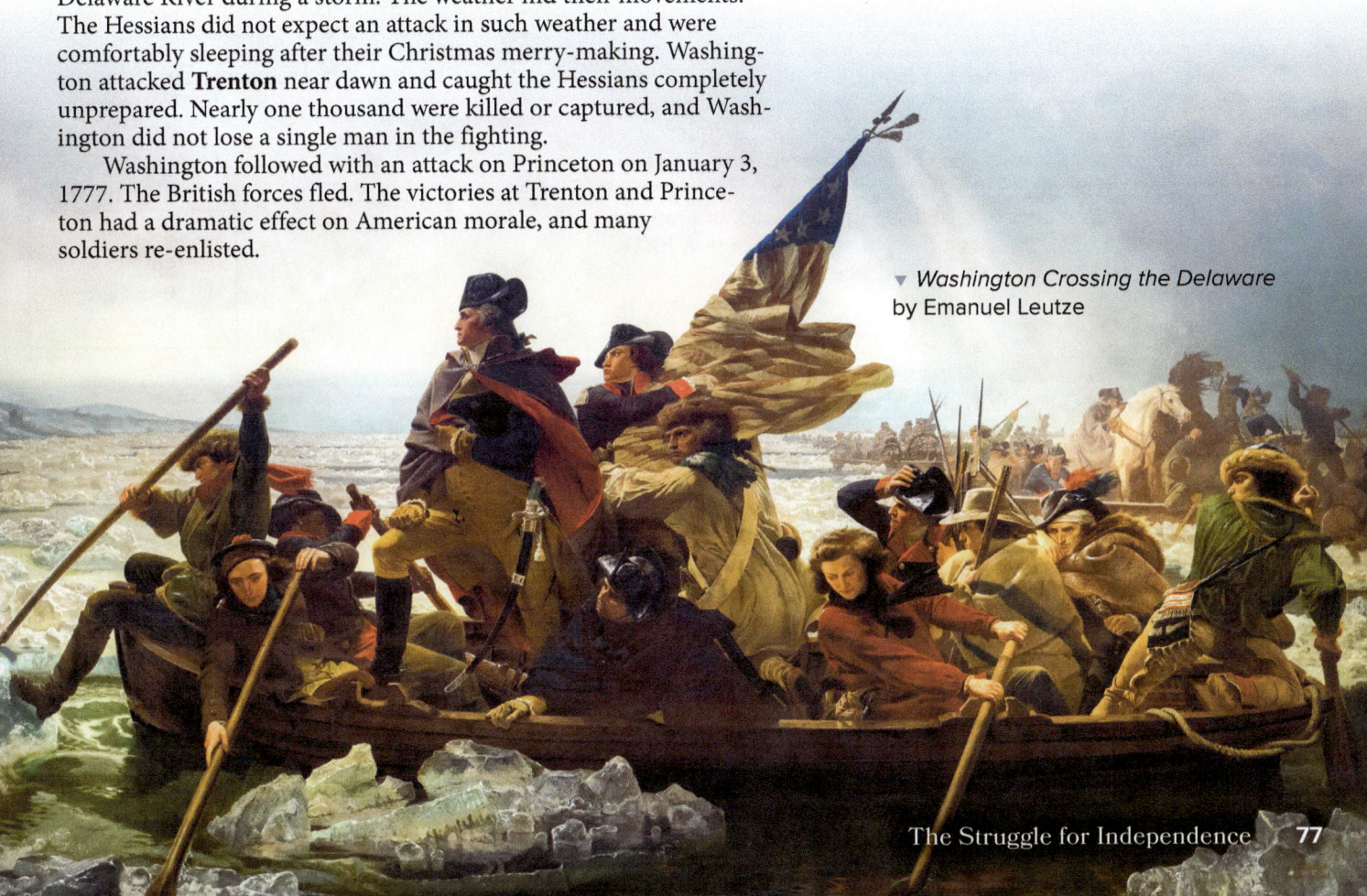

▼ *Washington Crossing the Delaware*
by Emanuel Leutze

## Fight for Philadelphia

Hoping to isolate New England from the other colonies, the British then planned a three-pronged assault on New York. One British force under General John Burgoyne would move south from Canada down Lake Champlain and through the wilderness of upstate New York, while General Howe would send a force north from New York City up the Hudson River to Albany. Meanwhile, a third British force would take a western route from Montreal, Canada, to Albany.

Fortunately for the Americans, Howe did not cooperate with the plan. Instead, he moved against the American capital of Philadelphia. On September 11, at the Battle of Brandywine Creek, Howe outmaneuvered Washington, and the Continental Army retreated. The British entered Philadelphia unopposed on September 26, but the Continental Congress was able to escape. On October 4 Washington made an attempt to recapture the city by attacking the British forces at Germantown, north of Philadelphia. The attack failed and the American capital remained in British hands.

## Victory at Saratoga

While Howe prepared to attack Philadelphia, General Burgoyne marched down Lake Champlain. He easily reseized Fort Ticonderoga, but the British plan for a three-pronged attack had begun to break down. Howe's decision to attack Philadelphia meant that only a small force would move up the Hudson River. The third British force marching toward Albany was pushed back by an American force.

In two separate battles south of **Saratoga**, New York, on September 19 and October 7, the Americans dealt heavy blows to the British. Over 1,000 British troops were killed in the battles. Much of the credit belonged to American General Horatio Gates' subordinates, General Benedict Arnold and Colonel Daniel Morgan. The British attempted to retreat to Canada, but the Americans overtook and surrounded them. On October 17, Burgoyne and his 5,000 remaining soldiers surrendered to Gates. The victory at Saratoga was a major turning point of the war.

Besides providing much needed munitions and supplies from the captured British army, the significance of the victory at Saratoga was that France, eager to see Americans win their independence from its rival, entered the war. The French had been providing supplies and loans to America. After the surprising American victory at Saratoga, France officially recognized the United States as a separate nation and entered the war against the British. America now had a powerful ally in its struggle for independence.

▼ *Surrender of General Burgoyne by John Trumbull*

### Northern Campaigns, 1776–78

Quebec

Montreal

*Lake Champlain*

St. Lawrence R.

Burgoyne

St. Leger

**FT. TICONDEROGA**
July 5, 1777

**SARATOGA**
Sept. 19 and
Oct. 7, 1777

Boston

Albany

Hudson R.

Delaware R.

West Point

**PRINCETON**
Jan. 3, 1777

New York City

Howe July 1776

**GERMANTOWN**
Oct. 4, 1777

**TRENTON**
Dec. 26, 1776

Valley Forge

**BRANDYWINE**
Sept. 11, 1777

Philadelphia

*ATLANTIC OCEAN*

Howe

→ British
✸ Colonial victory
✸ British victory
◇ Fort

## Benedict Arnold: The American Traitor

In a secluded spot on the site of the Battle of Saratoga stands a memorial with an inscription honoring "the most brilliant soldier of the Continental Army who was wounded on this spot, . . . winning for his countrymen the decisive battle of the American Revolution." The sculptor dared not mention the hero's name because that soldier was **Benedict Arnold**, one of the most infamous traitors in American history. Arnold's war record was one of the finest. He had captured Fort Ticonderoga with Ethan Allen. At Saratoga, Arnold had led a charge that broke the British lines and turned the tide of battle, all with an injured leg.

But Arnold was dissatisfied. He was often passed over for promotion. George Washington recognized Arnold's abilities and gave him command of Philadelphia after the British retreated. But politicians and jealous fellow officers criticized Arnold and worked against him. Arnold became bitter and began to look for ways to fill his purse and feed his ego. In 1779 he offered his services to the British.

When Washington attempted in 1780 to honor Arnold by giving him command of a section of the Continental Army, Arnold instead asked for West Point, an important fort on the Hudson River (now the site of the United States Military Academy). Washington was puzzled, but Arnold pleaded that the pain from his wound at Saratoga required an undemanding command. In reality Arnold had plotted with the British to turn the fort over for a large sum of money. Unaware of Arnold's treachery, Washington granted his request.

However, Arnold's plans went disastrously wrong. Americans captured his contact, British Major John André, with incriminating papers. Arnold fled to the British; André was hanged as a spy. Arnold spent the rest of the war leading raids for the British. After the war, he fled to Britain. Although he received a reward and a pension from the British, Arnold was shunned by British society. He died in London in 1801, no longer remembered as a hero of Ticonderoga and Saratoga.

## A Difficult Winter

Word of the French alliance did not reach America until the spring of 1778. Meanwhile, Washington and his army went through perhaps the hardest period of the war. With the British controlling Philadelphia, the American army made its headquarters for the winter of 1777–78 some twenty-five miles away at **Valley Forge**. The soldiers were hungry and ill-clothed. Few men had whole uniforms, and even fewer had shoes. Washington grimly observed that "you might have tracked the army from White Marsh to Valley Forge by the blood of their feet." Many soldiers deserted, and about 2,500 American troops died that winter.

Washington could do little to relieve the suffering of his men. Because the Continental Congress lacked the power to tax the colonies, Washington had only its worthless paper currency with which to buy supplies. Farmers and merchants found it far more profitable to sell their goods to the British in Philadelphia, who paid in gold and silver.

### Did You Know?

During the War for Independence, the Continental Congress issued paper currency known as the continental dollar. Inflation caused the dollars to lose their value rapidly. By 1779, one continental dollar was worth one or two cents in silver, thus the expression "not worth a Continental" began.

In February of 1778 the Prussian **Baron Friedrich von Steuben** came to Valley Forge to serve as a drillmaster for the Continental army. Although Von Steuben did not know English, he did know how to train men and how to instill pride and discipline. He taught them to march properly and showed them how to maneuver in battle. Von Steuben transformed the disorganized army that had fled New York into a fighting force.

▲ Baron von Steuben drilling troops at Valley Forge

When the French entered the war, the British decided to focus more attention on the southern colonies where more Loyalists lived. They also withdrew from Philadelphia to New York City in June 1778. Americans attacked them at Monmouth Court House in New Jersey. Although the battle was a draw, it showed how much Washington's army had improved.

## Lafayette, the Republican Aristocrat

Perhaps the most famous international hero during the War for Independence was the French aristocrat **Marquis de Lafayette** (1757–1834).

Because of his background, Lafayette seemed an unlikely candidate for a republican revolution. But the American cause fired his imagination. When a representative came to France in 1776 seeking officers for the Continental army, Lafayette enthusiastically volunteered. Because he was already wealthy, Lafayette declined to take a salary.

When General Washington learned that he was receiving a nineteen-year-old major general, he was initially unenthusiastic. Upon meeting the young officer, however, Washington's doubts melted. Lafayette was gracious, humble, and eager both to learn and to serve.

▲ Commemorative dollar coin with Washington and Lafayette (Lafayette on reverse)

Lafayette served bravely with the Continental army. He was wounded at the Battle of Brandywine, and a small force under his command constantly harassed Cornwallis and the British in Virginia. At Yorktown, he led an attack on a major British fortification.

When Lafayette returned to France after the war, he dreamed of making his native land like his adopted nation. When the French Revolution erupted in 1789, the marquis assisted in adopting a new constitution for France. The revolution turned ugly, however, and violence erupted. In dismay and disgust, Lafayette left France, but was imprisoned by the Austrians for five years. After his release, Lafayette returned to France. He made one last visit to America in 1824. To his astonishment, hordes of enthusiastic admirers and graying veterans greeted him as a hero.

# The War in the West and at Sea

A different kind of warfare took place on the frontier. There the fighting resembled the guerrilla tactics of the French and Indian War. A group of British soldiers and Iroquois engaged in a brutal struggle with hardy but scattered American frontiersmen.

One American leader, **George Rogers Clark**, arose in the West. In 1778 the twenty-five-year-old Clark led an attack on British trading posts in the region then known as the Northwest. With a tiny force of approximately 175 men, Clark won several strategically important victories in present-day Illinois and Indiana. They reduced Indian attacks and helped the United States lay claim to the territory north of the Ohio River.

The American navy in the War for Independence was pitifully small in contrast to the mighty British fleet. On September 23, 1779, Scottish-born Captain **John Paul Jones** was commanding the *Bonhomme Richard* (named in honor of Benjamin Franklin and his *Poor Richard's Almanac*) off the coast of Great Britain when he encountered two British warships, the *Serapis* and the *Countess of Scarborough*. The three-and-a-half-hour fight started poorly for the Americans when two of their largest cannons exploded, killing several men. Jones tried to overcome the British advantage by coming close to board the *Serapis*. The British guns tore gaping holes in the side of the American ship. At one point, an officer of the *Bonhomme Richard*, thinking Jones was dead, called out, offering surrender to the British. Jones refused to surrender, rose, and reportedly cried out, "I have not yet begun to fight!"

Although his ship was slowly sinking, Jones continued to pound the British. The captain of the *Serapis* finally surrendered. Jones and his crew boarded the British warship and watched the shattered *Bonhomme Richard* sink beneath the waves. John Paul Jones had given America its first great victory at sea.

▲ (top) George Rogers Clark maneuvering on the Wabash River; (bottom) John Paul Jones and crew boarding the *Serapis*

---

## Comprehension Check 3.4

1. All the following contributed to the capture of New York City by the British except ＿＿.

    A  the city's indefensible position

    B  the lack of American interest in the city

    C  the superiority of the British navy

2. One important result of the victories at Trenton and Princeton was ＿＿.

    A  the boost in re-enlistment of American troops

    B  the end to the British occupation of Philadelphia

    C  the replacement of General Gage with General Howe

3. France decided to enter the war and fight alongside the Americans after the victory at ＿＿.

    A  Brandywine Creek

    B  Saratoga

    C  Yorktown

4. Despite heroic fighting in the Continental Army, ＿＿ is best known as a traitor to the American cause.

    A  John André

    B  Benedict Arnold

    C  Horatio Gates

5. Baron von Steuben helped the Americans by ＿＿.

    A  introducing Washington to Marquis de Lafayette

    B  reclaiming New York from the British

    C  transforming the army through expert training at Valley Forge

6. ＿＿ gave America its first great victory at sea.

    A  George Rogers Clark

    B  John Paul Jones

    C  Daniel Morgan

### MAKING CONNECTIONS

7. How was the fighting on the western frontier different from the fighting in the East?

GUIDING QUESTIONS

- What were the important battles in the south during the War for Independence?
- What were the results of the War for Independence?

**3.5** # Winning the War for Independence

## The War in the South

During the early years of the war the British had generally concentrated on fighting Washington's Continentals and isolating New England. In late 1778 the British began a drive through the south, where they had more Loyalist support. By early 1779, all of Georgia—including Savannah, its chief city and port—had fallen into British hands. Georgia became a staging area for the siege of Charleston, South Carolina. In March 1780, British forces besieged Charleston. The British outnumbered the Americans more than two to one and cut their supply lines. The American troops were forced to surrender, and thousands were taken prisoner.

With the fall of Charleston, the Carolinas lay open to the British. General **Charles Cornwallis**, who now commanded the British troops, defeated Patriot forces in Camden, South Carolina, in August 1780.

General **Francis Marion**, the "Swamp Fox," led a small band of guerrilla fighters in the South Carolina low country. Marion and his men would attack British outposts and supply lines. Marion's successful hit-and-run operations pinned British troops, kept them from joining the main British force, and forced Cornwallis to constantly look over his shoulder.

Cornwallis sent more than a thousand Loyalists into western South Carolina. Their leader warned the frontier "over-mountain men" to pledge their loyalty to George III or he would lay waste their fields, burn their homes, and hang their leaders. The frontiersmen did not take kindly to threats. In October a force of nine hundred caught the Loyalists on the slopes of Kings Mountain. They killed the commander and killed, wounded, or captured almost his entire army. The victory at the Battle of Kings Mountain strengthened Patriot resolve.

▼ (left) Francis Marion, "the Swamp Fox," harassing British forces in South Carolina; (right) Battle of Kings Mountain

Toward the end of 1780, Congress appointed General **Nathanael Greene** commander of the Continental Army in the south. Greene divided his outnumbered army, hoping that Cornwallis would divide his force as well. Cornwallis sent Lieutenant Colonel Banastre Tarleton to catch the Continentals. On January 17, 1781, in Cowpens, South Carolina, the two armies clashed. In less than an hour, thanks to General Daniel Morgan's brilliant strategy, the battle was over. The British suffered over nine hundred casualties; the Americans had fewer than one hundred. The Battle of Cowpens was a major step toward eventual British defeat.

After the British losses at Kings Mountain and Cowpens, Cornwallis was determined to crush Greene, whose troops were the only serious obstacle to the British conquest of the Carolinas. In mid-March, Cornwallis faced the American army at Guilford Courthouse, a small crossroads in North Carolina. The British won, but Cornwallis lost one-quarter of his men there.

▲ General Nathanael Greene

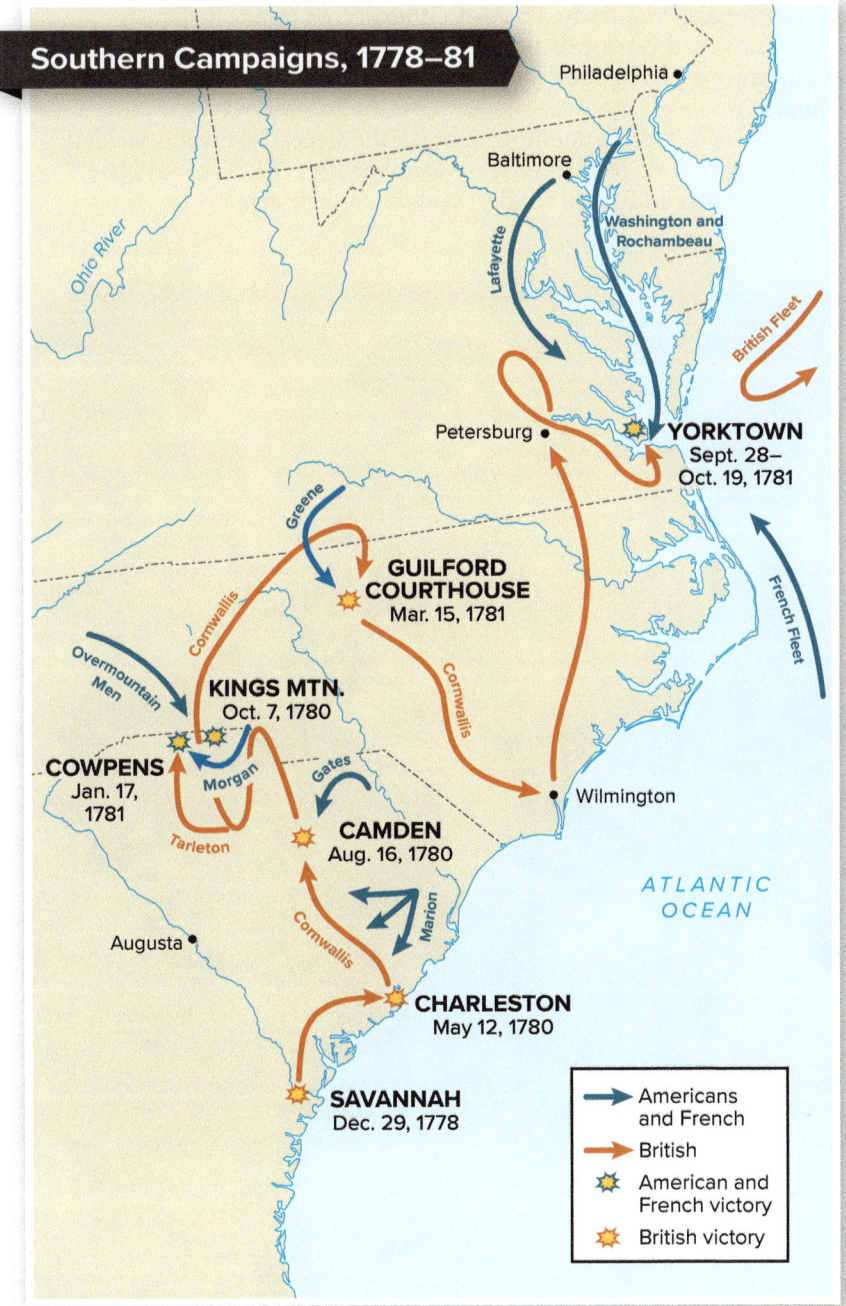

**Southern Campaigns, 1778–81**

Philadelphia

Baltimore

Lafayette

Washington and Rochambeau

British Fleet

Petersburg

**YORKTOWN**
Sept. 28–
Oct. 19, 1781

Ohio River

Greene

French Fleet

Cornwallis

**GUILFORD COURTHOUSE**
Mar. 15, 1781

Overmountain Men

**KINGS MTN.**
Oct. 7, 1780

Cornwallis

**COWPENS**
Jan. 17, 1781

Morgan

Tarleton

Gates

Wilmington

**CAMDEN**
Aug. 16, 1780

Augusta

Cornwallis

Marion

*ATLANTIC OCEAN*

**CHARLESTON**
May 12, 1780

**SAVANNAH**
Dec. 29, 1778

→ Americans and French
→ British
✴ American and French victory
✴ British victory

## Victory at Yorktown

After the exhausting battles in the Carolinas, Cornwallis decided to march north to Virginia where he was joined by reinforcements led by the traitor Benedict Arnold and where he planned to be resupplied by the British navy. Cornwallis established his headquarters at **Yorktown** on the York River. By late summer, Cornwallis had amassed a force of 7,200 troops. The Marquis de Lafayette, commanding the outnumbered Continental forces in Virginia, watched with alarm.

At the end of August, the French fleet sailed up the Chesapeake Bay, landed three thousand French troops to join Lafayette, and defeated the British fleet. Cornwallis found himself in trouble. Not only was he cut off by sea, but the arrival of Washington's Continentals and a large force of French regulars meant that he was outnumbered and surrounded.

Washington had been leaking false reports of an attack on the British in New York but was instead marching to Yorktown. The French naval victory had been an unexpected bonus for Washington who now had Cornwallis trapped. About 17,000 French and American troops surrounded the British and bombarded them day and night.

After desperate attempts to break the siege, Cornwallis yielded, asking for terms of surrender on October 17, 1781. Two days later, seven thousand British soldiers laid down their arms.

▼ Surrender at Yorktown

# Results of the War

The **Treaty of Paris of 1783** was finally signed almost two years later on September 3 of that year. It acknowledged that the colonies were indeed independent. The United States was awarded all the land east of the Mississippi River with the exception of Florida, which returned to Spanish control.

Besides independence, the war had many other effects on American society. After the war, America's population continued to grow, and settlers continued to push farther westward into lands acquired from the war. This growth brought more wealth and trade, but also led to continued conflict with Native Americans.

Traditional family roles changed, as many women ran the family farms or businesses while their husbands were away at war. There was a greater equality among family members, and women gained more legal rights, although they still could not vote. But this greater equality also led to a decline in parental authority, less respect toward the aged, and higher rates of divorce and out-of-wedlock births.

The war also began to change people's view of the relationship between church and state. The breakup with England weakened ties with the Anglican Church, and many states declared an end to established churches. In 1786 the **Virginia Statute for Religious Freedom** was passed which granted religious liberty, declared that the state had no official church and could not collect taxes to support churches, and removed religious tests for holding office. While disestablishment benefitted those from dissenting denominations such as Baptists and Methodists, it also decreased the role of religion in government and opened the door for people who taught false doctrines.

Many Americans began to change their view regarding slavery. They recognized that slavery contradicted the American ideals of liberty and equality expressed in the Declaration of Independence. Thousands of slaves gained freedom for fighting against the British. During the war Vermont had passed legislation outlawing slavery. In Massachusetts the new state constitution declared that all people were free and equal. Slaves began suing for their freedom, and the state supreme court ruled in their favor, declaring that slavery was inconsistent with the state's constitution. Pennsylvania passed a law for the gradual elimination of slavery. However, in states where slavery was more deeply entrenched, attempts to limit or end slavery were resisted. A costly war had secured independence; now the task of building a nation lay before them. In many ways, the challenges of peace would surpass the challenges of war.

1. By 1779 all of ____ was controlled by the British.
   - **A** Georgia
   - **B** South Carolina
   - **C** Virginia

2. The guerrilla tactics of ____ hurt British supply lines in the low country.
   - **A** Nathaniel Greene
   - **B** Francis Marion
   - **C** Banastre Tarleton

3. An American victory, the Battle of ____ ended in less than an hour with significant losses for the British.
   - **A** Cowpens
   - **B** Guilford Courthouse
   - **C** Kings Mountain

4. All the following factors contributed to an American victory at Yorktown except ____.
   - **A** the arrival of Washington's Continentals
   - **B** the delayed movements of Benedict Arnold
   - **C** the supply of troops by the French fleet

5. The Treaty of Paris ceded all land east of the Mississippi River except for Florida to the United States.

   True

   False

## MAKING CONNECTIONS

6. How did the War for Independence affect social and religious freedom in the United States?

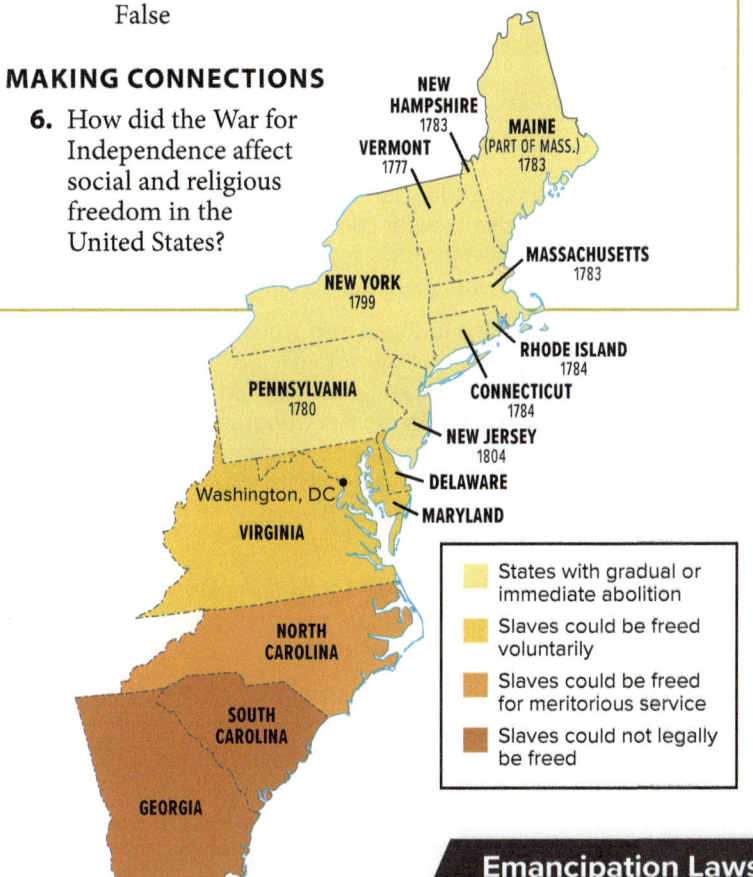

NEW HAMPSHIRE 1783
VERMONT 1777
MAINE (PART OF MASS.) 1783
MASSACHUSETTS 1783
NEW YORK 1799
RHODE ISLAND 1784
CONNECTICUT 1784
PENNSYLVANIA 1780
NEW JERSEY 1804
DELAWARE
Washington, DC
MARYLAND
VIRGINIA
NORTH CAROLINA
SOUTH CAROLINA
GEORGIA

States with gradual or immediate abolition
Slaves could be freed voluntarily
Slaves could be freed for meritorious service
Slaves could not legally be freed

**Emancipation Laws through 1805**

## Chapter Summary

### TERMS

French and Indian War
George Washington
Fort Duquesne
Albany Plan
Edward Braddock
Marquis de Montcalm
James Wolfe
Treaty of Paris of 1763
Pontiac

### 3.1 The French and Indian War

- The French and Indian War began as a conflict between Britain and France over control of land along the Ohio River.

- French advantages included alliances with many Native American tribes, the use of guerilla warfare tactics, and the isolated nature of the English colonies on the frontier. British advantages included colonists who had deeper roots than the French had in America, a far greater population in the colonies, and a strong navy. Britain's greatest disadvantage was disunity among the colonies.

- The French won a series of victories in the early years of the war. William Pitt adopted a new strategy, and the British had several victories, including the Battle of Quebec, which led to France's surrender.

- In the Treaty of Paris of 1763 Britain gained Canada and nearly all France's land east of the Mississippi River. Spain gained France's land west of the Mississippi River. In addition, Britain acquired Florida from Spain. The war also left Britain with a large debt.

### 3.2 The Growing Divide

- After the French and Indian War, the British began to exercise greater control over the American colonies through several acts that regulated trade and taxed the colonists.

- Colonial objections to these acts were based on the claim that the colonial legislatures, not Parliament, had the right to tax the colonies. The Stamp Act Congress met in protest of the Stamp Act. Tension between the colonists and British troops stationed in Boston led to the Boston Massacre.

- Colonists protested the Tea Act by dumping tea into Boston Harbor. Britain responded with the Coercive (Intolerable) Acts.

- The First Continental Congress met in response to the Intolerable Acts and adopted a declaration objecting to Parliament's actions but declaring their allegiance to the king. They also formed the Continental Association to enforce a boycott of British goods.

### TERMS

Proclamation of 1763
Navigation and Trade Acts
writs of assistance
Sugar Act
Stamp Act
Quartering Act
Patrick Henry
Stamp Act Congress
Sons of Liberty
Samuel Adams
Declaratory Act

Townshend Acts
*Gaspee*
Committee of Correspondence
Tea Act
Boston Tea Party
Coercive Acts
Quebec Act
First Continental Congress
Declaration of Rights and Grievances
Continental Association

## 3.3 The Road to Independence

- The British forces in Massachusetts attempted to seize the colonial stockpile of munitions in Concord. On the way, a skirmish in Lexington resulted in the first shots and casualties of the War for Independence.

- The Second Continental Congress began meeting in May 1775. It appointed George Washington as commander of the Continental Army. The colonists lost the Battle of Bunker Hill, but inflicted heavy casualties on the British, who eventually evacuated Boston.

- Colonists were divided over independence; some were Patriots who supported independence, some were Loyalists who favored maintaining a relationship with the king, and some were neutral. Thomas Paine, in his pamphlet *Common Sense*, argued for independence.

- On July 4, 1776, the Second Continental Congress voted to approve the Declaration of Independence, which reflected the political ideas of John Locke.

### TERMS

Concord

Lexington

Second Continental Congress

Fort Ticonderoga

Bunker Hill

Patriots

Loyalists

Olive Branch Petition

Proclamation of Rebellion

Prohibitory Act

*Common Sense*

Thomas Paine

John Locke

## 3.4 Fighting the War for Independence

- The British forced the Continental Army to retreat from New York City to New Jersey. Washington led a daring night-crossing of the Delaware River to defeat a force of Hessians at Trenton, New Jersey. He followed with another successful attack on Princeton.

- The British three-pronged assault on New York was not successful. American forces won a major victory at Saratoga, which led to France recognizing America's independence and entering the war against Britain.

- The Continental Army spent the winter of 1777–78 at Valley Forge, Pennsylvania. They lacked food and supplies. Baron Friedrich von Steuben from Prussia trained the soldiers there and turned them into a stronger fighting force. The Americans fought the British to a draw at the Battle of Monmouth.

- George Rogers Clark led a small band of guerilla fighters to several victories in the west. John Paul Jones won America's first major naval victory.

### TERMS

Trenton

Saratoga

Benedict Arnold

Baron Friedrich von Steuben

Marquis de Lafayette

George Rogers Clark

John Paul Jones

# CHAPTER **3** REVIEW

## Chapter Summary

### TERMS

Charles Cornwallis

Francis Marion

Nathanael Greene

Yorktown

Treaty of Paris of 1783

Virginia Statute for
Religious Freedom

### 3.5 | Winning the War for Independence

- The British shifted the focus of their fighting to the south. They successfully captured Savannah and Charleston. The British forces of Charles Cornwallis lost several battles to the forces of Francis Marion and Nathanael Greene.

- Cornwallis left the Carolinas for Virginia. At Yorktown, the French fleet defeated the British fleet and cut off Cornwallis by sea. In the Battle of Yorktown, the Americans and French defeated the British and Cornwallis surrendered.

- The Treaty of Paris of 1783 ended the war. The British recognized the colonies' independence, and the United States was awarded all land east of the Mississippi River except Florida. The war also resulted in a number of changes to American society.

## Chapter Review Questions

### RECALL

1. What British victory, in which both the British and French commanders were fatally wounded, led to the end of the French and Indian War?

2. How did the Boston Massacre begin?

3. What role did John Adams play in the aftermath of the Boston Massacre?

4. What was the purpose of Committees of Correspondence?

5. What were the Coercive Acts a response to, and what were the four Coercive Acts?

6. What were two actions of the First Continental Congress?

7. Why did the British troops march to Concord in April 1775?

8. Where were the first shots of the War for Independence fired?

9. What was the first action of the Second Continental Congress?

10. Why did the British military evacuate its position in Boston in March 1776?

11. What was the purpose of the Olive Branch Petition, and what were the responses of the king and Parliament to it?

12. What delegates of the Second Continental Congress were involved in drafting the Declaration of Independence?

13. What were two colonial victories in the south before Yorktown?

14. What was the last major battle of the War for Independence?

15. What did America gain as a result of the Treaty of Paris of 1783?

### UNDERSTAND

16. What caused the outbreak of the French and Indian War?

17. What advantages did the French have in the French and Indian War?

18. What advantages did the British have in the French and Indian War, and what was Britain's chief disadvantage?

19. Why did the colonists reject Benjamin Franklin's Albany Plan?

20. What were the results of the French and Indian War?

21. What was the purpose of Pontiac's war against the British and colonists?

22. Why were colonists opposed to the Proclamation of 1763?

23. How did the British respond to the burning of the *Gaspee*?

24. Why did the colonists protest the Tea Act?

25. Why were the colonists upset by the Quebec Act?

26. What was the difference between militia and regulars?

27. Why was George Washington a natural choice for commander of the Continental Army?

28. Why did some colonists choose to be Loyalists?

29. Why did some colonists choose to be Patriots?

30. Why did some colonists choose to be neutral?

31. What was Thomas Paine's argument in *Common Sense*, and what impact did it have in the colonies?

32. What was the significance of Washington's victories at Trenton and Princeton?

33. What was the significance of the colonial victory at Saratoga?

▼ Washington's entry in New York City, November 25, 1783

## THINK ABOUT IT

34. Why and how did British policies toward the American colonies change after the French and Indian War?

35. Why were the colonists opposed to the Stamp Act and the Townshend Acts?

36. What biblical arguments did some Patriots use to reconcile their position with the Bible's command to submit to their governing authorities?

37. In *Common Sense*, Thomas Paine analyzes 1 Samuel 8:4–22 and concludes, "These portions of scripture are direct and positive. . . . That the Almighty hath here entered his protest against monarchical government is true, or the scripture is false." Read the passage from 1 Samuel and evaluate Paine's argument. Does the Bible condemn monarchy? Explain your answer.

38. Which side would you have taken if you had lived during this time: Loyalist, Patriot, or neutral colonist? Defend your answer from Scripture.

39. How can John Locke's views be seen in the Declaration of Independence?

40. What were four effects of the War for Independence on American culture?

# 4 Confederation and Constitution

**4.1 Government by Confederation**
**4.2 Writing the Constitution**
**4.3 Ratifying the Constitution**

▲ Delegates to the Philadelphia Convention (1787) approaching Independence Hall to debate revising the Articles of Confederation

Having won their independence from Britain, Americans were deeply divided over how this new American nation should be governed. The Declaration of Independence referred to the former colonies as "United States," a term that some in England mocked as a contradiction in terms. In what sense could states who each claimed supreme political power ever truly be "united"? Many Europeans assumed that this American republican experiment would quickly fail as the states dissolved into regional alliances and conflicts with one another. Many of America's political leaders feared this as well. It did not take them long to realize that America's first form of government, the Articles of Confederation, would need to be replaced with a new Constitution which would create a national government capable of holding the republic together and preserving American nationhood.

## 4.1 Government by Confederation

What were the successes and weaknesses of the Articles of Confederation?

### Structure of the Confederation

On June 7, 1776, the Second Continental Congress voted to draw up a charter for joining the colonies into a **confederation**, a close alliance of sovereign states. Congress entrusted the task to a committee headed by John Dickinson of Pennsylvania, and a month later the committee presented its work. After more than a year of debate and revision, Congress adopted these **Articles of Confederation**. By 1781 all thirteen states had approved the Articles, which then went into effect.

Dickinson originally proposed establishing a strong central government. However, the same argument that the colonies had used against the British government, namely that the power to tax belonged to the colonial legislatures, was used by the states against a strong national government. A distant government strong enough to force the obedience of the states was exactly what the states had rebelled against. As a result, Dickinson's draft was weakened to the point that the Articles maintained the form of the loosely constructed Continental Congress and provided the minimum authority needed to conduct the war. Although the states pledged themselves to "perpetual union," they committed themselves only to "a firm league of friendship with each other." The Articles said plainly, "Each state retains its sovereignty, freedom, and independence." In effect, the central government was only as strong as the states allowed.

## GUIDING QUESTIONS

- How was the government under the Articles of Confederation structured?
- What were the achievements of the Articles of Confederation?
- What were the weaknesses of the Articles of Confederation?

"A Firm League of Friendship"

The legislature was the only branch of the Confederation government. The **Confederation Congress** was **unicameral** (having only one house). Each state legislature could elect two to seven representatives to attend, but each state had only one vote, regardless of how many representatives it sent or how many people they represented. Congress had power over foreign relations, Indian affairs, determinations of war and peace, disputes between states, borrowing and coining money, and running a postal system. Important legislation—such as declaring war, approving treaties, and coining money—had to be approved by at least nine states. Amending and ratifying the Articles required the unanimous consent of all thirteen states.

The chief executive, the president of Congress, was chosen by the legislature and was completely under its control. He was virtually powerless, and three officials (the superintendent of finance and the secretaries of war and foreign affairs) handled most administrative duties. A national judiciary did not yet exist.

The Articles simply formalized how the thirteen states were already functioning historically, politically, and economically. Therefore, the Articles reserved to the states every "power, jurisdiction, and right" that was not "expressly delegated" to Congress. States shared with Congress the power to coin money and deal directly with foreign governments. States had exclusive control of foreign and domestic trade and the right to act in economic matters involving debts, contracts, and family affairs. Among the most important powers reserved to the states was the power to tax. Unable to levy taxes, Congress was forced to ask the states for money, a request that the states could—and often did—ignore. For example, in 1781 Congress asked the states for $3 million but received $39,138. Government funds came primarily through printing paper money, receiving loans from other nations, selling public lands on the frontier, and earning profits from the government-owned post office.

## Successes of the Confederation

Despite the inherent weaknesses of the Articles, the Confederation Congress achieved some notable successes. Among these were the Treaty of Paris and the settlement of western lands.

### The Treaty of Paris

Having conducted a successful war against the British, the Confederation Congress's greatest foreign policy success was the negotiation of the Treaty of Paris which ended the war in 1783. America's primary negotiators were John Jay, Benjamin Franklin, and John Adams. America's ally France, exhausted by ongoing war with Britain in Europe, had offered terms of peace to Britain that would have confined the United States to the area east of the Appalachian Mountains and south of the Ohio River, so the Americans had decided to bargain directly with the British. The United States succeeded in getting Britain to recognize American independence and relinquish British claims to land east of the Mississippi River. Thus, Congress was able to acquire a vast amount of land and enhance America's reputation in the world.

▼ American commissioners of the Treaty of Paris (unfinished because the British refused to pose)

## Western Lands

Approval of the Articles of Confederation had been delayed until 1781 because Maryland had refused to ratify them until the matter of the western lands had been settled. The Treaty of Paris left the United States in control of all territory east of the Mississippi River and north of Florida. Several states, notably Virginia and New York, claimed large parts of that huge tract of land. States such as Maryland and New Jersey which had no western claims feared that unless the national government took over the western lands, the states with claims would have enormous economic and political advantages. Therefore, Maryland had refused to ratify the Articles unless the other states abandoned their claims and turned those lands over to the federal government. When those states agreed to yield their claims to the federal government, Maryland ratified the Articles.

**Western Land Claims**

Disputed between Britain and the United States

Disputed between Britain and the United States

Claimed by NH, NY, and MA

MASSACHUSETTS (MAINE)

Lake Superior

Claimed by VA

CANADA (BRITISH)

Lake Huron

Claimed by VA and NY

Lake Michigan

Lake Ontario

NEW HAMPSHIRE

Claimed by VA and MA

Claimed by VA, MA, and NY

Lake Erie

NEW YORK

MASSACHUSETTS

Claimed by VA and CT

Claimed by VA, CT, and NY

RHODE ISLAND

Claimed by VA

PENNSYLVANIA

CONNECTICUT

Mississippi River

Ohio River

NEW JERSEY

LOUISIANA (SPANISH)

Claimed by VA and NY

DELAWARE

VIRGINIA

MARYLAND

Claimed by VA

ATLANTIC OCEAN

Claimed by NC

Claimed by NC and NY

Claimed by NC

NORTH CAROLINA

South Carolina claimed a twelve-mile deep area between North Carolina and Georgia

SOUTH CAROLINA

Claimed by Georgia

GEORGIA

Disputed between Spain and the United States

| | Thirteen states |
| | Disputed |
| | State claims |
| | Ceded by New York |
| | Ceded by Virginia |

FLORIDA (BRITISH)

Confederation and Constitution  93

All lands north of the Ohio River that passed into the hands of the national government became known as the **Northwest Territory**. The question of how to develop and govern the Northwest Territory was settled by a series of ordinances. The first was the **Ordinance of 1784**, written by Thomas Jefferson. He proposed creating ten new states out of the territory (and four additional states south of the Ohio River), and once the number of free inhabitants in a territory equaled the free population of the smallest of the thirteen states, it would become a state equal to the other states in the Union. He also proposed banning slavery in the region. Congress approved the ordinance, but without the ban on slavery.

The **Land Ordinance of 1785** outlined how the government would distribute the land and how the land would be settled. The ordinance divided the new lands into orderly townships for sale and development. Each township contained thirty-six sections, or lots, of one square mile (640 acres). Each lot was to be sold for a dollar an acre ($640). The proceeds from the sale of lot sixteen in each township were to go toward building and maintaining schools in the area.

More sweeping was the **Northwest Ordinance of 1787**. Whereas the ordinance of 1785 concerned settlement, the ordinance of 1787 concerned government. The Northwest Territory was now to be divided into at least three but no more than five states. Each potential state went through three stages. In the first stage, the region remained almost completely under the direct control of the federal government, which appointed a governor and judges. When a region had at least five thousand free adult males, it entered the second stage and became a territory. The people could then elect a legislature and send a non-voting representative to Congress. In the third stage, once a territory had sixty thousand free inhabitants, it could draw up a state constitution and be admitted to the Union on an equal basis with the other states.

### Land Ordinance of 1785

Township
(6 miles square, or 36 square miles)

6 miles

| 6 | 5 | 4 | 3 | 2 | 1 |
| 7 | 8 | 9 | 10 | 11 | 12 |
| 18 | 17 | | 15 | 14 | 13 |
| 19 | 20 | 21 | 22 | 23 | 24 |
| 30 | 29 | 28 | 27 | 26 | 25 |
| 31 | 32 | 33 | 34 | 35 | 36 |

1 mile

16

Income from the sale of section 16 was reserved for education, but schools could be built on any of the sections.

Quarter section (160 acres)

Half section (320 acres)

Quarter of a quarter section (40 acres)

Half of a quarter section (80 acres)

Section (1 square mile)

Building on the educational provisions in the Land Ordinance of 1785, the Northwest Ordinance of 1787 explicitly emphasized the importance of education: "Religion, morality, and knowledge, being necessary to good government and the happiness of mankind, schools and the means of education shall forever be encouraged." The ordinance also guaranteed religious freedom, due process, trial by jury, and protection against cruel and unusual punishment years before the adoption of a national bill of rights. Regarding Native Americans, it stated that "their lands and property shall never be taken from them without their consent" and that laws were to be made "for preventing wrongs being done to them, and for preserving peace and friendship with them." Most importantly, the ordinance followed Jefferson's original suggestion and prohibited slavery in the new territories (although it included a provision for the return of runaway slaves).

These ordinances allowed orderly settlement of the territory based on republican principles, and the land sales they permitted provided income for the government. Eventually, the states of Ohio, Indiana, Michigan, Illinois, and Wisconsin were created from the Northwest Territory. Years later, in the third volume of his works, Daniel Webster recalled the significance of this law:

> [I doubt] whether one single law of any lawgiver, ancient or modern, has produced effects of more distinct, marked, and lasting character than the Ordinance of 1787. . . . It fixed for ever the character of the population in the vast regions northwest of the Ohio, by excluding from them involuntary servitude.
> — Daniel Webster

### Stages of the Northwest Ordinance of 1787

**1** **Under direct control of federal government**

**2** **Become a territory**
at 5,000 people

**3** **Become a state**
at 60,000 people

# Weaknesses of the Confederation

## Financial Weakness

Finances were perhaps the greatest threat to the new nation. The Confederation Congress faced a federal debt of $30 to $40 million. The continental dollars it was printing had no backing because states were ignoring Congress's requests for funds. In addition, the government had issued promissory notes, called certificates, to pay merchants and farmers for goods needed by the Continental Army. Compounding the problem was each state's ability to print its own currency. State currency was often as worthless as the Continental notes. Debtors tried paying their debts with this worthless paper, leaving their creditors bankrupt.

Superintendent of finance Robert Morris suggested a series of actions, including the creation of a national bank, new national taxes and duties, and the assumption of state debts by Congress, to improve the credit and financial health of the nation. However, these measures were met with objections from several states, who believed that Congress taxing the states was no better than Parliament taxing the colonies.

The financial weakness of the national government had threatened the Continental Army's ability to fight the British. Washington had expressed his frustration with Congress as his army went without pay, shoes, clothing, and adequate food for much of the war. Shortly before the Battle of Yorktown, Washington wrote in a letter:

▲ Paper currency issued by the states and the Continental Congress

*I am decided in my opinion, that if the powers of Congress are not enlarged, and made competent to all general purposes, that the blood which has been spilt, the expense that has been incurred, and the distresses which have been felt, will avail nothing and that the band, already too weak, which holds us together, will soon be broken; when anarchy and confusion will prevail.* — **GEORGE WASHINGTON**

### Analyzing Sources

What was Washington saying about the powers of Congress? What did he think the consequences would be for the nation if the powers of Congress were not expanded?

### Did You Know?

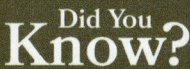

The Confederation Congress, which met in New York, passed the Northwest Ordinance the same summer (1787) that the Constitutional Convention was meeting in Philadelphia.

## Diplomatic Weakness

By the provisions of the Treaty of Paris, the United States was to restore the seized property of Loyalists and allow British subjects access to American courts to recover debts owed them. The Confederation Congress, however, had no means of enforcing those provisions in the states. Debts went unpaid, and Loyalists who returned to their homes were often prevented from regaining their land or possessions that had been confiscated during the war. Britain used these breaches of the treaty as an excuse to keep its forts in the Great Lakes region and thus protect the profitable British fur trade. When John Adams complained to the British about their violation of the treaty, the British pointed to the United States' failure to honor its obligations.

Congress also faced issues with Spain, who had been an ally of France but not of the United States during the war. One area of disagreement was the boundary between Georgia and Florida, which the British had returned to Spain in the Treaty of Paris. Spain also continued to control the land west of the Mississippi River, including the important port city of New Orleans. Americans west of the Appalachians frequently transported goods down the Mississippi River to New Orleans, but the Spanish at times denied the **right of deposit** (the freedom to stockpile goods until ships came to transport them overseas) or required Americans to pay a duty on goods brought to New Orleans. Spain also provided weapons to Native Americans and encouraged attacks on American settlements.

▲ The port of New Orleans

## Domestic Weakness

Another serious threat to the new republic was the national government's struggle to keep the peace within its own borders. In 1783 a group of officers in Newburgh, New York, grew frustrated by Congress's inability to pay salaries and pensions. In this **Newburgh Conspiracy**, the officers intended to force Congress and the states to grant them their back pay. Some conspirators wanted more; they wanted to establish a new government under a king or a dictator. Washington was their first choice as the leader; but if he refused, they would find someone else.

When Washington learned that the officers planned a mass meeting to discuss their grievances, he came as an uninvited guest. He spoke kindly to the men, sympathizing with their needs but urging them not to destroy the nation they had fought for. At the conclusion of the speech, Washington pulled out a letter of support. Before reading it, he paused and with deliberation took out his glasses and put them on. "Gentlemen, you will permit me to put on my spectacles," the general said, "for, I have grown not only gray, but almost blind in the service of my country."

As he finished reading, tears filled the eyes of many of the men who had great appreciation for Washington's service to his country. Before them stood the Patriot who had weathered the snows of Valley Forge and faced the bullets of the British by their side throughout the war. The Newburgh Conspiracy collapsed, but it had threatened the young and fragile government.

▼ George Washington speaking to the Newburgh conspirators

▲ Brawl between a Massachusetts government supporter and a rebel, during Shays's Rebellion

An even more serious problem arose in Massachusetts in 1786. Daniel Shays, a farmer and veteran of the Revolution, led an insurrection, known as **Shays's Rebellion**, against the courts in the western part of the state. Farmers who struggled to pay their debts began protesting tax increases and foreclosures on their land. When many of them were jailed, others retaliated by using force to close the courts. Shays and a group of 1,200 men attempted to seize a federal armory in Springfield in January 1787, but they were met by a large force of militiamen, and four farmers were killed. The rebels scattered, and many were soon captured. Most of them, including Shays, were later pardoned.

The insurrection ended just a few months before the delegates of the Constitutional Convention met at Philadelphia in 1787. Those who argued for a stronger national government pointed to Shays's Rebellion as a sign of the coming anarchy and dissolution of the United States if the Articles of Confederation were not revised to give the government more power of enforcement. Some suggested that the greatest flaw of the Articles was that they assumed that the people through their state and local governments would be more virtuous than a strong national government. However, the nation's experience under the Articles demonstrated that neither people nor governments were completely virtuous and that, in the words of George Washington, "we must take human nature as we find it." This meant revising the Articles so they could restrain both the "excesses of democracy" and the tendency of government to abuse its power.

## Comprehension Check 4.1

1. The Articles of Confederation created a form of government that included ____.

   A a single-house legislative body that had no power to tax

   B a two-house legislature, a judicial system, and a president

   C an annual election for the president and the representatives to the legislature

2. ____ refused to ratify the Articles of Confederation until other states dropped claims to western territory.

   A Delaware

   B Maryland

   C South Carolina

3. Jefferson introduced a proposal to ____ in the Northwest Territory, a measure that was upheld in the Northwest Ordinance of 1787.

   A aid Loyalists in recovering land

   B fund a national bank from sales

   C prohibit slavery

4. Each of the following describes Shays's Rebellion except that ____.

   A the insurrection involved farmers

   B the rebels were later pardoned

   C Washington's speech convinced the rebels to disperse

### MAKING CONNECTIONS

5. According to the Northwest Ordinance of 1787, how were the new states treated compared to the original thirteen states?

6. What were the weaknesses of the Confederation Congress?

- Why was a new constitution called for?
- What compromises were made at the Constitutional Convention?
- How did the Three-Fifths Compromise attempt to resolve sectional differences regarding slavery and representation?
- What principles are included in the Constitution?

## 4.2 Writing the Constitution

**What compromises and principles were written into the Constitution?**

### The Call for Change

The failures and weaknesses of the Confederation government caused thoughtful men to consider what could be done. Representatives from Maryland and Virginia met in 1785 to discuss trade disputes involving the Potomac River. The meeting was so profitable that the legislatures of Maryland and Virginia called for another trade convention in Annapolis, Maryland, in September 1786 to include all thirteen states. However, only five states sent representatives to the **Annapolis Convention**. Alexander Hamilton, a delegate from New York, wrote a resolution calling for another convention to remedy the weaknesses of the Confederation government. With a growing sense that revisions to the Articles of Confederation were necessary to preserve it, the Confederation Congress approved a convention in Philadelphia for May 1787.

### The Constitutional Convention

Delegates chosen by their respective states to attend the Philadelphia Convention (which became the **Constitutional Convention**) could be divided into three groups: radicals, who wished to replace the Articles of Confederation; moderates, who wished to revise the Articles; and conservatives, who wanted no changes at all, and who boycotted the convention. The fifty-five delegates who did attend were some of the best political thinkers and finest lawyers in America, well-read and well-educated. Their average age was forty-four. Thirty-five of them had served in the Continental Army as officers, and forty-two had served in the Continental or Confederation Congresses. Their experience gave them a first-hand knowledge of the weaknesses of the Articles.

The Constitutional Convention was more than a gathering of talent, however; it was also a collection of regional and individual interests. Twelve independent states (Rhode Island refused to participate) were represented. These states had united to fight against a common enemy, but that war was over. What united the states now? Diverse interests led to heated debates and threatened the success of the convention.

Once a quorum of seven states was present, the convention began its deliberations on May 25, 1787. Historian Joseph Ellis, in his book *The Quartet*, noted several significant decisions which were made in the first days of the convention. The first was a vote on a procedural motion that the one-state, one-vote rules of the Articles be applied to the convention. This gave small states the ability to block any plans that favored

▼ Independence Hall, Philadelphia

large states, thus forcing those who favored radical change to compromise with the small states. Second, the delegates voted to keep their deliberations secret to promote the free exchange of ideas and ensure confidentiality. Third, they chose to meet in the same room in Independence Hall where the Declaration of Independence was signed a decade earlier, linking the convention to the spirit of the American Revolution. Fourth, the delegates unanimously elected George Washington, whose very presence gave credibility to the meeting, president of the convention.

## Crucial Compromises

The question of whether the convention existed to revise the Articles of Confederation or replace them with something new was answered on May 30, when the convention approved Pennsylvania Delegate Gouverneur Morris's resolution that "a national government ought to be established, consisting of a supreme legislative, executive, and judiciary." This was already a radical change from the Articles, which had no executive or judicial branch.

The remainder of the convention focused on the details of how this new government would be structured, details upon which there was much disagreement. The disputes grew largely out of regional interests and would require compromises on three major issues: representation, slavery, and trade.

### THE GREAT COMPROMISE

How the states were to be represented was the first difficult question. The battle lines were drawn between the large states, such as Virginia, Pennsylvania, and New York, and the smaller states, such as New Jersey, Delaware, and Maryland. Virginia delegate James Madison, called "the Father of the Constitution," had spent months leading up to the convention studying confederacies and republics throughout history and compiling a list of the political failures of the Articles and problems with the state governments. Through his study, he believed that the solution to America's political weakness was to create a federal government that had supremacy over the states.

The culmination of Madison's study was his **Virginia Plan**, which was introduced to the convention by fellow Virginian Edmund Randolph. It advocated a three-branch form of government modeled on the state governments, and called for a **bicameral** (two-house) legislature, with the number of representatives in both houses to be based on state population. Members of the lower house, or House of Representatives, would be elected by direct popular vote. The lower house, in turn, would elect members of the upper house, or Senate, from nominees submitted by state legislatures. Compared to the Confederation Congress, the legislature would have greatly expanded powers. For example, the new Congress would be able to enforce its laws on the states and would elect both the chief executive and the national judiciary. Those two branches, the executive and the judicial, could unite to veto congressional and state legislation, but their veto could be overridden by a vote in both houses of Congress.

Since representation under the Virginia Plan was based on state population, it naturally favored the states with larger populations. The smaller states were quick to react, setting forth a proposal of their own known as the **New Jersey Plan**, presented by William Paterson of New Jersey. It called for maintaining the unicameral Congress of the Articles of Confederation, with each state having only one vote, but adding to it the power to tax the states and enforce federal laws. The plan would also amend the Articles by adding a federal judicial branch and declaring the Articles the supreme law of the land.

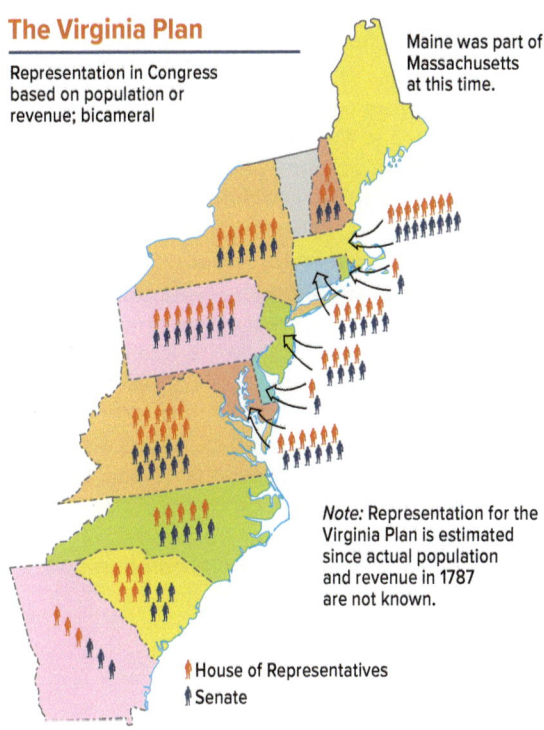

### Congressional Representation

**The Virginia Plan**

Representation in Congress based on population or revenue; bicameral

Maine was part of Massachusetts at this time.

*Note:* Representation for the Virginia Plan is estimated since actual population and revenue in 1787 are not known.

🧍 House of Representatives
🧍 Senate

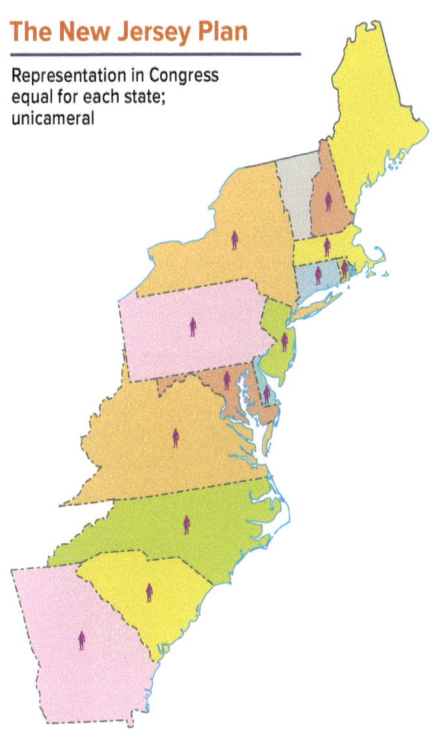

**The New Jersey Plan**

Representation in Congress equal for each state; unicameral

**The Great Compromise**

| House of Representatives | | Senate | |
|---|---|---|---|
| Virginia | New Jersey | Virginia | New Jersey |
| Based on population | | Same number from each state | |

## Roger Sherman

Roger Sherman was a devout Christian. John Adams referred to him as "that old Puritan, honest as an angel." Sherman favored state support of religion and opposed giving public offices to men who attacked Christianity. Despite having no formal education beyond grammar school, he held numerous public offices, including representative of the Connecticut House of Representatives, justice of the Connecticut Superior Court, treasurer of Yale University, and mayor of New Haven. After the Constitution was ratified, he was elected to the United States House of Representatives. He was the only founding father to sign all four of the significant documents of America's early years: the Articles of Association (establishing the Continental Association by the First Continental Congress), the Declaration of Independence, the Articles of Confederation, and the United States Constitution.

The convention was deadlocked over the issue of representation. The large states feared the diminishing of their power through lack of representation, arguing that basic democratic principles favored proportional representation. Madison argued that equal representation, even in only one house, would allow a majority of states, who may only represent a minority of the population, to "obstruct the wishes and interests of the majority, . . . extort measures repugnant to the wishes and interests of the majority, . . . [and] impose measures adverse thereto."

The small states feared domination by the large states. Connecticut delegate Oliver Ellsworth argued, "The capital objection . . . 'that the minority will rule the majority' is not true. The power is given to the few to save them from being destroyed by the many."

Many believed the convention would dissolve unless a compromise could be found. **Roger Sherman** of Connecticut offered the assembly a solution to the deadlock. His proposal, known as the **Great Compromise** (or Connecticut Compromise) recommended that representation in the House of Representatives be based on state population, and representation in the Senate be equal for all states regardless of size.

## Comparing the Articles of Confederation and the US Constitution

| Articles of Confederation | | US Constitution |
|---|---|---|
| • One House<br>• 2–7 delegates, but one vote per state | **Legislature** | • Two Houses<br>• House of Representatives: representation determined by population<br>• Senate: two senators per state |
| • No executive branch<br>• President of Congress chosen annually by Congress<br>• Administrative duties carried out by department heads | **Executive** | • Separate executive branch<br>• President chosen by the Electoral College for 4-year term<br>• Appoints heads of government departments |
| • No national judiciary | **Judicial** | • Separate judicial branch<br>• Federal judges appointed by the president and confirmed by the Senate |

## Three-Fifths Compromise: Representatives from Virginia

US Congress, 1793

| Free: 454,983 | Slaves: 292,627 |
|---|---|

**14** If none of the slaves were counted

**19** Counting three-fifths of the slaves

**23** If all of the slaves were counted

Based on the 1790 census and 1 representative per 33,000 people

## THREE-FIFTHS COMPROMISE

The next divisive issue that confronted the delegates of the Constitutional Convention was whether to count slaves in a state's population when determining representation. If slaves were not counted, the northern states' representatives would greatly outnumber those of the southern states in the House of Representatives. If slaves were counted, the southern representatives would outnumber those of the north. To resolve this impasse, Pennsylvania delegate James Wilson offered the **Three-Fifths Compromise**. Under this settlement, three-fifths of the total slave population of a state would be included for representation purposes in the House, but those states would also have to pay taxes on the slave population at the same rate.

## Slavery *and the* Constitution

Slavery was an issue that threatened the success of the Constitutional Convention. It was deeply ingrained in the life and economy of the states from Virginia to Georgia. Twenty-five of the delegates were slave owners.

By 1787 slavery had been outlawed in some New England states and put on the road to gradual extinction by middle states such as Pennsylvania. Delegates from some states argued that slavery was incompatible with the principles of the American Revolution as stated in the Declaration of Independence. Some called for an immediate end to the slave trade and the prohibition of slavery from all future western states. Maryland delegate Luther Martin called slavery "an odious bargain with sin, inconsistent with the principles of the revolution and dishonorable to the American character."

John Rutledge of South Carolina summed up the position of the delegates of South Carolina and Georgia: "Religion and humanity [have] nothing to do with this question. Interest alone is the governing principle with nations. The true question at present is whether the southern states shall or shall not be parties to the Union." The southern states wanted the continuation of the slave trade, no restrictions on slavery in new western states, and Constitutional protection of the property rights of slave owners. South Carolina delegate Pierce Butler said, "The security the [southern] states want is that their Negroes may not be taken from them." Virginians such as George Mason agreed with Luther Martin's view that slavery was immoral and supported an end to the slave trade; however, they were also opposed to creating a national government that was strong enough to take people's "property" from them.

The delegates saw no way to resolve the moral question of slavery in a way that could hold the thirteen states together. Moral condemnation of slavery in the Constitution would have caused the southern states to leave the convention. Those whose primary aim was to create a strong national government decided to set aside their moral objections to achieve their political goal.

Ultimately, the Constitution neither condemned nor permanently protected the institution of slavery. This ambiguity allowed the Constitution to be ratified by northern and southern states, but it also left a final resolution of the slave question to future generations.

▼ Slaves working in a field

## COMMERCE AND SLAVE TRADE COMPROMISE

Part of the motivation behind calling the Philadelphia Convention was the failure of the Confederation Congress to resolve interstate trade disputes and to direct international trade. Although most delegates agreed that Congress needed a role in commerce, regional interests kept them at odds over the extent of that role. Southern states worried that the new Congress would ban the slave trade and raise revenue through export duties. Such duties would hurt the economies of these states, which were dependent on the export of raw goods such as tobacco, rice, and indigo. The **Commerce and Slave Trade Compromise** settled the issue. The agreement gave Congress power over foreign and interstate commerce. However, the legislature was forbidden from imposing any export taxes on the states, and Congress was prevented from interfering with the slave trade for at least twenty years (until 1808).

# Principles in the Constitution

Despite disputes over details, the Constitution's framers agreed on certain basic principles. These principles have given the Constitution and the government durability. Many of the constitutional principles grew out of the founders' understanding of human nature. They recognized that people, both the governed and the governors, are inherently sinful. As John Adams, quoting Machiavelli, pointed out, "Whoever would found a state, and make proper laws for the government of it, must presume that all men are bad by nature."

This is not to say that the Constitution is a "Christian" document any more than its framers were all Christians. But what is clear is that the Constitution was written in a society where biblical principles were pervasive, and the document can be best understood in the light of those principles. These principles are not spelled out in the document itself, but they contribute to its fabric.

The key principles of the Constitution center on the issue of power—how to divide, balance, limit, and allot governmental power in view of human corruption. Madison underscored this point when he wrote his essay "Federalist 51."

### Analyzing Sources

What is James Madison, in "Federalist 51," saying about human nature? Because government is created by sinful humans for sinful humans, what difficulty is faced when creating a government?

*But what is government itself, but the greatest of all reflections on human nature? If men were angels, no government would be necessary. If angels were to govern men, neither external nor internal controls on government would be necessary. In framing a government which is to be administered by men over men, the great difficulty lies in this: You must first enable the government to control the governed; and in the next place, oblige it to control itself.* — JAMES MADISON

▶ (top) The United States Supreme Court (2022); (bottom left) the White House Oval Office; (bottom right) the House of Representatives in the US Capitol

**Checks and Balances**

**Judicial** Supreme Court

- Determines constitutionality of executive actions
- Interprets treaties
- Grants pardons
- Appoints federal judges
- Determines the number of Supreme Court judges
- Establishes lower federal courts
- Determines constitutionality of laws
- Interprets laws
- Impeaches judges
- Overrides vetoes
- Regulates types of appeals

**Executive** President

- Calls special sessions of Congress
- Approves or rejects treaties & presidential appointees
- Impeaches & removes officials, including the president
- Vetoes bills
- Suggests legislation

**Legislative** Congress

## Republican Philosophy

The Constitution established a **republic**, a government run by representatives chosen by and accountable to the voters. The founders opposed a monarchy or an aristocracy but also opposed a democracy, which they feared would devolve into rule by the mob. This republican philosophy was part of the founders' thinking when they decided how various government officials would be elected. The people were represented in the popularly elected House of Representatives. The states were represented in the Senate, whose members were originally chosen by the state legislatures. The election of the president not by the people directly but by the Electoral College (whose members were determined by each state) was also designed to distance the nation's chief executive from the changing whims of the people.

## Popular Sovereignty

**Popular sovereignty** is the idea that the ultimate source of governmental power lies in the people. The consent of the governed is a constitutional principle that is evident in several areas of the Constitution. The Preamble which introduced the charter reads:

> *We the people of the United States, in order to form a more perfect union, establish justice, ensure domestic tranquility, provide for the common defense, promote the general welfare, and secure the blessings of liberty to ourselves and our posterity, do ordain and establish this Constitution for the United States of America.*

The principle of popular sovereignty is best expressed in the Constitution through the document's provisions for representation and amendment. The proportional representation (representation based on population) of the House of Representatives allows the people to have a voice in their republican government through their elected officials. The challenge for the constitutional framers was to create a government based on the principle of popular sovereignty that also checked the excessive tendencies of "the people."

Constitutional amendments (changes to the Constitution) are also an expression of popular sovereignty. Amendments that survive the difficult ratification process often reflect widespread popular support and take precedence over the laws of Congress, the actions of the president, and the rulings of the courts. Chief Justice John Marshall later stated, "The people made the Constitution, and the people can unmake it. It is the creature of their own will, and lives only by their will."

### Did You Know?

An earlier draft of the Preamble read, "We the people of the states of New Hampshire, Rhode Island . . ." Gouverneur Morris, who was given the task of creating the final draft of the Constitution, revised the Preamble to read, "We the People of the United States."

## Democracy *or* Republic?

The United States is not a pure democracy such as could be found in ancient Athens. In fact, at the time of the Constitutional Convention, the term "democracy" was not considered a positive idea to many of the founding fathers. To them, democracy was associated with excess and mob rule, as evidenced by incidents such as Shays's Rebellion. Democracy that was unchecked, in Madison's view, was not compatible with a healthy republic because popularly elected leaders were more likely to cater to the immediate demands of the voters rather than the long-term interests of the nation.

Madison argued that the ideal solution was to create a democratic republic in which the will of the people could be "filtered" through layers that were increasingly distant from them and which could check their tendencies toward excess. The Constitution provided that filtering through the differing means of choosing representatives, senators, and the president.

Opponents of the Constitution argued that republics had only been attempted historically in small areas such as Greek city-states and had never been tried and would never succeed in an area as large and diverse as the United States. Madison responded that a large republic would actually be preferable to a small republic. He believed that large republics created "a greater variety of interests, of pursuits, of passions, which check each other." Madison later argued:

> As each representative will be chosen by a greater number of citizens in the large than the small republic, it will be more difficult for unworthy candidates to practice with success the vicious arts by which elections are too often carried; and the suffrages [elections] of the people being more free, will be more likely to center in men who possess the most attractive merit and . . . established characters. — "Federalist 10"

▲ Citizens of Athens, Greece, a democratic city-state, gathering at the Parthenon

## Limited Government

The underlying theme of the Constitution is limited government. The Philadelphia delegates desired to avoid what they saw as British tyranny—unlimited government and its consequences. The principle of limited government is expressed by the nature of a written constitution. Unlike the unwritten British constitution, which was an open-ended accumulation of laws and traditions subject to Parliamentary action, the American Constitution was a written charter which clearly defined the limits of governmental power and broadened the scope of individual liberty.

## Separation of Powers

To prevent any group or individual from gaining too much power, the founders designed the national government with the **separation of powers** in mind. That is the division of the government into three separate branches: the legislative branch, the executive branch, and the judicial branch. In broad terms, Congress makes the laws, the president executes and enforces the laws, and the courts interpret the laws. Although the three branches are separate, they are not fully independent. Their responsibilities intersect in many areas, and a certain amount of cooperation is necessary to make the national government work effectively.

## Checks and Balances

Although separation of powers is often thought to be synonymous with checks and balances, there is an important difference. If power were only divided or separated, then one branch could expand its powers within its rightful sphere and come to dominate the other branches. The principle of **checks and balances** is designed to prevent such an accumulation of power by not only balancing the power among the three but also giving each branch the ability to check, or limit, the power of the other branches. For example, Congress passes a bill to become law, but the president may reject, or veto, the bill. However, his veto may be overridden by a two-thirds vote in both houses of Congress. The Supreme Court may nullify acts of both Congress and the president if a majority of justices interprets a law as unconstitutional.

## Federalism

**Federalism** is the division of power between national and state levels of government. The Great Compromise, with equal votes for each state in the Senate, preserved a degree of control for the states, regardless of size. Many Americans in 1787 were not in favor of a national government that had total sovereignty over the states. The federal system struck a crucial balance between state and national demands. Many people believe that the genius of the Constitution is its ambiguity on the question of sovereignty. While state versus federal power would become a source of conflict in American history, federalism had provided needed flexibility in a large country of varying regions by giving citizens a greater voice in their affairs at the state and local level. Supporters of both limited government and a strong central government have ultimately accepted the Constitution.

---

### Comprehension Check 4.2

1. Within the first few days of the Constitutional Convention, the delegates agreed to the following measures for proceedings except ____.

   A meeting in Annapolis

   B one vote per state

   C secret deliberations

2. ____ introduced the Great Compromise between the Virginia and New Jersey plans for representation.

   A Alexander Hamilton

   B John Rutledge

   C Roger Sherman

3. The Three-Fifths Compromise dealt with ____.

   A abolishing the slave trade

   B representation on the basis of the slave population

   C slavery in future western states

4. A major difference between the American Constitution and the British constitution is that the American Constitution ____.

   A created a representative legislature

   B is a written document

   C never needed amendments

5. In addition to creating a separation of powers, the Constitution applies the principle of ____ by keeping powers from accumulating in any one branch.

   A checks and balances

   B federalism

   C popular sovereignty

#### MAKING CONNECTIONS

6. How did the Commerce and Slave Trade Compromise affect the powers of the federal and state governments?

7. Give two ways that the Constitution limited abuse of power by the government and two ways that it limited the excesses of democracy.

## 4.3 Ratifying the Constitution

**What arguments were made for and against the ratification of the Constitution?**

### Debate over Ratification

On September 17, 1787, Washington offered the final draft of the new charter to the convention. After the delegates signed and sent it to the Confederation Congress, the document would pass to the states for their **ratification** (consent). Although the Articles of Confederation had required all thirteen states to approve any changes, Article VII of the Constitution stated that it would take effect after nine states had voted to approve it.

While most delegates supported the final document, Edmund Randolph and George Mason of Virginia and Elbridge Gerry of Massachusetts objected to the expanded powers of the national government and the absence of a bill of rights. Mason declared that he "would sooner cut off his right hand than put it to the Constitution" because of the document's failure to guarantee civil liberties. Such objections foreshadowed a difficult ratification process.

After the signing, the delegates parted company. Their work would now be scrutinized by the nation. It would be up to the states to decide the fate of the Constitution, as they began to select delegates to their ratifying conventions. Privately some of the Constitution's framers worried about ratification because the stakes were so high. Washington wrote to Randolph saying, "This, or a dissolution of the Union, awaits our choice."

Shortly after the delegates departed, the text of the Constitution was published in the *Pennsylvania Packet* of Philadelphia. For the first time, Americans learned what had been devised behind the closed doors of Independence Hall, and not everyone was pleased. The battle lines were drawn between supporters of the Constitution, called **Federalists**, and opponents, called **Anti-Federalists**.

### GUIDING QUESTIONS

- Why did some Americans support and others oppose the Constitution?

- Why has the Constitution been successful?

### Franklin's Plea

Benjamin Franklin gave a written address to a colleague to read in hopes of swaying undecided delegates to sign. Franklin acknowledged:

> I confess that there are several parts of this constitution which I do not at present approve, but I am not sure I shall never approve them: For having lived long, I have experienced many instances of being obliged by better information, or fuller consideration, to change opinions even on important subjects. . . . Thus I consent, Sir, to this Constitution because I expect no better, and because I am not sure, that it is not the best.

▼ Delegates of the Philadelphia Convention signing the US Constitution, 1787

## Excerpt *from* "Cato," Essay VII

*Hitherto we have tied up our rulers in the exercise of their duties by positive restrictions—if the cord has been drawn too tight, loosen it to the necessary extent, but do not entirely unbind them.—I am no enemy to placing a reasonable confidence in them; but such an unbounded one as the advocates and framers of this new system advise you to, would be dangerous to your liberties; it has been the ruin of other governments, and will be yours.*

▼ Alexander Hamilton

## Excerpt *from* "Federalist 23"

*It is both unwise and dangerous to deny the federal government an unconfined authority in respect to all those objects which are entrusted to its management. . . . A government, the constitution of which renders it unfit to be trusted with all the powers which a free people ought to delegate to any government, would be an unsafe and improper depository of the national interests.*

 **Analyzing Sources**

According to "Federalist 23," how much power should the federal government be given? What would make a government unfit to be trusted with these powers?

It was clear to the Federalists that New York was going to be a battleground in the ratification debate. Governor George Clinton was strongly opposed to the new Constitution. Anti-Federalist articles began appearing in New York newspapers under pseudonyms such as "the Federal Farmer," "Brutus," and "Cato" in which arguments against the Constitution were presented. These included arguments that the executive would be too much like a king, that representation distant from the states was not able to truly represent the citizens, and that a large republic with consolidated power was a threat to liberty.

Alexander Hamilton, the only New York delegate who had supported and signed the Constitution, responded to the Anti-Federalist articles by writing several articles supporting ratification under the pen name "Publius" ("friend of the people"). Hamilton also enlisted the help of James Madison and John Jay. Together, the trio wrote eighty-five essays (Hamilton authored fifty-one, Madison twenty-nine, and Jay five) that were directed at the people of New York but were widely read throughout the country. The essays were compiled and published in two volumes in May 1788 as the ***Federalist Papers***. This work answered Anti-Federalist objections by carefully explaining and forcefully defending constitutional provisions of power. It also predicted dangers and dismemberment for the nation if the Constitution were rejected.

Delaware was the first state to ratify the Constitution, giving its unanimous consent on December 7, 1787. Within a month, four more states—Pennsylvania, New Jersey, Georgia, and Connecticut—followed. The toughest battles, however, were in Massachusetts, Virginia, and New York, where the Anti-Federalists were better organized and had leaders of considerable stature among their ranks.

In Massachusetts, one of the primary arguments against the Constitution was its lack of a bill of rights. A writer under the pseudonym "John DeWitt" wrote:

*That a Constitution for the United States does not require a bill of rights, when it is considered that a Constitution for an individual state would, I cannot conceive. The difference between them is only in the numbers of the parties concerned; they are both a compact between the governors and governed, the letter of which must be adhered to in discussing their powers.*

Massachusetts approved the Constitution in a close vote in February 1788 after John Hancock proposed a vote on ratification first, followed by a vote on recommendations for amending the Constitution.

Three more states—Maryland, South Carolina, and New Hampshire—joined to meet the requirement of ratification by nine states for the Constitution to become law. However, any hopes for a national union had to include both Virginia, the most populous state, and New York, the commercial center. If New York failed to ratify, then New England would be cut off geographically from the rest of the country. If Virginia refused to join, then the South would be severed geographically.

The Anti-Federalists of Virginia were led by Governor Edmund Randolph, George Mason, and fiery orator Patrick Henry. This trio expressed legitimate concerns: fear of consolidated political power in an overarching national government and the absence of guarantees of personal liberty, including religious freedom, in a bill of rights. Henry argued:

> *But we are told that we need not fear, because those in power being our representatives, will not abuse the powers we put in their hands. I am not well versed in history, but I will submit to your recollection, whether liberty has been destroyed most often by the licentiousness [lawlessness] of the people, or by the tyranny of rulers? I imagine, Sir, you will find the balance on the side of tyranny.*

**— PATRICK HENRY**

The Federalists argued that they were not opposed to personal liberty; rather, most of them thought that a bill of rights was unnecessary because the federal government's powers were restricted to only those items specifically granted in the Constitution and that it was too restrictive to limit rights to a written list. The Federalists also feared that the attempt to compose a bill of rights before ratification would derail the Constitution. After James Madison promised to introduce amendments for a bill of rights in the first session of Congress, the Virginia Federalists won a narrow victory for ratification, 89–79.

Once news of Virginia's ratification reached New York, Anti-Federalists there were faced with a decision: reluctantly join the union or try to exist independently. By a slim margin of 30 to 27, New York voted to ratify. North Carolina and Rhode Island held out for some time, but plans for the new government proceeded. Elections for the new Congress were set, and the opening session was scheduled for March 4, 1789, at the temporary national capital, New York City.

Benjamin Franklin wrote with satisfaction, "Our new Constitution is now established, everything seems to promise it will be durable; but, in the world, nothing is certain, except death and taxes."

## Analyzing Sources

Why does Henry not trust those who say the government will not abuse its power?

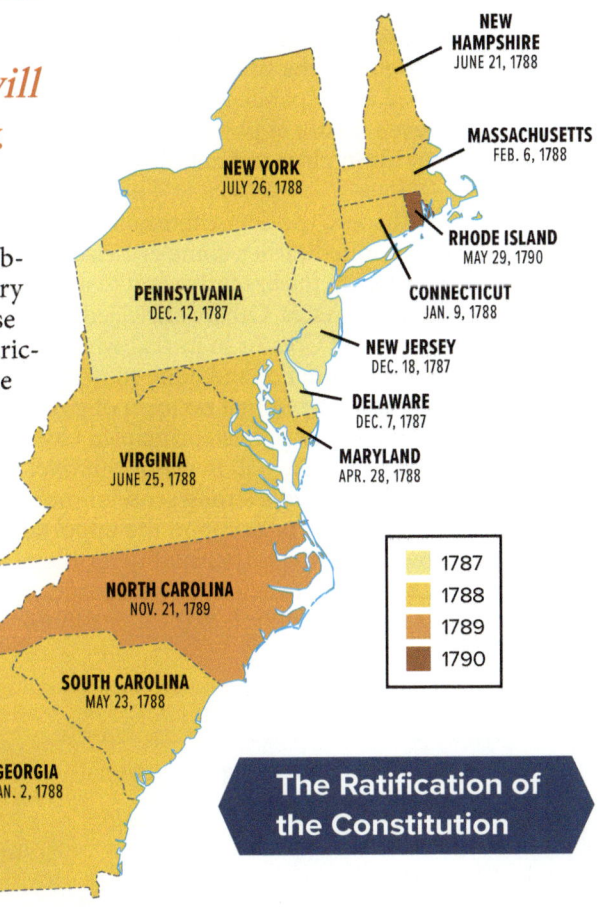

NEW HAMPSHIRE
JUNE 21, 1788

MASSACHUSETTS
FEB. 6, 1788

NEW YORK
JULY 26, 1788

RHODE ISLAND
MAY 29, 1790

PENNSYLVANIA
DEC. 12, 1787

CONNECTICUT
JAN. 9, 1788

NEW JERSEY
DEC. 18, 1787

DELAWARE
DEC. 7, 1787

VIRGINIA
JUNE 25, 1788

MARYLAND
APR. 28, 1788

NORTH CAROLINA
NOV. 21, 1789

SOUTH CAROLINA
MAY 23, 1788

GEORGIA
JAN. 2, 1788

| | |
|---|---|
| | 1787 |
| | 1788 |
| | 1789 |
| | 1790 |

**The Ratification of the Constitution**

## Baptists *and the* Bill *of* Rights

Many Protestants, including Baptists, had supported the War for Independence. One reason for their support was the anticipation of religious freedom that would result. However, when the text of the Constitution became known, Baptist leaders, including Pastor John Leland, expressed serious concerns because the document contained no guarantees of religious freedom. James Madison and others argued that these guarantees were unnecessary because the federal government could likely not attain a level of power that would threaten freedom of religion. However, Pastor Leland and many others insisted that their support for the Constitution was contingent on the addition of a bill of rights. When Pastor Leland convinced Madison to offer the suggested amendments, Leland and other Baptists supported the ratification of the Constitution and helped to ensure its passage.

# Success of the Constitution

The Constitution of the United States is now the longest-lasting and oldest written national constitution still in use. Because many nations have modeled their governments after the Constitution, some have referred to it as America's most important export.

One reason for the Constitution's success is that it is a flexible document. While it established foundational principles such as federalism, separation of powers, and checks and balances, its built-in ambiguity on issues such as the line between state and federal sovereignty has allowed for changing viewpoints over time. Its amendment process has allowed modifications without having to discard the entire Constitution, as many other nations have had to do. The fact that since the passage of the Bill of Rights in 1791 only seventeen amendments have been adopted is evidence that the Constitution has worked remarkably well.

Another reason for the Constitution's success is that the framers recognized the sinful nature of man. They purposely limited and separated the powers of the government to prevent abuse of power and corruption. They also put safeguards in place to limit the excesses of "the people."

Despite its success, the Constitution has had its share of critics. As mentioned earlier, some criticized it for giving too much power to the executive and to a consolidated government over the states. Others criticized it for failing to mention God or the Creator in its text whereas the Declaration of Independence had done so.

The framers recognized that no form of government is perfect. They knew that honest, principled citizens and rulers were necessary if the nation was to survive. Most Americans at that time had a strong sense of morality and religious convictions and understood the importance of obeying the law and taking responsibility for their actions.

Striking a balance between liberty and order was the great challenge and triumph of the Constitutional Convention.

## Comprehension Check 4.3

1. Anti-Federalists opposed the Constitution for the following reasons except that ____.
   A it lacked a bill of rights
   B the executive was like a king
   C the states had too much power

2. ____ wrote 51 essays of the *Federalist Papers* under the pen name "Publius."
   A Alexander Hamilton
   B Edmund Randolph
   C George Mason

3. ____ promised to introduce amendments that ensured civil liberties during the first session of Congress.
   A Elbridge Gerry
   B James Madison
   C Patrick Henry

4. Although nine states had already ratified the Constitution, the ratification by ____ helped provide unity in the south and the north.
   A Delaware and Pennsylvania
   B North Carolina and Rhode Island
   C Virginia and New York

5. The US Constitution is unique as a written document because it has never been ____.
   A copied by other countries
   B opposed by anyone since 1789
   C replaced since its ratification

### MAKING CONNECTIONS

6. What are three successes of the Constitution?

▼ The US Constitution housed in the National Archives in Washington, DC

# CHAPTER **4** REVIEW

## Chapter Summary

### 4.1 Government by Confederation

- After the United States declared independence from Britain, the Second Continental Congress adopted the Articles of Confederation as the form of government for the nation.

- The Articles of Confederation created a unicameral legislative branch (the Confederation Congress) which had limited power over the states. There was no federal judicial branch and a weak executive chosen by Congress.

- Achievements under the Articles included the negotiation of the Treaty of Paris of 1783 and the passage of ordinances dealing with the settlement and government of the Northwest Territory.

- Weaknesses under the Articles included financial weakness, the inability to enforce portions of the Treaty of Paris related to Britain and Spain, and domestic uprisings such as the Newburgh Conspiracy and Shays's Rebellion.

**TERMS**

confederation
Articles of Confederation
Confederation Congress
unicameral
Northwest Territory
Ordinance of 1784
Land Ordinance of 1785
Northwest Ordinance of 1787
right of deposit
Newburgh Conspiracy
Shays's Rebellion

**TERMS**

Annapolis Convention
Constitutional Convention
Virginia Plan
bicameral
New Jersey Plan
Roger Sherman
Great Compromise
Three-Fifths Compromise
Commerce and Slave Trade Compromise
republic
popular sovereignty
separation of powers
checks and balances
federalism

### 4.2 Writing the Constitution

- Congress called for a meeting in Philadelphia in 1787 to discuss changes to the Articles of Confederation. This meeting became the Constitutional Convention.

- The Virginia Plan proposed a bicameral legislature where representation in both houses would be determined by population. The New Jersey Plan proposed a unicameral legislature with equal representation for each state. The Great Compromise resolved this difference by proposing that representation in the House of Representatives be determined by population, and the Senate have equal representation for each state.

- The Constitution did not resolve the issue of slavery, but the Three-Fifths Compromise addressed the question of how to count slaves toward population for representation and taxation purposes, and the Commerce and Slave Trade Compromise gave the national government power to regulate trade without banning the slave trade for at least twenty years.

- Important principles of the Constitution include a republican philosophy, popular sovereignty, limited government, separation of powers, checks and balances, and federalism.

## 4.3 / Ratifying the Constitution

**TERMS**

ratification
Federalists
Anti-Federalists
*Federalist Papers*

- Nine states were required to ratify the Constitution for it to be adopted.

- The two sides in the ratification debates were the Federalists, who supported the Constitution, and the Anti-Federalists, who opposed it. Alexander Hamilton, James Madison, and John Jay wrote a series of essays known as the Federalist Papers to argue in favor of ratification.

- Despite nine states having ratified the Constitution, ratification in Virginia and New York was seen as crucial to a national union. After intense debate, both states voted to ratify.

- The United States Constitution is the longest-lasting and oldest Constitution still in use.

## *Chapter Review Questions*

### RECALL

1. What was the greatest foreign policy success of the Confederation Congress?

2. How was the land of the Northwest Territory to be distributed and sold according to the Land Ordinance of 1785?

3. How were schools to be funded according to the Land Ordinance of 1785?

4. What were the three stages for a region to become a state, according to the Northwest Ordinance of 1787?

5. Describe the financial problems the United States faced under the Articles of Confederation.

6. What potential act of rebellion did Washington end by listening to the leaders, sympathizing with them, and reminding them of his service to the country?

7. What state did not send delegates to the Constitutional Convention?

8. How many states needed to ratify the Constitution for it to take effect?

9. What was the purpose of the *Federalist Papers*? Who were the authors?

### UNDERSTAND

10. Describe the government that was created by the Articles of Confederation. What powers did the Confederation Congress have and what powers did the states have?

11. Why was John Dickinson's original draft of the Articles of Confederation, proposing a strong national government, rejected?

12. Why did some states refuse to ratify the Articles of Confederation until the western lands issue was resolved?

13. Besides prescribing a process for the establishment of new states, what were the other significant parts of the Northwest Ordinance of 1787?

14. What caused the foreign relations problems the United States had with England and Spain?

15. What did Shays's Rebellion demonstrate to critics of the Articles of Confederation?

16. Describe the government proposed by the Virginia Plan. Why did small states oppose it?

17. How did the Great Compromise resolve the deadlock between large and small states over the issue of representation?

18. How did the Three-Fifths Compromise address the issue of slaves and representation?

19. How did the Commerce and Slave Trade Compromise settle the issue of the government's power to regulate trade?

20. What is federalism? How has the Constitution's ambiguity on the issue of federal versus state power been both positive and negative?

21. What were the main arguments of the Anti-Federalists during the ratification debates?

22. What are two reasons the United States Constitution has been successful?

## THINK ABOUT IT

23. Summarize how financial, foreign, and domestic problems demonstrated to critics of the Articles of Confederation the need to change them. What type of change did they think was necessary?

24. What were the positions of the two sides on the issue of slavery during the Constitutional Convention? Do you think the Three-Fifths Compromise treated enslaved Americans equally with other Americans with regard to representation? Why or why not? Why did the Constitution not ultimately address the morality of slavery?

25. How could the founding fathers' view of human nature be seen in the basic principles of the Constitution?

26. What did many of the founding fathers think about democracy?

27. How did Madison's vision of a republic check the negative tendencies of "the people?" Why did he think large republics were better than small republics?

28. Why do you think the founders saw checks and balances as an important principle of government?

29. Which side would you have taken in the ratification debate and why?

30. Explain the following political cartoon. What is the cartoon about? What do the two columns that are not standing represent, and why were they important? [Note: Incipient Magni Procedere Menses is a quote from Virgil which translates to "Great Eras Begin" (literally "Great Months Begin to Proceed")]

The Ninth PILLAR erected !

"The Ratification of the Conventions of nine States, shall be sufficient for the establishment of this Constitution, between the States so ratifying the same." Art. vii.

INCIPIENT MAGNI PROCEDERE MENSES.

If it is not up' it will rise.

The Attraction must be irresistible

DEL. PEN. N·JER. GEOR. CON. MASSA. MARY. S·CARO. N.HAMP. VIRG. N.YORK

From the Independent Chronicle and Universal Advertiser, Boston, Thursday June 26, 1788.

# 5 Federalists and Democratic-Republicans

**5.1 The New Government under Washington**

**5.2 The Presidency of John Adams**

**5.3 Jeffersonian America**

**5.4 Challenges for Madison**

**5.5 The Era of Good Feelings**

▲ Federalist Roger Griswold (right) attacking Democratic-Republican Matthew Lyon (left), who had spat on him in the House of Representatives

# The New Government under Washington

**What occurred at home and abroad during the presidency of George Washington?**

GUIDING QUESTIONS

■ How was the first government under the Constitution established?

■ What were the significant domestic issues during George Washington's presidency?

■ What issues did America have with Britain, France, and Spain?

■ Why was Washington's farewell significant?

The early years of the young republic were not easy. Some of the nation's challenges included the establishment of a new government under the Constitution, the securing of the nation's finances, navigation of foreign and domestic threats, and differing visions for the identity of the nation. The question yet to be answered was whether the republic's Constitution and political leaders could see the nation through its infancy so that it could reach its potential.

## Washington Takes Office

George Washington was the natural choice for the nation's highest office. On February 4, 1789, Washington was unanimously elected president by the Electoral College and John Adams became the first vice president. On April 30, in New York City, Washington placed his hand on the Bible and promised to preserve, protect, and defend the Constitution.

The first order of business in 1789 was to organize the government in accordance with the new Constitution. The key features were the cabinet, the courts, and the Congress.

### Cabinet

With congressional approval, Washington organized three departments in the executive branch—State, Treasury, and War—and appointed their secretaries, or chief officers. Washington chose **Thomas Jefferson** as secretary of state, **Alexander Hamilton** as secretary of the treasury, and Henry Knox, a hero of the American Revolution, as secretary of war. In addition, Washington appointed fellow Virginian Edmund Randolph as attorney general.

Although the term "cabinet" was not in the Constitution, these department heads met regularly with the president to discuss policy decisions. Eventually, these advisors collectively took the name "**cabinet**"—this group played a key role in the first and future presidential administrations.

### Courts

The Constitution directly provided for only a Supreme Court but permitted Congress to establish lower federal courts. As a result, Congress passed the **Judiciary Act of 1789**. It organized thirteen district courts, established three circuit courts to handle appeals, and set the number of Supreme Court justices at six. Washington appointed **John Jay** to be the court's chief justice. Later, the number of courts and justices increased.

One significant section of the Judiciary Act of 1789 provided that state court decisions could be appealed to the federal court level if constitutional questions were involved. This provision clearly set the supremacy of the federal courts over the state courts.

▲ (top) Washington's first inauguration; (bottom) Washington and the first cabinet: (left to right) Henry Knox, Alexander Hamilton, Thomas Jefferson, and Edmund Randolph

## Congress

During the remarkable two-year session from 1789 to 1791, Congress drafted the Bill of Rights, organized the executive and judicial branches, and passed several crucial measures to put the country on a sound financial footing.

In the summer of 1789, Madison honored his pledge to his Anti-Federalist adversaries when he introduced amendments to the Constitution to protect individual rights. What emerged in 1791, after gaining the approval of three-fourths of the states, were the first ten amendments—the **Bill of Rights**.

The First Amendment protects the freedoms of religion, speech, press, assembly, and petition. The Second, Third, and Fourth Amendments protect the rights of the individual by guaranteeing the right to bear arms, prohibiting the forced quartering of troops in private homes during peacetime, and protecting against unreasonable searches and seizures. The Fifth, Sixth, Seventh, and Eighth Amendments guarantee fair treatment for those accused of crimes. The Ninth Amendment states that people's rights are not limited to those specifically mentioned in the Constitution. The Tenth Amendment reserved to the states those powers not delegated to the federal government. In summary, the Bill of Rights was specifically intended to restrict the power of the national government and to protect individual rights.

# Domestic Issues

## Finances and the Rise of Parties

### HAMILTON'S FINANCIAL PLAN

Treasury Secretary Hamilton presented his *Report on the Public Credit* to Congress, summarizing America's financial situation. He calculated that America's debt totaled over $77 million, which included $52 million in domestic and foreign debt owed by the national government and $25 million in debt owed by the states. His report also recommended actions to deal with the debt that had accumulated.

The first part of Hamilton's financial plan related to funding the debt. Some in Congress argued against repaying the full value of government certificates (promissory notes) or bonds used to finance the war, while Hamilton believed their full value plus interest should be paid. He argued that failure to pay would hinder America's ability to borrow money in the future. Another issue was that many war veterans and merchants who had been paid in certificates had sold them to speculators (short-term investors) for pennies on the dollar to get needed cash. Who should the government repay, the original holders or those who purchased them? Madison disliked the idea of speculation, which he perceived as taking advantage of desperate war veterans for profit. But Hamilton argued that the speculators had taken a risk and should be rewarded. If the debt was not repaid, no one would be willing to purchase government bonds and America's public credit would be weakened.

The second part of Hamilton's financial plan called for the assumption of all state debts by the federal government. He had several reasons: first, it would be more efficient to have one plan rather than thirteen individual plans for repaying the debt; second, it would cause creditors to have a greater interest in the success of the federal government and shift their loyalty from the states to the nation; and third, though some states (like Massachusetts) had made greater sacrifices than others during the war, yet all states had benefitted equally from the Revolution, so it was fair for all the states to share the cost of the war. Many southern states objected to the plan because they had already paid off much of their debt but would be asked to contribute taxes to pay the significant debt still owed by the New England states. Another objection was that the assumption plan would give the federal government control over the economies of the states.

The third part of Hamilton's plan called for raising revenue to pay the debt through tariffs (taxes on imported goods) and excise taxes (taxes on goods levied when manufactured) on whiskey and other spirits distilled in the United States. A revenue marine (later the Coast Guard) would be created to collect and enforce the tariffs.

The first Congress was at a standstill over Hamilton's financial plan, and some feared for the survival of the young republic. The legislative stalemate was broken by a major compromise. The site for a permanent national capital had not been determined. At a meeting mediated by Jefferson, Hamilton promised to get sufficient northern votes to locate the capital in the South, on the banks of the Potomac River, in return for southern votes favoring debt assumption. Shortly after that meeting, Congress passed the Residence Bill, which placed the site of the permanent capital on the Potomac River, and a few weeks later Congress approved Hamilton's assumption plan. The new capital was to be occupied in ten years; meanwhile, Philadelphia would serve as the temporary capital.

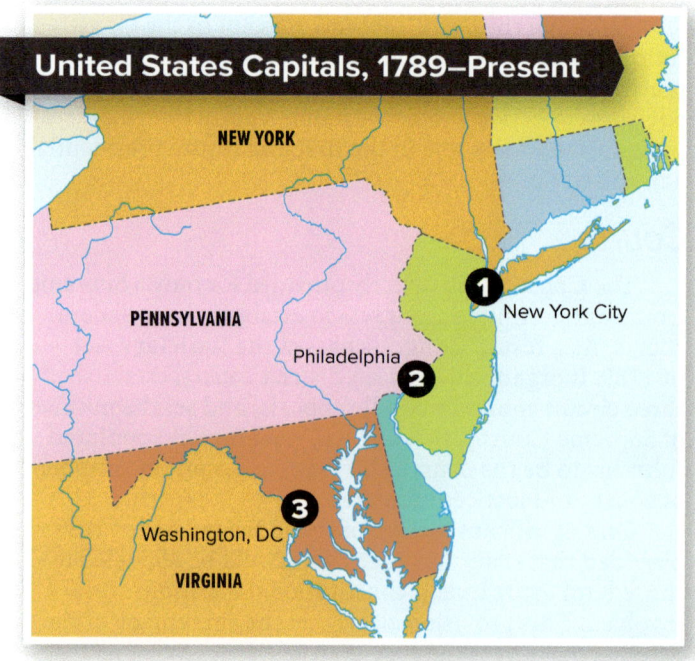

**United States Capitals, 1789–Present**

NEW YORK

PENNSYLVANIA

1 New York City

Philadelphia

2

3

Washington, DC

VIRGINIA

In a second report, Hamilton presented the final part of his financial plan—he proposed the formation of a national bank. He believed a national bank that would issue a uniform currency and grant business loans to encourage economic expansion was the centerpiece of a strong economy. The bill for a national bank with a twenty-year charter cleared Congress, but by the time it reached the president's desk to be signed into law, Madison and Jefferson were challenging its constitutionality.

Opponents argued that Congress had no specific authority to charter a national bank. Jefferson wrote that "to take a single step beyond the boundaries thus specially drawn around the powers of Congress, is to take possession of a boundless field of power." Expressing a strict interpretation, he believed that what the Constitution did not *permit*, it *prohibited*, and that according to the Tenth Amendment, those powers not delegated to the United States by the Constitution are reserved to the states. Others argued that a national bank would favor northern manufacturing and commercial interests over southern agricultural interests and that it might use its funds to influence elections and would thus be undemocratic.

Washington, concerned over the question of constitutionality, asked Hamilton to respond. Hamilton presented what has become the standard rationale for a loose interpretation of the Constitution. He argued that Article I, Section 8, Clause 18 of the Constitution gave Congress the authority to do whatever was "necessary and proper" to fulfill its duties. In other words, if the Constitution specified an end, then the government had the implied powers to do what was necessary to reach that end. Washington, persuaded by Hamilton's arguments, signed the bill into law, and the first Bank of the United States was created.

# Hamilton's Financial Plan

1. **REPAY WAR DEBTS**

2. **PAY STATE DEBTS**

3. **RAISE MONEY THROUGH TAXES**

4. **ESTABLISH A NATIONAL BANK**

▼ The First Bank of the United States, in Philadelphia

## THE RISE OF POLITICAL PARTIES

Division over Hamilton's financial plan demonstrated that there were two contrasting and competing visions for the United States. These differing visions led to the formation of America's first political parties.

Hamilton exemplified the principles of the **Federalist Party**. Federalists believed that America's future was in trade and industry and that economic growth occurs only under a strong national government. Hamilton believed that the government needed to establish the necessary conditions for the economy to thrive, and his broad interpretation of the Constitution gave the government the power to do so. He modeled his financial plan on Britain's, with a national bank, a strong finance minister, and government regulation of commerce.

Opponents of Hamilton's financial plan took the name Republicans, also known as Jeffersonian Republicans or the **Democratic-Republican Party** (not to be confused with the modern Republican Party which began in 1854). Like Jefferson, many Democratic-Republicans were southerners who believed that land, not money, was the ultimate measure of wealth. They had an agrarian rather than commercial vision for America's future. Many southern planters were in debt to British banks, and therefore despised credit, banks, and those who profited from lending money. The financial plan showed a growing difference between Hamilton's and Madison's visions of the power of the national government. Madison, who had been a staunch supporter of the Federalist cause, joined the Democratic-Republicans because he saw the power that was being concentrated in the federal government, especially the executive branch, as dangerous to liberty. Republicans wanted a small government limited by a strict interpretation of the Constitution and feared Hamilton's loose interpretation would give the government too much power.

The political division growing within the government alarmed President Washington. He had hoped to retire to his beloved home, Mount Vernon, after one term. But with the election of 1792 looming, all sides urged him to run again. The cabinet and Congress knew that no one could hold the fledgling nation together like Washington.

Reluctantly, Washington accepted the call for the sake of the nation and was unanimously reelected. His second term would be difficult, but his continuing leadership was crucial for the nation. Problems brewing in Europe were stirring unrest in America, and the new nation would need a steady hand to guide it.

## Differences between Federalists and Democratic-Republicans

| | Federalists | Democratic-Republicans |
| --- | --- | --- |
| **Party Representatives** | ▲ Alexander Hamilton | ▲ Thomas Jefferson |
| **Social Composition** | Commercial | Agrarian |
| **Governmental Views** | Loose interpretation of Constitution | Strict interpretation of Constitution |
| **Economic Views** | Support for National Bank | Opposition to National Bank |
| **Foreign Policy Views** | Strong national government | Small, limited government |

## The Whiskey Rebellion

Many backcountry farmers made their living raising corn and grain and often used part of their crop to make whiskey, which did not spoil on the trip to eastern markets as grain would. Because of the shortage of money, farmers sometimes used whiskey to purchase other items and were charged the excise tax. Farmers who refused to pay it were arrested and sent to distant federal courts for trial. In the summer of 1794, some Pennsylvania farmers attacked a federal marshal who attempted to arrest an individual for failing to pay the tax; they also burned the home of a tax inspector and tarred and feathered other officials.

President Washington offered amnesty to the rebels if they would agree to follow the law, but they refused. When Pennsylvania did not act against the rebels, Washington summoned thirteen thousand militiamen to end the **Whiskey Rebellion** and initially took command of them personally (the only time a president led troops while in office). When the army reached the western counties, the rebellion collapsed. Of the rebels that were arrested and tried, two were condemned to death, but Washington pardoned them. He had made his point: the national government possessed the strength and the will to enforce the law. In Washington's words, Americans had to "distinguish between oppression and the necessary exercise of lawful authority."

## Struggles on the Frontier

During Washington's presidency, American expansion into the Northwest Territory led to increasing conflict with the Native Americans. Washington desired to see westward expansion happen in a slow and orderly way where land belonging to Native Americans was purchased rather than taken by conquest. Despite Washington's hopes and the presence of many treaties, skirmishes occurred when settlers ignored the treaties, settled on land they did not own, and lived in isolated settlements that were vulnerable to attacks. Government attempts to keep settlers off Native American lands proved futile. Some Native American tribes also did not recognize the treaties, saying that the land could not be sold without the consent of all American Indians who lived there.

▲ The Battle of Fallen Timbers

The British, who had still not abandoned their forts in the Great Lakes region, urged local Native Americans to attack frontier settlements to slow America's expansion. In 1790 and 1791, they inflicted two humiliating defeats on the American army. Faced with an increasingly dangerous situation, President Washington appointed Revolutionary War hero "Mad Anthony" Wayne to defeat the British-allied Native Americans. Wayne marched his army from Fort Washington on the Ohio River (present-day Cincinnati) to a site near present-day Toledo. In the **Battle of Fallen Timbers** on August 20, 1794, Wayne's forces soundly defeated members of the Shawnee, Miami, Delaware, and Lenape tribes. In the resulting Treaty of Fort Greenville, the tribes surrendered all rights to the southern half of Ohio.

After Fallen Timbers, settlers began to pour into the Ohio region. By 1799 Ohio's population had grown so much that Congress, in accordance with the Northwest Ordinance, made it a separate territory. In 1803 Ohio was admitted to the Union as the seventeenth state (Tennessee had been admitted as the sixteenth state in 1796) and the first state from the Northwest Territory.

## Daniel Boone (1734–1820), Kentucky Backwoodsman

In 1792 Kentucky became the fifteenth state in the Union (Vermont, the fourteenth state, entered in 1791). Kentucky's admission was the result of the pioneering efforts of many men and women, the best known of whom was frontiersman **Daniel Boone**.

Born to a Quaker family on the Pennsylvania frontier, Boone learned to track and hunt from local Native Americans and gained a reputation as one of the region's best hunters. His family moved to North Carolina when he was sixteen, and he fought with the North Carolina militia during the French and Indian War.

Boone began exploring Kentucky in the 1760s to scout land for settlement. He blazed a trail called the "Wilderness Road" through the Cumberland Gap, and it became the main route of early settlers to Kentucky. He also helped establish some of the first settlements in Kentucky, one of which, Boonesborough, was named for him.

The Cherokees called Kentucky "the dark and bloody ground," and few other areas of the United States saw such fierce warfare between settlers and Native Americans. Boone's brother and two of his sons died in such clashes. During the Revolutionary War, Boone was elected as a representative in the Virginia General Assembly and served under George Rogers Clark in the western campaigns.

In 1799 Boone moved to Missouri (part of Spanish territory), because of legal and financial problems. Some reports state that in 1810, when he was seventy-six years old, he traveled up the Missouri River as far as the Yellowstone River and back, a two-thousand-mile round trip. He died in his son's home in Missouri in 1820.

▼ Storming of the Bastille

## Foreign Issues

### The French Revolution

The French Revolution erupted in 1789, just months after America inaugurated its new constitutional government. At first, most Americans rejoiced that the French were following their example in the struggle against tyranny. They could sympathize with the rallying cry of, "Liberty, Equality, Fraternity." But as the violence of the French Revolution worsened, some Americans began to express misgivings.

Jefferson, who had been serving as America's minister to France when the French Revolution began, viewed the Revolution with optimism. Believing the French deserved America's support because they had helped secure America's liberty and independence, Jefferson and other Republicans cheered when France declared itself a republic in 1792. When Louis XVI, the king who had aided the American Revolution, was executed in January 1793, Republicans welcomed the end of what they saw as a despotic French monarchy. Although Jefferson was bothered by the atrocities of the Reign of Terror (September 1793–July 1794), which brought the execution of more than 40,000 French citizens, he remained committed to the success of the Revolution:

> *The liberty of the whole earth was depending on the . . . contest, and was ever such a prize won with as little innocent blood? My own affections have been deeply wounded by some of the martyrs to this cause, but rather than it should have failed, I would have seen half the earth desolated.* — **THOMAS JEFFERSON**

Republicans feared that the failure of the French Revolution would lead to the failure of the American Revolution, in that America would return to monarchy, aristocracy, and tyranny if the democratic spirit of the people was crushed.

**Analyzing Sources**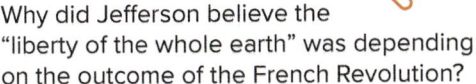

Why did Jefferson believe the "liberty of the whole earth" was depending on the outcome of the French Revolution?

Federalists, on the other hand, grew increasingly wary of the French Revolution as events unfolded. Hamilton believed the French Revolution sacrificed morality, religion, order, and property rights for the sake of liberty. He worried that the violence in France was a warning of what could happen in America if order were sacrificed for the sake of liberty. Hamilton wrote of the comparison between the two nations' revolutions:

> *Would to heaven that we could discern in the mirror of French affairs, the same humanity, the same decorum, the same gravity, the same order, the same dignity, the same solemnity, which distinguished the course of the American Revolution. . . .*
>
> *. . . When I perceive passion, tumult, and violence usurping those seats, where reason and cool deliberation ought to preside—*
>
> *I acknowledge, that I am glad to believe, there is no real resemblance between what was the cause of America and what is the cause of France—that the difference is no less great than that between liberty & licentiousness.* — **ALEXANDER HAMILTON**

▲ Execution of Louis XVI in January 1793

 **Analyzing Sources**

To Hamilton, what were the differences between the French and American Revolutions?

When France declared war on Britain, Holland, and Spain in 1793, America faced its first foreign policy crisis. Republicans like Jefferson believed the United States should support France in its war since France had supported the American Revolution. They argued that according to the 1778 Treaty of Alliance, America was obligated to come to the aid of France during wartime. Hamilton, arguing in favor of neutrality, said that the treaty was defensive in nature and did not apply since France was the aggressor in the war, and that the treaty had been made with a government and a king that the revolution had toppled, thus nullifying it. He also argued that America would need years of stability and prosperity before it would be prepared to fight a war, and that war with Britain would be foolish since over half of America's exports went to Britain and three-fourths of its imports came from Britain. Washington, agreeing with Hamilton, issued a **Proclamation of Neutrality** in April 1793. He declared that the United States would pursue a policy of friendliness and impartiality toward both nations.

The neutrality policy was threatened by the arrival of a new French ambassador, Edmond Charles Edouard Genêt, who in the egalitarian fashion of the French Revolution referred to himself as simply **Citizen Genêt**. Hamilton warned Washington that receiving Genêt on friendly terms might commit America to the French cause. Landing in Charleston, South Carolina, in April 1793, Genêt stirred up pro-French sentiment and gathered enthusiastic followers as he made his way to Philadelphia to meet Washington.

Genêt's agenda was to persuade the United States to provide funds, food, and military supplies to aid France in its war. He secretly recruited Americans to attack Spanish possessions in Louisiana and Florida and to convert private vessels into armed privateers to capture unarmed British merchant ships docked in American ports. Genêt overplayed his hand when he threatened to bypass Washington and appeal directly to the American people to support the French cause. At that point, even Jefferson agreed with Washington and Hamilton that Genêt was no longer welcome and drafted a letter asking the French government to recall him. However, because Genêt was in danger of the guillotine if he returned to France during the Reign of Terror, Washington graciously allowed him to remain in America.

Attitudes toward the French Revolution deeply divided the nation. At the same time, British attacks on American ships further complicated Washington's efforts to keep the country out of a European war.

## Trouble with Britain and Spain

In 1793 the British began attacking American ships trading in the French West Indies, denying the right of a neutral country to trade all goods except munitions with nations that were at war. Not only did the British seize more than 250 American ships and their cargo, but they also practiced **impressment**, seizing American sailors who they claimed were British deserters and forcing them into British naval service. These violations of American neutrality angered many, especially Republicans who already favored France over Britain.

In 1794 Washington dispatched John Jay to London to settle American and British differences. The resulting **Jay Treaty** seemed to benefit Britain at America's expense. The treaty granted Britain preferred trading status, imposed limitations on American shipping in the West Indies, and ignored the issue of impressment. The British promised only to abandon its forts in the Northwest Territory, pay reparations for past seizures of American ships (without a promise against future seizures), and agree to arbitration to settle disputes over seized American cargo. Given the United States' weak bargaining position (the nation lacked a navy), Washington considered the Jay Treaty to be the best agreement that could be reached. Republicans denounced the treaty as pro-British and said it would put America back into a colonial relationship with Britain; it barely received Senate approval in 1795. However, the Jay Treaty avoided war with Britain, and soon trade between America and Britain was booming.

Disputes with Spain continued over the boundary between Spanish Florida and the United States, and Spain continued to deny the right of deposit to American goods in New Orleans. Washington sent Thomas Pinckney of South Carolina to settle these disputes. The **Pinckney Treaty**, signed in 1795, settled the boundary of Florida and opened the port of New Orleans to American goods.

◄ (top) Washington with Citizen Genêt; (middle) British navy's impressment of Boston sailors; (bottom) Democratic-Republicans burning an effigy of John Jay

# Washington's Farewell

In 1796, after two terms as president, Washington announced his plans to retire. To those who accused the Federalists of being "monarchists," Washington's retirement showed that he still believed in the principles of republicanism and set the precedent for future presidents.

Washington left a remarkable legacy. The size of the nation by the end of his two terms had been enlarged with the addition of new states, and its power had been strengthened. Credit and commerce were stabilized, and the Constitution was proven to be a workable document.

In Washington's Farewell Address, however, he was looking not to the past but to the future. Washington urged Americans to lay aside partisan divisions. He encouraged commercial ties with Europe, yet he warned against political alliances with those nations.

◄ Washington, assisted by Alexander Hamilton, writing his Farewell Address

## Comprehension Check 5.1

1. Washington appointed John Jay as the first _____.
   A  ambassador to France
   B  chief justice
   C  secretary of state

2. Hamilton's financial report included a plan for the _____.
   A  assumption of state debts by the federal government
   B  reimbursement from Britain for the seizure of American ships
   C  sale of plots of land in the Ohio region for low down payments

3. As members of Washington's cabinet, Hamilton and Jefferson disagreed with each other on each of the following issues except _____.
   A  the ability of Congress to establish a national bank
   B  the location of the nation's capital on the Potomac
   C  the support of the United States for the French Revolution

4. After the Battle of Fallen Timbers, _____.
   A  farmers were pardoned for rebelling against a tax on whiskey
   B  Native American tribes surrendered their rights to lands in the southern half of Ohio
   C  Spain opened access to New Orleans

5. Washington's precedent for future presidents was to retire after one four-year term.
   True
   False

### MAKING CONNECTIONS

6. How did Federalists and Democratic-Republicans differ on politics, economics, and foreign affairs for the United States?

7. What were the reasons for America's position of neutrality regarding France and Britain?

# The Presidency of John Adams

**What happened during the presidency of John Adams?**

## Challenges for President Adams

### The Election of 1796

Despite Washington's warnings, partisan divisions were evident in the election of 1796, the first real contest in presidential politics. Nevertheless, the 1796 election demonstrated two features in the political maturing of the American republic that are remarkable even today: the peaceful transfer of power and the nonviolent competition between political parties.

The Federalists gave the presidential nomination to Washington's two-term vice president, John Adams of Massachusetts, and their vice-presidential nomination to Thomas Pinckney of South Carolina to balance the ticket geographically. Republicans nominated Virginian Thomas Jefferson for president and Aaron Burr of New York as his running mate.

Each elector cast two votes for president, and the candidate who received the most votes became president while the runner-up became vice president. Receiving the most votes, Federalist Adams was elected president, but Republican Jefferson (rather than Thomas Pinckney, Adams's running mate) received the second most votes and thus became vice president. An administration of political adversaries was certainly not what the constitutional framers had in mind.

John Adams's political experience made him well qualified for the job. Yet Adams faced the reality that he would never be as popular as the man he replaced. On Adams's inauguration day, there were cheers and tears for the departing Washington but little praise for the new president. Adams, however, had a strong sense that it was his duty to serve his nation regardless of personal and political cost.

GUIDING QUESTIONS

- What challenges did John Adams face during his presidency?
- How did Adams's appointment of John Marshall lead to the strengthening of the judicial branch?

▼ Artist's rendering of a White House reception in 1800

▲ 1798 cartoon "Cinque-Tetes or the Paris Monster"; the five-headed figure demanding "Money, Money, Money" represents the five Directors of the French government's executive branch, the Directory (1795-99). One of the three American diplomats replies, "Cease bawling, Monster! We will not give you six pence."

## The XYZ Affair

In foreign affairs, Adams had to maintain the delicate balance between protecting America's interests and avoiding war with either France or Britain. French hostility toward the United States following the Jay Treaty was intense. By 1797 the French had seized cargo on three hundred American ships. To make matters worse, the French refused to meet with America's minister to France, Charles Cotesworth Pinckney.

Adams responded to France's aggression in two ways: by maintaining American neutrality through negotiations, and by expanding the military in case those negotiations failed. In a May 1797 address to Congress, Adams denounced France's actions and announced plans to expand the navy and build up the nation's militia while at the same time sending two additional representatives to France to join Pinckney and attempt to open negotiations.

When the American delegation arrived in Paris, the French foreign minister, Charles Maurice Talleyrand, continually put off meeting with them, and then hinted through three of his agents, who did meet with the diplomats, that he would negotiate with the Americans for a price—a $250,000 bribe to France's leaders and a $12 million loan to the French government. Pinckney replied, "No, no, not a sixpence."

When word reached America that the delegation had failed to reach an agreement with France, Adams asked for additional military preparations. Pro-French Republicans in Congress, feeling the Federalists were overreacting, demanded to see the correspondence from the diplomats. Adams complied, substituting the letters X, Y, and Z for the names of the French agents, and the episode became known as the **XYZ Affair**. When evidence of the French demands for bribes became public, it raised a cry in America: "Millions for defense, but not one cent for tribute."

An undeclared naval war against the French was fought between 1798 and 1800. In this "Quasi War" (a conflict resembling war yet lacking a formal declaration), each side captured numerous ships from its opponent. In May 1798, amid growing fear of a French invasion, Congress created a separate Navy Department and authorized the creation of a 20,000 man "provisional" army, over the objections of Republicans who saw standing armies as tools used by repressive governments against the people. George Washington was called out of retirement to lead the army, with Hamilton as his second in command.

By 1799, Napoleon Bonaparte had risen to power in France and was willing to discuss peace with the United States. Adams sent a peace commission to France in late 1799, though he knew it would erode support from Federalists who wanted war with France. This decision contributed to his loss in the next election. Adams wanted to protect national honor and preserve freedom of the seas, but at the same time he believed that war would destroy the gains of the young American republic. Under Napoleon's terms, France promised to leave American ships alone and to suspend the Treaty of Alliance, signed in 1778, if America promised not to seek compensation for shipping damages from the Quasi War.

▲ Commemorative medal with the USS *Constellation*'s victory over *La Vengeance*

### The Alien and Sedition Acts

The anti-French sentiment that swept the country in the late 1790s influenced the passage of four acts, known as the **Alien and Sedition Acts**, in the summer of 1798. The Naturalization Act lengthened the period required for an immigrant to become a naturalized citizen with full voting rights from five to fourteen years. The Alien Act gave the president power to deport any foreign-born residents deemed dangerous to the peace. The Alien Enemies Act gave the president the power to declare as enemy aliens any residents who were citizens of a country at war with America. The purpose of these first three acts was to place restrictions on immigrants, who tended to be pro-French and supporters of the Republican party, by giving government the power to remove them and by making it harder for them to gain voting rights.

The fourth act, the Sedition Act, made it a crime to speak or publish anything "false, scandalous and malicious . . . against the government of the United States . . . or the President of the United States, with intent to defame . . . or to bring them, or either of them, into contempt or disrepute" and attached stiff fines and imprisonment for those convicted. Many were arrested under this law, and ten people were convicted. The Federalists put two-year expiration dates on the Sedition Act and the Alien Act.

While Federalists defended the Sedition Act as necessary to preserve order during the conflict with France, Republicans viewed the acts as a means for the Federalists to silence their political opponents. In November 1798 Jefferson drafted the **Kentucky Resolutions**, which were adopted by that state's legislature. In December Madison wrote the **Virginia Resolutions**. Both resolutions opposed the Alien and Sedition Acts as a violation of the First Amendment, held that the national government existed by consent of the states, and expressed the rights of the states to judge the constitutionality of a law. The Kentucky Resolutions went on to say that "whensoever the general government assumes undelegated powers, its acts are unauthoritative, void, and of no force." The Virginia Resolutions stopped short of declaring the right to **nullify** (declare void) federal law, declaring only that states had the right to "interpose for arresting the progress of the evil, and for maintaining within their respective limits, the authorities, rights, and liberties [pertaining] to them" without specifying what form that "interposing" might take. No other states joined in supporting these resolutions, and ten of the sixteen states officially opposed them.

Nullification would prove to be a contentious issue in future years (on topics including tariffs, slavery, and segregation), but as the election of 1800 grew nearer, the Republicans realized that the Alien and Sedition Acts were drawing more Americans to their side. Jefferson urged his supporters to make their views known through the ballot box. The upcoming election would determine the future of the acts as well as whether Federalists would maintain control of the government.

## Alien and Sedition Acts

| 1 **Naturalization Act** | 2 **Alien Act** |
|---|---|
| 3 **Alien Enemies Act** | 4 **Sedition Act** |

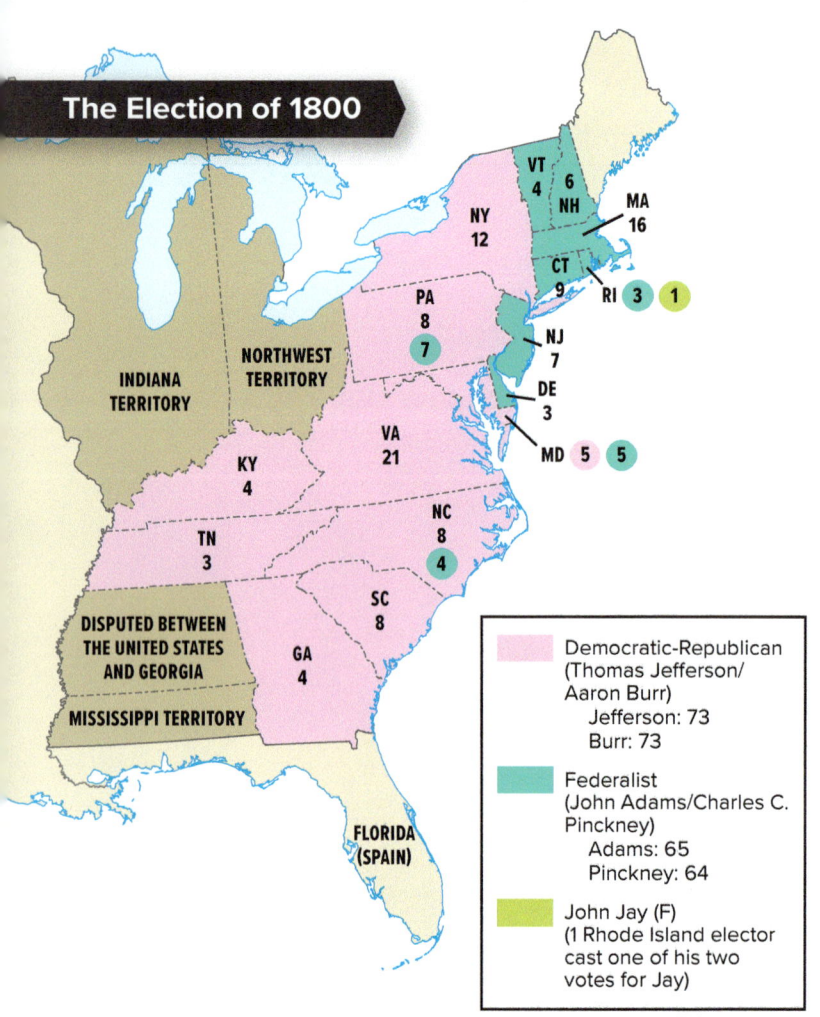

Democratic-Republican
(Thomas Jefferson/
Aaron Burr)
   Jefferson: 73
   Burr: 73

Federalist
(John Adams/Charles C.
Pinckney)
   Adams: 65
   Pinckney: 64

John Jay (F)
(1 Rhode Island elector
cast one of his two
votes for Jay)

## The Election of 1800

In the summer of 1800, John Adams moved to the new national capital, Washington, DC, named in honor of the first president (who had died in December 1799). Adams's stay in the executive mansion, however, would be brief. The election of 1800 was one of the most bitter ever. Adams's efforts to make peace with France had divided his own party, and the Alien and Sedition Acts had energized his opponents. Nevertheless, the Federalists picked him to run for reelection, with Charles Cotesworth Pinckney (the brother of Thomas Pinckney) as his running mate. The Republicans once again picked Jefferson and Burr as their candidates.

When the electoral votes were counted, Jefferson and Burr each had 73 votes. As stipulated in the Constitution, the tied election was decided by the House of Representatives. The Federalist-controlled House of Representatives was left to choose between the two Republican candidates. After a deadlock that lasted several days, Jefferson was elected president on the thirty-sixth ballot, and Burr became vice president.

Soon after the election, the Republicans supported the Twelfth Amendment to the Constitution. It called for electors to cast separate ballots for president and vice president. This prevented a recurrence of the complications of the 1796 and 1800 elections.

## Aaron Burr

Aaron Burr had a godly heritage. He was Jonathan Edwards's grandson, and the son of a Presbyterian pastor who was also president of Princeton University.

Burr became one of the most influential men in New York. In the deadlocked election of 1800, Burr denied being interested in the presidency, but rumors abounded that he was secretly hoping to win when the House of Representatives voted. Jefferson believed the rumors and never trusted his vice president again.

In 1804, while still vice president, Burr ran for governor of New York. Alexander Hamilton, who viewed Burr as a man without principles, opposed Burr's candidacy. Partly due to Hamilton's opposition, Burr lost. Angered, Burr challenged him to a duel. In the Burr-Hamilton duel, on July 11, 1804, Burr shot Hamilton, who died the following day.

# The Courts

## John Marshall

The Federalists lost control of both the executive and the legislative branches in the election of 1800. The only branch left to them was the judicial. After the election, but before Jefferson's inauguration, Adams took steps to strengthen Federalist control of the court system. In early 1801, he appointed Federalist **John Marshall** as chief justice of the Supreme Court. Marshall, who would serve as chief justice for thirty-four years, delivered some of the court's most important decisions. He was an enduring legacy of the Adams administration.

Marshall worked to strengthen the judicial branch by increasing the Supreme Court's influence. He reformed the practice of the court: instead of each justice writing an opinion for each case, the justices would discuss the case and issue one opinion, called the majority opinion. Justices who disagreed with the majority could write dissenting opinions. Marshall also encouraged the justices, who previously had been involved in party politics, to stay out of the political campaigns. He worked to build consensus with other justices, regardless of their political affiliation.

## The Midnight Judges

Before newly elected Republican congressmen took office, the Federalist-majority Congress passed the Judiciary Act of 1801, which increased the number of federal judges. Adams, of course, filled these appointments with Federalists. He was accused of staying up until midnight the night before Jefferson's inauguration on March 4, 1801, signing commissions for the new judges. The appointments were nicknamed the "midnight appointments."

The first major case before the Marshall Court involved the Judiciary Act of 1801. William Marbury had been granted one of Adams's "midnight appointments." However, Jefferson's secretary of state, James Madison, refused to deliver Marbury's commission, meaning that Marbury could not take office. Marbury asked the Supreme Court to issue a writ forcing Madison to deliver the commission. Marshall knew that he had no means of forcing Madison to obey, and some Republicans eagerly awaited the opportunity to disregard the authority of the Federalist judge.

Marshall cleverly handed down a ruling that preserved the authority of the Court without giving the Republicans an opportunity to defy it. Marshall said that although Marbury was right in his complaint, the power to issue such writs was not one of the powers delegated to the Court by the Constitution. The law that permitted such writs, then, was unconstitutional and therefore invalid. Thus, in ***Marbury v. Madison*** the Supreme Court established the principle of **judicial review**, the right of the Court to declare a law unconstitutional. As Marshall wrote in handing down the decision, "A legislative act contrary to the Constitution is not law. . . . It is emphatically the province and duty of the Judicial Department to say what the law is." Since that decision, the Supreme Court has declared well over a thousand state and federal laws unconstitutional.

## Comprehension Check 5.2

1. The XYZ Affair angered Americans because _____.

   A  Adams sent ambassadors to France while secretly negotiating a defense treaty with Britain

   B  American ambassadors called for deporting Irish immigrants who were pro-French

   C  French agents demanded a bribe from American ambassadors

2. The Kentucky and Virginia Resolutions claimed that the guaranteed rights of the First Amendment were threatened by the _____.

   A  Alien and Sedition Acts

   B  Quasi War

   C  Twelfth Amendment

3. The election of 1800 was the first election in which _____.

   A  a Federalist was chosen over a Republican for vice president

   B  a president was elected unanimously

   C  a tie between candidates was broken by the House of Representatives

4. In the election of 1800, Republicans secured power except in the _____ branch.

   A  executive

   B  judicial

   C  legislative

### MAKING CONNECTIONS

5. How did Adams's peacemaking efforts with France affect his political career?

6. What was the main difference between the Kentucky Resolutions and the Virginia Resolutions? What issue did these resolutions raise that would be contentious in future years?

- How did government policies change under the Democratic-Republicans?
- How did the Louisiana Purchase change America?

# Jeffersonian America

## What significant changes occurred during the presidency of Thomas Jefferson?

## Democratic-Republicans in Charge

### Differences between Parties

On March 4, 1801, Thomas Jefferson took the oath of office as the third president of the United States. This marked the beginning of the Jeffersonian era, which also included the presidencies of James Madison and James Monroe. It also marked the peaceful transition from one political party to an opposing party, a remarkable and enduring feature of American political history.

The Republican view of the economy contrasted sharply with the Federalist vision. Additionally, Jefferson believed the less government, the better, since he saw government as a corrupting influence on people who were by nature good. Republicans thought that shrinking the government could result in an ideal world without wars, standing armies, or debts.

Both parties wanted leaders who would govern with the common good, rather than personal gain, in mind; what they differed on was the basic assessment of human nature. The Federalists did not think that all people were equally capable of leading. They thought that government required the most educated individuals from the highest tier of society, finance, and trade. Republicans defended the common man as any man's equal.

Jefferson called his election "the revolution of 1800," suggesting that his victory marked a transformation as dramatic as that of 1776. While his election did bring change, it was no revolution. The Republicans did not destroy everything the Federalists had done during the early years of the republic, but they did alter the practices they disliked. The shift to Democratic-Republican control also signified a movement toward a greater emphasis on democracy, which would bring both positive and negative results.

### Did You Know?

Once political enemies, John Adams and Thomas Jefferson became close personal friends, frequently corresponding with one another. On July 4, 1826, the fiftieth anniversary of the signing of the Declaration of Independence, both men lay on their deathbeds. Adams's last words were about his old enemy and new friend; he whispered, "Thomas Jefferson survives." Ironically, his friend had died at his home in Virginia a few hours earlier.

▶ Thomas Jefferson

## Jefferson's Religion

Jefferson played a significant positive role in the founding of the United States. American believers can appreciate his rich contribution to the development of the country; however, his denial of Scripture's teaching about human sinfulness caused him to underestimate the depravity of man.

Jefferson admired the teachings of Jesus, calling them "a system of morals" that is "the most perfect and sublime that has ever been taught by man." However, Jefferson denied most of the scriptural teaching concerning Christ, such as the virgin birth. He also believed that much of the New Testament writings were corruptions of Jesus' teaching.

Jefferson compiled his own version of the four Gospels. Using scissors and paste, he pieced together an account of Jesus' life and teaching that excluded miracles and references to Christ as God. The result was a text limited mostly to the moral teachings of Jesus.

Baptists and other Christians from non-established churches supported Jefferson politically because, despite his beliefs, he championed religious liberty. In a letter to the Danbury Baptists in Connecticut in 1802, Jefferson affirmed his agreement with the First Amendment which said that Congress shall "make no law respecting an establishment of religion." He then added, "thus building a wall of separation between church and state." But Jefferson did not believe that the Constitution prohibited religion in public life. In fact, two days after writing that letter, he invited Baptist pastor John Leland to preach a sermon before Congress.

One of the first changes Jefferson made was to replace Federalists with Republicans. He also pardoned those convicted under the Sedition Act. The Republican-controlled Congress repealed the Naturalization Act, allowed the remaining Alien and Sedition Acts to expire, and repealed the Judiciary Act of 1801, thus eliminating many federal judgeships filled by Federalists.

Eager to downsize the national government, Jefferson had his secretary of the treasury devise a plan to both lower taxes and eliminate the national debt. By cutting expenses and reducing the size of the army and navy, the debt was cut in half and Jefferson was able to repeal the unpopular whiskey tax.

Yet the Republicans did not try to force change everywhere. For example, though Jefferson had opposed the creation of the National Bank because he believed it was unconstitutional, he left it intact because it was working well. He also continued the Federalist plan for repaying war debts.

## Fighting the Barbary Pirates

As part of his plan to cut federal expenses, Jefferson wanted to reduce the size of the navy. However, several small Muslim kingdoms in North Africa, known as the **Barbary States**, demanded tribute (a fee or tax) from ships sailing on the Mediterranean Sea. Ships that refused to pay were captured along with their crews and held for ransom. Most nations, including the United States, either paid the tribute to the Barbary pirates or avoided the area.

Jefferson wanted to end the tribute payments, so he sent a squadron of warships in 1801 to Tripoli to frighten the most important Barbary state with a show of force. In the war that followed, ships bombarded Tripoli's harbor.

The fighting ended with an agreement in 1805. The United States paid Tripoli a ransom of $60,000 for American prisoners but refused to pay additional tribute. Piracy in the other Barbary States continued for another decade. In 1815 the American navy, with help from European warships, ended all payment of American tribute along the Barbary coast.

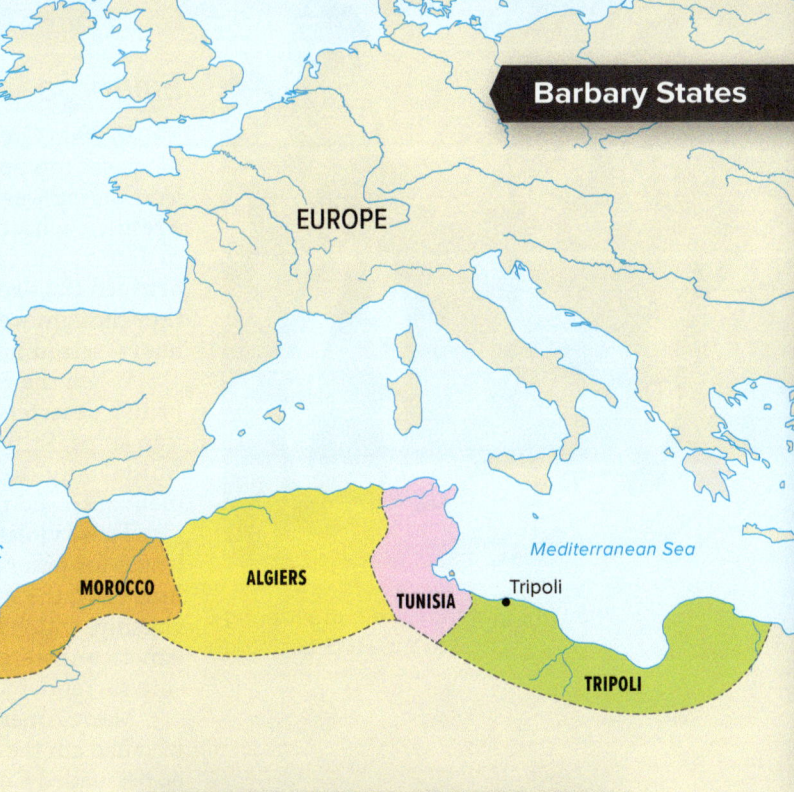

EUROPE

ATLANTIC OCEAN

*Mediterranean Sea*

MOROCCO

ALGIERS

TUNISIA

Tripoli

TRIPOLI

AFRICA

▼ Burning of the USS *Philadelphia* off the shore of Tripoli

## Did You Know?

The phrase "to the shores of Tripoli" in the Marine Corps hymn comes from the war against the Barbary pirates.

▲ The USS *Chesapeake* surrendering to the HMS *Leopard*

## Embargo

In 1803 Great Britain and France went to war again. The British navy was too powerful for Napoleon to invade Great Britain, and Napoleon's army was too strong for Britain to defeat France in land battle. As a result, each side tried to starve the other by restricting trade, hoping to destroy the enemy's economy. The neutral United States was caught between the two sides. Both Britain and France seized American ships they thought were bound for enemy ports, but Britain—with its powerful navy—seized more than the French.

When the British stopped American ships, they forcibly removed British deserters and returned them to service. While searching American ships, British officers—in desperate need of sailors—sometimes "mistakenly" took Americans as well. This renewed practice of impressment outraged the United States.

These violations of American shipping neutrality created great challenges for Jefferson, who had been reelected to a second term in 1804. In June 1807, the American warship *Chesapeake* was fired upon by a British warship, which had been informed that deserters were aboard. Three Americans were killed and eighteen were wounded. After the American ship surrendered, the British went aboard and seized four deserters.

Many Americans immediately called for war against Britain. Jefferson, who had cut the size of the army and navy, had few options. To avoid war, he persuaded Congress to adopt the **Embargo Act**, which ended all exports from the United States and all imports from Europe. Jefferson hoped the withholding of American goods would force Britain and France to stop violating American neutrality. The embargo failed miserably. Those most hurt by the embargo were Americans. Shipping dropped dramatically, and economic recession threw merchants, sailors, shipbuilders, and others out of work. Both political parties denounced the embargo.

## The Louisiana Purchase

New Orleans was vital to American interests; nearly half of all American trade passed through its port. In 1800 Spain signed a treaty returning the Louisiana Territory to France, who had controlled the area before the French and Indian War. Americans feared that France's dictator, Napoleon Bonaparte, who already had a large army in the French colony of Haiti, was planning to expand his empire to North America.

Jefferson sent James Monroe and Robert Livingstone, the ambassador to France, to Napoleon to offer him up to $10 million for New Orleans. France initially rejected the offer. But a yellow fever outbreak and a slave revolt in French Haiti caused Napoleon to abandon his plans for a North American empire. He also wanted money to resume his war against Britain and knew it was impossible to defend the vast Louisiana Territory. In May 1803 Napoleon's foreign minister astounded the Americans by offering to sell the entire territory—which was later determined to contain 530 million acres—for $15 million (or 2.8 cents per acre).

The American representatives sent word to Jefferson and urged him to accept the **Louisiana Purchase**. Jefferson was conflicted: he saw it would secure New Orleans and provide land for farmers, but as a strict constructionist he realized the Constitution gave the government no specific authority to purchase land. Jefferson briefly considered requesting a constitutional amendment to permit the purchase, but his ministers in France warned him to hurry before Napoleon changed his mind. Federalists objected to the purchase on constitutional grounds. They also favored closer relations with Britain than with France, feared their decreasing political influence as the nation expanded westward, and worried about the expansion of slavery in the territory. But when Jefferson submitted the treaty to the Senate, they quickly approved it in October 1803. With the Louisiana Purchase, the United States more than doubled its size.

## Lewis and Clark Expedition

To help determine the size of the territory and what it contained, Jefferson asked Congress to authorize **Meriwether Lewis** and **William Clark** to lead an expedition to explore the Louisiana Territory.

Jefferson instructed Lewis and Clark to study the geology, botany, and zoology of the territory; find the headwaters of the Missouri River; gather information on the Native Americans that they met; and report on any commercial possibilities. In preparation, Lewis went to Philadelphia, where he took classes on medicine, astronomy, navigation, botany, and fossils. He also spent time at Jefferson's home, Monticello, using the president's vast library to study geography and science.

On May 14, 1804, Lewis and Clark's group of about fifty men, known as the **Corps of Discovery**, left St. Louis. The group included scouts, interpreters, soldiers, sailors, carpenters, and a cook. York, a slave owned by William Clark, participated as an equal with the others in the party and was influential in negotiating with Native Americans, many of whom had never seen a black man before.

The party traveled up the Missouri River through the Dakotas and spent the winter of 1804–5 at a fort they built, Fort Mandan, in what is now North Dakota. There a French fur trapper named Toussaint Charbonneau, along with his Shoshone wife **Sacagawea**, joined the expedition. Sacagawea had been kidnapped from the Shoshones by another tribe as a young girl. The couple served as interpreters and smoothed relations between Native American tribes and the Corps of Discovery. When the expedition desperately needed horses, they met a group of Shoshones whose chief turned out to be Sacagawea's brother, who provided the much-needed animals.

▲ Entries from the Lewis and Clark journals

▼ The Corps of Discovery at the headwaters of the Missouri (Montana); (left to right) John Colter, York, Meriwether Lewis, William Clark, Sacagawea, and Charbonneau

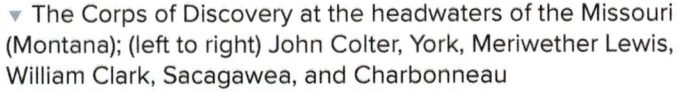

In spring the expedition set out and reached the headwaters of the Missouri River and the Rocky Mountains, crossed the Continental Divide, and sailed down the Snake and Columbia Rivers until they reached the Pacific Ocean in December 1805. They constructed Fort Clatsop on the Pacific coast in present-day Oregon, where they spent the winter. There Lewis filled his journals with information about the plants, animals, and people they had encountered.

On the return trip the Corps split, with Lewis's group exploring the Marias River and Clark's group exploring the Yellowstone River. They reunited near Fort Mandan and sailed down the Missouri River, arriving in St. Louis on September 23, 1806. The expedition had covered more than eight thousand miles over a period of twenty-eight months and had discovered nearly two hundred plants and more than one hundred animals. Lewis and Clark's journals sparked interest in westward expansion.

## Westward Expansion and Exploration

Legend:
- Louisiana Territory
- Pike (1805)
- Pike (1806–7)
- Lewis and Clark (1804–6)
- ◇ Fort
- ▲ Mountain

Map labels: Ft. Clatsop, Columbia R., Rocky Mountains, Snake River, Yellowstone River, Ft. Mandan, Ft. Snelling, Missouri River, Pikes Peak, St. Louis, Santa Fe, Arkansas River, Red River, Mississippi River, Rio Grande, PACIFIC OCEAN

## Zebulon Pike Expeditions

**Zebulon Pike** directed two important expeditions about the same time as Lewis and Clark's trip. The first, in 1805, went northward to the upper reaches of the Mississippi River. On his second trip, in 1806–7, he traveled up the Arkansas River to the Colorado Rockies, where he sighted the peak that now bears his name. He then turned southward into Spanish-held Mexico, where he planned to use the Rio Grande for his return trip, but he and a portion of his group were captured and held for a short time by the Spanish. As a result of these and other explorations, Americans learned more about the vast land they had acquired and began to envision a nation that stretched across the continent.

## Comprehension Check 5.3

1. The Democratic-Republicans thought the elite were the best leaders.

   True

   False

2. Jefferson sought to decrease the national debt by ____.

   A abolishing the National Bank

   B decreasing the army and navy

   C revising Hamilton's plans for repaying war debts

3. Jefferson sent warships to Tripoli in order to ____.

   A end paying tribute to the Barbary States

   B gain more territory from Spain

   C support the French against the British

4. Jefferson believed purchasing the Louisiana Territory was inconsistent with the federal government's constitutional powers, but he submitted the proposal for Congress's approval anyway.

   True

   False

5. Sacagawea and her husband helped the Corps of Discovery in all the following ways except ____.

   A establishing a good relationship with Native Americans

   B rescuing the explorers from captivity in Mexico

   C translating for the explorers

### MAKING CONNECTIONS

6. Why did Jefferson recommend the passage of the Embargo Act?

7. What effect did the explorations of Lewis and Clark and of Zebulon Pike have on the American public?

GUIDING QUESTIONS

- What challenges did James Madison face?
- What happened during the War of 1812?

**5.4** # Challenges for Madison

Why did the United States go to war with Britain again?

## Difficulties at Home and Abroad

In 1808 Jefferson refused to run for a third term, but he persuaded the Democratic-Republicans to nominate his secretary of state, James Madison, as his successor. Madison became the nation's fourth president in March 1809. Though Madison was a keen political philosopher and an experienced politician, he faced significant challenges from within and from outside the United States.

### Battle of Tippecanoe

One challenge Madison faced was conflict with Native Americans. American settlers felt that numerous attacks were being encouraged by the British in Canada. Native Americans blamed the attacks on violations of treaties by the settlers.

**Tecumseh**, the chief of the Shawnees, realized that individual tribes could never stand up to the United States. He therefore worked to form a confederacy of tribes whose goal was to halt the westward expansion of the United States. He traveled from Canada to the Gulf of Mexico recruiting tribes for his confederacy, and his persuasive speeches and strong personality were effective in gaining support.

Contributing to Tecumseh's success was a religious movement led by his brother, Tenskwatawa, who was also known as the Prophet. The Prophet urged his followers to return to their traditional way of life. Multitudes flocked to Tecumseh and the Prophet. They built a village called Prophetstown on the Tippecanoe River in the Indiana Territory.

**William Henry Harrison**, governor of the Indiana Territory, was alarmed by the growth of Tecumseh's following. He met with the brothers twice, but Harrison refused Tecumseh's demand that Native American lands be returned. In 1811, when Tecumseh was away in the south to rally the tribes to his cause, Harrison took nearly one thousand men and camped near Prophetstown. In his brother's absence, the Prophet ordered a night attack on the American camp. In the **Battle of Tippecanoe**, Harrison's forces drove off the attackers but took heavy losses. Prophetstown was abandoned, and Harrison burned the village.

When Tecumseh returned, he found his settlement destroyed. He and the Prophet moved to Canada and joined the British forces. Tecumseh later fought against the United States in the War of 1812.

▲ Tecumseh

▼ The Battle of Tippecanoe

### Trouble at Sea

Like Adams and Jefferson, Madison hoped to avoid war with France and Britain. At his request, Congress passed a bill which restored trade with those two countries. To encourage France and Britain to relax their stance, the act further stated that if either one would repeal its anti-trade regulations, the United States would trade fully with that side and stop trade with the other. Napoleon responded by repealing his restrictions in 1810, and the United States resumed trade with France and blocked all trade with Britain.

# The War of 1812

## Causes of the War

The congressional elections of 1810 nudged America closer to war. Even though France still seized American ships, Americans were angrier at Britain's continued violations of America's shipping rights. Newly elected representatives from western and southern states, led by Henry Clay of Kentucky and John C. Calhoun of South Carolina, pushed for war with Britain. These "**War Hawks**" said that British restrictions on American trade hurt southern planters and western farmers, who earned much of their income by shipping goods overseas. Some War Hawks wanted to seize Canada to stop British instigation of Native American attacks and to expand America's land. Above all, the group saw British actions, such as impressment, as insults to American honor. The War Hawks, who elected Clay to be Speaker of the House, denounced Britain and asked for a declaration of war.

On June 1, 1812, Madison asked Congress to declare war against Britain. Among the reasons he gave were (1) impressment of American sailors, (2) interference with American trade (e.g., seizure of American ships), and (3) inciting of Native American attacks on Americans.

Debate over the declaration of war was bitter. Federalists, especially New Englanders, generally opposed war. They depended on the sea and feared war would further disrupt trade. Some argued that the purpose of the war was to further the interests of the Republican Party and opposed its expansionist agenda. Others argued that France, not Britain, was the greater threat. Some Republicans opposed war, fearing it might strengthen the national government, increase the nation's debt, and possibly result in the loss of parts of the United States. On June 18 the House voted 79–49 and the Senate 19–13 for war, with no Federalists voting in favor. Two days before the vote Britain voted to end the seizure of American ships, but there were no quick means of communication and word did not reach the United States until after war was declared.

The United States entered what became known as the **War of 1812** divided and unprepared. The War Hawks were eager to fight but reluctant to pay the costs. Republicans had promoted a policy of small government and reduced budgets and were opposed to a large standing army. As a result, America went to war with Britain with only sixteen seagoing warships and an army of fewer than 5,000 men. The nation had an additional 50,000 to 100,000 state militiamen, but they were often poorly trained, and the New England states, dominated by Federalists, resisted giving money or men to the war effort, calling it "Mr. Madison's War." Additionally, most of the army's commanders were aged veterans of the War for Independence. Fortunately for Americans, Britain was fighting Napoleon and could not devote its full attention to the United States.

▲ James Madison

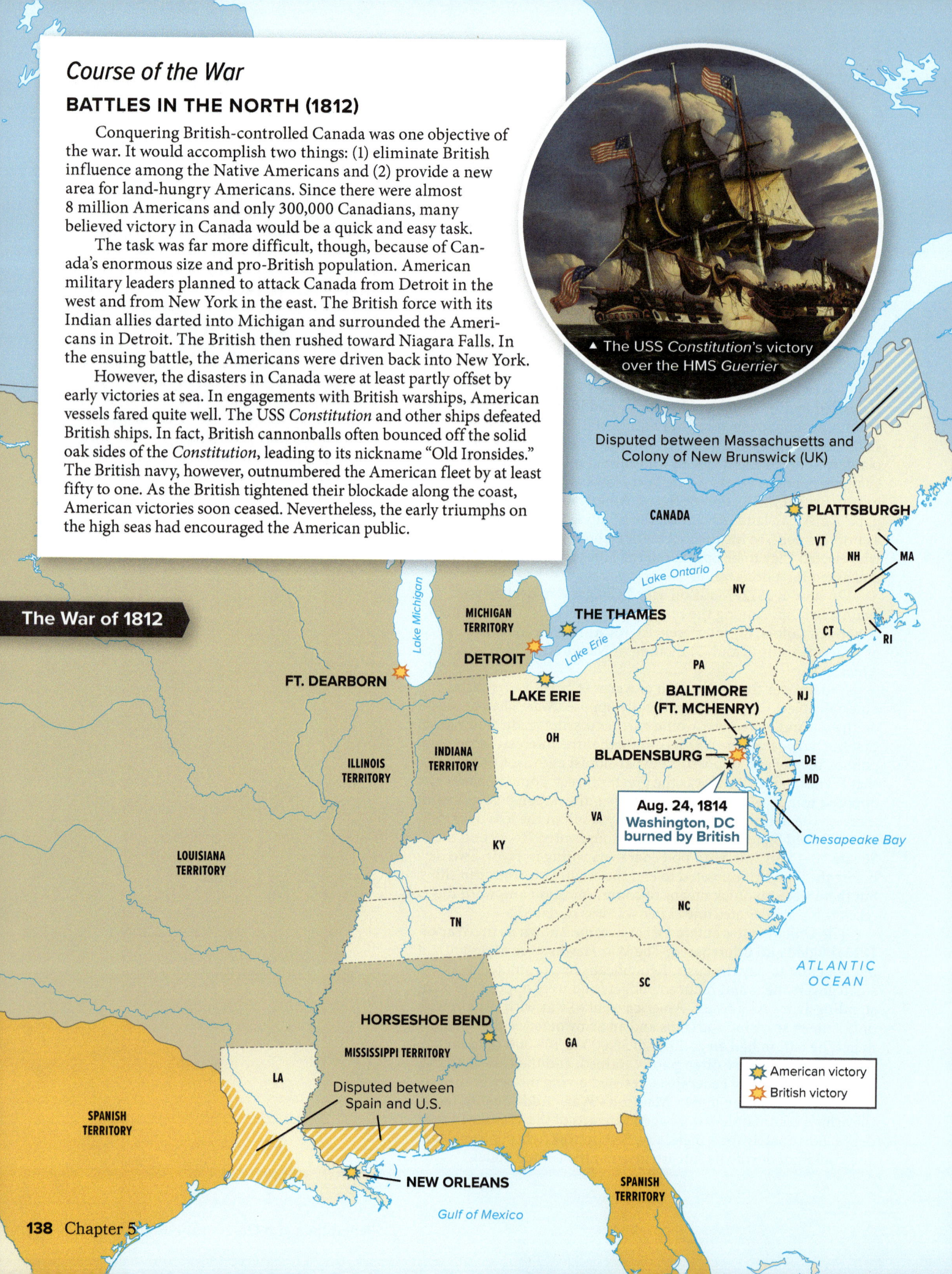

## Course of the War

### BATTLES IN THE NORTH (1812)

Conquering British-controlled Canada was one objective of the war. It would accomplish two things: (1) eliminate British influence among the Native Americans and (2) provide a new area for land-hungry Americans. Since there were almost 8 million Americans and only 300,000 Canadians, many believed victory in Canada would be a quick and easy task.

The task was far more difficult, though, because of Canada's enormous size and pro-British population. American military leaders planned to attack Canada from Detroit in the west and from New York in the east. The British force with its Indian allies darted into Michigan and surrounded the Americans in Detroit. The British then rushed toward Niagara Falls. In the ensuing battle, the Americans were driven back into New York.

However, the disasters in Canada were at least partly offset by early victories at sea. In engagements with British warships, American vessels fared quite well. The USS *Constitution* and other ships defeated British ships. In fact, British cannonballs often bounced off the solid oak sides of the *Constitution*, leading to its nickname "Old Ironsides." The British navy, however, outnumbered the American fleet by at least fifty to one. As the British tightened their blockade along the coast, American victories soon ceased. Nevertheless, the early triumphs on the high seas had encouraged the American public.

▲ The USS *Constitution*'s victory over the HMS *Guerrier*

Disputed between Massachusetts and Colony of New Brunswick (UK)

**The War of 1812**

CANADA

*Lake Ontario*

*Lake Michigan*

**PLATTSBURGH**

VT
NH
MA
NY
CT
RI

**MICHIGAN TERRITORY**

**THE THAMES**

*Lake Erie*

**DETROIT**

PA

NJ

**FT. DEARBORN**

**LAKE ERIE**

**BALTIMORE (FT. MCHENRY)**

OH

DE

**INDIANA TERRITORY**

**BLADENSBURG**

MD

**ILLINOIS TERRITORY**

VA

Aug. 24, 1814
Washington, DC
burned by British

KY

*Chesapeake Bay*

**LOUISIANA TERRITORY**

NC

TN

SC

*ATLANTIC OCEAN*

GA

**HORSESHOE BEND**

**MISSISSIPPI TERRITORY**

LA

Disputed between
Spain and U.S.

☆ American victory
☆ British victory

**SPANISH TERRITORY**

**NEW ORLEANS**

**SPANISH TERRITORY**

*Gulf of Mexico*

## BATTLES IN THE GREAT LAKES (1813)

Madison gave William Henry Harrison command in the Northwest. Harrison realized that the United States would need to control Lake Erie. American captain Oliver Hazard Perry rose to the challenge. Building his own ships and dragging cannons and ammunition through the wilderness, Perry defeated the British fleet in the Battle of Lake Erie (September 10, 1813). Perry sent a triumphant message to Harrison: "We have met the enemy and they are ours."

With Lake Erie secured, Harrison attacked the British army near the River Thames in Canada, on October 5, 1813. In the Battle of the Thames, Harrison crushed the British-Indian force and Tecumseh was killed. With these losses, Britain decided to focus its attention to the east and the south.

## BATTLES IN THE EAST (1814)

Despite Harrison's victory, the American situation remained grave early in 1814. Napoleon had surrendered, allowing Britain to turn its full attention to America. The British devised a three-pronged plan: (1) capture New York City to separate New England from the rest of the states, (2) attack major cities on the eastern coast, and (3) capture New Orleans.

The first stage failed when a small American naval squadron defeated a larger British fleet on Lake Champlain at the Battle of Plattsburgh on September 11, 1814. Without control of the lake, the British commander would not risk an invasion, and the force turned back.

The second prong was initially more successful. A British naval force landed in Maryland in August and marched toward Washington. In the Battle of Bladensburg, the British routed the militia and had a clear path to Washington. Before fleeing to safety with her husband, Madison's wife, Dolley, helped save important items from the Executive Mansion. British soldiers entered Washington and set fire to the Capitol, the president's mansion, and several other government buildings. Only heavy rain prevented the entire city from burning to the ground.

The British next turned to Baltimore, America's third largest city, protected by Fort McHenry. The British fleet began bombarding the fort on September 13, 1814, and continued for twenty-five hours.

During the bombardment, Baltimore lawyer **Francis Scott Key** was on board a British ship pleading for the release of a friend who had been captured by the British. The British commander agreed but kept the men aboard because the fleet was preparing to attack Fort McHenry. Straining to see the action, Key watched the British fleet shell the fort throughout the night. As dawn broke, he saw the American flag flying proudly above the fort, signaling that the bombardment had failed. Key wrote the first verse of the poem he called "The Defense of Fort McHenry" on the back of an envelope. Later set to music and renamed "The Star-Spangled Banner," the popular poem became the official national anthem in 1931.

After three days of fighting, during which the British commanding general was killed, the British abandoned the task. The entire force left Chesapeake Bay and joined the effort to capture New Orleans.

◄ (top) The British burning the White House; (bottom) Francis Scott Key observing Fort McHenry

## BATTLES IN THE SOUTH (1814)

As a result of Tecumseh's efforts among the southern tribes, civil war broke out between the pro-American Lower Creeks and pro-Tecumseh Upper Creeks, called Red Sticks, in the Mississippi Territory, and the war spilled over into white settlements. The government asked General Andrew Jackson to help the Lower Creeks and to defend the south against the British. Jackson won a series of victories against the Red Sticks, climaxing in the Battle of Horseshoe Bend (1814), in which he nearly wiped them out.

Jackson had little time to celebrate his victory, however. He marched quickly to New Orleans late in 1814 to meet the British attack. At New Orleans Jackson stationed his troops and artillery behind barricades and cotton bales. On January 8, 1815, the British marched directly on Jackson's lines. Jackson's artillery tore huge gaps in the British lines, and his frontier sharpshooters picked off those who managed to survive the cannons. The British had more than two thousand casualties; the Americans had fewer than one hundred.

The **Battle of New Orleans** was the most stunning victory of the War of 1812, but it was fought after the war was over. The treaty that ended hostilities had been signed in Europe some two weeks earlier. Slow communications kept that news from reaching America for several weeks. Nonetheless, the battle made Jackson the greatest hero of the war.

▼ The Battle of New Orleans led by General Andrew Jackson (on horseback)

## Results of the War

The **Treaty of Ghent**, signed in Belgium on December 24, 1814, was basically a cease fire, or agreement to stop fighting; neither side was victorious, and the treaty did not settle the disputes over impressment and the seizure of American ships, although both sides agreed to meet in the future to resolve their grievances.

The War of 1812 brought several changes to American society. First, it created a sense of national pride and unity. Many Americans developed a greater love for their country and increasingly identified with their nation rather than their state. Second, the war brought America greater respect around the world. Other countries recognized that the United States had the ability to fight to protect its interests. Third, the embargo and British blockade spurred the growth of American industry and manufacturing and decreased America's dependence on foreign countries for manufactured goods. Fourth, the war brought America a long period of freedom from European conflict, which allowed the nation to focus on its own affairs, including westward expansion. Fifth, the war influenced America's political parties. The Federalists lost influence and began to decline as a party because of their pro-British and anti-war positions, and some Democratic-Republicans began to support a stronger federal government that was more engaged militarily and economically.

▶ Signing of the Treaty of Ghent, 1814

---

### Comprehension Check 5.4

1. To resist expansion of white settlers into Native American territory, Tecumseh attempted to ____.

   A  convert Native Americans to Christianity

   B  join the Americans against the British

   C  unite the tribes into a confederation

2. Which was not a reason the War Hawks wanted war with Britain?

   A  impressment of American sailors

   B  interference with American trade

   C  prevention of American settlement in New Orleans

3. During the War of 1812, early American victories occurred on land.

   True

   False

4. ____ witnessed the failed attempt of the British to capture Fort McHenry.

   A  Francis Scott Key

   B  Oliver Hazard Perry

   C  William Henry Harrison

5. Andrew Jackson was victorious at the Battle of ____ after the War of 1812 was officially over.

   A  Lake Erie

   B  New Orleans

   C  Plattsburgh

6. The Treaty of Ghent made provisions for a ceasefire between the United States and Britain.

   True

   False

### MAKING CONNECTIONS

7. Why did many Federalists and some Republicans oppose the War of 1812?

8. What are three ways the War of 1812 changed American society?

## 5.5 The Era of Good Feelings

**How did America change during the Era of Good Feelings?**

Madison's secretary of state, James Monroe, won the presidential election of 1816. Monroe maintained Jeffersonian Republican philosophy into the 1820s. This period of both political peace and the end of American foreign conflicts led a Boston newspaper to call Monroe's presidency the "Era of Good Feelings."

▶ James Monroe

One cause of the Era of Good Feelings was the collapse of the Federalist Party. The Federalists had opposed the War of 1812, and during the conflict's darkest days in 1814, representatives of the New England states met in Hartford, Connecticut. The **Hartford Convention** opposed the war and the most radical Federalists proposed that New England secede (withdraw) from the Union. The convention was met with widespread public disapproval. News of the victory in New Orleans and of the Treaty of Ghent came soon after the meeting and eliminated its purpose. The Federalist Party, which was dying before the war, disappeared within a few years.

## Foreign Concerns

Britain and the United States began negotiations on a number of issues of mutual concern. One agreement they reached limited the number of British and American warships in the Great Lakes. Its provisions were eventually extended along the entire US-Canada border as the nations advanced westward. In 1818 the United States and Britain also agreed to occupy the Oregon Territory on the Pacific Ocean jointly until they could decide how to divide it.

## Florida

Americans had begun moving into Spanish West Florida (the part extending to the Mississippi River), and in 1810 those settlers revolted against Spanish rule and asked to become part of the United States. The United States government, claiming that the territory was part of the Louisiana Purchase, began taking control of parts of West Florida. Spain objected but took no action.

East Florida was also a source of conflict. It became a haven for smugglers and runaway slaves. Often, they joined the Seminoles in raiding American settlements in Georgia. Secretary of State John Quincy Adams warned Spain to control its territory or the United States would act. When Spain did not respond, Secretary of War John C. Calhoun asked Andrew Jackson to take the Tennessee and Georgia militias to the Florida border to stop the raids. Jackson, interpreting his orders loosely, invaded Florida, attacked the Seminoles and others who had helped in the raids, captured towns and forts, and overthrew Spanish officials. Monroe refused Spain's demands for payment for damages and for Jackson to be punished.

Spain, lacking the money or troops to defend Florida, decided to sell the region. Under the **Adams-Onís Treaty** of 1819, Spain sold East Florida to the United States for $5 million, allowed the United States to keep the portions of West Florida it had taken, and established the boundary of Spanish territory west of the Mississippi River. In 1821 Monroe appointed Jackson to serve as governor of Florida until a territorial government could be established.

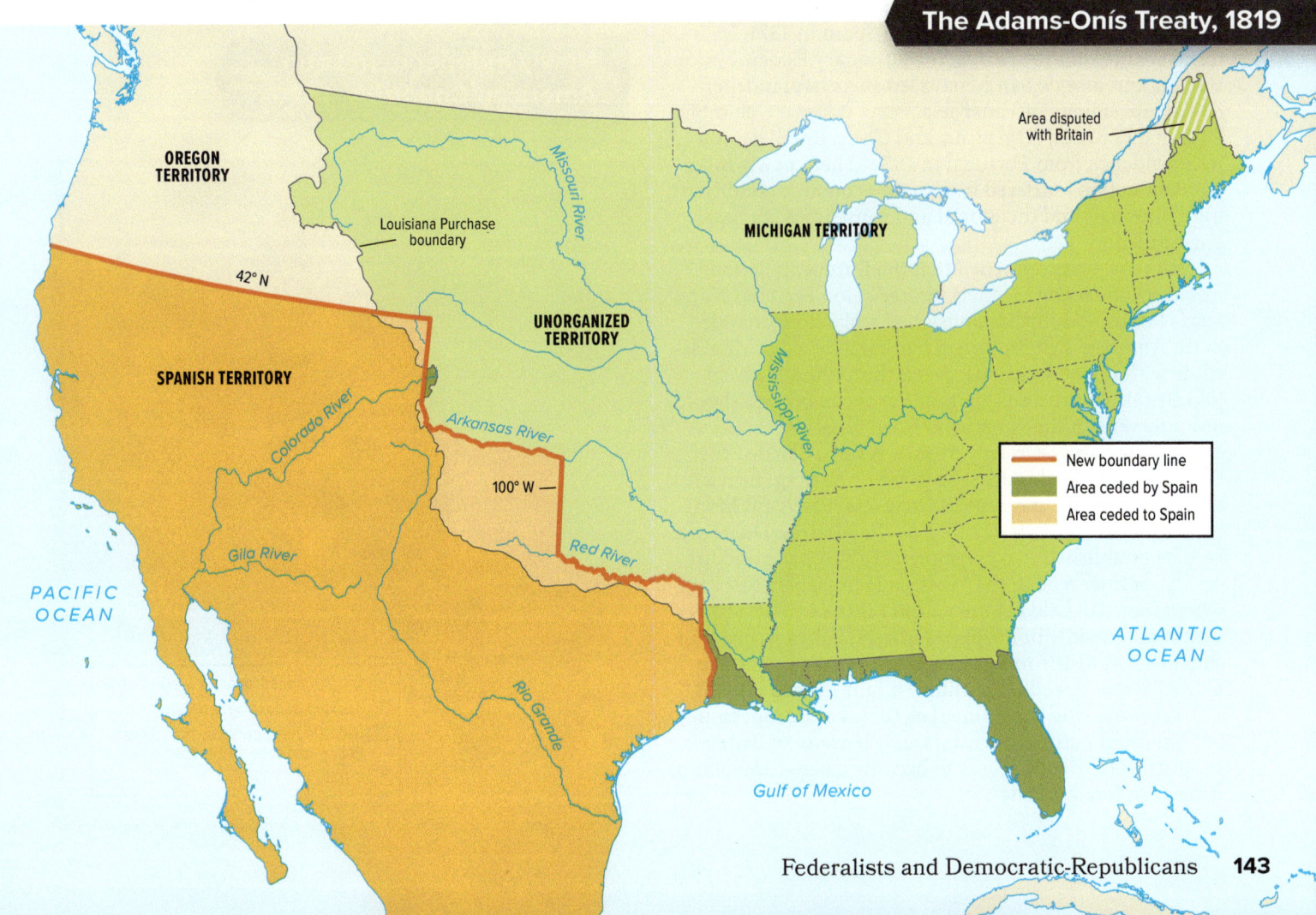

**The Adams-Onís Treaty, 1819**

OREGON TERRITORY

Louisiana Purchase boundary

42° N

SPANISH TERRITORY

Colorado River

Gila River

100° W

Arkansas River

Red River

Rio Grande

Missouri River

Mississippi River

UNORGANIZED TERRITORY

MICHIGAN TERRITORY

Area disputed with Britain

PACIFIC OCEAN

ATLANTIC OCEAN

Gulf of Mexico

New boundary line
Area ceded by Spain
Area ceded to Spain

## The Monroe Doctrine

As a result of Napoleon's conquest of Spain and Portugal, the Latin American colonies of those countries seized the opportunity to gain their independence. Mexico won its independence from Spain in 1821. In Central and South America, revolutionary leaders Simón Bolívar and José de San Martín led successful independence movements in Venezuela, Peru, Bolivia, Colombia, Panama, Ecuador, Argentina, and Chile. Brazil gained independence from Portugal in 1822. These newly independent nations suffered from poor economic conditions, high illiteracy, and dictatorial and sometimes corrupt governments.

Monroe was concerned that the European nations might try to reconquer their former colonies. After Napoleon's fall in 1815, Spain envisioned a plan to recolonize Latin America. Britain, which had established profitable trade with the new nations, asked the United States to join Britain in proclaiming that European powers should not intervene in the Americas.

Monroe and Secretary of State Adams decided that the United States should issue its own warning. In 1823, during his annual message to Congress, President Monroe issued what became known as the **Monroe Doctrine**. In it he established two principles: (1) European nations could not intervene in the Western Hemisphere (except where they still held colonies), and (2) the United States would not meddle in European affairs. When issued, the statement was little more than a paper pledge since the United States lacked the military might to back it up. It did, however, stop the immediate threat of European intervention in Latin America (largely because of Britain's support). This doctrine was to become a major element of American foreign policy.

▲ *The Birth of the Monroe Doctrine.* (Left to right) John Quincy Adams, William Crawford, William Wirt, President Monroe, John C. Calhoun, Daniel Tompkins, and John McLean.

**Newly Independent Latin American Countries, 1820s**

VENEZUELA
PANAMA
COLOMBIA
ECUADOR
PERU
BRAZIL
BOLIVIA
ARGENTINA
CHILE
PATAGONIA
Disputed by Chile and Argentina

- Led to independence by Simón Bolívar
- Assisted by José de San Martín
- Led to independence by both Simón Bolívar and José de San Martín
- Brazil

# Domestic Concerns

## *Economics*

The years immediately following the War of 1812 saw a growing spirit of nationalism (loyalty and devotion to one's nation). At the heart of that new nationalism was a concern for the economic strength of the nation. Speaker of the House Henry Clay and others proposed an ambitious program they called the **American System**, which included a new national bank, protective tariffs, and federal funds for internal improvements such as roads and canals.

The charter for the first Bank of the United States had expired in 1811, and the Republican government under Madison had not renewed it. State-chartered banks and private banks had begun issuing their own paper money, and without a national bank to regulate currency, prices rose rapidly. This inflation, along with the difficulties the country had faced in financing the War of 1812, began to convince many Republicans of the benefits of a national bank. In 1816 Congress approved a twenty-year charter on the Second Bank of the United States, which would assist economic growth by providing uniform currency, a source for loans to the public and private sectors, and a place to deposit government funds.

The embargo on trade and the War of 1812 had the unexpected benefit of stimulating the growth of American manufacturing. The British were quick to see the threat to their own interests posed by American industry and began flooding the market with imported goods. Congress passed the Tariff of 1816, America's first **protective tariff** (a high tariff designed to shield a nation's manufacturers from foreign competition). The tax imposed by the Tariff of 1816 increased the cost of foreign goods and thereby made domestic products more affordable than foreign imports.

Not everyone benefitted from the tariff. While it benefitted manufacturers, who tended to be in the north, by increasing sales, it hurt southern and western farmers and those who depended on foreign trade. Protective tariffs became a divisive issue between the regions.

Another key element of the American System was federal funding for internal improvements—roads and canals which would improve transportation and stimulate commerce. Such improvements would help link western goods with eastern markets and provide better routes for western settlement. Madison had vetoed a Republican internal improvement bill on the grounds that Congress lacked constitutional authority to fund such projects. Roads and canals were the responsibility of the state or local area they served. In the absence of federal funds, states and private businesses had to find their own financing to build roads and canals. Some Republicans complained that the president's narrow views were hindering economic growth.

After the War of 1812, America had experienced an economic boom as demand for its products increased around the world. As farmers received higher prices for their crops, more Americans moved west, buying farmland with money borrowed from state banks in hopes of reaping high profits. However, this economic boom did not last. As the economies of European nations recovered and demand for American goods decreased, prices began to fall, which made it difficult for farmers and speculators to pay back their bank loans. At the same time, the Second Bank of the United States, concerned over the health of the state banks, stopped loaning money to some banks and called in its loans, which caused many banks to fail. The resulting economic collapse was called the **Panic of 1819** and led to many Americans losing their homes, farms, businesses, and savings. The panic was particularly hard on southern and western farmers.

## The Missouri Compromise

As mentioned in the previous chapter, the Constitution did not resolve the issue of slavery. In 1819 America was comprised of eleven slave states and eleven free states. Westward expansion and the admission of new states raised questions regarding the status of slavery and the preservation of the balance between northern and southern interests. The southern states had lost control in the House of Representatives to the more populous North; balance in the Senate, therefore, remained critical to the South.

Missouri applied for statehood in 1819 as a slave state. Representative James Tallmadge of New York proposed an amendment to Missouri's statehood bill that would prohibit slaveholders from bringing new slaves into Missouri. It also stated that enslaved children born after Missouri received statehood would obtain freedom at age 25. In an impassioned speech he denounced slavery as immoral. The Tallmadge Amendment brought an outcry from slave states because it interfered with a state's laws. Voting along sectional lines, House members approved the Tallmadge Amendment despite southern objections. However, the amendment was defeated in the Senate.

When Maine (formerly part of Massachusetts) applied for statehood in the summer of 1819, a compromise solution became possible. Speaker of the House Henry Clay of Kentucky proposed the **Missouri Compromise**, which stated that Maine would be admitted as a free state and Missouri as a slave state, and that slavery would be prohibited in the rest of the Louisiana Territory north of 36°30′, Missouri's southern boundary. Even though over two-thirds of the former Louisiana Territory would be reserved for free states, many northern congressmen objected because that land was not open for settlement yet and was considered a desert unsuitable for farming, and because the compromise signaled that slavery was not declining but was expanding. By a narrow margin, Congress approved the Missouri Compromise in 1820. Yet the compromise was merely a reprieve in a growing argument over slavery and sectional power.

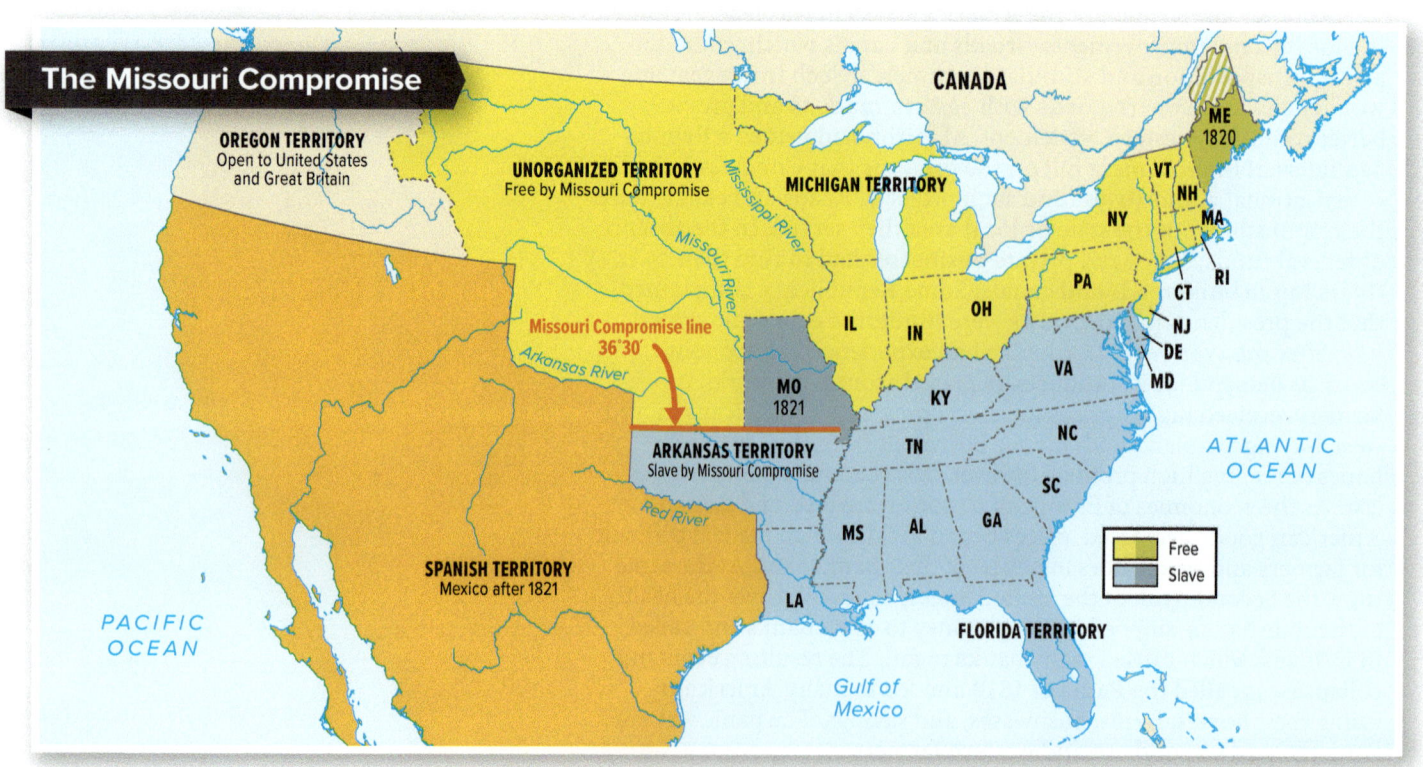

The Missouri Compromise

## The Supreme Court

Chief Justice Marshall's Federalist influence on the court continued throughout the period of Republican rule. In several important cases he protected an expanded view of the powers of Congress and the power of federal courts over the states.

When Congress created a second Bank of the United States in 1816, many states disliked the bank and began to tax its branches within their states. When Maryland taxed the Baltimore branch of the Bank of the United States, a lawsuit was filed and the court case *McCulloch v. Maryland* developed and eventually reached the Supreme Court in 1819. Claiming that "the power to tax involves the power to destroy," the Court overruled the state's action. The Constitution is the supreme law of the land, Marshall argued, referring to Article VI of that document. Therefore, the states had no authority to interfere with Congress's ability to enact legislation that is "necessary and proper" to carry out its delegated powers, and thus the Bank of the United States was constitutional.

An 1824 court case involved a New Jersey company's challenge of New York's granting of a monopoly to operate steamboat ferries between New York and New Jersey. In *Gibbons v. Ogden*, the Court upheld that Congress's power to regulate interstate commerce included the power to regulate navigation between states and said that where the Constitution entrusted Congress with a power, the states had no right to interfere with that power.

---

### Comprehension Check 5.5

1. One reason Monroe's presidency was described as the "Era of Good Feelings" was that the _____.

   A Federalist Party collapsed

   B Panic of 1819 had no serious long-term effects

   C issue of slavery was permanently resolved

2. The Hartford Convention proposed _____ during the War of 1812 but failed because of public disapproval.

   A compromise

   B expansion

   C secession

3. In addition to promising American neutrality in European affairs, the Monroe Doctrine stated that European nations _____.

   A should divide Canada into five regions among themselves

   B should not interfere with nations in the Western Hemisphere

   C should reclaim former colonies that had declared independence

4. The following measures were part of the American System except the _____.

   A Missouri Compromise

   B Second National Bank

   C Tariff of 1816

5. In both *McCulloch v. Maryland* and *Gibbons v. Ogden*, the Supreme Court upheld states' rights regarding economic power.

   True

   False

#### MAKING CONNECTIONS

6. How did the Missouri Compromise affect slavery in Maine, Missouri, and future states admitted from the Louisiana Territory?

## Chapter Summary

### 5.1 The New Government under Washington

- As the first president under the new Constitution, Washington established a cabinet of advisors. The first Congress established the federal courts and passed the Bill of Rights.

- Disagreements over Hamilton's financial plan led to the creation of two political parties—the Federalist Party and the Democratic-Republican Party.

- Washington faced domestic troubles including the Whiskey Rebellion in Pennsylvania and a war against Native Americans in Ohio.

- Republicans tended to support the French Revolution while Federalists tended to oppose it. Washington's Proclamation of Neutrality in the war between Britain and France was threatened when French ambassador Genêt came to America to gain support for France's war.

- Washington set a precedent for future presidents by stepping down after two terms. In his farewell address he warned America about the dangers of political factions and foreign alliances.

**TERMS**

Thomas Jefferson
Alexander Hamilton
cabinet
Judiciary Act of 1789
John Jay
Bill of Rights
Federalist Party
Democratic-Republican Party
Whiskey Rebellion
Battle of Fallen Timbers
Daniel Boone
Proclamation of Neutrality
Citizen Genêt
impressment
Jay Treaty
Pinckney Treaty

**TERMS**

XYZ Affair
Alien and Sedition Acts
Kentucky Resolutions
Virginia Resolutions
nullify
John Marshall
*Marbury v. Madison*
judicial review

### 5.2 The Presidency of John Adams

- Adams responded to France's seizure of American ships through negotiation and military preparation. The XYZ Affair referred to France's attempt to demand a bribe and loans from the American delegation to France. A Quasi War developed between the two nations, but Adams resisted his party's calls to declare war against France.

- The Federalist-controlled Congress passed the Alien and Sedition Acts to place restrictions on immigrants, who tended to be Republicans, and to stop the printing or speaking of anything against the Federalist government.

- The presidential election of 1800 ended in a tie, which the House of Representatives broke by choosing Thomas Jefferson as president.

- Adams appointed many Federalist judges in his last days in office, including Chief Justice John Marshall, who had a significant impact on the Supreme Court.

## 5.3 | Jeffersonian America

■ The election of Thomas Jefferson marked the shift from Federalist to Democratic-Republican rule. Democratic-Republicans tended to favor an agrarian economy and small government and believed in the goodness of human nature.

■ Jefferson went to war with the Barbary pirates to stop the payment of tribute for American shipping.

■ Britain and France both violated American shipping rights, and Britain practiced impressment of sailors. To avoid war, Jefferson imposed an embargo on all American trade, which hurt Americans more than it hurt Britain or France.

■ When France offered to sell the Louisiana Territory to the United States, Jefferson overcame his constitutional concerns and Congress approved the Louisiana Purchase. Jefferson appointed Lewis and Clark to head the Corps of Discovery in its exploration of the new territory.

**TERMS**

Barbary States
Embargo Act
Louisiana Purchase
Meriwether Lewis
William Clark
Corps of Discovery
Sacagawea
Zebulon Pike

**TERMS**

Tecumseh
William Henry Harrison
Battle of Tippecanoe
War Hawks
War of 1812
Francis Scott Key
Battle of New Orleans
Treaty of Ghent

## 5.4 | Challenges for Madison

■ Shawnee chief Tecumseh attempted to form a confederation of Native American tribes to resist American westward expansion. William Henry Harrison defeated the Native Americans at the Battle of Tippecanoe.

■ War Hawks in Congress pushed for war against Britain to stop British threats to American trade and shipping, to end British support of Native American attacks, and to gain land in Canada. Congress approved a declaration of war, although the American military was not prepared for war.

■ Both sides had limited success in the War of 1812. The British entered and burned Washington, DC, but Andrew Jackson led a major American victory at the Battle of New Orleans.

■ The Treaty of Ghent ended the War of 1812, but neither side was victorious. The war significantly changed American society.

## TERMS

Hartford Convention

Adams-Onís Treaty

Monroe Doctrine

American System

protective tariff

Panic of 1819

Missouri Compromise

*McCulloch v. Maryland*

*Gibbons v. Ogden*

### 5.5 The Era of Good Feelings

- The presidency of James Monroe was described as the "Era of Good Feelings" because it was a period of relative domestic and international peace for the United States.

- Andrew Jackson was sent to the Florida border to halt cross-border raids, but he invaded Florida instead. Spain agreed to sell East Florida to the United States and allowed the United States to keep the portions of West Florida it had already taken.

- The Monroe Doctrine said that European nations could not intervene in the Western Hemisphere and that the United States would not meddle in European affairs.

- Some Republicans supported more government involvement in the economy and proposed the American System, which included a Second Bank of the United States, protective tariffs, and federally-funded internal improvements.

- In the Missouri Compromise, Maine was admitted as a free state, Missouri as a slave state, and slavery was prohibited in the remainder of the Louisiana Territory above 36°30′.

## Chapter Review Questions

### RECALL

1. Whom did Washington appoint to each of the following positions: secretary of state, secretary of the treasury, secretary of war, and chief justice?

2. What was the debt of the United States when Washington took office?

3. What were the four parts of Hamilton's financial plan?

4. What compromise caused southern representatives to approve Hamilton's assumption plan?

5. Who initially led the troops who put down the Whiskey Rebellion?

6. What was the first state to be created out of the former Northwest Territory?

7. Which men were elected president and vice president in 1796, and what was unusual about this outcome?

8. What was the electoral outcome of the election of 1800? How was the winner decided? What amendment was passed to prevent this from happening again, and what did this amendment do?

9. What were the "midnight judges"?

10. Why was Monroe's presidency known as the "Era of Good Feelings"?

### UNDERSTAND

11. Why did Hamilton think it was important for the United States to fully fund its debt and pay the current holders rather than the original holders of debt certificates?

12. Why did Hamilton propose that the federal government should assume the debts of the states? What were the objections to this plan?

13. Why did Hamilton believe a national bank was important for America's economy?

14. What were the strict and loose interpretations of the Constitution that were related to Hamilton's bank proposal?

15. What were three differences between the views of the Federalist Party and the Democratic-Republican Party?

16. What was Washington's desire for how westward expansion would happen, and how did it actually happen?

17. What were two reasons why Jefferson and the Republicans supported the French Revolution at first, and two reasons why Hamilton and the Federalists opposed it?

18. In what two ways did Adams respond to France's aggression against American shipping?

19. In what way did Adams set aside his personal interests for the good of the nation?

20. What were the four Alien and Sedition Acts? What purpose did they serve according to supporters? What did opponents believe was the political purpose of these acts?

21. What changes did John Marshall make to increase the Supreme Court's influence? How did the *Marbury v. Madison* decision strengthen the judicial branch?

22. What were some changes Jefferson and the Republicans made to Federalist policies when he took office?

23. Why did Jefferson issue an embargo, and how well did the embargo work in achieving its goal?

24. Why was Napoleon willing to sell the Louisiana Territory to the United States? Why were some people opposed to the Louisiana Purchase? Why was the purchase significant for the United States?

25. Why did the War Hawks want war with Britain? Why did others oppose war?

26. What were five results of the War of 1812 for the United States?

27. What was happening in Latin America which led to the Monroe Doctrine?

28. How did Henry Clay's American System show a change in some Democratic-Republicans' attitudes toward the role of government?

29. Why did Missouri's application for statehood raise concerns among northern and southern states? How did the Missouri Compromise temporarily resolve this issue?

## THINK ABOUT IT

30. What was significant about Washington's stepping down from office after two terms? What two issues did Washington warn America against in his Farewell Address?

31. What was the main difference between the Kentucky Resolutions and the Virginia Resolutions? What issue did these resolutions raise that would be a source of conflict in future years? Why do you think this issue was a source of conflict?

32. How did the ruling of *Marbury v. Madison* counter the claim of the Kentucky and Virginia Resolutions?

▼ *Lewis and Clark on the Lower Columbia*
by Charles M. Russell

# 6 The Age of Jackson

**6.1 John Quincy Adams and Nationalism**

**6.2 Jacksonian America**

**6.3 Domestic Controversies**

**6.4 Party Politics**

▲ Chief Justice John Marshall administering the oath of office to Andrew Jackson, seventh president of the United States, March 4, 1829

# John Quincy Adams and Nationalism

What unique circumstances characterized the election and presidency of John Quincy Adams?

The "Era of Good Feelings" did not last beyond Monroe's two terms in office. With the collapse of the Federalist Party, the Democratic-Republicans were the only political party remaining. However, they were far from unified. Differences developed over issues such as the tariff, federal support for internal improvements, states' rights, and constitutional interpretation.

## The "Corrupt Bargain"

From 1796 to 1820, each party had selected its presidential and vice-presidential nominees through a **caucus** (a meeting of party leaders). But in 1824, because there was only one party, that meant that just one small group of people could potentially determine the next president. The reign of "King Caucus" came under fire by critics as an undemocratic process that took the election of the president out of the hands of the people. Nevertheless, congressional leaders led by Martin Van Buren called for a party caucus to meet in February 1824. Only one-fourth of the eligible members came to the caucus. They chose Monroe's secretary of the treasury, William Crawford from Georgia, as their candidate (even though he had suffered a debilitating stroke a few months earlier) because he was a strict constructionist who was opposed to protective tariffs and federally-funded internal improvements.

Van Buren had hoped the caucus would unite the party, but instead it showed that the party was hopelessly divided, and the selection of Crawford by the caucus did not dissuade others from campaigning for president. The other candidates were **John Quincy Adams** of Massachusetts, son of the former president and Monroe's secretary of state, who supported the American System of tariffs, internal improvements, and the National Bank; Henry Clay of Kentucky, speaker of the House of Representatives and the chief advocate for the American System; and **Andrew Jackson** of Tennessee, hero of the Battle of New Orleans and controversial leader of the military campaign in Florida.

William Crawford | John Quincy Adams | Henry Clay | Andrew Jackson

Jackson had returned from Florida in poor health, and while he was recuperating at the Hermitage, his home in Nashville, Tennessee, he spent time contemplating the troubles of the nation. He was concerned about corruption among government officials, the increased power of the federal government, and the abuse of patronage (the practice of giving government jobs to supporters). He also blamed the Second Bank of the United States for causing the Panic of 1819. His friends encouraged him to permit his name to be entered as a candidate for president. He responded that he would not seek the office, but if the people chose him, he would be bound to serve. In the meantime, his supporters had nominated him for a seat in the Senate, and he was elected in 1822.

The election of 1824 revealed the growing importance of the will of the people. States were beginning to drop the property ownership requirement for voting, thus expanding suffrage (voting rights) to most white males. In most states, the electors for president were now chosen by popular vote, while in six states the state legislatures still chose the electors. When the votes were counted, Jackson won the most popular votes (over forty-three percent) and the most electoral votes (thirty-eight percent) of any candidate. In the electoral vote Adams placed second, Crawford third, and Clay fourth. Since no candidate won over fifty percent of the electoral votes, the Twelfth Amendment required that the election be decided by the House of Representatives, where the president would be chosen from among the top three electoral vote winners.

Clay was placed in a unique position. He could not win the election, but as the powerful Speaker of the House, he could influence who would. Clay preferred the nationalist policies of Adams and considered Jackson unqualified. Clay gave his support to Adams, who was elected by the House of Representatives on the first ballot.

Jackson and his supporters were outraged. They felt the House had defied the will of the people, and rumors began swirling that Adams and Clay had made a secret agreement. Their suspicions were strengthened when Adams nominated Clay as secretary of state, a position which had become a stepping stone to the presidency. Jackson's supporters decried this "**corrupt bargain**." Adams denied that there had been any kind of bargain and said that he had chosen Clay for his qualifications and experience. True or not, the charges of corruption hurt the reputations of both Adams and Clay and confirmed in Jackson's mind that the government was corrupt and in need of reform to respect the people's will. He resigned his Senate seat and almost immediately began his campaign for election in 1828.

## The Election of 1824

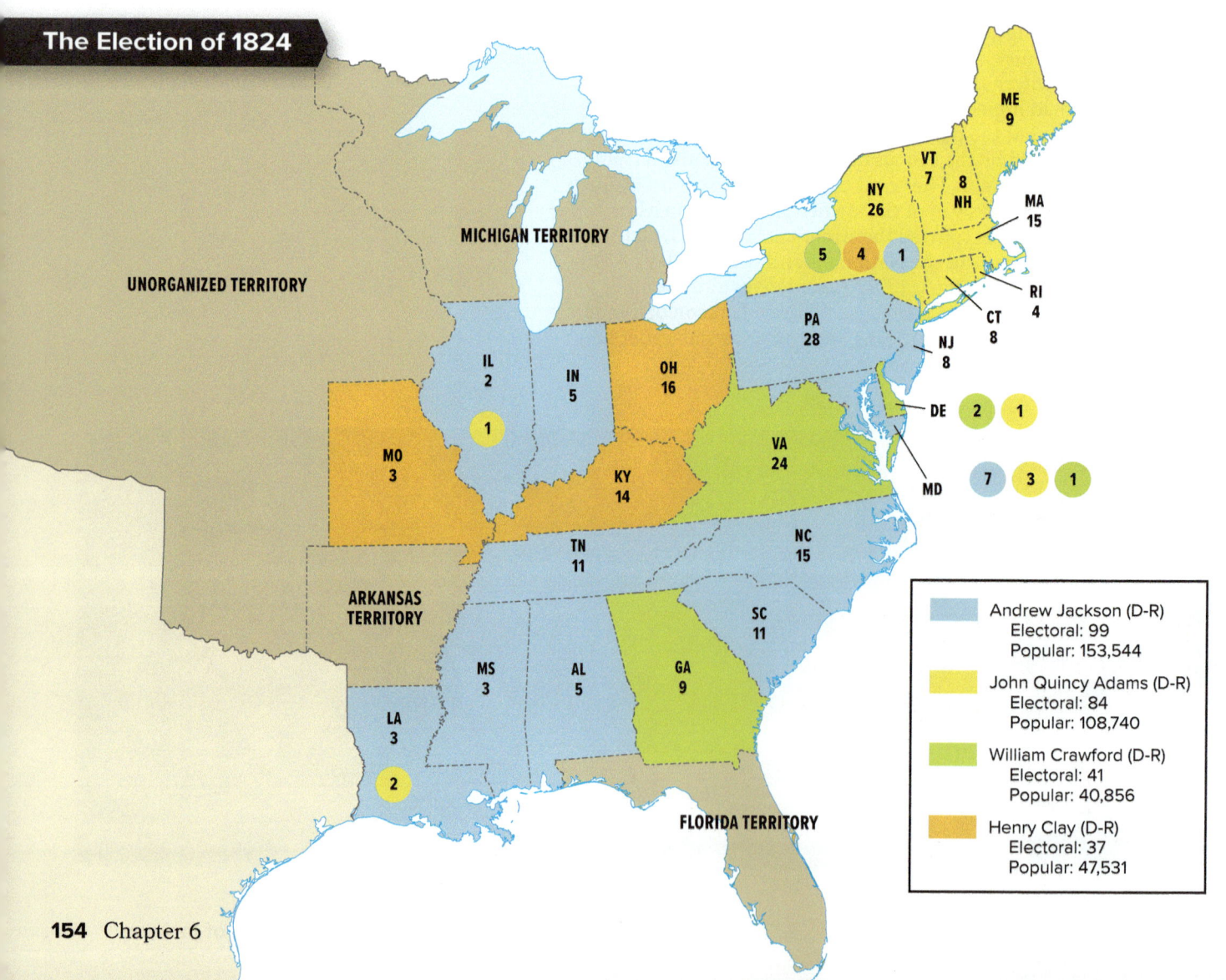

| | |
|---|---|
| Andrew Jackson (D-R) | Electoral: 99 / Popular: 153,544 |
| John Quincy Adams (D-R) | Electoral: 84 / Popular: 108,740 |
| William Crawford (D-R) | Electoral: 41 / Popular: 40,856 |
| Henry Clay (D-R) | Electoral: 37 / Popular: 47,531 |

# Challenges for Adams

John Quincy Adams had the intellect and experience that made him well-suited for the presidency. However, he came across as cold to some and had little patience for party politics.

In his first annual address to Congress, Adams urged the members to support his ambitious plan for internal improvements and the advancement of science, the arts, and education. Included in his plan were: funds for the building of roads and canals to be paid for from western land sales and tariffs; the creation of a national university, a naval academy, and an astronomical observatory; an improved patent system and a uniform system of weights and measures; and an extensive survey of America's land and resources. He urged Congress to not "fold up [their] arms and proclaim to the world that we are palsied [paralyzed] by the will of our constituents." To his critics, both his plan and his comments showed that he had little regard for the opinion of the people or for the constitutional limits placed on the federal government. While Congress did not approve all of Adams's plan, it did authorize funds for the surveying and building of several roads and canals.

Adams was committed to the westward expansion of the United States, but at the same time he was concerned about fair treatment of Native Americans through treaties that were mutually agreed upon and through payment for land. In 1825 a delegation of Creeks whose land bordered Georgia and Alabama traveled to Washington, DC, to protest a treaty that had ceded (given up) all Creek land east of the Mississippi River to the United States, claiming that those Creek leaders who signed the treaty lacked the authority to do so. Adams agreed that the treaty was not valid and negotiated a new treaty that allowed the Creeks to retain some of their land, angering many southerners and westerners. The governor of Georgia refused to recognize the new treaty, ordered the Creek land to be surveyed in preparation for white settlement, and began forcibly removing the Creeks. Adams threatened federal intervention but backed down when the governor mobilized the Georgia militia. Most of the remaining Creeks were removed from Georgia by the end of 1827 and from Alabama by 1837.

In foreign policy, Adams sought to expand American trade. He was able to reach trade agreements with several nations, which increased American exports.

◄ John Quincy Adams

— **Comprehension Check 6.1** —

1. All four candidates for president in 1824 were from what party?
   A  Democratic-Republican
   B  Federalist
   C  Whig

2. The candidate with the highest number of popular and electoral votes in the election of 1824 was ____.
   A  John Quincy Adams
   B  Henry Clay
   C  Andrew Jackson

3. Who selected the winner of the election of 1824?
   A  the House of Representatives
   B  the Senate
   C  the Supreme Court

4. Each of the following is true about John Quincy Adams's policies except ____.
   A  he wanted federal funding for internal improvements and advances in science, the arts, and education
   B  he was opposed to expanding American trade
   C  he believed Native American tribes should be treated with justice

**MAKING CONNECTIONS**

5. What was the "corrupt bargain" and how did it confirm in Andrew Jackson's mind what he already believed about the government?

GUIDING QUESTIONS

- Why was Jackson seen as the people's president?
- Why did Indian removal take place?

## 6.2 Jacksonian America

What were the strengths and weaknesses of Andrew Jackson's presidency?

## The People's President

Those Democratic-Republicans who favored limited government and a strict interpretation of the Constitution were dismayed over the nationalist agenda of President Adams. Leaders such as Martin Van Buren and Vice President John C. Calhoun shifted their allegiance from Adams to Andrew Jackson and began working towards his election in 1828. This led to the revival of the two-party system. Those who supported Adams became the **National Republican Party**, and Jackson's supporters became the **Democratic Party**.

## Andrew Jackson

Andrew Jackson was the first president from a state west of the original thirteen and the first to be born poor. The story of his rise from a log cabin to the White House appealed to the common people and demonstrated that in America anyone could overcome hardships and pursue their goals.

Andrew was born in the Carolina backcountry in 1767. His parents were Scots-Irish immigrants who had left Europe two years earlier. Frontier life was challenging and dangerous. Andrew's father was killed in an accident just three weeks before Andrew was born.

At thirteen Andrew joined Patriot forces against the British in the War for Independence, serving as a messenger. His brother Hugh died in battle at age sixteen. In April 1781 Andrew and his brother Robert were captured by British cavalry.

Both boys contracted smallpox while prisoners, and Robert died of the disease. His mother died of cholera (an intestinal disease) while nursing injured soldiers. Andrew, age fourteen, was now alone.

After the war Jackson studied law and moved to Tennessee. The frontier suited the fiery, energetic Jackson. He acquired land, slaves, horses, and a taste for politics. Jackson became a state judge and in 1796 was elected to a term in Congress, where he gained some respect for his straightforward, though sometimes harsh, manner. His temper and sense of honor led to numerous duels, one of which resulted in the death of his opponent and left a bullet in his own side for the rest of his life.

Jackson gained a national reputation on the battlefield as the hero of the Battle of New Orleans in the War of 1812. General Jackson was a strict disciplinarian who ordered the execution of several servicemen under his command. His troops said, "He's tough as hickory," and the nickname "Old Hickory" stuck. Despite demanding respect for his authority from his subordinates, he often challenged the authority of those above him. For example, when a Louisiana legislator criticized Jackson's declaration of martial law prior to the Battle of New Orleans, Jackson had the legislator arrested, as well as the judge who later ordered the legislator's release, and he went beyond his orders in his invasion of Spanish Florida.

He also gained notoriety as an "Indian fighter." His wars against the Creeks and Seminoles were brutal, and he often ignored treaties between the federal government and the Native Americans. Yet during the Creek War, when his troops discovered a ten-month-old Creek boy in the arms of his dead mother, Jackson took the child in and raised him as his own son.

Jackson did not remain a poor frontiersman. He became one of the wealthiest planters in Tennessee. Yet he continued to champion the cause of the common man throughout his political career.

## The Election of 1828

The presidential campaign of 1828 between Jackson and Adams was bitterly fought. Both sides used new methods in their campaigns, including posters, banners, parades, newspaper editorials, banquets, and rallies. They also engaged in extensive **mudslinging** (spreading negative information about opponents). Democrats accused Adams of elitism and reckless spending (including the purchase of a billiard table, often associated with gambling, for the White House) and reminded Americans of the "corrupt bargain" between Adams and Clay. They portrayed Adams as a man who did not care about the common people. The National Republicans denounced Jackson for killing at least one man in a duel and of sentencing numerous people to death during his military career. They also accused him of adultery and bigamy in his marriage to his wife, Rachel, in 1791. (The Jacksons claimed that before they married a divorce had been granted by Rachel's first husband, when in fact it had not been finalized. They obtained a new marriage certificate after the divorce was made official.)

The election of 1828 had far more popular participation than any previous election. States were expanding suffrage (the right to vote) by lowering or eliminating property requirements for voting, and twenty-two of the twenty-four states were now choosing their presidential electors by the popular vote rather than by the state legislatures. In total, over 1.1 million votes were cast in the 1828 election, compared to 350,000 in 1824. Jackson and his running mate, John C. Calhoun of South Carolina, won with an electoral tally of 178 to Adams's 83, and with 56 percent of the popular vote.

Unfortunately, between the election and the inauguration, on December 22, 1828, Jackson's beloved wife, Rachel, died. Jackson mourned the loss of his wife for many years and blamed her death on the attacks of his opponents.

### Did You Know?

After losing the election of 1828, John Quincy Adams was elected to the House of Representatives from Massachusetts. He served faithfully for the next twenty years and proposed a constitutional amendment which would have made every child born in the United States after July 4, 1842, free. He died in the Capitol from a stroke on February 23, 1848.

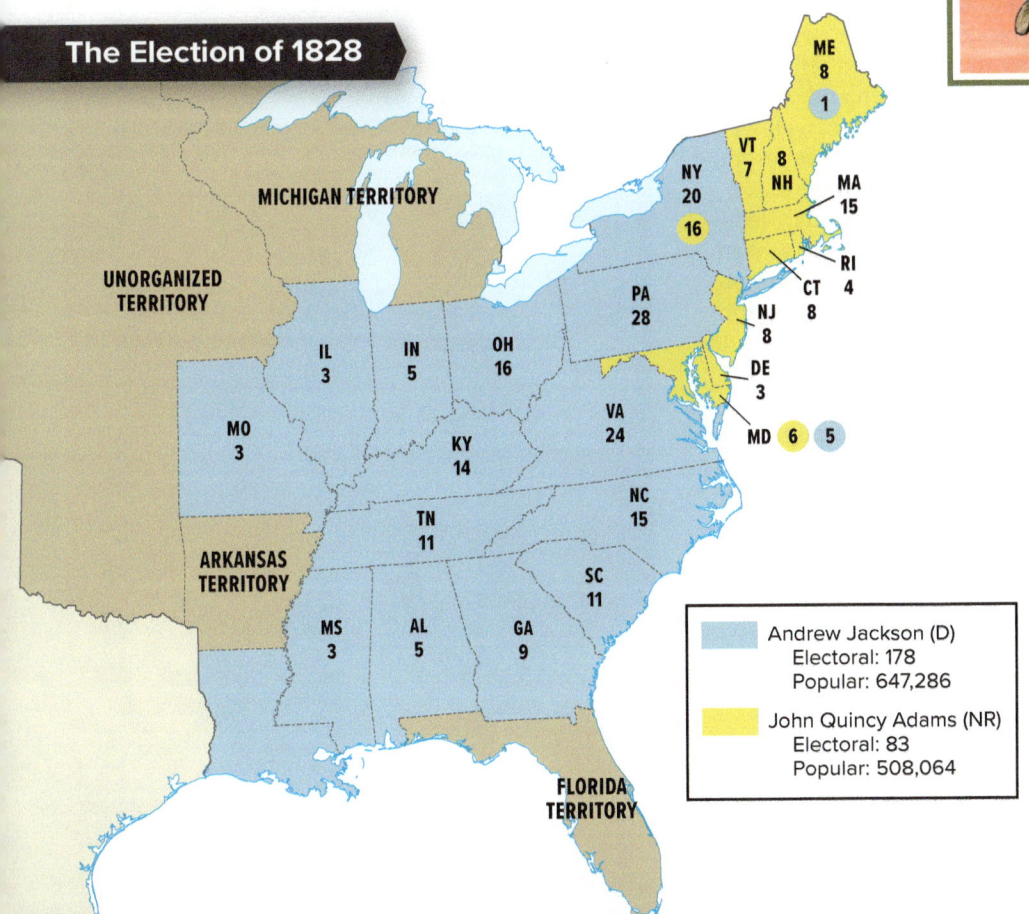

**The Election of 1828**

MICHIGAN TERRITORY

UNORGANIZED TERRITORY

ARKANSAS TERRITORY

FLORIDA TERRITORY

ME 8 / 1
VT 7
NH 8
NY 20 / 16
MA 15
RI 4
CT 8
NJ 8
DE 3
PA 28
MD 6 / 5
VA 24
OH 16
IN 5
IL 3
MO 3
KY 14
TN 11
NC 15
SC 11
GA 9
AL 5
MS 3

Andrew Jackson (D)
Electoral: 178
Popular: 647,286

John Quincy Adams (NR)
Electoral: 83
Popular: 508,064

In March 1829 an estimated 20,000 people attended Jackson's inauguration. After Jackson delivered his inaugural address and took the oath of office at the Capitol, the celebrating crowd followed him to the White House, where a modest public reception was planned. By the time the new president arrived, every room of the executive mansion was full of people of every social class. The reception quickly turned disorderly. The crowd stripped wallpaper for souvenirs, smashed furniture and glass, and gripped the hand of the new president just before he slipped out a back door. Mrs. Margaret Bayard Smith, a high-ranking member of Washington society, was in attendance and described the scene:

> *The President, after having been literally nearly pressed to death and almost suffocated and torn to pieces by the people in their eagerness to shake hands with Old Hickory, had retreated through the back way or south front and had escaped. . . . Cut glass and china to the amount of several thousand dollars had been broken in the struggle to get the refreshments, punch and other articles [that] had been carried out in tubs and buckets. . . . Ladies fainted, men were seen with bloody noses and such a scene of confusion took place as is impossible to describe. . . . Ladies and gentlemen only had been expected at this Levee [reception] not the [ordinary] people . . . but it was the People's Day and the People's President and the people would rule. God grant that one day or other, the people do not pull down all rule and rulers.*

## The Spoils System

In his first message to Congress, Jackson called for the elimination of the Electoral College, the system which he believed had deprived him of the presidency and negated the will of the people in 1824. As the "people's president" he also set out to remove from office the bureaucratic "elite" who he believed were corrupting the government. He argued that public service should not be a lifelong career, that those who stayed in office too long would begin to view their positions as a right, and that they would begin to act without regard for the will of the people. Jackson believed "rotation in office" (replacing government workers every few years) was a much-needed reform.

During his presidency, Jackson replaced between ten and twenty percent of government officeholders with political supporters. However, Jackson's policy did not necessarily make public servants more responsive to the public since the bureaucrats owed their jobs to their party leaders, not to the people, and it also removed some highly qualified individuals from office. Despite Jackson's intention to root out government corruption, the policy eventually became a source of corruption as people paid bribes for government jobs or politicians used the promise of jobs for their personal benefit. This practice became known as the **spoils system** from the saying, "To the victor belong the spoils."

Other than Van Buren, who was appointed secretary of state, Jackson's cabinet members were criticized for their lack of political or administrative skill. Almost from the outset, his administration was torn by infighting. As a result, Jackson began holding fewer cabinet meetings and began to rely on a circle of friends, newspaper editors, and politicians whom he trusted for counsel. Critics referred to these unofficial advisers as the "**Kitchen Cabinet**."

---

▶ (top) Crowd in front of the White House during Jackson's inaugural reception. (middle) 1877 political cartoon "To the Victors belong the Spoils" showing Jackson riding a hog. See Student Activities for a guided analysis of this cartoon. (bottom) Cartoon depicting Jackson's Kitchen Cabinet.

# Relations with Native Americans

Since early in its history, the policy of the federal government had been to acquire Native American lands east of the Mississippi River. Its strategy had been to do so by "civilizing" the Native Americans, assimilating them into "American" culture, respecting their tribal sovereignty and property rights until that assimilation could take place, and acquiring land only through legal treaties.

President Jackson proclaimed his policy toward the Native Americans in his first inaugural address:

> It will be my sincere and constant desire, to observe toward the Indian tribes within our limits, a just and liberal policy; and to give that humane and considerate attention to their rights and their wants, which is consistent with the habits of our government, and the feelings of our people.

Despite Jackson's expressed desire, the reality was that his policies toward Native Americans were widely regarded as unjust and inhumane.

Even before Jackson took office, he had come to several conclusions about how the United States should relate to the Native Americans. First, he concluded that the Native American tribes were subjects (but not citizens) of the United States, under its sovereignty and laws, and should not be treated as sovereign nations. Second, he thought that Native Americans who lived within the boundaries of states were a threat to the security of the nation. Third, he believed the policy that was in the best interest of both the United States and the Native Americans was their removal to the west of the Mississippi River, beyond the organized states and territories. In Jackson's view, American Indians had two choices: to remain where they were, adopting the white way of life, becoming United States citizens, and being subject to the states in which they lived, or to move west where they would be free to practice their traditional customs and way of life. Remaining where they were while attempting to live as Native Americans, he believed, would lead inevitably to their extinction.

When he took office, Jackson pursued this Indian removal policy vigorously. At his urging, Congress considered the **Indian Removal Act of 1830**, which would authorize the president to remove Native Americans from the states in which they resided to territory set aside for them west of the Mississippi River. He claimed that any treaties that had recognized the sovereignty of tribes within state borders violated the Constitution's prohibition of erecting a state within the jurisdiction of another state (Article IV, Section 3). There was considerable opposition to the Removal Act in both houses of Congress. Some objected on constitutional grounds, arguing the act gave the executive too much power. Others objected on religious and moral grounds and insisted that the Native Americans be given the right to refuse their removal. Christian mission organizations attempted to rally opposition to the act. Despite these objections, the Removal Act was passed. As a result, treaties that guaranteed new territory west of the Mississippi River were made, sometimes forcibly, with various tribes. Viewing the treaties as legal justification, the United States began moving the Native Americans westward and opening their former lands in the East to white settlement.

Not all tribes submitted meekly to this treatment. Some chose to fight for their lands. In 1832 a group of Sauk and Fox under Chief Black Hawk crossed the Mississippi River from present-day Wisconsin into northern Illinois to reclaim tribal land. A force of regular soldiers and Illinois militia moved to intercept them. In the resulting Black Hawk War, Black Hawk's warriors were defeated.

▼ Battle of Bad Axe (August 1–2, 1832), the final battle of the Black Hawk War

▲ Sequoyah

The Seminoles, led by Chief Osceola, also resisted efforts to move them west. In the Seminole War (1835–42), they hid in the swamplands and marshes of Florida as American troops attempted to track them down. Many battles and skirmishes occurred. Over 1,500 Americans and an unknown number of Seminoles died in the conflict. Most Seminoles were captured and sent west, but some remained hidden in the Florida swamps.

The Cherokee in the southeastern United States were not a military threat to the United States. Believing the promise that if they adopted white customs they would be left alone, they embraced many features of white civilization. They built towns with roads and schools and developed prosperous farms using European methods of agriculture. They welcomed Christian missionaries, and many of the Cherokee converted to Christianity. A brilliant Cherokee named **Sequoyah** developed a written syllabary (a writing system of symbols representing syllables), which led to the publishing of a newspaper and the Bible in the Cherokee language. In 1827 a constitution for the Cherokee Nation was written that was modeled on the United States Constitution.

▼ Replica of the Cherokee Council House at New Echota which served as the Cherokee National Capital

But in 1829 gold was found on Cherokee land in Georgia, and many white prospectors moved into the territory. The state of Georgia passed a series of laws aimed at stripping the Cherokee of their rights and forcing their removal. The Cherokee responded by suing the federal government for an injunction (a legal order that restrains an action) against the Georgia laws, claiming the laws violated previous treaties and that the Cherokee Nation was a foreign nation not owing allegiance to the United States or any state. The Supreme Court disagreed, ruling that the Cherokee Nation was a "domestic, dependent nation" subject to the United States but not to any individual state, and stated that because the Cherokee Nation was not a foreign nation the court did not have jurisdiction to rule on the case.

Several Christian missionaries who worked among the Cherokee helped organize opposition to removal. To stop this opposition, Georgia passed a law prohibiting any white person from residing in the Cherokee Nation without permission from the state. Several missionaries decided to challenge the law and refused to leave. Two missionaries, Samuel Worcester and Elizur Butler, were arrested and sentenced to serve four years of hard labor in a state prison. They appealed their conviction to the United States Supreme Court, which ruled in favor of the missionaries. In 1832, in the case **Worcester v. Georgia**, Chief Justice John Marshall ruled that the Georgia law was unconstitutional, and that the Cherokee were not subject to Georgia law. Marshall wrote,

*The Cherokee nation, then, is a distinct community, occupying its own territory, with boundaries accurately described, in which the laws of Georgia can have no force, and which the citizens of Georgia have no right to enter but with the assent of the Cherokees themselves, or in conformity with treaties and with the acts of Congress. The whole intercourse between the United States and this nation is, by our Constitution and laws, vested in the government of the United States.*

— **JOHN MARSHALL**

### Analyzing Sources

According to the Supreme Court, what power did individual states have over the affairs of the Cherokee?

The Cherokee hoped the court's decision would lead the federal government to intervene against the state, but Georgia and President Jackson refused to acknowledge the decision. Jackson's view of states' rights was that the states had sovereignty over all affairs within their border, including Native American lands, and that the federal government could not interfere. Jackson reportedly said, "John Marshall has made his decision. Now let him enforce it."

In 1835 a group of Cherokee signed a removal treaty exchanging their land in the southeast for $5 million and land in Indian Territory (present-day Oklahoma), but many Cherokee refused to leave. In 1838 (under President Van Buren), troops began forcibly removing those who remained. US soldiers dragged the Cherokee from their homes—sometimes at gunpoint—and placed them in detention camps until the marches west began.

These forced marches west began in the summer, and sickness and drought killed many of the travelers. Several groups waited until fall, but heavy rains became a problem. Travel was difficult and food was scarce. As winter set in, frigid weather and bad water caused more disease. About 4,000 of the 15,000 Cherokee died on the journey to Indian Territory. The Cherokee called the relocation the **Trail of Tears**.

▼ Arriving in Indian Territory at the end of the Trail of Tears

## Comprehension Check 6.2

1. Supporters of Andrew Jackson became known as the ___ Party before the election of 1828.

   **A** National Republican

   **B** Democratic

   **C** Whig

2. Significantly more people voted in the presidential election of 1828 than in the election of 1824.

   True      False

3. The spoils system was a less corrupt means of giving out government positions.

   True      False

4. In *Worcester v. Georgia*, the Supreme Court ruled that Georgia law applied in the Cherokee Nation.

   True      False

### MAKING CONNECTIONS

5. How did Jackson's treatment of the Cherokee result from his view of states' rights? What injustices resulted?

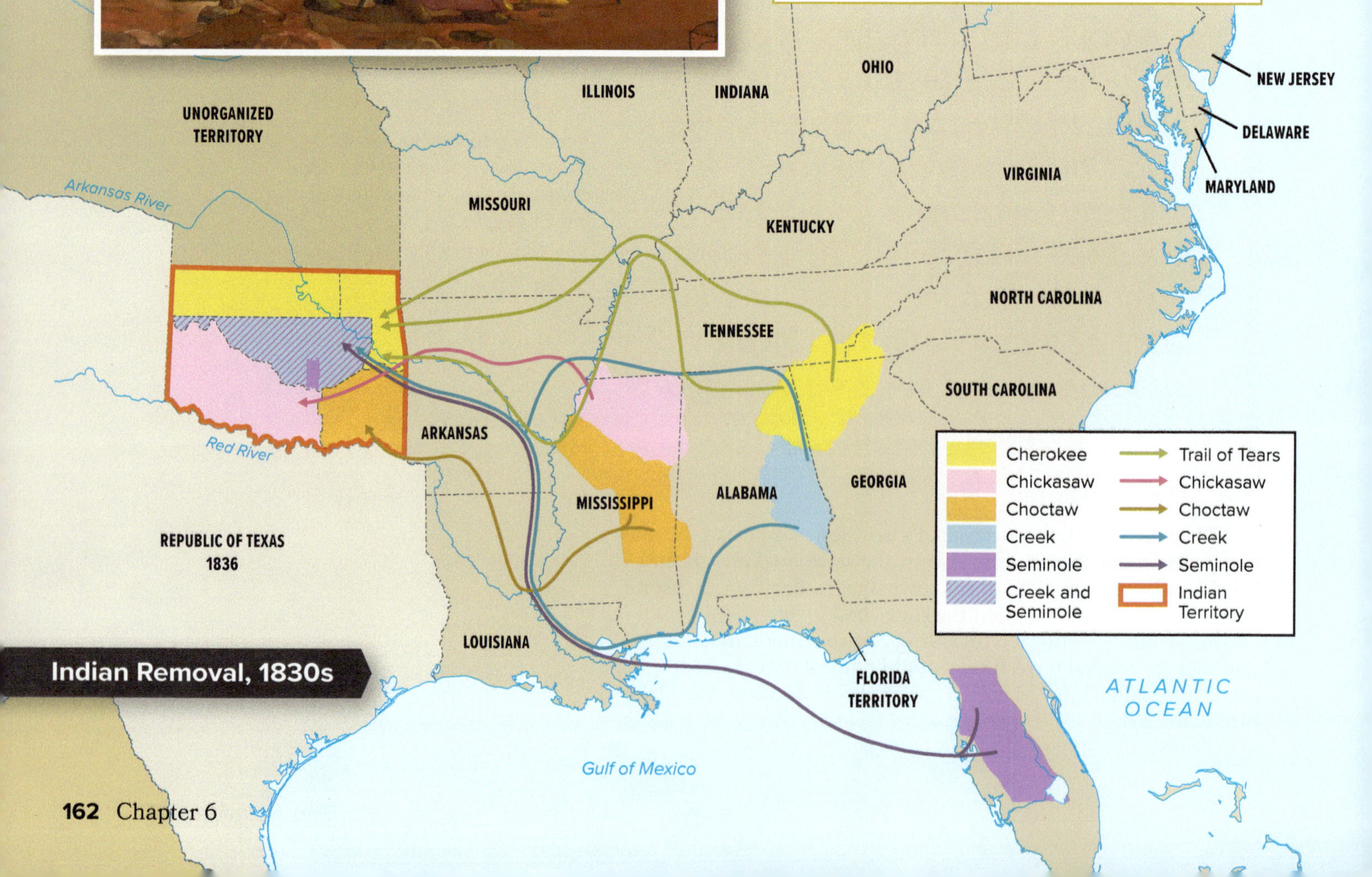

Indian Removal, 1830s

Legend:
- Cherokee
- Chickasaw
- Choctaw
- Creek
- Seminole
- Creek and Seminole
- Trail of Tears
- Chickasaw
- Choctaw
- Creek
- Seminole
- Indian Territory

OHIO
ILLINOIS
INDIANA
NEW JERSEY
DELAWARE
UNORGANIZED TERRITORY
VIRGINIA
MARYLAND
Arkansas River
MISSOURI
KENTUCKY
NORTH CAROLINA
TENNESSEE
ARKANSAS
SOUTH CAROLINA
Red River
GEORGIA
REPUBLIC OF TEXAS 1836
MISSISSIPPI
ALABAMA
LOUISIANA
FLORIDA TERRITORY
ATLANTIC OCEAN
Gulf of Mexico

**Domestic Controversies**

Why did controversies surround the tariff and the national bank?

GUIDING QUESTIONS

- Why did some states support nullification?
- What was the controversy concerning the National Bank?

## The Tariff and Nullification

### The Tariff of Abominations

As mentioned in the previous chapter, Congress passed its first protective tariff in 1816 to protect American manufacturers after the War of 1812. Congress increased the tariff in 1818 and again in 1824, benefitting factory owners, who were primarily in the northeast. Southerners opposed these higher tariffs because revenue the government received from the tariffs came largely from the South but was spent to fund internal improvements mostly in the North, and because tariffs increased the cost of manufactured goods which southern farmers had to buy from northern factories or from Europe, thus reducing their profits.

While John Quincy Adams was still in office, Congress passed an even higher protective Tariff of 1828. Northern states welcomed the tariff, while the southern states dubbed it the "**Tariff of Abominations**." Southern leaders recognized the constitutional right of Congress to levy modest tariffs to raise revenue. However, they claimed that this protective tariff supported the industry of the North but would lead to the ruin of the economy of the South as European countries retaliated with their own high tariffs or by reducing their purchase of American goods, particularly agricultural products from the southern states. Vice President Calhoun, a South Carolinian, said the tariff threatened his state's economic survival, which also depended on slavery.

▲ Slaves operating a cotton gin

*Because South Carolina, from her climate, situation, and peculiar institutions [a euphemism for slavery], is . . . dependent upon agriculture and commerce, not only for her prosperity, but for her very existence as a state— because the valuable products of her soil . . . are among the very few that can be cultivated with any profit by slave labor—and if by the loss of her foreign commerce, these products should be confined to an inadequate market, the fate of this fertile state would be poverty and utter desolation.*

— **JOHN C. CALHOUN**

▲ John C. Calhoun

### 🔍 Analyzing Sources

According to Calhoun, why would the tariff hurt South Carolina more than a northern state?

▼ Robert Hayne

Some southerners believed the tariff could be grounds for secession (withdrawing from the country). One of their concerns was that if the federal government could impose this tariff on their states, then one day it might impose the abolition of slavery on them as well. Vice President Calhoun drafted the *South Carolina Exposition and Protest* anonymously in response to the Tariff of 1828. In it, he echoed the arguments of the Kentucky and Virginia Resolutions, suggesting that states could interpret the constitutionality of national laws and had the duty to "interpose" to nullify an unconstitutional law and block its enforcement within the state. This doctrine of nullification was Calhoun's attempt to find a constitutional middle ground between submission and secession.

### The Webster-Hayne Debate

In January 1830 debate over nullification and states' rights came to the floor of the United States Senate. Senator Robert Hayne of South Carolina defended the states' rights position.

> *Who then . . . are the true friends of the Union? Those who would confine the federal government strictly within the limits prescribed by the Constitution . . . And who are its enemies? Those who are in favor of consolidation; who are constantly stealing power from the states and adding strength to the federal government. . . .*
>
> *. . . If this is to become some great "consolidated government," swallowing up the rights of the states, and the liberties of the citizen, . . . the Union will not be worth preserving.*
>
> — **ROBERT HAYNE**

 **Analyzing Sources**

Why did Hayne think states' rights supporters were better friends of the Union than his opponents were?

▼ The Webster-Hayne debate

Senator Daniel Webster from Massachusetts rose to oppose Hayne's argument. He said that the government of the United States was an agent of the people, not of the states.

> I hold it to be a popular government, erected by the people; . . .and itself capable of being amended and modified, just as the people may choose it should be. . . . The people brought it into existence, established it, and have hitherto supported it, for the very purpose, amongst others, of imposing certain salutary restraints on state sovereignties . . .
>
> "Liberty and union, now and forever, one and inseparable!" — **DANIEL WEBSTER**

### Analyzing Sources

According to Webster, what was one of the primary reasons, relating to states' rights, for replacing the Articles of Confederation with the Constitution?

## Calhoun and Jackson Clash

The issue of nullification also divided the White House. Calhoun supported nullification and made it known that he had authored the *South Carolina Exposition and Protest.* Jackson, who had long been a supporter of states' rights, could not support nullification or secession. He believed that only through a strong union could liberty be preserved.

At a banquet held by Democrats on April 13, 1830, to honor Thomas Jefferson, the difference between the president and vice president became apparent to the public. Jackson offered a toast, "Our Union: It must be preserved." Calhoun responded with his own toast, "The Union: Next to our liberty, most dear." With that, Jackson decided he could no longer support Calhoun, who resigned from the vice presidency and was elected by South Carolina as a senator in 1832.

## Nullification

Congress replaced the Tariff of Abominations with a new, lower **Tariff of 1832**, but it was not enough to satisfy South Carolina. The state legislature called a special convention which denounced the tariffs of 1828 and 1832, adopted an **Ordinance of Nullification** which declared those tariffs null and void, prohibited the collection of the tariff within the state after February 1, 1833, and declared that any attempt by Congress to enforce the tariff would lead to the state's immediate secession.

LIBERTY AND UNION, NOW AND FOREVER, ONE AND INSEPARABLE.

DANIEL WEBSTER

No other states joined South Carolina's action. Jackson threatened to have the leaders of the state hanged for treason and ordered his secretary of war to prepare to take military action against South Carolina. He also attempted to convince the American public of the dangers of nullification. In his Nullification Proclamation, Jackson said that the purpose of those who nullified the tariff was to destroy the Union:

> *I consider, then, the power to annul a law of the United States, assumed by one state, incompatible with the existence of the Union, contradicted expressly by the letter of the Constitution, unauthorized by its spirit, inconsistent with every principle on which it was founded, and destructive of the great object for which it was formed. . . .*

He said that states had surrendered "essential parts of sovereignty" when they became parts of the nation and did not have the right to secede because the Union was a perpetual entity. He then appealed directly to the people of South Carolina:

> *The laws of the United States must be executed. . . . Those who told you that you might peaceably prevent their execution, deceived you—they could not have been deceived themselves. . . . Their object is disunion, but be not deceived by names. Disunion, by armed force, is Treason. Are you really ready to incur its guilt? If you are, on the head of the instigators of the act be the dreadful consequences—on their heads be the dishonor, but on yours may fall the punishment—on your unhappy state will inevitably fall all the evils of the conflict you force upon the government of your country.*

Jackson then asked Congress to pass the **Force Bill**, which allowed the president to use the military to enforce the tariff.

## The Compromise Tariff of 1833

Although Jackson opposed nullification, he wanted to lower the tariff and avoid a possible civil war. Henry Clay, who was now a member of the Senate, proposed a new tariff that substantially, though gradually, reduced the Tariff of 1832, making it acceptable to South Carolina. Clay's proposed tariff, known as the **Compromise Tariff of 1833**, passed on March 1. South Carolina withdrew its nullification of the tariff, but it declared the Force Bill null and void, thus maintaining its claim to the right of nullification. Jackson ignored this action. Though the Union had been preserved through the crisis, the issue of states' rights remained unsettled.

▼ Merchant ships in Charleston Harbor

# The National Bank

## Jackson's Conflict with Biddle

The major campaign issue as Jackson faced reelection in 1832 was the future of the Second Bank of the United States. Jackson linked the Bank to corruption and saw it as dangerous to freedom. As mentioned previously, he blamed the Bank for causing the Panic of 1819.

Henry Clay, who was nominated as the National Republican candidate for president in 1832, saw the rechartering of the Second Bank of the United States as an issue which could help him win the election. He urged the president of the Bank, **Nicholas Biddle**, to ask Congress for a twenty-year renewal of the Bank's charter in the summer of 1832, though the existing charter did not expire until 1836. Clay hoped to use a Jackson veto of the Bank recharter to his political advantage.

The action of Clay and Biddle confirmed in Jackson's mind the corrupting influence of the Bank. He said, "The bank is trying to kill me, but I will kill it." The recharter bill passed Congress, but Jackson promptly vetoed it. In a written veto message, Jackson said that "some of the powers and privileges possessed by the existing bank are unauthorized by the Constitution, subversive of the rights of the states, and dangerous to the liberties of the people." Though the Supreme Court had ruled that the Bank was constitutional in *McCulloch v. Maryland*, Jackson disagreed.

▲ Nicholas Biddle

> *It is maintained by the advocates of the bank that its constitutionality in all its features ought to be considered as settled by precedent and by the decision of the Supreme Court. To this conclusion I cannot assent. Mere precedent is a dangerous source of authority, and should not be regarded as deciding questions of constitutional power except where the acquiescence of the people and the states can be considered as well settled.*
>
> **— ANDREW JACKSON**

### Analyzing Sources

Besides the Supreme Court, who else's agreement did Jackson say was necessary to determine the constitutionality of a law?

Jackson also presented his veto as a battle between the elites and the common people, even though both opponents and supporters of the Bank came from all classes of society:

> *It is to be regretted that the rich and powerful too often bend the acts of government to their selfish purposes. Distinctions in society will always exist under every just government. . . . But when the laws undertake to add to these natural and just advantages artificial distinctions, to grant titles, gratuities, and exclusive privileges, to make the rich richer and the potent more powerful, the humble members of society—the farmers, mechanics, and laborers—who have neither the time nor the means of securing like favors to themselves, have a right to complain of the injustice of their government.*

## The Election of 1832

Jackson concluded his veto message by putting his political fate in the hands of the people: "I have now done my duty to my country. If sustained by my fellow citizens, I shall be grateful and happy." In other words, if the people disagreed with Jackson's veto of the Bank, they could vote him out of office. The Senate failed to override the veto, and in November the people voted, and they overwhelmingly chose Jackson. Clay had miscalculated. The Bank was not a large enough issue to unseat the popular Jackson, who won 55 percent of the popular vote and 219 electoral votes to Clay's 49.

## Jackson and the "Pet Banks"

Jackson saw his reelection as a mandate from the people on the Bank issue. His veto of the recharter meant the Bank would dissolve in 1836, but he was determined to speed its collapse. He decided to begin withdrawing funds from the Bank of the United States to pay the government's expenses until its funds were depleted, but to deposit new government revenues in selected state banks. Two treasury secretaries refused to move the federal deposits, believing Jackson's order was illegal. When they refused to resign, Jackson fired both, and appointed Roger B. Taney as secretary of the treasury in September 1833. The next month Taney began placing federal deposits in state banks—Jackson's **pet banks**," as his enemies called them. In March 1834 the Senate passed a resolution censuring, or condemning, Jackson's actions as an abuse of presidential power.

Hundreds of new banks representing towns, canal companies, insurance agencies, railroads, and factories opened. These largely unregulated banks began issuing loans in the form of paper money, often without the gold or silver to back them. Biddle responded by reducing the lending of the Bank of the United States and demanding the repayment of loans owed by the state banks. Fearing a recession, business leaders begged Jackson to rescind his policy on the Bank, but he refused.

▼ Cartoon "Downfall of Mother Bank" (1833) depicting Jackson destroying the Second Bank of the United States

▲ Paper currency

## The Specie Circular

A flood of paper money issued by the nation's many banks led to severe inflation (a rise in prices often caused by an increase in the money supply). Jackson responded by issuing an executive order in July 1836 called the **Specie Circular** requiring that all purchases of public land be done in specie (silver and gold) rather than in paper money. He hoped the order would curb rampant land speculation that was occurring in the west, but it also rapidly reduced the money supply and the availability of credit, which caused bank closures, land and business foreclosures, and led to the Panic of 1837.

## Jackson's Legacy

Jacksonian democracy could be summarized in this way: the will of the people (meaning the majority) must be obeyed. Jackson had an unwavering belief in the virtue of the common man (as opposed to the view that the will of the people is suspect because of human sinfulness), who could be trusted to make decisions and whose will should therefore be supreme, and he was determined to be the "people's president." Jackson believed that the president represents the American people and is responsible to them. This went against the view of most of the nation's founders that Congress was the instrument of the popular will and that the president was an instrument of Congress. Jackson saw the presidency as the head of the government and therefore above, rather than equal to, the other branches. He also inserted the executive into the legislative process through his frequent use of the veto.

---

## Comprehension Check 6.3

1. Southerners tended to oppose the tariffs of 1828 and 1832 because protective tariffs _____.

   A lowered the cost of manufactured goods

   B funded internal improvements which primarily were built in the South

   C benefited northern industries while threatening the southern economy

2. What state voted to nullify the Tariff of 1832 and threatened to secede if the federal government attempted to enforce it?

   A Georgia

   B South Carolina

   C Kentucky

3. Jackson had Congress authorize the use of the military to enforce the tariff in the Force Bill.

   True

   False

4. The candidate for president who wanted to use the rechartering of the Second Bank of the United States as a campaign issue was _____.

   A Andrew Jackson

   B John Quincy Adams

   C Henry Clay

5. Each of the following is true about Jackson's actions toward the Second Bank of the United States except _____.

   A he said only the Supreme Court could declare the Bank constitutional

   B he vetoed the recharter of the Bank

   C he ordered all new government revenue be deposited in selected "pet banks" instead of the Bank of the United States

### Making Connections

6. How did the role of the presidency change under Andrew Jackson?

## GUIDING QUESTIONS

- How did Martin Van Buren continue Jackson's legacy?
- What was unusual about the presidencies of Harrison and Tyler?

▼ Cartoon "King Andrew" (1833) satirizing Jackson as an autocratic monarch trampling on the Constitution

## 6.4 Party Politics

**What were the presidents after Jackson like?**

Despite Jackson's popularity with the common people, opposition was beginning to grow over the expansion of executive power. National Republicans joined with Democrats who differed with Jackson over issues such as nullification, internal improvements, tariffs, or the Bank, and formed the **Whig Party**. The name was significant: in Britain the Whigs had been opposed to the strong executive power of the monarchy and believed in the supremacy of representative government. The Whig Party feared that "King Andrew the First" had created an "imperial" presidency where the executive had become the sole arbiter of the people's will.

## Van's Victory

The strategy of the Whigs in the election of 1836 was to run several candidates, each strong in his own region, who would carry enough states to prevent the Democratic candidate from gaining a majority of the electoral votes. The election would then go to the House of Representatives, where the Whigs hoped to be strong enough to maneuver one of their men into office. Daniel Webster from Massachusetts ran in New England; William Henry Harrison, popular Native American fighter from Ohio, ran in the West; and Tennessee's Hugh White ran in the South.

On the Democratic side, **Martin Van Buren**, who had become vice president in Jackson's second term, was Old Hickory's hand-picked successor. He was a skilled politician and a loyal supporter of Jackson. Van Buren won 170 of 294 electoral votes, thus avoiding a contested election.

▼ The inauguration of Martin Van Buren, March 4, 1837

Just weeks after Van Buren took office, the economy collapsed, plunging the country into a deep five-year depression known as the **Panic of 1837**. Banks and businesses failed, farmers lost their land, and unemployment grew across the nation. The economic hard times were caused by several factors: Jackson's economic policies, irresponsible practices among the state banks, a massive wheat crop failure, and the collapse of cotton prices.

Van Buren had few solutions for the problems he had inherited, but he set about to reorganize the government's financial structure. He proposed an independent treasury to replace the state banks as a depository for federal funds. The treasury was to have only federal funds deposited in it, and only government employees were to manage it. Subtreasuries were planned for major cities throughout the nation. This system would separate private banks from federal funds. Gold and silver, rather than paper money, would be used for all federal business. His plan was passed by Congress in 1840.

◄ Gold and silver coins and copper "hard times tokens" used as currency during the Panic of 1837

# Harrison and Tyler

## Tippecanoe

The Democrats renominated Van Buren in 1840 and hoped to capitalize on General Jackson's popularity for yet another election. The Whigs nominated **William Henry Harrison**, the hero of the Battle of Tippecanoe nearly thirty years earlier, as their candidate. They added John Tyler, a states' rights Virginian, as running mate to broaden the ticket's appeal.

The Whigs presented Harrison as a humble yet heroic backwoodsman symbolized by a log cabin, contrasted with the aristocratic Van Buren who lived in the White House, or the "Palace," as the Whigs referred to it. Actually, Harrison was born in a mansion belonging to his prominent political family. His father, a Virginia plantation owner, was a signer of the Declaration of Independence and later a governor of the state. Van Buren, who was the son of a New York tavern keeper, hardly had a luxurious upbringing.

Torch-light parades with banners, flags, and log cabin floats, and gallons of hard cider drew crowds for the Whigs. With slogans such as "Tippecanoe and Tyler too!"; "To guide the ship, we'll try old Tip!"; and "Van, Van is a used-up man!" the Whigs rode their log cabin theme to the White House, with an electoral landslide of 234 to 60.

Harrison was sixty-eight years old when he took the oath of office on the dreary, cold day of March 4, 1841. He stood on the east steps of the Capitol and read his inaugural address for nearly two hours, the longest in American history, while wearing neither overcoat nor hat. He developed pneumonia and died one month after taking office.

▼ Whig campaign poster

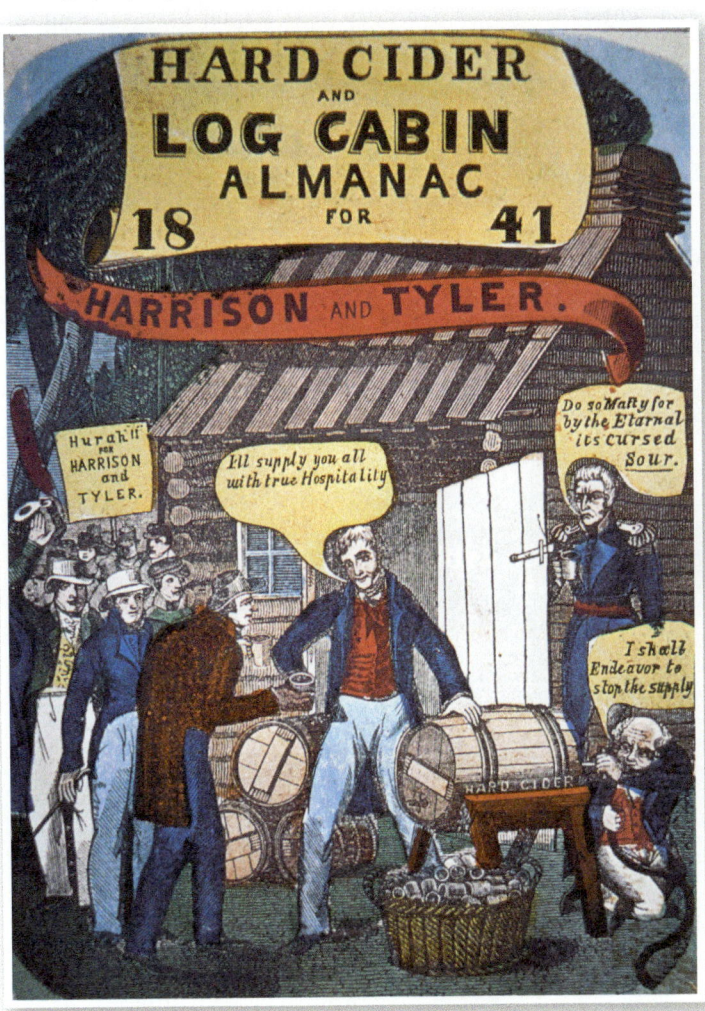

## And Tyler Too

The sudden death of President Harrison in 1841 created confusion in the Whig Party. Their leaders had chosen **John Tyler** of Virginia as their vice-presidential candidate in order to win votes in the South. They never expected him to become president. Since Harrison was the first president to die in office, some questioned Tyler's position. Was he simply "Acting President," or did he have the full powers of the presidency? At any rate, most Whig leaders in Congress and the cabinet assumed that Tyler should submit to their guidance and instruction.

Tyler left no doubt that he was president in the full sense of the term. Rather than follow the wishes of Congress, Tyler shocked the Whigs by his policies. At heart more of an anti-Jackson Democrat than a true Whig, Tyler vetoed bills for higher tariffs, a new national bank, and internal improvements—measures Clay supported. The Whigs responded to Tyler by voting him out of the party. Five of his six cabinet members—all except Secretary of State Daniel Webster—resigned in the fall of 1841. Embittered Whigs began to refer to Tyler as "His Accidency," and he became "a man without a party."

One reason Webster remained in the cabinet was his ongoing negotiations with Great Britain over the American-Canadian border. The northern border of Maine was the main point of controversy. Webster and the British representative, Lord Ashburton, sought to settle the issue. After much discussion, the pair hammered out the Webster-Ashburton Treaty (1842) which granted the United States seven-twelfths of the disputed area and gave the British the remainder. The diplomats also clarified the border between Minnesota and Canada, while the Oregon Territory (see Chapter 5) was to remain jointly occupied since no agreement had been reached for its boundary. After the treaty negotiations were complete, Webster joined the other Whig leaders and resigned his position.

One of Tyler's goals was to annex Texas into the United States, partly in hopes that it would aid his reelection (see Chapter 8). His early efforts at annexation failed, and he lost the election of 1844 to Democrat James K. Polk. However, during the months of his lame-duck period (the time between the election and his leaving office) he continued promoting the annexation. When a treaty to annex Texas failed to gain the two-thirds vote in the Senate required for ratification, he called for a joint resolution, which required only a simple majority. The joint resolution admitting Texas passed, and Tyler signed it just days before leaving office.

▲ John Tyler

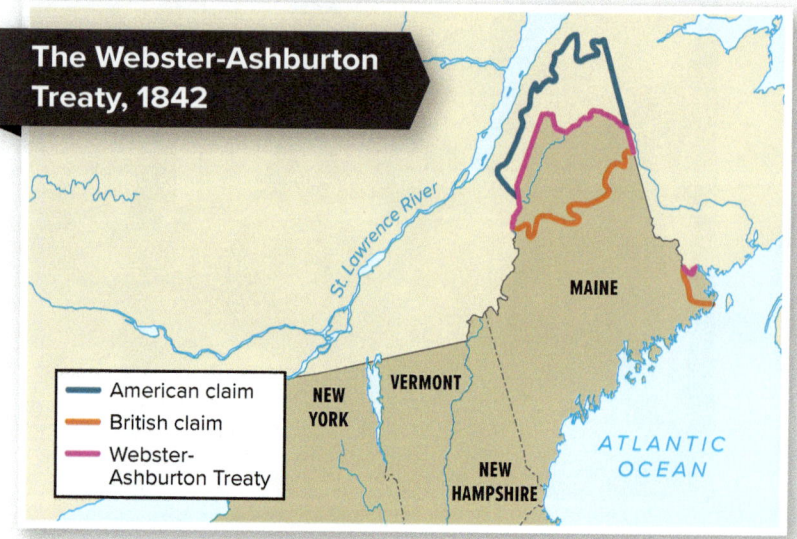

**The Webster-Ashburton Treaty, 1842**

- ■ American claim
- ■ British claim
- ■ Webster-Ashburton Treaty

MAINE

VERMONT

NEW YORK

NEW HAMPSHIRE

ATLANTIC OCEAN

St. Lawrence River

## Chapter Summary

**TERMS**

caucus

John Quincy Adams

Andrew Jackson

corrupt bargain

### 6.1   John Quincy Adams and Nationalism

- Four Democratic-Republicans ran for president in 1824. The party caucus selected William Crawford, but Andrew Jackson won the most electoral votes, but not over fifty percent, so the election went to the House of Representatives.

- When John Quincy Adams was chosen president by the House of Representatives and Adams then appointed Henry Clay as secretary of state, Jackson accused them of making a "corrupt bargain."

- Adams proposed an ambitious plan that included federal funding for internal improvements and the advancement of science, the arts, and education.

### 6.2   Jacksonian America

**TERMS**

National Republican Party

Democratic Party

mudslinging

spoils system

Kitchen Cabinet

Indian Removal Act of 1830

Sequoyah

*Worcester v. Georgia*

Trail of Tears

- The Democratic-Republicans split into two new parties before the election of 1828: the National Republican Party, which supported Adams and his nationalist agenda, and the Democratic Party, which supported Jackson and limited government.

- The election of 1828 was characterized by new campaign methods and mudslinging. The common people celebrated Jackson's election and saw him as the "people's president."

- Jackson believed government officials needed to be rotated out of office regularly to prevent corruption, but the spoils system also removed qualified people and became a source of corruption.

- Jackson pursued a policy of removing all Native Americans to west of the Mississippi River. The Cherokee adopted many white customs hoping to prevent their removal, and several Christian missionaries attempted to help them. Jackson ignored the Supreme Court's ruling that the Cherokee were not subject to Georgia law, and the remaining Cherokee were removed to Indian Territory in the Trail of Tears.

## 6.3 Domestic Controversies

- Southern states referred to the protective Tariff of 1828 as the "Tariff of Abominations" because they believed it favored northern industry but would ruin the southern economy.

- The Tariff of 1832 was lower than the Tariff of 1828, but South Carolina voted to nullify them both and threatened to secede. Congress passed the Force Bill authorizing Jackson to use the military to enforce the tariff. South Carolina agreed to the Compromise Tariff of 1833, thus avoiding civil war, but condemned the Force Bill, thus maintaining the right to nullify federal law.

- Henry Clay, wanting to make the Bank of the United States an issue in the election of 1832, pushed for the recharter of the Bank four years before its expiration. Jackson vetoed the recharter bill and was reelected in 1832.

- To shut down the Bank of the United States before its expiration, Jackson had all new federal revenue deposited in state-run "pet banks." He also issued the Specie Circular requiring that all purchases of public land be done in silver and gold rather than paper money. This led to financial problems for the country.

**TERMS**

Tariff of Abominations

Tariff of 1832

Ordinance of Nullification

Force Bill

Compromise Tariff of 1833

Nicholas Biddle

pet banks

Specie Circular

**TERMS**

Whig Party

Martin Van Buren

Panic of 1837

William Henry Harrison

John Tyler

## 6.4 Party Politics

- Jackson's opponents, believing he had gained too much power for the executive branch, created the Whig Party before the election of 1836.

- Democrat Martin Van Buren won the election of 1836, but his presidency was faced with the economic collapse of the Panic of 1837.

- Whig William Henry Harrison won the election of 1840 but died one month after taking office.

- John Tyler succeeded Harrison as president. He vetoed many Whig bills and was voted out of the party. Texas was annexed into the United States at the end of his term.

## Chapter Review Questions

### RECALL

1. Who were the four candidates in the election of 1824, and what party were they all from?

2. Who won the most votes (both electoral and popular) in the election of 1824?

3. Who decided the outcome of the election of 1824?

4. What Native American tribe did Georgia forcibly remove?

5. What Native American tribe from Florida fought against removal to the West during Jackson's presidency?

6. What state voted to nullify the tariffs?

7. What Democrat was elected president after Jackson in 1836? What economic crisis did the nation face during his presidency?

8. What happened to William Henry Harrison shortly after he took office?

9. Who succeeded William Henry Harrison as president?

10. What treaty settled the boundary between Maine and Canada?

11. What state was annexed into the United States just before Tyler left office?

### UNDERSTAND

12. Why did the caucus system come under fire in the election of 1824?

13. What was the "corrupt bargain" Jackson claimed prevented him from being elected in 1824?

14. What did John Quincy Adams's nationalist agenda include?

15. Why did the Democratic-Republican Party split into two parties before the election of 1828?

16. How were the presidential campaign methods of 1828 different from previous election campaigns?

17. Why was voter participation higher in 1828 than in previous elections?

18. What reasons did Jackson give for government officials to "rotate in office"? What were the drawbacks of this "spoils system"?

19. How did Jackson's policy toward Native Americans differ from that of the federal government before he was president?

20. How were the Cherokee culturally different from many other Native American tribes? Why did they believe this would keep them from being removed to the West?

21. What was the Supreme Court's decision in *Worcester v. Georgia*, and why did Jackson ignore the decision?

22. Why did southern states consider the Tariff of 1828 the "Tariff of Abominations"?

23. Contrast the views of Robert Hayne and Daniel Webster regarding nullification and states' rights.

24. What views did Jackson and Calhoun express regarding the union and states' rights in their toasts at the Jefferson Day banquet?

25. What did the Ordinance of Nullification say, and what was Jackson's response to it?

26. How did the Compromise Tariff of 1833 temporarily avoid civil war?

27. Why did Henry Clay push for Congress to vote on the rechartering of the Second Bank of the United States four years before it expired? What did Jackson do to the rechartering bill once it was passed?

28. After he was reelected in 1832, how did Jackson try to speed the collapse of the Bank of the United States?

29. How did Jackson change the role of the president?

30. Why was the Whig Party formed?

31. How did the Whigs portray the two candidates in the election of 1840? How did this compare to the truth about the two? Who won the election?

32. Why did the Whigs vote John Tyler out of their party?

### THINK ABOUT IT

33. Do you agree with Jackson that the Electoral College negates the will of the people? What are the benefits and weaknesses of the Electoral College system?

34. How did the events surrounding the inauguration of Andrew Jackson show that he was considered "the people's president"? Explain the warning of Margaret Bayard Smith, "God grant that one day or other, the people do not pull down all rule and rulers."

35. Were Jackson's policies toward Native Americans just? Explain.

36. What were the positive and negative aspects of the growing democratization of American politics?

# 7 The Growth of American Society

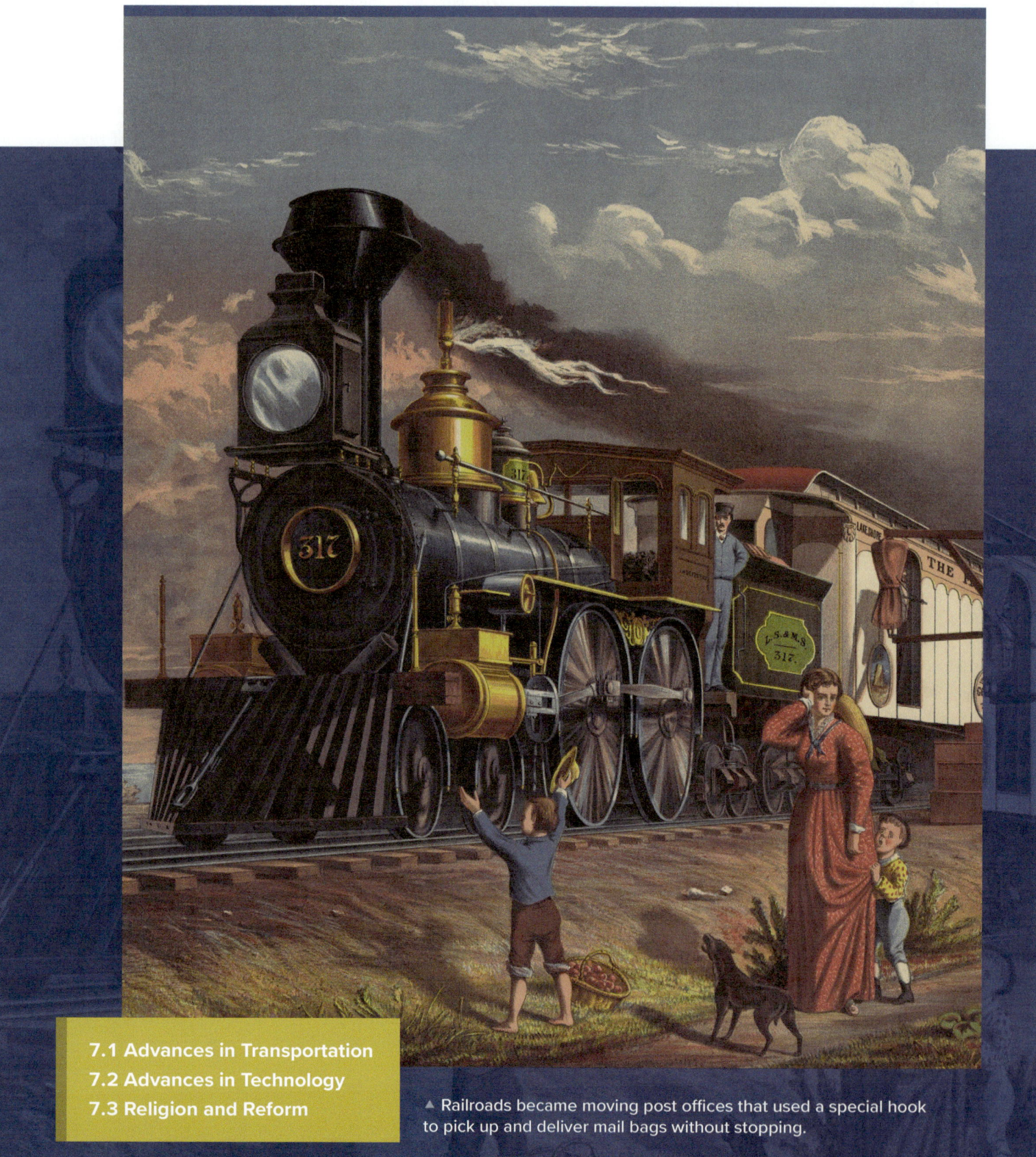

7.1 Advances in Transportation
7.2 Advances in Technology
7.3 Religion and Reform

▲ Railroads became moving post offices that used a special hook to pick up and deliver mail bags without stopping.

In just fifty years, from 1790 to 1840, the United States experienced tremendous growth, with its population increasing from under 4 million to over 17 million. During this time the United States also went through revolutions in transportation, communication, industry, and agriculture. These changes brought great opportunities but also many challenges, motivating some Americans to become involved in reform movements to address the ills of society. While the period was a time of great questioning concerning religion, it was also a time of great spiritual revival.

## 7.1 Advances in Transportation

How did advancements in transportation impact the nation during the period?

### GUIDING QUESTIONS

- What major roads were developed during the early 1800s?
- How did advances in water transportation impact trade?
- How did the early railroads develop?

As the United States expanded westward, economic development depended on the ability to move goods from one region of the country to another. Yet transportation was costly and time-consuming due to poor roads and slow waterways. The development of improved roads, the canal system, the steamboat and steamships, and the steam-powered locomotive in the period between 1810 and 1850 was known as the Transportation Revolution. It lowered the cost and time to move people and goods, encouraged western settlement, facilitated growth in manufacturing, and led to increased foreign trade.

## Roads

Most roads in the colonial era began as animal paths or Native American trails which were often made impassable by heavy rains. Gradually many of these trails were widened and improved to accommodate wagons and increased traffic. The Great Wagon Road (see Chapter 2) was the first major north-south road, stretching from Philadelphia to Georgia. In 1775 a group led by Daniel Boone (see Chapter 5) blazed the **Wilderness Road**, which carried travelers from southern Virginia, through the Cumberland Gap and into Kentucky, all the way to the Ohio River.

▲ Workers building a macadam road

Despite opposition by some to the use of federal money for internal improvements as proposed by congressman Henry Clay's American System, in 1808 Congress authorized funds to begin surveying a route for an east-west road. Construction began in 1811, and the first section of the road, from Cumberland, Maryland, to Wheeling (now in West Virginia), opened in 1818. This first phase of the **National Road** (also called the Cumberland Road) cost $1.7 million, or $13,000 per mile. It was the first federal highway and eventually linked Baltimore, Maryland, to Vandalia, Illinois. It became a major transportation route for early settlers moving west.

Many early American roads were built by private companies that paid for them by charging tolls (fees) for their use. These toll roads were often called turnpikes because the sharp sticks guarding the entrance to the roads would be turned upon payment of the toll.

Developments in road construction techniques gradually improved the quality of roads. In cities, cobblestones or bricks were used. Plank roads (built by laying a series of boards side by side) and corduroy roads (logs laid side by side) were built in the rural areas and enabled travel to continue in muddy conditions. Macadam roads (named for Scottish engineer John McAdam) were built of crushed stones placed in pre-dug roadbeds.

# Canals, Waterways, and Sea Trade

Despite gradual improvements in land transportation, water transportation was often faster, cheaper, and more efficient for moving people and goods. Most early American cities were built near rivers or other bodies of water. Moving goods downstream on barges or flatboats was inexpensive and relatively easy, but moving goods upstream was a challenge.

## Canals

Not all cities were naturally connected by water routes. The solution was to build canals, or man-made waterways, that allowed a vessel to travel from one body of water to another. The canal era began in 1817 when New York, at the urging of Governor DeWitt Clinton, began building a canal connecting Albany on the Hudson River to Lake Erie. Costing approximately $7 million, the 363-mile canal was a risk for the state. Critics called it "Clinton's Big Ditch," yet the **Erie Canal** proved such a success that it paid for itself from tolls in under ten years. Furthermore, the cost of shipping goods plunged. Before the canal opened, it cost $100 a ton to ship goods from Buffalo to New York City, and after, the price dropped to around $5 a ton.

The success of the Erie Canal encouraged other efforts. By the 1830s, one could travel from New York City to New Orleans completely by inland waterways. The weaknesses of canals were that they were expensive to build and maintain, travel along them was slow (from one to three miles per hour), and they froze over in winter.

▾ The illustrations below show a boat passing through a canal lock.

1. The boat approaches the lock.
2. The lock gate opens and the boat enters.
3. The gate is closed and the water level is raised until it is even with the upstream water.
4. The upstream lock gate is opened and the boat continues its journey.

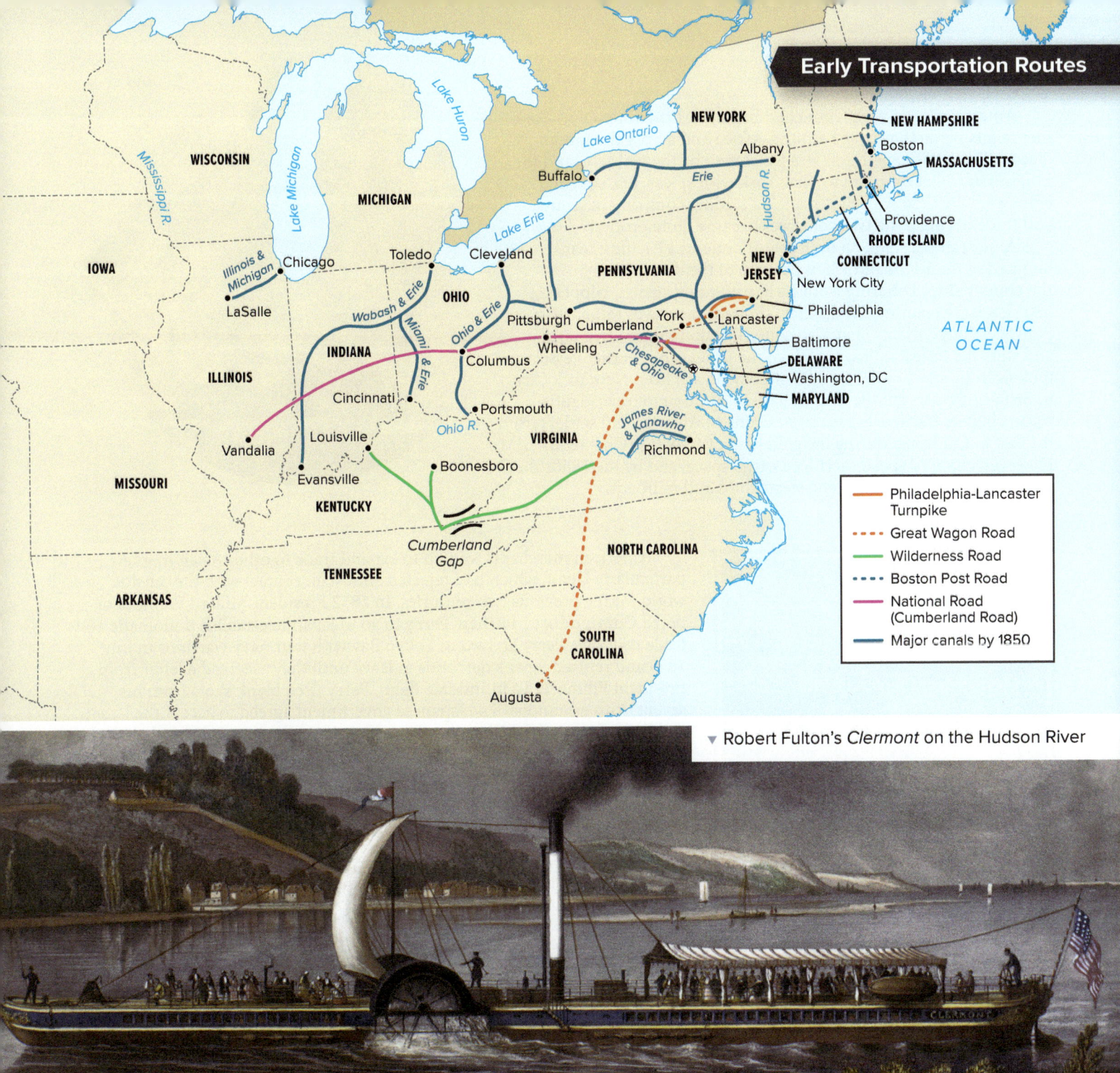

**Legend:**
- Philadelphia-Lancaster Turnpike
- Great Wagon Road
- Wilderness Road
- Boston Post Road
- National Road (Cumberland Road)
- Major canals by 1850

▼ Robert Fulton's *Clermont* on the Hudson River

## Waterways

By the late 1700s, inventors had developed vessels that were powered by steam engines. The steamboat solved the problem of upstream travel. The steamboat was perfected by Philadelphia inventor **Robert Fulton**, who in 1807 unveiled the *Clermont* on the Hudson River. Critics called it "Fulton's Folly," but it successfully sailed upstream to Albany in just thirty-two hours, a trip that would have taken four days with a wind-powered vessel. Rivers soon became busy highways moving goods and passengers cheaply and easily through the interior of the country. Cities such as

Pittsburgh and Cincinnati on the Ohio River and St. Louis and New Orleans on the Mississippi River grew into major transportation centers.

Steamboats also brought economic growth and improvements for settlers in the west. Trade between the east and the west grew more profitable as the cost of transportation decreased. Besides bringing settlers to the west, steamboats also brought newspapers and mail, allowing the settlers to remain connected to the east.

*The Growth of American Society*   **179**

## Sea Trade

American trade with China had begun in 1784 when New York merchants made the voyage around Africa and across the Indian Ocean. The trade expedition was welcomed by the Chinese, and the *Empress of China* returned to New York with spices, tea, silk, and chinaware. In 1786 America opened a trading company in China, and trade between the two countries became quite profitable.

American sea trade on both the Atlantic and Pacific oceans boomed in the 1840s and 1850s because of the development of the **clipper ship**. Differing from earlier seagoing vessels, clippers had slender, streamlined hulls that "clipped" the waves rather than plowed through them. They also contained up to thirty-five sails and were the fastest sailing vessels of the time. While earlier vessels took from twenty-one to twenty-eight days to sail from New York City to Britain, clippers cut the time in half. In addition to transatlantic trade, clippers transported tea from China to America and settlers from the east to California during the gold rush of 1849 (see Chapter 8). However, clippers' speed sacrificed cargo space, and by the 1850s they were supplanted by oceangoing steamships and railroads.

▼ Clipper ship

(see Chapter 8)

### Did You Know?

Perry brought many gifts for the Japanese government, including a small steam locomotive and tracks, weapons, telegraph instruments, and luxury items, introducing Japan to the Industrial Revolution. At the signing of the treaty establishing trade relations, the Japanese held a sumo wrestling demonstration for the American delegation.

American merchants wanted to expand trade to other Asian markets, particularly Japan, which had rejected almost all contact with the outside world for the previous two centuries. In 1852 President Millard Fillmore ordered **Commodore Matthew Perry** to go to Japan to establish diplomatic and trade relations. Perry arrived in Tokyo Bay with four navy warships in July 1853 and refused Japan's demands to leave until they accepted a letter from President Fillmore. To intimidate them, Perry fired blank shots from his seventy-three cannons. The Japanese government agreed to accept the letter, and Perry departed for China, promising to return the next year for their reply.

When Perry returned to Japan in 1854, he brought ten ships and 1,600 troops in a large show of force. Japan, realizing it could not withstand American power, agreed to a treaty establishing diplomatic and trade relations with the United States.

▼ Commodore Matthew Perry meeting with Japanese leaders

# Railroads

The transportation revolution continued with the development of the railroad, which combined the flexibility of canals and roads with the speed and dependable power of steam. The first economically successful railroad in America was the Baltimore & Ohio (B & O) Railroad. Originally, the B & O consisted of horse-drawn carriages on metal rails. Inventor Peter Cooper believed that the line could develop a steam-driven engine, like the ones British companies were using. Working mostly with scrap metal, Cooper constructed the *Tom Thumb*. This small but powerful steam engine was designed to handle the sharp curves and steep climbs of the B & O rail line. To display the engine's capabilities, Cooper agreed to run the *Tom Thumb* in a thirteen-mile race against a horse. Although the horse won narrowly because the engine had a mechanical problem, Cooper successfully demonstrated the potential of steam locomotives.

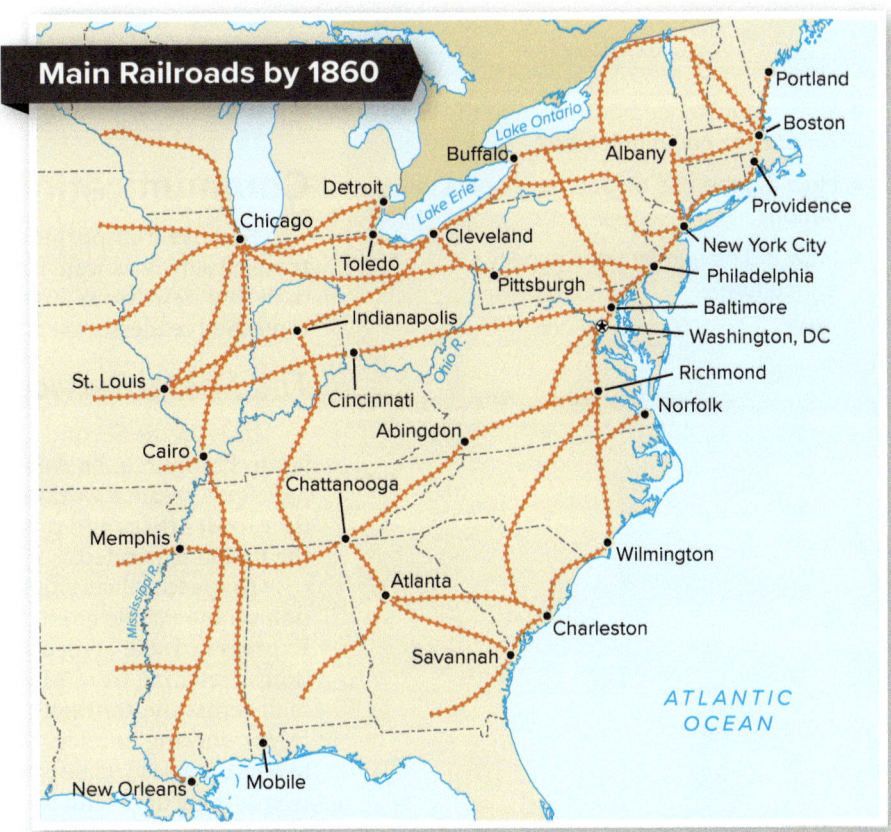

**Main Railroads by 1860**

▼ Peter Cooper's *Tom Thumb* locomotive

Several inventions accelerated the growth of railroads. Iron rails replaced wooden ones covered with iron strips. A cowcatcher attached to the front of an engine reduced damage from collisions with animals. Improvements to the steam engine made trains faster, safer, and more powerful. Railroads, particularly in the North and the West, began using a standard gauge (width) of track. This increased efficiency as trains from different companies could use the same tracks. The railroads' primary obstacle was the cost of constructing rail lines and bridges.

In 1840 the United States had about 3,000 miles of track. By 1860 about 31,000 miles of track fanned out across the country. Cities such as Chicago and Indianapolis became major centers of rail traffic. Chicago, for example, mushroomed from a population of about 4,000 in 1840 to more than 100,000 by 1860.

## Comprehension Check 7.1

1. What was the first federally funded road?

   **A** the Wilderness Road

   **B** the Great Wagon Road

   **C** the National Road

2. The Erie Canal connected Lake Erie with what other body of water?

   **A** Lake Ontario

   **B** the Hudson River

   **C** the Ohio River

3. Commodore Matthew Perry opened trade between the United States and ____.

   **A** Australia

   **B** China

   **C** Japan

4. "Fulton's Folly" was a ____.

   **A** steamboat

   **B** railroad locomotive

   **C** clipper ship

### MAKING CONNECTIONS

5. What were three effects of the Transportation Revolution on American society?

## 7.2 Advances in Technology

**How did communication, industry, and agriculture advance?**

# Communication

Because transportation was slow in early America, information traveled slowly as well. In larger cities, newspapers were published daily, but news from faraway places was often outdated by the time it reached readers, especially those in small towns or on the frontier.

## The Postal Service

In 1775 the Second Continental Congress had appointed Benjamin Franklin to be America's first postmaster general. In that role, he helped create a working postal system for the nation. Since that time, post offices and post roads were built, and the system grew as the nation expanded.

To speed delivery of the mail to the rapidly expanding population on the Pacific coast, three businessmen established the **Pony Express** in 1860. With a stable of 500 horses and a series of 190 stations stretching from Missouri to California, they promised to carry mail across the continent in the shortest possible time. A series of riders working in relays carried the mail from St. Joseph, Missouri, to San Francisco, California, in ten to twelve days, compared to twenty-four days with standard delivery. However, the company went bankrupt in 1861 after just eighteen months in service, a victim to the spread of the most important communications invention of the era, the telegraph.

## The Telegraph

The growth of railroads had created a new communication challenge. Trains traveling in opposite directions shared the same tracks and would use pull-offs to allow other trains to pass. To avoid head-on collisions, of which there were many, railroads needed a fast and dependable method of communication to keep track of moving trains.

The solution was the telegraph, invented by **Samuel F. B. Morse**, which used electricity to carry messages over wire using an alphabetic code. Tests of his method convinced Congress to authorize $30,000 to construct a model system. Stringing wire on poles from Baltimore to Washington, DC, Morse sent the first intercity telegraph message on May 24, 1844, before a group of political leaders in the United States Capitol. The first message was a Bible verse: "What hath God wrought!" (Num. 23:23).

Soon more than 23,000 miles of telegraph lines stretched across the nation, often alongside railroad tracks. By 1852 people living hundreds of miles apart could communicate almost instantly. In 1858 the first successful transatlantic telegraph cable was laid between North America and the British Isles. By 1861 the transcontinental line was also complete, making the Pony Express obsolete.

▼ Pony Express rider passing workers raising telegraph poles on the Great Plains

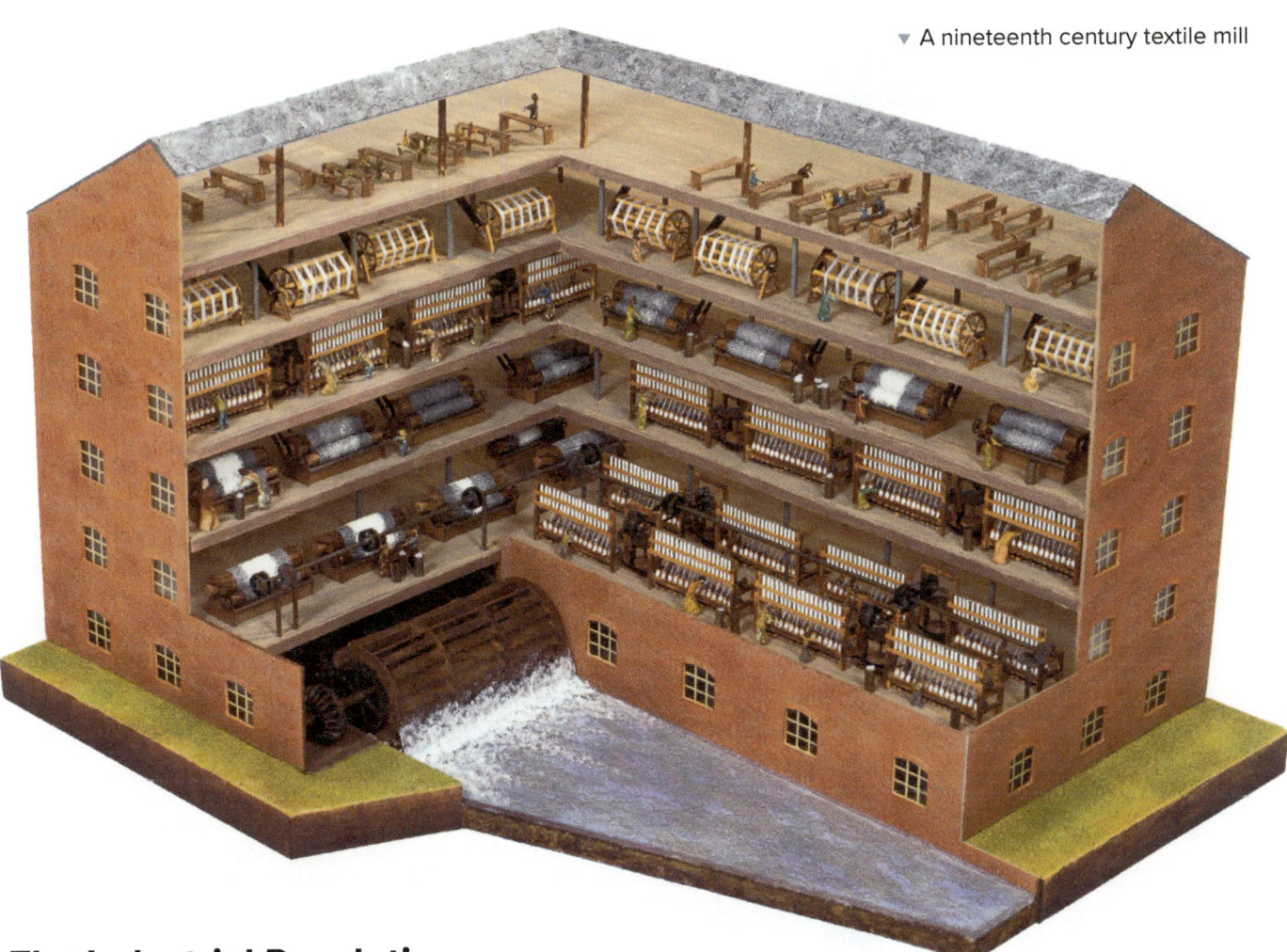

# The Industrial Revolution

## *Manufacturing and Industry*

The **Industrial Revolution** began in Great Britain in the mid-1700s. Production of goods by hand was replaced by machinery. The **factory system** developed to house machines powered by water or steam. Labor was done by unskilled factory workers who were paid a fixed wage. Labor was divided among the workers, with each worker responsible for one step of production. Factories were owned by one person, a group of people, or many investors. Owners bought the machinery and raw materials, paid the workers, took the risks, and received the profits.

Industrialization first developed in the textile industry, where cotton imported to Britain from America and elsewhere was spun into cloth, which would then be exported. In the late 1700s, Great Britain was the world's leader in manufacturing.

America's first attempts at factory production were not successful. America's machinery was not as good as Britain's, and American consumers preferred British products. The British government carefully guarded all machinery, including blueprints, related to its textile industry. Laws prohibited textile workers from emigrating. But that did not deter **Samuel Slater**. Although a successful apprentice in an English textile mill, Slater saw greater economic opportunities for himself in America. Slater carefully memorized the construction of the textile machines, disguised himself as a farm hand, and escaped to the United States in 1789.

In Pawtucket, Rhode Island, Slater—working entirely from memory—constructed an English-style mill with the financial support of American investors. This mill proved to be the first of a series of mills built across New England. Following the practice of British mills, Slater hired children as young as seven years old to work.

The factory system was critical in the establishment and growth of the fledgling American economy and New England was a natural site for the textile industry. Although its soil and climate were not suitable for large-scale agriculture, its numerous streams and rivers were ideal for driving water wheels used to power the machinery, and it had a large, readily available labor force. When steam replaced waterpower, New England's vast forests provided fuel for steam engines. In 1814 Francis Cabot Lowell created a textile mill in Waltham, Massachusetts. He hired many women to work in his mill and housed them in company-owned boarding houses, where they were provided educational and religious activities. After his death, the company built a larger mill to the north of Waltham, and the mill town of Lowell, Massachusetts, was established.

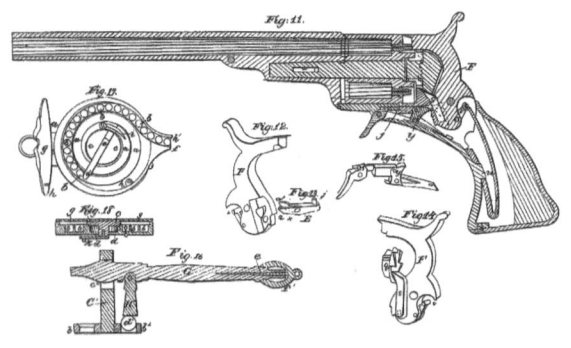

▲ Patent diagram for a Colt revolver

Productivity advanced further with **interchangeable parts**. Eli Whitney, better known for inventing the cotton gin (see p. 186), accepted an order to provide ten thousand rifles for the United States government. Until that time, guns were produced by craftsmen who individually made and fitted each part. Repairs also required making each replacement part by hand. Whitney designed a gun that was made of standardized, identical, machine-manufactured parts. When a piece broke, a new one could be easily inserted. Building on Whitney's process, other industries began to use interchangeable parts, which led to the mass production of products.

American inventors benefitted from the support of the United States government, which saw the importance of encouraging invention. The government established the patent system in 1790, which allowed inventors to secure patents for new devices and processes. As long as the patent was in effect, no one else could legally copy the inventor's work, and the inventor could reap the profits from a useful invention.

Spurred by the patent law and the promise of profits, inventors flooded the nation with new devices. Elias Howe perfected a mechanical sewing machine, which permitted the quicker, cheaper manufacture of clothing. Samuel Colt patented and manufactured a "six-shooter," a pistol with a revolving cylinder, which allowed a user to fire six times before reloading. His weapon became popular during the Mexican War (see Chapter 8) when it became the standard sidearm of the United States Army.

In early America most iron products had to be imported from England. In the 1790s large deposits of iron ore and anthracite, or "hard" coal, were discovered in western Pennsylvania. With this clean-burning, high-heating hard coal, American manufacturers could produce both more and better iron. As roads, canals, and railroads reached into the American interior, iron products also spread throughout the nation, and western Pennsylvania became a center of American heavy industry.

▼ A steel mill in Pittsburgh, Pennsylvania

Most iron went into the growing railroad industry to provide rails and engines. Smaller amounts went into producing items such as tools and cooking utensils. An efficient process of producing steel from iron was developed in the 1850s in Great Britain and spread to the United States.

As America became more industrialized, towns grew up around the factories. Urbanization (movement of people to cities) became a new way of life for many people. Workers who came from the countryside and emigrated from Europe found employment in the factories. To meet the needs of these workers and their families, some entrepreneurs opened stores, inns, and other retail establishments. Others offered much-needed services such as blacksmithing, carpentry, and saddle and harness making.

## Results of the Rise of Industry

Industrialization had many positive effects. New inventions made work easier, and mass production lowered the cost of many products. Factories brought job opportunities and an increased standard of living for unskilled workers, including new immigrants to the United States. For example, wages were often higher than what could be earned on the farm or in the immigrant's home country. Additionally, many workers were able to gain the knowledge and experience to rise to higher-paying jobs.

However, industrialization also created new problems. Working around machinery was dangerous, especially for children, and factory work limited children's educational opportunities. Workers often worked twelve hours a day, six days a week, and had little time to spend with their families. Some factory owners kept wages low to maximize their profits. As cities and mill towns became overcrowded from workers coming for factory jobs, living conditions deteriorated.

The first **labor unions** in America were organized by workers in the 1830s to address these problems. Workers pushed for shorter hours, higher wages, and the elimination of child labor. These early unions had limited success because workers often accepted wage cuts out of fear of losing their jobs, and new immigrants often found that even low wages were better than what they had earned in their native country.

## Technology *and* Faith

Advances in technology result from people being made in God's image. God has given people the ability to use their minds and creative capacities to develop new products that bring great benefits and help fill and subdue the earth (Gen. 1:26–28).

However, because humans are fallen, technological advances bring negative as well as positive effects. Every invention is designed from the worldview of its inventor. In addition, fallen people can put good inventions to bad use.

In this period of US history, some people began to view technology like a religion, believing that it could solve all of society's problems and bring about paradise on earth. Even those who did not go this far still put a great deal of faith in technology. Some believed that if something could be done, it should be done, without evaluating the technology using biblical principles.

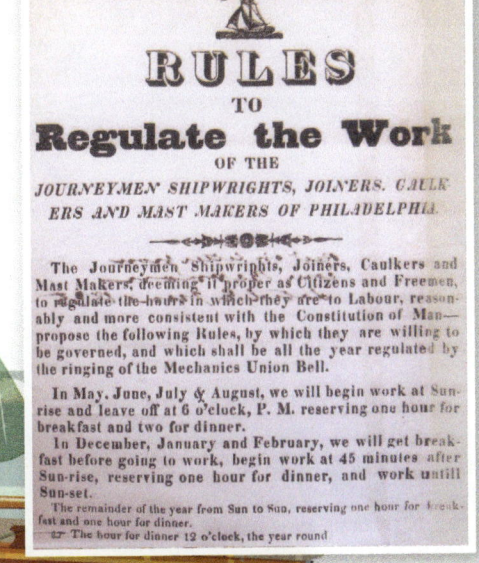

▲ The 1835 Ten-Hour Day Circular by Philadelphia carpenters and shipwrights called for a reduction in working hours from twelve to ten hours.

▲ Workers in the shipbuilding industry caulking a ship

# Agriculture

The United States had been predominantly agricultural since its founding. The first half of the 1800s saw important advances in technology which led to an increase in agricultural production. Farmers could now plow more land and plant, harvest, and process more crops. As a result, they could meet the needs of their own families as well as grow a surplus that could be bartered or sold. American grain became an important export to Europe. By 1861 the United States was producing nearly $2 billion worth of agricultural products each year.

Three inventions in particular transformed American agriculture: the steel plow, the mechanical reaper, and the cotton gin.

The rich soil of the northwest and of the plains west of the Mississippi was sticky and covered with a tough sod. In 1837 a blacksmith named **John Deere** designed an improved plow which proved ideal for the new lands of the middle and northwest regions. He put an edge of steel over the iron blade of the plow to cut through the sod and turn the soil without breaking the plow. His invention proved quite popular with farmers, and Deere eventually built a factory that produced thousands of plows per year.

Before advances in machinery, a farmer could typically harvest half an acre of wheat a day using hand-held tools. In 1834 **Cyrus McCormick** received a patent for a reaping machine, a horse-drawn device that allowed one man to cut and stack ten to twelve acres' grain in a single day.

The South differed from the North and the West in that, although food crops were important, the South did not produce the abundant grains of the West. Tobacco was important to some areas, particularly the states of the Upper South. Another cash crop, however, dominated the agriculture and economy of the region: cotton.

In 1789 cotton was a relatively unimportant crop. Most cotton grown in the South was a short-staple variety, the seeds of which clung to the cotton fibers. It took a worker (typically a slave) a whole day to clean just one pound of cotton. **Eli Whitney** changed that in 1793. While working as a tutor on a Georgia plantation, Whitney devised the **cotton gin**, a machine containing a series of metal teeth that were mounted on rollers and separated the cotton from the troublesome seeds. The cotton gin cleaned cotton fifty times faster than working by hand.

▼ Cyrus McCormick's reaping machine

▼ John Deere's steel plow

▼ Eli Whitney's cotton gin

Whitney's invention transformed the South's economy by making the growing of cotton more profitable. Strong demand for cotton in the textile mills of the North and Europe caused farmers in the Lower South to plant more cotton. In 1790 the United States produced two million pounds of cotton; in 1860 the nation produced more than two *billion* pounds—seven-eighths of the cotton produced in the world. Cotton was by far the most important US export. "Cotton is King," southerners proclaimed.

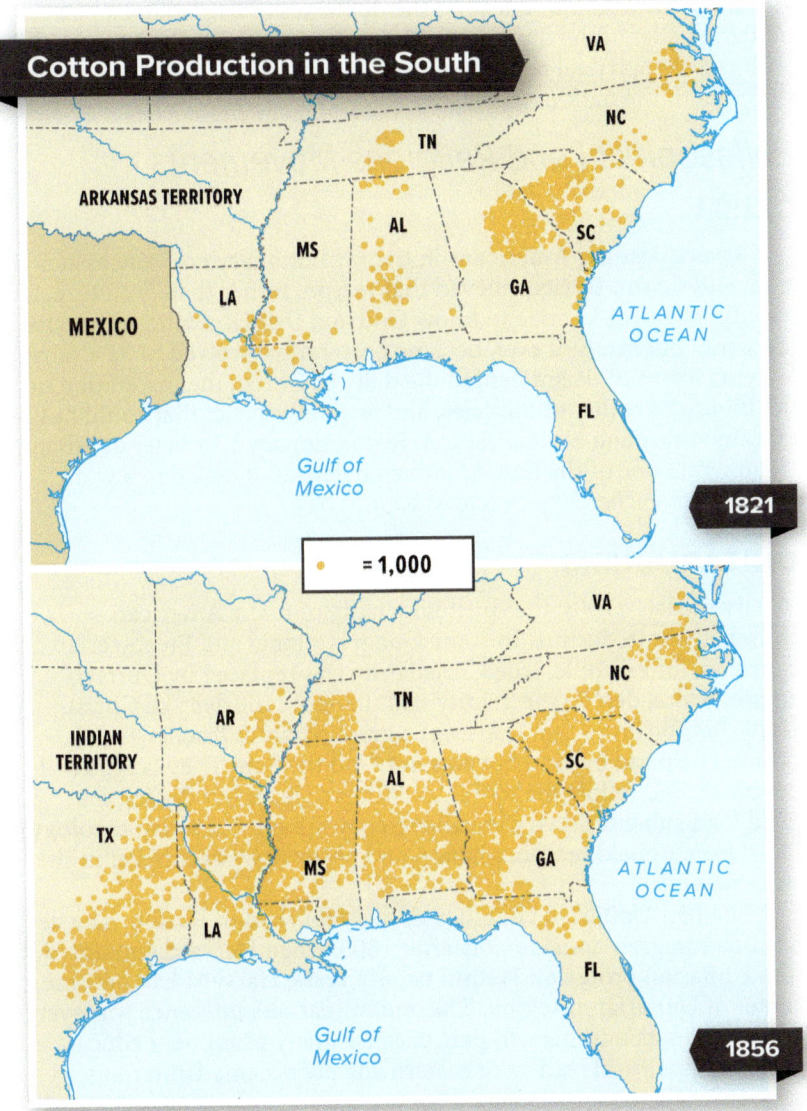

**Cotton Production in the South**

1821

• = 1,000

1856

In 1790 slavery had seemed an increasingly unprofitable and dying institution, but the increase in cotton production also increased the demand for slaves. In 1790 there were about 700,000 slaves in the South; by 1860 there were almost 4 million slaves. The Constitution's prohibition on the foreign slave trade, which went into effect in 1808, meant that new slaves were children born in slavery. Even though only one-fourth of southern families owned slaves, southerners became increasingly sensitive to northern criticism of slavery, which they saw as threatening the economic survival of the South. The overwhelming value of cotton also hampered southern industrial development, as profits and capital were invested in land and slaves instead of in resources for manufacturing.

## Cotton and Slavery (1790–1860)

| Year | Pounds of Cotton Grown | Slaves in the South |
| --- | --- | --- |
| 1790 | about 1.5 million | nearly 700,000 |
| 1810 | 89 million | about 1.2 million |
| 1850 | more than 1 billion | about 3.2 million |
| 1860 | almost 2 billion | almost 4 million |

### Comprehension Check 7.2

1. The invention of the ____ caused the Pony Express to go bankrupt eighteen months after it was started.

    A  railroad

    B  telegraph

    C  clipper ship

2. Industrialization took place first in what industry?

    A  textiles

    B  steel

    C  oil

3. The person who developed interchangeable parts and the cotton gin was ____.

    A  John Deere

    B  Samuel F. B. Morse

    C  Eli Whitney

4. The invention of the cotton gin led to a decrease in the number of slaves in the South.

    True

    False

### MAKING CONNECTIONS

5. What were two positive and two negative effects of industrialization on American society?

6. How should Christians view technology?

### GUIDING QUESTIONS

■ How did religious changes impact American society?

■ What were the goals of reform movements during the early 1800s?

## 7.3 Religion and Reform

How did religious and reform movements impact American society?

## Religious Changes

In the midst of the societal and technological change of this period, the United States experienced tremendous religious change as well. Some began to question the doctrines of Christianity, particularly belief in the divinity of Christ. Despite these challenges to faith, a large spiritual revival occurred which revitalized Christianity throughout the nation.

### *Philosophical and Religious Movements*

#### DEISM

Several leading Americans in the revolutionary era were associated with deism. Deists believed that reason, rather than Scripture, was the way people came to know God and that God Himself created the world but rarely, if ever, became personally involved in its affairs. Varying forms of deism denied the deity of Christ, the inspiration of the Bible, the reality of miracles, and any other belief that could not be explained through human reason. Revolutionary War veteran Ethan Allen wrote one of the first American defenses of deism in a work titled *Reason: The Only Oracle of Man*.

#### UNITARIANISM

By the late 1700s, the spiritual vitality of many American churches was in decline. In some Congregational and Presbyterian churches, for example, true Christianity was replaced by **Unitarianism**, which denied the Trinity and therefore the deity of Christ. Unitarians believed that Jesus was a great religious teacher and a prophet inspired by God but was not God the Son. They taught that people should follow the moral teachings of Jesus but denied the need for a substitutionary sacrifice to pay for sin. Unitarian theology, like deism, upheld reason, science, and philosophy over belief in the supernatural.

The first Unitarian churches were established in Boston. The denomination grew considerably after 1805, when Harvard appointed its first Unitarian professor. Within twenty years, Harvard had become a center of Unitarian teaching. The denomination's influence was even greater than its numbers, in part because many prominent educational and political leaders of eastern society became Unitarians.

#### TRANSCENDENTALISM

Founded by former Unitarians, **transcendentalism** denied the miraculous and taught that man was essentially good and ultimately perfectible. A form of romanticism, transcendentalism emphasized intuition and the senses over rationalism and logical reasoning. Its leading figure in America was Ralph Waldo Emerson. A graduate of Harvard, Emerson entered the Unitarian ministry but later developed his own optimistic, man-centered faith. Emerson denied a faith "in Christ" in favor of a faith "like Christ's," which Emerson defined as faith in man. Transcendentalism influenced author Henry David Thoreau and poet Walt Whitman.

◄ Ralph Waldo Emerson

## METHODISM

The Methodist church was founded by John Wesley (see Chapter 2). Methodism in America grew slowly at first, partly because of its association with Anglicanism and partly because of Wesley's opposition to the War for Independence. Later, however, the Methodist church was effective in reaching all classes of society with the gospel, including both free blacks and slaves, and gave women increased opportunities to participate in church activity. **Francis Asbury** was considered the father of American Methodism. Sent from England in 1772, Asbury found that the United States was too vast and its population too scattered to establish a minister in every community, so Asbury divided the land into sections, or circuits. One minister, called a "circuit rider," traveled on horseback from settlement to settlement throughout his assigned circuit, ministering to Christians and preaching to the lost. Asbury himself traveled nearly three hundred thousand miles on horseback in his lifetime.

▶ Francis Asbury statue

## Richard Allen

**Richard Allen** was a former slave who became a minister to African Americans. Allen, born in Pennsylvania, was converted under the preaching of a Methodist minister in 1777. Shortly thereafter, Allen's master allowed the young slave to purchase his freedom.

Allen chopped wood, worked in a brickyard, and delivered salt to make a living. He preached in the evenings and on Sundays. Allen became a circuit rider in New Jersey and Pennsylvania.

Allen enjoyed a fruitful ministry among African Americans in Philadelphia. Allen and his converts originally attended a white Methodist church, but some members resented the increased numbers of black Christians in their services. In 1787 Allen and the other African attendees started their own church. Francis Asbury dedicated the church in 1794 and ordained Allen. When several other black congregations expressed an interest in closer fellowship, they formed a new denomination, the African Methodist Episcopal (AME) Church, and Allen became their first bishop. Under his leadership, the denomination became one of the most effective means of reaching African Americans with the gospel.

## The Second Great Awakening

From 1795 to about 1840 the United States experienced a large spiritual revival known as the **Second Great Awakening**, in which many thousands of Americans became Christians, and which had a significant effect on American society.

### REVIVAL IN THE EAST

By the late 1700s colleges in New England had become battlegrounds between biblical belief and the growing influence of Unitarianism. In 1795 **Timothy Dwight**, a grandson of Jonathan Edwards, was named president of Yale College. Dwight confronted the unbelief of the student body by participating in public debates on the truths of the Christian faith. Dwight also preached a series of sermons in chapel on basic Christian theology. The fruit of Dwight's labors was a series of revivals in which at least a third of Yale's students were converted.

The revival at Yale spread to other colleges and churches in the East, led by men such as Asahel Nettleton, an evangelist from Connecticut. Nettleton's sermons were both doctrinal and practical, and his services emphasized order and restraint over the emotionalism of earlier revivals. He would not preach where he was not invited and refused to take credit away from God for any revival that happened during his ministry.

## REVIVAL IN THE WEST

The revival took a different form on the western frontier. The chief feature of the western revivals was the camp meeting. People would travel from great distances, pitch their tents, and attend religious services that often lasted several days. In 1800 Presbyterian minister James McGready and several other pastors, both black and white and representing several denominations, held an outdoor service in Logan County, Kentucky. During this and other services that followed, hearers began to profess a deep sense of their own sinfulness and to cry out for salvation. The results proved so remarkable that other preachers began to hold camp meetings. Probably the most significant camp meeting was held at Cane Ridge, Kentucky, in 1801, where it was estimated that over 10,000 people attended. One result of these meetings was the establishment of many new local churches in the western regions of America.

Camp meetings tended to be more emotional and sensational than the eastern revivals. At some meetings hearers shook, jerked, jumped, ran, barked, and fell. While some physical responses were the outward manifestation of inward conviction, several preachers began to encourage these outward displays. This led to a split between those ministers who cautioned against excesses that distracted from the gospel message and those who believed that these physical responses were signs of God's favor.

## CHARLES FINNEY AND THE "NEW MEASURES"

Some evangelists believed that revivals, rather than being special movements of the Holy Spirit, could be produced simply by using the right techniques. The leading proponent of this view was **Charles Finney**, a New York lawyer who in 1821 professed faith during a revival. Finney began preaching in small towns across New York, and reports of numerous dramatic conversions increased his reputation. By the 1830s he was preaching to huge crowds in New York City and was one of America's leading evangelists.

Revival, Finney said, was not a miracle but a "purely philosophical result of the right use of the constituted means." The "New Measures" he used included having an "anxious bench" in the front row to single out those who felt conviction, praying for the conversion of certain individuals by name, and holding "protracted meetings" which lasted several weeks in one location. When critics said that he put too much emphasis on man's action and not enough on God's work, Finney's response was that his methods were effective in creating professions of faith. Some questioned whether these were true conversions or merely emotional responses produced by Finney's methods.

Like Methodism, Finney's methods were reflective of the growing democratization of the period. He reached out to all classes of society and allowed women to participate in his services by praying publicly, giving testimonies, organizing volunteer societies, and leading Bible studies. While Finney was also correct to emphasize individual spiritual experience, this emphasis led some to a less doctrinal form of Christianity. Finney became one of the most dominant figures in American religion in this era.

▶ (top) Camp meeting; (bottom) Charles Finney preaching

## RESULTS OF THE AWAKENING

The Second Great Awakening, like the original Great Awakening of the colonial period, had a dramatic effect on American society. First, tens of thousands of people were genuinely converted to Christianity and joined churches. The Methodist church, for example, grew from 15,000 members in 1785 to 850,000 in 1840 and became the largest denomination in the United States. Second, the revival transformed the moral lives of many individuals, and social ills such as drunkenness declined dramatically. Third, the revival fueled the drive for social reform. Many of the leaders of social reform movements were converts of the revival and their newfound faith motivated their desire to improve society. Fourth, because the Second Great Awakening emphasized conversion and evangelism over theological doctrine, the number of denominations multiplied, including some that held to unbiblical teaching.

## FOREIGN MISSIONS

The effects of the Second Great Awakening reached beyond the shores of the United States. The first great American missions movement resulted from this revival. As a result of the revival on eastern college campuses, in 1821 a group of students from Williams College began to discuss the need to carry the gospel throughout the world. One member of that group, Samuel Mills, helped establish the American Board of Commissioners for Foreign Missions (ABCFM), America's first foreign mission board.

The ABCFM, a Congregationalist organization, sent many missionaries throughout the world, including Adoniram Judson and Luther Rice who went to India. On the way, however, sensing that their own theological views were more Baptist than Congregationalist, Judson remained in Asia while Rice returned to the United States to raise support among Baptists. Judson eventually moved to Burma, where his faithful translation work and preaching made him a leader of the American missions movement. Rice helped start a Baptist mission organization that became a major force in sending missionaries overseas.

## THE PRAYER MEETING REVIVAL

Another revival took place in the years just prior to the outbreak of the Civil War. It was known as the Prayer Meeting Revival, or the Businessmen's Revival, of 1857–59. The revival began during a financial crisis in 1857. In September of that year in New York City, Jeremiah Lanphier began holding a weekly prayer meeting for businessmen during the noon lunch hour. After a brief time of singing and a devotional, the remaining time was spent in prayer, particularly for the conversion of individuals. Attendance grew from six the first week, to twenty the next, to forty the next. After the stock market crash of October 10, 1857, attendance soared and the group began meeting daily. Other churches began to hold prayer meetings, and within months 10,000 people were gathering daily in New York City for prayer. The practice quickly spread to other cities.

The results of this revival were astounding. Nearly a million people were converted. Encouraged by the revival, Christians raised money to found Christian schools and support foreign missionaries. Established Christian organizations received floods of new volunteers whose lives had been transformed. For example, the Young Men's Christian Association (YMCA), established in 1844 in Great Britain, was able to expand its ministry of providing wholesome recreation and fervent religious instruction for young people, primarily in the cities. The Prayer Meeting Revival also marked perhaps the first time that non-clergy had dominated the leadership of a revival.

▼ Adoniram Judson

## Millerites

William Miller was a Baptist minister in New York who began to attract attention in the 1830s. Miller was a premillennialist, believing that Christ would return to the earth and establish the Millennial kingdom, a perfect kingdom of peace lasting a thousand years. Miller believed that Christ would return sometime between March 21, 1843, and March 21, 1844. Thousands of people in the Northeast heard Miller, and thousands became followers of his teaching. Some quit their jobs and sold their possessions as they waited for the Second Coming. When the date of Miller's prediction came and went, he prophesied a new date of October 22, 1844. When that date also passed, the Millerites were scorned. Miller gave up predicting the date of Christ's return and later helped form the Seventh Day Adventist Church.

▲ Horace Mann

## Reform Movements

Paralleling American efforts to improve technology were efforts to improve society. Reform movements, attempts to address society's ills, flourished in the first half of the nineteenth century. Some reformers were religiously motivated while others were guided by simple humanitarian ideals, but all believed that changes could and should be made to address the problems they saw.

### Education

Two important trends developed in the reform of American education: the growth of public education and teacher education. Most schooling since colonial days had been done at home or in small schools. Children often missed school when they were needed during the planting and harvesting seasons. Despite its sporadic nature, American education was remarkably successful. The 1840 census reported that 78 percent of the population was able to read and write. However, reformers were concerned that children working in factories and the children of immigrants were receiving little education. These reformers argued that the states should provide a free education to all children.

One of the leading reformers in the drive for public education was **Horace Mann**. In 1837 Massachusetts created a state board of education and appointed Mann as its secretary. Mann believed that ignorance was a threat to the freedom of the nation and therefore that the public should provide, control, and sustain universal, free education. He also believed in "common" schools that included children of all social, religious, and ethnic backgrounds. A Unitarian, Mann wanted children to be exposed to the moral teachings of Protestant Christianity without being indoctrinated to any particular denomination. Mann believed common schools would create virtuous citizens, an educated workforce, and a generation that could prevent moral and cultural decay. As a result of Mann's reforms, every child in the state could go to a free public school for six months out of the year. Other states soon followed Massachusetts in creating their own public schools.

Mann also believed in the importance of professionally trained teachers. Teacher colleges—called "normal schools" because they offered a uniform curriculum—developed, and more women were trained to become teachers.

William McGuffey was another person who saw the importance of public education. In a series of elementary reading books first published in 1836, McGuffey taught generations of Americans rules for living as well as rules for grammar. McGuffey believed that biblical values had a natural and necessary role for shaping character in the classroom. By the beginning of the twentieth century, 120 million copies of *McGuffey's Eclectic Readers* had been sold.

Another important figure in early American education was **Noah Webster**, who hoped to standardize American spelling and grammar usage. More than 100 million copies of his *American Spelling Book* (1782) were sold. He later published a grammar book and a reader. Webster also created *An American Dictionary of the English Language* (1828). In his dictionary, Webster frequently cited Bible passages to illustrate the meanings of words, and he emphasized the early American ideals of individual liberty and responsibility.

▶ Noah Webster

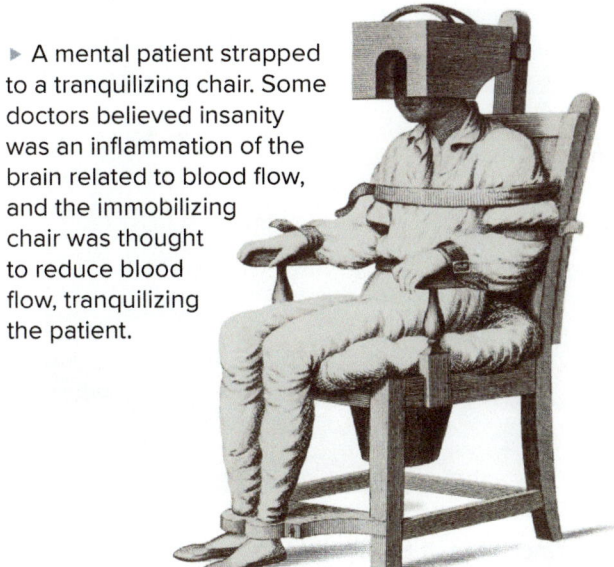

► A mental patient strapped to a tranquilizing chair. Some doctors believed insanity was an inflammation of the brain related to blood flow, and the immobilizing chair was thought to reduce blood flow, tranquilizing the patient.

## Institutional Reform

Some reformers were concerned with conditions in institutions such as insane asylums and prisons. One such reformer was **Dorothea Dix**, a quiet schoolteacher and writer. When she began teaching a Sunday school class at a Massachusetts prison in 1841, Dix found four mentally ill persons imprisoned there because officials did not know what else to do with them. At the time, mental illness was considered incurable, and facilities were designed to warehouse the mentally ill, not treat them. Secretly, Dix visited numerous prisons and insane asylums to get firsthand information about conditions for the mentally ill. She was appalled to find people chained to walls, left unclothed, and locked in underground cells. She wrote and lectured to inform the public about the situation. Through her efforts, legislatures in several states established state asylums and improved conditions for the mentally ill. Prison reformers worked to separate child prisoners from adults and move them into juvenile detention centers. Other reformers thought that prisons could become "perfected" institutions where prisoners were rehabilitated and reformed.

## Abolition

Slavery was the issue that motivated many reformers in the early 1800s. **Abolition**, the idea that slavery should be eliminated, was a growing movement. Many antislavery and abolition societies were formed, primarily in the North. Many Christians supported abolition on moral grounds. Quakers in particular had been leading advocates of abolition since colonial days.

However, not all abolitionists were religious. One important abolitionist leader was **William Lloyd Garrison**. In 1831 he launched a newspaper, the *Liberator*, dedicated to attacking the evil of slavery. Garrison's views were considered extreme by many. He was convinced that the Bible was a proslavery book, so he rejected it entirely. He also denounced the Constitution as "a covenant with death" and "an agreement with hell" because it did not condemn slavery, and he believed that the Union should be dissolved and the free states and slave states made separate countries. On one occasion he publicly burned a copy of the Constitution. Garrison alienated many Americans with his rhetoric, enraging many Northerners with his criticism of how free blacks were treated, and Southerners with his attacks on both slavery and those who owned slaves. But Garrison was unapologetic in his response:

▼ William Lloyd Garrison

> *I will be as harsh as truth, and as uncompromising as justice. On this subject, I do not wish to think, or speak, or write, with moderation. No! No! Tell a man whose house is on fire, to give a moderate alarm . . . but urge me not to use moderation in a cause like the present. I am in earnest—I will not equivocate—I will not excuse—I will not retreat a single inch—AND I WILL BE HEARD.*
>
> — **WILLIAM LLOYD GARRISON**

### Analyzing Sources

Why does Garrison insist that he cannot be moderate with his words?

Women also played prominent roles in the abolitionist movement. Foremost among them were the Grimké sisters, originally from a slave-holding family in Charleston, South Carolina. Sarah and Angelina both left the South as adults and moved to Philadelphia, where they became active with the Quakers and abolitionism. Angelina was the first woman to address the Massachusetts state legislature, promoting abolition.

Free blacks, including some former slaves, also promoted abolition, none more prominent than **Frederick Douglass.** Douglass had escaped from slavery in Maryland in 1838 and wrote his autobiography in 1845. He was invited to speak before numerous antislavery societies. Inspired by Garrison, Douglass began publishing his own abolitionist newspaper, the *North Star*, in 1847. However, Douglass later came to disagree with Garrison's view of the Constitution, holding that it was not a proslavery document and that it could be used on behalf of abolition.

▲ Frederick Douglass

▼ Sojourner Truth

Another important former slave in the abolitionist movement was Sojourner Truth, who in 1827 gained her freedom after forty years as a slave when New York enacted emancipation. She also spoke at many antislavery meetings.

Some antislavery reformers believed that gradual emancipation was a better solution than immediate abolition. They believed that slavery was a moral wrong and should be ended, yet they were concerned that freeing the slaves immediately would harm the economy for the whole nation (especially for the South), would make it difficult for freed slaves to find jobs because they lacked skills, and would raise racial tensions. Those who favored gradual emancipation believed that freeing slaves over time, as several northern states had done, would give the South time to adjust to the loss of enslaved labor without causing catastrophic economic problems, and some favored compensating slaveholders for freeing their slaves.

After studying the Bible, Baptist minister William Henry Brisbane freed the nearly thirty slaves he had inherited and exiled himself to Philadelphia. In 1847 he wrote *Slave Holding Examined in the Light of the Holy Bible* in which he stated that "slaveholding was incompatible with Christianity. If therefore, emancipation be a gradual work, it is gradual only because it is difficult to work Christianity into the hearts and the practice of mankind".

Another issue was that most Americans of the time did not believe in the equality of whites and blacks or that they could live side by side in a racially integrated society. Many reformers thought the best solution was for freed slaves to be returned to their ancestral homelands in Africa. The American Colonization Society was formed in 1816 for this purpose. The society purchased land in West Africa in 1821 in present-day Liberia. Richard Allen, who initially supported colonization, later said of America, "This land which we have watered with our *tears* and *our blood*, is now our *mother country*, and we are well satisfied to stay where wisdom abounds and the gospel is free." The colonization movement was largely unsuccessful, and only 15,000 former slaves moved to Africa between 1821 and 1860.

▶ Map of the West Coast of Africa including the colony of Liberia and its capital, Monrovia. The American Colonization Society named the city after President James Monroe, who supported African-American emigration to the colony.

## Women's Rights

In the early 1800s women were not allowed to vote, married women in some states could not own property in their names, and many women lacked the opportunity for higher education. However, many of the leading reformers in the early 1800s were women. Their activity in these movements caused some women, including abolitionist reformers Sojourner Truth and the Grimké sisters, to consider their own place in society and begin advocating for change. The first women's colleges in America were established in the 1830s. In 1848 three hundred women reformers led by Lucretia Mott and Elizabeth Cady Stanton met at the **Seneca Falls Convention** in New York, where they passed resolutions calling for women's suffrage (the right to vote) and for declaring the equality of women and men.

Industrialization had taken many men away from the home and into factories for long hours, which left women to care for house and children. This led some to separate life into two spheres, work and home, with home being considered the proper sphere for women. Some who opposed the Seneca Falls resolutions said that homemaking and raising children were noble and fulfilling tasks and that women could best affect society by modeling virtue and religious devotion in their own homes. Others were concerned with Stanton's beliefs that marriage was a form of bondage and that the church and the Bible were oppressive to women.

▼ "The First Wave" statue at the Women's Rights National Historical Park in Seneca Falls, New York, includes Elizabeth Cady Stanton (far left), Frederick Douglass, and other attendees of the Seneca Falls Convention.

THE
TEMPERANCE ALMANAC
FOR THE YEAR OF OUR LORD
1834;
CALCULATED GENERALLY FOR ALL PARTS OF THE
UNITED STATES AND CANADA;
CONTAINING, BESIDE THE USUAL ASTRONOMICAL CALCULATIONS,
MANY VALUABLE SUGGESTIONS AND IMPORTANT
STATEMENTS ON THE SUBJECT OF
TEMPERANCE.
PREPARED AND PUBLISHED UNDER THE DIRECTION OF
The Executive Committee of the New-York State
Temperance Society.
All the profits of the work, if any, are pledged to the gratuitous
diffusion of temperance intelligence.

THE GENIUS OF TEMPERANCE DESTROYING THE HYDRA.

Published and sold by L. D. [illegible], [illegible] Nassau st., New-York, and by the *N. Y. State Temperance Society,* 19 Green st. *Albany.* —Also, sold by W. C. [illegible] O. Steele, Webster & Skinner, and Hoffman & White, [illegible]—Hoyt, Porter & Co. *Rochester, N. Y.*—and by booksellers generally, in all the states.

Hoffman & White, [illegible] 71 State str[illegible]

*Price, $3 for 100 copies,—[illegible] for [illegible] cash.*

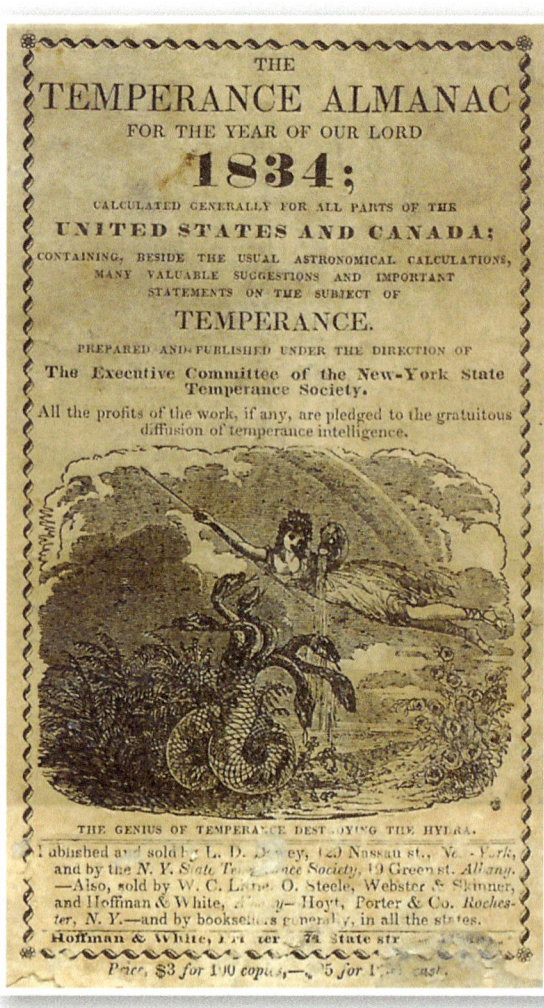

1834 Temperance Almanac

## Temperance

Alcohol was another social ill that reformers addressed. The average American adult in 1825 drank seven gallons of alcohol (mostly whiskey and hard cider) a year, and drunkenness created problems for drinkers, their families, and society generally. Employers supported the temperance movement, which opposed the consumption of alcohol, because drunkenness affected employee production and absence rates. Congregationalist minister and social reformer Henry Ward Beecher used speakers, tracts, and temperance plays to change people's attitudes toward drinking. The movement effectively reduced drunkenness and alcohol consumption and became a model for other reform movements. In 1851 Maine became the first state to pass a law prohibiting the sale or consumption of alcohol, and twelve other states followed by 1855.

## Utopian Reformers

Some Americans in the early 1800s believed that people were by nature good and that society had corrupted them. Some reformers believed that if people were placed in new, model societies that they could then achieve perfection and create heaven on earth, or **utopia** (an ideal society). While a few of these reformers operated from religious motives, others rejected Christianity and organized religion.

The Harmony Society was a religious community in Harmony, Indiana, founded in 1815 by George Rapp, who established a community based on mutual helpfulness and support. British industrialist and reformer Robert Owen purchased Harmony in 1825. Renaming it New Harmony, Owen sought to establish a perfect society based on education, science, technology, and the common ownership of property. He believed that poverty could be ended by gathering the unemployed in model communities featuring eight-hour workdays, cultural activities, and equal education for boys and girls. After two years of internal fighting and a loss of $200,000, Owen abandoned the New Harmony project.

New Harmony, Indiana

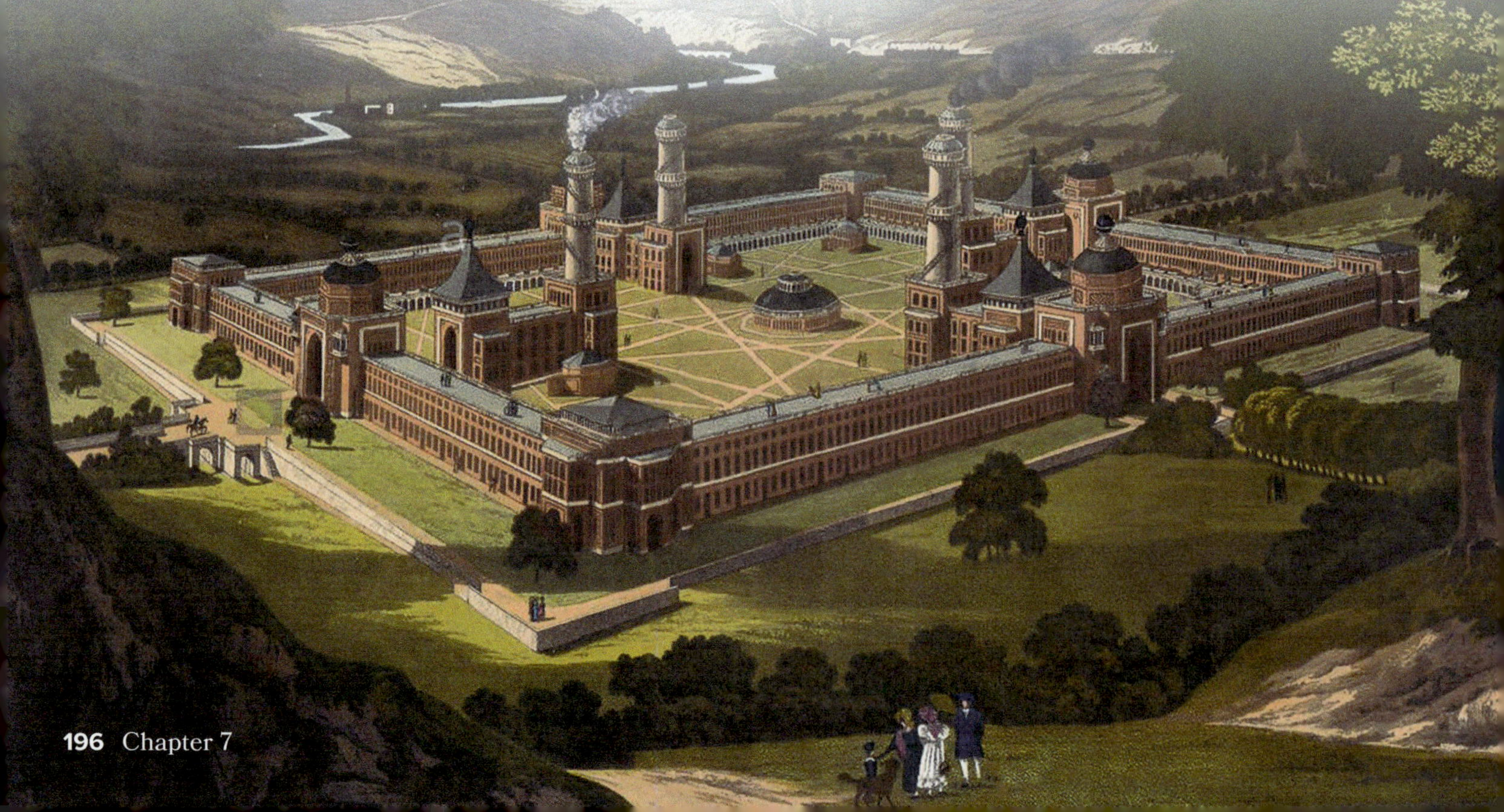

Another group that tried to develop a utopian society was the transcendentalists. Brook Farm was established in Massachusetts in 1841 as a transcendental experiment in communal living where members could do whatever work appealed to them and where study time and leisure activities were important. However, essential but unappealing tasks were left undone, and some members resented that they were doing more work than others, so leaders imposed a more structured system. The experiment at Brook Farm closed in 1847.

The Shakers, who began in England in the 1700s but enjoyed their greatest growth in America in the early 1800s, also attempted to create an ideal society. Shakers took their name from the shaking or dancing that accompanied their worship. They owned property in common and believed that their founder, Mother Ann Lee, was an incarnation of God, just as Jesus was. The Shakers built prosperous, well-ordered farms in New England, New York, Ohio, Indiana, and Kentucky. The group won many converts in the early 1800s, but it eventually died out because of its practice of celibacy.

The Oneida Community was established near Oneida, New York, in 1848 by John Humphrey Noyes. Believing that Jesus had already returned, he thought he could bring about the millennial kingdom on earth where people could reach perfection. The group practiced communal marriage and communal child-rearing, as well as "mutual criticism" in which members gathered to criticize other members as a means of individual improvement. The community came to an end in 1881.

The failures of these utopian experiments demonstrated that because man is not inherently good, creating heaven on earth is not possible.

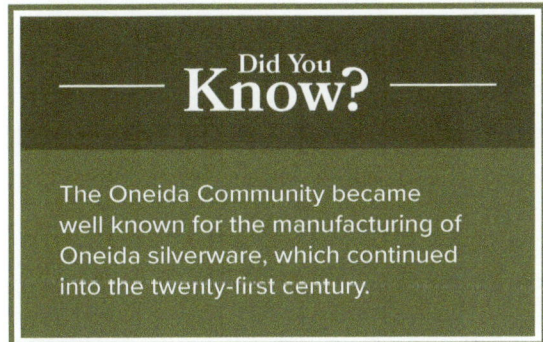

**Did You Know?**

The Oneida Community became well known for the manufacturing of Oneida silverware, which continued into the twenty-first century.

## Comprehension Check 7.3

1. What religious movement was a form of romanticism that emphasized intuition over logical reasoning?

   A deism

   B Unitarianism

   C transcendentalism

2. The eastern revival of the Second Great Awakening began at ___.

   A Harvard

   B Yale

   C a businessmen's prayer meeting

3. Each of the following is true about Horace Mann's beliefs about educational reforms except that ___.

   A education should be influenced by sectarian religion

   B the state should provide universal, free education

   C teachers should be trained in professional teacher colleges

4. Each of the following is true about William Lloyd Garrison except that he ___.

   A believed the Constitution was a "covenant with death"

   B published a newspaper which attacked slavery

   C upheld the Bible as an antislavery book

5. What former slave published an autobiography and an abolitionist newspaper?

   A Sojourner Truth

   B Frederick Douglass

   C Richard Allen

### MAKING CONNECTIONS

6. Name two "New Methods" of Charles Finney and one criticism of his methods.

7. What were three results of the Second Great Awakening on American society?

## Chapter Summary

### 7.1 Advances in Transportation

- Advances in transportation lowered the cost and time to move people and goods, encouraged westward expansion, facilitated growth in manufacturing, and increased foreign trade.

**TERMS**

Wilderness Road
National Road
Erie Canal
Robert Fulton
clipper ship
Commodore Matthew Perry

**TERMS**

Pony Express
Samuel F. B. Morse
Industrial Revolution
factory system
Samuel Slater
interchangeable parts
labor unions
John Deere
Cyrus McCormick
Eli Whitney
cotton gin

### 7.2 Advances in Technology

- Communication improved with the growth of the postal service and the creation of the Pony Express and was transformed by the invention of the telegraph.

- The Industrial Revolution began in Britain in the textile industry and led to the development of the factory system. British machinery was copied in the United States and the textile industry grew, particularly in New England.

- The development of interchangeable parts led to mass production, and the patent system encouraged invention. Industrialization brought benefits as well as new problems for society.

- Advances in agricultural technology led to an increase in production. The cotton gin made cotton production more profitable, which led to more cotton being planted and an increased demand for slaves.

### 7.3 Religion and Reform

- Some Americans questioned Christian doctrines, especially the divinity of Christ. However, the Second Great Awakening was a spiritual revival which revitalized Christianity throughout the nation.

- Reform movements developed to address society's ills. These movements included education reform, institutional reform, abolition, temperance, and women's rights. Some believed that eliminating social problems could create utopias.

**TERMS**

Unitarianism
transcendentalism
Francis Asbury
Richard Allen
Second Great Awakening
Timothy Dwight
Charles Finney
Horace Mann

Noah Webster
Dorothea Dix
abolition
William Lloyd Garrison
Frederick Douglass
Seneca Falls Convention
utopia

# Chapter Review Questions

## RECALL

1. What kind of roads, built by private companies, charged money for their use?

2. What two bodies of water did the Erie Canal connect?

3. What invention solved the problem of upstream river transportation?

4. With what two Asian nations did the United States establish trade relations in the late 1700s to mid-1800s?

5. What was the first economically successful railroad line in the United States?

6. What were two inventions that accelerated the growth of railroads?

7. What invention caused the Pony Express to go bankrupt after just eighteen months in service?

8. Where did the Industrial Revolution begin and in what industry?

9. What movement began among businessmen in New York City in 1857?

10. What country was established by the American Colonization Society for the relocation of freed slaves? What was its capital?

11. What issue did the temperance movement seek to reform?

## UNDERSTAND

12. What were three effects of the Transportation Revolution?

13. What was significant about the funding of the National Road?

14. What were two weaknesses of canals?

15. What were two effects of steamboat transportation?

16. How did clipper ships change sea trade?

17. How did Commodore Matthew Perry open trade relations with Japan?

18. How did advances in communication change American society?

19. Describe three features of the factory system.

20. How did Samuel Slater bring the Industrial Revolution to the United States?

21. What were three reasons New England was a natural site for the textile industry?

22. What was the significance of the development of interchangeable parts?

23. What were three positive and three negative effects of industrialization?

24. What was the purpose of the first labor unions?

25. What impact did the cotton gin have on cotton production and slavery in the South?

26. What were two of Charles Finney's "New Methods," and what were two criticisms of his methods?

27. What were three effects of the Second Great Awakening on American society?

28. What were two reforms Horace Mann believed were needed in education?

29. What was William Lloyd Garrison's view of the Constitution and the Bible?

30. How did Frederick Douglass's view of the Constitution differ from Garrison's?

31. Name two reasons some antislavery reformers favored gradual emancipation over immediate abolition.

## THINK ABOUT IT

32. How should Christians view technology?

33. Choose a technology from this chapter and evaluate how it helped humans wisely exercise dominion over Creation and how its use demonstrated the effects of the Fall.

34. Compare and contrast the eastern and western revivals of the Second Great Awakening.

35. What did most utopian reformers believe about human nature and the source of society's problems? Why did these utopian experiments fail?

# 8 Manifest Destiny

8.1 Texas
8.2 The Mexican War
8.3 Westward Expansion

▲ Pioneers on the Great Plains

Since the founding of the first settlements on the Atlantic coast, Americans had been pushing westward to settle the continent. The 1840s saw that pattern continue with a rush of expansion that stretched the United States to the Pacific Ocean. Supporting and motivating this growth was a controversial philosophy. In 1845 New York journalist John Louis O'Sullivan both named and described this philosophy when he wrote,

> *Our manifest destiny [is] to overspread and to possess the whole of the continent which Providence has given us for the development of the great experiment of liberty and federative self-government entrusted to us.* — JOHN LOUIS O'SULLIVAN

**Analyzing Sources**

On what basis did O'Sullivan justify westward expansion?

The idea of **Manifest Destiny**—that America was divinely ordained to possess the entire North American continent—dominated American thinking in the 1840s. Some, however, questioned this idea. They thought the United States should trade with and seek to convert Mexicans and Native Americans in the West, but that God had not given the right to take the land by force or by fraud.

The constant stream of pioneers along the trails began to populate the West. It also increased tension between the United States and both Mexico and Great Britain.

## 8.1 Texas

How did Texas become a state?

### Texas Attracts Settlers

The territory of Texas had been explored and claimed by Spain in the 1500s, but settlement of the area remained sparse into the 1800s. Only a few Catholic mission settlements were established by the Spanish, and Spain lacked power to control the Comanche and Apache and foreign settlers.

To attract settlers who would subdue the Native Americans and make Texas a buffer state between Mexico and the United States, Spain established the empresario system. Empresarios (Spanish for *contractors*) bought large tracts of land cheaply in Texas. In return, the empresarios promised to fill the land with settlers and govern their settlements. In 1821 Moses Austin from Missouri received permission from Spain to bring three hundred families to Texas, but he died before he could begin the journey. His son **Stephen Austin** became empresario in his father's place.

When Austin arrived in Texas in the fall of 1821, he learned that Mexico had gained its independence from Spain. The Mexican government continued the empresario system but established several conditions. Settlers would be free from paying taxes for ten years, but in return they agreed to become Mexican citizens, follow Mexican law, and convert to Roman Catholicism. The law allowed settlers to bring slaves to Texas but prohibited the buying and selling of slaves and declared the children born to slaves in Mexican territory free at age fourteen. Under Austin's leadership, his settlement prospered, and more Americans arrived to take advantage of the riches of the new land. Cotton growing and cattle raising became major businesses in Texas.

### GUIDING QUESTIONS

- Why did American settlers move to Texas while it belonged to Mexico?

- How did Texas become an independent nation?

- How did Texas become a state?

- What were the goals and achievements of the Polk administration?

▲ Stephen Austin

▼ Antonio López de Santa Anna

At first, Texans accepted Mexican citizenship, but few adopted Mexican customs or viewed Mexico as their country. In 1826 an American empresario attempted to declare his land independent of Mexico, but Mexican troops and militia from Austin's colony dispersed the rebels. By 1830 Texas had over ten thousand settlers from the United States, vastly outnumbering Mexican settlers. Fearing the growth of American settlement and attempts to break Texas away from Mexico, the Mexican government in 1830 closed Texas to additional American immigrants, instituted a tax on goods imported from the United States, and banned the import of slaves (although indentured servants were allowed).

These new laws angered many Texan settlers, who felt that slaves and new immigrants were necessary for the growth and success of their settlements, and the laws were often ignored. The number of settlers continued to increase, and slaves continued to be brought into Texas (sometimes renamed indentured servants to conform to Mexico's law). Austin, hoping to prevent a revolt against Mexico, traveled to Mexico City in 1833 to ask for lower taxes and for the American settlements to be made into a separate Mexican state. However, when Mexican authorities discovered that Austin had instructed the Texans to begin creating a state government regardless of the outcome of his meeting, he was arrested and imprisoned for over a year.

## Texas Fights for Independence

In 1833 General **Antonio López de Santa Anna** was elected president of Mexico. In 1834 he discarded the Mexican constitution of 1824 and declared himself dictator. When Austin was released from prison, he urged the Texans to prepare to fight to defend the Mexican constitution of 1824, which guaranteed them a degree of self-government within Mexico. However, when Santa Anna approached Texas with a large army, the Texans called for complete independence from Mexico.

The Texans enjoyed early military success. At Gonzalez the Texans forced the Mexican troops to retreat to San Antonio. The Texans also captured the Mexican supply base at Goliad. Following these victories, the Texans laid siege to San Antonio in December 1835, pushing the Mexican forces out of the area.

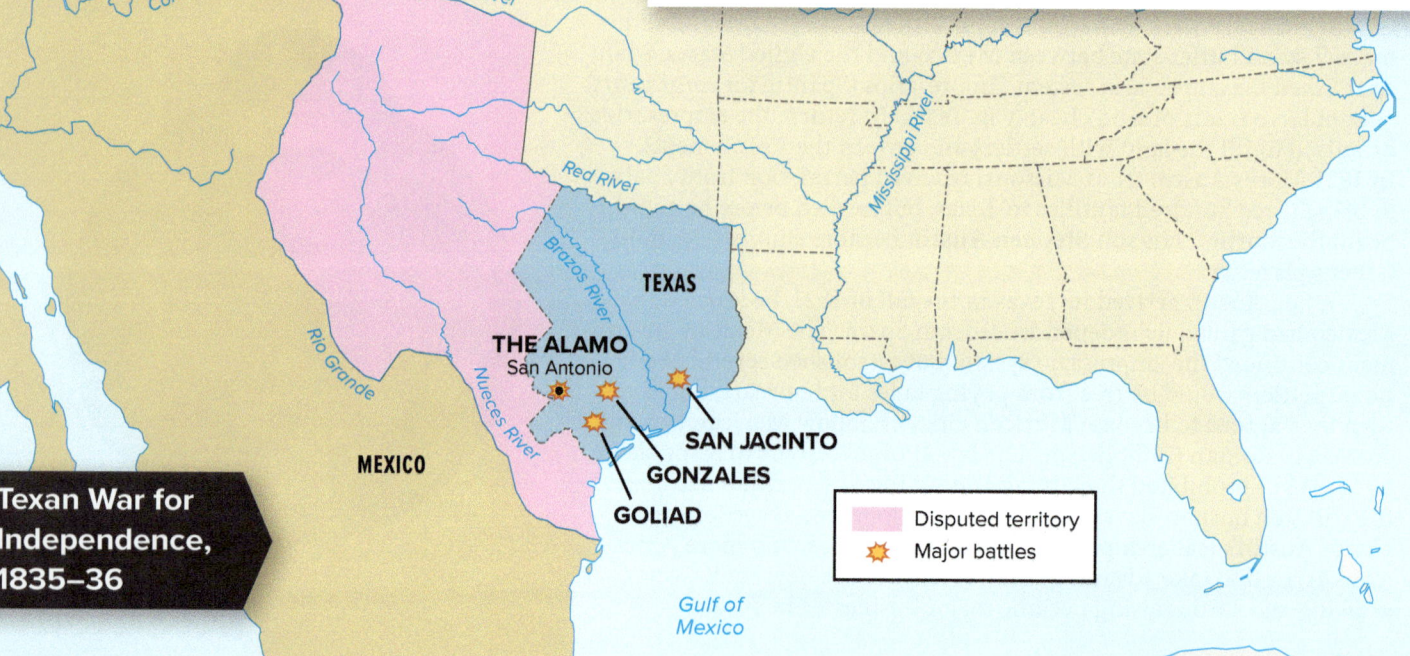

Colorado River

Arkansas River

Red River

Mississippi River

Brazos River

TEXAS

Rio Grande

Nueces River

THE ALAMO
San Antonio

SAN JACINTO

GONZALES

MEXICO

GOLIAD

Disputed territory

Major battles

Gulf of Mexico

**Texan War for Independence, 1835–36**

▼ Artist's rendering of the Battle of the Alamo

**Sam Houston**, a veteran of the War of 1812, joined the Texan forces. Houston ordered the forces in San Antonio, which were posted at a small abandoned Spanish mission called the **Alamo**, to destroy the post and fall back. But the commanders at the Alamo, Jim Bowie and William Travis, decided to hold the post to block a Mexican advance. In February 1836, Santa Anna marched into San Antonio with five thousand men and laid siege to the Alamo. Almost 190 defenders, including Bowie, Travis, and Davy Crockett, held out for thirteen days, and they inflicted about six hundred casualties on the Mexicans. On March 6 the Mexicans stormed the mission and all the occupants except for a few women, children, and slaves were killed.

## Did You Know?

**Davy Crockett**, famous frontiersman, fought in the Creek campaign of 1813–14 and served in the Tennessee legislature and the US House of Representatives as a Democrat. Because he disagreed strongly with President Jackson over Indian removal and other issues, Crockett switched to the Whig Party. Defeated for reelection to Congress in 1834, Crockett led a company of Tennessee riflemen to join the Texan War for Independence and was killed at the Alamo.

▲ The Dodson Tri-Color flag, the first flag of the Lone Star Republic

While the battle at the Alamo was occurring, delegates from throughout Texas were gathering more than 150 miles away. They declared independence from Mexico, adopted a constitution based on the US Constitution but with specific protection of slavery, and became the Republic of Texas, or the **Lone Star Republic**.

Just two weeks after the defeat at the Alamo, the Texans suffered another devastating defeat at Goliad, where the Texan forces were surrounded. The Texan commander surrendered, and the Mexican army executed over three hundred Texan prisoners.

After the defeats at the Alamo and Goliad, Houston was appointed commander of all Texan forces. Knowing he had limited troops, Houston moved his army east and avoided any large battle with Santa Anna until the time was right. Santa Anna divided his army into three parts: one to capture the Texan government, one to protect his supply line, and one to fight Houston's army. On April 21, 1836, Houston found his opportunity to fight Santa Anna in a surprise attack near the San Jacinto River. In the brief but bloody **Battle of San Jacinto**, eight hundred Texans—many shouting, "Remember the Alamo! Remember Goliad!"—defeated the Mexicans, killing about 630 and capturing 730 men, including Santa Anna. Houston forced Santa Anna to agree to remove his troops to south of the Rio Grande and to sign a treaty recognizing Texan independence. The Mexican legislature overthrew Santa Anna and refused to recognize the treaty, but they did not launch another military campaign against the Texans.

The Texans had won their independence, and Sam Houston was elected president of the Lone Star Republic in 1836. However, most Texans preferred to join the United States, and Texas applied for admission as a state in 1836. President Andrew Jackson realized that accepting it into the Union might spark a war with Mexico, which still claimed ownership of Texas. Jackson also knew that antislavery forces in the United States opposed annexing Texas because it would almost certainly enter as a slave state. Thus, Jackson recognized Texas as independent but did not support it becoming a new state. During its ten-year history as an independent republic, Texas grew to a population of 125,000, including 25,000 slaves.

## Sam Houston

Sam Houston was a soldier, statesman, and adventurer. As a teenager in East Tennessee, Houston ran away from home and lived with the Cherokee for three years, who gave him the name "the Raven" and later adopted him.

At the age of twenty-three, Houston served as a lieutenant under Andrew Jackson at the Battle of Horseshoe Bend. He received an arrow in the thigh and two bullets in the shoulder while leading a daring charge. In 1823 he was elected as one of Tennessee's representatives to Congress and became governor of Tennessee four years later. He remained an advocate for the Cherokee during his political career.

When his wife of only three months left him, Houston resigned as governor and moved to Texas, where he tried to drown his troubles in alcohol. The Native Americans gave him a new name: "Big Drunk." But the Texan War for Independence gave him new purpose and drive. His natural leadership and military talents won him the command of the Texan forces. After his decisive victory at San Jacinto, Houston was the most popular man in Texas. He served two terms as the president of the Republic of Texas. After Texas joined the Union, Houston was elected as a US senator and, later, governor of the state.

The final crisis of Houston's career came in 1860 when he was governor. Texans strongly favored joining the other Southern states in seceding from the Union, but Houston opposed secession. When the Texan government ordered all officials to take an oath of allegiance to the Confederacy, Houston refused and resigned as governor. He died in 1863. Texas's largest city bears his name.

# Texas Becomes a State

After Texas won its independence, the new republic still faced the possibility that Mexico would try to reclaim its lost territory. Houston sought security from the United States, but also approached Britain. Houston thought that the British, who already shared control of Oregon, might want to expand their influence in the hemisphere. He hoped that when the United States saw the potential for British influence in Texas, American lawmakers would be motivated to annex Texas to keep it out of British hands. Also, proslavery Americans feared that if Britain controlled Texas, it would abolish slavery there as it had in the rest of its empire. Houston had to convince American lawmakers that annexation would not lead to war with Mexico.

President Tyler (see Chapter 6) authorized the negotiation of a secret treaty with Houston for the annexation of Texas. When the treaty was brought before the Senate in 1844, Secretary of State John C. Calhoun wrote a letter stating that annexation was necessary to preserve the institution of slavery. His letter inflamed antislavery leaders, who were joined in opposition by those who feared annexation would lead to war, and the Senate voted to reject the treaty.

As the 1844 presidential election approached, the Whigs abandoned President Tyler and supported Henry Clay, who opposed the annexation of Texas. It was assumed by many that the Democrats would nominate former president Martin Van Buren, who also opposed annexation. Instead, at the urging of proslavery leaders and Andrew Jackson, the Democrats nominated **James K. Polk** of Tennessee as their candidate. Though not well-known nationally, Polk was politically experienced. He had served for fourteen years in the House of Representatives, including four years as Speaker of the House, and had been the governor of Tennessee. His close association with Jackson earned him the nickname "Young Hickory." Polk ran on a platform that called for "all of Oregon, all of Texas." This appealed to Northerners and Southerners who favored expansion in a way that balanced Northern and Southern interests.

As annexation gained support nationally, Clay changed his position, declaring that he could support annexing Texas if it would not result in war with Mexico. Opponents of slavery objected to Clay's shift, and many switched their support to third-party candidate James Birney of the antislavery Liberty Party. Polk, pledging to serve only one term, won the electoral vote by a count of 170 to Clay's 105. The popular vote was much closer, with Polk defeating Clay by only 39,000 votes out of 2.7 million cast.

## The Election of 1844

ME 9
VT 6
NH 6
NY 36
MA 12
RI 4
CT 6
PA 26
NJ 7
DE 3
MD 8
WISCONSIN TERRITORY
MI 5
IOWA TERRITORY
IL 9
IN 12
OH 23
VA 17
KY 12
MO 7
NC 11
TN 13
SC 9
AR 3
GA 10
MS 6
AL 9
LA 6
REPUBLIC OF TEXAS
FLORIDA TERRITORY

**James K. Polk (D)**
Electoral: 170
Popular: 1,337,243

**Henry Clay (W)**
Electoral: 105
Popular: 1,299,062

▲ James K. Polk

After the 1844 election but before Polk took office, President Tyler took the election results as a mandate for the annexation of Texas. Tyler realized that he could not obtain the two-thirds majority needed in the Senate to ratify a treaty of annexation, so he proposed to annex the region through a joint resolution of Congress, an action that required only a simple majority in both houses. The resolution passed, and Tyler signed it in March 1845, just days before leaving office. Texas became the twenty-eighth state in the Union. Outraged, the Mexican government severed diplomatic relations with the United States.

## Polk's Administration

Polk outlined four goals for his administration. He wanted to lower the tariff, restore the independent treasury system of Van Buren, settle the Oregon question, and acquire California from Mexico. The Democratic majority in Congress passed bills that accomplished Polk's first two goals.

As mentioned in Chapter 6, the United States and Great Britain occupied the Oregon Territory jointly until the two nations could decide how to divide the area. The Oregon Territory included the present states of Oregon, Washington, and Idaho, as well as parts of Wyoming and Montana. It also included a sizable portion of land in present-day Canada. At first, Britain did more toward developing the territory. Attracted by Oregon's abundance of beaver and other animals, British fur traders and trappers flocked to the region, but few permanent settlements were established. In 1840 the number of European settlers was only two hundred. As the 1840s proceeded, however, new settlers began entering the territory via the Oregon Trail (discussed later in this chapter). As a result, Oregon became far more American than British and joint occupation seemed less satisfactory to many Americans.

The Oregon country stretched from 42° latitude in the south to 54°40' latitude in the north. Many expansionists clamored for the United States to take the whole region. Their slogans were "Fifty-four, forty or fight!" and "All of Oregon or none!" The British, on the other hand, had long maintained that the proper boundary should be the Columbia River, a border that would have given most of the present state of Washington to Canada. Some felt only war with Britain would settle the Oregon issue.

Though Polk had campaigned on the promise of "All of Oregon," he was willing to compromise on the issue. He offered to extend the US-Canadian border along the 49th parallel, the line that formed the border from Minnesota to the Rockies. Because the fur trade had declined along the Columbia River, the British were more open to compromise as well. In 1846 the two nations signed a treaty that settled the Oregon question by making the 49th parallel the international boundary to the Pacific, but Britain retained all of Vancouver Island. Though Polk upset the most passionate expansionists, he made what most Americans considered a fair settlement.

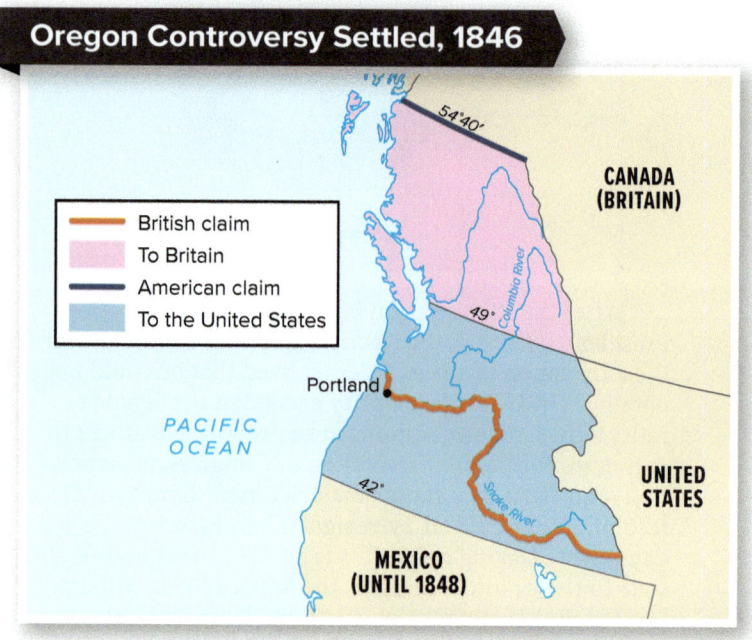

**Oregon Controversy Settled, 1846**

- British claim
- To Britain
- American claim
- To the United States

54°40'

CANADA (BRITAIN)

Columbia River

49°

Portland

PACIFIC OCEAN

42°

Snake River

UNITED STATES

MEXICO (UNTIL 1848)

## Polk's Goals

1. LOWER THE TARIFF
2. RESTORE INDEPENDENT TREASURY
3. SETTLE OREGON QUESTION
4. ACQUIRE CALIFORNIA

### Comprehension Check 8.1

1. Which of the following was an empresario who brought American settlers to Texas?
   - **A** Stephen Austin
   - **B** Sam Houston
   - **C** Davy Crockett

2. The battle in which the Texans captured Santa Anna and forced him to recognize Texas's independence was the Battle of ____.
   - **A** the Alamo
   - **B** Goliad
   - **C** San Jacinto

3. Texas was annexed into the United States in the last days of ____'s presidency.
   - **A** Van Buren
   - **B** Tyler
   - **C** Polk

4. Polk avoided war with Britain by agreeing to the ____ parallel as the boundary between Oregon and Canada.
   - **A** 45th
   - **B** 49th
   - **C** 54th degree 40 minute

### MAKING CONNECTIONS

5. What was Manifest Destiny, and why did some oppose this idea?

# The Mexican War

What were the causes and results of the Mexican War?

GUIDING QUESTIONS

- What caused the Mexican War?
- What happened in the Mexican War?
- What were the results of the Mexican War?

## Causes of the War

Polk hoped to achieve his fourth goal, acquiring California, through diplomacy if possible, but was willing to take it by force if negotiations failed. In 1845 the president of Mexico invited Polk to send a representative to negotiate with Mexico to settle the dispute over Texas. Polk sent John Slidell with instructions to offer $30 million to purchase California and New Mexico and gain Mexico's recognition of Texas's annexation. But when Slidell arrived, the Mexican president refused to meet with him because of political pressure from his opponents, who were against negotiating with the United States. The Mexican president was then overthrown in a military coup and replaced with a general who vowed to retake Texas from the United States.

The Mexicans claimed that the southern border of Texas was the Nueces River, which had been the southern boundary of Texas when it was a Mexican state. However, Texas claimed that the Rio Grande was the border, over one hundred miles further south, and this was the border that President Polk supported. Polk sent a force under General **Zachary Taylor** into the disputed area between the two rivers with orders to keep the Mexican forces from crossing the Rio Grande. Polk believed this action would provoke the Mexicans into war.

The Mexicans demanded that Taylor's forces leave the disputed territory and posted an army on the southern bank of the Rio Grande. On April 25, 1846, Mexican troops attacked a detachment of American cavalry on the northern side of the river. More than a dozen American soldiers were killed or wounded. Polk, who was already preparing to ask Congress to declare war on Mexico when news reached him of this incident, now had his justification for war. In his message to Congress asking for a war declaration, he said that Mexico had "shed American blood on American soil." On May 13, 1846, Congress approved the president's request and war was declared.

Many Americans welcomed news of the war. Some believed it was necessary to defend American territory against Mexican attacks. Some feared that if the United States did not take California and New Mexico, the British would. Others saw it as an opportunity to expand America's borders, and some Southerners hoped it would result in the addition of new slave states to the Union.

▶ Zachary Taylor, "Old Rough and Ready"

However, many Americans opposed the war. Antislavery leaders criticized the war because of its possible expansion of slave territory. Frederick Douglass said, "The war . . . was [begun] with no higher or holier motive than that of upholding and propagating (causing to spread) slavery." Pennsylvania congressman David Wilmot proposed an amendment to a bill appropriating funds for the war that would have prohibited slavery or involuntary servitude in any territory acquired from Mexico. The **Wilmot Proviso** (covered in more detail in Chapter 9) outraged proslavery Americans and was defeated in the Senate.

Others opposed the war because they believed Polk's justification for it was unfounded. James Waddel Alexander, a Presbyterian minister, writing to a friend about the Mexican War, said: "It is a war of pretexts. None of the alleged causes existed. . . . Never have I so much feared the judgments of God on us as a nation." Even Southerner John C. Calhoun spoke out against the war. He explained his reasons:

### Analyzing Sources

Why did Calhoun consider the war unjust and dangerous?

> *I opposed the war . . . not only because I considered it unnecessary, and that it might have been easily avoided; not only because I thought the President had no authority to order a portion of the territory in dispute and in possession of the Mexicans, to be occupied by our troops; not only because I believed the allegations upon which it was sanctioned by Congress, were unfounded in truth; but . . . because I believed it would lead to great and serious evils to the country, and greatly endanger its free institutions.* — JOHN C. CALHOUN

As the war dragged on, further opposition arose. Almost eighteen months after voting to declare war, the House of Representatives narrowly passed a resolution stating that the conflict had been "unnecessarily and unconstitutionally begun by the President of the United States." The Senate did not approve the resolution. Some opponents simply referred to it as "Mr. Polk's War." Young Whig congressman Abraham Lincoln of Illinois introduced a resolution in December 1847 that called for the administration to announce the exact spot of the Mexican attack. That way Congress could decide whether the war had actually begun on US soil. His motion, popularly known as the "**Spot Resolution**," was never acted upon. As some expansionists pushed for the acquisition not just of California and New Mexico, but all of Mexico, Calhoun feared that expansion into Mexico would strengthen the federal government and weaken the states. He warned that "Mexico is to us the forbidden fruit; the penalty of eating it would be to subject our institutions to political death."

## Two Views *of the* Mexican War

### Opposition to the War

Ulysses S. Grant, who later served as US president, was a lieutenant during the war. Almost four decades after the war ended, he wrote, "To this day [I] regard the war . . . as one of the most unjust ever waged by a stronger against a weaker nation. It was an instance of a republic following the bad example of European monarchies, in not considering justice in their desire to acquire additional territory."

US representative Nicholas Trist negotiated the treaty that ended the conflict. Just prior to the treaty signing, a Mexican representative commented to him, "This must be a proud moment for you; no less proud for you than it is humiliating for us." Trist responded, "We are making peace, let that be our only thought." Later, Trist wrote to his wife, "Could those Mexicans have seen into my heart at that moment, they would have known that my feeling of shame as an American was far stronger than theirs could be as Mexicans. For though it would not have done for me to say so there, that was a thing for every right minded American to be ashamed of, and I was ashamed of it, most cordially and intensely ashamed of it."

▲ Nicholas Trist

### Support for the War

In President James K. Polk's war message to Congress on May 11, 1846, he stated, "The strong desire to establish peace with Mexico on . . . honorable terms, and the readiness of this [US] Government to regulate and adjust our boundary and other causes of difference with that power . . . induced me . . . to seek the reopening of diplomatic relations. . . . An envoy [representative] of the United States repaired [went] to Mexico with full powers to adjust every existing difference. . . . The Mexican Government not only refused to receive him or listen to his propositions, but after a long-continued series of menaces have at last invaded our territory and shed the blood of our fellow-citizens on our own soil. . . .

Thus the Government of Mexico, though solemnly pledged by official acts in October last to receive . . . an American envoy, . . . refused the offer of a peaceful adjustment of our difficulties. Not only was the offer rejected, but the indignity of its rejection was enhanced by the manifest breach of faith in refusing to admit the envoy who came because they had bound themselves to receive him. . . . [The] Mexican Government refused all negotiation. . . .

As war exists, and, notwithstanding all our efforts to avoid it, exists by the act of Mexico herself . . .

. . . I invoke [ask] the prompt action of Congress to recognize the existence of the war, and to place at the disposition of the Executive the means of prosecuting the war with vigor, and thus hastening the restoration of peace."

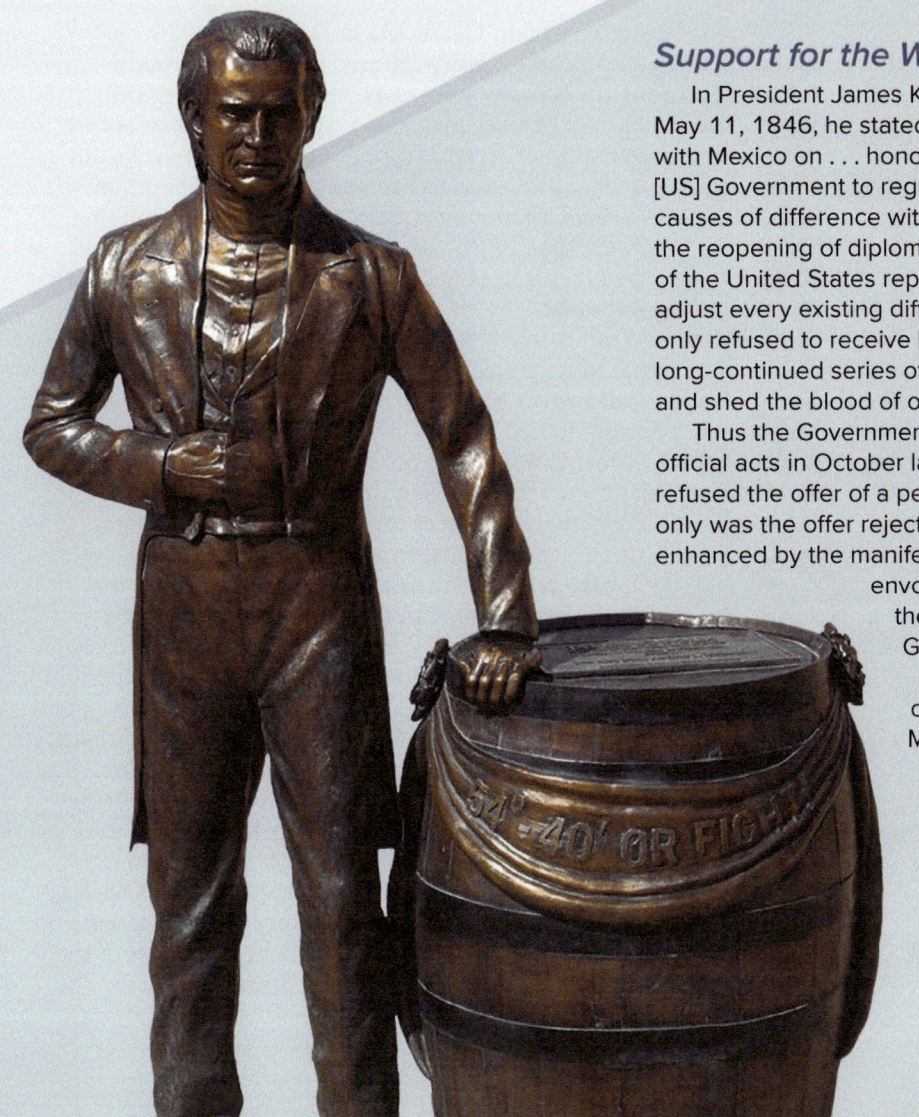

◀ Statue of James K. Polk in South Dakota

# Fighting the War

The US military was not well-prepared for the war. The regular army had only seven thousand men. Over 70,000 additional Americans volunteered to fight, but they often proved unruly and undisciplined. However, under the leadership of generals such as Winfield Scott and Zachary Taylor, American forces won decisive victories over the Mexican army.

The course of the Mexican War can be divided into four military campaigns: the New Mexico campaign, the California campaign, Taylor's campaign in northern Mexico, and Scott's campaign in central Mexico.

## In the West

### NEW MEXICO CAMPAIGN

Polk appointed General Stephen Kearny to lead a force of 1,500 men, mostly cavalry, down the Santa Fe Trail (discussed later in this chapter) to capture New Mexico. Kearny's army left Fort Leavenworth (in present-day Kansas) on June 5, 1846, and captured Santa Fe on August 18, encountering little resistance. Leaving most of his troops to occupy the newly conquered province, Kearny took part of his men west to aid in the conquest of California. Those who remained in New Mexico put down a number of uprisings by New Mexicans and Pueblo who resisted American rule.

### CALIFORNIA CAMPAIGN

When Kearny arrived in California in December 1846, he found that Americans had already claimed it. In 1845 Captain **John C. Frémont**, an explorer known as "the Pathfinder of the West," had led a group of sixty men into California on a surveying trip, but Frémont had instructions from Polk that if war broke out with Mexico, his expedition was to become a military operation. Frémont's party joined a group of American settlers near Sonoma, California, who were rebelling against Mexican rule. On June 15, 1846, they declared themselves to be an independent country called the "**Bear Flag Republic**."

Frémont had not received word that the United States had declared war against Mexico weeks earlier. In July an American naval fleet arrived at California's Monterey Bay with the news that war had started. Frémont joined forces with the naval commander, who declared that California was now a possession of the United States, and the short history of the Bear Flag Republic came to an end.

▼ California's state flag

The American forces quickly subdued California. Initially, most Californians greeted the Americans enthusiastically. The harsh treatment that some American soldiers displayed toward the Mexican Californians, however, quickly soured relations. The Mexicans recaptured Los Angeles. At this point, Kearny arrived from New Mexico with his men. With an army consisting of Frémont's "explorers," armed settlers, marines from the American fleet, and Kearny's cavalry, the Americans recaptured Los Angeles. By January 1847 California was under the control of the United States.

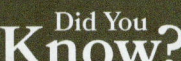

Map labels:

OREGON TERRITORY

UNORGANIZED TERRITORY

Sutter's Fort
San Francisco
Frémont 1846
Frémont 1845–46

CALIFORNIA

Bent's Fort
Kearny 1846
Ft. Leavenworth
St. Louis

Colorado River
Missouri River

**LOS ANGELES**

Stockton 1846

San Diego
Santa Fe
Kearny
Kearny 1846
**NEW MEXICO**

Red River
Pecos River
Brazos River

Sloat 1846
Rio Grande
Nueces R.
San Antonio
Mississippi River

PACIFIC OCEAN

Corpus Christi
New Orleans

**MONTERREY**
Taylor 1846
Saltillo
**PALO ALTO**
Matamoros
Scott 1846
Gulf of Mexico

**BUENA VISTA**

Mazatlán
Tampico
Scott 1847

Mexico City

**CHAPULTEPEC**
Veracruz
**CERRO GORDO**

## In Mexico

### TAYLOR IN NORTHERN MEXICO

Zachary Taylor, the commander of the troops on the Rio Grande, was a veteran of the War of 1812 and several Native American wars. Nicknamed "Old Rough and Ready" by his men, Taylor dressed sloppily and lacked the distinguished image of many generals. However, Taylor began the campaign in northern Mexico with two important victories, driving the Mexicans from the Rio Grande. Then, gathering his force of 6,600 men, Taylor marched to Monterrey, the main city of northern Mexico, and confronted a well-entrenched force of 7,000 Mexicans. For three days (September 21–23, 1846), the Americans assaulted Monterrey's fortifications. After the forts fell, fierce street fighting followed as the Americans battled house by house toward the city's central plaza. As the fighting became more desperate, the Mexican commander finally surrendered.

Despite Taylor's victory at Monterrey, the Mexican government refused to make peace. Polk decided to take the war to Mexico City to force the Mexicans to surrender. At the same time, many Whigs were speaking of running Taylor for president. To take the attention off Taylor, Polk—a Democrat—gave command of the Mexico City campaign to General **Winfield Scott**. To boost his own troop strength, Scott took the best of Taylor's men, leaving Taylor with only 4,500 volunteers. After Scott removed the troops, Taylor found himself facing an army of 15,000 Mexicans under the leadership of Santa Anna, who had returned as Mexico's president in August 1846. In the Battle of Buena Vista (February 22–23, 1847), Taylor's outnumbered army held out in a desperate defensive battle that brought the Americans as close as they came to defeat during the entire war. Finally, the exhausted Mexicans retreated to Mexico City to meet the next American attack.

### Did You Know?

New recruits often failed to recognize their poorly dressed, rumpled-looking general, Zachary Taylor. One new lieutenant, seeing Taylor sitting behind his tent cleaning his sword, unwittingly asked him if he would take a dollar to clean the lieutenant's sword too. "Sure thing," replied the general cheerfully.

Winfield Scott, "Old Fuss and Feathers"

## SCOTT IN CENTRAL MEXICO

Scott, called "Old Fuss and Feathers" by his men because of his love for military formality and discipline, was not as popular with the soldiers as Taylor, but he had a better grasp of strategy. Scott's army landed near the Mexican port of Veracruz in early March 1847 and captured the city in less than three weeks. Santa Anna, having recovered from his setback at Buena Vista, blocked the Americans' path to Mexico City. By quick movement and shrewd maneuvering, Scott drove the Mexicans back toward their capital. In August and September, the Americans and Mexicans engaged in a series of bloody battles outside Mexico City. As the Americans edged nearer, Santa Anna realized the hopelessness of his cause. With his army defeated, Santa Anna abandoned the city. Scott led the victorious Americans into Mexico City on September 14, 1847.

▼ Scott's forces entering Mexico City

## Results of the Mexican War

The loss of Mexico City was the final blow to Santa Anna's government. He resigned in disgrace, and a new government began negotiating with the United States. In the resulting **Treaty of Guadalupe Hidalgo**, Mexico ceded New Mexico and California to the United States. The **Mexican Cession** totaled over 500,000 square miles and included the future states of California, Utah, Nevada, and parts of New Mexico, Arizona, Colorado, and Wyoming. The treaty also recognized American claims to Texas southward to the Rio Grande. In return, the United States paid Mexico $15 million and agreed to pay $3.25 million in debts that Mexico owed to American citizens.

### Did You Know?

About 1,700 Americans died in combat in the Mexican War, but more than 11,000 perished from such diseases as dysentery (an intestinal disorder), malaria, measles, and mumps. Over 16,000 Mexican soldiers died from combat and disease.

Besides the vast expansion of territory, the Mexican War had several other important results. It opened the Pacific coast and its ports to trade, particularly with Asia. It made Zachary Taylor a hero and would eventually propel him to the White House (see Chapter 9). It was a training ground for American soldiers, many of whom became officers who would later fight against one another in the Civil War. And it reopened national controversy, as the status of slavery in the Mexican Cession would be fiercely contested. Author Ralph Waldo Emerson commented:

> *The United States will conquer Mexico, but it will be as the man [who] swallows the arsenic, which brings him down in turn. Mexico will poison us.* — **RALPH WALDO EMERSON**

Five years later, in 1853, the United States paid Mexico $10 million for land on the southern border of Arizona and New Mexico. The land, known as the **Gadsden Purchase**, was valued as a path for a possible transcontinental railroad. Ironically, the Mexican president who negotiated the purchase was Santa Anna, who had regained control of the government only months earlier. He was later overthrown, partly in reaction to the sale. The Gadsden Purchase finalized the continental United States at its current boundaries. It was in many ways the climax of Manifest Destiny.

## Mexico: Dress Rehearsal *for the* Civil War

The Mexican War was the first conflict in which graduates of West Point, the United States Military Academy, played a major role. The battlefields of Mexico furthered the training of West Point graduates who would soon be on the battlefields of the Civil War.

Among the young officers who gained distinction in Mexico was Captain Robert E. Lee, an engineer on General Scott's staff in central Mexico. While scouting the field at Cerro Gordo, Lee found a potential route for the Americans that would allow them to slip behind the Mexican position. As he scouted the route, Lee suddenly heard the voices of Mexican soldiers. After scrambling behind a log, he lay completely still while a party of Mexican soldiers gathered and talked. Some of them even sat on the log behind which Lee was hiding. After several hours, the Mexicans left, and Lee hurried back to Scott's headquarters. Using the information Lee supplied, the American army outflanked Santa Anna and won a decisive victory.

Other future generals served as lieutenants under Scott in Mexico. Ulysses Grant showed great ingenuity under Scott in central Mexico. Thomas J. Jackson also won praise for his bravery with an artillery unit in the attack on Mexico City. As bullets and shells whizzed around him, Jackson walked about in the open, calling, "There is no danger. See! I am not hit." Eventually, over two hundred US officers in the Mexican War later served as generals in the Civil War, often on opposing sides.

### Analyzing Sources

What did Emerson mean when he said "Mexico will poison us"?

### Comprehension Check 8.2

1. The United States claimed that the border between Texas and Mexico was the ____.
   - **A** Nueces River
   - **B** Rio Grande
   - **C** San Jacinto River

2. Who was the "Pathfinder of the West," who helped establish the Bear Flag Republic?
   - **A** John C. Frémont
   - **B** Zachary Taylor
   - **C** Stephen Kearny

3. Each of the following was a result of the Mexican War except ____.
   - **A** it trained American soldiers who fought in the Civil War
   - **B** it resolved the issue of slavery permanently
   - **C** it opened Pacific ports to American trade with Asia

4. The ____ Purchase completed the acquisition of the continental United States.
   - **A** Wilmot
   - **B** Guadalupe Hidalgo
   - **C** Gadsden

#### MAKING CONNECTIONS

5. What were two arguments for and two arguments against the War with Mexico?

GUIDING QUESTIONS

- Why did people go West?
- Who were the first pioneers to go West?
- What trails did settlers take to the West?

## 8.3 Westward Expansion

How did America expand to the West?

## Reasons to Go West

### Land

Three main factors in moving west were land, gold, and religion. The rich, inexpensive land drew farmers who struggled to make profits. Furthermore, the West offered an alternative to overcrowded cities for urban dwellers and for the increasing number of immigrants fleeing Europe for religious, economic, and political reasons.

### California Gold Rush

Swiss immigrant John Sutter arrived in California in 1839 while it was still under Mexican control. After obtaining a grant of fifty thousand acres of land from the Mexican government, Sutter began building a large ranch at the junction of the Sacramento and American Rivers (the site of the modern city of Sacramento). He also hired a foreman to build a sawmill to provide lumber for the extensive ranch. In the same year as the Mexican Cession of California, Sutter's foreman found some glittering stones below the mill's water wheel. The stones, he soon discovered, were gold.

Word spread first throughout the region and then back East and overseas. The **California gold rush** began with "gold fever" seizing thousands. The first wave of gold hunters came in 1849, so they became known as **forty-niners**. Most forty-niners followed the overland route to California. Others, particularly on the East Coast, went by sea. Some sailed to Central America, crossed the narrow bridge of land by mule and canoe, and found a ship on the Pacific side going to California. Some took the long and dangerous all-water route, around the southern tip of South America. In all, about eighty thousand people came to California in 1849, and over four hundred thousand came within the next decade.

Seeking gold was full of risks. Many sacrificed their savings and their occupations, believing that they would strike it rich. Some died in shipwrecks or on the trails without ever reaching California. Those who successfully staked claims found that standing in water all day and wielding a pick and shovel was hard, discouraging work. Some became wealthy by selling supplies to miners. The few miners who found gold became wealthy and inspired stories that encouraged others to come.

### Missions to Native Americans

As mentioned in Chapter 7, one of the effects of the Second Great Awakening was an increased interest in missions. In 1833 the *Christian Advocate and Journal* published a letter that described four Native Americans who had expressed interest in Christianity. Although the letter contained embellished details, it prompted missionary organizations to send workers to reach the Native Americans of the Pacific Northwest with the gospel. Many eagerly responded to the letter's appeal, the most famous of whom were two missionary couples: Henry and Eliza Spalding, and **Marcus and Narcissa Whitman**.

▼ Miners in California in 1850

▲ Marcus Whitman (above) and the Whitman Mission, Waiilatpu (below)

Alongside fur companies headed to the Pacific Northwest, the Spaldings and Whitmans journeyed to Oregon in 1836 and then parted ways. The Spaldings, who eventually settled in what is today northern Idaho, enjoyed some success among the Nez Perce and established both a church and a school. The Whitmans had less apparent success as missionaries but had greater impact on the settlement of Oregon. The Whitmans, soon joined by other missionaries, built a mission compound near the site of modern Walla Walla, Washington, and tried to reach the fiercely independent Cayuse. The Whitmans proved more successful at recruiting settlers than reaching the Cayuse. They sent back not only calls for more workers but also exciting descriptions of the rich, unsettled lands. Marcus Whitman even served as a scout for some parties of settlers from the East. The Whitmans had opened the door for a flood of migration. A thousand settlers came to Oregon in 1841; within two years the number had tripled and continued to grow.

The increasing stream of settlers caused the Cayuse to suspect that white settlers were more interested in taking the Native Americans' land than in preaching to them. Marcus Whitman wrote in a letter in 1844, "The Indians are anxious about the consequences of settlers among them, but I hope there will be no acts of violence on either hand." Whitman's hopes proved vain, especially when a measles epidemic, apparently carried into Oregon by settlers, wiped out nearly half the tribe, despite Whitman's efforts to treat the ill. In 1847 a party of Cayuse, believing that the Native American deaths were a result of Whitman's poisonous medicine, ambushed the mission compound, murdering Marcus, Narcissa, and twelve other settlers.

## The Mormons

As mentioned in Chapter 7, another result of the Second Great Awakening was an increase in unorthodox teaching. Probably the most significant unorthodox religious group to arise at this time was the **Mormons**, also known as the Church of Jesus Christ of Latter-Day Saints. Mormonism was founded by **Joseph Smith** in 1830. Smith claimed that, with an angel's help, he had found golden plates inscribed with ancient writing and had translated the plates to produce the Book of Mormon, which Smith and his followers believed took precedence over the Bible.

Opposition to Smith's teaching, attacks on Mormons, and the prospect of safe havens further west drove the Mormons from New York to Ohio to Missouri to Illinois. In Nauvoo, Illinois, Mormons stirred up controversy by their practice of polygamy, the taking of more than one wife at the same time. A group of Mormon dissenters published a newspaper which openly criticized Smith for his teaching and practice of polygamy. When Smith and the Nauvoo City Council suppressed the publication, conflict between Mormons and local residents led to the jailing of Smith in Carthage, Illinois. A mob attacked the jail and killed Smith. **Brigham Young** then assumed the leadership of the group. He led the Mormons on a prolonged trek west to Utah, where they founded Salt Lake City in 1847 in what was then Mexican territory. There the Mormons built the grand Salt Lake Temple, completed in 1893. The Mormons officially abandoned the practice of polygamy as one of the requirements in order for Utah to enter the union in 1896.

▼ Brigham Young

▼ Salt Lake Temple

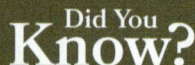

## Mountain Men and Trailblazers

As noted earlier in this chapter, Oregon first drew those interested in opportunities for trapping and trading. In 1808 John Jacob Astor established a fur company in Oregon Territory. Several trappers and traders, called mountain men, explored routes for the fur trade and later became guides for settlers from the East.

**Jedediah Smith**, who explored several regions as a trapper, was an important trailblazer for settlers to Oregon. Smith rediscovered the South Pass (in present-day Wyoming) through the Rockies, a path which trappers and traders working for Astor's fur company had used. In 1826 he and William H. Ashley blazed a path from the Platte River to the South Pass; this same route was used later by settlers on the Oregon Trail. In the same year Smith also discovered the first overland route to California.

Kit Carson, another famous mountain man, had worked as a trapper and explored parts of the West, including California. In the 1840s he helped guide John C. Frémont, who surveyed the West with the US Army's Topographical Engineers. In the California campaign Carson served as a guide for General Kearny and fought in battle. Joe Meek had worked as a trapper alongside Carson. With his knowledge of the land, Meek guided the Whitmans to Oregon.

## Trails West

### The Santa Fe Trail

As interest and opportunities in the West increased, four main trails had developed. The **Santa Fe Trail** was more of a commercial trade route than a means of pioneer transportation. During the era of Spanish domination, American merchants began a thriving trade between Santa Fe, New Mexico, and Independence, Missouri. Even after Mexican independence, trade flourished. Fear of growing American activity in Texas eventually caused the Mexican government to close the trail, but memories of earlier profits caused many Americans to covet New Mexico.

### The Oregon Trail

The **Oregon Trail** became the main route for pioneers and missionaries to the West. *Trail* is an accurate term, for this route was not a road. At best, it consisted of the ruts left by preceding wagons. Beginning in Missouri and extending two thousand miles to the west, the trail not only led to Oregon, but it also had branches ("cutoffs") that reached into California. After packing all their belongings into sturdy ox-drawn wagons, pioneers often had to lighten their loads along the difficult parts of the trail, leaving oak chests, chairs, trunks, and even grandfather clocks on the wayside. Pioneers could suffer from broken axles or the death of oxen, which could leave families stranded in the wilderness. Many who did survive the arduous journey settled in Oregon City on the banks of the Willamette River.

## The California Trail

Thousands of pioneers, many seeking the path to gold, used the **California Trail**, which followed the Oregon Trail for twelve hundred miles until it turned to the southwest after Fort Hall (in present-day Idaho). Desert land and rugged terrain through the Rockies and Sierra Nevada range made this particular route challenging. Probably the most horrible example of the dangers of the trail was the fate of the Donner Party. In 1846 a group under the leadership of George Donner was trapped for months in the Sierra Nevada range by the winter snows. About half of the eighty-seven members of the party survived. It appears many did so by resorting to cannibalizing the dead. Despite the dangers of the trail, gold seekers and other settlers continued to pour into California. Regardless of whether a prospector found gold, he seldom left. The trip home was too long and the beauty and potential of the region too appealing.

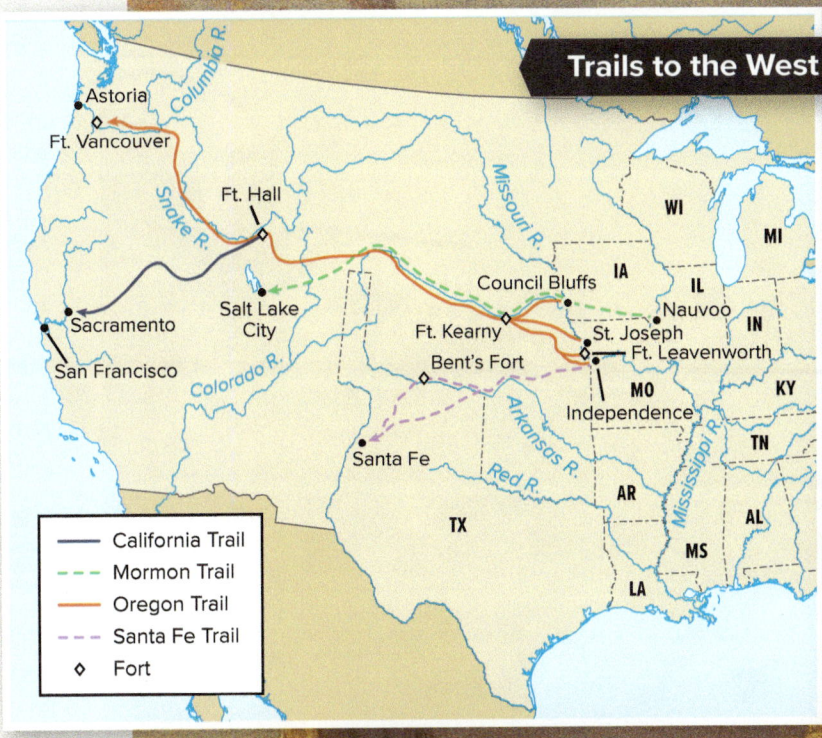

**Trails to the West**

- —— California Trail
- --- Mormon Trail
- —— Oregon Trail
- --- Santa Fe Trail
- ◇ Fort

## The Mormon Trail

The Mormons, under Brigham Young's leadership, blazed the **Mormon Trail** when they fled from Nauvoo, Illinois. The Mormons crossed through Iowa to Council Bluffs, one of the departure points of the Oregon Trail. From there, drawing from the publications of Frémont, Young guided a group of Mormons to eventually settle in Salt Lake City, Utah. Between 1847 and 1857 thousands of Mormons followed the trail, and some settled to the south and west of Salt Lake City. Eventually, non-Mormons found the Mormon Trail a convenient alternate route to California.

▼ *The Oregon Trail*, by Albert Bierstadt, 1869

▼ Native Americans attacking settlers

## Westward Expansion *and* Native Americans

Explorers, missionaries, and settlers had varying interactions with Native American tribes as westward expansion progressed. Many mountain men, such as Jedediah Smith, befriended and sheltered with Native American tribes. Crow guides had helped Smith to rediscover the South Pass through the Rockies. Native American guides also helped Frémont in his expeditions to California. The Comanche, however, were less friendly to mountain men. A group of Comanche attacked and killed Smith while he was traveling to St. Louis. In 1833 Kit Carson, Joe Meek, and seven others survived a Comanche attack of two hundred warriors.

The Spaldings attempted to help the Nez Perce learn different methods of agriculture. The Whitmans' mission in Oregon featured a thriving farm, but the missionaries increased tension with the Cayuse by suggesting that they abandon their traditions of hunting and fishing to become farmers.

The Mormons also attempted to promote farming among the Native Americans in Utah Territory. The Mormons established close ties with Native Americans rather than with other western settlers, who did not approve of the Mormons' religion. In the Mountain Meadows Massacre of 1857, a group of Native Americans and Mormons, acting without the approval of Brigham Young, attacked a group of pioneers on their way through Utah to California.

---

### Comprehension Check 8.3

1. Forty-Niners received their name because they came to _____ in 1849 to search for gold.

   A California

   B Oregon

   C Utah

2. Despite his best efforts to meet the medical needs of the Cayuse during a measles epidemic, _____ and his wife were murdered by a band of Cayuse in 1847.

   A Joe Meek

   B Henry Spalding

   C Marcus Whitman

3. After the founder of the Mormons was killed, Brigham Young led the Mormons to settle in _____.

   A Sacramento

   B Salt Lake City

   C Santa Fe

4. Jedediah Smith was a mountain man who rediscovered the South Pass, clearing the way for the Oregon Trail, and who _____.

   A established a mission school for the Nez Perce

   B fought the Mexicans in Santa Fe

   C traveled the first overland route to California

5. Unlike the pathways used by pioneers, the _____ Trail was formed mainly for trade.

   A Santa Fe

   B Mormon

   C California

### MAKING CONNECTIONS

6. How did religion influence settlement in the West?

## Chapter Summary

### TERMS

Manifest Destiny

Stephen Austin

Antonio López de Santa Anna

Sam Houston

Alamo

Lone Star Republic

Battle of San Jacinto

James K. Polk

### 8.1 Texas

- The idea of Manifest Destiny dominated American thinking in the 1840s and increased tension between the United States and both Great Britain and Mexico.

- American empresarios like Stephen Austin brought many settlers to Texas, who often violated Mexican laws regarding immigration and slavery.

- When Santa Anna became dictator of Mexico, the Texans fought at first to defend the Mexican constitution of 1824 but soon fought for independence from Mexico. The Texans suffered defeats at the Alamo and Goliad, but defeated Santa Anna at the Battle of San Jacinto in 1836.

- President Jackson recognized the independence of Texas but opposed annexation, fearing it would upset antislavery Americans and could lead to war with Mexico. When Democratic pro-annexation candidate James K. Polk won the election of 1844, Congress under President Tyler passed a joint resolution to annex Texas.

- President Polk avoided war with Britain by accepting a compromise border of the Oregon Territory at the 49th parallel.

### 8.2 The Mexican War

- Mexico refused to consider Polk's offer to purchase California. The United States claimed the southern border of Texas was the Rio Grande, while the Mexicans claimed it was the Nueces River. To provoke war, Polk sent forces to the disputed land between the rivers, where Mexican forces attacked the Americans, which led to an American declaration of war against Mexico. Many Americans felt the war was not justified.

- California briefly became the independent Bear Flag Republic but quickly came under the control of the United States. Zachary Taylor and Winfield Scott led decisive victories in Mexico.

- The Treaty of Guadalupe Hidalgo ended the Mexican War.

### TERMS

Zachary Taylor

Wilmot Proviso

Spot Resolution

John C. Frémont

Bear Flag Republic

Winfield Scott

Treaty of Guadalupe Hidalgo

Mexican Cession

Gadsden Purchase

## TERMS

California gold rush

forty-niners

Marcus and Narcissa Whitman

Mormons

Joseph Smith

Brigham Young

Jedediah Smith

Santa Fe Trail

Oregon Trail

California Trail

Mormon Trail

### 8.3 Westward Expansion

- Land, gold, and religion were the main reasons people came to the West. The discovery of gold in California drew thousands in 1849 and following years. Marcus and Narcissa Whitman, missionaries to the Cayuse in Oregon, promoted settlement there. Fleeing persecution, the Mormons settled in and around Salt Lake City, Utah.

- Mountain men were trappers in the West who discovered routes that later helped pioneers.

- The Santa Fe, Oregon, California, and Mormon Trails were the main routes taken by western settlers.

## Chapter Review Questions

### RECALL

1. At what battle were Sam Bowie, William Travis, and Davy Crockett killed?

2. At what battle did the Texans capture Santa Anna?

3. Who won the presidential election of 1844?

4. Who was president when Texas was annexed into the United States?

5. What were Polk's four goals as president? How many did he accomplish?

6. Who led the American forces that captured New Mexico?

7. What American general became a hero by winning the battles of Monterrey and Buena Vista and eventually rose to the presidency?

8. What American general defeated Santa Anna at Mexico City?

9. What was the purchase of land that completed the acquisition of the continental United States?

10. Who led the Mormons to Utah after Joseph Smith was killed?

11. Which trail was used mainly for trade rather than for settlers heading to the West?

### UNDERSTAND

12. What was the purpose of the empresario system?

13. What conditions did Mexico put on settlers in Texas?

14. Why did Mexico change the laws regarding immigration to Texas in 1830, and what laws did they put in place? How did Texans respond to these changes?

15. After being elected president, what did Santa Anna do and how did the Texans respond?

16. Why did President Jackson oppose annexing Texas?

17. Why did many antislavery voters abandon Henry Clay in the election of 1844?

18. Why was Oregon a source of conflict with Britain, and how was the issue resolved?

19. How did Polk provoke Mexico into war?

20. What were the terms of the Treaty of Guadalupe Hidalgo?

21. What were four results of the Mexican War?

22. What three main reasons did people have for traveling out west?

23. What did the Spaldings establish in Idaho? How did Marcus Whitman affect settlement in Oregon?

24. Why were the Whitmans killed?

25. How was the Mormon church started? Why is the Mormon church considered unorthodox?

26. Why did the Mormons migrate west?

27. What were Jedediah Smith's accomplishments?

28. Which people did Kit Carson and Joe Meek help guide?

29. What challenges did pioneers face on the trails to Oregon and California?

30. How was the route of the California Trail related to the Oregon Trail? What alternative route to California did some settlers take?

## THINK ABOUT IT

31. Was Manifest Destiny a biblical idea? Explain your answer.

32. What were the arguments for and against the Mexican War? Do you think the war was justified? Explain your answer.

33. Explain what Ralph Waldo Emerson meant when he said, "The United States will conquer Mexico, but it will be as the man [who] swallows the arsenic, which brings him down in turn. Mexico will poison us."

34. Trace the expansion of United States' territory after 1830, according to the map below. How does the map show the successes and failures of the idea of Manifest Destiny?

## United States Expansion to 1853

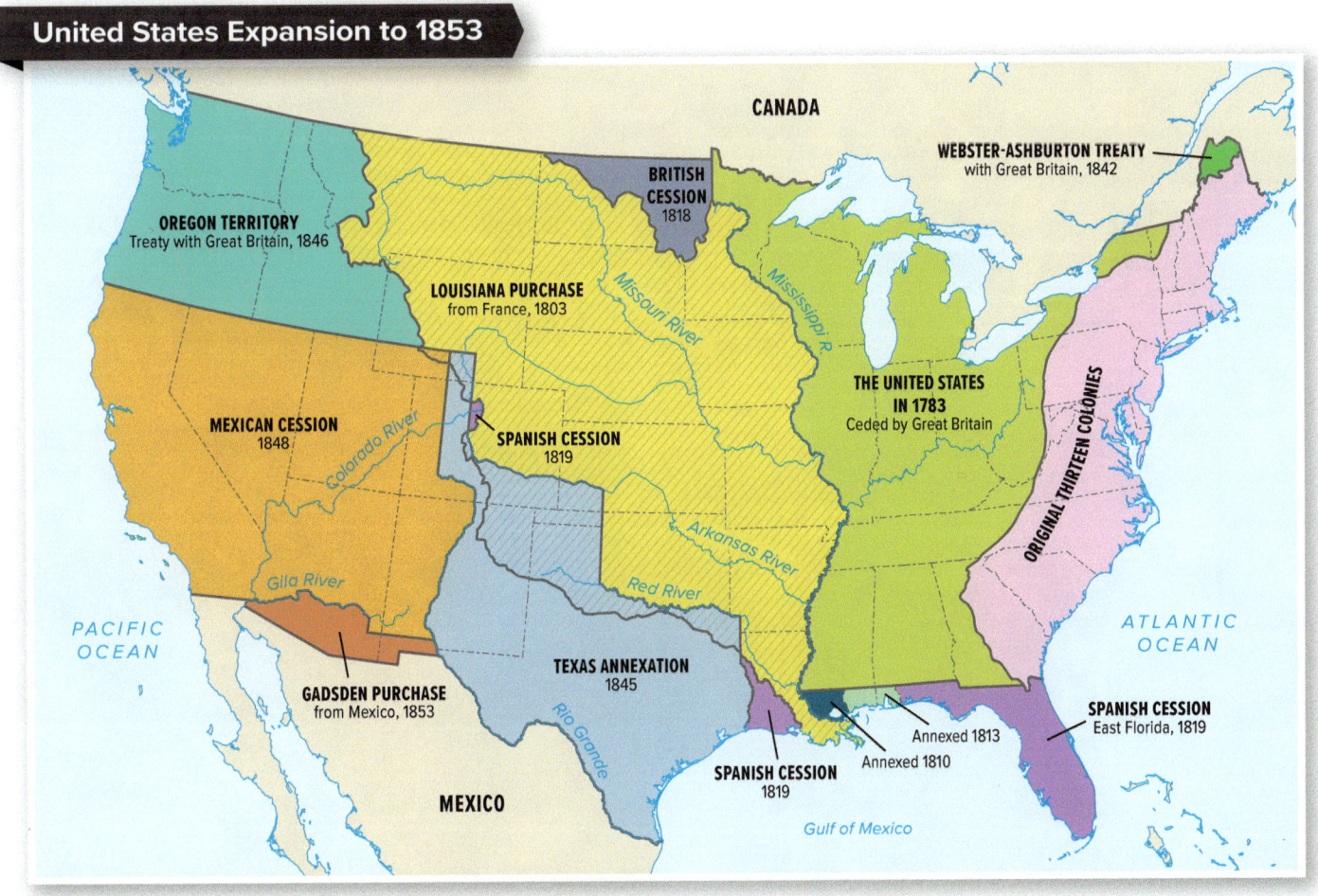

CANADA

WEBSTER-ASHBURTON TREATY
with Great Britain, 1842

BRITISH CESSION
1818

OREGON TERRITORY
Treaty with Great Britain, 1846

LOUISIANA PURCHASE
from France, 1803

Missouri River

Mississippi R.

THE UNITED STATES IN 1783
Ceded by Great Britain

MEXICAN CESSION
1848

Colorado River

SPANISH CESSION
1819

Arkansas River

ORIGINAL THIRTEEN COLONIES

Gila River

Red River

PACIFIC OCEAN

ATLANTIC OCEAN

GADSDEN PURCHASE
from Mexico, 1853

TEXAS ANNEXATION
1845

Annexed 1813

Annexed 1810

SPANISH CESSION
East Florida, 1819

Rio Grande

SPANISH CESSION
1819

MEXICO

Gulf of Mexico

# 9 A House Dividing

9.1 Sectional Differences
9.2 American Slavery
9.3 Sectional Conflict
9.4 Secession
9.5 Fort Sumter

▲ Lincoln at the Lincoln-Douglas Debates, 1858

What were the differences between the North and the South during the antebellum period?

GUIDING QUESTIONS

■ How did the economies of the North and South differ before the Civil War?

■ How did Northerners and Southerners view politics?

In the 1850s, rather than focusing on what Americans shared, such as their history, language, the Constitution, Protestant religion, and a republican government, Northerners and Southerners began to focus more on what divided them. These sectional differences showed in their economic development and political views. These years would become known as the antebellum (before war) period.

## Economics

As mentioned in Chapter 7, the South remained primarily agricultural as the North industrialized. In 1850, eighty percent of Southerners were engaged in agricultural production, growing cotton, sugar cane, rice, tobacco, and other crops. One result of the industrial and transportation revolutions was that farmers began producing not only for local consumption but also for national and international markets. Southern cotton accounted for sixty percent of all American exports.

In 1850 the population of the Southern states was about 9.4 million. Of those, 3.2 million were slaves and another 200,000 were free blacks. There were few large towns or cities in the South, and only ten percent of Southerners lived in towns of 2,500 people or more. The largest cities in the South were Baltimore and New Orleans.

About one-fourth of Southern families owned slaves, and less than two percent of slaveholding families (about 5,000) owned fifty or more slaves. A much larger number owned from five to forty-nine slaves, and most slaveholders owned fewer than five slaves. However, even the non-slaveholding Southern majority believed that slavery was necessary to the South's economic prosperity and stability.

In the South, plantation owners were the leaders politically, socially, and economically, although ordinary farmers made up most of the population. Doctors, lawyers, other professionals, and merchants made up the middle class. The lower class was made up of poor whites who lived on land too barren for successful farming or who owned no land. Below them were free blacks (primarily former slaves who had purchased or been given their freedom). At the bottom of the social ladder were slaves.

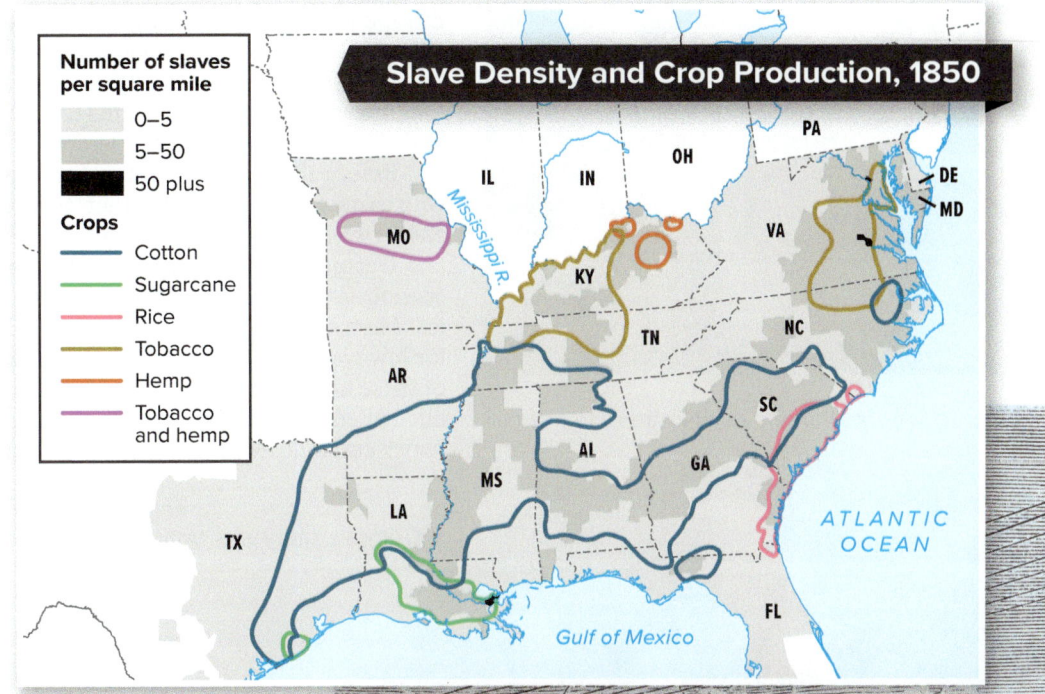

**Slave Density and Crop Production, 1850**

Number of slaves per square mile
- 0–5
- 5–50
- 50 plus

Crops
- Cotton
- Sugarcane
- Rice
- Tobacco
- Hemp
- Tobacco and hemp

▶ Bales of cotton being loaded by black stevedores in Charleston, South Carolina

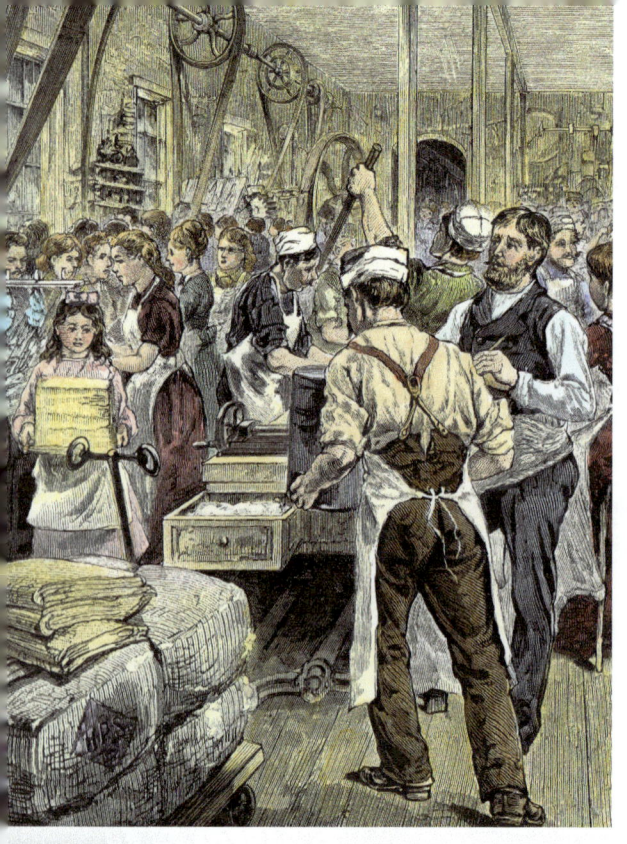

▲ Workers in a Northern textile mill

The North, with eighty percent of the nation's factories, was far more industrial than the South. However, agriculture remained important in the North, and about forty percent of its population were farmers.

In 1850 the population of the Northern states was about 14 million, with twenty-five percent living in urban areas. The largest northern cities were New York City, Boston, and Philadelphia.

Many owners of factories, railroads, and other industries became wealthy and influential in Northern society. Most of the population was composed of merchants, factory workers, and small farmers. There was also a significant population of free blacks, who did not have equality with whites.

America's rapid economic and territorial growth drew many from Europe who dreamed of higher wages and cheap land. During the 1820s, the United States had averaged fewer than 13,000 immigrants per year. By the 1840s over 70,000 immigrants were arriving annually. A total of five million immigrants came to the United States between 1820 and 1860, and nearly ninety percent of them settled in Northern states.

Before 1840, most immigrants to the United States were Protestants who came from Britain or other northern European countries. After 1840, two-thirds of immigrants were Roman Catholics from Ireland and Germany. The Irish potato famine of that decade, plus political and economic problems in those countries, pushed many to come to America. Most settled in large cities and took factory jobs working long hours for low wages. Living conditions were often filthy and miserable. Many of these new immigrants also faced mistreatment because of their Catholic beliefs. Despite these obstacles, many immigrant families adopted American culture and successfully improved their standard of living.

▼ German emigrants boarding a steamship bound for the United States

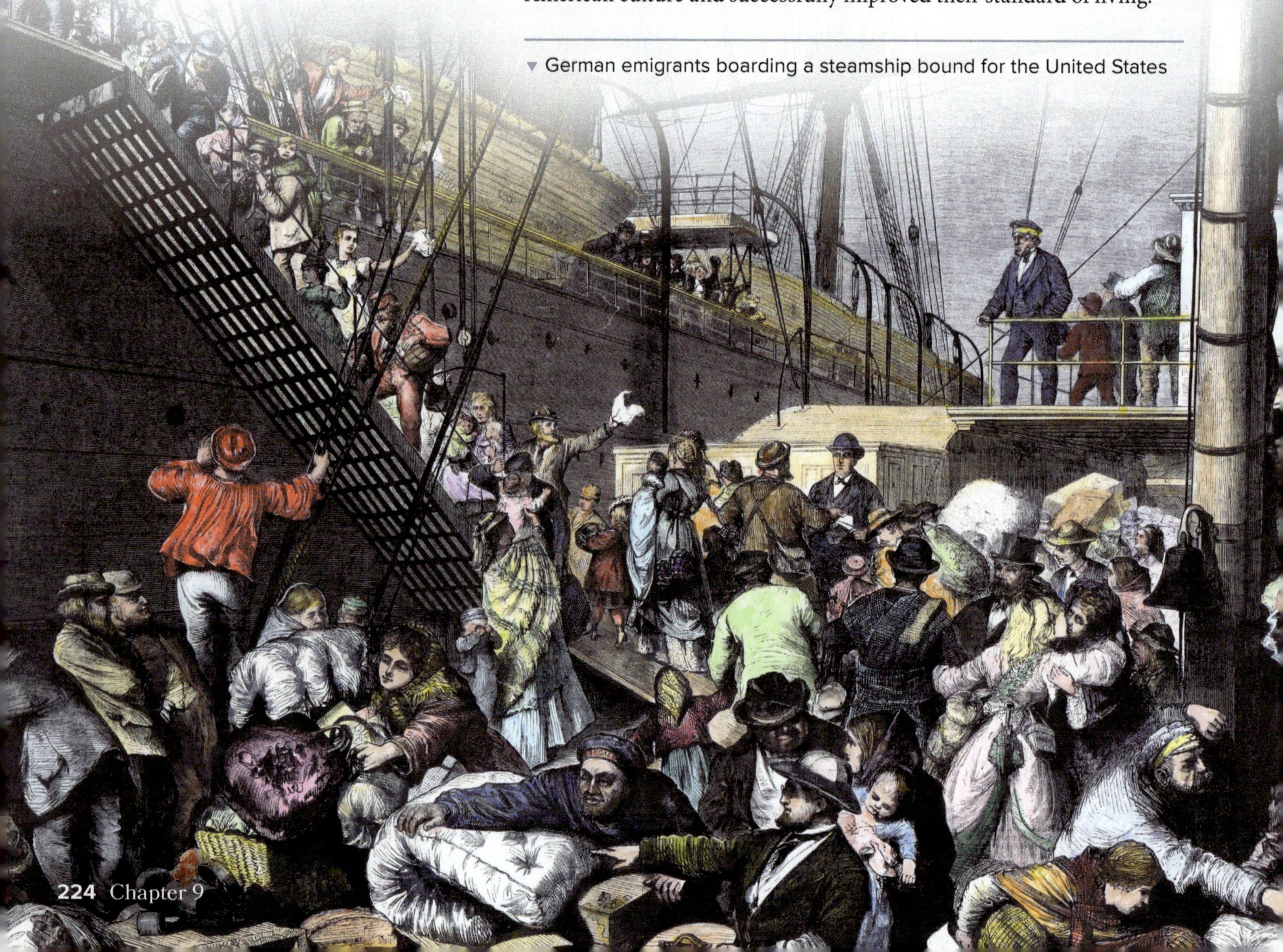

# Political Views

The North and South differed greatly on the interpretation of the Constitution. Most Northerners held that the federal government had the powers given to it by the Constitution along with those that were "necessary and proper" to carry out its expressed powers. Based on Article VI, Section 2, they held that the Constitution, laws, and treaties of the United States were the supreme law of the land and that states were bound to those laws. They also believed that the Constitution was formed by the people, not by the states, and that the Union was permanent.

Many Southerners held that the Constitution was created by the states, who contracted with one another to form a government. Therefore, according to the Tenth Amendment, the states maintained their sovereignty in areas that had not been delegated to the federal government and could overrule it on matters related to the Constitution through nullification or even through leaving the Union.

Not all political differences were sectional. Whigs were more prevalent in the North but were not exclusively Northerners. Whigs had generally opposed the Mexican War and supported internal improvements, tariffs to protect American industry and labor from low-wage foreign competition, a centralized banking system, temperance, and public schools that taught Protestant and republican ideals. Abraham Lincoln expressed the Whig view of government by saying it should "do for a community of people, whatever they need to have done, but cannot do, at all, or cannot, so well do, for themselves—in their separate and individual capacities."

Democrats, too, could be found in both the North and the South. They attracted factory workers, Catholic immigrants, Jacksonians who distrusted banks and corporations, and small farmers. They preferred a limited government and generally opposed federally funded internal improvements and protective tariffs. They had supported the Mexican War and the idea of Manifest Destiny.

However, there was one issue that divided the nation politically on sectional rather than party lines. That issue was slavery.

## Comprehension Check 9.1

1. While 80 percent of the southern population was agricultural, the North had 80 percent of the nation's ____.

   A  railroads

   B  banks

   C  factories

2. ____ were the leaders in the South economically, politically, and socially.

   A  Non-slaveholding farmers

   B  Plantation owners

   C  Merchants

3. Democrats included factory workers, small farmers, and ____.

   A  Catholic immigrants

   B  those who supported internal improvements

   C  factory owners

4. Whigs were found only in the North and Democrats were found only in the South.

   True

   False

### MAKING CONNECTIONS

5. What different views did the North and the South have regarding the Constitution?

◀ Antebellum politics reflect growing sectional division. This cartoon depicts the four candidates in the 1860 presidential election.

## GUIDING QUESTIONS

- What was the life of a slave like in America?
- How did the views of Northerners and Southerners differ regarding slavery?
- How did some misuse the Bible to defend slavery?

▼ Slaves picking cotton under the watch of a slave driver

## 9.2 American Slavery

**What was slavery like in antebellum America?**

Much of America's economic growth and industrial expansion was possible because of crops produced by slave labor. Northern and British textile mills depended on Southern cotton, which in turn fueled territorial expansion and the desire to extend slavery into those territories. Slaves bore the brunt of American economic progress but enjoyed almost none of its benefits.

## Life of Enslaved Peoples

### *Work and Family*

Southern plantations depended on slave labor. Most slaves worked in the fields while some worked in factories, mines, or as skilled workers or house servants. Field slaves, both men and women, often worked in gangs from dawn until dusk. They were managed by their masters or by drivers, often fellow slaves who kept them on task, sometimes brutally. Older slave women cared for the young children while the mothers worked in the fields or in the master's house, and children began field work around age ten. Solomon Northup, who had been a free black in the North but was kidnapped and sold as a slave, described his experience as a field hand:

> *The hands are required to be in the cotton field as soon as it is light in the morning, and . . . they are not permitted to be a moment idle until it is too dark to see. . . . They do not dare to stop even at dinner time . . . until the order to halt is given by the driver. . . . A slave never approaches the gin-house with his basket of cotton but with fear. If it falls short in weight . . . he knows that he must suffer. And if he has exceeded it by ten or twenty pounds . . . his master will measure the next day's task accordingly.*

— **SOLOMON NORTHUP,** *Twelve Years a Slave,* (Auburn, NY, 1853), 163–71.

### Analyzing Sources

According to Northup, how is a slave punished for both failure and success?

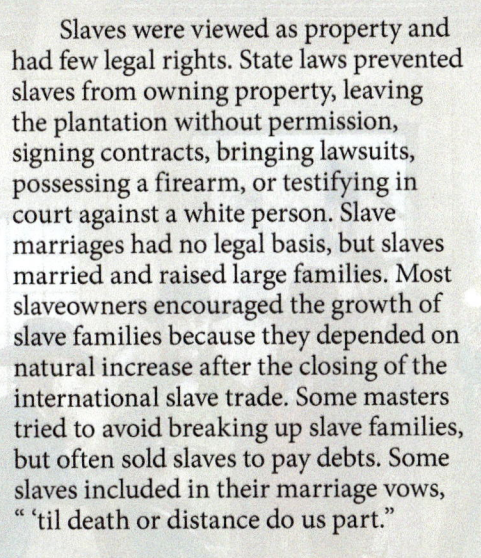

Slaves were viewed as property and had few legal rights. State laws prevented slaves from owning property, leaving the plantation without permission, signing contracts, bringing lawsuits, possessing a firearm, or testifying in court against a white person. Slave marriages had no legal basis, but slaves married and raised large families. Most slaveowners encouraged the growth of slave families because they depended on natural increase after the closing of the international slave trade. Some masters tried to avoid breaking up slave families, but often sold slaves to pay debts. Some slaves included in their marriage vows, " 'til death or distance do us part."

▶ A slave auction

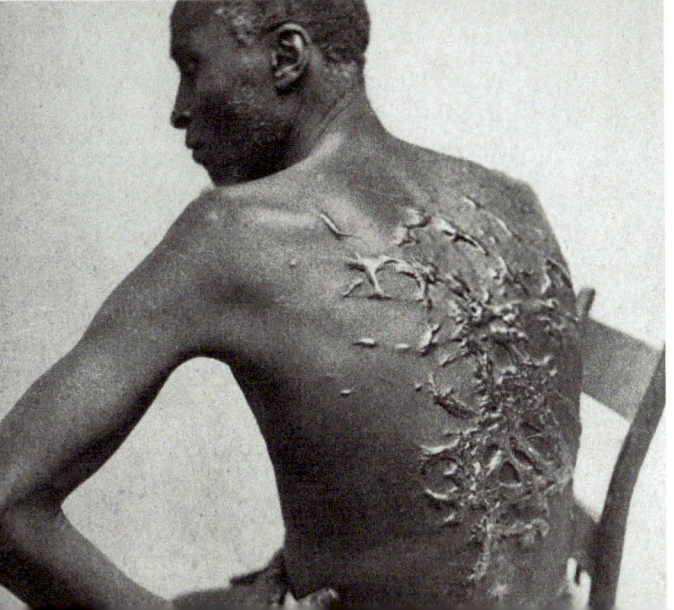

## Slave Responses

### AFRICAN AMERICAN CULTURE

Despite the harsh conditions slaves endured, they were able to develop a distinct African American culture. Religion often played a significant role in this culture, as some slaves were allowed to attend church with their masters or they attended black churches. Sometimes slaves created their own religion which blended Christianity and West African beliefs and practices. Music played an important role. Spirituals were songs created by slaves that often focused on freedom and deliverance from bondage, either in this life or in eternity.

### SLAVE REVOLTS AND RESISTANCE

One of the greatest fears of Southerners was the possibility of a slave insurrection. To prevent this, masters often prohibited slaves from reading, writing, or meeting together in groups. One of the first large slave revolts occurred in 1800 in Virginia. A slave named Gabriel Prosser and his followers made their own weapons and planned to capture Richmond and kill all supporters of slavery in the city. Prosser's plot was exposed, and he and several other organizers were arrested and executed.

In August 1831 a slave and radical preacher named **Nat Turner** led a slave rebellion in Southampton County, Virginia. Up to sixty white people and perhaps a hundred black people died in the rebellion and the bloody response that followed. Turner and other alleged leaders were hanged.

Slaves resisted in other ways short of insurrection. Some slowed the pace of their work, faked illness, injured themselves intentionally, sabotaged machinery, or destroyed crops. Thousands risked beatings or worse punishment by running away.

◀ (middle) Watercolor depicting the culture and music created by American slaves; (bottom) scars on the back of a Mississippi slave from being whipped

## THE UNDERGROUND RAILROAD

The **Underground Railroad** developed as a means of hiding fleeing slaves and leading them to safety and freedom in the North or in Canada. This "railroad" consisted of a secret network of safe houses and people who assisted escaping slaves with temporary housing and food and then "conducted" them to the next point in their journey toward freedom.

Perhaps the most famous member of the Underground Railroad was **Harriet Tubman**. Born a slave in Maryland in 1822, Tubman suffered much abuse at the hands of her masters until her escape in 1849. She made trips to the South to help lead dozens of slaves to freedom, including many of her family members. William Lloyd Garrison nicknamed her "Moses" after the prophet who led the Hebrews to freedom from Egypt.

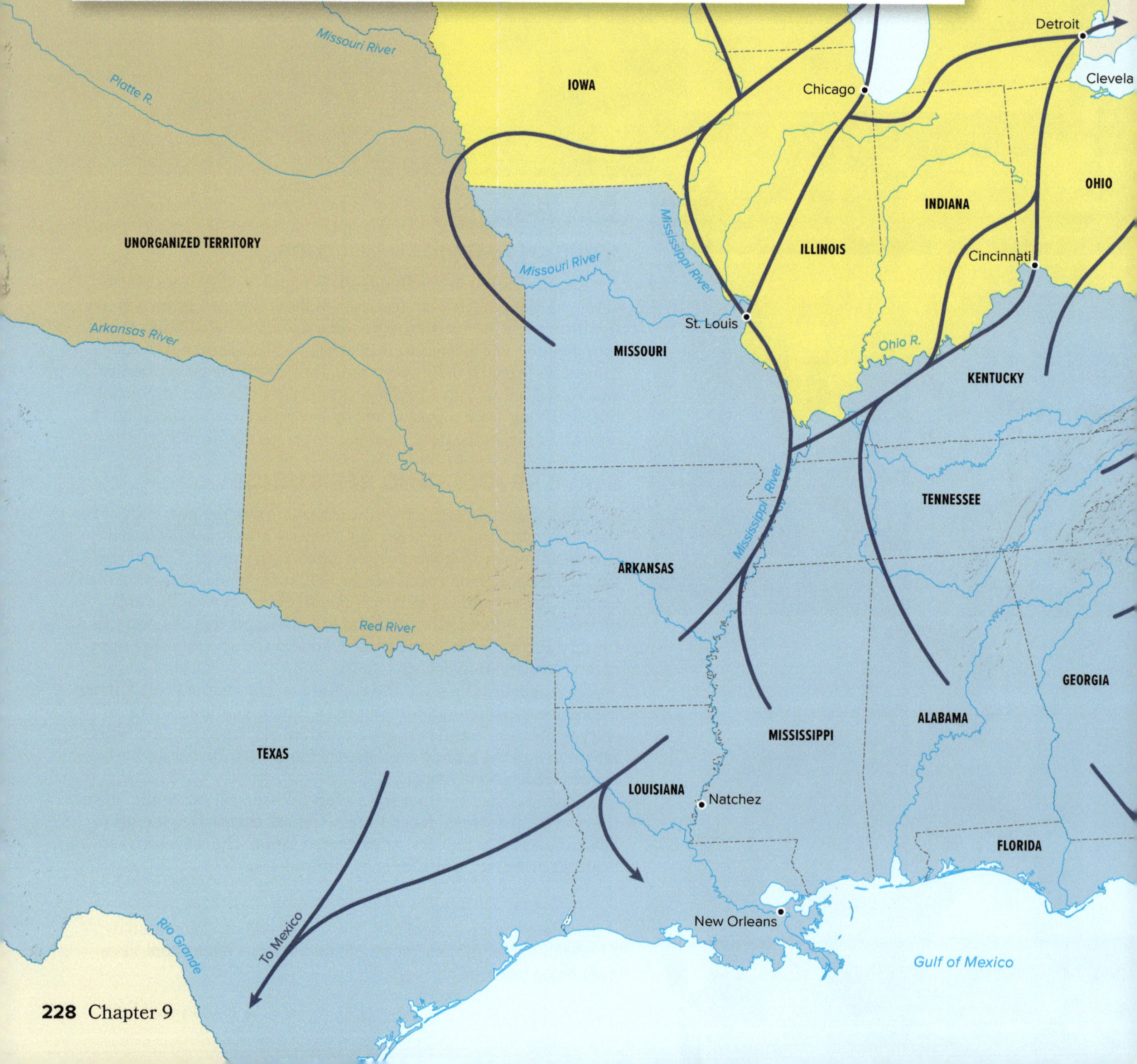

Missouri River

Lake Huron

MICHIGAN

Detroit

Clevela

IOWA

Chicago

Platte R.

OHIO

INDIANA

UNORGANIZED TERRITORY

Missouri River

Mississippi River

ILLINOIS

Cincinnati

Arkansas River

St. Louis

Ohio R.

MISSOURI

KENTUCKY

TENNESSEE

ARKANSAS

Mississippi River

Red River

TEXAS

MISSISSIPPI

ALABAMA

GEORGIA

LOUISIANA

Natchez

FLORIDA

Rio Grande

To Mexico

New Orleans

Gulf of Mexico

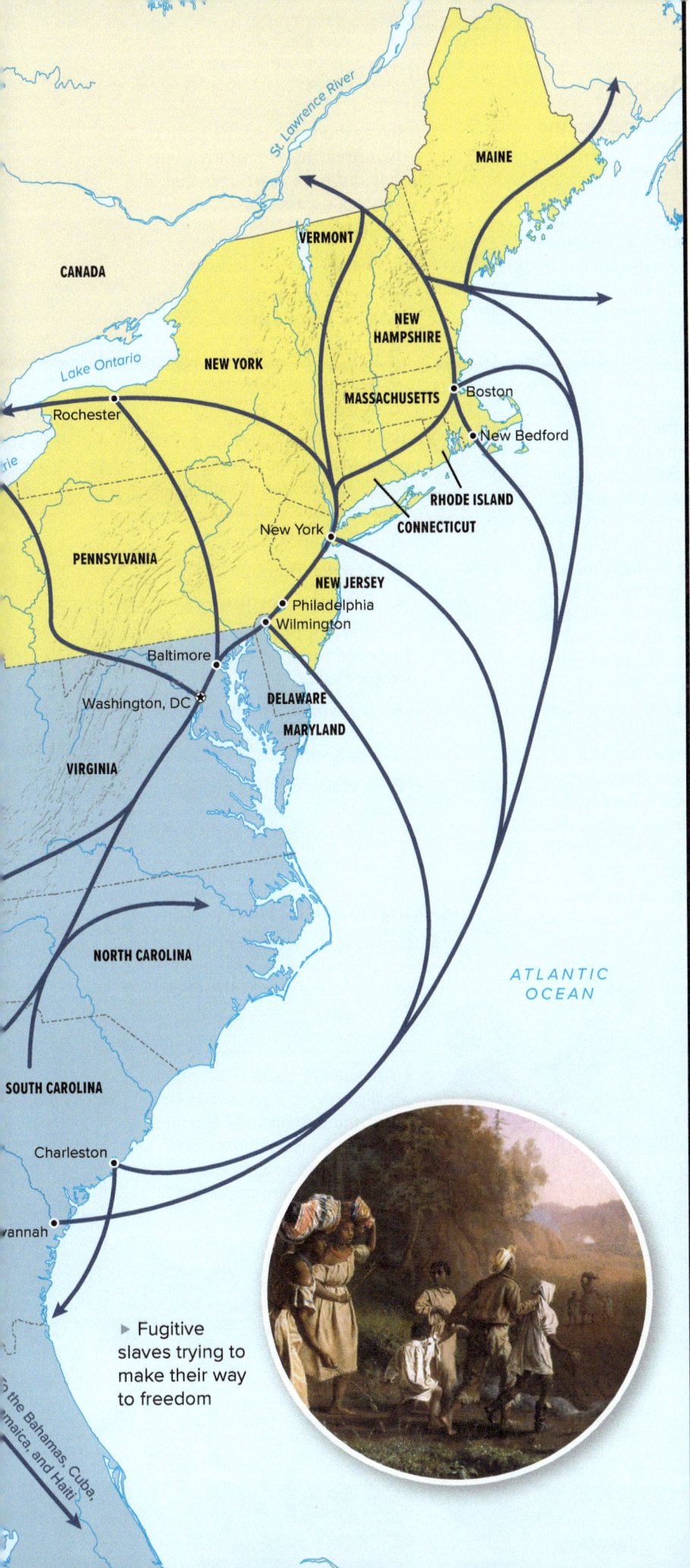

▶ Fugitive slaves trying to make their way to freedom

## Differing Views on Slavery

As mentioned in Chapter 7, most abolitionists believed that slavery was a moral evil, though not all based their position on the Bible, and some who opposed slavery supported gradual emancipation over immediate abolition. Other Northerners were opposed to slavery for economic and political reasons. They argued that slavery led to a lack of enterprise and improvement, discouraged education, and kept the South from progressing economically. Some recognized slavery as undemocratic and a violation of the principles of the Declaration of Independence. Still others were more concerned about the political impact of a possible coalition of proslavery states and territories that stretched from Maryland to New Mexico and the resulting decrease in influence of northern interests in Congress.

Early defenders of slavery had said that slavery was a necessary evil, but as opposition grew, Southerners began to argue that slavery was a positive good for both the masters and the slaves. Some slaveholders claimed that slavery promoted peace and prosperity, "civilized" the Africans, provided for their care from birth until death, prevented class and racial warfare by keeping whites and blacks from competing for jobs, and gave upper class slave owners time to pursue education, leisure, the arts, and public service.

Some Southerners defended slavery on constitutional grounds. They claimed the Constitution recognized slavery and did not allow the federal government to interfere with the right to own property in any state or in the territories.

Another defense was that the North was being hypocritical. New England shipping merchants had participated in and profited from the slave trade during the colonial period, and New England textile mills profited from the cotton grown by slave labor. Many Southerners also viewed Northern factory work as a form of "wage slavery" in which laborers were like machines, became slaves to the time clock, and were dependent on their bosses for wages, which kept them from being truly free. Southerners countered that slaves were treated with paternal care by their masters and were provided with food, clothing, and shelter, even in old age, unlike the urban factory worker.

While many Southern Christians defended slavery and opposed abolition, some spoke against the abuse of slaves and said that slave marriages should be legalized, that slave families should not be broken apart, and that resistance to educating and evangelizing slaves should end.

# The Bible's Role in the Slavery Debate

Most Americans at this time professed to be Christians, and the Bible played an important role in public debate. Both sides used the Bible to defend their positions on slavery, and the debate became increasingly heated as the nation's sectional divide deepened.

The issue of slavery divided some of America's largest denominations. The Methodist church split in 1844 when a bishop was suspended for marrying a woman who had inherited slaves. As a result, the Methodist Episcopal Church, South, was formed. That same year, the Baptists split when the denomination decided that slaveowners could not serve as missionaries or on mission boards. The Presbyterian church also divided into northern and southern branches at the outbreak of the Civil War. The Congregationalists, the majority of whom were in New England, were antislavery and remained unified. Some denominations avoided division by sidestepping the issue as much as they could.

Some defended slavery on religious grounds. Some pastors said that while cruelty toward slaves was wrong, slavery itself was not sinful because the Israelites were allowed to have slaves and in the New Testament the apostle Paul instructed slaves to obey their masters. However, those who attempted to use the Bible to defend slavery failed to recognize the differences between servitude in the Bible and American slavery. In Israel, servants were more like indentured servants, and their service was voluntary, primarily for paying off debts, and lasted a maximum of six years (unless the person volunteered to remain a servant for life). Those who ran away were to be given refuge and not returned to their masters (Deut. 23:15, 16). The Bible actually prohibited kidnapping people (manstealing) and enslaving them (Ex. 21:16; Deut. 24:7; 1 Tim. 1:10), and the Old Testament proscribed the death penalty for violators, including those who purchased the slaves. In the New Testament, slavery was a part of Roman society, and Christians were not in a position to end it. However, Paul told Christians who had authority over slaves to treat them as equals and forbade threatening (much less beating) servants (Col. 4:1, Eph. 6:9).

Opponents of slavery also pointed out the fact that all people were made in God's image and therefore had equal worth in God's sight, that Jesus commanded everyone to love their neighbor as themselves, and that all believers, whether Jew or Gentile, slave or free, male or female, are one in Christ Jesus (Gal. 3:28).

## Comprehension Check 9.2

1. Slaves did not have the right to own firearms or property, but they did have marriages that were legally recognized.

   True

   False

2. Gabriel Prosser and Nat Turner led slave revolts in ____.

   A Georgia

   B South Carolina

   C Virginia

3. William Lloyd Garrison called ____ "Moses" for leading slaves to freedom through the Underground Railroad.

   A Denmark Vesey

   B Harriet Tubman

   C Solomon Northrup

4. Northern opposition to slavery included the following reasons except that ____.

   A it enabled too much economic progress in the South

   B it violated the principles of the Declaration of Independence

   C it was a moral evil

### MAKING CONNECTIONS

5. Contrast the treatment of runaway slaves in America to runaway slaves in the Old Testament.

◀ Antislavery speaker Wendell Phillips giving a speech in Boston; (far left) an 1854 Boston poster announcing a public meeting to protest the arrest of a black man under the Fugitive Slave Law

## 9.3 Sectional Conflict

What led to the growing sectional conflict?

As a result of the annexation of Texas and the Mexican War, the United States had made the largest territorial acquisition in its history. This reopened the issue of slavery in the newly acquired territories.

The Wilmot Proviso (see Chapter 8) proposed that the United States prohibit slavery in any territory acquired from Mexico. The South viewed the proviso as an attack on the southern way of life. The proviso passed the House of Representatives but failed in the Senate, breaking across sectional rather than party lines, with Northern Democrats and Whigs in support and Southern Democrats and Whigs in opposition.

Senator John C. Calhoun responded to the Wilmot Proviso. In his Calhoun Resolutions, he argued that the territories were the common possession of the states and not of the federal government. Therefore, slave owners had the same constitutional protection of their property (including slaves) in the territories as in their home states, and neither Congress nor territorial legislatures had the right to limit slavery. Only when a territory became a state could it prohibit slavery. Although Congress had previously prohibited slavery in some territories under the Missouri Compromise, he claimed the South had permitted such measures to preserve the Union. He predicted that if Congress passed the Wilmot Proviso, the result would be revolution, anarchy, and war.

Neither the Wilmot Proviso nor the Calhoun Resolutions had enough support to pass Congress. Two compromise suggestions were raised. The first was to extend the Missouri Compromise line of 36°30' through the Mexican Cession. Polk supported this idea, but the House of Representatives rejected it. A second compromise known as **popular sovereignty** was suggested in 1848 by Senator Lewis Cass of Michigan. Cass proposed that the residents of a territory should decide for themselves the status of slavery.

The idea of popular sovereignty had enough support in the South that Cass won the Democratic nomination for the presidential election of 1848. The Whigs nominated the popular war hero Zachary Taylor as their candidate. Taylor owned over 100 slaves on his plantations in Mississippi and Louisiana, but his political views were unknown. He had the support of Whigs in the South as well as the support of the "Cotton Whigs" (Northern textile industrialists whose factories depended on Southern cotton).

In the North, many antislavery Whigs refused to support Taylor. These "Conscience Whigs," led by Senator Charles Sumner of Massachusetts, left the party. At the same time, many Northern Democrats who supported the Wilmot Proviso left the Democratic convention. The Conscience Whigs and Northern Democrats joined with the abolitionist Liberty Party to form the **Free Soil Party**. Under the slogan "Free Soil, Free Speech, Free Labor, and Free Men," the new party supported the Wilmot Proviso and nominated former president Martin Van Buren as its candidate. With Van Buren attracting dissatisfied Northern Democrats, Taylor narrowly defeated Cass in the election.

## GUIDING QUESTIONS

- Why did the Compromise of 1850 fail to resolve sectional conflict?
- How did the Kansas-Nebraska Act contribute to the growing divide in the country?
- What were the results of the Dred Scott decision?
- How did Lincoln and Douglas differ in their views?
- How did John Brown's raid intensify the conflict?

▼ Free Soil Party campaign platform pamphlet

Price 12½ Cents.

**CAMPAIGN OF 1848.**

**FREE SOIL**

**SONGS**

**FOR THE PEOPLE.**

IN UNION — THERE IS STRENGTH.

"Cheer up, cheer up, Free Soilers, all,
The time has come for action;
For Freedom's cause we must contend,
In spite of party faction."

BOSTON:
FOR SALE BY BELA MARSH,
No. 25 Cornhill.
WRIGHT'S STEAM PRESS, 3 WATER ST.

One Dollar per Dozen.

# The Compromise of 1850

The rush of people into California during the 1849 gold rush led to the need to establish a government there. California applied for admission to the Union as a free state in late 1849. Southerners opposed the admission of California because it would upset the balance between slave and free states in the Senate. Southern leaders known as "fire-eaters" threatened secession. Senator Robert Toombs of Georgia said, "If by your legislation you seek to drive us from the territories of California and New Mexico, . . . *I am for disunion.*"

Henry Clay, the "Great Compromiser" who had proposed the Missouri Compromise of 1820 and the Compromise Tariff of 1833, tried once more to find a compromise that would avoid secession and war. The **Compromise of 1850** proposed that (1) California be admitted as a free state and (2) the buying and selling of slaves be abolished in the District of Columbia. To the proslavery forces he offered (3) a new and more effective fugitive slave law, which required that all escaped slaves be returned to their masters, and (4) the protection of existing slavery in the District of Columbia. Clay offered the two sides a joint concession, proposing that (5) the new territories of New Mexico and Utah be organized and the slavery question there be decided by popular sovereignty.

The Compromise provoked intense debate from all sides. President Taylor opposed it for making concessions that might extend slavery into the territories. He thought debate on the Compromise would succeed only in deepening sectional division and delaying the admission of new territories.

The aging Calhoun came to the Senate on March 4 to present the South's position. Too weak to speak—he would be dead within three weeks—Calhoun gave his written remarks to a fellow senator to read. Calhoun declared that the Compromise would destroy the equilibrium in the Senate by adding free states. He argued that the only way to save the Union was for the North to give the South an equal right to the Mexican Cession, to stop agitating against slavery, and to give the South constitutional guarantees to protect its rights. Failure to do so, he said, would leave the South no choice but to secede.

Three days later, Daniel Webster rose to speak. "I wish to speak today, not as a Massachusetts man, nor as a northern man, but as an American. . . . I speak today for the preservation of the Union. Hear me for my cause." Webster opposed the Wilmot Proviso by noting that the bounds of slavery were already set by the Northwest Ordinance and the Missouri Compromise. He then turned his arguments in favor of union and compromise against the extremists in both sections. He agreed with the Southern complaint that Northern states were not fulfilling their constitutional obligation to return runaway slaves. Webster condemned the abolitionists in the North and scolded the secessionists in the South: "Secession! Peaceable Secession! Sir, your eyes and mine are never destined to see that miracle. . . . Peaceable secession is an utter impossibility." He implored, "Let us come out into the light of day; let us enjoy the fresh air of Liberty and Union."

▼ Senator Henry Clay urging passage of the Compromise of 1850

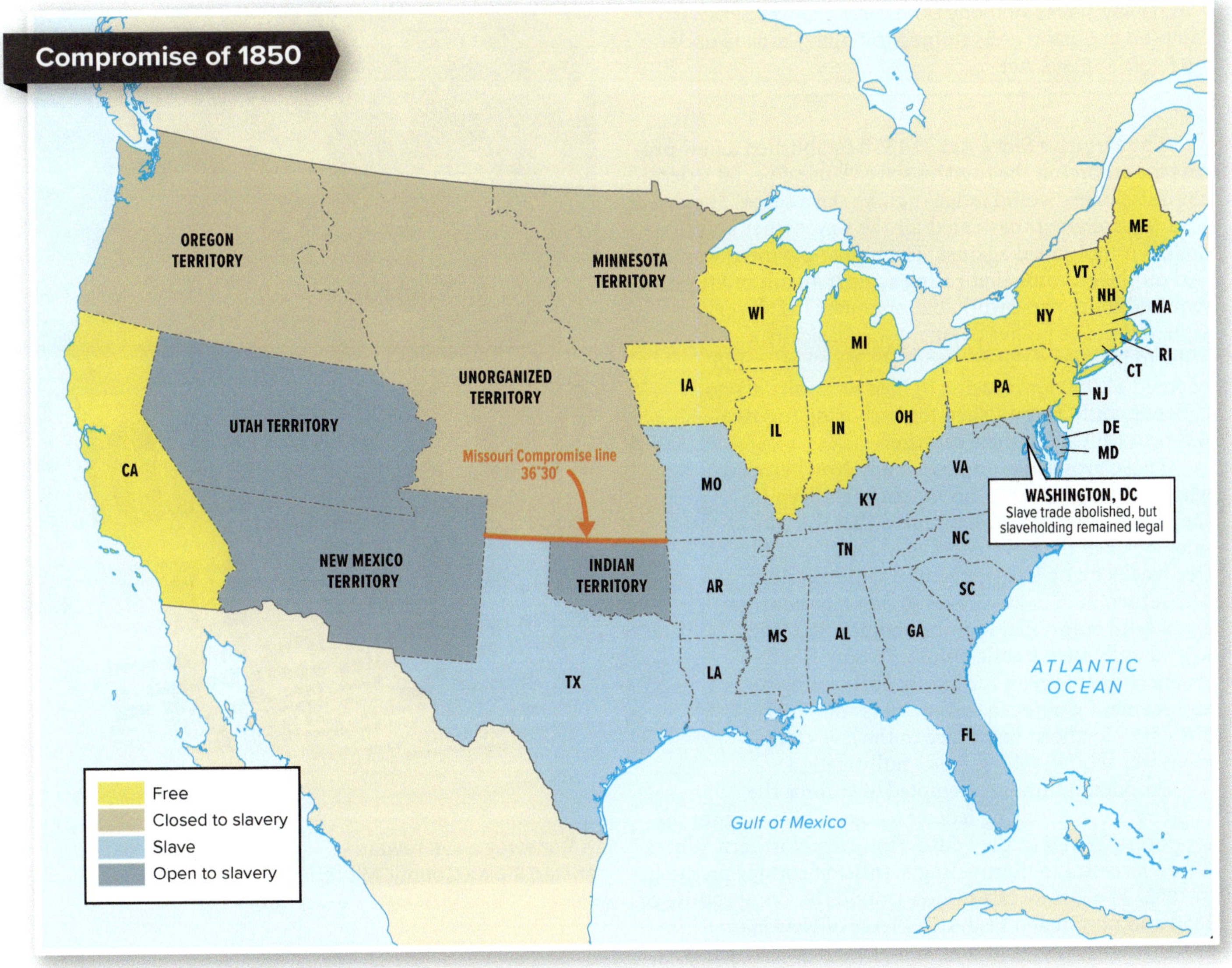

## Compromise of 1850

**Missouri Compromise line 36°30'**

OREGON TERRITORY

MINNESOTA TERRITORY

UNORGANIZED TERRITORY

UTAH TERRITORY

NEW MEXICO TERRITORY

INDIAN TERRITORY

CA

MO

AR

TX

LA

MS

AL

GA

FL

TN

KY

VA

NC

SC

WI

IA

IL

MI

IN

OH

PA

NY

ME

VT

NH

MA

RI

CT

NJ

DE

MD

**WASHINGTON, DC**
Slave trade abolished, but slaveholding remained legal

*ATLANTIC OCEAN*

*Gulf of Mexico*

Legend:
- Free
- Closed to slavery
- Slave
- Open to slavery

Abolitionists were outraged at both Calhoun's and Webster's positions. New York Senator William H. Seward condemned any compromise because slavery was unjust, saying. "there is a higher law than the Constitution," referring to the law of God.

The deadlock in Congress was broken with the sudden death of President Taylor. Vice President **Millard Fillmore**, who solidly backed the Compromise of 1850, succeeded to the presidency. By September it passed Congress and was signed into law.

The most controversial part of the Compromise of 1850 was the Fugitive Slave Act. The Constitution (in Article 4, Section 2, Clause 3) required that escaped slaves be returned to their masters but did not specify how this was to be enforced. An 1842 Supreme Court decision ruled that a slave-owner's right to his property superseded state laws against returning runaway slaves, but that the federal government had responsibility for enforcement of the fugitive slave clause and that the states did not have to cooperate. This led to many states passing "personal liberty" laws preventing state officials from assisting in the enforcement of the fugitive slave law, prohibiting kidnapping, and guaranteeing jury trials for runaway slaves.

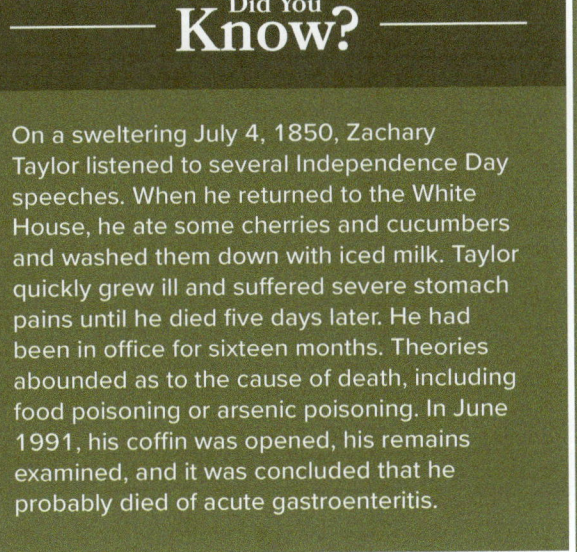

### Did You Know?

On a sweltering July 4, 1850, Zachary Taylor listened to several Independence Day speeches. When he returned to the White House, he ate some cherries and cucumbers and washed them down with iced milk. Taylor quickly grew ill and suffered severe stomach pains until he died five days later. He had been in office for sixteen months. Theories abounded as to the cause of death, including food poisoning or arsenic poisoning. In June 1991, his coffin was opened, his remains examined, and it was concluded that he probably died of acute gastroenteritis.

▶ Runaway slaves Anthony Burns and Thomas Sims, captured in Boston and returned to South Carolina under the Fugitive Slave Act

The **Fugitive Slave Act of 1850** established a new process for enforcing the fugitive slave clause. Special federal commissioners would judge fugitive slave cases. They were paid ten dollars if they ruled for the slaveowner and five dollars if they ruled against. The higher payment was justified on the grounds that ruling against an alleged fugitive required more paperwork, but opponents of slavery argued that the higher payment was basically a bribe to influence the decision. US Marshals could be fined $1,000 for refusing to help recapture slaves. Citizens could be punished for harboring fugitive slaves or hindering their capture.

These provisions angered many Northerners, who could be forced to aid slaveholders even if they opposed slavery. They feared that the lack of safeguards in the new federal law could result in free blacks being kidnapped and sent into slavery. The return of runaway slaves to bondage became a powerful emotional tool the abolitionists used to gradually turn public opinion. Many Northerners chose to break the law by obstructing its enforcement. Southern slaveholders were furious with Northern resistance to the law, claiming it was in effect the same as nullification.

President Fillmore attempted to enforce the Fugitive Slave Act using federal troops. This won him the support of Whigs in the South. However, Northern Whigs were successful in nominating Winfield Scott for president in 1852. The Democrats united around the Compromise of 1850 and nominated **Franklin Pierce** of New Hampshire as their candidate. Southern Whigs abandoned their party and supported Pierce, who won in a landslide.

▲ Runaway slave reward poster, Ripley County, Missouri

## Uncle Tom's Cabin (1852)

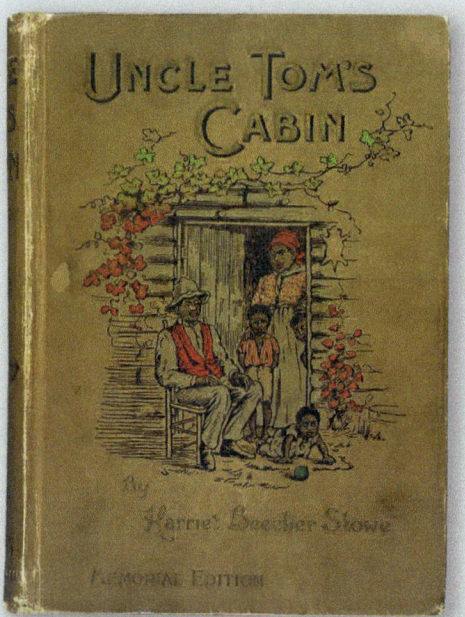

With the passage of the Fugitive Slave Act in 1850, Harriet Beecher Stowe brought the plight of slave families and runaways to public attention. The Stowes had lived in Cincinnati, Ohio, across the Ohio River from the slave state of Kentucky. There, she had met fugitive slaves. Based on their accounts, what she read in abolitionist papers, and her imagination, she wrote the novel **Uncle Tom's Cabin** in 1852. Within a year of publication, three hundred thousand copies had sold. Stowe tried to capture the wide variety of American experience with slavery. She showed both well-intentioned slaveowners caught in an unjust system as well as cruel masters. Both abolitionist and proslavery Northerners appeared in the book. Christian and non-Christian blacks were portrayed. But the point was consistent: the system of slavery was inescapably unjust. The book stirred opposition to slavery, but it angered many Southerners. Stowe's work had a huge impact. Some accounts say that when she visited the White House during the Civil War, Abraham Lincoln greeted her, "So you're the little woman who wrote the book that made this great war."

# Kansas-Nebraska Act

The Compromise of 1850 calmed talk of secession and war—for a time. But just four years later Democratic Senator **Stephen A. Douglas** of Illinois would reignite the sectional conflict. Douglas, like many Americans of his time, envisioned the construction of a transcontinental railroad linking the East Coast to California. The United States had arranged the Gadsden Purchase from Mexico as part of a potential southern route for such a line. Douglas owned real estate in Chicago and preferred a route that started in that city. A transcontinental route from Illinois, however, would have to go through the unorganized portion of the Louisiana Purchase above the 36°30' line. Southerners were not anxious to open this territory to settlement because of the Missouri Compromise's ban on slavery in this territory, and they preferred a southern route for the transcontinental railroad.

To win support in the South for the northern railroad route and the opening of settlement in the region, Douglas proposed the **Kansas-Nebraska Act** (1854), which organized two territories—the Kansas Territory and the Nebraska Territory. To settle the slavery issue, Douglas returned to the idea of popular sovereignty where each territory would decide the status of slavery for itself. To make popular sovereignty work and to please Southern congressmen, the act repealed the provision of the Missouri Compromise that banned slavery north of the 36°30' line.

The Kansas-Nebraska Act divided the Whig Party. Southern Whigs almost unanimously supported the act, while Northern Whigs opposed it, and the division killed the party. The Democrats in Congress held together enough to pass the bill. However, many Northern Democrats who voted in favor of the bill lost their seats in the next election, and several who voted against it left the party.

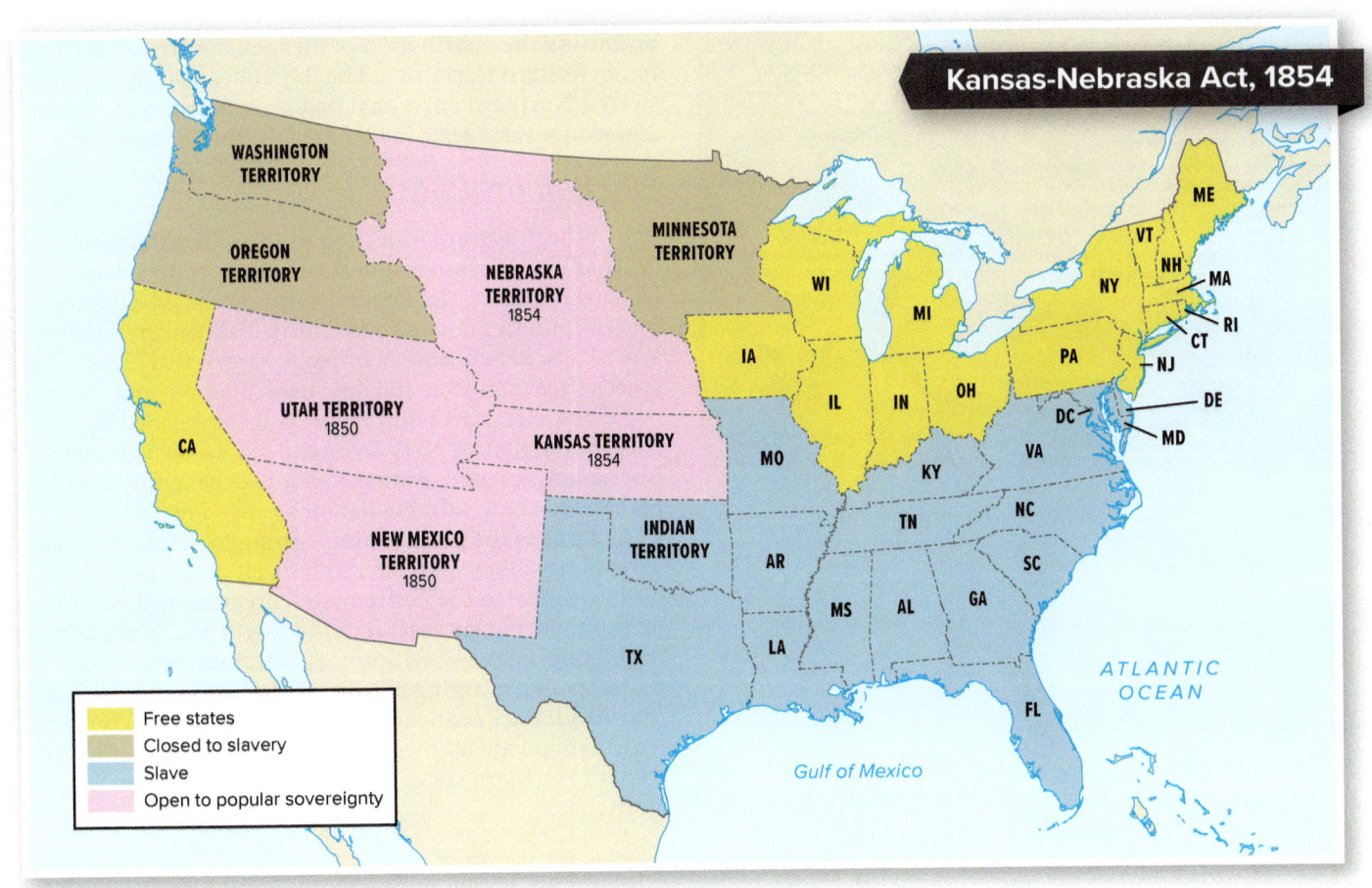

**Kansas-Nebraska Act, 1854**

Legend:
- Free states
- Closed to slavery
- Slave
- Open to popular sovereignty

▲ Know-Nothing Party banner

▲ 1856 Republican Party campaign poster

## The Know-Nothing Party

One group that sought to replace the Whigs was the American Party, better known as the **Know-Nothing Party**. The nickname came from secret societies that were forerunners of the American Party. When people asked members about their secret group, members replied that they knew nothing about it. The Know-Nothings arose in reaction to increasing immigration from Europe in the 1840s and 1850s. Many Americans feared that the immigrants would take jobs from native-born Americans. The fact that many of the immigrants were Irish and German Catholics also caused uneasiness among Protestants. They wanted to reduce the influence of foreign-born voters by increasing the waiting period for immigrants to become citizens and pledged to support only native-born Protestant candidates.

## The Republican Party

Many antislavery Whigs joined together to form the **Republican Party**. The party included abolitionists as well as Free Soilers who opposed the expansion of slavery. Soon, the Republican Party spread across the North.

The Republicans began as a generally antislavery party, but within the party was a wide range of beliefs. Some Free Soilers were more interested in preserving the territories for white settlers than in helping black slaves. The Republicans adopted many Whig principles, such as a protective tariff and federally funded internal improvements. Many Know-Nothings also joined the Republicans because they viewed the Democrats as the party of immigrants. Republicans appealed to the small farmer by promising the distribution of inexpensive land to settlers in the western territories. The Republicans were exclusively a Northern party that had no support in the South and won several seats in Congress in the 1854 election.

## Election of 1856

In the presidential election of 1856, the American Party (Know-Nothings) nominated former president Millard Fillmore. The Republicans nominated explorer-soldier John C. Frémont, the famed "Pathfinder of the West." The Republicans' campaign slogan was "Free speech, free press, free soil, free men, Frémont and victory."

The Democrats nominated an accomplished legislator and diplomat, sixty-five-year-old bachelor **James Buchanan**. A native Pennsylvanian yet generally sympathetic to the South, Buchanan seemed ideal to unite all factions of the party. Campaigning to defend popular sovereignty, Buchanan offered himself as the safe, sensible alternative to the "extremists," Frémont and Fillmore. Frémont proved successful in the North and West, carrying eleven states and winning 114 electoral votes. Fillmore, though winning many popular votes, carried only Maryland. Buchanan, as the head of the only party with a truly nationwide following, carried the entire South and enough Northern states to win 174 electoral votes and the election.

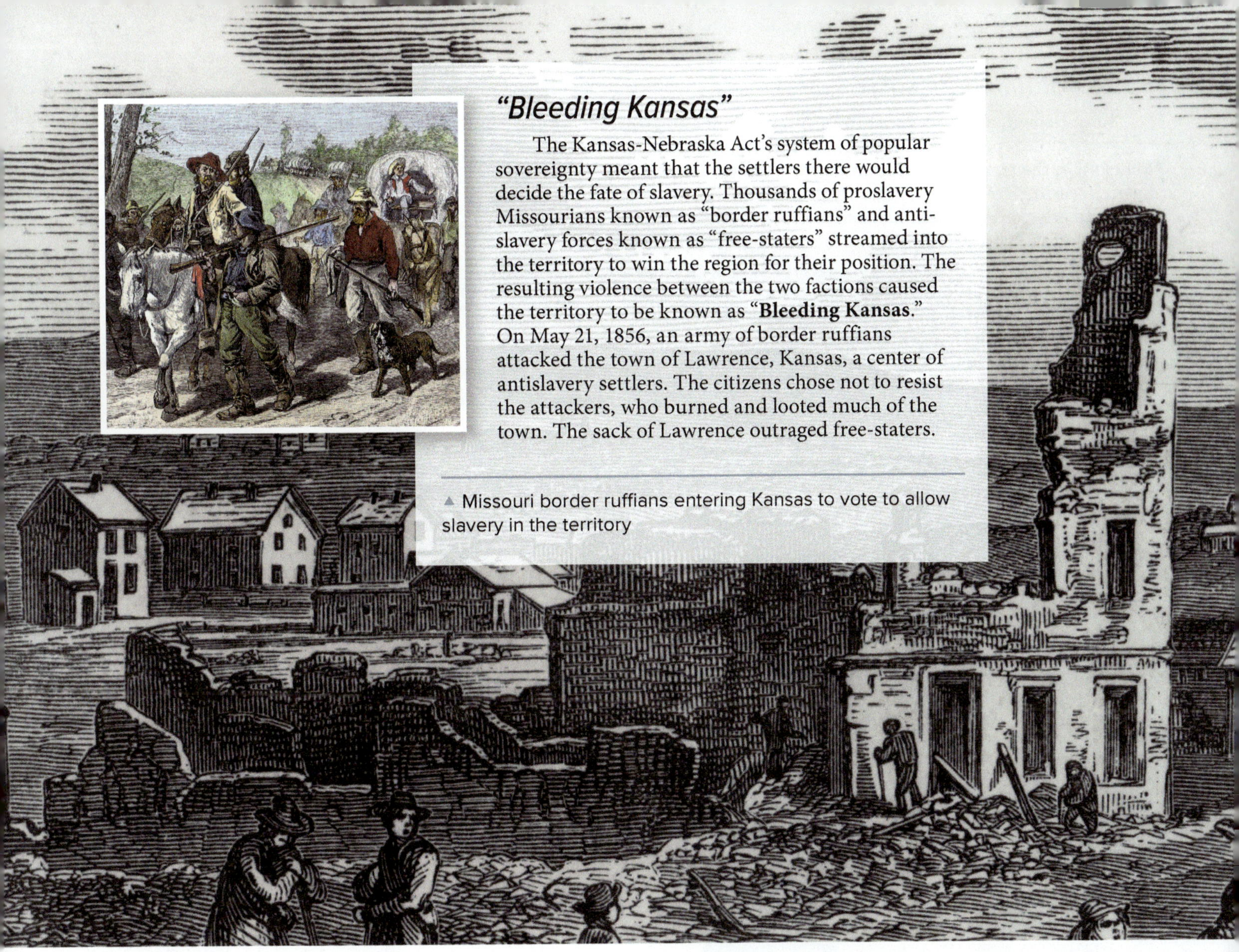

## "Bleeding Kansas"

The Kansas-Nebraska Act's system of popular sovereignty meant that the settlers there would decide the fate of slavery. Thousands of proslavery Missourians known as "border ruffians" and antislavery forces known as "free-staters" streamed into the territory to win the region for their position. The resulting violence between the two factions caused the territory to be known as "**Bleeding Kansas**." On May 21, 1856, an army of border ruffians attacked the town of Lawrence, Kansas, a center of antislavery settlers. The citizens chose not to resist the attackers, who burned and looted much of the town. The sack of Lawrence outraged free-staters.

▲ Missouri border ruffians entering Kansas to vote to allow slavery in the territory

▲ Ruins of the Free State Hotel, Lawrence, Kansas, destroyed by pro-slavery forces in 1856; (below) South Carolina Representative Preston Brooks beating Massachusetts Senator Charles Sumner with a cane on the floor of the US Senate

## Sumner-Brooks Episode

About the same time, Massachusetts Senator Charles Sumner, a fiery abolitionist, gave a heated Senate speech denouncing "the crime against Kansas." For two days, he verbally attacked his proslavery colleagues, especially South Carolina's Andrew Butler, who was not present. Two days later, just a day after the sack of Lawrence, Representative Preston Brooks of South Carolina, Butler's cousin, confronted Sumner in the nearly empty Senate chamber. As Sumner sat at his desk, Brooks struck him repeatedly with a cane. Because of his injuries, Sumner did not return to the Senate for over two years.

To Northerners, the Sumner incident joined "Bleeding Kansas" as a symbol of the South's violent defense of slavery. Southerners praised Brooks for his actions, and some sent him new canes. His district overwhelmingly reelected him to the House. Brooks was later convicted of assault and assessed a fine but received no prison sentence.

## Pottawatomie Massacre

**John Brown**, an abolitionist from Connecticut and father of twenty children, had come to Kansas with five of his sons to help win the territory for the antislavery forces. The sack of Lawrence infuriated Brown not only because the border ruffians had attacked the town but also because the free-staters had not fought back. Gathering his followers after receiving news of Brooks's beating of Sumner, Brown sought revenge. In the grisly Pottawatomie Massacre, Brown's men butchered five proslavery settlers with broadswords. Soon he returned East where he was hailed as a hero among some in the abolitionist movement. By the end of 1856, more than 200 people, including one of Brown's sons, were killed in Kansas during the dozens of bloody incidents of guerilla fighting.

◄ John Brown

▼ Dred Scott

## *Dred Scott* Decision

On March 6, 1857, only two days after Buchanan took office, the Supreme Court handed down a decision that heightened the conflict over slavery. The case revealed that even the Supreme Court could not provide a solution to the problems that so troubled the nation.

Dred Scott was the slave of army surgeon John Emerson from Missouri. During the 1830s, Emerson had taken Scott to Illinois and the unorganized territory of Wisconsin, which had been parts of the Northwest Territory where slavery was prohibited. Emerson later returned with Scott to Missouri, a slave state. After Emerson's death in 1843, Scott sued for his freedom on the grounds that he had become free by entering free territory. The case eventually found its way to the Supreme Court.

Southerners were optimistic that the Supreme Court, which had a Southern majority under Chief Justice Roger Taney, would settle the slavery question in their favor. The court considered three questions in the case. First, was a black man a citizen with the right to sue in federal court? Second, did Scott's residency in a free state and territory make him free? And third, did Congress have the authority to prohibit slavery in any territory?

In **Dred Scott v. Sandford** the court answered these questions by ruling that (1) black people were not citizens and had no right to sue. Taney said that the Declaration's statement that "all men are created equal" did not include blacks, that blacks were not citizens, and that the framers of the Constitution held that they were "so far inferior that they had no rights which a white man was bound to respect;" (2) Scott's residence in a free state did not make him free; and (3) neither Congress nor the territorial governments had the right to prohibit slavery in a territory and that the Fifth Amendment protected the right to property, including slaves. Therefore, the Missouri Compromise was unconstitutional. The decision implied that the doctrine of popular sovereignty, which could threaten the right to property if a state voted to prohibit slavery, was also unconstitutional.

The *Dred Scott* decision further deepened the sectional divide. Southerners praised it because it prevented Congress from prohibiting slavery in the territories, while Northerners denounced it and declared that it was not a binding precedent. Politically, compromise between the two sides seemed no longer possible.

◄ Chief Justice Roger Taney

# Lincoln-Douglas Debates

One man caught in the crossfire over the *Dred Scott* decision was Stephen Douglas, who maintained his belief in popular sovereignty but now had to reconcile it with the Supreme Court's ruling. In what became known as the Freeport Doctrine, Douglas argued that a territory could not deny a slaveowner the right to take his slaves into any territory, but the territories were not required to pass legislation enforcing and protecting that right. The Freeport Doctrine angered proslavery forces.

Republican **Abraham Lincoln** ran against Stephen Douglas for the US Senate seat from Illinois in 1858. Lincoln launched the campaign by giving his "House Divided" speech. He said,

> *"A house divided against itself cannot stand." I believe this government cannot endure permanently half slave and half free. I do not expect the Union to be dissolved—I do not expect the house to fall—but I do expect it will cease to be divided. It will become all one thing or all the other.*

Douglas immediately charged Lincoln with promoting conflict and discord. After all, Douglas argued, the nation had existed as half slave and half free since its founding. Why should it not continue to do so? Lincoln responded by challenging Douglas to a series of debates.

▲ Stephen Douglas

Douglas accepted, and the seven **Lincoln-Douglas debates**, held in different sites across the state, became a platform for not only the Illinois senate race but also the national debate on slavery.

In the debates, Douglas continued to promote popular sovereignty as the answer to the slavery question. Lincoln responded that popular sovereignty avoided the moral issue of slavery and made liberty an end unto itself rather than a means for all Americans, including blacks, to secure their unalienable rights. The heart of the controversy, Lincoln said, was the immorality and expansion of slavery. "The real issue in this controversy . . . is the sentiment on the part of one class that looks upon the institution of slavery *as a wrong*, and of another class that *does not* look upon it as a wrong."

Douglas replied, "I look forward to a time when each state shall be allowed to do as it pleases. If it chooses to keep slavery forever, it is not my business, but its own; if it chooses to abolish slavery, it is its own business—not mine."

When the state legislature voted, Douglas retained his Senate seat. Although Lincoln lost, he had gained national attention for his views.

▼ Lincoln speaking at one of the Lincoln-Douglas debates

## Abraham Lincoln

Abraham Lincoln was born into the family of a poor farmer living in Kentucky in 1809. The family moved to southern Indiana when Abraham was seven.

The Lincolns moved to Illinois in 1830. There Lincoln was able to find work as a store clerk, postmaster, and surveyor. Although he received infrequent formal education, Lincoln became an avid reader, eagerly consuming the works of Shakespeare, the poems of Robert Burns, and the Bible. He also began to study law on his own, and in 1836 he was licensed to practice.

Lincoln also developed a taste for politics. He joined the Whig Party, headed by fellow Kentuckian Henry Clay, and became an influential leader in the Illinois party. He served four terms in the Illinois state legislature (1834–42) and one term in the US House of Representatives (1847–49).

By 1850 Lincoln had left politics to devote himself to his profitable law practice in Springfield, Illinois. The Kansas-Nebraska Act brought Lincoln out of his political retirement. "I was losing interest in politics," Lincoln wrote in 1859, "when the repeal of the Missouri Compromise aroused me again." Lincoln denounced the act because it offered the possibility of slavery's expansion into the territories. Lincoln left the Whigs and joined the Republican Party. By 1858 he was the leading Republican in Illinois and the natural choice to oppose incumbent Stephen Douglas for the US Senate.

Douglas said that Lincoln "is as honest as he is shrewd." Lincoln's thoughtfulness, generosity, sense of humor, and talent for telling amusing stories charmed those who met him. The driving force behind his political thinking was that slavery was wrong.

▲ Young Abraham Lincoln cutting wood for his mother at their log cabin

Yet Lincoln knew that slavery could not be easily eliminated. He also believed that the federal government had no right to interfere with slavery in the states where it already existed but that slavery should not be allowed to expand any farther. He condemned popular sovereignty because it attempted to avoid the moral concerns about slavery. Lincoln believed the territories must be kept free so that slavery would eventually die out.

## John Brown's Raid

Events of the 1850s motivated an increasing number of abolitionists to abandon nonviolence in favor of more aggressive tactics. After his actions in Kansas, John Brown began planning a raid into the Shenandoah Valley of Virginia. In the fall of 1859, Brown and several followers moved secretly to a farmhouse near **Harpers Ferry, Virginia** (now West Virginia), the site of a federal arsenal. Brown's plan was to capture the arsenal and its large supply of weapons and begin a slave revolt by traveling down the Shenandoah Valley and freeing slaves. When Brown tried to recruit Frederick Douglass to his cause, Douglass refused, believing Brown's plan was a suicide mission that would turn the whole country against abolition.

Brown was only able to convince seventeen white men (including three of his sons) and five black men to join him. During the night of October 16, 1859, Brown's gang quietly seized the arsenal, which was guarded by only one night watchman, and cut the telegraph lines. Brown's men took several hostages. By the next morning, alarmed citizens and Virginia and Maryland militia surrounded the arsenal. As the day wore on, several people on both sides were mortally wounded, including two of Brown's sons. Ironically, the first person that Brown's raiders killed was a free black man working as a baggage handler.

▲ John Brown holding his dying son during the battle at the Harpers Ferry arsenal

Colonel Robert E. Lee received orders to take command of federal troops in the area and recapture the arsenal. On the morning of October 18, Lee ordered a detachment of marines under the command of Lieutenant J.E.B. Stuart to take Brown's stronghold. After a brief fight, Brown was injured, and he and his remaining raiders were captured.

Brown was quickly tried and convicted of murder and treason and was sentenced to be hanged. Initially, the Northern response to Brown's raid was to condemn it as the act of a madman. The majority did not support slave revolts or Brown's methods. Lincoln noted that although Brown "agreed with us in thinking slavery wrong, that cannot excuse violence, bloodshed and treason."

But Brown's words at his trial and hanging caused some to begin to view him as a martyr. Before his sentencing, Brown said,

> If it is deemed necessary that I should forfeit my life, for the furtherance of the ends [needs] of justice, and mingle my blood . . . with the blood of millions in this slave country, whose rights are disregarded by wicked, cruel, and unjust enactments—I say, LET IT BE DONE.

Abolitionists found Brown's death a useful symbol, and when he was hanged in Charlestown, Virginia, on December 2, 1859, some buildings in the North were draped with black, church bells were rung, and elegies were written for Brown.

The Southern reaction to Harpers Ferry was fear of more Northern plots to provoke slave insurrections. Further outrage was sparked by Northern expressions of admiration for Brown. Many Republicans tried to distance themselves from Brown's actions, but Southerners came to believe that if the Republicans came to power, the South would not be safe.

▲ John Brown being led to his execution

## Comprehension Check 9.3

1. Popular sovereignty proposed that ____.

   A outlawing slavery in the territories was unconstitutional

   B residents in the territories choose whether to allow slavery in the territory

   C the 36°30' line would extend through the Mexican Cession

2. The Great Compromise of 1850 included the following measures except ____.

   A a new fugitive slave law

   B California being admitted as a free state

   C New Mexico and Utah being admitted as slave states

3. The Supreme Court decided all of the following in *Dred Scott v. Sandford* except that ____.

   A a black man had the right to sue in federal court

   B Congress did not have authority to prohibit slavery in any territory

   C Scott was not free based on moving to free territories

4. John Brown attempted to seize a federal arsenal at ____ in order to incite a slave rebellion.

   A Washington, DC,

   B Pottawatomie Creek, Kansas,

   C Harpers Ferry, Virginia,

### MAKING CONNECTIONS

5. Which three parties formed after the Whigs split over slavery? What did each support?

6. How did Stephen Douglas propose handling the slavery issue in the Kansas-Nebraska Act, and how did that proposal lead to "Bleeding Kansas"?

## 9.4 Secession

**Why did some Southern states secede?**

## Election of 1860

As the Democratic Party convention began in 1860, dispute over the party's platform caused a serious rift. Supporters of Stephen Douglas wanted popular sovereignty in the territories. Deep South delegates called for protecting the rights of slaveowners in every territory. When the Northern delegates rejected the proposal, delegates from several Southern states left the convention. Each group reconvened, with Northern Democrats nominating Douglas, and Southern Democrats nominating Buchanan's vice president, John C. Breckinridge of Kentucky.

In addition, a new group emerged, made up of Southerners and Northerners, including many former Whigs, called the Constitutional Union Party. The Constitutional Union platform was "The Constitution of the Country, the Union of the States, and the Enforcement of the Laws." The party represented the sentiment in the Upper South and border states and offered a pro-Union alternative to those who believed that a Republican victory would bring disunion. They hoped to prevent secession by avoiding the slavery issue. They nominated John Bell from Tennessee for the presidency.

Republicans met in Chicago for their convention. The party platform opposed the expansion of slavery into the territories and supported a protective tariff for Northern business interests. It also endorsed a transcontinental railroad and opening of western lands to appeal to farmers and immigrants. The Republicans also tried to calm Southern fears by pledging not to interfere with slavery where it already existed. Abraham Lincoln won his party's nomination.

The presidential campaign was really two sectional races: Lincoln and Douglas competing in the North, Bell and Breckinridge in the South. With the Democrats hopelessly divided, Lincoln won with just under forty percent of the popular vote. Since his sectional strength was in the more populous North, however, he won a majority in the Electoral College.

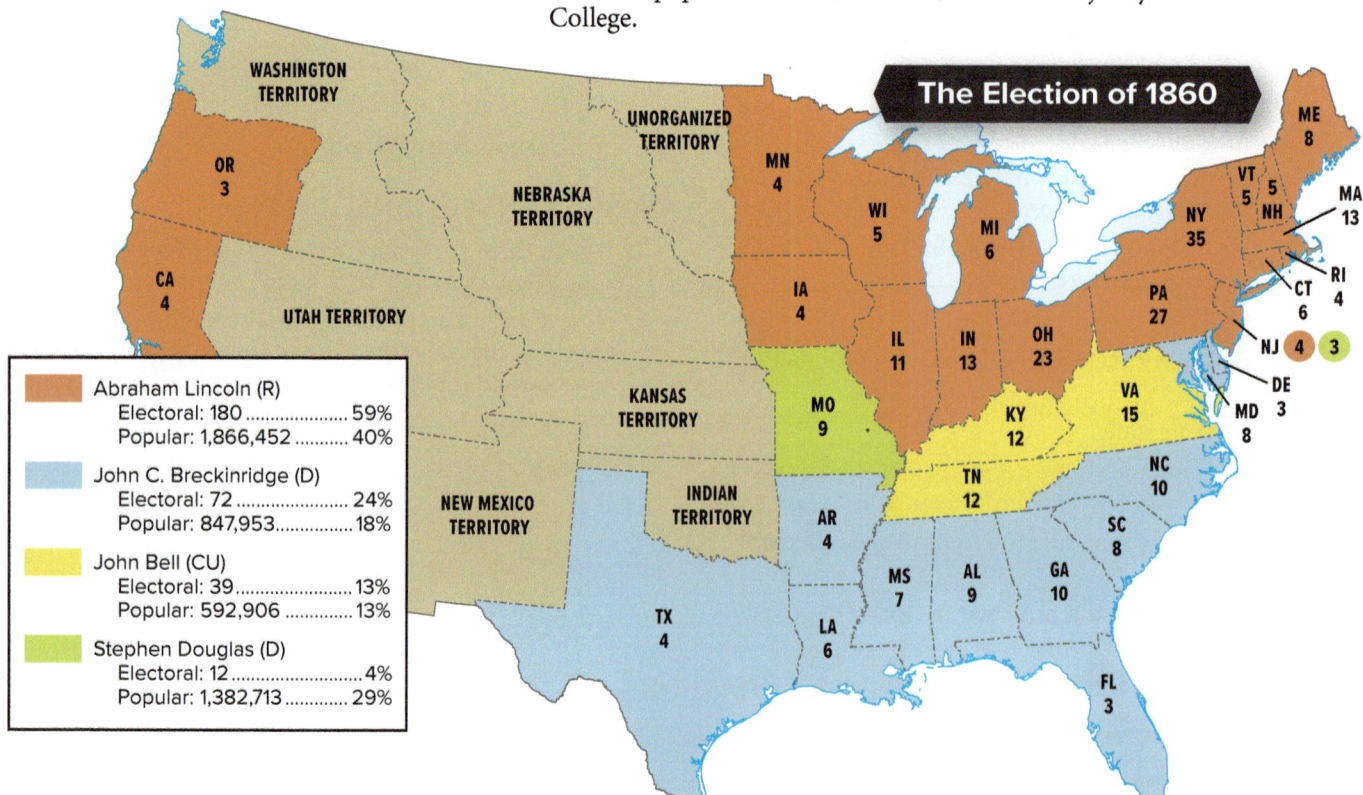

**The Election of 1860**

Abraham Lincoln (R)
Electoral: 180 .................... 59%
Popular: 1,866,452 .......... 40%

John C. Breckinridge (D)
Electoral: 72 ...................... 24%
Popular: 847,953 ............... 18%

John Bell (CU)
Electoral: 39 ...................... 13%
Popular: 592,906 ............. 13%

Stephen Douglas (D)
Electoral: 12 ...................... 4%
Popular: 1,382,713 ........... 29%

## Secession of the Deep South States

Many Deep South leaders had promised that if Lincoln won, they would not submit to what they considered a hostile, strictly Northern, antislavery government. South Carolina led the way on December 20, 1860, by unanimously approving an Ordinance of Secession. By February 1, 1861, six more Deep South states—Mississippi, Florida, Alabama, Georgia, Louisiana, and Texas—had also seceded. On February 8 in Montgomery, Alabama, those seven Southern states formed the **Confederate States of America** and elected **Jefferson Davis**, a former senator from Mississippi and secretary of war, as president, and **Alexander Stephens** of Georgia as vice president.

President-elect Lincoln repeated his campaign promise not to interfere with slavery in the states where it already existed, but he refused to commit himself to any course of action until he took office. President Buchanan denounced secession but declared he did not have the power to force a state into remaining in the Union.

▶ Crowd gathered at the capitol building in Montgomery, Alabama, at the announcement of the election of Jefferson Davis as president of the Confederate States of America

## Lincoln's View *of* Secession

In his first inaugural address, Lincoln stated why he believed states could not leave the Union.

> I hold that in contemplation of universal law and of the Constitution the Union of these States is perpetual. . . .
>
> If the United States be not a government proper, but an association of states in the nature of contract merely, can it, as a contract, be peaceably unmade by less than all the parties who made it? One party to a contract may violate it . . . but does it not require all to lawfully rescind [abolish] it? . . .
>
> It follows from these views that no state upon its own mere motion can lawfully get out of the Union; that resolves and ordinances to that effect are legally void, and that acts of violence within any state or states against the authority of the United States are insurrectionary or revolutionary. . . .
>
> I therefore consider that in view of the Constitution . . . the Union is unbroken, and to the extent of my ability, I shall take care, as the Constitution itself expressly enjoins upon me, that the laws of the Union be faithfully executed in all the States. . . .
>
> In doing this there needs to be no bloodshed or violence, and there shall be none unless it be forced upon the national authority.

 ### Analyzing Sources

How does Lincoln use the analogy of a contract to argue against secession?

## Comprehension Check 9.4

1. The Democratic Party was split between the nomination for Douglas in the North and ____ in the South.

   A  John Bell

   B  John C. Breckinridge

   C  James Buchanan

2. All of the following were included in the Republican Party platform except ____.

   A  abolishing slavery in the South

   B  endorsing a transcontinental railroad

   C  supporting a protective tariff

3. In reaction to Lincoln's election, seven states seceded and nominated ____ as president of the Confederate States of America.

   A  Alexander Stephens

   B  Jefferson Davis

   C  William Seward

4. James Buchanan opposed secession but claimed that he did not have power to prevent states from seceding.

   True      False

### MAKING CONNECTIONS

5. How did Lincoln counter the argument that the United States was an association of states that could be broken?

GUIDING QUESTIONS

- Why was Fort Sumter fired upon?
- Which slave states seceded, and which remained in the Union?

## 9.5 Fort Sumter

What resulted from the firing on Fort Sumter?

### Firing on Fort Sumter

In the last weeks of Buchanan's presidency, the Confederacy had seized federal property within its borders, except for Fort Pickens in Florida and **Fort Sumter** in Charleston, South Carolina. Having done nothing to interfere with secession, Buchanan did send a ship with supplies to Fort Sumter, but Confederate forces in Charleston fired on the ship before it could reach the fort.

In Lincoln's inauguration speech on March 4, 1861, he pledged again not "to interfere with the institution of slavery in the States where it exists. I believe I have no lawful right to do so, and I have no inclination to do so." On the other hand, Lincoln pledged to "hold, occupy, and possess" remaining federal property in the states that had formed the Confederacy. Lincoln also gave this promise and warning to the seceded states: "the government will not assail you, unless you first assail it."

Lincoln had no intention to surrender Fort Sumter, despite his cabinet's advice that he do so. He notified the governor of South Carolina of his intentions to send food, but not military supplies, to the fort. Lincoln also promised no military action would be taken unless the Confederates attacked Fort Sumter. Confederate leaders decided to stop the supplies from reaching Sumter. They believed that allowing federal troops to continue to occupy the fort would be a threat to the Confederacy's independence. They also hoped military action against the fort would convince Virginia to join the Confederacy.

▼ Lincoln taking the presidential oath of office at his first inauguration

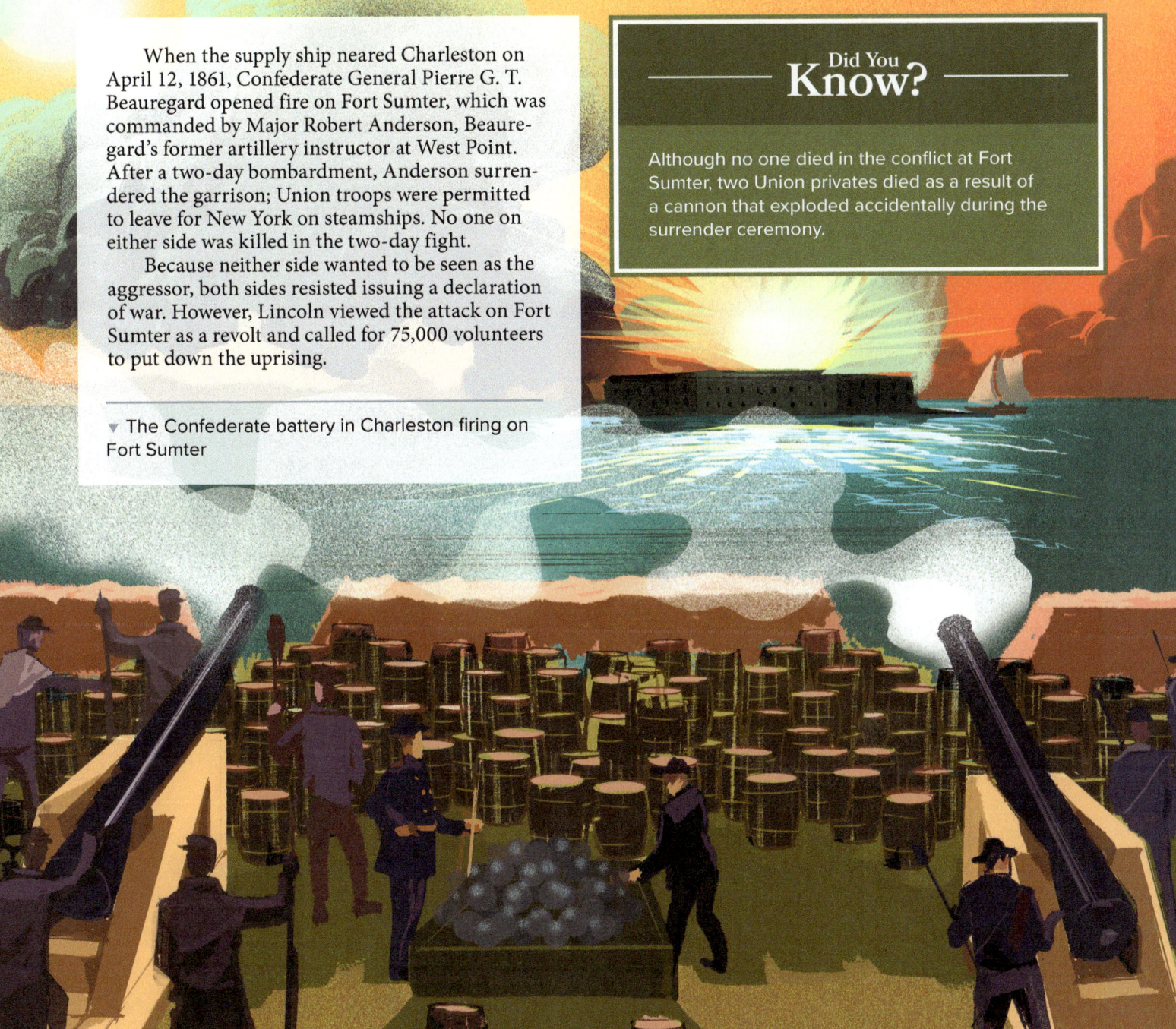

When the supply ship neared Charleston on April 12, 1861, Confederate General Pierre G. T. Beauregard opened fire on Fort Sumter, which was commanded by Major Robert Anderson, Beauregard's former artillery instructor at West Point. After a two-day bombardment, Anderson surrendered the garrison; Union troops were permitted to leave for New York on steamships. No one on either side was killed in the two-day fight.

Because neither side wanted to be seen as the aggressor, both sides resisted issuing a declaration of war. However, Lincoln viewed the attack on Fort Sumter as a revolt and called for 75,000 volunteers to put down the uprising.

▼ The Confederate battery in Charleston firing on Fort Sumter

### Did You Know?

Although no one died in the conflict at Fort Sumter, two Union privates died as a result of a cannon that exploded accidentally during the surrender ceremony.

## Robert E. Lee and Stonewall Jackson

Perhaps Robert E. Lee and Thomas J. "Stonewall" Jackson best illustrate the dilemma that many Southerners faced at the outset of the war. Lee had a great American heritage as the son of a Revolutionary War hero, and his wife was the step-granddaughter of George Washington. Lee had already given thirty years of distinguished service to his country as an officer in the army. In April 1861, Lincoln offered him the job as commander of the Union armies. Earlier, Lee had told a friend, "If Virginia stands by the old Union, so will I. But if she secedes (though I do not believe in secession as a constitutional right, nor that there is sufficient cause for revolution), then I will follow my native State with my sword, and, if need be, with my life." When Virginia left the Union, he declined Lincoln's offer, declaring, "Save in defense of my native state, I never desire again to draw my sword."

Thomas J. "Stonewall" Jackson was one of the South's best generals. He converted to Christ shortly after serving in the Mexican War, in which Lee had also fought. Like Lee, Jackson initially opposed secession. He believed Southerners should handle disagreements without leaving the Union. But when Virginia withdrew, he remained intensely loyal to his state.

# Secession of the Upper South States

In the Upper South, many people had hoped for reconciliation. When Lincoln called for volunteers to fight the South, the eight remaining slave states had to make the decision to either supply troops to fight against their fellow Southerners or join the Confederacy. Four states—Virginia, Arkansas, North Carolina, and Tennessee—voted to secede, making eleven states in the Confederate States of America.

The four remaining slave states, Missouri, Kentucky, Maryland, and Delaware, chose to remain in the Union and were called **border states**. Fifty counties in western Virginia, where slavery was less common and where resentment against eastern Virginia's dominance of the state was high, established their own government and applied for statehood. West Virginia entered the Union in June 1863 and was also considered a border state.

Lincoln was determined to keep the border states in the Union. Maryland was of particular concern—if it seceded, Washington, DC, would be surrounded by Confederate territory. Lincoln declared martial law in Maryland, placing the military in control of the state, and had a pro-secession state legislator imprisoned for hindering the movement of Union troops. When the legislator's attorney demanded a habeas corpus hearing in federal court to examine the charges, Lincoln suspended the writ of habeas corpus which said that a person could not be jailed without being charged with a crime. This action was allowed by the Constitution in cases of rebellion, though it did not specify whether it was a power of Congress or the executive branch. When Chief Justice Taney ruled that only Congress could suspend habeas corpus, Lincoln ignored his decision.

The stage was now set for the great conflict that nearly tore the nation apart.

## Comprehension Check 9.5

1. Both Buchanan and Lincoln attempted to send a supply ship to Fort Sumter.

    True      False

2. Lincoln issued a declaration of war on the Confederate States of America.

    True      False

3. Delaware, Maryland, Kentucky, and _____ were slave states that decided to remain in the Union.

    A  Missouri

    B  Tennessee

    C  Virginia

4. To keep the border states in the Union, Lincoln used the following measures except _____.

    A  declaring martial law in Maryland

    B  seizing the western counties of Virginia

    C  suspending habeas corpus

### MAKING CONNECTIONS

5. How did Lincoln's actions regarding Fort Sumter reflect his promises in his inauguration speech?

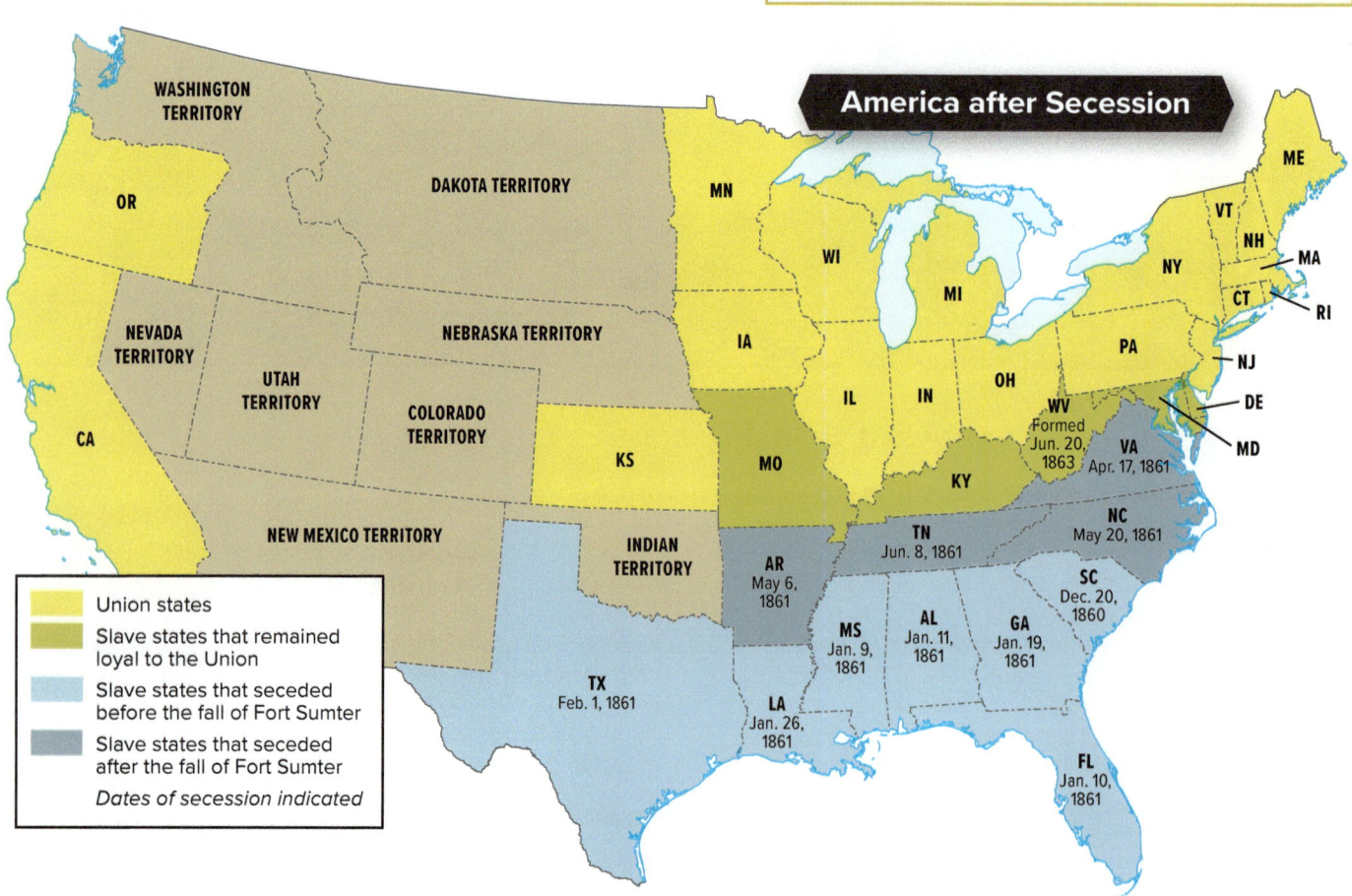

America after Secession

WASHINGTON TERRITORY

DAKOTA TERRITORY

OR

NEVADA TERRITORY

UTAH TERRITORY

NEBRASKA TERRITORY

COLORADO TERRITORY

CA

KS

NEW MEXICO TERRITORY

INDIAN TERRITORY

MN

WI

MI

IA

IL

IN

OH

MO

KY

TX
Feb. 1, 1861

AR
May 6, 1861

LA
Jan. 26, 1861

MS
Jan. 9, 1861

AL
Jan. 11, 1861

GA
Jan. 19, 1861

TN
Jun. 8, 1861

NC
May 20, 1861

SC
Dec. 20, 1860

FL
Jan. 10, 1861

ME

VT

NH

MA

NY

CT

RI

PA

NJ

WV
Formed Jun. 20, 1863

VA
Apr. 17, 1861

DE

MD

Union states

Slave states that remained loyal to the Union

Slave states that seceded before the fall of Fort Sumter

Slave states that seceded after the fall of Fort Sumter

*Dates of secession indicated*

# CHAPTER 9 REVIEW

## Chapter Summary

### 9.1 Sectional Differences

- Growing sectional differences between the economies and the political views of the North and South were apparent.

- Whigs and Democrats had support in both the North and the South, but the issue of slavery divided the nation politically along sectional rather than party lines.

**TERMS**

Nat Turner

Underground Railroad

Harriet Tubman

### 9.2 American Slavery

- Most slaves were field hands who worked in harsh conditions for long hours cultivating crops. Slaves were viewed as property and had no legal rights. Slave marriages were common but not recognized by law, and slave families were often broken up.

- Despite harsh conditions, slaves were able to create a distinct African American culture. Slaves also sometimes revolted, some resisted in other ways, and some ran away. The Underground Railroad helped many slaves escape to the North or to Canada.

- Northerners and Southerners used religious, moral, economic, constitutional, and political arguments to oppose or defend slavery. Some used the Bible to defend slavery, failing to recognize the differences between servitude in the Bible and American slavery.

### 9.3 Sectional Conflict

- The status of slavery in the Mexican Cession reopened sectional conflict. Both the North's Wilmot Proviso and the South's Calhoun Resolutions were defeated, and popular sovereignty was then proposed as a compromise. The question of slavery in the territory divided the Democratic Party and led to the election of Whig Zachary Taylor as president.

- California's application for statehood led to the Compromise of 1850. The Fugitive Slave Act of 1850 enforced the return of fugitive slaves, which angered many Northerners. Many Southerners were outraged at Northern resistance and obstruction of the law.

- Stephen A. Douglas proposed the Kansas-Nebraska Act which allowed popular sovereignty in those territories. This led to violence between proslavery and antislavery forces in "Bleeding Kansas," including the Pottawatomie Massacre led by abolitionist John Brown.

- The *Dred Scott* decision further deepened the sectional conflict.

- John Brown's failed attempt at Harpers Ferry to start a slave revolt and his treatment as a martyr by some Northerners caused many Southerners to believe that the South would not be safe if a Republican were elected president.

**TERMS**

popular sovereignty

Free Soil Party

Compromise of 1850

Millard Fillmore

Fugitive Slave Act of 1850

Franklin Pierce

*Uncle Tom's Cabin*

Stephen A. Douglas

Kansas-Nebraska Act

Know-Nothing Party

Republican Party

James Buchanan

Bleeding Kansas

John Brown

*Dred Scott v. Sandford*

Abraham Lincoln

Lincoln-Douglas debates

Harpers Ferry

## TERMS

Confederate States of America

Jefferson Davis

Alexander Stephens

## 9.4 / Secession

- The Democratic Party split into Northern and Southern branches in the election of 1860. The Constitutional Union Party formed. The Republican Party nominated Abraham Lincoln.

- Lincoln's election led to the secession of seven Southern states that joined together to form the Confederate States of America.

## TERMS

Confederate States of America

Jefferson Davis

Alexander Stephens

## TERMS

Fort Sumter

border states

## 9.5 / Fort Sumter

- Lincoln pledged to hold on to federal forts in the seceded states. When federal ships tried to resupply Fort Sumter, the Confederates opened fire. Lincoln called for volunteers to put down the rebellion.

- Four more Southern states seceded, and four other slave states chose to stay in the Union and were called border states. Virginia split and part of it became the state of West Virginia and joined the Union.

- Lincoln declared martial law in Maryland and suspended the writ of habeas corpus to prevent the state from seceding.

## *Chapter Review Questions*

### RECALL

1. What issue separated the nation politically along sectional rather than party lines?

2. What were three ways some slaves resisted slavery?

3. What proposed law would have prohibited slavery in the Mexican Cession?

4. What position for determining the status of slavery in the territories was supported by Lewis Cass and Stephen Douglas?

5. Who were the three candidates for president in 1848 and what party did each represent? Who won?

6. Who were the "fire-eaters"?

7. What president signed the Compromise of 1850 into law? How did he become president?

8. Who won the presidential election of 1852?

9. Who won the presidential election of 1856?

10. What abolitionist led the Pottawatomie Massacre and the attack on Harpers Ferry?

11. Who were the four candidates for president in 1860 and what party did each represent? Who won?

12. What federal fort in South Carolina did Lincoln vow to hold, occupy, and possess?

13. What states were border states?

## UNDERSTAND

**14.** Compare the economies of the South and the North in 1850.

**15.** Compare the Northern and Southern views of the Constitution.

**16.** How many immigrants came to the United States between 1820 and 1860? Where did most settle, and what was different about them compared to earlier immigrants?

**17.** What were three Northern arguments against slavery?

**18.** What were three Southern defenses of slavery?

**19.** What were three arguments from the Bible that opponents of slavery used?

**20.** What did John C. Calhoun predict the outcome would be if the Wilmot Proviso was passed?

**21.** What were three of the five parts of the Compromise of 1850?

**22.** Why was Calhoun opposed to the Compromise of 1850?

**23.** What did Daniel Webster say about those who argued for "peaceable secession"?

**24.** How did the Fugitive Slave Act of 1850 enforce the fugitive slave clause?

**25.** What three things did many Northerners dislike about the Fugitive Slave Act of 1850?

**26.** How did the Kansas-Nebraska Act affect the Missouri Compromise?

**27.** Why did Kansas become known as "Bleeding Kansas"?

**28.** Describe the Sumner-Brooks episode and the Northern and Southern responses to it.

**29.** What did the court decide on the three questions raised by the *Dred Scott* case?

**30.** In the Lincoln-Douglas debates, what was Lincoln's criticism of popular sovereignty?

**31.** Why did the first seven states secede from the Union?

**32.** What was President Buchanan's position regarding the seceded states?

**33.** What was Lincoln's view of a state's right to secede?

**34.** When and why was Fort Sumter bombarded?

**35.** What led Virginia, Arkansas, North Carolina, and Tennessee to secede?

**36.** Describe Lincoln's actions to keep Maryland in the Union. Why was the suspension of habeas corpus controversial?

## THINK ABOUT IT

**37.** What were four specific rules or actions which denied slaves justice and equality?

**38.** How does the Bible shape your own view of American slavery?

**39.** What did John Brown's actions at Pottawatomie and Harpers Ferry demonstrate about the relationship between the righteousness of a cause and the righteousness of a person's actions? How might this apply to a modern social issue?

▼ Federal forces retaking the arsenal at Harpers Ferry

# 10 The Civil War

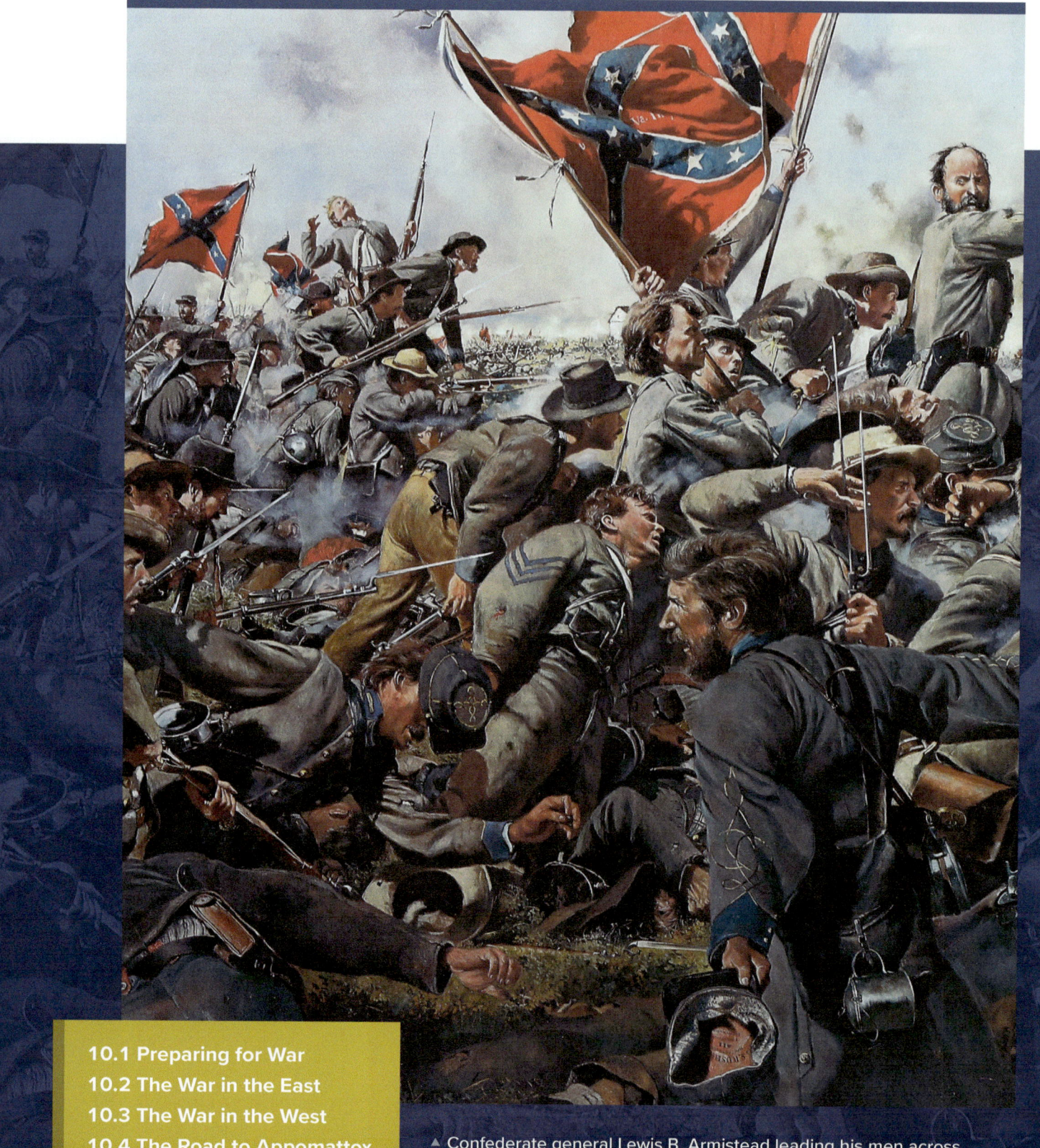

10.1 Preparing for War

10.2 The War in the East

10.3 The War in the West

10.4 The Road to Appomattox

▲ Confederate general Lewis B. Armistead leading his men across the stone wall during Pickett's Charge at Gettysburg, July 3, 1863

# Preparing for War

**How did the North and South prepare for war?**

After the firing on Fort Sumter and Lincoln's call for volunteers to put down what he saw as the Southern rebellion, the nation found itself in a state of war. In some families, brother fought against brother and father against son in this bloody conflict.

## GUIDING QUESTIONS

- What advantages did the North and the South have at the outset of the war?
- How did the North and the South recruit soldiers?
- How did life for those at home change during the war?
- How did each side fight the Civil War?

## Advantages & Disadvantages

### Southern

### Military Leadership

One area in which the South surpassed the North, particularly in the early years of the war, was in military leadership. The South had a strong military tradition, and many Southerners had attended West Point (the national military academy in New York) as well as Southern military academies such as the Citadel and Virginia Military Institute. As a result, many more of the Confederate officers were better trained than their Union counterparts at the outset of the war and had gained valuable experience in the Mexican War.

### Defensive War

Another Southern advantage was that, much like the American colonies in the Revolutionary War, the South only had to fight a defensive war to secure its independence. It would not need to invade and conquer the North but merely to outlast the North's will to fight. The North, on the other hand, would need to attack and occupy the South to bring it into submission. Fighting on Southern soil meant the South would be familiar with the terrain.

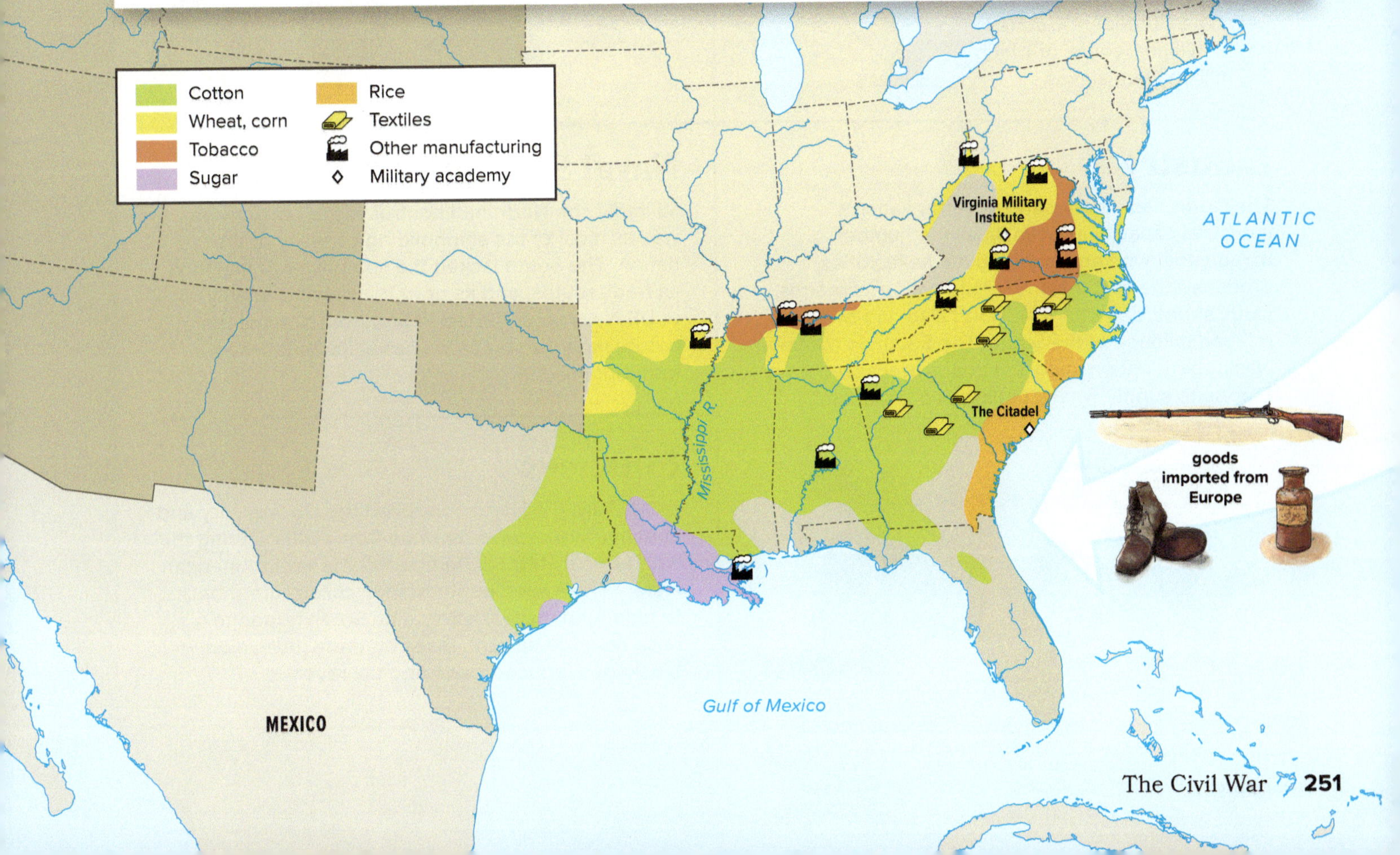

**Map Legend:**
- Cotton
- Wheat, corn
- Tobacco
- Sugar
- Rice
- Textiles
- Other manufacturing
- Military academy

Virginia Military Institute

The Citadel

ATLANTIC OCEAN

goods imported from Europe

Mississippi R.

MEXICO

Gulf of Mexico

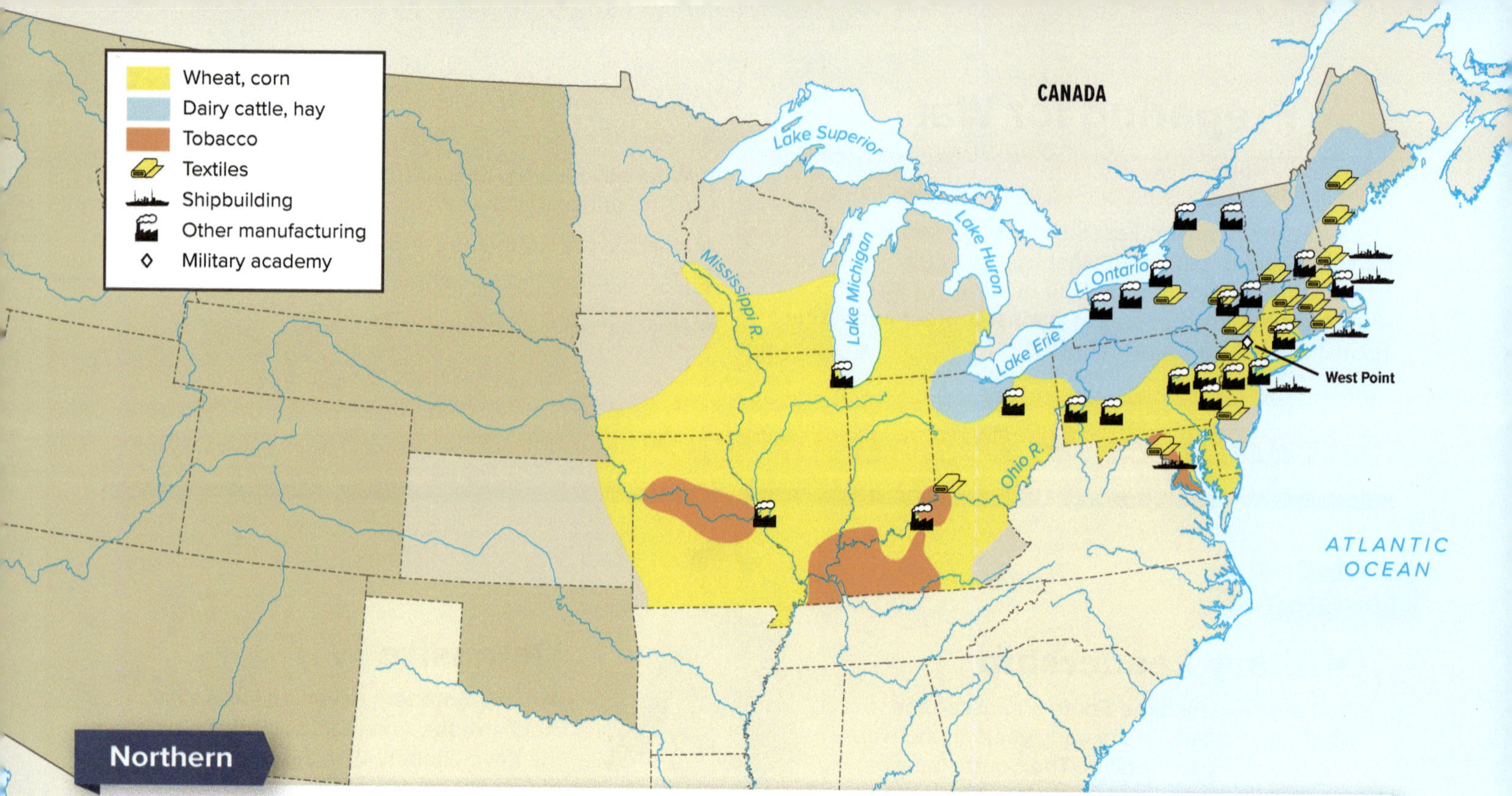

Legend:
- Wheat, corn
- Dairy cattle, hay
- Tobacco
- Textiles
- Shipbuilding
- Other manufacturing
- Military academy

CANADA

Lake Superior
Lake Michigan
Lake Huron
L. Ontario
Lake Erie
Mississippi R.
Ohio R.

West Point

ATLANTIC OCEAN

**Northern**

## Population

In 1860 the eighteen Northern states had a population of 22 million, more than twice that of the eleven seceding states, and were adding over 300,000 immigrants per year. The Confederate states had 9 million people, of which 3.5 million were slaves.

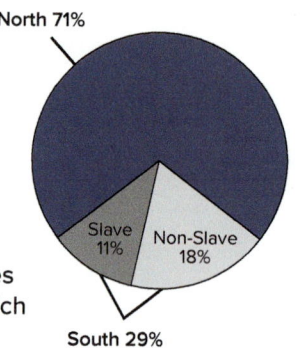

North 71%

Slave 11%  Non-Slave 18%

South 29%

## Food Production

The North dominated production of wheat, corn, and oats. While the South produced enough food to feed itself, its agriculture was geared toward the cash crops of cotton and tobacco, which would do little to sustain hungry troops.

## Industry

The North had ninety percent of the nation's industrial capacity and ten times the number of industrial workers as the South. Its factories produced the vast majority of the nation's firearms, cloth, shoes, and iron. The North also had twice the railroad mileage of the South. The South, in contrast, was dependent on imported goods purchased from Europe to supply what it could not produce.

## Naval Strength

Militarily, the North had control of the US Navy as well as most of the shipbuilding capacity of the nation. The South lacked the sea power to maintain its trade routes, and its navy consisted primarily of US Navy ships seized in Southern ports at the outbreak of the war as well as ships purchased from Britain.

## Finances

Financially, the North controlled the US Treasury and continued to receive revenue from tariffs. During the war it also instituted the first income tax in American history and issued paper money called "greenbacks" to help fund the war effort. The South hoped to raise revenue through taxes on trade, but Union blockades reduced trade and tax revenue.

# Assembling Armies

## Raising Northern Forces

Before the bombardment of Fort Sumter, the US Army had a total of 16,000 professional soldiers, mostly scattered in the West. As a result of secession, about one-fourth of those resigned to join the Confederacy. After Fort Sumter, believing the war would last only a short time, Lincoln called for 75,000 volunteers to serve a three-month enlistment. At first, there was little problem raising a force, as many were eager to fight. However, when it became apparent that the war would last much longer, Lincoln called for an additional one million volunteers to serve three-year enlistments. To encourage volunteers, recruits were paid a bounty, or bonus money, by the federal government.

It became harder for the Union to recruit volunteers as the war dragged on, enlistments expired, and casualties and desertions mounted. To raise troops, in March 1863 Congress passed a **conscription** (military draft) law which enrolled every white male ages twenty through forty-five. Those whose names were drawn could only be exempted from serving if they were disabled or if they were their family's sole means of support. Draftees could also pay money for exemption or hire a substitute. Hired substitutes were often recent immigrants and made up nearly one-fourth of all Union soldiers.

Conscription in the North led to fierce resistance in some places. The most violent example was the New York draft riot in July 1863. New York City was home to many immigrants, many of whom had no interest in fighting in the war. They resented having to enroll for the draft and that wealthy individuals could hire substitutes or pay not to be drafted. They also resented that free blacks could not be drafted and feared that as the war became a war of emancipation, freed slaves would take away their jobs. In four days of rioting, mobs attacked not only government officials but also the city's free black population. By the time the riots were suppressed, 119 people had died and about 300 had been injured.

Although free blacks initially could not serve in the army, they could enroll in the navy or assist in other capacities. However, in 1862 the army allowed free blacks and freed slaves to enlist in black army regiments. About 180,000 served in the Union army, making up about ten percent of the army's soldiers, and composed about one-fourth of the navy's sailors.

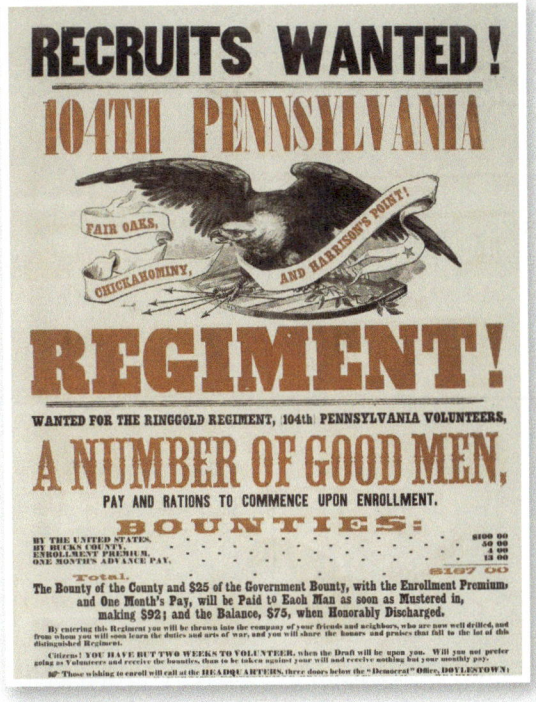

▲ (top) Union recruitment poster offering bounties (bonuses) for those who enlisted; (above) angry mob sacking a drug store during the New York City Draft Riots of July 13–16, 1863

▼ Black soldiers from Company E, 4th United States Colored Infantry

## Raising Southern Forces

When Lincoln called for volunteers to put down the rebellion in the South, many Southerners volunteered to fight the Northern invaders. The Confederate Congress created a War Department and brought the local and state militias under its control. These first volunteers signed up for one-year enlistments.

Like the North, the South had trouble recruiting volunteers as the war dragged on, casualties and desertions mounted, and enlistments expired. In April 1862 the Confederate Congress authorized a conscription law requiring all able-bodied white male citizens ages eighteen through thirty-five (later extended to fifty) to serve, and it lengthened current enlistments from one to three years. Certain professions, including teachers, civil officials, railroad workers, and others, were exempt, and anyone drafted could hire a substitute. Another provision said that for every twenty slaves on a plantation, one white person from that plantation would be exempt from service. These exceptions led to complaints that it was "a rich man's war and a poor man's fight."

Conscription was as unpopular in the South as it was in the North. Some dodged the draft. Others felt it violated the principles they were fighting for. Governor Joseph Brown of Georgia said the draft was a "dangerous usurpation by Congress of the reserved rights of the states" and contradicted the reasons for which Georgia seceded. Jefferson Davis responded that the Confederate constitution gave Congress the power to raise and support armies and that it could do everything necessary and proper to carry out those powers.

The South used some free blacks in nonmilitary roles such as driving wagons and constructing fortifications. As the war became more desperate for the South, some Confederate generals proposed using blacks, including slaves, in combat roles. Near the end of the war, Robert E. Lee even suggested granting slaves their freedom in return for fighting for the Confederacy, but these ideas met fierce resistance. As one Georgian said, "If slaves will make good soldiers our whole theory of slavery is wrong."

▲ Confederate recruitment poster

▼ General Nathan Bedford Forrest returning to his boyhood home of Chapel Hill, Tennessee, to recruit men to fight for the Confederacy

# Preparing at Home

## In the North

Northern industries grew as they manufactured uniforms, tents, cannons and other weapons, ammunition, wagons, blankets, and ships for the Union. Industrial workers who went to war were replaced by newly arriving immigrants, free blacks, and women in some industries.

Demand for food increased during the war. Even though many farmers went off to fight, agricultural production increased during the war years thanks to the use of machinery. Northern agricultural production was sufficient to feed the citizens and the army and to export wheat and flour to England.

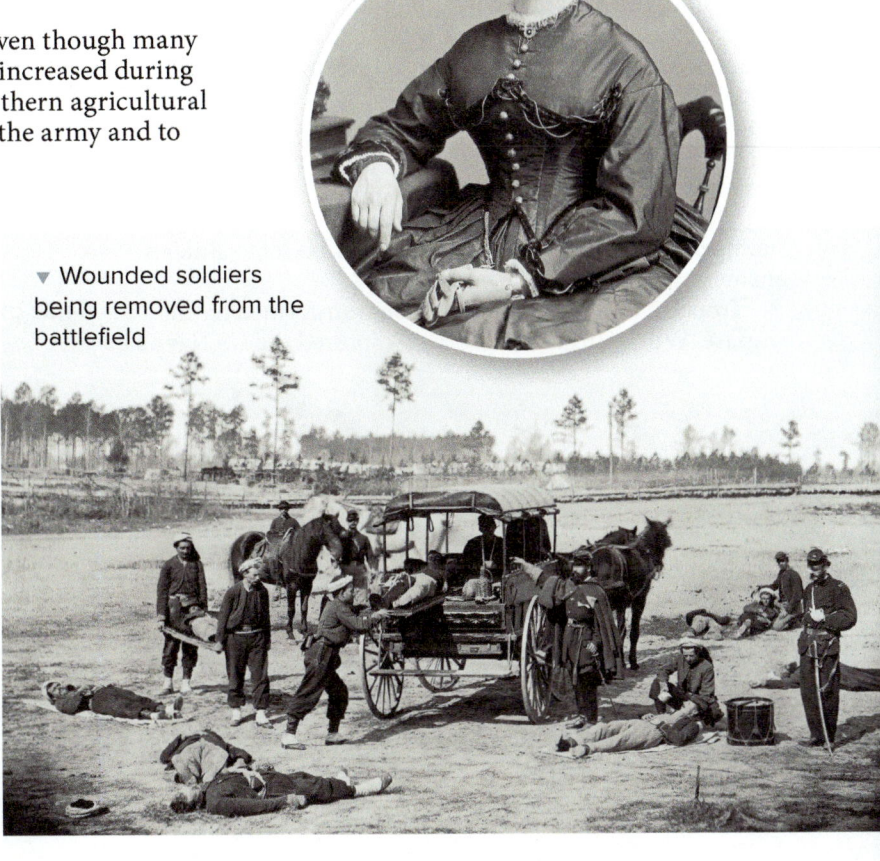

▼ Clara Barton

### Volunteer Work

Volunteer groups or commissions were popular on both sides, especially with women. Some purchased medicine or cut and rolled cloth for bandages, some provided Bibles and other reading materials for soldiers, some cared for the families of soldiers, some helped freed slaves find food and shelter, and some helped care for wounded veterans. Earning the nickname "angel of the battlefield," **Clara Barton** volunteered her services to the North and gained permission to visit the front lines as a nurse rather than serve only in the hospitals. After the war, she founded the American Red Cross and served as its first president for twenty-two years.

▼ Wounded soldiers being removed from the battlefield

## In the South

Since most battles occurred on Southern soil, life in the South was far more difficult than life in the North. As husbands and sons went off to fight, women were often left to run the farms or plantations. The war forced the South to develop its own industrial capacity.

Blockades of Southern ports, the destruction of transportation networks, including railroads, and the presence of Union troops in farming regions led to severe food shortages. Citizens competed with the Confederate army for what little food was available. In addition, as the Confederacy resorted to printing paper money to pay for the war, inflation skyrocketed. When soldiers heard of the hardships their families were facing, many deserted and returned to their homes. In April 1863, hungry women in Richmond started a riot because of bread shortages and high prices. Mobs smashed windows, broke into stores, and stole food and other goods. Only when Jefferson Davis personally confronted the rioters and persuaded them to disperse did the looting stop.

▶ Confederate paper currency (replica)

# Weapons and Strategies

Industrial and technological advancements made the Civil War the first modern war and required military leaders to adopt new strategies and tactics. Railroads enabled the armies to transport troops and supplies. Since telegraphs enabled the commanders-in-chief and war departments to communicate directly with battle-field commanders, both sides attempted to cut the other's telegraph lines throughout the war.

New, improved, and more lethal weapons led to high casualty counts. New rifled guns and cannons shot their projectiles with great velocity and accuracy, and repeating rifles enabled soldiers to fire several shots before reloading. Mines were placed in harbors to stop naval ships. The CSS *Hunley*, an experimental Confederate submarine, became the first underwater vessel to sink an enemy ship (before it, too, sank).

Ironclad (metal-sided) ships also transformed naval warfare. When Virginia seceded, it captured the US Navy's base in Norfolk, Virginia. The Confederates salvaged the hull of the USS *Merrimack* and converted it into the iron-armored CSS *Virginia*, with ten guns and an iron ram attached to its bow. On March 8, 1862, the *Virginia* sank two US Navy vessels in the Chesapeake Bay, with enemy shells bouncing off its iron sides. The next day the ironclad USS *Monitor* arrived in the Bay. Instead of the usual fixed guns on each side of the ship, the *Monitor* had two revolving guns that could fire in any direction. The two ironclads fought for nearly four hours. Both were damaged but neither sank. The battle was a draw, but it signaled the age of wooden ships was ending. Ironclads were used both at sea and on the rivers for the duration of the war.

▼ The USS *Monitor* (left) and the CSS *Virginia* (right) in a battle of ironclad ships

▼ (left) Confederate cavalry cutting telegraph lines; (right) Union mortar battery

## Northern Strategy

The two sides differed in their strategy for winning the war. General Winfield Scott, commander of the Union army at the beginning of the war, devised a plan not to conquer the South but to put down the rebellion and win back the loyalty of the Southern people. Scott believed a quick military victory over the South was unlikely, and his plan involved slowly eliminating the Confederacy's ability to wage war. First, he proposed a blockade of Southern ports to make it difficult for the Confederacy to obtain necessary supplies. Second, he called for the Union to take control of the Mississippi River. These actions would split the Confederacy and hamper its ability to move men and supplies from west to east and to import or export goods through New Orleans. The Northern press mockingly called Scott's scheme the **Anaconda Plan**, and the public demanded more aggressive offensive action to defeat the Confederate army. As a result, Scott's plan was modified to include two additional goals: to take the fight to the Southern heartland and to capture the Confederate capital, Richmond, Virginia.

**Northern Strategy**

1. Blockade the Confederate coasts
2. Control the Mississippi River
3. Divide/conquer the Southern heartland
4. Capture Richmond

▼ Cartoon depiction of Winfield Scott's Anaconda Plan

## Southern Strategy

The Confederate strategy was to fight a defensive **war of attrition** (war meant to wear out the opponent and exhaust its resources and will to fight by dragging it out) and to go on the offensive only when the opportunity was right.

Another aspect of the Southern strategy was to continue trade despite the blockade of Southern ports and to disrupt Northern trade. To bypass the Union blockade, **blockade runners** (low, fast ships) were built to keep trade flowing. These ships attempted to outrun the blockading ships in order to transport goods between Southern ports and Cuba, Bermuda, or the Bahamas. The South also built or purchased fast ships known as commerce raiders to attack Union merchant ships at sea. They burned whatever confiscated cargo they did not need and took Northern passengers and crew prisoner. The Confederate government also commissioned privateers to capture Northern ships, allowing the privateers to keep whatever ships and cargo they captured.

The final part of the Southern strategy was to gain recognition of its independence by Britain and France in the hope of procuring military and other assistance. France declared that it would not recognize the South's independence unless Britain did. To put pressure on England, many Southern planters chose to withhold sending cotton to England's textile mills. This "**cotton diplomacy**" failed because Britain was not eager to risk war with the United States over what seemed to be an internal American matter. Britain had warehouses full of cotton and could still get cotton from places such as India and Egypt. Britain would recognize the Confederacy only if it thought the South could win, which would have to be proven on the battlefield.

▼ Confederate blockade runner

## Comprehension Check 10.1

1. The South passed conscription laws to draft men to fight in the war, but the North did not.

    True        False

2. Men could avoid serving in the army by paying for an exemption or hiring a substitute.

    True        False

3. Each of the following was part of the Union strategy except ____.

    A   blockading Southern ports

    B   controlling the Mississippi River

    C   gaining support from European nations

    D   capturing Richmond

4. Each of the following was part of the Confederate strategy except ____.

    A   blockading Northern ports

    B   gaining support from European nations

    C   continuing trade using blockade runners and disrupting Northern trade using commerce raiders

    D   fighting a defensive war of attrition

### MAKING CONNECTIONS

5. What were two advantages each side had in the Civil War? Which advantages do you think had the greatest impact on the outcome of the war? Explain your answer.

## 10.2 The War in the East

What were the major Civil War battles in the East?

### Bull Run

In the spring of 1861 most Northerners and Southerners believed that a quick, decisive battle held somewhere between the two capitals of Washington, DC, and Richmond would end the war. With the Northern press clamoring "On to Richmond!" and the three-month enlistments of the first volunteers nearing an end, Lincoln felt pressure to take the offensive. General Irvin McDowell, commander of the Union forces, was ordered south toward Richmond. On July 18, McDowell's troops encountered Confederate forces under General Beauregard near Manassas Junction, a railroad intersection twenty-five miles southwest of Washington. Hundreds of spectators from the capital turned out in their finery with picnic baskets to watch "the greatest army in the world" smash the "Rebels."

The Confederates took position at a stream near Manassas called Bull Run. On Sunday morning July 21, McDowell launched his attack. At first the raw Union troops did well, pushing back the equally raw Confederates. But General Bernard Bee, whose troops were about to retreat, urged his men to hold the line. He reportedly pointed to General Thomas Jackson's brigade and shouted, "There stands Jackson like a stone wall! Rally behind the Virginians!" Jackson was thereafter known as **Stonewall Jackson**.

Troops under Joseph E. Johnston arrived by train to reinforce the Confederate lines, and by mid-afternoon McDowell's troops had been pushed back. The Union retreat turned into chaos as terrified troops and panicky picnickers scrambled toward Washington. The victorious Confederates, however, were too exhausted to attack the retreating Union forces.

After the victory at the **First Battle of Bull Run** (called Manassas by the Confederates), the South was confident, and the North was demoralized. The most significant result was that both sides realized that the war would not be over quickly. The Union determined to improve its ability to fight. The day after the battle, Lincoln replaced McDowell with General **George B. McClellan** and called for additional volunteers. In the months following Bull Run, McClellan took the remnants of McDowell's army and the flood of new recruits, organized and drilled them, instilled discipline and pride, and turned them into an impressive fighting force called the Army of the Potomac. Yet McClellan's army remained in Washington through the winter of 1861–62 without going on the offensive.

GUIDING QUESTIONS

- Why were the Battles of Bull Run important?
- Why was the Battle of Antietam important?
- What happened during the Battles of Fredericksburg and Chancellorsville?
- Why did the Battle of Gettysburg take place, and what were the results?

▼ General Thomas J. "Stonewall" Jackson

▼ Stonewall Jackson's Virginians attacking the Union forces at the First Battle of Bull Run

In the spring of 1862, Lincoln ordered McClellan to attack the Confederate forces in Manassas and move south to Richmond. The general offered an alternate plan to transport troops via the Chesapeake Bay and up the peninsula between the James and York Rivers to attack Richmond from the east before Johnston's troops could arrive. Johnston, however, anticipated McClellan's move and moved his troops from Manassas toward Richmond.

McClellan's plan also included the Union forces in the Shenandoah Valley marching from the west to assist in the attack on Richmond. However, during the Valley Campaign (March 23–June 9, 1862), Stonewall Jackson, with fewer than 20,000 men, defeated two separate armies, preventing 50,000 Union troops from assisting McClellan.

In April 1862 McClellan, with 100,000 troops, began the push toward Richmond. For two days Johnston struck McClellan, resulting in high casualties on both sides, including Johnston, who was severely wounded and replaced by General **Robert E. Lee**. Lee seized the initiative, launching what would be known as the Seven Days' Battles. From June 25 to July 1, the Confederates pushed McClellan's army back to the James River, with both sides taking heavy losses. McClellan abandoned the peninsula and returned to Washington, DC. He hoped to join General John Pope's forces in northern Virginia for a new drive on Richmond.

▲ General Robert E. Lee

## George B. McClellan— "Young Napoleon"

His men loved him, and some nicknamed him "Young Napoleon" or "Little Mac." Yet when called to put his army into action, McClellan consistently overestimated the enemy's strength and used that as an excuse not to fight. Lincoln, eager for aggressive action, commented, "If General McClellan does not want to use the Army, I would like to borrow it for a time."

▲ Union artillery during the Seven Days' Battles

Lee, however, had no intention of waiting to be attacked. He sent his cavalry commander, J.E.B. Stuart, to raid Pope from the rear and sent General Jackson around Pope's army. Jackson's men marched over fifty miles in forty-eight hours, capturing Union supplies at Manassas and attacking Pope's lines on the evening of August 28, 1862. Just as Pope was preparing to attack Jackson the next day, the remainder of Lee's army arrived. On the second day of the battle, Southern defenders counterattacked. The **Second Battle of Bull Run** forced Pope's army to retreat to Washington. After only two months in command, Lee had cleared practically all Union forces from Virginia.

## Antietam

After his victory at Bull Run, Lee decided to take the war into enemy territory. In September 1862 he crossed the Potomac River into Maryland, aiming to disrupt transportation and communication systems to Washington. He hoped that success would demoralize the North, bring Britain and France to recognize the independence of the Confederacy, and encourage **Peace Democrats**, or "Copperheads," (Northern Democrats who wanted to preserve the Union through negotiation, not victory over the South) in the upcoming congressional elections.

On September 13, a Union private found three cigars wrapped in papers. On the papers were Lee's orders to one of his generals revealing the battle plan. Lee soon learned that McClellan had his battle plan. Lee quickly gathered his army of about 30,000 and set up a defensive line at Antietam Creek near Sharpsburg, Maryland, where they awaited McClellan's 87,000 troops. At dawn on September 17, Union forces attacked the Confederate line at the **Battle of Antietam**. After a long day of intense fighting, more than 23,000 men had been killed or wounded. It was the bloodiest one-day battle in American history.

Unable to break through the Union lines, Lee slipped his battered army back across the Potomac into Virginia. While the two sides fought to a draw, the Union claimed victory because the Confederates had withdrawn and because the South's failure to win kept Britain and France from recognizing the Confederacy. It also gave Lincoln the opportunity he had been awaiting to issue his Emancipation Proclamation (see Section 4).

**War in the East, 1861–63**

GETTYSBURG July 1863
ANTIETAM Sept. 1862
PA
NJ
2ND BULL RUN Aug. 1862
Washington, DC
WV
DE
1ST BULL RUN (MANASSAS) July 1861
MD
Jackson's Valley Campaign
FREDERICKSBURG Dec. 1862
CHANCELLORSVILLE May 1863
VA
Jackson to the Peninsula
Richmond
Chesapeake Bay
THE SEVEN DAYS' June 1862
Petersburg
Monitor v. Virginia (Merrimack) March 1862
NC

→ Union movements
→ Confederate movements
☀ Confederate victory
☀ Union victory
☀ Indecisive
✪ Capital

## Did You Know?

More than twice as many Americans were killed in one day at the Battle of Antietam than those killed in combat in the War of 1812, the Mexican War, and the Spanish American War (see Chapter 14) combined.

▼ Bridge over Antietam Creek, Maryland

# Fredericksburg and Chancellorsville

After Antietam, Lincoln ordered McClellan to cross the Potomac and attack the Confederates before they could recover. When McClellan delayed yet again, Lincoln replaced him with General Ambrose Burnside. In November 1862 Burnside marched his army of 110,000 men to Falmouth, across the Rappahannock River from the town of Fredericksburg, Virginia. Burnside had to wait two weeks for supplies to build pontoon bridges to cross the river, giving Lee time to reinforce the town. On December 13, Union troops crossed the river and entered the town. Burnside ordered repeated attacks on the well-entrenched troops on Marye's Heights overlooking Fredericksburg. Wave after wave of brave Union troops marched up the hill only to be mowed down. The **Battle of Fredericksburg** claimed 13,000 Union casualties. One newspaper reporter said of the Union attack, "It can hardly be in human nature for men to show more valor, or generals to manifest [demonstrate] less judgment." Union morale dipped to its lowest point in the war. Lincoln replaced Burnside with yet another general, Joseph "Fighting Joe" Hooker.

With a huge force of 130,000 men, Hooker returned to the Fredericksburg area in April 1863 to crush Lee's army of 60,000. Hooker sent his cavalry to cut Lee's supply lines and conduct raids on Richmond. He left almost one-third of his army across the Rappahannock River from Fredericksburg to force Lee to keep a portion of his army there to protect the city, and he took his remaining troops west to attack Lee from the rear. Lee took the rest of his force to meet Hooker in the Wilderness, the dense woods near Chancellorsville. Though vastly outnumbered, Lee divided his army, sending Jackson's men on a flanking maneuver that surprised Hooker and drove his right flank back two miles.

That evening, Jackson and several officers returned from a scouting mission and were fired upon by their own men, who mistook them for the enemy. Jackson was hit twice in his left arm, which had to be amputated. Upon hearing of Jackson's wounds, Lee sent word, "Tell [Jackson] to make haste and get well, and come back to me as soon as he can. He has lost his left arm, but I have lost my right."

The **Battle of Chancellorsville** lasted for five days (May 2–6, 1863) and was a Confederate victory. Hooker withdrew his army across the Rappahannock after suffering 17,000 casualties. Lee lost 13,000 men, including Stonewall Jackson, who died of pneumonia eight days after being wounded.

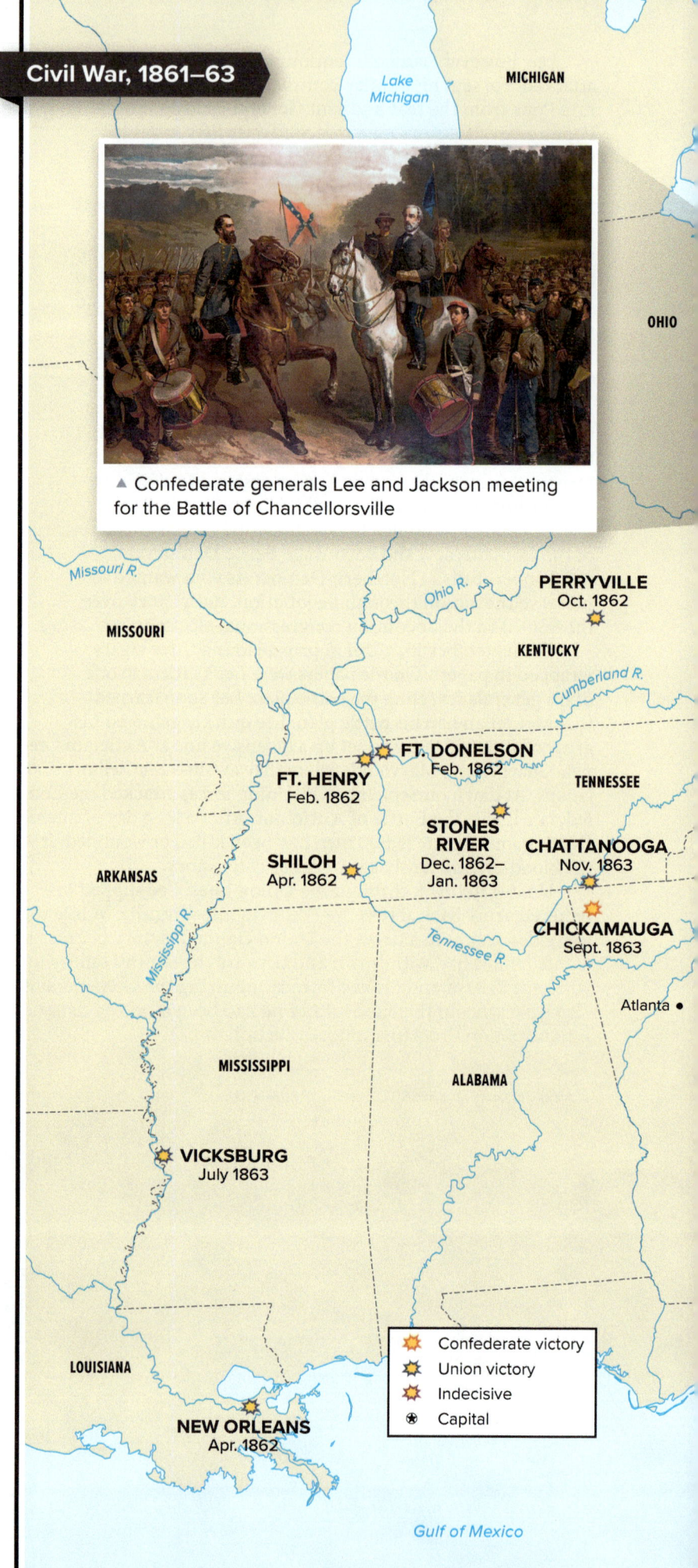

Civil War, 1861–63

▲ Confederate generals Lee and Jackson meeting for the Battle of Chancellorsville

**PERRYVILLE**
Oct. 1862

**FT. DONELSON**
Feb. 1862

**FT. HENRY**
Feb. 1862

**STONES RIVER**
Dec. 1862–
Jan. 1863

**CHATTANOOGA**
Nov. 1863

**SHILOH**
Apr. 1862

**CHICKAMAUGA**
Sept. 1863

Atlanta ●

**VICKSBURG**
July 1863

**NEW ORLEANS**
Apr. 1862

MICHIGAN
Lake Michigan
OHIO
MISSOURI
KENTUCKY
TENNESSEE
ARKANSAS
MISSISSIPPI
ALABAMA
LOUISIANA
Missouri R.
Ohio R.
Cumberland R.
Mississippi R.
Tennessee R.
Gulf of Mexico

☆ Confederate victory
☆ Union victory
☆ Indecisive
✹ Capital

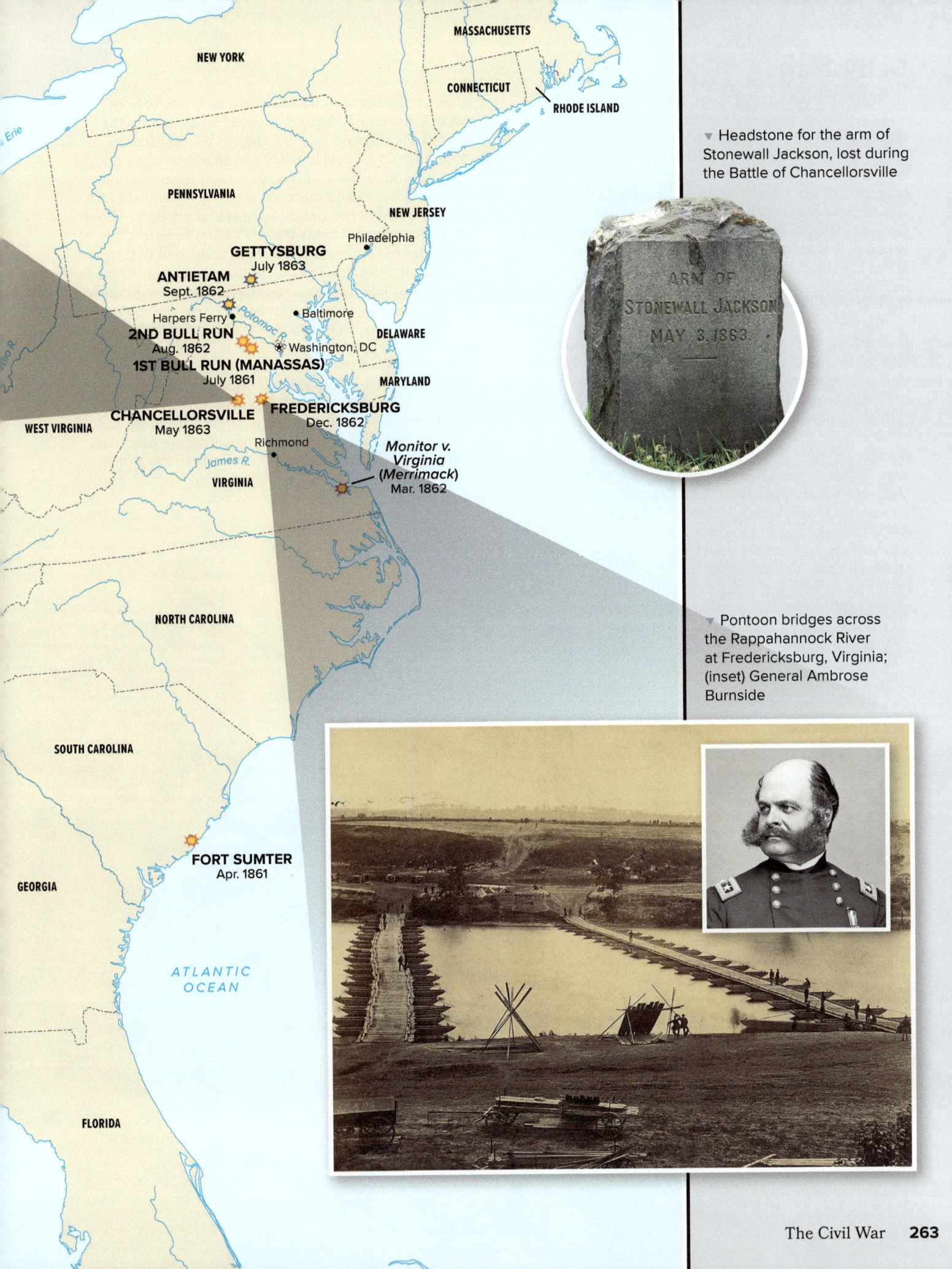

NEW YORK

MASSACHUSETTS

CONNECTICUT

RHODE ISLAND

PENNSYLVANIA

NEW JERSEY

Philadelphia

GETTYSBURG
July 1863

ANTIETAM
Sept. 1862

Harpers Ferry

Baltimore

2ND BULL RUN
Aug. 1862

DELAWARE

Washington, DC

1ST BULL RUN (MANASSAS)
July 1861

MARYLAND

CHANCELLORSVILLE
May 1863

FREDERICKSBURG
Dec. 1862

WEST VIRGINIA

Richmond

Monitor v.
Virginia
(Merrimack)
Mar. 1862

James R.

VIRGINIA

NORTH CAROLINA

SOUTH CAROLINA

FORT SUMTER
Apr. 1861

GEORGIA

ATLANTIC
OCEAN

FLORIDA

Lake Erie

Potomac R.

Ohio R.

▼ Headstone for the arm of Stonewall Jackson, lost during the Battle of Chancellorsville

ARM OF STONEWALL JACKSON MAY 3, 1863.

▼ Pontoon bridges across the Rappahannock River at Fredericksburg, Virginia; (inset) General Ambrose Burnside

# Gettysburg

After the convincing Confederate victory at Chancellorsville, Lee proposed a bold invasion into Northern territory. First, he hoped it would cause Lincoln to pull troops out of the Mississippi River and Tennessee campaigns (discussed later in this chapter), relieving pressure on Southern forces in those areas. Second, Lee hoped it would cause the British to reconsider recognition of the Confederacy. Third, the fertile farmland of Pennsylvania would provide much-needed food and supplies to his army. Fourth, he believed that if Northerners felt firsthand the effects of the war on their home soil, support for the war would decline.

In early June 1863, Lee marched his army of 75,000 men across the Potomac River into Maryland and then into southern Pennsylvania. When General Hooker was slow to respond to Lee's march north, Lincoln replaced him with General George Meade, who ordered his 90,000 soldiers to pursue Lee.

On July 1 the two armies established strongholds on the hills around Gettysburg: the Confederates on Seminary Ridge and the Union on Cemetery Ridge. Lee ordered General Richard Ewell, who had taken Stonewall Jackson's former command, to attack Cemetery Ridge if possible. Ewell, lacking Jackson's boldness, chose not to attack.

On July 2, Lee ordered attacks on the northern and southern ends of Cemetery Ridge. In a fierce day of fighting, the Confederates nearly captured Little Round Top on the southern end of Cemetery Ridge but were forced off the hill by a daring bayonet charge of the 20th Maine Regiment.

Believing the Union had shifted its forces to both ends of Cemetery Ridge, Lee ordered an assault on the center of the ridge on July 3. Cannons bombarded the Union lines for several hours. Then 14,000 troops under the command of General George Pickett formed a line nearly a mile long and marched across an open field into what remained of the Union soldiers and artillery. About half of the men who made **Pickett's Charge** were killed, wounded, or captured. When Pickett returned to the Confederate lines, Lee instructed him to rally his division for the expected Union counterattack. Pickett reportedly replied, "General, I have no division."

The **Battle of Gettysburg** was over; the South suffered 28,000 casualties and the North 23,000. It was the deadliest battle of the war. Two days later, Lee's retreating army crossed the Potomac into Virginia, and Meade, exhausted by his victory, failed to stop him. The Battle of Gettysburg was a turning point in the war. From this point on, the South would be primarily on the defensive. It also strengthened the Republican Party in the North, hurt the Peace Democrats, and meant that Britain would not recognize the South's independence.

▼ Union troops defending Little Round Top during the Battle of Gettysburg

On November 19, 1863, four months after the battle, a cemetery for the Union dead was dedicated at Gettysburg. More than 15,000 spectators were present. The first speaker, noted orator Edward Everett, spoke for two hours. Lincoln followed by speaking for only two minutes. In his **Gettysburg Address**, he noted the common courage and sacrifice of the soldiers who died defending freedom and called on those still alive to finish the task they were fighting to achieve.

◄ President Lincoln delivering the Gettysburg Address

## Gettysburg Address

*Four score and seven years ago our fathers brought forth on this continent, a new nation, conceived in Liberty, and dedicated to the proposition that all men are created equal. Now we are engaged in a great civil war, testing whether that nation, or any nation so conceived and so dedicated, can long endure. We are met on a great battlefield of that war. We have come to dedicate a portion of that field, as a final resting place for those who here gave their lives that that nation might live. It is altogether fitting and proper that we should do this. But, in a larger sense, we can not dedicate—we can not consecrate—we can not hallow—this ground. The brave men, living and dead, who struggled here, have consecrated it, far above our poor power to add or detract. The world will little note, nor long remember what we say here, but it can never forget what they did here. It is for us the living, rather, to be dedicated here to the unfinished work which they who fought here have thus far so nobly advanced. It is rather for us to be here dedicated to the great task remaining before us—that from these honored dead we take increased devotion to that cause for which they gave the last full measure of devotion—that we here highly resolve that these dead shall not have died in vain—that this nation, under God, shall have a new birth of freedom—and that government of the people, by the people, for the people, shall not perish from the earth.*

 **Analyzing Sources**

How does Lincoln's address encompass the past, the present, and the future of the nation?

## Comprehension Check 10.2

1. The First and Second Battles of Bull Run and the Battles of Fredericksburg and Chancellorsville were all Union victories.

   True     False

2. General George B. McClellan was often hesitant to put the army he trained and built into battle.

   True     False

3. Each of the following was a reason Lee invaded Maryland except _____.

   **A** to capture Washington, DC

   **B** to encourage the cause of the Peace Democrats

   **C** to gain European recognition of the Confederacy

4. The Battle of _____ was a draw, but resulted in the Union claiming victory and in Lincoln using the opportunity to issue his Emancipation Proclamation.

   **A** Fredericksburg

   **B** Antietam

   **C** Gettysburg

### MAKING CONNECTIONS

5. What were three reasons that Lee chose to attack Northern territory again after Chancellorsville?

6. What happened "four score and seven years" before Lincoln gave his Gettysburg Address? Why do you think he picked that occasion rather than the date of the Constitution as the start of the new nation?

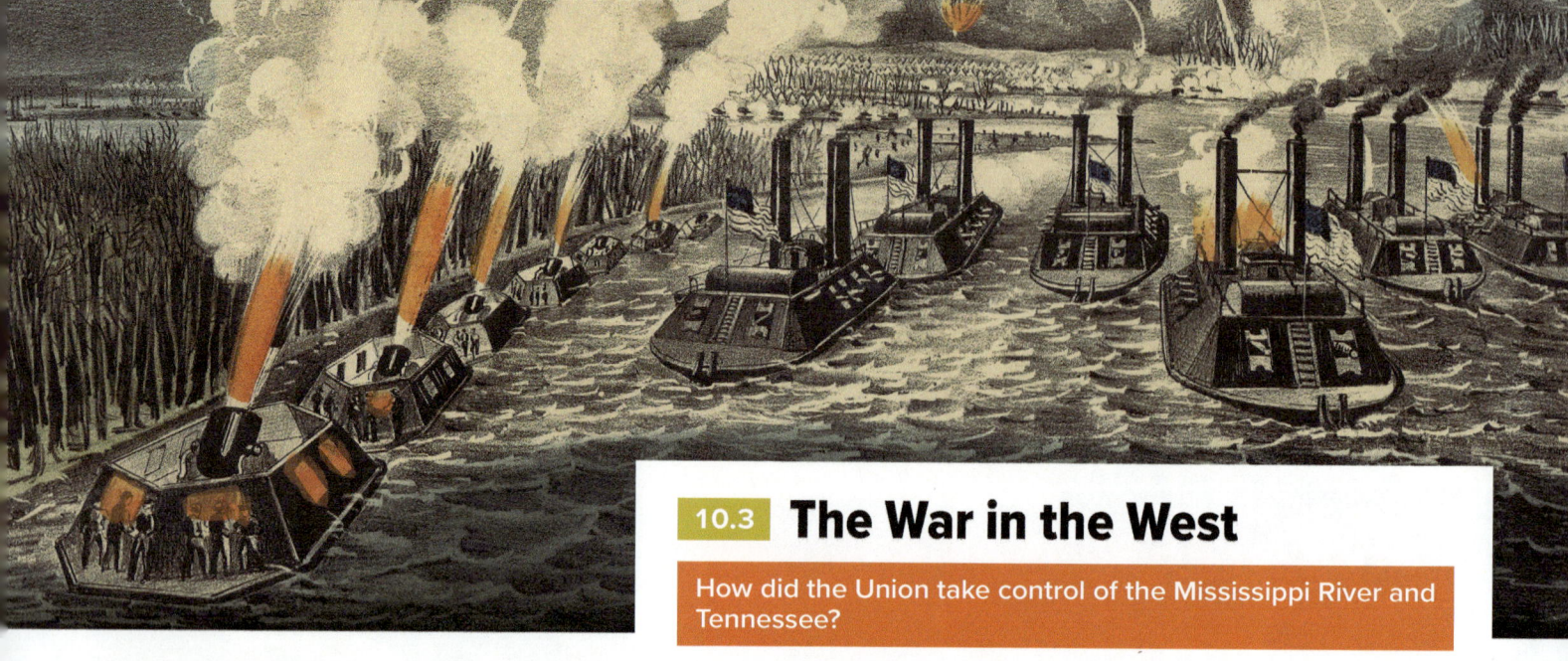

# The War in the West

How did the Union take control of the Mississippi River and Tennessee?

## Upper Mississippi

### Fort Henry and Fort Donelson

While war in the East centered in Virginia, war in the West consisted of the Mississippi River and Tennessee campaigns. Hoping to split the Confederacy, the Union sought control of the Mississippi River to stop the South from transporting goods and troops.

To maintain its grip, the Confederacy built fortifications along the Mississippi, Tennessee, and Cumberland Rivers which led through Kentucky; the latter two running deep into the state of Tennessee. To attack these fortifications, the Union built powerful ironclad gunboats, nicknamed "turtles" for their strange appearance and slow speed.

Union general **Ulysses S. Grant** knew an attack on the heavily cannon-fortified Columbus, Kentucky, would be foolish. Instead, he took his troops and the gunboat fleet to capture two important forts behind Columbus: Fort Henry on the Tennessee River and Fort Donelson on the Cumberland River. Grant easily captured the poorly designed Fort Henry on February 6, 1862. But Fort Donelson, only twelve miles to the east, was well designed and garrisoned with some 20,000 Confederate troops. The Union navy blocked the river, and the army surrounded the fort on three sides. Finally, on February 16, the Confederate commander sent a message asking for terms of surrender. Grant replied, "No terms except unconditional and immediate surrender can be accepted." The Northern public nicknamed him "Unconditional Surrender" Grant.

With Forts Henry and Donelson in Union hands, the Confederates abandoned Columbus. The fall of Fort Donelson allowed the Union to travel up the Cumberland River to Nashville, which became the first Southern state capital to fall.

### Shiloh

As Grant's army moved south to Pittsburg Landing along the Tennessee River, Confederate general Albert Sidney Johnston amassed 42,000 soldiers at nearby Corinth, Mississippi, to stop the Union advance. On April 6, 1862, Johnston's troops surprised the Union force of about equal size near an abandoned church called Shiloh. After a long day of intense fighting, the disorganized Union forces fell back toward the river. Both sides suffered heavy casualties, and General Johnston bled to death of a leg wound. As darkness fell, the Union army barely held its positions.

▲ (above) General Ulysses S. Grant; (top) Union gunboats on the Mississippi River

During the night, however, Union reinforcements arrived. At dawn on April 7, Grant counterattacked and drove the Confederates back. The **Battle of Shiloh** was a costly Union victory. Each side suffered more than 10,000 casualties. The Union then captured Corinth and Memphis on the Mississippi River.

## Lower Mississippi

### New Orleans

In April 1862 Union admiral David Farragut led the US fleet up the Mississippi from the Gulf of Mexico and, despite a noble Confederate defense, captured the South's largest city and critical seaport, New Orleans. From there, he took Baton Rouge, Louisiana, and Natchez, Mississippi. Only one city along the Mississippi River remained in Confederate control—Vicksburg, Mississippi.

### Vicksburg

**Vicksburg** was a natural fortress, situated on 200-foot-high bluffs above the river. Swampy lands near the city discouraged any approach by land. Jefferson Davis called Vicksburg "the nail head that held the South's two halves together." As long as the Confederates held the city, they could bring supplies and troops from their western regions. In late June 1862 the Union fleets bombarded the city, but the city's defenders drove the ships back.

Grant led the Vicksburg campaign in January 1863. Needing a path to bypass the guns of the forts, Grant first tried water routes, from digging a canal to using the various swamps and streams surrounding the city to float his gunboats and troops. All failed. Finally, he marched his men south of Vicksburg, then floated his fleet of gunboats and transports past the guns on the bluffs under cover of night. He then ferried his troops across below the city.

Grant's bold strategy stunned the Confederates, allowing his army to sweep north and surround Vicksburg by May 1863. The city's defenses were too strong to assault, so Grant laid siege to Vicksburg to starve it into submission. Finally, on July 4, 1863—the same day that Lee began his retreat from Gettysburg—Vicksburg surrendered. The Mississippi River was now completely in Union hands.

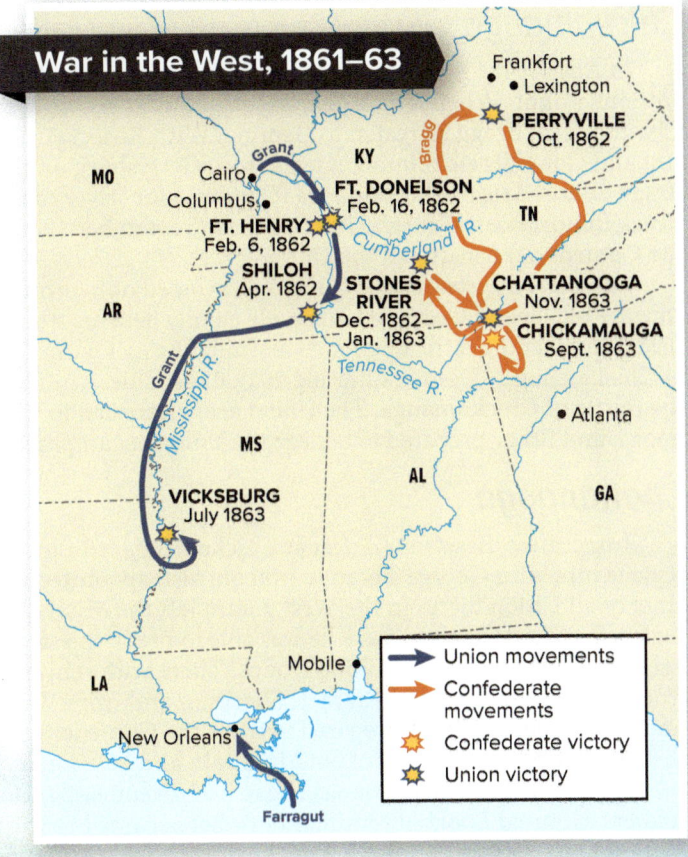

▼ The siege of Vicksburg, Mississippi

## Tennessee Campaign

After Albert Sidney Johnston died at Shiloh, President Davis appointed General Braxton Bragg to head the armies in the West. Bragg devised a plan to invade Kentucky, hoping to raise new troops from the pro-Confederate citizens and bring the state into the Confederacy. Bragg entered Kentucky in August 1862, but the campaign was a failure. Bragg's army retreated in late December to Murfreesboro, Tennessee, and then further back to Chattanooga by July 1863.

### Chickamauga

In August 1863 General Burnside's Union forces took Knoxville without a fight. When Union General William Rosecrans reached Chattanooga, Bragg retreated to Georgia. With Rosecrans in pursuit and Confederate reinforcements from Gettysburg on the way, Bragg attacked near Chickamauga (Cherokee for "river of death") Creek in northwest Georgia. For two days (September 19–20, 1863), the Confederates shattered the Union forces.

Complete disaster for the Union was avoided only through the courage of General George Thomas. He calmly held his troops on the field to protect the retreating forces, earning the nickname "the Rock of Chickamauga." Despite suffering 20,000 casualties, the South won the **Battle of Chickamauga**. The Union army retreated to Chattanooga, and Bragg prepared to besiege the Union encampment.

### Chattanooga

Rosecrans's disastrous defeat at Chickamauga led Lincoln to replace him with George Thomas. Lincoln also appointed Grant chief of all Union forces in the West. Grant left the Mississippi region for Chattanooga, where he was able to break the siege and get supplies to the hungry Union troops. Then, with reinforcements from Mississippi under **William T. Sherman** and from Virginia under Joe Hooker, Grant prepared to drive the Confederates from their strong positions on Lookout Mountain and Missionary Ridge.

As the **Battle of Chattanooga** began on November 24, Union soldiers captured Lookout Mountain in what became known as "the Battle Above the Clouds." But Bragg's men still held Missionary Ridge. On November 25 Grant sent General Thomas's men to capture enemy trenches at the base of Missionary Ridge. They not only captured the trenches, but also swarmed up the ridge, surprising the Confederates and taking Missionary Ridge. After Bragg retreated into Georgia, he resigned, and President Davis replaced him with Joseph E. Johnston. Three months later, President Lincoln promoted Grant to commander of all Union forces. The road to Georgia was now clear for invasion.

1. The Battles of Fort Henry, Fort Donelson, and Shiloh were Union victories.

   True    False

2. The last city on the Mississippi River to fall to the Union was ____.

   **A** Corinth, Mississippi

   **B** Memphis, Tennessee

   **C** Vicksburg, Mississippi

3. The Union won the Battle of Chickamauga but lost the Battle of Chattanooga.

   True    False

4. After Chattanooga, Lincoln named ____ commander of all Union forces.

   **A** Ulysses S. Grant

   **B** Joseph Hooker

   **C** George McClellan

#### MAKING CONNECTIONS

5. Why was the Union victory at Vicksburg significant?

▼ The Battle of Chattanooga

## 10.4 The Road to Appomattox

How did the Union win the Civil War?

### The Emancipation Proclamation

Lincoln's personal wish was that "all men everywhere could be free." However, any attempts to free the slaves had to be done constitutionally. Lincoln did not think he had the constitutional authority to free the slaves in the border states by presidential proclamation. Instead, Congress passed Lincoln's proposal that the border states would be compensated if they passed laws for gradual emancipation. The border states, however, passed no such laws.

As the Union began conquering slaveholding territory, the question quickly arose regarding the status of slaves who were captured or who sought refuge with the Union army. Slave owners demanded that their slaves be returned based on the Fugitive Slave Act, but some Union officers declared them to be contraband of war. Some generals went even further, declaring the freedom of all slaves in the territories they occupied. Fearing what these emancipation declarations would do to the loyalty of the border states, Lincoln revoked them, stating that the president alone could decide if and when military emancipation was necessary.

As the war continued, many abolitionists began to question Lincoln's goal of fighting to preserve the Union without forcing emancipation. Frederick Douglass said, "Fire must be met with water . . . and war for the destruction of liberty must be met with war for the destruction of slavery. *The simple way, then, to put an end to the savage and desolating war now waged by the slaveholders, is to strike down slavery itself*, the primal [main] cause of that war." Some argued that fighting to free slaves was a military necessity. The South depended on slave labor to feed and supply its people and could use a greater percentage of its white men in battle than the North because the slaves remained behind to work in the farms and industries.

In 1862 Congress passed several laws that moved toward abolition and emancipation, including prohibiting slavery in the western territories, abolishing slavery in Washington, DC, forbidding Union officers from returning fugitive slaves to their masters, and allowing blacks to serve as soldiers. Congress also passed a Confiscation Act enabling Union armies to seize Confederate property (including slaves) and declaring that slaves in conquered territory "shall be deemed captives of war and shall be forever free." Lincoln signed the bill but also notified his Cabinet that he intended to emancipate all slaves in the rebel states. He believed only the president could do this using his war powers as a "fit and necessary military measure."

On August 22, 1862, Lincoln wrote to newspaper editor Horace Greeley, expressing his dilemma:

> *My paramount object in this struggle is to save the Union, and is not either to save or to destroy slavery. If I could save the Union without freeing any slave I would do it; and if I could save it by freeing all the slaves, I would do it; and if I could do it by freeing some and leaving others alone, I would also do that.*

— **ABRAHAM LINCOLN**

### GUIDING QUESTIONS

- Why was the Emancipation Proclamation important?
- How did the North destroy much of the South?
- What happened in the election of 1864?
- How did the Civil War end?
- What impact did the Civil War have on the nation?
- Who assassinated Lincoln?

**Analyzing Sources**

According to this letter, what is Lincoln's goal in emancipation? How does his goal affect the scope of his plans for emancipation?

Lincoln was preparing the North for the possibility that he would free some or all of the slaves and that he had the authority to do so. But he was waiting for a military victory before making his announcement.

That victory came at the Battle of Antietam. On September 22, 1862, five days after the battle, Lincoln issued the first version of the **Emancipation Proclamation**, declaring that all slaves in states that were in rebellion as of January 1, 1863, would be freed. The Proclamation did not apply to the border states or those parts of the Confederacy already under Union control. Lincoln presented the Emancipation Proclamation as a war-time emergency act. Otherwise, he believed he had no power to make such a sweeping act without the consent of Congress.

▼ African Americans celebrating freedom in Washington, DC

# Emancipation Proclamation Accomplishments

| 1 | Prevented British recognition of the Confederacy |
| 2 | Encouraged blacks to fight for the Union |
| 3 | Inspired the North with a new, noble cause |
| 4 | Advanced abolition |

Some criticized Lincoln for freeing slaves in areas where he had no control and for not freeing them in regions where he did have control. However, the Confiscation Act had already declared slaves who were captured by Union forces to be free, and Lincoln, having failed to convince the border states to free their slaves voluntarily, believed he did not have the constitutional authority to interfere with slavery there. He also pursued legislative and constitutional enactment of emancipation, knowing that his proclamation could be declared unconstitutional (see Chapter 11).

The Emancipation Proclamation accomplished four things: it kept Britain from recognizing the South by appealing to the strong British antislavery feeling, encouraged blacks to join the war effort and fight for the Union, revived failing spirits in the North by giving Northerners another reason for fighting the war besides preserving the Union, and took another major step toward freeing slaves.

Despite its limitations, the Emancipation Proclamation was an important step toward eliminating slavery. The proclamation transformed the conflict from merely a war to save the nation to a war of liberation. "We shout for joy that we live to record this righteous decree," proclaimed Frederick Douglass.

# Destruction in the South

By 1863 some Northern commanders believed that winning the war would require waging total war, fighting not just the enemy's military and government but also the civilian population. When Union armies began invading the heart of the Confederacy, many used the policy of total war, focusing on destroying the enemy's ability and willingness to fight.

Some condemned the practice of total war. Northern theologian Charles Hodge said,

> *The aphorism [saying] that all things are lawful in war, is not only unchristian, but inhuman. . . . And yet we frequently hear . . . that the end of war is to inflict injury on your enemies, and the more injury you inflict the sooner and the more effectually will the war be brought to an end. We have heard men justify the burning of cities and laying waste the country by fire and sword. . . . The end sanctifies the means, is practically the creed of many. . . . Better let the rebels succeed than offend God by reverting to the cruel and wicked usages of former ages.*
>
> — **CHARLES HODGE**

Hodge said that noncombatants and their property should not be harassed and that if the military took provisions from civilians, they should compensate them in order to not violate God's command against stealing.

## The Shenandoah Valley

Hoping to capitalize on war weariness in the North, Lee ordered his cavalry to conduct raids from their base in the Shenandoah Valley into Northern territory. He did not expect to win battles but hoped to create anxiety in the North. Southern cavalry raided Maryland farms for supplies and livestock. In July 1864 they rode to the outskirts of Washington, DC, forcing Union troops to remain near the capital and out of the fight against Lee's army.

In response, Grant sent troops under General Philip Sheridan into the Shenandoah Valley to ruin Virginia "clean and clear . . . so that crows flying over it for the balance of the season will have to carry their own provender [food] with them." Sheridan's army defeated the Confederates in several battles in the valley. His soldiers also killed livestock, burned barns, mills, and houses, and destroyed crops. His army left the Shenandoah, which had been the "breadbasket of the South," desolate, depriving Lee's army as well as civilians of food and supplies.

▶ Wheat field

### Analyzing Sources

What philosophical argument does Hodge counter, and what is his ultimate concern in the waging of war?

## Atlanta

Grant gave his most trusted general, William Tecumseh Sherman, command of the Union troops in Chattanooga. Sherman's tasks were to destroy General Joseph Johnston's army and capture Atlanta, Georgia, one of the South's most important remaining railroad and manufacturing centers. Sherman approached the job with grim determination. "War is cruelty," he said, "and you cannot refine it."

Sherman began his 100-mile march from Chattanooga to Atlanta in May 1864. Between the Union forces and Atlanta stood Johnston's smaller but resolute force. A master of defensive tactics, Johnston carefully constructed fortifications of earth, timber, and stone and waited for his adversary to make a mistake. Sherman used his superior numbers to slip around the Southerners, forcing them to retreat or be overwhelmed.

Johnston's slow and skillful retreats frustrated Sherman, but they also irritated Jefferson Davis. The Confederate president thought that Johnston was afraid to fight and was risking the loss of Atlanta. In July Davis replaced him with the fiery, energetic John Bell Hood. True to his reputation as a fighter, Hood attacked the more numerous Union forces in the **Battle of Atlanta** (July 20–22, 1864). The attack surprised Sherman, but the Union troops recovered quickly. The Southerners suffered heavy casualties. Slowed but not halted, Sherman continued to encircle the city. Faced with destruction if he stayed, Hood abandoned Atlanta on September 2, setting fire to military facilities as he left. Sherman later ordered the destruction of all remaining military, industrial, and transportation facilities in the city, although many homes and businesses were destroyed as well.

▲ General William T. Sherman

## Sherman's March to the Sea

From Atlanta, Sherman proposed a march to cut a swath of destruction through Georgia all the way to the coast. He would wage total war on the South, destroying not only its armies but also its economy and its will. As he prepared his "**March to the Sea**," Sherman told his superiors in Washington, "I can make the march and make Georgia howl!" The march would destroy food, animals, and other supplies that supported the Confederate army and would show Southerners that the Confederacy was rapidly losing the ability to resist.

Sherman began his march on November 15. He divided his army into four columns and sent each on a different route toward Savannah, forming a 60-mile-wide, 250-mile-long band across Georgia to the Atlantic coast. Instead of establishing supply lines, he ordered his commanders to live off the land, taking what food and supplies they needed from what they could find. What they could not use themselves was to be destroyed. They burned houses and barns by the hundreds, destroyed cotton crops and gins, and tore up railroad lines, heating and twisting them into "Sherman neckties." Despite orders from Sherman to his commanders that Union soldiers were not to enter private dwellings or "commit any trespass" unless local citizens attacked them, much looting and destruction of private property resulted. Those responsible were regular Union troops as well as "bummers," a shabby collection of men including current soldiers and deserters from both armies. Sherman's inability or unwillingness to control these men left a bitter legacy long after the war was over.

▼ Union troops marching from Atlanta, Georgia

Sherman reached Savannah on December 10. Ten days later, the Confederate defenders abandoned the city and crossed into South Carolina. On December 21 the mayor surrendered Savannah to Sherman, who sent a telegram to President Lincoln presenting Savannah as a Christmas gift. Sherman then turned north and marched across South Carolina on his way to join Grant in Virginia. His policy of total war devastated the Carolinas just as it had Georgia.

▲ Sherman's March to the Sea through Georgia

## The Election of 1864

Sherman's success almost came too late for Abraham Lincoln. No end to the fighting had seemed to be in sight, and by the summer of 1864, Lincoln's chances for reelection had looked slim.

Opinion in the Democratic Party was split: War Democrats supported the war as a means of preserving the Union but disagreed with the Emancipation Proclamation and the recasting of the war as a fight to end slavery; Peace Democrats, some of whom claimed the war was a failure, wanted an immediate end to hostilities even if that meant recognizing the South's independence. All Democrats condemned what they believed were Lincoln's unconstitutional actions during the war, including restrictions on speech and the press, the draft, and the use of war powers to issue the Emancipation Proclamation. The Democrats eventually nominated pro-war former general George McClellan as their candidate, but their platform called for immediate peace negotiations with the South.

Lincoln also faced division within his own party. A group of "radical" Republicans, led by Senator Charles Sumner of Massachusetts, wanted the party to push for constitutional amendments to abolish slavery and guarantee racial equality. Other Republicans, concerned that Lincoln was not effectively leading the war effort, opposed his re-nomination. The fall of Atlanta, however, made victory now seem possible. The Republicans renamed themselves the National Union Party to appeal to border state voters and War Democrats, who ordinarily would never vote for a Republican. The new party nominated Lincoln as its presidential candidate and former Democratic Tennessee governor and senator Andrew Johnson as vice president. The party platform called for conducting the war until the unconditional surrender of the South was achieved and for an amendment to end slavery.

On Election Day, Lincoln won fifty-five percent of the popular vote and defeated McClellan 212 to 21 in the Electoral College. The election of 1864 guaranteed that the war to preserve the Union and end slavery would continue.

▲ National Union Party 1864 campaign poster

## Lincoln's Second Inaugural Address

On March 4, 1865, Lincoln delivered his second inaugural speech. In that address, he stated:

> Both [Union and Confederacy] read the same Bible and pray to the same God, and each invokes His aid against the other. . . . The prayers of both could not be answered—that of neither has been answered fully.
>
> The Almighty has His own purposes. "Woe unto the world because of offenses; for it must needs be that offenses come, but woe to that man by whom the offense cometh." [Then] we shall suppose that American slavery is one of those offenses which, in the providence of God, must needs come, but which, having continued through His appointed time, He now wills to remove, and that He gives to both North and South this terrible war as the woe due to those by whom the offense came. . . .
>
> Fondly do we hope, fervently do we pray, that this mighty scourge of war may speedily pass away. Yet, if God wills that it continue until all the wealth piled by the bondsman's two hundred and fifty years of unrequited toil shall be sunk, and until every drop of blood drawn with the lash shall be paid by another drawn with the sword, as was said three thousand years ago, so still it must be said "the judgments of the Lord are true and righteous altogether."

In describing both sides' prayers for victory, Lincoln declared that God may have designs that do not align with people's plans and proposed that the war may have been God's punishment on the nation for the evil of slavery. The president closed his speech with a plea for Americans to forsake sectional strife and assist in healing the nation from the devastations of war.

> With malice toward none, with charity for all, with firmness in the right as God gives us to see the right, let us strive on to finish the work we are in, to bind up the nation's wounds, to care for him who shall have borne the battle and for his widow and his orphan, to do all which may achieve and cherish a just and lasting peace among ourselves and with all nations.

◄ Battle of the Wilderness

# Confederate Collapse

## Toward Richmond

After being placed in command of the entire Union army, Grant marched toward Richmond with an army of over 120,000 men. Lee, with half that number, blocked his advance near the scene of his Chancellorsville triumph a year earlier. In the dense woods of the Wilderness, the two armies began a month-long series of battles. The Wilderness Campaign resulted in some of the costliest and most desperate fighting of the war.

In the Battles of the Wilderness (May 5–6, 1864), Spotsylvania Court House (May 8–12), and the North Anna River (May 16–23), the Confederates dealt punishing blows to the Union forces. Yet Grant kept up the pressure. Unlike previous Union commanders, Grant did not retreat after a major setback. At Spotsylvania he wrote, "I propose to fight it out along this line if it takes all summer."

The Wilderness Campaign climaxed at the **Battle of Cold Harbor** (June 1–3) with a massive assault on entrenched Confederate positions that left 7,000 Union soldiers dead or dying. When Grant ordered his men to renew the suicidal assault, they simply refused. Between the two armies lay acres of bodies, what soldiers from both sides dubbed "Grant's Slaughter Pen."

Cold Harbor capped a month of devastation for the battered Union army. In four weeks of nearly continuous fighting, Grant had lost more than 50,000 men. But though battle deaths and disease took their toll on both sides, Grant was receiving reinforcements and supplies while Lee was not.

Grant then laid siege to Petersburg, Virginia, the major railroad junction that led into Richmond from the south. For nine months (July 1864–March 1865), the two armies tested each other's defenses.

On April 1, 1865, when the fall of Petersburg was apparent, Lee believed his only hope was to move to North Carolina and link with General Johnston, whose soldiers were running from Sherman's advance. However, Sheridan's troops blocked Lee's retreat. Jefferson Davis and his cabinet abandoned Richmond. On April 7, Grant offered to discuss terms of surrender with Lee.

## Appomattox Court House

On April 9, 1865, Lee met Grant at **Appomattox Court House**, Virginia. After the two generals talked briefly about their service in the Mexican War, they agreed to terms of surrender for the Army of Northern Virginia. Grant's generous terms—that the Confederate soldiers would lay down their weapons and go home and that the officers could keep their swords and horses—gave Lee the opportunity to surrender with honor. Grant, recalling his impression of their meeting, later wrote that he felt "sad and depressed. I felt anything rather than rejoicing at the downfall of a foe who had fought so long and valiantly."

When word of Lee's surrender spread, the noise of celebration and gun salutes erupted throughout the Union lines. But Grant quickly ordered it stopped. "The war is over," he said. "The Rebels are our countrymen again." Within days, Joseph Johnston surrendered his forces to William Sherman near Durham, North Carolina. The remaining Confederate forces surrendered in May.

**Closing Campaigns, 1864–65**

Map labels:
NJ
Baltimore
OH
MD
Grant
DE
WV
Washington, DC
Lee
**WILDERNESS TO COLD HARBOR** May–June 1864
**APPOMATTOX (LEE SURRENDERS)** Apr. 9, 1865
KY
Richmond
VA
Danville
**PETERSBURG** 1864–65
Durham
Greensboro
TN
NC
Sherman 1865
Chattanooga
SC
Wilmington
**KENNESAW MT.** June 1864
**ATLANTA** Sept. 1864
Columbia
Charleston
Sherman 1864
GA
Savannah

Legend:
Union movements
Confederate movements
Confederate victory
Union victory
Indecisive

▼ General Lee surrendering to General Grant at Appomattox Court House, Virginia, April 9, 1865

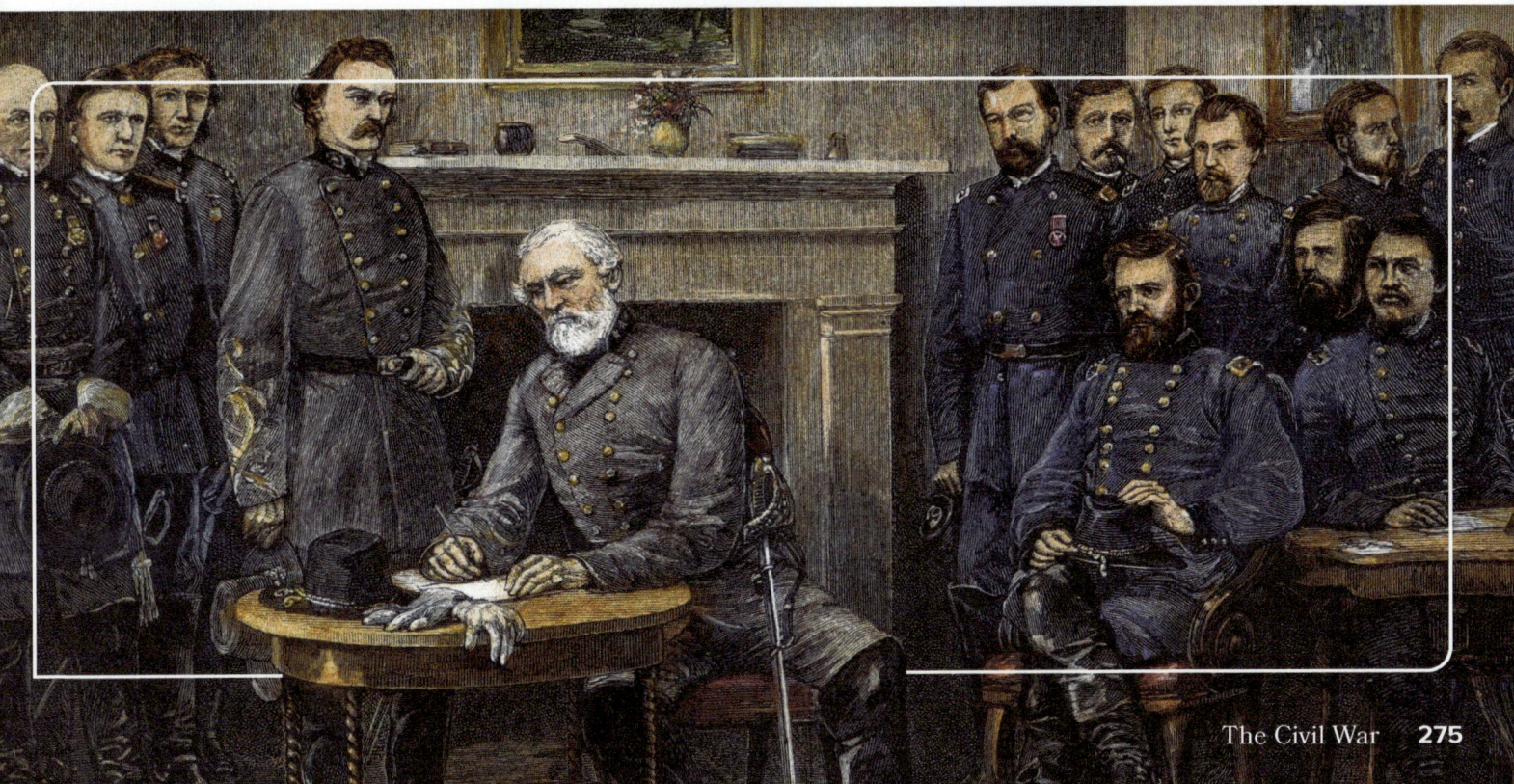

# The Bitter Harvest

## Costs of the War

    The surrender at Appomattox closed the bloodiest chapter in American history. Over 620,000 soldiers died in the four-year war. Of those deaths, almost 400,000 were from disease; about 30,000 soldiers on each side died as prisoners of war. Tens of thousands were disfigured for life.

    Much of the South lay in ruins, its economy devastated by the heavy fighting and destruction that had taken place throughout the region and its labor system based on slavery upended. Inflation was high, and morale was low. Deep bitterness and distrust between the North and South would last for decades. For former slaves, freedom had been achieved but they now faced a long struggle for equality.

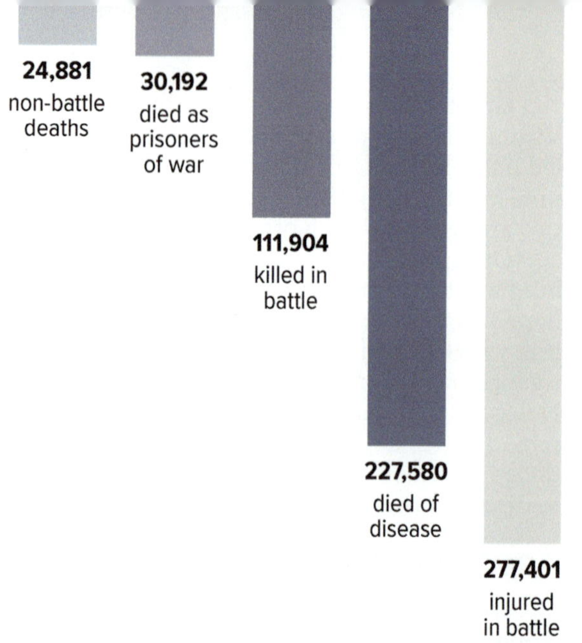

**24,881** non-battle deaths

**30,192** died as prisoners of war

**111,904** killed in battle

**227,580** died of disease

**277,401** injured in battle

### North

**394,557** total deaths

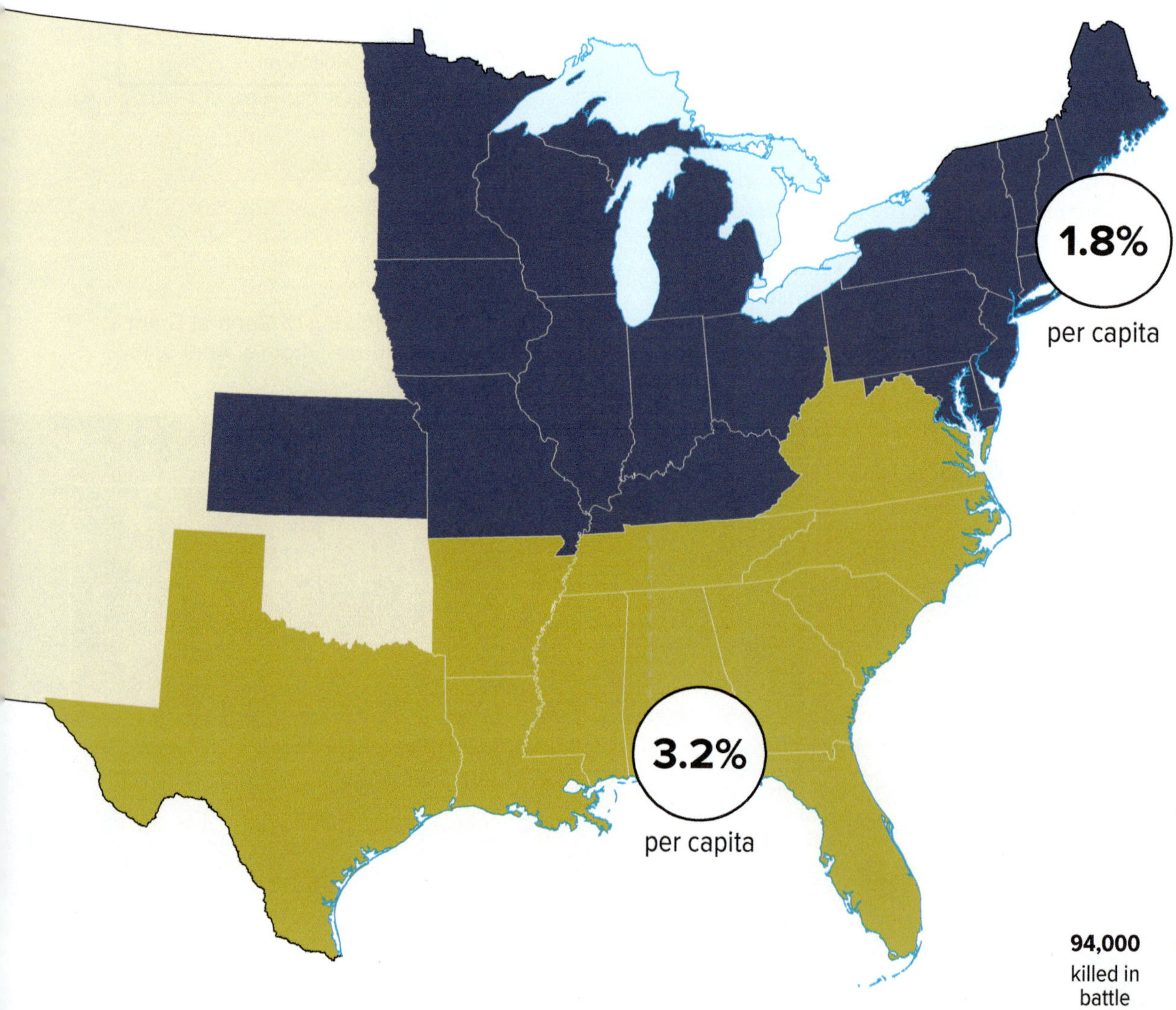

**Civil War Deaths and Injuries**

**1.8%** per capita

**3.2%** per capita

### South

**289,000** total deaths

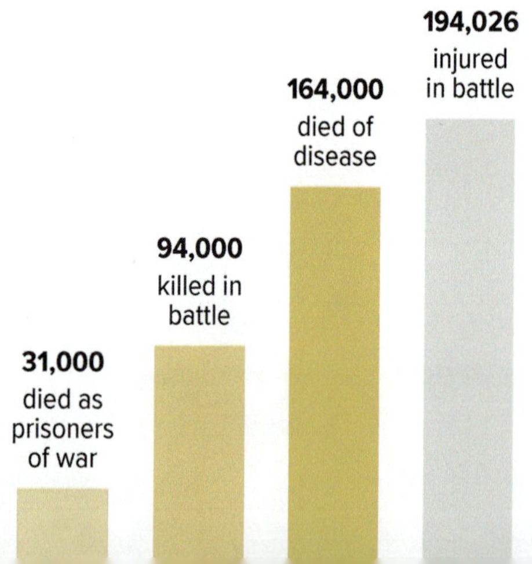

**194,026** injured in battle

**164,000** died of disease

**94,000** killed in battle

**31,000** died as prisoners of war

▼ (top) Richmond, Virginia, after the Civil War; (bottom left) dead Union soldiers on the Gettysburg battlefield; (bottom right) Civil War veterans who lost limbs in the war

The Civil War    277

## Lincoln's Assassination

Lincoln gave an address on April 11 in which he proposed a limited extension of the vote to black citizens as part of his reconstruction plan (see Chapter 11). **John Wilkes Booth**, an actor and Confederate sympathizer, after hearing Lincoln's second inaugural address and his plans for reconstruction, told a friend, "I'll put him through. That is the last speech he will ever make."

According to Secretary of War Edwin Stanton, on April 14 the president warned in his cabinet meeting that "there were men in Congress who . . . possessed feelings of hate and vindictiveness in which he did not sympathize and could not participate." In restoring the Confederate states to the Union, Lincoln called for "no persecution, no bloody work."

However, a national tragedy left the American public wondering whether Lincoln could have achieved the noble goals he expressed. On the night of the 14th, Good Friday, Booth entered Lincoln's private box in Ford's Theater in Washington, DC, and shot the president in the back of the head. Lincoln died several hours later on the morning of April 15. Almost two weeks later soldiers trapped Booth in a barn in Virginia, and a sergeant shot and killed Booth.

Ahead of the country lay a long and difficult road to rebuilding a nation. After Lincoln's assassination, the task of "binding up the nation's wounds" fell to Lincoln's vice president, Andrew Johnson.

▼ John Wilkes Booth shooting Abraham Lincoln, April 14, 1865, in Ford's Theater, Washington, DC

## Comprehension Check 10.4

1. General _____ waged total war throughout Georgia and into the Carolinas.
   A Ulysses S. Grant
   B Joseph Johnston
   C William T. Sherman

2. The National Union Party, whose platform included _____, nominated Lincoln for the election of 1864.
   A amending the Constitution to end slavery
   B ending the war immediately
   C preserving the Union without emancipation

3. Grant's costliest mistake in the Wilderness Campaign was at the Battle of _____.
   A Petersburg
   B North Anna River
   C Cold Harbor

4. On April 9, 1865 Lee agreed to the terms of surrender at _____.
   A Spotsylvania Court House
   B Appomattox Court House
   C Richmond

5. Who assassinated Abraham Lincoln?
   A John Brown
   B John Wilkes Booth
   C Jefferson Davis

### MAKING CONNECTIONS

6. What was a limitation of the Emancipation Proclamation? What were its achievements?

## Chapter Summary

### 10.1 Preparing for War

- Northern advantages over the South included population, the production of food crops, industrial production, a navy, and finances. Southern advantages included military leadership, having to fight only a defensive war, and fighting on home soil.

- Both sides depended on volunteers to fight, and both instituted conscription when they could not get enough volunteers. Draftees could pay for an exemption or hire a substitute. Many free blacks and former slaves served in the North, while the South would not use slaves as soldiers.

- The Northern economy grew during the war, while the South faced shortages of food and manufactured goods.

- New, improved, and more lethal weapons led to high casualty counts.

- The Northern strategy involved slowly eliminating the South's ability to wage war through blockading ports and taking control of the Mississippi River. The Southern strategy involved fighting a long, defensive war, continuing trade, disrupting Northern trade, and gaining European recognition of the South's independence.

**TERMS**

conscription
Clara Barton
Anaconda Plan
war of attrition
blockade runners
cotton diplomacy

**TERMS**

| | |
|---|---|
| Stonewall Jackson | Battle of Antietam |
| First Battle of Bull Run | Battle of Fredericksburg |
| George B. McClellan | Battle of Chancellorsville |
| Robert E. Lee | Pickett's Charge |
| Second Battle of Bull Run | Battle of Gettysburg |
| Peace Democrats | Gettysburg Address |

### 10.2 The War in the East

- The Confederates won the first battles of the war in Virginia.

- Lee attacked Northern territory in Maryland at the Battle of Antietam. It was the bloodiest one-day battle in American history and was a draw, although the South withdrew. The Union "victory" allowed Lincoln to issue the Emancipation Proclamation.

- The South won the battles of Fredericksburg and Chancellorsville, but General Stonewall Jackson was killed.

- Lee invaded Northern soil in Pennsylvania, hoping to force the Union to move troops from other campaigns, win British and French recognition of the Confederacy, gain needed food and supplies, and affect support for the war in the North. The Battle of Gettysburg was the bloodiest of the war, and Lee's army was defeated.

## Chapter Summary

### TERMS

Ulysses S. Grant

Battle of Shiloh

Vicksburg

Battle of Chickamauga

William T. Sherman

Battle of Chattanooga

### 10.3 The War in the West

- Victories in the west at Forts Henry and Donelson, Shiloh, New Orleans, and eventually Vicksburg (after a long siege) gave the Union control of the Mississippi River and much of Tennessee.

- The South won a major victory at the Battle of Chickamauga, but the Union won the Battle of Chattanooga, which opened the road to the invasion of Georgia.

### 10.4 The Road to Appomattox

- Lincoln issued the Emancipation Proclamation, which freed the slaves in states that were in rebellion as of January 1, 1863. It did not free slaves in the border states. The proclamation kept Britain from recognizing the South's independence, encouraged blacks to fight for the Union, made the end of slavery a reason for fighting the war, and took a major step in freeing the slaves in the Confederate states.

- The Union used the policy of total war in its destruction of fields, mills, homes, and towns in the Shenandoah Valley and Atlanta and during Sherman's March to the Sea.

- Lincoln faced opposition from Democrats as well as his own party but won re-election in 1864.

- As Union forces under Grant moved toward Richmond, they suffered high casualties and lost several battles, but because of greater numbers of soldiers and supplies, they forced Lee to surrender.

- The Civil War had a great cost in terms of soldiers killed or wounded, the destruction of the South's land and economy, the end of slavery as a labor system, lingering bitterness between the North and South, and the struggle for former slaves to gain equality.

- Lincoln was shot by John Wilkes Booth while watching a play at Ford's Theater and died the next day, changing the course of the nation's reunification.

### TERMS

Emancipation Proclamation

Battle of Atlanta

March to the Sea

Battle of Cold Harbor

Appomattox Court House

John Wilkes Booth

## Chapter Review Questions

### RECALL

1. What were three new, improved, or more lethal weapons which led to high casualties in the Civil War?

2. What was the South's strategy called that pressured Britain to recognize the Confederacy by withholding cotton?

3. What is a war called that is meant to wear out the opponent and exhaust its resources and will to fight?

4. At what battle did Thomas "Stonewall" Jackson get his nickname?

5. What Union general trained and disciplined the Army of the Potomac but often hesitated to use it in battle?

6. What Confederate general served as commander of the Army of Northern Virginia from the Seven Days' Battles until the end of the war?

7. What was the bloodiest one-day battle in American history?

8. What were two results of the Union "victory" at Antietam?

9. At what battle did wave after wave of Union troops get mowed down by Confederate forces on Marye's Heights?

10. At what battle did Stonewall Jackson receive his fatal wound?

11. What was the last city on the Mississippi River to be captured by the Union?

12. Who did the Democrats nominate for president in 1864?

13. Who assassinated Abraham Lincoln?

### UNDERSTAND

14. Give three advantages the North had over the South and two advantages the South had over the North during the Civil War.

15. How could people in the North and South avoid serving in the military, despite the draft?

16. Compare and contrast the use of black soldiers in the military in the North and South.

17. During the war, how was economic production affected in the North and South?

18. What were the four parts of the Union war strategy? Why did critics call it the Anaconda Plan?

19. How did the South attempt to keep trade flowing on the seas and to disrupt Northern trade?

20. What were three reasons why Lee invaded Maryland in 1862?

21. What were three reasons why Lee invaded Pennsylvania in 1863?

22. Why was the Confederate loss at Gettysburg a turning point in the war?

23. What did the Confiscation Act say about slaves captured by the Union army during the war?

24. Why did Lincoln not free the slaves in the border states in the Emancipation Proclamation?

25. What four things did the Emancipation Proclamation accomplish?

26. On what issues did the Peace Democrats and War Democrats agree and disagree?

27. How did Union success on the battlefield affect the election of 1864?

28. How was Grant able to force Lee to surrender despite losing many battles and men in the last year of the war?

29. What were the human and other costs of the Civil War?

### THINK ABOUT IT

30. To which political opponents of Lincoln do you think these words from the Gettysburg Address were aimed: "It is for us the living, rather, to be dedicated here to the unfinished work which they who fought here have thus far so nobly advanced. It is rather for us to be here dedicated to the great task remaining before us."? Explain.

31. Why did the achievement of Lincoln's personal wish for all men everywhere to be free require prudence (wisdom) on his part?

32. What is the purpose of total war and how was it demonstrated in the Shenandoah Valley and in Sherman's March to the Sea? Do you agree with Charles Hodge's criticisms of total war? Explain.

33. In his Second Inaugural Address, Lincoln said that the Civil War may have been God's judgment on the nation because of slavery. Why can we not always know why God allows certain things to happen? What might this teach us about interpreting current events in terms of God's providence?

# 11 Reconstruction

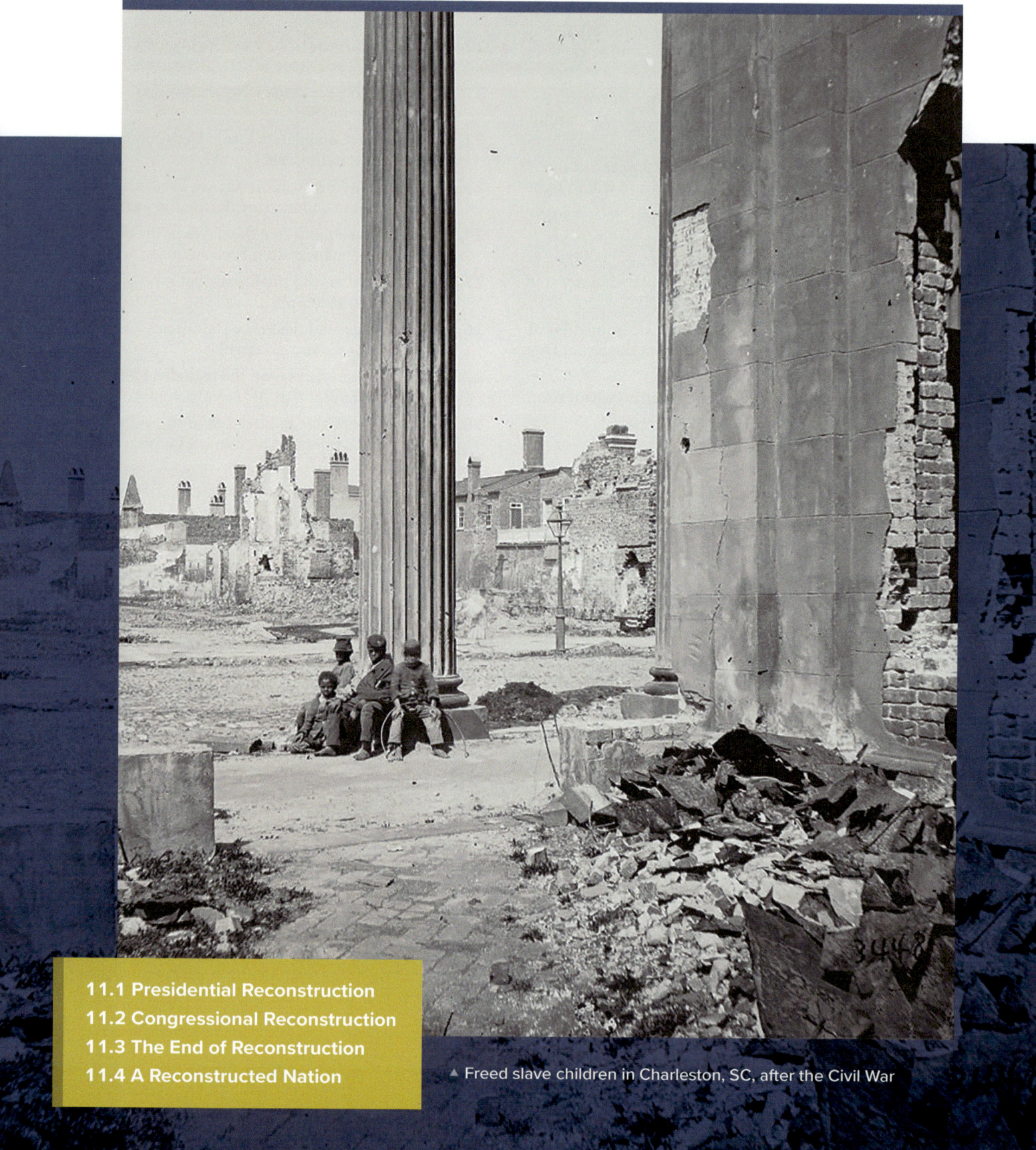

11.1 Presidential Reconstruction
11.2 Congressional Reconstruction
11.3 The End of Reconstruction
11.4 A Reconstructed Nation

▲ Freed slave children in Charleston, SC, after the Civil War

**Presidential Reconstruction**

What were Lincoln's and Johnson's plans to reconstruct the South?

- Why was the South in need of Reconstruction?
- Why did Congress object to Lincoln's plan?
- Why did Radical Republicans oppose Johnson's plan?

The period from the end of the Civil War to 1877 is known as the era of **Reconstruction**. In its narrowest sense, Reconstruction refers to the national government's attempts to rebuild the South after the war. Such recovery was not easy, and Southerners, black and white alike, struggled to make their way forward following the terrible devastation. In a broader sense, Reconstruction refers to changes in the whole country. The nation that emerged from Reconstruction in 1877 was very different from the nation that went into the war in 1861.

## America after the War

The war did not have a significant financial impact on the lives of Northerners. Despite losing thousands of men in combat or from disease, the population and labor force continued to grow because of immigration. Little Northern property was damaged, so soldiers could return to their previous lives with few obstacles. Industry continued to grow and the economy was strong.

In the South, however, the situation was much different. Thousands of young men had been lost. Property, including entire cities, farms, railroads, factories, homes, and businesses had been demolished. Confederate money was worthless. The plantation system was dead and the labor system of slavery was over. Formerly wealthy Southerners were now in poverty and the economy was in ruins. The mood of many Southerners was bitter and gloomy. Their land had been devastated and their way of life had been shattered. They resented the federal troops who were occupying their states, and they felt their liberties were being violated.

The over 4 million **freedmen** (former slaves) had gained liberty from slavery, but they still faced many challenges. Many white Southerners did not believe black Americans should be treated as equals. Most freedmen did not want to return to the fields where they had previously worked as slaves; instead, they hoped to own their own land and become independent and self-sufficient. However, most had no money and could not obtain credit to purchase land. Laws also limited the type of work they could do. Those who pushed for political or social equality often faced violence for doing so.

The states that had seceded also now had to establish new state governments. The Confederate state governments had been removed and new governments would have to be formed. The federal government would have to determine how the states would be readmitted.

One key question the United States government faced was who—the president or Congress—would control the process of Reconstruction.

▼ Newly freed slaves in the ruins of Richmond, VA

# Lincoln's Plan

Lincoln, who believed that secession was a constitutional impossibility, said that the Confederate states had committed an act of rebellion against the United States and that, as commander in chief, his duty was to crush the insurrection. Once that was complete, he believed he had the power to issue pardons and restore the seceded states. His goal was to make the terms of Reconstruction lenient to encourage the Southern states to stop resisting and to reconcile with the Union.

By 1863 the Union army had established control of large portions of Louisiana, Arkansas, and Tennessee, and a plan was needed to restore the relationship of these states with the United States. In December 1863 Lincoln issued his Proclamation of Amnesty and Reconstruction (also called the **Ten Percent Plan**). As the Union army pushed into the South, Lincoln appointed a military governor for each captured state. As soon as a number of citizens equal to ten percent of those who had voted in the 1860 election took an oath of allegiance to the Union, the governor could re-establish a civilian government. Once a government had been formed, it could send representatives to Congress. Further, states were encouraged to pass laws recognizing the permanent freedom of slaves and providing for their education. Lincoln also offered amnesty (a general pardon) and the restoration of property to those who had supported the Confederacy except for Confederate government officials or high-ranking military officers.

Opposing Lincoln in Congress was a group known as the **Radical Republicans**. The leading Radicals in Congress were Pennsylvania representative Thaddeus Stevens, who viewed the Southern states as "conquered provinces" under the direct authority of Congress, and Senator Charles Sumner of Massachusetts, who had survived his 1856 beating in the Senate. Sumner believed the Southern states had ceased to be states. Their readmission to the Union, he argued, should be determined by Congress.

Although they were only a minority within the Republican Party, the Radicals were highly influential. They believed Lincoln's plan did not do enough to punish the

▲ Representative Thaddeus Stevens

▲ Senator Charles Sumner

South for the rebellion or transform Southern attitudes. They also opposed the increase in presidential power that had taken place during the war. Lincoln had used his war powers and executive action several times without consulting Congress, and the Radical Republicans wanted to reassert the power of Congress over the president.

In 1864 the Radical Republicans proposed the **Wade-Davis Bill**, which would have given Congress more power to shape Reconstruction. It required military governors for each Southern state until over fifty percent of all adult white males signed an oath of allegiance. Before readmission, a state would also have to abolish slavery, give up claims for the federal government to pay its war debts, and prohibit former Confederate political or military leaders from voting or holding office. Also, only those who swore that they had never voluntarily borne arms against the United States or aided the Confederacy could participate in electing delegates to their state's constitutional convention. The bill passed both houses of Congress, but Lincoln vetoed it. He believed that it would slow the process of restoring the Union, that it rested on the faulty premise that the seceded states had left the Union and needed to be readmitted by Congress, and he thought that abolishing slavery would require a constitutional amendment.

## Thirteenth Amendment

Abraham Lincoln knew that his Emancipation Proclamation (see Chapter 10) could be overturned or be found unconstitutional at a later date, so he desired a legislative solution that would secure the abolition of slavery. The amendment abolishing slavery passed the Senate in April 1864 but failed in the House of Representatives. After a push to persuade representatives to support it, the **Thirteenth Amendment** passed the House narrowly in January 1865 and was sent to the states for their ratification.

The dispute between Lincoln and Congress had not been resolved when the president was assassinated in April 1865. The new president, **Andrew Johnson**, would have to battle Congress over who would control Reconstruction.

## Johnson's Plan

Sharing Lincoln's view that the Southern states had not left the Union, Johnson said that restoration, not reconstruction, was what was needed. Having grown up poor, Johnson hoped to restore the states in a way that would not radically affect most of Southern society, but he resented the "planter aristocracy" which he blamed for the war. While he supported abolition, he did not share the Radical Republicans' concern for the equality of black Americans. When Johnson became president in April 1865, Congress was in recess and would not return to session until December. During the first eight months of his presidency, Johnson began to implement his plans without congressional interference.

Like Lincoln's, Johnson's plan for Reconstruction included the ten percent oath of allegiance requirement and offered amnesty to Southerners who would swear loyalty to the Union. But Johnson excluded those whose property was worth more than $20,000. Unpardoned Southerners could not vote, hold office, or reclaim property seized by the government. Those individuals, mostly large-plantation owners, had to apply to him personally for a pardon. Next, each former Confederate state was required to hold a state convention to draft a new state constitution that would revoke its declaration of secession, refuse to pay Confederate debts, and ratify the Thirteenth Amendment.

Former Confederates were surprised and relieved at the lenient terms. By the winter of 1865 most of the former Confederate states had met Johnson's terms. As they organized their new governments and elected members to Congress, Johnson began granting pardons to thousands of Southerners. Ratification by the three-fourths of states needed for the Thirteenth Amendment to take effect was completed in December 1865, although some Southern states also passed declarations denying Congress's right to force any legislation on states regarding the political or civil rights of former slaves.

## Andrew Johnson

Andrew Johnson had been born in poverty in North Carolina. He was apprenticed as a tailor at age ten, but later ran away and eventually ended up in Tennessee. He was barely literate until he married a schoolteacher who tutored him. He established a successful business as a tailor, and his shop was a gathering place for locals, who often discussed politics. Johnson started his political career as an alderman, then as mayor of Greeneville, Tennessee. Next, he was elected to the Tennessee House of Representatives before being elected in 1843 to the US House of Representatives. In 1853 he was elected governor of Tennessee and then in 1857 to the US Senate where he was serving when the Civil War began.

When his state seceded, Johnson remained loyal to the Union and retained his Senate seat. Lincoln named him the provisional governor of Tennessee after the Union army captured it. Lincoln added Johnson to his ticket in 1864 hoping that, as a Southerner and a Democrat, Johnson would broaden the ticket's appeal and help promote unity when the war ended.

## Black Codes

Johnson's generous plan emboldened Southern states to defy efforts to transform Southern society. As states were restored under Johnson's plan, many of their legislatures also passed laws known as **black codes**. These laws severely limited the rights of black Americans, and though they varied from state to state, all seemed intended to keep African Americans in a condition similar to slavery.

No Southern state granted blacks the right to vote. In some states, black Americans could work only as household servants or farmers. Those who wanted to do anything besides farming had to be apprenticed and often had to obtain costly licenses which few could afford.

Blacks who were not employed could be arrested. Those who could not pay fines were often "hired out" to anyone who would pay their fines. Some black codes forbade them to carry weapons, and others limited where they could own property or even reside. Some states prohibited blacks from suing whites or serving on juries. These codes convinced Radical Republicans that Congress needed to do more to guarantee equality for black Americans.

▼ A freedman in Florida being auctioned to pay a legal fine in 1867

## Black Codes

The following codes were instituted in Opelousas, Louisiana, in 1865.

*No negro or freedman shall be allowed to come within the limits of the town of Opelousas without special permission from his employers. . . . Whoever shall violate this provision shall suffer imprisonment and two days' work on the public streets, or shall pay a fine of two dollars and fifty cents. . . .*

*No negro or freedman shall be permitted to rent or keep a house within the limits of the town under any circumstances. . . .*

*No negro or freedman shall reside within the limits of the town of Opelousas who is not in the regular service of some white person or former owner. . . .*

*No public meetings or congregations of negroes or freedmen shall be allowed within the limits of the town. . . .*

*No freedman who is not in the military service shall be allowed to carry firearms, or any kind of weapons. . . .*

### 🔍 Analyzing Sources

How do these codes compare with laws regarding slaves in the antebellum era (see Chapter 9)?

## Radical Republican Response

The Radical Republicans believed Johnson's plan was failing for several reasons. First, black Americans should not only be free from slavery but also given equality and the full rights of citizenship. Black codes had shown that Congress would have to act to secure those rights.

Second, Johnson's plan gave Southern states more political power in the national government, as the full population of freedmen was now counted in the census, thus raising their state populations and representation in Congress. Because those freedmen were not given the right to vote, those additional Southern representatives would presumedly be white Democrats, and Republicans feared losing control of the government.

Third, Southern states that had reinstituted their governments under Johnson's plan were electing former Confederates to office. Dozens of newly elected officials had been members of the Confederate Congress, six had served in the Confederate cabinet, four had been Confederate generals, and eight had been colonels in the Confederate army. Even Alexander Stephens, former vice president of the Confederacy, was elected as one of Georgia's two senators. All had obtained pardons based on Johnson's Reconstruction plan. Many Republicans were outraged that Southern voters had elected these officials, arguing that it was wrong for those who had led a rebellion against the Union to immediately return to power. Some argued that without changes in leadership, the South would not be much different than it had been before the war.

When it reconvened in December 1865, Congress refused to seat the newly elected Southern legislators. Instead, moderate and Radical Republicans established a Joint Committee on Reconstruction. This was the first step in Congress's attempt to take control of Reconstruction away from the president.

---

### Comprehension Check 11.1

1. The Radical Republicans opposed ____.

   A  Lincoln's Ten Percent Plan

   B  the Joint Committee on Reconstruction

   C  the Wade-Davis Bill

2. One way that Johnson's plan modified Lincoln's Ten Percent Plan was by ____.

   A  excluding owners of property worth over $20,000 from a general amnesty

   B  prohibiting former Confederate officers and officials from voting or holding office

   C  requiring fifty percent of a state's eligible voters to take an oath of allegiance

3. The ____ abolished slavery in all states.

   A  black codes

   B  Emancipation Proclamation

   C  Thirteenth Amendment

4. One major question concerning Reconstruction was whether Congress or the president would control the process.

   True

   False

**MAKING CONNECTIONS**

5. What were two reasons Radical Republicans believed Johnson's plan for Reconstruction was failing?

## 11.2 Congressional Reconstruction

**How did Radical Republicans in Congress control Reconstruction?**

## Radical Republicans

Johnson opposed the Joint Committee and believed Congress was consolidating too much power for itself and passing acts against the Southern states while preventing the seating of their representatives. Democrats in Congress, along with some moderate Republicans, were still willing to work with the president. But Johnson, known for his fiery temper, lashed out at his opponents. As Johnson's popularity sank, more Republicans drifted into the Radical camp. Johnson refused to negotiate.

Some Radical Republicans believed it was immoral for white men to deny black people the same rights and liberties. They therefore began working toward legal and constitutional protections for black Americans.

### The Freedmen's Bureau

In March 1865, while Lincoln was president, Congress had passed laws to establish a short-term agency that became known as the **Freedmen's Bureau**, officially known as the Bureau of Refugees, Freedmen, and Abandoned Lands. It issued rations of surplus army food and clothing and attempted to locate jobs for the freedmen and prevent employers from exploiting them. The bureau also sent agents into the South to establish hospitals and schools for black people of all ages. Additionally, the bureau was the steward of Confederate property seized under the Confiscation Act of 1862. After the war the agency supervised the restoration of land to the original owners.

In February 1866 Congress voted for a bill that would extend and enlarge the bureau. The bill dealt with the injustices of the black codes by empowering the agency to help freedmen negotiate fair work contracts and establishing special courts to protect the rights of freedmen. Many Southerners objected to these courts that had the power to overrule state courts. The bill also enabled the bureau to intervene if a court issued an unjust verdict or if civil rights were violated.

▼ Teachers and students outside the Freedmen's Bureau school, Beaufort, SC

President Johnson vetoed the bill, but the Radicals acted quickly to limit the power of the president. With the exclusion of Southern congressional representatives a few months earlier, Republicans controlled more than two-thirds of the votes in Congress and were able to override the president's veto.

The Freedmen's Bureau was headed by Union General Oliver O. Howard, who believed that education was the foundation for assisting former slaves. Consequently, the encouragement and oversight of schools for blacks occupied much of the agency's time. General Howard advocated for Congressional funding of a black university in Washington, DC, which was established as Howard University and named after the general. By 1869 thousands of schools, serving hundreds of thousands of students, were founded or supported by the Freedmen's Bureau, missionary groups, and black churches. In addition, more than forty hospitals were established by the bureau.

### Civil Rights Act of 1866

Congress, now led by the Radical Republicans, enacted several pieces of legislation to further control the Reconstruction process. In March 1866 it passed the Civil Rights Act which granted citizenship to black Americans. It also gave them "full and equal benefit of all laws." This act was intended to protect blacks from the black codes and other discriminating laws.

Andrew Johnson also vetoed this bill. He said the federal government did not have the power to enact such legislation. He believed individual states, not the national government, had the power to determine citizenship. In April 1866 Congress overrode the veto. Fearing that the Supreme Court might rule the Civil Rights Act unconstitutional or that it might be repealed by a future Congress, the Republicans proposed the Fourteenth Amendment in June.

▲ Frederick Douglass Hall at Howard University, Washington, DC

# The Fourteenth Amendment

While the Thirteenth Amendment had freed the slaves, the **Fourteenth Amendment** dealt with the legal status of freedmen and contained four important provisions.

**1** Black Americans were granted full citizenship and equal protection of the law, and states were prohibited from depriving a person of his life, liberty, or property without due process of law.

**2** All former slaves, not just three-fifths, were to be counted to determine the state's representation in Congress.

**3** Former senators, representatives, or other officeholders who had supported the Confederacy were barred from holding office. Congress (not the president) could, by a two-thirds vote, remove this restriction.

**4** Neither federal nor state governments could pay any of the Confederate debts or provide any compensation to former slaveholders for the loss of their slaves.

When ratified, the amendment would cancel not only black codes in the South but also laws against blacks in some midwestern states. But Johnson urged Southern states to vote against it. He believed it treated former Confederate leaders too harshly and that it was wrong to enact an amendment when the representatives of the Southern states, who had been barred from Congress, had had no part in its passage.

Realizing that he was powerless as long as the Radicals and the moderate Republicans had a two-thirds majority in Congress, Johnson traveled to the North and the Midwest, speaking against Radical candidates in the 1866 congressional races. But his efforts backfired when he lost his temper and responded harshly when audiences taunted him. Critics were skeptical of his leadership, and the Republicans that Johnson opposed won landslide victories over Democrats in the 1866 elections. Beginning in 1867 the Radical Republicans in Congress, now exercising even greater control, enacted their program speedily and with little resistance. When the president vetoed their legislation, Congress quickly overrode his vetoes.

## The Reconstruction Act of 1867

Congress passed the **Reconstruction Act of 1867** (also known as the Military Reconstruction Act). It ordered the army to ensure that the South complied with congressional mandates. First, the act divided the South into five military districts, each governed by a Union general. Second, it gave black Americans the right to vote and hold office. Third, it said that Southern states wanting to reenter the Union had to hold conventions that included both black and white voting delegates. (Those who had

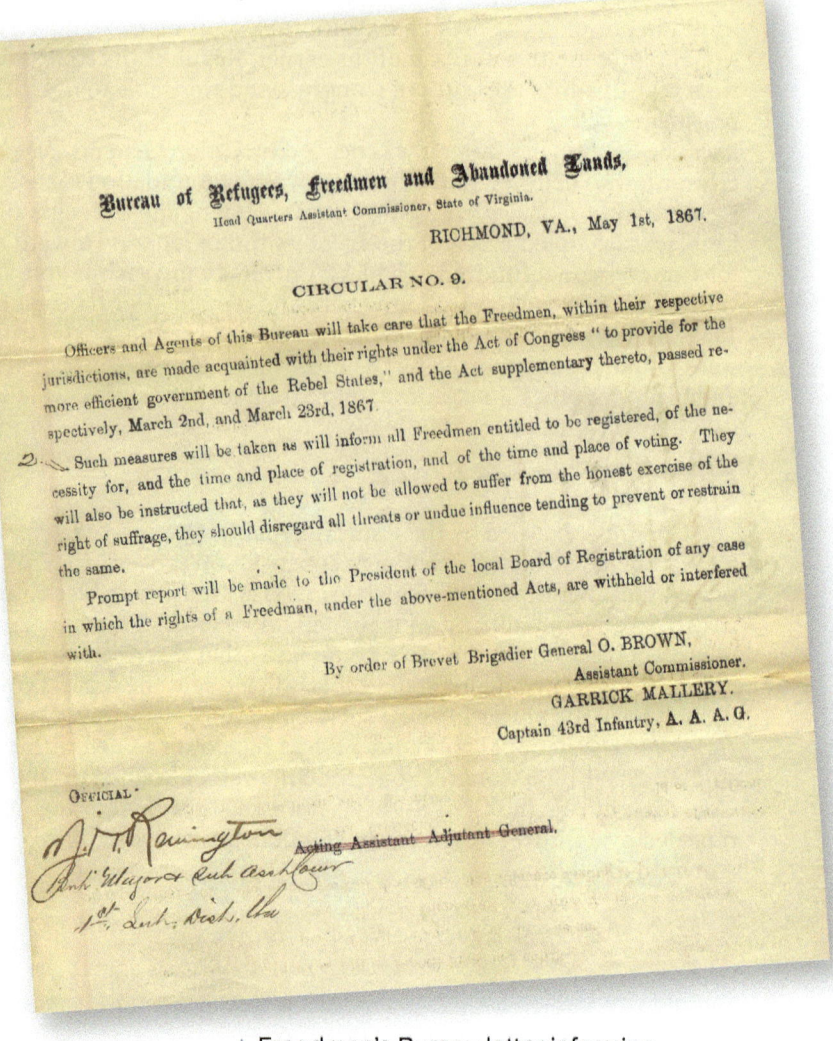

▲ Freedmen's Bureau letter informing freedmen of their right to vote

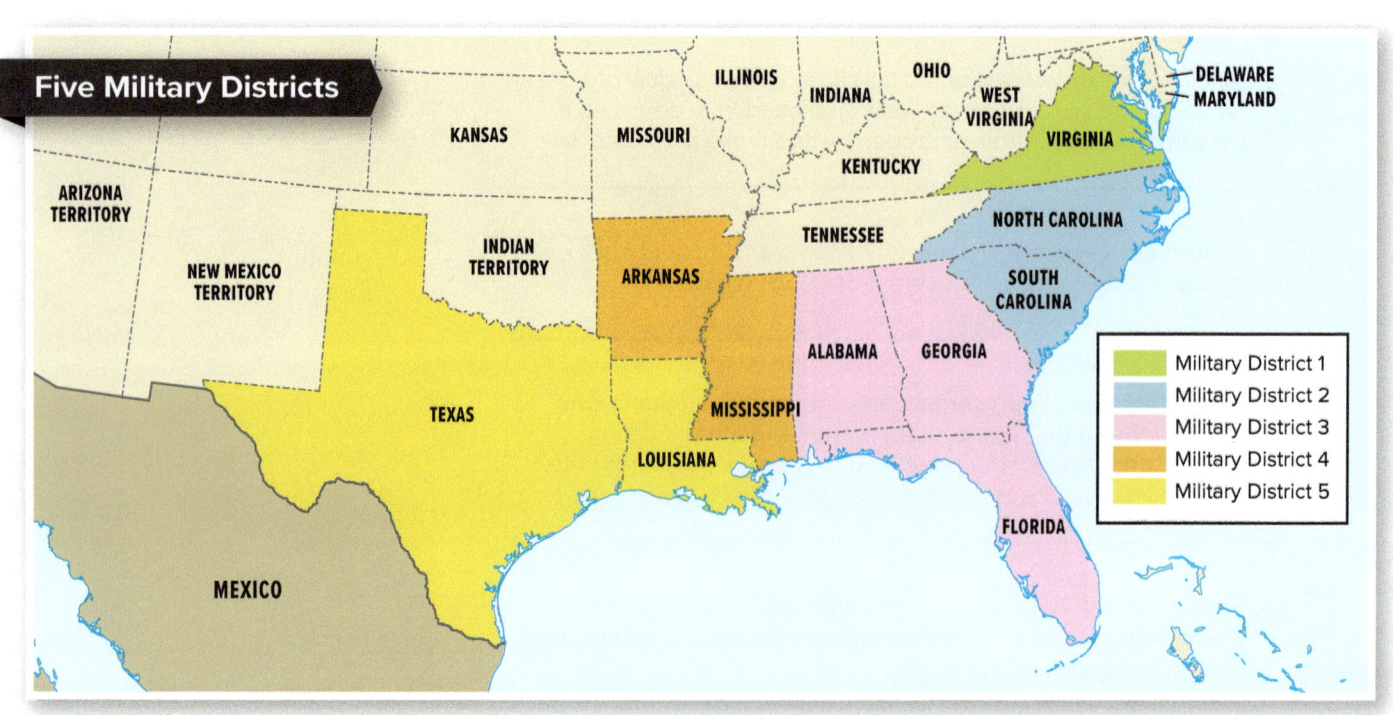

**Five Military Districts**

Military District 1
Military District 2
Military District 3
Military District 4
Military District 5

taken an oath, before the Civil War, to uphold the Constitution but had then supported the Confederacy were excluded from participation.) These conventions were to write new state constitutions, using the guidelines given by Congress. Fourth, the act required the Southern states to submit their new constitutions to Congress for approval. Fifth, the act required states to ratify the Fourteenth Amendment. Many Southerners resented the military occupation of the South.

When a state met all the requirements for reentry, it would be entitled to representation in Congress and troops would be withdrawn. Tennessee was exempt from this law because it had already ratified the Fourteenth Amendment.

The exclusion of former Confederate leaders from public office opened the way for Southern Unionists, Northerners, and black Americans to occupy such positions. These groups had formerly possessed little political power in the South. Six hundred black men served as state legislators, others were judges, and some were elected to Congress. Joseph Rainey of South Carolina was the first black man elected to the US House of Representatives, while **Hiram Revels** of Mississippi was the first black man elected to the US Senate.

Many white Southerners were angered that blacks now participated in the writing of the new state constitutions and held elective offices. Meanwhile, black delegates and legislators, who wanted political rights to be extended to black Americans without denying those rights to others, typically opposed efforts by some Southern Unionists to withhold voting and officeholding rights from former Confederates.

▲ Robert Smalls was born in slavery in Beaufort, SC, in 1839. He worked as a helmsmen on ships in Charleston Harbor. In 1862 he gained his freedom by commandeering a ship and helping his family and crew escape to the Union ships blockading the harbor. Smalls served in the Union army and navy for the duration of the war. During Reconstruction he was elected to the South Carolina House of Representatives, served in the state Senate, and was elected to the US House of Representatives, where he served for ten years. Smalls died in 1915.

## Hiram Revels

Hiram Revels was born to free black parents in Fayetteville, North Carolina, in 1822. Because of the lack of educational opportunities for blacks in North Carolina at the time, he moved to the Midwest, where he attended schools in Indiana, Ohio, and Illinois. Revels became a minister in the African Methodist Episcopal (AME) Church. He preached and taught in the Midwest and the border states, and at the outbreak of the Civil War was pastoring in Baltimore.

During the war, he recruited African Americans to fight for the Union and also served as a Union chaplain. Later, he preached to blacks in Mississippi and helped the Freedmen's Bureau establish schools there. He was elected to that state's senate in 1868 as a Republican. In 1870 he was elected to finish the last year of an unexpired US Senate term.

The first black man to serve in the US Congress, Revels persuaded the War Department to hire qualified black mechanics in the US Naval Yard and spoke out against segregation in the schools of Washington, DC. Although he supported the presence of troops in the South to protect the rights of blacks in the region, he opposed efforts to deprive former Confederates of the vote.

Revels returned to Mississippi after finishing his term and served as president of Alcorn College and briefly as Mississippi's secretary of state. After retiring from the presidency of Alcorn because of health problems, Revels returned to the ministry. He died in 1901.

## Carpetbaggers and Scalawags

Most white Southerners opposed the new Republican-controlled state governments. They called Northerners who moved to the South "**carpetbaggers**," a reference to the cheap luggage in which many of them brought all their belongings. Some carpetbaggers came to work with the Freedmen's Bureau, sincerely desiring to help freed slaves. Some came to make their fortunes by acquiring farmland or starting new businesses, factories, or railroads—business ventures which helped rebuild the South's economy. In some places Northerners took control of Southern politics. Bitterness against Northern interference increased when instances of corruption and electoral fraud occurred (discussed later in this chapter).

White Southerners who supported the new Reconstruction governments were called "**scalawags**," a term that basically meant "scoundrel" or "worthless person." Most scalawags had been pro-Union men since before the war, but former Confederate officers James Longstreet and John Mosby became Republicans and supported black rights. Both carpetbaggers and scalawags were despised by many white Southerners as treasonous, dishonest, and self-serving.

▲ Political Cartoon "The 'Strong' Government 1669–1877" by J. A. Wales. See Student Activities for a guided analysis of this cartoon.

▼ The impeachment trial of Andrew Johnson

# The Impeachment of Johnson

In March 1867 Congress passed the **Tenure of Office Act** which made it illegal for the president to remove any appointee who had been approved by the Senate unless the Senate also approved the dismissal. The Radicals intended the law to protect Edwin Stanton, the secretary of war appointed by Lincoln. Stanton often sided with Radicals in the cabinet against Johnson. Believing the act was unconstitutional, Johnson decided to test it by dismissing Stanton, who responded by literally barricading himself in his office. The president's actions gave the Radicals a potential opportunity to remove Johnson. The Constitution provides for a two-step process for removal. First, the House of Representatives, by majority vote, can bring charges, known as **impeachment**, against the president. After being impeached, the president must face trial in the Senate, and two-thirds of the Senate must declare the president guilty for him to be removed from office.

According to the Constitution, the only basis for removal of the president is "conviction of . . . treason, bribery, or other high crimes and misdemeanors" (Article II, Section 4).

In February 1868, the House voted 126–47 to impeach Johnson on eleven charges. The primary allegation was that he had violated the Tenure of Office Act by firing Stanton. The president's Senate trial began on March 13 and lasted until May 26. Johnson never attended the trial. He believed that he had done nothing wrong and that his attendance would only lend credibility to his accusers.

Senators had varied opinions about Johnson's guilt. They questioned whether the Tenure of Office Act was constitutional and whether it applied in Stanton's case. Stanton, after all, was Lincoln's appointee before the Tenure of Office Act was passed. Some questioned whether Radicals were trying to remove the president merely because they disagreed with him politically, which would set a dangerous precedent for the future.

Senators also knew that if Johnson were removed, Benjamin Wade, one of the most extreme Radicals, would become president. Wade was the president pro tempore of the Senate, and according to the law at the time, next in line since Johnson had no vice president. (In 1948 the law was changed to make the Speaker of the House the next in line after the vice president.)

When the final vote at the Senate trial was taken, thirty-five senators voted to convict Johnson. Nineteen, including seven Republicans, voted to acquit him. Because the Radicals were one vote short of the two-thirds needed to convict Johnson, the president was able to complete his term in March 1869. Years later, the Supreme Court declared the Tenure of Office Act unconstitutional.

## President Ulysses S. Grant

Despite Johnson's acquittal, he lost almost all influence with Republicans. As the nation approached the presidential election of 1868, the Republicans turned to war hero **Ulysses S. Grant** as their candidate. Despite having little political experience, Grant appeared to be the pillar of strength that the nation needed after the war and after the bitter struggle between President Johnson and Congress. The Republican campaign slogan was: "Let us have peace."

Grant won the election by defeating the Democratic candidate, former New York governor Horatio Seymour, whose party's slogan was "This is a White Man's Country; Let White Men Rule." About 500,000 black men voted for the first time in a presidential election, giving their support overwhelmingly to Grant.

### Did You Know?

Andrew Johnson is the second former president to serve in Congress after leaving the White House. Johnson served in the Senate and John Quincy Adams in the House of Representatives.

▼ (left) Republican campaign poster, 1868; (right) "This is a White Man's Government" political cartoon by Thomas Nast, 1868

LET US HAVE PEACE

GEN. U. S. GRANT.

African American men voting during Reconstruction

## The Fifteenth Amendment

Radical Republicans had long sought to secure voting rights for black Americans in the North. However, by 1868 only about half the Northern states had legalized black suffrage. In addition, although the Reconstruction Act of 1867 required that Southern states allow black men to vote and hold office in order to regain admission to the Union, Radicals feared that those laws could be changed. To prevent Southern states from possibly revoking this right in the future and to ensure that right nationwide, Congress passed the **Fifteenth Amendment**. It was adopted by Congress in 1869 and stated, "The right of the citizens of the United States to vote shall not be denied or abridged by the United States or by any state on account of race, color, or previous condition of servitude." It was ratified the following year.

## Scandals

Several scandals rocked the Grant administration. One of them, the Crédit Mobilier scandal, began before Grant took office. Crédit Mobilier was a construction company controlled by promoters and officers of the Union Pacific Railway. During the construction of the transcontinental railroad (see Chapter 13), Union Pacific received a substantial amount of money from the federal government. Crédit Mobilier overcharged Union Pacific for construction expenses and then paid the excesses to the stockholders. To discourage investigation into this illegal activity, Crédit Mobilier sold stock to congressmen and other government officials at prices far below the market value. An eventual congressional investigation in 1872 revealed that several prominent Republicans had received shares of the stock, including Vice President Schuyler Colfax.

Some scandals reached into Grant's inner circle of cabinet members and advisers. Secretary of War William Belknap was forced to resign for accepting bribes in return for granting special licenses to conduct trade with Native Americans. One of the worst scandals, revealed in 1875, was the Whiskey Ring, a group of whiskey distillers and distributors and federal tax collectors who conspired to cheat the government out of millions of dollars in revenue from taxes. Because his private secretary, Orville Babcock, was among those accused in the swindle, Grant was hesitant to demand a thorough investigation.

There is no evidence that Grant himself personally profited from any of the fraud. Despite the scandals during his administration, Grant had several positive accomplishments. He defended the rights of freedmen, signing legislation to combat the Ku Klux Klan and calling on states to give black Americans the rights that were lawfully theirs. Some of his appointments brought reforms to departments, such as improving tax collection, reducing the debt, and dismissing corrupt or incompetent employees. He also showed more concern for the plight of Native Americans than his predecessors had, and he approved the establishment of Yellowstone National Park, the first national park.

◄ "Whiskey Ring" political cartoon by Thomas Nast

## The Reconstruction Amendments

The Thirteenth Amendment (ratified 1865), the Fourteenth Amendment (ratified 1868), and the Fifteenth Amendment (ratified 1870) are often known collectively as the "Reconstruction Amendments."

## TAMMANY HALL

The most notorious political corruption in this period was found not in the Grant administration but in the government of New York City, which was run by the Democratic Tammany Hall under the direction of **William "Boss" Tweed**. Tammany Hall was a political organization founded after the Revolutionary War. Its influence grew until it controlled most of New York's political affairs during the last half of the nineteenth century. Under the leadership of Boss Tweed, its corruption in the 1860s and 1870s reached astonishing depths.

New York City's debt increased from $36 million in 1868 to more than $136 million in 1870, largely because Tweed and other Tammany leaders diverted city funds into their own pockets. In just one of his many frauds, Tweed charged New York taxpayers about $11 million to build a courthouse that actually cost about $3 million. (Thermometers for the building, for example, were listed as costing $7,500 each.) Tweed and his associates stole between $30 million and $200 million in taxpayer funds.

Tweed and his associates managed to stay in power by bribing people to vote for Democrats and by cheating during elections. Needing Tammany's help to win, many Democrats in the state ignored the corruption in New York City. Tammany politicians used bribes to persuade Republicans to leave them alone.

Reform efforts aimed at destroying Tammany Hall resulted in Tweed finally being arrested in 1871. Assisting the efforts was the gifted political cartoonist Thomas Nast, who repeatedly attacked Tweed and Tammany Hall. Tweed feared the cartoons more than any other opposition because, as Tweed himself said, his uneducated supporters could not read editorials, but they could understand Nast's drawings. Tweed was eventually convicted of his crimes. Later he managed to escape prison and flee to Spain. He was identified there through one of Nast's cartoons and was returned to prison in New York, where he died two years later.

## Thomas Nast

Thomas Nast, the cartoonist known for opposing Boss Tweed, was a man of firm principles with a fierce sense of right, and his political cartoons in *Harper's Weekly* had a sharp edge that made him the leading political cartoonist of the day.

A diehard Republican, Nast was not exactly unbiased. Even at the height of the Grant scandals, he defended the president. Yet even Nast's opponents could not deny the power of his work. When Tweed died, it was discovered that he had kept every cartoon Nast had ever drawn of him.

In addition to the Tweed drawings, Nast's cartoons made popular the symbols of the two parties—the Republicans' elephant and the Democrats' donkey.

THE "BRAINS"

THAT ACHIEVED THE TAMMANY VICTORY AT THE ROCHESTER DEMOCRATIC CONVENTION.

▲ (top) Thomas Nast 1871 political cartoon depicting William "Boss" Tweed; (bottom) Thomas Nast 1879 political cartoon featuring a donkey representing the Democratic Party and an elephant representing the Republican Party

## Election of 1872

The corruption of the Grant administration and disagreements with Radical Republicans led to the development of a splinter group within the Republican Party. Calling themselves the "Liberal Republicans," they decided to oppose Grant's reelection in 1872. They supported an end to military occupation of the South and an end to corruption in the national government. They had trouble finding an acceptable candidate. Eventually, they chose New York newspaper editor Horace Greeley.

The Democrats, still weakened by the war, decided their best hope for defeating Grant was to join forces with the Liberal Republicans. Thus, they also nominated Greeley. Although Greeley was well-known and thoroughly honest, he had long been a bitter critic of the South and aroused little excitement among Southern Democrats. Despite the scandals that surrounded Grant, the president defeated Greeley in the election and, in so doing, ended the Liberal Republican movement.

## Economic Boom and Bust

One of the reasons Grant won reelection so easily was the widespread prosperity of the nation, particularly in the North. For most voters, economic good times excused many of the failures of Grant's administration.

Prosperity came to a devastating halt, however, during Grant's second term. A financial collapse known as the **Panic of '73** touched off a six-year depression, the worst depression that the United States had endured up to that time. The stock market fell, and unemployment soared to 14 percent. By 1875 more than 18,000 companies, including many banks, had collapsed. Eighty-nine of the nation's 364 railroads also went bankrupt.

The Panic of '73 and the scandals under Grant hurt the Republicans. The Democrats retook control of the House of Representatives and gained seats in the Senate in 1874.

▼ Bank customers rushing to withdraw their money during the Panic of '73

## Comprehension Check 11.2

1. The Freedmen's Bureau established schools and hospitals as well as ____.

   A  banks for business investment

   B  courts for labor disputes

   C  funds for colonization in West Africa

2. The Fourteenth Amendment included the following provisions except ____.

   A  excluding former Confederate officials from voting or holding office until Congress removed the restriction

   B  guaranteeing citizenship to freedmen

   C  providing compensation to former slaveowners

3. The impeachment of Johnson failed because ____.

   A  Secretary of War Stanton supported Johnson

   B  Senate Democrats were in the majority

   C  Senate Republicans were one vote short of the necessary two-thirds majority

4. The Grant administration was plagued with all of these except ____.

   A  criticism from political cartoonist Thomas Nast

   B  financial collapse in the Panic of '73

   C  scandals involving cabinet members and advisors

5. William "Boss" Tweed was responsible for stealing taxpayer money and bribery in New York City's ____.

   A  Crédit Mobilier

   B  Tammany Hall

   C  Whiskey Ring

### MAKING CONNECTIONS

6. What were the five provisions of the Reconstruction Act of 1867?

7. Why did Republicans in Congress think it was necessary to create the Fourteenth and Fifteenth Amendments after the provisions in the Civil Rights Act and Reconstruction Act?

**The End of Reconstruction**

How did Reconstruction come to an end?

GUIDING QUESTIONS

- What did the Redeemers want to "redeem"?
- How did the election of Rutherford B. Hayes lead to the end of Reconstruction?

## The Redeemers

By the mid-1870s many Northerners had lost interest in Reconstruction and conditions in the South. Some were more concerned about the return to economic prosperity. Others were more interested in opportunities for expansion in the West. Some believed that ending Reconstruction policies would be better for business, while others were weary of the turmoil caused by some Radical Republicans and were willing to back away from controversial issues for the sake of peace. Many Americans seemed ready to move on from scandal and controversy.

In 1872 some Republicans convinced Congress to pass the General Amnesty Act. It removed the restrictions of Section 3 of the Fourteenth Amendment for all but a few hundred former Confederate leaders. As a result, most former Confederate leaders were now eligible to be elected to office again.

Although black people had gained some rights, many white Southerners found it difficult to accept them as equals. The Amnesty Act and growing Northern disinterest in Reconstruction paved the way for the **Redeemers**, white Southern Democrats who wanted to redeem (or save) their state governments from "Black Republican" rule. By the mid-1870s, Southerners were electing white Democrats to replace black officials and white Republicans. Only in areas still occupied by federal troops did Republican governments maintain control a bit longer. By 1876 federal troops remained only in Louisiana, Florida, and South Carolina.

The election of Redeemers had wide-ranging, long-term effects for black Southerners. Though black men continued to vote in significant numbers in the South into the 1880s, the effectiveness of their vote was hindered by episodes of fraud and violence. Sometimes ballot boxes were stuffed with more votes than there were voters or Republican ballots were removed. Congressional districts were sometimes drawn in strange shapes to ensure that black voters were not in a majority. In other cases, some freedmen had their votes determined by the employer for whom they worked. In many states Redeemers denied black children access to education and some of the old black codes were reestablished. Segregation, or separation of the races, was commonplace.

▼ Political cartoon "Of Course He Wants to Vote the Democratic Ticket!" depicting the intimidation of black voters

### Violence

Some Southerners who resented Congressional Reconstruction turned to violence. Some established secret societies. The largest of these was the **Ku Klux Klan** (KKK), which was organized in 1866 by some former Confederate soldiers in Pulaski, Tennessee. Many of them were determined to place black people firmly under white control. They targeted successful black businessmen and landowners and intimidated white people who did business with blacks. Schools and churches for blacks were burned to prevent them from gaining the education needed to become self-sufficient.

The Klan also targeted black officeholders, white Republican leaders, and Freedmen's Bureau agents. Some were beaten, and some were killed. Even voting made a black person a target. The violence severely damaged the Republican Party's organization in some parts of the South, and many blacks and Republicans were intimidated from voting or running for office. Some party leaders had to flee for their safety.

▲ 1866 race riot in Memphis, TN

The Klan included many prominent citizens—a fact that added to its power. Dressed in white hooded robes to conceal their identity, they usually terrorized at night. Many white citizens who opposed Klan violence kept silent publicly. Testifying against Klan members in court would make the witness a Klan target. Hundreds of freedmen were lynched (executed, often by hanging, without a legal trial). Many of them were dragged from their homes at night and killed in the presence of their families.

A group of Kentucky blacks sent a petition to Congress in 1871 pleading for the legislature to step in to stop the Klan.

> *We believe you are not familiar with the description of the Ku Klux Klan's riding nightly over the country, going from county to county . . . spreading terror wherever they go by robbing, whipping, ravishing, and killing our people without provocation [reason], compelling colored people to break the ice and bathe in the chilly waters of the Kentucky River. . . . We would state that we have been law-abiding citizens, pay our taxes, and in many parts of the state our people have been . . . refused the right to vote. Many have been slaughtered while attempting to vote. We ask, how long is this state of things to last?* — **GROUP OF KENTUCKY FREEDMEN**

Because local law enforcement could not or would not deal with the Klan, Congress stepped in to address the violence. The Enforcement Act, (1870), outlawed using force to prevent people from voting and gave the president power to use federal troops to enforce this legislation. The Ku Klux Klan Act (1871) imposed heavy penalties against terrorist groups like the Klan. Eventually thousands of Klansmen were arrested and hundreds of those were convicted for their actions. The Klan's power was diminished, but it was not destroyed and would reemerge in the twentieth century.

## The Election of 1876

Because of corruption in the Grant administration as well as at the local and state levels, both parties chose reform-minded candidates in the election of 1876. Republicans chose Rutherford B. Hayes, a Union general in the Civil War and three-time governor of Ohio with a reputation for unimpeachable honesty. The Democrats chose Samuel J. Tilden, railroad lawyer and former governor of New York with a national reputation for fighting the "Tweed ring" and reforming the state judiciary system.

When the election returns were tallied, Tilden won the popular vote by a margin of 250,000. He had 184 of the 185 electoral votes needed to win, and Hayes had 165. However, twenty electoral votes were disputed. Nineteen of these were in three Southern states—Florida, Louisiana, and South Carolina (all states that federal troops still occupied). Each state submitted conflicting election results with each side claiming victory (the twentieth disputed electoral vote was in Oregon). Tilden needed only one of the disputed electoral votes to win. Hayes needed to capture all twenty to become president.

▼ Rutherford B. Hayes

Congress created a commission of fifteen men—five each from the Supreme Court, the Senate, and the House—to resolve the disputed votes. Eight of the fifteen commissioners were Republicans, while seven were Democrats. By a vote of eight to seven, divided along party lines, the commission gave all the disputed votes, and thus the presidency, to Hayes. It is difficult to determine which candidate deserved to be elected because voting corruption by both parties had occurred.

As one might expect, the Democrats contested the commission's decision. The party threatened to prevent the official counting of the electoral votes in Congress to prevent Hayes from taking office. The deadlock was broken, however, when a group of Southern Democrats met secretly with the Republicans to make a deal known as the Compromise of 1877. The Democrats agreed to accept the election of Hayes and the Reconstruction Amendments, and the Republicans agreed to withdraw all remaining federal troops from the South.

Within weeks of taking office in April 1877, Hayes withdrew the last federal troops from the South. Troops were no longer present to monitor elections or enforce laws protecting black Americans. With the military gone, white Democrats were back in control in the South and Reconstruction was effectively over.

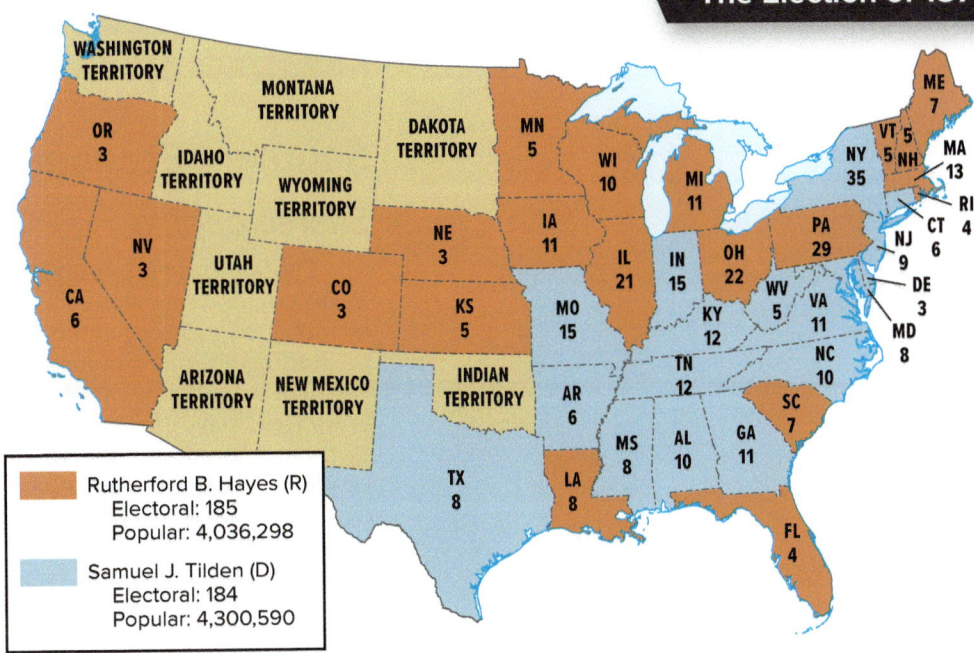

Rutherford B. Hayes (R)
Electoral: 185
Popular: 4,036,298

Samuel J. Tilden (D)
Electoral: 184
Popular: 4,300,590

## Readmission of Confederate States

| Order | State | Readmission | Local Rule |
|-------|-------|-------------|------------|
| 1 | TN | Jul 24, 1866 | Oct 4, 1869 |
| 2 | AR | Jun 22, 1868 | Nov 10, 1874 |
| 3 | FL | Jun 25, 1868 | Jan 2, 1877 |
| 4 | NC | Jul 4, 1868 | Nov 28, 1876 |
| 5 | LA | Jul 9, 1868 | Jan 2, 1877 |
| 6 | SC | Jul 9, 1868 | Nov 28, 1876 |
| 7 | AL | Jul 13, 1868 | Nov 16, 1874 |
| 8 | VA | Jan 26, 1870 | Oct 5, 1869 |
| 9 | MS | Feb 23, 1870 | Jan 4, 1876 |
| 10 | TX | Mar 30, 1870 | Jan 14, 1873 |
| 11 | GA | Jul 15, 1870 | Nov 1, 1871 |

### Comprehension Check 11.3

1. All of these statements apply to the Ku Klux Klan except that it _____.

   A included prominent white citizens

   B targeted black legislators and citizens as well as white Republicans

   C was permanently destroyed by the Ku Klux Klan Act

2. The Compromise of 1877 included _____.

   A Republicans accepting the election of Samuel J. Tilden as president

   B Republicans agreeing to withdraw federal troops from the South

   C Republicans overturning the Fourteenth and Fifteenth Amendments

### MAKING CONNECTIONS

3. Who were the Redeemers and what long-term effects did their election have on the South?

## 11.4 A Reconstructed Nation

**Was Reconstruction successful?**

## Southern Economy

### Sharecropping

The Southern economy had been devastated by the war, and recovery came very slowly. The freedmen generally returned to farming, the only occupation many knew, and agriculture remained the leading Southern industry. Some freedmen hoped that the government would seize the old plantations and from those lands give every freed slave "forty acres and a mule," but that did not happen. Without jobs, money, or land of their own, the freedmen often had no choice but to work for a landowner, sometimes their former masters. Those landowners needed laborers, but few owners had money to pay wages. With the shortage of cash and the absence of slave labor, the **sharecropping** system developed.

Not only blacks but also poor whites became involved in this new economic system. Sharecroppers farmed small plots owned by planters and paid an annual rent for seed, tools, a mule, a cabin, and the use of the land. They paid rent with a portion, or share, of the crop they grew. That share was typically one-half, or more, of the harvest. Since sharecroppers had little money, especially at the beginning of the season, they borrowed money to buy provisions for their family. Often, the landlord provided the loan and may have also owned the local store. The **crop-lien** system meant that people borrowing money pledged future crops as security for the loan. At harvest, each sharecropper settled his account. After paying his debts and interest, the sharecropper was fortunate if he broke even; more often he started the next season still in debt.

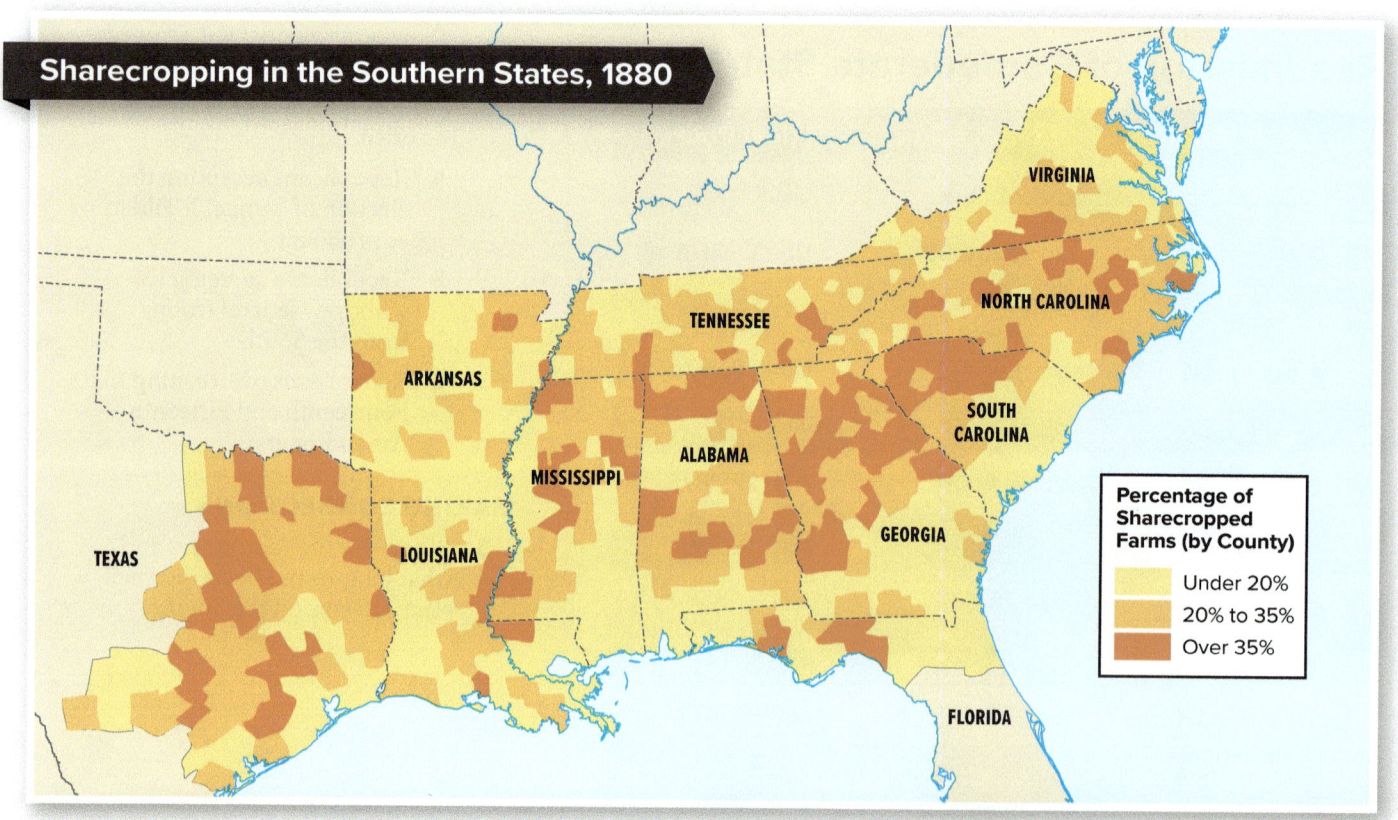

**Sharecropping in the Southern States, 1880**

Percentage of Sharecropped Farms (by County)

- Under 20%
- 20% to 35%
- Over 35%

▼ Sharecroppers in North Carolina planting a row of sweet potatoes

## "Life *of* Former Slaves"

In 1881 skilled orator and former slave Frederick Douglass wrote his third autobiography, *Life and Times of Frederick Douglass*. In it he gives the following description of the problems freed slaves faced after the Civil War:

> Though slavery was abolished, the wrongs of my people were not ended. Though they were not slaves, they were not yet quite free. No man can be truly free whose liberty is dependent upon the thought, feeling, and action of others, and who has himself no means in his own hands for guarding, protecting, defending, and maintaining that liberty. Yet the Negro, after his emancipation, was precisely in this state of destitution. . . . And yet the government . . . felt that it had done enough for him. It had made him free, and henceforth he must make his own way in the world. Yet he had none of the conditions for self-preservation or self-protection. He was free from the individual master, but the slave of society. He had neither money, property, nor friends. He was free from the old plantation, but he had nothing but the dusty road under his feet. He was free from the old quarter that once gave him shelter, but a slave to the rains of summer and to the frosts of winter. He was, in a word, literally turned loose, naked, hungry, and destitute, to the open sky.

Because of the need for profits, landowners usually insisted that sharecroppers grow crops that provided quick cash, such as tobacco or cotton. But those crops depleted the soil of nutrients and provided nothing for the sharecroppers to eat. Low prices for cotton and tobacco after the war only worsened the situation for both sharecroppers and landowners.

Sharecroppers worked as hard as slaves and often received less for their efforts, as their food and shelter were no longer provided. As years passed, the debts increased as interest accumulated and further debts were incurred. Some sharecroppers were able to save enough to purchase their own land and become independent, but many—both white and black—were trapped in a cycle of debt and poverty. While sharecropping allowed many Southerners to survive, it rarely enabled them to prosper. Most struggled just to provide food for their families.

Tenant farmers, those who had their own tools and mule but paid rent for farmland and a house, had slightly better conditions. They owned the crops they planted and received income after harvesting the crop. However, they faced many of the same challenges as the sharecroppers.

## The New South

Some Southern leaders, such as Henry Grady, editor of the *Atlanta Constitution*, began promoting the creation of a "**New South**" whose economy would be based on manufacturing and industry, not just agriculture, but would also be built on a view of white superiority and the denial of black political rights. Because the South lacked the capital to build factories and mills, Grady and others traveled to the North to encourage banks and businesses to invest in the South. Their effort was somewhat successful, as thousands of miles of new railroads, as well as many factories and textile mills, were built in the South between 1870 and 1900. However, the Southern economy remained highly dependent on agriculture.

 **Analyzing Sources**

According to Douglass, why was emancipation insufficient for black people to prosper?

▼ Steel mill in Birmingham, Alabama

US Army troops leaving New Orleans at the end of Reconstruction

# Results of Reconstruction

Reconstruction was one of the most difficult periods in American history. Black Americans were struggling to overcome black codes and violence as they sought their place as free and equal citizens. White Southerners were upset by the changes thrust upon them and hated being treated as a conquered nation.

The first result of Reconstruction was that black Americans gained civil rights for the first time. The adoption of the Thirteenth, Fourteenth, and Fifteenth Amendments ended slavery, granted citizenship, and gave the voting rights to blacks. A second Civil Rights Act, passed in 1875, provided equal treatment in public accommodations and transportation and prohibited the exclusion of blacks from juries. However, many of these gains proved temporary. The Supreme Court ruled the public accommodation portion of the Civil Rights Act of 1875 unconstitutional. When the Supreme Court ruled in 1876 that the Fifteenth Amendment did not confer the right to vote but only prevented discrimination in voting based on race, and also invalidated a law enforcing voting rights, some states made it more difficult for blacks to vote by requiring special voting fees called poll taxes. Literacy tests which required people to prove they could read before being able to vote were often unfairly administered and were designed to disqualify black voters. Many times, election officials were far less strict in collecting the poll tax or applying literacy requirements to white men. Furthermore, when Reconstruction ended, laws protecting black civil rights were rarely enforced.

Second, black Americans received greater opportunities for education. As a result of the work of the Freedmen's Bureau and private charities, thousands of schools for black children, many staffed by black teachers, were created. Reconstruction governments created comprehensive public school systems that included black and white students (in some cases in integrated schools, although they became segregated under the Redeemers). In addition, dozens of colleges, including Atlanta University (1865), Fisk University (1866), Howard University (1867), and Hampton Institute (1868), were formed to provide black Americans a higher education.

Third, a stronger, more centralized federal government emerged. Though some Southerners objected to this expansion of power, centralization occurred partly because local and state governments in the South had failed to treat freedmen in a just manner.

Fourth, white Southerners, many of whom bitterly opposed Republicans because of Radical Reconstruction, embraced the Democratic Party. The region became known as "the Solid South" for its commitment to Democrats. With few exceptions, the region elected only Democratic governors, state legislators, and congressmen for nearly a hundred years.

## Comprehension Check 11.4

1. Black and white families participated in the sharecropping system.

   True

   False

2. In the crop-lien system, freedmen received forty acres and a mule.

   True

   False

3. The "New South" sought to restore the Southern economy through industrialization.

   True

   False

### MAKING CONNECTIONS

4. What were two negative features of sharecropping?

5. What were the four results of Reconstruction?

## Chapter Summary

### 11.1    Presidential Reconstruction

- The period from the end of the Civil War to 1877 was called Reconstruction. The Southern economy, state governments, and labor system needed to be reconstructed after the war.

- Lincoln's Ten Percent Plan made states' return to the Union lenient. Radical Republicans in Congress wanted to punish the South and control Reconstruction. Their Reconstruction proposal was the Wade-Davis Bill, which Lincoln vetoed.

- Andrew Johnson's Reconstruction plan was much like Lincoln's. States would have to ratify the Thirteenth Amendment to be readmitted.

- Some Southern states enacted black codes which limited the freedom of black people, and many elected former Confederates to offices. As a result, the Radical Republicans refused to seat the newly elected southern legislators and moved to take control of Reconstruction from the president.

**TERMS**

Reconstruction

freedmen

Ten Percent Plan

Radical Republicans

Wade-Davis Bill

Thirteenth Amendment

Andrew Johnson

black codes

**TERMS**

Freedmen's Bureau

Fourteenth Amendment

Reconstruction Act of 1867

Hiram Revels

carpetbaggers

scalawags

Tenure of Office Act

impeachment

Ulysses S. Grant

Fifteenth Amendment

William "Boss" Tweed

Panic of '73

### 11.2    Congressional Reconstruction

- The Freedmen's Bureau was established to help former slaves by creating schools and hospitals and protecting their civil rights.

- Congress passed the Civil Rights Act of 1866 which gave citizenship to black Americans, and black citizenship was made part of the Constitution in the Fourteenth Amendment.

- The Reconstruction Act of 1867 divided the South into military districts; it required black people to be given the right to vote and hold office, established state constitutional conventions, required the new state constitutions to be approved by Congress, and required states to ratify the Fourteenth Amendment before being readmitted. As a result, many blacks and white Republicans were elected to office in Southern states.

- Johnson was impeached by Congress for violating the Tenure of Office Act but was acquitted by one vote.

- Ulysses S. Grant was elected president in 1868 and reelected in 1872. The Fifteenth Amendment was passed. His administration faced many corruption scandals, and the Panic of '73 created a six-year economic depression.

## Chapter Summary

### 11.3 The End of Reconstruction

- As Northerners lost interest in Reconstruction and former Confederates were given amnesty, Redeemers who wanted to save the South from "Black Republican" rule rose to power. As a result, many of the gains in civil rights that blacks had achieved were lost.

- The Ku Klux Klan and other groups used violence to keep black Americans under white control.

- The outcome of the election of 1876 was disputed. In the Compromise of 1877, Democrats agreed to accept Hayes as president and to accept the Reconstruction Amendments, and Republicans agreed to withdraw the remaining federal troops from the South, effectively ending Reconstruction.

**TERMS**

Redeemers

Ku Klux Klan

Rutherford B. Hayes

Samuel J. Tilden

Compromise of 1877

**TERMS**

sharecropping

crop-lien

New South

### 11.4 A Reconstructed Nation

- Landowners' lack of money and need for labor and freedmen's and poor whites' need for work led to the development of the sharecropping system. While some became independent, the crop-lien system kept most in debt and poverty.

- Some Southern leaders promoted a "New South" whose economy would be based on manufacturing and industry and encouraged Northern investment in the South.

- Reconstruction's results included gaining civil rights for blacks, although many of these proved temporary; greater opportunities for education for black Americans; a stronger, more centralized federal government; and Democratic control of southern politics for nearly a hundred years.

## Chapter Review Questions

### RECALL

1. Who became president after Lincoln's assassination?

2. What were laws that were created by states to severely limit the rights of black Americans called?

3. What were two accomplishments of the Freedmen's Bureau?

4. What was the outcome of Johnson's impeachment trial?

5. Who won the presidential elections of 1868 and 1872?

6. What were the three Reconstruction Amendments?

7. Who were the presidential candidates in the election of 1876?

8. What movement promoted the transformation of the Southern economy to manufacturing and industry?

### UNDERSTAND

9. Contrast Lincoln's Ten Percent Plan with the Wade-Davis Bill regarding the percentage of people who had to take an oath of allegiance and the status of former Confederates.

10. How did Lincoln's view of the seceded states differ from that of Radical Republicans such as Charles Sumner, and how did these views shape their answers on who was responsible for Reconstruction?

11. What was Johnson's plan for Reconstruction?

12. Why had Lincoln believed the Thirteenth Amendment was necessary?

13. Why did the Radical Republicans oppose Johnson's plan for Reconstruction?

14. What two steps did Congress take in December 1865 to take control of Reconstruction?

15. What did the Civil Rights Act of 1866 do?

16. What actions did Johnson take concerning the Civil Rights Act of 1866 and the Fourteenth Amendment?

17. What were the four important provisions of the Fourteenth Amendment?

18. What five things did the Reconstruction Act of 1867 impose on southern states?

19. Why was Johnson impeached, and why did some senators vote to acquit him?

20. Why did Congress feel the Fifteenth Amendment was necessary?

21. Name two scandals that took place during Grant's presidency. What were three positive accomplishments during his presidency?

22. How was William "Boss" Tweed able to stay in power in New York City until his arrest?

23. How did the Panic of '73 affect the economy?

24. What two things paved the way for Redeemers to gain control in the South?

25. What effects did the election of Redeemers have for black Southerners?

26. How did Congress attempt to address the violence of groups such as the Ku Klux Klan?

27. What was the dispute in the presidential election of 1876, and what was the decision of the commission that was formed to settle the dispute?

28. Relate the Compromise of 1877 to the end of Reconstruction.

29. Describe the sharecropping system and why it developed.

30. How did the crop-lien system often keep sharecroppers in a cycle of debt and poverty?

31. What were three results of Reconstruction?

### THINK ABOUT IT

32. What results of Johnson's plan for Reconstruction led to justice for freedmen being delayed or denied?

33. Read Deuteronomy 16:19 and Numbers 15:15–16. What principles are taught in these passages, and how did black codes violate these principles?

34. Relate the ideas of justice, freedom, and equality to southern attitudes toward Reconstruction and the role of Congress in securing the rights of black Americans.

# 12 The Gilded Age

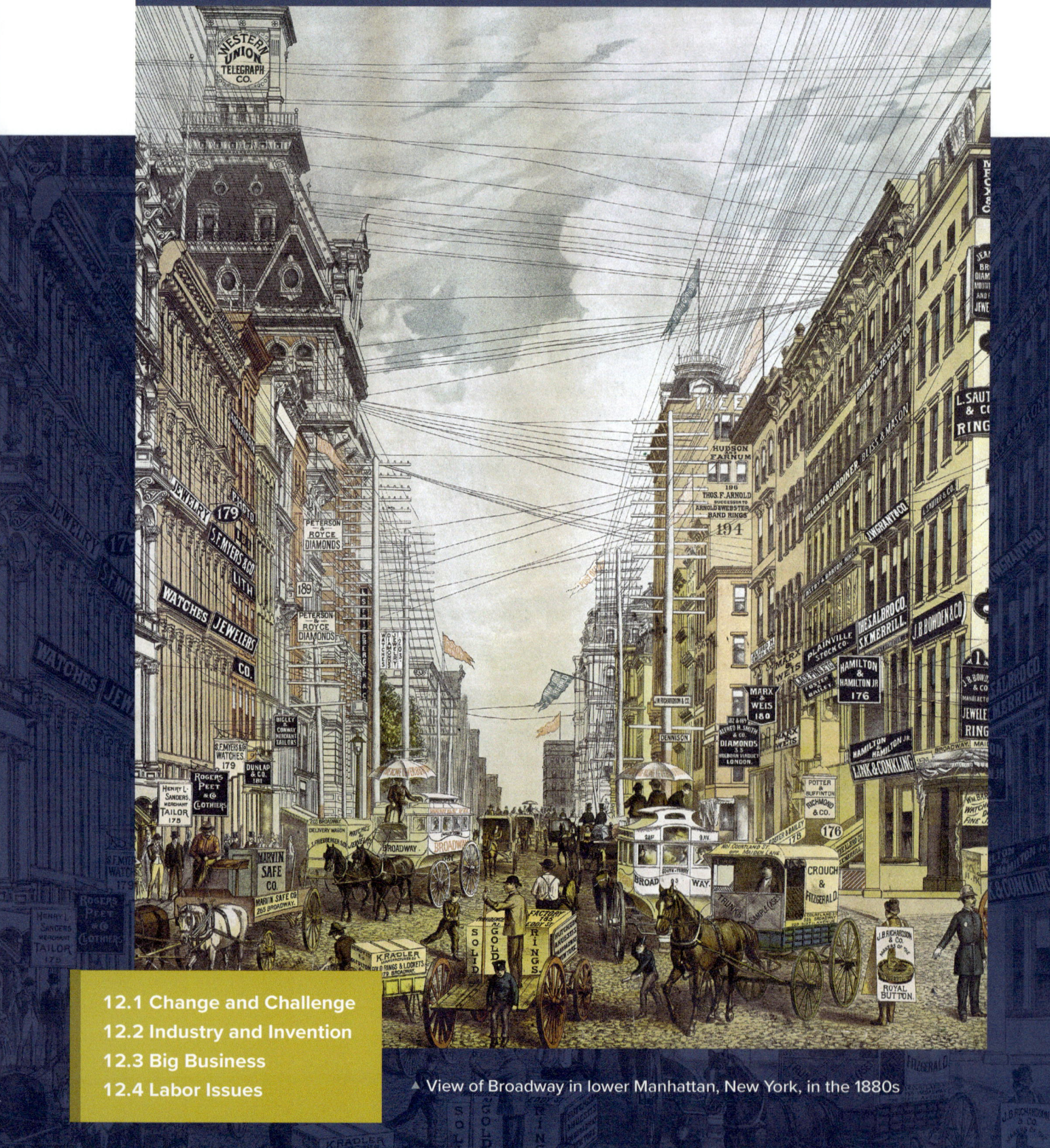

**12.1 Change and Challenge**
**12.2 Industry and Invention**
**12.3 Big Business**
**12.4 Labor Issues**

▲ View of Broadway in lower Manhattan, New York, in the 1880s

**Change and Challenge**

How did America change during the Gilded Age?

The period in America from the 1870s to about 1900 is often called the **Gilded Age** ("gilded" refers to something covered with a thin layer of gold). Taken from a novel by Mark Twain, the name describes a period in which prosperity, enabled by a flood of inventions and innovations, appeared on the surface. Yet behind the glitter of America's growing wealth were contrasts and divisions that would challenge national life. Where previous generations had protected freedom by limiting the power of government, a new generation began to believe that government needed to protect freedom by limiting powerful businesses.

## Urbanization and Immigration

The 1890 census revealed that for the first time, most Americans were in nonagricultural occupations. The concentration of industry and labor in cities made urbanization a significant social change during the Gilded Age.

The dramatic shift from rural to urban was reflected in the size and number of cities. For example, New York's population grew from 800,000 in 1860 to about 3.5 million in 1900, and Chicago grew from just over 100,000 to 1.6 million in the same period. From 1860 to 1910 the number of small cities with populations of 2,500 people or more grew from 400 to 2,200.

What was the attraction of city dwelling? The boom in manufacturing and service industries provided jobs for both immigrants and farm laborers who had been squeezed off the land by hard times or labor-saving machinery. People also found the services and attractions of city living, such as electric lights, streetcars, running water, and cultural attractions such as museums and theaters, alluring.

Yet urbanization also had an ugly side: overcrowding, high crime, pollution, and disease. In fact, the infant mortality rate in cities was double that in rural areas. In Chicago during the 1880s, for example, only half the children born lived past their fifth birthday.

The urban wealthy tended to live in large mansions in fashionable neighborhoods in the city center, waited on by servants. The working poor, on the other hand, lived in crowded tenements (multifamily apartment buildings). Those in the middle class often sought to escape the crowding and crime of the city and moved to suburbs that were connected to the city by rail lines or streetcars.

### GUIDING QUESTIONS

- How did immigration lead to the growth of cities?
- Who were the presidents during this period?
- What people and ideas influenced religion during the Gilded Age?

### US Population Growth, 1860–1910

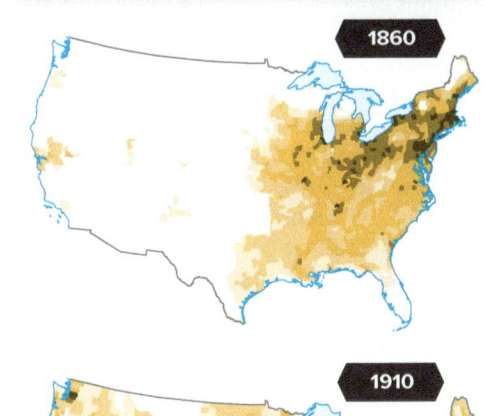

1860

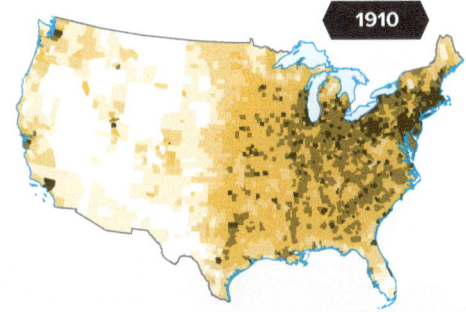

1910

▼ Tenement building in a Jewish neighborhood of New York City

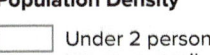

**Population Density**

| | |
|---|---|
| | Under 2 persons per square mile |
| | 2-6 |
| | 7-18 |
| | 19-45 |
| | 46-90 |
| | 91 and over |

One cause of the rapid growth of cities was a massive influx of immigrants. In addition to the immigrants from Ireland who came in the 1840s (see Chapter 9), waves of "new immigrants" came from southern and eastern European countries such as Italy, Greece, and Russia. Additionally, many Chinese immigrants began to settle on the West Coast. Many immigrants came to America for economic reasons, and others because of political or religious unrest in their native countries.

The largest port of entry in America for European immigrants was **Ellis Island** in New York Harbor. Between 1892 and 1954, over 12 million immigrants passed through Ellis Island. Most immigrants stayed there only a few hours. However, if there were problems or questions about their entry, some had to stay several days in dormitory-like facilities. Immigrants were screened for contagious diseases when they arrived, and some had to be quarantined in the medical facilities there until they were cleared. Only two percent of immigrants who arrived at Ellis Island were turned away, either because of a contagious disease (such as the eye disease trachoma) that was considered a danger to public health, or because the inspector believed the immigrant would become a "public charge" (a person dependent on government assistance).

Some of the more fortunate immigrants, particularly those from Scandinavia and Germany, moved directly to the Midwest and found work in farming, logging, or mining. Others joined relatives who had already settled in the United States. Some came under contracts with companies that paid their fare if the immigrants would work a specified length of time. Most immigrants, however, used their life savings to come to America and settled in the city of their arrival. Immigrants often clustered in neighborhoods where others of their nationality lived. These neighborhoods, with nicknames like Little Italy and Chinatown, retained much of the culture of their homeland.

### Lady Liberty's Light

More than a million immigrants a year passed through Ellis Island in New York Harbor alone. There in the harbor they saw a gleaming torch-bearer, a copper lady—the Statue of Liberty. Inscribed in the statue's pedestal were these words of welcome:

*Give me your tired, your poor,*
*Your huddled masses yearning to breathe free,*
*The wretched refuse of your teeming shore.*
*Send these, the homeless, tempest-tost to me,*
*I lift my lamp beside the golden door!*

▼ Ellis Island with the Statue of Liberty on Liberty Island in the background

As the number of new immigrants grew, so did opposition to immigration. American labor leaders feared that immigrant workers would take jobs from other Americans by agreeing to work longer hours for less pay. Many Americans branded immigrants as radicals and revolutionaries, even though only a tiny minority of immigrants held those views. Some were concerned that crime and disease would increase in impoverished ethnic neighborhoods. The large number of Catholic, Jewish, and Eastern Orthodox immigrants raised religious fears among America's predominantly Protestant population. With similar religious fears, Roman Catholics, who did not want their children to be taught Protestantism in the public schools, formed their own parochial (church-run) schools.

Chinese immigrants faced a great deal of hardship. Many Chinese people, who had faced famine, floods, and overpopulation in parts of China, came to America when word spread of the discovery of gold in California in the 1840s. These immigrants established service businesses, such as restaurants and laundries, for the gold miners. Later many Chinese laborers were hired to help construct the transcontinental railroad (see Chapter 13). As long as jobs were plentiful, Americans did not object to these workers. However, when the economy slowed, some began to resent the Chinese for taking jobs they believed non-immigrant citizens deserved. In 1882, Congress passed the **Chinese Exclusion Act**, which prohibited Chinese workers, with few exceptions, from entering the United States for ten years, and the act was extended in 1892 and again in 1902.

Despite the many obstacles immigrants faced, they continued to come with the hope of finding freedom and prosperity. Immigrants provided labor for construction projects and for factories; they built successful farms in the Midwest; some became prosperous shopkeepers and small businessmen. Immigrants, in short, provided much of the backbone and muscle in transforming the United States into an industrial giant. Assimilation (adopting the customs and priorities of the immigrants' new nation) into the broader American culture was not easy, but most immigrants gradually learned English and adopted American values and culture. At the same time, immigrants contributed parts of their native cultures to make America a "melting pot" in which diverse cultures blended. However, this large-scale cultural and religious pluralism (people of different cultures and beliefs coexisting in society) created other challenges for the nation.

▲ (top) Examination of immigrants' papers at Ellis Island; (above) poster depicting the prejudice against Chinese immigrants in the Chinese Exclusion Act

# Politics of the Gilded Age

Four issues dominated American politics from the mid-1870s to the end of the century: government corruption, civil service reform, tariff revision, and regulation of the trusts (see Section 3). Debate over these issues was intensified because the nation was evenly divided politically.

During the early part of Rutherford B. Hayes's administration, reform of the spoils system (see Chapter 6) was the pressing issue. Grant's administration (see Chapter 11) had been plagued by corruption, and the spoils system was considered partly to blame. Changes were needed to remove the potentially corrupting influence of politics and ensure competent, efficient government workers.

Hayes had been nominated largely because he was a reformer. He attacked political "machines" (groups that sought to control voters), even though it cost him political support. He particularly attacked a notorious New York Republican political machine controlled by Senator Roscoe Conkling, who believed that senators should have personal control of all federal appointments within their states. Conkling's machine controlled New York's tariff-collecting agency, the Custom House, which was

headed by future president Chester Arthur. In an effort to break the spoils system and Conkling's control, Hayes had Arthur removed from his position in 1878. The removal angered Conkling and other influential Republicans.

The clash between Hayes and Conkling reflected a growing division within the Republican Party. On one side was Conkling's faction, the "**Stalwarts**," who favored high tariffs, hard money (gold and silver coins rather than Greenbacks), and the spoils system. Opposing them were moderate Republicans, called "**Half-Breeds**," who favored civil service reform. The struggle between Stalwarts and Half-Breeds intensified over the Republican presidential nomination in 1880. When the convention deadlocked, the Republican factions eventually compromised by nominating Ohio's **James Garfield**, a Half-Breed, for president and New York's **Chester Arthur**, a Stalwart, for vice president.

---

▼ Political cartoon of Rutherford B. Hayes kicking Chester Arthur out of the New York Custom House

Although Garfield won the presidential election, his efforts at reform were short-lived. On July 2, 1881, just four months after the inauguration, Charles Guiteau, a disappointed office-seeker with a history of mental illness, shot Garfield at a railway station in Washington, DC. Upon his arrest, Guiteau declared "I am a Stalwart, and Arthur is now president." After enduring eleven weeks of pain and crude medical care, Garfield died on September 19, and Vice President Arthur became president.

Arthur's past attachment to New York's political machines led Conkling's supporters to rejoice, but Arthur turned out to be less of a Stalwart than many assumed. As president he refused to use his office to provide special favors for Conkling's associates. Arthur also backed civil service reform and favored lowering the tariff.

The corruption of the Grant administration and the assassination of President Garfield led many in Congress to support civil service reform. Senator George Pendleton, a Democrat from Ohio, introduced the Pendleton Civil Service Reform Act, which Congress enacted in January 1883. The **Pendleton Act** established an independent Civil Service Commission, made up of three presidential appointees who were responsible for seeing that only those who scored well on civil service examinations held offices. The intent of the act was to end the spoils system by preventing the awarding of political offices for no other reason than party loyalty. Within a few years, about twelve percent of federal positions were filled under these new procedures, and that number steadily increased.

In part because general prosperity and wartime taxes had led to government surpluses, Arthur recommended a general 25 percent tariff reduction. Congressmen who wanted to protect the trade interests of their regions, however, added many amendments to the proposed tariff. As a result, when the tariff passed in 1883, it only reduced tariffs by an average of 1.5 percent. Critics soon dubbed it the "Mongrel Tariff" for its mixture of competing elements.

▲ (top) Charles Guiteau shooting President Garfield; (above) Chester Arthur

▲ (top) Grover Cleveland
(bottom) Benjamin Harrison

In 1884 the Republicans bypassed Arthur for Maine's James Blaine, a long-time Republican leader tainted by an earlier railroad scandal. The Democrats nominated New York's former governor **Grover Cleveland**, noted for his honesty and for fighting the corruption of Tammany Hall. The 1884 election was a spirited, hard-fought affair in which Cleveland won a narrow victory. Had Blaine won the extremely close race in New York—he lost there by only 1,149 votes of more than a million cast—he would have won the election. Cleveland's election was the first Democratic presidential victory in twenty-eight years.

The Democrats renominated Cleveland in 1888. The Republicans nominated Indiana's **Benjamin Harrison**, the grandson of former president William Henry Harrison. Cleveland lost support in some northern states for favoring a reduction of protective tariffs. While Cleveland managed to win more popular votes (48.6 percent to 47.8 percent), Harrison won the majority of electoral votes and hence the election.

During Harrison's presidency, Republicans in Congress had sought to win favor with the voters and maintain control of the government through liberal spending. The Fifty-First Congress (1889–91) became known as the "Billion-Dollar Congress" because, for the first time in history, the annual budget exceeded one billion dollars.

A major goal of Harrison and the Republicans in Congress was to raise the tariff to further protect American industries. The Republican majority in both houses of Congress was bolstered by the admission of six new predominantly Republican states: North Dakota, South Dakota, Montana, and Washington in November 1889 and Idaho and Wyoming in July 1890. Ohio representative William McKinley introduced a bill that would impose higher duties on imports than had any previous tariff in history. When passed, the **McKinley Tariff** ended up lowering revenue by radically decreasing trade. This decrease in the government's income, combined with high congressional spending, reduced the Treasury's reserves significantly. The voters demonstrated their anger over the tariff in the congressional election of 1890, reducing the Republican majority in the Senate and giving the Democrats an overwhelming 235–88 advantage in the House.

The 1890 congressional elections were only a prelude to the 1892 presidential rematch between Benjamin Harrison and Grover Cleveland. Ex-president Cleveland made an ex-president of Harrison by recapturing the White House with a clear victory. Democrats also regained control of both the House and the Senate. Unfortunately for the Democrats, a financial collapse called the Panic of '93 occurred shortly after Cleveland's inauguration, plunging the nation into four years of the worst economic depression it had yet seen. The Democrats watched helplessly as banks and businesses failed and unemployment climbed to a record twenty percent.

Copies of *On the Origin of Species*; (inset) Charles Darwin

## Religious Influence

Another form of societal change during the Gilded Age was in the area of religion. The driving force for this change came from the publications of *On the Origin of Species* (1859) and *The Descent of Man* (1871) by **Charles Darwin**, an English naturalist (one who studies the natural world).

Darwin's theory was that plant, animal, and human life had evolved over millions of years by the process of natural selection. In his theory, species competed for survival under the cruel laws of nature, with some species adapting to the environment and surviving and thriving, and other species failing to adapt and dying out. He theorized that through this process species evolved into new, higher species.

Many devout Christians rejected Darwinism because it was contrary to the Bible's teaching on Creation and because it was atheistic—no God was required under this theory. Other Christians were reluctant to contradict modern scientific theories, and they suggested that God might have used the process of evolution in creating the species. These Christians divided on whether humans were the product of evolution or the result of special creation. These views did not satisfy Christian opponents to evolution. They believed that the theory could never be reconciled with the Bible's teaching that death entered the world because of Adam's sin.

Some Americans began to promote the idea of **Social Darwinism**, which applied Darwin's theory of natural selection to human society. Social Darwinism argued that humans and society improved through competition where only the fittest survived. Some industrial leaders used "survival of the fittest" to justify their actions in defeating weaker competition and to oppose any measures that would interfere with free competition in the business world and any public or private poor relief that they thought prevented natural competition.

Political cartoon in 1861 mocking Darwin's theory by showing an ape with the abolitionist's slogan "Am I a Man and a Brother?"

Just as Christians had different responses to Darwinism, their approaches to the challenges of urbanization and immigration varied. Some Christians, for example, confronted the poor conditions of city slums by establishing rescue missions, centers located in the middle of the slums for preaching the gospel and ministering to the physical needs of city dwellers (see Chapter 15). Others devoted themselves to the spread of the gospel by conducting large evangelistic campaigns in major cities. The leader of the urban evangelistic movement during this period was evangelist **Dwight L. Moody**.

Born in Northfield, Massachusetts, Moody accepted Christ when he was eighteen. In 1856 he moved to Chicago, where he thought great opportunities for wealth lay. In Chicago, Moody was influenced by the Prayer Meeting Revival (see Chapter 7) and became involved in Christian work. In the slums of Chicago, he began a Sunday school that grew under his leadership to more than one thousand students. In 1860 Moody quit his high-paying job with a shoe company and devoted himself to working with his Sunday school and with the Young Men's Christian Association (YMCA) and other Christian organizations.

After a successful speaking tour of Great Britain where he drew millions of listeners, Moody returned to the United States in 1875 and, despite some criticism for his lack of emphasis on doctrine and biblical exposition, was deluged with requests to hold citywide campaigns across the United States. Moody believed that reaching the major cities with the gospel would reach the whole nation. "Water runs downhill, and the highest hills in America are the great cities," he said. "If we can stir them we shall stir the whole country." Over the next twenty years, Moody preached to millions in the United States, Canada, the British Isles, and Mexico.

## Comprehension Check 12.1

1. Most immigrants came through New York's _____ upon arrival in the United States.
   - **A** Custom House
   - **B** Ellis Island
   - **C** Tammany Hall

2. The Chinese Exclusion Act refers to the _____.
   - **A** denial of entry into Catholic parochial schools for Chinese students
   - **B** exemption of Chinese immigrants from screening for disease upon arrival
   - **C** prohibition of Chinese workers from entering the United States for ten years

3. _____ was the first Democratic president in twenty-eight years.
   - **A** Grover Cleveland
   - **B** James Garfield
   - **C** Benjamin Harrison

4. Applying Darwin's theory of natural selection to human society, Social Darwinism referred to the improvement of humanity through the _____.
   - **A** "Half-Breeds" and "Stalwarts"
   - **B** "melting pot"
   - **C** "survival of the fittest"

### MAKING CONNECTIONS

5. What did the Pendleton Act intend to end, and what measure did it introduce?

6. How did Christians vary in responses to Darwinism and urbanization?

## Moody's Methodology

Moody's methodology was influenced by the business world. Like successful businessmen of his time, Moody was well organized. One minister noted, "As he stood on the platform, he looked like a businessman; he dressed like a businessman; he took the meeting in hand as a businessman would." Moody's services were informal but orderly. He carefully planned and organized each element of the massive meetings. He also incorporated "gospel in song" music into his services as a means of attracting and winning over his audiences. He recruited baritone Ira Sankey to serve as his song leader and soloist, and his methods popularized the gospel song in American church life. Many of these gospel songs were written by Fanny Crosby, who had been blinded when only six months old but, nevertheless, produced over eight thousand hymns.

◄ Dwight L Moody, accompanied by Ira D. Sankey at the organ, preaching at a revival meeting in Brooklyn, New York

**Industry and Invention**

How did industry expand during this period?

## The Rise of Industrialization

The postwar period witnessed a rapid rise of industry in the United States. From a few small iron factories and oil wells in the 1850s, American industry grew until the United States was a leader in the world's industrial community.

American industrial growth occurred for several reasons. First, the nation itself grew. The combination of immigration and a modest postwar baby boom nearly tripled the population from about 32 million in 1860 to 92 million in 1910. Increased population led to an increased demand for products and an increased work force to produce them. It also encouraged the movement westward and the accompanying development of farmland and mining in the resource-rich West.

Second, the innovative and entrepreneurial spirit of the times fostered new machines and methods that enhanced industrial expansion. This growth was encouraged by government policies, including a high tariff that protected American companies from foreign competition, and by the potential for high profits, and many were willing to take the risk to start new businesses.

Third, America had an abundance of natural resources that were necessary for an industrial economy. Gold, silver, iron ore, copper, coal, and oil were all readily available, especially in the West, and a growing transportation network enabled those goods to reach factories in the East. Waterpower continued to be an important source of energy as it could be converted to produce electricity, and coal and oil also soon fueled electric power plants.

**GUIDING QUESTIONS**

- How did America become more industrial?

- What new things were invented during this time?

- How did the number of railroads increase during the Gilded Age?

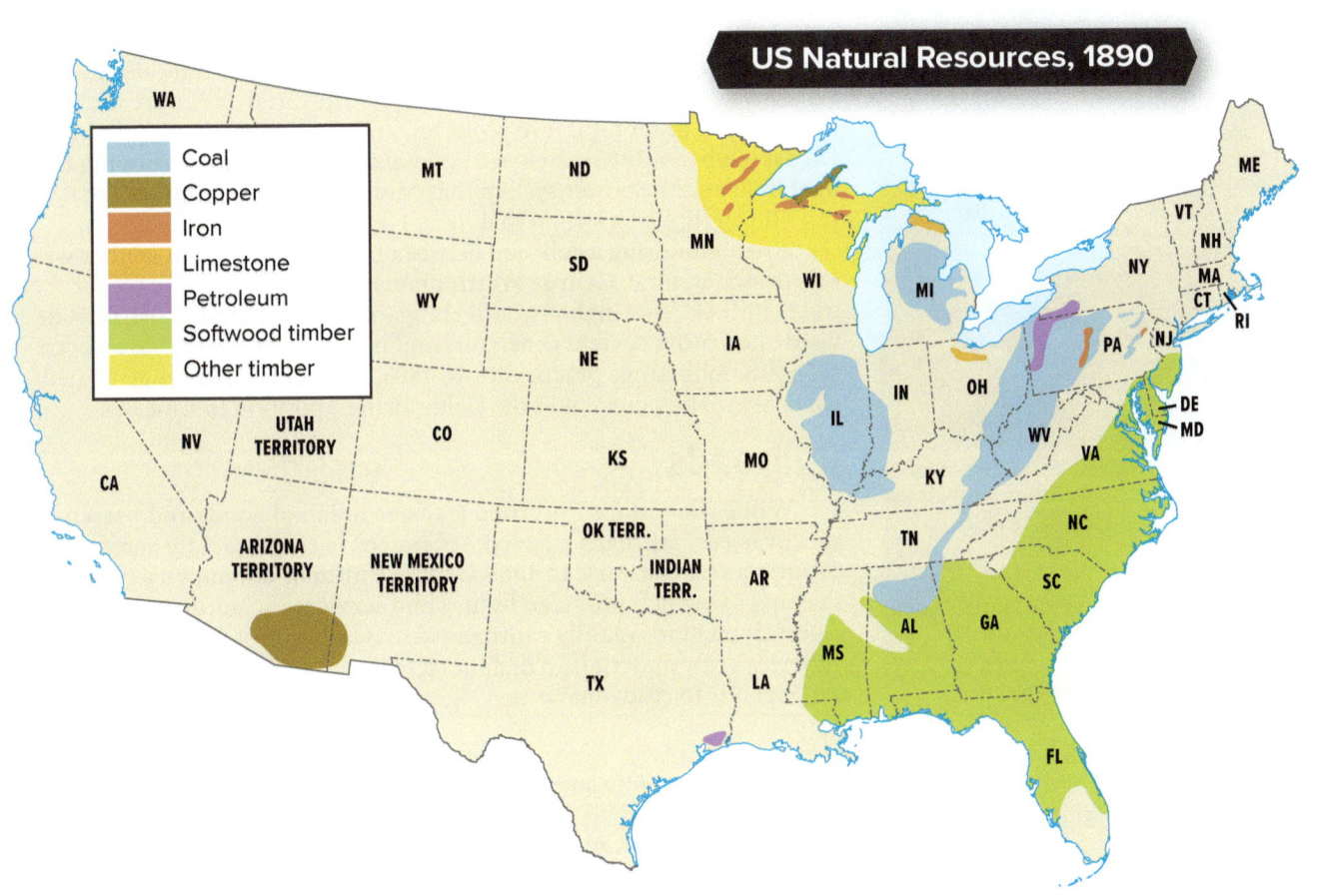

**US Natural Resources, 1890**

- Coal
- Copper
- Iron
- Limestone
- Petroleum
- Softwood timber
- Other timber

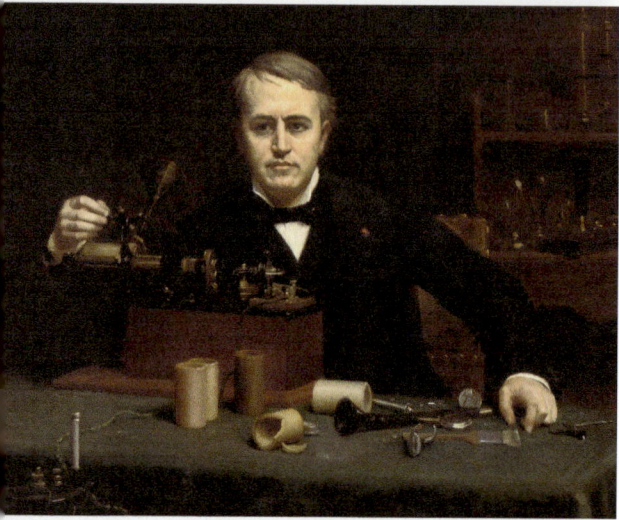

# Inventions and Innovations

Behind the rapid industrialization in America were new methods, ideas, and inventions that fueled expansion and created new markets. Thousands of inventions during the Gilded Age completely changed the way Americans lived.

Many Americans enjoyed changes in their standard of dress. The development of the sewing machine and its widespread use during the Civil War spawned a huge retail market for mass-produced clothing. For the first time, standardized sizes and designs were applied to clothing. Mass production of high-quality, fashionable clothing also decreased class distinctions. Ordering from a *Sears, Roebuck and Co. Catalogue*, men and women of middle and even lower classes could dress more stylishly.

Industrialization also created a communications revolution during the Gilded Age. The growth of businesses across the nation resulted in increased correspondence and more sophisticated recordkeeping. The invention of the typewriter (1867) met the new demands of the business world. The development of cheap paper from wood pulp and the invention of continuous-action roller presses resulted in the birth of mass media. Inexpensive newspapers, magazines, and books became available for an increasingly literate society.

The crowning communications achievement of the time came with the invention of the telephone by **Alexander Graham Bell**. Bell was a Scottish immigrant who arrived in the United States at the age of twenty-four to teach speech to the deaf. An innovative thinker who combined his interest in sound with his inclination for experimentation, Bell worked for three years on his invention that converted sound waves into electrical signals and back into sound on a receiving telephone. Finally, on March 10, 1876, he transmitted his first message by phone. Bell founded American Telephone and Telegraph (AT&T), and by 1905 there were 10 million phones in the United States.

America's most prolific inventor was **Thomas Edison**. Although he had little formal education, Edison had a knack for new ideas and a thirst for discovery. He established an "invention factory" at Menlo Park, New Jersey. Edison was responsible for more than a thousand inventions during his lifetime, but the most influential ones were the phonograph, the motion-picture projector, and the incandescent light bulb. On September 4, 1882, after years of experimentation in developing the light bulb and the power system that could make indoor lighting practical, Edison flipped a switch that lit up New York's financial district.

After witnessing a collision between two trains in which neither was able to stop in time, **George Westinghouse** invented the air brake for trains in 1869. Westinghouse and Hungarian immigrant Nikola Tesla devised alternating current generators and transformers which gave electrical power long-range practicality. In 1893, for example, power generated using alternating current lit the Columbian Exposition in Chicago.

# Railroads

While steamships improved transportation of goods and passengers overseas, railroads enabled Americans to travel rapidly across the country's vast territory. In 1864 **George Pullman** developed a railroad sleeping car which provided luxury and services including meals and entertainment to wealthy railroad passengers. Railroads also moved America's raw materials to distant factories and distributed manufactured goods to ready markets.

◀ (top to bottom) Alexander Graham Bell demonstrating the telephone; Thomas Edison with his phonograph; a Westinghouse brake coupling; Pullman Palace Sleeping Car

In 1850 most railroad tracks in the United States were in the East. There were no railroad bridges across the Ohio or Mississippi Rivers. In addition, railroads used different gauges (width between tracks), complicating long distance travel. For example, a passenger traveling from New York to Chicago had to change trains six times. The Civil War highlighted these problems and led to the adoption of a standard gauge—4 feet 8½ inches. The first transcontinental railroad was completed in 1869 (see Chapter 13).

One factor that improved the efficiency of rail transit was consolidation (combining several smaller railroads into a larger system). **Cornelius Vanderbilt**, who had developed a successful steamship line on the Great Lakes and eventually gained control of much of New York's waterborne shipping, desired to build a rail line from the Great Lakes to New York City. "Commodore" Vanderbilt purchased the railroads of his competitors, sometimes by exerting great pressure, and built a vast railroad empire.

Another railroad entrepreneur was **James J. Hill**. After starting a shipping business in St. Paul, Minnesota, he noted the need for an improved railroad system in the Great Lakes area. In 1865 he founded the James J. Hill Company, providing railroad tracks directly from the warehouses to the rail line. He then began buying up failing rail lines as well as land in Dakota Territory in preparation for building a rail line across the northern United States to the Pacific Northwest.

Hill innovated by shifting from wood fuel for his locomotives to coal and soon achieved stunning success in the trading of coal. He sought the best prices possible for coal and all other purchases for his companies. For example, he demanded more accurate weighing of carloads of coal, which led to more accurate billing for freight fees, and that in turn translated into savings and greater profits. He also identified products that were desired by Asia, such as cotton, textiles, and flour, and shipped them to Pacific ports so that his trains carried freight in both directions.

Hill built his **Great Northern Railroad** (see map on page 337) without any government land grants or funds, and his workers laid rails twice as fast as a nearby government-subsidized railroad had. He cut costs and passed the savings on to customers in the form of lower rates. He taught crop rotation to farmers along his route and provided free seeds and cattle to help farmers recover after a drought. He transported new immigrants to the Great Plains for a low fare if they would settle and farm along his rail lines. He even set up and operated model farms to demonstrate the latest improvements in farming science. The Great Northern became the most successful of the transcontinental railroad lines.

▲ Cornelius Vanderbilt

## Comprehension Check 12.2

1. American industrialization improved during the Gilded Age for each of these reasons except _____.

   **A** abundance of natural resources

   **B** increase in population and workforce

   **C** lack of government protection of industries

2. _____ invented the air brake for trains and helped develop alternating current generators and transformers for electrical power.

   **A** Alexander Graham Bell

   **B** Thomas Edison

   **C** George Westinghouse

3. _____ built the Great Northern Railroad.

   **A** James J. Hill

   **B** George Pullman

   **C** Cornelius Vanderbilt

### MAKING CONNECTIONS

4. Explain how two innovations or inventions improved the railroad industry during the Gilded Age.

▼ James J. Hill (fifth from right) and his associates in front of "William Crooks," the first locomotive of the Great Northern Railway Company

- How were businesses organized?
- What role did capitalism play during the rise of industry in America?
- Why were regulations needed?
- How did industrial and business changes impact America?
- How did the leaders of industry influence America?

## 12.3 Big Business

**How did the rise of big business change America?**

## Types of Business

The most basic business organization is a sole proprietorship, a business owned by one person. The owner receives all the profit, but also takes all the losses and often lacks the funds to expand the business. Other businesses are partnerships, owned by two or more people. Partnerships increase the amount of capital available, and the owners share both the losses and the profits.

Because larger businesses, such as factories, need greater amounts of capital, **corporations** were created. Corporations receive a legal charter from a state and can raise large amounts of capital quickly by selling stock (shares of ownership) to individual investors. When the business does well, the stockholders receive a dividend, or share, of the profit. If the business fails, the stockholders' risk is limited to the amount of their investment. A corporation must be chartered and is legally considered a "person" regarding business matters.

One of America's largest corporations was Carnegie Steel. **Andrew Carnegie** was born in Scotland, but hard times forced his poor family to immigrate to western Pennsylvania in 1848. His first job in America was as a bobbin boy in a textile mill, where he earned $1.20 a week. He then worked for a short time as a bookkeeper's clerk before becoming a telegraph delivery boy and then a telegrapher. Carnegie advanced rapidly to become superintendent of the Pittsburgh division of the Pennsylvania Railroad. He saved and invested heavily from his salary. By the early 1870s he began investing heavily in anything involving steel: sleeping-car construction, an iron company, and bridge building. Carnegie built his first steel mill in 1874, and with the profits he bought several other mills in the Pittsburgh area.

Through a method known as **vertical integration**, the control of every aspect of production in an industry, Carnegie bought coal and iron mines, railroads, steamships, and mills. Carnegie Steel soon became the largest steel company in the world, producing about one-fourth of America's steel. Carnegie pocketed nearly $226 million (over $7 billion in today's dollars) when financier J. P. Morgan bought Carnegie Steel in 1901.

▲ Andrew Carnegie

## Andrew Carnegie and the Gospel of Wealth

Carnegie was more than a financial genius; he was also a philosopher of big business. In 1889 he published "The Gospel of Wealth," revealing the influence of Social Darwinism on his thinking. He believed the accumulation of wealth simply illustrated the survival of the fittest. His version of Social Darwinism, however, said the wealthy should help create conditions in which the poor could help themselves. Wealth was not an end in itself. Carnegie wrote, "The man who dies rich dies disgraced. . . . Surplus wealth is a sacred trust which its possessor is bound to administer in his lifetime for the good of the community."

Although he disdained the word *philanthropy* (giving to charitable causes) because it implied a handout, Carnegie gave millions of dollars to causes that promoted self-improvement. Carnegie and other wealthy Americans founded or supported the building of libraries, concert halls, art museums, symphonies, and other cultural institutions. Philanthropists also founded several universities, including Vanderbilt, Carnegie-Mellon, Stanford, Johns Hopkins, and the University of Chicago (founded by John D. Rockefeller).

▼ Oil refinery in Richmond, California, that was a part of John D. Rockefeller's Standard Oil Company

▲ John D. Rockefeller

America's first billionaire was **John D. Rockefeller**, who founded Standard Oil Company in 1870. In 1859, when Rockefeller was still a young businessman, oil was discovered in Titusville, Pennsylvania, and the "black gold" rush began. He saw that his future was in oil, but he realized that drilling for it involved too much risk. He determined that a safer investment and greater profits would be in oil refining, turning raw petroleum into useful products. Soon others saw the profit potential in refining, too, and competition was stiff and chaotic. However, Rockefeller determined that he could succeed through efficiency and technological improvements.

Rockefeller waged a relentless war against waste in his company. When Rockefeller entered the oil industry, only half a typical barrel of oil was deemed useful in the production of kerosene, the source of lighting for the wealthy few who could afford it. The rest was thrown away—poured into rivers and lakes, polluting the water and surrounding lands. Through research and development, Rockefeller found ways to use that "useless" half barrel of oil and make money from it. His scientists developed petroleum jelly, paraffin, and about three hundred other useful products that increased both the quality of consumers' lives and his own profits. He continued to trim costs and improve production until he had cut the cost of refining to less than a penny a gallon by 1885. Rockefeller's efficiency reduced the cost of kerosene to the customer from fifty-eight cents to eight cents per gallon. Using **horizontal integration**, the control of one aspect of production (in this case, oil refineries), Standard Oil controlled ninety percent of American oil refining by 1879. Rockefeller combined horizontal with vertical integration, controlling every aspect of the oil-production process from barrel making to pipelines and transportation.

# Contrasting Business Models

*Andrew Carnegie and John D. Rockefeller built their wealth through different strategies.*

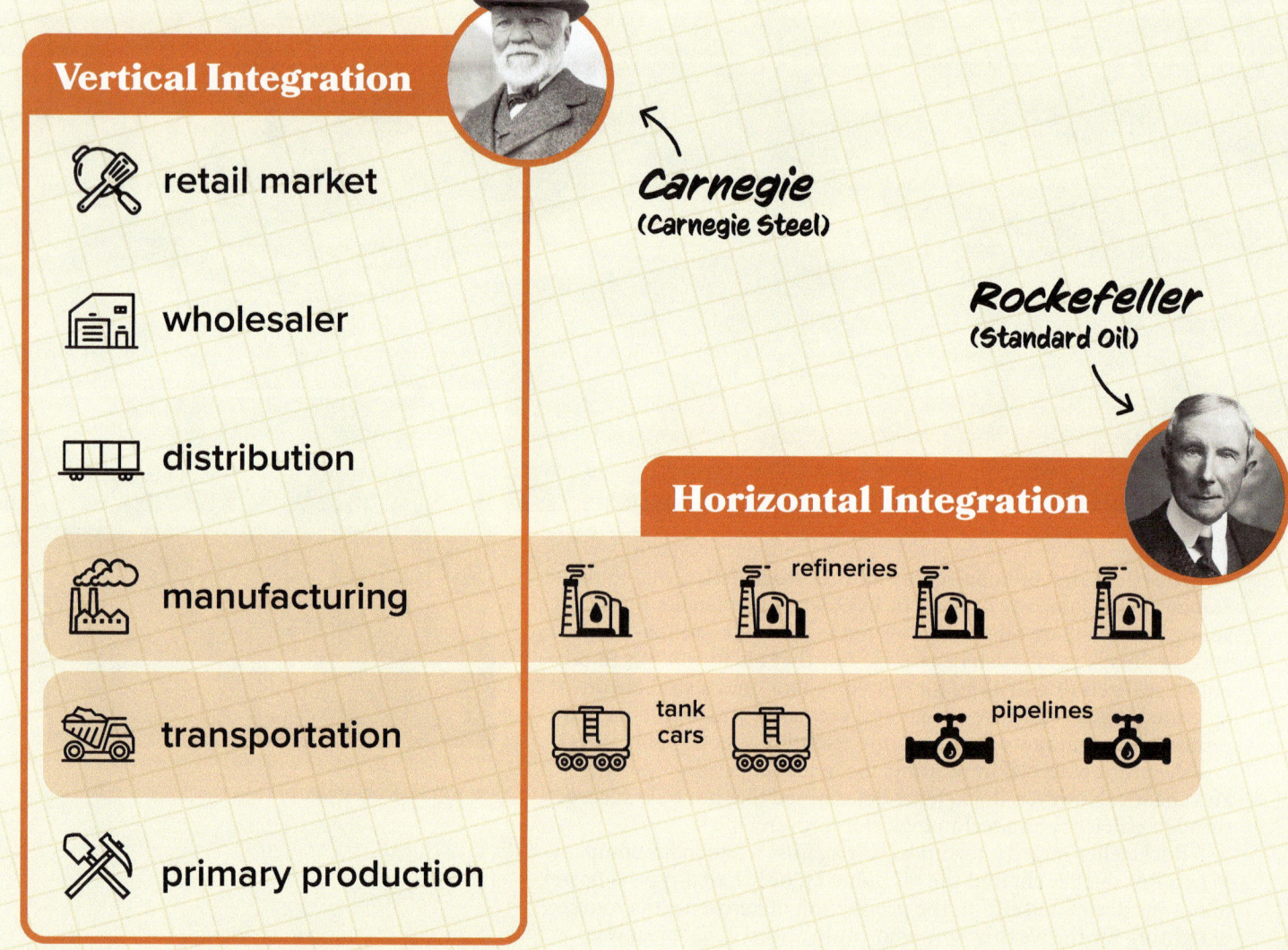

**Vertical Integration**

- retail market
- wholesaler
- distribution
- manufacturing
- transportation
- primary production

**Carnegie**
(Carnegie Steel)

**Rockefeller**
(Standard Oil)

**Horizontal Integration**

refineries

tank cars

pipelines

To prevent corporations from becoming too powerful, some states made it illegal for one company to own stock in another. In 1882 Rockefeller organized Standard Oil into a **trust**, a legal device by which a board of trustees is empowered to make decisions and control the operations of a whole group of companies. Instead of buying a company outright, stockholders gave their stocks to a group of Standard Oil trustees in return for shares in the trust. Since the trustees did not own stock but were merely managing it, they were not violating any laws. As a result, the Standard Oil Trust purchased twenty-seven competing oil companies. Rockefeller's trust became the pattern for the formation of other trusts by businessmen who also had the means to buy up competing companies.

In 1889 New Jersey changed its law to allow companies to own the stock of other companies. This change led to the creation of **holding companies**, which did not produce anything but owned stock in companies that did produce goods. Standard Oil's many subsidiaries (smaller companies) were organized under a holding company in 1899.

**J. P. Morgan** was the leading investment banker in America during the Gilded Age. To help corporations raise capital, investment bankers would buy large amounts of their stock at a discount, then find investors and sell the stock at a profit. Morgan began buying controlling interests in competing companies to reorganize them into more profitable corporations. He reorganized several major railroad lines, such as the Northern Pacific, Union Pacific, B & O, and Southern Railroads. Morgan's biggest move, however, was the consolidation of much of the steel industry. Through a series of purchases, the largest of which was Carnegie Steel, Morgan formed the first billion-dollar corporation, United States Steel Corporation, in 1901.

▲ J. P. Morgan

## Capitalism

America's rapid economic growth was based on the principles of **capitalism**, an economic system in which a nation's businesses are privately owned and operated. In this system, people are free to invest and seek profits, and anyone can go into business and compete with others. The market forces of supply and demand determine wages and prices. Capitalists believe that a free market with competing companies leads to greater efficiency and creates more wealth for everyone. They also believe that private individuals, not the government, should make most decisions about how the nation's wealth is spent.

The freedom of the capitalistic system enabled people to use labor and investments to help both the nation and its citizens and brought a higher standard of living to most Americans. However, some used that freedom to treat others unjustly. Some industrialists used ruthless tactics against competitors, neglected the health and safety of workers, ignored the environmental effects of industrialization, and focused on amassing huge personal fortunes while keeping employee wages low. However, others demonstrated genuine interest in workers and working conditions. The success of capitalism led to new questions about how to use both money and power. Americans wrestled with how to maintain the great benefits of capitalism while avoiding its abuses.

## Regulations

Most Americans embraced the idea of laissez faire (French for "let it alone") regarding government involvement in businesses. They believed the best way for a capitalist economy to develop was to operate without government interference and argued that government regulation would disturb the balance between supply and demand.

However, as abuses of free-market capitalism became apparent in some companies, many Americans came to believe that government intervention was necessary. They began to call for the federal government to regulate some business practices. However, controversy arose about how to balance the values of freedom and justice.

## Interstate Commerce Act of 1887

The first aspect of interstate commerce to be regulated was railroads. Many western farmers and smaller companies objected to the rates charged by railroads, claiming they were unfair because railroads often set rates based on the presence or absence of competitors. Thus it might be more expensive to transport goods a short distance on a route with no competition than a greater distance on routes with competition. Some railroad trusts were engaged in questionable activities, such as rate-fixing schemes and giving lower rates to larger companies. State railroad commissions had no authority to regulate activities outside the borders of their own states. Many Americans supported federal regulation of the railroads under the interstate commerce clause of the Constitution.

In February 1887 President Cleveland signed the **Interstate Commerce Act,** the first act which provided for federal regulation of commerce. The act (1) directed that railroad rates must be "reasonable and just," (2) required that railroad companies publish all rates and make financial reports, and (3) provided for the creation of the Interstate Commerce Commission (ICC), an independent regulatory agency, to investigate and stop alleged abuses. Though the ICC lost nearly every case it took to court from 1887 to 1906, railroads did begin changing their policies to avoid investigations and costly court battles. The ICC set a precedent for the creation of other independent regulatory agencies, and the power of these agencies became a matter of public debate.

## The Sherman Anti-Trust Act

The public had become increasingly wary of large businesses using trusts to create a **monopoly**, where a single company controls an entire industry. Competitors of companies such as Rockefeller's Standard Oil claimed that large companies were driving all competition out of business or forcing small companies to merge with their larger competitors. Some Americans feared that these huge companies would take advantage of their monopoly by raising prices to an exorbitant level or that they could exercise control over the government. Companies accused of being monopolies argued that they did face competition, often from foreign companies, which would keep them from raising prices and that their size led to greater efficiency, lower costs, and lower prices.

By 1880 both political parties supported regulation of trusts. Congress passed the **Sherman Anti-trust Act** in 1890 to make monopolizing illegal. It declared, "Every contract, combination in the form of trust or otherwise, or conspiracy, in restraint of trade or commerce . . . is hereby declared to be illegal." The act was difficult to enforce, however, because it offered no specific definitions of *contract, combination,* or *restraint of trade.* Therefore, the act was relatively ineffective until the passage of tougher federal regulations in the twentieth century, but it was eventually used to break up some large companies (see Chapter 15).

▼ Cartoon of the Standard Oil Company, depicted as an octopus strangling the US Capitol (left) and a state house (right) while attempting to grasp the White House

## Effects of Industry and Business

The growth of industry and business had a number of effects on American society, both positive and negative.

First, economic growth increased the standard of living for most Americans. Average wages rose sixty percent between 1860 and 1890; and even the average industrial worker's annual income rose by forty-eight percent, from $380 in 1880 to $564 in 1890. This growth also created a new class of wealthy Americans. The number of millionaires increased from about fifty in 1850 to five thousand by 1900. One downside of this increased wealth was that materialism, which emphasizes money and possessions, became the philosophy of a growing number of Americans.

Second, economic growth led to greater trade. The output of wheat and corn more than doubled between 1865 and 1900, and coal production increased 800 percent. Products from American farms and factories were traded around the globe.

Third, more Americans and new immigrants moved to urban centers. Mechanization of farming meant fewer farm workers were needed, and many moved from rural areas to cities. With the growth of these cities came many urban problems, such as air and water pollution, crime, overcrowding, and poor housing conditions.

Fourth, new labor-saving inventions and mechanization freed most Americans from certain types of work and created time for leisure activities. Americans sought new outlets for recreation and amusement. Organized sports became popular. Baseball became the national pastime beginning in 1869 when the Cincinnati Red Stockings, the first all-professional team, toured the country. Other sports, such as golf, tennis, and croquet, enjoyed an even broader appeal because both men and women could play them. The Ivy League colleges began playing football—without helmets or pads—in the fall of 1869. Canadian James Naismith introduced basketball as a YMCA (Young Men's Christian Association) winter sport in 1891. Bicycles were immensely popular during the 1890s. Other popular forms of entertainment included Wild West shows, circuses, and vaudeville shows featuring musicians, comedians, and other entertainers. Whereas reading books and newspapers and attending church had been the main free-time activities in rural America, the leisure options of the cities caused the entertainment culture to become an important part of American life in the late 1800s.

Fifth, industrialism affected family life. Child labor took children out of the home and kept them from receiving a consistent education. More women joined the workforce during and after the Civil War, and more went to work as industry expanded. This changed the lifestyle of many American families.

## 5 Impacts of Industrialism on America

 **HIGHER STANDARD OF LIVING**

 **GLOBAL TRADE**

 **URBANIZATION**

 **MORE LEISURE TIME**

 **WOMEN AND CHILDREN IN THE WORKFORCE**

▶ A high-wheel bicycle circa 1891

# Captains of Industry
## OR ROBBER BARONS?

At the top of America's growing industrial empire were men whose ideas, energy, and money dominated the age. Their lives often illustrated the best and worst aspects of industrialism and capitalism. Historians have often interpreted these men in one of two ways: as great "captains of industry" or as notorious "robber barons."

Historians who argue that these industrialists were captains of industry point out that their efforts helped forge America into a prosperous and productive nation. They created jobs that enabled workers to provide for their families. They made the United States the economic envy of the world and sparked a flood of immigrants seeking the "American dream." They became wealthy by efficiently providing what consumers needed and wanted. Moreover, many of them became great philanthropists, giving to numerous charitable causes. They were, indeed, aggressive, cost- and efficiency-conscious businessmen; yet those characteristics also accomplished enormous good for the average consumer, lowering prices on consumer goods and making goods available that once had been within reach of only the rich.

Supporters argue that the competition of free-market capitalism often creates winners and losers and that these men should not be criticized for coming out like captains—on top.

**H. J. Heinz** personified this interpretation. A devout Christian, he gave liberally to Christian works, particularly Sunday school organizations. Heinz was a leader in producing bottled and canned foods such as horseradish, ketchup, and pickles. While other producers added fillers such as ground turnips or wood pulp to their products and sold their goods in green-tinted bottles to hide the impurities, Heinz insisted on 100-percent-pure products sold in clear bottles so that consumers could see the purity for themselves. In addition, he treated his workers well and the H. J. Heinz Company never had a single strike during Heinz's life. He provided employees free medical care, gyms, swimming pools, gardens, and educational opportunities, such as libraries and free concerts and lectures. Heinz's workers enjoyed clean, well-lit, well-ventilated plants where dining halls provided food at discount prices. Heinz denied having any "secret" to his success other than honesty and hard work. "To do a common thing uncommonly well brings success," he often said.

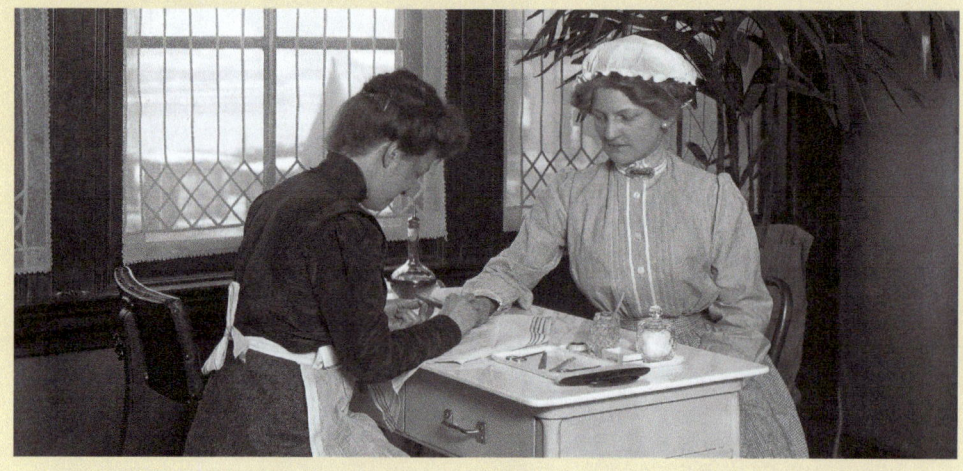

▲ (top) H. J. Heinz; (above) Manicure at the H. J. Heinz Company, a benefit and weekly requirement for all employees who handled food

Historians who call the industrialists "robber barons" imply that wealthy businessmen personified greed and callousness. Some of the industrialists were ruthless toward their competition and grew wealthy by exploiting their workers. Some sought success by special privileges or political advantages. They sought high tariffs to drive out competitors and asked for government subsidies (taxpayer dollars) to reduce costs to themselves. In fact, some of them found that they could make almost as much money by getting government grants and subsidies as they could by producing products or providing services. They pressured politicians to influence political decisions that might affect their businesses. Some even resorted to bribery to gain an advantage over competitors.

Examples of robber barons were James Fisk and Jay Gould, two unethical businessmen who tried to manipulate the gold market for their personal gain. They planned to buy gold on the New York Stock Exchange until the price of gold rose. They would then sell theirs and make an enormous profit. They bribed government officials to keep the US Treasury from selling gold so that their scheme would work. They also issued fraudulent stock in a railroad company, and in their association with "Boss" Tweed (see Chapter 11), bribed legislators and judges to ignore their actions.

The reality is that both interpretations have some truth. Many industrialists brought great benefits to the nation, but they sometimes used tactics that were morally questionable. Even the best of them reflected both the creative and fallen natures of humanity.

▼ James Fisk (left) and James Gould (seated right) plotting their gold scheme involving government bribery

## Comprehension Check 12.3

1. _____ refers to controlling one aspect of production.

   A corporation

   B horizontal integration

   C trust

   D vertical integration

2. _____ became a billionaire from his oil refining company.

   A Andrew Carnegie

   B J. P. Morgan

   C John D. Rockefeller

3. Both the Interstate Commerce Act and the Sherman Anti-trust Act reflected the principle of laissez faire in business.

   True       False

4. Historians interpret industrialists as "captains of industry" for the following reasons except that they _____.

   A asked for government subsidies to reduce costs

   B created jobs for workers

   C provided efficiently what consumers needed or wanted

### MAKING CONNECTIONS

5. What were two effects of the growth of industry and business on American society?

▼ Lewis Hine's photograph of child labor in a glass and bottle factory

- How did industrialization lead to the rise of labor unions?
- What led to conflict between industry owners and workers during this time?

## 12.4 Labor Issues

**Why did labor unions grow?**

# Rise of Labor Unions

## Labor Concerns

The laissez faire idea that the government should avoid regulating the economy had the drawback of leaving workers at the mercy of their employers. As mentioned in Chapter 7, working conditions were often difficult and dangerous for industrial laborers, working hours were long, and wages were low. Often the only recourse workers had was to quit their jobs in the hopes of finding a better one, but few could afford to do so because they had no savings to rely on.

By 1900 women made up nearly twenty percent of the labor force, with one third of those working in industrial jobs, while the remainder worked as domestic servants, teachers, nurses, clerks, and clerical workers. Women were typically paid lower wages than men doing the same jobs.

Child labor in factories also remained common. According to the 1900 census, more than 1,750,000 children ages ten to sixteen worked for wages in the United States, about twenty percent of the children in that age group. An additional 250,000 workers were under ten years old. Children as young as five worked as "breaker boys," picking debris, stones, and sulfur from the coal as it flowed through chutes beneath their feet. Breaker boys could fall into the coal chutes and be crushed by the coal. They often had a persistent cough from breathing the coal dust. At twelve, they went down into the mines. Those who entered the mines faced death or injury from cave-ins, explosions, or suffocation from poisonous gases or lack of oxygen. Children who worked in canneries, where they shucked oysters or peeled or sliced fruits and vegetables, risked slicing—or even cutting off—fingers or hands.

During this period many considered child labor to be acceptable or even necessary. One reason was the extensive loss of male workers in the Civil War. Another was that children were faster and more agile than adults in doing some tasks. They were also cheaper to hire. Families may not have wanted to send their children to work at dangerous jobs for low wages, but parents, especially new immigrants, often found it necessary for their children to work to provide for their families.

However, as reformers drew attention to the plight of child workers, state governments began to enact legislation limiting child labor. In 1879 only seven states had laws limiting the age of workers in manufacturing, but by 1909 forty-three of the forty-six states had such laws. These laws typically limited the age of the child who could work and the number of working hours a day and a week. The passage of compulsory school attendance laws further restricted child labor.

## Labor Unions

Chapter 7 mentioned that labor unions began in the 1830s but had limited success. The first unions in the United States represented craft workers—those who had special skills and training, such as shoemakers, machinists, stonecutters, and printers. These craft workers began to form trade unions such as the Knights of St. Crispin (for shoemakers) and the Iron Molders' International Union.

After the Civil War, workers occasionally held unorganized strikes in response to wage cuts, and the effectiveness and potential of labor organizations soon became apparent. Responding to the challenges and human cost of industrialization, organized labor became a powerful political and social force during the period. Because the unions represented workers whose skills employers needed, employers often had to negotiate with the unions, circumstances which enabled skilled workers to gain better wages and working conditions.

However, many companies tried to prevent unions from forming. Some even required workers to sign contracts promising not to join a union and fired workers who tried to unionize. Others hired detectives to identify union organizers, who were then fired and "blacklisted" (placed on a list of troublemakers that was passed around so no company would hire them).

One reason government and business leaders objected to unions was that unions were sometimes associated with radical ideas such as anarchism and Marxism, which were becoming popular in Europe. Anarchists were opponents of the established political order who sought change through violent means. Marxism was named for Karl Marx, a German philosopher and critic of capitalism, who co-wrote *The Communist Manifesto* in 1848 and published the first volume of *Das Kapital* in 1867. Marx said that history was the story of class struggle between the proletariat (workers) and the bourgeoisie (owners). He believed that eventually the workers would revolt against owners and against government and would take control of society. The result would be a communist society in which social classes did not exist. Marx also said that Christianity was the "opiate of the people," meaning that it was created by the bourgeoisie to suppress and control the proletariat and prevent revolution by telling the workers to be content with their miserable earthly existence while focusing on a heavenly reward. While not all union leaders in America agreed with anarchism or Marxism, Americans began to view unions, as well as European immigrants, with suspicion.

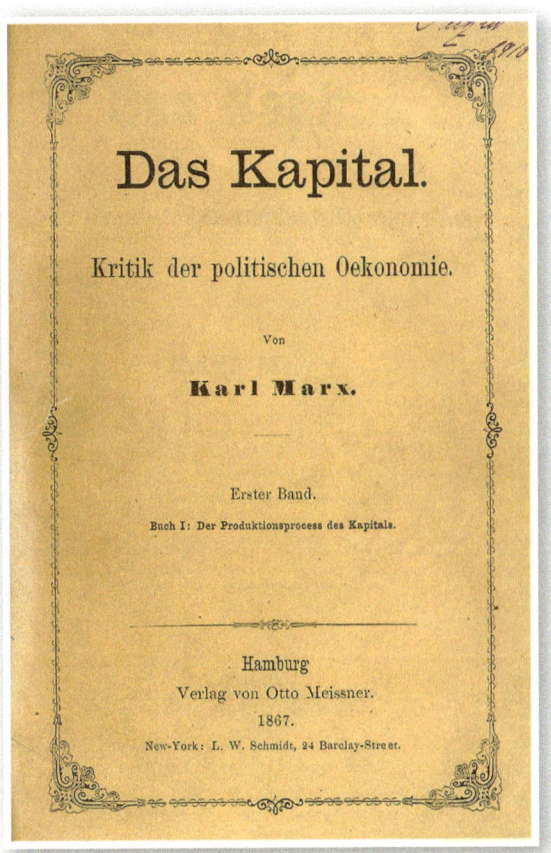

The **Knights of Labor** was formed in 1869 as a union for skilled and unskilled workers from various occupations. The Knights also welcomed women and African Americans. They called for an eight-hour workday, laws prohibiting child labor, equal pay for men and women, worker-owned factories, and compensation for loss due to injuries on the job. Its leader, Terence Powderly, favored boycotts and arbitration over strikes to settle wage disputes because strikes often resulted in violence. Several successful strikes, however, gained the Knights new influence and new members, and the group reached a peak of 700,000 members in 1886.

A more influential labor organization, the **American Federation of Labor** (AFL) was formed in 1886. The AFL was a confederation of several national trade unions for skilled laborers. Under the leadership of Samuel Gompers, the AFL pursued three primary goals: an eight-hour workday, recognition of a union's right of collective bargaining (the right of unions to represent workers in negotiations with owners and managers), and closed shops (factories that hired only union members). Gompers preferred to negotiate with owners but was willing to call for strikes when necessary. By 1900 the AFL had 500,000 members, although many of its member organizations did not allow women or African Americans to join.

## Strikes and Riots

During the late 1860s and the 1870s, only scattered, poorly managed strikes occurred over labor grievances. As unions grew, however, strikes—and violence—became more common. The government tended to support business owners over the unions. Courts often found that strikes were illegal restraints of trade, and union leaders were often fined or jailed.

One example of labor violence was the **Haymarket Riot**. Supporters of an eight-hour workday called for a nationwide strike to begin on May 1, 1886. On May 3, a fight broke out on the picket line (the line of striking workers outside the factory) in Chicago, and police who were called to intervene opened fire, killing four strikers. The next day, a large group including workers and anarchists met at Haymarket Square to protest the shooting. Someone threw a bomb into a group of policemen, touching off a riot. When the unrest ended, over 170 people had been injured and seven policemen had been killed. Eight people accused of being anarchists were convicted, including a member of the Knights of Labor, and four were executed. The Haymarket Riot discredited the Knights of Labor and its membership dropped significantly.

▲ Bombing in the Haymarket Riot

As a result of the Panic of '73 (see Chapter 11), the Baltimore and Ohio Railroad announced in July 1877 that it was cutting wages for the third time. B & O workers in Martinsville, West Virginia, walked off the job. Soon over 80,000 railroad workers nationwide joined what became known as the **Great Railroad Strike**, destroying equipment, tearing up tracks, and blocking rail service in several cities. Governors began calling their militias to put down the strike. President Hayes declared that the strike was an insurrection and sent federal troops to several cities. By the time order was restored, over 100 people had been killed.

In 1892 violence erupted during a strike at the Carnegie Steel mill in Homestead, Pennsylvania. Carnegie's chief executive officer, Henry Frick, who was determined to break up the steel workers' union, had proposed lowering wages by twenty percent. When the workers threatened to strike, Frick closed the plant, an action that became known as a "lockout." Frick hired guards from the Pinkerton Detective Agency to subdue picketers and protect replacement workers who were brought in. Fighting broke out between the locked-out workers and the guards on July 6, 1892, leaving several dead and wounded. The Pinkerton agents were forced to surrender, and the crowd abused many of the agents. The governor sent the militia to restore order and protect the strikebreakers. Four months later the **Homestead Strike** collapsed and many of the strikers went back to work. The union's power was broken, and Carnegie cut wages and jobs and implemented a twelve-hour workday.

▶ The Homestead Strike

### Did You Know?

Eugene V. Debs was a five-time candidate for president on the Socialist Party ticket. He ran in 1900, 1904, 1908, 1912, and 1920. In 1920 he became the first—and to date the only—candidate to campaign from a jail cell.

The **Pullman Strike** occurred in 1894. It began when the Pullman Palace Car Company in Chicago slashed wages by twenty-five percent but did not also reduce the rent on the houses it provided its employees or the cost of goods in the company stores. When the workers retaliated by striking, the Pullman Company withdrew the strikers' credit from the company stores. Facing starvation, the Pullman workers appealed to the American Railway Union, whose president was Eugene V. Debs.

On June 26, Debs ordered union members to cut all Pullman passenger cars out of trains and leave them standing on the side-tracks. The boycott of Pullman cars affected all western railroads. When boycotters were fired, the strike spread across the nation, and traffic, including the mail between the West and Chicago, came to a virtual standstill. Strikers and unemployed ruffians destroyed engines, cars, and equipment, causing owners to demand that federal troops be sent to break the strike. President Cleveland complied to keep the US mail moving. In addition, the federal courts issued an injunction, or court order, forbidding Debs and other strike leaders to further encourage the strike. Debs ignored the order and promoted the general strike; consequently, he spent six months in jail.

The violence of these strikes alarmed many Americans and further contributed to beliefs that unions were associated with radical ideas and that allowing workers to organize was dangerous to society.

## Comprehension Check 12.4

1. Reform in child labor resulted in the following changes except ____.

   A ensuring equal pay with adults

   B limiting the age of child workers

   C reducing work hours

2. ____ proposed that history was a clash between workers and owners and that class struggle would continue until workers overthrew the owners.

   A Eugene V. Debs

   B Samuel Gompers

   C Karl Marx

   D Terence Powderley

3. The Knights of Labor and the American Federation of Labor shared ____ as a goal.

   A closed shops

   B the eight-hour workday

   C equal pay for men and women

### MAKING CONNECTIONS

4. What effect did strikes and riots have on the general public?

## Chapter Summary

### 12.1 Change and Challenge

- The period from the 1870s to about 1900 is often called the "Gilded Age" because it was a period of great prosperity and innovation, but underneath the surface there were challenges.

- Cities grew dramatically during this period, partly as a result of a massive influx of "new immigrants."

- Presidents during this period attempted to deal with corruption in government. After Garfield's assassination, President Arthur signed the Pendleton Act which reformed the civil service. While the Republican Arthur and the Democrat Cleveland both wanted to lower the tariff, the Republican Congress during Harrison's presidency passed the high McKinley Tariff.

- Christianity faced challenges over how to respond to Darwinism, liberal theology, and urbanization.

**TERMS**

Gilded Age

Ellis Island

Chinese Exclusion Act

Stalwarts

Half-Breeds

James Garfield

Chester Arthur

Pendleton Act

Grover Cleveland

Benjamin Harrison

McKinley Tariff

Charles Darwin

Social Darwinism

Dwight L. Moody

**TERMS**

Alexander Graham Bell

Thomas Edison

George Westinghouse

George Pullman

Cornelius Vanderbilt

James J. Hill

Great Northern Railroad

### 12.2 Industry and Invention

- Industrial growth was made possible by a rapidly growing population, a spirit of innovation and entrepreneurship, and an abundance of natural resources.

- Innovations and inventions transformed American society in areas such as clothing, communications, and the use of electricity.

- Consolidation in the railroad industry led to railroad expansion and lower rates.

## Chapter Summary

**TERMS**

corporations
Andrew Carnegie
vertical integration
John D. Rockefeller
horizontal integration
trust
holding companies
J. P. Morgan
capitalism
Interstate Commerce Act
monopoly
Sherman Anti-trust Act
H. J. Heinz

### 12.3 Big Business

- Corporations were formed to raise large amounts of capital. Industrialists like Andrew Carnegie used vertical integration to control all aspects of production, and John D. Rockefeller added horizontal integration, the control of one aspect of production. Trusts and holding companies were formed to organize corporations that owned many businesses.

- America's economic growth was based on capitalism, and many Americans embraced the idea of laissez faire and opposed government regulation of businesses. Abuses of free-market capitalism led to the beginning of government regulation.

- Economic and industrial growth increased standards of living, materialism, trade, leisure time, and urbanization and changed family life.

- Industrial leaders were seen either as "captains of industry" or as "robber barons."

### 12.4 Labor Issues

- Labor unions developed to address labor issues such as wages, hours, working conditions, and child labor. Businesses and government often tried to prevent unions from forming, and some Americans associated unions with radical ideas such as anarchism and Marxism.

- Conflicts between labor and management sometimes led to violence, and government force was often used to put down strikes.

**TERMS**

Knights of Labor

American Federation of Labor

Haymarket Riot

Great Railroad Strike

Homestead Strike

Pullman Strike

## Chapter Review Questions

### RECALL

1. Which president of the Gilded Age was assassinated by a disappointed office seeker?

2. What act attempted to put an end to the spoils system?

3. What Democrat was elected president in 1884 and again in 1892?

4. Whose writings drove changes in the area of religion during this period?

5. What Christian preacher led the urban evangelistic movement in the late 1800s?

6. Which industrialist developed a successful steamship company before building a vast railroad empire?

7. What investment banker bought Carnegie's steel company and created United States Steel Corporation?

8. What French term describes the idea that government should leave the economy and businesses alone?

9. Which union, founded in 1869, was formed to help both skilled and unskilled labor?

10. Which union was a confederation of several national trade unions for skilled workers?

### UNDERSTAND

11. Why was the period from the 1870s to 1900 called the "Gilded Age"?

12. What were two advantages and two disadvantages of living in a city in the late 1800s?

13. What was different about the "new" immigrants who came to America in the late 1800s?

14. Why did some Americans oppose immigration in the late 1800s?

15. How did immigrants contribute to American society and culture?

16. What four issues dominated politics during the Gilded Age?

17. What did the McKinley Tariff do to tariff rates?

18. Why did many Christians reject Darwinism?

19. How did some industrialists attempt to apply Social Darwinism to business? How should a Christian evaluate Social Darwinism in light of Psalm 72:12–14?

20. What were three factors that contributed to America's industrial growth?

21. What were three things James J. Hill did that made the Great Northern Railroad the most successful transcontinental railroad line?

22. What are the differences between a sole proprietorship, a partnership, and a corporation?

23. Explain vertical and horizontal integration.

24. Explain Carnegie's "Gospel of Wealth."

25. What is a trust? What was its purpose in the Gilded Age? What is a holding company, and how is it different from a corporation that produces goods?

26. What are the strengths of capitalism? What were some of its abuses during the Gilded Age?

27. Why did many Americans oppose government regulation of businesses?

28. What were the complaints that led to the passing of the Interstate Commerce Act?

29. What were four effects of the growth of industry and business on American society?

30. Why did labor unions form, and how did many companies respond to attempts by labor to form unions?

31. What is Marxism, and why was it seen by many as a dangerous idea?

32. What side did the government take in the conflicts between unions and owners during this period?

### THINK ABOUT IT

33. Do you think government regulation of business is necessary? Explain, drawing on biblical principles.

34. Which do you think better describes the industrialists of the Gilded Age: captains of industry or robber barons? Explain.

35. Choose one of the following pairings of values and explain how they related to one another during the Gilded Age: gratitude and growth; freedom and justice. Be sure to include biblical considerations in your answers.

# 13 Westward Expansion

13.1 Rails, Miners, Cowboys, and Lawmen

13.2 Settlers and Sodbusters

13.3 Conflicts with Native Americans

▲ A pioneer homestead

# Rails, Miners, Cowboys, and Lawmen

What role did railroads, miners, cattlemen, and lawmen play in the West?

## GUIDING QUESTIONS

- What role did railroads play in the growth of the West?
- How did mining change the American West?
- What was it like to be a cowboy?
- What did the Wild West reveal about human nature?

Americans were restless and energetic. During the Gilded Age, they not only enlarged their cities and factories but also settled the western half of the nation. Since America's founding, the frontier had moved westward from the Appalachian Mountains to the Mississippi River to the Pacific coast, largely bypassing the area between the Mississippi and the Rocky Mountains known as the Great Plains. Going west appealed to people's rugged individualism and desire for growth. In the West a person could largely determine his own future. Railroaders, miners, cattlemen, and farmers—all pioneers—accepted the challenges of frontier life and pushed toward the Pacific in the last great wave of westward expansion in American history.

People of many backgrounds settled in the West. Some were laborers from the East, and many were recent immigrants from Germany, Ireland, and Scandinavia. More than 200,000 Chinese arrived between 1876 and 1900, most settling in California, along with thousands of Mexican miners, as well as immigrants from Chile and Peru. In addition, as many as 26,000 black Americans had moved to Kansas by 1880. These "Exodusters" were leaving discrimination in the South and hoping to start a new life in the West. Hundreds of thousands of black Americans settled west of the Mississippi River.

▲ African American "Exodusters" in Kansas

## Rails to the West

As mentioned in Chapter 12, most railroad tracks in the United States in 1860 were in the East. Prior to 1869 those who wished to travel from Missouri to California could go by covered wagon, a trip that would take four months, or by stagecoach, which would take twenty days. Another option for those traveling from the East Coast was a steamship which sailed around the southern tip of South America and up to California, which would take from three to six months.

The California gold rush of 1849 created a population explosion on the Pacific coast. California's population grew from 14,000 in 1848 to 250,000 by 1852. Americans began to dream of a rail line that would cross the continent. But the enormous cost of building a transcontinental railroad intimidated potential investors, and sectional division in the 1850s over the route the railroad would take kept Congress from acting.

After the southern states seceded, the sectional dispute over the route was no longer an issue, and Congress passed the Pacific Railway Act of 1862. The act gave the **Union Pacific Railroad** and **Central Pacific Railroad** permission to build a transcontinental line. The government provided subsidies (money granted by the government to assist an industry or business) to the railroads: $16,000 for each mile of track laid in the plains, $32,000 per mile in the foothills, and $48,000 per mile in the mountains. It also said that for each mile of track laid, the railroad company would receive land grants of alternating ten-square-mile sections of land along each side of the road. This land grant was expanded in 1864 to twenty-square-mile sections, ultimately giving the participating railroads about twenty million acres. Later, much of this land was sold by the railroad companies.

The Union Pacific began pushing westward from Omaha, Nebraska, in 1865. Its workers included Civil War veterans, frustrated miners and farmers, Irish immigrants, adventurers, and ex-convicts. At its height it employed 10,000 workers. The Central Pacific began in Sacramento, California, and pushed eastward. Because of a lack of available workers in the West, the Central Pacific hired 10,000 Chinese immigrant laborers.

▼ Workers laying tracks on the Central Pacific in Nevada, with telegraph lines running beside the tracks

▲ Chinese laborers working on the Central Pacific Railroad

**Photo Credit:** *Surviving Central Pacific Chinese Workers, Wong Fook, Lee Chao, Ging Cui* 1919. Gelatin silver print; Amon Carter Museum of American Art Archives, Fort Worth, Texas; A2010.092.DP1967.727

Both companies faced immense challenges. The Central Pacific faced the major, even potentially fatal, challenge of going over or blasting tunnels through the Sierra Nevada Mountains. The Union Pacific crossed the Plains and the Rockies, facing searing heat, the waterless and treeless prairie, and potential attacks by Plains Indians. An English visitor described the process of the Union Pacific track gangs:

 **Analyzing Sources**

How does this description of the rail workers reflect the age of industrialism?

*A light car, drawn by a single horse, gallops up to the front with its load of rails. Two men seize the end of a rail and start forward, the rest of the gang taking hold by twos until it is clear of the car. They come forward at a run. At the word of command the rail is dropped in its place, right side up. . . . Less than thirty seconds to a rail, and so four rails go down to the minute!*

— **ENGLISH OBSERVER**

The observer went on to note that there were "three strokes to the spike, . . . ten spikes to the rail, four hundred rails to a mile, eighteen hundred miles to San Francisco."

Over the four years of construction, the Central Pacific had completed 688 miles of track and the Union Pacific 1,086 miles. The two lines met on May 10, 1869, near Promontory Point, Utah. Officials drove in four special spikes—two gold, one silver, and one a mixture of gold, silver, and iron. On one of the gold spikes was inscribed, "May God continue the unity of our Country as this Railroad unites the two great Oceans of the world."

Within twenty-five years, four more transcontinental lines spanned the country: the Atchison, Topeka, and Santa Fe; the Southern Pacific (which crossed the Gadsden Purchase—see Chapter 8); the Northern Pacific; and the Great Northern. As mentioned in Chapter 12, the Great Northern line was the only transcontinental line that was completed without a penny of government subsidy. With these new rail lines, a person could travel from New York to California in ten days. These railroads brought new settlers by the thousands, and by 1880 San Francisco had a population of 234,000 people.

Some railroad companies were involved in scandals and corruption. Quality of construction was also a problem. In their rush to lay more track and thereby qualify for more subsidies, the companies often failed to prepare the roadbed properly before laying the track, so over time and under the weight of locomotives and loaded freight cars, the ties sank or tilted, twisting and misaligning the track. In such cases, the companies had to make costly repairs and often returned to the government seeking more financial help when this problem occurred.

▲ Driving the golden spike at Promontory Point, Utah, May 10, 1869, upon completion of the first transcontinental railroad

## Main Railroads from the Mississippi to the West Coast

# Miners

One of the reasons for the settlement of the West and the building of the transcontinental railroad was the mining of precious metals. Industrialization increased the demand for metals. The 1849 California gold rush was but the first of several western scrambles to dig wealth from the earth. One of the earliest gold strikes after California was the 1859 Pikes Peak gold rush in Colorado. Thousands of prospectors hoping to strike it rich streamed into Colorado. On their wagons, gold hunters boldly advertised, "Pikes Peak or Bust!" When the gold in Colorado gave out, however, many disappointed fortune seekers rode back with a new message: "Busted!"

Farther west, one of the largest and richest mines was the **Comstock Lode** in Nevada. It was named for Henry Comstock, an early prospector there. Miners eagerly dug gold out of the ground, but they were disappointed to find that it was contaminated by some other metal and therefore sold for less. Upon closer examination, the "other metal" turned out to be silver. In fact, more than half of the ore eventually mined from the Comstock Lode was silver; the rest was gold. Miners extracted some $400 million worth of gold and silver from the Comstock Lode between 1859 and 1900. The nearby town of Virginia City, Nevada, became a boomtown, growing to over 20,000 people by the 1870s. However, when all the precious metals had been taken out of the ground, the town shrank to a few hundred people. Other mining towns became "ghost towns" when their populations left completely.

In the 1870s gold was discovered in the Black Hills of the Dakota Territory, on land that had been given to the Sioux Indians by the US government in 1868. Prospectors ignored the Sioux ownership of the land. When the Sioux refused government attempts to buy the land, war ensued (discussed later in this chapter), and the miners took the land. The Homestake Mine near Deadwood, South Dakota, became one of the world's richest gold mines.

## Mining the West

Gold mining
Silver mining
Gold & silver mining
Black Hills

▼ The mining boom town of Deadwood, South Dakota, 1876

Miners often found more than gold in the West. For example, after a gold boom in Leadville, Colorado, ended in the early 1860s, the town shifted its emphasis and became a center for silver and lead mining. After the silver ran out, Leadville also became a center for mining zinc and copper. The Anaconda Mine in Montana began as a rather poor silver mine. But miners soon discovered that it included one of the richest veins of copper in the world. Nearby deposits of zinc and lead further enriched the region.

Mining techniques changed during the period. Early miners "panned" for gold in stream beds or diverted river water into a sluice where gold would be separated from sand and gravel. As mining grew in scale, companies began the environmentally harmful practice of hydraulic mining, where high-pressure water was used to wash away large amounts of soil to find veins of minerals. To access gold and other minerals deep below the surface, companies dug deep shafts and tunnels hundreds of feet into the earth and brought in huge drills, pumps, and other heavy machinery to extract the precious ores. Deep-shaft miners faced the constant danger of collapses and accidents.

▲ Hydraulic miners blasting soil away to reach "pay dirt"

## Cowboys and Ranchers

### Cattle Drives

In addition to mining, the cattle industry boomed after the Civil War. Cattle had roamed the southwest since the Spanish explorers first brought them to North America in the 1500s. Texas longhorn, descended from these Spanish cattle, were able to survive in the dry desert conditions. By 1865 millions of longhorn grazed freely on the open range, the unfenced public lands of the Plains.

With the large supply of cattle, each sold in Texas for only $3 or $4. After the Civil War, cattle in the growing cities of the East and West sold for $25 to $40 per head because of increasing demand. With the spread of railroads, ranchers began driving their cattle to railroad terminals in Missouri and Kansas from which they could be sold in the East and West for a huge profit.

In 1866 ranchers made the first "**long drive**" of 260,000 longhorn from Texas to Sedalia, Missouri, and other trails developed soon afterward. In 1867 a shrewd cattle broker named Joseph McCoy built large corrals, a bank, a hotel, and barns along the railroad line in Abilene, Kansas. He promoted his operation to cattlemen in Texas, and by 1871 over 700,000 head of cattle were traveling the **Chisholm Trail** from Texas to Abilene each year. However, the Chisholm Trail ran through Indian Territory (Oklahoma), and Native Americans began levying grazing taxes on cattle driven through their land. In addition, farmers began settling in the area, and they erected fences to keep the cattle off their farmland. As a result, new routes farther west developed, including the Western Trail to Dodge City, Kansas, and the Goodnight-Loving Trail (named after the men who blazed the trail) that went along the Pecos River in New Mexico to Colorado and eventually to Cheyenne, Wyoming.

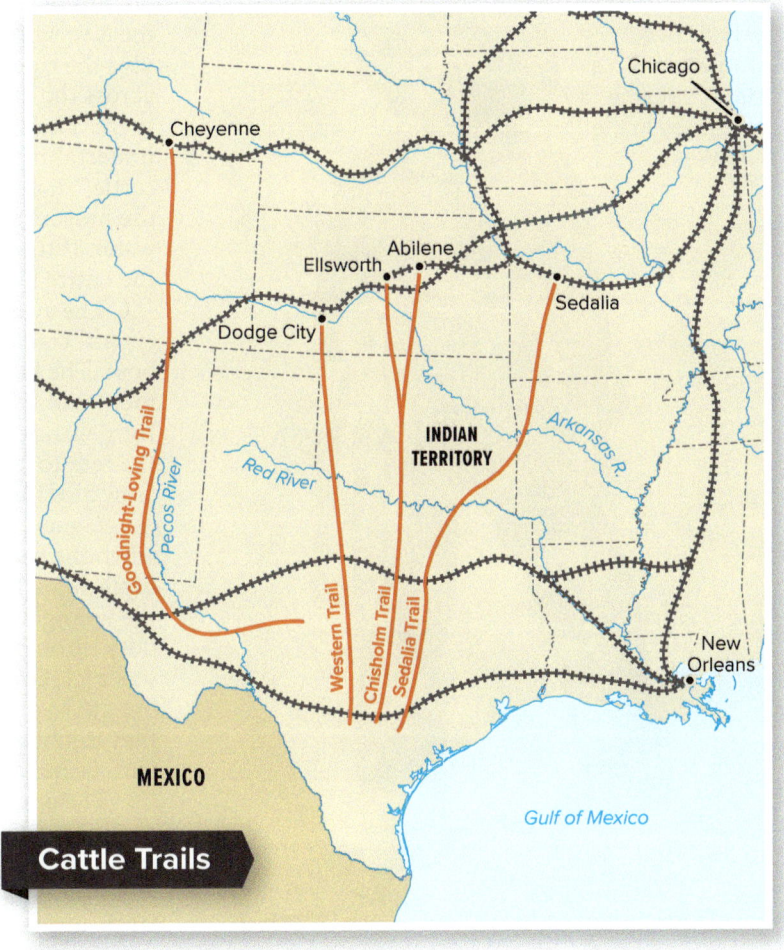

**Cattle Trails**

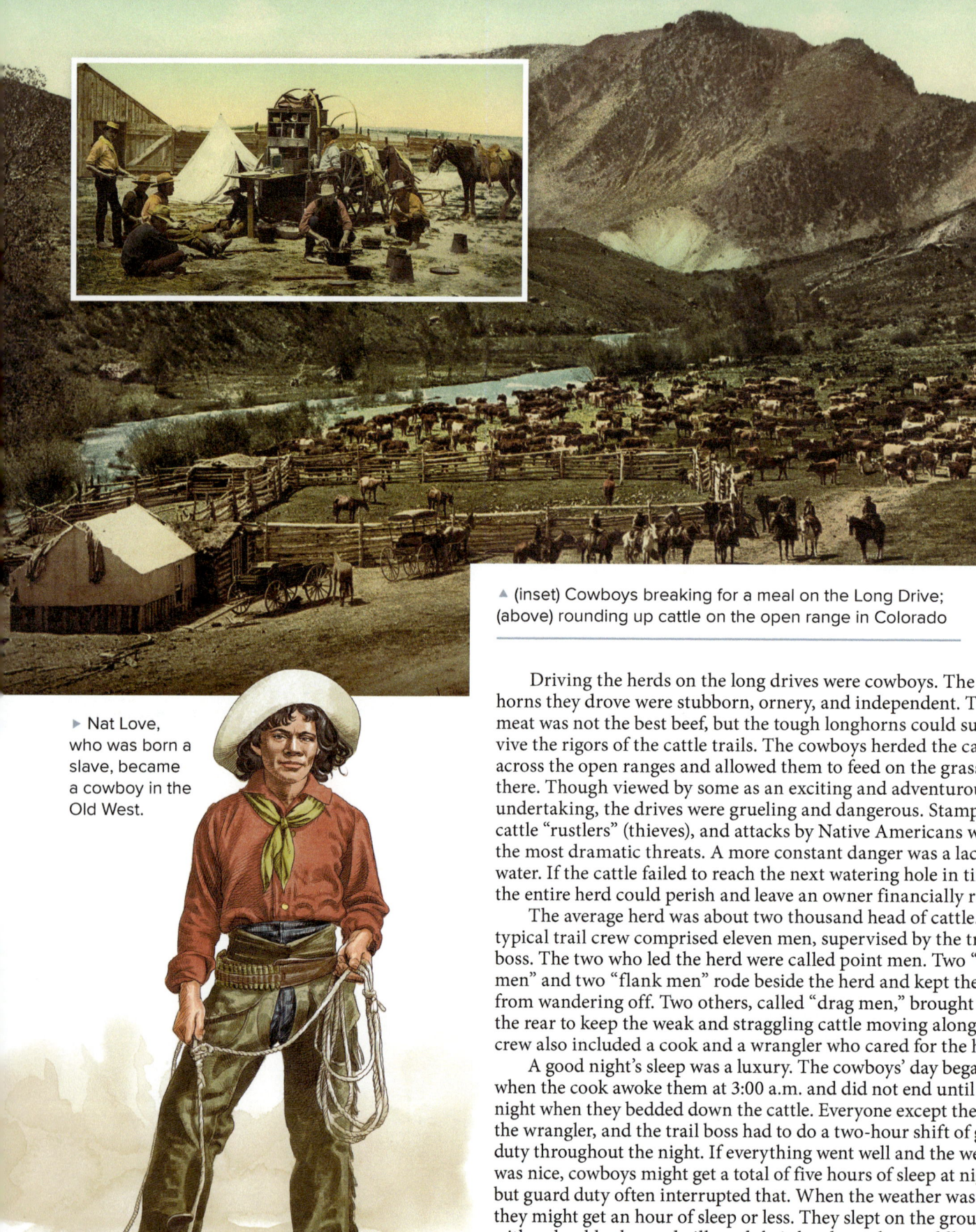

▲ (inset) Cowboys breaking for a meal on the Long Drive; (above) rounding up cattle on the open range in Colorado

► Nat Love, who was born a slave, became a cowboy in the Old West.

Driving the herds on the long drives were cowboys. The long-horns they drove were stubborn, ornery, and independent. Their meat was not the best beef, but the tough longhorns could survive the rigors of the cattle trails. The cowboys herded the cattle across the open ranges and allowed them to feed on the grasses there. Though viewed by some as an exciting and adventurous undertaking, the drives were grueling and dangerous. Stampedes, cattle "rustlers" (thieves), and attacks by Native Americans were the most dramatic threats. A more constant danger was a lack of water. If the cattle failed to reach the next watering hole in time, the entire herd could perish and leave an owner financially ruined.

The average herd was about two thousand head of cattle. The typical trail crew comprised eleven men, supervised by the trail boss. The two who led the herd were called point men. Two "swing men" and two "flank men" rode beside the herd and kept the stock from wandering off. Two others, called "drag men," brought up the rear to keep the weak and straggling cattle moving along. The crew also included a cook and a wrangler who cared for the horses.

A good night's sleep was a luxury. The cowboys' day began when the cook awoke them at 3:00 a.m. and did not end until late at night when they bedded down the cattle. Everyone except the cook, the wrangler, and the trail boss had to do a two-hour shift of guard duty throughout the night. If everything went well and the weather was nice, cowboys might get a total of five hours of sleep at night, but guard duty often interrupted that. When the weather was bad, they might get an hour of sleep or less. They slept on the ground with only a blanket and pillowed their heads on their saddles.

The era of cowboys was brief, lasting only from the 1860s to about 1890. During this period about 40,000 men drove an estimated 10 million head of cattle over the network of cattle trails. Almost one-fourth of the cowboys were African American, and a large number were Mexican.

## Meatpacking

The cattle industry owed at least part of its success to the development of a related business, meatpacking. The idea of meatpacking had first gained popularity during the Civil War when the Union army used treated meat packed in barrels or tins to feed its soldiers. After the war, city dwellers found the process convenient for purchasing and storing food. Meatpacking plants opened first in Midwestern cities such as Cincinnati, Chicago, Milwaukee, and Minneapolis. The use of railroads to ship live cattle from the Great Plains to the meatpacking plants meant cattle lost little weight on the journey and yielded hefty amounts of beef.

The invention of the ice-cooled refrigerator railcars by meatpacker Gustavus Swift allowed meat packers to slaughter the beef in the West and then ship the meat to the plants. Eventually, plants opened in the West too, shortening the process even further. Meatpackers such as Swift and Philip Armour became household names as their canned meat products stocked the shelves of American pantries. Armour also developed uses for the by-products, such as using the hides for shoes and gloves, the bones for glue, buttons, and fertilizer, and the fat to make soap.

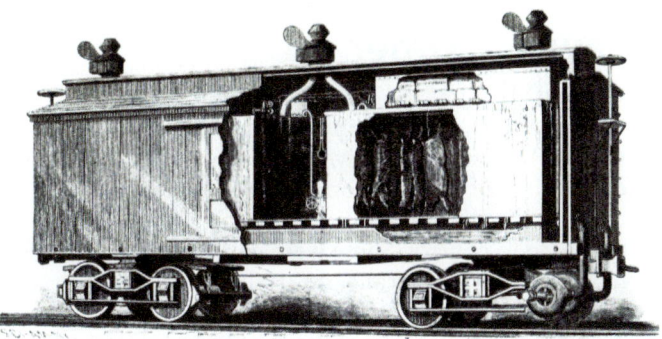

▲ Refrigerated railroad car

## The End of the Open Range

The open-range cattle industry ended in the 1890s for several reasons. One was that meat prices dropped because of the greater efficiency of meat production. This made meat more affordable for the consumer, but it was no longer as profitable for ranchers to raise huge herds of cattle. Another reason was that cattle overgrazed much of the land, ruining it for large herds. Grasses became shorter and scarcer, replaced by weeds, and frequent droughts made the problem worse. When it did rain, soil was eroded, and the hard ground could not absorb all the rainwater, causing flash floods. Also, bitterly cold winters in 1886 and 1887, where temperatures dropped to 40 degrees below zero, killed thousands of cattle and bankrupted many cattlemen. Blizzards covered the grasslands in the Great Plains with deep snow, and many cattle starved.

Open-range ranching also faced challenges from sheepherders, who wanted to raise their flocks on the prairie grasslands as well. Cattlemen resented the sheepherders and their "woolybacks" that grazed the grass down to the roots and fouled water holes. Cattlemen often tried to intimidate or attack sheepherders and their flocks. In addition, as farming spread in the Great Plains, farmers began to fence in their lands with barbed wire (discussed later in this chapter). Long cattle drives also became unnecessary as railroads expanded as far as Texas and the West.

As a result of the end of open-range ranching, cattlemen began fencing in their ranches and breeding smaller, meatier stock. Beef remained a profitable product, and related industries such as meatpacking continued to thrive; but the era of the long drive was over.

◀ Levi Strauss blue jeans label

# Law and Order

Settlement of the West occurred quickly, with boomtowns springing up almost overnight. Many wanted to live free from the constraints of city life. Some of the people who came to the West were tough, independent, and hard to control. Some were hardened and bitter Civil War veterans or criminals from the East who made bank robbery, cattle theft, and even murder, their way of life. The term "Wild West" came to describe the area during this time, although this perception was exaggerated by film and television in the 20th century.

Because of the rapid growth of the West, local governments had difficulty organizing fast enough to enforce the law. The West was also vast, and mining and cattle towns were often in remote places. Without law enforcement, human sinfulness showed itself more frequently. Vigilante groups and lynching were also problematic forms of justice that developed in areas that lacked official law enforcement. Outlaws portrayed the negative sides of individualism and growth. To control and punish lawbreakers, the national government appointed US marshals, and towns hired local lawmen, called sheriffs. Sometimes the lawmen had been lawbreakers themselves. Finding qualified, honest men was difficult, and turnover was high. Furthermore, the lawmen were given extremely large territories to cover. One county marshal in Wyoming was responsible for 16,800 square miles, an area larger than several individual eastern states. In addition, the absence of churches and their restraining effect on sinful behavior contributed to the lawlessness of parts of the West.

Many businesses on the frontier also wanted to bring law and order to the West. For example, after suffering more than two hundred stagecoach robberies in one month in 1877, the Wells Fargo stagecoach company hired the Pinkerton National Detective Agency to supplement the work of the government lawmen. Pinkerton detectives were used to guard factories during labor disputes (see Chapter 12), solve train robberies, pursue outlaws, and transport money and valuables. The Pinkertons developed America's first extensive "most-wanted" file on criminals, an idea that was later adopted by the Federal Bureau of Investigation. The list of criminals included such men as Black Bart, a well-dressed "gentleman bandit" who robbed twenty-eight stagecoaches but never hurt any passengers. He was finally apprehended by Pinkerton detectives after he dropped a handkerchief with markings on it at the scene of a crime.

**REWARD**
**($5,000.00)**
Reward for the capture, dead or alive,
of one Wm. Wright, better known as
**"BILLY THE KID"**
Age, 18. Height, 5 feet, 3 inches.
Weight, 125 lbs. Light hair, blue
eyes and even features. He is
the leader of the worst band of
desperadoes the Territory has
ever had to deal with. The above
reward will be paid for his capture
or positive proof of his death.
JIM DALTON, Sheriff.

**DEAD OR ALIVE!**
**"BILLY THE KID"**

▲ The James Gang circa 1870 (left to right): Cole Younger, Jesse James, Bob Younger, Frank James

Two of the most famous outlaws of the Wild West were brothers Frank and **Jesse James**, both Civil War veterans who had used guerilla tactics as members of the Confederate Quantrill Raiders. They claimed that misdeeds by Northerners during the war led them to a life of crime. They terrorized Missouri and neighboring states for fifteen years, robbing stagecoaches, trains, and banks. Jesse died in 1882 when he was shot in the back of the head at his home in St. Joseph, Missouri, by a "friend" who wanted the reward for capturing him "dead or alive." Frank James surrendered a few months later, was placed on trial, and was acquitted of all charges.

Billy the Kid, also known as William Bonney or Henry McCarty, was another notorious outlaw. He was accused of at least a dozen murders by the time he was eighteen. In late 1880 he was captured by Sheriff Pat Garrett in New Mexico. Billy was convicted of murder and sentenced to hang, but he managed to escape by killing two guards. Garrett tracked him down and killed him in July 1881. Billy was only twenty-one years old.

One of the best-known lawmen of the Wild West was **Wyatt Earp**, who had been a businessman with interests in mining, gambling, saloons, and horse racing. He became famous for participating in an 1881 gunfight near the OK Corral in Tombstone, Arizona, where he, two of his brothers, and his friend Doc Holliday engaged in a shootout with a group of outlaws, killing three. Earp also served as a lawman in Wichita and Dodge City, Kansas.

James Butler "Wild Bill" Hickok also became a folk hero of the Wild West, largely because of fabricated or exaggerated stories he told about himself. Hickok fled Illinois in 1855, thinking he had killed a man in a fight (the man survived), ended up in Kansas, and became friends with William "Buffalo Bill" Cody. He became a deputy US Marshal, then a sheriff, then was elected town marshal of Abilene, Kansas. He brought order to the town, but his methods involved frequent gun battles, one of which included him accidentally shooting his own deputy. After his career as a lawman, Hickok spent some time performing in Buffalo Bill's Wild West shows. He was killed by a fellow gambler while playing poker in Deadwood, South Dakota, in 1876.

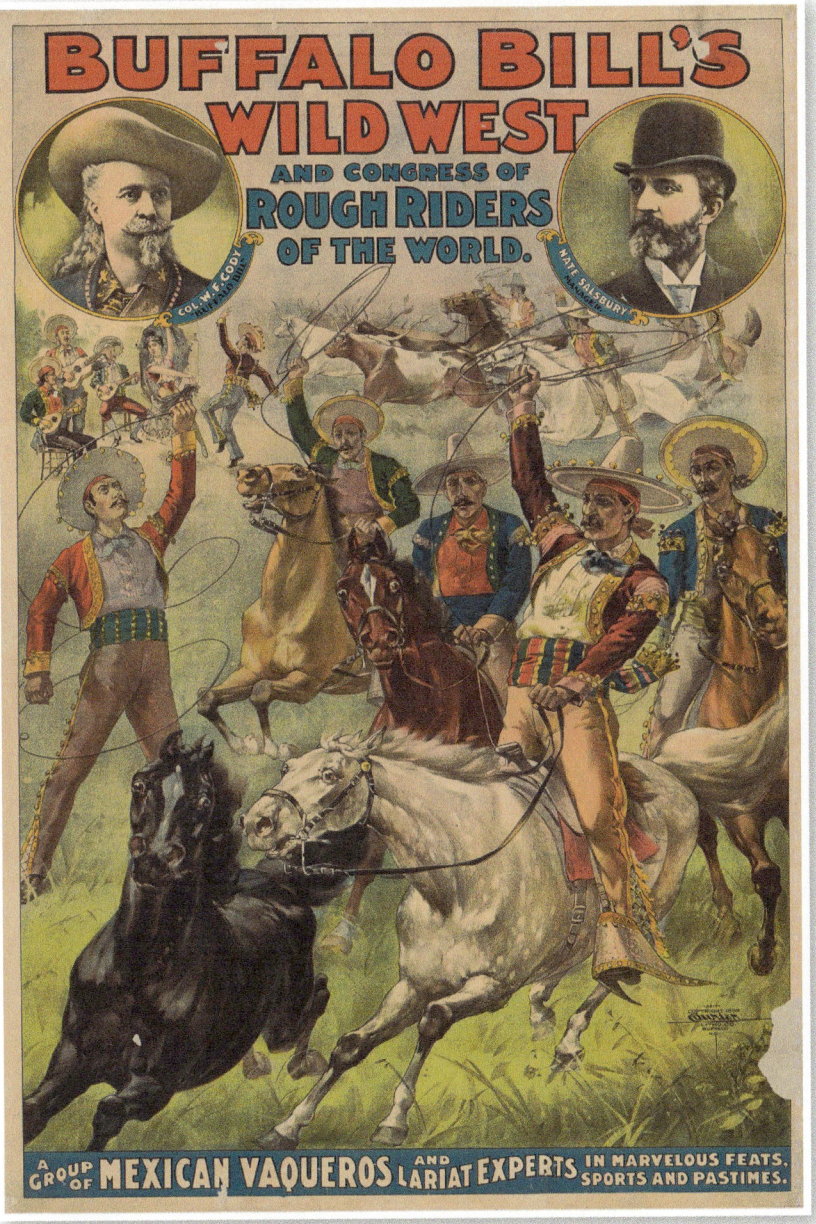

◄ Poster for Buffalo Bill's Wild West show

---

### Comprehension Check 13.1

1. The first transcontinental railroad was built without government subsidies.

   True

   False

2. Miners at the Comstock Lode found gold that was mixed with ____.

   **A** copper

   **B** silver

   **C** lead

3. Each of the following led to the end of open-range ranching except ____.

   **A** overgrazing

   **B** declining beef prices

   **C** farmers fencing their fields

   **D** the lack of railroads in the West

**MAKING CONNECTIONS**

4. How did freedom and individualism sometimes clash with justice in the Wild West?

- How did settlers acquire land in the Old West?
- How did settlers overcome the difficulties of settling the Great Plains?

◄ Advertisement announcing available land in Indian Territory (Oklahoma)

## 13.2 Settlers and Sodbusters

**What was life like for settlers on the Great Plains?**

Before the Civil War, Americans often called the Great Plains region the "Great American Desert." The grassy plains stretching north to south from Canada to southern Texas were nearly treeless and suffered from infrequent rainfall and extremes in temperature, and it was assumed that the land was not suitable for farming. The settlement of the Great Plains proved daunting to the pioneer farmers who moved to the region.

## Acquiring the Land

### Homestead Act

Railroads and the government began to encourage settlement on the Great Plains. Railroads which had received land grants from the government promoted life on the Plains to prospective settlers from the East and to new immigrants.

Government legislation furthered settlement and development in the Great Plains and the West. During the Civil War, Congress passed the **Homestead Act of 1862**. This act gave 160 acres of land to any individual who paid a small filing fee and promised to live on the land five years and make improvements to it. The goal was to open the land to small farmers rather than speculators or large corporations. The Homestead Act proved to be a tremendous success, and by 1900 nearly a million settlers had filed for homesteads under that law.

The **Morrill Land Grant Act of 1862** gave existing states 30,000 acres of federal land for every representative and senator they had. The land was to be used or sold for the purpose of establishing or supporting colleges that specialized in agricultural and mechanical education. The Timber Culture Act of 1873 granted an additional 160 acres to homesteaders if they planted 40 acres in trees, and the Desert Land Act of 1877 gave 640 acres of desert land to those who promised to irrigate and farm it.

### Oklahoma Land Rush

By the 1830s the national government had moved the Choctaw, Creek, Cherokee, Chickasaw, and Seminole tribes from the Southeast to Indian Territory. During the Civil War some of those tribes had signed treaties of friendship with the Confederacy. In 1862 Congress gave the president the power to cancel any treaties with tribes that sided with the Confederacy, and during Reconstruction the treaties were rewritten to reduce the territory allotted to those tribes. Some of their land was allotted to tribes from the Great Plains, upper Midwest, and Texas who had been moved there as well. Two tribes were persuaded to sell part of their allotment in Indian Territory to the US government. In addition, in 1887 the Dawes Act (discussed later in this chapter) allotted land to individual Native Americans rather than tribes. As a result of these changes, millions of acres of Indian Territory were now declared by the federal government to be "unassigned" and available for white settlement.

President Benjamin Harrison announced that three million acres in Indian Territory (Oklahoma) would be open to settlers beginning at noon on April 22, 1889. United States Army troops were stationed on the border to keep settlers out until the stated time. With the sounding of cannons, more than fifty thousand people (called "Boomers") rushed into the territory on the first day to claim their land. Some settlers illegally staked their claims before the appointed hour. They were called "**Sooners**." About 1.9 million acres were claimed in just a few hours. In 1893 an additional six million acres of land in Oklahoma were opened to settlement. In 1907 Oklahoma became the forty-sixth state.

## Developing the Land

Homesteaders faced many challenges as they sought to live on and farm the Great Plains. Even though the land itself may have been free, homesteaders had the expense of clearing, fencing, and plowing the land. It could be years before homesteaders saw any fruit from their labor. However, through individual hard work and determination, those obstacles were overcome, and the Plains became the agricultural heart of the country. By the 1880s the United States became the world's leading exporter of wheat and other grains.

### Hardships of the Prairie

Settlers on the prairie faced many hardships. One was a lack of resources. Because trees were scarce, building homes and fences was difficult, and there was a lack of fuel for building fires. Water was also not easily accessed on the Great Plains. Another hardship was the extreme weather of the Great Plains. Summers had temperatures over one hundred degrees and extended dry seasons; winters had temperatures below zero and blizzards. In addition, hailstorms and tornadoes threatened crops, livestock, and homes.

Problems also arose when farmers, sometimes called "sodbusters," plowed up the hard prairie grasslands. During dry periods, the wind blew the loosened topsoil and created dust storms and erosion, leaving some land infertile. Prairie fires were another challenge. A lightning strike or even a small spark from a campfire or chimney could easily cause dry grasslands to catch fire. Strong winds could spread these fires over hundreds of acres and destroy crops and homes.

Farmers also feared swarms of locusts and grasshoppers, insects that could destroy anything that grew. Some accounts reported that locusts covered the ground up to six inches deep in an 1870s invasion, eating crops, grass, tree bark, leather boots, and even fence posts and door frames. Their appearance and disappearance were unpredictable, but farmers dreaded them because they usually destroyed two years' worth of crops since the locusts laid eggs that hatched the next year.

Cattle ranchers often resented the homesteaders, whose presence threatened open-range grazing, so they sometimes threatened the homesteaders or destroyed their fences. While some homesteaders chose to live on the prairie for the sense of adventure, freedom, and wide-open spaces, others struggled with the isolation and loneliness of life on the Plains. Homesteads were often miles from the nearest town, and some settlers felt disconnected from society.

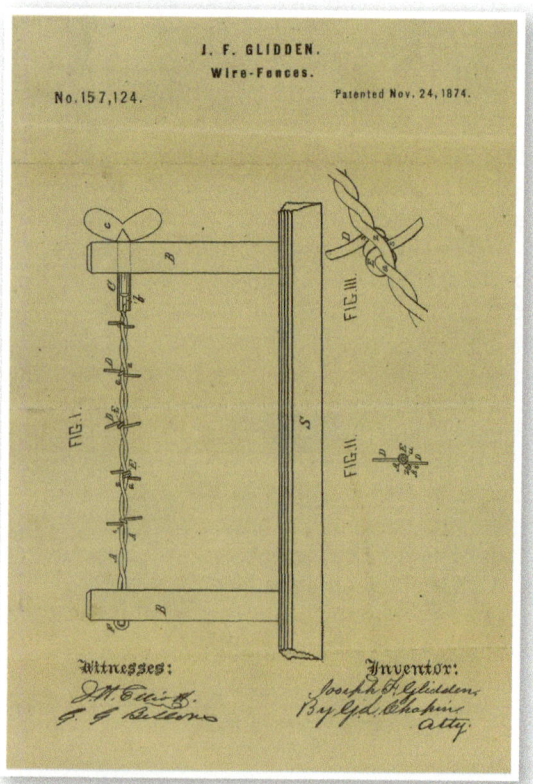

▲ A "soddie" on the Great Plains

## Overcoming the Hardships

Many early pioneers overcame the lack of trees on the Plains by living in "soddies," houses built of blocks of earth and sod. Soddies were warm in the winter and cool in the summer, but they were hardly luxurious. Rain was a particular menace to sod houses. If rains were heavy or prolonged, the sod house might collapse completely. At best, a soddie lasted only a few years, usually long enough for a settler to build another soddie or to import materials such as lumber by rail and build a more permanent house.

Fencing was likewise a problem on the treeless plains. Obviously, the split-rail fences used in the East were out of the question. A solution came in the 1870s when Joseph Glidden of Illinois patented barbed wire—two twisted strands of wire studded with sharp metal barbs at measured intervals. Pioneers strung the wire along posts, thus fencing their property more cheaply, easily, and quickly than they ever could have done with rail fences. The steel was more durable than wood, and the barbs kept wary livestock away from the fence so that they would not break it down.

To compensate for the lack of consistent rainfall, some farmers used rain barrels to catch rainwater. Some irrigated their fields from the region's rivers or creeks. Others dug wells to access water deep underground. Even with wells, farmers could not pump enough water by hand to irrigate their crops and water their livestock. Improved windmills allowed farmers to pump water up from the underground water table.

Farmers also developed new farming methods to adapt to the lack of rain. Dry farming, the cultivation of crops by careful conservation of water, was widespread, with farmers using ground covers (such as stubble from previous crops or a top layer of powdery soil) to hold in precious moisture. Because plants use more water while growing than when mature, farmers also planted crops such as winter wheat, which grew to maturity before the heat of summer increased the rate of evaporation.

◄ Joseph Glidden's barbed wire patent

New and improved tools, such as heavier steel plows that cut through the hard prairie sod, mechanical grain drills to plant seeds at the proper depth, and an improved reaper that cut and harvested the grain, made farming on the Great Plains more efficient and profitable. Steam-powered machines became more common, and by the 1890s the steam-driven tractor was in use.

Homesteaders dealt with isolation and loneliness in several ways. As railroads expanded to the Great Plains, farmers had more access to mail and freight from the East. Mail-order catalog companies, such as Montgomery Ward and Company, founded in Chicago in 1872, and Sears, Roe-buck and Company, founded in 1892, could deliver a wide range of products, including clothing, hardware, tools, and even kits to build an entire house, anywhere in the country.

Farmers also dealt with loneliness by forming their own organizations. Churches were often some of the first buildings erected in towns on the prairie and served a social as well as religious purpose. The Patrons of Husbandry, more commonly called the **Grange**, was founded in 1867 to encourage social contacts and scientific methods of farming. Beyond merely a social group, the Grange represented the economic and political interests of farmers. During the Panic of '73 (see Chapter 11) the Grange encouraged farmers to form coopera-tives in which farmers would work together to raise prices and lower costs rather than competing against one another. The Grange also made state regulation of railroads its chief goal. As a result, several midwestern states passed Granger Laws regulating railroads. Despite its success, the Grange lacked or-ganizational strength and declined in influence. In the 1880s the **Farmers' Alliance** took the lead in working for reforms to benefit farmers. Taking a lesson from industrial labor, the Farmers' Alliance united farm cooperatives across the country and looked to meet farmers' demands through political measures such as railroad regu-lation, favorable currency policies, and antitrust laws.

These innovations, along with the homesteaders' determination, allowed the plains farmers to transform the grasslands into America's agricultural heartland.

▶ A steam tractor being used to plow in the Great Plains

## Comprehension Check 13.2

1. The Great Plains were once considered the "Great American Desert" and unsuitable for farming.

   True      False

2. The ____ Act brought nearly a million settlers to the Great Plains by 1900.

   **A** Homestead

   **B** Morrill Land Grant

   **C** Desert Land

3. Settlers who entered Oklahoma before the appointed hour for staking a claim were called ____.

   **A** Boomers

   **B** Sooners

   **C** Sodbusters

### MAKING CONNECTIONS

4. What were three ways homesteaders overcame hardships on the Great Plains?

GUIDING QUESTIONS

- Why was there conflict between western settlers and Native Americans?

- How effective were reform efforts at resolving conflicts with Native Americans?

## 13.3 Conflicts with Native Americans

What efforts were made to resolve the conflicts between settlers moving to the West and Native Americans?

## Conflicts

As settlers moved to the West, they encountered Native Americans who had occupied the land for centuries as well as nations such as the Cherokee and Creek who had moved to Oklahoma after the Indian Removal Act of 1830. The US government made treaties with Native Americans which often created reservations, special tracts of land set aside, where they could theoretically live in peace. Some Americans thought this policy was a means of helping Native Americans and protecting them from further conflict with settlers and miners. Many others, instead, viewed it as an opportunity to move the Native Americans out of the way so that they could seize their rich lands. As more settlers and miners moved into the West and violated treaty terms by moving onto reservation land, conflict between Native Americans and settlers continued.

### Native American Land Loss, Pre-1850–1890

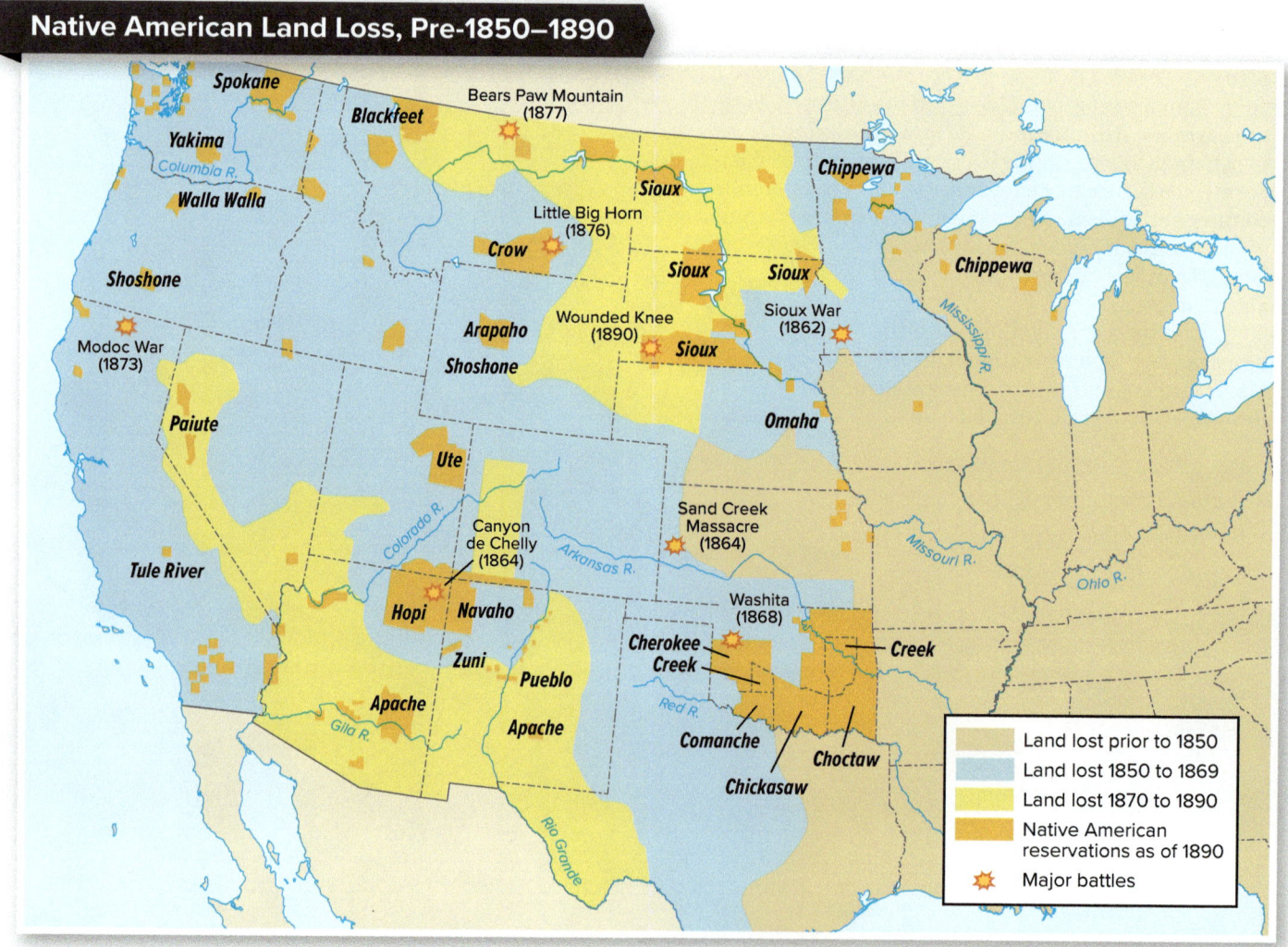

## Plains Indians

The **Plains Indians** included nations such as the Cheyenne, the Comanche, and the Sioux. The Plains Indians subsisted primarily on the bison that wandered the Great Plains in huge herds. The men of the tribes hunted the bison, riding on horses descended from those left by the Spanish centuries before. Bison provided meat as well as hides used for clothing, blankets, tent coverings, and other necessities. Bison tendons were used for bowstrings and thread for sewing coverings together.

Westward expansion contributed to the near extinction of bison in the West. Railroad crews shot bison for food and sport as well as to prevent them from damaging the tracks. Bison were so important to Plains Indians that during the Indian Wars the US government quietly encouraged the slaughtering of the herds to rob the Plains Indians of their means of livelihood. In 1867 an army colonel told a hunter, "Kill every buffalo you can. Every buffalo dead is an Indian gone." By 1900 the huge herds of the Great Plains had become nearly extinct. Some historians believe that the destruction of the bison was more important in the conquest of Native American land than any military campaign.

The Plains Indians were increasingly protective of their lands as frontiersmen encroached on them, and they soon learned that the government's word could not be trusted. Even when government officials intended to be fair, their unfamiliarity with Native American cultures sometimes caused them to make fatal errors. For example, they failed to understand that few chiefs had the authority to bind all their people to a treaty—treaties that the chiefs themselves often did not understand. Many Plains Indians did not want to abandon their tribal lands. Even those who agreed to move to the reservations rebelled when they saw the poor quality of the reservation land. (The government tended to establish reservations on arid, barren land that was often useless.) Misunderstanding, greed, force, and resistance resulted in bloody conflict on the Great Plains.

## Indian Wars

From the 1850s to the 1870s the US Army, sent to protect settlers from attacks, fought a series of campaigns against the Plains Indians. The Indian Wars were brutal, bloody affairs that illustrated tactics of total war. Both sides committed horrible deeds and slaughtered without mercy. In 1862 Dakota Sioux warriors killed hundreds of settlers—men, women, and children—in New Ulm, Minnesota. Some bands of Native Americans attacked wagon trains and settlements that crossed through their lands and hunting grounds. United States soldiers at times destroyed crops and livestock and killed Native American women and children. In 1864 conflicts broke out in Colorado between miners and the Cheyenne and Arapaho. A regiment under Colonel John Chivington killed over one hundred Native Americans, including women and children, who were seeking to live peacefully under Chief Black Kettle's leadership at Sand Creek.

▼ Native Americans on the Great Plains

▼ Sitting Bull

## Sitting Bull Speaks

*What treaty that the whites ever made with us red men have they kept? Not one. When I was a boy the Sioux owned the world. The sun rose and set in their lands. They sent ten thousand horsemen to battle. Where are the warriors today? Who slew them? Where are our lands? Who owns them? What white man can say I ever stole his lands or a penny of his money?*

### 🔍 Analyzing Sources

According to Sitting Bull, why have the Sioux declined during his lifetime?

Settlers and miners traveling through Wyoming to reach Montana disturbed Lakota Sioux and Cheyenne hunting grounds. During "Red Cloud's War" (1866–68) in the Wyoming-Montana region, Captain William Fetterman bragged that with eighty men he could ride through the entire Sioux nation; but when he was ambushed near Fort Phil Kearny by a large Sioux war party under Lakota Sioux chief Red Cloud, Fetterman and all his troops were killed. As the conflict continued, the Sioux won every battle. The US government ended the conflict with the **Treaty of Fort Laramie** (1868) that reduced Sioux lands established by previous treaties and created a new reservation that included the Black Hills (in present-day South Dakota), regarded by the Sioux as sacred. Additionally, the treaty guaranteed a portion of land outside the reservation to be free from white settlement and removed troops from the forts on that land. Some Sioux leaders signed the treaty and moved to the new Great Sioux Reservation, but some refused to sign the treaty and lived on the land outside the reservation.

### The Great Sioux War

The climax of the Indian Wars, commonly known as the **Great Sioux War**, occurred between 1876 and 1877. The fame of this war lies partly in the fact that it was the last great Indian War and partly in the personalities involved: cavalry Lieutenant Colonel **George Armstrong Custer** and Lakota Sioux leaders **Sitting Bull** and **Crazy Horse**.

Ohio-born George Armstrong Custer had risen from the rank of lieutenant to major general during the Civil War. Reduced to the rank of colonel when the army shrank after the war, Custer became a renowned fighter against the Native Americans. Typical of his method was the Battle of the Washita River (1868) in what is today Oklahoma. Coming upon a Cheyenne camp on the banks of the river, Custer divided his force and attacked, winning victory over the surprised Indians.

After a group led by Custer discovered gold in the Black Hills in 1874, settlers overran Sioux lands to mine for gold. The US government failed to stop these prospectors and instead unsuccessfully attempted to negotiate access to the Black Hills. By 1876 the Great Sioux War was underway. Military commanders, including Colonel Custer and General George Crook, attempted to subdue the Sioux living outside the reservation to pressure those on the reservation to give up the Black Hills. Opposing them were Cheyenne and Sioux under leaders Sitting Bull and Crazy Horse, who had refused to sign the Treaty of Fort Laramie. Sitting Bull was primarily a political leader, and Crazy Horse acted as the commander of the Sioux warriors. Under Crazy Horse's leadership, the Sioux and Cheyenne warriors fought a unified, well-organized campaign.

▼ The Crazy Horse Memorial in the Black Hills, South Dakota

In present-day Montana, General Crook fought the Cheyenne and Sioux at the Battle of the Rosebud and withdrew afterward to his army camp in Wyoming for supplies and reinforcements. The major battle of the Sioux War took place about a week later. On June 25, 1876, Custer's cavalry regiment came upon a huge camp of Sioux and Cheyenne on the banks of the Little Bighorn River in Montana. Sitting Bull and Crazy Horse had noted his approach and were prepared to meet him. Custer's scouts from the Crow and Arikara, tribes that were enemies of the Sioux, had seen glimpses of the camp and warned the colonel that the Sioux had more warriors than the soldiers had bullets. Custer brushed these warnings aside. As he had done at the Washita River eight years before, Custer divided his forces to attack the Indians from two directions. One force attacked the camp head-on and was soon driven back with heavy losses. Custer took some two hundred men and swept north of the camp. The Native Americans fought with overwhelming numbers. Approximately 1,500 warriors attacked the two hundred soldiers. Custer and all his force lost their lives in the **Battle of the Little Bighorn** in less than an hour's time. That defeat became known as Custer's Last Stand.

▼ (inset) George Armstrong Custer; (below) Custer's last stand at the Battle of the Little Big Horn

Shocked by the defeat, the US government quickly sent more men and supplies west to defeat the Native Americans. Within months of Custer's defeat, the army had forced the resistant groups to accept peace on the government's terms. Most Sioux went sadly to the reservation, which because of a new negotiation, no longer included the Black Hills. Crazy Horse, after giving himself up, died in a scuffle with soldiers as they attempted to put him in a guardhouse. Sitting Bull fled to Canada for a time but eventually returned to live on a reservation. In 1890 he was accused of encouraging Indians to rebel in the Ghost Dance movement, in which Native Americans envisioned the restoration of the bison and Native American lands. Some who participated in this movement claimed that they received special powers to kill whites, and some claimed that the ghost shirts worn at the dance could stop bullets. Sitting Bull was killed in a fight between Native American police, who had arrested him, and Sioux warriors who attempted to rescue him.

On December 29, 1890, just two weeks after the death of Sitting Bull, the army tried to disarm and capture a band of Sioux near Wounded Knee Creek in South Dakota. In the process, someone fired a shot. Versions of the story vary, and it is still unclear how the fighting began. When it was over, twenty-five soldiers and more than one hundred fifty Native Americans (half of them women and children) were dead. The **Wounded Knee Massacre** was a tragic conclusion to the Indian Wars.

▲ The dead being buried after the massacre at Wounded Knee

The fate of the Sioux was typical of what happened to other nations of the West. Some Native Americans still resisted the idea of living an impoverished life on the barren reservations. Some fought, such as the Apache leader Geronimo, who with a small band of warriors for several years frustrated the army's attempts to force them onto a reservation. Eventually, he surrendered and died several years later in captivity. Although considered a prisoner, he was allowed to participate in Wild West shows and expositions.

◄ Chief Joseph

## Chief Joseph Speaks

In an interview published in 1879, Chief Joseph explained his perspective on the US government's handling of Native American lands.

> *If we ever owned the land we own it still, for we never sold it. In the treaty councils the commissioners have claimed that our country had been sold to the Government. Suppose a white man should come to me and say, 'Joseph, I like your horses, and I want to buy them.' I say to him, 'No, my horses suit me, I will not sell them.' Then he goes to my neighbor, and says to him: 'Joseph has some good horses. I want to buy them, but he refuses to sell.' My neighbor answers, 'Pay me the money, and I will sell you Joseph's horses.' The white man returns to me, and says, 'Joseph, I have bought your horses, and you must let me have them.' If we sold our lands to the Government, this is the way they were bought.*
>
> *On account of the treaty made by the other bands of the Nez Perces, the white men claimed my lands. We were troubled greatly by white men crowding over the line. Some of these were good men, and we lived on peaceful terms with them, but they were not all good.*

In 1877 the government tried to force the Nez Perce leader **Chief Joseph** and his followers onto a reservation. Chief Joseph and his tribe lived in the Wallowa Valley in what is now Idaho. Joseph did not want to leave his land, but he hated war. While he was trying to organize his people for the move, a handful of young warriors attacked and killed some white settlers. With little hope of peace now, Joseph prepared to flee and—if necessary—to fight. Joseph took his people east, eventually deciding to escape to Canada. In 108 days, Joseph marched more than 700 Indians—most of them women, children, and old men—nearly 1,400 miles. In eight separate battles and skirmishes, the Nez Perce defeated contingents of four separate cavalry units. Joseph refused to fight a savage war, however. He forbade the killing of women and children and the taking of scalps from the dead. Finally, on September 30, 1877, the US cavalry, led by General Oliver O. Howard, former head of the Freedmen's Bureau, overtook Joseph's band just forty miles from the Canadian border. Outnumbered and numbed by a chilling cold, Chief Joseph surrendered. Joseph was eventually settled on a reservation in Washington State, where he died on September 21, 1904.

## Reforms

In 1881 Helen Hunt Jackson published *A Century of Dishonor*, a work portraying the government's ruthless and often dishonorable dealings with the Indians. Jackson's book, combined with the decreasing threat of the Plains Indians, inspired some sympathy for the Native Americans' plight.

Some believed it would be in the best interest of the Native Americans for them to assimilate into "American" culture by learning English, giving up traditional cultural practices, becoming US citizens, and supporting themselves on individual farms. In 1887 Congress passed the **Dawes Act**, which allowed Native American lands to be parceled out to Native American heads of households and individuals. Heads of households received 160 acres, while single adults received 80, and minors 40. Participants were granted land and US citizenship if they "adopted the habits of civilized life." Supporters of the act hoped that its promotion of citizenship, with an emphasis on individualism and Western civilization, would help end the abuses that had occurred under the treaty system and that Native Americans would no longer need to rely on the federal government's protection. However, one critic, Senator Henry M. Teller from Colorado, asserted that "the real aim of this bill is to get at the Indian lands and open them up to settlement. The provisions for the apparent benefit of the Indian are but the pretext to get at his lands and occupy them. . . . [If] this were done in the name of greed, it would be bad enough; but to do it in the name of humanity . . . is infinitely worse."

Attempting to absorb Native Americans into mainstream American life, the Dawes Act reflected a continued misunderstanding of Native American cultures and was problematic for several reasons. Most tribes who were given lands had been hunters and gatherers, not farmers. The allotted lands were undesired by settlers because they were dry and could not support a family. The act tended to break down the unity of the tribes. Many Native Americans were not used to private ownership of land and relied on extended family and the tribe for social structure. Included in the Dawes Act was a provision for opening surplus land to settlers.

Some settlers also bought land from Native Americans who were unhappy with the conditions of the land. Dealings often involved cheating the Native Americans, impoverishing many. When oil was discovered on Native American land, speculators bought even more of the land. In the 1920s several wealthy Osage in Oklahoma were murdered for access to their oil holdings.

## Treatment *of* Native Americans

In 1877 President Rutherford B. Hayes said, "Many, if not most, of our Indian wars have had their origin in broken promises and acts of injustice on our part." In 1878 General Philip Sheridan commented, "We took away their country and their means of support, broke up their mode of living, their habits of life, introduced disease and decay among them, and it was for this and against this that they made war. Could anyone expect less?" General Nelson A. Miles sent a telegram from South Dakota to Washington, DC, on December 19, 1890. He described problems facing the Sioux, the Cheyenne, and other groups in the area by stating, "It [The difficult Indian problem] requires the fulfillment by Congress of the treaty obligations that the Indians were entreated and coerced into signing. They signed away a valuable portion of their reservation, and it is now occupied by white people, for which they have received nothing. They understood that ample provision would be made for their support; instead, their supplies have been reduced, and much of the time they have been living on half and two-thirds rations. . . . The [dissatisfaction] is wide spread."

◀ Native American boys at the Carlisle Indian School, 1890

The effort at "Americanization" included the establishment of a number of boarding schools, where children were required to speak English, adopt an English name, and wear American-style clothing and hair styles. Like the Dawes Act, many missionaries and reformers had good intentions, but the results often hurt the Native Americans. Although the schools provided Christian teaching, many equated conversion and adherence to the Christian life with adoption of Western customs. Native American children, often separated from parents, were coerced to give up traditional languages and customs, and tribal unity continued to break down. Additionally, many of the schools lacked sufficient resources for the children, leading to neglect and abuse.

In the twentieth century, the US government tried to remedy some of the wrongs done to the Native Americans. In 1924 Congress gave Native Americans full citizenship. In 1934, to preserve the remaining Native American lands, the **Indian Reorganization Act** halted the allotment program of the Dawes Act and gave the tribes limited self-government on their reservations. Congress also made it easier for Native Americans to seek damages for past violations of treaties and other agreements. These acts, however, failed to address all the injustices that Native Americans had suffered.

### Comprehension Check 13.3

1. All of the following are true of conflicts with Native Americans except ____.
   A US Army leaders sometimes used brutal tactics on Native Americans
   B Native Americans refused to attack white settlers
   C settlers and miners encroached on Native American lands

2. Native Americans, under leaders Sitting Bull and ____ defeated Colonel George Custer's troops at the Battle of the Little Bighorn.
   A Crazy Horse
   B Geronimo
   C Red Cloud

3. The ____ granted acres of land to Native Americans to farm.
   A Treaty of Fort Laramie
   B Indian Reorganization Act
   C Dawes Act

### MAKING CONNECTIONS

4. What was a motivation for attempts to "Americanize" Native Americans? What were the shortcomings of the Dawes Act and boarding schools for Native American children?

# CHAPTER 13 REVIEW

## Chapter Summary

### 13.1 Rails, Miners, Cowboys, and Lawmen

- Population growth in the West as a result of the California gold rush led to demand for the construction of a transcontinental railroad. The Union Pacific and Central Pacific Railroads received government loans and land grants to construct the first transcontinental line, which greatly reduced travel times to the West.

- Miners searching for gold, silver, and other valuable minerals were some of the first to move to the West. Mining towns developed quickly but also disappeared when all the minerals were gone.

- After the Civil War, the value of Texas longhorn cattle increased, and cattle ranchers profited by having cowboys take their herds on the "long drive" to the railroads in the Great Plains. The meatpacking industry developed to process beef and other meats. Open-range ranching ended for many reasons, including a drop in beef prices, overgrazing, cold winters, challenges from sheep herders, the fencing of land by farmers, and new railroads in Texas and the West.

- The rapid development of western towns and the individualism of many of its settlers demonstrated man's sinful nature and made maintaining law and order difficult in the "Wild West."

**TERMS**

Union Pacific Railroad
Central Pacific Railroad
Comstock Lode
long drive
Chisholm Trail
Jesse James
Wyatt Earp

**TERMS**

Homestead Act of 1862
Morrill Land Grant Act of 1862
Sooners
Grange
Farmers' Alliance

### 13.2 Settlers and Sodbusters

- To encourage settlement on the Great Plains, the Homestead Act of 1862 gave 160 acres to those who promised to live on and improve the land. The Morrill Land Grant Act of 1862 provided land for establishing schools.

- The government opened land in Indian Territory (Oklahoma) to white settlement, resulting in the Oklahoma land rush.

- Homesteaders on the Plains faced many hardships but were able to overcome them through hard work and determination.

## Chapter Summary

**13.3  Conflicts with Native Americans**

- To protect settlers and miners from attack by Plains Indians, the US Army fought Native Americans and negotiated treaties that attempted to move them onto reservations. During the Great Sioux War, Lieutenant Colonel George Custer's entire force died in the Battle of the Little Bighorn. The army eventually forced Plains Indians onto reservations.

- Inspired by Helen Hunt Jackson's *A Century of Dishonor*, reform efforts attempted to improve conditions for Native Americans. The Dawes Act sought to "Americanize" Native Americans by offering citizenship to those who farmed plots of land and adopted "civilized" habits. The act often distributed poor-quality land and tended to break down tribal unity. In the twentieth century, Native Americans were granted full citizenship, and the Indian Organization Act ended the measures of the Dawes Act.

**TERMS**

Plains Indians

Treaty of Fort Laramie

Great Sioux War

George Armstrong Custer

Sitting Bull

Crazy Horse

Battle of the Little Bighorn

Wounded Knee Massacre

Chief Joseph

Dawes Act

Indian Reorganization Act

## Chapter Review Questions

### RECALL

1. Where did the people who settled in the West come from?

2. What two railroad companies built the first transcontinental railroad?

3. What were three important mining sites in the West that were discovered after the California gold rush?

4. What agency was hired by the Wells Fargo freight company to protect its stagecoaches?

5. Name three famous outlaws and two lawmen of the Wild West.

6. What was the difference between "Boomers" and "Sooners"?

7. What were two organizations that were founded to represent the needs and interests of farmers?

8. Who were the two Lakota Sioux leaders who were involved in the Great Sioux War against the US Army?

9. At what battle were George Armstrong Custer and his force killed?

10. What Apache leader fought to keep from being forced onto a reservation?

### UNDERSTAND

11. How did the government support the construction of the first transcontinental railroad?

12. How did the transcontinental railroad affect settlement of the American West?

13. What effects did miners have on the settlement of the West?

14. What was the purpose of cattle drives, and why did they develop after the Civil War?

15. What was the role of the cowboys on a cattle drive, and what difficulties did they face?

16. What innovations to meatpacking were made by Gustavus Swift and Philip Armour?

17. What were three causes of the end of open-range ranching?

18. How did the Homestead Act of 1862 distribute land to settlers? What other government acts encouraged settlement and farming in the Great Plains and the West?

19. What caused the Oklahoma land rush in 1889?

20. What were two character traits that helped settlers overcome hardships on the Great Plains?

21. What were four hardships that settlers on the Great Plains faced?

22. How did settlers on the Great Plains overcome the shortage of trees and water?

23. What were two new tools that made farming on the Great Plains easier?

24. What were two ways homesteaders on the Great Plains dealt with isolation and loneliness?

25. How did settlement by miners and farmers in the Great Plains and the West lead to conflicts with Native Americans?

26. What uses did the Plains Indians have for bison, and how was the bison population affected by western settlement?

27. What led to the Great Sioux War? What was the outcome of the war?

28. What was the Ghost Dance movement?

29. Who was Chief Joseph? What led to war between the Nez Perce and the US cavalry?

30. What belief about what was best for Native Americans led to the Dawes Act? How did the Dawes Act attempt to impose that belief on Native Americans?

31. How did the US government attempt in the twentieth century to remedy some of the wrongs done to Native Americans?

## THINK ABOUT IT

32. What positive aspects of freedom and individualism can be seen in the settlement of the Old West? How did freedom, individualism, and justice clash in the Wild West?

33. What do you think may have been positive effects of the Dawes Act and other reforms for Native Americans? What were three reasons these reforms failed to meet their expectations?

▼ A miner moving to the West

# 14 Age of Imperialism

14.1 Populism
14.2 International Expansion
14.3 The Spanish-American War
14.4 The Turn of the Century

▲ Battle of Manila Bay

As a result of the westward growth of the late 1800s, some declared that the American frontier was now closed and that Manifest Destiny had been fulfilled. As the nation grew and became stronger, some Americans wanted to extend its influence to more distant lands. However, seeking such growth challenged the equality, freedom, and individualism of other peoples.

## 14.1 Populism

**What was the Populist Party?**

Industrialism and innovation caused important changes in American agriculture. Improved farm machinery and methods increased production and made agricultural commodities an important export. Yet, such innovations also created problems for farmers. They could not adjust quickly to supply and demand because of the seasonal nature of farming. Too much or too little rain affected harvests. Railroads, the essential link between farmers and markets, charged high shipping costs, taking away a large portion of the farmers' profits. Abundant production itself became a problem because high yields kept prices low. High tariffs also affected farmers as many countries who exported their products to the United States would retaliate by raising their own tariffs on imports from America, and those items were often farm products.

### The Populist Party

By the late 1880s, farmers felt that both the Republicans and the Democrats favored industry and banks over farmers and that neither party adequately addressed their concerns. The Farmers' Alliance (see Chapter 13) had been successful in promoting Democratic and Republican candidates who supported its goals; however, it had been unable to get legislation passed in Congress to achieve those goals. Farmers believed the solution was to form their own party. In 1892 over 1,000 delegates representing farmers and laborers met in Omaha, Nebraska, and formed the People's Party, also called the **Populist Party**. Its goals were based on **populism** (appealing to the common people). They supported a long list of reforms such as government ownership and regulation of railroads and telegraphs, the direct election of US senators by the people rather than by state legislatures, government loans for farmers, and a graduated income tax (where higher earners pay a higher percentage of their income in taxes than lower earners). To broaden their appeal to include unions and industrial workers, they also supported an eight-hour workday for factory workers and immigration restrictions to decrease competition with immigrant labor.

However, the main issue that dominated the Populist movement was currency policy. Prior to the Civil War, the government had minted both gold and silver coins. During the Civil War, Congress issued paper money called "greenbacks" (see Chapter 10). These greenbacks were not backed by gold or silver, but simply by the government's promise to honor them. Therefore, most Americans saw greenbacks as less valuable than "hard money" (gold and silver or notes redeemable in gold or silver). In addition, the more greenbacks that were printed, the less valuable they became, causing inflation. After the war, bankers wanted to get rid of the greenbacks and return to basing money entirely on gold. Yet "easy money" advocates wanted not only to continue using greenbacks but also to print more. Struggling with debt, farmers and the lower classes liked greenbacks and silver, because the more money that was in circulation, the more everybody would have. Wages would rise, so it would be easier to pay debts.

**GUIDING QUESTIONS**

- What were the goals of the Populist Party?
- How did the Populist Party impact the election of 1896?

▲ A $1 "greenback" issued 1862–1863

▲ US silver dollars (discontinued after 1934)

But in 1873 the government had stopped buying silver to make coins. Just when the demand for silver had dropped, the available supply of it had climbed due to silver mining in the West. The result was that the value of silver plummeted, hurting western silver miners. The government had also reduced the number of greenbacks in circulation, although it pledged to begin redeeming them for their face value in gold. When these government actions reduced the amount of currency in circulation, farmers were negatively affected.

In an attempt to alleviate the depression that had begun in 1873 (see Chapter 11), Congress passed the Bland-Allison Act in 1878, which required the US Treasury to purchase $2–$4 million per month in silver, returning the nation to a bimetal (silver and gold) standard. However, farmers continued to struggle with debts and falling prices, and along with the mining industry, pressed Congress for further action. In 1890 Congress passed the Sherman Silver Purchase Act, which required the Treasury to purchase an additional 4.5 million ounces of silver a month. This was the result of a compromise: the Republicans agreed to the Silver Purchase Act favored by Democrats, and the Democrats supported the highly protective McKinley Tariff (see Chapter 12) favored by Republicans.

Populists felt that these acts did not go far enough toward increasing the money supply. They advocated for "**free silver**," the unlimited production of silver coins. Such purposeful inflation would make more money available to the hard-pressed workingman, result in higher prices for crops, and make it easier to pay debts. However, inflation would also raise prices on goods that farmers needed to buy.

Although the party was new, the Populists' presidential candidate, James B. Weaver, polled more than a million votes in the election of 1892. In fact, the new third party carried four western states and showed remarkable strength in the otherwise solidly Democratic South.

## The Election of 1896

The depression that had begun with the Panic of '93 (see Chapter 12) was still underway as the parties met to nominate their candidates for the election of 1896. The Republicans nominated former congressman and governor **William McKinley** from Ohio. McKinley had the support of most business and finance leaders because of his support for the gold standard and high tariffs (having sponsored the highly protective McKinley Tariff of 1890).

Grover Cleveland's chances of being renominated by the Democrats in 1896 were hurt by the depression as well as his pro-gold standard position. When the Democrats arrived in Chicago for their convention, the place was abuzz with talk of free silver and the inevitable question of who would get the nomination and stamp out the "goldbugs." The answer was a thirty-six-year-old former Nebraska congressman named **William Jennings Bryan**.

▲ William McKinley

Bryan was called "the Great Commoner" because of his genuine sympathy for the common man. In Chicago he made a fiery appeal for economic deliverance through free silver. Bryan stood before the convention and declared to a sea of rapt faces, "I come to speak to you in defense of a cause as holy as the cause of liberty—the cause of humanity." The government must have a social conscience, he cried. Its voice must be the people's voice, and the people would be heard. Bryan and other Populists, like Andrew Jackson in the previous era, saw the world as a struggle between the "righteous" people and those who supposedly threatened the people, including bankers and industrialists. He concluded,

> *Having behind us the producing masses of this nation and the world, supported by the commercial interests, the laboring interests, and the toilers everywhere, we will answer their [the business interests'] demand for a gold standard by saying to them: "You shall not press down upon the brow of labor this crown of thorns; you shall not crucify mankind upon a cross of gold."*

Bryan's "Cross of Gold" speech helped him win the Democratic nomination. The Populist Party also gave its support to Bryan. The campaign that followed was a study in contrasts. Leading a cash-poor campaign (Republicans outspent Democrats as much as twenty to one), Bryan went on a whirlwind tour of the country. He made hundreds of stops during an 18,000-mile trek and was seen and heard by audiences totaling nearly five million. McKinley, however, stayed home. In a carefully orchestrated effort, McKinley ran a "front porch campaign" from his home in Canton, Ohio. Trainloads of select audiences were given all-expense-paid trips to Canton to hear McKinley read a prepared script, while hundreds of speakers fanned out across the country to promote him.

▲ William Jennings Bryan

▼ (left) Bryan, speaking from the train, at a whistlestop on his campaign trail; (right) William McKinley's "front porch" campaign in Canton, Ohio

On Election Day, Bryan polled six and a half million votes, but McKinley got more than seven million. The influence of the Populist Party declined, but other groups would take up many of its reforms in the coming years.

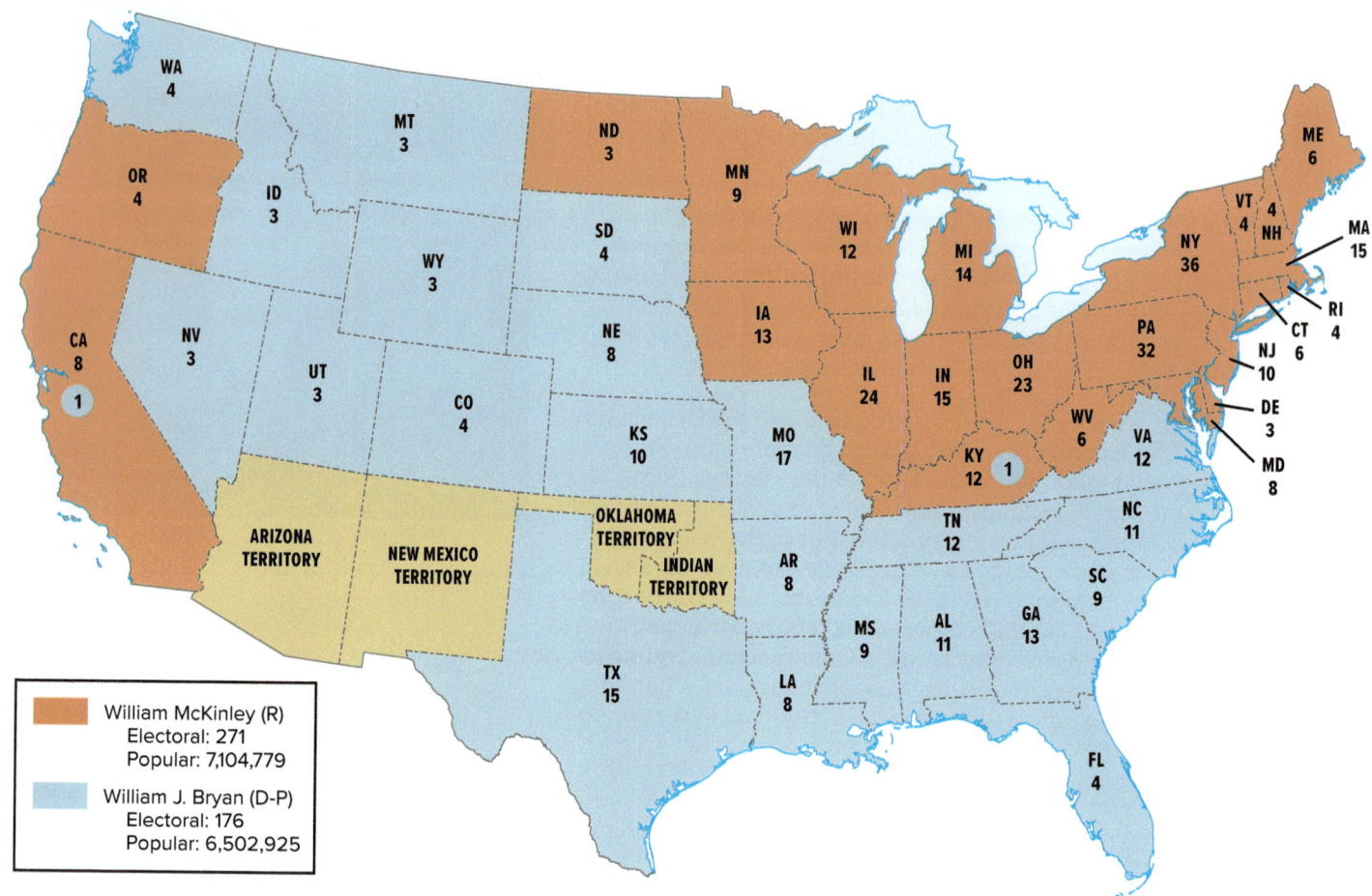

William McKinley (R)
Electoral: 271
Popular: 7,104,779

William J. Bryan (D-P)
Electoral: 176
Popular: 6,502,925

## Comprehension Check 14.1

1. The People's or Populist Party represented the interests of laborers and _____.

   A bankers

   B farmers

   C immigrants

2. The Populist Party supported the following measures except _____.

   A direct election of senators

   B government ownership and regulation of railroads

   C reduction of greenbacks in circulation as currency

3. _____ won the Democratic nomination with Populist support in the election of 1896.

   A William Jennings Bryan

   B Grover Cleveland

   C William McKinley

   D James B. Weaver

### MAKING CONNECTIONS

4. Explain one reason some people wanted to decrease greenback and silver currency and one reason others wanted to increase these currencies.

# International Expansion

GUIDING QUESTIONS

- Why did the United States begin to acquire new territories?
- What new Pacific territories did the United States gain?
- How were foreign missions and America's international expansion related?

After the Mexican War in 1848 (see Chapter 8), the United States was focused more on sectional conflict, the Civil War, Reconstruction, settlement of the West, and industrialization than on foreign affairs and international expansion. There were some foreign issues, however, that arose during the time of the Civil War that the United States had to address.

During the Civil War, France had mounted one of the most serious challenges to the Monroe Doctrine in American history. France, Great Britain, and Spain had sent soldiers to Mexico in the 1860s to force Mexico to repay its debts to those nations. After Mexico repaid the debts, the British and Spanish had withdrawn their troops while the French troops had remained. Napoleon III (nephew of Napoleon Bonaparte) installed the Austrian archduke as the Mexican ruler in 1864 and gave him the name Maximilian I. Napoleon III ignored American protests, particularly since the United States was distracted by the Civil War. After the war, however, President Johnson stationed 50,000 troops by the Rio Grande. Secretary of State William Seward then gave Napoleon III an ultimatum to withdraw the French soldiers from Mexico. The French, worried by the American troops and plagued by troubles in Europe, quietly withdrew. The United States had successfully upheld the Monroe Doctrine. Having lost the support of the French, Maximilian was executed by a Mexican firing squad in 1867.

▲ French attack on the Mexican Fort San Xavier in 1863

After its confrontation with France, the United States sought to settle three longstanding differences with Great Britain. First, the United States sought compensation for the damages its merchant fleet had suffered during the Civil War from commerce raiders. Because many of these ships had been built in British shipyards, the US government considered Britain partly responsible for the damage caused by these raiders. Second, the United States and Britain had been arguing since the 1840s over who owned a group of islands between Vancouver Island and the state of Washington. Third, the United States and Canada had long disagreed over fishing rights off both coasts of North America.

The Treaty of Washington (1871) settled these matters by setting up international tribunals to deal with each question. One tribunal awarded the United States more than $15 million in damages from Britain for the destruction caused by the commerce raiders. Another tribunal awarded possession of the islands off Vancouver to the United States. A third required the United States to pay Canada more than $5 million for special fishing privileges. The treaty promoted greater friendship and cooperation between the United States, Britain, and Canada.

# Imperialism

While the United States was focused on its own domestic issues, in the late 1800s the Germans, Dutch, French, and British were establishing more colonies around the world. The process of larger, more powerful nations gaining economic and political control over weaker nations (which usually became colonies) was called **imperialism**. This process brought greater wealth and power to those strong nations. British imperialism in the late 1800s was so extensive that it was rightly said that "the sun never sets on the British Empire," which included possessions on six continents.

As Americans witnessed the benefits of empire for European powers, some made several arguments in favor of creating an American empire. First, it would enhance the nation's prestige and pride. Because other nations were creating empires, and the United States wanted to be seen as an important nation, it too should create an empire. Second, an empire would increase the nation's power. A strong military would be needed to subdue and govern those under America's rule and protect the empire from foreign adversaries. For an overseas empire, a strong navy as well as military bases overseas would be of particular importance. US naval officer Alfred Thayer Mahan wrote an influential book promoting the need for naval power to protect the nation's merchant fleet and expand its trade interests around the world.

**Major World Empires, 1914**

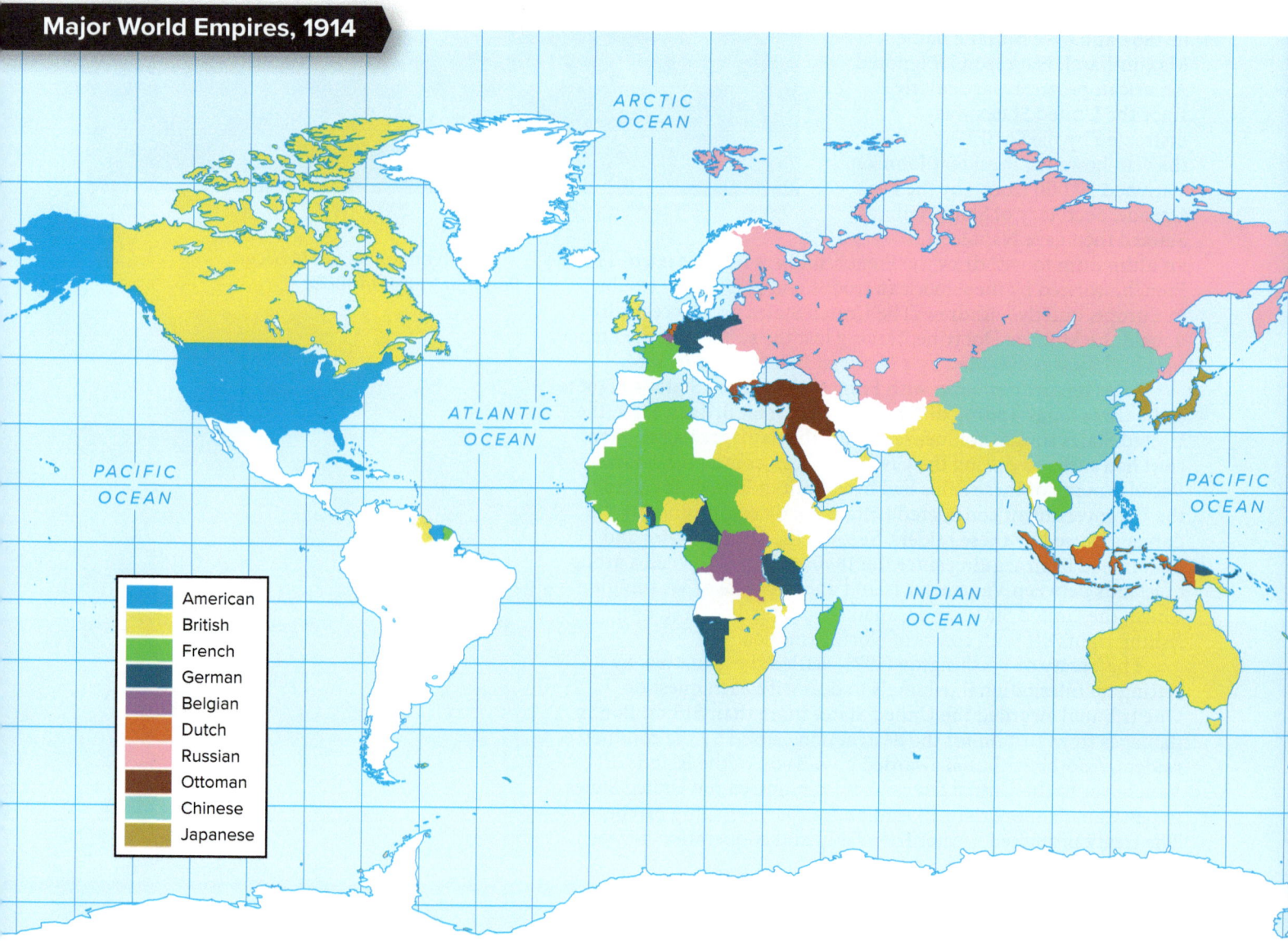

American
British
French
German
Belgian
Dutch
Russian
Ottoman
Chinese
Japanese

Third, an empire would increase the nation's wealth. By 1880 American farmers and industries were producing more than they could sell at home and wanted markets for their products. Some began looking for new sources of raw materials as well. Just as America had served as a source of raw materials and a market for goods when it was a British colony, new American colonies could serve as a source of raw materials and markets for goods for the United States. Fourth, many saw imperialism as a way to bring Western civilization to other nations of the world. British author Rudyard Kipling referred to the "white man's burden" to share the fruit of his culture—education, medical care, industry, better farming methods, and technology—with "less civilized" nations. Fifth, some argued that imperialism allowed for the spread of Christianity by opening countries to missionaries.

Others were opposed to American imperial expansion. They questioned the motives of prestige and power, which were often based on the principles of Social Darwinism. Was it right to apply "survival of the fittest" to justify one nation taking over another? Did it contradict the American values of equality and freedom? They also questioned whether an empire was necessary for increasing the nation's wealth. The United States lacked few natural resources in its own territory. It could purchase materials it lacked without needing to dominate other nations for their resources. Also, imperialism often led to exploitation of the colonies, as the mother country would send its own citizens to oversee the colonies' industries, hire local workers for low wages, and send the profits back to the mother country. The weaker nation often lost its land, its independence, and sometimes its national identity.

Finally, while imperialism sometimes brought improvements to the colonies, including better medical treatment, development of natural resources, improvements in education, and better roads, bridges, and railroads, the work of civilizing others often included treating those receiving aid as inferiors and was sometimes based on ideas of racial superiority. The subtitle of Darwin's *On the Origin of Species* was "The Preservation of Favoured Races in the Struggle for Life." He believed that civilized nations, composed of superior races, would replace uncivilized and inferior ones through natural selection. American minister Josiah Strong, echoing Darwin, argued that Anglo-Saxons were a race of unequaled energy and wealth and that it was their duty to spread their institutions, as well as his misguided version of Christianity, across the world.

▲ Political cartoon depicting imperialism, 1885 with "The World's Plunderers"—Germany, England, and Russia—grabbing what they can of Africa and Asia

## Arguments For and Against Imperialism

| For Imperialism | Against Imperialism |
| --- | --- |
| Enhances prestige and pride Increases power | Reflects Social Darwinism |
| Acquires natural resources | Resources could be purchased |
| Spreads Western civilization | Leads to exploitation |
| Spreads Christianity | Interferes with mission work |

Pacific Islands

ALASKA

CONTINENTAL USA

MIDWAY ISLANDS

HAWAII

PACIFIC OCEAN

AMERICAN SAMOA

# Pacific Expansion

## *Alaska*

Through a variety of circumstances, the United States began acquiring foreign land shortly after the Civil War. The largest American acquisition came with Russia's sale of Alaska in 1867 during the presidency of Andrew Johnson. When Secretary of State William Seward announced the purchase, many Americans—believing Alaska to be only an empty wasteland of snow and ice—called the area "**Seward's Folly**" or "Seward's Icebox." Still, at a cost of only $7.2 million (less than two cents an acre), Alaska seemed a bargain, and the treaty of purchase passed the Senate easily.

Within a few years, Alaska had proved its value to the United States. First, gold was discovered in 1896 near the Yukon River, bringing thousands of miners to the area. Later prospectors found silver, copper, and oil, making it a source of enormous wealth for the nation. Fishing also became important to Alaska's economy. In 1959 Alaska became the forty-ninth state.

## *The Midway Islands and Samoa*

Increased trade with Asia required the United States to find ports in the Pacific for refueling merchant ships. In 1859 American sailors discovered and claimed some uninhabited islands approximately halfway between North America and Asia, and they became known as the Midway Islands. The United States annexed the Midway Islands in 1867.

By the late 1800s many American, British, and German ships were stopping in Pago Pago in the Samoa Islands for refueling. In 1889 the United States joined Britain and Germany in a joint protectorate of the Samoan islands. Disagreements among the three nations, however, led to the division of the islands between Germany and the United States in 1899. The eastern islands later became the US territory of American Samoa.

## Queen Liliuokalani *on* US Annexation *of* Hawaii

After the overthrow of the monarchy, Queen Liliuokalani and others met with President Cleveland and senators to petition against annexation. A few months before the annexation was approved by Congress, under McKinley's administration, the queen published *Hawaii's Story by Hawaii's Queen*, which she concluded with this appeal to the American people:

*Is this [imperialistic] prospect satisfactory to a people who rely upon self-government for their liberties, and whose guaranty of liberty and autonomy to the whole western hemisphere . . . has made any attack upon it practically impossible to the statesmen and rulers of armed empires? There is little question but that the United States could become a successful rival of the European nations in the race for conquest. . . . But is such an ambition laudable [praiseworthy]? Is such a departure from its established principles patriotic or politic [wise]? . . .*

*. . . I have had the opportunity to know the real American people, quite distinct from those who have assumed this honored name when it suited their selfish ends. . . .*

*Oh, honest Americans, as Christians hear me for my down-trodden people! . . . Do not covet the little vineyard of Naboth's, so far from your shores, lest the punishment of Ahab fall upon you, if not in your day, in that of your children, for "be not deceived, God is not mocked." The people to whom your fathers told of the living God, and taught to call "Father," and whom the sons now seek to despoil and destroy, are crying aloud to Him in their time of trouble; and He will keep His promise, and will listen to the voices of His Hawaiian children lamenting for their homes.*

## Hawaii

Another Pacific addition to the United States was Hawaii. The Hawaiian Islands had been an important supply point for whalers, merchant ships, and warships since the 1700s. In the early 1800s, American missionaries had come to the islands, and in 1840 Christianity became the official religion of the kingdom. Soon Americans set up sugar plantations and created a thriving sugar industry that dominated the economy of Hawaii and helped the islands to prosper. In 1875 the United States eliminated tariffs on sugar imported from Hawaii; in 1887 the United States was granted the right to use Pearl Harbor as a naval base.

In 1887 American businessmen forced the Hawaiian king to accept a new constitution greatly limiting the king's power, taking voting rights away from most Hawaiians and immigrants from Asia, and giving voting rights to wealthy Americans and Europeans who were not Hawaiian citizens.

The McKinley Tariff of 1890 eliminated tariffs on all foreign sugar, but also subsidized US farmers two cents per pound of sugar produced, giving an advantage to sugar grown in the United States. American sugar producers in Hawaii pushed for annexation by the United States so that their sugar would be considered domestic in order to compete successfully.

In 1891 Queen Liliuokalani took the throne. She tried to reestablish native control of the islands and limit the power of the Americans by revoking the voting privileges of noncitizens. In 1893 the business owners revolted against "Queen Lil." With the help of a US Marine force, she was overthrown. The new government, led by Sanford Dole, asked to be annexed to the United States. President Grover Cleveland, however, refused to support the uprising, and he and the majority in Congress blocked annexation of the islands because they believed the queen had been removed illegally. Hawaii therefore existed for several years as an independent republic, with Sanford Dole as its president.

In 1898 the United States was at war in the Pacific with Spain (discussed later in this chapter), and Pearl Harbor was a key supply station. Fearing Japanese annexation of Hawaii, Congress voted to annex the islands and Hawaii became an American territory. In 1959 Hawaii became the fiftieth state.

### Did You Know?

Wealthy sugar planters in Hawaii included American Sanford Dole, the son of missionaries in Hawaii. Dole's cousin established a pineapple business in Hawaii that became known as the Dole Food Company, which is still in business today.

1. The United States applied the Monroe Doctrine in Mexico by forcing the ____ troops to withdraw.

   A British

   B French

   C Spanish

2. The purchase of ____ was known as "Seward's Folly," but gold was later discovered there.

   A Alaska

   B Pago Pago

   C Vancouver Island

3. After the overthrow of the native monarchy, the United States annexed the ____ Islands.

   A Midway

   B Hawaiian

   C Samoan

**MAKING CONNECTIONS**

4. What were two arguments for American imperialism?

5. What were two problems with American imperialism?

# Foreign Missions

As noted earlier, one argument for imperialism was the opportunity for Christian missions in other lands. While some used missions as a justification for the annexation or conquest of other nations, many missionaries opposed the negative effects of imperialism on native peoples. For example, Hiram Bingham, one of the first Congregationalist missionaries to go to Hawaii in 1820, clashed with Americans and others who were determined to exploit the Hawaiians. When Bingham helped end prostitution among the native women, outraged white sailors armed with knives and clubs assaulted him.

In the nineteenth century missionaries went to all corners of the globe, including China. One leader of Chinese missions was Lottie Moon, a Southern Baptist missionary who bravely traveled into the dangerous interior of China to minister to the Chinese people during plagues, famines, and the Boxer Rebellion (discussed later in this chapter).

One of the most important movements in foreign missions was the Student Volunteer Movement for Foreign Missions (SVMFM). This organization began in 1886 at a Bible conference in Massachusetts hosted by Dwight L. Moody (see Chapter 12). Spurred by an appeal to consider foreign missions, one hundred college students pledged themselves to become missionaries. Taking as its motto "The evangelization of the world in this generation," the SVMFM grew rapidly. Although its influence declined in the early twentieth century after trying to make room for both doctrinally conservative and doctrinally liberal Christians, it is credited with ultimately sending twenty thousand missionaries to the mission field. Another important mission group in America was the Christian and Missionary Alliance (C&MA), founded by A. B. Simpson in 1887. Some missionaries suffered martyrdom; thirty-five C&MA missionaries to China, for example, died in the Boxer Rebellion.

▼ Peter Parker, an American medical missionary to Guangzhou (formerly Canton), China, trained Chinese physicians and introduced medical treatments for eye diseases.

# The Spanish-American War

## Causes of the War

The height of American imperialism came in 1898, when the United States went to war with Spain in a conflict involving Cuba, one of Spain's oldest colonies. Cuba had become a major producer of sugarcane, and slaves labored on the plantations of wealthy landowners until Spain abolished slavery in 1886. Cuba, less than one hundred miles from Key West, Florida, exported much of its sugar to the United States. American businesses also invested heavily in Cuban railroads, mines, and sugar plantations.

### Cuban Revolt

Cuban rebels had launched an unsuccessful revolt against the Spanish government in 1868. When that revolt collapsed, many of its leaders fled to the United States, where they worked to gain sympathy for the plight of the Cuban people and to raise support for another attempt at revolution. In 1895 a depression in Cuba with its resulting unemployment provided ideal conditions for a new insurrection. Bands of guerrillas destroyed sugar mills, plantations, and anything else the people loyal to Spain valued. To stop the destruction, Spain sent General Valeriano Weyler to Cuba. Weyler ordered Spanish troops to round up the Cuban peasants, who were providing food and support to the rebels, and put them in barbed-wire "reconcentration" camps, where tens of thousands died of starvation or disease. The United States under President Cleveland offered to mediate between Spain and the rebels, but Spain refused the offer.

### Yellow Journalism

As the Cuban revolt continued and news of conditions in the reconcentration camps reached the United States, American newspapers began to play a greater role in pushing the government to intervene in Cuba. Two of the leading newspapers were William Randolph Hearst's *New York Journal* and Joseph Pulitzer's *New York World*. Each paper practiced "**yellow journalism**," or sensationalized news reporting aimed more at attracting readers than reporting the truth. Each attempted to outdo the other in reporting shocking stories that would boost sales. The papers sent well-known writers and artists, including Stephen Crane and Frederick Remington, to Cuba to report on the war from the rebel's side. The yellow journals often printed accounts of Spanish atrocities that were greatly exaggerated or completely fabricated.

American public opinion began to favor war with Spain to establish Cuba's independence. Despite journalistic propaganda, President McKinley, like his predecessor President Cleveland, intended to avoid hostilities. The Spanish government showed willingness to meet McKinley's call for better treatment of the Cubans, and recalled General Weyler to Spain, hoping to prevent American intervention in Cuba. However, two incidents gave Americans who supported the war new reasons to demand military action.

▶ Cartoon portraying William Randolph Hearst as a jester tossing headlines, such as "Appeals to Passion," "Venom," and "Attacks on Honest Officials," that are eagerly grabbed by the public

- What caused the Spanish-American War?
- What were the major battles of the Spanish-American War?
- What were the results of the Spanish-American War?

▼ Cuban victims of starvation

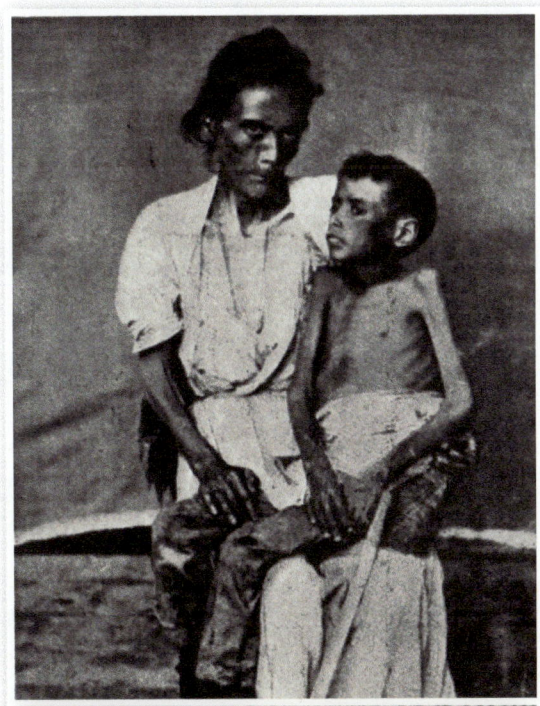

Age of Imperialism   **371**

## De Lôme Letter

First, on February 9, 1898, the *New York Journal* published a personal letter written to a friend by Enrique Dupuy de Lôme, the Spanish ambassador in Washington, DC. The letter had been stolen by Cuban rebels and given to the American press. In the **de Lôme letter**, the ambassador denounced McKinley as, among other things, "weak and catering to the rabble, and besides, a low politician." Americans were outraged at the insult to their president. De Lôme resigned and the Spanish government apologized; despite this, Spanish-American relations worsened.

## The USS Maine

A second incident pushed America further toward war against Spain. The battleship **USS *Maine*** had been sent to Cuba in January 1898 to protect American interests on the island. On February 15, the *Maine*, anchored in Havana Harbor, suddenly exploded and sank, killing 260 American sailors. Possible explanations for the explosion included the spontaneous ignition in the coal bunkers of the ship, causing the ship's ammunition magazine to erupt, or a mine placed in the harbor detonating, causing the ship to explode. One day after the explosion, before an investigation could even commence, the yellow-press headlines proclaimed that the Spanish were responsible. An investigation in the next weeks by the American government concluded that a mine had sunk the *Maine*.

Despite Spain's denial of responsibility and the possibility of other explanations, many Americans wanted to blame Spain and demanded that the government act. The battle cry became "Remember the *Maine*!"

McKinley faced tremendous political pressure to declare war against Spain. In his message to Congress on April 11, 1898, McKinley outlined the suffering of the Cuban people, the damage to American business interests, and the sinking of the *Maine*, and asked Congress for authorization to use force if necessary to end the war between Spain and the people of Cuba, to secure the establishment of a stable government for Cuba, and to protect American interests. Congress passed a joint resolution on April 19 recognizing the independence of the people of Cuba, demanding Spain's withdrawal from the island, and directing the president to use force, if necessary, to establish Cuba's independence. The Senate added to the resolution the **Teller Amendment**, which stated that the United States had no intention to exercise sovereignty over Cuba but only desired an end to conflict and the independence of the Cuban people.

The **Spanish-American War** began on April 21, 1898, and the US Navy's Atlantic fleet was immediately sent from Key West to begin a blockade of Cuba.

▼ Headline of Hearst's *New York Journal* on the destruction of the USS *Maine*

# The War against Spain

When the war began, the US Army lacked weapons and supplies and consisted of only 26,000 troops, mostly stationed in the West. But when President McKinley called for an additional 125,000 volunteers, over 1 million tried to enlist, and most had to be turned away.

## *The Philippines*

The United States Navy was a powerful, modern fleet and was reasonably well prepared for war. Ironically, the war over Cuba started in the Pacific Ocean, where one of Spain's major fleets was located. Assistant Secretary of the Navy Theodore Roosevelt sent secret orders to Commodore George Dewey, who was in Hong Kong as commander of America's Pacific fleet, to prepare an attack on the Spanish fleet in the Philippines (a Spanish colony) in case war developed. Dewey left Hong Kong on April 27 and fought the Spanish fleet in Manila Bay, the main harbor of the Philippines, on May 1. The Americans engaged the outdated Spanish fleet, sinking eight ships, and killing or wounding almost 400 men. American losses were slight—one warship damaged, one sailor dead (of heatstroke), and nine others wounded. The **Battle of Manila Bay** destroyed Spanish sea power in the Pacific. McKinley ordered 25,000 troops to sail from San Francisco to the Philippines. On the way they stopped at Guam in the Mariana Islands, captured the small Spanish garrison there, and claimed the island for the United States.

While Dewey was waiting for the US troops to arrive, Filipino revolutionary leader Emilio Aguinaldo led guerilla operations on land and took control of much of the Philippines. Dewey took control of Manila when the American forces arrived.

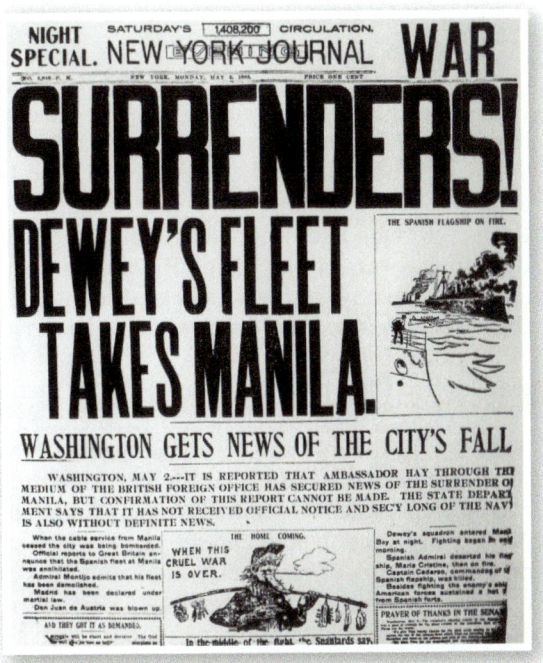

▲ Headline of victory in the Philippines

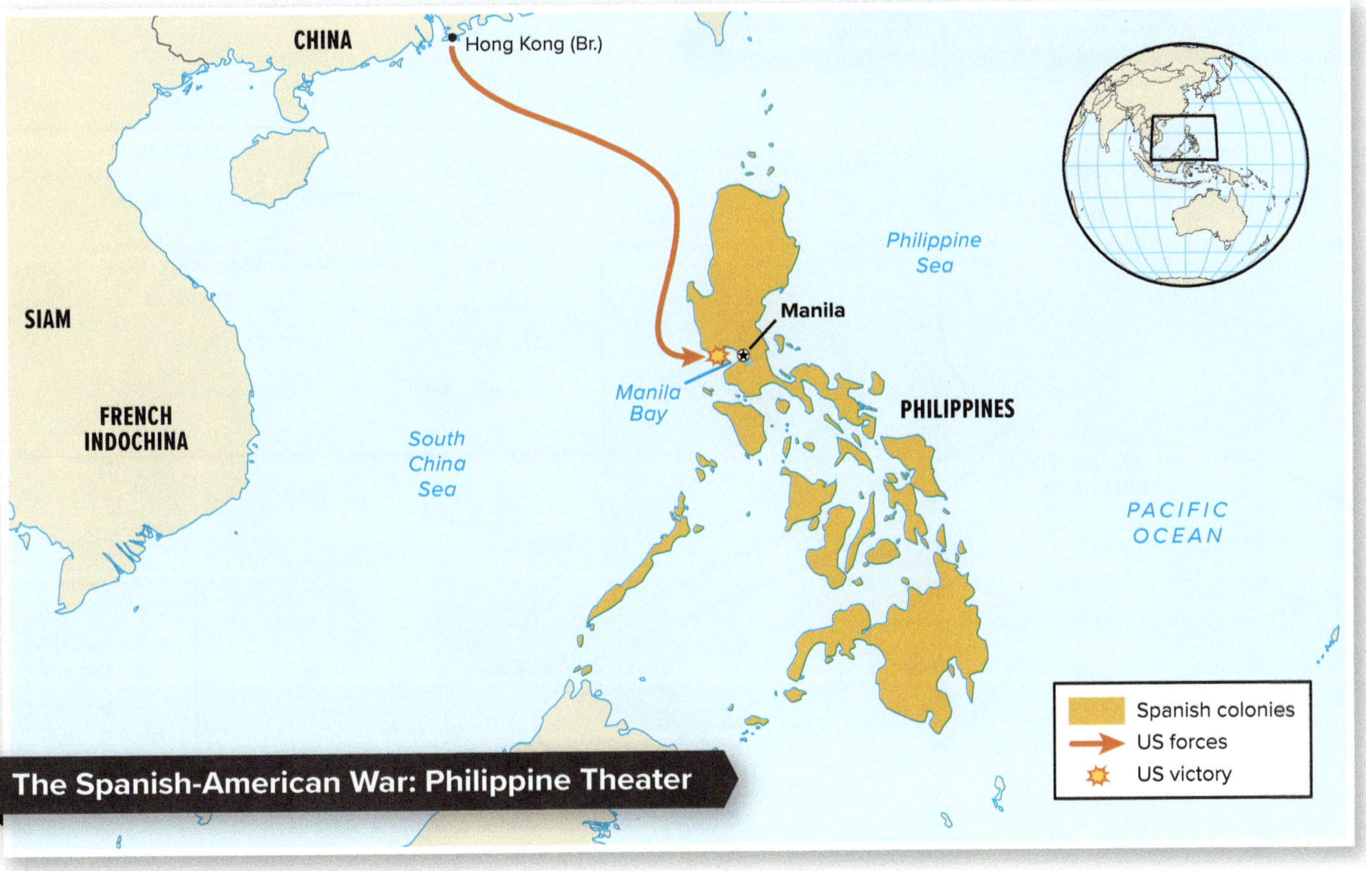

**The Spanish-American War: Philippine Theater**

CHINA
Hong Kong (Br.)
SIAM
FRENCH INDOCHINA
South China Sea
Manila Bay
Manila
Philippine Sea
PHILIPPINES
PACIFIC OCEAN

Spanish colonies
US forces
US victory

## Cuba

On May 19, 1898, Spain's Atlantic fleet entered Cuba's Santiago Harbor. McKinley ordered the US Army to capture Santiago. In late June, 17,000 American soldiers landed in Cuba and pushed the Spanish troops back to defenses on **San Juan Hill** outside Santiago. Colonel Leonard Wood and Lieutenant Colonel **Theodore Roosevelt**, who had resigned as Assistant Secretary of the Navy to fight in the war, led the Rough Riders, a group of volunteers which included cowboys, miners, college students, and adventurers from the West. On July 1, 1898, Roosevelt led a daring charge up San Juan Hill against the Spanish fortifications. After fierce fighting, the defenders fled their position. The US Army then laid siege to Santiago.

On July 3, the Spanish fleet tried to escape the blockade of Santiago Bay. In the resulting naval battle, the US Navy suffered three ships damaged while the Spanish had three ships sunk, three others run aground, and 474 sailors killed or wounded. Surrounded by American forces on land and sea, the Spanish surrendered Santiago on July 17. Shortly thereafter, American forces captured Spain's other colony in the Caribbean, Puerto Rico. With the losses of Cuba, Puerto Rico, and the Philippines, the Spanish asked for peace.

The **Treaty of Paris of 1898** officially ended the Spanish-American War. Spain ceded Guam and Puerto Rico to the United States, and Cuba became independent. The United States also purchased the Philippines from Spain for $20 million.

Theodore Roosevelt called the Spanish-American War "a splendid little war." The war had lasted a total of sixteen weeks. Fewer than 400 American soldiers died in combat, but over 5,000 died of yellow fever, malaria, and other tropical diseases. Over 60,000 Spanish soldiers and sailors died in combat or from disease.

▲ "Rough Riders" charging San Juan Hill. Roosevelt was the only one on a horse because the other "riders" were still waiting for their horses to come from Florida.

## The Spanish-American War: Caribbean Theater

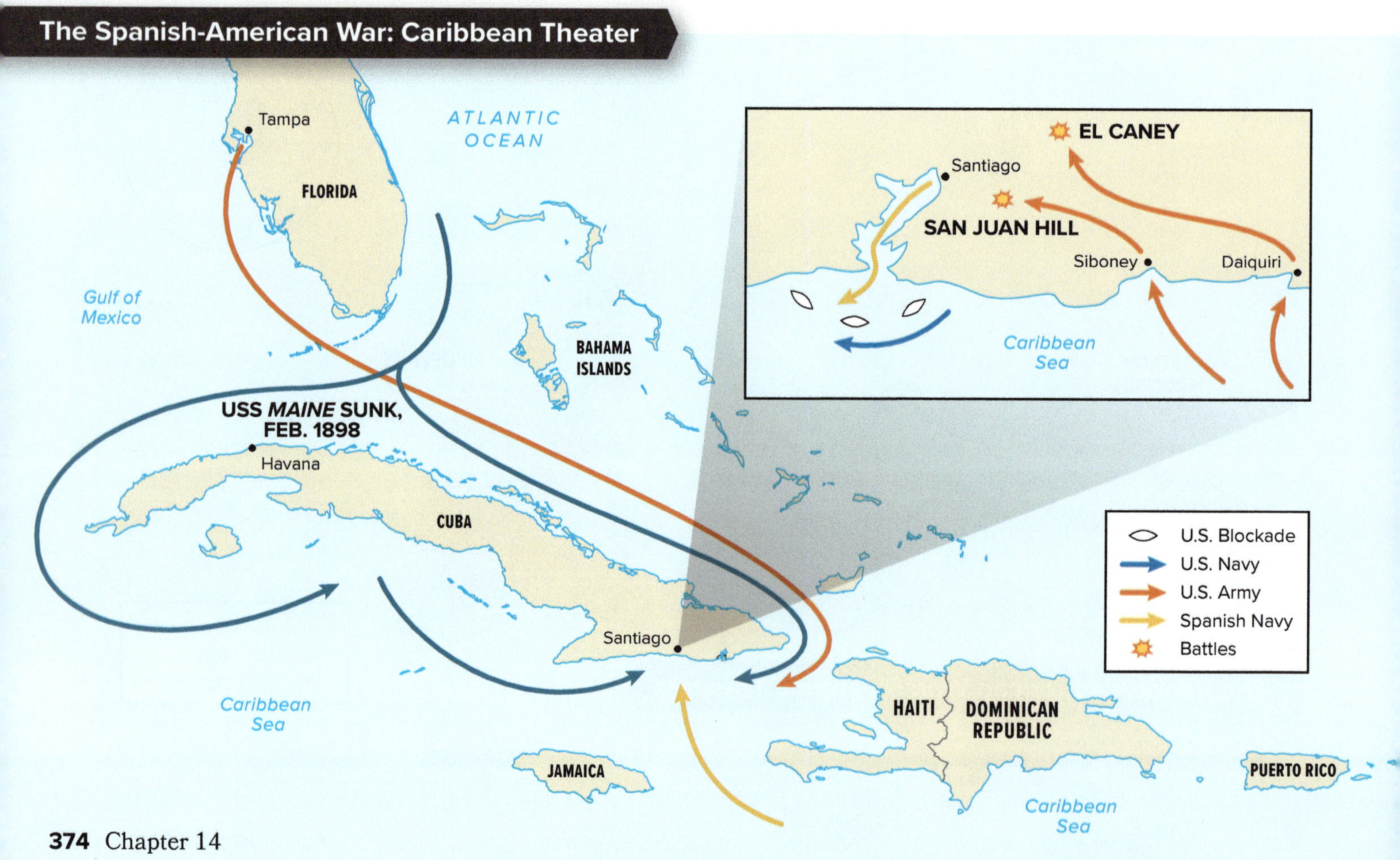

Tampa

ATLANTIC OCEAN

FLORIDA

Gulf of Mexico

BAHAMA ISLANDS

**USS *MAINE* SUNK, FEB. 1898**

Havana

CUBA

Santiago

Caribbean Sea

JAMAICA

HAITI    DOMINICAN REPUBLIC

PUERTO RICO

Caribbean Sea

**EL CANEY**

Santiago

**SAN JUAN HILL**

Siboney    Daiquiri

Caribbean Sea

- U.S. Blockade
- U.S. Navy
- U.S. Army
- Spanish Navy
- Battles

# Impact of the War

## Debate over Imperialism

One result of the Spanish-American War was that it widened the debate about American imperialism. The acquisition of these new territories led several prominent Americans, including author Mark Twain and industrialist Andrew Carnegie, to speak out against an American empire. The Anti-Imperialist League was formed with a platform that stated that imperialism is "hostile to liberty and tends toward militarism," that governments "derive their power from the consent of the governed," and that "subjugation of any people is 'criminal aggression.'" Senator George F. Hoar from Massachusetts, a League member, stated:

> *If this be the first step in the acquisition of dominion over barbarous archipelagoes in distant seas; if we are to enter into competition with the great powers of Europe in the plundering of China, in the division of Africa. . . if our commerce is hereafter to be forced upon unwilling peoples at the cannon's mouth; if we are to govern subjects and vassal States, trampling as we do it on our own great Charter which recognizes alike the liberty and dignity of individual manhood, then let us resist this thing in the beginning, and let us resist it to the death.*
>
> — **GEORGE F. HOAR**

**Analyzing Sources**

What characteristics of imperialism does Hoar condemn? What document does he refer to as "our own great Charter"?

▼ Political cartoon showing McKinley measuring Uncle Sam for new clothes, while Carl Schurz, an anti-imperialist, offers him "Anti-Expansion Policy" medicine, with journalists Joseph Pulitzer and Oswald Ottendorfer also carrying the remedy

Supporters of imperial expansion argued that America was justified in competing for world markets and should not be left behind by European empires. Others saw imperialism as an opportunity to spread Protestant Christianity to places like the Philippines (where Roman Catholicism was prevalent). President McKinley admitted that he embraced imperialism reluctantly. He said,

> The truth is I didn't want the Philippines.... When I next realized that the Philippines had dropped into our laps I confess I did not know what to do with them.... I walked the floor of the White House night after night until midnight; and I am not ashamed to tell you ... that I went down on my knees and prayed Almighty God for light and guidance....
>
> And one night late it came to me this way ... (1) that we could not give them back to Spain—that would be cowardly and dishonorable; (2) that we could not turn them over to France or Germany—our commercial rivals in the Orient—that would be bad business and discreditable; (3) that we could not leave them to themselves—they were unfit for self-government—and they would soon have anarchy and misrule over there worse than Spain's was; and (4) that there was nothing left for us to do but to take them all, and to educate the Filipinos, and uplift and civilize and Christianize them, and by God's grace to do the very best we could by them, as our fellow-men for whom Christ also died. And then I went to bed, and went to sleep, and slept soundly.

## Cuba

The Teller Amendment had promised Cuba its independence. However, after the war the United States decided that Cuba was not ready to govern itself completely, and it became a US protectorate (a nation that is technically independent but must submit to some control by another nation). In 1901 Congress passed the **Platt Amendment** which prohibited Cuba from making alliances with other countries besides the United States, allowed American oversight of Cuba's finances, and authorized the United States to send troops to Cuba to keep order if necessary. Cuba also allowed the United States to establish and keep a naval base on the island, and Guantanamo Bay is still used by the US Navy today.

The United States did much to help Cuba, including helping to combat yellow fever. A Cuban physician, Dr. Carlos Finlay, believed that mosquitoes carried the dreaded and often fatal disease. US Army doctor Walter Reed proved that Finlay was correct. As a result, army engineers under Major William Gorgas drained swamps and other low-lying areas in Cuba to eliminate mosquito breeding grounds. The United States also built roads, schools, railroads, and hospitals on the island and provided food and clothing for the poor.

## Puerto Rico

The United States helped Puerto Rico in similar ways. In 1917 Puerto Rico was made a US territory with a governor appointed by the president and a two-house legislative assembly. Puerto Ricans were also granted US citizenship.

## The Philippines

Americans discovered that empires can be extremely costly. For the first time in its history, the United States had to maintain a large peacetime standing army and navy to protect the newly annexed areas. Filipino leader Emilio Aguinaldo believed that after the Spanish were overthrown, the Filipinos would receive independence immediately. He rejected trading Spanish control for American control. In 1899 his revolutionaries tried to overthrow the Americans and establish Philippine independence. For two years the United States struggled to subdue the Filipinos at a cost of over 4,200 American casualties from wounds or disease. Even after the capture of Aguinaldo in 1901, the Filipinos insisted on independence.

McKinley appointed William Howard Taft to be the civilian governor of the Philippines in 1901. Taft did not think the Filipinos were ready for self-government, but he tried to establish institutions and conditions that could lead to their eventual independence. He worked to improve education, transportation, and healthcare in the Philippines.

American leaders feared that if the islands were granted independence too quickly, they might fall prey to another major power, such as Japan. In 1917 the United States enacted a law promising eventual independence for the Philippines. Over the next thirty years, the United States gradually gave the Filipinos increasing amounts of self-rule. Two world wars would interrupt further progress, but eventually the Philippines were given their independence in 1946.

---

### Comprehension Check 14.3

1. All of the following contributed to arguments for US involvement in the Spanish-American War except the ____.
   - **A** Anti-Imperialist League
   - **B** de Lôme letter
   - **C** sinking of the USS *Maine*
   - **D** "yellow journalism"

2. ____ led the famous charge of the Rough Riders up San Juan Hill in Cuba.
   - **A** Commodore George Dewey
   - **B** Major William Gorgas
   - **C** Lieutenant Colonel Theodore Roosevelt

3. Revolutionary leader Emilio Aguinaldo led forces against the United States in ____.
   - **A** Cuba
   - **B** Puerto Rico
   - **C** the Philippines

### MAKING CONNECTIONS

4. What lands did the United States acquire at the end of the Spanish-American War?

5. What was the Teller Amendment, and how did the Platt Amendment modify it?

How did America relate to the rest of the world during the presidency of Theodore Roosevelt?

GUIDING QUESTIONS

- How did Theodore Roosevelt become president?
- What were the results of Roosevelt's Big Stick policy?
- How did the United States relate to China and Japan during the Age of Imperialism?

## Reelection and Assassination

For the 1900 presidential election, many Republicans embraced imperialism, renominating McKinley and enlisting Spanish-American War hero Theodore Roosevelt as their vice-presidential candidate. The Democrats also focused on the issue of imperialism, renominating William Jennings Bryan, who opposed American imperialism. The Republican ticket won an electoral landslide over Bryan and the Democrats.

On September 6, 1901, President McKinley visited the Pan-American Exposition in Buffalo, New York. A young man in the line to greet the president appeared to have a bandage on his right hand, and McKinley stretched out his left toward the man's unbandaged hand. However, the young man, an anarchist named Leon Czolgosz, pushed the president's outstretched hand aside, and shot the astonished president. The Pan-American Exposition featured a new invention—an x-ray machine—but the doctors, fearing unknown side effects, did not use it and could not find the bullet. Eight days later, after infection set in, President McKinley died.

▼ McKinley's assassination by Leon Czolgosz

For the third time, the nation's president had been assassinated. Vice President Theodore Roosevelt took office as the nation's twenty-sixth president, at age forty-two, the youngest person ever to do so. Though they had shared the presidential ticket, two presidents of the same party could hardly have been more different. McKinley had been quiet, reserved, and calm; Roosevelt was energetic, active, and outgoing. Furthermore, McKinley had been a political conservative who took a cautious approach to American expansion, while Roosevelt favored vigorous expansion of American influence overseas.

## Roosevelt and the Big Stick

Theodore Roosevelt's foreign policy involved the United States more actively in international affairs. He was known for saying, "Speak softly and carry a big stick." Called **big stick diplomacy**, his foreign policy relied on military strength to protect American interests. He considered the expansion of a "civilized power," such as the United States, into world affairs to be "a victory for law, order, and righteousness."

▼ Theodore Roosevelt

Age of Imperialism   **377**

## Panama Canal

For years people from various countries had discussed the possibility of a canal somewhere across the narrow isthmus of Central America to connect the Atlantic and Pacific Oceans. Most American engineers who studied possible routes preferred a route through Nicaragua. From 1881 to 1889 Frenchman Ferdinand de Lesseps, whose previous company had built the Suez Canal connecting the Mediterranean Sea to the Red Sea, attempted to build a canal through Panama, which at the time was part of Colombia. Due to the terrain, climate, engineering obstacles, lack of funds, and diseases such as yellow fever which killed 20,000 laborers, the project failed, and the company went bankrupt.

Roosevelt believed it was crucial for both commercial and military reasons that the United States build and control a canal to move ships quickly from ocean to ocean to expand trade and protect its newly acquired empire. When Roosevelt became president, members of Congress disagreed about the best route—Nicaragua or Panama. The French company, needing to sell its rights of construction so it could pay its creditors, sent a representative, Philippe Bunau-Varilla, to negotiate with the United States. In 1902 Congress passed an act authorizing purchase of the French rights to construction of a canal in Panama for $40 million, and in 1903 the Senate passed a treaty with Colombia agreeing to purchase perpetual control of the Canal Zone for $10 million initially, with annual payments of $250,000 thereafter. But the Colombian senate, believing the price was too low, rejected the treaty.

Infuriated by the decision of their senate, Roosevelt denounced the Colombians as "foolish and homicidal corruptionists" who were attempting to blackmail the United States. Bunau-Varilla, who was still trying to promote the sale of his company's rights, quickly pointed out to the president that a revolution in Panama was imminent; many Panamanians resented the Colombian government and wanted to break away. Officers of the French company, led by Bunau-Varilla, helped finance and organize the revolt. Roosevelt, for his part, ordered the US Navy to prevent Colombian troops from landing in Panama to crush the rebellion.

Mainly because of that American support, Panama's revolt succeeded on November 3, 1903. Three days later, President Roosevelt recognized Panama's independence, and the Panamanians then appointed Bunau-Varilla as their minister to the United States. He and Secretary of State John Hay signed an agreement on November 18 promising Panama the same payment for the canal that the United States had offered to Colombia. In return, the United States would build, control, and perpetually defend both the canal, which would be open to all nations equally through the payment of tolls, and the 10-mile-wide canal zone.

Construction of the Panama Canal began in 1904 and took about ten years. To combat yellow fever and malaria among canal laborers, lessons learned in Cuba during the Spanish-American War were applied in Panama. William Gorgas became chief sanitary officer of the Panama Canal project. He improved sanitary conditions in Panama by draining swamps, pouring oil on standing water where mosquitoes bred, clearing away mosquito-infested underbrush, and using mosquito netting. By the time the canal was completed, Gorgas had reduced malaria and yellow fever deaths by over 80 percent.

▼ Ships in the Panama Canal

Building the canal, which included dams, locks, and a cut through the mountains of central Panama, was an immense feat of engineering and construction. More than 75,000 workers from ninety-seven countries, many from the Caribbean islands, were employed on the project. The canal cost about $400 million, but its financial benefits to world shipping outweighed the cost. In August 1914 the canal opened and linked ocean to ocean. In 1922 Colombia formally recognized Panama after the US government paid Colombia $25 million in compensation.

## Roosevelt Corollary

Roosevelt's actions in Panama represented his general approach to affairs in Latin America. He envisioned the United States as the leader in the Western Hemisphere, protecting the region and regulating its behavior. Complicating Roosevelt's position was the conduct of some Latin American nations. In 1902 Venezuela came into conflict with Great Britain and Germany when it proved unable to repay loans from those nations. Likewise, a bloody revolution in the Dominican Republic in 1904 worried the European powers that had sizable investments in that nation. Fearing European intervention in the hemisphere, Roosevelt devised an addition to the Monroe Doctrine that became known as the **Roosevelt Corollary**.

The president addressed Congress in 1904:

> Chronic wrongdoing . . . [may] ultimately require intervention by some civilized nation, and in the Western Hemisphere the adherence of the United States to the Monroe Doctrine may force the United States, however reluctantly, in flagrant cases of such wrongdoing or impotence [weakness], to the exercise of an international police power.

To the Monroe Doctrine's assertion that European nations could not intervene in the Americas, Roosevelt's corollary placed the United States in the position of "policeman" to maintain economic and political stability in Latin America. During the next decade, the United States intervened in Haiti, Honduras, Nicaragua, and the Dominican Republic in attempts to collect debts or maintain order. As a result, European and Latin American resentment toward the United States intensified.

▲ The traditional route around South America compared to the route through the Panama Canal

◀ Political cartoon depicting Roosevelt bearing a truncheon labeled "the New Diplomacy" and standing as policeman of the world

# China and Japan

## An Open Door in China

Opening Japan to American trade in 1854 (see Chapter 7) was a major step in Japan's expansion into other parts of Asia, including areas in and controlled by China. By the 1890s Japan had adopted Western technology and transformed itself into a modern industrial and military power. Along with Japan, European powers, such as Britain, France, Germany, and Russia, had each set up a "sphere of influence" in China, where the foreign nation could dominate Chinese trade. Besides claiming these "spheres of influence," some of these foreign powers seized Chinese territory and established colonies. As a result, the United States found itself in the middle of intense competition when attempting to trade with China. The United States was interested only in trading in China, not in establishing a colony.

In 1899 Secretary of State John Hay, desiring to open Chinese trade to all countries, proposed the **Open Door Policy**, which called for all nations trading in China to refrain from interfering with one another and to allow free trade in China. Although the United States could do little to enforce such a policy, the idea fit well with what some European powers—notably Great Britain—already wanted to do in China. Because the policy suited the inclinations of the major powers, it succeeded.

▲ Political cartoon, "China--the Cake of Kings . . . and Emperors," showing a distressed China while Britain, Germany, Russia, France, and Japan seek portions of China

## Spheres of Influence

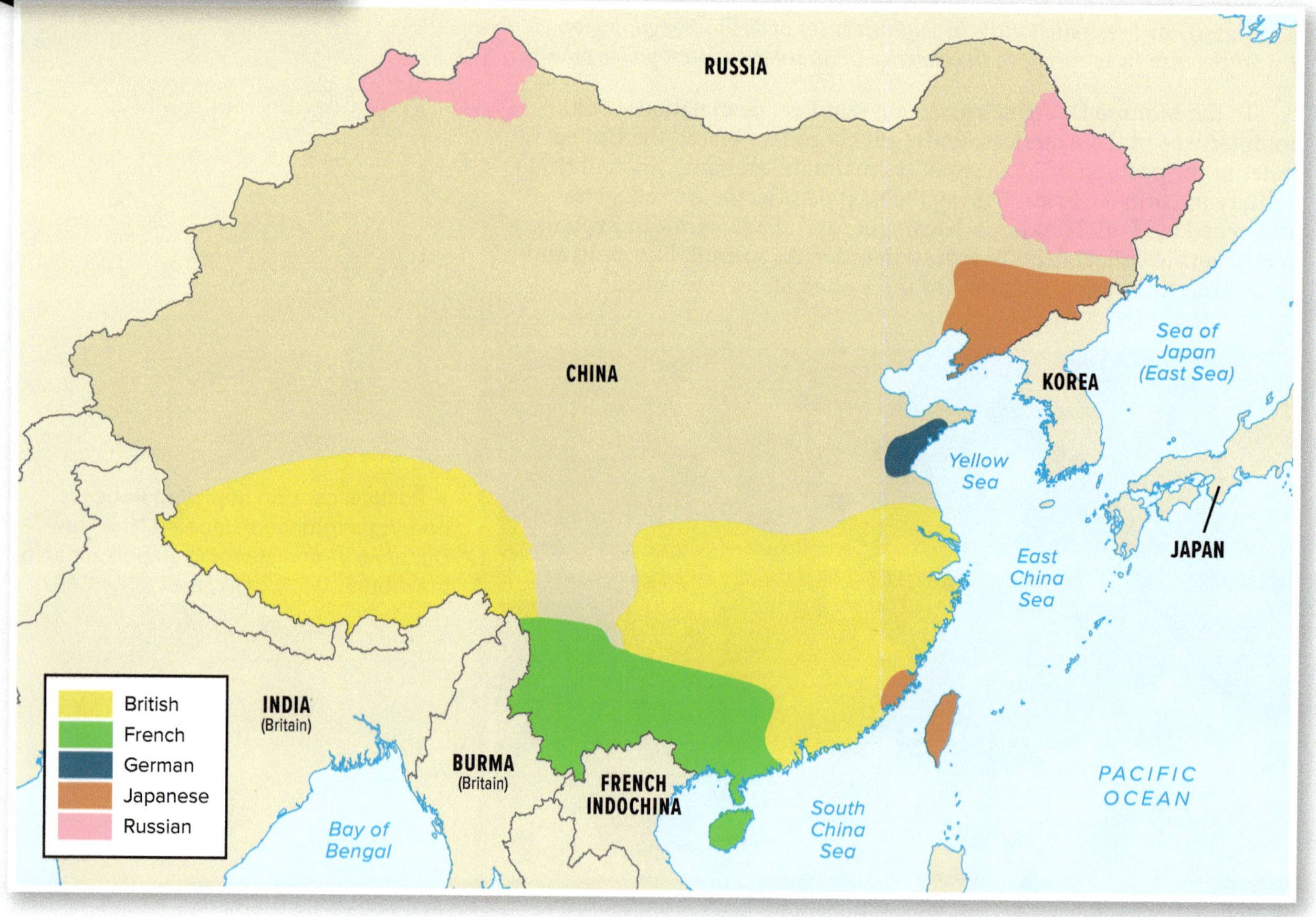

RUSSIA

CHINA

KOREA

Sea of Japan (East Sea)

Yellow Sea

East China Sea

JAPAN

INDIA (Britain)

BURMA (Britain)

FRENCH INDOCHINA

Bay of Bengal

South China Sea

PACIFIC OCEAN

- British
- French
- German
- Japanese
- Russian

But Hay nearly saw his open door close as soon as it had opened. The Chinese resented *all* attempts by foreign powers to determine the future of their country. In 1900 an anti-foreign movement known as the **Boxer Rebellion** erupted in China. (The name "Boxer" comes from a leading organization in the rebellion, "the Society of Righteous and Harmonious Fists.") The movement wanted foreigners and foreign influence expelled from the nation. Boxers destroyed anything foreign and killed missionaries, diplomats, foreign merchants, and Chinese converts to Christianity (which Boxers considered a "foreign" religion).

In August several European nations, Japan, and the United States sent 20,000 soldiers to protect foreigners and Chinese Christians in Peking (present-day Beijing). Approximately 2,500 Americans were among the international military force that intervened and crushed the rebellion. Thousands of Chinese Catholics, Protestants, and Russian Orthodox as well as about 200 missionaries had been killed in the uprising.

Although some countries wanted to receive land as compensation for the losses caused by the Boxer Rebellion, Secretary Hay opposed dividing China among the victors. He and British diplomats persuaded the other nations to accept payments from the Chinese rather than insist on territorial concessions. The nations involved accepted Hay's proposal, and required China to pay $333 million for damages, divided among the nations that had sent forces, over the next forty years. The United States was promised approximately $25 million. After the Chinese diplomat and Secretary Hay negotiated to reduce the amount owed to the United States, Roosevelt supported the measure in his State of the Union address in 1907, acknowledging that the promised amount was more than the cost of damages in the rebellion. Congress passed a bill a year later reducing the amount to approximately $13.5 million. China voluntarily used the portion no longer owed to educate Chinese students in American preparatory schools and universities through a scholarship program. American efforts to help China, although not free from self-interest, helped improve relations between the two countries.

## Relations with Japan

Trade with China and American possessions in the Pacific, such as the Philippines and Guam, brought the United States into closer contact with Japan's modernized navy. Throughout the Roosevelt years, relations with the increasingly powerful Japanese were a sensitive issue.

In February 1904 war broke out between Japan and Russia over conflicts of interest in Manchuria (a province of China). The Japanese won a series of quick naval and land victories that worried the other great powers, who feared growing Japanese power in the Pacific. The war, known as the Russo-Japanese War, strained the finances of both nations, and the Japanese invited Roosevelt to mediate. In 1905, at a conference in Portsmouth, New Hampshire, Roosevelt negotiated the **Treaty of Portsmouth** that preserved most of Japan's gains yet allowed Russia to escape with some of its honor intact. Roosevelt later received the Nobel Peace Prize for his services. Unfortunately, both Russia and Japan were unhappy with the compromises, and American relations with both nations soon cooled.

By the late 1860s the Japanese had loosened their laws by allowing some Japanese citizens to emigrate to other countries. Japanese immigrants began coming to the United States, settling primarily in California. An 1894 agreement guaranteed the Japanese the right to immigrate to the United States. However, as Japanese immigration to California increased, anti-Asian feelings grew. In 1906 the San Francisco Board of Education passed a rule that required all Japanese, Korean, and Chinese students to attend a separate segregated school, and an anti-Japanese race riot occurred in the city in 1907. The Japanese were understandably offended at the discriminatory legislation and treatment. Roosevelt finally negotiated a "**Gentlemen's Agreement**" (verbal agreement) with the Japanese government. Japan agreed to restrict emigration to the United States, and Roosevelt was able to win better treatment for Asians in California, including allowing Japanese students to attend public schools. The agreement slowed Japanese immigration, and tensions eased.

▼ Chinese Boxers fighting an international military force

▼ Chinese Christian refugees in Tianjin (formerly Tientsin) during the Boxer Rebellion

1. Roosevelt's big stick diplomacy advocated
   ___.

   A  deferring to European powers in China

   B  relying on military strength to protect
      American interests

   C  seizing Japanese possessions in the
      Pacific

2. The United States supported a revolution
   in ___ to secure the rights to build a canal
   connecting the Atlantic to the Pacific.

   A  Haiti

   B  Nicaragua

   C  Panama

3. The United States proposed the Open
   Door Policy, which called for ___ in
   China.

   A  colonization

   B  free trade

   C  the overthrow of foreign influences

### MAKING CONNECTIONS

4. How did the Roosevelt Corollary expand
   on the Monroe Doctrine?

## Great White Fleet

Japanese-American relations also sparked the climax of Roosevelt's foreign policy, a grand display of American naval power. Roosevelt desired to use American influence to keep a **balance of power** (preventing any one nation from gaining enough power to dominate other nations) in Asia. In December 1907, sixteen battleships, referred to as the "**Great White Fleet**," steamed from Virginia, heading around South America, out into the Pacific, and on to Japan. Roosevelt's goal for the fleet, which got its name from the fact that the ships were painted white, was to impress the Japanese with American strength. In 1908, partly because of that "battleship diplomacy," the two countries signed an agreement pledging to respect each other's territorial claims in the Pacific and to maintain the "open door" for trade in China. The fleet itself imitated Magellan by sailing around the world and symbolized American power wherever it went.

Roosevelt's foreign policy did have its critics, including William Jennings Bryan. Americans were still essentially isolationists, whereas Roosevelt was clearly an internationalist. But Roosevelt succeeded in convincing Congress that the nation had to be more involved internationally because of strategic concerns; it needed to expand the market for its exports. Roosevelt set the nation on the road to growing international involvement.

▼ The "Great White Fleet" on its circumnavigation

# CHAPTER **14** REVIEW

## Chapter Summary

### 14.1   Populism

- The Populist Party was formed to address many of the issues that farmers and laborers faced. The party pushed for several reforms, including government ownership of railroads and telegraphs, the direct election of US senators, and free silver.

- William Jennings Bryan, a Populist, won the Democratic nomination for president in 1896. He was defeated by Republican William McKinley.

**TERMS**

Populist Party

populism

free silver

William McKinley

William Jennings Bryan

**TERMS**

imperialism

Seward's Folly

### 14.2   International Expansion

- In the late 1800s strong nations practiced imperialism, or the exercise of economic and political control over weaker nations, leading to arguments over whether America should form an empire.

- The United States purchased Alaska and annexed the Midway Islands and American Samoa. Americans in Hawaii helped overthrow Queen Liliuokalani, and Hawaii was annexed to the United States.

- Foreign missions grew as a result of American expansion.

### 14.3   The Spanish-American War

- Cuban rebels attempted to overthrow Spanish rule in Cuba. American newspapers practicing "yellow journalism" promoted the cause of the rebels, influencing popular opinion. The printing of the de Lôme letter, which criticized President McKinley, and the explosion of the USS *Maine* in Havana Harbor led the United States to go to war against Spain.

- In the Spanish-American War, the US Navy destroyed the Spanish fleet at the Battle of Manila Bay in the Philippines. The US Army and Navy defeated the Spanish forces at Santiago, Cuba, and captured Puerto Rico.

- In the Treaty of Paris of 1898, Spain ceded Guam and Puerto Rico to the United States, Cuba became independent, and America paid Spain $20 million for the Philippines. After the war, the acquisition of the Philippines led Americans to again debate American imperialism.

- Cuba became an American protectorate, while the Filipinos fought against American control.

**TERMS**

yellow journalism

de Lôme letter

USS *Maine*

Teller Amendment

Spanish-American War

Battle of Manila Bay

San Juan Hill

Theodore Roosevelt

Treaty of Paris of 1898

Platt Amendment

# CHAPTER **14** REVIEW

## Chapter Summary

### 14.4 The Turn of the Century

- McKinley was reelected in 1900 but was assassinated in 1901, and Theodore Roosevelt became president. Roosevelt practiced big stick diplomacy in foreign affairs.

- When Colombia refused an American offer for building a canal in Panama, the United States assisted a revolt in Panama. America recognized Panama's independence and negotiated a canal treaty. The Panama Canal took over ten years to build and opened in 1914.

- The Roosevelt Corollary said that the United States would police the Western Hemisphere, which led to American intervention in numerous Latin American countries.

- When China was divided into spheres of influence by other imperial powers, the United States proposed the Open Door Policy. Chinese resentment of foreign influence led to the Boxer Rebellion. The United States and other nations sent troops to put down the rebellion and accepted money rather than land in return for damages from the rebellion.

- Roosevelt helped negotiate the Treaty of Portsmouth after a war between Russia and Japan over territory in China. The growing number of Japanese immigrants to California led to anti-Japanese sentiment and treatment, but Roosevelt's "Gentlemen's Agreement" helped ease tensions between the two countries. Roosevelt sent the "Great White Fleet" around the world to impress other nations, including Japan, with American strength.

### TERMS

big stick diplomacy
Roosevelt Corollary
Open Door Policy
Boxer Rebellion
Treaty of Portsmouth
"Gentlemen's Agreement"
balance of power
Great White Fleet

## Chapter Review Questions

### RECALL

1. What political party was formed to represent the needs of farmers?

2. Whose "Cross of Gold" speech led to his nomination for president by the 1896 Democratic convention?

3. Who won the elections of 1896 and 1900?

4. What American land acquisition was called "Seward's Folly"?

5. What were four island groups in the Pacific that were acquired or annexed by the United States?

6. What was the name for sensationalized news reporting aimed at attracting readers?

7. What is a nation called that is technically independent but has to submit to some control by another nation?

8. Who became president when McKinley was assassinated?

9. What was Roosevelt's foreign policy called?

10. What war did the Treaty of Portsmouth end, and what award did Theodore Roosevelt receive for his part in the treaty?

### UNDERSTAND

11. What were two problems facing farmers during this period?

12. What were three reforms proposed by the Populist Party?

13. According to the Populists, how would free silver benefit farmers and laborers?

14. How did the Treaty of Washington (1871) resolve each of the longstanding differences with Britain?

15. What were four arguments in favor of American imperialism?

16. What were four arguments against American imperialism?

17. What role did Americans play in the revolt in Hawaii, and why did they revolt? Why did President Cleveland oppose its annexation? How and why did the United States annex Hawaii?

18. What were the four primary causes of the Spanish-American War?

19. In what battle did the US Navy defeat the Spanish in the Philippines?

20. How did the US Army and Navy defeat the Spanish in Cuba?

21. What lands did the United States acquire in the Treaty of Paris of 1898? What was Cuba's status?

22. What were four arguments against an American empire by the Anti-Imperialist League?

23. How did the Platt Amendment modify the Teller Amendment? What restrictions did the Platt Amendment place on Cuba?

24. How did the Filipinos respond to American control?

25. Why did the United States want a canal across Central America? What role did the United States play in Panama's gaining independence from Colombia?

26. What was the Roosevelt Corollary, and how did it affect relations between the United States and Latin America?

27. What was happening in China that led to the Open Door Policy, and what did the Open Door Policy say?

28. Who were the Boxers and how were foreigners in China affected by the Boxer Rebellion? How did the United States attempt to deal fairly with China after the rebellion?

29. What was the situation that led to the "Gentlemen's Agreement," and how did the agreement try to resolve it?

30. What was the Great White Fleet, and what agreement did it help to create with Japan?

## THINK ABOUT IT

31. What four things did McKinley consider as he made the decision to keep the Philippines? Choose one of his points and evaluate whether it was justifiable.

32. Explain what William Jennings Bryan meant when he said "you shall not crucify mankind upon a cross of gold." What biblical allusion is being made? Who is doing the crucifying, and who is being crucified? What does that imply about his view of the common man? Do you agree with this view of human nature? Do you think this was an appropriate analogy? Explain.

33. How do the details in this political cartoon reveal the artist's view of Bryan? Do you agree with the artist's assessment? Explain.

▲ Political cartoon depicting William Jennings Bryan as "the sacrilegious candidate" for his "Cross of Gold" speech

# 15 The Progressive Era

15.1 Society of the Progressive Era
15.2 Goals of the Progressive Era
15.3 Presidents of the Progressive Era

▲ President Theodore Roosevelt and naturalist John Muir at Yosemite National Park, California, in 1903

The period of American history from the 1890s to about 1920 is often referred to as the Progressive Era. The root word of progressive is "progress." Several factors in the late nineteenth century led many people to believe that humans were making progress toward a better society. Darwinian evolution taught that species were evolving to higher species. Economic growth and technological advances led many to believe that the application of science and technology could solve all of society's ills.

**Progressivism** was not a single organized movement. It was a collection of people and ideas that favored achieving political and social reform through education, wider political participation, and direct government action. While some operated from an evolutionary point of view, others were traditional Christians. Some progressives had been Populists while many were members of the middle and upper classes who were upset by the abuses of some industrialists, by corruption in government, and by the plight of the poor. Progressives of this period included both Democrats and Republicans. Sometimes supporters disagreed about which changes needed to be made, and they differed regarding how best to implement change. However, they all advocated reform.

## 15.1 Society of the Progressive Era

How did American society change during the Progressive Era?

### Life during the Progressive Era

As mentioned in Chapter 12, the urbanization and industrialization of the late 1800s had both positive and negative effects. By 1920 more than half of Americans lived in cities and towns (though in the South less than thirty percent) and the standard of living was increasing for most people. Increased income and shorter working hours gave many Americans more time to spend with their families and enjoy leisure activities.

Organized sports such as baseball, basketball, and football, continued to gain popularity. The first baseball World Series was held in 1903 between the Boston Americans (later the Red Sox) and the Pittsburgh Pirates. Boxing was the second-most popular sport of the era with fights attracting thousands of spectators.

Interest in opera and classical music surged, especially in cities with large numbers of European immigrants. Many symphony orchestra members and conductors were born in Europe. Immigrants who could afford tickets packed concert halls to hear the music of European composers.

Newspapers continued to be popular. Features such as comic strips and crossword puzzles were introduced to the papers, which increased their readership even more. Magazines which originally covered news soon branched out into the arts, literature, fashion, and culture. *Harper's*, the *Atlantic, Ladies' Home Journal*, and the *Saturday Evening Post* were some of the popular magazines of the era.

▶ Magazine covers, circa 1910–1920

▲ Henry Ford driving a Model T (with Thomas Edison riding in the back seat)

# Transportation Transformation

The application of science and technology to daily life brought great changes to society. Two inventions—the automobile and the airplane—transformed transportation in the twentieth century, bringing greater speed, power, and mobility.

## Automobiles

Numerous inventors in America and Europe were experimenting with automobiles in the late 1800s, and one of the first gasoline-powered cars was created by German inventor Karl Benz in 1885. In 1896 **Henry Ford** of Detroit unveiled his automobile, which led to the establishment of the Ford Motor Company in 1903.

In 1908 Ford produced the Model T, a plain but remarkably sturdy car. Although the Model T was well designed, Ford's genius lay more in the manufacture of his vehicle. By using standardized, interchangeable parts and the assembly line, Ford achieved a high degree of efficiency and speed in auto manufacturing. This allowed Ford to lower costs and make the Model T affordable through mass production. The price of a new Model T dropped steadily from more than $800 when it was first sold to $360 by 1916 and to $260 by 1925. Lower costs led to higher sales, and by the 1920s more than half the cars on America's roads were Fords.

## Airplanes

The first successful airplane was the work of brothers **Orville and Wilber Wright.** The Wrights had first become interested in flight as boys when their father gave them a toy helicopter powered by rubber bands. Later, the popularity of bicycling led them to open a bicycle sales and repair shop that eventually became a successful bicycle-manufacturing firm.

The profits of their bicycle company enabled the Wrights to pursue their dream of flight. They read all the literature on flying they could find, and they experimented with homebuilt kites and gliders. Needing more room for their work, they decided to use the treeless, windswept dunes of Kitty Hawk, North Carolina. On December 17, 1903, after years of tiring work, Orville climbed into their flying machine. The 12-second, 120-foot trip was the first powered, sustained, and controlled flight in history. From this humble beginning at Kitty Hawk, the airplane developed quickly into a faster means of transporting people and goods and soon became an important military weapon.

▶ The Wright brothers' flyer at Kitty Hawk, North Carolina, December 17, 1903

## The *Titanic*

Ocean-going steamships were the primary means of travel between Europe and the United States. In 1912 the new British luxury liner *Titanic* was the largest ship of its kind. It was 882 feet long, and its hull was divided into sixteen watertight compartments. People called the ship "unsinkable." On April 10, 1912, the ship left Southampton, England, for New York City on her maiden voyage.

About 11:40 p.m. on April 14, a lookout sighted an iceberg. The side of the ship hit the iceberg, and five hull compartments ruptured. Despite the damage, the ship remained afloat for almost three hours. The crew sent distress signals, and passengers began to board lifeboats—but there was room for only 1,178 of the 2,224 passengers. Some lifeboats entered the water only half full, leaving about 1,500 people to drown or freeze to death in the 28°F water. The *Titanic* sank off the coast of Newfoundland, Canada.

Another ship, the *Californian*, had been less than twenty miles from the sinking *Titanic*, but its radio operator was off duty that night and did not receive the distress calls. One of Congress's last acts during the Taft administration was to pass a law requiring the presence of two radio operators on passenger liners so one could always be on duty.

The *Titanic* remained untouched until 1984, when Robert Ballard's underwater research team discovered the wreckage.

▲ Poster (replica) advertising *Titanic*'s maiden voyage

▼ Passengers on lifeboats look on as the *Titanic* sinks.

# Education

Progressives saw education as an important means of changing society. Public elementary schools, high schools, and colleges funded by taxpayers were becoming common. More women and African Americans were able to attend college. Colleges had traditionally been small, religiously affiliated institutions that taught the philosophy and ancient languages of Western civilization. By the late 1800s more colleges were large, secular universities focused more on modern languages, social science, industrial arts, and practical studies.

One effect of changes in education was that people began to see Christian teaching as old-fashioned. Instead of pastors and theologians being the best educated and most trusted members of a community, scientists and other experts displaced them. Most Christians valued the growing educational opportunities and embraced the benefits of modern science and technology but were concerned by the unbiblical philosophy behind what was taught. As a result, some Christians worked to preserve or establish distinctly Christian colleges.

▼ Progressive education reformer John Dewey

## *John Dewey*

A leader of progressive education during this period was John Dewey, a professor at Columbia University and the University of Chicago. Dewey criticized American education, saying that it created passive students who memorized facts and that it trained students to submit to authoritarian social and political structures. He stated that students learn best in an environment where they are active learners who experience and interact with the content through hands-on activities. But he also said that the purpose of education is less about learning content and more about students realizing their full potential, and he believed that education should serve as a means of social change.

The philosophy behind some of Dewey's educational philosophy is secular humanism, which denies the existence of God and affirms the goodness and perfectibility of humanity. Secular humanism also replaces absolute standards of truth with relative standards based on human experience. Humanists believe that human nature can be improved, often through education. Such belief ignores the biblical teaching that people are sinful by nature and can ultimately be improved only through the saving work of Christ.

## Booker T. Washington

One of the most famous schools for black Americans was the Tuskegee Institute, founded in Alabama in 1881. Its first teacher and president was **Booker T. Washington**, who had been born a slave in Virginia in 1856. After emancipation, Washington attended Hampton Institute, where he later became a teacher. When Hampton's founder received a letter asking for someone to run a school for black students in Tuskegee, Alabama, he recommended the twenty-five-year-old Washington.

The institute focused on practical trades and farming. Students helped construct buildings on campus and care for the school's crops and livestock. Washington recruited wealthy industrialists, including Andrew Carnegie, John D. Rockefeller, and Julius Rosenwald (chairman of Sears, Roebuck and Company) to support Tuskegee Institute.

▲ Mathematics class at Tuskegee Institute

◄ Booker T. Washington

## George Washington Carver

A leader in southern agricultural education during and after the Progressive Era, **George Washington Carver** had been born a slave in the early 1860s. Carver had an insatiable curiosity about nature, especially plants. He taught himself so much about plants and soils that neighbors nicknamed him "the plant doctor." After initially being turned away from a college because he was black, Carver persevered and was able to attend and graduate from Iowa's State Agricultural College (later Iowa State University) in 1894. Booker T. Washington offered him a teaching position at Tuskegee Institute. When Carver arrived in 1896, the school had little more than its land and a few ramshackle buildings. Carver stocked his laboratory by making his own equipment with what was at hand.

Cotton production had depleted the soil of the South. Carver found that certain plants—particularly peanuts—replenished the nitrogen that cotton removed from the soil. Farmers complained, however, that although peanuts might help the soil, they brought little profit to the growers, so Carver worked to find uses for peanuts. After much experimentation, he developed more than two hundred uses for the peanut, including dyes, a milk substitute, ice cream, livestock feed, fertilizer, and flour. Although most of these did not prove to be financially profitable, Carver's work helped southern farmers become less dependent on cotton production.

▼ George Washington Carver working in his lab

▲ Segregated drinking fountain in the South

# Discrimination

Not all Americans enjoyed the progress of this era equally. African Americans faced discrimination that kept them from being treated as equals in society. Though African Americans made some gains politically and economically after Reconstruction, including holding elective office (for example, in every session of Congress from 1869 to 1901 except one, there was at least one black member of the House of Representatives), discrimination remained a common part of life for many. After Reconstruction ended, states began passing **Jim Crow laws** which required the forced segregation, or separation, of blacks and whites in trains, restaurants, hotels, schools, restrooms, and other public facilities. (Jim Crow was a stereotyped black character in a nineteenth-century minstrel, or comedic variety, show.)

As mentioned in Chapter 11, Southern states began to deprive black people of their right to vote by establishing **literacy tests** (which were often unfairly administered to prevent black Americans from passing them) or requiring **poll taxes** in order to vote. Later, many states also passed **grandfather clauses** which typically said a person who could not pay the poll tax or pass the literacy test could still vote if he or his father or his grandfather was eligible to vote before 1867. No black citizens met this requirement. As a result of these laws, the number of black voters

plummeted. For example, the number of registered black voters in Louisiana was 130,000 in 1896 but only about 1,300 in 1904.

Segregation was strengthened when the Supreme Court issued a series of decisions that made the enforcement of the Reconstruction civil rights legislation difficult. The most famous of these cases was ***Plessy v. Ferguson***, whose decision in 1896 decreed that "separate but equal" facilities for blacks and whites (in this case, on trains) were constitutional. These decisions gave state legislatures the legal justification they needed to pass additional Jim Crow laws.

Some progressives attempted to use science to justify discrimination and segregation. During the Progressive Era, faith in evolutionary ideas led to a rise in the "science" of eugenics, a set of beliefs and practices whose goal was to "improve" the genetic quality of the human population. People who were considered "inferior," such as the disabled or criminals, were discouraged or prevented from reproducing. In some areas marriages between people of differing races was illegal, partly because some believed certain races were inferior. Furthermore, those who believed white people were superior to other races often used eugenics and social science to defend Jim Crow laws.

African Americans reacted to increased discrimination in differing ways. One approach was offered by Booker T. Washington. He urged African Americans not to risk strife by insisting on their political rights. Instead, they should concentrate on bettering themselves economically through vocational education and the establishment of black businesses and trades. As black people became more economically powerful, Washington argued, white people would be forced to accept them and grant them political equality. In 1895 in Atlanta, Georgia, he delivered a speech that became known as the "Atlanta Compromise." He explained his view:

> *No race can prosper till it learns that there is as much dignity in tilling a field as in writing a poem. It is at the bottom of life we must begin, and not at the top. Nor should we permit our grievances to overshadow our opportunities. . . .*
>
> *The wisest among my race understand that the agitation of questions of social equality is the extremest folly, and that progress in the enjoyment of all the privileges that will come to us must be the result of severe and constant struggle rather than of artificial forcing. No race that has anything to contribute to the markets of the world is long in any degree ostracized [excluded]. It is important and right that all privileges of the law be ours, but it is vastly more important that we be prepared for the exercises of these privileges. The opportunity to earn a dollar in a factory just now is worth infinitely more than the opportunity to spend a dollar in an opera-house.*
>
> — **BOOKER T. WASHINGTON**

 **Analyzing Sources**

What did Washington believe Black Americans should be primarily focused on at this time?

Where Washington sought an economic solution to the problem, **W. E. B. Du Bois** pursued a political solution. Du Bois was the first African American to receive a PhD from Harvard University. He and his supporters argued that blacks could not truly improve themselves economically until they enjoyed equal participation in the political process as American citizens. They opposed Washington's emphasis on technical and industrial education over liberal arts, fearing that it would force black Americans into an economically inferior laboring class and discourage higher education among them. In his 1903 essay criticizing the Atlanta Compromise, Du Bois said,

> Mr. Washington represents in Negro thought the old attitude of adjustment and submission. . . . [It developed into] a gospel of Work and Money to . . . almost completely [disregard] the higher aims of life. . . . Mr. Washington's programme [of industrial education] practically accepts the alleged inferiority of the Negro races. . . . Mr. Washington withdraws many of the high demands of Negroes as men and American citizens. . . .
>
> [He] asks that black people give up, at least for the present, three things,—first, political power, second, insistence on civil rights, third, higher education of Negro youth,—and concentrate all their energies on industrial education. . . .
>
> What has been the return?
>
> 1. The disfranchisement [loss of voting rights] of the Negro.
>
> 2. The legal creation of a distinct status of civil inferiority for the Negro.
>
> 3. The steady withdrawal of aid from institutions for the higher training of the Negro.

In 1905 Du Bois and other African American leaders met at Niagara Falls. The resulting Niagara Movement demanded full rights, and especially voting rights, for African Americans. The Niagara Movement soon merged with the **National Association for the Advancement of Colored People (NAACP)** which was formed in 1909 by a group of black and white leaders. The goal of the NAACP was to seek equality for blacks and to focus on fighting legal battles to achieve that objective. During Washington's lifetime, his views influenced relations between blacks and whites; afterward, however, because many white people continued to refuse recognition of the equality of African Americans, the NAACP's approach gained strength.

Some progressives made attempts to improve relations between black and white Americans. For example, Theodore Roosevelt invited Booker T. Washington to dine with him at the White House over the objection of many of his aides. However, those progressives who opposed racial discrimination were unable to deliver meaningful reform for the majority of black Americans.

◄ (top) W. E. B. DuBois; (bottom) founding members of the Niagara Movement

# Challenges to Christianity

## Modernism

Orthodox, or traditional, Christianity faced challenges from related movements that grew during this period. One was a theological movement known as **modernism**. Modernists were attempting to "save" Christianity and keep secular and liberal people in the church by adapting Christianity to modern ideas. Influenced by Darwin's emphasis on natural processes, modernists (also called liberal theologians) said that all claims to theological truth must be based on reason or experience alone, not on an external authority. They denied the inspiration of the Bible (that the Bible was written by men who were guided by the Holy Spirit) and treated it as a purely human book. Modernists contended that the Israelites preserved a series of stories, legends, and myths and that the priests and royal scribes gradually shaped those tales into the biblical books. Thus, they rejected the idea that Moses wrote the first five books of the Old Testament. Additionally, they denied biblical teachings such as the deity of Christ, His virgin birth, and atonement for sin through His blood. This movement came first to American colleges and seminaries and soon spread to American churches through graduates who became pastors. Instead of "saving" Christianity, modernists created an alternative religion under the name of Christianity.

## Reform Darwinism and the Social Gospel

In the late nineteenth century, a movement known as **Reform Darwinism** emerged. Lester Frank Ward and other Darwinists were not satisfied with the assertions of Social Darwinism (see Chapter 12). Ward argued that human progress was best achieved not through competition but through cooperation. He believed that government was best equipped to promote human progress through this cooperation. As a result, government—as an active agent for social change—could remove what he saw as the two great barriers to a better world: poverty and ignorance. Ward's ideas would have a tremendous impact on social thinking and public policy in the twentieth century.

As noted in Chapter 12, many orthodox Christians tried to reach the urban poor through the reform efforts of various organizations. The YMCA continued to expand in cities during the Gilded Age. The Salvation Army, originally from Great Britain, was active in providing relief for the poor and establishing rescue missions in many of the slums of US cities. These rescue missions met spiritual needs by presenting the gospel and physical needs by offering food and shelter. Others outside of the Salvation Army also started rescue missions. Jerry McAuley, who had served jail time for robbery and who had converted to Christianity, established the Water Street Mission in New York City in 1872. He wanted to reach the "down-and-outers" who lived in the worst parts of the city. In 1877 Colonel George Clarke and his wife, Sarah, founded the Pacific Garden Mission in Chicago.

## Unorthodox Religions

In addition to modernist teachings, two unorthodox religious groups emerged in late nineteenth-century America. Mary Baker Eddy founded Christian Science, which teaches that matter, death, disease, pain, and sin were mental illusions. Christian Science emphasizes spiritual healing, but denies the Trinity, the inspiration of the Bible, and the atonement of Christ.

The Watch Tower Society (Jehovah's Witnesses) was founded in 1872 by Charles Taze Russell. While Jehovah's Witnesses believe in the inspiration of the Bible, they deny the Trinity and eternal punishment in hell and believe that 144,000 will rule with Jesus in heaven while remaining believers live eternally on the new earth.

▼ Salvation Army workers providing doughnuts to arriving immigrants at Ellis Island

But a movement related to Reform Darwinism presented what many saw as an unorthodox alternative to traditional Christian outreach: the **social gospel** movement. It replaced an emphasis on regeneration of individuals with an emphasis on "regeneration" of society through social and political reform. The social gospel often grew out of a genuine concern to relieve the misery of the slums and was based on the belief that the essence of Christianity was the command "Thou shalt love thy neighbor as thyself." This love, however, embraced primarily the present life. Although some of their reforms were worthwhile, advocates of the social gospel joined with the modernists in rejecting the orthodox teachings of Christianity. Social gospel leaders departed from correct doctrine and emphasized "soup and soap"—feeding and cleaning people and society.

## Christian Responses

Orthodox Christians responded vigorously to modernist attacks on their faith. One of the centers for the defense of orthodox Christianity was Princeton Theological Seminary. Perhaps the greatest defender of orthodox Christianity at the time was Benjamin B. Warfield, professor at Princeton from 1887 until his death in 1921. Countering modernist claims that there were errors in the Bible, Warfield argued that Christians must accept what the Bible teaches about itself, namely that it is inspired (breathed out) by God. He noted that the prophets, beginning with Moses, repeatedly said that they were writing a message received from God and that Jesus accepted the Old Testament as being without error. Warfield then demonstrated that the Bible's authors believed that Jesus is God. By his careful scholarship, Warfield contended that modernist attempts to reinterpret the Bible were not legitimate.

Some Christians opposed unbiblical teachings by thoroughly educating other believers in the truths of Scripture. One educational method was the Bible institute, a school similar to a college but whose curriculum usually consisted almost entirely of courses in Bible or church-related subjects. One of the earliest major Bible institutes was Nyack Missionary College in New York City, founded by A. B. Simpson of the Christian and Missionary Alliance in 1882. Another was D. L. Moody's Chicago Bible Institute, founded in 1889 and renamed Moody Bible Institute after its founder's death. In 1908 the Bible Institute of Los Angeles (present-day Biola University) was established.

Another educational method was the Bible conference. Not all Christians could attend Bible institutes, so many of them spent their vacations at Bible conferences, held in resort spots for a week or more during the summer. These sessions featured noted preachers and Bible teachers. Three important American Bible conferences were the Niagara Conference in Ontario, D. L. Moody's Northfield Conference in Massachusetts, and the Winona Lake Bible Conference in Indiana.

▶ (top) Baptist reformer and social gospel advocate Walter Rauschenbusch; (bottom) Benjamin B. Warfield

1. Henry Ford's Ford Motor Company featured the following characteristics except ____.

   **A** the assembly line method of production

   **B** high prices for its Model Ts

   **C** standardized, interchangeable parts

2. ____ was the first president of the Tuskegee Institute.

   **A** George Washington Carver

   **B** John Dewey

   **C** Booker T. Washington

3. The Supreme Court case *Plessy v. Ferguson* decreed that ____ were constitutional.

   **A** literacy tests and poll taxes

   **B** marriages between people of different races

   **C** separate but equal facilities for blacks and whites

4. ____ sought equality for black people through legal battles.

   **A** The National Association for the Advancement of Colored People (NAACP)

   **B** The "Atlanta Compromise"

   **C** Eugenics

5. Reform Darwinism thought human progress was best achieved through ____.

   **A** Christianity

   **B** competition

   **C** cooperation

### MAKING CONNECTIONS

6. What were three effects of secular humanism on education during the Progressive Era?

7. How did Booker T. Washington and W. E. B. Du Bois differ in their reactions to discrimination?

One notable orthodox means of defending and furthering the Christian faith was the continuation of the urban revivals popularized by D. L. Moody. After Moody's death in 1899, the most important urban evangelist was former professional baseball player William "Billy" Sunday. In 1886, while drinking with his teammates, Sunday heard a group of workers from the Pacific Garden Mission singing in the street and followed the singers back to the mission. After attending several services there, Sunday became a Christian.

Leaving baseball and working for a time at the YMCA, Sunday later became an evangelist. His popular style of preaching, characterized by dramatic gestures as well as illustrations drawn from his baseball career, brought in large crowds. When church and city auditoriums proved too small, he used the tabernacle, a wide, low, wooden, barn-like structure built especially for the campaigns. His most famous campaign was in New York City in 1917. In that ten-week campaign, nearly one and a half million people attended his meetings, and almost one hundred thousand responded to his invitations for salvation.

Gradually, an orthodox alliance was forming in the United States. Theologians such as Warfield, popular preachers such as Sunday, and other Christians were finding that they had a common interest in defending Christianity against modernism. From 1910 to 1915, Christian businessmen sponsored the publication and distribution of *The Fundamentals*, a series of essays by some of the leading Christian scholars of the day to defend key doctrines such as the authority of the Bible and Christ's deity, vicarious (substitutionary) atonement, resurrection, and second coming. In 1920 a Christian editor suggested the name **"Fundamentalists"** for those who defended these fundamental doctrines. These Fundamentalists would face continuing challenges in the 1920s (see Chapter 17).

▼ Satirical drawing of Evangelist Billy Sunday

- How did Progressives want to reform government?
- How did Progressives want to reform society?
- How did the Progressive amendments meet Progressive goals?

## 15.2 Goals of the Progressive Era

### What were the goals of Progressivism?

One assumption of progressivism was that people and their behavior were primarily shaped by their environment. Therefore, they believed, people's lives could be improved through reforms meant to change the environment in which they lived. Social improvement, however, was often brought about through the exercise of social control by means of legislation, regulation, reliance on experts and social scientists, and the establishment of government agencies.

## Government Reforms

Most progressives believed that government should take an active role in solving the problems of society, but that the government itself needed reforming before it could do so. These reforms had both populist and elitist elements. Generally, the progressives favored reform through (1) advocating government intervention for fighting corruption, (2) promoting direct democracy, and (3) increasing government efficiency through hiring unelected experts.

### Fighting Corruption

The progressives strongly believed that they could best achieve reform by direct government action or government intervention. However, they did not always agree about which action to take. For instance, progressives were united in attacking the alleged corruptions of trusts and abuses of big business. But they differed on how to deal with the problem. Some progressives favored "trust-busting," breaking up the monopolies and restoring competition to the marketplace. Others favored leaving the trusts intact but regulating their operations.

For some progressives, government ownership of businesses was the answer. The most extreme progressives—the socialists—wanted the government to take over major businesses. Most reformers, however, preferred only limited government ownership. The most widely accepted form of control was "gas-and-water socialism," city or state control of utilities such as gas and water companies. The progressives argued that a monopoly was the most efficient way to operate a utility and that the safest monopoly was one owned and operated by the government.

Progressives also promoted government intervention on behalf of labor. They favored legislation that was sympathetic to labor unions and that would force businesses to negotiate fairly with the unions. In this way, unions could provide a check to the power of big business.

### Increasing Democracy

Many progressives believed "the cure for the ills of democracy is more democracy." Progressives thought that direct democracy, or placing power in the hands of the people, would naturally result in better government. William Jennings Bryan, an orthodox Christian, said that he favored "anything that makes the government more democratic, more popular in form, anything that gives the people more control over government."

Progressives tried to further the growth of democracy through several specific reforms. They favored the secret ballot for elections. Before this time, Americans had to indicate publicly which candidate they preferred as they voted. The secret ballot reduced the possibility of influencing or intimidating voters, and it frustrated corrupt politicians who now could not be sure whether their bribery had secured votes.

Progressives also wanted to discard the system of nomination of candidates by party conventions and caucuses and replace it with a system of direct primaries where a party nominated its candidates by popular vote. In theory, the direct primary took power from party bosses and gave it directly to the people.

Progressives also called for greater popular participation in legislation through the initiative and the referendum. **Initiative** is a process in which voters initiate legislation. After a certain number of signatures is collected on a petition, the proposed laws are sent to the state legislature or directly to the people to be accepted or rejected. A **referendum** allows the people to vote directly on whether a law passed by the legislature should be enacted.

Closely related to these two processes is **recall**, in which voters petition to hold a special election to decide whether to remove an elected official from office before his term expires. Although the national government accepted none of these innovations except the secret ballot, many state and city governments embraced them.

## Progressive Voting Reforms

| Initiative | Voters initiate legislation. |
|---|---|
| Referendum | Voters decide whether passed legislation should be enacted. |
| Recall | Voters petition to hold a special election to decide on removing an official. |

◄ 1912 political cartoon showing an overwhelmed Oregon voter (far right) with a complex voting ballot, an unintended consequence of progressive political reforms that put an increasing number of decisions in the hands of the voting public

## *Improving Efficiency*

Progressives sought to make government more efficient by putting qualified technical experts in positions of responsibility. City governments showed the greatest zeal for such improvements. Some cities adopted the city manager form of government, under which the city council either removed the office of elected mayor or reduced the mayor's power and hired a qualified city manager who served as the administrator of the city government. Other cities adopted the city commission form of government. This plan divided city government into several departments, each one under an expert commissioner's control. For example, a city's water or street commissioner could be a trained civil engineer.

The emphasis on technical experts grew from the increased trust in social scientists to address difficult problems. Progressives thought experts would be guided by impartial science and would therefore develop the best policies. While relying on specially trained individuals was sometimes helpful, experts were not always impartial, and their solutions did not always benefit society.

# Social Reforms

As mentioned in Chapter 7, reformers sought solutions to problems created by industrialization and urbanization. The work of reformers in areas such as labor, temperance, and women's rights continued in the Progressive Era with many successes.

▼ The Triangle Shirtwaist Factory fire in New York City, March 25, 1911

## Labor Issues

Employees in the steel, meatpacking, and textile industries faced unsafe working conditions. For example, workers in Southern textile mills inhaled cotton lint because of a lack of filtering systems. Some of these workers developed brown lung disease and later died from the condition. In March 1911 unsafe conditions in New York City's Triangle Shirtwaist Company led to one of the worst urban disasters in the early twentieth century. A fire broke out and spread in the top three stories of the building in which the company was located. Because doors had been locked to keep the workers on the job until the end of the shift, nearly 150 workers, mostly women and teenage girls, died in the fire. After the tragedy, the state set up a commission to investigate factory conditions throughout New York, and many new laws were established to improve health and safety among workers.

Whereas the AFL (see Chapter 12) had often excluded women and African Americans from participation, new unions established during the Progressive Era welcomed them. The Women's Trade Union League was founded in 1903 and participated in calling for regulations after the Triangle Shirtwaist Company fire. The Industrial Workers of the World (IWW), also called "Wobblies," was founded in 1905 and included socialists such as Eugene V. Debs. Unlike the AFL, the organization welcomed unskilled workers, women, and African Americans.

Progressives favored legislation directly helping the worker. For example, progressives on the city, state, and national levels sponsored laws establishing minimum wage levels, prohibiting child labor, limiting the number of hours in a workday, and mandating safety standards for factories.

## Quality of Life

Many tenements lacked indoor plumbing or running water while some had toilet facilities that large numbers of residents shared. Epidemics often spread in the crowded, unsanitary conditions. Some reformers responded to these conditions by founding **settlement houses**, where they "settled" in slum areas and provided childcare, clothing, medical care, and food as well as recreational and educational opportunities for the urban poor, who were often immigrants. One of the most famous settlement houses was Chicago's Hull House, founded in 1889 by Jane Addams and Ellen Gates Starr. These women and others at Hull House advocated for improvements in wages and working conditions and child labor laws.

Other reformers worked to improve living conditions in prisons and mental hospitals, where filth and cruelty were common. Reform efforts included some states establishing juvenile courts and ending the convict lease system in which convicts, many of whom were African American, were "hired out." However, many states later replaced convict leasing with chain gangs.

Some progressives, advocating eugenics, urged states to pass laws that led to sterilizing criminals and those with mental illness. Eugenics advocates claimed they were using science to help society progress. Critics argued they were unjustly denying due process to prisoners and establishing cruel and unusual punishments.

◄ Hull House founder Jane Addams with children

## Temperance

The abuse of alcohol continued to be a problem in many areas of the country, especially cities. Alcoholism contributed to increased crime, poverty, and violence toward family members. Social workers visiting the slums saw families in which drunken parents neglected or even abused their children and spent money on alcohol that should have been spent on food and clothing. Prison reformers spoke to inmates who blamed alcohol for leading them into crime.

Many religious Americans formed temperance societies, such as the Women's Christian Temperance Union and the Anti-Saloon League, that were dedicated to ending the consumption of alcohol. Along with temperance societies, evangelists such as Billy Sunday preached against the sin of drunkenness, and secular progressive businessmen advocated for temperance as a means of increasing production by eliminating worker absences and accidents caused by drunkenness.

These different groups concluded that eliminating alcohol would reduce crime and poverty. They sought temperance through the political means of the prohibition movement, which called for laws prohibiting alcohol. By 1915, fifteen states had outlawed alcoholic beverages.

## Women's Suffrage

"Women suffragettes" had begun campaigning for the right to vote before the Civil War (see Chapter 7) and continued their crusade at the state and national levels into the twentieth century. Some, such as Susan B. Anthony, also labored for the right of women to control their own property and to receive custody of children in divorce cases. However, it was their campaign for the vote that garnered the most attention. Additionally, black leaders such as Ida B. Wells-Barnett and Mary Church Terrell advocated for women's suffrage as part of their efforts to improve the lives of African Americans.

As a result of the crusade for women's suffrage, many western states as well as New York and Michigan allowed women to vote by 1920. Additionally, some states in New England, the Midwest, and the South gave women limited suffrage by allowing them to vote only in presidential elections. In 1916 Montana elected the first female member of Congress, Jeannette Rankin, to the US House of Representatives. One of her first actions was introducing a bill for a Constitutional amendment that guaranteed women's right to vote in every state.

▲ (top) Temperance reformer Carrie Nation, holding an ax and a Bible. Nation often used an ax to break liquor containers in saloons across the country; (bottom) 1912 women's suffrage parade, New York City

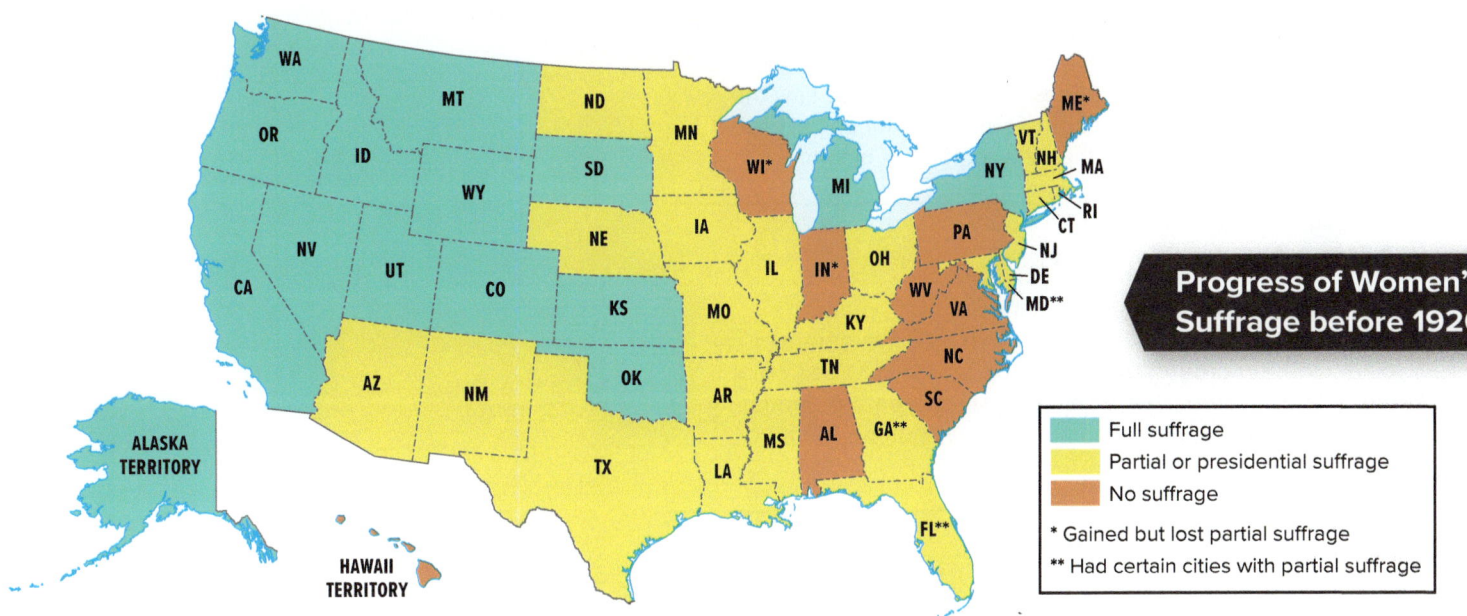

### Progress of Women's Suffrage before 1920

- Full suffrage
- Partial or presidential suffrage
- No suffrage
- \* Gained but lost partial suffrage
- \*\* Had certain cities with partial suffrage

# Progressive Amendments

Four progressive ideas eventually became a part of the US Constitution by the amendment process. These four additions to the Constitution were also known as the "progressive amendments."

## 16th Amendment

The **Sixteenth Amendment** established the federal income tax and was ratified in 1913. Progressives had two reasons for favoring the tax. First, income taxes would provide the government with funds to initiate reforms and provide the expanded social services that the progressives wanted. Second, the tax rate was graduated, that is, the more money one made, the higher percentage of income one must pay in taxes, and money would be redistributed from the wealthy to benefit all Americans.

## 17th Amendment

Another progressive effort to increase democracy was to have US senators directly elected by the people rather than by state legislatures (as directed by Article I, Section 3 of the Constitution). Progressives charged that senatorial elections had become corrupt auctions in which the wealthy sometimes bribed state legislators to elect them. Direct election, they believed, would end this abuse by giving the decision to the voters of each state. The **Seventeenth Amendment** was passed by Congress in 1912 and ratified in 1913. Opponents argued that senators directly elected by the people would be more interested in reelection than in making the best decisions for the nation and that direct election would destroy an important aspect of federalism by removing the state legislatures' check on federal power.

## 18th Amendment

The **Eighteenth Amendment** (ratified in 1919) established Prohibition, which banned the manufacture, sale, or transportation of alcoholic beverages. The progressives saw the amendment as a simple means of solving major social problems resulting in part from the consumption of alcohol.

## 19th Amendment

The **Nineteenth Amendment** (ratified in 1920) granted women suffrage nationwide and climaxed a movement much older than the progressive movement. Although Susan B. Anthony died fourteen years before the Nineteenth Amendment was ratified, it was sometimes called the "Anthony Amendment" in her honor.

---

## Comprehension Check 15.2

1. The following measures were intended to increase democracy except ____.

   A initiative

   B recall

   C prohibition

   D referendum

2. The fire in ____ led to the passage of several laws mandating health and safety regulations for factories.

   A the Hull House

   B the Triangle Shirtwaist Company

   C the Women's Trade Union League

3. The Sixteenth Amendment ____.

   A banned the sale, manufacture, and transportation of alcohol

   B established a federal income tax

   C granted women the right to vote

   D set up the direct election of US senators

### MAKING CONNECTIONS

4. What were two ways progressive city governments tried to increase efficiency through technical experts?

5. What was one positive result and one negative result of progressive prison reform?

# Presidents of the Progressive Era

**Who were the presidents of the Progressive Era?**

## GUIDING QUESTIONS

- How did Roosevelt's domestic policies reflect the goals of progressivism?
- How did Taft's progressivism differ from Roosevelt's?
- What were Wilson's domestic policies?

## Roosevelt

Three US presidents governed during the Progressive Era: Theodore Roosevelt (1901–1909), William Howard Taft (1909–1913), and Woodrow Wilson (1913–1921). Though each of them endorsed progressive ideas, Theodore Roosevelt was probably the president most closely associated with the movement. A member of a moderately wealthy New York family, a Harvard graduate, and an accomplished historian, Roosevelt was in some ways the most "aristocratic" president since John Adams. Yet by living as a cowboy on his cattle ranch in the Dakotas and through his heroics with the Rough Riders in Cuba, "Teddy" Roosevelt shed much of his upper-class image and displayed a great appeal to the common man. Roosevelt had a reputation as a friend of reform and served as a New York state legislator, member of the US Civil Service Commission, New York City police commissioner, and governor of New York. In 1900 he was elected vice-president. The stage was set for a dramatic change in American government when Roosevelt became president in September 1901.

### Square Deal

Upon McKinley's assassination, conservative Republicans urged Roosevelt to carry on the slain president's pro-business policies. However, Roosevelt wanted to balance his allegiance to the Republican Party with his desire to address the problems of society. Central to his philosophy was his belief that every man and woman should receive fair treatment and equal opportunity, a "Square Deal," as he put it.

### Muckrakers and Regulation

#### MUCKRAKERS

Roosevelt enlisted the help of progressive journalists to persuade the public of the need for reform. He nicknamed these writers who exposed abuse and corruption "**muckrakers**" (muck means "filth, dirt, or mud"). The name came from a character in John Bunyan's *Pilgrim's Progress* who uses a muckrake and ignores everything but filth.

The golden age of muckraking began in 1902 when *McClure's* magazine published an article by Lincoln Steffens on local corruption in St. Louis. Then came Ida Tarbell's *History of the Standard Oil Company* (1904), a scathing portrait of the alleged unscrupulous and dishonest methods John D. Rockefeller used to build his oil empire.

Other muckraking articles and books followed—such as attacks on insurance fraud and on impure and worthless medicines. For the most part, muckrakers did not call for any specific action; they contented themselves with describing corruption in graphic detail and trusting the disgust of the American people to motivate reforms.

▶ Teddy Roosevelt as a Rough Rider

## Teddy Bears

On a 1902 hunting trip in Mississippi, Roosevelt refused to shoot a bear his companions had caught for him. A reporter recounted the story, which caught the public's fancy. One toy maker wrote to Roosevelt, asking permission to market stuffed toy bears under the name "teddy bear." Roosevelt replied saying that he doubted whether his name would make a difference but granted his permission nonetheless. Soon, toy makers were selling stuffed bears in all sorts of attire, including one in a Rough Rider uniform.

▲ Workers at a meatpacking plant

In many cases, their attacks resulted in legislation addressing abuses. One example is Upton Sinclair's *The Jungle*, published in 1906. Sinclair had spent weeks secretly investigating the working conditions and food purity in Chicago's meatpacking plants. Sinclair wrote,

> There was never the least attention paid to what was cut up for sausage. . . . There would be meat that had tumbled out on the floor, in the dirt and sawdust, where the workers had tramped and spit uncounted billions of consumption germs. There would be meat stored in great piles in rooms; and the water from leaky roofs would drip over it, and thousands of rats would race about on it. . . . These rats were nuisances, and the packers would put poisoned bread out for them; they would die, and then rats, bread, and meat would go into the hoppers together. . . . the meat would be shoveled into carts, and the man who did the shoveling would not trouble to lift out a rat even when he saw one—there were things that went into the sausage in comparison with which a poisoned rat was a tidbit. . . . All of their sausage came out of the same bowl, but when they came to wrap it they would stamp some of it "special," and for this they would charge two cents more a pound.

*The Jungle* shocked the nation. After Roosevelt read the book, he appointed officials to investigate packing plants. They issued a scathing report that confirmed most of Sinclair's disgusting account. Sinclair's original intent in writing the book was to focus on the dreadful living conditions of immigrant packing plant employees. Though these were mentioned throughout the book, it was his graphic descriptions of how meat products were manufactured that captivated the public. As a result, in 1906 Congress passed the **Pure Food and Drug Act**, which outlawed the interstate sale of impure food and drugs and required honest labeling of food and drug products, and the **Meat Inspection Act**, which required the Department of Agriculture to oversee the preparation and packaging of meat and to inspect the health of animals before they were slaughtered.

## TRUST-BUSTING

The growing power of large corporations and trusts worried Roosevelt. He did not oppose all trusts but made a distinction between "good" trusts which improved efficiency, lowered prices, and provided better service, and "bad" trusts which eliminated competition and led to higher prices for consumers. Congress created the Department of Commerce and Labor in 1903 to monitor and investigate business practices. Roosevelt preferred to deal with the trusts through regulation by government agencies rather than through antitrust lawsuits.

Early in his presidency, however, Roosevelt signaled that he was willing to use the Sherman Antitrust Act to fight the abuses of the "bad" trusts. In 1902 the federal government charged the Northern Securities Company, a holding company formed by the merger of the Great Northern, Northern Pacific, and other railroads and shipping companies, with violating the act, and the government filed a lawsuit to break it apart. Northern Securities fought the suit, but the Supreme Court agreed with the government's action. The Northern Securities case was a milestone in confirming the government's authority to regulate trusts. His action against "bad" trusts won Roosevelt widespread public approval as a "trustbuster."

▲ Political cartoon of Roosevelt hunting "bad trusts" and leashing "good trusts"

## REGULATION

Roosevelt wanted to regulate the conduct of business and industry for what he viewed as the public good. He gave the most attention to railroads. Consumers often complained that the railroads, which operated as monopolies in some areas, charged excessively high rates and granted special concessions to businesses they favored. The Hepburn Act (1906) gave the Interstate Commerce Commission (ICC) the ability to set "just and reasonable" maximum railroad rates and to view the railroads' financial records. The act also said that ICC orders were binding and could only be overturned by federal courts.

## COAL STRIKE

Roosevelt's dedication to a "square deal" for labor and business was severely tested by a coal miners' strike in 1902. Coal was the major source of fuel for steam-operated machinery, including railroad locomotives, and the major source of heat for the nation. As winter drew near and the public grew concerned, Roosevelt tried to break the stalemate. He arranged a meeting between the owners and the union leaders at the White House, but the owners refused even to speak to the union men assembled there. Losing his patience, Roosevelt threatened to use federal troops to operate the mines. For the first time, the threat of federal force was used against owners rather than against workers. Reluctantly, the owners consented to a ten percent pay raise and a nine-hour day. This was the first instance of the federal government's acting as the mediator in a labor dispute, and the success of the effort increased Roosevelt's popularity among labor leaders.

▲ Roosevelt meeting with J. P. Morgan and others to seek a resolution to the 1902 coal strike

## Conservation

Roosevelt, the rugged outdoorsman, promoted the conservation of natural resources, seeking to balance development and preservation. The Reclamation Act of 1902 took funds from the sale of public land to construct dams, reservoirs, and other irrigation projects in the West. In 1905 he convinced Congress to establish the US Forest Service to manage the millions of acres already set aside for national forests. During his last year in office, Roosevelt established the National Conservation Commission, which was tasked with compiling a record of the nation's water, timber, land, and mineral resources. Roosevelt also established five new national parks during his presidency.

▼ Crater Lake, Oregon

▲ William Howard Taft

▼ Roosevelt on an African safari after leaving office

# Taft

Roosevelt chose not to run for president in 1908. Instead, he encouraged his close friend **William Howard Taft** to campaign for the Republican presidential nomination. Taft had enjoyed a distinguished public career as an attorney and judge and in appointed positions such as governor of the Philippines and secretary of war. His ambition was to become chief justice of the Supreme Court, but Roosevelt convinced him to set that dream aside to run for president. With Roosevelt's support, Taft comfortably defeated William Jennings Bryan in the 1908 presidential election.

Taft did not pursue progressive reforms as vigorously as Roosevelt had, yet he accomplished several progressive goals, including Congressional passage of the Sixteenth and Seventeenth Amendments, increased power for the Interstate Commerce Commission to regulate railroads, post office reform, and regulation of telegraph and telephone companies.

## Tariff Dispute

Taft wanted to lower tariff rates—a controversial issue that Roosevelt had avoided during his two terms. Conservative Republicans favored high tariffs while progressives favored lowering the rates. The House drafted a bill lowering the tariff moderately, but by the time the Senate was finished with the bill, rates remained virtually unchanged. Progressives urged Taft to veto the bill, but the president accepted it as the best he could get. When Taft tried to defend the new tariff as "on the whole . . . the best [tariff] bill that the Republican party ever passed," progressives were dismayed.

## Dollar Diplomacy

Taft also adopted a less confrontational foreign policy than Roosevelt's "big stick" diplomacy. Taft preferred to influence foreign affairs through the investment of American dollars in foreign countries, a policy nicknamed "**dollar diplomacy**." Concerned by Japan's efforts at expansion in China, he encouraged American companies to build railroads in China and establish themselves as competitors there. Taft also backed similar efforts in Latin America, particularly in Nicaragua.

Taft's dollar diplomacy intended to bring mutual economic benefit and to build better foreign relations between the United States and other nations. American investment helped Latin American countries establish industries and build infrastructure. But if those countries violated the interests of the United States, American investments could be halted.

## Split with Roosevelt

After helping Taft reach the presidency, Roosevelt traveled to Africa and Europe. But even overseas, he heard complaints about Taft from progressives. One issue that divided the two men was conservation. In reality, Taft was just as concerned with conservation as Roosevelt; however, Taft believed it should be accomplished through legislation rather than executive orders. As a result, Taft clashed with the head of the US Forest Service, Gifford Pinchot, who was worried about the future of some of the public lands that Taft was returning to private use. Taft eventually removed Pinchot from his position for his public criticism of the president's actions. After Pinchot's removal, Roosevelt expressed concern over Taft's devotion to conservation.

The final break between Roosevelt and Taft came over antitrust proceedings. Taft, unlike Roosevelt, believed that all monopolistic trusts were bad and that the courts, rather than a large federal bureaucracy, should deal with them. Taft initiated more antitrust suits in one term than Roosevelt had in two. But one suit in particular upset Roosevelt. In 1907, during Roosevelt's second term, US Steel had wanted to purchase the Tennessee Coal and Iron Company. Roosevelt had agreed that the move was acceptable and given his unofficial blessing to the purchase. Taft, however, viewed the transaction as a step toward building an illegal monopoly and filed suit against US Steel. Since the charges suggested that Roosevelt had been fooled by the corporation, the former president was angry and offended.

# Wilson

## Election of 1912

Roosevelt's frustration with Taft led him to announce his own campaign for the Republican nomination in 1912. Roosevelt was still popular with the voters; however, Taft won the nomination. Declaring that Taft had not only betrayed progressivism but also stolen the nomination, Roosevelt and his followers formed a third party, the Progressive Party (popularly known as the Bull Moose Party because Roosevelt had told a reporter that he felt "as strong as a bull moose"). Roosevelt ran on a platform that he called the "New Nationalism."

## The Bull Moose Platform

The Progressive Party platform called for federal agencies rather than courts to regulate businesses, a federal securities commission to supervise the sale of stocks and bonds, revision of the tariff, direct primary elections for nomination of candidates, easier amendment of the Constitution, and numerous social reforms, including women's suffrage and labor reforms.

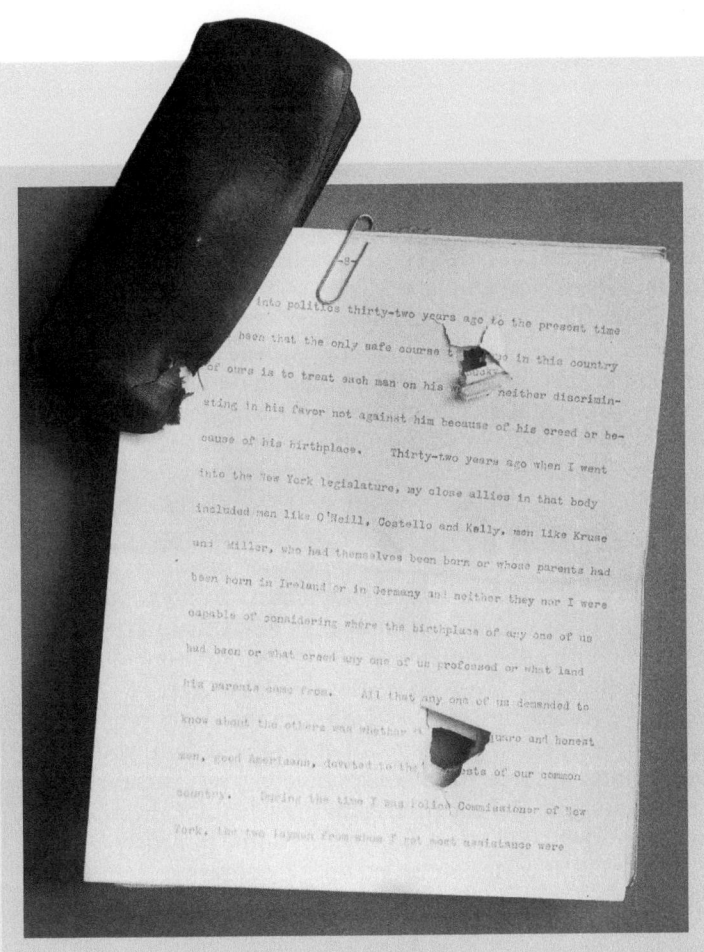

## Assassination Attempt

*"Friends, I shall ask you to be as quiet as possible. I don't know whether you fully understand that I have just been shot; but it takes more than that to kill a Bull Moose. But fortunately I had my manuscript, so you see I was going to make a long speech, and there is a bullet—there is where the bullet went through—and it probably saved me from it going into my heart. The bullet is in me now, so that I cannot make a very long speech, but I will try my best."* —Theodore Roosevelt, Address at Milwaukee, WI, October 14, 1912

On that day, John F. Schrank shot the former president when he was campaigning in Milwaukee, Wisconsin. In addition to the fifty page manuscript of his speech, the bullet was also slowed by his overcoat and a steel-reinforced eyeglass case. Despite his comment above, Roosevelt delivered a ninety-minute speech. But at times, he spoke only in a whisper.

Later in the day, doctors located the bullet lodged against one of Roosevelt's ribs. They determined it was more dangerous to attempt to remove it than to leave it in his chest. It remained there until his death in 1919.

◀ Roosevelt's speech and glasses case from the day he was shot

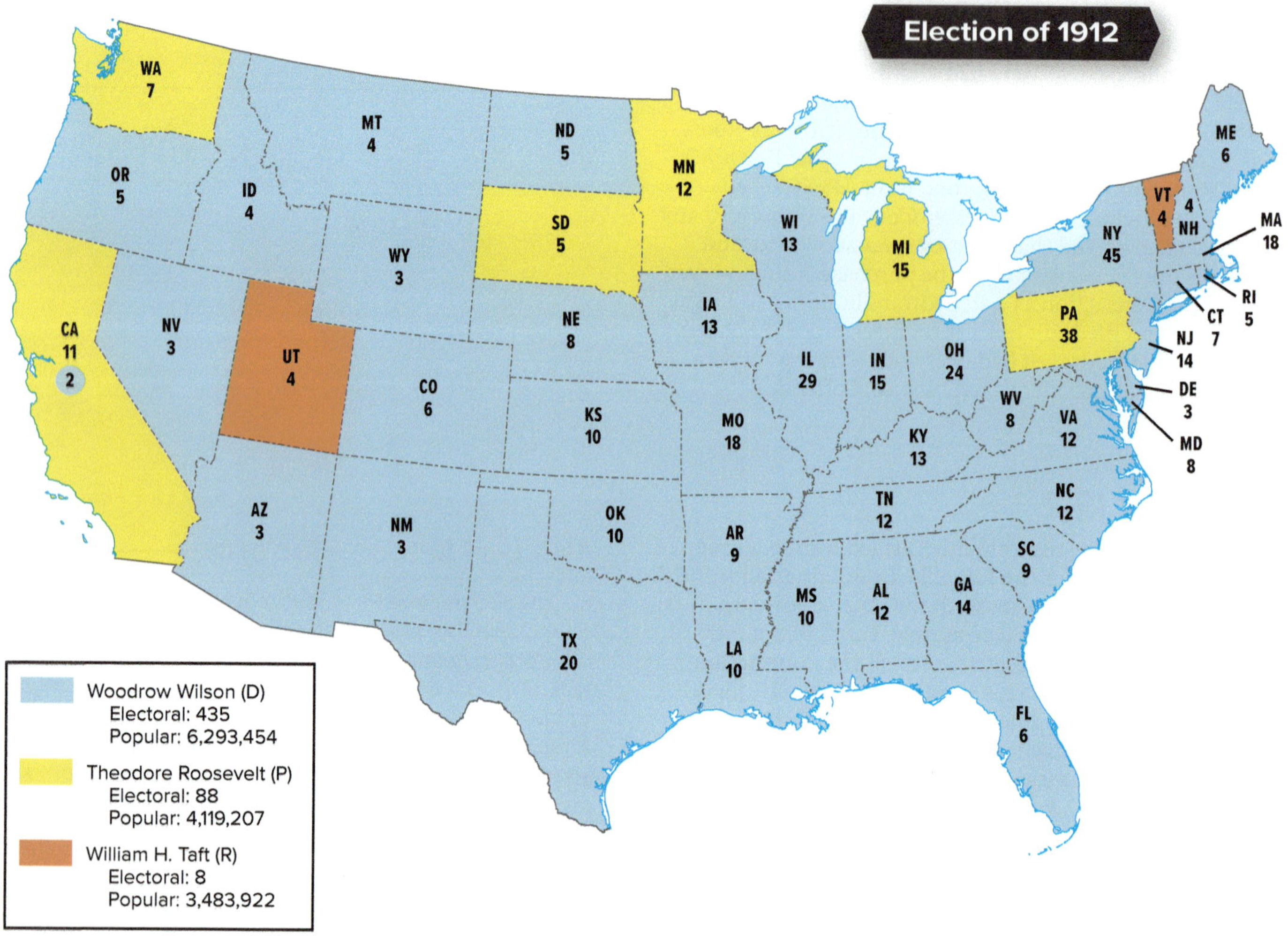

## Map: Election of 1912

WA 7
OR 5
ID 4
MT 4
ND 5
MN 12
SD 5
WI 13
MI 15
ME 6
VT 4
NH 4
NY 45
MA 18
RI 5
CT 7
NJ 14
DE 3
MD 8
CA 11 (2)
NV 3
UT 4
WY 3
CO 6
NE 8
IA 13
IL 29
IN 15
OH 24
PA 38
WV 8
VA 12
KY 13
AZ 3
NM 3
KS 10
OK 10
MO 18
AR 9
TN 12
NC 12
SC 9
MS 10
AL 12
GA 14
TX 20
LA 10
FL 6

**Legend:**

Woodrow Wilson (D)
Electoral: 435
Popular: 6,293,454

Theodore Roosevelt (P)
Electoral: 88
Popular: 4,119,207

William H. Taft (R)
Electoral: 8
Popular: 3,483,922

▲ Woodrow Wilson

The Democrats also nominated a progressive candidate, Governor Woodrow Wilson of New Jersey. As a historian, professor, and president of Princeton University, Wilson had both studied and written about the American system of government. As governor of New Jersey, he had initiated reforms such as the direct primary, state regulation of utilities, and legislation designed to drive monopolies out of the state. Wilson campaigned under the motto "New Freedom." His platform sounded much like the progressive principles of Roosevelt's earlier years in the presidency. For example, Wilson called for increased competition through trust-busting rather than the greater regulation for which Roosevelt was now campaigning.

In the election all three candidates supported progressivism. Roosevelt and his Progressive Party made the best third-party showing in presidential history. Roosevelt won 4.1 million votes to 3.5 million for Taft, and he won 88 electoral votes to Taft's 8. With the Republicans divided, however, Wilson won the election with 6.3 million votes (42 percent of the total) and 435 electoral votes, and the Democrats captured both houses of Congress. Socialist Party candidate Eugene Debs, running for president for the fourth time, received over 900,000 votes. For the first time in nearly twenty years, the Democrats controlled both Congress and the White House.

# Wilson and the New Freedom

Wilson's first term was the climax of the progressive movement in America. For example, three of the four "progressive amendments" to the Constitution (the Seventeenth, Eighteenth, and Nineteenth) reached final ratification during Wilson's time in office. Wilson's "New Freedom" agenda included tariff and tax reform, banking reform, and business reform.

## REVENUE REVISION

One of the first important reforms of the Wilson administration was the **Underwood Tariff Act of 1913**, which enacted the first genuine tariff reduction since the Civil War, slashing overall rates by about a third from what they had been. Even more important, the act compensated for the loss of tariff revenue by adopting the first income tax (allowed by the recently ratified Sixteenth Amendment). Those who earned less than $4,000 a year, which included most factory workers and farmers, paid no income tax. Tax rates rose from one percent for those earning between $4,000 and $20,000 to six percent for those earning above $500,000.

## FEDERAL RESERVE ACT

In 1907 the latest in a series of financial panics left American businessmen desiring a better system of regulating currency and banking practices. These businessmen envisioned something similar to the Bank of the United States that Andrew Jackson had destroyed. They argued that the country needed a centralized, privately owned national bank that could easily set standards for local banks and regulate the flow of currency throughout the country.

Wilson and the progressives in Congress, however, developed a different system in the **Federal Reserve Act** (1913). This act divided the nation into twelve banking districts, each served by a private regional Federal Reserve Bank. Over these district banks was a central, government-run organization, the Federal Reserve Board. This system was a compromise between a totally private banking system (as businessmen wanted) and a totally government-controlled system (as many progressives wanted). The Federal Reserve is still in operation today. The twelve branches function as "bankers' banks." They and the Board influence the nation's monetary policy and the amount of money in circulation by setting interest rates for loans between banks. The "Fed" also exercises control over many banking operations throughout the country.

| District number | Federal Reserve Bank location |
|---|---|
| 1 | Boston, MA |
| 2 | New York, NY |
| 3 | Philadelphia, PA |
| 4 | Cleveland, OH |
| 5 | Richmond, VA |
| 6 | Atlanta, GA |
| 7 | Chicago, IL |
| 8 | St. Louis, MO |
| 9 | Minneapolis, MN |
| 10 | Kansas City, MO |
| 11 | Dallas, TX |
| 12 | San Francisco, CA |

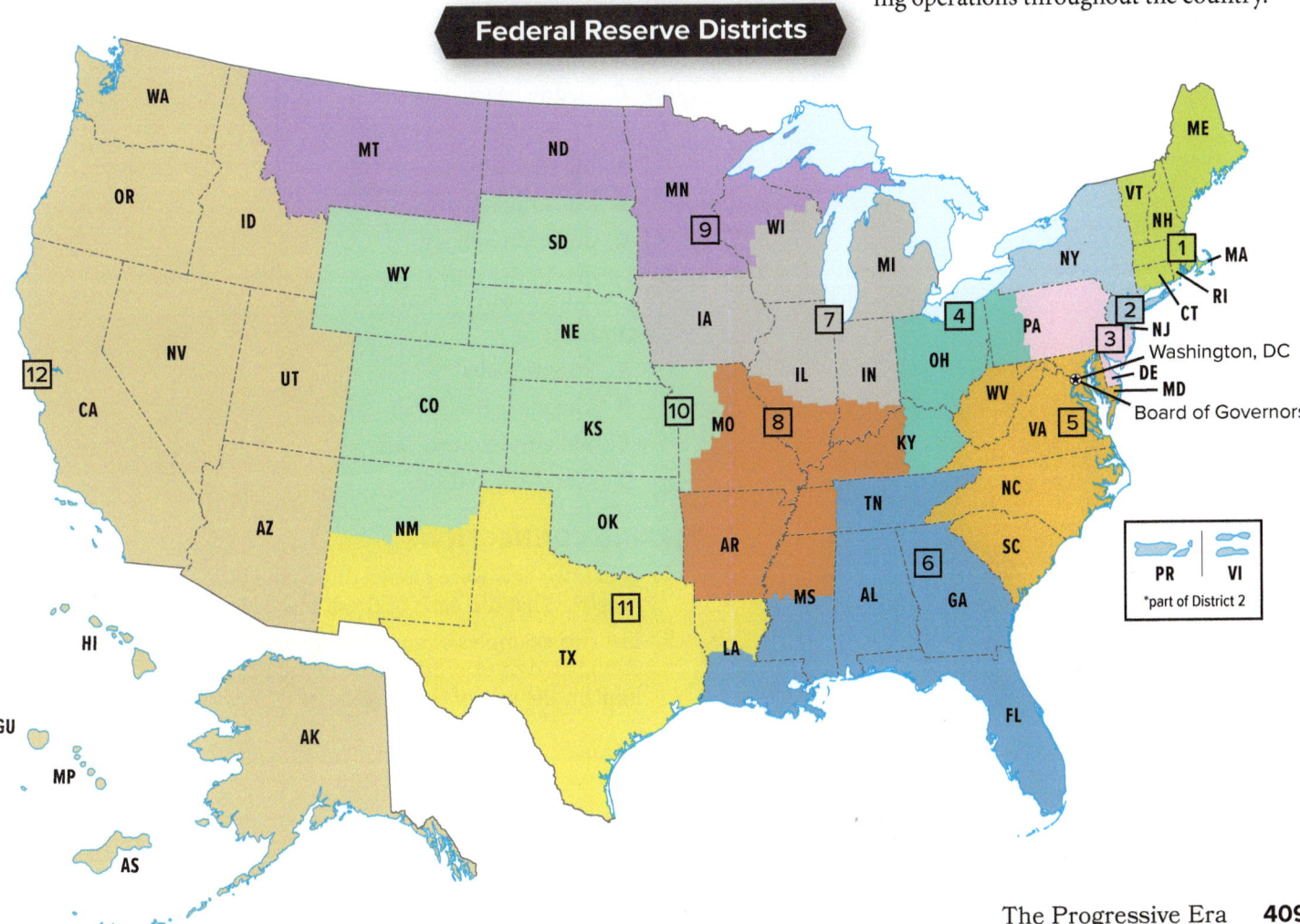

**Federal Reserve Districts**

## BUSINESS AND LABOR

Wilson signed two important pieces of legislation in 1914 concerning the regulation of business and labor. The **Clayton Antitrust Act** strengthened the Sherman Antitrust Act by expanding the list of practices prohibited to corporations. Because businesses had tried to use antitrust laws to target unions, the Clayton Act exempted labor unions from antitrust legislation and legalized practices such as strikes, picketing, and boycotts.

Even more sweeping was the Federal Trade Commission Act. That act established the **Federal Trade Commission** (FTC), a board of five people authorized to help define and halt unfair business practices. The FTC Act marked a growing tendency for government regulation of business practices. Increasingly, the determining of unfair practices, the establishment of regulations, and the enforcement of policies were being left to regulatory agencies such as the FTC instead of to Congress or the courts.

As Wilson's first term as president neared an end, however, events in Europe and Mexico would force him to shift his focus from his domestic agenda to foreign affairs.

## Wilson's Progressive Legislation

| Legislation | Date | Effect |
| --- | --- | --- |
| Underwood Tariff Act | 1913 | Lowered tariffs and enacted a federal income tax |
| Federal Reserve Act | 1913 | Established the Federal Reserve Board and Federal Reserve Banks to carry out the nation's monetary policy and oversee other banks |
| Federal Trade Commission Act | 1914 | Created the Federal Trade Commission to define and halt unfair business practices |
| Clayton Antitrust Act | 1914 | Expanded the Sherman Antitrust Act's list of practices prohibited to corporations |

### Comprehension Check 15.3

1. Roosevelt enlisted the help of the ____, who were journalists exposing abuse and corruption.

    A "Fed"

    B "muckrakers"

    C "teddy bears"

2. Taft's foreign policy was called ____.

    A big stick diplomacy

    B muckraking

    C dollar diplomacy

3. Because of the split between Republicans in the election of 1912, ____ won as the Democratic candidate.

    A Eugene Debs

    B Theodore Roosevelt

    C William Howard Taft

    D Woodrow Wilson

### MAKING CONNECTIONS

4. What two acts were passed due to the influence of *The Jungle*? What did each of these acts do?

5. List two examples of government agencies that were established or expanded during the Progressive Era. Explain the role of these agencies.

## Chapter Summary

### 15.1 Society of the Progressive Era

- Progressivism was a collection of people and ideas which favored achieving political and social reform through education, wider political participation, and direct government action. The period from the 1890s to around 1920 was called the Progressive Era.

- Life for many Americans was transformed through new leisure activities and advances in faster transportation, including air travel. Education, not the Bible, was viewed as the best way to improve society.

- African Americans faced discrimination in the form of Jim Crow laws and voting restrictions. Responses varied from Booker T. Washington's advocacy of industrial education and economic progress to W. E. B. Du Bois's advocacy for voting and other political rights.

- Modernism attempted to adapt Christianity to modern ideas by rejecting doctrines such as the inspiration of the Bible and the deity of Christ. Reform Darwinism and the social gospel emphasized the physical rather than the spiritual needs of people.

- Christians responded to these challenges by defending the authority of the Bible, establishing Bible institutes and conferences, and evangelizing.

**TERMS**

progressivism

Henry Ford

Orville and Wilber Wright

*Titanic*

Booker T. Washington

George Washington Carver

Jim Crow laws

literacy tests

poll taxes

grandfather clauses

*Plessy v. Ferguson*

W. E. B. Du Bois

National Association for the Advancement of Colored People (NAACP)

modernism

Reform Darwinism

social gospel

Fundamentalists

**TERMS**

initiative

referendum

recall

settlement houses

Sixteenth Amendment

Seventeenth Amendment

Eighteenth Amendment

Nineteenth Amendment

### 15.2 Goals of the Progressive Era

- Progressives sought to reform government by fighting corruption through trust-busting and government ownership of utilities; increasing democracy through secret ballots, initiative, referendum, and recall elections; and improving efficiency by hiring experts as city managers or commissioners.

- Progressives achieved reforms in areas such as labor hours and working conditions, living conditions, temperance, and women's voting rights.

- The Sixteenth through Nineteenth Amendments accomplished four progressive goals: an income tax, the direct election of US senators, prohibition of alcoholic beverages, and women's suffrage.

## Chapter Summary

### 15.3 | Presidents of the Progressive Era

■ Theodore Roosevelt pursued a progressive agenda. Muckrakers exposed corruption and problems in society, which sometimes led to legislation to address abuses. Roosevelt used the Sherman Antitrust Act against trusts he saw as bad but preferred to use government agencies to regulate businesses. He sided with unions in labor disputes and promoted conservation of America's natural resources.

■ Republican William Howard Taft succeeded Roosevelt in 1908. He pursued a foreign policy known as "dollar diplomacy." He achieved several progressive goals, but his actions on tariffs, conservation, and trust-busting angered Roosevelt and other progressives.

■ Democrat Woodrow Wilson defeated Taft and Roosevelt in the 1912 election. Wilson's progressive agenda was called "New Freedom" and included lower tariffs, an income tax, the creation of the Federal Reserve Bank, new antitrust legislation, and the creation of the Federal Trade Commission to regulate businesses.

**TERMS**

muckrakers

Pure Food and Drug Act

Meat Inspection Act

William Howard Taft

dollar diplomacy

Underwood Tariff Act of 1913

Federal Reserve Act

Clayton Antitrust Act

Federal Trade Commission

## Chapter Review Questions

### RECALL

1. What were two inventions that transformed transportation during the Progressive Era?

2. What industrial college was founded by Booker T. Washington?

3. What organization was formed in 1909 to seek equality for African Americans?

4. What Princeton Seminary professor defended orthodox Christianity from modernism?

5. What former professional baseball player became a leading urban evangelist?

6. What did progressives believe primarily shaped people and their behavior?

7. What tragedy in New York City led to new laws to improve health and safety among factory workers?

8. What party did Roosevelt create to oppose Taft in the election of 1912?

9. Who were the four major candidates and their parties in the election of 1912? Who won the election?

### UNDERSTAND

10. What is progressivism? What were two reasons people believed that society was progressing?

11. What were two ways people spent their leisure time during this era?

12. How was Henry Ford able to lower the cost of the automobile?

13. What were three ways education changed during the Progressive Era?

14. What contributions did George Washington Carver make to the field of agriculture?

15. What were two ways African Americans faced discrimination during this period?

16. What did the Supreme Court rule in *Plessy v. Ferguson*?

17. How did some people use science to defend discrimination?

18. How did modernists attempt to adapt Christianity to modern ideas?

19. How did Reform Darwinism differ from Social Darwinism?

20. What was the social gospel movement? What aspect of Christianity did it embrace, and what aspect of Christianity did it neglect?

21. What were four ways orthodox Christians responded to modernism and the problems of society during the Progressive Era? How did these efforts differ?

22. What were three ways progressives attempted to fight corruption?

23. What were three ways progressives attempted to increase democracy?

24. What were two ways progressives tried to improve government efficiency?

25. What acts were the result of the publication of the muckraking book *The Jungle*?

26. How did Roosevelt distinguish between "good" trusts and "bad" trusts?

27. What were Roosevelt's actions during the coal strike of 1902? How did his actions differ from previous government actions involving labor issues?

28. What were three ways Taft's domestic and foreign policies differed from Roosevelt's?

29. What were four progressive policies enacted by Woodrow Wilson?

## THINK ABOUT IT

30. Contrast the views of Booker T. Washington and W. E. B. Du Bois regarding how African Americans should respond to discrimination.

31. Why do increased democracy and reliance on experts not always lead to better government?

32. How did each of the progressive amendments accomplish a goal of progressivism?

33. Why could progressivism's goal of changing society by changing man's environment never be fully successful?

▼ Roosevelt on the campaign trail in 1912

# 16 World War I

16.1 The Powder Keg of Europe
16.2 American Neutrality
16.3 The War to End All Wars
16.4 Aftermath of World War I

▲ Aerial combat in World War I

# The Powder Keg of Europe

**What led Europe into World War I?**

- What circumstances led to war in Europe?
- What event caused Europe to go to war?
- What was modern warfare like during World War I?

"It would be an irony of fate if my administration had to deal chiefly with foreign affairs," Woodrow Wilson privately remarked before his inauguration in March 1913. Such irony would indeed be his "fate." The Progressive Era's optimism about the advancement of mankind was soon to be shattered by conflict that began in Europe but eventually drew America in.

## Factors Leading to War

### Militarism

After a war between France and Prussia in 1870, the balance of power in Europe was disrupted. The Prussians captured French emperor Napoleon III, besieged Paris, and defeated the French army. Prussian Chancellor (prime minister) Otto von Bismarck used the war to unify a collection of small independent states into the German Empire. In the peace treaty, Germany received the French territories of Alsace and Lorraine along the Rhine River, and France was forced to pay for war damages.

Having lost the Franco-Prussian War, France adopted a policy of **militarism** (buildup of military might). It reformed its strategies and training, adopted universal conscription (a requirement that all males serve in the army for a period of time) and modernized its weapons to prevent another humiliating military defeat. Germany noted France's increased military preparation and pursued its own military modernization as well, especially the enlargement of its navy.

### Alliances

In 1879 Austria-Hungary entered into an alliance with Germany. In 1882 Italy joined, forming the **Triple Alliance**. Alarmed by this alliance, Russia made a treaty with France in 1894. Britain, which felt threatened by Germany's naval buildup, entered into an "*entente cordiale*" (friendly understanding) with France and Russia in 1907, and the three countries came to be known as the **Triple Entente**. This system of alliances, in which countries promised mutual military support, meant that once any European country entered a conflict, the others were likely to be drawn in as well.

### Imperialism and Nationalism

As mentioned in Chapter 14, many European powers engaged in imperialism in the late nineteenth and early twentieth centuries. The British, Ottoman, Austro-Hungarian, Russian, and German empires gained control of other nations or peoples through annexation, military conquest, or economic control. Some of those nations or peoples who had been brought under imperial control responded with a growing sense of **nationalism** (a feeling of loyalty or devotion to one's country or cultural group that surpasses other loyalties). Many of these people began to demand independence and the right of **self-determination** (the ability of people to form their own countries and governments). Nationalism in the late 1800s and early 1900s often went beyond devotion to a belief in the superiority of their nation and to competition among nations over military and imperial strength.

Nationalism was particularly powerful in the Balkan Peninsula (the area of southeastern Europe between the Black, Mediterranean, Aegean, and Adriatic seas), a region comprised of people from many ethnic groups with differing religions and cultures. The Balkans had been part of the Ottoman Empire until the nineteenth century, when Ottoman power began to decline. A developing nationalism in the 1800s led to Greece, Bulgaria, Montenegro, and Serbia gaining their independence. The imperial powers of Europe all had interest in the region. Russia saw Serbia as important for checking Austria-Hungary's power and expansion. Austria-Hungary annexed Bosnia-Herzegovina in 1908, which aroused new nationalist movements among Slavic people (Bosnians, Serbs, Croats, and Slovenes) in the region. Russia, also a Slavic nation, supported these movements.

## The Spark

On June 28, 1914, Austrian archduke **Francis (Franz) Ferdinand**, heir to the throne of the Austro-Hungarian Empire, and his wife, Sophie, traveled to Sarajevo, the capital of Bosnia which was now part of Austria-Hungary. As the archduke's motorcade traveled through the city streets, seven young Serbian nationalists, members of the terrorist group Black Hand which wanted an independent Slavic nation, launched a coordinated attack. After narrowly escaping one assassin's bomb, the archduke's driver took a wrong turn into a side street, slowing the car to make the turn and coming within five feet of one of the assassins, Gavrilo Princip. Princip raised his pistol and fired two quick shots, killing both Franz Ferdinand and his wife. The archduke's assassination became the "spark" that led to what was soon called the Great War or the World War (later called World War I, after the outbreak of World War II).

◀ Archduke Francis Ferdinand of Austria and his wife, Sophie, in Sarajevo before the assassination

## Warfare and Weapons

### The Spread of World War

When officials in Austria-Hungary learned that the conspirators had been aided by Serbians, they issued an ultimatum on July 23, 1914, demanding that Serbia condemn all anti-Austrian propaganda in the country, remove from office any officials who promoted anti-Austrian sentiment, and allow Austria-Hungary to send officials to investigate matters relating to the archduke's death. Serbia replied that it was willing to accept some but not all of Austria-Hungary's demands. Austria-Hungary was not satisfied and declared war on Serbia on July 28. Both Austria-Hungary and Serbia began mobilizing (assembling) their troops for war.

Russia, fearing that Austria intended to establish control of Serbia, began mobilizing its troops on July 30. Germany, Austria's ally, declared war on Russia two days later. Since Russia and France were both members of the Triple Entente, Germany demanded to know France's intentions. The French, concerned about Germany's preparation for war, mobilized their troops, an act that the Germans interpreted as aggressive.

On August 2 the German emperor, Kaiser Wilhelm II, asked neutral Belgium for permission to pass through its country in the event of a war with France. The following day, the Belgian king denied the request, saying "Belgium is a nation, not a road." That same day, August 3, Germany declared war on France. On August 4 German troops invaded Belgium.

▶ Kaiser Wilhelm II of the German Empire

▼ German recruitment poster saying, "Your Fatherland is in danger, register!"

▲ British recruitment poster

Britain, which had a treaty with Belgium promising to protect the neutrality of that nation, demanded that Germany withdraw its troops. The German chancellor sneered at Britain's commitment to a "scrap of paper" (its treaty with Belgium) and ignored the British demand. Britain declared war on Germany on August 4.

Within a week of the war beginning, all members of the Triple Alliance and Triple Entente joined the war except Italy, which although a member of the Triple Alliance, felt that Germany and Austria-Hungary had acted too hastily in declaring war. Italy would later join the **Allied Powers**, which also included the original Triple Entente: Britain, France, and Russia. The **Central Powers** included two of the original Triple Alliance nations: Germany and Austria-Hungary, and later Bulgaria and Turkey (or the Ottoman Empire). Eventually 135 countries from around the world would participate in the war.

As confident German troops marched into Belgium, the words of their kaiser rang in their ears: "You will be home before the leaves have fallen from the trees." By the end of August, the Germans had approached the outskirts of Paris, but the British and French forces were able to drive the Germans back at the Battle of the Marne. In the first month of war, the French alone lost two hundred thousand troops in battle. By the end of 1914, a long, bloody stalemate had settled over the frontlines along Germany's Western Front (the line between German and French forces) as both sides dug opposing trenches that stretched from Belgium to Switzerland.

## World War I in Europe

**Legend:**
- Central Powers
- Allied Powers
- Neutral nations

German submarine blockade, 1917

British blockade

*Lusitania* torpedoed, May 1915

ATLANTIC OCEAN

NORWAY
SWEDEN
UK
North Sea
DENMARK
Baltic Sea
RUSSIAN EMPIRE
NETHER- LANDS
GERMANY
BELGIUM
LUX.
FRANCE
SWITZ.
AUSTRIA-HUNGARY
Caspian Sea
PORTUGAL
SPAIN
ITALY
MONT.
SERBIA
Sarajevo
ROMANIA
BULGARIA
Black Sea
ALBANIA
GREECE
OTTOMAN EMPIRE
Mediterranean Sea

# Modern Warfare

## Life in the Trenches

**Trench warfare** became a major part of World War I. The trench system included frontline trenches, support trenches (for men and supplies to assist those on the frontlines), and communication trenches (which assisted with the movement of messages as well as supplies). Beyond the frontline trenches were barbed wire and "no man's land," a neutral zone that varied in size from a few yards to more than a mile between the Allied and German lines. This system made advancing difficult.

Trench life was not for the fainthearted. Soldiers faced severe discomfort. Trenches were often filled with water and pests—rats and lice. Food was also a problem, both in availability and desirability. Beside discomfort, soldiers faced disease. Unsanitary conditions caused dysentery, a flu-like disease. Waterlogged trenches could lead to trench foot, an infection that, if left untreated, could result in toes or the entire foot having to be amputated. Lice carried a disease that came to be known as trench fever, which was not life-threatening but was disabling.

## Modern Weapons

Modern weapons were utilized by both sides. Trucks and automobiles were used to transport military goods and personnel. Machine guns, grenades, mines, and improved artillery made warfare far more efficient and deadly. Britain developed the tank, an armored vehicle whose caterpillar tracks could traverse rugged terrain, and which could shoot its guns while moving. The German navy effectively used **U-boats** (from *Unterseeboot*, German for a submarine), and soon other countries were using them as well.

▼ Allied tank

▼ Surfaced German U-boat

The Germans first used poison gas on April 15, 1915, at the Second Battle of Ypres in Belgium. Soon both sides were launching shells filled with chlorine or mustard gas at one another. The gas, if breathed in, harmed noses, throats, and lungs, and often caused soldiers to choke to death. As a result, the gas mask was developed to protect troops from the fearsome poison.

◄ German gas mask

Aviation was also an important military development during World War I. Airplanes were first used to scout enemy positions, but soon became weapons themselves. They were used to bomb targets or attack enemy planes. Fighter pilots became "aces" after recording at least five "kills" (enemy planes shot down). The most famous World War I ace was German pilot Manfred von Richthofen (also known as the Red Baron because of his scarlet-red triplane) who shot down eighty planes. On April 20, 1918, he scored his seventy-ninth and eightieth kills. The next day, he was mortally wounded in combat.

▶ Model of the Red Baron's plane

## Comprehension Check 16.1

1. Imperialism led to a growing nationalism and desire for self-determination by those who had been brought under imperial control.

   True      False

2. Britain, France, and Russia were members of the _____.

   **A** Triple Entente

   **B** Triple Alliance

   **C** Central Powers

3. Archduke Franz Ferdinand was assassinated by a _____ nationalist.

   **A** Serbian

   **B** Polish

   **C** Austrian

4. Britain declared war against Germany because Germany had invaded _____.

   **A** Russia

   **B** Serbia

   **C** Belgium

### MAKING CONNECTIONS

5. What were four modern weapons used in World War I, and how did modern weapons change warfare?

- How did Wilson's foreign policy differ from Roosevelt's and Taft's?

- Why was it difficult for America to remain neutral?

### 16.2 American Neutrality

**How was America pulled into World War I?**

## Wilson's Foreign Policy

### Idealism

In his foreign policy, Wilson, along with his secretary of state William Jennings Bryan, sought to make the United States the moral leader among nations, believing that America's role in the world was to promote democracy and peace by example and persuasion. He was called an idealist because he was optimistic that people and nations would set aside their own interests for the good of others. Wilson saw America as having a new Manifest Destiny, not of territorial expansion but of sharing political ideals. In a key foreign policy address delivered in 1913 in Mobile, Alabama, Wilson said:

> *I want to take this occasion to say that the United States will never again seek one additional foot of territory by conquest. She will devote herself to showing that she knows how to make honorable and fruitful use of the territory she has. . . .*
>
> *We dare not turn from the principle that morality and not expediency is the thing that must guide us and that we will never condone iniquity because it is most convenient to do so.*
>
> **— WOODROW WILSON**

Wilson wanted to expand the United States economically by promoting trade with other nations. In helping American companies make profits, he advocated **moral diplomacy**, a policy that promoted freedom and democratic ideas and help for other countries to improve economically. For example, Wilson supported countries that provided the right to free elections and pressured those that did not provide that freedom. Despite his noble goals, global realities soon challenged Wilson's ability to enact his proposals.

### Caribbean Conflict

At the beginning of his administration, Wilson denounced both Taft's dollar diplomacy and Roosevelt's "big stick" policies as contrary to the new moral leadership of the United States. He hoped to mend fences with America's southern neighbors, but the desire to protect the strategic Panama Canal and Wilson's eagerness to see America's neighbors form orderly democratic governments actually led him into more military interventions in the Caribbean than his predecessors.

**Analyzing Sources**

According to Wilson, what principles should govern the United States in its foreign policy?

▲ Political cartoon depicting Woodrow Wilson as a teacher to the leaders of Venezuela, Nicaragua, and Mexico

More than a half-dozen presidents in Haiti were killed or overthrown between 1911 and 1915. Fearing both the loss of American lives or property and the threat of European intervention, Wilson ordered US Marines to occupy Haiti. American forces were there from July 1915 until 1934. They built roads and schools and established order, but the Haitian people began to resent America's dominance of its affairs.

Next door to Haiti, in the Dominican Republic, civil war erupted in 1916. A US Marine police force occupied that area until 1924. As in Haiti, the Dominican Republic benefited materially during the US occupation, but resentment of the "Colossus of the North" remained high in Latin America.

## Trouble in Mexico

Wilson's idealism was also put to the test in Mexico. From 1876 to 1911 Porfirio Díaz had ruled Mexico ruthlessly but welcomed foreign investors. Díaz and European and American businessmen all profited from the oil and mining resources of Mexico but left the Mexican people impoverished. In 1911 a popular revolt led by Francisco Madero drove Díaz out of office, but the rebellion also unleashed violent rivals for power, groups that had previously been suppressed by Díaz's stern rule.

Just weeks before Wilson's inauguration, President Madero was murdered by his own military commander, General Victoriano Huerta. Many countries quickly extended diplomatic recognition to the new Mexican government in hopes of reestablishing profitable business relations. Previously, most countries, including the United States, traditionally extended such recognition if a government simply held power, without concerning themselves with how it obtained that power. But this time Wilson refused to recognize "government by murder." "Mexico has a great and enviable future before her, if only she choose and attain the paths of honest constitutional government," he told Congress. He later declared, "I am going to teach the Latin American republics to elect good men!"

Determined to drive Huerta out of office, Wilson began supplying weapons to Huerta's challengers, Venustiano Carranza and **Pancho Villa**. In April 1914, a group of American sailors in Tampico, Mexico, were arrested. Although they were soon released and the local commander expressed regret to the American naval commander, the US government was outraged. Wilson, citing national honor, went to Congress and requested authority to use force against the Huerta regime. On April 20, 1914, Congress granted the request. American marines landed in the city of Veracruz. Following a bloody clash between US troops and Mexicans there, the "ABC powers" (Argentina, Brazil, and Chile) mediated a truce between the United States and Mexico. The accumulated internal and international pressure encouraged by Wilson eventually toppled Huerta, bringing Carranza to power.

◄ (top) American marines with captured Haitian outlaws outside Port-au-Prince; (bottom) Francisco "Pancho" Villa

World War I    **421**

Peace, however, did not come with Huerta's exit. Villa soon rebelled against Carranza. Wilson at first supported Villa, believing he wanted to improve the lives of poor Mexicans. As the fight between Villa and Carranza intensified, Wilson decided to withdraw his support. Villa was furious with the Americans. In January 1916, Villa had a train stopped in northern Mexico, and his men murdered eighteen Americans. Two months later, his men led a raid into New Mexico, where his band killed seventeen more Americans and burned the border town of Columbus. In response, Wilson sent General **John J. "Black Jack" Pershing** into Mexico with eleven thousand troops to capture Villa. After months of searching fruitlessly for the elusive Villa, and as problems in Europe loomed ever larger, Wilson ordered Pershing to cancel the expedition in early 1917.

## Challenges to Neutrality

When news of the war in Europe reached the United States, President Wilson issued a proclamation of neutrality. He urged Americans not to take the side of either the Allied Powers (also called Allies) or the Central Powers. Sentiment in America was divided, and numerous factors challenged the country's neutrality.

### Favoring the Allies

Many Americans had been born in Germany or were descended from German immigrants. Many Irish immigrants and their descendants also favored Germany, mainly because the Irish opposed Britain's rule of Ireland. Most Americans, however, had their roots in Great Britain, and the nation's language, legal system, and form of government were English in origin. Some also favored France because of its aid in America's Revolutionary War, while others tended to view Germany as the aggressor for invading neutral Belgium.

While American businesses sold goods to both sides, America's strong economic ties with the Allies, particularly Britain, increased during the war. Early in the war, both Britain and France purchased grain, cotton, and other supplies in cash. When the Allies ran out of cash, Wilson allowed American banks to grant loans to the Allies. Germany protested that these loans were being used to purchase American-made guns and ammunition which were being used to kill Germans. Wilson chose not to end the loans, and by early 1917 the United States had loaned the Allies over $2 billion but only $27 million to Germany.

### Propaganda

American neutrality was also challenged by **propaganda** (information spread to advance a cause or damage an opponent's cause) coming from both sides of the conflict in Europe. When the war began, Britain cut the German transatlantic telegraph cable. As a result, most news that reached the United States about the war in Europe came from Britain, who hoped to win American public support. The British portrayed the Allies in the best possible light and presented only negative information, and even lies, about Germany.

RED CROSS OR IRON CROSS?

WOUNDED AND A PRISONER OUR SOLDIER CRIES FOR WATER.

THE GERMAN "SISTER" POURS IT ON THE GROUND BEFORE HIS EYES.

THERE IS NO WOMAN IN BRITAIN WHO WOULD DO IT.

THERE IS NO WOMAN IN BRITAIN WHO WILL FORGET IT.

▲ British propaganda poster vilifying German nurses of the Red Cross

## Submarine Warfare

The most significant threat to America's neutrality was the violation of American rights at sea. As the land war in Europe ground to a stalemate, both sides sought to gain an advantage by stopping the flow of goods to the enemy. Both sides declared that all grain and flour shipments to the enemy would be contraband (goods prohibited from shipment) and subject to seizure. Britain blockaded ships from traveling to or from German ports and seized an American freighter headed to Germany with a shipment of grain.

A starving Germany countered by declaring the seas around Britain to be a war zone in which any ship would be subject to destruction. According to international law, warships could not sink a merchant or passenger ship until (1) the presence of war materials aboard those vessels had been confirmed, and (2) the crew and passengers on the ships had been evacuated. When Germany announced in February 1915 that it intended to use unrestricted submarine warfare, it declared that because Britain was using merchant and passenger ships to carry war materials, all ships entering the war zone would be subject to attack without warning. President Wilson warned the Germans that this abandoning of international law was unacceptable.

In late April 1915, the German government placed advertisements in American newspapers, including the *New York Times*, warning American citizens not to travel into the war zone. The British passenger ship **Lusitania** left New York on May 1, 1915, with many Americans aboard. When the liner entered the war zone near Ireland on May 7, the commander of a German submarine spotted the ship and fired a torpedo. Within eighteen minutes, the large liner sank, and 1,198 passengers and crewmen, including 128 Americans, perished.

# NOTICE!

TRAVELLERS intending to embark on the Atlantic voyage are reminded that a state of war exists between Germany and her allies and Great Britain and her allies; that the zone of war includes the waters adjacent to the British Isles; that, in accordance with formal notice given by the Imperial German Government, vessels flying the flag of Great Britain, or any of her allies, are liable to destruction in those waters and that travelers sailing in the war zone on ships of Great Britain and her allies do so at their own risk.

**IMPERIAL GERMAN EMBASSY**
WASHINGTON, D. C., APRIL 22, 1915

▲ German warning to American passengers to avoid traveling on British ships

"All the News That's Fit to Print."

# The New York Times.

**EXTRA**
5:30 A. M.

VOL. LXIV...NO. 20,923.          NEW YORK, SATURDAY, MAY 8, 1915.—TWENTY-FOUR PAGES.          ONE CENT

## LUSITANIA SUNK BY A SUBMARINE, PROBABLY 1,260 DEAD; TWICE TORPEDOED OFF IRISH COAST; SINKS IN 15 MINUTES; CAPT. TURNER SAVED, FROHMAN AND VANDERBILT MISSING; WASHINGTON BELIEVES THAT A GRAVE CRISIS IS AT HAND

**SHOCKS THE PRESIDENT**

Washington Deeply Stirred by the Loss of American Lives.

**BULLETINS AT WHITE HOUSE**

Wilson Reads Them Closely, but Is Silent on the Nation's Course.

**HINTS' OF CONGRESS CALL**

Loss of Lusitania Recalls Firm Tone of Our First Warning to Germany.

**CAPITAL FULL OF RUMORS**

Reports That Liner Was to be Sunk Were Heard Before Actual News Came.

**SOME DEAD TAKEN ASHORE**

Several Hundred Survivors at Queenstown and Kinsale.

**STEWARD TELLS OF DISASTER**

One Torpedo Crashes Into the Doomed Liner's Bow. Another Into the Engine Room.

**SHIP LISTS OVER TO PORT**

Makes It Impossible to Lower Many Boats, So Hundreds Must Have Gone Down.

**ATTACKED IN BROAD DAY**

Passengers at Luncheon—Warning Had Been Given by Germans Before the Ship Left New York.

**Only 650 Were Saved, Few Cabin Passengers**

The Lost Cunard Steamship Lusitania
X Where the First Torpedo Struck.   XX Where the Second Torpedo Struck

World War I   **423**

President Wilson was deeply moved by the tragedy but resisted the calls of some Americans to declare war. Wilson demanded that the Germans apologize, provide financial compensation for American families affected by the *Lusitania's* sinking, and cease attacking the citizens of neutral countries even if sailing on British ships. Germany expressed regret for the loss of life but asserted that the sinking was justified since the passenger vessel was also carrying war materials. Secretary of State Bryan, who believed the British blockade of food shipments to Germany was equally as offensive as German U-boat attacks, later resigned because he feared Wilson's words would lead to war with Germany.

The *Lusitania* incident caused a change in many Americans' attitudes toward the Germans. As one newspaper stated, "The torpedo that sank the *Lusitania* also sank Germany in the opinion of mankind." Realizing that American opinion was shifting toward war against Germany, the Germans temporarily halted unrestricted submarine warfare. But on March 24, 1916, a German submarine attacked an unarmed French passenger ship, the *Sussex*, in the English Channel. Among those killed and injured were several Americans. The furor over the *Sussex* caused Wilson to warn the Germans that another attack on passenger or merchant vessels would likely mean a break in diplomatic ties. In May 1916 Germany issued the "*Sussex* pledge" promising not to target passenger ships and not to sink merchant ships until the presence of war materials onboard had been verified and provisions had been made to evacuate crew members.

Back on land, the Great War was going badly for both sides. New technology gave the armies mass-produced weapons for mass-produced death. One tragic illustration of this was the British offensive at the Somme. On the opening day, July 1, 1916, the British suffered sixty thousand casualties—the bloodiest day in modern history. By the end of the Somme campaign, the British had gained four or five miles of mud, but the price was steep, with almost half a million British soldiers killed or wounded. In addition, there were about 700,000 German and French casualties.

▼ Wounded men during the Battle of the Somme

## Election of 1916

The presidential election of 1916 occurred amidst the foreign crises in Mexico and Europe. The Democrats nominated Wilson for a second term, cheering, "He kept us out of war." On the Republican side, Supreme Court Justice Charles Evans Hughes resigned his position to run for president. In many ways, the election mirrored the nation's mood regarding the war. In the East, where war fever was highest, Hughes won the states handily. However, the German-Americans and Irish-Americans of the Midwest supported Wilson, and on the Pacific coast Wilson's neutrality was popular. The election was very close, and the outcome was in doubt while the nation awaited California's results. Wilson won that state by fewer than 4,000 votes, giving him an electoral victory of 277 to 254.

After the election, Wilson appeared before the Senate and issued a historic declaration. In that January 1917 speech, he warned the deadlocked nations of Europe that only "peace without victory" could provide a lasting solution:

> The question upon which the whole future peace and policy of the world depends is this: Is the present war a struggle for a just and secure peace, or only for a new balance of power? . . . There must be, not a balance of power, but a community of power; not organized rivalries, but an organized common peace.
>
> [There] must be a peace without victory. . . . Victory would mean peace forced upon the loser, a victor's terms imposed upon the vanquished. . . . Only a peace between equals can last. . . .
>
> The equality of nations upon which peace must be founded if it is to last must be an equality of rights; the guarantees exchanged must neither recognize nor imply a difference between big nations and small, between those that are powerful and those that are weak. Right must be based upon the common strength, not upon the individual strength, of the nations upon whose concert [agreement] peace will depend.

A week after Wilson's speech, the Germans, suffering under the British blockade, declared the resumption of unrestricted submarine warfare. All ships in the war zone—passenger or merchant, from a nation at war or a neutral one—would be sunk without warning. Wilson reluctantly severed diplomatic ties with Germany on February 3, 1917. Many Americans, including the president, still hoped that war could yet be avoided.

## The Zimmermann Telegram

On March 1, 1917, tensions increased with the revelation of a secret German diplomatic plot. The German foreign minister, Arthur Zimmermann, sent a telegram to the German ambassador in Mexico stating if the resumption of unrestricted submarine warfare caused the United States to enter the war, Germany offered to ally with Mexico to reconquer Texas, New Mexico, and Arizona. He also asked Mexico to influence Japan to join the Central Powers. The British intercepted and decoded the telegram and forwarded it to the United States. When the details of the **Zimmermann telegram** were first revealed, some people thought the entire affair was a British hoax. But when the message was verified, Americans were outraged.

▼ The Zimmermann telegram

TELEGRAM RECEIVED.

FROM 2nd from London # 5747.

"We intend to begin on the first of February unrestricted submarine warfare. We shall endeavor in spite of this to keep the United States of America neutral. In the event of this not succeeding, we make Mexico a proposal of alliance on the following basis: make war together, make peace together, generous financial support and an understanding on our part that Mexico is to reconquer the lost territory in Texas, New Mexico, and Arizona. The settlement in detail is left to you. You will inform the President of the above most secretly as soon as the outbreak of war with the United States of America is certain and add the suggestion that he should, on his own initiative, invite Japan to immediate adherence and at the same time mediate between Japan and ourselves. Please call the President's attention to the fact that the ruthless employment of our submarines now offers the prospect of compelling England in a few months to make peace." Signed, ZIMMERMANN.

The receipt of this information has so greatly exercised the British Government that they have lost no time in communicating it to me to transmit to you, in order that our Government may be able without delay to make such disposition as may

Two weeks later, German submarines sank four unarmed American merchant vessels, killing more than thirty civilians. On April 2, Wilson appeared before a joint session of Congress and requested that the House and Senate formally recognize that Germany had thrust a state of war upon the United States:

> *The world must be made safe for democracy. Its peace must be planted upon the tested foundations of political liberty. We have no selfish ends to serve. We desire no conquest, no dominion. . . . We are but one of the champions of the rights of mankind. We shall be satisfied when those rights have been made as secure as the faith and the freedom of nations can make them. . . .*
>
> *. . . It is a fearful thing to lead this great peaceful people into war, into the most terrible and disastrous of all wars, civilization itself seeming to be in the balance.*
>
> *But the right is more precious than peace, and we shall fight for the things which we have always carried nearest our hearts—for democracy, for the right of those who submit to authority to have a voice in their own Governments, for the rights and liberties of small nations, for a universal dominion of right by such a concert of free peoples as shall bring peace and safety to all nations and make the world itself at last free.* — **WOODROW WILSON**

Within days, the Senate voted 82 to 6 to declare war on Germany, the leading member of the Central Powers. The House of Representatives agreed by a vote of 373 to 50. On April 6, 1917, the president signed the declaration, and America entered World War I on the side of the Allies.

 **Analyzing Sources**

According to Wilson, what is the main reason the Unites States must fight in the war? What does he hope will be the final result of the war?

**Comprehension Check 16.2**

1. Wilson's foreign policy was called _____ diplomacy.
   A  big stick
   B  moral
   C  dollar

2. Wilson refused to recognize Huerta's government in Mexico because it took power by murder.
   True
   False

3. America loaned more money to Germany than to the Allies.
   True
   False

4. Each of the following led to Wilson's request for a declaration of war against Germany except _____.
   A  the Zimmermann telegram
   B  the sinking of four American merchant vessels by German U-boats
   C  Pancho Villa's attack on Americans in New Mexico

**MAKING CONNECTIONS**

5. What was Wilson's view of America's new Manifest Destiny?

# The War to End All Wars

**What was World War I like for Americans?**

GUIDING QUESTIONS

- How did America prepare to fight the war?
- How did life in America change during the war?
- What happened during America's involvement in World War I?

## Preparation

America found itself ill-prepared to answer Wilson's call to war. At the time of the war declaration, the peacetime army and National Guard numbered around 300,000 men. In 1917 George M. Cohan wrote the popular song "Over There," which was used to encourage young men to enlist in the army. In a propaganda crusade led by the newly founded **Committee on Public Information**, artists used their pens and paints in the war effort, producing posters to recruit men and raise money. Religious motivations were often given for young men to fight. Some Americans pointed to the rejection of orthodox Christianity by some German theologians and philosophers and argued that the kingdom of God could be advanced by fighting Germany. This view equated warfare with the spread of God's kingdom; when soldiers died, their sacrifice for the nation was often viewed as sacrifice for God.

Although hundreds of thousands voluntarily enlisted, the **Selective Service Act** introduced a national draft to meet the tremendous manpower demands of modern war. In 1917 all men ages 21 to 30 were required to register for the draft, and in 1918 the bracket was expanded to include men 18 to 45 years old. Altogether, 2.8 million men were drafted into the military. The total number of Americans in the military during the conflict exceeded 4 million. About half of those were transported to France to fight.

▲ (left) US recruitment poster; (right) draft sign in 1918

▲ Airplane production in the Lowe, Willard & Fowler Engineering Company of Queens, New York

▼ Poster promoting victory gardens

"I see we're fighting the war together"

FOOD FIGHTS FOR VICTORY

PLANT A *Victory* GARDEN

PENNSYLVANIA RAILROAD

BUY UNITED STATES WAR BONDS AND STAMPS

# On the Home Front

America's entry into the war had both positive and negative effects. For Americans young and old, the war was "fought" in backyard gardens and factory assembly lines and touched every area of life. American involvement reflected the changing face of modern war. As President Wilson said, "In the sense in which we have been [conditioned] to think of armies, there are no armies in this struggle; there are entire nations armed."

## Effect of War on the Economy

Americans saw their national government take unprecedented control of the economy. The Wilson administration did not think the free market could respond quickly or efficiently enough to meet the demands of war. The president also wanted to prevent what he considered "excessive" profiteering. Thus, Wilson created numerous government agencies to control the economy. Among these were the War Industries Board, the Railroad Administration, and the Fuel Administration.

The draft could provide the men but not the machinery of war. The United States needed to produce uniforms and medical supplies and build weapons and equipment such as tanks, aircraft, and ships to carry the equipment. The War Industries Board retooled factories to produce the needed war materials and set price standards for certain items. It took almost a year for the nation's industry to convert to full wartime production.

Industrial production increased by more than a third between 1916 and 1919. The Gross National Product (GNP), the annual value of all goods and services that a nation produces, increased from $49.6 billion to $78.3 billion during the same period. The labor shortage due to soldiers' joining the war and a drop in immigration opened more industrial jobs to women and African Americans. During the war over 500,000 African Americans moved to northern cities. Thanks to the labor shortage, wages increased significantly as well. The average full-time manufacturing worker saw his annual earnings climb from $751 to $813 in that period.

The Railroad Administration took control of all railroads. It set rates and schedules and established shipping priorities to ensure that items reached ports for shipment to Europe. National control of railroads included standardization of design for locomotives that were built to keep up with the high demand of freight.

The Fuel Administration controlled fuel prices and directed national conservation of fuel by adding "gasless day." These days were intended to conserve fuel for the trucks that were transporting national goods.

## Rationing and Victory Gardens

One of the key needs was an adequate food supply for both the American forces and the beleaguered Allies. To address that need, the **Food Administration** was established. Future president Herbert Hoover became its leader and gained international attention for organizing methods of saving and producing food. Through a voluntary program of "Hooverizing," citizens were invited to join in "Meatless Tuesdays" and "Wheatless Wednesdays." Many people, encouraged by the slogan "Food Will Win the War," raised their own food in "liberty gardens," or "victory gardens," so that more of the nation's commercial agricultural production could be sent to ease shortages in Europe. The amount of food sent to Europe was more than double the amount that had been exported before the war.

## War Bonds

In addition to raising food, patriotic Americans raised money. The federal income tax (see Chapter 15) and other taxes supplied about $8 billion, but the nationwide effort to invest in war bonds, specifically the $50 "Liberty Loan," reaped $17 billion in revenue. Those who purchased bonds loaned money to the government and later earned interest when they redeemed those bonds. Movie celebrities appeared at huge rallies to boost bond sales. Others, even schoolchildren, who could not afford to buy the $50 loan upfront saved their pennies to fill a card with 25¢ "thrift stamps." They could exchange a filled card (16 stamps) for a $5 War Savings Stamp. Ten of these stamps collected on a certificate could then be exchanged for the $50 "Liberty Loan."

## Espionage and Sedition Acts

The national zeal for the war effort contributed toward widespread anti-German sentiment, as well as suspicion against those who objected to the war. Many high schools dropped German language courses, and "liberty" replaced virtually everything connected with that nation—German measles became "liberty measles," German shepherds were renamed "liberty dogs," and sauerkraut was called "liberty cabbage." Some Americans, including German Americans, were arrested for being conscientious objectors, those who refuse to fight because of various beliefs such as pacifism (the religious belief that killing is always wrong—even in war).

This nationalistic fervor influenced the passage of new laws, often at the cost of constitutionally guaranteed liberties such as freedom of speech and the press. For example, the **Espionage and Sedition Acts** made it a criminal offense to criticize the war effort in any way. A number of German spy plots, including the successful sabotage of a New Jersey munitions plant in 1916, prompted lawmakers to enact stiff laws to safeguard national security. Some of the enforcement of the Espionage and Sedition Acts, which resulted in more than a thousand convictions, was the result of unfounded fears and hysteria. Despite examples of excessive enforcement, however, the Supreme Court ruled in the 1919 landmark decision *Schenk v. United States* that Congress could limit free speech, particularly during wartime, if such speech presented "a clear and present danger" to national interests. In the ruling, Justice Oliver Wendell Holmes noted, "Free speech would not protect a man in falsely shouting 'fire' in a theater and causing a panic."

# American Forces in Europe

## "Lafayette, We Are Here"

The US Navy's chief function was to get troops and supplies to Europe. To defend against attacks from U-boats, US ships carrying soldiers overseas used the **convoy system**. These ships traveled in groups called convoys and were protected by navy destroyers equipped with antisubmarine weapons. The system was effective; none of the convoys were sunk.

The American entry was crucial for the Allies. Morale among the struggling Allies was miserable. They had already suffered seven million casualties in the war. Weary in the face of death, some French troops staged mutinies in May and June of 1917.

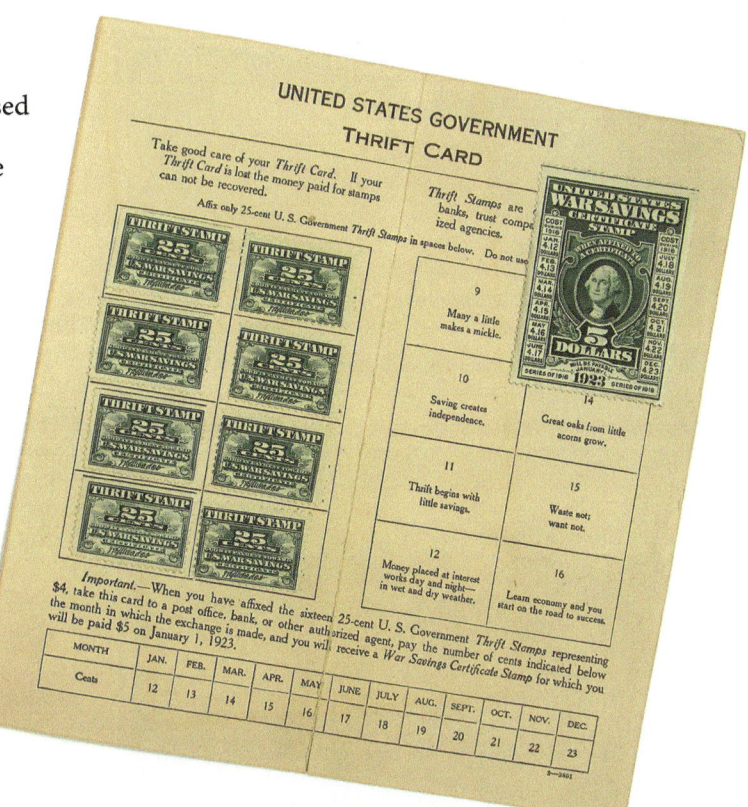

▲ War Savings Thrift Card with 25-cent thrift stamps and a $5 war savings certificate

▼ US convoy passing through New York Harbor

## The American Red Cross

The American Red Cross played a significant role during the First World War. Many women worked near the front lines as nurses or ambulance drivers. Members cared for the wounded at places such as American base hospitals and hospital trains. In addition, they manned canteens that provided food, beverages, and various supplies and that gave soldiers a place to socialize. Almost half of the eighteen thousand Red Cross nurses were active on the home front, proving especially invaluable during the influenza epidemic of 1918–19. After the war, Red Cross workers set up hospitals, convalescent homes, health centers, clinics, and mobile dispensaries to meet postwar needs around the world.

As the Allied armies languished on Germany's Western Front, the arrival of American soldiers beginning in June 1917 revived the Allied spirit. Led by the tough "Black Jack" Pershing, US troops, known as the **American Expeditionary Force** (AEF), marched through the streets of Paris on July 4th. The French were delighted. American colonel Charles E. Stanton, recalling the French alliance during the American Revolution, declared simply, "Lafayette, we are here."

Additionally, the arrival of US troops was important because of a crisis that occurred on Germany's Eastern Front (facing Russia). In November 1917 the bloody Bolshevik Revolution, headed by Vladimir Lenin, had swept the Communists to power in Russia. Lenin, who had been a vocal opponent of Russia's involvement in the war, negotiated a separate peace with Germany early in 1918, freeing hundreds of thousands of German troops to join their comrades on the Western Front. The Germans hoped this would deal a final blow to the Allies.

### Holding the Line

The German commander Erich von Ludendorff knew that Germany could not prolong the war when the forces of the United States were added to those of the rest of the Allies. He decided to wage a full offensive against the British and French, hoping to force them to surrender before the United States could give substantial support. Germany began the British phase (attacking British troops) of the offensive in northern France and Belgium on March 20, 1918, with the heaviest artillery fire ever used. Some 6,000 German guns, answered by 2,500 British guns, pounded the front with tons of steel and explosive shells for more than four hours. Then the German infantry charged across "no man's land." Flamethrowers, poison gas, hand grenades, and machine guns were used by both sides. The Germans, covered by a fog, successfully broke through in some places, but the drive slowed and faltered. After several days of intense battle, the British, aided by recently arrived American troops, prevented a general collapse of the line.

Having failed to break the British line completely, the Germans opened an attack on the French line to the south on May 27. The German assault broke the lines by May 30 and reached the Marne River, only fifty miles from Paris. But in June American and French troops rushed into the gaps, halting the German drive at Château-Thierry. The US troops continued to withstand the German advance and then countered at Belleau Wood, driving the German troops from the area and keeping Paris out of danger. Although American soldiers (also called "Yanks" or "doughboys") were initially inexperienced, by the spring of 1918 they had become a critical factor in the Allied recovery and ultimately in the Allied victory.

### Push to Victory

On July 18 the Allies began a counterattack, slowly pushing the Germans back. The doughboys won an impressive victory at Saint-Mihiel in mid-September, but the largest effort was the Meuse-Argonne offensive (in France's Argonne Forest) that began on September 26. It was one of the costliest military campaigns in American history. One and a quarter million US troops, concentrated on a twenty-five-mile front, fought for six weeks to press toward the central German rail center at Sedan.

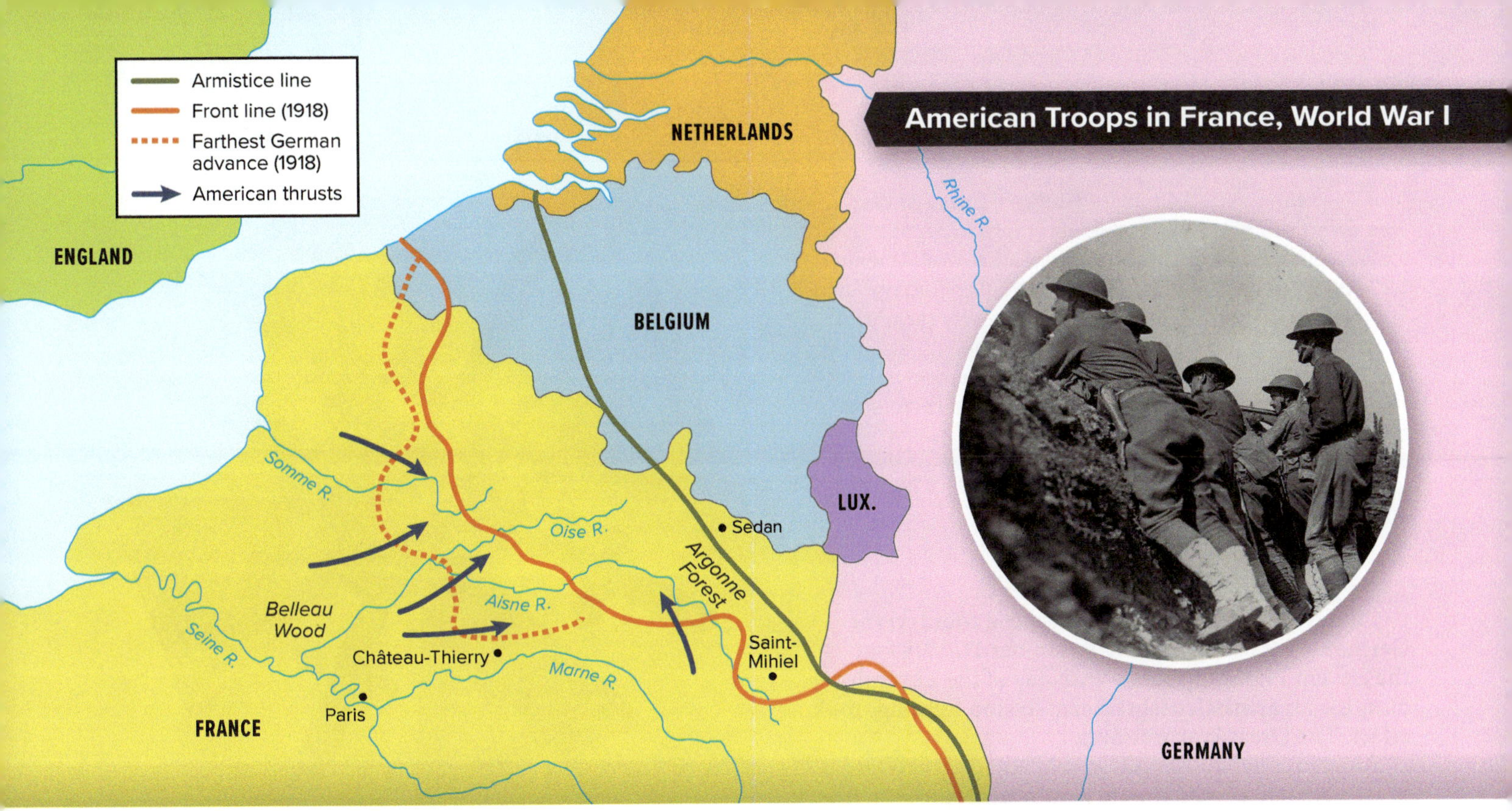

## Map Legend

- —— Armistice line
- —— Front line (1918)
- ‑‑‑‑ Farthest German advance (1918)
- → American thrusts

ENGLAND

NETHERLANDS

BELGIUM

LUX.

Rhine R.

Somme R.

Oise R.

Aisne R.

Argonne Forest

• Sedan

Belleau Wood

Seine R.

Château-Thierry •

Marne R.

Saint-Mihiel •

Paris •

FRANCE

GERMANY

One of the most distinguished units in the Meuse-Argonne offensive was the 369th Infantry Regiment, an all-black unit from the Harlem district of New York City. Beginning in April 1918 they fought on the front lines for six months, longer than any other Americans in an offensive during the war. During that time, they did not surrender any territory to the enemy nor were any of the soldiers captured. German soldiers, recognizing their courage and determination, nicknamed them the "Hellfighters."

Corporal Alvin C. York earned fame for his bravery in the Argonne Forest. Having converted to Christianity a few years before the United States entered the war, he almost registered as a conscientious objector because his church taught pacifism. However, he decided to enlist and joined the 82nd Division. On October 8, 1918, York's unit was exploring an enemy position in the Argonne when they found themselves behind enemy lines. They surprised a group of encamped Germans and took them prisoner. But a nearby machine gun nest opened fire on the Americans, killing several of York's companions. York took command of the remaining seven American soldiers. One by one, as the Germans peered over the embankment to take aim, York shot and killed them until the Germans finally surrendered. When York, his men, and his 132 prisoners reached the Allied lines, a lieutenant asked, "York, have you captured the whole German army?" York answered that he had "a tolerable few." In addition, York had single-handedly killed numerous other Germans and silenced the German machine guns. As a result, York was promoted to sergeant.

US troops suffered 117,000 casualties during the Argonne offensive, including 26,000 killed in action, but the effort turned the tide. In October, the German leadership began to negotiate for peace. Germany's allies were also withdrawing from the war. Bulgaria did so on September 29; Turkey on October 30; and Austria-Hungary on November 3.

33 USA

Alvin C. York

▶ (top) Soldiers of the 369th infantry ("Harlem Hellfighters") who received the Croix de Guerre; (bottom) stamp with Alvin York

## The Croix de Guerre *and the* Congressional Medal *of* Honor

The distinguished Croix de Guerre ("Cross of War") medal was awarded by the French government to regiments and individuals for their bravery in the war. Several American individuals and units received this medal, including Alvin York, Eddie Rickenbacker, the 369th Infantry (awarded to both the regiment as a whole and to individuals), and the 5th and 6th US Marine Regiments (awarded to both regiments three times). Additionally, several recipients of the Croix de Guerre and other individuals were awarded the US Congressional Medal of Honor, the highest US military award.

▼ French Croix de Guerre medal

On November 9, the kaiser fled the country; the German lines collapsed. On November 11, 1918—at the eleventh hour of the eleventh day of the eleventh month—an **armistice** (agreement to stop fighting) took effect. The Great War was over.

Approximately 10 million soldiers died in World War I, 116,000 of which were Americans. Additionally, about 200,000 Americans were wounded. Beginning in 1919, the United States observed November 11 as Armistice Day (known today as Veterans Day) to honor veterans of the war.

▼ Signing of the armistice

### Comprehension Check 16.3

1. The United States instituted a draft to enlist men for the war.

   True     False

2. The Food Administration encouraged a voluntary program of saving food.

   True     False

3. The Espionage and Sedition Acts _____.

   **A** made criticizing the war a criminal act

   **B** removed German language courses from public high schools

   **C** were ruled unconstitutional in a 1919 Supreme Court case

4. The US entry into the war came at a crucial time for the following reasons except that _____.

   **A** morale was extremely low among the Allies

   **B** Paris had fallen to the German army

   **C** Russia's peace treaty with Germany freed German soldiers to join the Western Front

### MAKING CONNECTIONS

5. What was one religious motivation for fighting in the war?

6. What were two effects of the war on the US economy?

# Aftermath of World War I

How did the end of World War I affect America?

## GUIDING QUESTIONS

- What did Wilson hope to accomplish with his Fourteen Points?
- What were the results of the Paris Peace Conference?
- What happened in America as a result of World War I?

## Wilson's Fourteen Points

In January 1918, months before most American troops had arrived in Europe, Wilson made a speech before Congress in which he outlined his peace proposal. Known as the **Fourteen Points**, he proposed freedom of the seas, an end to secret treaties, free trade, and reduction of every nation's military. It also called for self-determination for Europe's various nationalities. Wilson's Fourteenth Point called for the formation of a **League of Nations,** "a general association of nations . . . for the purpose of affording mutual guarantees of political independence and territorial integrity to great and small states alike." An idealist, Wilson believed that nations would set aside their own interests and act unselfishly to resolve conflicts, and that the League of Nations would prevent a recurrence of the events that had ignited the 1914 conflict. Wilson's Fourteen Points were widely published in Europe for everyone from kings to common laborers on both sides to consider.

## The Paris Peace Conference

### Wilson as Diplomat

Just one week after the armistice with Germany was signed, Wilson announced that he would personally lead the American peace delegation in Europe. Wilson believed that, given his tremendous prestige in Europe, a personal appearance would ensure that the victors would accept and preserve his Fourteen Points. He was particularly concerned that the League of Nations, which he believed would ensure a just and lasting peace, be included in the peace settlement.

### Big Four, Big Differences

Allied leaders from twenty-seven countries met outside Paris at the Palace of Versailles on January 18, 1919. The Paris Peace Conference lasted from January to June and was dominated by the "Big Four"—President Wilson of the United States, Premier Georges Clemenceau of France, Premier Vittorio Orlando of Italy, and Prime Minister David Lloyd George of Britain. Each nation had distinct aims. Wilson made clear that the United States wanted no territory in return for its participation in the war. What Wilson wanted was acceptance of the Fourteen Points. However, his Allied colleagues, whose nations had suffered far more greatly than America had during the war, were determined to make Germany, who had no representation at the conference, pay for the destruction of their countries and to hurt Germany militarily and economically.

In addition to wanting to weaken Germany to ensure France's future security, Clemenceau wanted the return of Alsace-Lorraine which Germany had taken in 1871, as well as a buffer zone, or neutral zone, east of the Rhine River. Italy, which had changed alliances at the outset of the war partly because of British promises of territory in Austria, wanted significant territorial gains in the peace settlement.

Lloyd George was a master politician, willing to do whatever was necessary to maintain British control of the seas. Although he professed to support the terms of the armistice, he had campaigned for reelection in December 1918 on the promise that the Germans would be made to bear the cost of the war. His party won a landslide victory just weeks before the peace conference began. His supporters used such slogans as "Make Germany Pay" and "Hang the Kaiser."

▼ Paris welcoming Wilson

▲ The "Big Four" at Versailles—(from left to right) David Lloyd George of Great Britain, Vittorio Emanuele Orlando of Italy, Georges Clemenceau of France, and Woodrow Wilson of the United States

## The Treaty of Versailles

Five separate treaties were signed between the Allies and the defeated countries during 1919 and 1920. The **Treaty of Versailles**, between the Allies and Germany, was signed on June 28, 1919, exactly five years after the assassination of Archduke Franz Ferdinand. The peace treaties drastically changed the map of Europe and had far-reaching consequences.

The Germans, in signing the Treaty of Versailles, were forced to accept a "war guilt" clause stating that Germany and its allies were entirely responsible for the damages caused by the war. Since Germany was deemed responsible, it was required to pay **reparations**, money a defeated nation pays for the cost of the war. The huge sum assigned to Germany, more than $30 billion, deepened poverty in Germany. The treaty also required Germany's army to demilitarize, reducing its size to no more than 100,000 troops. Its navy was also restricted in size (and was forbidden to have submarines), and it was prohibited from having an air force. It was also stripped of 25,000 square miles of territory, which was ceded to various countries, and had to renounce sovereignty over its overseas colonies. The terms of the treaty led to resentment among many Germans.

Ultimately, most of Wilson's Fourteen Points were not incorporated into the Treaty of Versailles. Freedom of the seas and free trade were ignored. However, concerns about self-determination did lead to the creation of the nations of Poland, Czechoslovakia, and Yugoslavia, as well as the Baltic countries of Lithuania, Latvia, and Estonia. While the new national identities satisfied millions, they also created problems. Many of the new countries encompassed a number of ethnic groups whose own nationalist desires were further awakened by the changes. For example, Yugoslavia, composed of six major groups, was originally called the Kingdom of the Serbs, Croats, and Slovenes. In addition, thousands of German-speaking people found themselves living under foreign flags. Adolf Hitler would use that point to justify expansion of his country's borders when he gained control of Germany in the 1930s.

Wilson and others were aware of the problems of the Treaty of Versailles. But Wilson believed that the League of Nations would fix those flaws. Its establishment was one of the conditions of the Treaty of Versailles. First, however, if the United States were to take the lead in the newly formed League, Wilson would have to convince the US Senate to ratify the treaty.

The Hall of Mirrors during the signing of the Treaty of Versailles

## Territorial Changes in Europe after World War I

**Legend:**
- From Germany
- From USSR
- From Austria-Hungary
- From the Ottoman Empire
- From Bulgaria

NORWAY
SWEDEN
FINLAND
ESTONIA
LATVIA
LITHUANIA
DENMARK
GREAT BRITAIN
NETHER-LANDS
East Prussia
Berlin
GERMANY
Rhineland
POLAND
UNION OF SOVIET SOCIALIST REPUBLICS (USSR)
BELGIUM
LUXEMBOURG
River
Saar
CZECHOSLOVAKIA
ATLANTIC OCEAN
SWITZ.
AUSTRIA
HUNGARY
ROMANIA
Caspian Sea
FRANCE
YUGOSLAVIA
Black Sea
ITALY
BULGARIA
PORTUGAL
SPAIN
ALBANIA
GREECE
TURKEY
Mediterranean Sea
Baltic Sea
North Sea
Cyprus (Britain)

# Rejection, Retreat, and Results

When Wilson returned from Europe, his most formidable opponent against the Treaty of Versailles and his most cherished part, the League of Nations, was Republican Senate majority leader Henry Cabot Lodge of Massachusetts.

Most Democrats in the Senate naturally sided with Wilson, but the Republicans held the majority and many expressed concerns or outright opposition to the treaty, particularly the article in the League covenant stating that in the case of a covenant-breaking member all members would contribute to the armed forces used to protect the covenants of the League. The "irreconcilables" refused to support the treaty under any circumstance. The "**reservation-ists**," led by Lodge, would ratify the treaty only if it was amended to address their reservations. They feared that unqualified support of the League could drag the United States into future conflicts without Congress's consent. The hard-bargaining Lodge dismissed Wilson's idealism by describing the Versailles Treaty as "the beautiful scheme of making mankind virtuous by a statute or a written constitution." America's security, Lodge believed, was best protected by two oceans and a strong military force. Wilson refused to consider any modifications to the treaty.

As the debate over treaty ratification continued, public opinion, which had initially favored ratification, began to shift in Lodge's direction. Wilson decided to take the issue to the people. In a marathon trip of eight thousand miles in twenty-two days, the president delivered forty speeches in favor of the treaty and membership in the League of Nations. The president declared, "America does not want to feed upon the rest of the world. She wants to feed it and serve it. America . . . is the only national idealistic force in the world, and idealism is going to save the world."

▼ Woodrow Wilson promoting the League of Nations in San Francisco

▲ Woodrow Wilson with his wife, Edith

Wilson's crusade, however, nearly killed him. On September 25, 1919, after an enthusiastic rally in Pueblo, Colorado, the president slumped with exhaustion. His aides canceled the rest of the tour and took Wilson back to Washington, where he suffered a serious stroke that paralyzed him on one side. Wilson's wife and a few close friends shielded his condition from the public, but his fighting days were over. For seven critical months, Wilson did not meet with his cabinet. Most executive functions were performed by his wife and closest advisors. In November, the Senate vote on the treaty fell short of the two-thirds required for ratification.

When public and administrative pressure brought a reconsideration of the treaty in March 1920, it seemed that the amended treaty would finally pass. But Wilson, who had regained some of his strength, bitterly fought any changes. Ironically, Wilson sided with the irreconcilables to defeat his own treaty in the interest of keeping it intact.

The United States never joined the League of Nations nor ratified the Treaty of Versailles. The League was formed without the participation of the United States. Not until October 1921, after Wilson's term, did the Senate ratify a new agreement with Germany ending the official state of war between the two countries.

World War I was one of the deadliest conflicts in human history. Total casualties were around 37 million dead and wounded, including military personnel and civilians. Cities and nations were ruined economically. The German, Russian, Austro-Hungarian, and Ottoman empires were destroyed.

This devastation led many Americans to change their view of humanity. Before the war most Americans were generally optimistic about the prospects for world peace and human progress. But the horrors of World War I began a process of despair and disillusionment as many realized that mankind was no less brutal or destructive than before.

The war also caused some to become disillusioned with religion. European nations with rich Christian histories slaughtered one another barbarically. Church attendance declined and some Americans rejected biblical morality. They failed to understand that the brutality of World War I was not caused by Christianity but by the rejection or distortion of Christianity's teachings. The war demonstrated that sinful man was capable of committing and defending horrible deeds.

## Comprehension Check 16.4

1. The Treaty of Versailles did all the following except _____.

   A blame Serbia for starting the war

   B limit the size of Germany's army and navy

   C strip Germany of territory and its overseas colonies

2. German reparations payments to the Allies deepened poverty and resentment among the German people.

   True

   False

3. The United States became a member of the League of Nations.

   True

   False

### MAKING CONNECTIONS

4. What did Wilson think the League of Nations would do? Why did the reservationists have concerns about America's participation in the League?

5. After World War I ended, what did Americans realize about human nature and progress?

## Chapter Summary

### 16.1 The Powder Keg of Europe

- Factors in Europe that led to World War I included growing militarism, the formation of alliances, and imperialism which provoked nationalism among those under imperial rule.

- World War I was sparked by the assassination of Archduke Franz Ferdinand by Serbian nationalists. The war spread throughout Europe as the Allied Powers fought the Central Powers.

- The war on Germany's Western Front was a stalemate for the majority of the war, and trench warfare was used by both sides. Modern weapons made warfare more efficient and deadly.

**TERMS**

militarism
Triple Alliance
Triple Entente
nationalism
self-determination
Francis (Franz) Ferdinand
Allied Powers
Central Powers
trench warfare
U-boats

**TERMS**

moral diplomacy
Pancho Villa
John J. "Black Jack" Pershing
propaganda
*Lusitania*
Zimmermann telegram

### 16.2 American Neutrality

- Wilson's foreign policy, called moral diplomacy, promoted freedom and democratic ideas in other countries.

- Wilson intervened in Haiti and the Dominican Republic. He also sent troops to Mexico to attempt to capture Pancho Villa, who had attacked Americans in Mexico and New Mexico.

- Wilson proclaimed neutrality in the war in Europe, but trade, Allied propaganda, and German submarine warfare led many Americans to support the Allies.

- Wilson was narrowly reelected in 1916. Germany's resumption of unrestricted submarine warfare and the Zimmermann telegram led Wilson to ask Congress for a declaration of war in April 1917.

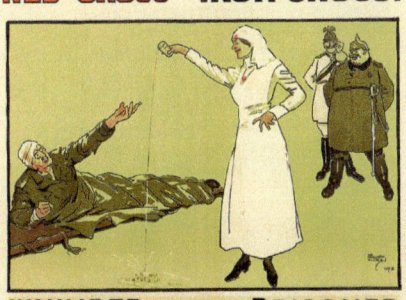

RED CROSS OR IRON CROSS?

WOUNDED AND A PRISONER
OUR SOLDIER CRIES FOR WATER.
THE GERMAN "SISTER"
POURS IT ON THE GROUND BEFORE HIS EYES.
THERE IS NO WOMAN IN BRITAIN
WHO WOULD DO IT.
THERE IS NO WOMAN IN BRITAIN
WHO WILL FORGET IT.

## Chapter Summary

### 16.3 The War to End All Wars

- In addition to recruiting soldiers through propaganda from the Committee on Public Information, the Selective Service Act established a national draft.

- Several newly created government agencies oversaw the war effort on the home front in areas such as factory production, railroads, and fuel and food conservation. The Espionage and Sedition Acts made criticism of the war a criminal offense.

- The convoy system protected US ships carrying troops and supplies to Europe. The American Expeditionary Force (AEF) began arriving in France by June 1917, a crucial time when morale was low among Allies and before the Russians pulled out as a consequence of the Bolshevik Revolution. American soldiers joined the Allies in withstanding a German offensive and counterattacking in an Allied offensive. An armistice ended the war on November 11, 1918.

**TERMS**

Committee on Public Information

Selective Service Act

Food Administration

Espionage and Sedition Acts

convoy system

American Expeditionary Force (AEF)

armistice

**TERMS**

Fourteen Points

League of Nations

Treaty of Versailles

reparations

reservationists

### 16.4 Aftermath of World War I

- Wilson's peace proposal, the Fourteen Points, included freedom of the seas, the end of secret treaties, free trade, military reductions, self-determination, and the creation of a League of Nations.

- Wilson attended the Paris Peace Conference to ensure his Fourteen Points would be the basis for peace, but other countries had other goals. In the Treaty of Versailles, Germany accepted a war guilt clause, taking responsibility for the war, was required to pay reparations and accept limits to its military, and lost territory and overseas colonies.

- The US Senate, led by Republican "reservationists," would not accept the Treaty of Versailles without changes. Wilson traveled the country to promote the treaty but suffered a stroke. The Senate did not ratify the treaty, and the League of Nations was formed without American participation.

- World War I began a process of despair and disillusionment regarding human progress and caused some to become disillusioned with religion.

## Chapter Review Questions

### RECALL

1. What were four factors that led to war in Europe?

2. Who were the members of the Triple Alliance? Which of the three members switched sides during the war?

3. Who were the members of the Triple Entente?

4. Who led the American forces fighting against Pancho Villa as well as the American Expeditionary Force in Europe?

5. What system was used to protect ships carrying soldiers and supplies between the United States and Europe from U-boat attacks?

6. At what hour, day, month, and year did the armistice between the Allies and Germany take effect?

7. What happened to Wilson physically after he took the issue of the ratification of the Treaty of Versailles to the people?

8. About how many total casualties resulted from World War I?

### UNDERSTAND

9. What did those European nations that were under imperial control begin to demand?

10. Whose assassination was the spark that led to World War I? What group was responsible for the assassination? Why did group members assassinate him?

11. What caused each of the following nations to mobilize their troops for war: Austria-Hungary, Serbia, Russia, Britain?

12. What were four modern weapons that changed warfare in World War I? What effect did modern weapons have on warfare?

13. Why did Wilson not recognize the Huerta government in Mexico?

14. What were three factors that threatened American neutrality?

15. What did Wilson mean when he called for "peace without victory" and making the world "safe for democracy"?

16. What did the Zimmermann telegram offer Mexico in exchange for its support? What was the result when the United States learned of it?

17. What was the purpose of the Committee of Public Information?

18. What did the Selective Service Act do and why was it considered necessary?

19. What were three American agencies established during World War I to control the economy, and what did each do?

20. What were two ways the Food Administration involved American citizens in the war effort?

21. How did American citizens help fund the war effort?

22. What happened in Russia in 1917 and how did that affect the Allies?

23. How did America's entry into the war affect the outcome of the war?

24. What were four of Wilson's Fourteen Points?

25. What were two parts of the Treaty of Versailles that may have caused the German people to be resentful?

26. What concern did the reservationists have about the Treaty of Versailles?

27. What was the US Senate's final decision regarding the Treaty of Versailles and the League of Nations?

28. What did the disillusionment resulting from World War I lead many Americans to believe? What was incorrectly blamed for this?

### THINK ABOUT IT

29. Contrast Wilson's moral diplomacy with Roosevelt's big stick diplomacy and Taft's dollar diplomacy.

30. How did the Espionage and Sedition Acts limit free speech? What did the Supreme Court rule in *Schenk v. United States* about these laws? Do you agree with that decision? Explain.

31. How did Wilson's vision for a League of Nations reflect his idealism? Why was this not a realistic vision?

32. Why do you think the rest of the "Big Four" did not share Wilson's goals for the Paris Peace Conference?

# 17 The Twenties

17.1 Postwar Difficulties

17.2 The Growth of Consumer Society

17.3 The Roaring Twenties

17.4 Harding and Coolidge

▲ A mixture of old and new in traffic on Fifth Avenue, New York City, 1920s

It was the age of flappers, foxtrots, Freud, and all that jazz. The generation coming of age in the 1920s enjoyed postwar prosperity. Participation in moral crusades and reform movements waned in the pursuit of fun and frivolity, as attention was diverted to celebrities on the silver screen, the athletic field, and the radio waves. The roar of the 1920s seemed to drown out problems both at home and abroad.

## 17.1 Postwar Difficulties

**What challenges did America face after World War I?**

### Problems at Home

In 1920 America was readjusting to the challenges of peacetime. The nation's industries and manpower were no longer demanded by the war effort. Americans' energies and emotions were no longer focused on defeating a foreign enemy. When the war ended and the doughboys returned and the parades down main street were over, the soldiers often found that America held few opportunities for them. War industries closed, but peacetime industries did not resume production quickly because they had to retool to make consumer goods. With more than two million men returning from the American Expeditionary Force, unemployment climbed to a staggering 11.9 percent in 1921.

Soldiers returning to farms found their prospects no less bleak. Agriculture had been a profitable business during the war since American farms were feeding both the nation and also the war-torn regions. With the war over, however, exports of farm products declined as Europeans began to farm their own lands again. Farmers had to rely on the ordinary peacetime needs of the nation for their livelihoods. The huge surpluses caused food prices to plunge by the end of 1920. Low prices devastated farmers, especially since many farmers were heavily in debt for land and equipment purchased during the years of high demand. Continued overproduction and low prices kept the agricultural market depressed for the entire decade, and this problem remained a major domestic issue throughout the 1920s.

### GUIDING QUESTIONS

- What problems did Americans face at home after World War I?

- How did America relate to the rest of the world after World War I?

- Why were many Americans afraid of communism during the 1920s?

▼ 1920s citrus farm workers

▲ Poster encouraging employers to hire soldiers returning from the war

# World Relations

On the campaign trail in 1920, Republican Warren G. Harding preached the political philosophy that carried the United States into the new decade: "America's present need is not heroics but healing; not nostrums [favorite but usually ineffective remedies] but normalcy; not revolution but restoration; . . . not surgery but serenity." **Normalcy**, the return to life as it was before the war, became the goal of a people wishing to distance themselves from wartime pressures and problems.

## Isolationism

The general theme of American foreign policy in the 1920s was **isolationism**, or the desire to stay out of foreign entanglements and wars. The taste of war had left many Americans disillusioned with idealistic efforts to change the world. Wilson's failure to persuade the United States to join the League of Nations illustrated the preference of Americans to focus on things at home rather than on foreign matters. Nonetheless, by the end of World War I, America had become a world leader that sought to influence other countries.

The United States faced two basic foreign policy tasks in the 1920s: to maintain world peace and to stabilize the world economy. Americans undertook both of those tasks with special attention to how any action would affect the peace and prosperity of the United States. They did not want foreign conflicts to draw their sons into battle again, and they did not want foreign economic problems and policies to endanger American business and prosperity.

## Washington Naval Conference

Although the United States sent "unofficial observers" to meetings of the League of Nations, America pursued world peace through independent activities. The first such activity was the **Washington Naval Conference** of 1921. The buildup of sea power fueled by the war continued after the armistice. Japan and Britain strengthened their navies to acquire military advantages over potential enemies. France and Italy also were determined to enhance their naval strength. To keep these powers in check, the United States felt pressured to expand its own navy. Concerned by the escalating arms race, the United States called the Washington Naval Conference, which brought foreign diplomats to Washington, DC, to negotiate an agreement limiting the growth of naval power. The result was a plan that called for Japan, Britain, and the United States to scrap some of their vessels, limit battleship construction, and establish a cap for naval tonnage: the United States and Britain 500,000 tons, Japan 300,000 tons, France and Italy 175,000 tons.

Idealists praised the treaties devised at the Washington Naval Conference, yet the agreements had some notable flaws that contributed later to a war in the Pacific. Although the treaties limited the buildup of battleships, they did not restrict the buildup of cruisers, destroyers, or submarines—vessels that would prove more valuable in future naval warfare. They also did nothing to limit land forces. In addition, Japan resented being given an inferior standing to Britain and the United States. Japan had expansionist goals that relied on a strong navy; for this reason, it did not sign an extension of the treaty in 1936.

▲ The Japanese battleship *Tosa*, whose construction was halted after the agreement at the Washington Naval Conference

## Kellogg-Briand Pact

After the widespread destruction of World War I, the American secretary of state, Frank B. Kellogg, and the French foreign minister, Aristide Briand, proposed an international agreement that would outlaw war. On August 27, 1928, fifteen nations signed the **Kellogg-Briand Pact** in Paris, and more nations signed later, making a total of sixty-two countries. The signers agreed to abandon war as a means of settling disputes and to seek peaceful means instead. Its flaw was that it had no means of enforcement. In fact, World War II would start just eleven years later.

## International Economics

The United States also modified its relationship with Latin American nations to promote peace with its closest neighbors. Presidents Harding and Coolidge continued Wilson's policy of intervention in Latin America and the Caribbean (see Chapter 16). By 1925 the United States had marines stationed in several of those nations and controlled the financial policies of at least ten countries in the region. Naturally, such interventionism created resentment toward the United States in Latin America. Harding's secretary of state, Charles Evans Hughes, began softening the policies of the Roosevelt Corollary to the Monroe Doctrine—where the Corollary had asserted the police power of the United States in the Western Hemisphere, Hughes instead urged the withdrawal of troops from Latin American countries.

In Europe, World War I had wreaked havoc on the economies of many nations. Not only were its farms and factories devastated by warfare, but also its surviving governments faced an incredible burden of debt. Although the war had depleted the economic resources of Europe, the United States had escaped relatively unscathed with its finances in order and its factories intact. The Allies were frustrated that America insisted they repay over $22 billion in war loans plus interest.

The Allies had received aid in the form of war materials and foodstuffs, yet America required that their debts be repaid in cash (gold). The war had drained the Allied coffers, so the logical means for them to acquire the needed sums was by trading European goods for the needed gold. However, intent on protecting America's own reviving industries, Congress passed the Fordney-McCumber Tariff in 1922. This high tariff (replaced by an even higher tariff in 1930) established a nearly insurmountable wall restricting European trade with the United States.

Trade with America being blocked, the Allies' only other source for paying their debts was the German reparations payments awarded by the Treaty of Versailles. Germany, however, was in ruins, its economy was in shambles, and it had little with which to rebuild its industry, much less to make the colossal reparations payments. Germany's only means of obtaining the needed cash was through loans, and the only country willing and able to loan Germany money was the United States. Thus began a dangerous circular flow of money: money lent by American financial institutions to Germany was passed on by Germany to the Allies in reparations, who in turn, used the money to repay the United States for war debts. The result of this cycle was that Germany fell heavily into debt to the United States without having funds to improve its own economy. As the debts mounted, Germany could not make payments to the Allies. The Allies, deprived of reparations payments, could not make their loan payments to the United States. American investors grew alarmed by unpaid foreign loans.

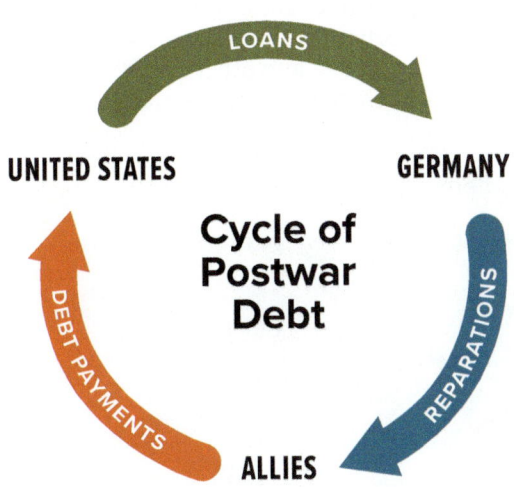

**Cycle of Postwar Debt**

UNITED STATES — LOANS → GERMANY — REPARATIONS → ALLIES — DEBT PAYMENTS → UNITED STATES

In 1924 an American banker, Charles Dawes, led a panel of economic experts from the involved countries to resolve the impending crisis. The Dawes Plan reduced German reparations payments significantly and encouraged private American institutions to continue lending money to help Germany rebuild. The American government also reduced the interest charged on the Allied war debts and offered more generous terms for repayment. Despite these efforts, the cycle of debt continued.

## The Red Scare

As mentioned in Chapter 12, Karl Marx in his writings promoted communism and worldwide revolution. After the Communists in Russia led the Bolshevik Revolution in November 1917, Russian leaders organized the Third International and called for worldwide revolution. They attempted to export communism to other nations and began to gain followers in Europe and the United States. Because Communists envisioned a worldwide revolution led by workers against owners, Americans began to view labor organizations, especially the socialistic Industrial Workers of the World (IWW), strikes, and other signs of worker discontent as part of the Communist plot.

The threat of communism alarmed many Americans and led to the **Red Scare** (a time of increased public concern about communism in America, so named because red was associated with revolutions, including the Bolshevik Revolution). The Red Scare began in 1919 when anarchists mailed small packages containing bombs to more than thirty government officials and businessmen, including industrialist John D. Rockefeller and Supreme Court Justice Oliver Wendell Holmes. One of the bombs blew up in the hands of a senator's maid, injuring her and the senator's wife. Although the other mail bombs were discovered before they exploded, the violence set off a wave of bombings that resulted in death and great property destruction. Even the house of Wilson's attorney general, A. Mitchell Palmer, was bombed. The following year a bomb exploded in front of the New York Stock Exchange, killing thirty and injuring hundreds.

Believing the bombings were carried out by Communists, Attorney General Palmer called for investigations. Beginning in late 1919, the government began tracking down Americans and foreigners with objectionable political views. Thousands were arrested in the "Palmer Raids," and others, especially Russians, were deported. Many who were jailed were later released for lack of evidence.

▼ Aftermath of the 1919 Wall Street bombing

## Comprehension Check 17.1

1. The American economy immediately after World War I ____.

   A thrived with the invention of new consumer products

   B suffered from a lack of agricultural production

   C struggled as it transitioned from war production to peacetime levels of production

2. Presidential candidate Warren Harding pledged to return America to ____.

   A normalcy

   B prosperity

   C democracy

3. The general theme of American foreign policy in the 1920s was ____.

   A moral diplomacy

   B isolationism

   C interventionism

4. In the Kellogg-Briand Pact, nations agreed to ____.

   A limit the number of warships in their navies

   B reduce German reparations payments

   C abandon war as a means of settling disputes

### MAKING CONNECTIONS

5. Who were Americans afraid of during the Red Scare? Why did they feel threatened?

# The Growth of Consumer Society

## GUIDING QUESTIONS

- How did the automobile impact America?
- How did air transportation advance?
- How did new products influence American society?

**How did America become a consumer society?**

After the economic downturn that followed the war, businesses recovered and expanded throughout the decade as taxation and government regulation decreased. Secretary of the Treasury Andrew Mellon influenced Congress to cut taxes to encourage economic growth. The administrations of both Harding and Coolidge favored minimal government interference in the market. Due to reduced taxation and mass production of goods lowering costs, many Americans had more of their earnings to spend or invest.

As the 1920s progressed, Americans grew accustomed to the comforts of the most prosperous decade in American history to that point. Thriving business and wealth created a growing middle class and improved standards of living. Even the lower class benefited through new jobs, new inventions, and expanding opportunities.

## Automobiles

America was fast becoming a consumer society that was spending money on new goods, including the newest models of automobiles. In 1920, there were only about nine million automobiles in the United States. During the 1920s, that number nearly tripled. Although Henry Ford's black Model Ts were affordable and commonplace thanks to his use of the assembly line and interchangeable parts (see Chapter 15), General Motors and other competitors attracted buyers who wanted something different, forcing Ford to introduce the Model A in 1927. Ford and other manufacturers also set up credit corporations to help consumers who did not have the money for a car to buy one on credit. With advertising to make the product known and **installment plans** (making small weekly or monthly payments until the item is paid for) available to finance the price, Americans eagerly stepped into the driver's seat. Two-thirds of all cars sold in 1927 were sold on the installment plan. New service industries developed around consumer products such as the automobile. Gas stations, motels, and drive-in restaurants were built along busy highways. Stores and other businesses were built intentionally with large parking lots.

The automobile had social as well as economic influence. Workers with automobiles no longer had to live within walking distance of their jobs and could now reside in the suburbs on the edge of cities and commute to and from work by car. Rural families could visit the city often rather than just a few times a year, and tourism boomed as the average family could travel for vacations.

▼ 1920s Texaco gasoline advertisement

No extra price

▼ An automobile passing a wagon in rural America

## Airplanes

World War I had boosted aviation, and the US government began providing airmail service between major cities. Pilots called "barnstormers" transported passengers over short distances and performed stunts for crowds. These "barnstormers" included former World War I pilots and Bessie Coleman, the first female African American pilot.

Additionally, record-setting pilots pushed aviation to new levels. At 7:52 a.m. on May 20, 1927, twenty-five-year-old **Charles A. Lindbergh** took off in a small silver airplane named *Spirit of St. Louis* from Roosevelt Field on Long Island, New York. With his single-engine craft he was attempting the first nonstop solo transatlantic flight, from New York to Paris. Relatively unknown before his historic flight, Lindbergh captured the attention of both the United States and western Europe as they awaited news of his fate, which came on the night of May 21. Lindbergh had flown over 3,000 miles in thirty-three-and-a-half hours. After returning home, "Lucky Lindy" was showered with acclaim and received numerous awards, including the Distinguished Flying Cross from President Calvin Coolidge.

Although Lindbergh claimed to be only a stunt flyer, his solo flight riveted the world's attention on the potential of air power. Beginning in 1927, Pan American Airline's "Clippers" transported passengers internationally. Additionally, domestic airlines connected major cities.

(top) Charles Lindbergh's *Spirit of St. Louis*; (bottom) Pan American Airlines clipper

## Consumer Products

Americans acquired many more new material possessions in the 1920s. With electricity becoming increasingly available in both small towns and large cities, electric appliances multiplied. Radio, using a sound transmitter instead of telephone or telegraph lines, became the greatest mass media device until the invention of television after World War II. On November 2, 1920, station KDKA in Pittsburgh made its first broadcast announcing the election results for Warren G. Harding. Harding's was the first inauguration to use a public address system for amplification, and Harding became the first president to make a speech over radio when he dedicated the Francis Scott Key Memorial at Fort McHenry on June 14, 1922. By 1930 over twelve million households had a radio. Rural and urban Americans tuned in to the news, sermons, music, sports, and other entertainment that it offered. Along with the electric radio, electric refrigerators, stoves, irons, washing machines, and other devices brought pleasure, comfort, efficiency, and more leisure time into many homes.

A kitchen with 1920s appliances

## The Golden Age *of* Radio

The 1920s and 1930s have been called "the golden age of radio." Many radio personalities—musicians, comedians, advertisers, and news reporters—became household names. During that time, many "firsts" were accomplished.

First religious broadcast, Calvary Episcopal Church, KDKA

First broadcast of World Series baseball game, (New York Giants defeated New York Yankees), KDKA

First government regulation of radio broadcasting, Federal Radio Commission

**1921**  **1922**  **1923**  **1924**  **1925**

First commercial ad time sold, $9 for a 30-second spot, WEAF (Albany, NY)

First business-sponsored program, variety show "The Ever-Ready Hour," WEAF

▲ An early radio broadcast studio

For companies to profit, mass production required mass consumption. Through increased newspaper, magazine, and radio advertisements, businesses coaxed people to buy from the seemingly unlimited array of desirable products even if they did not need them or have the money. Advertising emphasized youth, glamour, happiness, luxury, and keeping up with one's neighbors. Consumers were encouraged to spend rather than save, to enjoy the present rather than prepare for future needs or emergencies. Materialism replaced values of thrift and productivity as advertisers elevated consuming goods above producing them. Buying on credit through installment plans fueled this materialism. By 1929 credit purchases for all sorts of major products made consumer loans the tenth largest industry in the nation.

▶ 1920s advertisement for a Franklin luxury automobile

*The greatest luxury of today!*
**AIR-COOLED MOTORING in the World's Fastest Road Car** ···· *now at new, low prices!*

THE most luxurious motoring you have ever known! Luxury in every line and detail of the smart bodies and interiors; luxury in the smooth, riding comfort of the flexible, shock-absorbing chassis; luxury in the matchless performance of the record-breaking air-cooled motor!

And now—through Franklin's great Expansion Program—this new luxury of air-cooled motoring is available to you, at the highest point in its develop-

ment to date, at prices as much as $600 less than any previous prices of corresponding Franklin types.

Following the many recent speed and hill records, which have won for Franklin the title of "the world's fastest road car"—these new models create revolutionary new standards of quality motor car values. You owe it to yourself to inspect the complete line—now on display throughout the country.

FRANKLIN AUTOMOBILE COMPANY ... SYRACUSE, N.Y.

| THE ONE-THIRTY-FIVE | ALL PRICES F. O. B. SYRACUSE | THE ONE-THIRTY-SEVEN |
| Sedan $2485   Sport Sedan $2625   Coupe $2510 | THE ONE-THIRTY | Sedan $2775   Limousine $2970   Touring-7 $2870 |
| Convertible Coupe $2610   Victoria Brougham $2595 | Sedan $2180        Coupe $2160 | Sport Touring $2785        Sport Runabout $2785 |

# FRANKLIN

THE ONE-THIRTY SEDAN
**$2180**

THE ONE-THIRTY-FIVE SEDAN
**$2485**

THE ONE-THIRTY-SEVEN SEDAN
**$2775**

Perpetually in debt for their purchases, many Americans searched for ways to acquire the money they needed to maintain their comfortable lifestyles. Some resorted to fraud, to selling alcohol (which was prohibited), or to other illegal activities. Others turned to **speculation**, buying or selling that involved unusually high risks for the chance to gain an unusually large profit from anticipated, but unreliable, fluctuations in price rather than earning steadily from normal profits on trade or investment.

Land in Florida, especially around Miami, became a popular item for speculation in the 1920s. Billed as a tropical paradise, acreage there began to sell, with some speculators not even viewing the property, and the more buyers expressed interest, the higher land prices climbed. Speculators bought large tracts of land and subdivided them for sale. As the land boom progressed, they resold the properties for higher and higher amounts. Much of the land was marshland or otherwise undesirable, but promises of future golf courses, shopping areas, and other developments tempted many people to buy lots for $20,000 or more (ten times more than the average American's annual income). Some borrowed money in order to purchase these tracts. Then in 1926 a severe hurricane hit the Miami area, killing four hundred people and destroying thousands of houses. The disaster brought a sudden end to the land boom as people realized the hazards of their speculation. The credit that had sustained the boom collapsed as land prices plummeted. Many fortunes made in the boom were lost overnight, and thousands of unwary Americans were left with heavy debts and worthless land deeds.

Prosperity led to higher wages for many, and some Americans invested their money in the stock market. A great **bull market** (a stock market characterized by optimism and rising stock prices) began in 1927 as stock prices rose due to prosperity in industries. Stock became a prime choice for American speculation, with prices climbing dramatically. Low interest rates made it easy for people to buy stocks with borrowed money. **Buying on margin** meant investors could purchase stock through a broker but pay only ten percent of the purchase price. The broker would finance the remaining amount with money he had borrowed from a bank or other sources, and the investor would pay the broker back with interest. As long as the stock's value increased, the investor could pay the broker and still make a profit, and the broker was assured he could cover the loan. However, if the stock price dropped, the broker would call in the investor's loan and force him to increase his margin or pay for the stock immediately.

From March 1928 to September 1929, prices of many favored stocks doubled, and nearly every stock rose. The possibilities of profits from stock speculation fueled tremendous activity on Wall Street. The progressive attitudes, prevalent before the war, that favored more business regulation were replaced with admiration and favorable expectations for American business. President Coolidge disapproved of speculation, but encouraged Americans to have faith in business, stating, "The chief business of the American people is business." The economy was improving so much that when Herbert Hoover accepted the Republican nomination in 1928, he predicted a total eradication of poverty in the land. At the time, Hoover's declaration seemed possible.

## Comprehension Check 17.2

1. Charles Lindbergh's 1927 feat was historic as the first ____ flight.

   A "barnstormer"

   B international passenger

   C solo nonstop transatlantic

2. The 1920 presidential election result was the first to be transmitted through ____.

   A radio

   B telegraph

   C television

3. All of the following characterized the US economy during the 1920s except that ____.

   A a bull market began in 1927

   B consumers had more of their earnings available to spend or invest

   C Harding and Coolidge continued progressive policies of regulating businesses

### MAKING CONNECTIONS

4. How did consumer products influence the social lives of Americans? How did increased availability of these products change American values?

5. How did Americans buy goods on credit, and how could they buy stock without paying the full price?

# The Roaring Twenties

How did society change during the Roaring Twenties?

The economic growth and prosperity and great social change that took place during the decade earned it the label the "Roaring Twenties." The decade was marked by breaking with tradition, including traditional values and morality.

## Arts and Leisure

Modern literature, art, and music in the early twentieth century revealed the influence of new ideas, and traditional standards yielded to modern ones. The destruction of World War I caused many to become disillusioned and full of despair, and the literature of the era reflected these attitudes. T. S. Eliot's poetry criticized the emptiness of modern society and characterized society as a "waste land." Novelist William Faulkner—with his creative and complex sentence structure, departure from traditional narrative, and emphasis on man's evil—created a meaningless world from which the old values had been removed. Ernest Hemingway wrote stories in which characters fail to find meaning in life. F. Scott Fitzgerald's novel *The Great Gatsby* tells the story of a man corrupted by the new morals of the era. The disillusionment of American writers in the 1920s was evident from the number of prominent authors, including Hemingway and Fitzgerald, who chose to live and write in Europe (particularly Paris) rather than in the United States. These authors are often referred to as "the lost generation."

▼ *The Great Gatsby* depicted fashionable society in the Roaring Twenties.

GUIDING QUESTIONS

- What did Americans do with their new leisure time?
- How did American culture shift during the 1920s?
- How effective was Prohibition?
- What caused growing racial and ethnic tensions during the 1920s?
- Why did Fundamentalism develop during this time?

The spread of daily newspapers, the advent of radio, and the shift from vaudeville to motion pictures allowed people across the nation to keep tabs on rising stars in sports, entertainment, and politics. Movies became the biggest source of entertainment for many Americans. In 1922 about 40 million Americans attended movies each week. By 1929 that number was 90 million (out of 121 million Americans). Movies were big moneymakers and reflected the changing values of the culture. They also changed the way the world viewed America, as Hollywood films were shown in many countries around the world.

Americans went to the movies to see famous comedians such as Charlie Chaplin and the duo Laurel and Hardy or dramatic stars such as Rudolph Valentino, Clara Bow, and Gloria Swanson. "Talkies" replaced silent films in 1927, and the more than twenty thousand movie palaces in the nation rivaled churches as the most important downtown buildings. Many middle-class Americans had become obsessed with Hollywood, not only by the world portrayed on the screen but also by the glamorous offscreen lives of the stars.

Many young people began to emulate what they saw in the movies. "**Flappers**" were young women who captured attention by their shocking behavior, such as wearing shorter skirts, short haircuts, and heavy makeup, as well as using slang, drinking, and smoking. In reality, most young women did not pursue this lifestyle, but fashion was nonetheless influenced by the flappers.

When World War I broke out in Europe, industries faced a shortage of laborers. Looking for economic opportunity and hoping to escape segregation and discrimination, hundreds of thousands of African Americans moved from the South to the North and Midwest between 1914 and 1930 in what was known as the **Great Migration**. The northern urban setting offered social and cultural opportunities for black Americans. The Harlem neighborhood of New York City became the center of African American culture. In the **Harlem Renaissance**, African American culture flourished as black intellectuals and writers including James Weldon Johnson, Alain Locke, and Langston Hughes achieved prominence. Black actors and singers such as Paul Robeson and Josephine Baker starred in Broadway musicals.

▼ Langston Hughes

▼ Movie theater

▼ 1920s fashion

◄ Paul Robeson

The decade of the 1920s is also known as the Jazz Age. Trumpeter Louis Armstrong, a New Orleans native, brought jazz music (music influenced by the syncopated rhythms of ragtime and other musical styles) to Chicago in 1922. Bandleader and composer Edward "Duke" Ellington, as well as other jazz musicians, brought innovative music to New York City. Soon white audiences were coming to the Cotton Club in Harlem (where black Americans were not allowed as customers) to watch these African American musicians perform and to dance the Charleston, the foxtrot, and other popular dances.

Jazz music, with its emphasis on improvisation, experimentation, and individual performances, was a reflection of its time. Some saw it as a form of music which broke away from the rules and values of previous generations. While jazz broke down some barriers between white and black Americans, some disapproved of jazz and associated it with alcohol and immoral behavior.

Organized sports became major entertainment in the 1920s. In 1921 fans overflowed a sixty-thousand-seat stadium near Jersey City to watch boxer Jack Dempsey knock out the French boxer Georges Carpentier. It was the first "million-dollar gate" (paid attendance) for sports in the United States and the first major sports event to be broadcast by radio. Babe Ruth thrilled huge crowds at baseball games in Yankee Stadium, and in the 1927 season he hit sixty home runs. Fans filled college football stadiums to thrill in the exploits of athletes such as Red Grange of Illinois and the Four Horsemen of Notre Dame, coached by the legendary Knute Rockne. Fans got a glimpse of the lives of their favorite athletes on and off the field in newsreels shown before the movies. Horse racing and auto racing also drew large crowds.

Other sports heroes gained wealth, fame, and admiration during the 1920s while popularizing their sports for the enjoyment of millions of Americans. In 1926 Gertrude Ederle became the first woman to swim the twenty-one miles across the English Channel. Bobby Jones became the king of the golf links, and William Tilden and Helen Wills rose to the heights of the tennis world. Golf courses and tennis courts multiplied across the land as their popularity soared.

▼ Jazz band

◄ Singer Bessie Smith

▼ Babe Ruth on set of baseball cards

► Sulky (buggy) racing

## Culture Clash

Modern ideas challenged American society in the 1920s. Although the writings of Charles Darwin (evolution) and Karl Marx (communism) had appeared in the nineteenth century, their full impact did not become apparent in the United States until after World War I. Darwin's theory contradicted the scriptural account of Creation, and Marx's economic philosophy denied the sinfulness of man. Although these ideas had been too radical for most nineteenth-century Americans, evolution and communism gained influence in the 1920s.

The ideas of Austrian psychologist Sigmund Freud also became popular in the 1920s. While Freud acknowledged that religion had helped maintain civilization by restraining immorality, he believed that religion reflected a stunted emotional development, as the adult held onto emotions from childhood and a kind of irrational wishful thinking. Freud claimed that science would do a better job than religion in bringing happiness to mankind. Freud also believed that traditional restrictions on sexual behavior were too severe, yet he said that those restrictions helped civilization as people channeled their unfulfilled sexual desires into other activities such as art and music. Psychologists would later use Freud's work to argue that sexual self-restraint (or "repression") led to emotional disorders and that immoral conduct was acceptable.

## Prohibition

The Eighteenth Amendment, which prohibited the manufacture, sale, or transportation of intoxicating liquors, had been ratified in 1919 (see Chapter 15). The amendment stipulated that it would take effect one year after ratification. The period during which alcohol was illegal in the country, from 1920 to 1933, is known as **Prohibition**.

Congress passed the **Volstead Act** in October 1919 to provide for the enforcement of Prohibition. It defined illegal beverages as those that contained more than 0.5% alcohol by volume and established the Bureau of Prohibition to enforce the law. However, the law proved difficult in practice. While many Americans, including many Christians, supported Prohibition, others, especially certain immigrant groups, considered alcoholic drink an important part of their cultures. They resented attempts to restrict alcohol and were unwilling to participate in its enforcement.

▲ Sigmund Freud

▼ 1920s anti-prohibition parade

▲ Al Capone (center) at his federal tax evasion trial, 1931

Illegal activity increased as government struggled to enforce the law. **Bootlegging** (making and selling illegal liquor) became common. Illegal taverns and bars, called "speakeasies," sprang up across the nation. Liquor was smuggled into the country across the border with Canada or through American ports, and the Bureau of Prohibition lacked the budget and manpower to stop it.

Violent crime increased as gangsters competed for control of illegal alcohol trade in their territories. Chicago was headquarters for the most infamous gangster of the era—**Al Capone**, also known as Scarface. Several gangs entered the bootlegging business in Chicago during the 1920s, but Capone soon established himself as the king of Chicago's underworld. People who stood in his way were killed. The most infamous example of gang violence was the "Saint Valentine's Day Massacre" in 1929, when members of Capone's gang, disguised as policemen, gunned down members of a rival gang in a garage. Authorities struggled to find evidence that would put Capone behind bars. His subordinates were too well paid, too loyal, or too afraid to testify against him. He often bribed judges, police officers, and government officials. Finally, federal investigators uncovered evidence of about $1 million in income on which Capone had paid no taxes. Prosecutors brought Capone to trial for income tax evasion in 1931. The court found him guilty and sentenced him to eleven years in prison. He was released in 1939 and died in 1947.

When enforcement of Prohibition proved to be a problem, President Hoover appointed the Wickersham Commission to investigate the lax enforcement. The commission found that Prohibition was impossible to enforce because a large part of the nation was willing to violate the law. Although the commission did not recommend repeal, vocal opposition to Prohibition grew, especially among Democrats. When Franklin Roosevelt, who favored repeal, was elected in 1932, Prohibition's days were numbered. The end of the "noble experiment," as Hoover once called it, came in December 1933 with the ratification of the **Twenty-First Amendment**, which repealed the Eighteenth Amendment. Despite its problems, Prohibition contributed to a significant decline in alcohol consumption that lasted for several decades.

▲ Entrance to a speakeasy

▲ A bootlegger truck with a hidden compartment for transporting alcohol

Average net paid circulation | DAILY ◆ NEWS | FINAL EDITION
of THE NEWS, July, 1927.
Sunday, 1,317,467
Daily, 1,177,817
NEW YORK'S ◆ PICTURE NEWSPAPER
Vol. 9. No. 50. 82 Pages ** New York, Tuesday, August 23, 1927. 2 Cents

# DEAD!

Story on Page 3

## SACCO          VANZETTI

SACCO AND VANZETTI PAY SUPREME PENALTY!—Nicola Sacco, Massachusetts shoemaker, and Bartolomeo Vanzetti, fish-monger and philosopher, were put to death early today in the electric chair at the Charlestown, Mass., state prison. After seven years of legal delays, during which their cause was taken up by millions of sympathizers and became a matter of international importance. Massachusetts justice exacted its penalty for the South Braintree payroll murders on April 15, 1920. Until the last moment the execution of the sentence remained in doubt. The two men, waiting in their death cells, did not know positively that the governor would not intervene until they were ready to be led to the chair.—Story, p. 3; other pictures, pp. 16 and 17.

EUROPE

3%

GATE

# Pride and Prejudice

While immigration had dropped sharply during World War I, by 1921 it had returned to prewar levels. As mentioned previously, soldiers returning from the war came home to an economic recession and had difficulty finding jobs. Many blamed the immigrants and African Americans, who had filled industrial jobs while the soldiers were in Europe, for taking jobs that they believed should have gone to them. Many Americans also had lingering animosity toward Germans and a fear of radical groups such as Communists after the war. A general anti-immigrant sentiment spread across the country.

The public largely associated labor unrest, strikes, and crime with immigrants, and this association was evident in the famous Sacco-Vanzetti case. In 1920 two Italian immigrants, Nicola Sacco and Bartolomeo Vanzetti, were arrested and tried on suspicion of murdering two shoe company employees during a payroll robbery in South Braintree, Massachusetts. Both Sacco and Vanzetti were associated with radical anarchist activities. Their case received mounting publicity, and they both were convicted and in 1927 were executed. Their defenders argued that they had been convicted not because of the evidence, which was disputed, but because they were Italian-born immigrants and anarchists.

The increased fear of foreign radicals coming to the United States, particularly from southern and eastern Europe, led to a growing nativist movement (protecting the interests of native-born or established inhabitants against those of immigrants). To limit immigration from these regions, Congress passed the Emergency Quota Act of 1921. This act set an annual cap on immigrants of any nationality at three percent of the number of people from that nation living in the United States in 1910.

The **Immigration Act of 1924**, which included the Asian Exclusion Act and the National Origins Act, further restricted immigration. The Asian Exclusion Act, which was pushed for by California and other western states, barred immigrants from Japan. The National Origins Act reduced the quota of immigrants to two percent of the number of people of that nationality living in the United States as of the 1890 census, effectively reducing still further the number of immigrants from southern and eastern Europe. The act capped total annual immigration at 165,000 for countries outside the Western Hemisphere—an eighty percent reduction from the average before World War I. Some union leaders supported these restrictions because they would limit the amount of cheap labor competing for jobs. Others believed the act would preserve America's ethnic identity, and some believed southern and eastern Europeans, many of whom were Roman Catholic or Jewish, and Asians were "undesirables" who were unable to assimilate into American culture.

◀ (top) Headline announcing the executions of Sacco and Vanzetti; (bottom) "The Only Way to Handle It" political cartoon on the Emergency Quota Act of 1921

The leading nativist group during the 1920s was the Ku Klux Klan (KKK), which had reappeared in 1915 and was patterned after the original group founded during Reconstruction. The Klan promoted "100% Americanism" and limited membership to native-born white Protestants. Through skillful promotion, the Klan expanded nationally through the early 1920s, becoming a strong social and political force in many northern cities, where immigrant and black populations were rising. Feeding on prejudice and racism, the Klan's organizers resorted to intimidation and violence against African Americans, Roman Catholics, immigrants, and people of Jewish descent.

Klan members in the 1920s sought to justify their movement by appropriating the symbol of the cross and the cause of moral reform. Klan membership in the 1920s may have reached several million. In August 1925 over 50,000 KKK members openly paraded through Washington, DC. Membership declined after the passage of the 1924 immigration law but would increase again in the 1950s.

African Americans who fought in World War I hoped that when they returned home they would be treated like every other citizen. Instead, they found that Jim Crow laws and racial discrimination continued. Across the country, black veterans pushed to have their civil rights recognized but were met with resistance. In 1919 race riots occurred in more than three dozen cities. One of the worst race riots of the time was the Tulsa race massacre in Oklahoma in 1921 in which over 100 people were killed when a white mob attacked black citizens and the upscale black area of Tulsa known as "Black Wall Street" was looted and burned.

▲ Ku Klux Klansmen on parade in Washington, DC, 1926

The National Association for the Advancement of Colored People (see Chapter 15) continued to battle against segregation and discrimination against African Americans. The NAACP challenged state laws that violated the Fourteenth and Fifteenth Amendments. It also started a journal, the *Crisis*, to educate Americans about racial problems. The NAACP claimed that 3,436 known lynchings had taken place between 1889 and 1922, the majority occurring in the South, yet in only a small number of cases were the lynchers punished. From 1919 to 1925 the NAACP promoted an anti-lynching bill that would punish both those who participated in lynching and local officials who failed to punish lynchers. The bill passed the House of Representatives in 1922 but failed in the Senate because of opposition from many Southern senators who protested that the bill unconstitutionally imposed federal control over state law enforcement. However, the publicity surrounding the legislation brought public attention to lynching and helped reduce its frequency.

Leaders in the black community differed over how to address the challenges of racism. Marcus Garvey, a native Jamaican, founded the Universal Negro Improvement Association (UNIA). He disagreed with the NAACP's approach of working with white Americans to bring about social change. Garvey claimed that whites were incapable of overcoming their racial prejudices and argued that black Americans should develop their own cultures that would be entirely separate from those of white Americans. Instead of seeking equality in America, he urged emigration to Africa. Many African Americans rejected Garvey's vision of racial separation, but his call for black nationalism and black pride would reemerge in later decades.

▲ 1925 NAACP banner reminding New Yorkers that lynching was still occurring

◄ Marcus Garvey

▼ A Universal Negro Improvement Association (UNIA) parade in Harlem, 1920

THE NEW NEGRO HAS NO FEAR

# Fundamentalism

## Rise of Fundamentalism

As mentioned in Chapter 15, orthodox Christian theologians in the Progressive Era resisted the theological errors of modernism, the social gospel, and the inroads of Darwinian evolution. These Fundamentalists argued that theological modernism was a different religion from Christianity and that the social gospel was no gospel at all. They believed the Bible taught that there could be no Christian unity with those who promoted a false gospel (2 John 1:7, 10 and 2 Corinthians 6:14, 17). These Christians fought to remove modernists from their denominations.

The battle in the North between Fundamentalists and modernists, called the Fundamentalist-Modernist controversy, raged over doctrine and the control of the major denominations' schools, mission boards, and institutions. Such men as William Bell Riley fought for the orthodox faith in the Northern Baptist Convention. J. Gresham Machen, a professor at Princeton Seminary, and others battled the liberals for the historic Christian faith in the northern Presbyterian church, also known as the PC(USA). Machen's book, *Christianity and Liberalism*, written in 1923, forcefully pointed out that modernism was not Christianity but another religion.

◄ J. Gresham Machen (front row, center) and the faculty of Westminster Theological Seminary, 1931

For a time, orthodox Christians remained the majority in the major denominations. However, many church leaders were unwilling to expel modernists from their denominational institutions if such action risked a major split, and they prevented Fundamentalists from removing false teachers from key leadership positions. Fundamentalists then left or were forced to leave the major denominations, colleges, and seminaries. They founded denominations, churches, and schools that were faithful to the gospel. Fundamentalists in the Northern Baptist Convention left to form the General Association of Regular Baptist Churches (GARBC) in 1932. Machen led a group of Presbyterian Fundamentalists to form the Orthodox Presbyterian Church in 1936.

Fundamentalism flourished in the 1920s. By 1930 more than fifty Fundamentalist Bible institutes, colleges, and seminaries existed, some of which had been long established while others were newly formed. Fundamentalists also published books, newspapers, and magazines, and produced radio programs that linked like-minded Christians.

---

## Focus of the Fundamentalists in the 1920s

**1** INSPIRATION AND INERRANCY OF SCRIPTURE

**2** VIRGIN BIRTH AND DEITY OF JESUS CHRIST

**3** SUBSTITUTIONARY ATONEMENT ON THE CROSS

**4** RESURRECTION OF JESUS' BODY FROM THE DEAD

**5** MIRACULOUS NATURE OF BIBLICAL EVENTS

## The Scopes Trial

In 1925 the Tennessee legislature passed a law forbidding public school teachers from teaching evolution. Wanting to challenge such laws, the American Civil Liberties Union (ACLU) offered to defend any teacher in the state who would violate that law. Believing the nationwide publicity of a big trial would be good for business, some town leaders of Dayton, Tennessee, coaxed a high school teacher, John T. Scopes, to challenge the law. Scopes had been a substitute for the regular biology teacher for a few weeks, and though he did not recall teaching evolution, he agreed to be arrested for doing so.

The resulting **Scopes trial**, also called the Monkey Trial, became a media event as national attention focused on Dayton for the summer of 1925. Two hundred reporters descended on the town, and the trial was the first to be covered by radio. The ACLU hired Clarence Darrow, a famous trial lawyer and an agnostic (one who claims it is impossible to know if God exists), to defend Scopes. Former presidential candidate and secretary of war William Jennings Bryan helped the prosecution. Bryan was also a witness and was called by the defense as an authority on the Bible. Famous journalist H. L. Mencken, a well-known atheist, was present at the trial, and in his reporting he described Bryan as a "buffoon." Although Bryan showed courage in his defense of the faith, he was no Bible scholar and did not make the best case for the cause. While Scopes was convicted, Bryan and the other antievolutionists lost the publicity battle.

Bryan remained in Tennessee after the trial, making speeches and writing about the event. He died five days after the trial ended, at age sixty-five. Later, Scopes's attorney appealed the case to the Tennessee Supreme Court, which upheld the law that banned the teaching of evolution, but overturned Scopes's conviction based on a technicality.

▲ Attorney Clarence Darrow (left) and William Jennings Bryan (right) at the Scopes trial

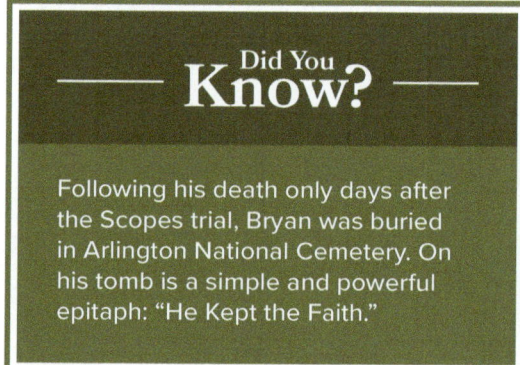

### Did You Know?

Following his death only days after the Scopes trial, Bryan was buried in Arlington National Cemetery. On his tomb is a simple and powerful epitaph: "He Kept the Faith."

---

### Comprehension Check 17.3

1. The Great Migration refers to the movement of ____.

   A immigrants from southern and eastern Europe to the United States

   B African Americans from the South to the North and Midwest

   C rural farmworkers to large cities

2. The center of African American culture in the 1920s was ____.

   A Chicago

   B New Orleans

   C Harlem

3. The Volstead Act ____.

   A enforced Prohibition

   B outlawed the teaching of evolution in public schools

   C limited immigration

4. All of the following were evidence of a growing nativism in the United States except ____.

   A the reappearance of the Ku Klux Klan

   B the passage of laws restricting immigration

   C the Sacco-Vanzetti case

   D the Scopes trial

### MAKING CONNECTIONS

5. How did the literature and music of the 1920s reflect the ideas of the decade?

6. Why did Fundamentalists believe they could not be unified with modernists?

# Harding and Coolidge

**What were the presidencies of Harding and Coolidge known for?**

- What scandals occurred during the presidency of Warren G. Harding?
- What was Calvin Coolidge like as president?

Republicans easily won the White House in not only 1920 but also 1924 and 1928 as their party received credit for the apparent peace and prosperity of the decade. Government regulation and activism were minimal, and laissez-faire capitalism was thriving.

## Harding

A former newspaper editor in Marion, Ohio, **Warren G. Harding** became involved in politics with the assistance of Harry Daugherty, the leader of a group of state politicians called the "Ohio Gang." Harding became a US senator in 1914. At the Republican convention in 1920, Harding received the nomination. President Wilson's ill health left the Democratic Party in need of a new leader, and the convention chose progressive Governor James M. Cox of Ohio, and his running mate, Franklin D. Roosevelt of New York. During the campaign, Harding's theme of a return to "normalcy" pleased the nation, and he won decisively.

Harding was a pro-business president who favored lower taxes, higher tariffs, and less government involvement in the economy. The American public generally liked Harding and approved of his policies, but his presidency later became associated with scandals in his cabinet. He had rewarded his friends in the Ohio Gang with high offices, and the improprieties of those friends soon put the president under extreme strain. To a journalist he noted, "I have no trouble with my enemies. I can take care of [my enemies] all right. But my . . . friends, . . . they're the ones that keep me walking the floors nights!"

The most infamous of the scandals, the **Teapot Dome scandal**, involved the secretary of the interior, Albert B. Fall. Fall had won Harding's approval to take control of the US Navy's oil reserves at two locations, Teapot Dome in Wyoming and Elk Hills in California. Fall accepted bribes to lease the oil rights on those properties to two oil businessmen, who were later found to have also given Fall sizable "loans." The scandal also implicated various other members of the administration. Following Harding's death from a heart attack in August 1923, the incident became public knowledge and brought his name into disrepute. Fall was later fined $100,000 and sentenced to one year in prison, the first cabinet official to receive a prison sentence for misdeeds in office.

Teapot Dome was not the only scandal of that era. For example, Charles Forbes, head of the Veterans' Bureau, defrauded that agency of more than $200 million. And Harding's old friend, Attorney General Harry Daugherty, was brought to trial twice after being implicated in bribery schemes. Daugherty escaped conviction, although the Senate investigations revealed that he had burned the records of his account in his brother's bank. Daugherty refused to give his reason for destroying the records but implied that the revelation would further harm the memory of the late President Harding.

Although Harding appointed some officials who turned out to be disreputable, he made better choices in Herbert Hoover as secretary of commerce and Andrew Mellon as the secretary of the treasury. Their leadership helped the free market to adjust without interference, and this adjustment enabled the American economy to overcome the postwar economic downturn.

▲ Warren G. Harding

▲ Secretary of the Interior Albert Fall

▲ Calvin Coolidge

# Coolidge

A man of few words from rural Vermont, **Calvin Coolidge**, nicknamed "Silent Cal," had first gained national fame in 1919 as governor of Massachusetts by putting down a Boston police strike. When Samuel Gompers of the AFL (see Chapter 12) asked Coolidge to acknowledge the right of the police to express their grievances, the governor declared, "There can be no right to strike against the public safety by anybody, anywhere, anytime." That strong statement elicited admiration from many, as the country was immersed in the Red Scare at that time.

When Coolidge, the vice president, took office upon Harding's sudden death, the cabinet scandals were just beginning to unfold. Harding had failed to deal with his officials' misdeeds as soon as they occurred, but Coolidge immediately made clear that thorough investigations into the underhanded dealings would be conducted and that the guilty would be punished. For example, he forced Daugherty to resign in March 1924. As a result, Coolidge distanced himself from the corruption of his predecessor's administration.

After winning the 1924 election, President Coolidge continued Harding's pro-business, hands-off approach to government. He was content to let the market have free rein. When Congress twice passed a bill that was intended to help farmers through pricing and government purchase of surplus crops, Coolidge vetoed the bill both times. As prices on the stock market climbed, Americans credited the president for the country's unprecedented prosperity. In light of his popularity, Coolidge surprised the nation when he announced in 1927, "I do not choose to run for president in 1928."

## Comprehension Check 17.4

1. The scandals during Harding's presidency involved ____.

   **A** political opponents James M. Cox and Franklin D. Roosevelt

   **B** labor leaders of the AFL

   **C** cabinet members from the Ohio Gang

2. In the Teapot Dome Scandal, Albert B. Fall took "loans" in return for ____.

   **A** election results

   **B** oil reserves

   **C** crop surpluses

3. Coolidge distanced himself from the following except ____.

   **A** pro-business policy

   **B** government corruption

   **C** labor strikes

### MAKING CONNECTIONS

4. How were Harding and Coolidge similar in their views on the economy?

## Chapter Summary

### 17.1 Postwar Difficulties

- The American economy declined after World War I as war production ceased, and unemployment was high. Farmers were hurt by low prices after demand for food declined after the war.

- President Harding pledged to return America to "normalcy." America's foreign policy was isolationism but still promoted international peace through the Washington Naval Conference and the Kellogg-Briand Pact. The United States also tried to improve relations with its Latin American neighbors and attempted to resolve an impending financial crisis in Europe over war debts and reparations payments.

- The Red Scare displayed America's growing fear of the spread of communism.

**TERMS**

normalcy

isolationism

Washington Naval Conference

Kellogg-Briand Pact

Red Scare

**TERMS**

installment plan

Charles A. Lindbergh

speculation

bull market

buying on margin

### 17.2 The Growth of Consumer Society

- Millions of automobiles were bought during the 1920s, with many Americans using installment plans to purchase vehicles. The automobile enabled city dwellers to move to the suburbs, rural families to visit the city more frequently, and families to travel for vacations.

- After the airplane was used in World War I, many saw new potentials. Charles Lindbergh successfully made the first nonstop solo transatlantic flight in 1927. The US government provided airmail service, and international and domestic airlines grew.

- Economic prosperity encouraged Americans to spend more on consumer products such as cars and electric appliances to increase efficiency and pleasure. Businesses used advertising to promote products, influencing Americans to elevate consuming. Consumers made purchases through installment plans, and many in debt tried to gain money through illegal means or speculation in land or the stock market. A bull market beginning in 1927 further boosted confidence for those who invested in stock.

## Chapter Summary

### 17.3 The Roaring Twenties

- The literature, art, music, and movies of the 1920s reflected the new ideas, disillusionment, and changing standards of the era. The Harlem Renaissance featured prominent African American writers, actors, and musicians, and jazz music became popular with both black and white audiences. Organized sports were popular leisure activities, and many athletes gained wealth and fame.

- Prohibition began in 1920, but enforcement was difficult. Organized crime was led by gangsters like Al Capone. Prohibition ended with the ratification of the Twenty-First Amendment in 1933.

- Sentiment against immigrants from southern and eastern Europe and Asia led to restrictions on immigration and the reappearance of the Ku Klux Klan. African Americans continued to face discrimination.

- Fundamentalists defended orthodox Christianity from modernism, which they believed was not Christianity but false religion. In the Scopes trial, the law preventing the teaching of evolution was upheld, but the reputation of those defending biblical teaching was hurt.

### TERMS

| | |
|---|---|
| flappers | bootlegging |
| Great Migration | Al Capone |
| Harlem Renaissance | Twenty-First Amendment |
| Prohibition | Immigration Act of 1924 |
| Volstead Act | Scopes trial |

### TERMS

Warren G. Harding

Teapot Dome scandal

Calvin Coolidge

### 17.4 Harding and Coolidge

- Although Warren G. Harding appointed some qualified cabinet members who helped the economy recover, his administration was mainly associated with the scandals of cabinet members who had been close friends in the Ohio Gang. In the Teapot Dome Scandal, the secretary of the interior leased rights to naval oil reserves in exchange for bribes. These scandals became public knowledge after Harding's death.

- Calvin Coolidge, Harding's vice president, took office after Harding's death in 1923. Coolidge promised thorough investigations into the scandals and effectively distanced himself from the corruption. Like Harding, Coolidge favored limited government regulation of business, and many Americans credited the president with the decade's prosperity.

## Chapter Review Questions

### RECALL

1. What did Warren G. Harding pledge he would restore to America if elected?

2. What was the period of increased public concern about communism in America called?

3. Who was the first person to fly solo nonstop from New York to Paris?

4. What is buying or selling something that involves unusually high risk for the chance to gain an unusually high profit called?

5. What were young women who captured attention by their shocking behavior and dress called?

6. What psychologist's beliefs about the repression of sexual desires encouraged some Americans to believe that immoral behavior was acceptable?

7. What gangster controlled the bootlegging business in Chicago in the 1920s?

8. What amendment ended Prohibition?

9. What scandal led to the imprisonment of Harding's secretary of the interior?

### UNDERSTAND

10. What were two problems at home that soldiers returning from World War I faced?

11. Why was isolationism the general theme of American foreign policy in the 1920s?

12. What two basic foreign policy tasks did the United States face in the 1920s, and what did they want to avoid while accomplishing those tasks?

13. What was the purpose of the Washington Naval Conference? What agreement resulted? What were two flaws of or objections to the resulting treaties?

14. What did the signers of the Kellogg-Briand Pact agree to? What made the pact ineffective?

15. Why did the Allies have trouble paying back their war debts to the United States? Why did Germany have trouble paying its reparations to the Allies? How did the Dawes Plan attempt to solve these problems?

16. Why were Americans concerned about the spread of communism in the 1920s?

17. What government policies contributed to economic growth during the 1920s?

18. What were three ways automobiles changed American society?

19. How did advertising and installment plans contribute to increasing materialism in American culture?

20. What was the Great Migration? What caused it?

21. What was the Harlem Renaissance?

22. What were two reasons for the growing nativist movement in America? What were three evidences of this nativism?

23. How did Marcus Garvey's UNIA differ from the NAACP in its approach to dealing with racial discrimination?

24. Why did Fundamentalists believe they could not be united with modernists? How did Fundamentalists respond when the major denominations would not remove modernists from leadership positions?

25. What was the Scopes trial about? What was its outcome? What affect did it have on those who defended the biblical view of Creation?

26. What approach to government did Harding and Coolidge practice?

### THINK ABOUT IT

27. What benefits did the growth of consumer society bring to Americans? What were some negative effects of the growth of consumer society?

28. How did the arts and leisure activities of the 1920s reflect the changing ideas and values of the era?

29. Why was Prohibition difficult to enforce? Do you think this "noble experiment" should have been tried? Explain.

# 18 Depression and New Deal

**18.1 The Great Depression**
**18.2 Hoover Responds**
**18.3 Roosevelt and the New Deal**
**18.4 Responses to the New Deal**

▲ Men in Chicago advertising their willingness to work, 1934

Coolidge's announcement that he would not seek reelection in 1928 opened the door for **Herbert Hoover**, a fellow Republican, to seek the presidential nomination. After earning a fortune as an engineer, Hoover had headed the Food Administration under Wilson, organized American food relief for Belgium during World War I, and served with distinction as secretary of commerce in the cabinets of both Harding and Coolidge. After winning the Republican nomination, Hoover faced New York governor Al Smith in the 1928 election. There were two reasons that many Americans opposed Smith—he was Roman Catholic and he opposed Prohibition. In the early twentieth century, mainstream American culture was Protestant, and most Americans were concerned about electing a Roman Catholic to the presidency. In addition, Prohibition had become a moral crusade that united both conservative and liberal Protestants. Satisfied with the prosperity of the 1920s and trusting that Hoover would continue the hands-off government policies of Harding and Coolidge, Americans elected Hoover, who received 58% of the popular vote and won the electoral vote 444 to 87.

However, prosperity under Hoover lasted only a short time. Within a year of his inauguration, the stock market crashed, and America began to fall into the most severe economic depression in its history.

▲ Herbert Hoover

## 18.1 The Great Depression

**Why was there a Great Depression?**

## The Depression Begins

### The Crash

While Wall Street was booming, many Americans had focused their attention on the excitement and affluence that resulted. The stock market continued to reach new highs throughout the first half of 1929, despite warnings by the Federal Reserve and others that excessive speculation was causing a "bubble" (inflated prices that did not reflect the true value of the stocks) in the market.

The stock bubble began to leak in mid-September as investors began to sell. When they had difficulty finding buyers, they had to sell at reduced prices. On October 24 ("Black Thursday"), the bubble burst. Fear began to fuel panic selling. Millions of shares were offered for sale, but virtually no one bought. Prices dropped dramatically until New York's leading financiers pooled their resources to buy stock and halt the devastating decline. The attempt to prop up the market worked for that day, but not before stock prices had taken a significant fall. A record-breaking 13 million shares changed hands that day, and the market lost 11 percent of its value, with investors losing over $9 billion.

Banks began to pressure brokers, and brokers began to pressure investors who had bought stock on the margin (see Chapter 17) to pay up. Because most of these speculators did not have the extra cash, they opted to sell the stock, which resulted in a new wave of selling at the stock exchange and an accompanying drop in prices. On Black Tuesday, October 29, the market crashed and more than 16 million shares were sold. Stocks continued to drop until they reached their lowest point on November 13—by that point investors had lost $30 billion.

### GUIDING QUESTIONS

- What were the causes of the Great Depression?
- What was America like during the Depression?

▼ News report, issued the day before Black Tuesday, of the continuing drop in stock prices

Americans hoped that the stock market crash was only a temporary "readjustment" of the inordinately high stock prices caused by speculation. Instead, a **bear market** (a stock market characterized by pessimism and declining stock prices) dominated the economy for the next several years. The stock market crash signaled the beginning of the worst economic crisis in American history, known as the **Great Depression**, which lasted for over ten years.

Because Hoover was intent on keeping public morale high, he avoided the standard historical term for an economic decline—*panic*—and instead chose to call the downturn by a term that, at the time, evoked less emotion. He called it a "depression." Although that economic term seemed less alarming at the time, the word came to strike fear in the hearts of Americans in the decades that followed and would bring to mind painful memories for the remainder of the century.

## Causes of the Great Depression

The stock market crash alone did not cause the Great Depression. Several other factors in the economy were also at work that set off the long-lasting downturn.

First, the Federal Reserve System (see Chapter 15) had expanded credit throughout most of the 1920s by lowering interest rates. This contributed to economic expansion but also created inflation. Consequently, prices of real estate and stocks rose. More people borrowed money at low rates, dramatically increasing the volume of farm and personal mortgages. The low rates led banks to make risky loans, such as margin loans, to stockbrokers. State and local governments also increased their own indebtedness. When the Fed in 1929 finally decided to raise interest rates to slow inflation, businesses borrowed less and decreased spending, and the economy began to readjust itself to match the true economic situation. The resulting collapse of credit devastated America's financial market.

The combination of the Fed tightening interest rates and the stock market crash had a devastating effect on the banks. Some banks had invested their depositors' funds in the stock market. Others had lent their depositors' money to stockbrokers or real estate speculators. When the value of stocks and real estate collapsed, many borrowers could not pay their loans, and the banks could not absorb all the losses. Depositors, worried that they might lose their money, rushed to the banks to remove some or all of their funds, creating bank runs. In turn, the banks were then short of cash and did not have funds to make additional loans. As a result, many banks were forced to close, sometimes permanently. When this happened, depositors lost all their savings. By 1931 more than four thousand banks had closed across the country. By the end of the decade, that number was more than nine thousand.

Additionally, the booming economy of the 1920s had led to overproduction. As explained in Chapter 17, farmers were already dealing with overproduction in agriculture because of falling demand overseas. Factories that had been turning out products to meet demand were soon producing more than they could sell as the economy began to slow. As demand declined, employers began to cut workers' hours or lay them off, reducing incomes. This led to workers cutting back their spending, which lowered demand even further, which led to further layoffs.

▼ Bank run at New York's American Union Bank

Another cause of the Great Depression was the government's tariff policy. Hoover had pledged in the 1928 presidential campaign to help farmers by increasing tariffs on agricultural imports. However, after the stock market crash some Republicans demanded that tariffs on industrial imports be increased as well. As a result, Congress passed the **Smoot-Hawley Tariff** in 1930. It was one of the highest tariffs in American history. Hoover initially opposed the bill, and over one thousand economists signed a letter pleading with him to veto it. However, under pressure from fellow Republicans, he signed it. Foreign governments retaliated with their own high tariffs, greatly reducing foreign trade. As mentioned in Chapter 17, Allied nations and Germany depended on trade to make debt and reparations payments, and the inability of these nations to make their payments only further increased economic difficulties for the United States and Europe.

## Life during the Depression

A nation that had become one of the wealthiest and most powerful in the world was thrown into a confusing economic situation, trapping millions of its people in poverty and despair. Although most Americans escaped severe deprivations, few of them passed through the 1930s without some hardship and anxiety. There were unwanted reminders everywhere that the prosperity of the 1920s was gone and that the future was doubtful.

### The Family

Once the Depression struck, almost anything that President Hoover said was used to mock him, especially when he told reporters, "Nobody is starving. The hoboes [beggars, drifters], for example, are better fed than they have ever been. One hobo in New York got ten meals in one day." Soon a flood of newspaper headlines refuted the president's point. Ninety-five cases of starvation were reported in New York City during 1931. That report is probably inflated because substantiated reports were few, but some starvation did occur and lack of food was commonplace among the poor. In 1932 the New York City Health Department declared that more than 20 percent of the city's public school children were suffering from malnutrition. Jobless men who happened to find work were sometimes too weak from hunger to labor.

Private charities had maintained rescue missions and soup kitchens for the down-and-out in the past, but they were not prepared to continue helping the vast numbers of the unemployed. The federal funds given to states for relief were partly used to provide needed extra provisions for the hungry. Soon "breadlines" formed along city streets as the desperate sought food in the soup kitchens. Local agencies were established to provide some cash for relief to those who applied and met all the requirements. Even then, the sums given were hardly enough to feed a family, much less clothe and house them.

Often it was the parents' concern for their children that finally brought the family to apply for relief, but that concern could not cover the sense of humiliation that the adults felt. Husbands and fathers who had trudged from business to business trying to find work blamed themselves for their inability to gain and hold a job. Some left home to look for work and stayed away for long periods of time if they found it. Wives struggled with their own cares, trying to keep the ragged clothes that their families wore from falling apart and even searching for housecleaning jobs or other employment that might bring in some money.

# Some Causes of the Great Depression

**1** STOCK MARKET CRASH

**2** EXPANSION OF CREDIT

**3** OVERPRODUCTION

**4** TARIFF POLICY

▼ Breadline at a soup kitchen in New York City, 1932

## Homelessness

About two million people were uprooted from their homes in the 1930s. Some became hoboes, usually young, unmarried men and teenage boys who had lost hope of finding a job and settling down. They rode in, on, or even under boxcars on freight trains from place to place, eating in soup kitchens, sleeping in city parks, camping in "hobo jungles," and perhaps dreaming that the next stop might hold promise for a job.

Countless thousands of families faced the threat of homelessness. Some of them had mortgages on their homes, but now, without income, they could not make their payments. Banks were seldom quick to foreclose, but many institutions eventually had to repossess the houses. Other people rented houses or apartments for which they now had no money to pay. Rent in those days was typically low (often around $10 to $12 per month), but even that was beyond the means of many families.

▲ Hobo

People were quick to blame Hoover for the Depression. His name was soon linked with the hardships of the era because he was the president when the crisis began. As conditions grew bleaker, cardboard shacks sheltering homeless people in parks and vacant lots of American cities were called "**Hoovervilles**." Newspapers used as covering on cold nights were "Hoover blankets," and empty pockets turned inside out became "Hoover flags." The frayed sacks in which the jobless carried their belongings were called "Hoover bags." Broken-down cars pulled by horses or mules were "Hoover carts," and the jackrabbits that farmers killed for food were "Hoover hogs." A popular joke of the day was that Hoover went to Secretary of the Treasury Andrew Mellon one day and asked him for a nickel to phone a friend. Mellon replied, "Here's a dime; telephone both of them." Hoover, saddened by the animosity of the nation, commented, "Democracy is not a polite employer."

▼ Hooverville in Seattle, Washington, 1933

## The Dust Bowl

Farmers who had poured into the Great Plains region in the late nineteenth and early twentieth centuries converted millions of acres from prairie grassland to fields of fertile, powdery soil. They had been able to build a sustainable life for themselves and their families.

But falling farm prices in the 1920s dropped even lower during the Depression. To make matters worse, a devastating drought in the Great Plains began in 1932. For four years, rainfall was rare, and the region's produce all but vanished. Adding to the woes that the farmers were experiencing, the prairie winds began to pick up the powdery dust from the plains and carry it across the land. Billowing black clouds of dust sometimes engulfed the region, the dirt sifting through every crack in a farmer's house, piling in huge drifts against buildings and fences, obscuring sunlight, and nearly suffocating anyone who ventured outdoors. Even indoors the people often slept with wet cloths over their faces to keep from breathing the dust.

The **Dust Bowl**, a term coined by a newspaper reporter in 1935, reached as far north as Colorado and Kansas and as far south as Texas and New Mexico, but its most brutal effects were felt in Oklahoma. Some farmers gave up and moved away. Called "**Okies**," thousands of them loaded their cars or trucks with all their possessions and headed west to California. There they sought jobs as migrant farm workers, harvesting various crops as they came in season. The uprooted farm families generally remained in poverty until the end of the Depression, but at least they had opportunities for work.

Those who remained on the land soon learned to adjust their farming methods to the needs of their arid land. Much acreage was returned to grassland and used as pasture for livestock, and soil conservation techniques prevailed on the remaining fields. Those efforts continue today to keep the dust of the plains settled, thereby averting any recurrence of the Dust Bowl.

▶ "Okie" family en route to California

## Minority Groups

The hardships of the Depression fell heavily on black Americans, although economic struggles were not new to them. In 1932 about half of all African American workers were unemployed, a rate of joblessness double that of the general population. Farm problems and government policies drove sharecroppers in the South, many of them black, off the land. Many moved to cities in the North and West, continuing the migration of African Americans that had begun with World War I. With unemployment wracking America's cities, the North was hardly a promised land for jobless black Americans.

Hispanic migrant farm workers and their families in the Southwest who were not US citizens generally returned to Mexico when the Depression hit, or they were deported. Jobs were not available for Americans, much less immigrants. Those who remained faced the same problems that other Depression-era families encountered, but they also had to deal with prejudice and even violence because they were competing for the same jobs. Most migrated to urban areas, hoping to find employment as unskilled workers.

▲ Family gathered around a radio

## Entertainment

Although a quarter or more of the population was deeply affected by the Depression, 80 million Americans (of a population of about 123 million) still had jobs, food on their tables, clothes on their backs, and roofs over their heads.

In the midst of hard times and great challenges, life continued, and the people found ways to cope and even laugh in the face of difficulty. Many Americans seemed intent on forgetting their troubles during the rough times. Some found escape in reading books such as Margaret Mitchell's epic Civil War novel *Gone with the Wind*, which appeared in 1936 and became a popular movie in 1939. Hollywood produced more than five thousand feature films of fantasy and drama, providing escape and entertainment for millions of Americans. Walt Disney's first full-length animated presentation, *Snow White*, debuted in 1938, and many new movie stars began to draw wide admiration, among them a little girl named Shirley Temple, who became the darling of the nation.

Families continued to be entertained at home through radio programs such as "Amos and Andy," "The Lone Ranger," and "Little Orphan Annie" and music by crooner Bing Crosby as well as musician Benny Goodman, who introduced "swing music" in 1935 and whose big bands broadcast jazzy orchestra numbers. Radio created one of the most dramatic episodes of the 1930s when Orson Welles presented his radio dramatization of H. G. Wells's *War of the Worlds* on a major network in 1938. So realistic was his version of the story of invasion from Mars that some listeners who tuned in to the program as it was in progress were terrified, unaware that the frightening account of a spaceship landing in New Jersey was only fiction.

Sports continued to attract many fans. One of the decade's biggest sports heroes was **Jesse Owens**. In the 1936 Olympics in Berlin, Germany, Owens, an African American sprinter, won four gold medals in track events. His performance was an irritation to Adolf Hitler, the leader of the host country. Hitler believed that Aryans, including Germans, were the master race. Owens won his first gold medal in the 100-meter dash with a time of 10.3 seconds. In his next event, the long jump, he competed against German Luz Long. Owens won by landing a jump of 26 feet and 5.5 inches, gaining his second gold medal. Owens's third gold medal came in the 200-meter race and the fourth in the 4x100 relay.

▶ US athletes (from left to right) Jesse Owens, Ralph Metcalfe, Foy Draper, and Frank Wykoff in the men's 4x100 meter relay at the 1936 Berlin Olympics

▲ RCA TRK (television receiver kinescope)-12 television model shown at the 1939 World's Fair

World's fairs also became a big attraction in the decade. In 1934 Chicago hosted one that featured, among other "Century of Progress" innovations and wonders, an exhibit of premature babies in incubators and the Burlington Route's *Zephyr*, a streamlined diesel locomotive that set the record for a Denver-to-Chicago trip. The Chicago fair was surpassed by the spectacular New York World's Fair in 1939. From its opening to its closing two years later, the New York fair attracted 45 million visitors to its 1,500 exhibits. People marveled at the technological innovations on display at this event christened "The World of Tomorrow," and they delighted in the breathtaking carnival rides. One of the most popular attractions, General Motors' "Futurama," carried fairgoers on a fifteen-minute tour of America in 1960. The 1939 prophets provided breathless audiences with 100-mph highways traveled by Americans in radio-controlled, raindrop-shaped cars, who enjoyed their two months of vacation each year.

## 1930s Comic Strips

Entertainment, comedy, drama, and adventure during the Great Depression were as near as the daily newspaper—the comic strip. Comic strips had been appearing in newspapers since the 1890s. The 1930s, however, proved to be a golden age of comics. One of the most popular strips was *Little Orphan Annie*. Along with her dog Sandy, Annie, an orphan, overcame the challenges of the Depression with backbone and courage. Annie was a reflection of her creator's philosophy. Harold Gray, who began the strip in 1924, was a Republican and dedicated opponent of FDR's New Deal (discussed later in this chapter). Through Annie and her friends, Gray advocated his views of self-help through hard work. As her adopted father Daddy Warbucks says in one early strip, "Annie doesn't need charity—just give her an even break and she'll do the rest—Charity!!—BAH!" The lawlessness of the 1920s and 1930s gave birth to one of the toughest detectives in comics—*Dick Tracy*. Created by Chester Gould in 1931, *Dick Tracy* brought a realism to police comics never before seen. In the best "crime does not pay" tradition, villains in *Dick Tracy* often died realistically (and sometimes gruesomely). Those who wanted to escape the problems of the 1930s could travel by comic strip to exotic, faraway places, or even the future. Two popular science fiction strips were *Flash Gordon* and *Buck Rogers*. But the ultimate superhero comic was *Superman*. For pure humor, one could read *Popeye*, *Krazy Kat*, *Blondie*, *Li'l Abner*, or *Nancy*. The "funnies" became one small means of temporarily escaping the hard times of the Depression.

## Crime

Real-life drama also captured the nation's attention during the 1930s. The "crime of the century" was the 1932 kidnapping of the infant son of aviation hero Charles Lindbergh. A ransom note was left demanding a payment of $50,000 for his return. All across the nation, people were eager to hear of any developments in the case. Seventy-two days after the disappearance, a dead baby was found in the woods near the Lindbergh's house. An autopsy confirmed that it was the Lindberghs' baby, who had died of a fractured skull and had been dead since the night of the kidnapping. The search for the murderer required more than two years of intense detective work and ended in the conviction and execution of Bruno Hauptmann, a German immigrant.

Other crimes gained wide attention during the Depression, particularly those of bank-robbing gangs. Although those desperate criminals sometimes were portrayed as modern-day Robin Hoods who stole from the rich to give to the poor, in reality they were brutal. John Dillinger topped the "most wanted list," but he was joined by bandits such as "Pretty Boy" Floyd, "Machine Gun" Kelly, "Baby Face" Nelson, and couple-in-crime Bonnie Parker and Clyde Barrow. Most of these criminals died in a hail of gunfire or spent long stints in jail. Lawmen, especially agents of the newly formed Federal Bureau of Investigation (FBI), led by director J. Edgar Hoover, were viewed by some as heroes as they tracked down criminals.

DAILY NEWS
NEW YORK'S PICTURE NEWSPAPER
FINAL
New York, Wednesday, March 2, 1932
LINDY'S BABY KIDNAPED
Story on Page 3
The most famous baby in the world, Charles A. Lindbergh Jr., son of the world renowned Lone Eagle and the former Anne Morrow, who was kidnaped from his crib at the Lindbergh home at Hopewell, N. J., last night. Biggest police hunt in years is now under way. This picture of the boy—now one year and eight months old—was made by his father just after his birth in June, 1930, at his mother's home in Englewood, N. J.

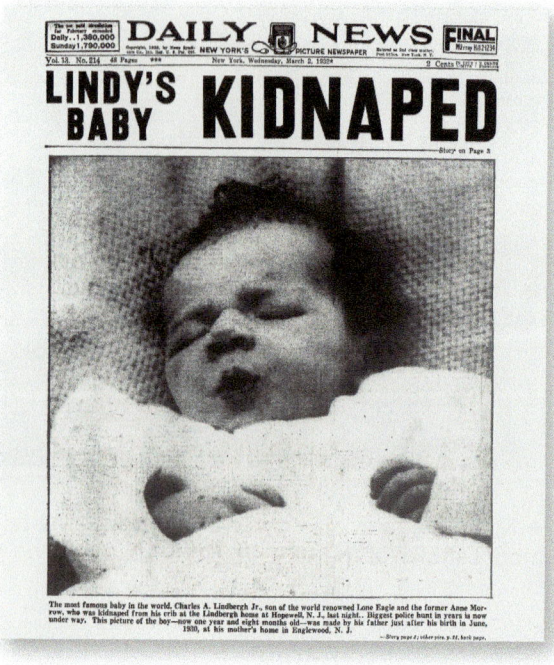

▲ *Daily News* headline about the kidnapping of Charles Lindbergh's son

▼ 1934 news report of the death of criminals Bonnie and Clyde

THE vanity of human life is like a river, constantly passing away, and yet constantly coming on. —Pope.
49TH YEAR NO. 236
The Dallas Morning News
DALLAS, TEXAS, THURSDAY, MAY 24, 1934—TWENTY PAGES
Section One General News
5c PER COPY
Posse Kills Clyde Barrow and Bonnie Parker
Manchukuan Farm Villages Wrecked By Japanese Bombs
Chinese Sources Claim 1,000 Dead as Planes Drop Explosives on Twenty Towns
Fires Still Raging
Refusal of Settlers to Give Up Arms Alleged Cause of Reprisals
Salutatorian at Rusk Not Only Gets Diploma, But Check for $11,600
Dillinger's Girl And Doctor Aiding Him Get 2 Years
Another Woman in Conspiracy Also Convicted and Third Acquitted
Leading Principals in Slaying of Outlaws
Church Must Aid New Deal Because Taught by Christ
Praise for Program of Roosevelt Government Given Presbyterians
Dallas Deputy Tells Of Ending Long Chase
Planes Complete 1,000-Mile Flight To Aid Newlywed
Surgeons Go Prepared to Help Appendicitis-Stricken Bridegroom
Bob Alcorn Says All He Has Done for Months Is Hunt for Bandits
Elusive Dallas Desperadoes Shot to Death in Louisiana
Failure of Clyde To Pay for Guns' Delivery Is Fatal
Henchman, Caught by Officers, Gives Valuable Information
Long Hunt Over Three States Is Ended as Six Officers Ambush Pair in Speeding Auto
Comrades Praise Men That Trapped Barrow and Parker
Job Done, Message Sent by Ex-Rangers, Now on Highway Patrol
New Australian Flight Mark Set By Plucky Girl
Relief Is Promised For Drouth Sections
The Weather
Arcadia Sheriff

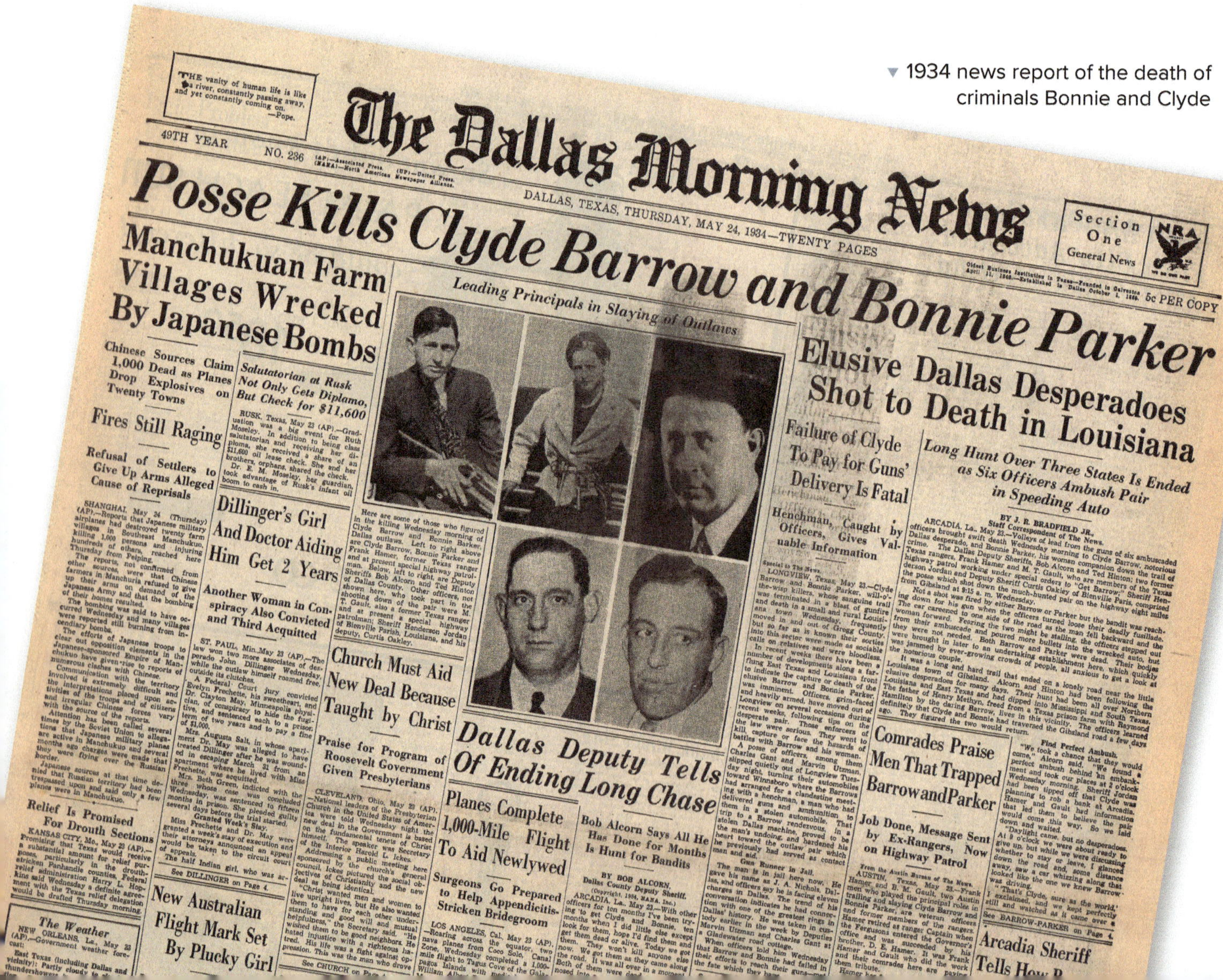

▲ Amelia Earhart

## Flight

**Amelia Earhart** became America's flying heroine when, in 1932, she became the first female pilot to fly solo across the Atlantic. But in 1937, during an adventurous round-the-world flight, she disappeared somewhere over the Pacific. Hers was not the only air tragedy of the 1930s, however. Popular humorist Will Rogers perished in an airplane crash while on a tour of Alaska with Wiley Post, the first man to fly solo around the world.

The most dramatic of the 1930s air tragedies was the explosion and crash of the zeppelin *Hindenburg*. At 803 feet long and 135 feet wide, the giant, blimp-like craft was one of the largest aircraft ever built. It contained passenger cabins, a dining room, a reading room, a lounge, and a promenade from which passengers could view the earth below. The *Hindenburg* could travel up to eighty-four miles an hour and had made several trips between Germany and the United States between 1936 and 1937. However, during its flight on May 6, 1937, as it began its final descent near Lakehurst, New Jersey, flames appeared near its tail. Within seconds the whole aircraft burst into flames as the hydrogen used to fly it ignited, killing thirty-five of the airship's ninety-seven passengers.

▶ The *Hindenburg* explosion

— **Comprehension Check 18.1** —

1. The stock market crash occurred within a year of the inauguration of ____.
   A  Calvin Coolidge
   B  Herbert Hoover
   C  Franklin Delano Roosevelt

2. After the crash of 1929, a ____ market followed for several years.
   A  bear
   B  black
   C  bull

3. Farmers who moved to California during the Dust Bowl were called ____.
   A  "Futurama"
   B  "Hoovervilles"
   C  "Okies"

4. ____ won four gold medals at the 1936 Olympics.
   A  Amelia Earhart
   B  Bruno Hauptmann
   C  Jesse Owens

**MAKING CONNECTIONS**

5. Other than the stock market crash, what were three causes of the Great Depression?

GUIDING QUESTIONS

- How did Hoover attempt to help during the Depression?
- How did Hoover's actions lead to declining popularity?

## 18.2 Hoover Responds

**Were Hoover's actions to alleviate the Great Depression effective?**

In 1928 Hoover's election campaign advertised him as the candidate who promised "a chicken in every pot and a car in every garage." The Republicans gladly accepted credit for the prosperity of the 1920s and promised more, a promise that the American people wanted to believe. But when the Great Depression began, blame for the end of prosperity began to fall on Hoover's shoulders.

### Government Involvement

After the stock market crash, Hoover projected an optimistic attitude for the American public. He predicted that the Depression would be short-lived and tried to restore confidence in the nation's financial system. However, as conditions worsened, few people listened.

## *Hoover's Strategy*

 ### Job Security

Shortly after the crash, in December 1929, Hoover called a meeting of four hundred of the nation's leading business executives. He urged them to voluntarily keep their workers and maintain satisfactory wage levels. He also asked that they continue to invest in new construction and equipment rather than cut industrial growth. Although the businessmen tried to cooperate, by the end of 1930 economic realities made their support impossible. To abide by the agreement would have sent many firms into bankruptcy, so businesses cut jobs and wages, and unemployment rose to 8.7 percent in 1930 (from 3.2 percent in 1929).

 ### Work and Relief Programs

Hoover signed legislation in 1929 to cut taxes and increase spending for federal public works (government-financed construction of public facilities) to create jobs. Although Hoover adamantly opposed any form of dole (an unearned government handout) to meet the needs of impoverished Americans, he believed that work relief was acceptable. Employment in a government relief job would at least discourage idleness and preserve the self-respect of the needy. In 1932 the Emergency Relief and Construction Act was passed, which authorized funds for public works projects across the country. It also gave federal money to state governments to provide some assistance to the unemployed and other needy individuals. Hoover also wanted to keep most of the relief efforts under the control of state and local government rather than creating large federal relief agencies. That way the measures taken could be adapted more easily to the specific needs in each local area.

▼ Hoover Dam, constructed from 1931 to 1936, on the border of Arizona and Nevada

## 3 Private Sector Stimulation

Hoover believed that it was the duty of private individuals, not the government, to help the needy. However, when voluntary cooperation did not provide the desired results quickly enough, Hoover initiated several government measures to hasten recovery. With unemployment still rising, Hoover established the President's Emergency Committee for Employment (PECE) in October 1930. This committee tried to encourage the private sector to create new jobs and coordinate the efforts of state and local charities as they provided relief to the poor. About a year later, PECE was replaced by the President's Organization for Unemployment Relief (POUR). It attempted to raise private funds to provide unemployment relief, but the amount raised was far short of what was needed, as unemployment rose to 15.9 percent in 1931.

## 4 Farm Assistance

Hoover also acted to help farmers. The Federal Farm Board, which had been established before the crash, instituted public stabilization corporations chartered by the states rather than by the federal government. These corporations attempted to bolster the prices of farm products by buying surpluses and persuading farmers to cut back production voluntarily. Hoover also asked Congress for a $25 million loan to the Department of Agriculture for the provision of seed and feed to impoverished farmers. Hoover hoped that these efforts would ease the farm problems, but they failed as overproduction continued and funds for stabilizing farm prices were used up. The price for wheat fell from $1.03 per bushel in 1929 to 38¢ in 1931. Other farm prices dropped similarly, throwing farmers deeper into debt and despair.

## 5 International Relations

The increase in the tariff (see Section 1) undoubtedly contributed to an economic collapse in Europe in 1931. Hoover was especially concerned about this international crisis because he believed that America's foreign economic ties contributed to the Depression. He soon declared a moratorium, or suspension, of European debt payments to the United States. He also called for an international economic conference to solve international economic problems. Even so, no action was taken to lower the tariff until 1934.

## 6 Taxation

With the large increase in government spending, Hoover also was determined to keep the federal budget in balance. He declared that "the course of unbalanced budgets is the road to ruin." Most Americans shared Hoover's view that deficit spending (spending more money than is received) would jeopardize confidence in the nation's financial stability and further discourage industrial recovery. To pay for additional government spending, Hoover pressed Congress to pass the Revenue Act in 1932. This law imposed a sales tax on gasoline, tires, cars, electricity, and other items. It taxed stock transfers and phone, telegraph, and radio messages. It raised the personal income tax, the corporate income tax, and the gift tax.

## 7 Business Loans

In 1932 when unemployment in the country reached 23.6 percent, Hoover approved the creation of the **Reconstruction Finance Corporation (RFC)**. The RFC was authorized to lend $2 billion to struggling banks, railroads, agricultural organizations, and other large businesses that were facing bankruptcy. Some criticized the RFC for helping the wealthy—bankers and businessmen—rather than the needy. However, Hoover believed the RFC loans to businesses on the brink of bankruptcy would help those businesses maintain their workforces and create new jobs.

**Unemployment, 1929–40**

Despite Hoover's intentions, the spread of poverty and despair took a toll on the American people, and many urged for more government programs to ease their suffering. By late 1932 the situation was bleak. The nation's measure of productivity, its gross national product (GNP) fell to $41 billion, down from $104 billion in 1929. More than five thousand American banks had failed, eighty-six thousand businesses had closed, and a quarter of a million families had been evicted from their homes. In September of that year, *Fortune* magazine estimated that 28 percent of the population—about 34 million men, women, and children—were without any income whatsoever.

## The Bonus Army

In 1924 Congress had passed legislation providing a bonus to each World War I veteran. The bonuses averaged about $1,000 and would be paid in 1945. In the spring and summer of 1932, a large group of unemployed veterans made their way to Washington, DC, to ask for an early payment of that bonus. These veterans called themselves the **Bonus Army**. The House of Representatives approved partial early payment, but the Senate defeated the measure. Veterans turned to Hoover for help, but he would not meet with them. Most of the fifteen to twenty thousand veterans returned home, and Congress, at Hoover's request, provided money for the protestors' travel. However, about two thousand of the veterans, some with their wives and children, refused to accept defeat. Some lived in hastily built shanties on the edge of the city, while others occupied vacant buildings near the Capitol. As weeks passed, Hoover became more and more frustrated by their embarrassing presence in Washington, DC.

On July 28, government agents informed the Bonus Army that they must move out of the downtown buildings, but they refused. Police with nightsticks in hand were sent to force the illegal occupants from the buildings, but the veterans, reinforced by those from the shanties, met the officers with a volley of bricks. In the clash, some of the policemen began to fire on the veterans, killing two and wounding two others. Hoover learned of the trouble and sent troops under General Douglas MacArthur to quell the disorder and destroy the shantytown. MacArthur, contrary to Hoover's orders, determined to use all necessary force to drive the veterans completely from the capital city. After an hour's warning, the general's forces marched in with tear gas, tanks, and bayonets. Once the downtown buildings were cleared, MacArthur moved on to the main camp, driving out the veterans who remained and burning their shacks.

Although the action had been much harsher than he intended, Hoover took full responsibility for the affair. In doing so, he appeared more heartless than ever to the needs of struggling Americans.

### Comprehension Check 18.2

1. The following statements reflect Hoover's attitudes about poor relief except that ____.

   **A** it was the duty of private individuals to provide for the needy

   **B** government should not provide work relief programs

   **C** state and local governments should control relief efforts

2. The Reconstruction Finance Corporation ____.

   **A** declared a moratorium on European debt payments

   **B** lent $2 billion to banks, railroads, agricultural corporations, and large businesses

   **C** tried to support farmers by buying surpluses

3. Two thousand members of the Bonus Army ____.

   **A** clashed with police and troops by refusing to leave the capital

   **B** defended Hoover from attacks by angry citizens

   **C** received jobs on public works projects

### MAKING CONNECTIONS

4. Why did Hoover oppose the dole? How did this opposition and his treatment of the Bonus Army affect people's perception of him?

▼ Bonus Army March, June 1932

# Roosevelt and the New Deal

What did Franklin Delano Roosevelt do to try to end the Great Depression?

## The Election of 1932

As the 1932 presidential election approached, Republican prospects for reelection were bleak. Hoover had lost his appeal to the impatient public, and voters held his whole party responsible for the continuing Depression. Though Hoover won renomination easily, the Republicans entered the fall campaign with little confidence.

The Democrats, however, did have a popular candidate for the 1932 campaign. **Franklin Delano Roosevelt (FDR)** had long desired the office once held by his Republican cousin Theodore, but that ambition seemed lost in August 1921 when polio paralyzed him from the waist down for life. However, Roosevelt's struggle to overcome his disability added appeal to his public image. In 1928 he won the governorship of New York, despite overwhelming public support for Republicans in that year, and was reelected easily in 1930 as Republicans lost popular support.

In 1932 Roosevelt won the Democratic nomination for president and flew from Albany to Chicago, site of the Democratic Convention, to make his acceptance speech in person. This unprecedented action helped to portray Roosevelt as a daring man who was willing to challenge tradition.

Tradition versus innovation became the central issue of the campaign between Hoover and Roosevelt. Hoover highlighted that theme when he said, "My countrymen! The fundamental issue that will fix the national direction for one hundred years to come is whether we shall go in fidelity to American traditions or whether we shall turn to innovations." Many needy Americans were critical of Hoover's insistence on tradition and were ready to support a candidate willing to try innovations.

Roosevelt brought assurance of action to meet the crisis. Even his campaign song, "Happy Days Are Here Again," renewed hope in a change for the better. With so many Americans dissatisfied with Hoover's response, Roosevelt would easily win unless he foolishly antagonized the public. Therefore, he carefully avoided explaining the details of his economic plans. In his July acceptance speech at the Chicago convention, Roosevelt stated, "I pledge you, I pledge myself, to a new deal for the American people." That promise of a "**New Deal**" (a name that would soon be permanently attached to his efforts to conquer the Depression) was what the people wanted to hear. Roosevelt won more than 57 percent of the popular vote in November and 472 electoral votes to Hoover's 59.

During the months between the November election and the March 4 inauguration of Roosevelt, the defeated president was left to struggle with the continuing problems of the Depression. Hoover was not only somewhat bitter about his fate but also deeply concerned that Roosevelt would take government intervention too far. Nonetheless, Hoover tried to enlist Roosevelt's help in a cooperative effort to deal with the difficulties arising in the early weeks of 1933. For any new effort to gain acceptance, Hoover believed it must have the approval of the popular president-elect. Roosevelt, however, avoided approving any of Hoover's programs for fear that the people would transfer the blame for any failures to himself. Roosevelt wanted to start his job without any ties to the unpopular moves of the outgoing administration.

Despite Hoover's efforts, the banking crisis worsened. The nation's banking system was on the brink of total collapse. By the time Hoover's term ended, 80 percent of the nation's banks were closed. Governors in some states had ordered closures, which they hoped would be only temporary, until the banking crisis could be addressed.

GUIDING QUESTIONS

- Why did Roosevelt (FDR) win the election of 1932?
- What were FDR's first actions to help with the Depression?
- What were the "alphabet agencies" designed to do?

▲ Franklin Delano Roosevelt in a rare photograph showing him in his wheelchair

## The Twentieth Amendment

The **Twentieth Amendment**, which moved presidential inaugurations from March 4 to January 20, was not ratified until early 1933; thus, it did not take effect until the 1936 election.

# Fighting Fear

In his first inaugural address, Roosevelt sought to calm apprehensions caused by the banking crisis by stating: "First of all, let me assert my firm belief that the only thing we have to fear is fear itself." The banking crisis had brought the financial markets of the nation to a virtual standstill. In order to restore confidence in the banking system, on March 6, just two days after taking office, Roosevelt called for a "**bank holiday,**" a temporary closing of all banks to calm the fears of a nervous public. The banks that proved to be basically sound would be allowed to reopen.

Roosevelt also called for a special session of Congress, which convened on March 9 and remained in an emergency session until June 16. Roosevelt said in his inaugural address, "I shall ask the Congress for the one remaining instrument to meet the crisis—broad Executive power to wage a war against the emergency, as great as the power that would be given to me if we were in fact invaded by a foreign foe." In those first one hundred days of Roosevelt's presidency, Congress, with a new Democratic majority after the recent election, passed fifteen major pieces of New Deal legislation.

On the first day of the emergency session, Congress approved the Emergency Banking Act, a measure that endorsed Roosevelt's bank holiday and authorized measures to deal with an impending currency shortage due to the bank closures and people holding on to their money rather than depositing it in banks. To keep the nation informed and inspired, and to ensure that public support remained behind him, Roosevelt used the radio. He began his frequent "**fireside chats**" on March 12. His personal charm and fatherly manner carried over the airwaves and persuaded most Americans that they could trust him to make the government work for their benefit. In his first fireside chat, some sixty million Americans heard him say, "I assure you it is safer to keep your money in a reopened bank than under the mattress." When banks began reopening the following day, deposits far exceeded withdrawals. Over the next few weeks many Americans returned their savings to banks.

## Begging Directly to the President and Mrs. Roosevelt

Thousands of people wrote letters to President Roosevelt, and even more wrote to his wife, Eleanor, telling them of their trials and needs and asking for some help. Some women pleaded with Mrs. Roosevelt to send them clothing for their children or old clothes discarded by the first lady for themselves.

▼ (left) FDR giving a fireside chat in December 1941; (right) First Lady Eleanor Roosevelt

# Alphabet Agencies

New Deal legislation created a vast array of programs and agencies that came to be known by their initials. The nation's conversations were soon filled with talk of the CCC, the AAA, the NRA, the TVA, and other "alphabet agencies." These various agencies fell under three broad categories which corresponded to the goals of the New Deal—recovery, relief, and reform, or the "three Rs" of the New Deal.

◄ President Roosevelt portrayed as Dr. New Deal, trying several remedies for an ailing Uncle Sam, with Congress portrayed as a nurse following the doctor's orders

## Recovery

Recovery focused on helping the nation's farms and industries survive and recover from the Great Depression. The **Agricultural Adjustment Act (AAA)** established a new method of subsidizing farm products and aided debt-ridden farmers who were in danger of losing their farms to foreclosure. To reduce the huge farm surpluses expected in the 1933 harvest, the AAA offered benefit payments to farmers who destroyed crops and livestock rather than bringing them to market. Farmers responded by slaughtering and burying six million piglets and destroying ten million acres of cotton. Many farmers supported the AAA because of the subsidies they received from the government for planting less and producing less. Lower production led to a 50 percent increase in farm income over the next three years. Some criticized the AAA's policies since they led to higher food prices at a time when many were already struggling to pay for food, clothing, and shelter. Also, not all farmers benefited from the AAA. For example, sharecroppers received no benefits since the payments went to the landowners rather than those who worked the land.

▶ Poster from the Agricultural Adjustment Administration, created by the Agricultural Adjustment Act (AAA)

The National Industrial Recovery Act (NIRA) attempted to organize guidelines for industries to increase employment, maintain wages, and reduce unwanted competition. The act established the **National Recovery Administration (NRA)**, which established over five hundred codes or regulations for businesses to follow. These codes assigned businesses a share of the national market of their industry along with annual production quotas, maximum work hours, and minimum wages. The NRA also required businesses to recognize a labor union if its employees chose to form one. Businesses that complied with the codes were allowed to display the blue eagle symbol of the NRA. Some Americans opposed this government attempt at industrial planning. The NRA's fixed prices and codes of fair competition helped NRA-compliant businesses be profitable but eliminated some smaller businesses. The act also led to higher costs for the customer and financially burdened many who struggled to survive during the Depression.

## Relief

Another set of New Deal agencies was focused on providing relief to the millions of needy unemployed. Relief came in the form of federal jobs programs that would provide income for those who worked for one of these agencies. For example, the **Civilian Conservation Corps (CCC)** put young, unmarried men ages 18 to 25 to work in planting trees, building roads, developing parks, and assisting with soil conservation projects under the supervision of the army. It proved to be one of the most popular New Deal agencies, lasting until after American entry into World War II. About three million young men were part of the CCC. It emphasized rigid discipline and team effort. CCC workers wore uniforms and marched like soldiers, carrying not rifles but shovels, rakes, and hoes.

Another provider of work relief was the Public Works Administration (PWA), which built schools, courthouses, hospitals, bridges, and other public facilities all over the country. The PWA also built ships and planes for the nation's military. The Federal Emergency Relief Administration (FERA) gave state and local governments funds to create their own relief programs. Concerned that the unemployed would suffer during the winter of 1933, the Civil Works Administration (CWA) was created to put the jobless to work. The CWA employed four million people, including three hundred thousand women, to build roads, playgrounds, and airports. It also supported teachers, artists, and writers in public enrichment activities. The CWA spent nearly $1 billion in less than five months, and Roosevelt shut the program down in the spring of 1934.

Two other programs were designed to bring relief to rural areas by promoting economic development. The **Tennessee Valley Authority (TVA)** was established in 1933 to bring electricity, flood control, navigation, and development to the Tennessee River Valley, which included Tennessee and portions of Alabama and Kentucky, an area that suffered from extreme poverty during the Depression. The TVA built dams and reservoirs along the Tennessee River and its tributaries and became the nation's first federally owned utility provider. The Rural Electrification Act (REA), passed in 1936, gave federal loans to electric power companies to extend electricity to rural areas.

▶ (top) Blue Eagle symbol of the National Recovery Administration (NRA); (middle) Civilian Conservation Corps (CCC) project in Homedale, Idaho; (bottom) Norris Dam, the first hydroelectric dam of the Tennessee Valley Authority (TVA)

## Reform

The purpose of some New Deal agencies was to reform those parts of the economy that were considered causes of the Depression to prevent another economic crisis from happening in the future. The Banking Act of 1933 separated commercial banks from investment banks and prevented commercial banks from investing their depositors' money in risky investments. It also created the **Federal Deposit Insurance Corporation (FDIC)**, which insured the bank deposits of millions of Americans against loss. Because deposits up to a certain amount were protected, the FDIC greatly increased public confidence in the banking system. The Securities Act of 1933 established the **Securities Exchange Commission (SEC)** to regulate the stock market and prevent fraud in investments. These reforms brought an end to the laissez faire attitude of the previous decade's government toward the economy and ushered in greater government involvement and regulation.

## The Second New Deal

Despite the efforts of the New Deal to ease poverty and put people to work, unemployment remained over 20 percent in 1935. Facing criticism from those who said he was not doing enough to ease suffering (see Section 4), in 1935 Roosevelt launched another series of programs, sometimes referred to as the Second New Deal.

One of those new programs was the **Works Progress Administration (WPA)**. The WPA employed almost anyone in almost any kind of job. More than 8 million jobs had been created by the time it was disbanded in 1943. It built and repaired roads; constructed public buildings and recreational areas; supported actors, directors, writers, and artists in art programs; and manufactured a wide variety of other jobs. Critics considered the WPA "make-work"— unnecessary jobs done with lackluster efforts, remarking that WPA stood for "We Piddle Around."

▼ Artists from the Works Progress Administration (WPA) painting murals for the Arsenal Building in Central Park, New York

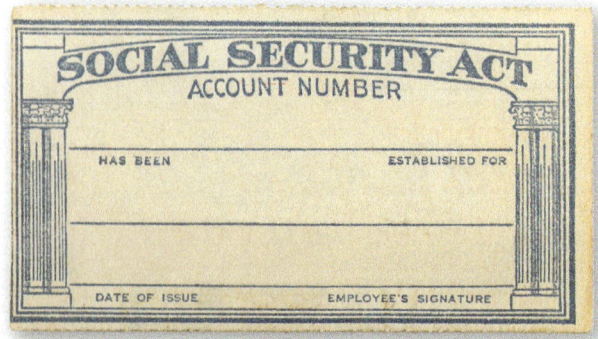

▲ Social Security card

▲ Sit-down strike of United Auto Workers at General Motors in Flint, Michigan

Congress also passed the **Social Security Act (SSA)** in 1935, instituting pensions for retirees and unemployment insurance (temporary payments to those who had lost their jobs). It also gave small payments to people with disabilities, widows, and poor mothers with dependent children. Social Security was paid for through a federal payroll tax paid by both employers and employees.

Another significant piece of legislation in the Second New Deal was the National Labor Relations Act, also known as the **Wagner Act**. This act prohibited unfair labor practices such as employers firing or discriminating against employees who organized or joined a union. It also guaranteed workers the right to collective bargaining (negotiations between an employer and representatives of the workers to establish conditions of employment). The act established the National Labor Relations Board (NLRB) to enforce its provisions.

As a result of the Wagner Act, labor unions gained strength in the late 1930s. John L. Lewis, president of the United Mine Workers and an organizer for the AFL (see Chapter 12), recognized that the recent legislation had provided the opportunity to organize the workers in large industries, so he formed the Congress of Industrial Organizations (CIO) to accommodate both skilled and unskilled workers, unlike the AFL. Breaking from the AFL in 1936, the CIO quickly made the headlines with successful strikes at Firestone and Goodyear rubber plants and at General Motors. One tactic was sit-down strikes, where workers simply sat down on the job, refusing either to work or to leave the factories until their point was made with the management. Some strikes, such as the 1937 Republic Steel strike in Chicago, turned violent. The Supreme Court ruled that sit-down strikes were unlawful in 1939. This decision eliminated the CIO's most effective weapon, but the union remained powerful, eventually reuniting with the AFL to become the AFL-CIO.

## Comprehension Check 18.3

1. Roosevelt's _____ plans for legislation attempted to overcome the Depression.

   A "fireside chat"

   B "Happy Days"

   C "New Deal"

2. All of the following were goals and "Rs" of Roosevelt's agencies except _____.

   A recovery

   B reform

   C relief

   D response

3. The Tennessee Valley Authority (TVA) brought _____ to Tennessee, Alabama, and Kentucky.

   A banks

   B electricity

   C food

4. All of the following were programs that created federal jobs for the unemployed except the _____.

   A Civilian Conservation Corps (CCC)

   B National Recovery Administration (NRA)

   C Public Works Administration (PWA)

   D Works Progress Administration (WPA)

### MAKING CONNECTIONS

5. How did the Agricultural Adjustment Act (AAA) reduce farm production? What were two shortcomings of the AAA?

6. What three measures did the Banking Act of 1933 and Securities Act of 1933 take to help prevent depressions in the future?

# Responses to the New Deal

Roosevelt's extensive New Deal activities sought to meet the nation's demand for change. He had stated during his 1932 campaign that "the country needs and, unless I mistake its temper, the country demands bold, persistent experimentation. It is common sense to take a method and try it: If it fails, admit it frankly and try another. But above all, try something." Because he was boldly taking action, he received widespread praise from many Americans, especially the poor, regardless of whether their lives were improved.

## Roadblocks and Pitfalls

Government relief efforts were slow to reach needy black Americans, and some aspects of the AAA and NRA were actually harmful to the interests of black citizens. At first, Roosevelt was reluctant to press for needed steps for fear of angering southern Democrats. However, Eleanor Roosevelt helped to turn attention to problems of discrimination by openly befriending African American leaders. FDR then began to try to prohibit racial discrimination in some federal programs, beginning in 1935 with the Works Progress Administration. The Public Works Administration also constructed a large share of its public housing projects for black Americans.

### Opposition from the Right

People to the political right of Roosevelt, including most Republicans and a few Democrats, found much in the New Deal to criticize. First was its great expense. The government was using deficit spending to fund the various New Deal programs, sending the nation heavily into debt—something that had initially contributed to the Depression. Also, many of the programs brought increased government involvement and regulation of American businesses, a tendency that looked suspiciously socialistic to some. Finally, the New Deal was not bringing full recovery. American businesses were still in the doldrums, and millions of people were still unemployed.

Roosevelt's opponents rejoiced in 1935 when the Supreme Court, still dominated by conservative Republican appointees, began to reject some New Deal legislation. On May 27, 1935, the Court declared unanimously that the National Industrial Recovery Act (NIRA) was unconstitutional because the Constitution did not allow Congress to delegate its powers to the executive branch, as the NIRA had done when it allowed the National Recovery Administration to set codes for businesses. Early in 1936, the Supreme Court, in a 6–3 decision, struck down the Agricultural Adjustment Act as well.

### Opposition from the Left

Those to the political left of Roosevelt complained that he was not doing enough to alleviate suffering. Three different men gained wide followings by advocating bolder governmental action to combat the Depression. One was Senator **Huey Long**, the powerful and popular former governor of Louisiana. His "Share Our Wealth" scheme proposed that the government heavily tax the rich and redistribute that wealth to the poor, guaranteeing a minimum annual income of $2,500 for every American family. Long seemed to be stealing some support from Roosevelt prior to the 1936 election, but the rise of the Louisiana "Kingfish" ended suddenly with his assassination in September 1935.

## GUIDING QUESTIONS

- Why did some people not like the New Deal?
- What was significant about the election of 1936?
- What were the dangers of court-packing?
- How did the New Deal change Americans' attitude toward government involvement?

▼ Louisiana senator Huey Long, known as the "Kingfish"

Another liberal critic of Roosevelt was Dr. **Francis Townsend**, a retired doctor from California. He proposed that the government pay a pension of $200 a month to each citizen over sixty, provided that they agreed to hold no job and to spend every penny they received. This pension would be financed by a two percent national sales tax. He believed his plan would lead to increased spending and would open jobs for the younger unemployed.

Another challenger who promoted his own brand of government action was Father **Charles Coughlin**, a Roman Catholic priest from Royal Oak, Michigan. Coughlin turned his weekly radio program of sermons into a national political broadcast. At one point, over thirty million people were listening to his radio program. By 1934 the eloquent priest, using populist rhetoric, was telling his huge audience that the nation needed to abandon the "pagan god of gold" and coin large amounts of silver, thereby inflating the money supply. He also began to propose that capitalism be replaced with his own system of "social justice," which included government ownership of banks and other industries.

While none of the programs advocated by these liberal critics were adopted, their appeal to a large number of Americans motivated Roosevelt to introduce some of the Second New Deal programs that called for more active government involvement.

## The Election of 1936

Roosevelt remained widely popular across the country in 1936. The Great Depression showed signs of easing, with unemployment dropping to 16.9 percent. Democrats chose FDR overwhelmingly as their candidate in the 1936 election.

The Republicans nominated Alfred Landon, the governor of Kansas. A Midwesterner, he was free of the image of Wall Street and big business, an image that had plagued the Republican Party since the Depression had begun. Although Landon had a progressive record and supported much of the New Deal, Republicans hoped that he would be "the Kansas Coolidge," bringing a return of business prosperity to the nation. They used the slogan "America is in peril" to criticize the New Deal.

One effect of Roosevelt's policies was the winning of African American voters to the Democratic Party. This group had strongly supported Republicans ever since they had achieved the right to vote—approximately 70 percent voted for Herbert Hoover in 1932. But Hoover's perceived inaction toward their plight, contrasted with Roosevelt's public attempts to alleviate the effects of the Depression, caused many black Americans to support FDR and the Democrats. In 1936 Roosevelt gained more than 70 percent of the black vote, initiating a long-term political trend of black Americans voting for Democrats.

On Election Day, Roosevelt won with over 60 percent of the popular vote. Landon won only two states, Maine and Vermont, garnering only 8 electoral votes to Roosevelt's 523. Republicans also held less than one-quarter of the seats in the Senate and the House of Representatives.

▲ (top) Dr. Francis Townsend presenting his plan of government pensions; (bottom) Father Coughlin at a Cleveland rally

## Court-Packing

Roosevelt believed that his overwhelming election victory had given him a clear mandate to proceed with his New Deal. The decisions of the Supreme Court in 1935 and 1936 declaring various New Deal measures unconstitutional, however, disturbed the president greatly. At first, he thought about pushing for a constitutional amendment to protect New Deal legislation but dismissed the strategy because it could be defeated easily and would take too long. On February 5, 1937, he announced instead a plan to enlarge the Court. For each justice over age seventy (the average retirement age at the time and the mandatory retirement age for judges in some states) who did not retire, he wanted the right to appoint an additional justice up to a maximum of six. Roosevelt argued that the new members would make the Court more efficient.

The president's proposal generated opposition from many directions and for many reasons. Some people attacked the plan because it threatened the American tradition of an independent judicial system and the balance of power among the three branches of government. They believed that Roosevelt wanted to "pack the Court" with justices who supported his New Deal programs. Conservatives also argued that more justices would actually delay Court proceedings rather than making them more efficient. Politicians who before had not dared oppose Roosevelt publicly because of his popularity spoke out against the court-packing plan.

Because of the extensive opposition to the plan, Court reform failed to win approval even in the Democrat-controlled Congress, but Roosevelt won the "war." One of the justices announced his retirement from the Court, giving the president the opportunity to replace him with a more liberal justice. Meanwhile, another justice left the conservative bloc on the Court and voted with a new majority that approved New Deal programs in several decisions. Roosevelt eventually was able to nominate several members of the Supreme Court because of deaths or retirements of justices. By 1940 five of the nine justices were his appointees.

## The Legacy of the New Deal

Despite Roosevelt's impressive victory in the 1936 election, the United States still faced major problems. When FDR took his oath of office again in 1937, he said, "I see one-third of a nation ill-housed, ill-clad, ill-nourished." Conditions worsened later in the year when the nation experienced another sharp decline—a depression within the Depression.

In May 1939, FDR's trusted secretary of the treasury, Henry Morgenthau, lamented, "We have tried spending money. We are spending more than we have ever spent before, and it does not work. . . . We have never made good on our promises. . . . I say after eight years of this Administration we have just as much unemployment as when we started. . . . And an enormous debt to boot!" The national debt had soared from $22 billion in 1933 to $40 billion in 1939, and despite this government spending the unemployment rate at the beginning of 1939 was 19 percent.

▲ Political cartoon for FDR's court-packing plan, with the donkey (Democratic Party) creating a dust storm, opposing the plan

1. The following illustrate the Left's opposition to Roosevelt's policies except for ____.

   A Dr. Francis Townsend's government pension proposal

   B Father Charles Coughlin's "social justice" system

   C Huey Long's "Share Our Wealth" scheme

   D Supreme Court decisions concerning New Deal legislation

2. Each of the following is true about Roosevelt's court-packing plan except that ____.

   A Roosevelt was disturbed that the Supreme Court was declaring New Deal programs unconstitutional

   B Roosevelt claimed more justices would make the Court more efficient

   C the plan passed Congress with Republican and Democratic support

3. In the election of 1936, ____.

   A Landon won the popular vote, but Roosevelt won the majority of electoral votes

   B Roosevelt won the popular and electoral votes

   C Landon won the popular and electoral votes

**MAKING CONNECTIONS**

4. What significant change occurred among black voters in the 1936 election? Why did this happen?

5. What were two reasons critics opposed the New Deal, and what were two reasons supporters championed it?

Had the New Deal succeeded? Critics would argue that the New Deal failed to solve the crisis of the Great Depression and that it left the nation deep in debt. It also increased the power of the government to regulate and intervene in the economy, which critics said threatened the freedom of individuals and businesses. Critics also argued that the New Deal shifted the emphasis from individual responsibility to dependence on the federal government in times of difficulty. Additionally, people primarily turned to the government for care rather than to the traditional institutions, such as the family and the church.

▼ Political cartoon "What We Need Is a New Pump," showing FDR pouring money into the leaking New Deal pump while a burdened taxpayer looks on

Supporters of the New Deal pointed to a number of successes. The gross national product grew in almost every year between 1932 and 1939, and the annual average income rose from $678 in 1933 to $925 in 1939. Government programs brought electricity to rural areas and produced roads, bridges, parks, and countless other facilities that benefited the public. New Deal reforms also put systems in place to limit the effects of future economic downturns and created a social safety net to help the elderly, disabled, and unemployed. Perhaps the greatest achievement of the New Deal was that it restored people's confidence and faith in America and showed that the government cared not just for the business interests but also for ordinary citizens. A number of New Deal agencies and programs, including Social Security, the TVA, the SEC, and the NLRB, still exist today.

The Great Depression was a significant challenge for Americans, but they continued to embrace democracy and freedom. In contrast, in several other countries that faced their own depressions during this time, democratic governments were overthrown and dictators came to power, threatening freedom in those countries and in the United States as well.

# CHAPTER 18 REVIEW

## Chapter Summary

### 18.1 The Great Depression

- Many factors contributed to the Great Depression. After excessive speculation formed a bubble, the stock market crashed in October 1929, resulting in a dramatic fall in prices and losses in investment. A bear market followed for several years. The Federal Reserve's adjustment of interest rates to slow inflation resulted in a collapse of credit. Because of the market crash and runs on the banks, many banks closed. Overproduction in factories led to layoffs and cuts in hours, which reduced worker spending. The Smoot-Hawley Tariff led to retaliation in foreign trade.

- Millions of Americans were faced with poverty and hunger as effects of the Great Depression. Two million Americans lost homes. Some set up Hoovervilles in cities. Several farmers in the Dust Bowl left their farms to find work in California after dust storms destroyed their crops. Many African Americans and Hispanic immigrants moved off farms and tried to find work in the cities. Many Americans turned to entertainment to cope with their struggles. Several crimes and criminals gained national attention, as did the disappearance of pilot Amelia Earhart and the explosion of the *Hindenburg*.

**TERMS**

Herbert Hoover

bear market

Great Depression

Smoot-Hawley Tariff

Hoovervilles

Dust Bowl

Okies

Jesse Owens

Amelia Earhart

**TERMS**

Reconstruction Finance Corporation (RFC)

Bonus Army

### 18.2 Hoover Responds

- Hoover wanted relief to come primarily from individuals and state and local governments rather than federal government. Hoover increased spending for federal public works to create jobs and established the Federal Farm Board to help farmers with crop prices. He tried to encourage maintaining workers and creating jobs through the Reconstruction Finance Corporation. However, conditions continued to worsen, and many desired more government programs to deal with economic challenges.

- When a group of unemployed veterans, known as the Bonus Army, came to Washington, DC, to press for early payments of bonuses, the Senate voted against the measure. After Hoover refused to meet with the veterans, some stayed to protest. After violence broke out between protesters and police, Hoover ordered General MacArthur to control the situation. MacArthur's harsh treatment went beyond Hoover's orders, but Hoover's reputation suffered as a result.

## Chapter Summary

- Because Hoover was unpopular for his handling of the Depression, many supported Roosevelt in the 1932 election. They were encouraged by his promises of action in his New Deal.

- Roosevelt worked to restore confidence in the banks by declaring a "bank holiday" and using fireside chats on the radio to encourage investment. He also called a special session of Congress to approve his New Deal legislation.

- Roosevelt's New Deal legislation created several new programs and "alphabet agencies." To help farming recover, the AAA subsidized farm products and paid farmers to reduce surpluses. To help industry recover, the NRA established codes and regulations to protect businesses and workers. Several agencies, such as the CCC, the PWA, the CWA, and the WPA, provided work relief through federal jobs programs. The TVA and the REA brought electricity to rural areas. Congress passed legislation regulating banking and investment to help prevent future depressions. Social Security was established to provide pensions and unemployment insurance. Workers and labor organizations gained protections in the Wagner Act.

**TERMS**

Franklin Delano Roosevelt (FDR)

New Deal

Twentieth Amendment

bank holiday

fireside chats

Agricultural Adjustment Act (AAA)

National Recovery Administration (NRA)

Civilian Conservation Corps (CCC)

Tennessee Valley Authority (TVA)

Federal Deposit Insurance Corporation (FDIC)

Securities Exchange Commission (SEC)

Works Progress Administration (WPA)

Social Security Act (SSA)

Wagner Act

**TERMS**

Huey Long

Francis Townsend

Charles Coughlin

- Roosevelt's New Deal efforts had shortcomings and faced opposition. Some measures were harmful to black Americans, but their condition was improved by some efforts of Roosevelt and his wife. Conservatives criticized the New Deal for its reliance on deficit spending, increase in government regulation of business, and failure to bring significant recovery. Liberals criticized the New Deal for not going far enough in distributing wealth to needy citizens, and some offered their own solutions to the economic problems.

- Roosevelt remained popular and was reelected in 1936.

- Roosevelt tried to overcome the resistance of Supreme Court justices with a proposal to add justices to the Court. Many opposed his plan, but Roosevelt was able to appoint several justices after some justices died or retired.

- The nation was still suffering the effects of the Depression by the end of the 1930s. Critics believed the New Deal had failed and dangerously increased government regulation and citizens' reliance on the government for aid. Supporters argued that the gross national product and income increased consistently, programs improved rural areas and public works, systems were established to protect the economy from future collapse, and faith in the government was restored.

## Chapter Review Questions

### RECALL

1. What term describes a stock market characterized by pessimism and declining stock prices?

2. What was one of the highest tariffs in American history, passed during Hoover's presidency?

3. What were the groups of shanties for homeless people during the Great Depression called?

4. Who won four gold medals for track in the 1936 Olympics?

5. What group came to Washington, DC, to receive part of the promised payment for their services in World War I?

6. Which amendment changed the date of presidential inaugurations?

7. What was the nickname for Roosevelt's radio programs?

8. What were the "three Rs" of the New Deal?

9. Which New Deal legislation established pensions and unemployment insurance?

### UNDERSTAND

10. What were two factors that contributed to the stock market crash in 1929?

11. What were three causes of the Great Depression other than the stock market crash of 1929? How did each of the four causes contribute to economic decline?

12. What were three negative circumstances that many families faced during the Great Depression? What were two ways they tried to fill those needs?

13. What happened in the Dust Bowl, and how did farmers respond?

14. What two minority groups faced economic hardships in the Depression, and how did many in those groups seek to overcome those struggles?

15. What were three forms of popular entertainment that helped distract Americans from the hardships of the Depression?

16. What were two of the accomplishments and two of the tragedies in flight during the Depression?

17. Why did Hoover want to limit the role of the federal government in providing aid during the Depression? What were two efforts by Hoover that reflected this limited role of the federal government?

18. What did the RFC do, and what was its purpose? Why was it criticized?

19. What was the government response to the veterans who stayed in Washington, DC? How did this response affect Hoover's reputation?

20. What two ideas were contrasted in the presidential campaigns of 1932?

21. What did the "bank holiday" do? Why did Roosevelt call for it? What did he want Americans to do when the bank holiday ended?

22. What did the AAA do for farms and the NRA do for industries? What were the benefits for farmers and businesses? Who did not benefit from these measures, and why did they not?

23. What were three of the New Deal agencies that provided work for the unemployed, and what work projects were involved?

24. What were the measures of the Banking Act of 1933 and the Securities Act of 1933? Why were these measures established?

25. What were two measures of the Wagner Act? What was one effect of the Wagner Act on labor unions?

26. What did the Supreme Court decide concerning some New Deal programs, including the National Industrial Recovery Act and the Agricultural Adjustment Act?

27. Who were the three liberal critics of Roosevelt's New Deal? What did all three believe about the New Deal? What did each propose as an alternative to the New Deal?

28. How did the Roosevelts help black Americans? How did their actions affect black voters in the 1936 election?

29. What was Roosevelt's initial plan to enlarge the court? Did Congress pass his plan? Why was Roosevelt eventually able to nominate several justices for the Supreme Court?

30. What were two reasons some criticized the New Deal? What were two reasons some supported it?

### THINK ABOUT IT

31. Why did many blame Hoover for the Great Depression? Do you think their assessment is fair? Explain.

32. What dangers did critics point out concerning Roosevelt's plan to enlarge the Supreme Court? Do you agree with this criticism? Explain.

33. How would you assess the legacy of the New Deal in terms of the following American values: growth, freedom, and individualism?

# 19 World War II

**19.1 The Coming of War**
**19.2 Isolation and Infamy**
**19.3 The European Theater**
**19.4 The Pacific Theater**

▲ United States Marines raising the American flag atop Mt. Suribachi during the Battle of Iwo Jima

# The Coming of War

**How did World War II start?**

- What led to the rise of dictatorships after World War I?
- What lands did Nazi Germany want to control?

Although politicians attempted to ensure that no international conflict would follow "the war to end all wars," events in Europe shattered America's uneasy peace and isolation. In addition, Japan and the United States increasingly disagreed over trade issues. Tensions in Europe and Asia soon reached a boiling point. The coming global conflict would change the face of the world for the rest of the century.

## Rise of Dictators

In the 1920s and 30s, as Americans experienced prosperity followed by economic depression, storm clouds were building on the world horizons in both Asia and Europe. Militant nationalism grew in Japan, fascism overtook Italy and Germany, and the Communist Party in Russia, which had become the Union of Soviet Socialist Republics (USSR), or the Soviet Union, consolidated its power under a new leader.

## Japan

The Japanese had extended their power throughout Asia and the Pacific since the turn of the century, but their expansionistic goals, fueled by ideas of racial superiority, desire for territory, and need for natural resources, were checked in part by American power in the Pacific (see Chapter 14).

Although **Hirohito** became emperor of Japan in 1926, historians disagree about Hirohito's direct involvement in government and military decisions. Beginning in the 1930s and continuing until the end of World War II, it was military leaders who increasingly gained influence in the Japanese government. General Hideki Tojo, the most important of these, was prime minister from 1941 to 1944.

In 1931 Japan invaded Manchuria, a province of China that had been a "sphere of influence" under first Russia and later Japan. The League of Nations condemned the invasion but took no other action, and Japan withdrew from the League. With the distraction of the Great Depression at home and an ongoing desire to remain isolated from the rest of the world, the United States did little to stop Japanese aggression other than strengthening its defenses in the Philippines. In 1934 Japan canceled the Washington Naval Treaty (see Chapter 17), and US-Japanese relations continued to deteriorate during Roosevelt's first term. Encountering no real opposition, Japan continued to lay plans for greater gain. In 1937 the Japanese launched a full-scale war against China that would not end until 1945. As US trade policies tightened in an effort to halt the Japanese brutalization of China, Japanese leaders developed an animosity toward the United States, their chief rival in the Pacific.

▼ Emperor Hirohito

▲ Benito Mussolini

## Italy

Profiting from the discontent created by economic hardships in Europe, **fascism**, a political and economic system promoting extreme nationalism and emphasizing militarism, was gaining ground. Fascism is characterized by dictatorial, one-party rule, and by totalitarianism, a system of government that regulates every aspect of life. Opposing communism, fascists permitted private property, but they heavily regulated all individual or business activity and resulting profits. Fascists believe that the government and the common good supersede individual interests, demanding ultimate allegiance to the state from all individuals and groups. Leaders justify such control by claiming to provide economic equality for all, but to deliver on that pledge, they use force. When they fail to establish equality, they provide scapegoats on whom to heap the blame—another nationality, ethnic group, or economic class. Such blame shifting tactics, in turn, lead to suppression of and violence against the targeted group. Two forms of fascism developed in Italy and Germany.

The Fascist Party came to power in Italy in 1922 when **Benito Mussolini** was appointed prime minister. Called *Il Duce* (the leader) by his Black Shirt followers, Mussolini crushed opposition by declaring all rival political parties illegal. He gained popular support by building efficient railroads and major highways and providing housing and land for thousands of peasants.

Italy was disappointed that it had not gained all the territory it was promised when joining the Allies in World War I (see Chapter 16). Mussolini assured the masses that he would establish a "Second Roman Empire," restoring Italy to the imperial greatness that existed in the days of Roman caesars.

With this dream, Mussolini set out to acquire foreign territories and markets. In 1935–36 Italy quickly conquered and annexed resource-rich Ethiopia. The League of Nations condemned the invasion and banned the sale of some materials to Italy; however, that did not deter Mussolini. In 1939 Italy invaded Albania.

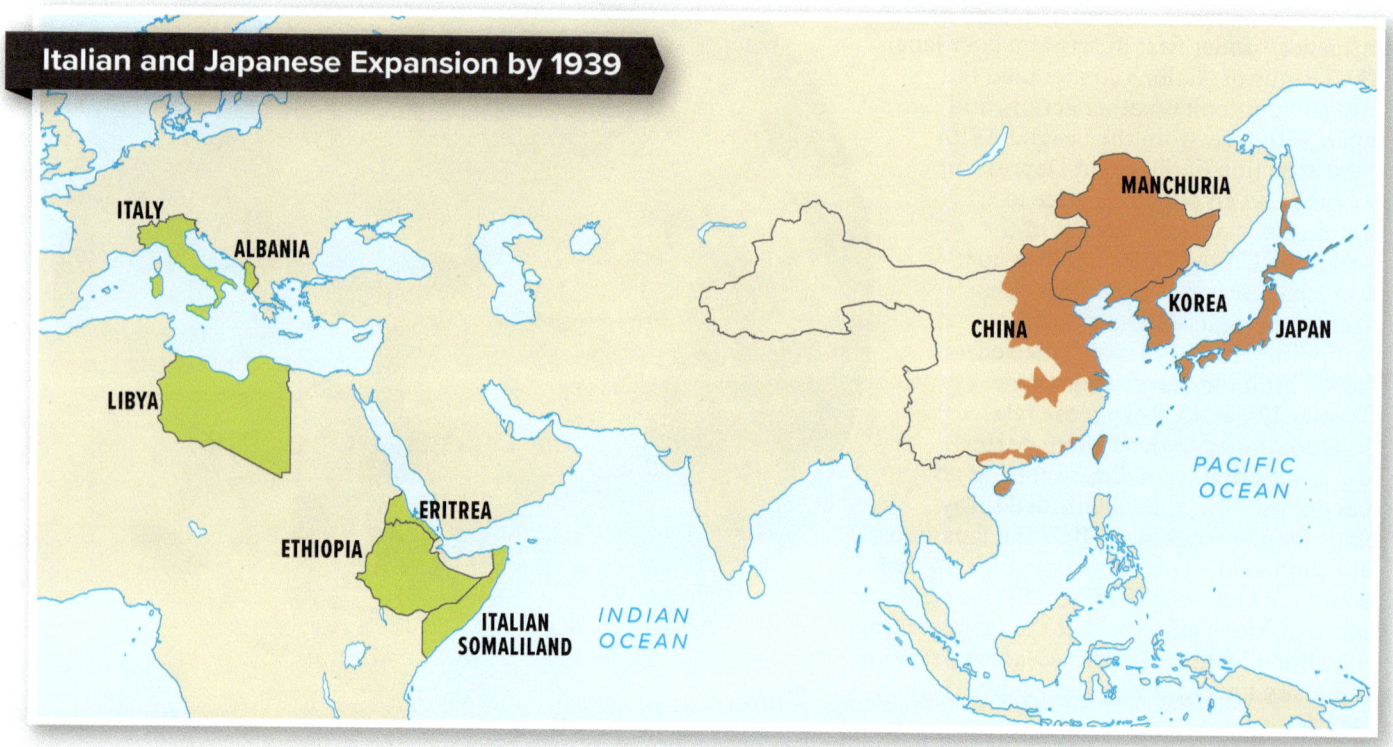

**Italian and Japanese Expansion by 1939**

## Germany

Meanwhile, in 1923 **Adolf Hitler,** a German World War I veteran and radical seeking to avenge Germany's earlier defeat, tried to overthrow the government in Munich. The failed attempt landed him in jail, where he wrote an autobiography, *Mein Kampf* (*My Struggle*), which set forth his ideas for a new Germany. He advocated abandoning the League of Nations, ridding Germany of the "weakening" influence of democracy, uniting all Germans, and eliminating all Communists and Jews. After his release from prison, he preached his doctrines to growing audiences of all classes. Hitler, who had taken leadership of the National Socialist German Workers', or Nazi, Party came to power in Germany in 1933 when he was appointed chancellor, the leading minister of the nation. Hitler withdrew Germany from the League of Nations later that year. Eventually given the powers of a dictator, he used his new authority to eradicate opponents and establish himself as the *Führer*, (leader). He called the Nazi regime the Third Reich (realm or empire) and promised that it would last a thousand years.

The Nazis in Germany, with unquestioning nationalism and totalitarianism, governed much like the Fascist Party in Italy. Hitler's version of fascism emphasized the dominant ethnic group of the "Aryans" (Germans) at the expense of all other ethnic groups, laying the blame for Germany's problems on German Jews, leading to anti-Semitism (anti-Jewish feelings) in government policies and national sentiment. For years, in violation of the Versailles agreement, he secretly rebuilt the German navy, army, and air force and ordered the development of new weapons, providing jobs for workers who had suffered through Germany's economic collapse after World War I. In 1936 Italy initiated the Rome-Berlin Axis, an alliance of the two fascist nations. In 1940 Japan joined Italy and Germany to form the Rome-Berlin-Tokyo Axis. During World War II the three nations were known as the **Axis Powers**.

---

▼ Adolf Hitler at a Nazi party rally

Joseph Stalin

## Soviet Union

The decades of the twenties and thirties were among the most brutal years of the Soviet Union. Communist leader and dictator, **Joseph Stalin,** oversaw systematic terror and bloodshed, eliminating those who disagreed with him, both in and out of the Communist Party. In 1928 he ordered the destruction of all resistance to his agricultural "reforms," or collectivization, in which the government seized all private lands and crops and forced farm workers to labor under government order. Millions who resisted were shot, starved, or worked to death in labor camps. With chilling ruthlessness, Stalin pushed the USSR into the industrial age and fortified his own power. He also trampled any perceived threat or opposition by organized religion. Many Christians and Jews were killed. Most historians estimate that he was responsible for the deaths of ten to twenty million of his own countrymen during those two decades.

# German Aggression

Despite Hitler's violations of the Treaty of Versailles and the growing threat he represented, the rest of Europe allowed Hitler to make numerous territorial gains unopposed. He assured other nations that he was interested only in consolidating German territory and reestablishing German control over areas "stolen" by the World War I victors.

## Rhineland, Austria, Sudetenland

▼ German infantry occupying the Rhineland

In March 1936 German troops moved into the Rhineland, an industrial region of Germany near Alsace-Lorraine. This move was an open violation of the Treaty of Versailles, which stated that the region was to remain demilitarized (free of soldiers and military equipment). The League of Nations protested Hitler's action, but the Nazis were not concerned. In the Rhineland the Germans then began building the Siegfried Line, a series of fortifications along the German bank of the Rhine River from the Swiss border to the North Sea. Hitler claimed that the Siegfried Line was a response to the Maginot Line, a similar French line of fortifications on the west side of the river; however, his actions were another violation of the Versailles Treaty.

Hitler next moved toward Austria. He had long dreamed of Germany's union, or *Anschluss*, with Austria, a German-speaking land and Hitler's birthplace. Despite explicit prohibitions against such unification in the World War I peace treaties, in March 1938 Hitler took control of Austria unopposed.

Czechoslovakia was next on Hitler's agenda. He declared that Germany had a right to annex the Sudetenland, a province in western Czechoslovakia with approximately three million Germans. Czech leaders appealed to the British and French to protect them from such blatant aggression.

In September 1938 Britain's prime minister, Neville Chamberlain, France's premier, Édouard Daladier, and Italy's Benito Mussolini, Hitler's ally by this point, met with Hitler in Munich. Czechoslovakia was not allowed to send a representative to the Munich Conference. Hitler was determined to get the Sudetenland, even if it meant going to war. In a policy of **appeasement** (yielding to an aggressor's demands in order to preserve peace), Chamberlain and Daladier agreed to allow Hitler to take the Sudetenland—but nothing more. Hitler promised, "This is the last territorial claim I have to make in Europe." Believing him, Chamberlain returned to England proclaiming "peace for our time." Six months later, in March 1939, Hitler openly violated his promise and annexed the remainder of Czechoslovakia. International outrage over Hitler's betrayal forced the British and French leaders to wake up to the Nazi threat. Anticipating Hitler's next move, they promised to protect Poland and Romania if those nations were attacked.

◄ Neville Chamberlain holding the paper signed by himself and Hitler after the Munich Conference

## Nazi-Soviet Pact

Hitler knew that to continue his expansion eastward, he would have to deal with the Soviet Union. Stalin, lacking a security agreement with France and Britain and aware of their failure to defend Czechoslovakia, desired to protect the USSR from German advancement. On August 23, 1939, Hitler and Stalin signed a non-aggression pact, an agreement that the USSR and Germany would not attack each other for a period of ten years. The pact was surprising considering that fascism and communism opposed each other. Secretly, the two nations agreed that Stalin could control the Baltic countries (Lithuania, Latvia, Estonia), Finland, and a slice of eastern Poland. In exchange, Hitler would invade Poland from the west.

## Blitzkrieg!

Hitler lost little time taking advantage of the secret agreement. The Munich Conference had emboldened him to ignore British and French threats to intervene. The swift assault, called **blitzkrieg** (lightning war), began on September 1, 1939, when sixteen hundred Luftwaffe (Nazi air force) aircraft bombed military and civilian targets while 1.5 million German soldiers rolled across the Polish border. Forty-eight hours after the initial invasion, the Polish defenders had suffered 100,000 casualties, but continued resisting. On September 17 Soviet troops attacked Poland from the east. By the end of September, the conquest of Poland was complete. The Germans and Soviets would kill six million Polish citizens, half of them Jews, by the end of the war.

On September 3 Britain and France, known as the Allies, or **Allied Powers**, declared war on Germany. However, preparation for war kept fighting minimal for the next eight months. Americans watched with growing concern but maintained neutrality.

Hitler attacked again on April 9, 1940. In another blitzkrieg, the powerful German armored divisions, or panzers—assisted by fighters, bombers, and paratroopers—occupied neutral Denmark in a matter of hours. That same day, Germany attacked neutral Norway to gain naval bases and access to iron-rich Sweden. Norway resisted fiercely for sixty-two days before surrendering.

On May 10 Germany launched a coordinated attack on Belgium, Luxembourg, and the Netherlands—countries on its western border from the northern end of France's Maginot Line to the North Sea. Against the overwhelming German force, resistance was short-lived. Luxembourg fell after only a day, Holland in five days, and Belgium in eighteen days.

By May 14 the Germans had bypassed the Maginot Line and entered France through the Ardennes Forest. The French army, reinforced by the British, was quickly trapped in northern France. The Luftwaffe destroyed French fortifications far ahead of German armored divisions and infantry. German Stuka dive-bombers dominated the air. These new weapons and tactics were a total departure from the trench warfare of World War I. For the French, who relied on the old methods of the last war, blitzkrieg was disastrous.

The German forces drove the Allied troops northward to the French port of Dunkirk on the English Channel and surrounded them. Hitler had ordered his army to stop its advance and allow the Luftwaffe to destroy the enemy. But a dense fog settled over the Channel, preventing the Luftwaffe from bombing. Even though the air force was grounded, the usually efficient Wehrmacht (German army) continued to wait. Using a fleet of 850 fishing boats, yachts, lifeboats, and almost anything else that would float across the English Channel, the Allies rescued about 338,000 of the 400,000 trapped men, leaving behind almost all their weapons and equipment.

◄ (top) German dive bombers; (bottom) British soldiers wading to a ship during the Dunkirk evacuation

▲ German troops on parade in June 1940 after occupying Paris

🔍 **Analyzing Sources**

According to Churchill, what would be the consequence if Hitler were to conquer Britain?

▲ Aftermath of a German bombing raid on London

In June Italy declared war on the Allies and attacked southern France. The German army entered Paris on June 14. In the same railroad car in which the Germans had signed the humiliating armistice terms ending World War I on November 11, 1918, France submitted to Germany's terms of surrender on June 22, 1940.

## The Battle of Britain

Several weeks before the French surrender, Chamberlain had been replaced as prime minister by **Winston Churchill**, who had opposed appeasement of Germany. The new leader, with "nothing to offer but blood, toil, tears, and sweat," inspired the British with his grand defiance and fighting spirit. Britain now faced the Nazi menace alone. Hitler planned to bomb the island extensively, hoping to "soften" it before landing troops. Churchill, anticipating the attack, declared:

> *Hitler knows that he will have to break us on this Island or lose the war. If we can stand up to him, all Europe may be free and the life of the world may move forward into broad, sunlit uplands. But if we fail, then the whole world, including the United States, including all that we have known and cared for, will sink into the abyss of a new Dark Age. . . . Let us therefore brace ourselves to our duties, and so bear ourselves that, if the British Empire and its Commonwealth lasts for a thousand years, men will still say: "This was their finest hour."*

— **WINSTON CHURCHILL,** Excerpt from "This was their finest hour" speech 18 June 1940 reproduced with permission of Curtis Brown, London on behalf of the Estate of Winston S. Churchill © The Estate of Winston S. Churchill.

Throughout the late summer and fall of 1940, the Battle of Britain took place between the Luftwaffe and the British Royal Air Force (RAF) in the skies above southern England and the Channel. Thanks to newly invented radar, the British were able to successfully repel the German attack. Germany lost 1,733 aircraft, while the RAF lost 915 planes. In August 1940 Churchill, referring to the RAF, stated that "never in the field of human conflict was so much owed by so many to so few," When bombing during the daylight hours became too costly, the Luftwaffe changed its tactics and began night bombing with fire bombs. London and several other cities were heavily damaged, and tens of thousands of civilians were killed or injured. Yet during the months of "the blitz," British resolve in the face of the enemy was firm. In late 1940 Hitler indefinitely postponed his intended invasion of Britain.

## Operation Barbarossa

In the wake of the fall of France, continued bombing of Britain, and conquests in the Balkans, Hitler again seized the initiative. Distrusting Stalin and needing oil and other resources, Hitler disregarded the non-aggression pact and launched a massive surprise attack, code-named Operation Barbarossa, on the Soviet Union. On June 22, 1941, three million troops of the Wehrmacht rolled into the USSR, covering five hundred miles of territory within two months on a front that stretched from the Black Sea to the Arctic. The Germans launched attacks at three strategic cities—Leningrad (St. Petersburg) to the north, Moscow in the center, and Kiev, Ukraine, to the south—engulfing the Soviet heartland in some of the fiercest, costliest fighting of the war.

By October 1941 the Soviets had suffered enormous losses, and German supply lines were stretching thin in the vast interior as the Russian winter approached. The Soviets, able to withstand the harsh weather, pushed back and kept Hitler's troops from victory. Now on the side of the Allies, the Soviet Union continued fighting Germany for more than two years.

▲ Russian troops defending their homeland from the German invasion

**Operation Barbarossa**

Legend:
- Axis territory
- USSR territory
- → Operation Barbarossa objective

Leningrad
Baltic Sea
Moscow ⊛
E. PRUSSIA
POLAND
UNION OF SOVIET SOCIALIST REPUBLICS (USSR)
Kiev
Attack on Stalingrad 1942–43
Stalingrad
Black Sea

---

### Comprehension Check 19.1

1. Fascist governments took over the following countries except _____.

   **A** Germany

   **B** Italy

   **C** the USSR

2. Hitler's violations of World War I treaties included all of the following except _____.

   **A** building the Siegfried Line

   **B** moving troops into the Rhineland

   **C** rebuilding the German army, navy, and air force

   **D** union with France

3. The Allies declared war after Germany's invasion of _____.

   **A** Ethiopia

   **B** Manchuria

   **C** Poland

4. The Allies successfully repelled the Germans _____.

   **A** by sea, using the Maginot Line

   **B** in the air, during the Battle of Britain

   **C** on land, defending Paris

### MAKING CONNECTIONS

5. What was the international response to the territorial expansions of Japan, Italy, and Germany?

6. What were the agreements in the Nazi-Soviet Pact, and what event ended this pact?

- Why was it difficult for the United States to remain neutral at the beginning of World War II?

- What caused America to enter World War II?

- How did America prepare for war?

▲ Charles Lindbergh speaking at an America First Committee meeting

## 19.2 Isolation and Infamy

### Why did America eventually enter World War II?

While war was devastating much of Europe, America sat safe across the ocean. Leaders in Washington were more concerned with economic recovery from the Great Depression than with events in Europe and Asia, and most Americans wanted to avoid involvement in another European war.

Despite a policy of isolationism, the sympathies of most Americans were with the Allies and the nations victimized by the Nazi war machine. But although Americans felt strong cultural ties to Britain, they hoped that the Allies would crush the German aggressors without direct US military support.

## The Struggle to Remain Neutral

Hoping to avoid similar issues that had brought America into World War I, Congress passed the Neutrality Act of 1937 which forbade US citizens from traveling on the ships of belligerent nations (nations at war) and forbade the sale of arms and war materials to those nations. It also prevented the arming of American merchant ships and prohibited those ships from transporting arms, even those produced outside the United States, to nations at war. These nations could purchase all other items from the United States on a cash basis and transport them on non-American ships. This "**cash and carry**" policy was set to expire in two years.

After Congress had rejected the renewal of the cash and carry provision in March 1939 and the Germans and Soviets had invaded Poland in September, President Roosevelt called Congress into special session. After intense debate, Congress passed the Neutrality Act of 1939, which extended cash and carry but now allowed for it to include the sale of arms to belligerent nations.

Some American isolationists who were outraged at this law organized the America First Committee in 1940. Charles Lindbergh and Henry Ford were prominent members. The committee argued that no foreign power could successfully attack the United States, that a Nazi defeat of Britain would not endanger American national security, and that arms sales would lead to America's entrance into the war.

Despite the isolationist views of many Americans, there was an increasing sense of the need for preparedness. In September 1940 Congress instituted a peacetime draft—the first in American history—which required men ages twenty-one to thirty-five to register. Of these, some 375,000 men were drafted and sent to training in preparation for a possible attack on the United States.

Also, in September Roosevelt agreed to a "destroyers for bases" deal with Britain. The United States sent Britain fifty outdated destroyers. In return, the British gave the United States ninety-nine-year leases for the establishment of air and naval bases on British possessions in the Caribbean, Bermuda, and Newfoundland.

During the election of 1940, Roosevelt, running for an unprecedented third term, promised, "I have said this before, but I shall say it again and again and again: Your boys are not going to be sent into any foreign wars." FDR defeated Republican opponent Wendell Willkie, a former Democrat who had never held political office, by a wide margin.

◄ FDR campaign button used in the 1940 election

When Roosevelt addressed Congress in January 1941, he stressed that the democratic way of life was being threatened around the world, that the United States should increase its armament production so that it could become the "arsenal of democracy," and that America looked forward to a day when the "four freedoms"—freedom of speech and of worship, and freedom from want and from fear—could be enjoyed around the world.

FDR, fearful that Britain was in danger of falling to Germany, asked for and received from Congress all-out aid to the Allies in early 1941. "They do not need manpower," the president stated. "They do need billions of dollars' worth of the weapons of defense." On March 11, 1941, he signed the **Lend-Lease Act**, which empowered the president to lend or lease, rather than sell, food and armaments to Britain and other allies. Eventually, the United States distributed nearly $50 billion worth of military supplies to thirty-eight Allied countries, with most going to Britain and the USSR.

The United States also sent China one hundred fighter planes. Claire Chennault, a retired Army Air Force captain, served as an advisor to the Chinese air force. He helped organize a group of pilots known as the American Volunteer Group (AVG), or the "Flying Tigers." Although always outnumbered, the Flying Tigers became a formidable force, downing almost three hundred

Japanese planes in the seven months the group existed. In mid-1942, the AVG became part of the US military.

The alliance between the United States and Britain was strengthened in August 1941 when Churchill and Roosevelt secretly met in Newfoundland. There the two leaders devised the Atlantic Charter, a list of common principles or goals of the anti-Axis nations, such as self-determination, freedom of the seas, and economic cooperation. It sought to provide "a better future for the world" and expressed America's moral commitment to the Allied cause. By late September, more than a dozen additional nations signed the charter.

Escalating tensions in the Atlantic brought America to the verge of war. In May 1941, a German submarine attacked and sank an American merchant vessel in the waters off Brazil. In September another German submarine fired on the US destroyer *Greer,* after which Roosevelt ordered the fleet to "shoot on sight" German or Italian attack vessels. In October the destroyer *Reuben James* was sunk west of Iceland, with the loss of more than a hundred Americans. Yet in the waning days of 1941 war came not in the Atlantic, surprisingly, but in the Pacific.

▼ Flying Tigers fighting with the Chinese against Japan

# Pearl Harbor

Japan's expansionist policies placed increasing strain on US-Japanese relations. In the summer of 1941 Japan seized the strategic oil fields and rubber plantations of French Indochina in Southeast Asia (present-day Vietnam, Laos, and Cambodia). Roosevelt responded by placing an oil embargo on the Japanese and freezing Japanese assets. He named General Douglas MacArthur commander of all American forces in the Far East.

Japan, though, had bigger plans than simply taking French Indochina. With England being pounded by Hitler and the Netherlands under Nazi occupation, the Japanese eyed the resource-rich British and Dutch colonies of the Pacific. The chief obstacle to their plans was the US Navy's Pacific fleet, which was stationed at **Pearl Harbor**, Hawaii.

Shortly before 8:00 a.m. on Sunday, December 7, 1941, Japanese warplanes swept across the blue Hawaiian sky over Pearl Harbor. Commander Mitsuo Fuchida signaled, "Tora! Tora! Tora!" ("Tiger! Tiger! Tiger!") to indicate that the Americans had been caught by surprise. A second wave of Japanese aircraft attacked an hour later. The Japanese destroyed more than three hundred US planes and sank or damaged eight battleships and thirteen other warships. The two-hour attack killed 2,403 Americans and wounded about 1,200. On the same day as Pearl Harbor, Japanese forces also attacked bases in Malaya, Hong Kong, Guam, the Philippines, Wake Island, and Midway Island.

Despite the heavy American losses, Pearl Harbor was not a complete success for the Japanese. First, they had missed the vital American aircraft carriers, which were at sea at the time of the attack. Second, by not sending a third wave of planes to attack, Japan failed to completely destroy the American naval base. The Americans would rebuild with the facilities that remained. Third, with one blow, the Japanese had done what Hitler's accumulated aggressions had not—united the American nation to enter the war.

Declaring that December 7, 1941, was a date that would "live in infamy," Roosevelt addressed a joint session of Congress on December 8, and Congress declared war on Japan, as did Britain that same day. On December 11, Germany and Italy declared war on the United States, which responded by declaring war on them. Pearl Harbor had triggered war on a global scale.

▼ The USS *Arizona* Memorial at Pearl Harbor

▼ The USS *Arizona* sinking after being attacked at Pearl Harbor

# Mobilizing the Nation

The entire nation mobilized for war, and families sacrificed ordinary comforts for the cause of victory. Millions of Americans joined the military, while those at home contributed by working in factories, reducing consumption of items like food and gasoline, and volunteering in service organizations.

## Men and Women

Over 60,000 volunteers enlisted in the first month after the attack on Pearl Harbor. Eventually about 16 million Americans, more than ten percent of the population, joined the armed forces.

More than 2.5 million African Americans registered for the draft. Although they served in every military branch, about 909,000 black Americans served in the US Army. No matter in which branch they served, they were segregated from white soldiers, usually with a white officer in command. Brigadier General Benjamin Davis was the first black general in the US Army. His son Lieutenant Colonel Benjamin Davis, Jr., commanded the all-black **Tuskegee Airmen** of the US Army Air Corps. This unit trained 1,000 pilots and 14,000 navigators, bombardiers, aircraft mechanics, and other flight personnel at airfields near Tuskegee Institute in Alabama. The Tuskegee Airmen made over 15,000 combat flights over North Africa and Europe. Their 332nd fighter squadron, known as the "Red Tails" for the red-painted tails of their P-51 Mustangs, escorted bombers on missions deep over enemy territory. They earned numerous awards and commendations for their service during the war.

Native Americans also contributed significantly to the war effort. About 540 Navajos served in the US Marines, about 400 of them as "**Navajo code talkers**," who by creating code in their native language frustrated Japanese code breakers throughout the entire war. Japanese intelligence forces were never able to "decode" the language. Other Native Americans served in the US Army, most of them Cherokees, Choctaws, and Comanches. Several Native Americans received the Medal of Honor for their bravery in the war.

▲ Families put blue star flags in their windows to represent family members fighting in the war. Blue stars were replaced with gold stars if the family member was killed in the war.

▲ (Left) Tuskegee Airmen; (right) Navajo code talkers

▲ (top) Female pilots from the WASPs delivering bombers to their bases; (above) Rosie the Riveter poster

Although the overwhelming majority of those in the military were men, about 68,000 women served as nurses in the army or navy, and about 268,000 women joined the various women's auxiliary units of the service branches. The largest such unit was the Women's Army Corps (WAC), which enlisted 150,000 women. The Navy enlisted 86,000 women in its WAVES (Women Accepted for Volunteer Emergency Service) program. The 2,000 WASPs (Women Air Service Pilots) flew new warplanes to their frontline bases for the Army Air Corps. Other women volunteered with the Red Cross or the United Service Organizations (USO), which provided entertainment and encouragment to the troops.

The war increased the demand for industrial production and workers while most able-bodied men left for military service. Consequently, women filled many of those jobs. The number of employed women jumped from 25 percent in 1941 to 36 percent by 1944. In addition, female workers filled many traditionally male-oriented jobs, particularly in the defense industry. Working on the assembly line and in the shipyard, women played a vital role in the war on the home front. Posters featuring "Rosie the Riveter" were used to recruit women for industrial work.

Unemployment resulting from the Great Depression had been over 14 percent in 1940, but it dropped to 4.7 percent in 1942 and 1.2 percent in 1944. For a time it looked as if black Americans would not benefit from the improved job market, as many industries proclaimed that they would not hire black workers. However, when African-American labor leader A. Philip Randolph pressured Roosevelt to take action to promote equality, the president signed an executive order prohibiting employers who had contracts with the federal government from excluding workers because of their ethnicity.

## Japanese Americans

After the attack on Pearl Harbor, American military leaders worried that Japan was preparing an invasion of the West Coast. Some Americans suspected that Japanese Americans were spies or that they would be disloyal to the United States. Responding to that wartime hysteria, President Roosevelt on February 19, 1942, issued an executive order authorizing the War Department to declare any part of the country a military zone and to remove anyone from that zone if necessary. Most of California, Oregon, and Washington were declared military zones, and 120,000 Japanese Americans, most of whom were "Nisei" (American-born Japanese) with US citizenship, were forced from their homes and placed in internment camps farther inland, where they lived for most of the war. None was ever charged with or convicted of treason or espionage. In the 1944 case *Korematsu v. United States*, the Supreme Court upheld that the internment was justified. The Supreme Court many years later denounced the ruling as a bad decision, and in 1988 Congress authorized reparations payments to those who were wrongfully held in these camps.

Beginning in 1943, Japanese Americans were allowed to leave internment to enlist for military service, and over 30,000 Nisei demonstrated their patriotism, despite the violation of their civil liberties, by serving in combat units in Europe. The first all-Nisei unit formed was the 100th Infantry Battalion, which became known as the "Purple Heart Battalion" because about 4,000 of its men were wounded in combat. The most famous unit was the 442nd Regimental Combat Team, which became the most decorated combat unit in the war.

◄ Japanese Americans in an internment camp

▲ B-24 bombers being produced at Ford's Willow Run factory

## The Home Front

The War Powers Act of 1941 authorized the president to get the nation's economy ready for war. The **War Production Board** (WPB), which began operation in January 1942, immediately halted nearly all domestic building construction to conserve materials for war production. Production of many consumer goods was discontinued through much of the war because the WPB ordered factories to convert from civilian to military production. For example, civilian automobiles were not produced from February 1942 to July 1945. Instead, the government ordered Ford Motor Company to build B-24 bombers, General Motors to produce tanks, and its Cadillac division to build P-51 fighter planes and engines for tanks. Clothing manufacturers made uniforms, blankets, and parachutes. Even small manufacturers, such as the Hoover vacuum company, switched to producing helmets and bomb fuses.

Conserving vital goods such as foodstuffs, rubber, and gasoline for the war effort required a system of nationwide rationing. In addition to rationing gasoline, the government issued every man and woman ration books containing stamps needed to purchase various goods such as meat, sugar, coffee, and shortening. Even shoes and nylon stockings (since nylon was needed for parachutes) were limited. A new generation of "victory gardens" also sprang up in backyards across America to offset the shortages created by the war. By 1943 those gardens produced one-third of the nation's vegetables.

Besides rationing, recycling was an important part of the national war effort. Boy Scouts went through their neighborhoods collecting cooking grease and discarded metal and rubber goods. Farm boys scoured the fields for old plow tips and even junk cars, doing their part to help "scrap" the Axis.

Paying for the war posed an enormous challenge. America's war bill totaled about $350 billion, a figure that Roosevelt believed should be paid with increased taxes rather than allowing the nation to lapse into debt. With elections looming in 1942, Congress was less enthusiastic about raising taxes and supported only half the tax increase that FDR recommended. Altogether, taxes covered only about 45 percent of the war's cost, and thus the national debt increased sixfold. The government also sold war bonds, as it had in World War I. Individuals, banks, and other businesses bought a total of $185 billion in bonds to help fund the war.

Don't Let That Shadow Touch Them
*Buy* WAR BONDS

▲ A US war bonds poster

### Did You Know?

Famous actors such as Jimmy Stewart and Clark Gable paused their careers to serve in the military. Others, such as singer Bing Crosby and comedian Bob Hope, entertained troops stationed overseas, both on the radio and at USO shows near the front lines.

1. During neutrality the United States helped the Allies in the following measures except the ____.

   A  America First Committee

   B  "cash and carry" policy

   C  Lend-Lease Act

2. Congress declared war the day after the ____.

   A  introduction of a peacetime draft

   B  German submarine attacks on US ships

   C  Japanese attack on Pearl Harbor

   D  signing of the Atlantic Charter

3. The War Production Board ____.

   A  converted factories from civilian to military production

   B  introduced the highest taxes in American history

   C  organized propaganda for the war effort

**MAKING CONNECTIONS**

4. What were the three reasons why the Japanese attack on Pearl Harbor was not completely successful?

5. How were the civil liberties of Japanese Americans violated during the war years?

- How was World War II fought in North Africa and Italy?

- How was victory in Europe achieved?

- How did the Holocaust reflect Hitler's worldview?

In 1942 Roosevelt created the **Office of War Information** (OWI) to inform Americans about the war and to create propaganda to rally support for the war effort. The OWI created posters to encourage enlistment, the purchase of war bonds, and rationing. Radio programs, comic strips, and Disney cartoons carried messages meant to shape the mood of the public toward the Allied cause. Hollywood director Frank Capra created a film series for the army, *Why We Fight*, to illustrate the danger of fascism.

▼ An American propaganda poster

## 19.3  The European Theater

How did the war in Europe progress?

Hitler's occupation of Europe was seemingly invincible. Yet by 1942 faint cracks in his empire could be detected. Deep within Russia, German forces were locked in bitter cold and bitter fighting. German casualties had mounted to a million since the invasion was launched.

Allied leaders held a series of meetings to discuss war strategy. They agreed to prioritize defeating Nazi Germany before focusing on Japan. The United States decided to help first by invading North Africa to support the Allies facing Axis forces there.

In a conference in Casablanca, Morocco, Roosevelt and Churchill met with French general Charles de Gaulle to develop a strategy for the assault on Hitler's Europe. Stalin, who was not present, had been urging for a second front in France to relieve German pressure on the Soviet front. Both Roosevelt and Churchill refused to commit themselves to such an invasion, citing a lack of troops and preparedness for such a grand assault. The leaders did agree, however, to open a front in Italy, which Churchill described as Europe's "soft underbelly." A successful invasion there would not only thrust into the heart of Europe but also reopen Mediterranean sea lanes.

# North Africa and Italy

Mussolini, seeking to expand his African empire, had invaded Egypt, but the British, who controlled Egypt and the Suez Canal, sent troops to halt the Italian advance. By February 1941 the British had defeated the Italian army in Libya and taken 130,000 prisoners. But the triumph was short-lived: the British had exhausted their resources, and German panzers led by the famed General Erwin Rommel arrived by the end of February. Nicknamed "the Desert Fox" for his superb military strategy, Rommel took command of the Axis forces in North Africa and moved his Afrika Korps (an elite armored division) eastward toward the Suez Canal. After a string of stinging British defeats at the hands of Rommel, Churchill ordered Field Marshal Bernard "Monty" Montgomery to take command. By early November 1942, Montgomery's forces had pushed the Axis forces westward.

On November 8, 1942, Operation Torch, commanded by US General **Dwight D. Eisenhower** used 850 ships to land troops on the west coast of Africa at Casablanca, Oran, and Algiers. In a three-day advance, the American tanks raced eastward toward Tunisia. With Montgomery coming west, the German and Italian tank corps were caught in the middle. After suffering repeated defeats and numerous shortages, the last German outpost at Tunis fell on May 13, 1943.

▶ British general Bernard Montgomery in North Africa

**World War II, 1942–44**

Legend:
- Axis occupied (end of 1944)
- Allied liberated territory (end of 1944)
- Allies
- Neutral
- → Allied advance

The invasion of Italy began in July 1943 with an attack on Sicily, the island just off the Italian coast. In Operation Husky, 3,000 ships and landing craft carried troops and equipment to the island. Shortly after the invasion, the Italian government removed Mussolini from power. Although the Allies suffered heavy casualties, the Italian and German armies withdrew to the mainland by August, leaving Sicily as an Allied base. From there, Montgomery's Eighth Army landed at Calabria, the "toe" of the Italian "boot," on September 3. A few days later Italy surrendered. The following day, the 5th Army landed at Salerno. The Germans, refusing to recognize the Italian surrender, fought furiously to stop the Allied advance northward. However, the Allies finally marched into Rome on June 4, 1944. Despite this successful capture, the Italian campaign was far from over. Northern Italy was the scene of intense, deadly fighting. Not until the closing days of the war did the Germans surrender Italy.

# From France to Germany

In November 1943 Stalin, Roosevelt, and Churchill met in Tehran, Iran. Stalin again urged the other two to invade northern Europe to take pressure off the Soviet front. In exchange for the promised invasion, to be carried out mid-1944, Stalin promised to assist in fighting the Japanese once Hitler was defeated.

In January 1944 General Eisenhower was appointed Supreme Allied Commander and tasked with his greatest challenge ever—coordinating a cross-channel, amphibious (sea and land) assault on occupied France. Three million Allied soldiers, sailors, and airmen—half of them Americans—were readied in southern England for the grand invasion while Allied bombers targeted German aircraft and transportation lines.

After the loss of North Africa, Hitler had assigned Rommel to defend France from the expected Allied invasion. On June 4, 1944, after looking at the threatening skies and impressive coastal defenses on the French side of the English Channel, Rommel thought no Allied invasion was possible in the next few days. He traveled to Germany to celebrate his wife's fiftieth birthday, which was on June 6.

▼ American troops landing on the beaches of Normandy during the D-Day invasion

## *D-Day*

Code-named Operation Overlord, the invasion of Normandy began early on the morning of "**D-Day**," June 6, 1944. Over 20,000 paratroopers and soldiers in gliders landed behind German lines in the darkness. They cut vital transportation and communication lines and captured key bridges and roads for miles around the invasion site. On the shore, the Germans had assembled miles of fortifications with barbed wire, machine guns, and heavy artillery in front of the steep cliffs. Allied battleships, cruisers, and destroyers hurled tons of high explosives onto the German defenses.

The invaders encountered mines and pilings along the beaches and under the water level. Despite the bad weather and deadly opposition, the Allied Expeditionary Force (AEF), composed of more than 150,000 troops in landing crafts, established a beachhead along a sixty-mile stretch of the coast. Racing through the surf under intense enemy fire, Americans landed on beaches code-named Utah and Omaha while British and Canadian troops landed on beaches code-named Gold, Sword, and Juno.

The D-Day operation was costly in lives, but the Germans could not stop the surprise invasion. The Allies controlled the skies and bombed roads, bridges, and supply depots to prevent German reinforcements from reaching the front. This invasion, the largest in history, was a crucial success.

## Paratroopers *in* Normandy

To distinguish between friend and foe in the darkness, paratroopers used clicking toy "crickets" as a signaling device. When anyone approached, a soldier clicked his cricket and knew it was a friend if the person responded with a similar click. American General Maxwell Taylor, commander of the 101st Airborne Division, later recalled in his memoir *Swords and Plowshares* his own experience in the invasion:

> At the last moment, a gust of air caused me to drift away from my comrades. . . . And only by a mighty tug on the shroud lines did I manage to escape becoming entangled in the top of a tall tree. Then I came down with a bang in a small Norman field. . . .

> . . . [I] used my parachute knife to cut my way out [of my parachute]. . . . I started out, pistol in one hand and identification cricket in the other, to find my troops. . . .
>
> . . . I heard someone just around the corner of the hedge and veered toward the sound ready to shoot. But then there was the welcome sound of a cricket to which I quickly responded in kind and jumped around the corner. There in the dim moonlight was the first American soldier to greet me. . . . We embraced in silence and took off together to round up others of our comrades who were beginning to appear.

▼ American paratroopers on D-Day

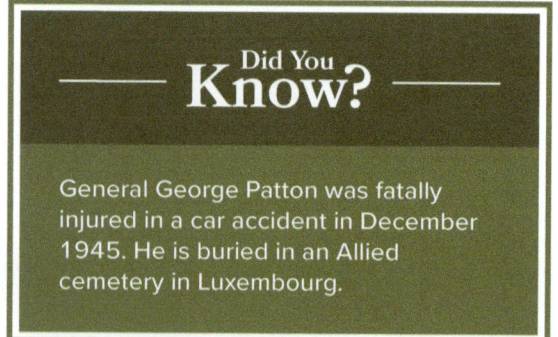

After intense fighting inland and throughout the countryside, the Allies pushed toward Paris. Beginning on August 1, the determined American General George Patton, who had served in World War I and distinguished himself in North Africa and Sicily, led the rapid advance. Allied soldiers liberated Paris on August 25. An additional invading army landed in southern France, opened new ports and supply bases, and pushed quickly up the Rhône Valley to join the forces in northern France. By the end of 1944, territory in France, Belgium, Luxembourg, and the Netherlands had been freed of German armies. The Allied force was at Germany's border, ready to break the famous Siegfried Line and move on to Berlin.

## Battle of the Bulge

At 5:00 a.m. on December 16, 1944, Hitler unleashed a stunning counteroffensive out of Belgium's Ardennes Forest against the weakest point in the Allied line, surprising the troops. The thrust created a "bulge" fifty miles deep into the Allied lines, dividing the forces and giving the battle its name. By Christmas Day, the Germans had captured thousands of troops and had surrounded American forces in the city of Bastogne. When the German commander ordered General Anthony McAuliffe to surrender, the defiant American refused.

Eisenhower ordered Montgomery to attack from the northern portion of the bulge while he sent Patton against the southern part to free Bastogne. Together, they squeezed the bulge back. The **Battle of the Bulge** cost Hitler one hundred thousand casualties, nearly one thousand aircraft, and eight hundred tanks. By the end of January 1945, American troops, who had borne the brunt of the attack and suffered heavy losses, were ready to cross the Rhine River for the final push into the German heartland.

---

**Battle of the Bulge**

December 24, 1944

Axis-controlled territory
Allied-controlled territory
German attack
Allied resistance

North Sea
Amsterdam
NETHERLANDS
BELGIUM
Brussels
FRANCE
Bastogne
LUXEMBOURG
Paris

▼ US troops fighting in the snow during the Battle of the Bulge

## V-E Day

In February 1945 the Big Three—Roosevelt, Churchill, and Stalin—met at the Soviet Union's Black Sea resort of Yalta. With German power crumbling, the Big Three laid plans for postwar Europe. They agreed to support democratically elected governments in all the liberated nations. The conference participants also decided to divide Germany into four zones to be administered by the Soviet Union, the United States, Britain, and France. Within the Soviet zone, Germany's capital city, Berlin, would also be divided into four zones among the four nations.

Roosevelt, who had won a fourth term the previous November, came to Yalta enjoying the wide support of the American people. He believed that if the United States corrected what he saw as the mistake of not joining the League of Nations then the postwar world would be secure. As a result, formation of an international organization for peace, known as the United Nations, was a major part of his Yalta agenda. With Americans bogged down in costly fights in the South Pacific, Roosevelt also wanted Soviet help against the Japanese. Stalin promised to join the fight within three months of Germany's defeat, but he wanted territory controlled by Japan in return. Roosevelt agreed. On April 12, just eight weeks after Yalta, Roosevelt died of a cerebral hemorrhage. After fewer than three months as vice president for Roosevelt's fourth term, **Harry Truman** was the new commander in chief.

▲ Churchill, Roosevelt, and Stalin meeting at the Yalta Conference

▲ Roosevelt's funeral procession

▲ Harry Truman

By April 1945 British and US bombers had targeted key German cities such as Dresden, in which approximately 25,000 civilians died, and the capital, Berlin. Allied forces in the west under Eisenhower had pushed as far as the Elbe River in central Germany, while the Soviets advanced to Berlin from the east. As Allied forces freed Europe from Nazi control, they came across unexpected horrors. In Nazi prison camps they found evidence of the mass murder of millions of people, known as the **Holocaust**.

# The Holocaust

Nazis believed in "Aryan" superiority. Hitler used his ruthless Gestapo (secret police) and SS (*Schutzstaffel*, special security) forces to control, isolate, and exterminate those considered "undesirables" in Germany and in the countries the Nazis conquered. "Undesirables" included political opponents, Jews, prisoners of war, Poles, Roma, the disabled, and others, but Hitler directed special attention against Jews.

In March 1933, less than two months after Hitler was appointed chancellor, the first concentration camp was opened in Dachau, Germany. The *Reichstag* (German parliament) then began passing laws against Jews, which included forcing Jewish government workers to retire, excluding Jews from the army, defining "Jew" as anyone with two Jewish grandparents, revoking citizenship rights for Jews, and requiring Jews to wear yellow stars of David as identification badges.

▶ A Jewish couple in the Warsaw ghetto

▲ Jews being rounded up by German soldiers after an uprising in the Warsaw ghetto

The Nazis encouraged Germans to boycott all Jewish businesses. On November 9, 1938, the Nazis vandalized thousands of Jewish businesses, burned scores of synagogues, and robbed, shamed, and arrested thousands of Jews all across Germany in the *Kristallnacht*, "the night of broken glass."

Next, Hitler ordered that all Jews be segregated into areas called ghettos. There they lived in crowded, unsanitary conditions, often with several families in one apartment. They had little food or fuel for warmth. The Warsaw ghetto in Poland was the most infamous.

In May 1940, the Nazis opened a concentration camp at Auschwitz, Poland, and began to transport thousands of Polish Jews there by train in filthy, unheated, and overcrowded cattle cars. Hundreds died en route. As the war progressed, Hitler ordered the implementation of the "Final Solution"—the mass extermination of all Jews.

▼ Train tracks leading to the Auschwitz concentration camp

Execution in gas chambers was commonly used to carry out the Nazi plan. The guards expelled the gas with ventilators; other prisoners removed the bodies, placing them in ovens for cremation.

Concentration and extermination camps existed all across Nazi-controlled areas, including Mauthausen and Gusen in Austria, Belzec and Treblinka in Poland, and Bergen-Belsen and Buchenwald in Germany. One American soldier related that as US troops neared Dachau, they "could smell the camp from at least five miles away."

▶ (right) Starving prisoners at the Ebensee, Austria concentration camp; (below) the crematory of the Majdanek concentration camp

An estimated six million Jews alone were killed in Hitler's program of state-supported mass murder. Combining this number with the number of non-Jews, an estimated 11 to 17 million people died at the hands of the Nazis.

◀ Prisoner identification photos. In addition to the Star of David patch to identify Jews, various colored triangle patches were used to identify criminals, political prisoners, homosexuals, Jehovah's Witnesses, and other groups.

1. The Allies determined to invade ____ first as Europe's "soft underbelly".

   A  Belgium

   B  Holland

   C  Italy

2. As Supreme Allied Commander, ____ organized the D-Day invasion.

   A  Anthony McAuliffe

   B  Dwight D. Eisenhower

   C  Erwin Rommel

3. In the Battle of the Bulge, ____.

   A  the Allies invaded Normandy

   B  the Germans counterattacked the Allies

   C  the Soviets took Berlin

**MAKING CONNECTIONS**

4. What were two of the proposals at the Yalta Conference?

Eisenhower had ordered his troops to allow the Soviets to take Berlin. On April 30, as the Battle of Berlin raged, Hitler, his wife (of only one day), and other Nazi leaders along with their wives and children committed suicide in his bunker more than fifty feet beneath the city. The Third Reich was no more. A few days earlier, Mussolini had attempted to flee Italy disguised as a German soldier. He was arrested and shot by Italians.

On May 7, the Nazis surrendered. News of victory in Europe triggered joyous celebrations. **V-E Day** (Victory in Europe Day) was commemorated from Times Square in New York City to Red Square in Moscow. In his victory address to the nation, President Truman pointed to the unfinished task:

> *We must work to bind up the wounds of a suffering world—to build an abiding peace, a peace rooted in justice and law. We can build such a peace only by hard, toilsome, painstaking work—by understanding and working with our Allies in peace as we have in war.*

In July 1945 Truman traveled to Berlin to meet with Churchill and Stalin to plan the conclusion of the war in the Pacific. The Potsdam Conference lasted from July 17 to August 2. Truman was not the only new face among the Big Three. Elections in Britain during the conference had swept Churchill's party out of power, and Churchill was replaced by Clement Attlee.

▼ Newspaper headline on V-E Day

## 19.4 The Pacific Theater

How was the war in the Pacific different from the war in Europe?

GUIDING QUESTIONS

■ What was the extent of Japan's territorial gains in the Pacific?

■ What happened in the Pacific during World War II?

While war raged in Europe and North Africa, the United States was also fighting the Japanese. After the attack on Pearl Harbor, the Japanese advanced rapidly across the Pacific. The Allies finally stopped the advance and began the bloody task of pushing the Japanese back.

## Japan Advances

After the Japanese invaded the Philippines on December 7, 1941, they forced the American and Philippine forces to retreat to the Bataan Peninsula by early January 1942. Slowly, the huge Japanese force advanced in the face of stiff American resistance. In March Roosevelt ordered General **Douglas MacArthur**, commander of the US Army forces there, to leave to avoid capture. MacArthur, vowing "I shall return," left for Australia, where he laid plans for stopping the Japanese advance and reversing Japanese gains in the Pacific. In April the surviving American defenders on Bataan surrendered to the Japanese, who forced the American and Filipino prisoners to make a brutal sixty-five-mile march to prison camps, known as the **Bataan Death March**. The Japanese shot or bayoneted anyone who fell behind, paused for water or rest, or tried to help those who did; approximately 10,000 of 78,000 prisoners died. On May 6, the last American troops, holding out on the island fortress of Corregidor, surrendered. The Japanese conquest of the Philippines was complete.

The Japanese also captured most of Southeast Asia and many Pacific islands. In June 1942 they also captured two of the Aleutian Islands, American possessions located off the tip of southern Alaska.

## America Pushes Back

With American forces suffering one defeat after another, the American people badly needed positive news. They needed to know that US forces were fighting back. To boost American morale, Roosevelt ordered his military leaders to formulate a plan to bomb Japan as soon as possible. However, the range of typical navy planes was limited, and aircraft carriers could not get close enough to Japan to allow the planes to operate. Army bombers could travel farther but required longer takeoff distances. The plan they devised was to launch B-25 medium bombers from an aircraft carrier to bomb Japanese cities.

### Doolittle Raid

After intense special training, volunteer crews under Lieutenant Colonel Jimmy Doolittle set out with sixteen B-25s aboard the carrier USS *Hornet*, which secretly sailed within 625 miles of Japan. The **Doolittle Raid** was successful in bombing Tokyo and three other Japanese cities. But bad weather and other circumstances foiled the landings on the Chinese mainland that the American raiders had planned. Eleven crews had to parachute out, and four crash-landed. Of the eighty men involved, three were killed and eight were captured by the Japanese (four of those died in captivity). Although the raid did little damage to the factories, military installations, and oil storage facilities that the Americans hit, it boosted American morale. It also shocked the Japanese, who were bewildered as to where the planes had originated. As a result of the attack, Japan's military leaders determined to destroy the US aircraft carrier fleet and to keep a large military force on the home islands to defend against future attacks.

▲ Filipino and American prisoners on the Bataan Death March

▲ A B-25 bomber taking off from the USS *Hornet* during the Doolittle raid

## The Battles of the Coral Sea and Midway

With the fall of Corregidor in May 1942, the Japanese controlled a huge Pacific empire stretching from Burma to the Bering Sea. The Japanese navy planned to cut supply routes to Australia by occupying New Guinea and the Solomon Islands. British and American code breakers deciphered Japanese messages, and US Admiral **Chester Nimitz** ordered two carriers to the Coral Sea to stop the Japanese advance. In the Battle of the Coral Sea (May 4–8, 1942) the Japanese and American fleets never saw one another. The battle was conducted entirely by navy planes attempting to attack the enemy's ships. The United States lost the carrier *Lexington* in the battle, but the Japanese invasion force was turned back without achieving its objectives.

Having failed to destroy the valuable American carriers at Pearl Harbor, Japanese Admiral Yamamoto believed an attack on Midway Island would lure them into battle in hopes of destroying them. However, the United States again intercepted a Japanese message detailing the plan and prepared for the attack. In the **Battle of Midway** (June 4–7, 1942) Admiral Nimitz skillfully directed his carrier forces, which destroyed four Japanese carriers. More than 3,000 Japanese died. American losses included the aircraft carrier *Yorktown* and about 300 American sailors. The Battle of Midway turned the tide of the war as the Allies now went on the offensive in the Pacific.

## Island Hopping

In August 1942, the drive to defeat Japan began when US Marines landed on Guadalcanal, a jungle island in the Solomon Islands. After several months of fighting, Japanese troops abandoned the island in February 1943. Because it was impossible to capture all of the thousands of Pacific islands, American forces used an "**island hopping**" strategy, bypassing some Japanese-occupied islands and establishing air bases after securing others. Launching from runways on these islands, bombers attacked Japanese fortifications on other islands and cut supply lines. For the next year, US Army forces under MacArthur and US Navy and Marine forces under Nimitz slowly reduced the area of Japanese control in the South and Central Pacific.

▼ The USS *Yorktown* on fire during the Battle of Midway

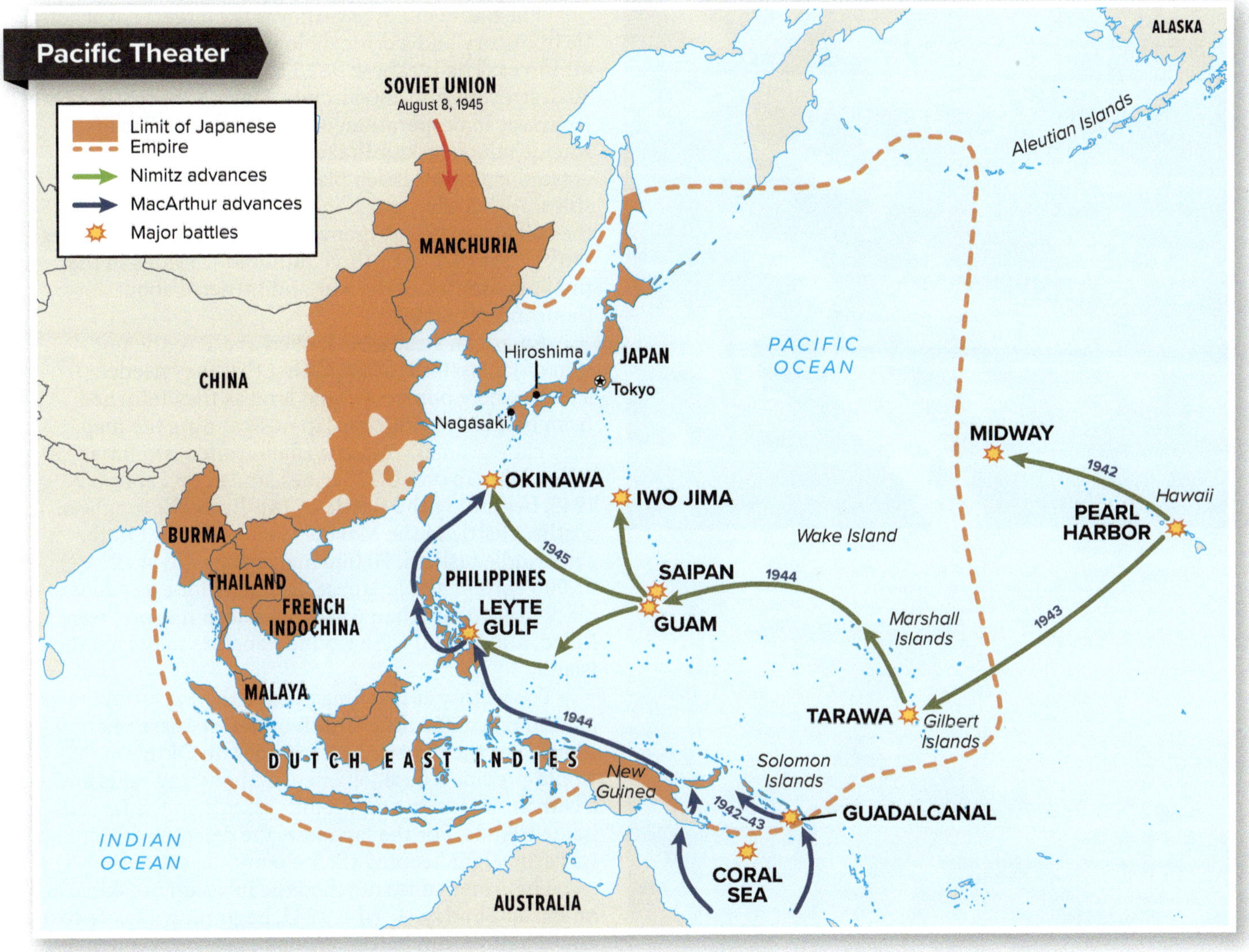

## Pacific Theater

**Map legend:**
- Limit of Japanese Empire
- Nimitz advances
- MacArthur advances
- Major battles

ALASKA

SOVIET UNION
August 8, 1945

Aleutian Islands

MANCHURIA

CHINA

Hiroshima

JAPAN

Tokyo

Nagasaki

PACIFIC OCEAN

OKINAWA

IWO JIMA

MIDWAY

1942

Wake Island

Hawaii

PEARL HARBOR

BURMA

PHILIPPINES

LEYTE GULF

1945

SAIPAN

GUAM

1944

THAILAND

FRENCH INDOCHINA

Marshall Islands

1943

MALAYA

DUTCH EAST INDIES

New Guinea

1944

Solomon Islands

TARAWA

Gilbert Islands

INDIAN OCEAN

1942–43

GUADALCANAL

CORAL SEA

AUSTRALIA

---

Nimitz's first target, in November 1943, was Tarawa in the Gilbert Islands, which was well-defended. After pounding the island with naval guns for hours, the Americans expected little resistance. However, the heavily fortified Japanese fought fiercely, killing or wounding over 3,000 US Marines. Only seventeen of the over 4,500 Japanese defenders survived the battle, which taught the Americans that their enemy would not surrender easily. The island hopping continued as the United States also retook the western Aleutian Islands in the summer of 1943, captured the Marshall Islands in early 1944, and attacked New Guinea in April 1944.

The Japanese resistance became desperate during the summer of 1944. The most significant fighting was in the Mariana Islands, which included Saipan and Guam. While the amphibious assault on Saipan was under way, a massive air battle took place between carrier-based fighters. US fighter planes knocked 346 Japanese warplanes from the sky, a victory that Americans dubbed "the Great Marianas Turkey Shoot." The capture of the Marianas enabled Allied bombers to target both the Japanese home islands and the Japanese bases in the Philippines.

In October US forces were ready to retake the Philippines. The first major assault, involving more than 700 ships carrying over 160,000 troops, was on the central island of Leyte. MacArthur declared, "I have returned." By March 1945, US forces, with the help of Filipino guerillas, recaptured the capital, Manila.

▼ General Douglas MacArthur coming ashore in the Philippines

The Battle of Leyte Gulf was the largest naval battle in history and a critical blow to Japanese naval and air forces. The Japanese lost 3 battleships, 9 cruisers, 10 destroyers, and 180 aircraft. During the battle, the Japanese, in desperation, organized squadrons of suicide pilots, or **kamikazes**. Their mission was to crash their bomb-laden planes into American warships. Although American gunners stopped most of the suicide missions, many still succeeded. Kamikazes sank or crippled over three hundred US ships in the final ten months of the war and inflicted about ten thousand casualties.

American strategists looked ahead to the invasion of Japan itself, determining that they needed a place where bombers could land as they returned from bombing raids over Japan. Scanning the map, they chose a small volcanic island called Iwo Jima, 750 miles from Tokyo. US Marines landed on February 19, 1945, beginning the **Battle of Iwo Jima**, the toughest, costliest battle of the Marine Corp's history. On the cave-riddled island, 70,000 marines fought against 21,000 entrenched Japanese defenders for every foot of black sand. More than 6,800 American marines were killed, and 20,000 were wounded before they took the island.

The victory at Iwo Jima opened the way to Okinawa, an island just 350 miles south of the Japanese main island. For the Americans, a victory on Okinawa would provide a base for intensive bombing raids and a launch site for an amphibious assault on the Japanese home islands. For the Japanese, the defense of Okinawa was crucial for keeping their enemy at a distance.

The Americans launched the invasion of Okinawa on Easter Sunday, April 1, 1945, beginning a fierce two-and-a-half-month battle. While the infantry fought for the island, the US Navy was locked in combat with an equally determined foe. Nearly two thousand kamikazes attacked the American fleet, killing five thousand American sailors and sinking thirty-eight US ships. But by mid-June, Okinawa had been captured.

The **Battle of Okinawa** was the bloodiest battle in the Pacific theater; 12,000 American servicemen were killed and 50,000 wounded. Of the estimated 117,000 Japanese casualties, 110,000 were deaths, many by suicide which was an honorable death in Japanese military culture. Additionally, tens of thousands of Okinawan civilians died. Survivors testified that before the invasion began, Japanese soldiers distributed grenades to civilians, ordering them to throw all but one at the American soldiers and to use the last one to commit suicide. Other Okinawans jumped from cliffs onto jagged rocks or into the sea to avoid surrender.

◄ (top) A kamikaze attack on an American aircraft carrier; (middle) US Marines fighting at Iwo Jima; (bottom) US Marines destroying a Japanese underground position during the Battle of Okinawa

## Atomic Bombs

The grim tale of Okinawa was an indication of the difficulty America would face when invading Japan; US leaders feared hundreds of thousands of Americans would die in such an endeavor. As in Okinawa, by the summer of 1945 civilians on the main islands of Japan were joined to the war effort by a government order drafting millions of men and women. As Truman, Stalin, and Atlee met at Potsdam in July 1945, they agreed to a declaration demanding Japan's unconditional surrender. After the defeat at Okinawa, Emperor Hirohito had urged his senior government officials to find a way to end the war, but he would not agree to unconditional surrender if it meant the emperorship would be abolished.

The day before the Potsdam Conference opened, Truman had received a top-secret message which read:

> *TO SECRETARY OF WAR FROM HARRISON. DOCTOR HAS JUST RETURNED MOST ENTHUSIASTIC AND CONFIDENT THAT THE LITTLE BOY IS AS HUSKY AS HIS BIG BROTHER. THE LIGHT IN HIS EYES DISCERNIBLE FROM HERE TO HIGH HOLD AND I COULD HAVE HEARD HIS SCREAMS FROM HERE TO MY FARM.*

The coded words meant that the test of the atomic bomb on July 16 had been successful; the noise of the blast could be heard for over a hundred miles. The "big brother" was the bomb that had been tested in the New Mexico desert. The "little boy" was a second atomic bomb that was ready, if approved by Truman, to be used against Japan.

The atomic bombs were the result of the highly classified **Manhattan Project**. Physicist Albert Einstein, a German Jew who had fled to the United States, had written President Roosevelt in 1939 warning him that the Germans were trying to develop an atomic bomb. FDR and his advisors established the Manhattan Project to design and assemble such a weapon before Germany. Sworn to secrecy and led by physicist Robert Oppenheimer, thousands of scientists, engineers, and chemists worked at research laboratories and testing facilities in Oak Ridge, Tennessee, and Los Alamos, New Mexico. The successful test in July 1945 was the culmination of their work.

The Allies issued an ultimatum to Japan—surrender or face destruction. No mention was made of the atomic bomb. The Japanese premier refused to surrender. On the morning of August 6, Colonel Paul Tibbets piloted a B-29 Superfortress (named *Enola Gay* in honor of his mother) and dropped the first atomic bomb over **Hiroshima**, a military headquarters city and military supply depot. The extraordinary weapon destroyed half the city in a single blast. It is estimated that more than 70,000 of 280,000 residents died that day. Tens of thousands later died from injuries and the results of radiation exposure.

The next day, August 8, the Soviet Union officially declared war on Japan, sending more than one million soldiers into Japanese-occupied Manchuria and the Korean peninsula. Despite not entering the war against Japan until its final days, Stalin would demand extensive Asian territorial concessions from the Allies.

Despite the first atomic bomb and Soviet entrance into the war, Japan refused to surrender. On August 9 the United States dropped a second bomb on **Nagasaki**. About 40,000 of the 200,000 residents were killed that day.

## Should *the* Atomic Bombs Have Been Used?

For more than seventy years, people have debated whether the atomic bombs should have been dropped on Japan. Opponents have questioned the ethics of using a bomb that intentionally killed thousands of civilians. They believe that targeting civilians is wrong because it is intentionally putting to death innocent people. They argue that there were alternative ways of ending the war. Some think that Japan could have been defeated by continued use of traditional bombing, blockading the coast of Japan, and with the help of Soviet troops who entered the war in August 1945.

Supporters have argued that an invasion of Japan would have cost hundreds of thousands of American lives, and perhaps even more Japanese lives. They also note that Hiroshima was full of military targets and personnel and that the bombing of Tokyo and other Japanese cities with incendiary bombs (those designed to start fires) in March 1945 had already killed over 100,000 civilians, yet the Japanese government had refused to surrender.

▶ Atomic bomb explosion over Hiroshima

## V-J Day

On August 14, the Japanese agreed to surrender. On August 15, the Japanese people, hearing their emperor's voice for the first time, listened to Hirohito's recorded announcement that the war was over. The official surrender ceremony took place on September 2, 1945 (proclaimed **V-J Day** for Victory over Japan), aboard the battleship *Missouri* anchored in Tokyo Bay. General MacArthur stood on deck and addressed victor and vanquished alike:

> *We are gathered here, representatives of the major warring powers, to conclude a solemn agreement whereby peace may be restored. The issues, involving divergent ideals and ideologies, have been determined on the battlefields of the world and hence are not for our discussion or debate. Nor is it for us here to meet . . . in a spirit of distrust, malice, or hatred. . . . It is my earnest hope . . . that from this solemn occasion a better world shall emerge . . . a world dedicated to the dignity of man. . . . Let us pray that peace be now restored to the world, and that God will preserve it always. These proceedings are closed.*

Throughout the world the wounds of war ran deep. Worldwide, fifty million men, women, and children were killed during World War II, including 400,000 American soldiers, sailors, and airmen. While Americans returned to peacetime with great relief, the postwar world would pose new challenges to the United States and the world.

▼ Japanese surrender ceremony aboard the USS *Missouri*; (inset) newspaper headline on V-J Day

### Comprehension Check 19.4

1. American pilots used the _____ strategy to bypass certain Japanese territories and establish air bases on others.

   **A** Doolittle

   **B** island hopping

   **C** kamikaze

2. The Battle of _____ was the turning point of the war in the Pacific.

   **A** Saipan

   **B** Leyte Gulf

   **C** Midway

3. The Allies used atomic bombs on _____ and Nagasaki.

   **A** Hiroshima

   **B** Okinawa

   **C** Tokyo

### MAKING CONNECTIONS

4. What are two arguments for and against the use of atomic bombs in Japan?

Oshkosh Daily Northwestern

## JAPAN SURRENDERS TO END WORLD WAR

## Chapter Summary

### 19.1 The Coming of War

- Military leaders gained influence in Japan under Emperor Hirohito. Japan's growing militarism was demonstrated in its invasion of Manchuria and later full-scale war in China. Italy, Germany, and the Soviet Union were controlled by powerful dictators. Italy under Mussolini sought to expand the Italian empire in North Africa. In Germany Hitler wanted to unite all Germans and establish a Third Reich, and he rebuilt the German military. Italy, Germany, and Japan formed an alliance as the Axis Powers. Stalin eradicated opposition to his government programs in the Soviet Union.

- In violation of the Versailles Treaty, Hitler moved troops into the Rhineland and built German fortifications and united with Austria. Although he promised to end expansion after taking the Sudetenland, Hitler took the rest of Czechoslovakia. He and Stalin signed a non-aggression pact shortly before Hitler's invasion of Poland, after which Britain and France declared war. Swiftly taking countries in northern Europe (including France), Germany prepared for an invasion of Britain, but the British air force defeated the Germans in the Battle of Britain. Hitler invaded the USSR in Operation Barbarossa, driving the Soviets to the Allies.

**TERMS**

Hirohito

fascism

Benito Mussolini

Adolf Hitler

Axis Powers

Joseph Stalin

appeasement

blitzkrieg

Allied Powers

Winston Churchill

**TERMS**

cash and carry

Lend-Lease Act

Pearl Harbor

Tuskegee Airmen

Navajo code talkers

War Production Board

Office of War Information

### 19.2 Isolation and Infamy

- The United States hoped to avoid involvement in World War II but supported the Allied Powers through policies such as "cash and carry" and Lend-Lease.

- Japan's expansion in the Pacific led to its attack on the US naval base at Pearl Harbor, Hawaii, as well as bases at Guam, the Philippines, and other areas. In response, President Roosevelt asked Congress for a declaration of war.

- The entire nation mobilized for war as sixteen million Americans joined the military. Others contributed by working in factories, serving in women's auxiliary units, and volunteering in service organizations. Many Japanese Americans, who were suspected as spies or disloyal citizens, were sent to internment camps.

- The War Production Board oversaw the transition of industries from civilian to military production, and rationing of vital goods was implemented. The war was funded through higher taxes and war bonds, although the nation's debt also increased. The Office of War Information informed Americans about the war and produced propaganda to rally support for the war effort.

# CHAPTER 19 REVIEW

## Chapter Summary

### 19.3   The European Theater

- US troops under Dwight D. Eisenhower helped the Allies in North Africa against Italian and German forces there. Next, they helped invade Italy, the "soft underbelly" of Europe. After the beginning of the invasion of Italy and the overthrow of Mussolini, Italy surrendered, but Germany continued resisting.

- The Allies planned an invasion of France to help take pressure off the Soviet front. Supreme Allied Commander Eisenhower organized the D-Day invasion of Normandy, the largest amphibious assault in history. The Allies moved into France and quickly liberated Paris and other territory in surrounding countries. Despite Germany's counteroffensive in the Battle of the Bulge, the Allies pushed through to Germany, and the Soviets took Berlin. The Nazis surrendered on May 7, 1945, marking V-E day.

- Hitler's policies as chancellor targeted Jews and others considered undesirable. Jews, especially, faced discrimination and persecution before finally being sent to concentration or death camps. As the Allies freed Europe from Nazi control, they came across these camps. An estimated six million Jews died during the Holocaust.

**TERMS**

Dwight D. Eisenhower

D-Day

Battle of the Bulge

Harry Truman

Holocaust

V-E Day

---

**TERMS**

Douglas MacArthur

Bataan Death March

Doolittle Raid

Chester Nimitz

Battle of Midway

island hopping

kamikazes

Battle of Iwo Jima

Battle of Okinawa

Manhattan Project

Hiroshima

Nagasaki

V-J Day

### 19.4   The Pacific Theater

- Japan completed conquering the Philippines in 1942. To boost American morale, the Doolittle Raid bombed Japan.

- The United States stopped the Japanese advance at the Battle of the Coral Sea and the Battle of Midway and then went on the offensive in the Pacific. United States military leaders employed an island-hopping strategy in the Pacific. Fighting on the islands was fierce and resulted in high casualties for both sides.

- President Truman made the decision to drop atomic bombs, which the Manhattan Project had developed, on Japan to speed its surrender. The war ended on September 2, 1945, known as V-J Day.

- Over 50 million people were killed in World War II, including 400,000 American military personnel.

## Chapter Review Questions

### RECALL

1. Who was the emperor of Japan during World War II?

2. Who were the Axis Powers?

3. What was the name of the policy for selling goods other than arms to nations at war that had to be transported on non-American ships?

4. What event brought the United States into the war?

5. Who was the Supreme Allied Commander in Europe?

6. What was the largest amphibious invasion in history?

7. Who replaced Roosevelt as president in the final months of the war?

8. What was the 65-mile journey made by American and Filipino prisoners of war called?

9. What were kamikazes?

### UNDERSTAND

10. What were Japan's, Italy's, and Germany's acts of aggression and expansion in the 1930s?

11. What was the Nazi-Soviet Pact?

12. What policy did Britain and France follow at first in dealing with Hitler's expansion? What was the effect of this policy, and why did they eventually change their response?

13. Why did Stalin eventually join the Allied side?

14. Other than selling or leasing materials to the Allies, what were two ways the United States indicated its readiness to join the war?

15. What organization protested American sale of arms to the Allies? What was one reason they gave?

16. What were two ways women and minority groups participated in the war?

17. Why did Japan seize China, French Indochina, and British and Dutch colonies? What was the chief obstacle to Japan's expansion?

18. What was the cause of the Supreme Court case *Korematsu v. United States*? What was the Court's decision?

19. What were three ways supplies were conserved for the Allied troops?

20. What were two means by which the OWI spread war information and propaganda?

21. What were the three areas in the European theater where the United States was involved in invasions?

22. Who met at the Yalta Conference? What was one of the conference decisions that affected postwar Europe?

23. What were two examples of Nazi persecution of Jews before the implementation of the "Final Solution"? What was the "Final Solution"? When did Allied troops discover it?

24. What happened to Hitler and Mussolini about a week before V-E Day?

25. Who was the commander of the US Army forces in the Philippines? Why did he leave?

26. What was the Doolittle Raid, and how did it influence Japanese military strategy?

27. What enabled Admiral Nimitz to prepare for the Japanese attacks in the Battles of the Coral Sea and Midway? What type of ship was crucial to his strategy?

28. What was the largest naval battle in history? What desperate strategy did the Japanese begin to use during this battle?

29. Why did Americans want to capture Iwo Jima and Okinawa? How was Japanese resistance on these islands similar?

### THINK ABOUT IT

30. Why do you think people were willing to follow Hitler and Mussolini? What did fascism turn into an idol, and how did fascism violate biblical principles regarding equality and the importance of the individual?

31. How did Roosevelt help African Americans with an executive order? Explain how this order succeeded in upholding the American ideal and biblical principle of equality.

32. How did Roosevelt hurt Japanese Americans with an executive order? Explain how this order failed to uphold the biblical principle of justice.

33. What were two arguments for and against using the atomic bombs against Japan? Why would the use of the atomic bomb have been a difficult decision for a president to make?

# 20 The Postwar Era

**20.1 The Postwar Era**
**20.2 The Cold War Begins**
**20.3 Life in Postwar America**

▲ Schoolchildren practicing an atomic bomb drill

**The Postwar Era**

**What was different about America and the world after World War II?**

- How did America transition to peacetime after World War II?
- What were conditions in Asia and Europe like after the war?

On April 12, 1945, the day Franklin Roosevelt died, Harry Truman took the presidential oath of office. Truman confided to reporters the next day that he felt "like the moon, the stars, and all the planets had fallen on me." Taking office after serving less than three months as vice president, Truman had little experience in foreign policy. He was told nothing about the project to develop the atomic bomb until he became president.

Prepared or not, Truman proceeded to make his mark on American policy at home and in the world. After involvement in wars, previous presidents typically had resumed an isolationist position. Truman, however, led the United States into membership in, and even sponsorship of, international organizations. In a further departure from tradition, he pushed for a peacetime buildup of US armed forces, a buildup anchored by atomic weapons.

## Postwar Politics

### The GI Bill

Many Americans feared another economic decline would follow World War II, as it had followed the First World War. To help returning veterans transition into civilian life and to express gratitude for their service, Congress had passed the **GI Bill** in 1944. It provided benefits such as tuition grants, job training, and government assistance with home loans. As a result, millions of veterans purchased homes and enrolled at educational institutions by 1956, the year the bill expired. One result of the GI Bill was that it reduced the risk of economic depression from unemployment, as many veterans pursued their education. Although the educational benefits extended to black veterans, many were often denied home loans by banks or turned away from certain educational institutions.

▲ A veteran studying for a course at Pennsylvania State College in a trailer home he rents, while his wife and daughter play nearby

### Truman and the Fair Deal

Signaling that his domestic program would be an expansion of the New Deal, President Truman sent Congress a list of proposals shortly after the war. His legislative goals, soon known as the **Fair Deal**, included a government commitment to full employment (federal spending designed to ensure jobs for the unemployed), an increase in the minimum wage, subsidized medical insurance, and an act that protected Americans from racial or religious discrimination in hiring. But opposition from economic conservatives and from southern Democrats killed most of his agenda. Truman settled instead for the Employment Act of 1946, which created the Council of Economic Advisers to guide the president on economic matters.

That year Congress also created the Atomic Energy Commission, which gave control over atomic energy to civilian rather than military authorities. It was later abolished, and the Department of Energy was created in 1977 to oversee nuclear energy.

Truman faced economic problems, such as labor strikes in the auto, steel, coal, and railroad industries. There were also allegations that Communists held government positions. As a result, Truman's approval ratings sank, and Democrats lost public support. In the 1946 elections, "To err is Truman" and "Had enough?" were effective Republican slogans, and Republicans captured both houses of Congress for the first time since 1928. With control of Congress, Republicans pushed through the **Taft-Hartley Act** of 1947. This anti-union measure, passed over Truman's veto, permitted states to pass "right-to-work" laws banning the "union shop," which required union membership as a condition for hiring. The act also required an eighty-day cooling-off period before strikes in businesses that the president thought were crucial to maintaining the health and safety of the nation. Additionally, union officials were required to swear that they were not Communists.

Congress also passed the National Security Act in 1947, which changed the American military establishment. World War II, especially the Pearl Harbor disaster, had revealed the need for greater coordination among the armed forces. This act eliminated the position of secretary of war and created the post of secretary of defense, a civilian cabinet position that supervised the army, navy, and air force. It also established the **Central Intelligence Agency (CIA)** to gather and analyze information about foreign countries, often by using spies. To assist the president in foreign policy matters, the National Security Council, composed of the vice president, the secretary of defense, the secretary of state, and others, was also created.

## Election of 1948

When Truman faced the voters in the 1948 election, prospects for victory looked dim. The left wing of the Democratic Party was enraged over the president's firing of Secretary of Commerce Henry A. Wallace for his criticism of Truman's policies. These liberal Democrats left the party and nominated Wallace, who had served as FDR's second vice president, on the Progressive ticket (a different Progressive Party from the one in 1912 that had nominated Theodore Roosevelt). Southern Democrats, upset over Truman's support of civil rights for black Americans (see Chapter 22), walked out of the Democratic National Convention and eventually nominated Governor Strom Thurmond of South Carolina to represent the States' Rights Party, more commonly known as "Dixiecrats." Confident because of the division among Democrats, Republicans chose Thomas Dewey, the popular governor of New York, as their candidate.

▲ CIA headquarters in Langley, Virginia

A triumphant Truman holding the *Chicago Tribune*'s incorrect headline which had proclaimed his opponent's victory before the final votes came in

Truman campaigned vigorously. After he called the Republican-controlled Congress back into a special session and it refused to act on several of his proposals, he dubbed it the "do-nothing" Congress and used it as a campaign issue. Truman targeted his appeals to labor union members and African Americans in the cities as well as to farmers in the Midwest and West in hopes of keeping the old New Deal coalition alive. On a 31,000-mile "whistle-stop" train tour, Truman spent four months campaigning across the country, leading up to election night. Many Americans went to bed thinking that Dewey had won, but the ballot count the next morning revealed that Truman had beaten Dewey in one of the biggest upsets in the history of presidential elections. After his election victory, Congress, which now had a Democratic majority, passed many of the president's Fair Deal proposals, which updated the New Deal. Congress raised the minimum wage, extended Social Security coverage, and gave more aid to farmers. Congress, however, rejected civil rights bills, federal aid to education, and national health insurance.

In 1951 the **Twenty-Second Amendment** to the Constitution was adopted. It declared that no one could be elected president more than two times. Many supported it because they felt that FDR had set a dangerous example by being elected to a third and fourth term. Previously, no president had been elected more than two times but had instead followed George Washington's precedent.

## The Postwar World

### *Nuremberg Trials*

After World War II, the Allies, seeking justice for the atrocities of the war, placed many leaders of the Axis powers on trial. They faced such charges as conspiring to commit crimes against peace, planning and waging wars of aggression, and committing war crimes and crimes against humanity.

Some of the Nazi party's highest officials, including Adolf Hitler, had escaped prosecution because they had committed suicide. The trials of several other Nazi war criminals (including Hermann Göring) were held in Nuremberg, Germany, beginning in the fall of 1945. Robert Jackson, the chief United States prosecutor present, observed in his opening statement, "The wrongs which we seek to condemn and punish have been so calculated, so malignant and so devastating, that civilization cannot tolerate their being ignored because it cannot survive their being repeated."

In the first of the **Nuremberg Trials**, twenty-four individuals were charged. Twelve were sentenced to death, seven received prison sentences ranging from ten years to life, three were found innocent, one committed suicide early in the proceedings, and one was released without going to trial.

Beginning in 1946 similar proceedings were held in Tokyo for important Japanese officials. Of the twenty-eight defendants, two died of natural causes during the lengthy trial, one was declared insane, eighteen received prison sentences, and seven were sentenced to death, including Hideki Tojo.

In later trials thousands of other individuals faced charges. These included both Japanese prison camp guards who had brutalized Allied soldiers they supervised and also Nazi guards who had been ruthless at the Jewish concentration camps in Europe.

▲ Hermann Göring, Marshal of the Greater German Reich, taking the oath at the Nuremberg Trials, March 1946

## United Nations

One effort to maintain peace was the formation of the **United Nations** (UN). Born out of wartime cooperation among the Allies, the UN began on April 25, 1945, in San Francisco with delegates from fifty nations meeting to write a charter for the organization. The United States Senate ratified the UN charter in 1945 by an overwhelming margin, and eventually the United Nations made its permanent home in New York City. Proponents of the United Nations hoped it would provide an avenue for rational discussion and a means of furthering world peace.

The United Nations includes two major bodies. The General Assembly consists of delegates from all member nations and provides a forum in which those nations can express their views. The Security Council currently includes five permanent members—the United States, Russia, Britain, France, and China—and ten members elected by the General Assembly for two-year terms. Permanent members have veto power. If any of those five members votes against a Security Council resolution, it does not pass. The highest official in the UN is the Secretary-General, who is appointed by the General Assembly.

## Postwar Japan

With Japan's navy and cities in ruins, the United States sent billions of dollars in aid to rebuild Japan under the direction of General MacArthur. In addition to recovery efforts, MacArthur headed the formation of a new Japanese constitution. Hirohito was not placed on trial in Tokyo because the peace settlement terms stated that he would remain emperor and would not be charged with any crimes; however, he was required to renounce a long-standing Japanese tradition—the belief that the emperor was divine. The Japanese government would become democratic, with the emperor as a symbolic figurehead. The new constitution gave women the right to vote for the first time. Additionally, it changed the nature of the military by designating civilian government officials to oversee the military, forbidding military leaders from taking government positions, and limiting the Japanese military to a defense force.

◄ (top) General Assembly of the United Nations in New York; (bottom) General Douglas MacArthur with Emperor Hirohito

### Did You Know?

Hirohito remained the emperor until his death at age 87 in 1989, more than four decades after the war ended.

## Postwar Europe

Like Japan, war-torn Europe needed help to rebuild. In many cities millions of destitute refugees had homes turned to rubble. Farms, businesses, and industries had been destroyed. In many of these nations, economic challenges led the people to call for reform or to join radical political parties.

In accordance with the Yalta Conference (see Chapter 19), the United States, Britain, and France occupied the three western zones of Germany while the Soviet Union occupied the fourth (eastern) zone. The German capital, Berlin, was located entirely within the Soviet zone, and it too was divided similarly into three western zones and one eastern Soviet zone. Stalin broke the promise he made at Yalta to support free elections and democratically elected governments in the liberated nations of Europe. Instead, he established pro-Soviet governments throughout Eastern Europe. Before World War II ended, the Soviet Union had installed "puppet" governments in Poland and Romania. Soon, East Germany, Hungary, Bulgaria, Albania, and Yugoslavia were under Communist control. In 1948 Czechoslovakia was the last Eastern European country that succumbed to Soviet control.

### Occupation of Germany after WWII

▼ Ruins of Dresden, Germany, at the end of the war

### Comprehension Check 20.1

1. The National Security Act of 1947 created the following, except the ____.

   A CIA

   B National Security Council

   C secretary of defense

   D UN

2. The Taft-Hartley Act ____.

   A enabled states to pass laws that challenged unions

   B limited presidents to two terms

   C punished Nazi and Japanese officials for war crimes

3. After the war, the USSR ____.

   A established a new democratic government and led recovery in Japan

   B refused to join the United Nations

   C set up puppet governments in Eastern European countries

### MAKING CONNECTIONS

4. What were two Fair Deal measures that Congress passed, and what was one measure that did not?

▲ Test in the Marshall Islands of the first hydrogen bomb, 1952

### GUIDING QUESTIONS

- Where did early Cold War conflicts begin?
- How did China become Communist?
- How did the Korean War result from Cold War tensions?

## 20.2 The Cold War Begins

How did the Cold War affect postwar foreign affairs?

## Soviet Conflicts

A cold war is a period of tension between countries that consists of threats and other measures short of actual warfare. The period from the end of World War II until the early 1990s became known as the **Cold War** era because of the tension and intense competition between the United States and its allies and the Soviet Union and its allies. Both sides tried to avoid direct military conflict because they feared a third world war. Yet the conflict occasionally flared into actual military conflict (i.e., a "hot war").

The relationship between the United States and the Soviet Union had been difficult ever since the Bolshevik Revolution in 1917. The United States government did not officially recognize the Communist government of the Soviet Union until 1933 and was alarmed by the Nazi-Soviet Pact, by the USSR's invasion of Poland and Finland in 1939, and by the USSR's annexation of the Baltic States in 1940. However, when Germany invaded the Soviet Union in 1941, the Americans and Soviets set aside their ideological differences to defeat Nazi Germany.

What ultimately launched the Cold War was the realization that the USSR intended to spread its power throughout the world. The Cold War was waged as the forces of democracy and communism confronted each other in nation after nation.

The existence of nuclear weapons heightened Cold War tensions. In August 1949, the Soviet Union successfully tested its first atomic bomb and forced Truman to reevaluate America's defense policy. He called first for increasing conventional military forces since the Soviets possessed "the bomb." He also ordered development of a more powerful weapon, the hydrogen bomb. When the "H-bomb," as it was popularly known, was finally developed in 1952, it had an explosive power hundreds of times greater than the bomb dropped on Hiroshima. Within a year, the Soviet Union revealed that it, too, had developed a hydrogen bomb.

## The Iron Curtain

Winston Churchill described the unfolding events in Europe as the descent of an "**iron curtain**" separating Communist Eastern Europe from the free nations of Western Europe. In a speech given at Westminster College in Fulton, Missouri, in 1946, Churchill said:

▲ Winston Churchill delivering his "Sinews of Peace" speech, in which he described the "Iron Curtain"

> *From Stettin in the Baltic to Trieste in the Adriatic, an iron curtain has descended across the Continent. Behind that line lie all the capitals of the ancient states of Central and Eastern Europe. Warsaw, Berlin, Prague, Vienna, Budapest, Belgrade, Bucharest and Sofia, all these famous cities and the populations around them lie in what I must call the Soviet sphere, and all are subject in one form or another, not only to Soviet influence but to a very high and, in many cases, increasing measure of control from Moscow. . . .*
>
> *The Communist parties, which were very small in all these Eastern States of Europe, have been raised to pre-eminence and power far beyond their numbers and are seeking everywhere to obtain totalitarian control. . . .*
>
> *I do not believe that Soviet Russia desires war. What they desire is the fruits of war and the indefinite expansion of their power and doctrines.*
>
> — **WINSTON CHURCHILL,** Excerpt from "Sinews of Peace" speech delivered at Westminster college in Fulton, Missouri, 5 March 1946.

 **Analyzing Sources**

Why do you think Churchill used the term "iron curtain" to describe what was happening in Eastern Europe? How do you think the Communist parties in these countries were able to exercise "power far beyond their numbers"?

Soon the term "East" or "Eastern" was used to refer to Communist-controlled areas throughout the world, and "West" or "Western" referred to democratic nations. The term "Third World" referred to nations that did not align themselves with either the East or West. (Today, "Third World" refers to underdeveloped, or developing, nations—especially those with widespread poverty.)

## The Truman Doctrine and the Marshall Plan

Though unhappy with the expansion of communism, Truman feared that trying to force the Communists to withdraw from Eastern Europe might cause another war. He responded to the Soviet presence in Eastern Europe with the policy of **containment**, declaring that further Communist expansion would be resisted and that communism must be contained within its new boundaries.

Truman's policy of containment was put to the test in 1946 when Communist-led guerillas attempted to take control of Greece. The Soviet Union also pressured Turkey for territory and the right to establish naval bases on the Bosporus, the strategic waterway providing access between the Black Sea and the Aegean Sea. To prevent the spread of Soviet influence in the Mediterranean, Truman asked Congress for $400 million in economic aid for Greece and Turkey, and both countries successfully pushed back Communist threats. This policy of giving money or other assistance to support pro-Western, anti-Communist governments became known as the **Truman Doctrine**.

In Western Europe, economic ruin from World War II created a sense of desperation and hopelessness for many. The opportunity was ripe for Communist advances in these war-torn countries. France and Italy, for example, already had strong left-wing parties that could lay a foundation for a Communist takeover. To reduce the appeal of communism, Secretary of State George C. Marshall in 1947 offered a plan for massive economic and agricultural aid to all European countries, including those already under Communist control. The Soviet Union and its satellite countries in Eastern Europe refused the aid, but Western European nations welcomed it. In 1948 Congress passed this European Recovery Program, better known as the **Marshall Plan**. By 1951 the United States had spent $13 billion on restoring the economies of Western Europe, whose production soon surpassed prewar levels. The Marshall Plan stabilized the region and thereby diminished the appeal of communism. It also restored those European countries as trading partners with the United States. Meanwhile, the Soviet satellites remained in economic despair for decades.

▲ German poster, "The Marshall Plan helps Europe"

## Berlin Airlift

The Soviets were not pleased with the arrangement of occupied Germany. Because they had twice been invaded by Germany in recent memory, the Soviets did not want to see Germany reunified and did not want to lose control of East Germany. In 1948 the Americans, the British, and the French consolidated their occupied zones in western Germany and began the process of forming a government. They also created a single new currency for all of their occupation zones. Threatened by the prospect of a unified western Germany and a unified, anti-Communist West Berlin deep within the Soviet occupation zone, the Soviets blocked highway, water, and rail traffic into West Berlin. By blocking all access to that area, Stalin hoped to take over the entire city or force the West to stop the unification of western Germany.

Stalin's action left two million residents of West Berlin without access to food, fuel, and other necessities. Truman faced a difficult decision. Using military force to reopen the routes to West Berlin risked war with the Soviets. Surrendering West Berlin would allow communism to expand, contrary to the policy of containment. Truman decided on a massive airlift of food and supplies to West Berlin. The **Berlin airlift** continued for eleven months. British and American planes departed and landed every few minutes. Some 277,000 flights brought 2.3 million tons of cargo—food, fuel, medicine, and other essentials—to the city.

▶ A plane delivering food and supplies during the Berlin Airlift, 1948

In May 1949 the Soviets ended the blockade. Afterward, the Federal Republic of Germany (West Germany) was created from the American, British, and French zones. The Soviets responded by creating the German Democratic Republic (East Germany). Berlin remained divided: East Berlin was part of East Germany, while West Berlin was part of West Germany. Germany would remain divided until 1990.

## NATO and the Warsaw Pact

Reacting to the Soviet military threat to the West, the Western nations forged a military alliance to defend themselves. In April 1949, representatives from ten Western European countries (United Kingdom, France, Italy, Portugal, the Netherlands, Denmark, Norway, Belgium, Luxembourg, and Iceland), along with the United States and Canada formed the **North Atlantic Treaty Organization (NATO)**. Greece and Turkey joined in 1952, and West Germany joined in 1959. The member nations agreed to provide military support for any member that was attacked. General Dwight D. Eisenhower became the first supreme commander of NATO forces.

In 1955 the Communist countries of Eastern Europe reacted to NATO by creating their own military alliance, the **Warsaw Pact**. It included Poland, Albania, East Germany, Bulgaria, Romania, Czechoslovakia, Hungary, and the Soviet Union.

## NATO and Warsaw Pact Countries

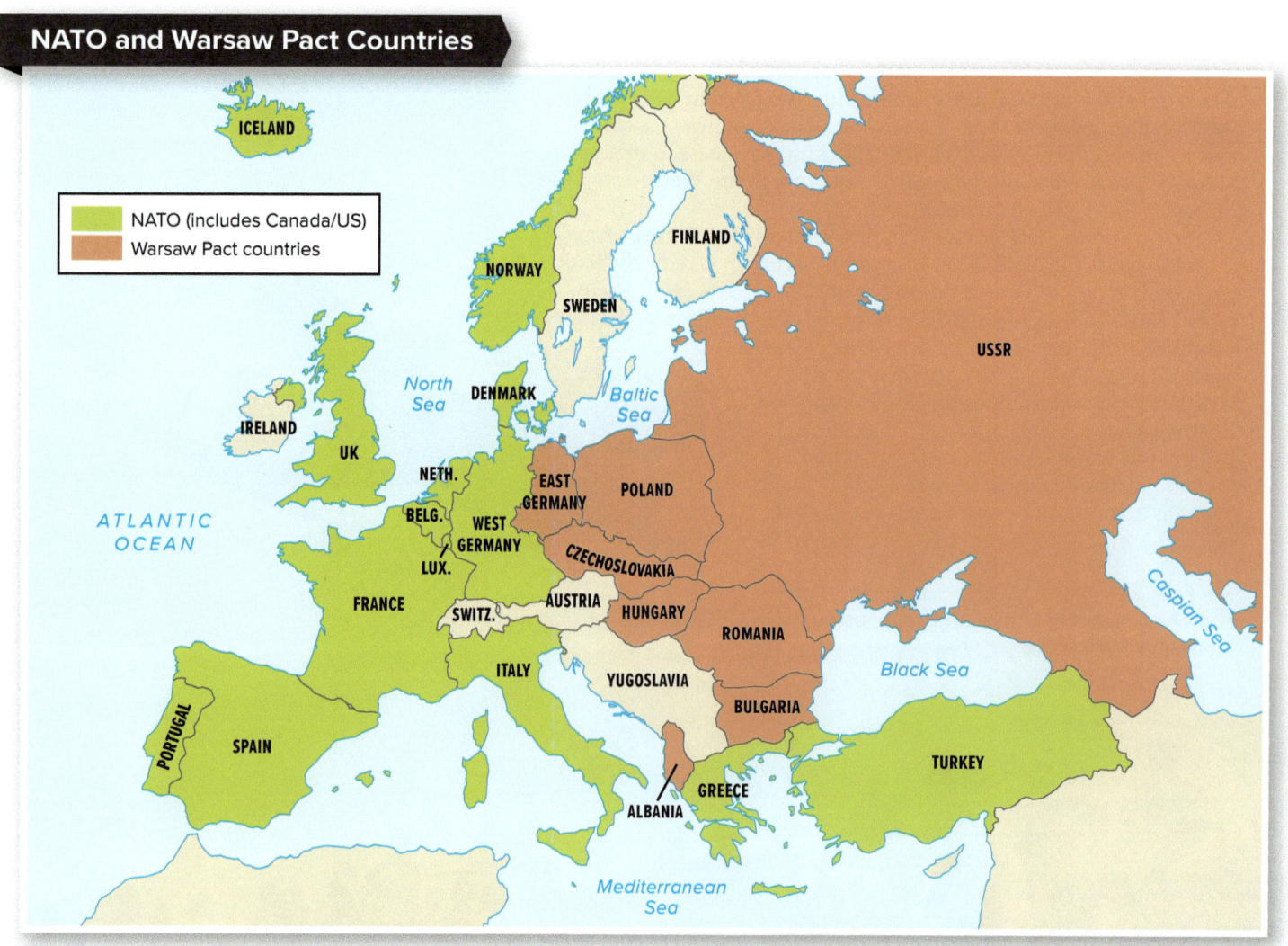

## Communist China

Since the 1920s China had endured civil war between the Nationalists, led by **Chiang Kai-shek**, and the Communists, led by **Mao Zedong**. World War II interrupted their fighting as they both battled the Japanese, but after 1945 civil war resumed.

Corruption and conflicts within the Nationalist group and public disapproval of many of Chiang Kai-shek's policies hurt the Nationalist cause. Despite significant financial aid from the United States, the Nationalists lost control of mainland China to the Communists in 1949. Chiang Kai-shek and his forces fled to the island of Taiwan (Formosa), about a hundred miles off the coast of China, and there they established the Republic of China (also called Nationalist China or Free China). Mao Zedong ruled mainland China, called the People's Republic of China (also called Communist China).

In 1950 the People's Republic of China and the Soviet Union signed the Sino-Soviet Treaty of Friendship, Alliance, and Mutual Assistance. It provided security guarantees and increased economic cooperation between the two countries. It also raised American fears that the two Communist nations would work together against the free world. The United States and the United Nations continued to recognize the Nationalists in Taiwan as China until the 1970s (see Chapter 23).

▲ Nationalist General Chiang Kai-shek (left) with Mao Zedong (right), leader of the Chinese Communists

## The Korean War

The most serious military conflict of the early Cold War occurred in Asia on the Korean peninsula. After the Soviet Union had joined the war against Japan in August 1945, its troops occupied the northern portion of the Korean peninsula. After the war, the Allies agreed that the Soviets could remain in the portion of Korea north of the 38th parallel of latitude, and the Soviets agreed to hold free elections. Instead, the Soviets established a Communist government in North Korea. South of the 38th parallel, South Korea held elections and established the free Republic of Korea, with Seoul as its capital.

Diplomats attempted to find a peaceful resolution to the Korean situation, hoping to unify the country, but talks broke down. Then on June 25, 1950, more than eighty thousand North Korean soldiers invaded the South in a surprise attack to unite the peninsula under Communist rule. The UN Security Council called an emergency session to respond to this act of aggression. It called for a resolution demanding North Korea's immediate withdrawal from South Korea. The USSR, which could have vetoed the Security Council action, was boycotting UN meetings in protest of America's refusal to recognize the government of Communist China. The remaining members passed the resolution.

The Security Council called for the UN to provide military aid to South Korea. Truman committed American planes and ships to support South Korea and moved troops stationed in Japan to Korea. The UN voted to send peacekeeping troops to Korea to help end the conflict, which was called the **Korean War** (though war was never declared). Although sixteen other nations sent troops, the United States contributed over 80 percent of the fighting force, and Truman placed General Douglas MacArthur, who was overseeing the rebuilding of Japan after the war, in charge of the UN military forces.

**China and Taiwan**

CHINA

KOREA

Yellow Sea

East China Sea

TAIWAN

PACIFIC OCEAN

South China Sea

0   100   200 mi

0   200 km

Initially, the North Korean forces, who were well supplied by the Soviets, penetrated deeply into the South, easily brushing aside both disorganized South Korean resistance and the first American units sent to Korea. Within three months, North Korea controlled 90 percent of the peninsula and was on the verge of bringing all Korea under communism. Only the small southeastern corner of the peninsula near Pusan remained under UN control.

MacArthur, however, reversed the situation by taking advantage of his superior air and naval power to launch an amphibious invasion behind North Korean lines at Inchon, a seaport halfway up the western coast of Korea. In that September 1950 attack, MacArthur cut the North Korean supply lines and began destroying the North Korean forces. Before long, the UN forces had pushed the Communists back across the 38th parallel and into the North, hoping to unify the peninsula under a non-Communist government. But MacArthur's success had an unexpected effect. In October Communist China sent 260,000 troops into North Korea to rescue the North's Communist government. The Chinese forces then pushed the UN forces reeling back down the peninsula past the 38th parallel. Soon, the two well-entrenched sides were fighting each other desperately for a few square miles of land. The Korean conflict had become a stalemate.

North Korea invades South Korea (June–September 1950)

UN forces counterattack (September–November 1950)

Chinese and North Korean troops push back UN troops (October 1950–January 1951)

Retreat of UN troops (November–December 1950)

CHINA

Farthest advance of UN forces (November 1950)

Pyongyang

NORTH KOREA

Armistice Line (July 1953)

38th parallel

Inchon

Seoul

Farthest advance of Communist forces (January 1951)

SOUTH KOREA

Farthest advance of North Korean forces (September 1950)

Pusan

JAPAN

▼ US radio-photo crew in the Korean War, 1951

Hawaii Calls

MacArthur—who later declared "In war there can be no substitute for victory"—argued for breaking the deadlock by expanding the war into China. He believed that victory in Korea would require full-scale war, including attacking military bases and supply lines in China with nuclear weapons if necessary. Truman, however, wanted only a limited war, one with a limited objective short of total victory over the enemy. Truman thought it more acceptable to restore the original boundary with North Korea and refused to expand the conflict into a war against China. One reason is that Truman feared that if the UN forces attacked China, the Soviets might enter the conflict, since Stalin and Mao Zedong had signed the Sino-Soviet Treaty. This fear was heightened by the fact the Soviets had successfully tested their own atomic bomb in 1949.

MacArthur disagreed publicly with the president's views and voiced his opposition to the press and to members of Congress. He stated that limited war was a mistake and was nothing more than appeasement. Despite repeated warnings, MacArthur continued to criticize Truman. In early April 1951, Truman fired MacArthur as commander.

Cease-fire talks began in July 1951; however, the fighting continued and the talks stalled. Campaigning for the presidency in 1952, Dwight Eisenhower pledged to go to Korea personally to end the war. Upon his election, Eisenhower did travel to Korea and revived the stalled talks. An armistice (cease-fire) was signed on July 27, 1953, which established a new boundary between North and South Korea near the 38th parallel. It also created a demilitarized zone (DMZ) between Communist North Korea and free South Korea. The boundary and the DMZ still exist today, and no peace treaty has formally been reached between the two sides. The United States continues to have over 20,000 troops permanently stationed in South Korea today to defend against another attack by North Korea.

It is estimated that three million people died in the Korean War, most of them civilians. Of the over 1.7 million American soldiers who served in the Korean War, more than 54,000 were killed and over 100,000 wounded.

▲ General Douglas MacArthur giving a speech at Soldier's Field, Chicago, Illinois, in 1951

▶ The Korean Demilitarized Zone (DMZ) between North and South Korea

## Frozen Chosin

The influx of Communist Chinese forces into the Korean War surprised MacArthur's army. The US 1st Marine Division, holding a position by the Chosin Reservoir not far from the Yalu River (the boundary between North Korea and China), was nearly surrounded by the oncoming Chinese. The division's only hope of escape was to break out to the south toward the seaport of Hungnam.

One colonel told his men, "All right, they're on our left, they're on our right, they're in front of us, they're behind us. . . . They can't get away this time." The commanding general of the division, Oliver P. Smith, denied that the action was a retreat. "We're just advancing in another direction," he said. The marines' escape involved combat just as fierce as any offensive operation.

Bitterly cold weather complicated the situation as weapons froze. Marines joked that Chosin rhymed with frozen, but the subzero temperatures were no laughing matter. Something as simple as tossing a grenade meant removing a glove and risking frostbite.

The breakout produced countless individual acts of bravery. One sergeant, his legs paralyzed from a bullet wound, died holding off the enemy on a hilltop for ten minutes so his comrades could escape. Others used shovels like baseball bats to return grenades that the enemy tossed at them. A private was being treated for severely frostbitten feet when he discovered his unit was in danger. Without hesitation, he ran toward his buddies, his feet leaving bloody footprints in the snow.

▲ The US 1st Marine Division breaking out from the Chosin Reservoir in North Korea

Fox Company, holding the heights of Toktong Pass south of the Chosin Reservoir, fought against overwhelming odds to keep the enemy from stopping the withdrawal. For five days, the company survived the waves of attacking Chinese soldiers. Of Fox Company's 240 men, 115 of them were killed or wounded, including all but one of its officers. Even when relief arrived, the rest of the unit stayed until the last truck was safely through Toktong Pass. The peak they defended was thereafter known as Fox Hill.

The withdrawal took fourteen days, and the Chinese contested almost every foot of the more than fifty miles from the reservoir to Hungnam. The marines suffered nearly 13,000 casualties from both battle and the bitter cold; the Chinese took even heavier losses—37,500 casualties.

---

### Comprehension Check 20.2

1. All of the following were features of the Cold War except the ____.
   - **A** confrontation between democracy and communism
   - **B** development of nuclear weapons
   - **C** forging of military alliances in both West and East
   - **D** restoration of democratic governments in Soviet Europe

2. Both the Truman Doctrine and the Marshall Plan ____.
   - **A** dictated a full-scale war in China and Korea
   - **B** promoted economic aid to help prevent the spread of communism
   - **C** supported East Berlin against German unification

3. The Berlin Airlift ____.
   - **A** dropped tons of supplies to counter a Soviet blockade
   - **B** removed a hydrogen bomb from detonating
   - **C** transported thousands of refugees to West Germany

**MAKING CONNECTIONS**

4. How did the results of the Korean War reflect the policy of containment?

**Life in Postwar America**

How did postwar prosperity change American society?

## An Affluent Society

The postwar era brought unprecedented economic prosperity for the United States. The biggest reason for the economic improvement was defense spending because of the Cold War. With Europe and Japan devastated by the war, America had little competition as a major supplier of industrial goods to the world. With newer industries (such as aerospace, electronics, and chemicals) and technological improvement in automation and computers, industry output jumped dramatically. Also, many American consumers, after sacrificing and saving during the war, went on a buying spree. People made money and spent it to improve their standard of living. They bought homes, automobiles, washing machines, refrigerators, and televisions. By the mid-1950s the number of Americans in the middle class was about twice as many as before World War II. Never before had Americans been so well off.

▲ (left) A comedian holding a wallet with four credit cards; (right) ad for the Buick Roadmaster

The economic growth altered American culture as well. Businesses carefully orchestrated the growing "consumer culture." Borrowing from the 1920s, advertisers influenced the public to forget the problems of the Depression and war years and to increase spending. Manufacturers continually offered different models and styles so that earlier models were outdated or out of style. Such "planned obsolescence," or purposely making items obsolete quickly, fueled the urge to buy. Marketing specialists appealed to self-gratification, social status, and materialism. In 1950, Diners Club released its first charge card, which an owner could use for dining out and pay the full balance by the end of the month. By the 1960s many Americans had either a Diners Club or American Express charge card, or the first modern credit cards, (which later were called Visa and MasterCard). Consumers, less thrifty and less concerned about debt, readily used their credit cards when they did not have the money. Shopping became a leisure activity for millions.

## Baby Boom

Postwar America witnessed enormous changes in the family. Young adults had postponed marriage and having children during the war, but with the prosperity of the '40s and '50s, more couples were having more children. Americans had one of the highest marriage rates in the world for the period 1944 to 1948. Many of the fifteen million returning soldiers became new fathers, contributing to the "**baby boom**," a massive rise in the birth rate lasting until 1964. Between 1945 and 1960 America's population increased by almost thirty percent.

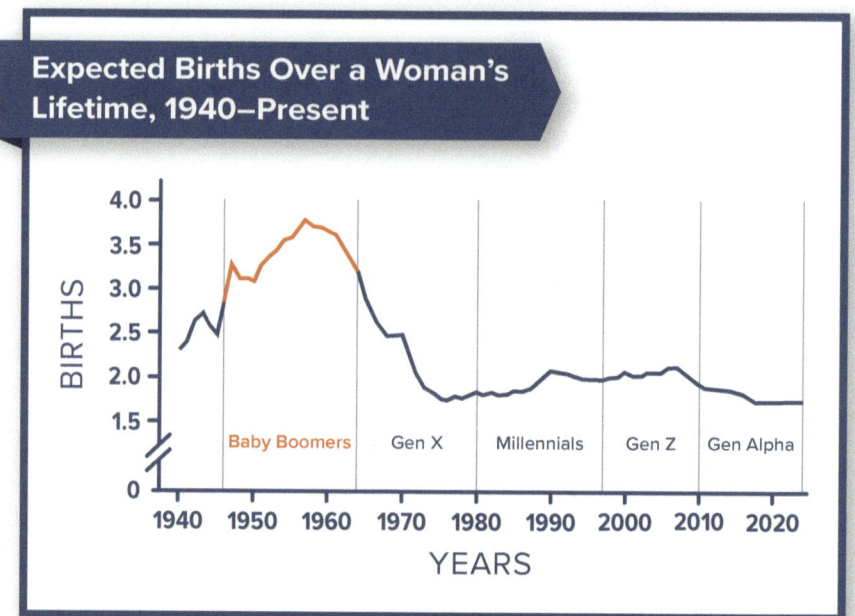

**Expected Births Over a Woman's Lifetime, 1940–Present**

## Suburbs

Thanks in part to the GI Bill, the number of homeowners in the United States increased significantly between 1945 and 1960. Architects such as William Levitt, creator of "Levittowns," constructed rows of identical, affordable houses on the edges of cities. As more Americans, mainly young white families, moved to the suburbs, retail activity in the postwar period shifted from downtown to suburban malls, and the number of malls mushroomed from eight in 1945 to almost four thousand by 1960.

▼ Postwar suburban neighborhood

## TV, Music, and Culture

Television replaced radio as the main medium of information and entertainment. By 1960, 90 percent of American homes had televisions. Many shows celebrated the American middle-class family. The Andersons of *Father Knows Best*, the Cleavers of *Leave It to Beaver*, and the Nelsons of *Ozzie and Harriet* were models of the ideal family, presided over by a patient and dutiful father.

Rock and roll music, which developed from earlier musical forms including gospel, blues, country, and jazz, exploded on the scene in the 1950s. Rock and roll appealed to American youth, and radio and television stations made celebrities of rock and roll singers such as Elvis Presley, Little Richard, and Buddy Holly. Businessmen capitalized on this new genre by selling transistor radios, phonographs, and records. Critics argued that rock and roll, with its suggestive lyrics and movements, led to the sexualization of youth culture and symbolized rebellion against the values of traditional American society. This music would become a driving force in the coming cultural revolution.

Mass media decreased regional differences as Americans throughout the country read, listened to, or watched the same materials, creating a nationally shared culture. However, many argued that music, television, movies, and magazines were often negative influences in society, driving consumers to mass conformity as they sought to imitate television figures. Ironically, the new media could also drive consumers to extreme individualism as many disconnected from family relationships and some replaced reality with fantasy. Rather than challenging Americans intellectually, the media usually focused on entertaining. Some blamed juvenile delinquency on rock and roll music, crime comic books, television, and movies such as *Rebel Without a Cause*, starring actor James Dean.

Two other factors contributed to changing family dynamics in the postwar era. Divorce rates climbed in 1946, leveled off for several years, and then increased substantially in the 1970s. With the increase in divorce, the number of single-parent heads of household rose dramatically. Although television showcased the image of the ideal housewife, some women, accustomed to work that had been encouraged during the war, continued to work, not only in traditionally female jobs but in male ones as well. By the 1960s, a large percentage of married women were in the work force.

▲ (top) The cast of the television sitcom "Leave It to Beaver"; (bottom) Elvis Presley in rehearsal for "The Ed Sullivan Show"

**Divorce Rate, 1940–80**

DIVORCE RATE (per 1000 married women)

YEAR

**Married Women in Workforce, 1940–80**

MARRIED WOMEN IN WORKFORCE (percentages)

YEAR

Source: pbs.org/fmc/book/2work8.htm

Americans displayed a renewed interest in religion after World War II. In 1952 Dwight Eisenhower promoted religion, stating, "Our form of government has no sense unless it is founded in a deeply felt religious faith, and I don't care what it is. With us, of course, it is the Judeo-Christian concept, but it must be a religion that all men are created equal." Congress, in 1954, added "under God" to the pledge of allegiance. The following year, President Eisenhower signed a law mandating that the phrase "In God We Trust," first appearing on coins during the Civil War, be printed on all paper currency. In 1956 the president signed a bill making the statement the national motto. However, these actions were not necessarily a sign that Americans were embracing orthodox Christian beliefs. In the Cold War period the nation was engaged in a bitter struggle with communism, which identified itself with atheism. Thus, these actions were motivated in part by a desire to contrast America's general religious values with those of the enemy.

Membership in religious groups rose significantly. The number of conservative Protestant Christians expanded through large local churches and other ministries in the 1940s and 1950s. Charles E. Fuller preached to millions on his popular "Old Fashioned Revival Hour" radio program. Youth rallies during the war led to the creation in 1944 of a large evangelistic outreach called Youth for Christ. **Billy Graham** was the first full-time evangelist of Youth for Christ and, in his own ministry, soon received national attention during his 1949 Los Angeles crusade and became the world's most prominent evangelist. He preached to millions in televised crusades that were conducted around the world. Roman Catholicism also grew; by 1960 Roman Catholics made up approximately a quarter of the American population.

▼ Billy Graham

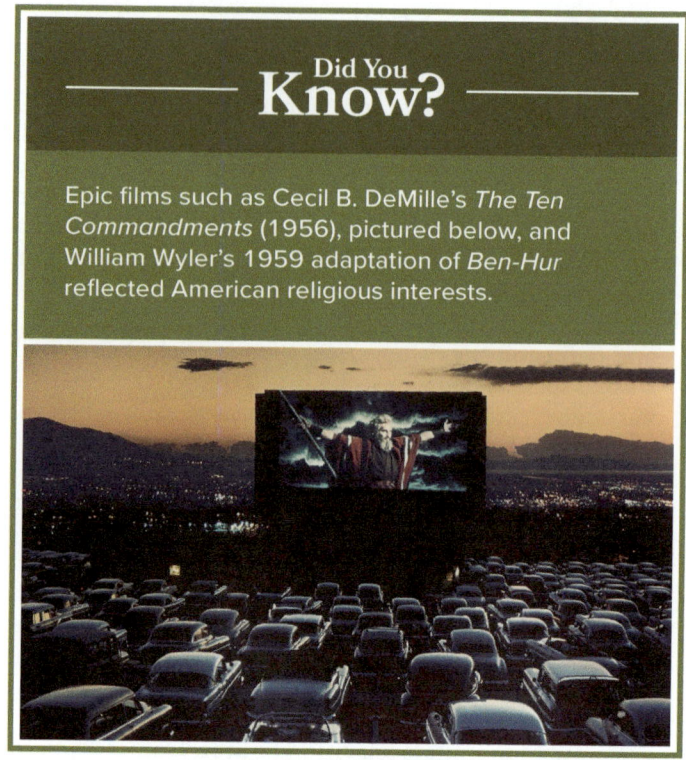

The ecumenical movement, promoting universal Christian unity, became popular during the postwar period. Its goal was to develop understanding and cooperation among Christian churches. Many supporters wanted to unite Christian denominations into a single church. Though that objective was not fully realized, some denominations with similar backgrounds united. American Methodists, for example, had healed their 1844 North-South split in 1939, and in 1968 they merged with the Evangelical United Brethren to form the United Methodist Church. Work toward greater cooperation was also facilitated by organizations like the National Council of Churches and the World Council of Churches. These groups—which included representatives from various denominations—met, dialoged, and often sought to reach agreement on debated issues. While they were able to resolve practical differences in this way, when it came to resolving theological differences the natural result was that these two organizations embraced liberal theology rather than fundamental Christian beliefs.

Evangelicals who upheld traditional biblical beliefs formed two factions. Some, who identified themselves as New Evangelicals, argued that in order to maintain cultural influence, they should seek to join and influence organizations and denominations that had embraced liberal theology. Others, who retained the name Fundamentalist, opposed this move, and responded that those who denied the fundamentals of the faith were not Christians. As the twentieth century progressed, the New Evangelicals became the largest religious group and eventually dropped "new" from their name. Though the evangelicals did not manage to take over the liberal mainline denominations, the liberal mainline withered nonetheless. And though evangelicals also never gained the cultural position once held by the mainline, they did come to gain political influence.

# Anticommunism in America

A growing fear of communism in the United States led to a second "Red Scare" after World War II. Many Americans suspected that there were Communist supporters in the US government, particularly in the State Department and the military. In 1947 President Truman instituted a loyalty review program to screen federal employees for Communist sympathies.

At the urging of FBI director J. Edgar Hoover, the House Committee on Un-American Activities (HCUA) conducted extensive investigations and held public congressional hearings about Communist activity in America. One hearing focused on the Hollywood film industry. When some Hollywood directors and screenwriters refused to cooperate with the committee or pled their Fifth Amendment right against self-incrimination, they, along with anyone who was suspected of Communist sympathies, were blacklisted, or kept from being hired on film projects.

One case of espionage involved Alger Hiss, a former State Department official. In 1948 Whittaker Chambers, a former Communist and Soviet spy, testified before the HCUA, accusing Hiss of passing secret documents to him ten years earlier. Hiss denied the accusation. Since the statute of limitations had expired (meaning the actions were too long ago to prosecute), Hiss could not be tried for espionage. But the court found him guilty of perjury, believing he lied under oath (about whether he had spied for the Soviets). The Hiss case elevated the political career of Congressman Richard Nixon, whose aggressive work eventually sent Hiss to jail.

Another case, in 1950, revealed the existence of a Communist spy ring in America. Through a British investigation, scientist Klaus Fuchs, who had been one of the developers of the atomic bomb, confessed that he was a Soviet spy. Using information gained from him, the FBI located other Soviet agents, including David Greenglass, who worked at the atomic bomb research center in Los Alamos, New Mexico. To save himself, Greenglass became a witness for the government and turned in his sister and brother-in-law, **Ethel and Julius Rosenberg**. Julius, a talented engineer, had held a civilian job with the US Army during World War II. He had secretly turned to communism and married Ethel who was also a Communist. In 1944 and 1945, Rosenberg, apparently with his wife's knowledge and support, helped funnel classified information concerning the atomic bomb to the Soviets. The Rosenbergs were arrested, tried, and convicted of espionage and were sentenced to death in the electric chair. They were executed in 1953.

In 1950 Congress also passed an act which made it easier for the government to combat espionage. One provision of this act required Communists and their organizations to register with the Justice Department.

In a 1951 speech, Senator **Joseph McCarthy** of Wisconsin declared boldly that the State Department had over two hundred Communists working there and claimed to have a list of their names. A Senate committee investigated his claims and concluded that his charges were "a fraud and a hoax." McCarthy continued his attacks, however, and he headed a Senate subcommittee that investigated the presence of Communists in the government and the military. Despite his investigations and well-publicized hearings, many of which were televised, the senator never found a single Communist in the government. By the end of 1954, McCarthy's charges had become increasingly irresponsible, and his Senate colleagues passed a vote of censure, or formal disapproval, against McCarthy. His opponents coined the word "McCarthyism," which became synonymous with "witch hunt," or attacking someone by distorting facts, casting unfounded suspicion, or making outright false accusations. McCarthy's reckless tactics set back the legitimate cause of those who were concerned about the threat of communism within the United States.

▲ (left) Senator Joseph McCarthy (standing) in the Senate hearings for the army; (right) news report of Julius and Ethel Rosenberg's sentencing for their role as Soviet spies

# America under Eisenhower

Truman, whose low popularity was due largely to the Korean War, declined to run for reelection in 1952. The Republicans chose war hero Dwight Eisenhower as their candidate. Eisenhower, considered a moderate Republican, balanced the ticket by choosing thirty-nine-year-old Senator Richard Nixon, a conservative, as his vice-presidential running mate. The Democrats nominated the governor of Illinois, Adlai Stevenson. An intellectual, Stevenson could not match the popularity and charm of Eisenhower, captured in the slogan "I like Ike" (a popular nickname for Eisenhower). Eisenhower promised to end corruption in Washington and the war in Korea. Elected in a landslide, Eisenhower was the first Republican president since Herbert Hoover.

The new president described his philosophy as "dynamic conservatism," calling himself "conservative when it comes to money and liberal when it comes to human beings." In 1954 his new budget cut expenditures by nearly ten percent as he sought to balance the budget. To the frustration of many conservative Republicans, however, Eisenhower supported expansion of Social Security to cover professionals, farm workers, armed services personnel, and other groups that had previously been excluded. He also supported an increase in the minimum wage, federal funds for education and public housing, and the creation of a new cabinet-level department—the Department of Health, Education, and Welfare (renamed Health and Human Services in 1979)—to coordinate federal social programs.

Eisenhower's presidency spanned the early years of the civil rights movement, in which black Americans pushed for equality (see Chapter 22). Eisenhower proved to be very popular with the American public and easily defeated Democratic candidate Adlai Stevenson again in the election of 1956.

In 1959 Congress admitted the forty-ninth and fiftieth states to the Union: Alaska and Hawaii. These two non-contiguous states (not physically connected to the other forty-eight on the North American continent) greatly added to the cultural diversity of the nation.

▲ President Dwight D. Eisenhower with Vice President Richard Nixon

## Seaways and Highways

In 1954 Canada and the United States undertook a joint project to create the St. Lawrence Seaway, which deepened the St. Lawrence River and created locks and dams where necessary. The seaway allowed modern oceangoing vessels to sail from the Atlantic Ocean to the Great Lakes and provided hydroelectric power to the region, benefiting the economies of both nations.

Eisenhower was convinced of the need for better highways across the United States to handle increased vehicle traffic as well as for national defense purposes. He recommended the construction of an **interstate highway system**, a national system of limited-access highways, or "interstates." The Interstate Highway Act of 1956 committed the federal government to pay most of the cost of construction of the highway system, with the states paying the remainder. These interstates became the main arteries of highway transportation in the United States.

▼ US interstate highway in the 1950s

## Cold War Continues

In foreign policy, Eisenhower faced a different kind of tyranny than the fascism he had fought against in World War II. Communism was still expanding, this time into Southeast Asia and Cuba (see Chapter 21), and Cold War conflicts with the Soviet Union continued in Europe. In 1954 the Southeast Asia Treaty Organization (SEATO) was created. This defensive alliance, similar to NATO in Europe, included the United States, Great Britain, France, New Zealand, Australia, the Philippines, Thailand, and Pakistan, with the purpose of protecting Southeast Asia from Communist expansion.

Eisenhower sought to balance the need for both military and economic strength. He said that nuclear weapons provided the best deterrence to war, and a strong nuclear capability would also be less expensive than a conventional force (an army, navy, and air force with non-nuclear weapons) large enough to counter communism. Therefore, Eisenhower devoted the military budget to building long-range strategic bombers, land-based intercontinental ballistic missiles (ICBMs), and submarines—all of which could deliver nuclear warheads. The American stockpile of nuclear bombs increased from 1,000 in 1953 to around 18,000 in 1961, and an arms race developed as the Soviets increased their nuclear capability too. Eisenhower also used the CIA to conduct covert (secret) operations in foreign countries to undermine Communist governments.

### SOVIET UNION

In the Soviet Union, Joseph Stalin died in 1953, triggering a power struggle, and by 1956 **Nikita Khrushchev** emerged as the new Communist leader. While Khrushchev indicated a softening of Stalin's harsh policies, not all his changes were positive, as he launched a campaign against religion in the Soviet Union, enforcing state-sponsored atheism throughout the USSR by ordering the mass closing of churches and restricting the rights of parents to teach religion to their children.

In international affairs, Khrushchev expressed the idea of "peaceful coexistence," the belief that Communist and democratic nations could exist side by side without constant threat of conflict. While there were continued "hot spots" during the Cold War, there were attempts by the Soviets and Americans to improve relations. In September 1959 Khrushchev became the first Soviet leader to visit the United States.

### EUROPE

Most people in the Soviet satellites were not happy under Communist rule. In June 1953 workers in East Berlin began protesting. As discontent spread, more than one million people joined demonstrations throughout East Germany. Soviet troops crushed the protest in East Berlin, killing about one hundred Germans. Fear of further Soviet reprisals ended the remaining protests in the country.

On October 23, 1956, in Budapest, Hungary, approximately 20,000 people gathered to protest the Soviet-controlled government, and soon the crowd grew to over 200,000. The protest quickly became a revolution. Using shortwave radio broadcasts, the rebels pled for help from the West, but none came. The USSR sent troops and tanks to Hungary to crush the revolt. The Hungarian rebels were no match for the powerful Soviet forces, and they suffered over 20,000 casualties, including 2,500 deaths. Thousands more were imprisoned, and almost 200,000 fled the nation before the Communist government sealed the borders to prevent others from leaving. The United Nations condemned the Soviets' invasion of Hungary but took no real action, leaving the Soviets free to ruthlessly crush the revolution with no fear of interference by the free world.

▲ (top) Intercontinental ballistic missile (ICBM) at Cape Canaveral, Florida, 1959; (bottom) protest in East Berlin, 1953

The Postwar Era   **543**

## U-2 INCIDENT

An incident in 1960, the last year of Eisenhower's presidency, threatened US-Soviet relations. A Four Powers summit meeting between the United States, Britain, France, and the USSR was scheduled to take place in May. However, on May 1, just two weeks before the summit was to begin, the Soviets shot down an American U-2 spy plane, piloted by Francis Gary Powers, over Soviet territory. Powers parachuted out and was quickly captured by Soviet troops. Not knowing that Powers had survived, American officials tried to cover up the story by saying that the plane was a NASA weather research aircraft that had experienced a malfunction. Khrushchev then revealed that the Soviets had captured Powers and that most of the camera equipment from the U-2 had survived, exposing the attempted American cover-up.

Powers was tried and convicted of spying and was sentenced to three years in a Soviet prison and seven years of hard labor. However, in 1962 he was exchanged in a prisoner swap for a Soviet spy. The U-2 incident hurt US-Soviet relations. The Four Powers summit was cut short by Khrushchev over the incident, and the Soviet leader canceled a prior invitation for Eisenhower to visit the Soviet Union.

▼ Francis Gary Powers, US pilot, with his U-2 reconnaissance plane

# CHAPTER 20 REVIEW

## Chapter Summary

### 20.1 The Postwar Era

- After World War II the GI Bill helped returning veterans with tuition grants, job training, and home loans. Truman's domestic program, the Fair Deal, called for an expansion of New Deal programs, but Congress did not pass most of his proposals until after the election of 1948. Republicans in Congress passed the Taft-Hartley Act, which weakened the power of unions, and the National Security Act, which replaced the secretary of war with a civilian secretary of defense and established the CIA. Despite a three-way division of the Democratic Party, Truman won the election of 1948.

- The Nuremberg Trials were held to bring Nazi war criminals to justice, and similar proceedings were held in Japan. The United Nations was formed in 1945 to further world peace. The United States helped rebuild Japan and created a new Japanese constitution with a democratic government. Germany and its capital, Berlin, were divided into zones of occupation. Instead of supporting free elections in Soviet-occupied nations, Stalin established pro-Soviet governments throughout Eastern Europe.

**TERMS**

GI Bill
Fair Deal
Taft-Hartley Act
Central Intelligence Agency (CIA)
Twenty-Second Amendment
Nuremberg Trials
United Nations

### 20.2 The Cold War Begins

**TERMS**

Cold War
iron curtain
containment
Truman Doctrine
Marshall Plan
Berlin airlift
North Atlantic Treaty Organization (NATO)
Warsaw Pact
Chiang Kai-shek
Mao Zedong
Korean War

- After World War II, the Cold War began between the United States and its allies and the Soviet Union and its allies. Truman promoted a policy of containment to keep communism from spreading beyond its existing boundaries, and his Truman Doctrine supported pro-Western governments with money and other assistance. The Marshall Plan helped European countries rebuild in an effort to prevent communism from spreading. Fearing a reunified Germany, the Soviets blockaded West Berlin. The Berlin airlift supplied the people there until the blockade was lifted. The Western nations formed the NATO military alliance, and the Soviets countered with the Warsaw Pact.

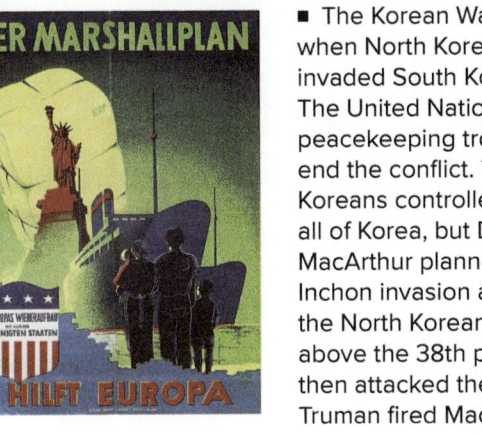

- The US-supported Nationalists in China lost the civil war against the Communists and fled to Taiwan.

- The Korean War began when North Korean troops invaded South Korea. The United Nations sent peacekeeping troops to end the conflict. The North Koreans controlled nearly all of Korea, but Douglas MacArthur planned the Inchon invasion and drove the North Koreans back above the 38th parallel. China then attacked the UN forces. Truman fired MacArthur over a disagreement about whether to attack China. The war ended with a cease-fire agreement in 1953.

## *Chapter Summary*

### 20.3 / Life in Postwar America

- The postwar years brought economic prosperity for most Americans, and the nation experienced a baby boom. Television and music reflected both traditional family values and rebellion against those values. There was a renewed interest in religion. Evangelistic programs and crusades led many to faith. The ecumenical movement encouraged universal Christian unity but embraced liberal theology rather than fundamental Christian beliefs.

- A fear of spreading communism within the United States led to Congressional investigations of Communist activity. Some Americans were found guilty of spying for the Soviets. Senator Joseph McCarthy conducted investigations which often featured false accusations and distorted facts, hurting the cause of anti-Communism in the nation.

- Republican Dwight Eisenhower was elected president in 1952. He was conservative with money but liberal in social programs. He recommended construction of the St. Lawrence Seaway and the interstate highway system. He built up America's nuclear capability to deter war. Cold War conflicts continued. US-Soviet relations were hurt when an American spy plane was shot down over Soviet territory.

### TERMS

baby boom

Billy Graham

Ethel and Julius Rosenberg

Joseph McCarthy

interstate highway system

Nikita Khrushchev

## *Chapter Review Questions*

### RECALL

1. What was Truman's legislative agenda called?

2. What amendment prohibited a president from being elected more than two times?

3. What was the period of tension and intense competition between the United States and its allies and the Soviet Union and its allies called?

4. What phrase did Winston Churchill use to describe the division in Europe between the Communist East and the free West?

5. What was the term for countries who were not aligned with either the East or the West?

6. What military alliance of Western nations was created in 1949? What alliance of Communist nations was created in reaction to this?

7. After UN forces drove the North Korean army north of the 38th parallel after the Inchon invasion, what country attacked the UN forces?

8. Who was the world's most prominent evangelist, whose first crusade was in 1949?

9. What married couple was executed for espionage in 1953?

10. What two states were added to the Union in 1959?

### UNDERSTAND

11. How did the GI Bill help World War II veterans? How were black veterans denied some benefits?

12. What was the purpose of the Taft-Hartley Act? What were its three provisions?

13. What changes were made by the National Security Act in 1947?

14. What groups split from the Democratic Party before the election of 1948 and who were their candidates? Who was the Republican candidate? Who won the election?

15. What was the purpose of the Nuremberg Trials?

16. What was the purpose of the United Nations? What is the UN General Assembly?

17. Who comprises the UN Security Council? What power do permanent members have?

18. How did the United States help Japan after World War II? What changes were made to the Japanese government and military?

19. What was Europe like after the war? How was Germany divided? How did Stalin break the promise he had made at Yalta?

20. What did Truman's policy of containment mean? How did the Truman Doctrine attempt to contain communism?

21. What did the Marshall Plan do for Europe, and how did it relate to containment?

22. Why did the Soviets blockade West Berlin? What difficult decision did Truman have to make? What solution did Truman use to break the blockade?

23. Who won the Chinese civil war? Where did the losing side go?

24. What caused the Korean War? What organization led the effort to defend South Korea?

25. What was the significance of General MacArthur's Inchon invasion?

26. What was the disagreement between Truman and MacArthur during the Korean War? Why did Truman fire MacArthur?

27. How did the Korean War end? What is the status of the two Koreas today?

28. What were three causes of the economic growth in America in the postwar years?

29. What did Eisenhower mean by "dynamic conservatism"? How was that reflected in his policies?

30. Why did Eisenhower favor building America's nuclear weapons capability? What actions did he take to accomplish this?

31. What did Khrushchev mean by "peaceful coexistence"? What actions did the Soviets take in East Berlin and Hungary against protestors?

32. What was the U-2 spy plane incident? How did the United States and the Soviet Union respond? How did it affect US-Soviet relations?

## THINK ABOUT IT

33. Choose two changes to American society during the postwar years and evaluate the positive and negative effects of those changes.

34. What did Joseph McCarthy claim about the US government? What was "McCarthyism"? How did McCarthyism relate to the core value of justice?

◄ Private G. David Schine (left) of the US Army at a McCarthy hearing in 1954, while Senator McCarthy (center), with his counsel Roy Cohn (right), holds up a transcript of one of Schine's phone calls

# 21 Struggles of the Sixties

**21.1 The Kennedy Years**

**21.2 The Johnson Administration**

**21.3 The Vietnam War Era**

▲ Antiwar protesters at the US Capitol, May 1971

The period from 1960 to the early 1970s was one of the most tumultuous in American history. Cold War tensions in Cuba, Europe, and Southeast Asia drew the United States into conflicts over communism. Domestic issues, including the assassinations of important leaders, the fight for civil rights (discussed in more detail in Chapter 22), and conflicts over America's involvement overseas showed that Americans were deeply divided over important questions.

## 21.1 The Kennedy Years

How did America almost get involved in nuclear war with Cuba?

### GUIDING QUESTIONS

- What was Kennedy's domestic agenda?
- How did Kennedy's policies toward Cuba affect Soviet-American relations?
- What was the significance of the Berlin Wall?

### Domestic Affairs

#### Election of 1960

In the election of 1960, Eisenhower's vice president, Richard Nixon, was the Republican nominee. The Democrats chose forty-three-year-old Massachusetts senator **John F. Kennedy (JFK)** as their candidate. Long-time Texas senator Lyndon B. Johnson was chosen as his vice-presidential running mate to appeal to southern Democrats. Kennedy's Catholic faith was an issue in the election, but he confronted concerns openly by stating that he believed in the absolute separation of church and state and that no Roman Catholic church official would influence his actions if he were elected.

Television played an important role in the presidential campaign, as both sides spent millions of dollars on TV advertisements. The 1960 election was also the first to feature televised debates. In the first debate, JFK came across as youthful, handsome, and charming, while Nixon, who was suffering from the flu and had recently been hospitalized, appeared pale and tired. A poll of those who listened to the debate on the radio felt Nixon did slightly better than Kennedy, but those who watched the debate on television overwhelmingly thought Kennedy won the debate.

▲ John F. Kennedy

▲ The live televised debate between Richard Nixon and John F. Kennedy

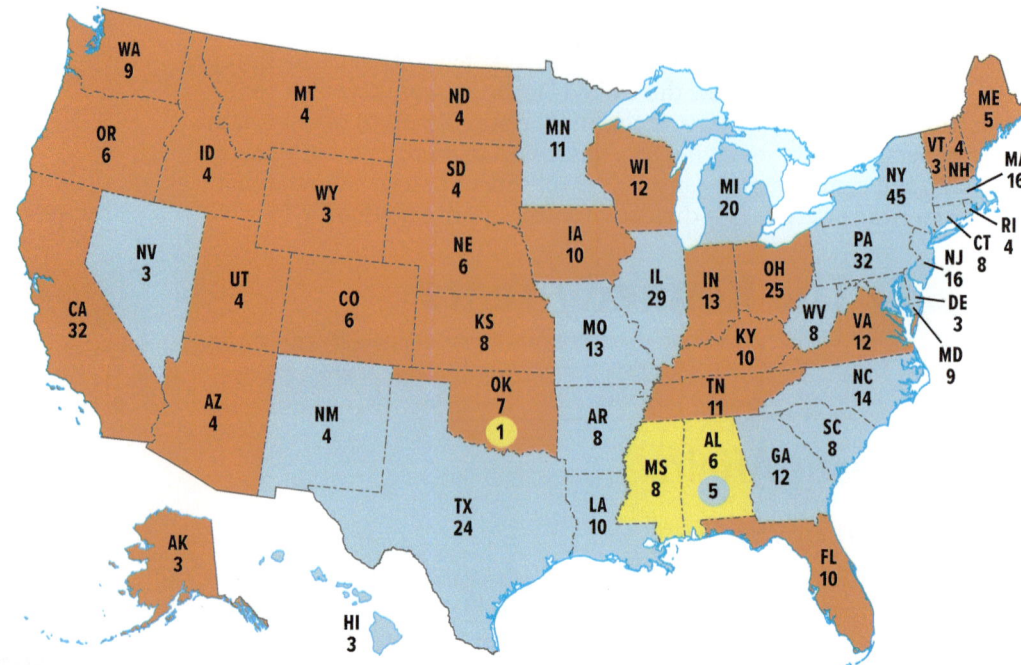

John F. Kennedy (D)
Electoral: 303
Popular: 34,227,096

Richard M. Nixon (R)
Electoral: 219
Popular: 34,107,646

Harry F. Byrd (D)
Electoral: 15
Popular: 116,248

▲ President Kennedy with his wife Jacqueline and children John Jr. and Caroline

Kennedy won the electoral vote 303 to 219, but the popular vote was much closer, 49.7 percent to 49.5 percent, a margin of only 118,574 votes out of more than 68 million cast. Kennedy seemed to embody a dramatic change in government. People admired the handsome, articulate Kennedy, his lovely wife, Jacqueline (Jackie), and their two young children. Kennedy himself proclaimed a change in emphasis. In his inaugural speech the president said, "Let the word go forth from this time and place . . . that the torch has been passed to a new generation of Americans." He went on to tell the people that they needed to take a more active role in making America better, saying, "Ask not what your country can do for you—ask what you can do for your country."

## The New Frontier

In his speech upon acceptance of the Democratic nomination, Kennedy had said,

> We stand today on the edge of a New Frontier—the fronter of the 1960s— a frontier of unknown opportunities and perils, a frontier of unfilled hopes and threats. . . . Beyond that frontier are the uncharted areas of science and space, unsolved problems of peace and war, unconquered pockets of ignorance and prejudice, unanswered questions of poverty and surplus. . . . I am asking each of you to be pioneers on that New Frontier.

To address the challenges and opportunities of the decade, Kennedy proposed economic aid to poor areas, medical insurance for the elderly, civil rights legislation (see Chapter 22), and federal financial aid for higher education. He also proposed an ambitious space program, pledging to put a man on the moon by the end of the decade (discussed later in this chapter).

The economy had entered a recession by the end of the 1950s. To stimulate the economy, Kennedy persuaded the Democrat-controlled Congress to increase spending on public works, housing, the military, and the space program. Congress also agreed to financial aid for distressed areas, an increase in Social Security benefits, and an increase of the minimum wage. Believing that boosting prosperity would help eliminate some social problems, Kennedy pushed Congress to pass the Trade Expansion Act to stimulate trade with several European nations and to pass significant tax cuts and tax credits for businesses.

Liberal Democrats criticized Kennedy for failing to get passage of the more ambitious parts of his program in education, healthcare, and civil rights. However, Kennedy believed that his narrow victory over Nixon dictated caution in the White House, and he also had to work with southern Democrats in Congress who opposed those parts of his program.

Another distraction to Kennedy's domestic agenda was his focus on foreign affairs. One of Kennedy's most popular programs, the **Peace Corps** was a government project designed to send skilled volunteers overseas to help under-developed nations. Kennedy also initiated the Alliance for Progress in 1961 to thwart the threat of communism in Latin America. Through the Alliance, the United States granted economic aid to strengthen economic cooperation between North and South America. The program aimed at increasing the income of Latin Americans, decreasing illiteracy, establishing democratic governments, and avoiding extremes of inflation and deflation. Although some of the economic goals were reached in some countries, the program failed to prevent the establishment of dictatorships in about a dozen governments.

▲ A Peace Corps worker helping to build a house in Sierra Leone, Africa

▲ Fidel Castro

▲ Bay of Pigs invaders captured by Cuban forces

## Cuba

Cuba had gained its independence after the Spanish-American War (see Chapter 14), but the United States periodically intervened in its affairs. In 1959 **Fidel Castro** overthrew Fulgencio Batista, the corrupt dictator of Cuba. Many hoped that conditions within Cuba would improve; instead, they soon worsened. Castro proved to be another cruel dictator. He refused to allow elections, imprisoned or executed opponents, and placed restrictions on the press. Castro, who resented American interference in Cuba, began confiscating foreign-owned property and signed a trade agreement with the Soviet Union. Instead of installing the democratic government that many Cubans had anticipated, he announced he was Communist and established a totalitarian government. Many Cubans fled to Florida, only ninety miles away, by any means possible to escape Castro's harsh regime.

In response to Castro's actions, President Eisenhower restricted trade with Cuba, broke diplomatic relations with the nation, and secretly authorized the CIA to plan an attack to overthrow Castro. The CIA project culminated during the Kennedy administration when some 1,400 Cuban exiles invaded their homeland. Assisted by the CIA, they landed at the **Bay of Pigs** on April 17, 1961. The operation was a disaster. Castro had learned of the "secret" attack and had begun preparing his troops for it. When some of the invading ships ran aground on coral reefs and it appeared that the invasion would fail, Kennedy canceled air force support for the attack. An anticipated civilian and military uprising against Castro never occurred. Within two days, almost all the invaders were killed or captured. The incident was a great embarrassment for Kennedy, who had been president for only three months.

An even more dramatic confrontation with the Soviets over Cuba occurred the next year. The Soviets, concerned that America had supported the plan to overthrow Castro, began secretly installing missiles in Cuba that could carry nuclear warheads and reach the United States within minutes. On October 22, 1962, after American spy planes confirmed that missile sites were under construction, President Kennedy described the situation to Americans in a televised speech. He demanded that the Soviets dismantle the sites immediately, and then he established a naval blockade around the island to prevent the delivery of any more missiles. Kennedy also stated that any missile attack from Cuba would result in the United States launching a full-scale nuclear attack on the Soviet Union.

Soviet leader Khrushchev denounced the blockade as illegal and said his ships would not stop for it. Both sides placed their military forces on high alert. For several days the world faced the possibility of nuclear war in what became known as the **Cuban missile crisis**. The crisis ended when, through secret negotiations, Khrushchev agreed to remove the missiles in exchange for Kennedy's public promise not to invade Cuba. In addition, the president privately pledged to remove American missiles from Turkey, near the Russian border.

In the wake of the Cuban missile crisis, the United States and the Soviet Union established a "hot line," a means of communication for sending urgent messages between the two nations, in hopes of easing tensions and averting future crises.

▼ (top) Map showing distances from Cuban missile sites to American cities; (bottom) US spy plane image of a Cuban missile site, October 1962

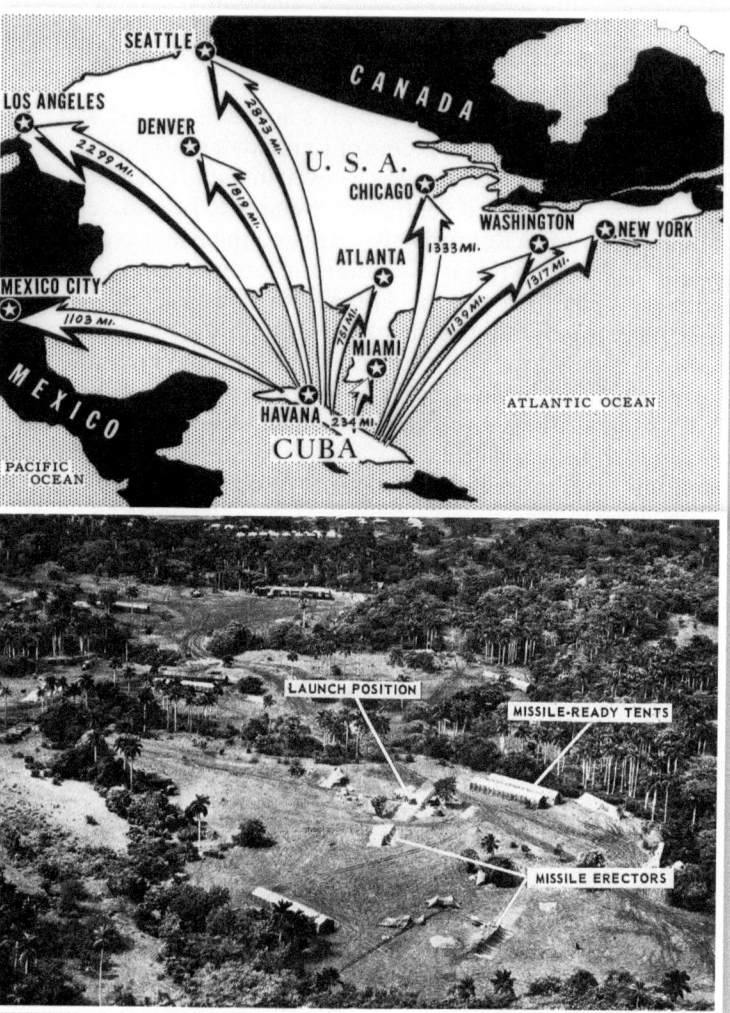

## The Berlin Wall

West Berlin had become a "showcase of democracy" and a haven for refugees fleeing from East Germany. By 1961 almost three million East Germans (nearly 15 percent of the population) had fled communism by crossing into West Berlin. Most of those who departed East Germany were under age forty-five. Such a loss of workers dramatically weakened the nation's economy.

In June 1961 Khrushchev and Kennedy held a summit in Vienna, Austria. Khrushchev wanted Britain, France, and the United States to withdraw their troops from West Berlin. Kennedy, fearing this would lead to a Communist takeover of the city, refused. The Soviet leader then threatened to restrict access to West Berlin, just as Stalin had done in 1948.

◄ President Kennedy and Soviet leader Nikita Khrushchev meeting in Vienna, Austria

In August 1961 the Communists began erecting the **Berlin Wall**, which prevented movement between the two parts of the city. Soon, the wall was topped with barbed wire and accompanied by guard towers and minefields. The wall made it nearly impossible for East Germans to escape to West Berlin (though some succeeded, many others died in the attempt), but it also demonstrated the failure of communism—an immense barrier had to be constructed to keep people from leaving.

In 1963 President Kennedy visited West Berlin. In his speech there, he said:

▲ The Berlin Wall

> *There are many people in the world who really don't understand . . . what is the great issue between the free world and the Communist world. Let them come to Berlin. There are some who say that communism is the wave of the future. Let them come to Berlin. . . .*
>
> *Freedom has many difficulties and democracy is not perfect, but we have never had to put a wall up to keep our people in, to prevent them from leaving us. . . . While the wall is the most obvious and vivid demonstration of the failures of the Communist system, for all the world to see, we take no satisfaction in it, for it is . . . an offense not only against history but an offense against humanity, separating families, dividing husbands and wives and brothers and sisters, and dividing a people who wish to be joined together. . . .*
>
> *All free men, wherever they may live, are citizens of Berlin, and, therefore, as a free man, I take pride in the words "Ich bin ein Berliner (I am a Berliner)."* —JOHN F. KENNEDY

## Analyzing Sources

What does Kennedy mean by saying that he is a Berliner?

## Kennedy's Assassination

On November 22, 1963, President Kennedy and his wife, Jackie, were in a motorcade in Dallas, Texas. As the president's convertible limousine drove through the city streets, **Lee Harvey Oswald** fired three shots from the sixth floor of a nearby building, killing the forty-six-year-old president. Texas governor John Connelly was also shot but survived. Vice President Lyndon Johnson, who had been in a separate car, took the presidential oath of office the same day aboard the airplane that returned the president's body to Washington, DC. Only two days later, Oswald was gunned down by Dallas nightclub owner Jack Ruby as the assassin was being transferred from the Dallas police headquarters to the county jail. While many theories have been suggested, no clear motivation for Kennedy's assassination has been proven. The government's 1964 Warren Commission investigation concluded that Oswald acted alone and that he was not part of a larger conspiracy to kill the president.

▼ (top) President and Mrs. Kennedy in the motorcade in Dallas moments before his assassination, November 22, 1963; (bottom left) Kennedy assassin Lee Harvey Oswald being approached by Jack Ruby, who shot and killed Oswald as he was being escorted from the Dallas police headquarters; (bottom right) Lyndon B. Johnson taking the presidential oath of office aboard Air Force One shortly after Kennedy's death

## Twenty-Fifth Amendment

The Constitution states "In case of the removal of the President from office, or his death, resignation, or inability to discharge the powers and duties of the said office, the same shall devolve on the Vice President" (Article II, Section 1, Clause 6). This provision did not make clear whether the vice president *became* the president in those circumstances or merely assumed the powers and duties of the president. It also did not make clear what defined inability. This issue has come up a number of times in American history: for example, four presidents have died in office and four have been assassinated, leaving the vice president to assume the presidency. Others were incapacitated for a time because of surgery or another medical condition (such as Woodrow Wilson after his stroke).

After JKF's assassination, Congress proposed an amendment to clarify the procedure. The Twenty-Fifth Amendment was ratified in 1967. In four sections it states:

> Section 1: In case of the removal of the President from office or of his death or resignation, the Vice President shall become President.
>
> Section 2: Whenever there is a vacancy in the office of the Vice President, the President shall nominate a Vice President who shall take office upon confirmation by a majority vote of both Houses of Congress.
>
> Section 3: Whenever the President transmits to the President pro tempore of the Senate and the Speaker of the House of Representatives his written declaration that he is unable to discharge the powers and duties of his office, and until he transmits to them a written declaration to the contrary, such powers and duties shall be discharged by the Vice President as Acting President.
>
> Section 4: Whenever the Vice President and a majority of either the principal officers of the executive departments or of such other body as Congress may by law provide, transmit to the President pro tempore of the Senate and the Speaker of the House of Representatives their written declaration that the President is unable to discharge the powers and duties of his office, the Vice President shall immediately assume the powers and duties of the office as Acting President. . . .

▲ The presidential coat of arms, a symbol of the presidency itself, was included on the reverse of the half dollar, redesigned in 1964, to commemorate the late President Kennedy.

## Comprehension Check 21.1

1. The Peace Corps was an organization in which volunteers ____.
   A helped underdeveloped nations overseas
   B protested Kennedy's actions in Cuba
   C advocated for a unified Berlin

2. Soviet actions during Kennedy's administration include the following except ____.
   A building the Berlin Wall
   B secretly negotiating the removal of missiles from Cuba
   C overthrowing Fidel Castro's regime

3. Kennedy was assassinated by ____.
   A John Connelly
   B Lee Harvey Oswald
   C Jack Ruby

**MAKING CONNECTIONS**

4. What was the intention of the Bay of Pigs invasion, and what was one reason it failed?

5. How did Kennedy respond to the presence of missiles in Cuba, and what was established after the end of the crisis?

### 21.2 **The Johnson Administration**

Who won the space race?

## The Great Society

### War on Poverty

**Lyndon B. Johnson** of Texas was well prepared for political leadership. He had spent twelve years in the Senate, including five years as majority leader. In his first State of the Union message in 1964, Johnson declared a "War on Poverty," stating "Our aim is not only to relieve the symptom of poverty, but to cure it and, above all, to prevent it." The "**Great Society**" was his legislative program aiming to end poverty and inequality and help all citizens gain the opportunity to better themselves politically, socially, and economically.

Congress passed the Economic Opportunity Act of 1964, which created the Office of Economic Opportunity (OEO). At the signing of the act, Johnson explained that his goal was to help people become self-sufficient and not dependent on the government, stating, "We are not content to accept the endless growth of relief rolls or welfare rolls. We want to offer the forgotten fifth of our people opportunity and not doles (handouts)." Through the OEO, the government attacked poverty through job-training and job-placement programs, such as the Job Corps and Neighborhood Youth Corps. A domestic version of the Peace Corps called Volunteers in Service to America (VISTA) helped the poor in areas throughout the United States through educational and social services. The OEO also began Project Head Start, a comprehensive preschool program for children in poor families.

▲ Johnson giving his 1964 "War on Poverty" speech before Congress

### 1964 Election

In 1964 Johnson ran against the Republican nominee, Senator Barry Goldwater of Arizona. Goldwater and Johnson advocated opposing philosophies of government. The Arizona senator believed that the nation would benefit from less government activity and regulation and opposed legislation that gave the federal government what he viewed as too much power. Johnson, on the other hand, supported a more active government to help those in need and favored more regulation.

Goldwater's campaign suffered because he often failed to understand his audience. For example, he denounced the Social Security system in front of senior citizens in Florida and suggested in a speech in Knoxville, Tennessee, that the government sell the Tennessee Valley Authority. Black Americans objected to Goldwater's vote against the Civil Rights Act of 1964 (see Chapter 22), and Goldwater alarmed many voters by his statements about how he would conduct Cold War conflicts, including the possible use of nuclear weapons. On Election Day, Johnson scored an overwhelming victory with 61 percent of the vote. He garnered 486 electoral votes to only 52 for Goldwater.

### A Flood of Legislation

The 1964 elections also gave the Democrats huge majorities in Congress. In 1965 Johnson used his victory and Democratic majorities to push eighty-nine bills through the legislature. On the first day of the session, Johnson delivered the first televised evening State of the Union address, calling attention once again to his vision for America. "The Great Society asks not how much, but how good; not only how to create wealth but how to use it; not only how fast we are going, but where we are headed."

### Did You Know?

Johnson's campaign used Goldwater's reputation to run negative TV ads, including one showing a little girl in a field plucking petals from a daisy, while a voice-over gave a countdown, which was followed by a photo of a nuclear explosion.

In this first wave of legislation, two influential education bills were signed. Johnson signed the Elementary and Secondary Education Act, which provided funding for schools with students from low-income families and for educational materials and other educational programs. Congress also passed the Higher Education Act providing federal aid for educational institutions as well as aid for middle- or low-income students seeking higher education.

Congress also passed bills seeking to improve cities and the environment. One act created the Department of Housing and Urban Development (HUD). Johnson appointed Robert Weaver, the first African American cabinet member, as secretary. Through additional legislation, federal funding for public housing and urban renewal was increased. The Water Quality Act sought to fight pollution by improving and enforcing standards for water quality.

Two government health insurance programs were established in 1965 to help people pay for medical care. **Medicare** was designed to ensure that the nation's elderly, those 65 or older, would be able to afford proper medical treatment (later the program included those younger than 65 with disabilities). The federal government pays for this program through taxes. **Medicaid** was designed to provide health care for low-income citizens of all ages. It is state-administered with federal regulation and partial federal funding.

How effective was Johnson's War on Poverty? Supporters point out that poverty rates declined from 19 percent in 1964 to 11 percent in 1973, lifting millions of Americans out of poverty. Critics respond that the poverty rate, which was 32 percent in 1950, had already been falling rapidly before the War on Poverty, and contrary to Johnson's hope that his policies would lead to greater self-sufficiency, the poverty rate continues to be around 13 percent despite increased government spending on welfare programs. They express concerns that some recipients of aid have become dependent on the government.

## Supreme Court

Led by Chief Justice **Earl Warren**, the Supreme Court, known as the Warren Court from 1953 to 1969, pursued a policy of judicial activism, interpreting the law and the Constitution broadly to address what the judges perceived as major social problems.

Not all of the justices agreed with the court's practice. In a dissenting opinion in 1964, Justice John Harlan warned:

> The Constitution is not a panacea [cure] for every blot upon the public welfare, nor should this Court, ordained as a judicial body, be thought of as a general haven for reform movements. . . . This Court . . . does not serve its high purpose when it exceeds its authority, even to satisfy justified impatience with the slow workings of the political process.

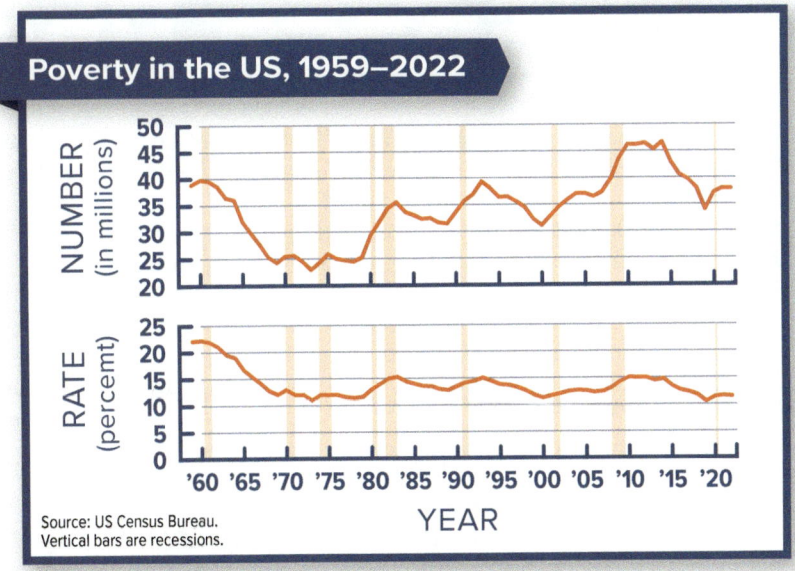

**Poverty in the US, 1959–2022**

Source: US Census Bureau.
Vertical bars are recessions.

▼ Chief Justice Earl Warren

## The Warren Court

The Warren Court is probably best known for its civil rights decisions. In *Brown v. Board of Education of Topeka, Kansas* (1954), the court ordered an end to segregated schools (see Chapter 22). Many who favored the court's decision pointed to its protection of minority rights. The court also ruled in favor of greater protection for accused criminals in cases such as *Gideon v. Wainwright* (1963), which determined that the state must provide an attorney for defendants who could not afford one. Both *Brown* and *Gideon* overturned previous Supreme Court rulings. Additionally, in *Miranda v. Arizona* (1966), the court ruled that criminal suspects must be informed of their constitutional rights before they may be questioned, resulting in tighter restrictions on law enforcement officials.

By 1964 certain states had repeatedly failed to redraw legislative districts after each census. The Supreme Court ordered the redrawing of legislative districts according to population in a series of "one man, one vote" decisions. In these cases, the justices ruled that districts that were unequal in population violated the guarantees for "equal protection of the law" in the Fourteenth Amendment. The court eventually extended the "one man, one vote" principle to city councils and local school boards. In *Engel v. Vitale* (1962), the court banned state-sponsored voluntary prayers in public schools as an alleged violation of the Establishment Clause of the First Amendment. In *Roth v. United States* (1957) the Supreme Court ruled that obscenity was not protected by the First Amendment's guarantee of freedom of speech, but it defined *obscenity* so narrowly that the decision actually struck down many obscenity laws.

# The Space Race

Americans were shocked when they learned that on October 4, 1957, the Soviets successfully launched Sputnik I, the first man-made satellite in space. It orbited the earth at 18,000 miles per hour and circled the globe every 96 minutes. A month after the launch of Sputnik I, a second Soviet rocket carried the first living creature, a dog named Laika, into orbit. Americans were trailing the Soviets in what was soon called the space race, seen as an extension of the Cold War competition between the US and the USSR.

In December 1957 America attempted to place a US satellite into orbit. The launch failed when the rocket exploded. Nevertheless, the following month an attempt succeeded. A few months later, Congress established the **National Aeronautics and Space Administration (NASA)** to conduct the new space program. Rising to the challenge, NASA scientists overcame many of the complex problems of space travel in a series of projects. Today, satellites are a vital part of communications, travel, and everyday life. Among other things, they transmit television and cell phone signals, assist in the navigation of ships, airplanes, and cars, and can spy on other countries.

In April 1961 Soviet cosmonaut Yuri Gagarin became the first person to orbit the earth. A month later the Mercury project succeeded in sending the first American astronaut, **Alan Shepard**, into space. Then in February 1962 **John Glenn** became the first American to orbit the earth. In a 1961 address to Congress, President Kennedy declared, "I believe that this nation should commit itself to achieving the goal, before this decade is out, of landing a man on the moon." In a later speech he said, "We choose to go to the moon in this decade and do the other things, not because they are easy, but because they are hard."

After the Mercury project, the Gemini missions successfully tested the technology needed to dock two craft in outer space. The third program, Apollo, culminated in beating the Soviets in the race to the moon. On July 20, 1969, **Neil Armstrong**, the commander of Apollo 11, stepped from the ladder of the Eagle lunar module to become the first person to set foot on the moon. As he did so, he said, "That's one small step for a man, one giant leap for mankind." Over the next few years, a dozen Americans walked on the moon, but the space program soon turned to such projects as Skylab, the International Space Station, and the Hubble space telescope. The space race has seen some tragedies. Three astronauts were killed during a simulated launch of Apollo I. In 1986 the space shuttle *Challenger* exploded seventy-three seconds after liftoff, killing its seven-person crew. And in 2003, the space shuttle *Columbia* burst into flames upon reentry, killing all seven people aboard. The space shuttle program, from its beginning in April 1981 until its end in July 2011, completed 135 missions. Recent NASA projects include exploration of Mars using the Curiosity rover, Artemis missions to the moon and planning for a possible manned mission to Mars, and the Double Asteroid Redirection Test (DART)'s deflection of asteroids.

▼ (left to right) Katherine Johnson, an African American NASA mathematician, John Glenn, Alan Shepard

▼ The Russian Sputnik satellite

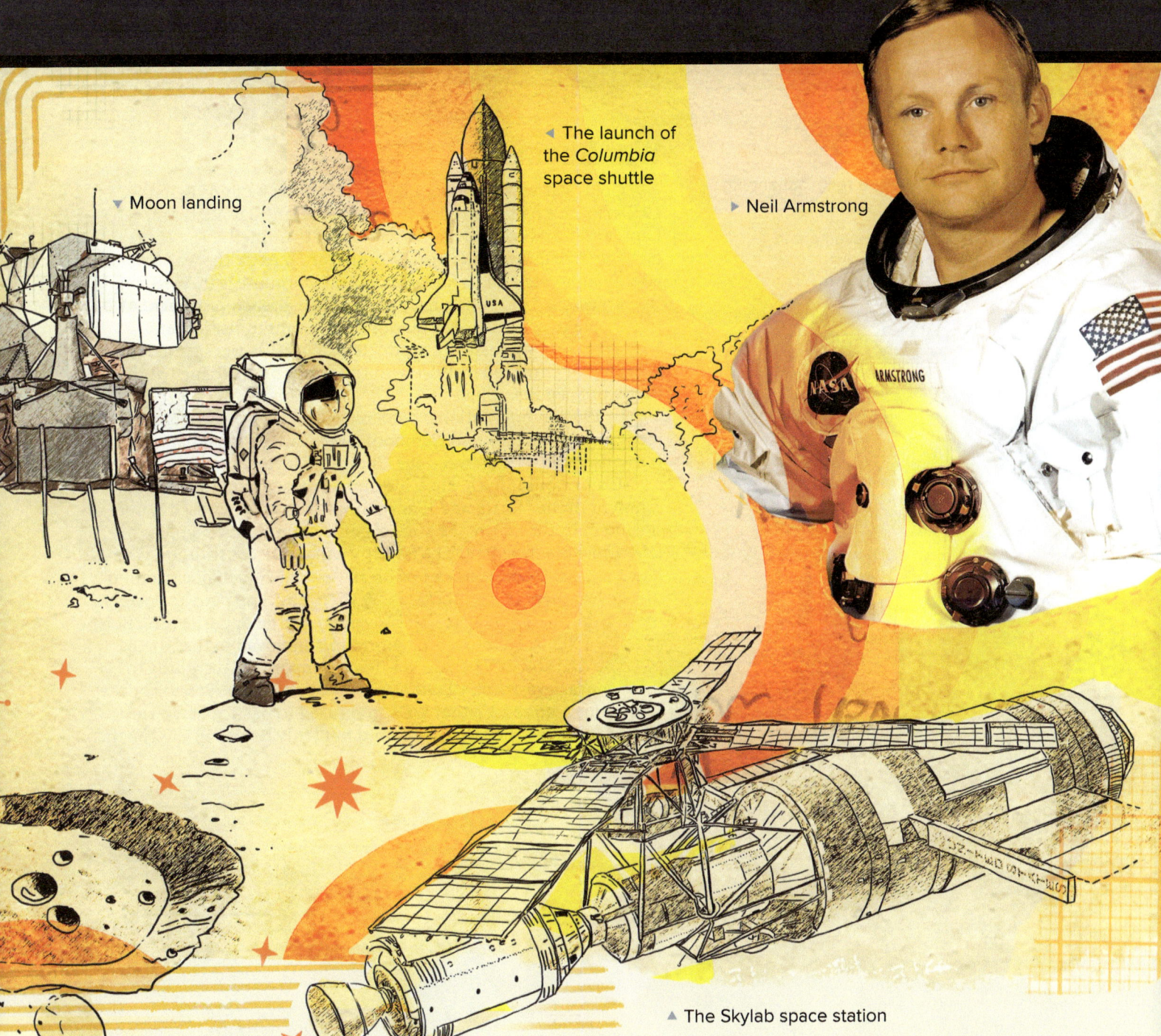

▼ Moon landing

◄ The launch of the *Columbia* space shuttle

► Neil Armstrong

ARMSTRONG

NASA

▲ The Skylab space station

---

## Comprehension Check 21.2

1. After Kennedy's assassination, Lyndon Johnson served as president but was defeated in the 1964 election.

   True    False

2. The "Great Society" legislation included the following measures except ____.

   **A** creation of the Department of Housing and Urban Development

   **B** decreasing federal funding for education

   **C** establishing Medicare and Medicaid

3. The Soviets were first to launch a satellite and orbit the earth.

   True    False

### MAKING CONNECTIONS

4. What was one defense and one criticism of the War on Poverty?

5. How did the Apollo mission fulfill Kennedy's vision for the space race?

- How did the Vietnam War begin?
- How did American participation in Vietnam increase?
- How did counterculture reflect changing attitudes in American society?
- How did America's involvement in Vietnam end?

▲ Ho Chi Minh

## 21.3 The Vietnam War Era

**Why were Americans divided over the Vietnam War?**

## War Begins

Cold War tensions flared up in Indochina beginning in the 1950s. France had controlled that area (present-day Vietnam, Laos, and Cambodia) from the middle of the nineteenth century until Japan captured it during World War II. After the war, France attempted to reclaim its former colony. Communists in Vietnam, the largest part of Indochina, used the anti-French sentiment of the people to organize a revolution. The Communist leader, **Ho Chi Minh**, successfully conducted a guerrilla war against the French that climaxed in 1954 with the defeat of the French at the Battle of Dien Bien Phu.

In 1954 an international conference in Geneva, Switzerland, recognized that Laos and Cambodia were independent nations. It divided Vietnam between the Communist North and the non-Communist South. Ho Chi Minh imposed a totalitarian government in the North, and tens of thousands who opposed it were executed. In the South, the strongly anti-Communist Ngo Dinh Diem became president. The South Vietnamese constitution gave Diem almost absolute power. With the establishment of a Communist government in the North, more than a million people moved to the South. There was a smaller movement in the opposite direction as some 130,000 supporters of communism moved to the North.

The division of Vietnam was to be temporary. According to the Geneva agreement, elections were scheduled for 1956 to choose leaders for a united Vietnam. Diem refused to participate in the elections because he said they would not truly be free in the North.

**Southeast Asia, 1954**

President Eisenhower supported Diem's decision. The United States, which had not signed the Geneva agreement, understood that Vietnamese elections might result in a victory for Ho Chi Minh. He was a nationalist hero to many Vietnamese because he had not only fought to free Vietnam from French rule but also battled the Japanese when they controlled the area during World War II. Communists in South Vietnam formed a group called the **Viet Cong** to try to overthrow the non-Communist government there. Both the North Vietnamese army and the Viet Cong received supplies and military equipment from China and the USSR.

To support the anti-Communists in South Vietnam, Eisenhower sent 2,000 military advisers to aid Diem in training and organizing his forces. Eisenhower's rationale for helping anti-communism in Vietnam became known as the **domino theory**—if one non-Communist nation in Southeast Asia fell to communism, then other nations would fall like a row of dominoes.

President Kennedy increased the number of American advisers in Vietnam to 16,000 by 1963, but the situation there was worsening. Diem's government was becoming increasingly unpopular among his own people. Diem was a Roman Catholic in a predominately Buddhist nation, his government had grown increasingly corrupt, and many wanted him to redistribute land from the rich to the poor. Several South Vietnamese generals plotted against Diem and launched a coup, or overthrow, against his government in November 1963. He was executed shortly afterwards. The new government, though anti-Communist, was unstable. Meanwhile, the Viet Cong increased their guerrilla warfare in the South.

▲ Political cartoon depicting the domino theory

## Johnson Escalates the War

### *Escalation*

During his campaign against Goldwater, Johnson had said, "We are not about to send American boys nine or ten thousand miles away from home to do what Asian boys ought to be doing for themselves." Yet an incident occurred off the coast of Vietnam during the campaign that changed the complexion of the war. On August 2, 1964, the American destroyer USS *Maddox*, which had been assisting the South Vietnamese in gathering intelligence and conducting raids on North Vietnamese radar systems, repulsed an attack by North Vietnamese patrol boats in the Gulf of Tonkin, an attack the US government presented to the American public as "unprovoked." On August 4 the *Maddox* and another destroyer reported being under attack again. Johnson denounced this as another unprovoked attack in a televised address to the American people and asked Congress to pass a joint resolution giving him authority to respond to Communist aggression. On August 7 Congress overwhelmingly approved the **Gulf of Tonkin Resolution**, empowering the president "to take all necessary measures to repel any armed attack against the forces of the United States and to prevent further aggression." However, more recent information released by the government has led many to conclude that the August 4 incident was not an attack by North Vietnam.

The resolution was not a declaration of war but authorized the president to increase American involvement in Vietnam. Johnson approved Operation Rolling Thunder, a bombing campaign over North Vietnam to destroy supply lines and military sites in that nation, which began in March 1965 and continued until October 1968. The number of American troops on the ground also grew rapidly as Americans began to take over a large part of the fighting from the South Vietnamese army. By November 1965 the number of US troops in Vietnam increased to 120,000 and grew to over 500,000 by 1968.

▼ A B-52 bomber dropping bombs over North Vietnam during Operation Rolling Thunder

# Difficulties of the Vietnam War

## 1 Difficulty Identifying the Enemy

The war in Vietnam proved to be quite difficult for many reasons. It was not a clear-cut conflict between two separate nations. Americans were fighting both the North Vietnamese and the Viet Cong. The Viet Cong looked, dressed, and acted just like the South Vietnamese civilians—until they opened fire. There were no clear fronts or lines of battle; enemy forces emerged suddenly from the jungle, attacked, and then faded out of sight, into the thick forests or even into networks of tunnels that honeycombed some areas. American helicopters armed with machine guns and carrying troops swooped like war birds over the jungles; napalm, Agent Orange, and other chemicals were used to burn away or kill the jungle foliage in which the enemy hid; American fighter planes and bombers pounded their opponents' positions. Yet the enemy kept coming back. The United States resorted to a war of attrition, trying to wear down the enemy rather than gaining territory. Generals began measuring success by how many enemy soldiers had been killed.

▾ Viet Cong guerrillas rowing through a swamp before a surprise attack on US troops, 1966

## 2 Complexities Related to Neutral Nations

Supplies for the Communist forces from North Vietnam flowed not only across the north-south border but also through the neighboring and supposedly neutral countries of Laos and Cambodia on the west, along the Ho Chi Minh Trail. Such supply lines would be impossible to cut without attacking those nations, and American political leaders were hesitant to do so.

### The Vietnam War, 1961–73

CHINA
Hanoi
LAOS
NORTH VIETNAM
Gulf of Tonkin
HAINAN (CHINA)
Mekong R.
DMZ (Demilitarized Zone)
17th parallel
Khe Sanh
Hue
THAILAND
CAMBODIA
Mekong R.
SOUTH VIETNAM
Saigon
South China Sea

- ◼ Countries allied with US
- ◼ Communist countries
- ◼ Neutral countries
- → Ho Chi Minh Trail

## 3 Strategy Directed by Political Agendas

America's leaders often allowed political considerations to affect how the war was conducted. For example, President Johnson was committed to the idea of a limited, defensive war. He did not want to risk an outright war against North Vietnam—a war that might draw in the Soviet Union or Communist China, divert dollars from his Great Society domestic program, and prove politically damaging. These limits affected the military's ability to defeat the enemy.

## 4 Public Dislike of the War

The war was increasingly unpopular at home. Dislike of the war was fueled by distrust of the government. Opinion polls in 1965 showed that 25 percent of Americans believed it was a mistake to send troops to Vietnam; in December 1967 that number had risen to 45 percent. President Johnson feared that if Americans knew how the war was really going, he would lose even more support. Therefore, setbacks and casualty counts were often downplayed. The government generally shared only optimistic reports of how well the war was going, yet media coverage showed increasing American casualties which seemed to contradict the government's message. Many began to doubt that the government was telling the truth to the American public, creating a "credibility gap" (a difference between what is said and what is true).

## 5 Resistance to the Draft

In addition, many Americans were angered over the draft. The peacetime draft had continued between 1954 and 1964, drafting around 120,000 people per year into the military. As American involvement in Vietnam escalated, that number increased. Between 1964 and 1973, 2.2 million men were drafted. Draftees made up about 25 percent of Americans who served in Vietnam, but they were more likely than volunteers were to be assigned to combat units; thus, they made up a disproportionately high percentage of casualties. Also, since those in college could defer military service, some claimed the draft system was unfair toward poorer individuals. "Draft dodgers" burned their draft cards in protest or fled the country to avoid being drafted. To address accusations of favoritism, in 1969 a draft lottery was introduced in which numbers representing dates of birth were pulled at random, and all those registered who had that birthday were called to serve.

▼ Men burning their draft cards

## Tet Offensive

▲ US troops retaking an area of Saigon after the Tet Offensive

In November 1967 General William Westmoreland, commander of US forces in Vietnam, declared in a speech that the enemy was on the run and that the end of the war was in view. Just ten weeks later, on January 31, 1968, during the South Vietnamese celebration of Tet, the lunar new year, 85,000 Communist troops launched attacks on nearly every major city and strategic point in South Vietnam. One force even captured part of the US embassy in Saigon for a time. In the weeks that followed the attacks, American and South Vietnamese forces drove back the enemy, recapturing what had been lost and inflicting massive casualties on the enemy.

Militarily, the **Tet Offensive** was a major failure for the Communists, but it had a dramatic effect on the American public. Television newscasts emphasized only the negative aspects—the suddenness of the attack and the heavy losses—leading many Americans to believe that Tet was a Communist victory. Having misled the American people and media about the course of the war, the US government now faced the wrath of a public who wanted to know how things could come so close to disaster so suddenly. After Tet, many Americans no longer looked to win the war; they only wanted a way out.

## Paris Peace Talks

As antiwar sentiment at home grew among politicians, other public figures, and young people, Johnson showed willingness to negotiate with the Communists in Vietnam. In May 1968 the North Vietnamese offered to hold peace negotiations, and the United States accepted. The Paris Peace Talks got off to a rocky start as the two sides engaged in a heated discussion over what shape of table to use. After that, the peace talks dragged on for nearly five years while the fighting continued. The United States wanted out but also wanted to preserve South Vietnam as a non-Communist nation. North Vietnam wanted the reunion of the two nations under Communist rule.

# Radical Youth

By the late 1960s half the population of the United States was under the age of twenty-five. Many of these young people had grown up in the midst of prosperity and affluence, but some began to question and then rebel against values such as militarism and materialism while also rejecting Christian values. However, even among young people, the radicals were a minority.

## Antiwar Movement

The rallying point for dissatisfied youth was opposition to the Vietnam War. Antiwar demonstrations grew in proportion to the number of troops Johnson was sending overseas. In a rally in Washington, demonstrators chanted, "Hey! Hey! LBJ! How many kids did you kill today?" Antiwar radicals seized control of college buildings, barricaded themselves inside, and dared police to come after them; a number of young men fled to Canada to avoid being drafted into the army. Some Vietnam veterans joined antiwar protests upon their return to the United States.

One force behind the antiwar movement was the "**New Left**," radical groups that harnessed many young people's discontent and resistance to authority and hoped to use resentment of the war as a means of overthrowing established American institutions. The Students for a Democratic Society (SDS) was the largest New Left group, with more than five thousand members on more than two hundred campuses. An even more radical group, the Weathermen, engaged in terrorist bombings of buildings, including the Capitol and Pentagon, to "bring the war home." Some demonstrators went beyond protesting US involvement in the war and actually supported the Communists. The North Vietnamese and Viet Cong flags became common symbols at antiwar demonstrations even as protestors burned the American flag. Others waved Chinese leader Mao Zedong's "little red book" of maxims.

The antiwar movement entered a lull when Nixon took office (discussed later); protesters waited to see what the new president would do. Events at home, however, stirred up further controversy over the war.

▲ Antiwar protesters marching in Washington, DC

### "Aid and Comfort" *to the* **Enemy?**

Jane Fonda, a popular actress of the sixties, traveled to North Vietnam and had her picture taken on an antiaircraft gun used to down American planes, thereby encouraging the Communists there and demoralizing American POWs housed in the nearby prison known as the "Hanoi Hilton."

One situation involved the revelation of the My Lai massacre. In March 1968, the US Army's C Company, which had suffered many casualties from the Viet Cong in the area, was angry and on edge when it entered the village of My Lai. There, Lieutenant William Calley and some of the company killed more than three hundred apparently unarmed civilians whom they suspected of aiding the Viet Cong. When news of the massacre leaked out, the army launched an investigation and a series of courts-martial lasting from 1969 to 1971. Only Calley was convicted of murder; he received a sentence of life in prison. His sentence was later reduced, and he was released in 1974. Many Americans were appalled that American troops could commit such a slaughter, but others sympathized with Calley. They believed that either the army was making him a scapegoat to cover for other officers or the antiwar movement was persecuting him in anger over the whole war effort. Calley himself publicly apologized for My Lai in 2009.

Another event was the publication of the "Pentagon Papers" in 1971. Pentagon staff analyst Daniel Ellsberg stole a number of confidential documents concerning the progress of American involvement in Vietnam and released them to the *New York Times*. The Nixon administration tried vainly to block publication in the interest of "national security." But the documents were more embarrassing to the government than they were dangerous to the nation. They revealed the blunders and deceptions of primarily the Kennedy and Johnson administrations in the conduct of the war. Readers learned, for example, that Johnson had drafted what became the Gulf of Tonkin Resolution months before the actual incident in the Gulf of Tonkin took place. These revelations of government deceit prompted even more antiwar sentiment.

◀ Jane Fonda in North Vietnam

Struggles of the Sixties    **565**

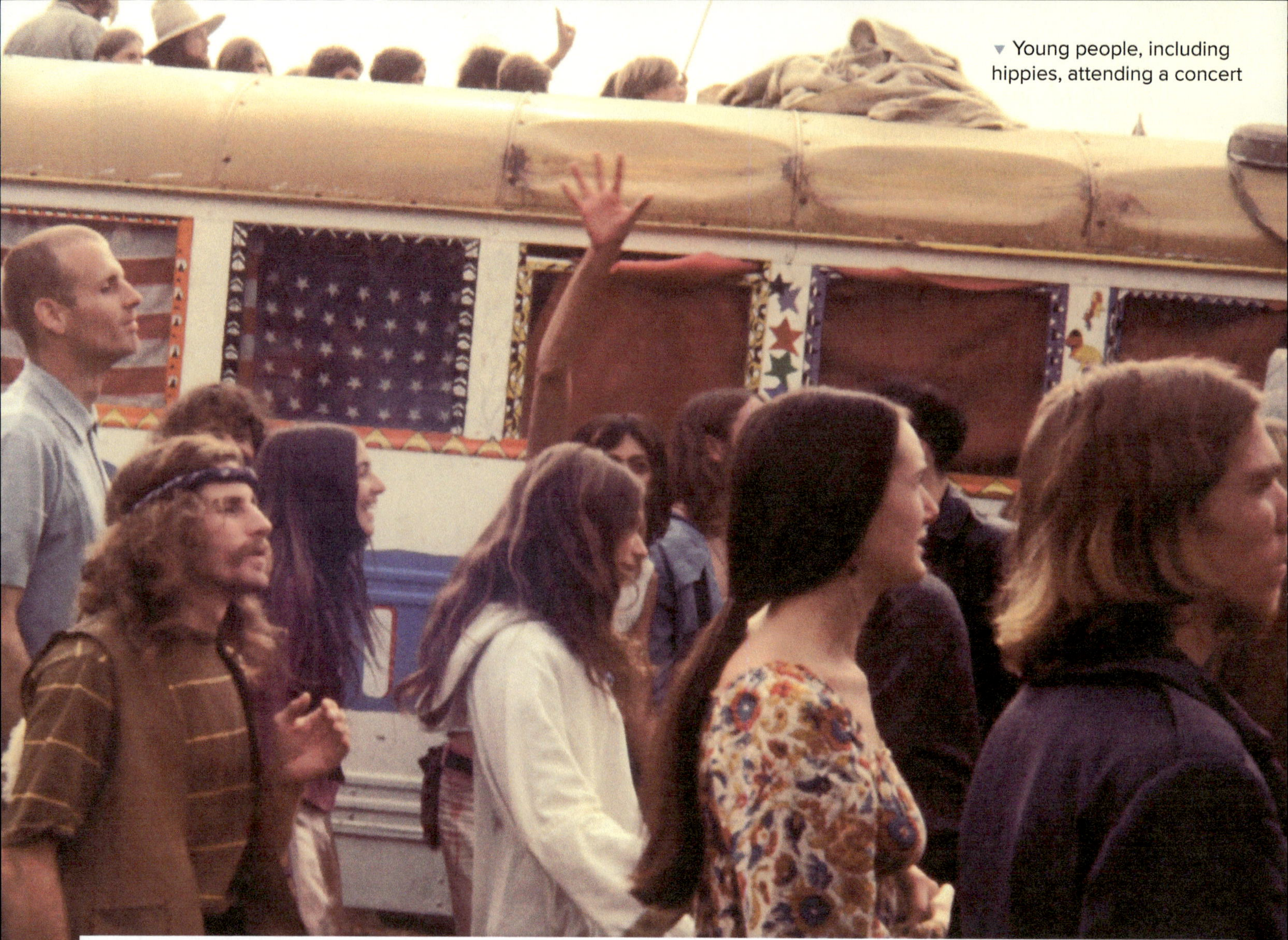

▼ Young people, including hippies, attending a concert

## *Counterculture*

The antiwar movement was itself only a part of an overall youth movement known as the counterculture. More an attitude than an ideology, the counterculture of the 1960s and early 1970s had its roots in rebellion—specifically a rejection of the materialism, morals, and values of the previous generation—and the belief that material possessions and moral restrictions corrupted people rather than people being corrupt by their sinful nature.

Proponents of the counterculture believed that the solution to society's problems included self-expression and espousing a philosophy of love and sharing. "Do your own thing" and "All you need is love" were simplistic expressions of the counterculture creed. The counterculture also praised youth as having the answers to society's problems, as illustrated by the popular saying "Don't trust anyone over thirty."

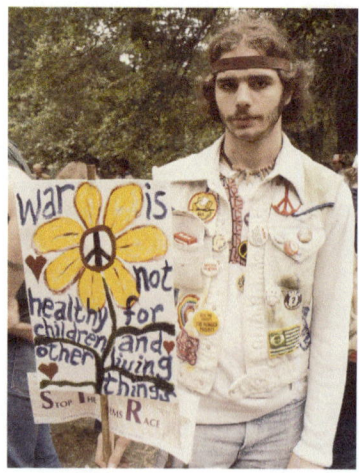

▲ A hippie with peace sign

The popular expression of the counterculture was the "hippie" movement (derived from the slang term *hip*, "approving of current tastes and attitudes"). Hippies made a virtue of nonconformity. As a sign of protest, young men grew their hair and beards long, and some men and women wore jeans and t-shirts that were dirty or patched. Further rejecting traditional standards, they repudiated marriage and advocated unrestricted sexual activity. They embraced rock music which, with its provocative lyrics, symbolized their rebellion. Hippies were also leaders in the drug culture and experimented with numerous illegal hallucinogenic drugs, such as LSD and marijuana.

The social upheaval shocked many Americans, however, especially after the relative calm of the Eisenhower and Kennedy years. They wondered how a nation so advanced and so wealthy could experience such disorder.

# The End of the War

## Election of 1968

### JOHNSON BOWS OUT

Johnson and the war in Vietnam were becoming increasingly unpopular, yet it was assumed he would win renomination by the Democrats. However, an antiwar Democrat, Minnesota senator Eugene McCarthy, declared that he would run against Johnson for the Democratic nomination. Johnson's advisers at first dismissed McCarthy as a threat, but the Tet Offensive in January reinvigorated the antiwar movement. In the New Hampshire primary in March, McCarthy nearly upset the president. Seeing that Johnson was vulnerable to defeat, New York senator **Robert F. Kennedy**, who had served as his older brother JFK's attorney general, suddenly announced that he, too, would compete for the Democratic nomination. After Johnson was advised that he could lose badly in the upcoming Wisconsin primary, he stunned the nation by withdrawing from the race.

After Johnson's withdrawal, Vice President Hubert H. Humphrey also joined the race, representing a continuation of Johnson's positions. McCarthy and Kennedy, both advocating against the war, competed in the primaries to win the right to challenge Humphrey, who ignored the primaries hoping to win delegates from nonprimary states, at the convention in Chicago.

### TWO TRAGEDIES

Two assassinations in 1968 shocked the nation and influenced the presidential campaign. First, in April 1968, while the candidates fought over the nomination, civil rights leader Martin Luther King Jr. (see Chapter 22) was shot and killed in Memphis, Tennessee. Second, Robert Kennedy, who had won a major victory in the California primary and appeared likely to win the Democratic nomination, was assassinated after greeting supporters in a Los Angeles hotel. The assassin was a young Arab nationalist who opposed Kennedy's support of Israel. Within a period of two months, two major American leaders had died violently.

▲ Robert Kennedy giving a speech in Los Angeles minutes before his assassination

### NIXON TAKES THE CENTER

The favorite to win the Republican nomination was **Richard Nixon**. Despite his loss to JFK in 1960 and a failed bid in the California governor's race in 1962, the former vice president won a series of primaries in 1968 that made him the Republican front-runner. Nixon tried to take the "middle of the road" on political issues to appeal to the general public. At the Republican convention in Miami, he beat back challenges by both liberal Nelson Rockefeller and conservative Ronald Reagan to win the nomination. Sensing America's dismay over the ongoing war in Vietnam and the violence that racked America, Nixon pledged to bring peace but did not give out details about how he would accomplish that. His message of "law and order" and a firm response to the chaos appealed to what Nixon called the "silent majority" of Americans whose voices had been drowned out by social unrest (see Chapter 23).

IT TAKES COURAGE!

# WALLACE
### HAS IT!

### DO YOU?

### Stand Up for America!

P.P.A. Wallace Campaign
P.O. Box 1968, Montgomery, Ala.
Seymour Trammell, Chm.

▲ George Wallace campaign poster

## DEMOCRATIC DISARRAY

The violence in American society carried over to the Democratic convention in Chicago, where thousands of anti-war protestors clashed with police outside the convention hall. These clashes were broadcast live on television for the public to see. Inside, the delegates nominated Hubert Humphrey as their candidate, though many antiwar Democratic delegates opposed his nomination.

## THE WALLACE FACTOR

Further complicating the election of 1968 was the third-party candidacy of Alabama governor George Wallace. The former Democrat ran as the candidate of the newly formed American Independent Party. Wallace had risen to fame as a pro-segregation governor during the civil rights struggles of the early 1960s and sought to draw on popular discontent in the south with the civil rights movement, and national opposition among conservatives to urban violence, rampant immorality, rising crime rates, and the seemingly endless war in Vietnam.

## ELECTION: NIXON'S THE ONE

The election reflected the fragmented state of American society. Nixon received 43.4 percent of the popular vote to Humphrey's 42.7 percent and Wallace's 13.5 percent. Nixon's lead in the Electoral College, however, was more substantial: 301 for Nixon, 191 for Humphrey, and 46 Deep South electoral votes for Wallace. The voters had repudiated Johnson's policies but did not give Nixon an overwhelming mandate.

### The Election of 1968

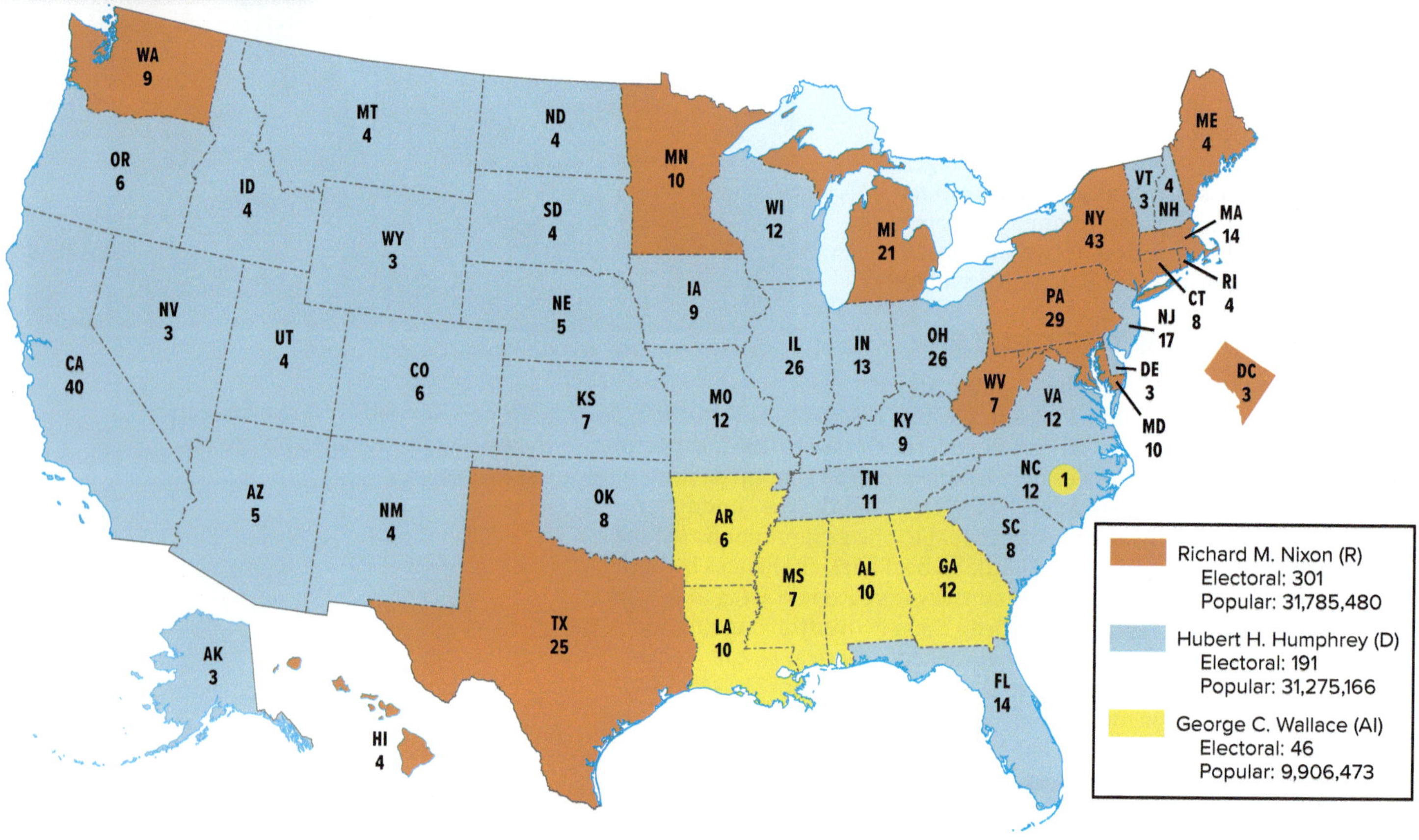

| | | | |
|---|---|---|---|
| WA 9 | | | ME 4 |
| OR 6 | MT 4 | ND 4 | VT 3 / 4 NH |
| | ID 4 | MN 10 | NY 43 / MA 14 |
| NV 3 | WY 3 | SD 4 | WI 12 / RI 4 |
| CA 40 | UT 4 | NE 5 | MI 21 / CT 8 |
| AZ 5 | CO 6 | IA 9 | PA 29 / NJ 17 |
| | NM 4 | KS 7 | IL 26 / IN 13 / OH 26 / DE 3 |
| | | MO 12 | KY 9 / WV 7 / VA 12 / MD 10 / DC 3 |
| AK 3 | OK 8 | TN 11 / NC 12 (1) |
| | TX 25 | AR 6 / MS 7 / AL 10 / GA 12 / SC 8 |
| HI 4 | | LA 10 / FL 14 |

Richard M. Nixon (R)
Electoral: 301
Popular: 31,785,480

Hubert H. Humphrey (D)
Electoral: 191
Popular: 31,275,166

George C. Wallace (AI)
Electoral: 46
Popular: 9,906,473

## Vietnamization

After his election, Nixon sought to disengage American forces from the fighting in Vietnam without appearing to abandon South Vietnam. Nixon's policy, termed **Vietnamization**, called for improving the South Vietnamese army's fighting ability through increased training and equipment and the gradual withdrawal of American combat forces. The number of American forces in Vietnam decreased from more than 500,000 when Nixon took office to fewer than 140,000 by the beginning of 1972 and only 24,000 by December 1972.

However, as American soldiers began leaving Vietnam, the Communists increased their forces and stockpiled supplies. North Vietnamese and Viet Cong forces established bases in neighboring Cambodia, a neutral country. To destroy these bases, the United States began bombing Cambodia between March 1969 and April 1970, but these missions failed to accomplish their objective. Nixon's military advisers told him it would be impossible to remove additional American troops if the bases remained intact, so Nixon authorized raids by ground forces into Cambodia in April 1970.

On April 30 Nixon gave a televised address to the American people explaining his reasons for the invasion of Cambodia. After his speech, antiwar protesters demonstrated across the country, and one of these protests turned deadly. On May 1, thousands of students from Kent State University, near Cleveland, Ohio, along with other antiwar protestors, began a demonstration on campus against the Cambodia invasion. On May 2, protestors set fire to the Army ROTC building on campus, and the governor called in the National Guard. On May 4, protestors continued to demonstrate, and the guardsmen ordered the crowd to disperse. Some students taunted the guardsmen and hurled rocks at them; the guardsmen responded by using tear gas canisters, which failed to disperse the crowd. A few of the soldiers, who later stated they feared for their lives, began firing their weapons at the crowd, killing four students, two of whom were bystanders on their way to class, and wounding nine others. The **Kent State shooting** led to more protests and student strikes across the country, and many universities temporarily closed to avoid further violence.

## "Peace" and Aftermath

The peace negotiations which had begun in Paris in 1968 dragged on. Hoping to pressure the Communists into making a deal, Nixon ordered a massive bombing campaign over North Vietnam in December 1972. Finally, in January 1973, a cease-fire was signed. According to the terms of the agreement, the United States would withdraw its remaining 24,000 troops from South Vietnam, and North Vietnam would release nearly 600 POWs (prisoners of war). Despite America's withdrawal, the conflict in Vietnam was not over. The United States continued to provide South Vietnam huge amounts of arms to protect itself, and North Vietnam still maintained troops and guerrillas in the South. Nixon hoped that the supply of arms and the threat of future American intervention would protect South Vietnam.

In the spring of 1975 North Vietnam launched a massive offensive, and South Vietnamese resistance collapsed with astonishing speed. Nixon was no longer in office (see Chapter 23), and his successor, Gerald Ford, was unable to persuade Congress to help South Vietnam. With no outside help and torn by internal dissension and corruption, the South fell. Vietnam was finally united and at "peace"—under Communist rule.

▼ A student shot during antiwar protests at Kent State University

▼ (below) American POWs lined up prior to their release from a North Vietnamese prison camp; (bottom) Vietnamese refugees fleeing South Vietnam

## 26th Amendment

The **Twenty-Sixth Amendment** was passed in 1971. It granted voting rights to citizens age eighteen and older. Prior to 1971 only a few states allowed individuals under age twenty-one to vote. The Vietnam War brought greater attention to the issue of voting age since eighteen-year-olds could be drafted into the military. Many argued that those individuals should have the right to vote for the people who have the power to send them into war.

The results of the war at least partially proved the "domino theory." One after another, South Vietnam, Laos, and Cambodia fell to the Communists. Fears of Communist atrocities in the fallen nations also proved justified. The worst example was the cruel Communist regime in Cambodia called the Khmer Rouge. Led by dictator Pol Pot, the Khmer Rouge slaughtered 1.2 million Cambodians—one-fifth of the nation's population.

The cost of the Vietnam War for the United States was high. Over 58,000 Americans were killed, 300,000 wounded, and over $150 billion spent. But beyond these statistics, war veterans returned home to a disillusioned country. Instead of being hailed as heroes, they were ignored or even harassed by war opponents. Even veterans who were not physically wounded came home emotionally scarred, with many suffering from post-traumatic stress disorder (PTSD) after witnessing the horrors of the war.

Although Congress had given the president power to conduct the war, it was upset with how Johnson and Nixon had run the conflict. As a result, Congress adopted a joint resolution called the **War Powers Act** of 1973, which limited the president's power to use American troops abroad. The act requires that the president notify Congress within forty-eight hours of his committing US troops to military action and withdraw such troops within ninety days unless Congress specifically approves continued use of those forces. Since its passage, the executive branch has disputed the constitutionality of the act and Congress's power to restrict the authority of the president as commander in chief. Congress has maintained that the act was necessary to check the president's power to use the US military in armed conflict and that Congress has the power to make laws necessary and proper for any departments and officials to carry out their constitutional duties.

---

## Comprehension Check 21.3

1. The Viet Cong was a group of ____.
   - **A** anti-Communists fighting against Communists in North Vietnam
   - **B** Communists in South Vietnam seeking to overthrow the non-Communist government
   - **C** Communists and non-Communists seeking a unified Vietnam

2. All the following illustrated rebellion against traditional values and protested the Vietnam War except the ____ movement.
   - **A** New Left
   - **B** "hippie"
   - **C** Vietnamization

3. The War Powers Act ____.
   - **A** agreed to Johnson's resolution to commit troops in Vietnam
   - **B** attempted to limit the president's power to use American troops abroad
   - **C** set up an investigation of the president's confidential papers regarding Vietnam

4. All the following occurred by the end of the Vietnam War except ____.
   - **A** a cease-fire
   - **B** the creation of a new boundary between North and South Vietnam
   - **C** the withdrawal of American troops

**MAKING CONNECTIONS**

5. What were two factors that made fighting in the Vietnam War difficult for the United States?

6. What was the domino theory, and how did the aftermath of the war in Southeast Asian countries demonstrate that theory?

## Chapter Summary

### 21.1 The Kennedy Years

- John F. Kennedy was elected president in 1960. He described the challenges and opportunities of the 1960s as a New Frontier and proposed a number of social programs and the space program, as well as tax cuts to stimulate the economy. Only some of his programs were passed by Congress.

- Fidel Castro became dictator of Cuba in 1959. Kennedy carried out a plan by the CIA to use Cuban exiles to invade Cuba at the Bay of Pigs to overthrow Castro, but the mission failed. The Cuban missile crisis began in 1962 when the United States found that the USSR had begun installing nuclear missiles in Cuba. Kennedy ordered a blockade of Cuba, which Khrushchev denounced. The crisis ended when the USSR agreed to remove the missiles and the United States agreed not to invade Cuba and to remove missiles from Turkey.

- In 1961 the Communists in East Germany erected the Berlin Wall to keep people from escaping from East Berlin to West Berlin.

- Kennedy was assassinated on November 22, 1963 in Dallas, Texas, and Lyndon Johnson became president.

**TERMS**

John F. Kennedy (JFK)
Peace Corps
Fidel Castro
Bay of Pigs
Cuban missile crisis
Berlin Wall
Lee Harvey Oswald

**TERMS**

Lyndon B. Johnson
Great Society
Medicare
Medicaid
Earl Warren
National Aeronautics and Space Administration (NASA)
Alan Shepard
John Glenn
Neil Armstrong

### 21.2 The Johnson Administration

- Lyndon Johnson declared a "War on Poverty." His "Great Society" legislation included programs to help the poor through job training and job placement, education, housing and urban development, water quality, Medicare, and Medicaid. Johnson won the election of 1964 over Barry Goldwater.

- The Supreme Court under Chief Justice Earl Warren pursued a policy of judicial activism to address what the justices perceived as major social problems.

- The Soviets put the first satellite in space in 1957. The United States attempted to catch up to the USSR in the space race by establishing NASA. In 1961 President Kennedy declared the goal of putting a man on the moon by the end of the decade. Neil Armstrong became the first man to set foot on the moon in 1969.

## Chapter Summary

### 21.3 The Vietnam War Era

- Ho Chi Minh led Vietnam to defeat France in 1954. Vietnam was divided between the Communist North and the non-Communist South. To prevent all of Vietnam from becoming Communist, President Eisenhower sent military advisers to help South Vietnam, and Kennedy sent additional advisers, believing the domino theory that if Vietnam became Communist, neighboring countries would as well.

- After an alleged attack on an American destroyer, Congress passed the Gulf of Tonkin Resolution, giving the president power to increase American involvement in Vietnam. The war was difficult because of circumstances both in Vietnam and at home. In the Tet Offensive the North Vietnamese and the Viet Cong attacked nearly every city and strategic point in South Vietnam simultaneously, causing many Americans to want to get out of the war.

- Many young people opposed the war, and the New Left hoped to overthrow established American institutions. Revelations of the My Lai massacre and the publishing of the "Pentagon Papers" led to further antiwar sentiment. The youth counterculture rejected the values of the previous generation.

- Johnson withdrew from the 1968 election, Robert Kennedy was assassinated, and Nixon won the election. Nixon's policy of Vietnamization called for withdrawing US forces and improving South Vietnam's army's ability to fight. Nixon bombed and invaded Cambodia, which led to protests in America, including one at Kent State University where National Guard troops killed four students. The remaining American troops in Vietnam were withdrawn after a ceasefire was signed in 1973. In 1975 all of Vietnam became Communist, along with neighboring countries. Congress passed the War Powers Act, attempting to limit the president's use of troops in future conflicts.

### TERMS

Ho Chi Minh

Viet Cong

domino theory

Gulf of Tonkin Resolution

Tet Offensive

New Left

Robert F. Kennedy

Richard Nixon

Vietnamization

Kent State shooting

Twenty-Sixth Amendment

War Powers Act

## Chapter Review Questions

### RECALL

1. What president famously said, "Ask not what your country can do for you—ask what you can do for your country"?

2. Who overthrew Cuba's government in 1959 and became a Communist dictator?

3. What tragic event occurred on November 22, 1963?

4. Who became president after Kennedy?

5. Who was the first man to walk on the moon?

6. What Communist leader led Vietnam to defeat the French in 1954?

7. What was the name of the Communist forces in South Vietnam who were trying to overthrow the non-Communist government?

8. What was the term for radical groups that harnessed the young people's discontent, resistance to authority, and antiwar sentiment to encourage the overthrow of established institutions?

9. What Democratic candidate for president was assassinated in 1968?

10. According to the Twenty-Sixth Amendment, by what age must citizens be allowed to vote?

## UNDERSTAND

**11.** What role did television play in the outcome of the election of 1960?

**12.** What did Kennedy call the unknown opportunities and perils of the 1960s? What were three parts of Kennedy's domestic agenda that Congress passed?

**13.** What was the purpose of the Peace Corps? What was the purpose of the Alliance for Progress, and what were two ways it accomplished its purpose?

**14.** What failed CIA operation in Cuba led to the Soviets installing nuclear-capable missiles in Cuba?

**15.** How did the Cuban missile crisis bring the world close to nuclear war? What was the compromise that ended the Cuban missile crisis?

**16.** Why did the Communists erect the Berlin Wall? How did the wall symbolize the failures of communism?

**17.** What were the goals of President Johnson's Great Society? What were four pieces of legislation that were enacted as part of his agenda?

**18.** What Soviet accomplishments demonstrated that America was initially behind the Soviet Union in the space race? What agency was created to conduct the United States space program? What goal did Kennedy set for the space program by the end of the 1960s?

**19.** Why did the United States first get involved in the conflict in Vietnam under President Eisenhower? How did American involvement increase under President Kennedy?

**20.** What power did the Gulf of Tonkin Resolution give the president? How did American involvement in Vietnam escalate under President Johnson?

**21.** What were four reasons the war in Vietnam was difficult for the United States?

**22.** Why was the Vietnam draft a source of anger for many Americans?

**23.** What was the Tet Offensive? Why did it lead to many Americans no longer supporting the war?

**24.** How did the My Lai massacre and the publication of the "Pentagon Papers" contribute to antiwar sentiment?

**25.** Why did Johnson withdraw from the presidential race in 1968? Which Democrat won his party's nomination? Who were the candidates for the American Independent Party and the Republican Party? Who won the election?

**26.** What was Nixon's Vietnamization policy?

**27.** Why did Nixon order an attack on Cambodia in 1970? How did the antiwar movement respond to this action? What tragedy in the United States happened during this response?

**28.** How did America's involvement in Vietnam end? What happened in Vietnam after the United States withdrew its forces?

**29.** How did the aftermath of the war confirm the domino theory?

**30.** What was the cost in lives and dollars of the Vietnam War for the United States? What were the effects for many Vietnam veterans?

**31.** What was the purpose of the War Powers Act? What requirements did it place on the president? Why is it considered unconstitutional by some?

## THINK ABOUT IT

**32.** According to the following passages, what are some common causes of poverty? Ruth 1:1–5, Prov. 24:30–34, Prov. 21:17, Amos 5:11

Based on the following passages, what are some principles that should be considered when helping the poor? Lev. 23:22; Deut. 14:28–29; 1 Tim. 5:4, 8; Acts 2:44–45; 2 Thess. 3:10; Prov. 14:31

What are some ways Christians can help the poor today? What are some dangers to avoid?

How might these biblical principles inform an evaluation of the War on Poverty?

**33.** What ideas did the counterculture reject? What ideas did it embrace? What effects do you think the counterculture had on God-ordained institutions such as family, church, and government?

# 22 The Civil Rights Movement

**22.1 Early Civil Rights Movement**
**22.2 Advances in Civil Rights**
**22.3 Civil Rights Struggles**

▲ Civil rights leaders Martin Luther King Jr. and Ralph Abernathy in jail after a civil rights demonstration in St. Augustine, Florida, 1964

# Early Civil Rights Movement

What caused attitudes toward civil rights to begin changing?

- What gains were made in civil rights after World War II?

- Why was *Brown v. Board of Education* important?

- Why was the Montgomery bus boycott successful?

- What significant events in the civil rights movement occurred during Eisenhower's presidency?

The term "civil rights" refers to the rights of every citizen to receive equal treatment under the law. Discrimination occurs when the civil rights of individuals are denied or lessened because of their membership in a particular group or class. In American history the **civil rights movement** refers primarily to the period after World War II in which African Americans struggled to secure the exercise and protection of their basic rights as citizens.

## Roots of the Movement

The equality that black Americans had hoped would come from emancipation had not been realized. As mentioned in previous chapters, since Reconstruction individuals and groups such as Booker T. Washington, W. E. B. Du Bois, and the NAACP had been working toward equality for black Americans. The NAACP had supported court cases aimed at overturning discrimination. They achieved a notable victory in 1935 when the Supreme Court ruled in *Norris v. Alabama* that exclusion of African Americans from juries violated their Fourteenth Amendment right to equal protection under the law. This decision led to a gradual change in laws which had kept black citizens from serving on juries.

Despite some court victories, progress toward civil rights was slow. Black World War II veterans returned from overseas hoping to be able to participate in the political process in the country whose freedom they had fought to defend. Yet in many places they were prevented from registering to vote, or if they could register, were met with threats of violence if they attempted to exercise their right to vote.

▼ A segregated battalion of black soldiers in the Aleutian Islands during World War II

Segregation was practiced in both the South and the North. In the South, Jim Crow laws (see Chapter 15) which enforced segregation in restaurants, schools, theaters, public transportation, and many other areas were still in effect. These laws meant that black Americans typically had access only to inferior facilities and accommodations.

Outside the South, segregation was not always required by law but commonly occurred. In the practice known as **redlining**, a bank might refuse to offer mortgages or might charge higher interest rates for homes located in minority neighborhoods. Throughout the country some white neighborhoods had rules preventing black families from living there, and some real estate agents agreed among themselves not to sell homes in white neighborhoods to black families. These practices created segregated neighborhoods, which also resulted in creating segregated schools and school districts. Whether by law or by practice, these forms of discrimination made it difficult for black Americans to enjoy the benefits of home-ownership and the prosperity of the postwar years.

Harry Truman was the first twentieth-century president to give considerable attention to civil rights for African Americans. He stated in a speech given May 17, 1952, "No citizen of this great country ought to be discriminated against because of his race, religion, or national origin. That is the essence of the American ideal, and the American Constitution."

In 1946 Truman established the President's Committee on Civil Rights. The committee released a report in 1947 documenting nationwide discrimination in areas such as education, housing, public accommodations, and voting rights. In February 1948 Truman asked Congress to pass a broad civil rights bill which would protect African Americans' right to vote, abolish poll taxes, and make lynching a federal crime. He also called for an end to discrimination in employment and in public transportation. Truman's push for civil rights led to a splintering of the Democratic Party months before the 1948 presidential election (see Chapter 20). Truman won reelection, but most of his legislative efforts failed as a coalition of Republicans and southern Democrats defeated most of his proposals. Looking for other ways to advance his civil rights agenda, Truman used executive orders, including prohibiting discrimination in federal employment and ending segregation in the armed forces.

Truman also appointed African Americans to federal courts and other important government positions. In 1949 he appointed William Hastie to the Third Circuit Court of Appeals, making him the highest-ranking black judge in the federal court system up to that time. Edward Dudley became the first black US ambassador when he was named the ambassador to Liberia.

◀ William Hastie, first African American federal judge

# Jackie Robinson

Professional sports, like most areas of American life before the 1950s, were racially segregated. Baseball, one of America's national pastimes, was no exception. The best white players joined the major league teams of the National and American Leagues. Black players participated in leagues composed of all-black teams, including the Negro League. But a brave and talented ballplayer, **Jackie Robinson**, broke that color barrier.

Robinson was born in Georgia but moved with his family to California while still a child. A gifted athlete, Robinson earned a scholarship to UCLA, where he starred in football, basketball, track, and baseball. After serving in the army during World War II, Robinson joined the Kansas City Monarchs of the Negro League. There he came to the attention of Branch Rickey, president of the Brooklyn Dodgers.

Rickey was determined to integrate the major leagues. But the first player to do so would not only have to be talented but also have the strength of character to withstand intense public scrutiny and even open prejudice. Rickey observed Robinson and became convinced that Robinson met the requirements to become baseball's black pioneer.

Robinson joined the Dodgers in 1947 as their second baseman. From his first time at bat, he heard racial slurs and insults from not only hecklers in the crowd but also opposing players. Some players tried to start fights with him or, when sliding into second, purposely tried to injure him with the spikes on their shoes. In many cities, Robinson had to stay in a separate hotel from his white teammates. Aware that the nation's eyes were on him, Robinson curbed both his natural competitiveness and his resentment of the treatment he received. He knew that—fairly or not— many Americans would judge all black Americans by his behavior. For Robinson, Branch Rickey later wrote, "there could be but one direction of dedication—the doctrine of turning the other cheek. There came in the greatness of Jackie Robinson."

In his first season, Robinson won Rookie of the Year. In 1949 his .342 batting average and thirty-seven stolen bases helped him win the league's Most Valuable Player Award. In Robinson's ten seasons with Brooklyn, the Dodgers won six pennants and one World Series. After his retirement, he was elected to baseball's Hall of Fame. In 1997, as a permanent acknowledgement of Robinson's achievements, Major League Baseball retired his uniform number, 42, across all major league teams.

Robinson opened the door for other talented black players who would follow him in baseball and other sports. The National Football League, which had signed its first four African American players in 1946, one year before Robinson joined the Dodgers, continued to add black athletes, and the National Basketball Association signed its first African American player in 1950.

## Did You Know?

Even into the 1960s, black major league baseball players faced discrimination. In many cities in Florida, where several teams held their spring training, black players were not allowed to stay in the same hotels, eat at the same restaurants, or swim at the same beaches as white players. Some cities and businesses changed their policies after teams threatened to relocate their spring training unless black and white players were treated equally.

## Brown v. Board of Education

In Kansas, as in many states, the law called for separate schools for black and white children. Despite numerous legal challenges, the Kansas Supreme Court did not overturn the state's school segregation law. In 1950 the NAACP's Topeka chapter organized another legal challenge by taking up the case of Linda Brown, a young African American girl who was forced to attend an all-black school across town rather than the all-white school close to her house. When her case reached the US District Court, it ruled that the law segregating schools was not unconstitutional and, citing the 1896 case *Plessy v. Ferguson* (see Chapter 15), ruled that the black and white schools were "separate but equal" with respect to buildings, curriculum, and teacher qualifications.

The NAACP's chief legal counsel, African American attorney **Thurgood Marshall**, appealed the case to the US Supreme Court. The Supreme Court combined the Topeka case with four other NAACP-sponsored cases from other states. Marshall argued in the case ***Brown v. Board of Education of Topeka*** (1954) that having separate schools for black and white children, regardless of the quality of the facilities or education, was itself an unconstitutional violation of the Fourteenth Amendment's equal protection clause. In a unanimous decision, Chief Justice Earl Warren, writing for the court, stated,

> We conclude that, in the field of public education, the doctrine of "separate but equal" has no place. Separate educational facilities are inherently unequal. Therefore, we hold that the plaintiffs and others similarly situated for whom the actions have been brought are, by reason of the segregation complained of, deprived of the equal protection of the laws guaranteed by the Fourteenth Amendment.

Though the *Brown* decision applied only to public schools, the ruling threatened the entire system of racial segregation by challenging the principle of "separate but equal" established by *Plessy.* The decision convinced many black Americans that the time had come to challenge segregation in other areas.

The reaction by many white Southerners to *Brown* was anger and defiance. While some school districts in the Upper South obeyed the court and integrated their schools, most in the Deep South defended segregation and vowed to resist. Senator Harry F. Bird of Virginia called on Southerners to adopt "massive resistance" against the ruling. White Citizens' Councils were formed across the South to pressure local governments and school boards to resist integration. Some districts closed their public schools rather than integrate, while others used delaying tactics or created attendance zones or other requirements to prevent black students from attending white schools. Many communities established private academies where only white students were allowed to enroll.

A year after the *Brown* decision, the Supreme Court followed up with a second decision called *Brown v. Board of Education II* (*Brown 2*), which dealt with questions about how and when school districts must comply with desegregation. In *Brown 2,* the court ordered school districts to end school segregation with "all deliberate speed." The vague and contradictory language (since *deliberate* can mean a long and thoughtful rather than speedy process) allowed many districts to keep their schools segregated for many more years.

▲ (top) The children of the lawsuit *Brown v. Board of Education of Topeka*, with Linda Brown in the center; (bottom) Thurgood Marshall, NAACP lawyer for *Brown v. Board of Education of Topeka*

A group of 101 southern members of Congress who opposed the *Brown* decision signed the "Southern Manifesto" in 1956. In it they attacked the decision as a "clear abuse of judicial power" that violated states' rights and the separation of powers and pledged themselves to use "all lawful means" to reverse the decision and prevent its implementation.

## Rosa Parks and the Montgomery Bus Boycott

On city buses in Montgomery, Alabama, the back rows of seats were reserved for black passengers and the front rows were reserved for whites. The middle rows were available for black or white passengers, but black passengers were required to give up their seats in those rows to white customers and stand if the buses became crowded. On December 1, 1955, a black seamstress named **Rosa Parks**, who was also the secretary of the local NAACP chapter, refused to give up her seat in the middle section to a white man. She was arrested and fined for disobeying the bus driver's order to stand.

▼ Rosa Parks sitting in the front of a bus in Montgomery, Alabama; (inset) Rosa Parks getting fingerprinted after her arrest during the Montgomery Bus Boycott

Parks's small act of defiance energized the black community in Montgomery. The Women's Political Council, a group of black women working for civil rights in the city, called for a one-day boycott of the Montgomery bus system. A meeting was held for local black ministers and leaders on December 2 at Dexter Avenue Baptist Church to discuss and publicize the **Montgomery bus boycott**. On Monday, December 5, 90 percent of Montgomery's black bus riders refused to use the buses. Seeing the popularity of the boycott, the leaders met again that afternoon to discuss making the boycott a long-term campaign. At that meeting they formed the Montgomery Improvement Association (MIA) and chose Dexter Avenue's twenty-six-year-old minister, **Dr. Martin Luther King Jr.**, who had recently moved to Montgomery, as its president. At a meeting later that evening, over 5,000 African Americans gathered and voted to extend the boycott. At that meeting, King said,

> *There comes a time when people get tired of being trampled over by the iron feet of oppression. . . .*
>
> *We are here . . . because we're tired. . . . We are not here advocating violence. . . . We are Christian people. . . . The only weapon that we have . . . is the weapon of protest. . . .*
>
> *We're going to work . . . to gain justice on the buses in this city. . . .*
>
> *We are not wrong in what we are doing. If we are wrong, the Supreme Court . . . is wrong. . . . If we are wrong, God Almighty is wrong. . . . If we are wrong, justice is a lie.*

◄ Martin Luther King Jr. speaking at his church during the civil rights movement

The MIA presented a list of demands to the city commissioners for changes in the bus system, including first-come, first-served seating for all passengers, the hiring of black bus drivers, and more courteous treatment by drivers. The city refused these demands, and the boycott continued. The city's leaders tried to defeat the boycott by fining black taxi drivers who helped the boycotters by driving them for reduced rates. The MIA responded by organizing a carpool system where those with cars, both blacks and whites who were sympathetic to their cause, drove the boycotters where they needed to go. Opponents used intimidation and the law to try to end the boycott. The homes of King and the local NAACP leader were bombed along with four black Baptist churches. The city received a court injunction ordering the end of the boycott, and over eighty black leaders, including King, were arrested for violating a law prohibiting conspiracies or boycotts that interfered with businesses. King spent two weeks in jail, and after losing the appeal of his conviction, paid the $500 fine.

The boycott and King's arrest drew national attention to the civil rights movement in Montgomery. It also financially devastated the city bus system. A federal court ruled in June 1956 that laws requiring racially segregated seating violated the Constitution. The city challenged the ruling, but the Supreme Court upheld the lower court's decision on December 20, 1956. The city ended its segregated seating policy the next day, and the MIA voted to end the boycott, which had lasted 381 days.

▲ Black citizens of Montgomery walking to work in the third month of the bus boycott

Capitalizing on the success of the boycott, King, along with other African American leaders including Rev. Ralph Abernathy and Rev. Fred Shuttlesworth, formed the **Southern Christian Leadership Conference (SCLC)** in 1957 to spread and organize the civil rights movement across the South. King was elected its first president. With the support of black churches, many of which hosted mass meetings, the SCLC encouraged marches, boycotts, and other nonviolent protests against laws that violated the civil rights of African Americans. It also worked to register African Americans to vote and supported legal challenges to segregation laws across the South.

King's approach to the battle for civil rights was influenced by the nonviolent resistance of Mohandas (Mahatma) Gandhi, the leader of India's independence movement in the 1930s and 1940s. Gandhi had used nonviolence, including civil disobedience (peaceful refusal to obey unjust laws), to bring change to India's society. The Fellowship of Reconciliation (FOR) and the Congress of Racial Equality (CORE), two groups founded in the northern US states in earlier decades, had embraced Gandhi's methods and advised King and others in the civil rights movement on how to apply nonviolent strategies. King expounded on his philosophy of nonviolence in a 1962 speech given at Cornell College in Iowa:

### Analyzing Sources

What is King's justification for disobeying "unjust laws"? According to King, what effect does nonviolence have on the opponents to civil rights?

> *This is what we try to teach in the struggle for freedom and justice in the nonviolent movement in the South. We have come to the point where we are able to say to those who will even use violence to block us, we will match your capacity to inflict suffering with our capacity to endure suffering. . . . Do to us what you will, and we will still love you. We cannot in all good conscience obey your unjust laws, because noncooperation with evil is as much a moral obligation as is cooperation with good. And so throw us in jail, and we will still love you. Bomb our homes and threaten our children, and, as difficult as it is, we will still love you. . . . Be ye assured that we will wear you down by our capacity to suffer, and one day we will win our freedom. We will not only win freedom for ourselves, we will so appeal to your heart and your conscience that we will win you in the process.*

— **MARTIN LUTHER KING JR.** Excerpt from "A Realistic Look at the Question of Progress in the Area of Race Relations, Address at Cornell College" reprinted by arrangement with The Heirs to the Estate of Martin Luther King Jr., c/o Writers House as agent for the proprietor New York, NY. Copyright © 1962 by Dr. Martin Luther King, Jr. Renewed © 1990 by Coretta Scott King.

## The Case *of* Emmett Till

In August 1955 fourteen-year-old **Emmett Till**, an African American from Chicago, traveled to visit relatives in Money, Mississippi. Shortly after his arrival in Mississippi, he and a group of black teenagers entered Bryant's Grocery and Meat Market to buy candy after spending most of the day picking cotton. What happened next is not certain, but Till was accused of whistling at, flirting with, or touching the hand of Carolyn Bryant, the white twenty-one-year-old wife of the store owner, who was working at the store. Four days later, on August 28 at around 2:30 in the morning, Carolyn's husband Ron Bryant, and Ron's half-brother J. W. Milam went to the home of Emmett's great uncle, Mose Wright, where Till was staying. They grabbed Till, tied him up, put him in the back of their pickup truck, and drove him to a barn where they beat him until he was unconscious. They then took him to the bank of a river, shot him in the head, tied his body to a large cotton gin fan, and threw his body in the river, where it was found three days later. His body was so badly disfigured that some questioned whether the body was really Emmett Till's.

Till's murder drew national attention. His body was returned to Chicago for his funeral, where his mother insisted on an open casket so the public could see Emmett's badly mutilated body. Pictures of his corpse were published across the country, and many across the nation were enraged after seeing the impact of racial violence for the first time.

Mississippi's governor urged that the perpetrators of Till's murder be prosecuted vigorously. Bryant and Milam were indicted for murder and put on trial. Because blacks and women were barred from jury duty in the county, an all-white, all-male jury heard the case. Despite strong evidence of their guilt, Bryant and Milam were found not guilty of all charges. A few months later, they admitted that they had committed the crime, and were paid by *Look* magazine for a story in which they told how they had kidnapped and killed Till. Carolyn Bryant admitted in a 2007 interview that Till had not touched or harassed her and that "nothing that boy did could ever justify what happened to him."

The case of Emmett Till was one of the events that motivated the civil rights movement. One hundred days after Till's murder, Rosa Parks was arrested for refusing to move to the back of a Montgomery bus. She later said, "I thought of Emmett Till, and I couldn't go back." In 2022 Congress passed the Emmett Till Antilynching Act which made lynching a federal crime.

▼ Mamie Till-Mobley, grieving at the open casket at her son's funeral

# Eisenhower and Civil Rights

## *Civil Rights Act of 1957*

In 1956 only 20 percent of eligible black Americans were registered to vote. Discriminatory registration and voting laws, including literacy tests and poll taxes, were keeping black Americans from exercising their right to vote. That year President Eisenhower proposed a broad civil rights bill that would empower the federal government to prosecute anyone who violated African Americans' civil rights under the Fourteenth Amendment or their voting rights under the Fifteenth Amendment. Eisenhower sent the bill to Congress, knowing that it would be opposed by southern Democrats. Eisenhower wanted to see civil rights legislation passed, and politically he knew the bill would also divide the Democratic Party and hopefully cause more black Americans to vote for him and other Republicans in the election of 1956.

Eisenhower's bill met fierce resistance in Congress. However, Texas Democrat Lyndon Johnson, who was the Senate majority leader at the time, worked out a compromise which enabled the **Civil Rights Act of 1957** to pass in a watered-down form. The act, the first civil rights legislation to pass Congress since Reconstruction, created the Civil Rights Division of the Department of Justice, authorized the US attorney general to prosecute individuals that attempted to deny another citizen's right to vote, created the US Commission on Civil Rights to investigate claims of voting rights violations, and allowed African Americans to serve on federal court juries regardless of state jury laws.

## Little Rock Central High School

▲ Elizabeth Eckford, one of the "Little Rock Nine," facing harassment, September 4, 1957

▼ Soldiers escorting some of the "Little Rock Nine"

In response to the *Brown* decision, the school board of Little Rock, Arkansas, decided to implement a plan to gradually integrate the school district, starting with Central High School. Black students would be allowed to attend Central High starting in the fall of 1957. White parents with children at the school began a petition to stop the integration plan. Governor Orval Faubus supported the petition, but a federal court ordered the board's integration plan to proceed. Nine black students registered to attend the school that fall. On September 2, Governor Faubus announced that he would call in the Arkansas National Guard to prevent the black students from attending, claiming it was for the students' safety and to prevent violence and bloodshed. When the **"Little Rock Nine"** arrived for the first day of school on September 4, they were met by a crowd of hostile adults and students and state National Guard troops who prevented them from entering the building. Because of this, a federal judge began legal proceedings against Governor Faubus. President Eisenhower met with Faubus to try to convince him to remove the National Guard troops, but Faubus continued to deny entry to the students. The federal judge ordered the guardsmen to be removed on September 20, and the Little Rock police attempted to escort the nine students into the school on September 23; however, over one thousand protesters met them and prevented their attendance. Eisenhower then signed an executive order federalizing the Arkansas National Guard and deploying over one thousand troops from the US Army's 101st Airborne Division to Little Rock to escort the students and maintain order. The Little Rock Nine attended classes at Central High for the first time on September 25.

At the end of the 1957–58 school year, Faubus asked the federal court for a two-year delay in the implementation of school integration. When that request was denied, Faubus signed an act ordering all Little Rock high schools closed for the 1958–59 school year. He planned to lease the buildings to segregated black and white private schools. In a city-wide referendum, Little Rock voters supported his plan to prevent integration. A federal judge blocked the private school plan, but the high schools remained closed, meaning that no free public Little Rock high schools were opened during what became known as the "lost year."

▲ Arkansas governor Orval Faubus holding up a headline covering Eisenhower's intervention at Central High School

## Comprehension Check 22.1

1. President Truman used executive orders to ____.
   A desegregate public schools
   B end discrimination in federal employment and segregation in the military
   C end segregation on city buses

2. Both Truman and Eisenhower faced opposition in Congress to their civil rights agendas.
   True     False

3. Each of the following is true about *Brown v. Board of Education of Topeka* except that ____.
   A it ruled that separate schools violated the Fourteenth Amendment
   B some Southerners called for massive resistance to the decision
   C all schools were desegregated within a year of the decision
   D the decision convinced black Americans to begin challenging segregation in other areas besides schools

4. Each of the following is true about the Little Rock Central High School episode except that ____.
   A the Little Rock school board refused to create a plan to integrate the schools after the *Brown* ruling
   B many white families and the governor opposed allowing black students to attend Central High School
   C Eisenhower used US Army troops to help protect the black students as they attended school
   D Governor Faubus closed all Little Rock high schools the following year rather than allowing them to be integrated

### MAKING CONNECTIONS

5. What did Martin Luther King Jr. say the effect of the strategy of nonviolence would be? How did the Montgomery bus boycott demonstrate this effect?

▲ A sit-in at Woolworth's lunch counter in Little Rock, Arkansas

## 22.2 Advances in Civil Rights

**What successes were achieved in the civil rights movement?**

During the 1960s more and more Americans supported the demand for equal rights for all citizens. Black Americans often led the way, and a growing number of white Americans stood with them in their effort to secure rights that included improved educational opportunities for their children, integration of public facilities, and the right to vote. In 1962 James Meredith enrolled as the first black student at the University of Mississippi after federal marshals and troops overcame a defiant governor and mob. After the successes of the 1950s, the civil rights movement marched on through the 1960s as King, the Southern Christian Leadership Conference, and others effected change in many southern states through nonviolent protests, believing that in their quest for justice that they must continue to employ just means.

## Strategies

In the 1940s CORE had begun staging **sit-ins** in Chicago restaurants and recreational facilities to challenge the segregationist practices of local businessmen. Before a sit-in, organizers contacted the police, informing officers of their intentions. During the sit-in, black participants entered and sat in a restaurant or business; if the staff refused to serve the participants and asked them to leave, they continued to sit, drawing attention to the discrimination. In a Chicago sit-in, a business owner contacted the police to expel the participants, but the police officer cited that there was no legal basis for removal and upheld the actions of the protesters.

**GUIDING QUESTIONS**

- Were the resistance strategies used to advance civil rights effective?
- What led to the passage of the Civil Rights Act of 1964?
- How did the Voting Rights Act of 1965 achieve significant goals of the civil rights movement?

In February 1960 four freshman college students from North Carolina A & T College planned and executed a sit-in at a Woolworth's store in Greensboro, North Carolina. After making purchases, they sat down at the "whites only" lunch counter and refused to leave when the owner demanded; the police did not arrest the students. In the next few days, other students from the college as well as white female students from a nearby college joined in. Soon after, students in other cities throughout several southern states were staging sit-ins and in some areas were arrested. As a result of the sit-ins, Woolworth's lunch counter became integrated as did several other establishments throughout the South. Another result of this student-led strategy was the creation of the **Student Nonviolent Coordinating Committee (SNCC)** in April of 1960 that organized additional student sit-ins and other forms of nonviolent protest, such as the Freedom Rides.

Despite recent Supreme Court decisions which ruled against segregation in interstate transportation and facilities, many interstate bus terminals remained segregated. Black and white **Freedom Riders** traveled in buses across the Deep South in 1961, hoping to secure federal enforcement of desegregated interstate travel. Despite the Supreme Court rulings, Freedom Riders faced brutal opposition. Ku Klux Klansmen threw a firebomb into a bus stopped in the station in Anniston, Alabama. Riders were beaten at stations in South Carolina and Alabama and arrested in Mississippi. As the Freedom Rides became a national point of interest, the Interstate Commerce Commission (ICC) banned segregation on interstate buses and terminals by the fall of that year.

King, Abernathy, and others supported Shuttlesworth and his organization, the Alabama Christian Movement for Human Rights (ACMHR) to protest segregation in Birmingham, Alabama, strategically targeting local businesses during a peak sales season. Protesters used the same nonviolent tactics of sit-ins, mass meetings, and boycotts, and hundreds were arrested. After an Alabama court issued an order to stop the protest, King and Abernathy purposefully continued the campaign as an act of civil disobedience, knowing they would go to jail. King, Abernathy, and other protesters were arrested on Good Friday, April 12, 1963. While in solitary confinement, King wrote "Letter from Birmingham Jail" in reaction to clergy who supported civil rights but had urged moderation. King argued that direct action was necessary because of the ongoing persecution of black Americans and that the nonviolent movement was a moderate course between the status quo of segregation and the extremes of the emerging black nationalists (discussed later in this chapter). After King's release on bond and concessions from business leaders to end segregation practices, the protest ended in May.

Opponents of the civil rights movement often used violence against nonviolent protesters. Protest demonstrations, such as the Freedom Rides, sometimes ended with assaults on the demonstrators by angry mobs of whites. In Birmingham, policemen used tear gas, police dogs, and firehoses against protesters, including hundreds of children. Violent reactions to the end of segregation in Birmingham continued after the protest ended, including the bombing of Sixteenth Street Baptist Church, where four young African American girls were killed.

Television had become an ally of the civil rights movement. As news cameras showed police dogs and fire hoses being used against children and adults, many white Americans began to realize the need to protect the rights of black Americans.

---

▾ (left) Freedom Riders, escorted by members of the Alabama National Guard, May 26, 1961; (right) a black high school student in Birmingham, Alabama, being attacked by a police dog

# Civil Rights Act of 1964

In August 1963 more than 200,000 people—both black and white—gathered in the nation's capital for a civil rights protest known as the **March on Washington for Jobs and Freedom**. Two months before the march, President Kennedy had promised a historic civil rights bill. The march from the Washington Monument to the Lincoln Memorial focused attention on the proposed bill and called for federal legislation to end job discrimination.

The speakers at the Lincoln Memorial included A. Philip Randolph, who was the director of the march and had influenced FDR's executive order during World War II (see Chapter 19), and John Lewis, the chairman of the SNCC and one of the Freedom Riders. The highlight was Martin Luther King's address, later called his "I Have a Dream" speech because of his repeated phrases that captured his vision for the country.

> *I have a dream that one day this nation will rise up and live out the true meaning of its creed, "We hold these truths to be self-evident, that all men are created equal." I have a dream that one day on the red hills of Georgia, sons of former slaves and the sons of former slave owners will be able to sit down together at the table of brotherhood. . . . I have a dream that my four little children will one day live in a nation where they will not be judged by the color of their skin, but by the content of their character.*

— **MARTIN LUTHER KING JR.** Excerpt from "I Have a Dream" reprinted by arrangement with The Heirs to the Estate of Martin Luther King Jr., c/o Writers House as agent for the proprietor New York, NY. Copyright © 1963 by Dr. Martin Luther King, Jr. Renewed © 1991 by Coretta Scott King.

▲ March on Washington for Jobs and Freedom, August 28, 1963

## Analyzing Sources

How does King tie elements of American history to his hopes for the future?

▼ Martin Luther King Jr. at the Lincoln Memorial

After the march President Kennedy and Vice President Johnson discussed the civil rights legislation with King and other leaders. The bill was not passed, however, until the following year. By that time, President Kennedy had been assassinated. Soon after becoming president, Johnson ensured passage by dedicating the legislation to recently slain President Kennedy. Congress passed the **Civil Rights Act of 1964**, which established fairer procedures for voter registration, forbade racial discrimination in public buildings such as restaurants and stores, promoted the desegregation of public schools, authorized withholding federal funds from projects or institutions that discriminated against minorities, and created the Equal Employment Opportunity Commission (EEOC) to ensure that job seekers did not encounter discrimination.

## Voting Rights Act of 1965

Both the Civil Rights Acts of 1957 and 1964 included measures intended to protect voting rights of black citizens in keeping with the Fourteenth and Fifteenth Amendments. A minor civil rights bill in 1960 gave the attorney general access to voter registration records as part of the larger investigation into voter discrimination against black citizens in southern states. These records shed light on discriminatory practices such as different applications of literacy tests for white and black voters, and influenced further measures to protect black citizens against voter suppression.

### Twenty-Third Amendment

Ratified in 1961, the **Twenty-Third Amendment** allowed Washington, DC, to gain electors for presidential elections, giving residents the ability to vote in federal elections, although the district did not have a voting member of Congress. At the time of the amendment's ratification, the majority of the district's population was black. Residents voted for the first time in the 1964 election.

### Twenty-Fourth Amendment

Passed in 1962 and ratified in January 1964, the **Twenty-Fourth Amendment** outlawed the use of poll taxes in federal elections. The Supreme Court ruled in 1966 that poll taxes in state elections violated the 14th Amendment.

### The Struggle for Voting Rights

Despite the passage of amendments and civil rights legislation, the federal government struggled with enforcement of protections, and black citizens continued to face intimidation to keep them from voting. In 1964 in a coordinated effort later called **Freedom Summer**, volunteers from various civil rights organizations worked to help thousands of black Americans register to vote in Mississippi. Members of the Ku Klux Klan brutally murdered three civil rights workers, two white men and one black man. Other violent demonstrations included burning and bombing homes, churches, and businesses.

That same year, the Mississippi Freedom Democratic Party (MFDP) was created in opposition to the all-white Democratic Party of the state. Speaking on behalf of the MFDP, Fannie Lou Hamer, a key organizer, described the death threats and police brutality she and others had endured in their attempts to register for the vote. At the end of her speech she asked, "Is this America, the land of the free and the home of the brave, where we have to sleep with our telephones off the hooks because our lives be threatened daily, because we want to live as decent human beings, in America?" Television broadcasts of her testimony and other news of the violence in Mississippi helped ensure the passage of the Civil Rights Act of 1964.

▲ Lyndon B. Johnson signing the 1964 Civil Rights Act

## Selma

Like many areas of Mississippi, only a small percentage of black citizens could vote in Selma, Alabama. After the shooting of a young African American demonstrator named Jimmie Lee Jackson by an Alabama state trooper in a February 1965 protest, hundreds marched from Selma toward Montgomery, the state capital, to protest voter discrimination. The march began on March 7 and ended at the Edmund Pettus Bridge, where police attacked the protesters, using tear gas and beating several, including John Lewis, one of the leaders of the march. The police attack marked what became known as **"Bloody Sunday"** and influenced President Johnson to press Congress for a new voting rights bill. The attack also prompted him to send federal troops to protect both King, who arrived in Selma after "Bloody Sunday," and thousands of marchers in a renewed effort beginning on March 21. Four days later, they reached the capitol building in Montgomery, where King delivered a rousing speech. Hundreds of marchers had been beaten, and three white civil rights advocates involved in Selma died in separate incidents at the hands of Klansmen and other extremists.

In August President Johnson signed "an act to enforce the fifteenth amendment," titled the **Voting Rights Act of 1965**. The act outlawed literacy tests for voters and allowed federal officials to be sent into states to oversee and ensure fairness in voter registration and elections. Additionally, any changes to voting procedures made after November 1, 1964, in any areas where voter discrimination had previously occurred were required to obtain approval from a district court or the attorney general. The act also augmented the Twenty-Fourth Amendment's ban on poll taxes in federal elections by giving the attorney general the power to challenge poll taxes used in state and local elections. After the passage of the Voting Rights Act, the numbers of black voters and black elected officials increased significantly. Congress has since extended the provisions of the act several times since its initial passage. In the twenty-first century, a Supreme Court ruling struck down the provision of the Voting Rights Act which indicated which states must seek approval for changes in voting policies and procedures. Some in Congress have attempted to pass additional legislation designed to protect provisions of the Voting Rights Act.

▼ Martin Luther King Jr. with his wife, Coretta Scott King, and John Lewis in the Selma March

### Comprehension Check 22.2

1. Nonviolent strategies in the 1960s included all of the following except ____.

   **A** boycotts

   **B** firehoses

   **C** freedom rides

   **D** sit-ins

2. The highlight of the March on Washington was a speech by ____.

   **A** A. Philip Randolph

   **B** John Lewis

   **C** Martin Luther King Jr.

3. All of the following were provisions of the Civil Rights Act of 1964 except ____.

   **A** allowing residents of Washington, DC, to vote in presidential elections

   **B** establishing the Equal Employment Opportunity Commission (EEOC)

   **C** forbidding segregation in public buildings

   **D** withdrawing federal funds from institutions practicing discrimination

#### MAKING CONNECTIONS

4. How did television aid the civil rights movement?

5. Which amendment was the Voting Rights Act of 1965 intended to enforce, and why was the act necessary?

# 22.3 Civil Rights Struggles

Why was the Black Power movement appealing to some?

## Urban Issues

While many celebrated the passage of the Voting Rights Act, daily life for many African Americans had not changed much. In urban areas, where over 70 percent of the African American population lived, there was anger and frustration over poverty, discrimination, inadequate schools, and a lack of economic opportunity. The average income of black families was considerably lower than that of white families, and nearly half of all African Americans lived in poverty. Poor neighborhoods in large cities had higher rates of unemployment, crime, illness, infant mortality, single-parent households, juvenile delinquency, and school dropouts than the affluent neighborhoods.

Less than a week after Johnson signed the Voting Rights Act, one of the worst race riots in American history erupted in the predominantly black neighborhood of Watts in Los Angeles. In addition to the problems facing most large cities, African Americans in Los Angeles were frustrated when California voters passed a proposition in 1964 which overturned a state law preventing housing discrimination. Housing segregation was widespread in Los Angeles and most African Americans were prevented from moving to the suburbs, leaving them confined to urban ghettos. Anger boiled over on August 11, 1965, when a white policeman in Watts pulled over a young black man for drunk driving. Crowds began to gather, and the situation escalated rapidly as the police struggled to place the driver under arrest. Some accused the police of brutality, and the tension exploded as the crowd began throwing rocks at the police. The unrest became a riot overnight with the burning and looting of businesses. It took six days for the police and the National Guard to restore order. By the end of the Watts riots, thirty-four people had been killed, nearly nine hundred wounded, and $45 million in property had been destroyed.

### GUIDING QUESTIONS

- Why did riots occur in some places?
- How was the Black Power movement different from nonviolent civil rights strategies?
- How did King's assassination change the civil rights movement?

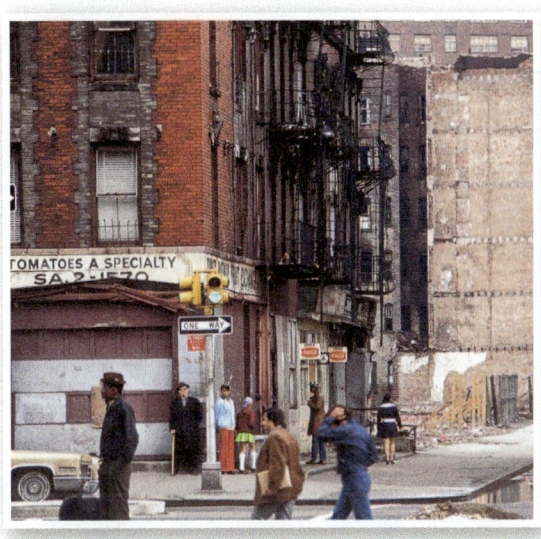

▲ 101st Street in East Harlem, New York City, 1967

▼ Watts neighborhood of Los Angeles after the riot

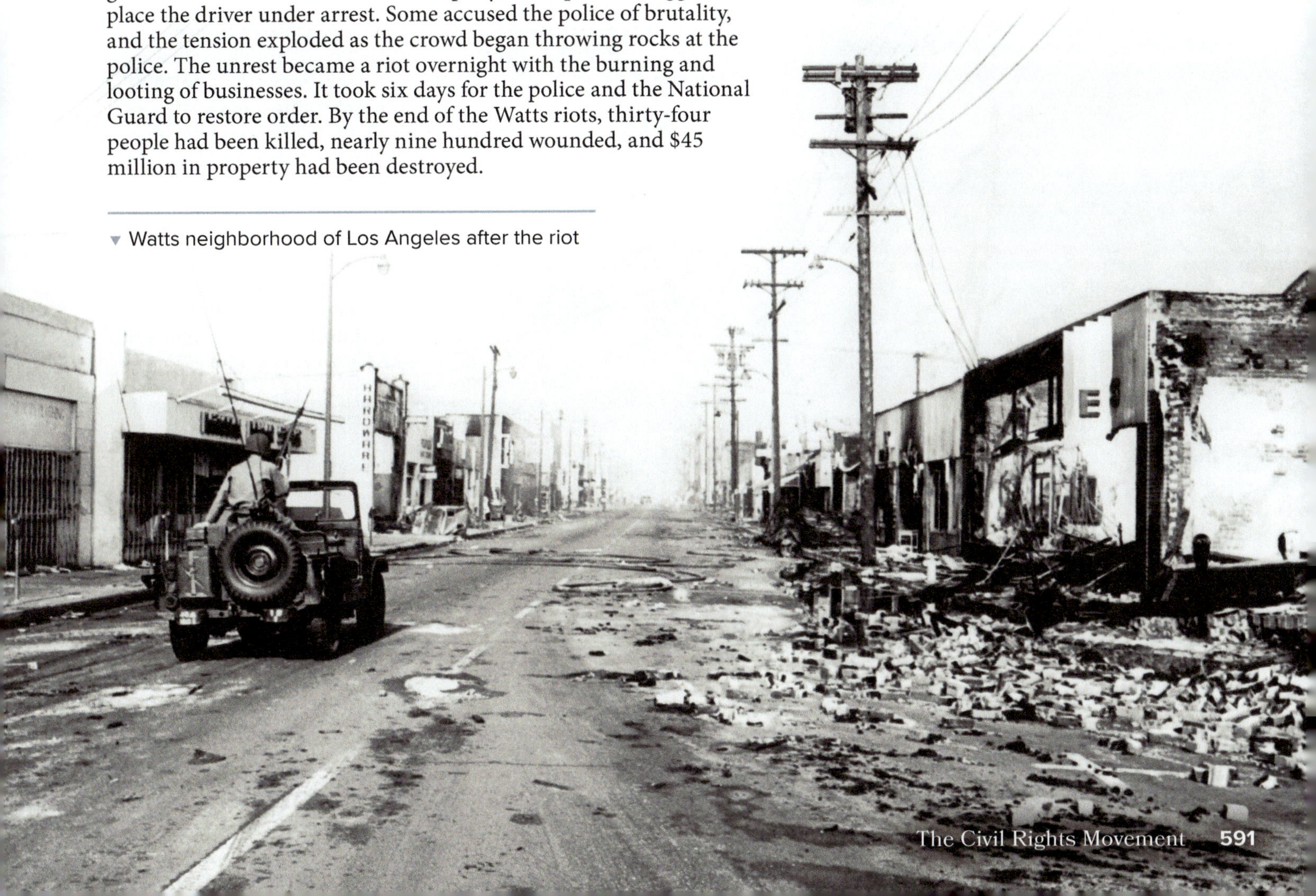

After the Watts riot, more than thirty other riots occurred across the nation as the frustration of black Americans over economic and other inequalities erupted, often sparked by arrests or allegations of police brutality against blacks. In Detroit forty-three people died in 1967 while looters ransacked shops and arsonists set hundreds of fires. Another major riot occurred in Newark, New Jersey, the same year. Tragically, black Americans felt the brunt of the destruction; their homes and businesses suffered most of the damage, and most of the casualties were black. When the televisions had shown nonviolent demonstrators being brutally treated by police, most Americans had sympathized with black Americans who were suffering to gain justice and equality. But these violent urban outbursts alienated many formerly sympathetic white Americans, who became increasingly fearful and suspicious of the protesters' actions and motives. Even the peaceful Martin Luther King Jr. lost some popularity among white Americans. By the end of the 1960s, ethnic tensions had reached a new high. As a result, progress on civil rights issues slowed considerably.

## Black Power

While most African Americans continued to embrace the strategy of nonviolence and saw the successes it brought in ending segregation, an increasing number of younger black people felt that this strategy did not go far enough to address the problems of poverty and the lack of economic opportunity in the African American community. They also objected to the Vietnam War and argued that it disproportionately affected blacks, who were drafted and were being killed in combat in high numbers. Dr. King and Stokely Carmichael, who became the chairman of the SNCC after John Lewis, both spoke out against the war. However, many young African Americans began to call for more aggressive strategies.

One person who rejected King's strategy of nonviolence was **Malcolm X**. Born Malcolm Little in Omaha, Nebraska, Malcolm experienced a difficult upbringing and spent time in prison for burglary. While in prison he joined a radical group called the Nation of Islam, founded by Elijah Muhammed, an African American convert to Islam, that preached black nationalism. Malcolm gave up the last name he said white society had given him and changed his name to Malcolm X (the X symbolized the unknown family name of his enslaved African ancestors).

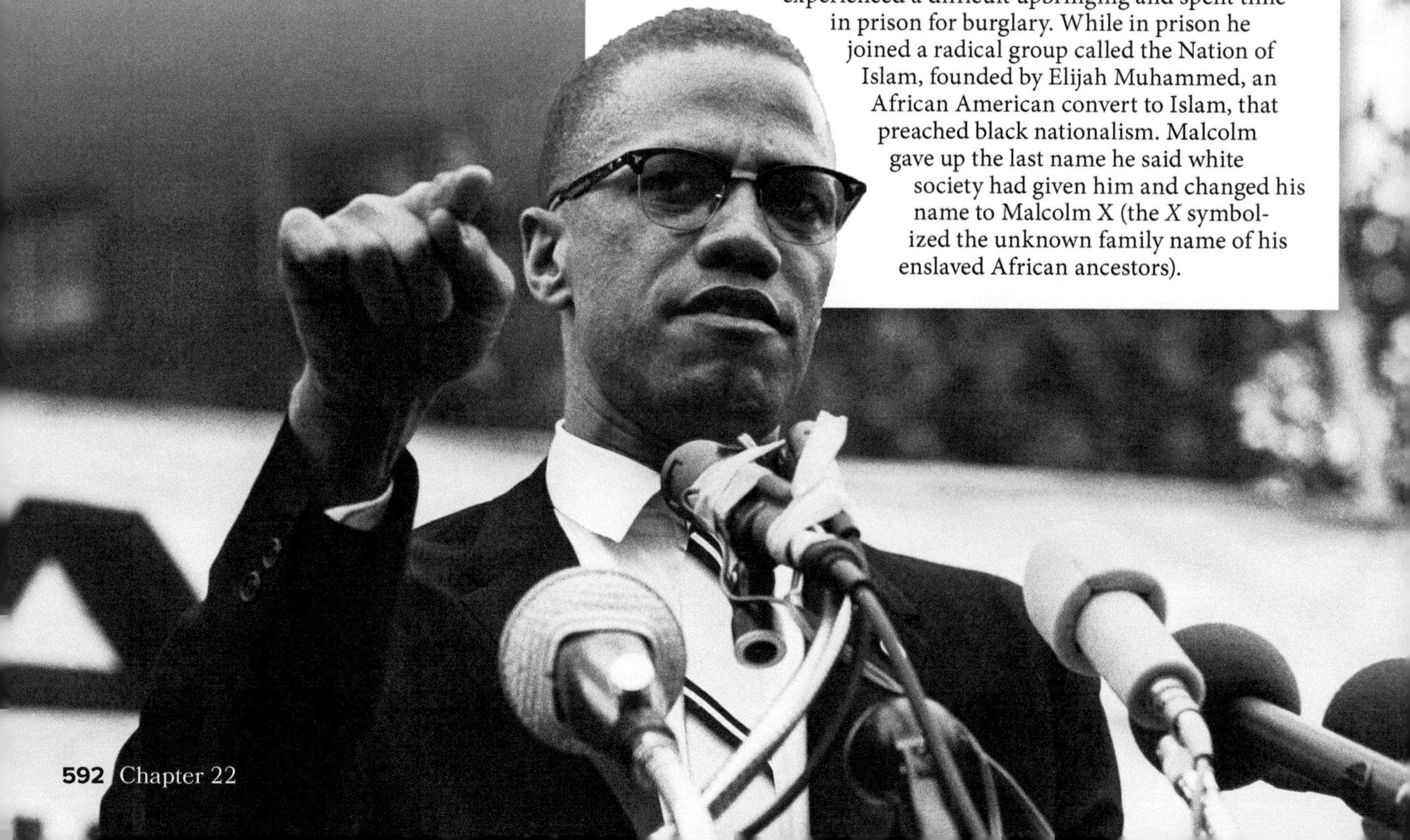

▼ (below) Stokely Carmichael speaking in support of the Viet Cong, 1967; (bottom) Malcolm X speaking on separation of whites and blacks

While King and others in the civil rights movement called for integration and political involvement through voting, the Nation of Islam called the white race inherently evil, said that total separation was the only way to achieve racial equality, and prohibited its members from participation in the political process. By 1964 Malcolm X had broken with the Nation of Islam over disagreements about the group's activities and moral concerns about Elijah Muhammed's personal life. Malcolm went on a pilgrimage to the Muslim holy city of Mecca, and when he returned, he seemed more willing to work with moderate civil rights leaders, although he still advocated a more aggressive approach than King. In a 1964 speech entitled "The Ballot or the Bullet," he called on his audience to use the ballot before resorting to the bullet to enact change. He said that black men were growing tired of turning the other cheek and that if politicians failed to keep their promises to African Americans, violence could result. His break with the Nation of Islam and his criticism of its policies led that organization to call for his death, and in February 1965 Malcolm X was shot and killed by three Nation of Islam members.

After Malcolm X's murder, a new militant group called the Black Panthers was formed in 1966 in Oakland, California. They organized armed citizen patrols in several large cities and, drawing on socialist ideas, began several programs, including one that provided free breakfasts for poor children. They called for an end to racial oppression and for black control of major institutions in the African American community, including schools, hospitals, law enforcement, and housing. However, the group lost the support of many African Americans because of its reputation for violence, including incidents where police officers were killed.

By 1966 Stokely Carmichael had grown impatient with the slow progress that resulted from nonviolent protest. As leader of the Student Nonviolent Coordinating Committee, he called for a new "**Black Power**" movement in which black Americans took control of the social, political, and economic direction of the civil rights movement. He began to advocate black separatism and discouraged white membership in the SNCC.

Carmichael eventually broke with King's doctrine of nonviolence and the goal of racial integration. He met with Communist leaders in Cuba, China, and North Vietnam, and eventually left the SNCC and became a leader in the Black Panthers. He moved to Guinea, West Africa, and changed his name to Kwame Ture.

King criticized black power as a philosophy of hopelessness and despair born out of hurt and the failure of white Americans to deliver on their promises to African Americans. The emphasis of the Black Power movement and the Black Panthers on violence frightened many white Americans and angered many black Americans, who feared that violence would hinder the progress of the civil rights movement.

## Black Pride

Along with black power came "black pride," where African Americans expressed pride in their African heritage and the distinctiveness of black culture. Stokely Carmichael wrote that black people must develop a sense of pride, not shame, in blackness, and that the roots of their identity would be found in Africa, not America. African Americans showed "black pride" by adopting African names, African clothing styles, and "Afro" hair styles.

▶ 1970s ad for hair care products designed for black women

## Identity Politics

The Black Power movement is an example of what has been called identity politics. *Britannica* defines identity politics as "political or social action by or on behalf of a racial, religious, gender, or other group, usually undertaken with the goal of rectifying injustices suffered by group members because of differences or conflicts between their particular identity and the dominant identity of larger society." However, rather than eliminating injustice, identity politics can sometimes promote injustice because its definition of justice is based on group power rather than on universal moral principles.

Many civil rights leaders expressed concern over this form of identity politics. NAACP leader Roy Wilkins said that Black Power viewed "every other ethnic group [as] an antagonist" and that achieving "racial dignity" did not require one race to be pitted against another. Martin Luther King stated that most black Americans wanted to share power, "in order to bring about a community in which neither power nor dignity will be black or white."

Black Power and identity politics influenced later rights movements, including women's rights and homosexual and transgender rights. As historian George Marsden writes,

> "[A]lthough some of the rhetoric of justice and equality was similar, it was now reshaped by the frameworks of identity politics. Whatever the merits of these causes, rather than grounding reforms in a universalized moral order, their outlooks were often frankly shaped on perceptions and experiences unique to their group."

George Marsden, *The Twilight of the American Enlightenment: The 1950s and the Crisis of Liberal Belief* (New York: Basic Books, 2014), 67.

▶ Stokely Carmichael speaking at the University of California at Berkeley to the Students for a Democratic Society (SDS)

Marsden goes on to say that these movements claimed to be built on American ideals such as freedom and equality, but that they were no longer connected to a common understanding of morality. Rather than appealing to biblical justice, as King and other nonviolent leaders did, radicals in the Black Power movement abandoned the true sense of justice by rationalizing violent tactics. The abandonment of a biblical understanding of justice would later be illustrated in the radical element in the women's rights movement that advocated for abortion rights and in the LGBTQ movement that desired acceptance for unbiblical expressions of sexuality (see Chapter 23).

## King's Assassination

Despite the gains the civil rights movement had achieved in voting rights and ending segregation, many African Americans felt that more needed to be done to address economic inequality. In the spring of 1968, King and the Southern Christian Leadership Conference prepared for the Poor People's Campaign in Washington, DC, to lobby Congress for billions of dollars to end poverty and unemployment in the United States. However, before that campaign took place, a tragedy in Memphis, Tennessee, struck the cause of civil rights.

As part of the effort to address economic issues, in April 1968 King and other SCLC members went to Memphis to support a strike by African American sanitation workers who were asking for better pay and working conditions after two of their coworkers were crushed to death by a malfunctioning machine.

On the night of April 3, King, aware of recent death threats, gave a speech in which he expressed the possibility that he would not live to see the fulfillment of all the goals of the civil rights movement.

> *We've got some difficult days ahead. But it doesn't matter with me now. Because I've been to the mountaintop. And I don't mind. Like anybody, I would like to live a long life. Longevity has its place. But I'm not concerned about that now. I just want to do God's will. And He's allowed me to go up to the mountain. And I've looked over. And I've seen the promised land. I may not get there with you. But I want you to know tonight, that we, as a people, will get to the promised land. And I'm happy tonight. I'm not worried about anything. I'm not fearing any man. Mine eyes have seen the glory of the coming of the Lord.*

— **MARTIN LUTHER KING JR.** Excerpt from "I've Been to the Mountain Top," reprinted by arrangement with The Heirs to the Estate of Martin Luther King Jr., c/o Writers House as agent for the proprietor New York, NY. Copyright © 1968 by Dr. Martin Luther King, Jr. Renewed © 1996 by Coretta Scott King.

**Analyzing Sources**

What biblical allusion does King make in this speech? To what biblical figure does he compare himself?

The next day, April 4, 1968, a white man named James Earl Ray shot and killed thirty-nine-year-old King while he stood on the balcony of his Memphis motel.

◄ The assassination of Martin Luther King Jr. at the Lorraine Motel in Memphis, Tennessee, 1968

▲ Black Panther demonstration at the capitol building in Olympia, Washington

King's assassination sparked a new wave of urban violence, with riots breaking out in over a hundred cities. President Johnson called for calm and urged Americans to reject violence and to continue to embrace King's commitment to nonviolence. Johnson also called on Congress to pass the Civil Rights Act of 1968, also known as the **Fair Housing Act**, to honor King's legacy. The act prohibited discrimination based on race, religion, color, or national origin in the sale, rental, or financing of housing, and Johnson signed it into law on April 11, 1968.

After King's assassination, the civil rights movement lost some of its unity. Some black Americans wanted to continue King's strategy, while others saw King's murder as evidence that his message of nonviolence was being met with violent resistance by white Americans. This belief that nonviolence was ineffective led more young African Americans to join radical groups that promoted violence, such as the Black Panthers.

The civil rights movement of the 1950s and 1960s was successful in achieving many of its goals. Segregation laws were overturned, employment and housing discrimination based on race was outlawed, and barriers to African American voting were knocked down. One sign of progress for black Americans was the appointment by President Johnson of Thurgood Marshall, the NAACP lawyer who had argued the *Brown* case, to be the first African American Supreme Court justice in 1967. However, many felt that more work needed to be done, especially in the area of economic opportunity, for African Americans to achieve equality.

## Comprehension Check 22.3

**1.** The civil rights movement dramatically improved the daily lives of urban black Americans by the 1960s.

　　　　True　　　　False

**2.** Urban riots caused many white Americans to become more fearful of and less sympathetic toward the civil rights movement.

　　　　True　　　　False

**3.** Each of the following is true about Malcolm X except that ____.

　**A** he joined the Nation of Islam group while in prison

　**B** after breaking from the Nation of Islam group he was more willing to work with moderate civil rights leaders

　**C** he was killed by a white segregationist

**4.** The Civil Rights Act of 1968 prohibited discrimination in ____.

　**A** housing

　**B** the military

　**C** employment

### MAKING CONNECTIONS

**5.** How did the views of the leaders of the Nation of Islam group and the Black Power movement differ from those of Martin Luther King Jr.?

## Chapter Summary

### 22.1 Early Civil Rights Movement

- African Americans faced both legal and informal discrimination, including Jim Crow laws and redlining. When President Truman's attempt to pass a broad civil rights bill was opposed in Congress, he instead used executive orders to end discrimination in federal employment and segregation in the armed forces.

- Jackie Robinson broke the color barrier in Major League Baseball in 1947.

- In *Brown v. Board of Education*, the Supreme Court ruled that separate schools were inherently unequal, and in *Brown 2* the Court said that desegregation must proceed with "all deliberate speed." Many in the South resisted the ruling.

- The arrest of Rosa Parks led to the Montgomery bus boycott and the rise of Martin Luther King Jr. as a leader in the Civil Rights Movement. The strategy of nonviolent protest led to an end to segregated seating on Montgomery buses.

- The kidnapping and murder of Emmett Till and the trial in which his murderers were acquitted helped spark the civil rights movement.

- Under President Eisenhower, the Civil Rights Act of 1957 became the first civil rights legislation to pass Congress since Reconstruction. When the governor of Arkansas refused to allow nine black students to attend Central High School, Eisenhower used the US Army to enforce integration.

**TERMS**

civil rights movement

redlining

Jackie Robinson

Thurgood Marshall

*Brown v. Board of Education of Topeka*

Rosa Parks

Montgomery bus boycott

Dr. Martin Luther King Jr.

Southern Christian Leadership Conference (SCLC)

Emmett Till

Civil Rights Act of 1957

Little Rock Nine

**TERMS**

sit-ins

Student Nonviolent Coordinating Committee (SNCC)

Freedom Riders

March on Washington for Jobs and Freedom

Civil Rights Act of 1964

Twenty-Third Amendment

Twenty-Fourth Amendment

Freedom Summer

"Bloody Sunday"

Voting Rights Act of 1965

### 22.2 Advances in Civil Rights

- Through sits-ins, Freedom Rides, boycotts, and marches to challenge segregation, businesses and interstate buses and facilities were desegregated. Sit-ins throughout the South also resulted in the creation of the student-led SNCC. Although protestors sometimes faced violent opposition, television coverage helped direct white sympathy toward the civil rights movement.

- President Kennedy proposed civil rights legislation in 1963. The March on Washington for Jobs and Freedom focused attention on the legislation as well as on job discrimination. A year later President Johnson signed the Civil Rights Act of 1964.

- In the 1960s black citizens still faced discriminatory voting practices, such as poll taxes and literacy tests, and intimidation to discourage blacks from voting. Civil rights activists in Mississippi and in Selma, Alabama, increased national attention on voting rights. Several measures extended and protected voting rights, including the Twenty-Third and Twenty-Fourth Amendments and the Voting Rights Act of 1965.

## Chapter Summary

### 22.3 Civil Rights Struggles

- Urban African Americans still faced many difficulties. Frustration led to riots in Los Angeles (Watts) and other cities and led white Americans to become fearful of and less sympathetic toward protesters.

- Some young black Americans felt King's nonviolent strategy did not go far enough to address poverty and pushed for more aggressive action. Malcolm X joined the radical group Nation of Islam, which pushed for black nationalism and separation from white society. He later broke with that group and expressed willingness to work with moderate civil rights leaders but was killed in 1965.

- Some groups such as the Black Panthers began to promote violence to achieve their goals. Stokely Carmichael called for a "Black Power" movement in which black Americans took control of the social, political, and economic direction of the civil rights movement.

- Martin Luther King Jr. was assassinated in Memphis on April 4, 1968, sparking riots in over a hundred cities. Congress passed the Civil Rights Act of 1968 (Fair Housing Act) the next week, which prohibited discrimination in the sale, rental, or financing of housing.

- While the civil rights movement achieved the end of segregation laws and employment and housing discrimination and secured voting rights for black Americans, many felt more needed to be done in the area of economic opportunity.

**TERMS**

Malcolm X

Black Power

Fair Housing Act

## Chapter Review Questions

### RECALL

1. Who was the first African American to break the color barrier in major league baseball?

2. Who was the NAACP chief legal counsel who argued *Brown v. Board of Education* and who later became the first African American Supreme Court justice?

3. Whose arrest led to the beginning of the Montgomery bus boycott?

4. What organization was formed after the Montgomery bus boycott to spread and organize the civil rights movement across the South?

5. What fourteen-year-old African American's kidnapping and murder in 1955 helped motivate the civil rights movement?

6. What civil rights group was formed as a result of the student-led sit-ins of 1960?

7. What amendment gave electoral votes to Washington, DC?

8. What did the Twenty-Fourth Amendment outlaw in federal elections?

9. Who joined the radical group Nation of Islam while in prison and supported black nationalism until shortly before his murder in 1965?

10. What movement did Stokely Carmichael call for as leader of the SNCC?

### UNDERSTAND

11. What was redlining? What effects did the practice have for black Americans?

12. What civil rights reforms did President Truman hope to accomplish? Why was he unsuccessful in achieving most of these reforms? What were two executive actions he took related to civil rights?

13. What was the issue that the Supreme Court had to decide in *Brown v. Board of Education*? What did the court decide? What prior court decision did it overturn?

14. What were three ways some Southerners showed resistance to the *Brown* ruling?

15. What did the Supreme Court order in the *Brown 2* decision? Why did this ruling not lead to immediate action?

16. What strategy did the black community in Montgomery use to end segregation on city buses? What opposition did they face? What brought an end to the action?

17. What was the first civil rights legislation passed by Congress since Reconstruction? What were three things this law did?

18. What prevented the "Little Rock Nine" from attending Central High School at the beginning of the 1957–58 school year? How did President Eisenhower respond? Why was the 1958–59 school year in Little Rock known as the "lost year"?

19. Who were the Freedom Riders? What did they accomplish?

20. Why was King arrested in Birmingham in 1963? In his "Letter from Birmingham Jail," how did he respond to clergy who called for moderation?

21. What was the purpose of the 1963 March on Washington for Jobs and Freedom? What famous speech did Martin Luther King Jr. give at that march?

22. What were three things the Civil Rights Act of 1964 accomplished?

23. What was the goal of Freedom Summer in 1964? What opposition did it face?

24. What was the purpose of the march from Selma to Montgomery in 1965? What happened on "Bloody Sunday"?

25. What were three reforms enacted by the Voting Rights Act of 1965?

26. What were three issues urban African Americans continued to face despite the passage of civil rights legislation?

27. What occurred in the Watts neighborhood of Los Angeles and other major cities between 1965 and 1967? What effects did these events have on the civil rights movement?

28. What did the Fair Housing Act accomplish?

29. How did Martin Luther King's assassination change the civil rights movement?

30. What had the civil rights movement achieved, and what work did African Americans feel still needed to be done?

## THINK ABOUT IT

31. Explain Martin Luther King Jr.'s strategy of nonviolence. Give two examples during the civil rights movement when this strategy was effective in bringing about change and upholding justice.

32. How did the ideas of the Nation of Islam and the "Black Power" movement differ from those of Martin Luther King Jr.? Give an example of how these ideas helped or hurt the civil rights movement in establishing justice. Compare these ideas with the Bible's view of authority and justice.

▼ Funeral procession of Martin Luther King Jr. in Atlanta, Georgia

# 23 Challenges of the Seventies

**23.1 The Nixon Administration**

**23.2 The Ford Administration**

**23.3 The Carter Administration**

**23.4 Issues of the Seventies**

▲ President and Mrs. Nixon in Shanghai, China, 1972

# 23.1 The Nixon Administration

**Why did Nixon resign?**

As mentioned in Chapter 21, Richard Nixon was elected president in 1968. The nation was in the midst of the turmoil of the Vietnam War and the struggle for civil rights, and many radical voices were questioning America's values. In a speech during his first year in office, Nixon appealed to "the great silent majority of . . . Americans" for support. With the term **silent majority**, the president affirmed his belief that most Americans were not violent radicals wholly discontent with America. The bulk of the population, he believed, were quiet, decent, respectable, and hard-working citizens who wanted peace and order. Nixon claimed that he represented the interests of that silent majority and that his administration would represent their values.

## Foreign Affairs

As Nixon was seeking to end America's involvement in the Vietnam War (see Chapter 21), he also sought friendlier relations with the Communist nations of China and the Soviet Union. He introduced a new era of **détente** (an easing of tensions) between the United States and those two countries. Nixon relied heavily on Henry Kissinger, a Harvard professor born in Germany, who served as a special advisor and in 1973 became secretary of state.

### China

One of Nixon's biggest decisions was establishing relations with the Communist government of the People's Republic of China (PRC). Since the flight of China's Nationalist government to Taiwan in 1949 (see Chapter 20), the United States had recognized the Nationalist Republic of China (ROC) as the legitimate government of China. The PRC became allies with the Soviet Union, but by the 1960s disagreements emerged between the two nations. Seeing an opportunity to drive a wedge between the two Communist countries and hoping China could pressure North Vietnam to negotiate to end the war there, Kissinger and other advisors encouraged Nixon to end America's isolation of the PRC. The United States quietly reached out to the Chinese, who were receptive to a meeting between the two countries. In July 1971 Kissinger secretly traveled to China to ask for the PRC to approve an official visit from Nixon. In return, the United States offered to lift a trade embargo with China, not pursue independence for Taiwan, and support representation of the PRC alongside the ROC in the United Nations. The Chinese agreed, and Nixon announced that he would visit the People's Republic the following year. Contrary to Nixon's wishes, the United Nations voted to expel Taiwan when it admitted the PRC into its membership in 1971, giving Communist China a permanent seat on the UN Security Council and leaving Taiwan without UN representation.

## GUIDING QUESTIONS

- What significant events in foreign affairs occurred during Nixon's presidency?
- Why did certain countries stop exporting oil to America?
- Why did Americans become less trusting of government after Nixon's resignation?

◄ Richard Nixon

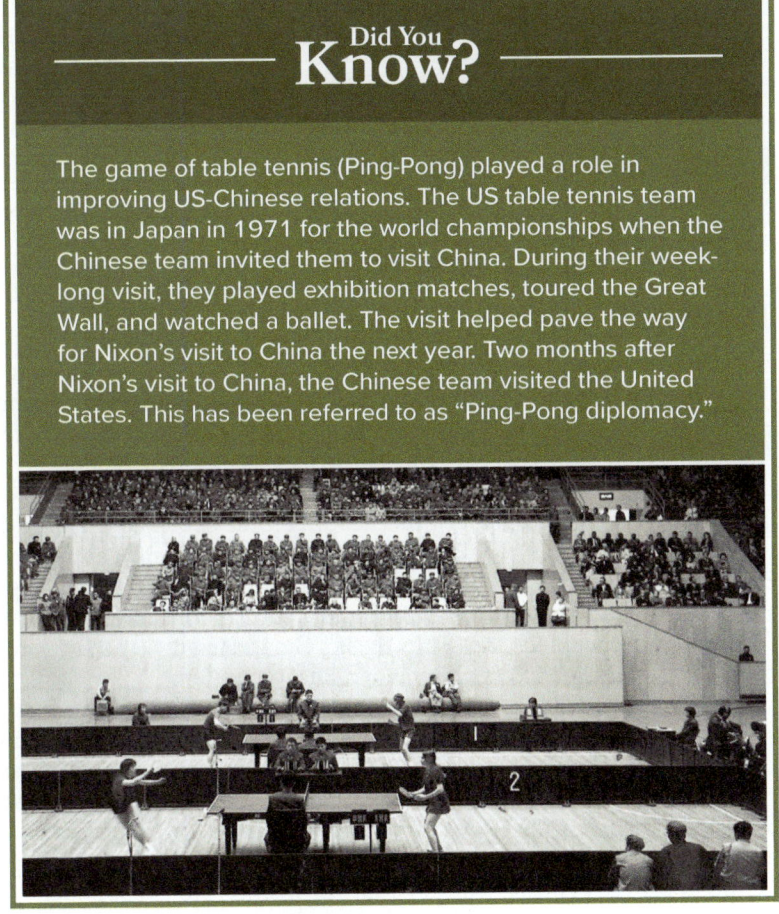

### Did You Know?

The game of table tennis (Ping-Pong) played a role in improving US-Chinese relations. The US table tennis team was in Japan in 1971 for the world championships when the Chinese team invited them to visit China. During their weeklong visit, they played exhibition matches, toured the Great Wall, and watched a ballet. The visit helped pave the way for Nixon's visit to China the next year. Two months after Nixon's visit to China, the Chinese team visited the United States. This has been referred to as "Ping-Pong diplomacy."

▲ US and Chinese table tennis teams playing a friendly match in Beijing, China, April 1971

Nixon's visit in February 1972 was an enormous public relations success. He met with Chinese premier Zhou Enlai and Chairman Mao Zedong and exchanged messages of good will with them. Television cameras followed the president as he toured the Great Wall and other sites long closed to foreigners, portraying Nixon as an astute diplomat and able statesman. He laid the groundwork for establishing normalized relations and trade with mainland China. Nixon also agreed to a statement in which the United States acknowledged that there was only one China, which included mainland China and Taiwan, and called for a peaceful settlement of the Taiwan issue. In 1978 President Carter (see Chapter 24) formally recognized the PRC and severed official diplomatic ties with Taiwan. However, the United States maintained support for Taiwan's security from Chinese threats. In the Taiwan Relations Act, the United States promised to "provide Taiwan with arms of a defensive character."

▶ Nixon eating with Chinese premier Zhou Enlai during Nixon's visit to China

## Soviet Union

On May 22, 1972, Nixon traveled to Moscow for a summit with Soviet leader Leonid Brezhnev. At least in part because of his interactions with China, Nixon was able to win some concessions from the Soviet Union. In the **Strategic Arms Limitation Talks Agreement (SALT I)**, the United States and the USSR agreed to limit the number of strategic land- and submarine-based nuclear missiles each nation had. The agreement also included an Anti-Ballistic Missile (ABM) treaty in which both sides agreed to limit missile systems that could shoot down incoming ballistic missiles. As a further sign of détente, Nixon also arranged the sale of large amounts of grain to the Soviets, and the two sides agreed to cooperate in scientific and space projects. Some Democrats and Republicans were concerned that he was too accommodating to these Communist regimes.

◀ Nixon with Soviet leader Leonid Brezhnev in Moscow

## The Middle East

After becoming a nation in 1948, Israel was in constant conflict with its Arab neighbors, most of whom opposed the existence of an independent Israeli state. The nations fought a series of wars, and the region suffered from constant unrest and violence. In 1956, after Egypt took unilateral control of the Suez Canal, the Israelis seized the Sinai Peninsula, but withdrew under international pressure. A UN peacekeeping force occupied Sinai until 1967, when Egypt coerced it to leave as Egypt prepared for a new attack on Israel. Before Egypt could attack, Israel launched a preemptive strike on Egypt. In the Six-Day War (June 5–10, 1967), Israel captured the Sinai Peninsula and the Egyptian-occupied Gaza Strip, Syria's Golan Heights, and the Jordanian-controlled West Bank (which included East Jerusalem).

In October 1973, Egypt and Syria, armed with modern weapons supplied by the Soviets, launched a surprise attack on two fronts simultaneously against Israel to take back their lost territory in what became known as the Yom Kippur War (Yom Kippur is the holiest day of the year for Jews). The invading forces experienced early success, but Israel launched a counteroffensive deep into Syria and across the Suez Canal into Egypt. Nixon approved sending a large supply of weapons to assist Israel. After three weeks of fighting, the warring nations agreed to a cease-fire, but a joint effort by the United States and the USSR to create a long-term peace agreement between the sides was not successful.

▲ Israeli troops raise their flag after occupying Syrian territory during the Six-Day War

# Recession and Crisis

## Economic Problems

Nixon inherited a deteriorating economic situation. Johnson had tried to pay for both the Great Society and the Vietnam War without raising taxes. The result was a growing budget deficit which, in turn, led to inflation. Nixon tried to control inflation by getting American troops out of Vietnam, trimming the federal budget by vetoing funding for a number of Great Society programs, raising taxes, and supporting the raising of interest rates. However, inflation remained unchanged, unemployment rose, and a recession (an economic slowdown not as severe as a depression) set in. In an effort to slow inflation, Nixon responded with his New Economic Policy (NEP). First, he imposed a ninety-day freeze in 1971 on all wages and prices. Then he established a board to regulate all wage and price increases. Finally, in 1973, he replaced the mandatory guidelines with voluntary ones. These policies brought temporary reductions to inflation, but when the controls were lifted, inflation returned at an even higher rate.

## Energy Crisis

In retaliation for America's support of Israel in the Yom Kippur War, the **Organization of Petroleum Exporting Countries (OPEC)**—which consisted mostly of Arab nations that produced the greatest amounts of oil—proclaimed an oil embargo in October 1973 against the United States (and other nations that supported Israel). When the embargo started, the United States was still under President Nixon's wage and price controls. With a shrinking supply of gasoline, gas stations stayed open fewer hours and limited the amount of gas each customer could buy. Motorists often waited in long lines to buy the gas that was available. When price controls were finally lifted, the price of gasoline shot up.

Nixon asked Americans to conserve energy by carpooling or buying smaller, more efficient vehicles. Congress mandated a 55-mile-per-hour speed limit on all interstate highways (for fuel efficiency) and authorized construction of the Trans-Alaskan Pipeline to transport oil from wells in the Arctic Circle to the port at Valdez in southern Alaska.

OPEC lifted the embargo in March 1974, but it steadily increased the price for oil. The prices for all petroleum products—from heating oil and fuels to asphalt and plastics—rose even more.

▼ (below) An oil pump in the Middle Eastern country of Bahrain; (bottom) long lines at the gas pumps during the 1970s energy crisis

# Watergate

### 1972 Election

In the 1972 presidential election, Nixon's chances of reelection, strengthened by détente with China and the USSR and the de-escalation of the Vietnam War, looked good. The Democrats, furthermore, were again divided. Alabama's George Wallace campaigned for the Democratic nomination and, by crusading against busing (discussed later in this chapter), was able to win primaries not only in the South but also in northern industrial states such as Massachusetts and Michigan. However, a would-be assassin shot him in Maryland, cutting short his campaign and leaving him paralyzed for the remainder of his life. The Democratic nomination eventually went to anti-war liberal South Dakota senator George McGovern.

### Watergate Break-In

Despite indications that he would win reelection, Nixon was often suspicious and almost paranoid of his critics. He kept an "enemies list" of political opponents. The **Committee to Re-Elect the President (CRP)** was formed to raise funds for Nixon's campaign, but it also engaged in activities such as spying on and spreading false rumors about his opponents.

One of the CRP's plans involved breaking into the headquarters of the Democratic National Committee in the Watergate complex in Washington, DC, to plant listening devices on the telephones of Democratic staff members. On May 28, 1972, a team of burglars successfully broke in and planted the devices. However, the wiretaps were not working properly, so in the early hours of June 17, 1972, the five burglars broke in again to replace them. This time they were caught and arrested by police. The incident drew little attention at first. However, at their hearing, when the judge asked their occupations, one of the burglars indicated he was a retired CIA agent. This drew the attention of *Washington Post* reporter Bob Woodward, who was in the courtroom. Woodward and fellow journalist Carl Bernstein began investigating what became known as the **Watergate scandal**.

As Woodward and Bernstein investigated, the *Washington Post* printed their stories which began to make connections between the break-in, the CRP, and the White House. On August 29, Nixon held a news conference in which he vigorously denied that anyone in his administration had any connection with the incident.

Most voters believed Nixon when he said he was not involved, and the president defeated McGovern in November in a landslide, with 61 percent of the popular vote and an electoral victory of 520–17, winning every state except Massachusetts and the District of Columbia.

## Cover-Up

After the election, however, more information about the Watergate affair was revealed. Relying on anonymous sources with code names such as "Deep Throat," Woodward and Bernstein reported that the FBI had made connections between the Nixon administration and the break-in. They also uncovered a number of other questionable and illegal CRP activities. For example, some aides had sent letters to newspapers, accusing Democratic candidates of racism and immorality. Others had burglarized the office of Daniel Ellsberg's psychiatrist (Ellsberg had released the "Pentagon Papers" [see Chapter 21] to the *New York Times*), trying to find material with which to discredit Ellsberg.

The trial of the five Watergate burglars and two accomplices began in federal court in January 1973. During the trial the judge pressed the defendants and witnesses on White House involvement in the break-in. Five of the defendants pleaded guilty, and the other two were found guilty by the jury. Sentencing was scheduled for March. In the meantime, the Senate voted to establish a Select Committee on Presidential Campaign Activities to conduct its own investigation. Before his sentencing, one of the convicted burglars told the judge that the defendants had been pressured by the White House to plead guilty and to lie about the involvement of "higher ups" in the break-in. The judge gave the defendants heavy jail sentences but offered to reduce them if they cooperated with investigations by a federal grand jury and the Senate committee.

As the defendants began cooperating, revelations began to pour forth in the press and to the grand jury and Senate committee. These included accusations that officials in the Nixon administration had attempted to cover up the White House's involvement in the break-in, destroyed documents, made payments to the burglars to keep them from cooperating with the investigations, and ordered the CIA to interfere with the FBI's investigation. On April 30 Nixon made a televised address to the nation in which he continued to deny any advance knowledge of the break-in while also announcing the removal or resignation of several top aides from his administration.

Huge audiences watched the televised Senate committee hearings during the spring and summer of 1973. Despite all the testimony, no evidence had come to light that implicated Nixon himself in the Watergate scandal. That changed on July 26, when a former White House aide testified that Nixon had installed a secret recording system in the Oval Office that taped every conversation there. Immediately, both the court and Congress pressed Nixon to release the tapes. The president refused, claiming executive privilege (the principle that the president's conversations should remain private) and that turning over the tapes would endanger national security.

Nixon's refusal began a long struggle over control of the tapes. Nixon tried to satisfy investigators by first releasing edited transcripts of the tapes and then by releasing just some of the tapes. One of the released tapes included a gap of over eighteen minutes. Meanwhile, he maintained his complete innocence of wrongdoing. The president's approval rating plummeted. The tapes and judicial and congressional inquiries exposed a disturbing side of politics—the political "dirty tricks," subtle lies, and outright deceit that some politicians, including Nixon, practiced.

---

▼ (left) US senators questioning witnesses during the Watergate investigation; (right) James McCord testifying before the Senate Watergate Committee and demonstrating the device used to bug the phones in the Democratic National Headquarters

## Resignation of Agnew

Another problem that plagued Nixon's administration was the allegation that Vice President **Spiro Agnew** had taken bribes when he had been the governor of Maryland. By negotiating an agreement with prosecutors, Agnew was allowed to plead no contest (which meant he did not plead guilty or not guilty) to one count of failing to report income on his taxes, and he received only a fine and probation. He resigned as vice president in October 1973. Although Agnew's crimes were unrelated to Watergate, they increased the perception that the Nixon administration was thoroughly corrupt.

Using the procedure outlined by the Twenty-Fifth Amendment (see Chapter 21), President Nixon nominated House minority leader **Gerald Ford** of Michigan to succeed Agnew as vice president. Both houses of Congress confirmed the nomination by overwhelming margins. Nixon hoped that Ford's popularity in Congress and reputation for honesty would help deflect criticism from his administration.

▶ Vice President Spiro Agnew

## Resignation of Nixon

On July 24, 1974, the Supreme Court ruled unanimously that Nixon must release all the tapes. The tapes did not indicate Nixon knew about the Watergate break-in beforehand, but they proved that he participated in attempts to cover up the involvement of his White House subordinates. The House Judiciary Committee passed three articles of impeachment for obstruction of justice and other charges to send to the full House for its consideration. With impeachment by the House a virtual certainty and with conviction (and removal from office) by the Senate likely, Nixon announced on August 8 that he would resign. He left office at noon on August 9.

Eventually, about two dozen members of the Nixon administration were convicted and jailed for offenses relating to Watergate. The Watergate scandal damaged the prestige of the presidency and undermined the American people's faith in their political leaders. Yet it also showed that the Constitution's system of checks and balances worked and that the president was not above the law.

## A President Resigns

Nixon's resignation speech was broadcast live on radio and television at 9 p.m. on August 8, 1974. The following is an excerpt from his remarks.

*In all the decisions I have made in my public life, I have always tried to do what was best for the Nation. Throughout the long and difficult period of Watergate, I have felt it was my duty to persevere, to make every possible effort to complete the term of office to which you elected me. . . .*

*From the discussions I have had with Congressional and other leaders, I have concluded that because of the Watergate matter I might not have the support of the Congress that I would consider necessary to back the very difficult decisions and carry out the duties of this office in the way the interests of the Nation would require. . . .*

*Therefore, I shall resign the Presidency effective at noon tomorrow. Vice President Ford will be sworn in as President at that hour in this office. . . .*

*I regret deeply any injuries that may have been done in the course of the events that led to this decision. I would say only that if some of my judgments were wrong, and some were wrong, they were made in what I believed at the time to be the best interest of the Nation. . . .*

*I shall leave this office with regret at not completing my term, but with gratitude for the privilege of serving as your President for the past five and a half years.*

▲ Nixon giving the victory sign as he boards the presidential helicopter after resigning the presidency

---

### Comprehension Check 23.1

1. Nixon's foreign policy was characterized by _____ between the United States and major Communist countries.

   A  an arms race

   B  an end to the Cold War

   C  an era of détente

2. Nixon's successful trip to _____ improved relations between the two countries.

   A  China

   B  Israel

   C  Taiwan

3. An energy crisis resulted from _____ placing an oil embargo on the United States.

   A  CRP

   B  OPEC

   C  ROC

4. SALT I included limits on the following except _____

   A  anti-ballistic missile (ABM) systems

   B  land- and submarine-based strategic nuclear missiles

   C  scientific and space projects

**MAKING CONNECTIONS**

5. How was Nixon involved in the Watergate scandal, and what did he do after Congress learned of his involvement?

GUIDING QUESTIONS

- Why did Ford pardon Nixon?
- What economic conditions caused stagflation?

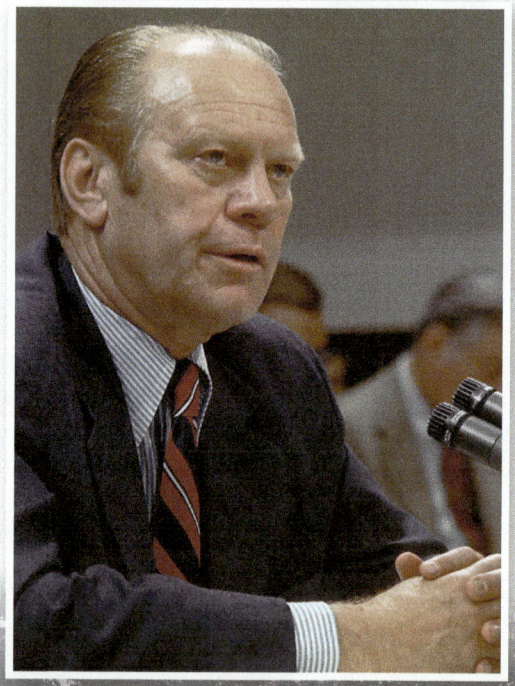

▼ (below) President Gerald Ford explaining his pardon of Nixon to Congress; (bottom) crowds protesting Ford's pardon of Nixon

## 23.2 The Ford Administration

**What problems did Ford face during his presidency?**

Gerald Ford took the presidential oath of office on the day Nixon resigned. Having been appointed vice president upon Agnew's resignation, Ford was the only person to serve as both vice president and president who was not elected to either office. Ford then appointed former New York governor Nelson Rockefeller to be his vice president. In Ford's first speech as president, he said,

> *My fellow Americans, our long national nightmare is over. Our Constitution works; our great Republic is a government of laws and not of men. Here the people rule. But there is a higher Power, by whatever name we honor Him, who ordains not only righteousness but love, not only justice but mercy.*

Ford enjoyed a flood of goodwill when he took office. The American people indeed wanted to put the "long national nightmare" behind them. Furthermore, Ford's reputation as a decent, honest man was a welcome contrast to the Watergate scandal and Nixon's bitter struggle with Congress.

### Pardon of Nixon

After Nixon's resignation, Congress and the federal courts began pursuing criminal charges against the former president. Only a month into his presidency, Ford made the controversial decision to grant Nixon a full pardon for any crimes he "may have committed" while in office. The president maintained that a trial of the former president would have only prolonged the nation's agony over the Watergate scandal and further divided the nation. Ford's decision angered many Democrats, who accused him of making a "buddy deal" with the former president in exchange for his nomination as vice president (although no evidence exists that such a deal was made). Many critics thought it unfair that Nixon should escape punishment while his subordinates suffered. Many of Ford's supporters also abandoned him. As a result, Ford's popularity dropped dramatically. Nevertheless, many historians today agree that Ford's decision was best for the nation, even though it cost him politically.

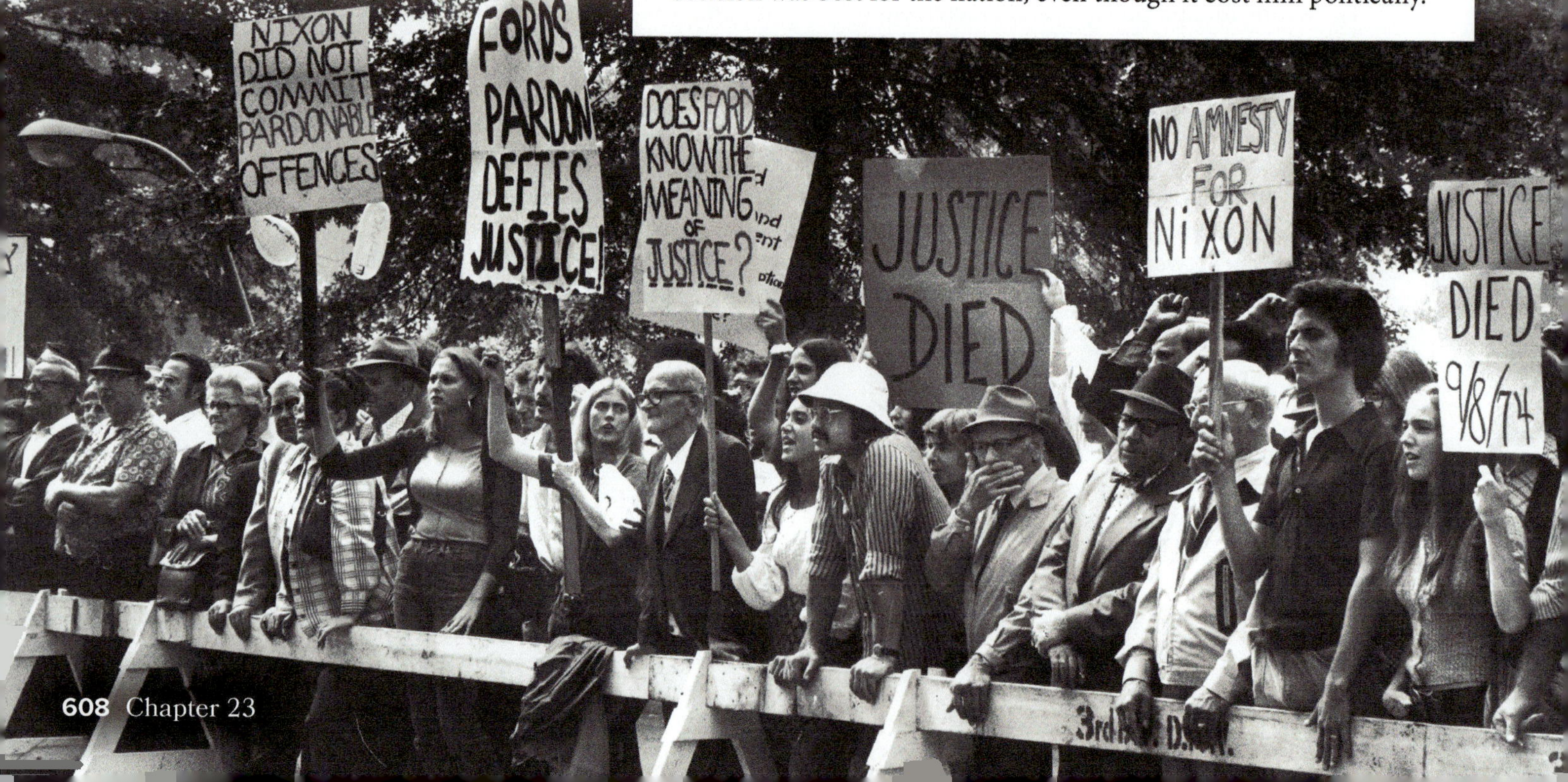

During his presidency, Ford had to deal with a hostile Congress. The Democrats held comfortable majorities in both houses, and they were determined to control the government after the controversies of the Nixon administration. Ford's sole means of steering the nation was the veto; he vetoed sixty-six bills in fewer than three years in office while attempting to limit government spending and protect the powers of the presidency. Congress, however, overrode twelve of his vetoes. The standoff between Ford and Congress often created a legislative deadlock.

Other factors also hurt Ford's popularity. In 1975 America tasted final defeat in Southeast Asia as South Vietnam, Cambodia, and Laos fell to the Communists (see Chapter 21). A sluggish national economy also worried voters.

## Stagflation

Nixon's efforts to end inflation had been unsuccessful. When Ford took office, the inflation rate reached 12 percent. However, inflation was not the only problem with America's economy. Normally, when inflation is high, unemployment is low; and when unemployment is high, inflation is low. During much of the 1970s, however, the United States experienced high inflation and high unemployment at the same time, a condition that economists called **stagflation** (a stagnant economy coupled with inflation).

Three key factors contributed to stagflation. First, the energy crisis created a scarcity of many products, causing price increases. Second, the Vietnam War and social programs had created a large budget deficit. As a result, the government had to print more money to cover the deficit, further fueling inflation. Third, increased competition in international trade caused the United States to experience trade deficits (meaning the nation imported more goods than it exported) throughout the 1970s.

▼ A Whip Inflation Now (WIN) button

Stagflation left Congress and President Ford in a dilemma. Ford asked Congress to cut taxes and spending. Congress chose to cut taxes but did not cut spending. As a result, budget deficits increased. Ford called for a voluntary anti-inflation crusade called WIN ("Whip Inflation Now"), which urged consumers to stop buying high-priced goods and to save money instead. The plan also asked workers not to seek wage increases and urged people to plant gardens to offset rising food costs. However, most workers ignored WIN. While inflation did begin to decline during Ford's presidency, most Americans listed the economy as their main concern going into the election of 1976.

---

### Comprehension Check 23.2

**1.** Ford was never elected as either vice president or president.

    True    False

**2.** Ford's popularity rose after he granted a pardon to Nixon.

    True    False

**3.** Ford responded to stagflation by _____.

    **A** calling for a voluntary anti-inflation crusade

    **B** freezing and regulating prices and wages

    **C** working with the Democratic Congress on legislation

#### MAKING CONNECTIONS

**4.** What is stagflation, and what were two factors that contributed to it?

▲ (top) Jimmy Carter; (above) Carter and Ford debating

## 23.3 The Carter Administration

### What was Carter's greatest success?

Ford entered the 1976 presidential race burdened by numerous weights. Although he was the incumbent, he was an unelected incumbent. Inflation, unemployment, and the Nixon pardon all hampered the president's campaign. Furthermore, Ford was not even the preferred choice of many members of his own party. Former California governor Ronald Reagan, favored by the Republican conservatives who dominated the party, mounted a strong challenge to the more moderate Ford in the primaries. The president won the Republican nomination but only by a narrow margin.

One of the Democratic candidates was **Jimmy Carter**, a successful peanut farmer from Georgia. He later became a local school board member, working for school desegregation. His political experience consisted of serving two terms in the Georgia state senate, and one term as governor. Carter placed himself in the political center where he could attract the most voters. Representing the "New South" that emerged after the civil rights movement, Carter won the Democratic nomination.

At first the 1976 election looked as though it would be an easy victory for Carter. Ford, however, fought back. The incumbent hammered away at Carter's vagueness on the issues. "Jimmy Carter will say anything anywhere to be president of the United States," Ford said. "He wavers, he wanders, he wiggles, and he waffles." But Ford hurt himself by proclaiming in a televised debate that he did not believe Eastern Europe was under Soviet domination, despite the presence of Soviet-imposed governments in those nations. This blunder merely reinforced the perception of some people that Ford was the weaker candidate.

Carter ran as an "outsider," a candidate untainted by the corruption in Washington and therefore supposedly better able to clean it up. Carter also campaigned as a "born-again" Christian who wanted a government "as filled with love as are the American people." After the trauma of Watergate, Americans were attracted to a candidate who said plainly, "I'll never tell a lie" to the American people.

In the end, Carter won narrowly—50.1 percent to 48 percent in the popular vote. The vote in the Electoral College, 297 to 240, was the closest since Woodrow Wilson defeated Charles Evans Hughes in 1916.

## Election of 1976

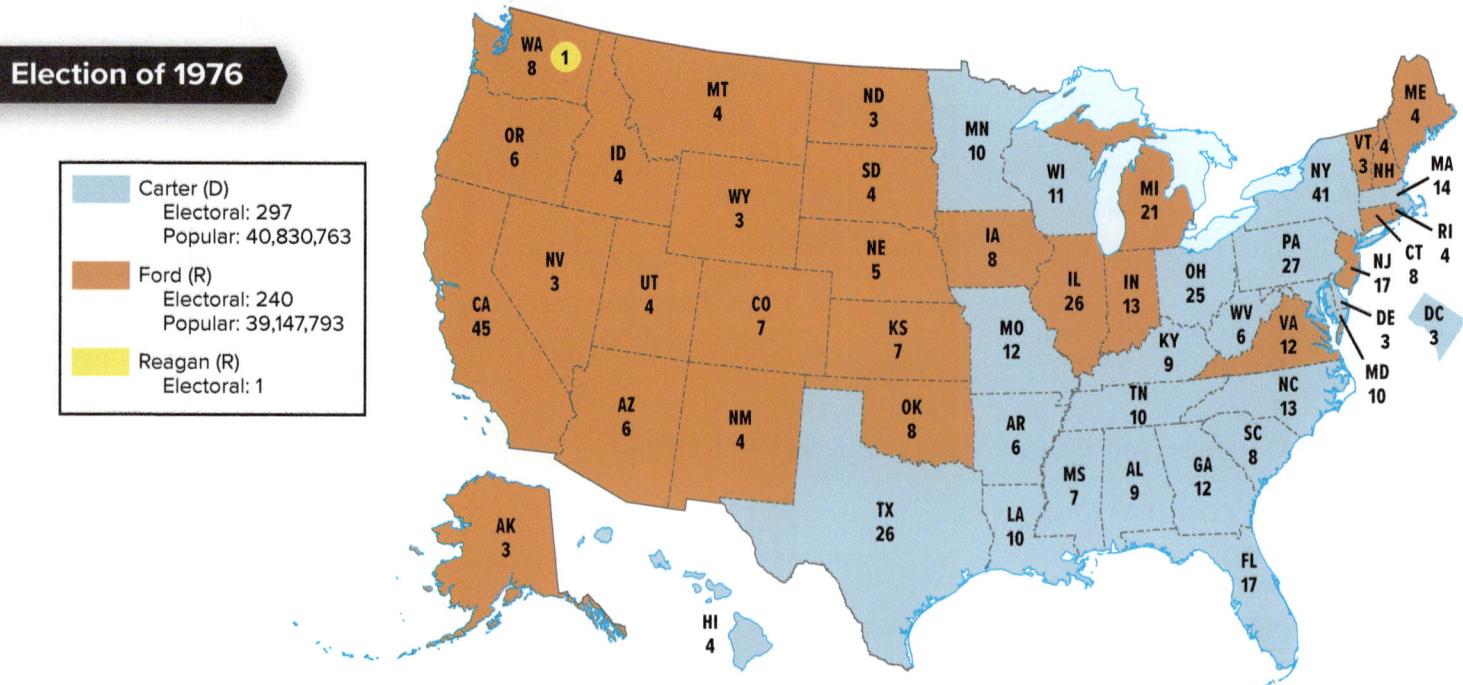

Carter (D)
Electoral: 297
Popular: 40,830,763

Ford (R)
Electoral: 240
Popular: 39,147,793

Reagan (R)
Electoral: 1

## Domestic Affairs

Carter entered office professing his desire to be a "people's president" with an open, honest, and compassionate administration. Carter appointed record numbers of women and minorities to government positions. He surprised and delighted the American people by abandoning his armored limousine and walking down Pennsylvania Avenue after his inauguration. Later, he made some televised addresses wearing a sweater instead of a suit, and many photographs showed him relaxing in blue jeans. He calculated that all of these "down-home" images would endear him to the American people as "one of them."

But one decision affecting hundreds of thousands of individuals was less well-received. In 1977 he granted amnesty (a general pardon) to those who had fled the country or failed to register for the draft to avoid fighting in Vietnam. Mercy to "draft dodgers" was not popular with many veterans who had fulfilled their obligation and fought in the war, nor with relatives of veterans who had died in the war.

◀ Carter and his family walking during his inauguration parade

▼ Vietnam War draft dodgers

DRAFT RESISTERS

The economy was the primary domestic difficulty. Ford had managed to get the rate of inflation down to about 5.5 percent, but the result was a recession and an unemployment rate of almost 8 percent by the time he left office. In his four-year term, Carter was able to lower unemployment only slightly. Inflation, however, soared. By 1980 the annual inflation rate had risen to over 14 percent. Depositors and investors worried about how inflation was devastating their hard-earned savings. Consumers complained loudly about rising prices for food, clothing, fuel, and other necessities as well as high interest rates on loans that made payment on home mortgages difficult. The American economy seemed out of control, and Carter appeared ineffective.

## Unemployment and Inflation Rates, 1970–80

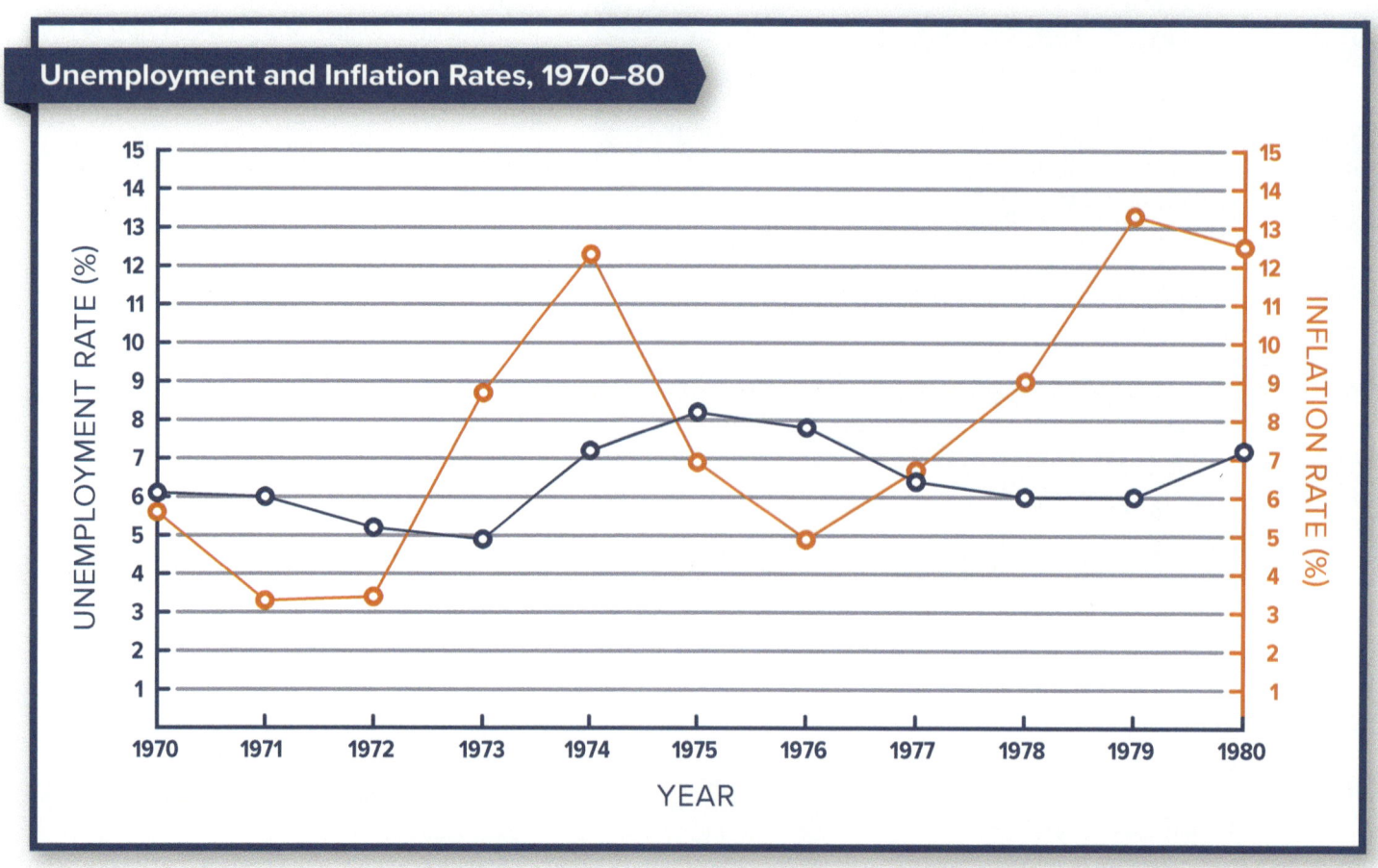

Carter's "outsider" status in Washington made it hard for him to work with Congress, despite large Democratic majorities in both houses. Carter was also perceived as a micromanager of the government, bogged down by details that could have been delegated to subordinates. Additionally, Congress's continued determination to be independent after the abuses by the executive branch during Watergate often paralyzed legislation. A growing number of Americans became frustrated as President Carter and a Democratic majority in Congress could not agree on how to help the nation.

Due to the ongoing energy crisis, Carter attempted to end dependence on foreign oil. In April 1977 he presented his National Energy Plan that promoted nationwide conservation and development of alternative energy sources. Later that year, Congress passed an act that created the Department of Energy and the following year, passed the National Energy Act that directed various government bureaucracies on energy conservation measures.

Carter's energy plan suffered as a result of an accident at the Three Mile Island nuclear plant in Pennsylvania in 1979. Carter had supported nuclear power as an alternative energy source, but the accident increased concerns over nuclear hazards. In addition, the Iranian revolution in 1979 (discussed later) diminished oil supplies in the United States again, reviving the long lines and high prices at gas stations that had characterized the early 1970s.

As American anger rose, Carter's popularity dropped. By December 1979 only 19 percent of the American people approved of Carter's performance—a rating lower than that of Richard Nixon during the depths of the Watergate affair. Yet, since his presidency, Carter has been credited for economic policies that contributed to the economic recovery in the 1980s, including appointing a new Federal Reserve chairman who raised interest rates to lower inflation, deregulating the transportation industries, and lowering tariffs to introduce more foreign competition in the auto industry.

▼ The Three Mile Island nuclear plant

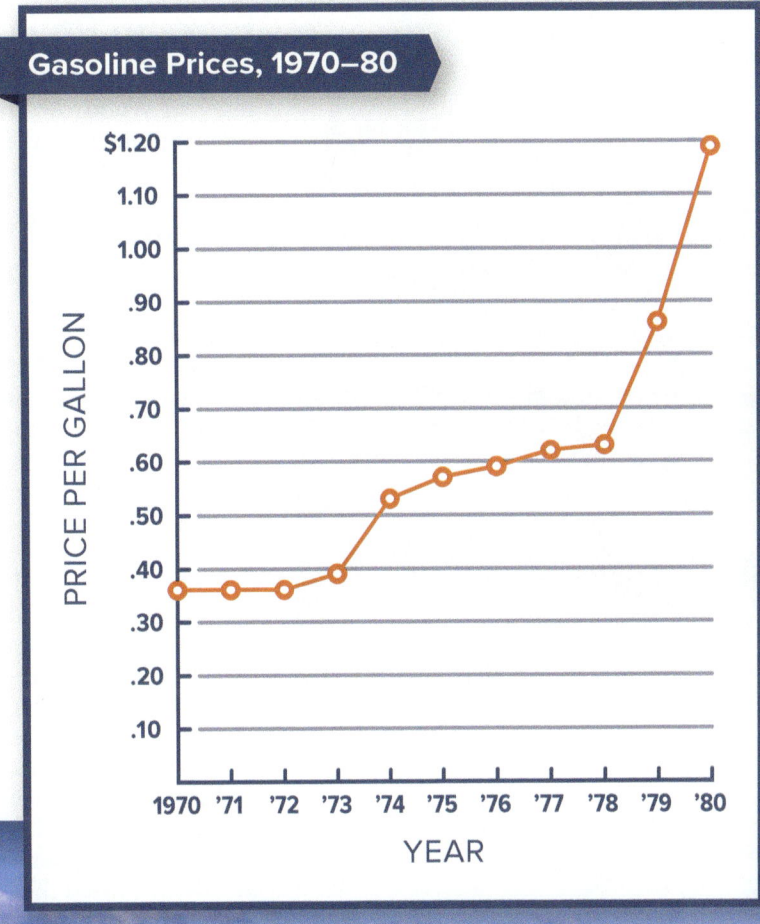

**Gasoline Prices, 1970–80**

PRICE PER GALLON

$1.20
1.10
1.00
.90
.80
.70
.60
.50
.40
.30
.20
.10

1970 '71 '72 '73 '74 '75 '76 '77 '78 '79 '80

YEAR

▲ Carter and President Omar Torrijos of Panama signing the Panama Canal Treaty

## Foreign Policies

Carter tried to pursue a foreign policy based on fairness and morality, much as Woodrow Wilson had tried to do. The cornerstone of Carter's foreign policy was the defense of human rights—protecting people from government oppression and ensuring that people had basic freedoms..

### Panama Canal Treaty

Carter's first great challenge in foreign affairs concerned the Panama Canal. Although the United States paid Panama for perpetual control of the Canal Zone (see Chapter 14), Panamanians had resented American control of the canal for many years. The Nixon and Ford administrations had begun negotiations to give the canal to Panama; Carter completed the process. He signed the **Panama Canal Treaty** in 1977. The new treaty allowed Panama and the United States to operate the canal jointly until December 31, 1999, when Panama would take over the operation completely.

The treaty created controversy in the United States. Administration officials, numerous leading Democrats, and even some Republicans defended the treaty. They argued that the canal's narrow width and the growth of air power made the canal less important militarily and economically to the United States. They noted, for example, that aircraft carriers and oil tankers were too wide to use the canal. Supporters also hoped that the US action would improve relations with Latin America.

Opponents of the treaty contended that the waterway was still vital to American interests and should not be handed over to the authoritarian and sometimes unstable government of Panama. As for its narrowness, it could be widened to accommodate larger ships. (Panama did complete a decade-long widening project in 2016.) Despite opposition, the Senate narrowly ratified the treaty in 1978.

### Camp David Accords

President Carter's most significant moment of diplomacy came in the Middle East. Egypt, one of Israel's most powerful opponents, was tired of the fighting in previous decades, which had brought it no gain and much loss. In 1978 Carter invited Egypt's president, Anwar Sadat, and the prime minister of Israel, Menachem Begin, to meet with him at Camp David, the presidential retreat in Maryland. After thirteen days of difficult negotiations, the three men reached an uneasy agreement known as the **Camp David Accords**. In return for Egypt's recognition of Israel's right to exist (which no other Arab nation had done) and a guarantee of peace, Israel returned to Egypt the Sinai Peninsula, which it had taken in the Six-Day War (1967). The agreement marked one of the greatest advances for peace in the Middle East. Egypt and Israel have not gone to war since that agreement. Both Sadat and Begin received the Nobel Peace Prize that year. A year later at the White House, Egypt and Israel signed a peace treaty that solidified the agreements made at Camp David. Sadat paid a heavy price for signing the Camp David Accords. On October 6, 1981, he was assassinated by Muslim extremists who opposed Sadat's agreement to recognize Israel's right to be a nation.

▶ (left to right) Presidents Anwar Sadat and Jimmy Carter, and Prime Minister Menachem Begin shake hands after the Camp David Agreement

### Did You Know?

President Carter later explained that because of tension between Sadat and Begin the world leaders were close to leaving Camp David without signing an agreement. When Carter signed a photograph of the world leaders for each of Begin's grandchildren, using the name of each grandchild in the message (Carter's secretary had researched the names), Begin was so moved that he reconsidered.

▲ (top) Afghan Mujahideen standing on a destroyed Russian helicopter; (above) the 1980 Olympic Games in Moscow

## Soviet Relations

Carter's success with the Camp David Accords, however, was overshadowed by several setbacks in foreign policy. His dealings with the Soviet Union are one example. Like Nixon and Ford before him, Carter pursued a policy of détente with the Soviet Union. The key to good relations, Carter decided, would be passage of the SALT II Treaty, a follow-up to the Strategic Arms Limitation Talks (SALT I), to further limit the number and kinds of nuclear weapons of each superpower. Brezhnev, who had signed SALT I, and Carter signed the treaty in June 1979, but some in the Senate opposed ratification. Conservatives charged that the treaty would put the Soviet Union ahead of the United States in nuclear weaponry and that, given the Communists' consistent treaty violations, the United States could not be sure that the Soviets would maintain the agreement.

In late December 1979 all chance of passing the treaty vanished with the Soviet invasion of its neighbor Afghanistan. The Soviets claimed that they were helping Afghanistan's Communist ruler against Afghan groups that opposed the Communist government. However, the Soviet invasion also overthrew that leader, who was quickly assassinated, and replaced him with another Soviet puppet. Denouncing the invasion, Carter placed an embargo on sales of grain to the Soviets and called for an American boycott of the 1980 summer Olympic Games in Moscow. He also withdrew the SALT II Treaty from the Senate's consideration and called for a new registration of young men for the discontinued draft (although he did not revive the draft itself). In his State of the Union address for 1980, he announced the "Carter Doctrine," that declared the United States would resist, by military force if necessary, any Soviet attempt to push farther south to the Persian Gulf. The United States supplied funds and military equipment to the Afghan resistance, support that continued until the Soviets withdrew in 1989.

Carter's actions brought a storm of criticism. Liberals described the Carter Doctrine, draft registration, and withdrawal of the SALT II Treaty as harsh, provocative overreactions that threatened world peace. Farmers complained about their financial losses from the grain embargo. Conservatives claimed that Carter's response was weak—too much talk and too little action.

## Iran Hostage Crisis

The Camp David Accords gave Carter his greatest triumph, but the Middle East also gave him his worst defeat when revolution erupted in Iran. The shah (king) of that nation, Mohammed Reza Pahlavi, was long known to be pro-West in his outlook but dictatorial in his rule. In January 1979, after months of violent disorder, the shah fled the country, and an Islamic extremist, the Ayatollah Ruhollah Khomeini, took power. Khomeini denounced everyone who was not as zealous as he and his followers were—the shah, other Arab nations, the Soviet Union, and especially "the great Satan" who had supported the shah, the United States. In November, when Carter allowed the exiled shah to enter the United States to receive cancer treatments, enraged Iranian students stormed the American embassy in Tehran, Iran. They took more than sixty Americans hostage (although some were later released, bringing the number to fifty-two). They offered to free the Americans in exchange for demands, including the shah's return to place him on trial in Iran. Carter refused to accept their conditions.

▼ Ayatollah Khomeini

The **Iranian hostage crisis** became Carter's foreign policy nightmare. Carter, with few options open to him short of military invasion, tried vainly for months to use economic sanctions, negotiations, and world opinion to move the Iranians to release the hostages. Resisting these efforts, the Iranians threatened to kill the hostages or place them on trial as spies. Television networks almost daily broadcast footage of Iranians burning American flags and chanting anti-American slogans. As the weeks and months dragged on, the American public's frustration and anger partially turned from Iran to the president himself. Carter's failed efforts made him seem weak and indecisive. In April 1980 an attempted military rescue of the hostages was a disaster. In addition to helicopters breaking down, one helicopter collided with an American transport plane in the desert of Iran, killing eight American soldiers who never got near the hostages.

The crisis continued and became a major issue in the 1980 presidential election. Many Americans voted against Carter because of his inability to obtain freedom for the hostages. After the beginning of the Iran-Iraq War (1980–88) and pressure from the United Nations, Iran entered into final negotiations. Release finally came after 444 days of captivity on January 20, 1981—the day Americans inaugurated a new president, Ronald Reagan. For much of the 1970s, some believed the United States suffered a "leadership crisis" and looked for a reversal under the new president.

◄ (top) An American hostage in Iran; (bottom) American hostages arriving at a US Air Force base in West Germany after their release from Iran

## News Coverage *of the* Iran Hostage Crisis

An average American watching the CBS Evening News in 1980 would have noticed a difference from earlier broadcasts on that network. Each night, Walter Cronkite, anchor of the program, still closed with his trademark line "And that's the way it is. . . ." But by January viewers heard Cronkite add a final phrase to his remarks: "on the eightieth day of captivity for the American hostages in Iran." Each night Cronkite added another day to the total—one hundred, two hundred, and still more with no end in sight. The nightly broadcasts became a reminder of the inability of the nation to resolve the Iranian situation.

## Comprehension Check 23.3

1. Carter surprised the public with his formal manners and dress.

   True    False

2. Carter's reputation suffered as a result of high inflation rates.

   True    False

3. Carter received criticism for his handling of these foreign policy matters except the _____.

   A  Camp David Accords

   B  Panama Canal Treaty

   C  Soviet invasion of Afghanistan

### MAKING CONNECTIONS

4. What were two of Carter's responses to the Soviet invasion of Afghanistan?

5. What key demand of the hostage takers would Carter not meet, and what were two things Carter did to try to free the hostages?

**Issues of the Seventies**

How does modern life reflect the social issues of the 1970s?

## Environmentalism

During this time, a growing number of people voiced concern about the effects of industrial development on the environment. Beginning in the 1960s, the environmental movement began to sound warnings about industrial pollution of the water and air.

Severe smog, particularly in large cities, posed health risks to many Americans. By the late 1970s, tests showed that air quality in Los Angeles was unhealthy for the majority of the year. Automobile emissions were also a serious concern in many parts of the nation. Water quality issues due to pollution existed in every region of the country. The Great Lakes, because of the discharge of large amounts of waste from factories and cities, were seriously affected. Many rivers were not safe for swimming or fishing. In 1969 in Cleveland, Ohio, a spark caused the Cuyahoga River to catch fire because of all the industrial and chemical waste that had been dumped in the river.

Due to increased concerns and under pressure from environmentalists, President Nixon urged Congress to pass a number of laws regulating pollution. In 1970 Congress established the **Environmental Protection Agency (EPA)** to oversee and coordinate environmental regulations. Key acts to combat air and water pollution were the Clean Air Act (1963) and the Clean Water Act (1972). The Comprehensive Environmental Response, Compensation and Liability Act (1980), also called "Superfund" was aimed at cleaning up hazardous waste sites.

▼ Smog blanketing the Los Angeles skyline, 1975

**GUIDING QUESTIONS**

- How should Christians care for the earth?
- What changes were made in civil rights for African Americans and Native Americans during the 1970s?
- How has society's attitude toward women changed over time?
- How did *Roe v. Wade* attempt to achieve certain goals of the women's liberation movement?

▼ A cloth covered in oil after being dipped in the Cuyahoga River in Cleveland, Ohio

## Christians *and the* Environment

Some secular academics blamed the widespread pollution on Christian teaching. In his 1967 essay, historian Lynn White specifically attacked the Creation Mandate in Genesis 1:26–28 as a main cause for environmental problems because of its "human-centered" view of nature. Viewing humanity's exercise of dominion as necessarily harmful to the environment, White and others proposed alternatives, including living in harmony with nature (as the counterculture emphasized). Extreme environmentalists rejected the idea that nature was made primarily for the benefit of humans, seeking to minimize humans' impact on the earth and expressing the need to reduce what they considered human "overpopulation."

Many in the 1970s were concerned about addressing pollution and other environmental concerns from a biblical worldview. Theologians defended the Creation Mandate in Genesis 1:26–28 which requires humans to exercise dominion over God's creation. They critiqued other worldviews that could not find a sufficient reason for humans to care for their environment. These theologians affirmed that humans were given responsibility over the environment, but pointed out that exercising dominion did not mean—nor did it justify—exploiting nature. The proper human role remained as a ruler over nature, but this role demanded stewardship that included taking reasonable steps to protect the environment. Since pollution harms both nature and humans, Christians should combat it to obey both the Creation Mandate and Christ's command to love one's neighbor.

Those actions helped reduce pollution of the environment, but they also increased demands on the nation's energy resources. Many industries, for example, began to switch from highly pollutant coal to oil as a power source, further straining American oil resources. Likewise, regulations to reduce air pollution by cars required adding emission-control devices, which reduced pollution but also lowered fuel efficiency. Additional costs led many industries to plead for delays in implementing the environmental regulations to give them time to make the adjustments.

▼ (below) An inspector checking a car's emissions; (bottom) a catalytic converter (a device to reduce emissions) being replaced on a car

# Civil Rights Struggles Continue

## Busing

Despite Supreme Court orders for the desegregation of schools since the 1950s, the integration of schools had proceeded slowly. One of the main obstacles to integration was that nearly all schools drew their students from surrounding neighborhoods. Most neighborhoods, however, tended to be segregated by ethnic group. As a result, black students went to predominantly black schools in their own neighborhoods, and white students went to predominantly white schools in their own neighborhoods. To overcome this fact, the courts ordered the **busing** of students out of their neighborhoods to other schools until all schools reflected the overall ethnic makeup of the community.

Forced busing was controversial. Some parents opposed busing because they opposed racial integration or because they feared their children would be sent to lower performing schools than those in their own neighborhoods. Others thought that it was too costly and too hard on children to bus them to a school many miles away from home. Many, including some black Americans, believed the money spent on busing would be better used to improve underperforming schools in black neighborhoods. Angry protesters—mostly blue-collar and middle-class white Americans—demonstrated against court-ordered busing. Sometimes violence resulted, as in Pontiac, Michigan, where protesters fire-bombed empty school buses. Nixon tried to placate anti-busing forces by slowing the process of integration. The courts, however, pressed the issue, and busing continued. In the 1980s and 90s, the practice of forced busing declined as courts ruled that most schools were adequately desegregated.

▼ Protesters in Boston demonstrating against forced busing policies

## Affirmative Action

Another controversial measure that sought to correct past racial discrimination was affirmative action, a phrase originating during Kennedy's administration. **Affirmative action** describes a broad range of policies designed to make improvements for minority groups in jobs, college admissions, and other areas. Both Johnson and Nixon supported affirmative action programs intended to increase hiring of minorities in businesses funded by the government. Many universities in the late 1960s and 1970s created policies to increase their admissions of minorities. Ford and Carter championed affirmative action in businesses and education.

President Johnson's 1965 speech at Howard University gives the rationale for affirmative action:

> You do not take a person who, for years, has been hobbled by chains and liberate him, bring him up to the starting line of a race and then say, "you are free to compete with all the others," and still justly believe that you have been completely fair.
>
> Thus it is not enough just to open the gates of opportunity. All our citizens must have the ability to walk through those gates.
>
> This is the next and the more profound stage of the battle for civil rights. We seek not just freedom but opportunity. We seek not just legal equity but human ability, not just equality as a right and a theory but equality as a fact and equality as a result.

Critics have referred to affirmative action as "reverse discrimination," pointing out instances where minorities were favored above those with better qualifications. Others have said that it actually hurts minorities because it casts doubt on their achievement since people assume they were chosen because of their race rather than their accomplishments, or because it creates a mismatch between students' ability and the difficulty of the college that accepted them. Several court cases have challenged affirmative action in higher education. In a 1978 case the Supreme Court ruled that quotas may not be used in college admissions but determined that race could be used as one of many factors in selecting students.

## Native American Relations

While African Americans were making gains in securing their civil rights, many other minorities attempted, with varying degrees of success, to broaden their own legal rights. Native Americans, for example, protested to reveal their plight: a high rate of unemployment and lower life expectancy. Protests included a 1972 march on Washington, called the Trail of Broken Treaties, which started with caravan travel from the West Coast and ended with marchers in Washington, DC, occupying the Bureau of Indian Affairs (BIA). Another protest over broken treaties occurred at Wounded Knee, South Dakota, in 1973, on the hundredth anniversary of the Wounded Knee massacre (see Chapter 13). Some Native American groups sued the government for violating numerous treaties, and the courts often granted Native Americans financial compensation and sometimes returned lands they had lost.

# Other Rights Movements

## Women's Rights

One of the largest and most influential movements in the 1960s and 1970s was the women's rights movement. Although not a minority numerically, women as a group suffered from various forms of discrimination. For instance, women often received less pay than men working at the same job or were discriminated against in attaining certain jobs. In some states, a married woman could not own property in her own name. In addition, widows sometimes discovered after the death of a spouse that the excellent credit rating they had built with their husbands no longer existed; however, a widower's credit rating continued unimpaired. With such injustices as illustrations, advocates of women's rights successfully appealed to the public's sense of fairness to address these problems.

The radical element within the women's movement became known as the women's liberation movement. Some within this group portrayed modern American marriage as a form of slavery in which wives labored in the "demeaning" roles of mother and homemaker. In the 1963 best-seller *Feminine Mystique*, Betty Friedan argued that many middle-class homes had become "a comfortable concentration camp" for women. To achieve their vision of freedom, some women's liberation activists advocated a platform of "free love" (premarital and extramarital sex), easier divorce laws, recognition of lesbian marriages, and, above all, a woman's unquestioned "right" to abortion on demand.

Although radicals seized much of the public's attention, the movement actually included many women who were uninterested in or even opposed to the demands of the liberation activists yet were very interested in pursuing economic equality. Both higher inflation and rising divorce rates drove more women out of the home and into the workplace to make a living and support their families. In addition, a large number of women were pursuing career opportunities. Congress and the states began to address economic inequality by passing legislation to give women equal access to employment and equal pay. However, one downside of the demand for equal pay meant that male heads of households could not earn more than their coworkers, thereby pushing many women, who would have otherwise preferred to stay at home as mothers, into the workforce to help financially support their families.

▲ A member of the American Indian Movement (AIM) standing guard after approximately 200 members of AIM took the reservation village of Wounded Knee, South Dakota, by force, February 1973. The village was immediately surrounded by federal marshals and a siege began, which ended in May 1973.

## EQUAL RIGHTS AMENDMENT

The most controversial and divisive piece of women's rights legislation was the **Equal Rights Amendment (ERA)**. Introduced in 1923, the amendment was finally passed by Congress in 1972. Section 1 of that proposed amendment said briefly, "Equality of rights under the law shall not be denied or abridged by the United States or by any state on account of sex." Proponents of the amendment claimed that it would reinforce the basic rights as citizens that women held under the Constitution. A key leader in support of the ERA was First Lady Rosalynn Carter. Conservative activist Phyllis Schlafly led the fight against the ERA by visiting the states that had not yet ratified it. Opponents argued that sufficient laws were already in effect to guarantee those rights. Some feared that the amendment would break down the God-given biological distinctions between men and women, emphasizing that women were designed to have children. They worried it would threaten traditional protections that women enjoyed, such as exemption from the military draft and a husband's provision for his family, or child support from a divorced husband. The amendment failed to garner the necessary approval of three-fourths of the state legislatures before its deadline for ratification expired in 1982. It had been approved by thirty-five of the needed thirty-eight state legislatures. However, by 1979, five of those thirty-five had revoked earlier support. Supporters of the ERA have attempted to revive ratification in the 21st century, but many of the original provisions of the ERA have since been codified separately into law.

---

▼ (left) Activist Phyllis Schlafly wearing a "Stop ERA" badge; (right) anti-abortion and pro-abortion activists facing off on the steps of the New Jersey State House

## ROE V. WADE

A major issue for the radical element of the women's rights movement was abortion rights. State laws had long restricted or even prohibited abortion to preserve the life of the unborn child and to protect the life of the mother. Radical feminists and their supporters claimed that having a child would interrupt a woman's education or career, and that childbearing reinforced what they saw as antiquated views of the importance of marriage and motherhood. Further, they argued, freedom and equality for women meant that they should be free to reject an unwanted pregnancy, that they had the right to control their own bodies, and that forcing a woman to carry an unwanted child to term treats her unequally from a man. These arguments viewed the unborn child not as a distinct person with unique DNA with a right to life, but only as a "potential" person with no legal protections. However, the Bible clearly declares that life begins at conception (Ps. 139:13, Jer. 1:5)

In the landmark case *Roe v. Wade* (1973), the Supreme Court declared that most state laws that restricted abortion were unconstitutional. The ruling was based on an interpretation of a right to privacy implied in the Fourteenth Amendment. The Court further determined that a state could not prohibit abortions within a pregnancy's first trimester. Women's liberation activists celebrated the decision. Consequently, the death of unborn children by abortion rose to more than one million per year by 1977; over 63 million abortions have been performed since 1973.

In recent years several factors, such as improved technology, crisis pregnancy centers, and new laws, have corresponded to a decline in the number of abortions. *Roe* would later be overturned in the 2022 case *Dobbs v. Jackson Women's Health Organization* (see Chapter 25).

## Gay Rights

Another movement that gained supporters and coverage during this period was the gay rights movement. One of its goals was to remove the many legal prohibitions to practicing homosexuality. Later, a major objective was to redefine marriage to include same-sex unions.

The push for homosexual rights was presented as a struggle for freedom. Proponents compared the issue to the civil rights struggle of African Americans. Whereas African Americans faced discrimination because of their skin color, homosexuals claimed to be victims of bigotry because of their sexuality. Beginning in 1970, activists organized Gay Pride Week in June. In the early years of the movement, supporters argued homosexuality was a "sexual preference," not a mental illness, as listed by the American Psychiatric Association until 1973. Later, many asserted it was not a preference or choice but that it was a "sexual orientation" that was biologically determined.

Opponents of the gay rights movement voiced a number of concerns. Conservative Christians said that homosexuality was immoral. They observed that the Bible forbids homosexual desires and practices (Leviticus 18:22; Romans 1:27; and Jude 1:7) and noted that from Creation God had ordained marriage to be an institution between one man and one woman. Though Christians believed that the Bible taught that homosexual behavior was immoral, it was difficult to present biblical teaching in a public forum. As a result, Christians and many non-Christians pointed to the need for children to have both a mother and father. They noted that this traditional family structure had been an important part of most civilizations and that it was a foundation of American society. Critics of the gay rights movement also highlighted differences between the civil rights struggle for black Americans and the gay rights movement. They stated that neither a person's ethnicity nor skin color can be changed and that neither are moral matters, whereas sexual behavior is a moral issue and a matter of choice.

Christians debated the degree to which homosexuality was a choice or a condition that people were born with. Orthodox Christian theology has always taught that everyone is born with sinful desires; however, those who trust in Christ are made new and empowered by the Holy Spirit to resist sinful desires.

### Comprehension Check 23.4

1. All of the following were congressional measures to deal with the environment except for the ____.

   A creation of the BIA

   B creation of the EPA

   C Clean Air Act

   D Clean Water Act

2. Measures for civil rights for African Americans in the 70s included the following except ____.

   A affirmative action

   B busing

   C the Equal Rights Amendment

3. In *Roe v. Wade*, the Supreme Court ruled that ____.

   A quotas could not be used in college admissions

   B state laws banning abortions in the first trimester were unconstitutional

   C the federal government had to return land to Native Americans

**MAKING CONNECTIONS**

4. What were two examples of civil rights protests among Native American groups?

5. What was an argument for and an argument against the Equal Rights Amendment?

## Chapter Summary

### 23.1 The Nixon Administration

- Richard Nixon sought to appeal to the silent majority of Americans who desired peace and order. In foreign affairs he sought détente with China and the Soviet Union, resulting in increased trade with both countries and a treaty limiting nuclear missiles with the USSR. He also supported Israel in its wars against Egypt and Syria.

- The economy suffered from a budget deficit and inflation. OPEC proclaimed an oil embargo against the United States for its support of Israel, creating an energy crisis.

- During the election campaign of 1972, the Committee to Re-Elect the President authorized the break-in of the Democratic National Committee headquarters in the Watergate complex in Washington, DC. The White House denied involvement, and Nixon was reelected. After the election, investigations revealed that the CRP planned the break-in and that the White House covered up its involvement. Tapes from the Oval Office revealed Nixon's involvement in the cover-up, and he resigned from office on August 9, 1974.

**TERMS**

silent majority

détente

Strategic Arms Limitation Talks Agreement (SALT I)

Organization of Petroleum Exporting Countries (OPEC)

Committee to Re-Elect the President (CRP)

Watergate scandal

Spiro Agnew

Gerald Ford

**TERMS**

stagflation

### 23.2 The Ford Administration

- Gerald Ford, who was not elected as vice president or president, replaced Nixon. He made the controversial decision to pardon Nixon for any crimes he may have committed, saying it was in the nation's best interest, hurting his own popularity.

- The economy entered a period of stagflation with high inflation and high unemployment.

**TERMS**

Jimmy Carter

Panama Canal Treaty

Camp David Accords

Iranian hostage crisis

### 23.3 The Carter Administration

- Democrat Jimmy Carter from Georgia won the election of 1976. He granted amnesty to Vietnam War draft dodgers and faced inflation and a recession. He created a National Energy Plan, but the Three Mile Island nuclear accident hurt his plan for alternative energy sources.

- Carter signed the Panama Canal Treaty in 1977, giving control of the canal to Panama in 1999. He successfully negotiated peace between Israel and Egypt in the Camp David Accords and worked on a new nuclear treaty with the USSR, but the Soviet invasion of Afghanistan halted that effort. In Iran, revolutionaries overthrew the shah and installed Islamic extremist Ayatollah Ruhollah Khomeini as leader. The revolutionaries took more than sixty American hostages. Carter's efforts to release the hostages failed, and they were held 444 days, not being released until the day Ronald Reagan was inaugurated in January 1981.

## 23.4 Issues of the Seventies

- Environmental concerns, including air and water pollution, led to the creation of the Environmental Protection Agency and the passage of the Clean Air and Clean Water Acts.

- Because school integration had slowed due to neighborhoods being highly segregated, the courts ordered busing programs to send students to schools outside their neighborhoods. Affirmative action programs attempted to increase hiring of minorities and minority admissions to universities. Native Americans sought greater legal rights and action by the government to address past wrongs.

- The women's rights movement pushed to end discrimination against women. Some radical elements in the movement rejected biblical morality and distinctions between men and women. The Equal Rights Amendment failed to gain the approval of the necessary number of states for ratification. The Supreme Court decision in *Roe v. Wade* declared that women had a constitutional right to privacy and that state restrictions against abortion early in pregnancy were unconstitutional. Gay rights activists pushed for equal rights, but the movement rejected biblical morality related to homosexuality and failed to recognize the differences between the civil rights movement for African Americans and the gay rights movement.

**TERMS**

Environmental Protection Agency (EPA)

busing

affirmative action

Equal Rights Amendment (ERA)

*Roe v. Wade*

## Chapter Review Questions

### RECALL

1. What term did Nixon use to describe decent, hardworking Americans who wanted peace and order?

2. Nixon's presidency was characterized by détente with which two countries?

3. What agreement reduced nuclear missiles for the Unites States and USSR during Nixon's administration?

4. What organization was responsible for the break-in and wiretapping of the Democratic National Committee in the Watergate complex?

5. What term describes a period of high inflation and high unemployment at the same time?

6. Which president was known as a "born-again" Christian, a Washington "outsider," and "the people's president"?

7. What agreement do many consider to be Carter's greatest triumph in diplomacy?

8. What organization did Congress establish to oversee and coordinate environmental regulations?

9. What minority group protested in a march on Washington called the Trail of Broken Treaties?

10. What women's rights legislation failed to gain ratification by the states?

### UNDERSTAND

11. What agreements did Nixon make concerning China and Taiwan? How did Carter complete what Nixon began?

12. What contributed to inflation beginning with Nixon's administration? How did Nixon attempt to deal with inflation?

13. What led to the Energy Crisis beginning in Nixon's administration? What measures did Nixon and Congress take to meet the crisis?

14. What did Nixon deny regarding the Watergate scandal? What did he refuse to do during the investigation? What did the Supreme Court order Nixon to do, and what information came to light as a result?

15. Who resigned as vice president in 1973? Who was selected as the new vice president by the procedure of the Twenty-Fifth Amendment?

16. Why did Nixon resign as president?

17. What controversial decision did Carter make related to the Vietnam War? Who criticized this decision?

18. What two measures did Carter's National Energy Plan promote? What two events hurt his energy plan efforts?

19. What were the terms of the Panama Canal Treaty? What was one reason given for supporting the treaty and one reason for opposing it?

20. What did the Soviet Union do in 1979 to preserve the Communist government in Afghanistan? Who supported the Afghan resistance? What treaty was withdrawn as a result of the Soviet Union's action?

21. The "Carter Doctrine" was aimed at what country's actions? What did this doctrine declare?

22. What was the Iranian hostage crisis? How did Carter respond? How did the crisis impact the 1980 election?

23. What did courts order to help increase school integration? Why did some see this as a necessary measure, and for what reasons did some oppose it?

24. In what two areas was affirmative action intended to increase the number of minorities? What value were proponents desiring to support with affirmative action measures? Why did some oppose affirmative action?

25. What was one example of economic inequality that women's rights advocates protested? How did Congress and states begin to address this inequality?

26. What was the radical element of the women's rights movement? What institution was attacked by some within this radical group? What were some of the proposals offered by radicals in opposition to this institution?

27. What happened to the proposed Constitutional amendment for women's rights? What were the objections to the amendment?

28. How did state laws handle abortion before the 1970s? What was the ruling in *Roe v. Wade*?

29. What were two goals of the gay rights movement? How was the gay rights movement different from the civil rights movement?

## THINK ABOUT IT

30. How did the actions of Congress during the Watergate scandal illustrate the system of checks and balances? How did they exemplify justice?

31. Why did Ford pardon Nixon? What happened to Ford as a result of the pardon? Do you agree with his decision? Explain.

32. How does extreme environmentalism view humans in relation to nature? How does the Creation Mandate in Genesis 1:26-28 relate to environmental measures? What actions did the government take to protect the environment?

33. How did the push for abortion rights relate to the radical element of the women's rights movement? What impact did *Roe v. Wade* have? How did this ruling fail to uphold justice?

▼ Women reading newspaper coverage of Nixon's resignation

# 24 The Turn of the Century

**24.1 The Reagan Era**

**24.2 George H. W. Bush and the End of the Cold War**

**24.3 The Clinton Administration**

**24.4 George W. Bush and the World**

▲ Vice President George H. W. Bush and President Ronald Reagan with Soviet leader Mikhail Gorbachev

Why did conservatives approve of Reagan?

**GUIDING QUESTIONS**

- How did the rise of conservatism lead to Reagan's election?
- How did Reagan's domestic agenda reflect conservative ideas?
- How did Reagan attempt to halt communism around the world?

## The Election of 1980

Political conservatives were concerned with the course that America had taken in the 1960s and 1970s. Traditional conservatives believed firmly in limited powers for the national government and staunch resistance to the growth of communism. They opposed increased government spending, especially since the nation's budget deficit was growing at an alarming rate. They also feared that the United States was growing weaker militarily and in foreign affairs.

### New Right

Joining the traditional conservatives was a faction called the **New Right**, which shared many beliefs of the traditionalists, notably opposition to communism and belief in limited government. But the New Right was also motivated by numerous social and moral issues, particularly abortion. The *Roe v. Wade* decision spurred a Right-to-Life movement that opposed abortion and sought to use such means as a constitutional amendment to overturn *Roe*. Other New Right activists emphasized the need to reduce the increasingly heavy burden of taxation by national, state, and local governments. The campaign to defeat the ERA also gained much support from the New Right.

### Religious Right

An important component of the New Right was the **Religious Right**, composed of various conservative Christian leaders and organizations concerned primarily with moral issues such as widespread drug abuse, abortion, the increasing secularization of American culture, and increased toleration and advocacy of homosexuality. The Religious Right hoped to stem the tide of immorality through political action that would reestablish America's traditional moral standards.

The Religious Right, which included Protestants, Catholics, and Mormons, also feared that the government was undercutting the nation's religious freedoms, pointing to Supreme Court decisions against prayer and Bible reading in public schools. Some of the movement's most prominent leaders were television evangelists who motivated many Christians to become active politically. Pat Robertson established the first Christian television station in the United States and was a host on a Christian talk show. Baptist pastor Jerry Falwell of Virginia founded a religious political action group called the Moral Majority to help elect conservative candidates and to further conservative causes.

Some Christians who supported many of the goals of the Religious Right were concerned about some of its methods. Because Catholics and Mormons had joined with Protestants for political purposes, there were efforts to downplay differences in the religious teachings of these groups. Some Christians pointed out that members of the Religious Right were placing too much faith in politics and treating certain conservative political positions as though they were Christian doctrines. These critics said that rather than offering political solutions, Christians should focus on loving their neighbors, influencing society through living a consistent Christian life, and reaching non-believers with the gospel.

▲ TV evangelist Jerry Falwell in front of his local church

### The Election

With the support of the New Right, the Republicans nominated **Ronald Reagan**, a former Hollywood actor and governor of California, as their candidate in 1980. Reagan used his oratorical skills to energize conservatives with his defense of free enterprise, the shrinking of the federal government, and opposition to communism. He chose politically moderate George H. W. Bush to be his running mate.

Despite opposition from the Democratic Party's liberal wing, Carter won his party's nomination to run for reelection. John Anderson of Illinois ran for president as an Independent.

The Republicans hoped that popular discontent with Carter's failure to obtain the release of hostages in Iran and the dangerously high inflation rate would help them. In his closing statement during a televised debate only a week before the election, Reagan asked the public,

> *Are you better off than you were four years ago? Is it easier for you to go and buy things in the stores than it was four years ago? . . . Is America as respected throughout the world as it was?*

On Election Day, Reagan won 50.7 percent of the popular vote to Carter's 41 percent and Anderson's 6.6 percent. In the Electoral College, however, Reagan carried forty-four states for a 489–49 victory. Furthermore, the Republicans won twelve additional seats in the Senate, capturing control there for the first time since 1954.

## The Reagan Revolution

Reagan believed that with Communist threats from Central America to Central Asia, the United States needed to maintain a firm grip on the reins of free-world leadership. He wanted to reduce the size of the federal government and the amount of taxes, believing that both of these hindered growth and opportunity. Reagan wanted to restore and strengthen traditional American values by curbing government intrusion into the home, the church, and the school.

### Did You Know?

Reagan survived an assassination attempt on March 30, 1981. John Hinkley shot Reagan, White House press secretary James Brady, and two law enforcement officers. The bullet that hit Reagan stopped about an inch from his heart. Hinkley, who claimed he was trying to impress actress Jodie Foster, was found not guilty by reason of insanity and spent thirty-five years in a psychiatric facility before being released in 2016.

▼ The assassination attempt on Ronald Reagan, outside the Hilton Hotel in Washington, DC

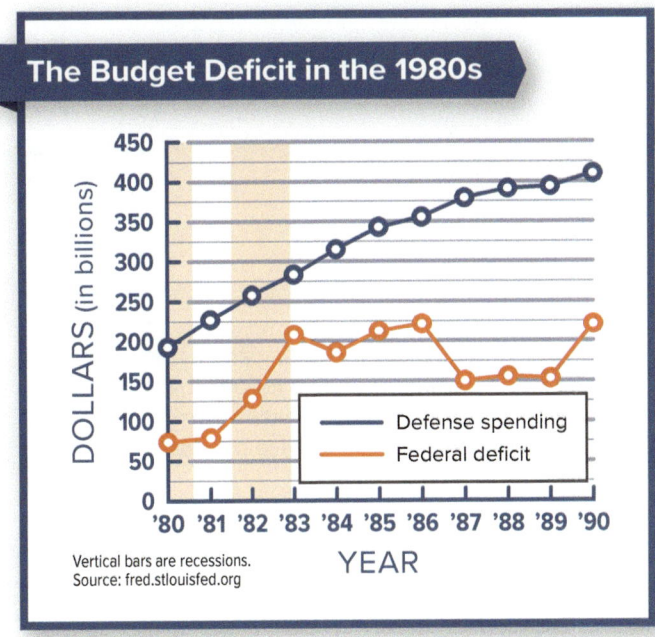

## Reaganomics

First on Reagan's agenda was tackling the nation's economic woes. Reagan's prescription for America's inflation was **supply-side economics** (also known as Reaganomics). This approach cut taxes to increase the incentive for citizens to earn, save, and invest; it also reduced government regulations on business and provided corporate tax breaks to encourage economic expansion. In general, the supply-side approach seeks to increase the supply of goods in order to lower prices and seeks to use deregulation to energize the economy in order to boost employment. In his inaugural address, Reagan declared an end to a "tax system which penalizes successful achievement and keeps us from maintaining full productivity." Calling Reagan's approach "trickle-down economics," critics argued that it would help wealthy Americans and large businesses but that little money would "trickle down" to middle- or lower-class Americans.

Reagan took his cause to Congress, which passed the Economic Recovery Tax Act of 1981. It cut income taxes by about 25 percent over three years, reduced maximum tax rates for upper incomes, and lowered business taxes.

Another important part of Reagan's economic plan was budget cuts. In 1981 Congress approved cuts of $35 billion, reducing funding for transportation, education, welfare, and arts assistance. Opponents claimed such cuts unfairly affected the poor. For example, forced cutbacks in Aid to Families with Dependent Children (AFDC) ended welfare benefits for 400,000 households.

One budget area that did receive a boost by the Reagan administration was defense. Believing in "peace through strength," Reagan added $12 billion to defense programs in 1982, and the buildup continued through the end of the decade. Given Communist expansion in Asia, Africa, and Central America and the need to protect vital oil interests in the Middle East, Reagan continued throughout his administration to advocate for military spending.

After an economic slump in 1982, in which unemployment grew to more than 10 percent, along with a drop in his approval rating and concerns over growing budget deficits, Reagan abandoned his antitax policies and pushed through a tax increase aimed mainly at businesses. By 1983 the economy rebounded. The nation enjoyed lower interest rates and lower oil prices. Eighteen million new jobs were created during the 1980s, and unemployment dropped to about 5 percent. The housing market, an important indication of American economic strength, expanded rapidly.

However, tax cuts, increases in defense spending, and unwillingness by Congress to make further budget cuts produced huge budget deficits. The national debt increased from $827 billion at the end of the 1970s to $2.9 trillion a decade later.

### The Budget Deficit in the 1980s

DOLLARS (in billions) — 0, 50, 100, 150, 200, 250, 300, 350, 400, 450

YEAR — '80 '81 '82 '83 '84 '85 '86 '87 '88 '89 '90

Defense spending
Federal deficit

Vertical bars are recessions.
Source: fred.stlouisfed.org

Sandra Day O'Connor sworn in as Supreme Court justice

## The Courts

Reagan made several appointments to the Supreme Court. In 1981 he appointed the first female Supreme Court justice, Sandra Day O'Connor. In 1986 when Warren Burger retired, Reagan nominated Justice William H. Rehnquist as chief justice, and appointed Antonin Scalia to fill Rehnquist's former position. A year later Reagan nominated Anthony Kennedy. Reagan's appointments moved the court generally in a more conservative direction.

## The Drug War and AIDS

First declared by Nixon in the 1970s, the war on drugs became a major part of Reagan's domestic agenda. During the 1980s the Drug Enforcement Administration led several operations targeting drug trafficking of marijuana and cocaine. Drug-prevention efforts continued as the introduction of crack cocaine, a form cheaper than powder cocaine, in the United States led to an increase in drug addictions and drug-related violence. First Lady Nancy Reagan led a drug-prevention program for children and teenagers, using the slogan "Just Say No." In 1986 Congress passed the Anti-Drug Abuse Act, which increased the penalties for drug distribution and established mandatory minimum sentences for drug possession and other crimes.

In addition to the drug epidemic, the AIDS (acquired immunodeficiency syndrome) crisis concerned American society. In the 1980s the newly discovered disease had been observed in the United States mostly in homosexual men, leading many Americans to associate it with that lifestyle. Later, doctors discovered the source of the disease and that it was often sexually transmitted, affecting both homosexual and heterosexual men and women. Because of the lack of treatment options in the 1980s, thousands with the disease died.

## The 1984 Election

As the 1984 election approached, Democrats claimed that Reagan's social policies ignored the working class and ignored civil and women's rights. Walter Mondale, former vice president under Jimmy Carter, won the Democratic nomination. Mondale chose as his running mate New York congresswoman Geraldine Ferraro, the first female vice-presidential candidate for a major party. The president's personal popularity and a strong economy produced a landslide victory, with Reagan winning 58 percent of the popular vote and a 525 to 13 electoral vote.

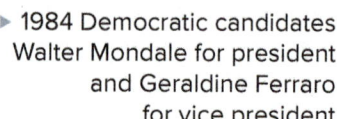

1984 Democratic candidates Walter Mondale for president and Geraldine Ferraro for vice president

# Around the World

Reagan was not satisfied with previous administrations' efforts to merely contain communism; he was determined to defeat it. A key aspect of Reagan's foreign policy was the **Reagan Doctrine**, which pledged America's support to groups fighting Communists in the Third World. As a result, military and economic aid flowed to anti-Communist fighters in Latin America, Africa, and Asia.

## Soviet Union

Addressing a group of religious leaders, Reagan referred to the Soviet Union as an "evil empire." Critics groaned that Reagan's harsh words might renew and worsen Cold War tensions. In 1983 Reagan announced plans for a space-based defense shield of satellites, missiles, and lasers designed to safeguard the country from nuclear attack. This Strategic Defense Initiative (SDI), called "Star Wars" (after the popular science fiction movies), would have needed years of technological developments and several billions of dollars and has thus not yet become reality.

**Mikhail Gorbachev** became the new Soviet leader in 1985. In contrast to his recent predecessors, he called for *perestroika*, or "restructuring," of the stagnant Communist economy, shifting to more free-market policies and some private ownership. Gorbachev also advocated *glasnost*, or "openness," in Soviet society. He allowed more freedom of speech, press, and religion.

During his second term, Reagan met with Gorbachev five times to improve diplomatic ties. The summit meetings between the two leaders were called Strategic Arms Reduction Talks (START). START aimed primarily at reaching an agreement to substantially reduce the number of nuclear weapons the two nations possessed. Reagan insisted that all treaties include enforcement procedures. At the Washington Summit in 1987, Reagan and Gorbachev signed the Intermediate Nuclear Forces (INF) Treaty, which eliminated most medium-range missiles from Europe. The superpowers' agreement was heralded as a symbol of friendlier relations.

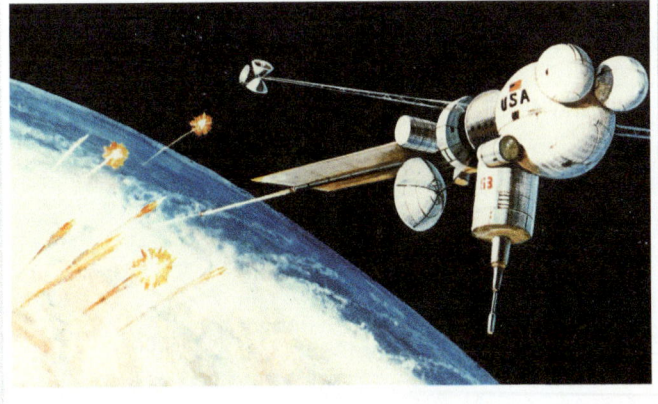

▲ Artist's conception of an electromagnetic railgun intercepting nuclear weapons in space, as part of Reagan's Strategic Defense Initiative (SDI)

In June 1987, a few months before the Washington Summit, Reagan had visited Berlin and delivered a speech beside the Berlin Wall. The speech included his famous challenge to the Russian leader:

> *General Secretary Gorbachev, if you seek peace, if you seek prosperity for the Soviet Union and Eastern Europe, if you seek liberalization: Come here to this gate! Mr. Gorbachev, open this gate! Mr. Gorbachev, tear down this wall!*

While Reagan continued negotiations for arms reductions, he proposed developing the SDI program. Gorbachev knew that SDI would force the Soviet Union to develop its own costly defense shield. With the Soviet economy on the verge of collapse, Reagan's SDI development brought increased pressure on Gorbachev's government as the 1990s began.

▼ Reagan's address at the Brandenburg Gate in Berlin, in which he challenged Gorbachev to "tear down this wall"

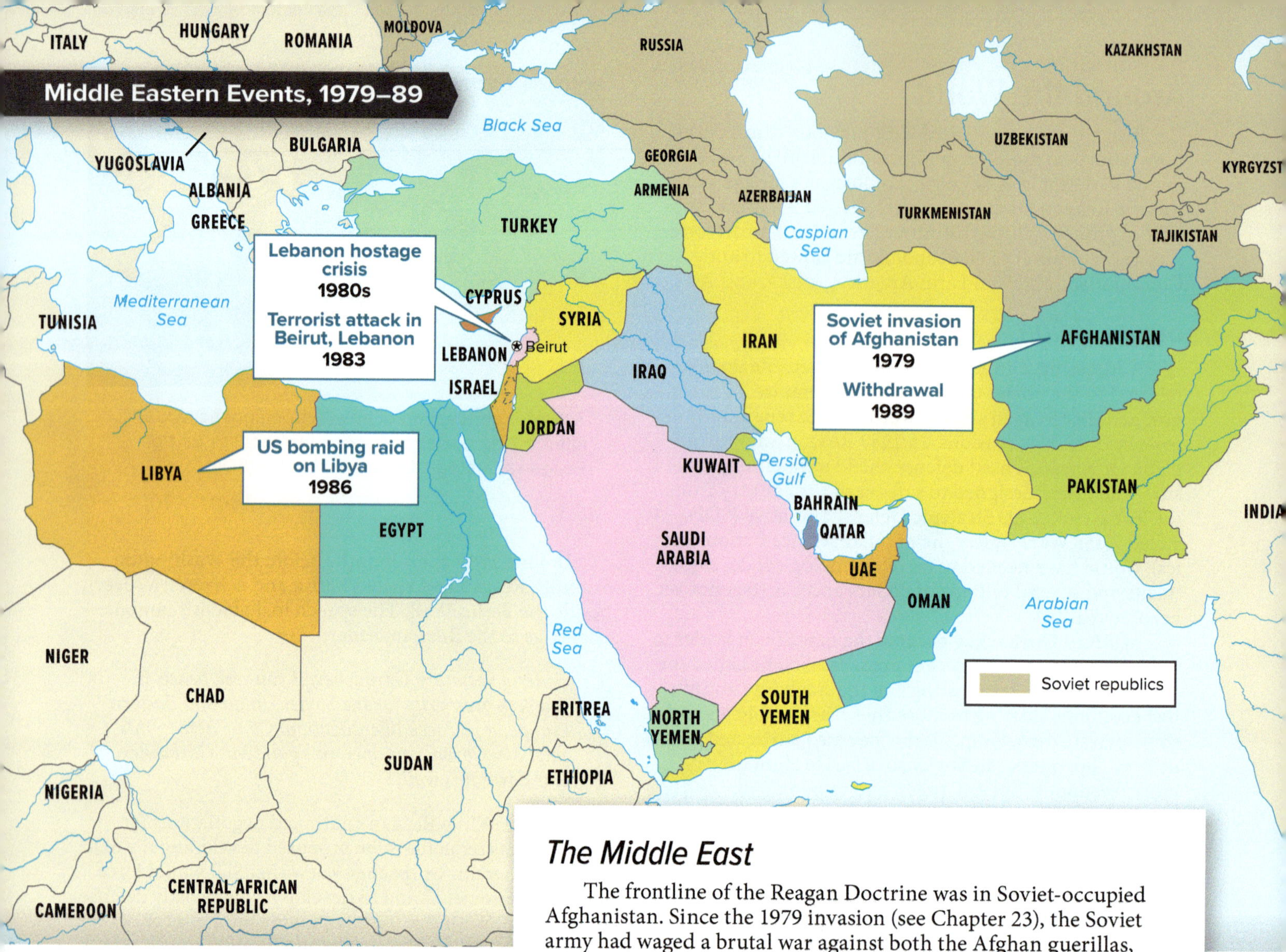

## Middle Eastern Events, 1979–89

ITALY
HUNGARY
ROMANIA
MOLDOVA
RUSSIA
KAZAKHSTAN

BULGARIA
Black Sea
YUGOSLAVIA
ALBANIA
GEORGIA
UZBEKISTAN
KYRGYZST
GREECE
ARMENIA
AZERBAIJAN
TURKMENISTAN
TAJIKISTAN
TURKEY
Caspian Sea

**Lebanon hostage crisis 1980s**

**Terrorist attack in Beirut, Lebanon 1983**

CYPRUS
SYRIA
IRAN
**Soviet invasion of Afghanistan 1979**

**Withdrawal 1989**

AFGHANISTAN

Mediterranean Sea
TUNISIA
LEBANON ✷ Beirut
ISRAEL
IRAQ

**US bombing raid on Libya 1986**

JORDAN
KUWAIT
Persian Gulf
PAKISTAN
LIBYA
BAHRAIN
QATAR
INDIA
EGYPT
UAE
SAUDI ARABIA
OMAN
Arabian Sea

NIGER
CHAD
Red Sea

SUDAN
ERITREA
NORTH YEMEN
SOUTH YEMEN

NIGERIA
ETHIOPIA

CENTRAL AFRICAN REPUBLIC
CAMEROON

Soviet republics

▼ Afghan mujahideen soldier with a stinger missile near a rebel base in the Safed Koh Mountains, 1988

## The Middle East

The frontline of the Reagan Doctrine was in Soviet-occupied Afghanistan. Since the 1979 invasion (see Chapter 23), the Soviet army had waged a brutal war against both the Afghan guerillas, known as mujahideen, and Afghan civilians. America supplied military advisors and state-of-the-art weapons, including surface-to-air missiles, to the determined rebel resistance. The Soviet army withdrew in the spring of 1989, and many Americans viewed the Soviet retreat as a great triumph for the Reagan Doctrine. The United States did not commit resources to rebuild Afghanistan. Following the ten-year war, radical elements took control, and future US administrations would expend immense human and financial resources to combat Islamic radicalism in the country.

In other areas of the Middle East, Islamic extremism led to terrorist attacks, including suicide bombings, and hostage crises. Responding to terrorist attacks sponsored by Libyan leader Muammar al-Qaddafi, the US conducted a surprise bombing raid on Libya in 1986.

In Lebanon a civil war had begun in the 1970s and involved multiple factions, including Islamic extremists. Reagan sent US Marines to join a multinational peacekeeping force there. In April 1983 a terrorist used a truck to bomb the US embassy in Beirut, and in October a terrorist drove a bomb-laden truck into the marine barracks in Beirut, killing 241 Americans. A few months later, the peacekeeping force, including US troops, withdrew. Several US citizens, some working in Beirut as teachers and journalists, were taken hostage during the 1980s. The American public watched in helpless anger. Eventually some hostages were released, but others died in captivity.

## Latin America

In 1981 Communist rebels and the government of El Salvador were involved in a civil war. Reagan responded to the aggression of the Soviet- and Cuban-backed rebels by supplying arms, military advisors, and economic aid to the Salvadoran government.

By 1983 the government of Grenada, a tiny Caribbean island, was increasingly threatened by Communists who had close ties with Cuba, and a new Communist government had been established in October. Responding to calls for help from the governments of neighboring islands (who also feared the spread of communism), Reagan sent nearly 2,000 US troops to Grenada. The October 1983 invasion defeated the Cuban and Grenadian soldiers there, and a new, anti-Communist government was established.

In Nicaragua a group known as the Sandinistas had established a Communist government in 1979 and then began sending military supplies to the Communists in El Salvador. Under the direction of the CIA, groups of anti-Sandinista guerrillas known as Contras (from the Spanish word for counterrevolutionary) were organized in Nicaragua to fight communism there.

Reagan's support for anti-Communist forces in Nicaragua ignited fierce debates in Congress. Critics warned that reviving "big stick" policies would renew anti-Americanism throughout the region. They urged compromising with the Sandinistas and increasing economic aid to the region. Reagan, however, believed that the Sandinistas posed a threat to not only the democratic elements within Nicaragua but also the security of all Central America. With the Soviets supporting Nicaragua's Communist government, Reagan argued that US support of the Contras also represented a vital test of American commitment to the Monroe Doctrine. At first, Congress agreed to support the Contras. Reagan hoped that his actions in El Salvador, Grenada, and Nicaragua would send a clear message to Communists regarding his desire to stop their expansion.

▲ Contras in Nicaragua

**Latin American Events**

## Iran-Contra Affair

In November 1986, an underground newspaper in Beirut, Lebanon, reported that the Reagan administration had secretly sold weapons to Iran, which was locked in a costly war with neighboring Iraq. The weapons were exchanged for Iran's help in obtaining the release of the American hostages in Lebanon, who were held by terrorist groups sympathetic to Iran. As the story unfolded, it revealed that members of the White House National Security Council (NSC) had established this arrangement.

Investigations into what happened to the money from the arms sales to Iran widened the scandal. The funds, funneled through Swiss banks, had been used to supply the Nicaraguan Contras battling the Communist Sandinistas, giving the matter the name **Iran-Contra affair**.

The support to the Contras came after Congress had stopped military aid to that group. The Reagan White House was already embarrassed about the disclosure of selling weapons to Iran as part of the attempt to obtain freedom for hostages, as this violated the long-stated US policy of not negotiating with terrorists. Congress conducted televised hearings regarding the affair. The president's public approval rating dropped significantly. On March 4, 1987, in a speech to the nation, the President took responsibility for the actions of those who served in his administration.

Throughout 1987 the investigations and congressional hearings continued to uncover more details, and much of the responsibility for the events was placed on Reagan's loose management style and his failure to properly supervise subordinates. President Reagan had approved the weapons sales to Iran, but no evidence was found that he knew about the money being sent to the Contras. Nevertheless, the scandal tainted Reagan's second term and his reputation.

▼ Lieutenant-Colonel Oliver North at the House Foreign Affairs Committee hearings on the Iran-Contra Affair

1. The New Right wanted limited government but was not concerned about moral issues.

   True

   False

2. Reagan's economic policies included all of the following except ___.

   **A** cutting taxes

   **B** decreasing military spending

   **C** reducing government regulation

3. Reagan and Gorbachev signed a treaty that reduced the number of nuclear weapons.

   True

   False

4. Terrorists bombed the US embassy and US Marine barracks and took Americans hostage in ___.

   **A** Afghanistan

   **B** Lebanon

   **C** Libya

5. All of the following are true concerning the Iran-Contra affair except that ___.

   **A** money from secret weapons sales to Iran went to the Contras in Nicaragua

   **B** the United States hoped to gain Iran's help with the release of hostages in Lebanon

   **C** the scandal did not hurt Reagan's reputation

### MAKING CONNECTIONS

6. What was the Reagan Doctrine, and how did it influence foreign policy in Latin America?

# George H. W. Bush and the End of the Cold War

## "A New World Order"

### Election of 1988

Reagan supported his vice president, **George H. W. Bush**, for the Republican nomination for president in 1988, believing he was the best candidate to continue the "Reagan Revolution." The Democrats nominated Governor Michael Dukakis of Massachusetts. In the campaign, Bush rallied support largely by promoting strength at home and abroad and by stating "Read my lips: no new taxes." Bush won decisively with 53 percent of the popular vote, and he won the electoral vote 426 to 111.

▼ George H. W. Bush speaking to the press, 1991

### Panama

General Manuel Noriega, who at one time had been an ally of the United States in anti-Communist efforts in Central America, became ruler of Panama in 1983. However, Noriega became involved in drug trafficking, and he began to shift his allegiance toward the Soviets and Cuba. Determined that Panama would have a stable, pro-American government when it took control of the canal in 1999, Bush ordered US troops to invade Panama in December 1989. Noriega was captured and sent to the United States where he stood trial and was convicted on drug charges. Panama then held elections to establish a new government. Noriega was later extradited and tried on further charges abroad.

◄ US Marines in Panama

## The Fall of Communism

During the Bush administration, the world witnessed the final collapse of the Iron Curtain and the end of the Cold War. In 1989 protests began to mount in numerous Communist countries in Eastern Europe. Poland elected a non-Communist prime minister for the first time in over forty years. Hungary reopened its borders and its ruling party abandoned communism. East Germans began protesting as well. Pro-democracy pressure caused the East German Communist leader to resign. In October Soviet leader Mikhail Gorbachev, who was facing a growing pro-democracy movement in his own country, told the West that his nation would no longer use force to keep the governments of Eastern Europe under Communist control. This opened the door for more countries to challenge Communist rule.

On November 9, 1989, the Communist East German government announced that it would begin allowing its citizens to freely cross from East Berlin into West Berlin. In the following days, hundreds of thousands of East Germans gathered at the Berlin Wall. Not knowing how to handle the matter, government leaders and border guards watched as the protestors began dismantling the wall. For the first time in many years, Germans on both sides of the wall could connect with one another. East and West Germans urged reunification of their countries. Although some European countries feared the power of a reunified Germany, Bush supported this movement and worked with world leaders to bring about a peaceful reunification in 1990.

▼ Berliners celebrating the fall of the Berlin Wall, November 12, 1989

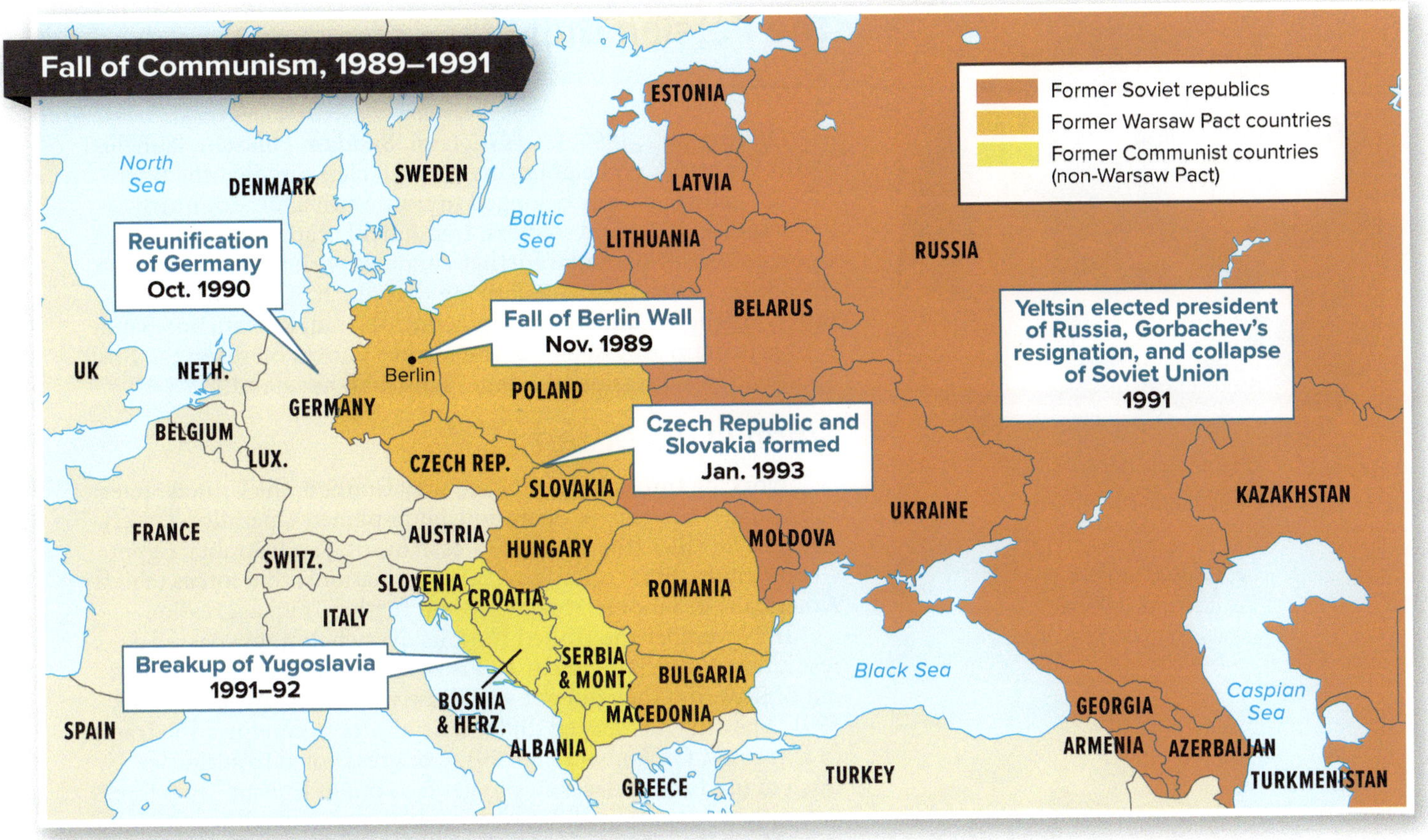

## Fall of Communism, 1989–1991

**Legend:**
- Former Soviet republics
- Former Warsaw Pact countries
- Former Communist countries (non-Warsaw Pact)

**Reunification of Germany Oct. 1990**

**Fall of Berlin Wall Nov. 1989**

**Czech Republic and Slovakia formed Jan. 1993**

**Yeltsin elected president of Russia, Gorbachev's resignation, and collapse of Soviet Union 1991**

**Breakup of Yugoslavia 1991–92**

*Map labels: North Sea, DENMARK, SWEDEN, ESTONIA, LATVIA, Baltic Sea, LITHUANIA, RUSSIA, BELARUS, UK, NETH., Berlin, GERMANY, POLAND, BELGIUM, LUX., CZECH REP., SLOVAKIA, KAZAKHSTAN, FRANCE, AUSTRIA, HUNGARY, UKRAINE, MOLDOVA, SWITZ., SLOVENIA, CROATIA, ROMANIA, ITALY, SERBIA & MONT., BULGARIA, Black Sea, Caspian Sea, BOSNIA & HERZ., MACEDONIA, GEORGIA, ARMENIA, AZERBAIJAN, SPAIN, ALBANIA, TURKMENISTAN, GREECE, TURKEY*

Between 1989 and 1991 Communist governments also fell in Czechoslovakia, Bulgaria, Romania, Albania, and Yugoslavia. In the Soviet Union, Gorbachev faced growing criticism both from those who favored democracy and from Communist Party loyalists. In 1991 pro-democracy candidate Boris Yeltsin was elected president of the Russian Republic (the largest republic of the USSR). In August of that year, pro-Communist officials attempted a coup to overthrow the government. Yeltsin stood up to the coup leaders, and Bush pledged his support for Yeltsin. The coup ended and the fifteen Russian republics declared their independence from the USSR. In December 1991, Gorbachev resigned and announced that the Soviet Union no longer existed.

President Bush responded to the fall of communism in the Soviet Union and Eastern Europe with cautious optimism. He realized that if he boasted that America had won the Cold War that it might humiliate the Communists and provoke a counterreaction from them or from extreme nationalists. Instead, he worked quietly behind the scenes to help the transition to democracy in those countries, even though this meant that at home he did not capitalize politically for this success as much as he could have.

### Tiananmen Square

After witnessing the initial pro-democracy movements in Europe, Chinese workers and students held demonstrations in the spring of 1989 in Beijing's Tiananmen Square. However, the Communist government was determined to stay in power and used tanks and soldiers to put down the demonstrations. Many demonstrators were killed, and protest leaders were arrested and sentenced to death. The United States and other nations responded with some economic sanctions against China, but Bush resisted calls for a stronger response.

▼ Protesters crowding around the "Goddess of Democracy" statue, which was sculpted for the protest in Tiananmen Square, with Mao Zedong's portrait in the background

# The Persian Gulf War

## Confrontation

On August 2, 1990, Iraq's dictator, **Saddam Hussein,** launched a military attack on neighboring Kuwait, claiming that the tiny, oil-rich nation actually belonged to Iraq. With a force of nearly one hundred thousand soldiers, Iraq quickly captured Kuwait and stood poised for potential further conquest with troops located on the border of Saudi Arabia. Fearing that much of the world's oil supply might fall under Hussein's control (Iraq, Kuwait, and Saudi Arabia contain almost half of the world's known oil reserves), Bush opposed the aggression, vowing, "This shall not stand."

## Storm in the Desert

Working through the UN Security Council, the United States coordinated a defensive operation, code-named Operation Desert Shield. The allies (the United States, Kuwait, Saudi Arabia, Egypt, Great Britain, France, and several other nations) sent forces (chiefly American) to Saudi Arabia to prevent further Iraqi aggression.

In November the United Nations overwhelmingly passed a resolution authorizing the use of military force to push the Iraqis out of Kuwait if they did not withdraw voluntarily by January 15, 1991. The allies exhausted diplomatic efforts to convince the Iraqis to withdraw. On January 12, 1991, Congress voted to authorize Bush to use force if necessary to get Iraq out of Kuwait. Iraqi forces defiantly refused to withdraw by the January 15 deadline. On January 16, Bush ordered a massive military assault on Iraqi military targets. Code-named Operation Desert Storm, the **Persian Gulf War** for the liberation of Kuwait began. The allied commander, American general Norman Schwarzkopf, told his forces, "Now you must be the thunder and lightning of Desert Storm."

▲ Oil well on fire in southeastern Kuwait

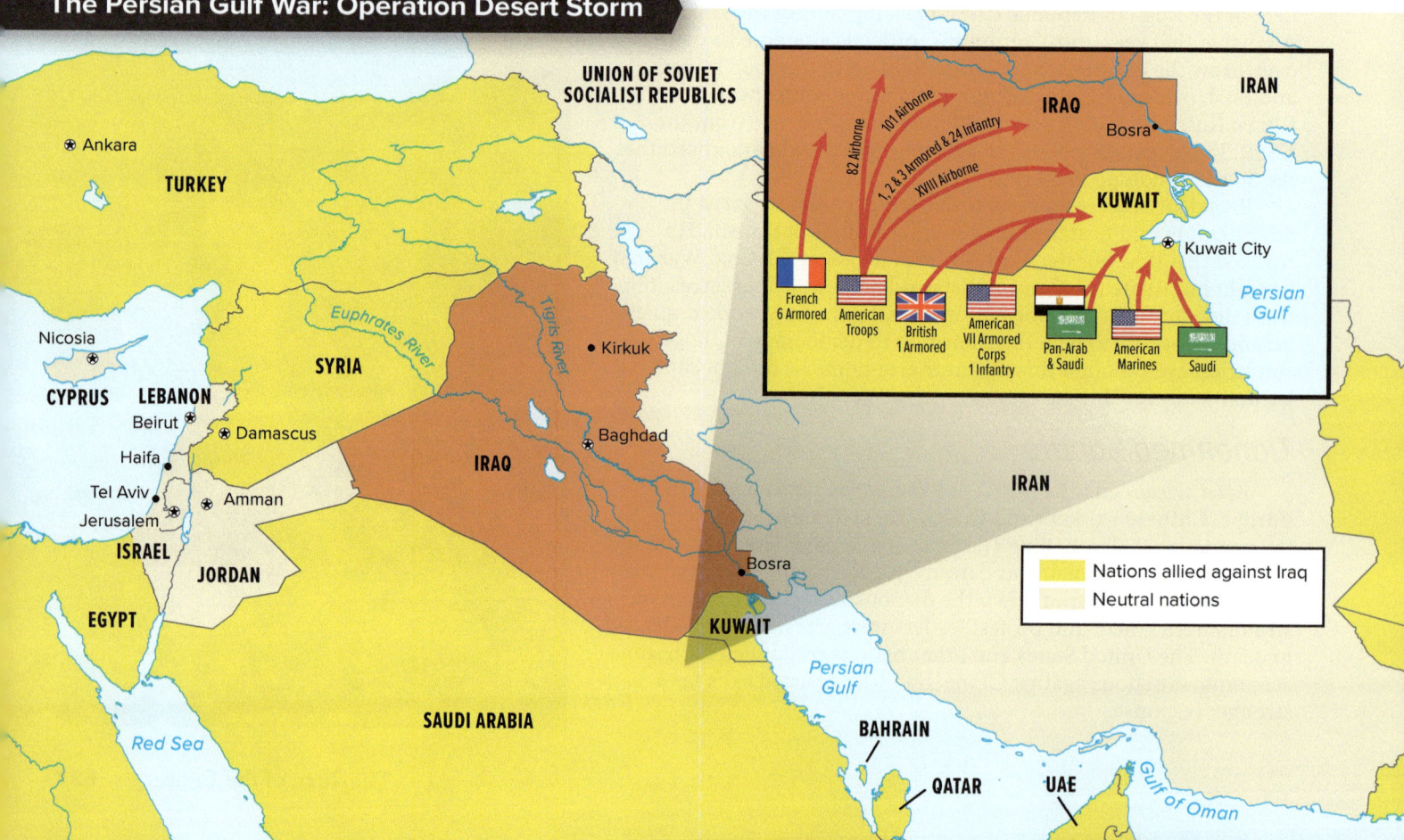

The Persian Gulf War: Operation Desert Storm

In the first stage, Allied cruise missiles, bombers, and fighters, including the new stealth fighters (aircraft that use technology to avoid detection) conducted massive, around-the-clock bombing and air strikes on military targets in Iraq and Kuwait. Enjoying almost complete air superiority, the allies destroyed much of Iraq's military capability—communications networks, airfields, bridges, roads, and missile launch sites. Thousands of Iraqi soldiers deserted.

## The 100-Hour War

The second stage of the war was a ground attack on the Iraqis. On February 24 a coalition of allied troops assaulted enemy positions in southern Kuwait, pinning down the Iraqis, who thought this attack was the main thrust. But while the battle was raging, a separate allied coalition moved into southern Iraq, west of Kuwait. With amazing speed, armored and infantry forces encircled and entrapped the main Iraqi forces in Kuwait and southern Iraq. With their lines of communication severed, Iraqi units fought fiercely but ineffectively. On February 27—just one hundred hours after the ground war began—Bush declared Kuwait's liberation and a UN victory in a televised address.

## Aftermath

The Persian Gulf War was an intensive military effort. Allied planes flew more than 100,000 missions during the six-week war, losing about 75 aircraft. The American-led coalition wrecked nearly 4,000 enemy tanks and killed between 20,000 and 35,000 Iraqi soldiers. Only about 300 allied soldiers died. Victory in the war was a great achievement for George H. W. Bush, and his approval rating rose to 89 percent.

Although defeated, Saddam Hussein still ruled Iraq and threatened the stability of the Middle East. He resisted efforts by UN officials to inspect his military sites and defied the economic sanctions that the victors imposed on him.

Trouble continued to simmer in the Middle East long after Desert Storm ended. Many Muslims resented the presence of US troops in Saudi Arabia, a nation with some of Islam's holiest sites. This resentment led to terrorist attacks by radical Muslims on American targets throughout the world.

▶ US tanks in the ground war stage of the Persian Gulf War

## A War *of* Precision

Because of technological advances, military and civilian casualties were less than those in any other war on that scale. The United States used precision-guided missiles and "smart bombs" that pinpointed targets to within a few feet. Numerous videos show pilots delivering camera-carrying bombs right into air ducts of targeted military installations.

# Domestic Issues

## Economic Concerns

One sign of economic trouble was the failure of many of the nation's savings and loan (S&L) banks. Unsound investments and declining oil prices drove several of the S&Ls into bankruptcy. Because the federal government guarantees the deposits in banks, approximately $125 billion in taxpayer funds was spent to cover the debts of the collapsing institutions.

Probably the most politically damaging moment was when Bush signed a budget deal that sought to tame the federal deficit by raising taxes. He had campaigned on the phrase "Read my lips—no new taxes." But pressure from Congress and budget deficits, worsened by the S&L crisis, made him rethink his vow. Consequently, many voters were upset with Bush, and it cost him votes in the next election.

## New Legislation

Bush signed the **Americans with Disabilities Act** in 1990. This legislation prohibited job discrimination based on disabilities. It also required local governments and businesses to improve and alter their accommodations (e.g., provide special parking places and install ramps for wheelchairs) for the disabled. Other significant legislation passed included the Clean Air Act of 1990, which tightened air pollution standards, and the Immigration Act of 1990, which increased overall immigration to allow 700,000 immigrants per year.

▼ George H. W. Bush signs the Americans with Disabilities Act

## The Twenty-Seventh Amendment

When James Madison originally proposed the Bill of Rights, he offered twelve amendments, although only ten were passed. One which did not originally pass read, "No law, varying the compensation for the services of the senators and representatives, shall take effect, until an election of representatives shall have intervened." In other words, if Congress votes itself a pay raise, it will not take effect until after another congressional election takes place. In the 1980s many taxpayers were outraged when Congress voted itself pay raises, even when the national economy was in a downturn. The resulting furor gave a fresh push to the old Madison amendment, and the **Twenty-Seventh Amendment** was ratified in 1992.

---

## Comprehension Check 24.2

1. All the following accompanied the end of the Cold War except the ____.
   - **A** fall of the Berlin Wall
   - **B** independence of the fifteen republics from the USSR
   - **C** overthrow of Boris Yeltsin in Russia
   - **D** reunification of Germany

2. Bush broke his campaign promise to resist ____.
   - **A** attempts to raise taxes
   - **B** calls for a stronger response to the Tiananmen Square incident
   - **C** the overthrow of Noriega in Panama

3. The Twenty-Seventh Amendment ____.
   - **A** ensured the government would never have a budget deficit
   - **B** made any pay raise that was voted on by Congress take effect after the next election
   - **C** prohibited discrimination against Americans with disabilities

### MAKING CONNECTIONS

4. What was the cause of the Persian Gulf War, and what was the military outcome of the war?

# The Clinton Administration

Should Clinton have been impeached?

## The Election of 1992

After the success of the Persian Gulf War, President Bush looked unbeatable as he prepared to run for reelection. As a result, some major Democratic candidates hesitated to enter the presidential race. Their hesitancy allowed relatively unknown Arkansas governor **Bill Clinton** to win the nomination. Marketing himself as a "New Democrat," Clinton said he would not promote big government and would end the tax-and-spend policies that many Democrats had supported in the past. Complicating the campaign was third-party candidate Ross Perot. A blunt-speaking Texas billionaire, Perot promised to put an end to "politics as usual" and to trim the budget deficit. He made a virtue of the fact that he was no politician.

With the Cold War won and no immediate foreign threats facing the country, Americans worried more about domestic issues such as education, health care, and especially the economy. Bush emphasized Clinton's rumored sexual immorality, marijuana use, draft dodging during the Vietnam War, and questionable financial transactions as governor of Arkansas. Clinton's campaign shrewdly leveraged the recession after the Gulf War as well as Bush's broken promise not to raise taxes, making the economy his central issue.

By Election Day 1992, Bush's approval rating had dropped to less than 40 percent, and Clinton defeated Bush with 43 percent of the popular vote to Bush's 37 percent. Perot won 19 percent of the vote (but no electoral votes), the largest total for a third-party candidate since Theodore Roosevelt's Bull Moose Party in 1912. In the Electoral College, Clinton defeated Bush 370 to 168.

### GUIDING QUESTIONS

- What factors led to Clinton's election in 1992?
- What happened in America during the Clinton administration?
- What foreign challenges faced Clinton's administration?

▲ George H. W. Bush (left), Ross Perot (center), and Bill Clinton (right) at one of the presidential debates

◄ Bill Clinton

## The Election of 1992

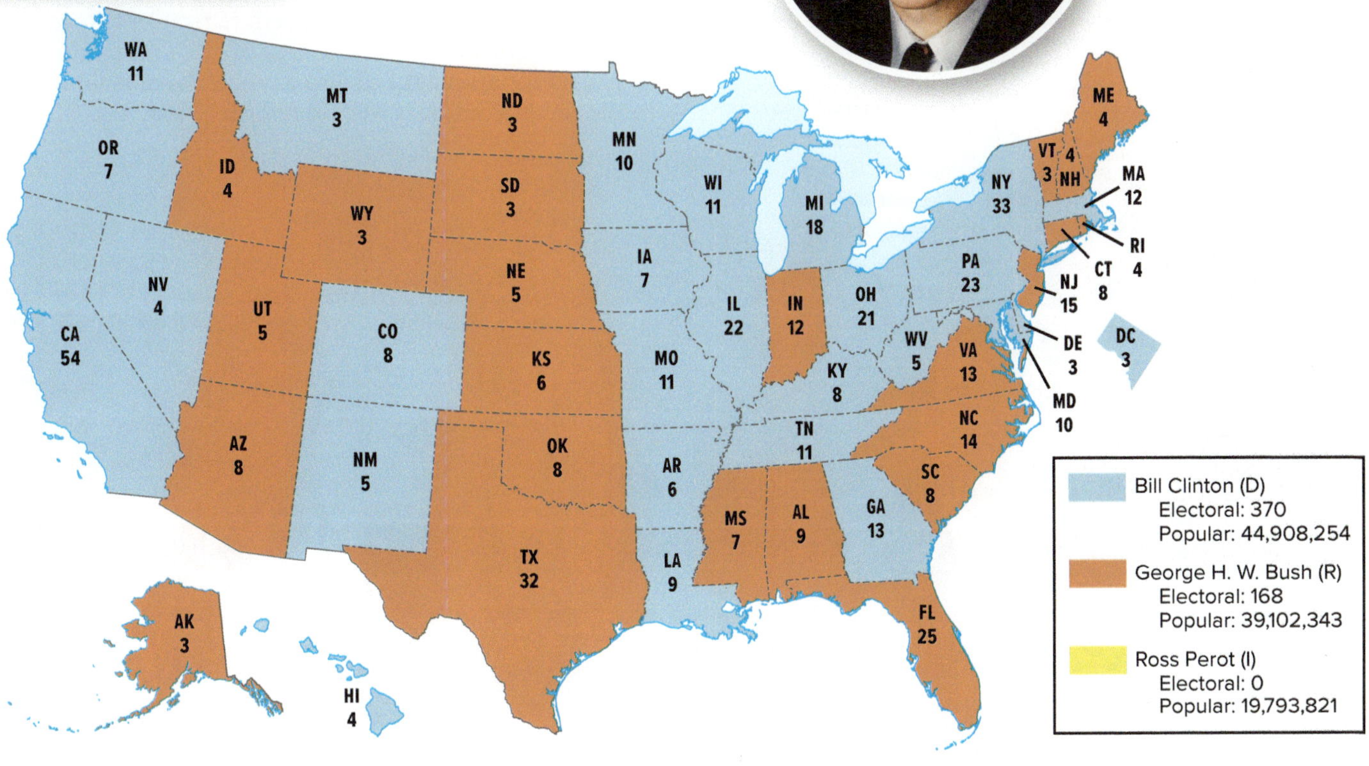

**Bill Clinton (D)**
Electoral: 370
Popular: 44,908,254

**George H. W. Bush (R)**
Electoral: 168
Popular: 39,102,343

**Ross Perot (I)**
Electoral: 0
Popular: 19,793,821

Map states and electoral votes:
WA 11, MT 3, ND 3, MN 10, ME 4, OR 7, ID 4, SD 3, WI 11, MI 18, VT 3, NH 4, NY 33, MA 12, WY 3, IA 7, PA 23, RI 4, NV 4, UT 5, NE 5, IL 22, IN 12, OH 21, NJ 15, CT 8, CA 54, CO 8, KS 6, MO 11, WV 5, VA 13, DE 3, DC 3, MD 10, AZ 8, NM 5, OK 8, AR 6, KY 8, TN 11, NC 14, SC 8, GA 13, MS 7, AL 9, TX 32, LA 9, FL 25, AK 3, HI 4

## Domestic Issues

### Legislative Agenda

After his inauguration, Clinton pursued his domestic agenda, which promoted social change as well as economic change. He began a discussion about lifting the ban on homosexuals in the military, but this was met with an uproar of opposition from military leaders and much of the public. Quickly, Clinton backed down and adopted a compromise policy of "don't ask, don't tell" in which military personnel could not ask whether a military member was homosexual, but those who told about their homosexuality could be discharged from the service.

With a Democratic majority in Congress, Clinton was able to enact significant legislation. The Family and Medical Leave Act required businesses to give employees up to twelve weeks of unpaid leave to care for newborn children or seriously ill family members. The Brady Bill (named for the press secretary who was wounded in the Reagan assassination attempt) mandated a five-day waiting period and a background check before an individual could purchase a firearm at a gun store. The National Voter Registration Act, commonly called the "Motor Voter Act," required states to allow voters to register to vote when they applied for or renewed a driver's license.

However, even with a Democratic majority, Clinton was unable to achieve one of his primary goals, universal healthcare for all Americans. First Lady Hillary Rodham Clinton took the lead in the attempt to pass the program. Many argued that the plan was too expensive and complicated and that it would give government too much power over healthcare. Because of intense disagreements, Congress did not vote on the proposal.

### Republicans Respond

Religious and economic conservatives joined forces during the Clinton administration in an attempt to preserve and restore traditional American values. The Religious Right expressed growing concern over parts of the Clinton agenda related to homosexuality and to abortion (Clinton had vetoed a ban on a procedure known as partial-birth abortion), as well as Clinton's two Supreme Court appointments, Ruth Bader Ginsburg and Stephen Breyer, who were liberals. Economic conservatives were concerned about rising taxes, regulations on businesses, and wasteful government spending.

As the 1994 congressional elections approached, House Republican candidates issued what they called a "**Contract with America**," promising to introduce ten bills within their first hundred days in office if elected, including bills on term limits and a balanced federal budget. Opposition to Democratic policies, the efforts of the Religious Right, and the Contract with America all contributed to Republican victories in the fall elections. The Republicans captured control of both houses of Congress for the first time since Eisenhower's first term. Under the leadership of Speaker of the House Newt Gingrich, House Republicans passed much of their promised legislation, although most measures failed in the Senate or were vetoed.

Aware that many voters had begun to view him as too liberal, Clinton moved to the moderate stance that had gotten him elected. In his 1996 State of the Union address, Clinton presented himself again as a New Democrat—tough on crime, supportive of family values, and ready to reform welfare. He declared, "The era of big government is over."

Clinton followed through by signing the **Defense of Marriage Act** in 1996, which secured federal benefits, such as health insurance, for spouses in traditional marriages only, denying any status to homosexual unions. Then he signed the **Welfare Reform Act of 1996**. This Republican-sponsored legislation required welfare recipients to go back to work within two years and set a lifetime maximum of five years for assistance. It also gave blocks of federal funds to the states to address welfare reform as they saw fit.

▼ Speaker of the House Newt Gingrich holding a copy of the "Contract with America" after the first hundred days of the 104th Congress

CONTRACT WITH AMERICA
★ ★ ★ ★ ★

## Election of 1996

In the 1996 presidential election, the Republicans nominated Senate Majority Leader Bob Dole of Kansas, and Ross Perot ran again with the Reform Party. Clinton cruised to reelection, although he failed again to get a majority of the popular vote, with 49 percent to Dole's 41 percent and Perot's 8 percent. In the Electoral College, the president defeated Dole 379–159; however, the Republicans retained control of Congress.

## Economic Prosperity

One of the reasons for Clinton's easy reelection was the nation's booming economy. The United States was enjoying extraordinary economic growth, and citizens generally credited the president for their prosperity. A strong economy bolstered the president's popularity as most Americans remained generally satisfied, even optimistic, about the nation's financial status. Inflation remained low. Unemployment fell steadily to its lowest level in thirty years. Businesses had to offer higher salaries and benefits not only to attract but also to retain skilled employees. The stock market soared to record levels. Throughout Clinton's second term, the government had budget surpluses instead of the deficits that had been characteristic since the Vietnam War.

## Scandal and Impeachment

Despite the period of economic prosperity, past controversies plagued Clinton's presidency. The Whitewater scandal took its name from Clinton's earlier investment while governor in the failed Whitewater Development Corporation, a resort in northeastern Arkansas. Rumors surfaced that Clinton had unethically used his influence as governor to promote the Whitewater scheme for his private benefit. Eventually, the Justice Department launched an investigation that led to the trials and convictions of several friends of the president, including the governor of Arkansas who succeeded Clinton, although the evidence never touched the president himself.

While digging deeper into Whitewater, Kenneth Starr, the independent counsel, broadened his investigation to include a sexual harassment claim against then-governor Clinton by Paula Jones, a former Arkansas government employee. During that investigation, Starr found evidence that the president had been having a sexual relationship with a young White House intern named **Monica Lewinsky**. After months of denial and stalling, Clinton agreed to testify before a grand jury. During his testimony, he eventually admitted to wrongdoing with Lewinsky but insisted he had done nothing illegal.

At the end of his investigation, Starr sent evidence to the House outlining Clinton's impeachable offenses. They included perjury (lying under oath) for his denying having a relationship with Lewinsky and obstruction of justice for hiding evidence from the court. In December 1998 the House of Representatives passed two articles of impeachment against the president. For the second time in American history (the first being Andrew Johnson), a president had been impeached and would stand trial before the US Senate.

The trial before the Senate took place in January and February 1999. Members of the House served as prosecutors while Chief Justice William Rehnquist presided over the trial. The two-thirds requirement for conviction was not reached on either charge.

Though Clinton remained in office, his reputation suffered serious damage. Although Christian leaders disagreed about whether impeachment was the right course of action for Congress, they were concerned about the moral impact of the scandal on the nation, noting that the US system of government requires that its officials be principled. Even some of the president's supporters denounced his actions as immoral.

▲ Headline of Clinton's impeachment

▲ The US Senate voting on the perjury charges during Clinton's impeachment trial

## Domestic Terrorism

The 1990s saw some surprising violence on the home front. On February 29, 1993, the Bureau of Alcohol, Tobacco, and Firearms (ATF) had raided the compound of a group known as the Branch Davidians near Waco, Texas. The ATF had suspicion that the group was involved in criminal activity and was stockpiling illegal weapons. The raid was poorly organized, resulting in a standoff, and four ATF agents and six Branch Davidians were killed. Federal agents then surrounded the compound for the next fifty-one days, until Attorney General Janet Reno ordered them to storm the compound with tear gas and tanks. When they did, the compound caught fire, killing over seventy members of the Branch Davidians.

On April 19, 1995, the second anniversary of the end of the Waco disaster, Timothy McVeigh and two accomplices, angry at the government for Waco and other issues, loaded a rental truck with explosives and detonated it in front of the federal office building in Oklahoma City. The explosion killed 168 people, including nineteen children who were in the building's day care center. The **Oklahoma City bombing** was the deadliest act of terrorism in America to that point. McVeigh was executed in 2001.

## Foreign Issues

### NAFTA

The idea for a North American free trade zone began under President Reagan, was negotiated during Bush's presidency, and finally came to fulfilment when the **North American Free Trade Agreement (NAFTA)** was ratified by the United States, Canada, and Mexico in 1993 during Clinton's administration. NAFTA reduced or eliminated tariffs on most goods exported from one North American country to another. As a result, trade between the three countries increased.

▲ Alfred P. Murrah Federal Building after the Oklahoma City bombing

### International Issues

In Haiti, military leaders overthrew a democratically elected president in 1991. When he took office, Clinton began to pressure the Haitian regime to allow the ousted president to return to office. When Clinton threatened armed intervention, the Haitian military backed down. The United States succeeded in putting the former president back in office.

In the 1990s the UN decided that warring factions in Somalia needed to be disarmed. When a powerful warlord fought back, the UN and the United States tried unsuccessfully to capture him. During a raid by US Army Rangers in October 1993, the Somalis shot down two American helicopters and dragged the dead body of an American soldier through the streets. Eighteen Americans were killed in the failed mission. Within six months, Clinton ordered the withdrawal of American forces from Somalia.

In Europe, the nation of Yugoslavia split apart after communism collapsed in 1991. In Bosnia, a brutal civil war erupted between Orthodox Serbs, Catholic Croats, and Bosnian Muslims. The Serbs practiced ethnic cleansing—the killing or expelling of an ethnic group from an area—against the other ethnicities in their attempt to control the area. The United Nations sent peacekeepers, but they were unable to stop the bloodshed. The United States then sent bombers against the Serbs, causing the Serbs to agree to negotiations to end the conflict. The sides met in 1995 in Dayton, Ohio, and came to an agreement called the **Dayton Accords** which made Bosnia into a confederation in which the Serbs, Croats, and Muslims shared power. US and other NATO troops were sent into the region to enforce the agreement.

▼ American Blackhawk helicopter shot down in Somalia

## Islamic Terrorism

On February 26, 1993, a truck bomb exploded in an underground parking garage beneath the World Trade Center in New York City, killing six people and injuring over a thousand. A federal investigation traced the bombing to a radical Muslim terrorist who had hoped to bring down both the twin towers. The mastermind of the bombing, Ramzi Yousef, was captured in Pakistan in 1995. He had been involved in other terrorist activities around the world and was plotting more attacks when he was captured. He was sent to the United States for trial and was sentenced to life in prison.

On October 12, 2000, a US Navy destroyer, the USS *Cole*, was anchored at a port in the Middle Eastern country of Yemen. Suicide bombers sailed a small boat alongside the *Cole* and detonated explosives that ripped a hole in the ship, killing seventeen US sailors and wounding thirty-nine. It was determined that the attackers were members of the al-Qaeda terror network (discussed later in this chapter).

▼ Aftermath of the 1993 World Trade Center bombing

## Comprehension Check 24.3

1. Clinton enacted a compromise policy concerning ____.
   A homosexuals in the military
   B partial-birth abortions
   C universal healthcare

2. In 1995 Timothy McVeigh bombed the ____.
   A compound of Branch Davidians in Waco, Texas
   B federal office building in Oklahoma City, Oklahoma
   C World Trade Center in New York City, New York

3. All the following are examples of legislation illustrating Clinton as a "New Democrat" except the ____.
   A "Contract with America"
   B Defense of Marriage Act
   C Welfare Reform Act of 1996

4. One foreign policy success under the Clinton administration was ____.
   A the overthrow of a drug lord in Somalia
   B the signing of NAFTA
   C the unification of Yugoslavia

### MAKING CONNECTIONS

5. What was one impeachment charge against Clinton, and what was the result of his impeachment trial?

## GUIDING QUESTIONS

- Why was the election of 2000 controversial?
- How did the War on Terror progress?
- What were Bush's domestic policies?

## 24.4 George W. Bush and the World

**Should some liberties be limited to prevent terrorism?**

## The Election of 2000

In the presidential election of 2000, the Democrats nominated Clinton's vice president, Al Gore, as their candidate. The Republicans turned to Texas governor **George W. Bush**, the son of former president George H. W. Bush. The younger Bush ran on a theme of "compassionate conservatism." He promised educational reforms and promised to restore honor and dignity to the White House.

▼ 2000 presidential candidates Al Gore and George W. Bush

The two sides ran the closest presidential campaign in a generation. Gore narrowly won the popular vote by a little more than 500,000 votes out of more than 105 million cast, a margin of about one-half of one percent. In the electoral vote, Gore won 267 electoral votes (out of 270 needed to win) and Bush won 246, but the crucial state of Florida (with 25 electoral votes) was in dispute. Bush led after the initial count in that state by only about 1,800 votes out of some six million cast. A recount of the votes in Florida (required by Florida law because the result was so close) cut Bush's lead to about 300 votes.

◄ Headlines covering the contested vote in Florida

With the presidency at stake, both sides began to plead their cases before the American people and especially before the courts. The Democrats claimed that many of the computer-read ballots should be recounted by hand, but they initially asked for those recounts only in heavily Democratic counties where the results would favor Gore. Republicans replied that such hand-counting was done by arbitrary standards and therefore was unfair. Some counties began recounting the ballots. Weeks dragged by as state and federal courts rendered decisions, some favoring Bush and others favoring Gore. Finally, on December 12—exactly five weeks after Election Day—the Supreme Court ruled in **Bush v. Gore** in favor of Bush, halting all recounts and, by default, making him the victor in Florida (by 537 votes) and therefore the winner of the presidency.

## The Election of 2000

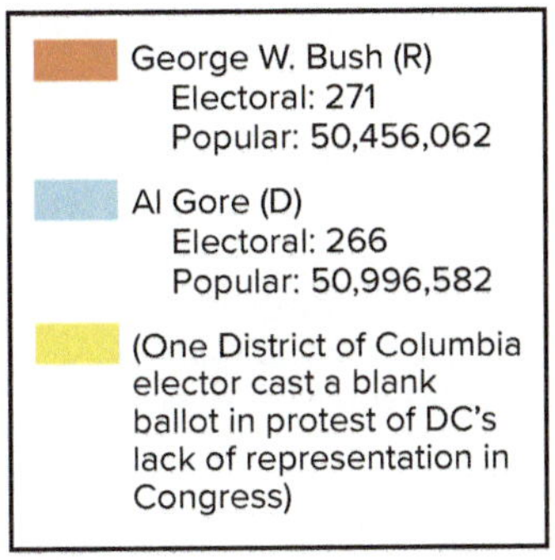

George W. Bush (R)
Electoral: 271
Popular: 50,456,062

Al Gore (D)
Electoral: 266
Popular: 50,996,582

(One District of Columbia elector cast a blank ballot in protest of DC's lack of representation in Congress)

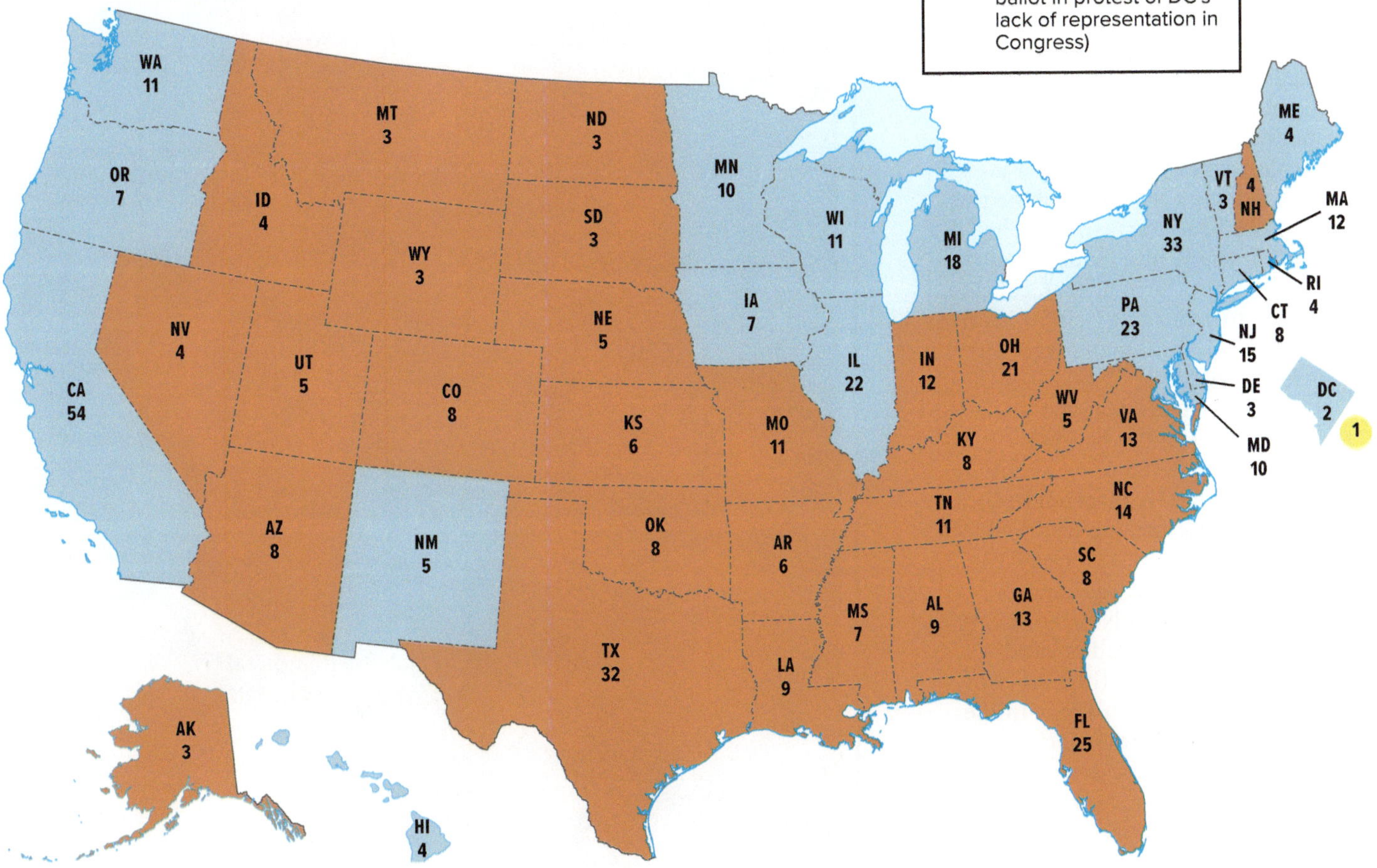

WA 11
MT 3
ND 3
MN 10
ME 4
OR 7
ID 4
WY 3
SD 3
WI 11
MI 18
VT 3
NH 4
NY 33
MA 12
NV 4
UT 5
CO 8
NE 5
IA 7
IL 22
IN 12
OH 21
PA 23
RI 4
CT 8
NJ 15
DE 3
MD 10
DC 2  1
CA 54
KS 6
MO 11
KY 8
WV 5
VA 13
AZ 8
NM 5
OK 8
AR 6
TN 11
NC 14
SC 8
GA 13
MS 7
AL 9
TX 32
LA 9
FL 25
AK 3
HI 4

## The War on Terror

When Bush took office in 2001, he called for a major tax cut to stimulate the economy. Democrats opposed it, arguing that the plan favored the wealthy and would reduce the budget surplus. Compromising, Bush and Congress agreed on a smaller tax cut. But arguments over the budget disappeared when tragedy suddenly struck the nation.

## September 11, 2001

On the morning of September 11, 2001, radical Muslim terrorists hijacked four airliners. Two of the planes were flown into the twin towers of the World Trade Center in New York City. The resulting fires caused both towers to collapse. Over 2,700 people were killed, including plane passengers, people working in the Trade Center, and over 400 New York City firefighters and police officers who were trying to rescue survivors.

Less than an hour after the first plane struck the World Trade Center, terrorists crashed the third plane into the Pentagon in Washington, DC, the headquarters of the Department of Defense, killing 59 passengers and crew and 125 people who were working in the building. When passengers in the fourth plane realized that their plane had been hijacked, many made desperate phone calls to loved ones who told them about the other attacks. Deducing that their plane was going to be used to crash into the US Capitol or the White House, they heroically fought the hijackers, causing the plane to crash in a field in rural Pennsylvania, killing all forty-four people on board.

The **9/11 attack** was the worst terrorist attack in the nation's history, killing 2,966 people. The terrorists purposely targeted innocent civilians and intentionally struck at symbols of America—the World Trade Center was a major financial complex in New York City and a symbol of capitalism; and the other targets were the homes of the government and military in the nation's capital. More Americans were killed by the 9/11 attacks than the number of Americans who died at Pearl Harbor.

▶ (top) The crash of Flight 175 into the South Tower of the World Trade Center, approximately fifteen minutes after the attack on the North Tower; (bottom) New Yorkers, covered in ash, evacuating after the attacks on the World Trade Center

◄ Officials examining the crash site of Flight 93 in Shanksville, Pennsylvania

◄ The 9/11 attack on the Pentagon, resulting in the collapse of part of the outer ring

That evening, President Bush addressed the nation:

*Today our fellow citizens, our way of life, our very freedom came under attack in a series of deliberate and deadly terrorist acts. . . .*

*These acts of mass murder were intended to frighten our nation into chaos and retreat, but they have failed. Our country is strong. A great people has been moved to defend a great nation. Terrorist attacks can shake the foundations of our biggest buildings, but they cannot touch the foundation of America. These acts shattered steel, but they cannot dent the steel of American resolve. America was targeted for attack because we're the brightest beacon for freedom and opportunity in the world. And no one will keep that light from shining.*

*Today our nation saw evil, the very worst of human nature, and we responded with the best of America. With the daring of our rescue workers, with the caring for strangers and neighbors who came to give blood and help in any way they could. . . .*

*The search is underway for those who are behind these evil acts. I've directed the full resources of our intelligence and law enforcement communities to find those responsible and to bring them to justice. We will make no distinction between the terrorists who committed these acts and those who harbor them. . . .*

## Analyzing Sources

How was the enemy different in the War on Terror than in previous wars? How would this difference affect who and where the United States would fight this war?

▼ Bush delivering his "bullhorn speech" in praise of first responders, September 14, 2001

▶ Osama bin Laden

## The War on Terror Begins

Intelligence experts, including the FBI, learned that the nineteen hijackers were members of an international terrorist network called **al-Qaeda**. Its leader was **Osama bin Laden**, a radical Muslim from Saudi Arabia. The organization was linked to several other terrorist attacks around the world. Al-Qaeda hated Israel and America, considering them obstacles to the expansion of Islam. Its members trained for terrorist activities at bases in Afghanistan, where the government was controlled by the **Taliban**, a radical Muslim group composed of some who had been part of the mujahideen that the United States had supported in Afghanistan's war against the Soviet Union (see Chapter 23). But now the Taliban, which had taken control of the country in 1996, protected bin Laden and his supporters as he commanded al-Qaeda's worldwide terrorist network.

The Turn of the Century   **651**

When the Taliban refused Bush's demands to turn over bin Laden and his supporters to the United States and to shut down all terrorist camps, the president assembled a multinational coalition to oust the Taliban. On October 7, 2001, those allied forces invaded Afghanistan. The coalition received help from the anti-Taliban Northern Alliance in Afghanistan and from Pakistani volunteers. Within two months, Taliban forces fled into the mountains on the Afghan-Pakistani border. Afghan leaders of several anti-Taliban factions met in Germany in December and signed a peace agreement. They established a temporary government and began working to rebuild their country. However, bin Laden escaped capture, and almost ten years would pass before he was located.

To protect Americans at home, Congress created the **Department of Homeland Security**. It regulated security issues related to US borders, transportation (especially at airports), and preparations for emergencies. Congress also overwhelmingly passed the **Patriot Act** to improve the government's ability to detect and prevent terrorism. The act allowed law enforcement to use surveillance and wiretapping (in some cases without a search warrant) to investigate terror-related crimes and suspected terrorists. It also enabled law enforcement to seek federal court permission to obtain bank and business records to aid in national security terror investigations and prevent money laundering for terrorism financing. Additionally, the act attempted to improve information and intelligence sharing between government agencies, provided tougher penalties for convicted terrorists and those who gave them shelter, and made it harder for foreigners with suspected links to terrorist activities to enter the United States.

Most Americans agreed with Bush's approach at the time. But critics contended that the government, in its zeal to protect citizens from terrorism, had gone too far and was infringing on the rights of Americans. The Supreme Court later declared some provisions of the Patriot Act unconstitutional, and Congress eventually allowed the remainder of the law's provisions to expire.

## The War with Iraq

President Bush was also greatly concerned about the government of Iraqi dictator Saddam Hussein. Hussein continued to threaten peace in the Middle East, and his development of chemical and biological **weapons of mass destruction (WMDs)** was well-known. He had used chemical weapons against the Kurds, citizens of his own country, in the late 1980s.

One of the conditions of the cease-fire at the end of the Persian Gulf War in 1991 had been that Iraq would get rid of its WMDs. Furthermore, it would not build any additional ones and would allow UN weapons inspectors to verify its adherence to these agreements. Throughout the 1990s, Iraq only partly cooperated with UN weapons inspectors, and by December 1998, it was no longer allowing inspectors into the country. In September 2002, President Bush gave a speech to the United Nations in which he demanded that Hussein surrender his WMDs, readmit inspectors, provide more freedoms for Iraqi citizens, and stop supporting terrorism. The UN later adopted a resolution supporting Bush's demands.

Iraq admitted that it had possessed WMDs before the Persian Gulf War but stated they no longer had them. Hussein agreed to allow the resumption of UN inspections, but he did not fully cooperate with the inspection process. American, British, and Spanish officials then pushed for a UN resolution authorizing force against Iraq. Germany, France, Russia, China, and other countries opposed military action.

▲ (top) US Marines in Afghanistan; (middle) agents of the Transportation Security Administration (TSA), formed in response to the 9/11 attack, checking airline passengers; (bottom) Iraqi president Saddam Hussein

On March 19, 2003, a coalition which included the United States and other allied nations invaded Iraq, defeating that country's military forces in only two weeks, and Saddam Hussein went into hiding. In December 2003, Hussein was captured and charged with crimes against humanity and other offenses. His trial before a tribunal of Iraqi judges began in October 2005. He was convicted and on December 30, 2006, was executed by hanging.

Despite the quick military victory, some issues involving both Americans and Iraqis made the transition of regimes challenging. First, between 2004 and 2007, the United States did not send more soldiers to help ensure stability after the collapse of Hussein's government. The resulting power vacuum gave Iran and its allies an opportunity to further destabilize Iraq. Second, the provisional government, led by US ambassador Paul Bremer, prevented all members of Hussein's Ba'ath party from working in government jobs, which affected many Iraqis, including teachers. Third, the provisional government disbanded the Iraqi army, which sent armed men home with little prospect of finding a job, a potentially dangerous combination. After the overthrow of Hussein, Muslim factions clashed over the establishment of the new government. Members of the Sunnis and Shiites, major divisions within Islam, attacked each other. Amid the chaos, some Iraqis, desiring freedom, held elections and approved a constitution.

After the defeat of their military, some Iraqis, aided by extremists from other Muslim countries, continued the fight as guerillas, launching terrorist attacks, encouraging suicide bombings, and setting improvised explosive devices (IEDs) beside roads. Over 3,000 American troops died in Iraq between 2003 and 2007, and thousands more were injured.

Americans were deeply divided over the Iraq War. Many were upset when the US military found no evidence of the WMDs. They noted that the invasion made radical Muslims hate America more, and that Iraq had not directly attacked the United States. Supporters of the war argued that the war in Iraq was part of the war on terror, and that a preemptive strike was necessary to keep Iraq from attacking the United States or other nations.

▲ US Army raid in Mosul, Iraq, that killed two of Saddam Hussein's sons

## Other Foreign Affairs

Bush enjoyed some other diplomatic successes. He convinced Libya to renounce terrorism and seek closer ties to the West. He also obtained a promise from Pakistan that it would work closely with the United States in rooting out terrorism. In Asia, Bush forged closer economic and diplomatic ties with China, and he tried to get China's assistance, along with that of Japan and South Korea, to keep North Korea from developing nuclear weapons.

# Domestic Affairs

## The Election of 2004

Bush ran for reelection in 2004 against Democratic candidate John Kerry, a senator from Massachusetts. Although Kerry was a decorated Vietnam veteran, he had opposed that war after he returned home. That opposition led many veterans to oppose him in the 2004 election.

Bush's reelection campaign was affected by mixed economic news, mounting casualties in Iraq, and scandals over US mistreatment of Iraqi prisoners of war at a prison camp at Guantanamo Naval Base in Cuba and at Abu Ghraib prison in Iraq. Consequently, his approval ratings were falling. However, when the votes were counted, Bush won the electoral vote 286–251.

▲ Bush with children in the computer lab of "The Fishing School," a faith-based community program in Washington, DC

## Domestic Matters

In 2002 Congress passed a significant piece of education legislation called No Child Left Behind. The act sought to ensure that every child could read and write and required testing and school accountability to make certain that schools were attaining these goals. The act continued until 2015, when Congress passed new education legislation.

During his presidency, Bush made religion a prominent issue. He embraced cooperation between evangelical Christians and the government by enlisting faith-based organizations to administer government social programs that put into practice what he called "compassionate conservatism." He believed that these organizations' programs were often more effective and efficient than those run by the government, and they became an important part of his domestic plan to combat problems in the inner cities. These organizations faced the challenges of working with the government without compromising their beliefs and of allowing some federal oversight of their programs.

Bush also signed a ban on federal funding for stem cell research that required the destruction of human embryos (unborn babies in the first eight weeks of development). Scientists believed that embryonic stem cells, which can be grown into different kinds of cells, such as nerve or muscle cells, could be used to treat diseases like Alzheimer's—but they would have to kill the embryo to get the stem cells. President Bush believed that killing an embryo was killing a human. He later wrote, "My faith and conscience led me to conclude that human life is sacred. God created man in His image and therefore every person has value in His eyes." The ban allowed federal funding to continue for research on stem cells from embryos that had already been destroyed, but prohibited research that would involve the destruction of embryos after that point.

▲ A scientist conducting stem cell research

Bush nominated two conservative justices to the Court. The president nominated John G. Roberts Jr. to replace Sandra Day O'Connor, who retired in 2005. Before the Senate could vote on the nomination, however, Chief Justice William Rehnquist died. Bush chose Roberts to replace Rehnquist, and Roberts was confirmed in September 2005. Bush then nominated Samuel Alito Jr. to replace O'Connor.

The United States faced one of its worst natural disasters when **Hurricane Katrina** hit the Gulf Coast of Louisiana, Mississippi, and Alabama on August 29, 2005. In New Orleans, where much of the city lies below sea level, floodwaters broke the levees which protected the low-lying areas, and soon 80 percent of the city was under water. Gulf residents suffered greatly from the hurricane; about 1,800 people were killed and $100 billion in damages occurred. Bush received blame for the government's response to the disaster. The Federal Emergency Management Administration (FEMA) was slow to respond, and local and state officials failed to effectively evacuate citizens in the storm's path.

▲ John Roberts sworn in as Chief Justice

▲ Samuel Alito sworn in as Supreme Court justice

▼ Flooding in New Orleans from Hurricane Katrina

Throughout the early 2000s, housing prices rose rapidly. As prices rose, banks provided more mortgage loans to allow and even encourage people to buy homes. Some loans were "sub-prime," meaning they were made to people who did not meet income requirements or who had poor credit histories. The banks often sold their mortgages to investment firms. Eventually, a bubble occurred in the housing market. That bubble burst in 2007 and housing prices dropped dramatically. Many people owed more on their homes than they were worth. Banks and businesses that had invested in real estate lost billions of dollars, creating a financial crisis. As a result, some of America's largest banks and corporations filed for bankruptcy, including the investment firm Lehman Brothers and auto manufacturers General Motors and Chrysler. Layoffs resulted in home foreclosures, and many small businesses closed permanently. The **Great Recession** had begun and would last from late 2007 into 2009.

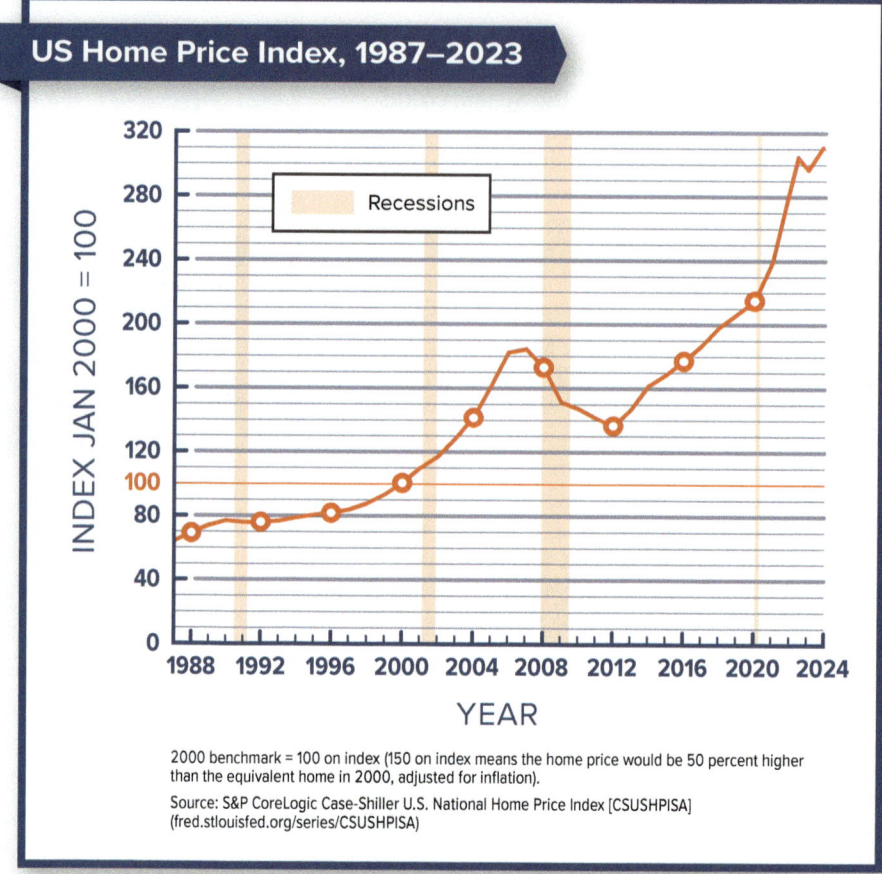

**US Home Price Index, 1987–2023**

INDEX JAN 2000 = 100

YEAR

2000 benchmark = 100 on index (150 on index means the home price would be 50 percent higher than the equivalent home in 2000, adjusted for inflation).

Source: S&P CoreLogic Case-Shiller U.S. National Home Price Index [CSUSHPISA] (fred.stlouisfed.org/series/CSUSHPISA)

---

### Comprehension Check 24.4

1. All the following are true of the election of 2000 except that _____.

   A  Bush won the popular vote

   B  Florida's electoral votes were in dispute

   C  the Supreme Court ruled in favor of Bush

2. The 9/11 attack was _____.

   A  directed by Saddam Hussein

   B  directed at symbols of America's economy, military, and government.

   C  unsuccessful in targeting any government buildings

3. Congress created the _____ in response to the 9/11 attack.

   A  Department of Homeland Security

   B  Federal Emergency Management Administration (FEMA)

   C  Guantanamo Naval Base

4. All the following occurred after the United States invaded Iraq except _____.

   A  Saddam Hussein was captured and executed

   B  some Iraqis held elections and adopted a constitution

   C  the United States found weapons of mass destruction (WMDs)

5. The Great Recession resulted from the _____.

   A  cuts in federal funding for stem cell research

   B  destruction on the Gulf Coast from Hurricane Katrina

   C  the housing market bubble bursting

**MAKING CONNECTIONS**

6. What was the purpose of the Patriot Act, and what were two of its provisions?

7. Why did the United States invade Afghanistan, and what did the invasion accomplish within two months?

## Chapter Summary

### 24.1 The Reagan Era

- The New Right and the Religious Right helped to elect Ronald Reagan in 1980. Reagan practiced supply-side economics to tackle inflation and unemployment, and he cut taxes while raising defense spending, which created budget deficits. He later increased some taxes. The economy grew rapidly, and Reagan was reelected in 1984.

- Determined to defeat communism, Reagan pledged to help groups fighting communism in Third World countries. He announced plans for the Strategic Defense Initiative which put pressure on the Soviet government. Mikhail Gorbachev allowed more free-market activity and openness in the Soviet Union, and the US and USSR agreed to some arms limitation treaties. Reagan supported anti-Communists in Nicaragua, but a scandal developed when it was revealed that the government sold arms to Iran in return for Iran's help releasing American hostages in Lebanon, and that the funds from the arms sales were used to aid the Contras in Nicaragua.

**TERMS**

New Right

Religious Right

Ronald Reagan

supply-side economics

Reagan Doctrine

Mikhail Gorbachev

Iran-Contra affair

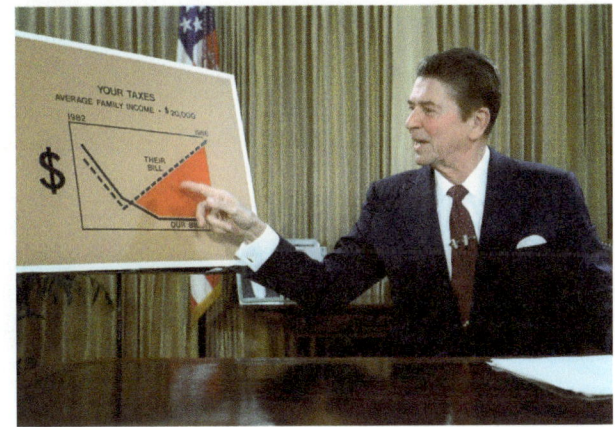

**TERMS**

George H. W. Bush

Saddam Hussein

Persian Gulf War

Americans with Disabilities Act

Twenty-Seventh Amendment

### 24.2 George H. W. Bush and the End of the Cold War

- George H. W. Bush won the election of 1988 and continued many of Reagan's policies. Pro-democracy movements in Eastern Europe led to the fall of communism in many countries, the reunification of Germany, and the fall of the Soviet Union.

- Iraqi dictator Saddam Hussein invaded Kuwait in 1990. The UN and the United States authorized the use of force to liberate Kuwait. The Persian Gulf War (Operation Desert Storm) began with air strikes on Iraqi targets and finished with a 100-hour ground attack. Kuwait was liberated, but Hussein remained in power. Many Muslims resented the American presence in Saudi Arabia, leading to terrorist attacks on American targets around the world.

## Chapter Summary

### 24.3 | The Clinton Administration

- Democrat Bill Clinton won the election of 1992. The Democratic Congress passed much of Clinton's legislative agenda, but not national healthcare.

- Conservatives united over concern about Clinton's agenda, and the Republicans regained control of Congress. Clinton took a more moderate stance, signing the Defense of Marriage Act and the Welfare Reform Act. Economic prosperity led to Clinton's reelection.

- An investigation into Clinton's dealings as governor led to revelations of his immoral relationship with White House intern Monica Lewinsky. The House of Representatives voted to impeach Clinton, but the Senate did not convict him. Angry at the federal raid on the Branch Davidian compound in Waco, Texas, Timothy McVeigh bombed the federal building in Oklahoma City.

- Clinton signed NAFTA, and the United States was involved in ending the conflict in the former nation of Yugoslavia. The bombing by terrorists of the World Trade Center failed to destroy the towers, and Islamic terrorists attacked the USS *Cole* in Yemen.

**TERMS**

Bill Clinton

Contract with America

Defense of Marriage Act

Welfare Reform Act of 1996

Oklahoma City bombing

North American Free Trade Agreement (NAFTA)

Dayton Accords

**TERMS**

George W. Bush

*Bush v. Gore*

9/11 attack

al-Qaeda

Osama bin Laden

Taliban

Department of Homeland Security

Patriot Act

weapons of mass destruction (WMDs)

Hurricane Katrina

Great Recession

### 24.4 | George W. Bush and the World

- The Supreme Court ended a recount of the vote in Florida in the disputed election of 2000, giving the win to George W. Bush over Al Gore.

- On September 11, 2001, terrorists hijacked four airliners, crashing two into the World Trade Center and one into the Pentagon. Passengers fought the hijackers on the fourth plane, causing it to crash. The 9/11 attacks were the worst terrorist attacks in US history. The terrorist group al-Qaeda was discovered to be responsible. Because the Taliban in Afghanistan allowed the terrorists to train there and refused to turn over al-Qaeda leader Osama bin Laden, the United States and other allied countries invaded Afghanistan and overthrew the Taliban.

- The Department of Homeland Security was formed to regulate US security, and the Patriot Act was passed to give the government greater ability to detect and prevent terrorism.

- The United States and other allied nations invaded Iraq in 2003 after Saddam Hussein did not cooperate with UN inspectors looking for WMDs. After Hussein was overthrown, Iraqi guerilla fighting continued against US forces for several years.

- The Great Recession began in 2007 after the housing market crashed, causing many large corporations and small businesses to declare bankruptcy.

## Chapter Review Questions

### RECALL

1. What Republican candidate did conservatives, including the New Right and the Religious Right, help elect to the presidency in 1980?

2. What Soviet leader did Reagan meet with to negotiate an arms treaty and also implore to tear down the Berlin Wall?

3. What Central American country did George H. W. Bush order US troops to invade to remove its pro-communist leader?

4. What amendment put rules on Congress's ability to raise its own pay?

5. What was the name of the series of legislation proposed by House Republican candidates in 1994?

6. What was the name of the 1993 free trade agreement between the United States, Canada, and Mexico?

7. What was the name of the terrorist group responsible for the 9/11 attack? Who was its leader?

8. What federal department was formed after the 9/11 attack?

9. What natural disaster hit the Gulf Coast in August 2005?

### UNDERSTAND

10. What did each of the following conservative groups of the 1980s believe: traditional conservatives, the New Right, the Religious Right?

11. What were the goals of the "Reagan Revolution"?

12. What is supply-side economics? Why is it sometimes referred to as "trickle-down economics"?

13. How did Reagan's approach to communism differ from his predecessors? What was the Reagan Doctrine? What actions did Reagan take in Latin America to demonstrate this doctrine?

14. What space-based defense program did Reagan propose? How did this affect Gorbachev?

15. What was the Iran-Contra affair? What were its consequences?

16. What were two factors that led to the fall of communism in Eastern Europe and the Soviet Union between 1989 and 1991?

17. What caused the Persian Gulf War? What was the military result of the war? What were the long-term results of the war?

18. What issue did Clinton make the primary focus of his campaign, and how did that help lead to his victory over Bush in the 1992 election?

19. What were three pieces of legislation passed in Clinton's first term in office? What was one piece of his legislative agenda that did not get passed?

20. Why did Timothy McVeigh bomb the Oklahoma City federal building in 1995?

21. Describe America's economy under Clinton.

22. On what charges was Bill Clinton impeached? What was the outcome of the trial?

23. What actions did the United States take in Somalia and Bosnia during Clinton's presidency?

24. What two incidents of Islamic terrorism happened during Clinton's presidency?

25. Why was the presidential election of 2000 controversial? How was the outcome decided?

26. What happened in the 9/11 attack? Why was this attack significant?

27. What did President Bush pledge to the American people regarding those who were responsible for the 9/11 attack?

28. Why did the United States and other nations invade Afghanistan in 2001?

29. What was the purpose of the Patriot Act? What were three powers it gave the government? Why did some criticize the act?

30. Why did the United States invade Iraq in 2003? What arguments were made by Americans for and against this invasion?

31. What pieces of legislation related to education and stem cell research were passed under George W. Bush?

32. What caused the Great Recession?

### THINK ABOUT IT

33. Why were some Christians concerned about the methods of the Religious Right? Why should Christians be careful about associating Christianity with a particular political party or movement?

34. How did the Defense of Marriage Act and the Welfare Reform Act of 1996 show Clinton's shift to a more moderate stance?

35. Do you think Clinton should have been impeached? What factors should guide American Christians in their assessment of political candidates or those currently in office (see Ex. 18:21, Prov. 16:12, 17:7, 29:2)? Explain your answers.

36. How did George W. Bush enlist evangelical Christians to help put into practice "compassionate conservatism"? Give an example of a way Christian organizations and the government might be able to work together today to address a social issue. What cautions should Christian organizations take when working with the government?

# 25 America and the Modern World

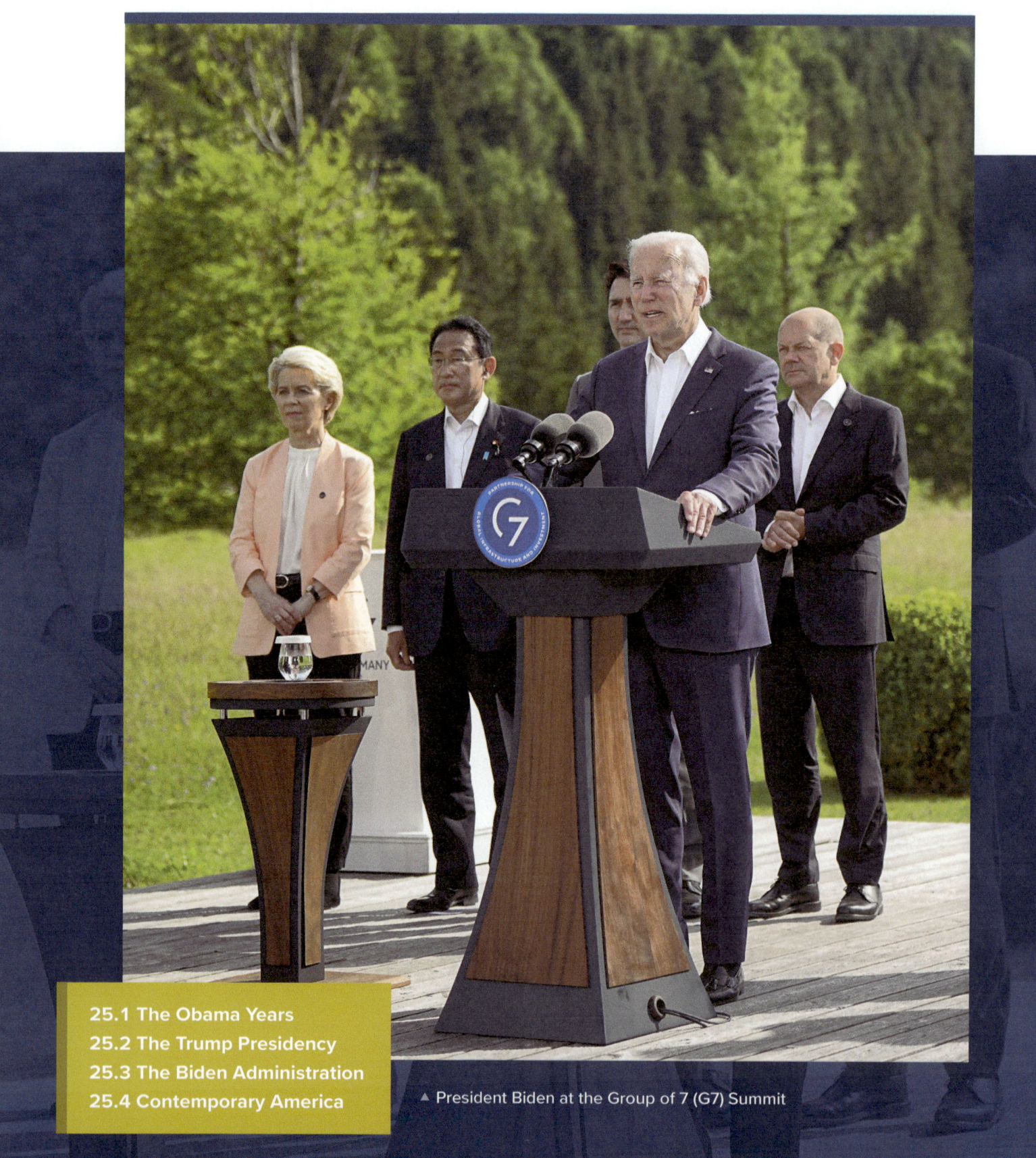

**25.1 The Obama Years**
**25.2 The Trump Presidency**
**25.3 The Biden Administration**
**25.4 Contemporary America**

▲ President Biden at the Group of 7 (G7) Summit

**The Obama Years**

How did society change under Obama?

GUIDING QUESTIONS

- How did Obama's policies change American society?
- How did Obama address conflicts in the Middle East?

In 2008 the Democrats chose Senator **Barack Obama** from Illinois as their candidate for president. He chose Delaware senator Joe Biden as his vice-presidential running mate. The Republicans nominated long-time Arizona senator and former Vietnam War POW John McCain, who chose Alaska governor Sarah Palin as his running mate.

◄ Barack Obama on the campaign trail

Obama was the first African American candidate to win the nomination of a major party. He defeated McCain by almost 10 million popular votes and by an electoral margin of 365–173.

**The Election of 2008**

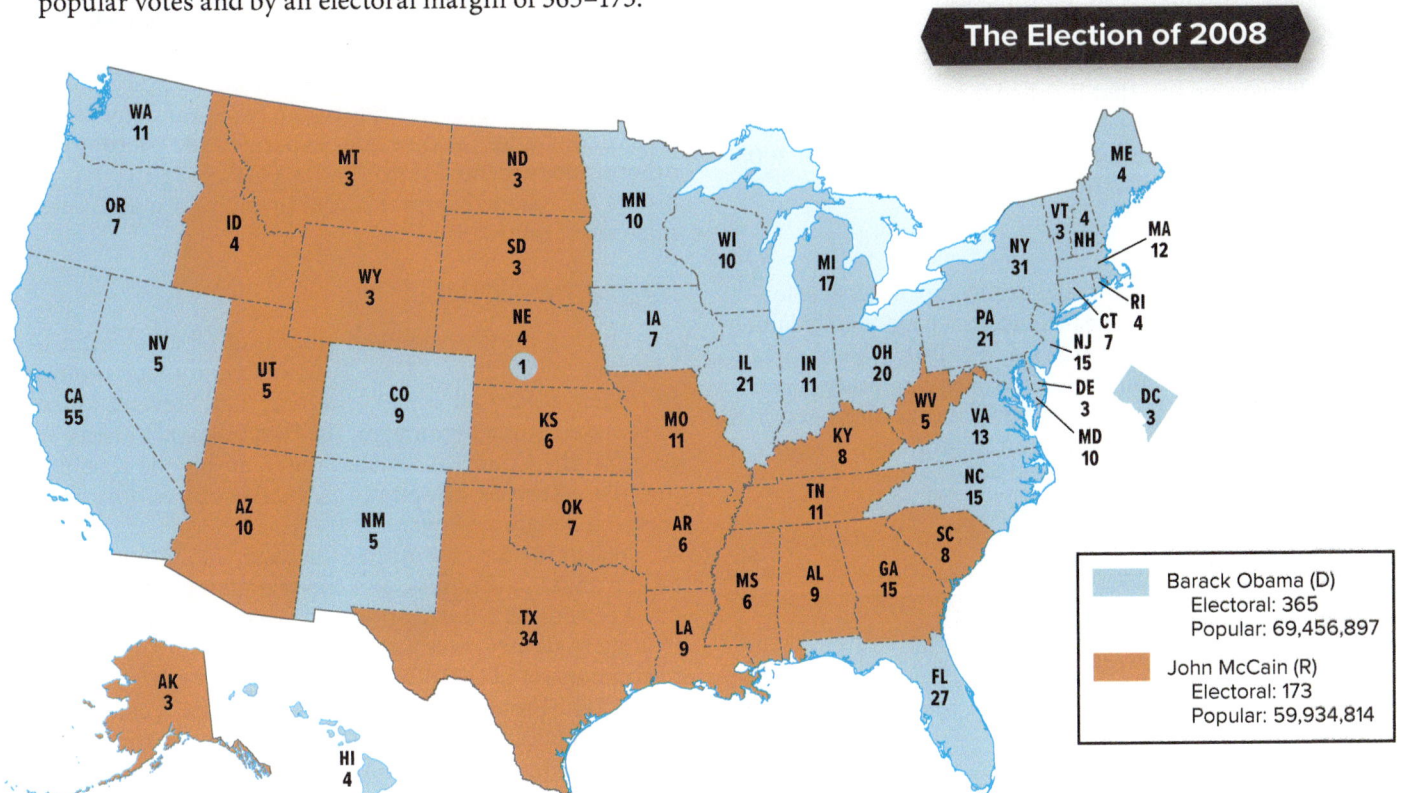

| | Barack Obama (D) |
| --- | --- |
| | Electoral: 365 |
| | Popular: 69,456,897 |
| | John McCain (R) |
| | Electoral: 173 |
| | Popular: 59,934,814 |

# Domestic Issues

## Stimulus and Response

When Obama was elected, the nation was in the midst of the Great Recession. In October 2008 Congress had passed the **Troubled Asset Relief Program (TARP)**, which provided $700 billion in government assistance to prevent some of the nation's largest financial institutions and other large corporations from collapsing. President Bush had signed the bill, and Obama continued TARP once he took office. In many cases, the government purchased shares of ownership in corporations which were near bankruptcy. Some of those businesses closed for good; others eventually rebounded, and the government was able to sell its shares for a profit, recouping most of the expense of the program. TARP drew criticism from those who believed it was inappropriate to use government funds to "bail out" these corporations. Others applauded it as a brave and necessary move to prevent economic catastrophe, comparing it to Hoover's Reconstruction Finance Corporation during the Great Depression (see Chapter 18).

By early 2009, unemployment passed 8 percent and was continuing to climb. More than five million Americans had lost their jobs in the past two years. President Obama called for more government action. In February 2009, Congress passed the American Recovery and Reinvestment Act, which provided approximately $800 billion in federal funds to attempt to stimulate the economy. The measure included money for the states, additional funds for food stamps and unemployment benefits, and financing for construction projects (such as bridges, roads, and government buildings). A portion of those funds, $200 billion, was designated to give tax rebates to individuals and businesses. Supporters praised this legislation, though some thought the amount allocated should have been larger. Opponents, which included most Republicans in Congress, argued that the bill was too expensive and that it called for too much government intervention in the economy. Partly as a result of these programs, the national debt grew from $10 trillion in 2008 to nearly $20 trillion by 2016.

## Obamacare

Obama also sought to make health care accessible for all Americans by making health insurance more affordable. The **Affordable Care Act (ACA)**, also called "Obamacare," prevented insurance companies from denying health coverage due to a person's preexisting medical conditions, required all Americans to obtain health insurance or incur a higher tax, and offered government subsidies to help lower-income Americans pay for coverage.

Congress, whose houses both had Democratic majorities, passed the bill. Obama praised the bill as a huge step toward providing insurance for the millions of uninsured Americans and improving health care for everyone. Critics said it allowed the government to intrude into the health-care and insurance industries.

As the 2010 congressional elections neared, many conservatives expressed their dissatisfaction with Obama's legislative agenda. They called for a significant reduction in the government's size and scope. Republicans regained control of the House of Representatives by winning more than sixty seats. They won six additional Senate seats, but Democrats maintained control of that chamber.

Several progressive groups had a goal of overturning the "Don't Ask, Don't Tell" policy regarding homosexuals in the military. After much debate in Congress and despite concerns raised by some military leaders, Congress passed the repeal of this policy, and Obama signed it in December 2010. Homosexuals were now free to serve openly in the military. Conservatives raised this as a campaign issue during the 2012 election.

## Election of 2012 and Obama's Second Term

In the 2012 election, the Republicans nominated former Massachusetts governor Mitt Romney to challenge Obama. The president was easily reelected, with 51 percent of the popular vote to Romney's 47 percent, and an electoral victory of 332 to 206. Congress remained divided, with Republicans controlling the House and Democrats the Senate.

Obama began his second term by emphasizing issues such as climate change, immigration, gun control, and wealth inequality. He promised to work with Congress when possible, but knowing that getting legislation through a divided Congress would be difficult, he also expressed willingness to bypass Congress by using executive orders. Opponents saw the president's broad use of executive orders as a means to push his political agenda regardless of congressional support.

Some of Obama's executive orders restricted the ability of local, state, and federal officials to apprehend, detain, or deport thousands of illegal immigrants. His **Deferred Action for Childhood Arrivals (DACA)** order stated that undocumented aliens who arrived in the United States as children could receive renewable two-year deferments from deportation, and he later expanded the program to other undocumented immigrants. Critics argued that these orders encouraged further illegal immigration and were misuses of presidential power.

## Supreme Court

During the first eighteen months of Obama's administration, two Supreme Court justices announced their retirements—David Souter and John Paul Stevens. Obama nominated Sonia Sotomayor, the first Hispanic justice to serve on the Court, to replace Souter, and Elena Kagan to replace Stevens. Despite conservative opposition, both received Senate approval.

When Justice Antonin Scalia died, the 2016 presidential race was in progress, and the selection of a replacement quickly became a heated political issue. Democrats wanted Obama to name a new justice, while Republicans hoped to regain control of the White House and have the new president make the selection. Obama nominated a candidate, but the Republicans, who had regained control of the Senate in the 2014 midterm elections, refused to schedule confirmation hearings before Obama left office.

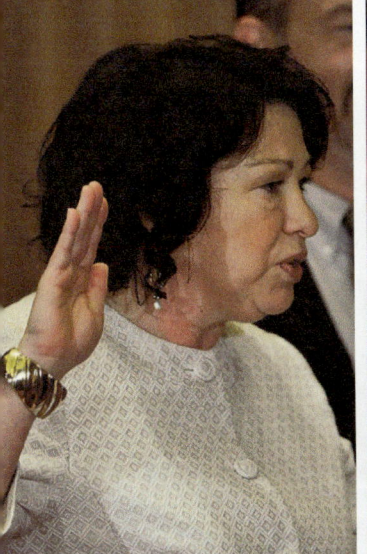

During the 2008 presidential campaign, Obama had advocated for the repeal of the Defense of Marriage Act (see Chapter 24). In 2011 Obama's attorney general, Eric Holder, announced that his department would no longer defend DOMA in the growing number of court cases seeking to declare it unconstitutional. In 2015, in the case ***Obergefell v. Hodges***, the Supreme Court declared in a 5–4 decision that key sections of DOMA were unconstitutional. The court decreed that the due process and equal protection clauses of the Fourteenth Amendment required all states to recognize same-sex marriages.

This Supreme Court decision established a new right for same-sex couples to marry. It was praised by President Obama and many on the Left, yet the dissenting opinions of the conservative justices reflected the thoughts of many by noting the questionable basis for and drastic effect of this decision on the traditional—and many would say biblical—view of the family.

The Supreme Court also handled cases dealing with Christians' exercise of free speech and religious liberty. In two cases the Supreme Court ruled in favor of Christians who had resisted the Affordable Care Act's mandate for providing certain contraceptives (birth control) to employees, stating the mandate violated their religious beliefs. Additionally, the Supreme Court reviewed a case in which a Christian bakery owner refused to make a wedding cake for a same-sex couple. The Colorado Civil Rights Commission had determined that he was guilty of discrimination based on a Colorado law. Although the Supreme Court ruled in favor of the bakery owner in *Masterpiece Bakery v. Colorado Civil Rights Commission*, the case did not provide clarification for the tension between religious liberty and laws protecting same-sex couples from discrimination.

◄ (top left) Justice Sonia Sotomayor; (top right) Justice Elena Kagan; (left) the White House lit in rainbow colors after the *Obergefell* decision

## Foreign Challenges

In 2009 Secretary of State Hillary Clinton proposed a "reset," or new beginning, for US-Russia relations. Obama helped Russia join the World Trade Organization, and the Senate approved a treaty limiting nuclear arms for both countries in 2010. Yet, in 2014 Russians seized Crimea (part of Ukraine) and then made several military intrusions into Ukraine, ignoring protests from the United States and its allies. Many Americans argued that little had changed regarding the tense relationship between the two nations.

Following a build-up of troops in Iraq and Afghanistan under President George W. Bush in 2007, Obama promised to complete the defeat of enemy forces in Afghanistan, a war he considered just, and withdraw American forces from Iraq, a war he considered unjust. Obama achieved a long-standing goal in the War on Terror when 9/11 attack planner Osama bin Laden, who had been located in Pakistan, was killed by Navy SEAL Team Six on May 1, 2011. Nevertheless, the war in Afghanistan proved to be a difficult conflict to end. Radical Muslims were resilient and able to reconstitute their military forces. Obama sent more US troops to Afghanistan to train Afghan soldiers to defend against Taliban forces. After this surge, Obama significantly reduced the number of troops by 2015.

▲ Osama bin Laden's compound in Abbottabad, Pakistan

Beginning in December 2010, a series of protests and uprisings known as the Arab Spring spread across several Arab countries, including Tunisia, Egypt, Yemen, Libya, and Syria. Although many regimes were overthrown, some protests resulted in civil war. In many of these countries, Muslim radicals used the unrest to incite violence and expand their control over citizens. After Obama removed virtually all American forces in Iraq by December 2011, a power vacuum resulted, creating a struggle between Sunni and Shiite Muslims for control of Iraq.

A group of radicals known as the **Islamic State of Iraq and Syria (ISIS)** rushed to seize power during the war in Iraq and the Syrian Civil War. Following the capture of key Iraqi cities by ISIS and many reports of atrocities against the Iraqi people, the United States led airstrikes against ISIS in Iraq and Syria. Obama sent special forces back to Iraq in order to train Iraqi forces. By 2017 Iraqi forces and their allies had pushed ISIS out of Iraq. However, the terrorist group continued to be a threat in the Middle East.

▲ An ISIS leader and fighters

## US-Cuba Relations

In December 2014 President Obama and Cuban president Raul Castro, brother of Fidel Castro (who had died that November), announced that their two nations would restore full diplomatic ties for the first time in more than a half century. In March 2016 Obama made a historic trip to Cuba to meet with the Cuban president.

In 2012, on the anniversary of the 9/11 attacks, terrorists attacked the US diplomatic compound in Benghazi, Libya. The US ambassador and three other American officials were killed. Many Americans viewed the attack as a tragic example of Islamic radicals taking advantage of perceived American weakness and blamed the Obama administration for not protecting American diplomats abroad. The Benghazi tragedy was an issue in both the 2012 and 2016 presidential elections.

Negotiations with Iran that had begun under George W. Bush concluded during the Obama administration. In 2015 the United States and other countries reached an agreement with Iran known as the Joint Comprehensive Plan of Action (JCPOA). The agreement loosened sanctions on Iran in exchange for Iran's promise to limit its nuclear weapons program. Critics stated that it could not ensure enforcement and that money Iran received because of the lowered sanctions would be used to fund terrorism.

---

### Comprehension Check 25.1

1. _____ was the Great Recession program that was designed to prevent some of the nation's largest financial institutions from collapsing through government purchase of their stocks.
   - A  PPACA
   - B  TARP
   - C  DACA

2. An executive order Obama issued related to immigration was _____.
   - A  DACA
   - B  TARP
   - C  Obergefell

3. In Obergefell v. Hodges, the Supreme Court ruled that _____.
   - A  abortion was constitutional
   - B  Obamacare was unconstitutional
   - C  states must recognize same-sex marriage

4. Each of the following is true of foreign issues during Obama's presidency except _____.
   - A  US troops were significantly reduced in Afghanistan and Iraq before returning to help stabilize the countries
   - B  terrorists in Iran attacked a US embassy
   - C  Osama bin Laden was killed

5. The Obama administration concluded an agreement with _____ over its nuclear weapons program.
   - A  China
   - B  North Korea
   - C  Iran

**MAKING CONNECTIONS**

6. What two changes regarding the recognition of homosexuality were made during the Obama administration?

# 25.2 The Trump Presidency

## Why was Trump impeached twice?

In 2016 Hillary Clinton, former first lady, New York senator, and US secretary of state, won the Democratic presidential nomination, pledging to continue Obama's policies. The battle for the Republican nomination was heated. Wealthy real estate entrepreneur and television personality **Donald Trump** surprised many by rising to the top of the field of candidates. Trump's sometimes crude remarks, his earlier liberal positions on social issues, and rumored marital infidelity concerned many, including many evangelical Christians. But his populist positions, his pledge to embrace conservative social views, and his promises to "Make America Great Again" (MAGA) and to shake up the political establishment in Washington, DC, echoed with enough voters for him to win the nomination. Trump selected Indiana governor Mike Pence, who described himself as a born-again, evangelical Catholic, as his running mate.

As the election neared, polls and political observers overwhelmingly predicted a Clinton victory. But Election Day brought a surprise. Although Clinton received about 48 percent of the popular vote to Trump's 46 percent, Trump won in the Electoral College 304 to 227. Furthermore, Republicans maintained control of both houses of Congress.

## GUIDING QUESTIONS

- How well did Trump's domestic policies succeed?

- How were Trump's foreign policies different from those of previous presidents?

- What caused Trump's second impeachment?

▲ Donald Trump and Hillary Clinton debating

## The Election of 2016

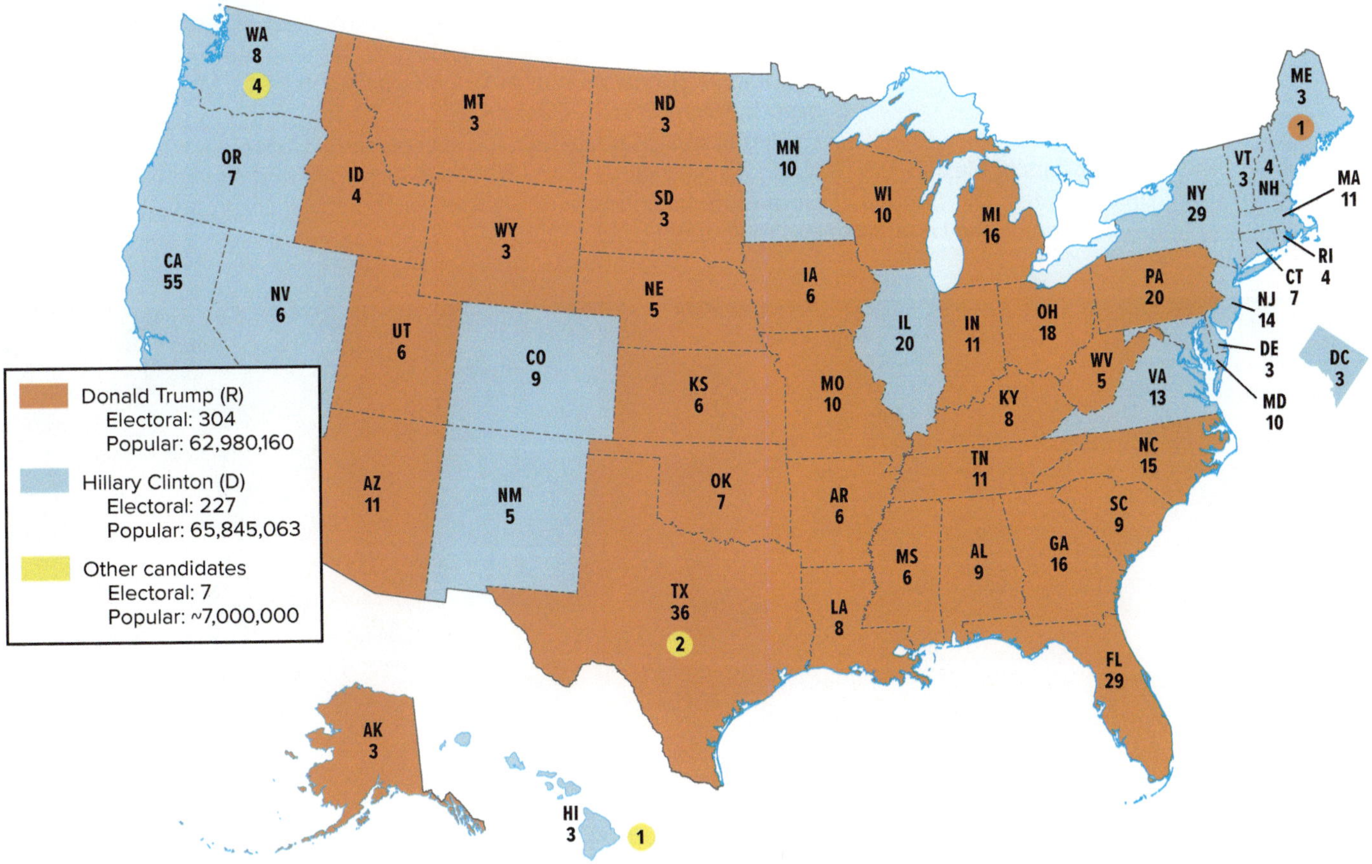

| | | |
|---|---|---|
| Donald Trump (R) | Electoral: 304 | Popular: 62,980,160 |
| Hillary Clinton (D) | Electoral: 227 | Popular: 65,845,063 |
| Other candidates | Electoral: 7 | Popular: ~7,000,000 |

WA 8 — 4
ME 3 — 1
MT 3
ND 3
OR 7
ID 4
MN 10
VT 3
NH 4
NY 29
MA 11
CA 55
WY 3
SD 3
WI 10
MI 16
PA 20
RI 4
CT 7
NV 6
UT 6
CO 9
NE 5
IA 6
IL 20
IN 11
OH 18
WV 5
VA 13
NJ 14
DE 3
DC 3
MD 10
AZ 11
NM 5
KS 6
MO 10
KY 8
NC 15
SC 9
TN 11
OK 7
AR 6
MS 6
AL 9
GA 16
TX 36 — 2
LA 8
FL 29
AK 3
HI 3 — 1

In his inaugural address, Trump declared his "America First" agenda:

> The oath of office I take today is an oath of allegiance to all Americans. For many decades, we've enriched foreign industry at the expense of American industry; subsidized the armies of other countries while allowing for the very sad depletion of our military; we've defended other nations's borders while refusing to defend our own; and spent trillions of dollars overseas while America's infrastructure has fallen into disrepair and decay.
>
> We've made other countries rich while the wealth, strength, and confidence of our country has disappeared over the horizon. One by one, the factories shuttered and left our shores, with not even a thought about the millions upon millions of American workers left behind. The wealth of our middle class has been ripped from their homes and then redistributed across the entire world.
>
> But that is the past. And now we are looking only to the future.
>
> We assembled here today are issuing a new decree to be heard in every city, in every foreign capital, and in every hall of power. From this day forward, a new vision will govern our land. From this moment on, it's going to be America First.

# Domestic Issues

## Economics

During Trump's first year in office, Congress passed a new tax plan lowering taxes on individuals and businesses. As additional money flowed into the economy, the unemployment rate dipped significantly. Trump also signed an executive order to remove the tax penalty for Americans who did not obtain health insurance as required by the Affordable Care Act.

Trump frequently criticized free-trade agreements for benefitting America's trade partners more than the United States. Three days after his inauguration, Trump withdrew the United States from the Trans-Pacific Partnership trade deal. He also pushed for modification or elimination of NAFTA (see Chapter 24). After lengthy negotiations, Mexico, Canada, and the United States agreed to the **United States-Mexico-Canada Agreement (USMCA)**, which modified NAFTA's provisions. The USMCA was passed and signed by each member nation, receiving support from both Republicans and Democrats, and took effect in July 2020.

▼ The leaders of Mexico, the United States, and Canada signing the USMCA

## Court Appointments

Trump appealed to conservatives, including many evangelical Christians, largely because of his promise to appoint conservative judges to the federal courts. The Republican-controlled Senate confirmed about 230 Trump-nominated federal judges, comprising nearly 30 percent of all federal judgeships. Because federal judges serve for life and thereby have impact for many years, this would prove to be one of Trump's most lasting accomplishments.

Trump was also able to appoint three justices to the Supreme Court. Within his first two weeks in office, he nominated Neil Gorsuch to take the place of deceased justice Antonin Scalia. He also appointed Brett Kavanaugh to replace retiring justice Anthony Kennedy. Then in September 2020, associate justice Ruth Bader Ginsburg died, and Trump chose Amy Coney Barrett to replace her. Democrats attempted to block Barrett's nomination as Republicans had done to Obama's last Supreme Court nominee four years earlier, but the Senate confirmed her nomination in October. These three appointments gave conservatives a solid majority on the Supreme Court.

## The Mueller Investigation

Evidence emerged that the Russian government had attempted to sabotage the 2016 election using social media and hacking emails from leading Democrats. Former British intelligence officer Christopher Steele created a report (called the Steele Dossier) that alleged the Trump campaign colluded, or conspired, with the Russians to affect the election. A further complication arose when Trump fired the FBI director who was investigating the allegations. In May 2017 the Department of Justice appointed Robert Mueller, a former FBI director, as special counsel to investigate possible collusion between Russia and the Trump campaign.

In March 2019, the **Mueller Investigation** noted that the Russians had in fact interfered during the campaign and that several Trump associates had been in communication with Russia, but "the investigation did not establish that members of the Trump Campaign conspired or coordinated with the Russian government in its election interference activities." Throughout the investigation, Trump insisted that the allegations were "fake news." It was later revealed that Steele had been enlisted by a company hired by the Clinton campaign to conduct opposition research on Trump. The media, which had widely reported the allegations contained in the Steele Dossier as true, began to acknowledge around 2020 that the report had been deeply flawed and that its allegations could not be verified. An investigation into the origins of the probe into Trump's campaign led to the 2023 release of the Durham Report, which concluded that the FBI's handling of the matter was seriously flawed.

The controversy surrounding Trump helped the Democrats to regain the majority in the House of Representatives in the 2018 congressional elections, while the Republicans maintained control in the Senate.

## First Impeachment

In 2019 a government source revealed that President Trump, in a conversation with the president of Ukraine, had threatened to withhold military funds that Congress had designated for Ukraine unless the Ukrainians investigated Hunter Biden, the son of former vice president Joe Biden. Trump suspected Hunter Biden of unethical dealings in his role as a board member of a powerful Ukrainian energy corporation. Democrats accused Trump of using the withholding of funds from Ukraine for political purposes, namely to harm Joe Biden, Trump's likely rival in the 2020 election.

The House of Representatives investigated and voted to impeach the president on charges of abuse of power and obstruction of justice, making Trump the third president to be impeached. After the impeachment trial of January 2020, the Senate failed to reach the two-thirds majority necessary to convict the president.

▼ (top to bottom) Supreme Court Justices Neil Gorsuch, Brett Kavanaugh, and Amy Coney Barrett

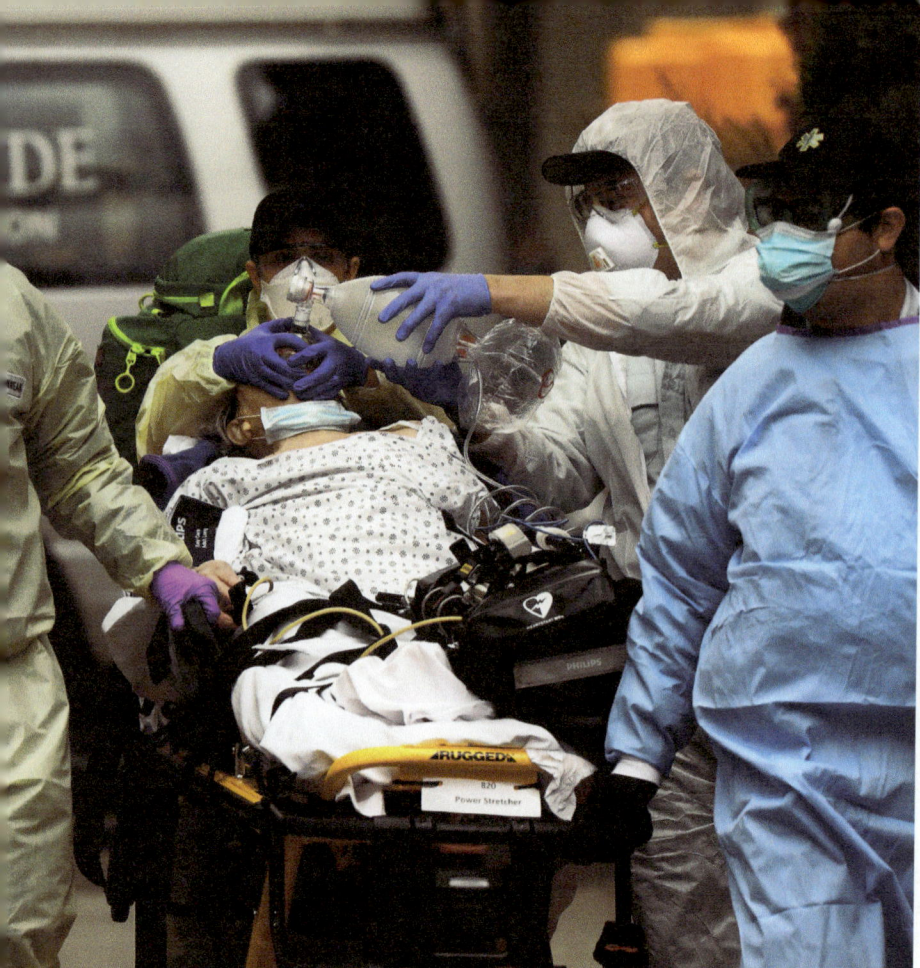

## Global Pandemic

Shortly after the impeachment trial, the world's attention shifted to a new challenge, a global pandemic. A new coronavirus was first reported in Wuhan, China, in December 2019. Quickly spreading to millions of people around the world, the virus caused an illness called **COVID-19**, which caused severe respiratory symptoms for many patients. The death rate for those infected was significantly higher than that of the flu, especially for those with preexisting medical conditions. In the United States, reports indicate that hundreds of thousands died of COVID-19, and over 1.5 million worldwide in 2020.

Businesses were ordered to close, schools sent children home and switched to online learning, and many people stayed home to try to stop the spread of the disease. Some states and cities placed restrictions on public meetings, including church services, and some churches challenged those restrictions in court. Most churches suspended in-person meetings for at least a few weeks and began streaming their services over the internet.

There was much heated debate in America about COVID-19 restrictions. Some Americans believed that state and local governments were abusing power by introducing COVID-19 policies, while others accepted the mandates as necessary to protect the health of citizens. Some questioned the effectiveness of these public health measures and whether they were worth the risks to the economy and to the social and emotional health of Americans.

▲ (top left) A COVID-19 patient being wheeled into the hospital; (top right) students being checked for fevers before entering school during the COVID-19 pandemic; (bottom right) a restaurant closed during the COVID-19 pandemic

The first vaccines for COVID-19 became available in December 2020, and even those caused controversy. The federal government, the military, and many private businesses began to mandate the vaccine, and some employees were fired for not getting vaccinated.

Closures related to COVID-19 caused great disruption to the economy. People stopped traveling, affecting airlines and the tourist industry. Entire factories closed for extended periods if a worker tested positive for the virus, creating shortages of certain goods. In January 2020, prior to the pandemic, unemployment was 3.6 percent. By April 2020 unemployment climbed to 14.7 percent. To deal with the economic crisis, Congress passed the **Coronavirus Aid, Relief, and Economic Security (CARES) Act** in March 2020. The CARES Act provided $2.2 trillion in economic stimulus, including direct payments to individuals, loans to corporations, forgivable loans to small businesses, and funds for state and local governments. Congress passed another $900 billion stimulus bill in December 2020 which gave additional payments to individuals and extended unemployment benefits.

## Immigration Policy

Trump had promised during his campaign to crack down on illegal immigration, pledging to build a wall along the Mexican border to prevent illegal entry into the United States. Tension between Trump and Congress over the amount of federal funds designated for the border wall led to a partial government shutdown, affecting several government agencies, between December 2018 and January 2019. In February, citing threats to security from criminal activity, Trump declared a national emergency, an action that enabled him to use funds from the military budget for the border wall. While some supported his efforts to fulfill his campaign promise, others criticized his calling of a national emergency to bypass Congress.

To further restrict both legal and illegal immigration, Trump signed executive orders banning people from several countries where terrorism was widespread from entering the country, and reducing the number of visa applications that would be accepted, as well as requiring asylum seekers who tried to enter the United States through Mexico to remain in Mexico until their case could be heard in court. Trump also attempted to repeal Obama's DACA executive order but his action was blocked by the Supreme Court. After a surge of unaccompanied minors and families with children began arriving at the border, the attorney general announced a "zero tolerance" policy in which anyone who crossed the border illegally would be detained and prosecuted, even if it resulted in children being separated from their parents. This controversial policy, meant to deter immigrants from entering illegally, resulted in thousands of children being placed in shelters or temporary homes while their parents were detained. Under criticism from both Republicans and Democrats, Trump issued an order reversing the policy.

## Sanctuary Cities

In March 2020, after the outbreak of the COVID-19 pandemic, the Centers for Disease Control (CDC) issued a public health order, allowing for the rapid removal of those entering the country, with the stated purpose of slowing the spread of the disease. Some Democrat-controlled cities declared themselves to be "sanctuary cities" where local government officials pledged not to assist immigration officials in enforcing federal immigration laws and deporting those in the country illegally.

## Racial Tension *in* 2020

Two incidents illustrated racial tension in 2020. In February a young black man named Ahmaud Arbery was jogging through a neighborhood in Georgia when three white men, thinking he had been involved in a recent burglary, pursued him in a truck, shot, and killed him. The district attorney chose not to bring charges against the men, but when video of the incident was released in May and shared on social media, the state attorney general reassigned the case, and a grand jury indicted the men. All three were convicted of murder.

In late May another black man, George Floyd, died while a police officer knelt on his neck for a prolonged time during an arrest in Minnesota. Video footage of the incident shared on social media spread quickly, sparking protests and demonstrations across the country. While some protests were peaceful, others turned into violent riots. The officer was tried and convicted for murdering Floyd. While some Americans called for evaluation of certain police procedures, some progressive groups began to demand that police departments be defunded and the money be spent on social services instead. Violence against police officers also increased.

▼ A portion of the border wall between the United States and Mexico being constructed; (inset) a memorial to George Floyd

▲ (top) Trump and North Korean dictator Kim Jong-un meeting in Vietnam; (bottom) pro-democracy supporters protesting in Hong Kong

# Foreign Issues

## Challenges in the Far East

Trump became the first president to visit Communist North Korea while still in office. Seeking an arrangement that would decrease North Korea's ability to create nuclear weapons, he held a series of meetings with North Korean dictator Kim Jong-un beginning in 2018. Negotiations to denuclearize North Korea failed, and North Korea continued to develop its nuclear capability and to launch missiles in tests of its nuclear program.

Trump's relationship with China proved complicated. Trump believed previous trade agreements with China had created unfair competition because of China's lower wages and its practice of intellectual property theft (stealing individuals' and companies' ideas and inventions). Trump drastically raised tariffs with China, up to a 25 percent rate on certain products, which led to China's retaliation with its own tariffs on American goods.

As previous presidents had done, Trump reiterated America's "one China" policy (see Chapter 23) while still selling defensive weapons to Taiwan. In 2020, Hong Kong, which the British had ceded back to Chinese control in 1997, lost much of its remaining autonomy (self-government) to mainland China, as many had feared. Since then, the Chinese government has arrested several members of pro-democracy groups.

## Successes in the Middle East

In 2018 Trump withdrew from the Obama-era Iran nuclear agreement. Believing Iran was sponsoring terrorism around the world, Trump reimposed economic sanctions on the country. Tensions increased further in January 2020 when a strike by a US drone (unmanned aircraft) targeted and killed an Iranian commander in Iraq who had planned attacks on US and Iraqi forces. The Iranians responded with missile strikes a few days later on bases in Iraq that housed US soldiers.

In 1995 Congress had passed a law to recognize Jerusalem as Israel's capital. Because of unrest between Israel and the Arabs, presidents Clinton, Bush, and Obama had deferred moving the US embassy from Tel Aviv. In December 2017 Trump officially recognized Jerusalem as Israel's capital and moved the US embassy there in 2018.

Although Trump sought to end American involvement in the long-running war in Afghanistan against the Taliban, he briefly sent more military troops as Obama had done. In 2020 the United States and the Taliban signed an agreement in which all US and allied troops would leave by May 1, 2021, in exchange for the Taliban's promise to oppose terrorism in Afghanistan and negotiate a cease-fire and other arrangements with Afghan government officials. By January 2021, American troops had been reduced to 2,500, the lowest number since the beginning of the war, despite the Taliban not upholding all of its commitments.

Trump also negotiated peace agreements between Israel and several Arab nations. Before 2020, Egypt (see Chapter 23) and Jordan had been the only Muslim-majority countries to formally recognize Israel. In September 2020, the United Arab Emirates (UAE) and Bahrain signed peace agreements, known as the **Abraham Accords**, to establish political relations with Israel and have further discussions to open trade. By the end of the year, Sudan and Morocco had also signed agreements with Israel.

# The Election of 2020

▲ Joe Biden and Kamala Harris

The Republicans renominated Trump in 2020. He campaigned on a record of economic success (though the economy had stumbled significantly during the COVID-19 crisis), his America First policy, and his promise to continue combating illegal immigration. Former senator and former vice president **Joe Biden** won the Democratic nomination and chose as his running mate California senator Kamala Harris.

Largely because of COVID-19, many states changed their voting rules for the 2020 election to allow early voting and mail-in voting, or they mailed ballots to voters who could return them to a polling drop box. The certified election results indicated that Biden had won the popular vote by more than 7 million and electoral vote 306 to 232. However, Trump and many of his supporters claimed that a substantial amount of voter fraud had occurred. Numerous legal challenges were made about election fraud, but judges dismissed most of the cases. In the end, none of the legal challenges changed the election results of any state. The Justice Department also concluded from its own investigations that fraud was minimal and did not affect the election's outcome.

## The Election of 2020

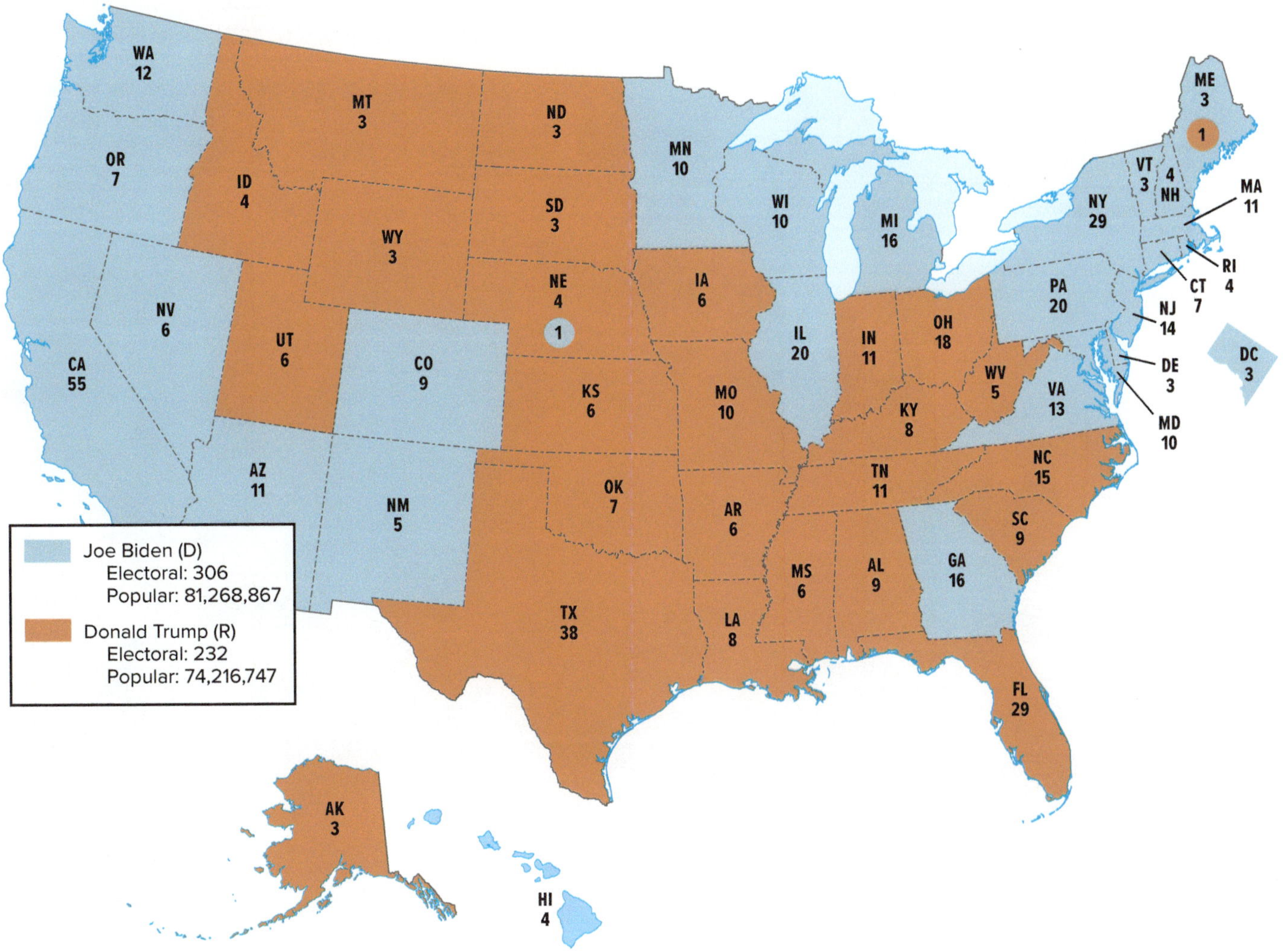

| State | Electoral Votes |
|-------|-----------------|
| WA | 12 |
| OR | 7 |
| CA | 55 |
| NV | 6 |
| ID | 4 |
| MT | 3 |
| WY | 3 |
| UT | 6 |
| AZ | 11 |
| NM | 5 |
| CO | 9 |
| ND | 3 |
| SD | 3 |
| NE | 4 (1) |
| KS | 6 |
| OK | 7 |
| TX | 38 |
| MN | 10 |
| IA | 6 |
| MO | 10 |
| AR | 6 |
| LA | 8 |
| WI | 10 |
| IL | 20 |
| MI | 16 |
| IN | 11 |
| OH | 18 |
| KY | 8 |
| TN | 11 |
| MS | 6 |
| AL | 9 |
| GA | 16 |
| FL | 29 |
| WV | 5 |
| VA | 13 |
| NC | 15 |
| SC | 9 |
| PA | 20 |
| NY | 29 |
| ME | 3 (1) |
| VT | 3 |
| NH | 4 |
| MA | 11 |
| RI | 4 |
| CT | 7 |
| NJ | 14 |
| DE | 3 |
| MD | 10 |
| DC | 3 |
| AK | 3 |
| HI | 4 |

Joe Biden (D)
Electoral: 306
Popular: 81,268,867

Donald Trump (R)
Electoral: 232
Popular: 74,216,747

## Capitol Riot

After the Electoral College results were announced, Trump called for supporters to assemble for a rally in Washington, DC, on January 6, 2021—the day that Congress was scheduled to certify the Electoral College votes. Normally the certification of an election is a formality in which the state-certified electoral vote results given to Congress are merely officially opened and counted. But because of the controversy surrounding the 2020 election, there was much debate about certifying the electoral vote. Thousands gathered for the rally. Speakers, including Trump, called on Congress and Vice President Pence to not certify the results. Before the electoral vote count began, Pence said, "My oath to support and defend the Constitution constrains me from claiming unilateral authority to determine which electoral votes should be counted and which should not."

At the rally Trump told supporters to march from the White House to the Capitol to make their views known to Congress. Thousands marched to the Capitol grounds. Hundreds swept past barricades, overwhelming Capitol police officers, some of whom were injured in their attempts to keep back the crowd. Still, hundreds of protesters entered the building, some after smashing windows or breaking through doors. Some protesters roamed the halls of the Capitol making threatening remarks as they sought to locate members of the House and Senate and Vice President Pence in the **January 6 Capitol riot** Congressional proceedings were disrupted as law enforcement officials evacuated Congress members and their staffs to safe locations.

▼ Trump speaking to supporters on January 6, 2021

▼ Rioters climbing the Capitol on January 6, 2021

Eventually order was restored, and Congress reconvened. They certified the electoral vote and declared Joe Biden the winner of the election.

On January 20, 2021, Joe Biden was inaugurated as the nation's 46th president. Kamala Harris became the first female, the first African American, and the first Asian American to hold the office of vice president.

## Second Impeachment

Many members of Congress argued that Trump was responsible for the Capitol riot and began calling for his impeachment. On January 13, a week before Biden took office, the House voted 222 to 197 to impeach Trump for a second time, charging that he had incited insurrection. The Senate trial did not begin until February 9, almost three weeks after Trump's term ended. Many Republican members of the Senate declared an impeachment trial unconstitutional since Trump was no longer in office; however, they did not have enough votes to stop the trial. Chief Justice John Roberts declined to preside over the trial because the person charged was no longer president.

The trial lasted five days. Prosecuting senators argued that Trump's repeated claims of election fraud and his speeches (including the one delivered at the January 6 rally) led the mob to attack the Capitol. The defense noted that Trump never called for violence and that his January 6 speech had urged citizens to march peacefully. Fifty-seven senators voted guilty, falling short of the two-thirds required to convict.

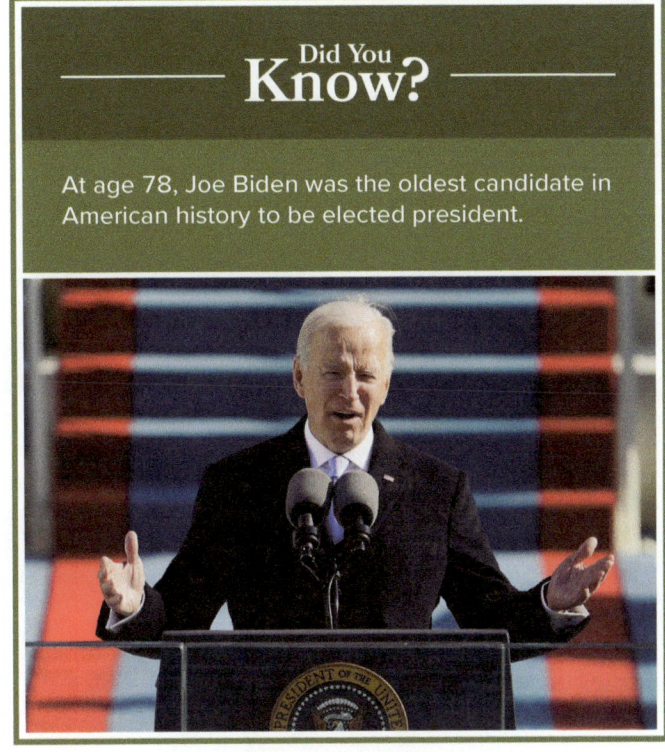

**Did You Know?**

At age 78, Joe Biden was the oldest candidate in American history to be elected president.

▲ Biden speaking at his inauguration

---

## Comprehension Check 25.2

1. Trump's economic policies included all of the following except ____.

   A reducing taxes

   B signing the Trans-Pacific Partnership free trade agreement

   C signing the US-Mexico-Canada Agreement to replace NAFTA

2. The Mueller Investigation investigated ____.

   A the January 6 Capitol riot

   B Trump's threat to withhold military aid from Ukraine

   C accusations that the Trump campaign colluded with Russia to affect the 2016 election

3. Trump's first impeachment was related to ____.

   A the January 6 Capitol riot

   B Trump's threat to withhold military aid from Ukraine

   C accusations that the Trump campaign colluded with Russia to affect the 2016 election

4. In foreign policy, Trump did each of the following except ____.

   A pledge to keep US troops in Afghanistan indefinitely

   B recognize Jerusalem as the capital of Israel

   C withdraw from the Iran nuclear agreement

   D negotiate peace agreements between several Arab nations and Israel

**MAKING CONNECTIONS**

5. How did the COVID-19 pandemic change American society? Why did some Americans disagree with the government's COVID-19 policies?

6. What was the relationship between the 2020 election, the January 6 Capitol riot, and Trump's second impeachment?

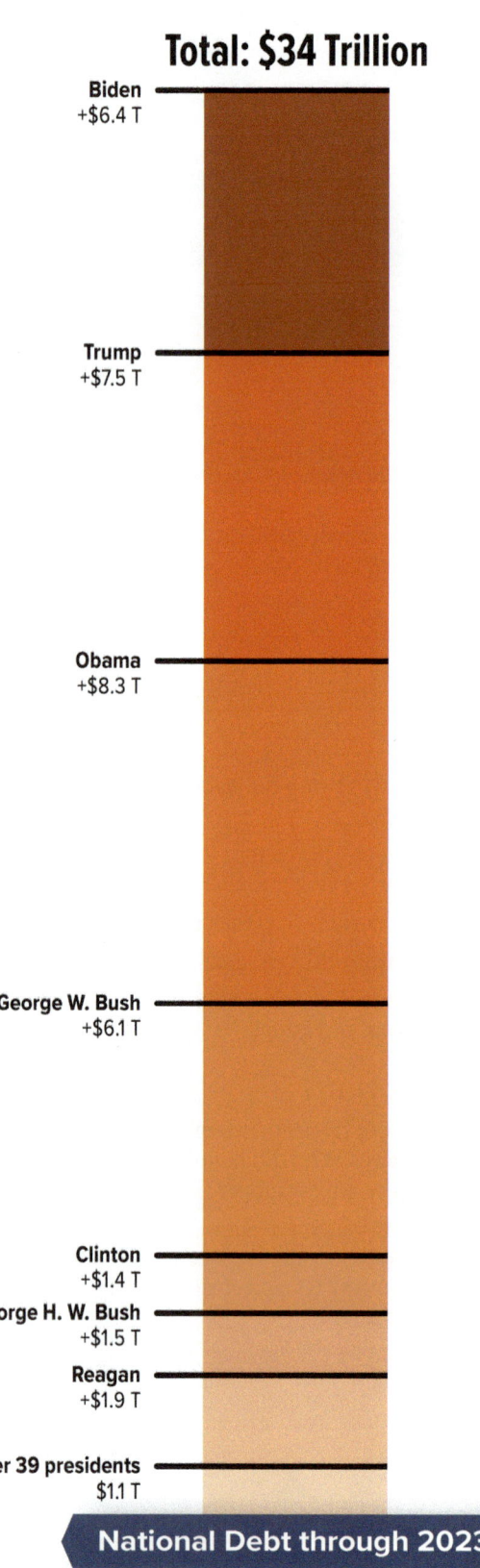

## Total: $34 Trillion

Biden
+$6.4 T

Trump
+$7.5 T

Obama
+$8.3 T

George W. Bush
+$6.1 T

Clinton
+$1.4 T

George H. W. Bush
+$1.5 T

Reagan
+$1.9 T

All other 39 presidents
$1.1 T

**National Debt through 2023**

How did Biden's policies differ from previous presidents?

# Domestic Issues

Amidst division over the election, racial tensions and the ongoing COVID-19 pandemic, Biden emphasized unity and the preservation of democracy in his inaugural address. Biden prioritized appointing a diverse administration.

## COVID-19 and the Economy

In March 2021 Congress passed an additional $1.9 trillion stimulus bill, called the **American Rescue Plan**, to help counter the economic effects of the second year of the pandemic. In addition to giving direct payments to Americans, the bill funded vaccine distribution.

As COVID-19 receded, and Americans returned to work, the unemployment rate dropped, reaching under 4 percent by 2022. However, economists pointed out that inflation rates, caused by supply-and-demand issues related to the pandemic and other factors, continued to rise. In August 2022 Congress passed the **Inflation Reduction Act**, which placed a minimum tax rate on certain corporations, allocated funds to expand the IRS, introduced a measure intended to reduce Medicare drug costs, and introduced tax credits for clean energy solutions. Some were concerned that it would hurt Medicare in the long term and would increase, not reduce, inflation.

Another controversial decision was Biden's announcement of a plan to cancel hundreds of billions of dollars of federal student loans by executive order for those affected by the COVID-19 pandemic. The plan was ruled unconstitutional by the Supreme Court in 2023.

## Infrastructure

During his presidential campaign, Biden had proposed a new infrastructure plan. In November 2021, Congress passed the **Infrastructure Investment and Jobs Act**. The bill designated approximately $1 trillion for projects to improve roads, bridges, railways, and public transportation in cities and states. It also funded projects such as improving drinking water by replacing water pipelines and increasing electric vehicles and access to broadband internet.

## Immigration

Biden took a drastically different approach to immigration and border security. He stopped all funding and construction of the border wall and appointed Vice President Harris to work with Mexico, Honduras, Guatemala, and El Salvador to address root causes of migration. He also lifted Trump's restrictions on the number of visas issued.

Biden's policy changes dramatically increased the number of migrants being encountered at the border. Republicans blamed the president's policies for the growing number of illegal immigrants being allowed into the country. Republican governors in Texas and Florida began busing migrants to New York City, Chicago, Washington, DC, and other "sanctuary cities" to bring greater attention to the issue. Facing mounting criticism even from his own party, Biden visited the border city of El Paso, Texas, in January 2023 and announced that he would begin deporting 30,000 illegal immigrants a month under the COVID-19 public health order. He also announced programs that would require those from Cuba, Nicaragua, and Haiti who wanted to migrate to the United States to apply from their home countries and remain there until accepted; if they attempted to enter through Mexico, they would be expelled. Further, he called on Congress to pass comprehensive immigration reform. Bipartisan reform bills have since been introduced in Congress, although Congress remains deeply divided over the issue.

## Overturning Roe v. Wade

Pro-life supporters had been advocating for the overturning of *Roe v. Wade* since the court handed down that decision in 1973 (see Chapter 23). After Trump's three appointments had given conservatives a clear majority on the Supreme Court, many pro-life Americans believed the time was right to challenge *Roe*. Several states passed laws restricting access to abortion, hoping that challenges to those laws would reach the Supreme Court. In the 2022 case ***Dobbs v. Jackson Women's Health Organization***, a Mississippi abortion clinic challenged a state law that banned most abortions after the first fifteen weeks of pregnancy. In a 6–3 ruling, the Supreme Court ruled that the Constitution did not protect abortion as a right, thus overturning *Roe*. The decision meant that each state could make its own laws regarding abortion, returning the power to determine the status of abortion to the state legislatures and state supreme courts. Since *Dobbs*, some states have passed laws banning almost all abortions, while others have passed laws permitting abortion until the moment of birth. President Biden denounced the *Dobbs* ruling and called for Congress to pass a federal law allowing abortion nationwide.

## Respect for Marriage Act

The Supreme Court's decision in *Dobbs* led many supporters of same-sex marriage to fear that the conservative court might overturn *Obergefell v. Hodges* next. In December 2022, Congress passed the **Respect for Marriage Act**, reversing the Defense of Marriage Act and strengthening federal recognition of same-sex and interracial marriages. In both the House and the Senate, some Republicans joined the Democrats to pass the act. Many Christians were concerned about religious freedom for business owners who opposed recognition of same-sex marriage.

Inflation, budget deficits, and concerns over Biden's agenda affected the 2022 midterm elections. The Republicans narrowly took back the House, while Democrats maintained a slight majority in the Senate.

## Affirmative Action Challenged

In 2023 the Supreme Court handed down a significant decision related to the consideration of race in college admissions. The conservative-majority court ruled in two separate cases that race-based admission practices meant to increase diversity on college campuses were a violation of the equal protection clause of the Fourteenth Amendment.

▲ Justice Ketanji Brown Jackson, who was appointed by Biden to the Supreme Court in 2022

## Investigations and Indictments

Donald Trump announced in 2022 that he was running for president again in 2024. Since leaving office, Trump faced numerous investigations into his actions before, during, and after his time in office. A congressional committee continued to consider whether to refer Trump for criminal charges for his actions on January 6, 2021. In March 2023 a Manhattan district attorney announced that a grand jury (a jury that hears a case for the possibility of indicting, or charging, for a crime) had indicted Trump with falsifying business records, making Trump the first former president to be indicted for a crime. In June 2023 Trump was also indicted by a federal grand jury for his handling of classified documents found at his Florida home after he left office. (Just weeks after the FBI conducted a raid on Trump's home, it was revealed that classified documents had also been found at Biden's Delaware home from his time as vice president). In July 2023 a federal grand jury indicted Trump for conspiring to overturn the 2020 election, and in August 2023 a Georgia grand jury indicted Trump and eighteen others for attempting to overturn the election results in that state. In each of these cases, the former president pled not guilty to all charges. Trump and his supporters argued that the cases against him were weak and were politically motivated to keep him from being elected in 2024.

Meanwhile, congressional Republicans pushed for investigations into possible links between President Biden and his son Hunter's international financial dealings. The House of Representatives opened an impeachment investigation into Biden's role from his time as vice president.

# Foreign Policies

## Afghanistan

Continuing with Trump's agreement to withdraw all troops from Afghanistan by 2021, Biden announced in April 2021 a new date of September 11, despite concerns over the Taliban's failures to fulfill its part of the agreement. Biden soon accelerated the evacuation dates, asserting that US withdrawal would not necessarily result in the Taliban's takeover of the country; however, the Taliban swiftly reclaimed territory during the remaining months of evacuation, taking over Kabul, the capital, by August 15. An attack on the Kabul airport by an ISIS group killed 13 US troops and over 150 Afghans on August 26. The final US plane departed on August 30, leaving behind hundreds of US citizens and thousands of Afghan allies seeking to flee. Biden's handling of the evacuation and denials of the threat the Taliban posed drew sharp criticism from both parties.

▲ (above) Afghans in Kabul, Afghanistan, waiting to board a plane to flee the country

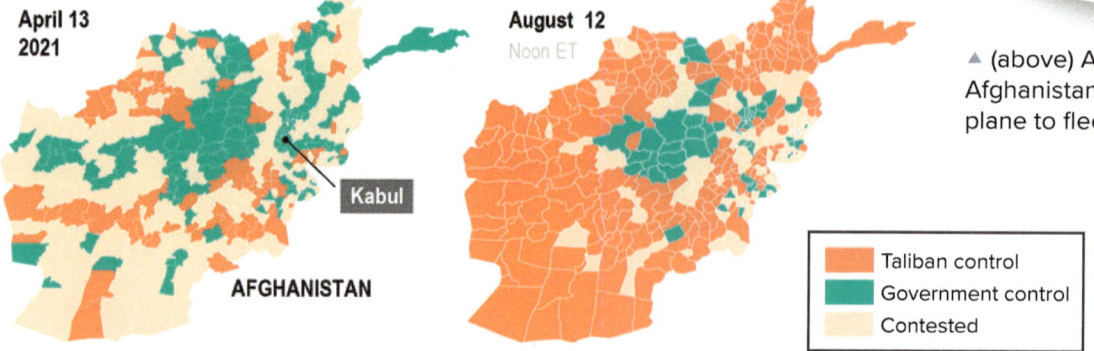

April 13 2021

August 12 Noon ET

Kabul

AFGHANISTAN

- Taliban control
- Government control
- Contested

## Europe

Ukraine, led by President **Volodymyr Zelensky**, began expressing interest in joining NATO. To prevent this, in February 2022 Russian president **Vladimir Putin** launched an invasion of Ukraine. The United States and its NATO allies responded by placing economic sanctions on Russia, supplying money and weapons to Ukraine, and training Ukrainian soldiers. Despite rising inflation throughout the year, many Americans supported American aid to Ukraine, which continued to resist the invasion and by the end of the year had reclaimed some of the territory overtaken by the Russians. However, the war continued into 2024 with no apparent end in sight.

---

### Comprehension Check 25.3

1. Congress passed an additional stimulus bill called _____ to help with the pandemic.

    **A** American Rescue Plan

    **B** Inflation Reduction Act

    **C** Infrastructure Investment and Jobs Act

2. The Supreme Court case *Dobbs v. Jackson Women's Health Organization* reversed an earlier decision regarding _____.

    **A** Medicare drug costs

    **B** homosexual marriage

    **C** abortion

3. All of the following occurred in Afghanistan during Biden's administration except _____.

    **A** final withdrawal of all US troops

    **B** ISIS bombing on airport in Kabul

    **C** moving the final evacuation date from September to August

    **D** successful defense against the Taliban's attempted takeover

4. The United States provided military and economic support to _____ after it was invaded.

    **A** China

    **B** Russia

    **C** Ukraine

### MAKING CONNECTIONS

5. Why was the Respect for Marriage Act passed and what did it accomplish?

▲ (top) Ukrainian president Volodymyr Zelensky (center) after the Russian invasion of Ukraine; (middle) Russian president Vladimir Putin; (bottom) Ukrainian residents fleeing their homes after a Russian bombing

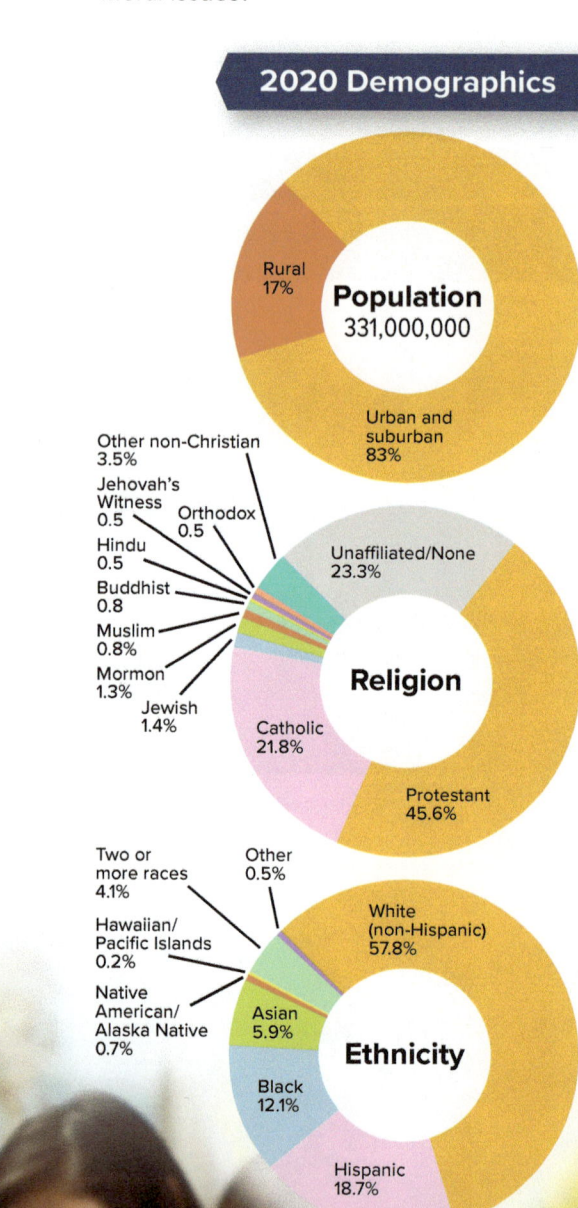

**2020 Demographics**

Population
331,000,000

Rural
17%

Urban and
suburban
83%

Religion

Other non-Christian
3.5%

Jehovah's
Witness
0.5

Orthodox
0.5

Hindu
0.5

Buddhist
0.8

Muslim
0.8%

Mormon
1.3%

Jewish
1.4%

Unaffiliated/None
23.3%

Catholic
21.8%

Protestant
45.6%

Ethnicity

Two or
more races
4.1%

Other
0.5%

Hawaiian/
Pacific Islands
0.2%

Native
American/
Alaska Native
0.7%

Asian
5.9%

White
(non-Hispanic)
57.8%

Black
12.1%

Hispanic
18.7%

## 25.4 Contemporary America

### How can people with differing ideas and cultures share core values?

The challenge for historians in dealing with contemporary issues is one of perspective. Historians normally write about events that took place many years ago, which gives them the opportunity to sort out what was important, what an event meant, and what effects it had on later events. One could argue that the study of current events is not history. However, the following contemporary issues are worthy of mention because they directly impact the nation today and undoubtedly will in the future. As we approach these issues, we want to keep in mind what was said in Chapter 1 about how the worldview of a person will determine how he or she evaluates an issue or event. As we discuss these contemporary issues, we want to consider them from a biblical worldview.

## Social Issues

### Diversity

At the time of the establishment of the United States, much of the country shared English heritage and culture. They generally valued principles of morality as taught in the Bible. They also valued certain core principles such as liberty, equality, individualism, and growth. As a result of rights and ideals codified in the Constitution, America became a leader in promoting political, religious, and economic freedom around the world.

The nation's core values brought tremendous economic and population growth, as many people from other nations desired the freedom and possibility of economic prosperity that America offered. Immigrants came and continue to come to the United States in large numbers.

American culture has been influenced by the cultures of many places. However, this diversity has also brought challenges. Is America a "melting pot" where people of various cultures come together and adopt a common set of values and beliefs, or is it a "salad bowl" in which people live side by side but hold on to the values, beliefs, and practices of their native cultures? Whether a culture composed of people from many places and with different histories and beliefs can agree to a common set of values is one of the most difficult questions facing America today.

## RACE

Since the early days of its history, issues of race have challenged America's core beliefs. Native Americans and African Americans were often denied the justice and liberty that others enjoyed. How did the ideas of liberty and equality relate to these groups? Americans struggled over that question and often failed to treat others as fellow humans made in God's image or to love their neighbor as they loved themselves.

The struggle for justice and equality for black Americans has been difficult. The civil rights movement brought progress, and with the election of an African American president many Americans hoped that racial conflict would diminish. However, racial tension continued.

In 2012 Trayvon Martin, a black teen, was shot and killed in Florida by a neighborhood watch captain. The man was charged with murder, but was acquitted after pleading self-defense. The verdict led to protests, some of which turned violent. The next year, the Black Lives Matter (BLM) organization was formed. The BLM organization had position statements calling for the disruption of the traditional idea of the nuclear family because it was "Western-prescribed" and affirming LGBTQ+ identities. Not all who used the phrase "Black lives matter" were associated with the organization, and many who were concerned about racial injustice did not hold to the extreme views that the organization held.

In 2014 a black man named Michael Brown was shot and killed by a police officer in Ferguson, Missouri. Brown had robbed a convenience store and resisted arrest. When Brown tried to take the officer's gun, the officer shot him. A grand jury chose not to charge the officer, saying the shooting was justified. Public protests soon turned into riots in cities across the country. Although the Department of Justice determined that there was not enough evidence to charge the officer with violating federal law, it did find evidence of racial bias in some police departments which created distrust between law enforcement and the community.

▲ (top) A memorial to Trayvon Martin; (bottom) Black Lives Matter protesters

## Thinking *about* Race *and* Racism

Coinciding with increased racial tension were debates over Critical Race Theory (CRT), which had been introduced in American universities in the last decades of the twentieth century. Debates over CRT and related approaches to racism took place in the halls of government, in universities, and at public school board meetings. This theory and related approaches have argued that racism is a pervasive and inherent component of American culture. They oppose a "colorblind" society and argue that the goal is not the integration of minorities into a majority culture but the redistribution of power from white Americans to minority Americans. These approaches tend to divide society into the oppressed and oppressors.

A secular approach to racism that contrasts with CRT is the majority conformity approach. This approach holds that racism is no longer a significant problem in the United States and that racial discrimination no longer holds ethnic minorities back from achievement. The majority conformity approach says the responsibility for solving unequal outcomes for various ethnicities lies mainly with the minority groups. It says that if people would stop talking about race and if minority groups would conform to majority norms, they would become upwardly mobile.

Christians should recognize that both of these contrasting secular approaches fail to recognize the depth of human sinfulness. The majority conformity approach tends to deny the ongoing effects of long-term national sins. This can lead to an unwillingness to even consider historical and contemporary accounts of such injustice, instead insisting that America must "move past" such things. Critical race theory and related approaches fail to recognize that sin and the misuse of power are universal among humans. Transferring power from one identity group to another will not end injustice; it will only shift which group has the power to sin against others. Neither approach has a biblical standard for right and wrong; instead, they determine right and wrong by looking to the values of the various groups themselves.

Christians have resources to address these questions that secular approaches do not have. Scripture teaches not only that there is one human race but also that ethnic diversity (not ethnic segregation) is part of God's plan for mankind. It celebrates the ability for variety God designed in the human race and affirms that all peoples share a fundamental unity because they are all made in the image of God. Christian approaches to injustice will recognize the universality of sin and will apply God's standards for what is just and unjust. Christians will understand that no group can be trusted with unchecked power and that all groups need to be ready to forgive and work together toward resolving real injustices, as God defines them, when they occur. Best of all, Christians have the hope of redemption and the confidence that Christ will return to set all things right.

America and the Modern World    **679**

## IMMIGRATION

Immigration is another heated social issue in the United States today. Currently there are nearly 12 million undocumented people living in the United States. In 2022 there were over 2.7 million encounters with undocumented immigrants crossing the border from Mexico. The stark contrast between Trump's and Biden's immigration policies has raised questions about the proper course the country should take.

Americans have differed on the proper balance between extending freedom to aliens and ensuring the security of the nation. Those who propose looser immigration policies point out that America has always welcomed immigrants and that it is inhumane to close the nation's borders, especially to those seeking asylum from crime, war, and oppression in their native countries. Those who propose stricter immigration policies point out that illegal immigration drains tax resources, results in the loss of jobs for American citizens, leads to the exploitation of undocumented laborers, and makes it easier for criminals, even terrorists, and dangerous illegal drugs to enter the country. They argue that immigrants, including asylum-seekers, should seek to enter the country through legal means.

Christians have disagreed over this issue as well. Some emphasize the Bible's commands to show mercy to aliens and strangers and to care for the poor and needy while others emphasize the commands to respect the rule of law, to obey those in authority, and the Bible's teaching on government's responsibility to punish wrongdoers and protect those who do right.

▲ Volunteers giving out water to migrants waiting to enter the United States

## Technology and Information

America and the world are in the midst of a technology and information revolution which began with the computer revolution of the 1950s to 1980s and exploded with the internet revolution of the 1990s. This revolution has created many benefits for society. People around the world can communicate with one another through phone calls, texts, and emails; they can access virtually any information they are seeking via the internet, spreading news, ideas, and even the Gospel globally and almost instantaneously.

The information revolution has also created many challenges. Social media, for example, has brought people together, but it has also distracted them for hours a day, affecting their ability to concentrate on a task or even to speak with one another. It has also created shallow views of "friendships" and relationships, and the constant need for affirmation through "likes" of social media posts. The advent of artificial intelligence (AI) has raised even more significant questions about the role of technology in society.

Another danger is the power that information technology companies have. Companies like Google, Apple, Microsoft, Facebook, X (formerly Twitter), Amazon, and TikTok have a wealth of personal information on their millions of users, raising concerns over privacy and the potential sharing of that information with governments, advertisers, or other parties without a person's knowledge or consent.

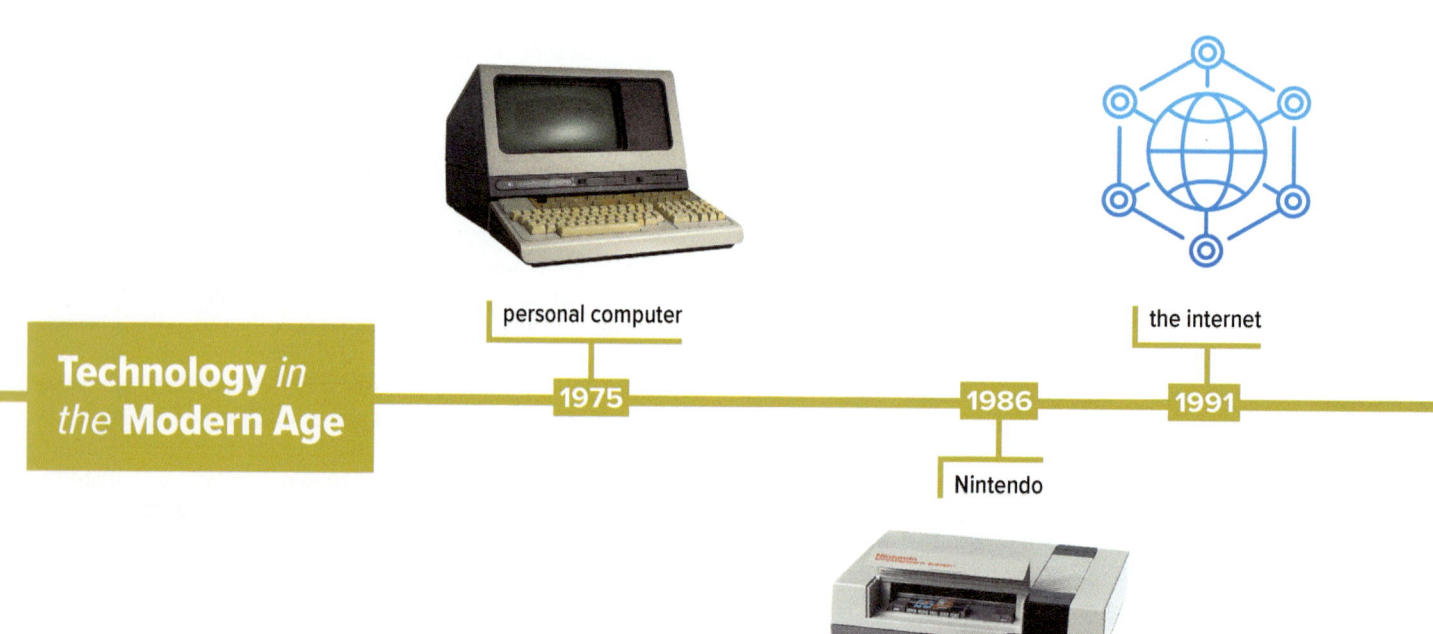

**Technology** *in the* **Modern Age**

personal computer

1975

the internet

1986

1991

Nintendo

Because these technology companies control so much of the way people access information today, they also can control what information is allowed on their platforms. Because they are private companies and not government agencies, they are not bound by the First Amendment's guarantee of free speech. Finding the proper balance between allowing free speech and a diversity of opinions while also preventing agents of foreign governments from spreading false information to undermine the stability of America's institutions and prohibiting posts that promote violence against others or obscenity is challenging. The worldview of those making such decisions has a significant effect on where the line between censorship and freedom is drawn.

## Thinking *about* Technology

Technologies such as AI, robotics, and virtual reality offer almost unlimited potential, yet even some leading creators of these technologies have warned about their potential dangers. New technologies raise questions, such as: just because something *can* be done, does it mean it *should* be done? Are people putting too much faith in technology? Do all of society's problems have technological solutions? How has technology contributed to the belief that individuals can create their own realities? What effects do the worldviews of those who are creating these technologies have on the end products and their uses?

## *Gun Violence and Gun Control*

Another social issue facing America today is violent crime, particularly gun violence. News of murders is in the news daily. The issue of guns challenges the nation's values. Many Americans desire freedom from government restrictions on their constitutional right to own guns, but they also desire safety in their communities. Solutions to the issue of gun violence have been difficult to find.

The Second Amendment states, "A well-regulated militia, being necessary to the security of a free state, the right of the people to keep and bear arms, shall not be infringed." Since its ratification, the meaning of the Second Amendment has been debated. Some have argued that the right to bear arms applies only to state militias, while others have argued that it protects the rights of private individuals. In the 2008 case *District of Columbia v. Heller*, the Supreme Court ruled that the Second Amendment gives individuals, not just militias, the right to own firearms. In a case two years later, the Court ruled that state laws must recognize the right of individuals to bear arms.

Several mass shootings within a decade drew greater attention to the issue of gun violence, including school shootings at the Sandy Hook Elementary School in Connecticut in 2012 and at a high school in Parkland, Florida, in 2018. These incidents have led to intense debates over gun control laws. Some argue that the best way to reduce gun violence is to pass stronger laws such as bans on assault-style weapons. Others say that such laws would violate the Second Amendment and that those intent on committing crimes would likely not obey such laws. The issue of gun violence also raises issues related to mental health, portrayals of violence in mass culture, the breakdown of families, and the decreasing influence of churches and biblical virtues in America, individual responsibility, and the need for people's hearts to be changed through the gospel.

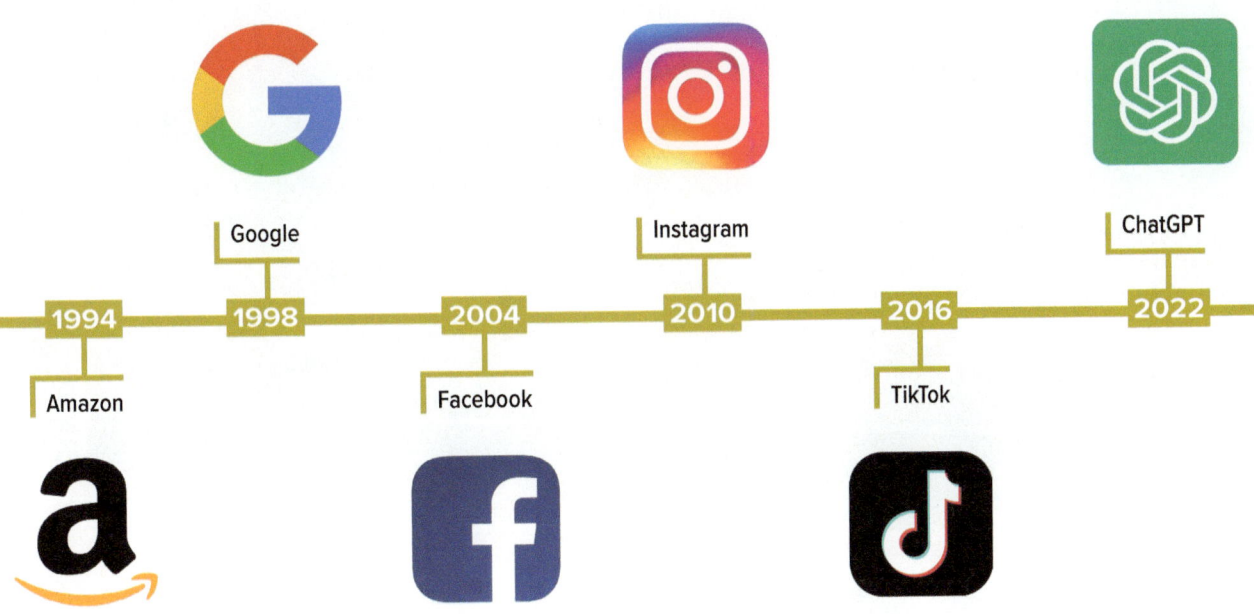

Google 1998

Instagram 2010

ChatGPT 2022

1994

2004

2016

Amazon

Facebook

TikTok

## Thinking *about* Climate Change

In 2021 Biden's secretary of defense, Lloyd Austin, said, "Today no nation can find lasting security without addressing the climate crisis. [Few threats] truly deserve to be called existential. The climate crisis does." Climate change raises several questions for Christians: Does climate change really threaten human existence? How much of climate change is the result of human activity, and how much is from natural climate cycles? What solutions are proposed to limit climate change and what effect will they have on earth's climate? What are the human and economic costs of those solutions?

▼ A Tesla electric vehicle (EV) being charged

## Climate Change

One of the biggest debates of modern American culture is over climate change. President Biden appointed former senator, secretary of state, and presidential candidate John Kerry as Special Presidential Envoy for Climate. Melting glaciers, forest fires, hurricanes, tornadoes, floods, droughts, and other natural disasters have been blamed on climate change, and some say that those changes have been caused by human activity. The burning of fossil fuels to create electricity and power vehicles, it is argued, is the main source of climate change. Billions of dollars have been spent to switch from coal and natural gas to wind and solar power to create electricity. Electric cars and trucks are being built to replace gasoline and diesel-powered ones, and some states have passed laws to eventually ban the sale of non-electric vehicles.

The issue of climate change has challenged Christians as well. The view that humans are a blight on nature is not consistent with a biblical understanding of man's place in Creation. Humans have been given dominion over Creation to use it for their benefit but have also been commanded to be good, wise stewards of it. Some Christians argue that wise stewardship of Creation must also consider the demands of human well-being, such as the elimination of poverty. They say that some proposals aimed at reducing climate change, such as eliminating the use of fossil fuels, will result in keeping people in underdeveloped nations in poverty, while it is unknown what the effects of these policies would be on reducing temperatures.

# Moral Issues

## *Abortion*

While the *Dobbs* decision in 2022 was celebrated by those who believe in the Bible's teaching that life begins in the womb, the debate over abortion in America has shifted to individual states, where the outcomes have varied widely. Some state supreme courts have overturned their states' laws banning abortion, while others have upheld them, and some states have added amendments to the state constitutions to restrict abortion, while others have added a right to abortion to their constitutions. In states where abortion bans have taken effect, the number of clinical abortions performed dropped dramatically. However, some women seeking abortions traveled to other states or received abortion medications through the mail.

▼ Pro-life demonstrators celebrating the Supreme Court's *Dobbs* decision

With such a varied political landscape regarding this issue across America, pro-life Christians have debated strategies for further reducing abortions. Some questions include: How can Christians engage the culture to change people's attitudes on issues related to life? Can Congress be persuaded to pass legislation to ban abortion nationwide? Would allowing exceptions for difficult cases such as rape and incest be an acceptable compromise to gain passage of bans on most abortions? How can Christians show compassion to women in unwanted pregnancies and help both them and their children before and after birth?

▲ LGBTQ+ activists

## LGBTQ+

LGBTQ+ activists have convinced many to champion their cause as an outflowing of American values, often tying the movement to the earlier civil rights movement. Gradually, American culture shifted from objections to homosexuality to increasing acceptance of open homosexual behavior to eventual legalization of same-sex marriage.

In recent years, transgenderism (understood as a mismatch between a person's biological sex and the gender with which that person identifies) has become another prevalent social and political issue. As more young Americans, including school-age children, identified as transgender, some states passed legislation requiring public schools to allow students to compete in men's and women's athletics and to access bathrooms according to their chosen gender identity. Transgender advocates supporting these laws cite federal protection against gender discrimination. In contrast, several states have introduced or passed legislation that requires transgender students to compete in sports events and to use bathrooms according to their biological (at birth) gender. Supporters of this legislation argue that they maintain fairness in competition for sports and protect the right to privacy in bathrooms.

Many states have also attempted to restrict minors' access to what advocates refer to as gender-affirming care (which includes mental health therapy and medical solutions such as puberty blockers, hormone therapy, and gender-reassignment surgeries). These state laws sought to protect young people from potentially damaging psychological and physical effects of hormonal and surgical treatments. Believing such laws discriminated against transgender youth, Biden signed an executive order in 2022 designed to ensure access to transgender healthcare at any age.

Many Christians have voiced concerns about the rejection of biblical teaching on gender, marriage and sexuality, and about the compromise of some professing Christians who have come to accept and even support the LGBTQ+ community. Many Christians express concern that same-sex marriage minimizes the importance of both mothers and fathers in raising children and sees marriage as a temporary arrangement for personal fulfillment rather than as a covenant commitment for the raising of families. Many who hold to biblical teachings desire to obey the Bible's command to love their neighbors, including members of the LGBTQ+ community, as themselves while remaining firm in their convictions and in their freedom to express their beliefs and to implement church and school policies that reflect biblical principles. They believe that caring about these neighbors includes not only treating them with dignity as image-bearers but also speaking the truth in love (Eph. 4:15), firmly declaring what is sinful while offering the hope of the gospel.

Americans can be grateful for the liberty and economic prosperity that have been manifest throughout the nation's history. The culture of the United States reflects core American values: freedom, individualism, equality, and growth. While these provide a degree of unity, Americans often have differing worldviews that lead them to disagree on the definitions and expressions of those core values. This tension continues to shape public discourse in contemporary America.

---

### Comprehension Check 25.4

1. All of the following are true about technology and information today except ____.

   A access to information globally has become easier

   B private companies are not allowed to censor information on their platforms

   C technology companies have access to the personal information of users

2. Humans have been given dominion over Creation and the responsibility to be wise stewards of it.

   True

   False

#### MAKING CONNECTIONS

3. What is one positive aspect of America's diversity? What is a challenge that this diversity creates?

4. What are two arguments for and two arguments against stricter immigration policies?

## Chapter Summary

### 25.1 The Obama Years

- Barack Obama won the election of 2008, becoming America's first African American president. Obama continued the TARP program begun under Bush and pushed for additional stimulus spending to help American corporations and individuals during the Great Recession. Congress passed healthcare reform, nicknamed "Obamacare." Republicans regained control of the House in 2010, and Obama was reelected in 2012. In 2015 the Supreme Court ruled that all states must recognize same-sex marriages.

- Foreign challenges under Obama included Russia seizing Crimea, the Arab Spring in the Middle East, the rise of ISIS, and an attack on the US embassy in Libya. Obama withdrew American forces from Iraq and increased American forces in Afghanistan, and Osama bin Laden was killed in a US raid in Pakistan. The United States and other nations made an agreement with Iran, lifting sanctions in return for Iran's agreement to limit its nuclear weapons program.

**TERMS**

Barack Obama

Troubled Asset Relief Program (TARP)

Affordable Care Act (ACA)

Deferred Action for Childhood Arrivals (DACA)

*Obergefell v. Hodges*

Islamic State of Iraq and Syria (ISIS)

**TERMS**

Donald Trump

United States-Mexico-Canada Agreement (USMCA)

Mueller Investigation

COVID-19

Coronavirus Aid, Relief, and Economic Security (CARES) Act

Abraham Accords

Joe Biden

January 6 Capitol riot

### 25.2 The Trump Presidency

- Donald Trump won the election of 2016 with the promise to "Make America Great Again" (MAGA) and a pledge to put "America First." He pushed Congress to lower taxes and replace NAFTA with the USMCA. He appointed numerous federal judges, including three conservative Supreme Court justices. The Mueller Investigation looked into alleged collusion between Russia and the Trump campaign to interfere with the 2016 election. Trump was impeached for abuse of power and obstruction of justice over allegations related to Ukraine but was not convicted in the Senate trial.

- Trump enacted policies to reduce illegal immigration and declared a national emergency to use funds to begin building a wall along the Mexican border. He raised tariffs with China, met with North Korea's dictator, withdrew from the Iran nuclear agreement, recognized Jerusalem as Israel's capital, began negotiations to withdraw from, and helped negotiate peace agreements between several Arab nations and Israel.

- Joe Biden was elected president in 2020, but Trump claimed the election was stolen from him because of fraud. Trump called on supporters to gather in Washington, DC, on January 6, 2021, the day the electoral vote would be certified. A riot broke out when protestors stormed the US Capitol. The House voted to impeach Trump for inciting insurrection. The Senate trial began after Trump left office, and the Senate did not vote to convict him.

## 25.3 | The Biden Administration

- As the COVID-19 pandemic continued, Biden introduced the American Rescue Plan to give stimulus payments to Americans and fund vaccine distributions. His Infrastructure Investment and Jobs Act designated funds for improving roads, bridges, and transportation as well as investing in alternative energy. To meet rising inflation, Congress passed the Inflation Reduction Act which, also included alternative energy measures. The *Roe v. Wade* decision protecting abortion was overturned in *Dobbs v. Jackson Women's Health Organization*. Congress passed the Respect for Marriage Act that strengthened federal recognition of homosexual and interracial marriages.

- After twenty years of American presence in Afghanistan, Biden withdrew all US troops. However, the Taliban quickly took over the country as the US troops withdrew. The United States supported Ukraine after a Russian invasion in 2022, supplying weapons and money. Biden continued the tariffs on Chinese trade and banned imports because of human rights abuses.

### TERMS

American Rescue Plan

Inflation Reduction Act

Infrastructure Investment and Jobs Act

*Dobbs v. Jackson Women's Health Organization*

Respect for Marriage Act

Volodymyr Zelensky

Vladimir Putin

## 25.4 | Contemporary America

- Ethnic diversity has made America unique, but it raises questions regarding how people of various cultures and beliefs can share common values.

- Contemporary America is facing a number of social and moral issues, including race, immigration, technology and information, gun violence, climate change, abortion, and LGBTQ+. Positions on these issues are determined by one's worldview, and debates over these issues have often been heated and divisive.

## Chapter Review Questions

### RECALL

1. Who was the first African American president of the United States?

2. "Obamacare" was a nickname for what act?

3. What radical group sought to seize power in Iraq and Syria after the Iraq War?

4. Who won the popular vote in the 2016 election? Who won the electoral vote?

5. What trade agreement replaced the North American Free Trade Agreement (NAFTA)?

6. What was the name of the investigation that looked into alleged collusion between Russia and the Trump campaign?

7. What virus caused the global pandemic which began in 2020?

8. What nations made peace agreements with Israel in the Abraham Accords?

9. What act reversed the Defense of Marriage Act and strengthened federal recognition of same-sex marriages?

### UNDERSTAND

10. What were two government programs that were passed to deal with the Great Recession? What did each do? What was the negative consequence?

11. What was the purpose of the Affordable Care Act? What were its provisions? Why did some criticize the act?

12. What happened to "Don't Ask, Don't Tell" and the Defense of Marriage Act under Obama? What was the decision in *Obergefell v. Hodges*?

13. What did Obama's Deferred Action for Childhood Arrivals (DACA) executive order do? What were the objections to it?

14. What were the issues in the religious liberty cases related to the Affordable Care Act and the *Obergefell* ruling?

15. What was a significant foreign policy event during the Obama administration in each of the following countries: Russia, Cuba, Iraq, Pakistan, Afghanistan, Libya, Iran?

16. What did Trump mean by his "America First" agenda?

17. Why did Trump criticize free trade agreements such as NAFTA?

18. How did the federal courts change under Trump?

19. What led to the Mueller Investigation? What were the conclusions of the investigation?

20. What led to Trump's first impeachment? What was the outcome of the impeachment trial?

21. What were the effects of the COVID-19 pandemic on businesses, churches, schools, and the overall economy? What were the varying responses to the restrictions placed on society during the pandemic?

22. How did Congress respond to the economic disruption of the pandemic during Trump's presidency?

23. What were three changes Trump made to US immigration policy?

24. What were American relations with China and North Korea like under Trump?

25. What significant foreign policy events took place between the United States and each of the following countries during the Trump administration: Iran, Israel, Afghanistan?

26. What was the outcome of the 2020 election? What claims did Trump and his supporters make about the election? How did the courts and Justice Department respond to these allegations?

27. What significant action was Congress to take on January 6, 2021? What happened on that date that disrupted this action?

28. Why was Trump impeached a second time? What was unusual about this impeachment? What was the outcome of the trial?

29. What were four significant acts or proposals under the Biden administration related to the economic effects of the pandemic?

30. How did Biden change American immigration policy from that of Trump?

31. What was the significance of the Supreme Court decision in *Dobbs v. Jackson Women's Health Organization*? How did abortion policy change in America after this?

32. Why was Trump indicted in 2023?

33. When were the final US troops removed from Afghanistan? Describe the withdrawal.

34. What happened in Ukraine in February 2022? What was America's role in the conflict?

## THINK ABOUT IT

35. What are some benefits and challenges of America's ethnic and cultural diversity? Do you think it is possible for a culturally diverse nation to share a common set of values? Explain.

36. How do you think a Christian should approach issues of race and racism? Use biblical principles in your response.

37. What are some benefits that the computer and information revolutions have brought? What are some negative consequences or dangers of these changes? How should Christians view technology?

38. What are the arguments for and against gun control? Which do you find more persuasive? What other steps do you think can be taken to reduce gun violence?

39. How should Christians view environmental issues such as climate change? Do you think climate change threatens human existence? How should the needs of people factor into environmental considerations?

40. How have views on LGBTQ+ issues changed in America in the last decade? What concerns have Christians raised regarding these changing views and their effects on children and families and religious freedom?

41. On social issues such as those discussed in this chapter, how do the opposing sides each view American values (individualism, freedom, equality, and growth) differently? Based on a Christian worldview, how would you define these terms as they relate to these controversial social issues?

42. How do you think Christians should live in an increasingly secular culture? See Genesis 41:37–57; Jeremiah 29:1–9; Daniel 1, 3, and 6; and 1 Peter 1:13–25 for examples from the Bible of believers living in a hostile culture. What lessons can be taken from these examples?

# Appendix A. *Map of the United States*

Olympia

Mt. Rainier

Mt. St. Helens

WASHINGTON

*Columbia R.*

Salem

OREGON

Boise

IDAHO

NEVADA

Sacramento

Carson City

CALIFORNIA

*Sierra Nevada*

Great Salt Lake

Salt Lake City

UTAH

*Colorado R.*

Grand Canyon

ARIZONA

PACIFIC OCEAN

Phoenix

Helena

MONTANA

NORTH DAKOTA

*Badlands*

Bismarck

SOUTH DAKOTA

*Black Hills*

Pierre

WYOMING

*Rocky Mountains*

Cheyenne

*Platte R.*

NEBRASKA

Lincoln

Denver

COLORADO

Pikes Peak

KANSAS

*Arkansas R.*

Santa Fe

NEW MEXICO

*Red R.*

OKLAHOMA

Oklahoma City

TEXAS

Austin

*Rio Grande*

ALASKA

*Yukon R.*

Juneau

Honolulu

HAWAII

0   200 mi

0   200 km

0   100 mi

0   100 km

688

# In CONGRESS, July 4, 1776.

## The unanimous Declaration of the thirteen united States of America.

When in the course of human events, it becomes necessary for one people to dissolve the political bands which have connected them with another, and to assume among the powers of the earth, the separate and equal station to which the laws of nature and of nature's God entitle them, a decent respect to the opinions of mankind requires that they should declare the causes which impel them to the separation.

We hold these truths to be self-evident, that all men are created equal, that they are endowed by their Creator with certain unalienable rights, that among these are life, liberty and the pursuit of happiness.—That to secure these rights, governments are instituted among men, deriving their just powers from the consent of the governed,—That whenever any form of government becomes destructive of these ends, it is the right of the people to alter or to abolish it, and to institute new government, laying its foundation on such principles and organizing its powers in such form, as to them shall seem most likely to effect their safety and happiness. Prudence, indeed, will dictate that governments long established should not be changed for light and transient causes; and accordingly all experience hath shewn, that mankind are more disposed to suffer, while evils are sufferable, than to right themselves by abolishing the forms to which they are accustomed. But when a long train of abuses and usurpations, pursuing invariably the same object evinces a design to reduce them under absolute despotism, it is their right, it is their duty, to throw off such government, and to provide new guards for their future security. — Such has been the patient sufferance of these colonies; and such is now the necessity which constrains them to alter their former systems of government. The history of the present king of Great Britain is a history of repeated injuries and usurpations, all having in direct object the establishment of an absolute tyranny over these states. To prove this, let facts be submitted to a candid world.

He has refused his assent to laws, the most wholesome and necessary for the public good.

He has forbidden his governors to pass laws of immediate and pressing importance, unless suspended in their operation till his assent should be obtained; and when so suspended, he has utterly neglected to attend to them.

He has refused to pass other laws for the accommodation of large districts of people, unless those people would relinquish the right of representation in the legislature, a right inestimable to them and formidable to tyrants only.

He has called together legislative bodies at places unusual, uncomfortable, and distant from the depository of their public records, for the sole purpose of fatiguing them into compliance with his measures.

He has dissolved representative houses repeatedly, for opposing with manly firmness his invasions on the rights of the people.

He has refused for a long time, after such dissolutions, to cause others to be elected; whereby the legislative powers, incapable of annihilation, have returned to the people at large for their exercise; the state remaining in the meantime exposed to all the dangers of invasion from without, and convulsions within.

He has endeavoured to prevent the population of these states; for that purpose obstructing the laws for naturalization of foreigners; refusing to pass others to encourage their migrations hither, and raising the conditions of new appropriations of lands.

He has obstructed the administration of justice, by refusing his assent to laws for establishing judiciary powers.

He has made judges dependent on his will alone, for the tenure of their offices, and the amount and payment of their salaries.

He has erected a multitude of new offices, and sent hither swarms of officers to harass our people, and eat out their substance.

He has kept among us, in times of peace, standing armies without the consent of our legislatures.

He has affected to render the military independent of and superior to the civil power.

He has combined with others to subject us to a jurisdiction foreign to our constitution, and unacknowledged by our laws; giving his assent to their acts of pretended legislation:

For quartering large bodies of armed troops among us:

For protecting them, by a mock trial, from punishment for any murders which they should commit on the inhabitants of these states:

For cutting off our trade with all parts of the world:

For imposing taxes on us without our consent:

For depriving us in many cases, of the benefits of trial by jury:

For transporting us beyond seas to be tried for pretended offenses:

For abolishing the free system of English laws in a neighboring province, establishing therein an arbitrary government, and enlarging its boundaries so as to render it at once an example and fit instrument for introducing the same absolute rule into these colonies:

For taking away our charters, abolishing our most valuable laws, and altering fundamentally the forms of our governments:

For suspending our own legislatures, and declaring themselves invested with power to legislate for us in all cases whatsoever.

He has abdicated government here, by declaring us out of his protection and waging war against us.

He has plundered our seas, ravaged our coasts, burnt our towns, and destroyed the lives of our people.

He is at this time transporting large armies of foreign mercenaries to complete the works of death, desolation and tyranny, already begun with circumstances of cruelty and perfidy scarcely paralleled in the most barbarous ages, and totally unworthy the head of a civilized nation.

He has constrained our fellow citizens taken captive on the high seas to bear arms against their country, to become the executioners of their friends and brethren, or to fall themselves by their hands.

He has excited domestic insurrections amongst us, and has endeavored to bring on the inhabitants of our frontiers, the merciless Indian savages, whose known rule of warfare, is an undistinguished destruction of all ages, sexes and conditions.

In every stage of these oppressions, we have petitioned for redress in the most humble terms: our repeated petitions have been answered only by repeated injury. A prince whose character is thus marked by every act which may define a tyrant, is unfit to be the ruler of a free people.

Nor have we been wanting in attentions to our British brethren. We have warned them from time to time of attempts by their legislature to extend an unwarrantable jurisdiction over us. We have reminded them of the circumstances of our emigration and settlement here. We have appealed to their native justice and magnanimity, and we have conjured them by the ties of our common kindred to disavow these usurpations, which, would inevitably interrupt our connections and correspondence. They too have been deaf to the voice of justice and of consanguinity. We must, therefore, acquiesce in the necessity, which denounces our separation, and hold them, as we hold the rest of mankind, enemies in war, in peace friends.

We, therefore, the representatives of the united states of America, in general congress, assembled, appealing to the Supreme Judge of the world for the rectitude of our intentions, do, in the name, and by authority of the good people of these colonies, solemnly publish and declare, that these united colonies are, and of right ought to be free and independent states; that they are absolved from all allegiance to the British Crown, and that all political connection between them and the state of Great Britain, is and ought to be totally dissolved; and that as free and independent states, they have full power to levy war, conclude peace, contract alliances, establish commerce, and to do all other acts and things which independent states may of right do. And for the support of this declaration, with a firm reliance on the protection of divine Providence, we mutually pledge to each other our lives, our fortunes and our sacred honor.

 of the United States, in order to form a more perfect union, establish justice, insure domestic tranquility, provide for the common defense, promote the general welfare, and secure the blessings of liberty to ourselves and our posterity, do ordain and establish this Constitution for the United States of America.

★ ★ ★

## Article I: The Legislative Branch

### SECTION 1

All legislative powers herein granted shall be vested in a Congress of the United States, which shall consist of a Senate and House of Representatives.

### SECTION 2

1. The House of Representatives shall be composed of members chosen every second year by the people of the several states, and the electors in each state shall have the qualifications requisite for electors of the most numerous branch of the state legislature.

2. No person shall be a representative who shall not have attained to the age of twenty-five years, and been seven years a citizen of the United States, and who shall not, when elected, be an inhabitant of that state in which he shall be chosen.

3. Representatives and direct taxes shall be apportioned among the several states which may be included within this Union, according to their respective numbers, *which shall be determined by adding to the whole number of free persons, including those bound to service for a term of years, and excluding Indians not taxed, three-fifths of all other persons.* The actual enumeration shall be made within three years after the first meeting of the Congress of the United States, and within every subsequent term of ten years, in such manner as they shall by law direct. The number of representatives shall not exceed one for every thirty thousand, but each state shall have at least one representative; *and until such enumeration shall be made, the state of New Hampshire shall be entitled to choose three, Massachusetts eight, Rhode Island and Providence Plantations one, Connecticut five, New York six, New Jersey four, Pennsylvania eight, Delaware one, Maryland six, Virginia ten, North Carolina five, South Carolina five, and Georgia three.*

4. When vacancies happen in the representation from any state, the executive authority thereof shall issue writs of election to fill such vacancies.

5. The House of Representatives shall choose their speaker and other officers; and shall have the sole power of impeachment.

### SECTION 3

1. The Senate of the United States shall be composed of two senators from each state, chosen by the legislature thereof, for six years; and each senator shall have one vote.

2. Immediately after they shall be assembled in consequence of the first election, they shall be divided as equally as may be into three classes. *The seats of the senators of the first class shall be vacated at the expiration of the second year, of the second class at the expiration of the fourth year, and of the third class at the expiration of the sixth year,* so that one-third may be chosen every second year; *and if vacancies happen by resignation, or otherwise, during the recess of the legislature of any state, the executive thereof may make temporary appointments until the next meeting of the legislature, which shall then fill such vacancies.*

3. No person shall be a senator who shall not have attained to the age of thirty years, and been nine years a citizen of the United States, and who shall not, when elected, be an inhabitant of that state for which he shall be chosen.

4. The vice president of the United States shall be president of the Senate, but shall have no vote, unless they be equally divided.

5. The Senate shall choose their other officers, and also a president pro tempore, in the absence of the vice president, or when he shall exercise the office of president of the United States.

6. The Senate shall have the sole power to try all impeachments. When sitting for that purpose, they shall

[Note: Words in *italics* are sections of the Constitution that are no longer in force.]

be on oath or affirmation. When the president of the United States is tried, the chief justice shall preside: And no person shall be convicted without the concurrence of two-thirds of the members present.

7. Judgment in cases of impeachment shall not extend further than to removal from office, and disqualification to hold and enjoy any office of honor, trust or profit under the United States: but the party convicted shall nevertheless be liable and subject to indictment, trial, judgment and punishment, according to law.

## SECTION 4

1. The times, places and manner of holding elections for senators and representatives, shall be prescribed in each state by the legislature thereof; but the Congress may at any time by law make or alter such regulations, except as to the places of choosing senators.

2. The Congress shall assemble at least once in every year, *and such meeting shall be on the first Monday in December, unless they shall by law appoint a different day.*

## SECTION 5

1. Each house shall be the judge of the elections, returns and qualifications of its own members, and a majority of each shall constitute a quorum to do business; but a smaller number may adjourn from day to day, and may be authorized to compel the attendance of absent members, in such manner, and under such penalties as each house may provide.

2. Each house may determine the rules of its proceedings, punish its members for disorderly behavior, and, with the concurrence of two-thirds, expel a member.

3. Each house shall keep a journal of its proceedings, and from time to time publish the same, excepting such parts as may in their judgment, require secrecy; and the yeas and nays of the members of either house on any question shall, at the desire of one-fifth of those present, be entered on the journal.

4. Neither house, during the session of Congress, shall, without the consent of the other, adjourn for more than three days, nor to any other place than that in which the two houses shall be sitting.

## SECTION 6

1. The senators and representatives shall receive a compensation for their services, to be ascertained by law, and paid out of the treasury of the United States. They shall in all cases, except treason, felony, and breach of the peace, be privileged from arrest during their attendance at the session of their respective houses, and in going to and returning from the same; and for any speech or debate in either house, they shall not be questioned in any other place.

2. No senator or representative shall, during the time for which he was elected, be appointed to any civil office under the authority of the United States, which shall have been created, or the emoluments whereof shall have been increased during such time; and no person holding any office under the United States, shall be a member of either house during his continuance in office.

## SECTION 7

1. All bills for raising revenue shall originate in the House of Representatives; but the Senate may propose or concur with amendments as on other bills.

2. Every bill which shall have passed the House of Representatives and the Senate, shall, before it become a law, be presented to the president of the United States; if he approve he shall sign it, but if not he shall return it, with his objections to that house in which it shall have originated, who shall enter the objections at large on their journal, and proceed to reconsider it. If after such reconsideration two-thirds of that house shall agree to pass the bill, it shall be sent, together with the objections, to the other house, by which it shall likewise be reconsidered, and if approved by two-thirds of that house, it shall become a law. But in all such cases the votes of both houses shall be determined by yeas and nays, and the names of the persons voting for and against the bill shall be entered on the journal of each house respectively. If any bill shall not be returned by the president within ten days (Sundays excepted) after it shall have been presented to him, the same shall be a law, in like manner as if he had signed it, unless the Congress by their adjournment prevent its return, in which case it shall not be a law.

3. Every order, resolution, or vote to which the concurrence of the Senate and House of Representatives may be necessary (except on a question of adjournment) shall be presented to the president of the United States; and before the same shall take effect, shall be approved by him, or, being disapproved by him, shall be repassed by two-thirds of the Senate and House of Representatives, according to the rules and limitations prescribed in the case of a bill.

## SECTION 8

*The Congress shall have power*

1. To lay and collect taxes, duties, imposts and excises, to pay the debts and provide for the common defense and general welfare of the United States; but all duties, imposts and excises shall be uniform throughout the United States;

2. To borrow money on the credit of the United States;

3. To regulate commerce with foreign nations, and among the several states, and with the Indian tribes;

4. To establish a uniform rule of naturalization, and uniform laws on the subject of bankruptcies throughout the United States;

5. To coin money, regulate the value thereof, and of foreign coin, and fix the standard of weights and measures;

6. To provide for the punishment of counterfeiting the securities and current coin of the United States;

7. To establish post-offices and post-roads;

8. To promote the progress of science and useful arts, by securing for limited times to authors and inventors the exclusive right to their respective writings and discoveries;

9. To constitute tribunals inferior to the Supreme Court;

10. To define and punish piracies and felonies committed on the high seas, and offenses against the law of nations;

11. To declare war, grant letters of marque and reprisal, and make rules concerning captures on land and water;

12. To raise and support armies, but no appropriation of money to that use shall be for a longer term than two years;

13. To provide and maintain a navy;

14. To make rules for the government and regulation of the land and naval forces;

15. To provide for calling forth the militia to execute the laws of the Union, suppress insurrections and repel invasions;

16. To provide for organizing, arming, and disciplining, the militia, and for governing such part of them as may be employed in the service of the United States, reserving to the states respectively, the appointment of the officers, and the authority of training the militia according to the discipline prescribed by Congress;

17. To exercise exclusive legislation in all cases whatsoever, over such district (not exceeding ten miles square) as may, by cession of particular states, and the acceptance of Congress, become the seat of the government of the United States, and to exercise like authority over all places purchased by the consent of the legislature of the state in which the same shall be, for the erection of forts, magazines, arsenals, dock-yards, and other needful buildings; and

18. To make all laws which shall be necessary and proper for carrying into execution the foregoing powers, and all other powers vested by this Constitution in the government of the United States, or in any department or officer thereof.

## SECTION 9

1. The migration or importation of such persons as any of the states now existing shall think proper to admit, shall not be prohibited by the Congress prior to the year 1808, but a tax or duty may be imposed on such importation, not exceeding ten dollars for each person.

2. The privilege of the writ of habeas corpus shall not be suspended, unless when in cases of rebellion or invasion the public safety may require it.

3. No bill of attainder or ex post facto law shall be passed.

4. No capitation, or other direct tax shall be laid, *unless in proportion to the census or enumeration herein before directed to be taken.*

5. No tax or duty shall be laid on articles exported from any state.

6. No preference shall be given by any regulation of commerce or revenue to the ports of one state over those of another: nor shall vessels bound to, or from one state, be obliged to enter, clear, or pay duties in another.

7. No money shall be drawn from the treasury but in consequence of appropriations made by law; and a regular statement and account of the receipts and expenditures of all public money shall be published from time to time.

8. No title of nobility shall be granted by the United States: and no person holding any office of profit or trust under them, shall, without the consent of the Congress, accept of any present, emolument, office, or title, of any kind whatever, from any king, prince or foreign state.

## SECTION 10

1. No state shall enter into any treaty, alliance, or confederation; grant letters of marque and reprisal; coin money; emit bills of credit; make any thing but gold and silver coin a tender in payment of debts; pass any bill of attainder, ex post facto law, or law impairing the obligation of contracts, or grant any title of nobility.

2. No state shall, without the consent of the Congress, lay any imposts or duties on imports or exports, except what may be absolutely necessary for executing its inspection laws; and the net produce of all duties and imposts, laid by any state on imports or exports, shall be for the use of the treasury of the United States; and all such laws shall be subject to the revision and control of the Congress.

3. No state shall, without the consent of Congress, lay any duty of tonnage, keep troops, or ships of war in time of peace, enter into any agreement or compact with another state, or with a foreign power, or engage in war, unless actually invaded, or in such imminent danger as will not admit of delay.

# Article II: The Executive Branch

## SECTION 1

1. The executive power shall be vested in a president of the United States of America. He shall hold his office during the term of four years, and, together with the vice president, chosen for the same term, be elected as follows.

2. Each state shall appoint, in such manner as the legislature thereof may direct, a number of electors, equal to the whole number of senators and representatives to which the state may be entitled in the Congress; but no senator or representative, or person holding an office of trust or profit under the United States, shall be appointed an elector.

*The electors shall meet in their respective states, and vote by ballot for two persons, of whom one at least shall not be an inhabitant of the same state with themselves. And they shall make a list of all the persons voted for, and of the number of votes for each; which list they shall sign and certify, and transmit sealed to the seat of the government of the United States, directed to the president of the Senate. The president of the Senate shall, in the presence of the Senate and House of Representatives, open all the certificates, and the votes shall then be counted. The person having the greatest number of votes shall be the president, if such number be a majority of the whole number of electors appointed; and if there be more than one who have such majority, and have an equal number of votes, then the House of Representatives shall immediately choose by ballot one of them for president; and if no person have a majority, then from the five highest on the list the said House shall in like manner choose the president. But in choosing the president, the votes shall be taken by states, the representation from each state having one vote; a quorum for this purpose shall consist of a member or members from two-thirds of the states, and a majority of all the states shall be necessary to a choice. In every case, after the choice of the president, the person having the greatest number of votes of the electors shall be the vice president. But if there should remain two or more who have equal votes, the Senate shall choose from them by ballot the vice president.*

3. The Congress may determine the time of choosing the electors, and the day on which they shall give their votes; which day shall be the same throughout the United States.

4. No person except a natural born citizen, *or a citizen of the United States, at the time of the adoption of this Constitution,* shall be eligible to the office of president, neither shall any person be eligible to that office who shall not have attained to the age of thirty-five years, and been fourteen years a resident within the United States.

5. *In case of the removal of the president from office, or of his death, resignation, or inability to discharge the powers and duties of the said office, the same shall devolve on the vice president, and the Congress may by law provide for the case of removal, death, resignation, or inability, both of the president and vice president, declaring what officer shall then act as president, and such officer shall act accordingly, until the disability be removed, or a president shall be elected.*

6. The president shall, at stated times, receive for his services, a compensation, which shall neither be increased nor diminished during the period for which he shall have been elected, and he shall not receive within that period any other emolument from the United States, or any of them.

7. Before he enter on the execution of his office, he shall take the following oath or affirmation:—"I do solemnly swear (or affirm) that I will faithfully execute the office of president of the United States, and will to the best of my ability, preserve, protect and defend the Constitution of the United States."

## SECTION 2

1. The president shall be commander in chief of the army and navy of the United States, and of the militia of the several states, when called into the actual service of the United States; he may require the opinion, in writing, of the principal officer in each of the executive departments, upon any subject relating to the duties of their respective offices, and he shall have power to grant reprieves and pardons for offenses against the United States, except in cases of impeachment.

2. He shall have power, by and with the advice and consent of the Senate, to make treaties, provided two-thirds of the senators present concur; and he shall nominate, and by and with the advice and consent of the Senate, shall appoint ambassadors, other public ministers and consuls, judges of the Supreme Court, and all other officers of the United States, whose appointments are not herein otherwise provided for, and which shall be established by law; but the Congress may by law vest the appointment of such inferior officers, as they think proper, in the president alone, in the courts of law, or in the heads of departments.

3. The president shall have power to fill up all vacancies that may happen during the recess of the Senate, by granting commissions which shall expire at the end of their next session.

## SECTION 3

He shall from time to time give to the Congress information of the state of the Union, and recommend to their consideration such measures as he shall judge necessary and expedient; he may, on extraordinary occasions, convene both houses, or either of them, and in case of disagreement between them, with respect to the time of adjournment, he may adjourn them to such time as he shall think proper; he shall receive ambassadors and other public ministers; he shall take care that the laws be faithfully executed, and shall commission all the officers of the United States.

## SECTION 4

The president, vice president, and all civil officers of the United States shall be removed from office on impeachment for, and conviction of, treason, bribery, or other high crimes and misdemeanors.

# Article III: The Judicial Branch

## SECTION 1

The judicial power of the United States shall be vested in one Supreme Court, and in such inferior courts as the Congress may from time to time, ordain and establish. The judges, both of the Supreme and inferior courts, shall hold their offices during good behavior, and shall, at stated times, receive for their services a compensation, which shall not be diminished during their continuance in office.

## SECTION 2

1.  The judicial power shall extend to all cases, in law and equity, arising under this Constitution, the laws of the United States, and treaties made, or which shall be made, under their authority; to all cases affecting ambassadors, other public ministers and consuls; to all cases of admiralty and maritime jurisdiction; to controversies to which the United States shall be a party; to controversies between two or more states; *between a state and citizens of another state*; between citizens of different states, between citizens of the same state claiming lands under grants of different states, and between a state, or the citizens thereof, and foreign states, citizens or subjects.

2.  In all cases affecting ambassadors, other public ministers and consuls, and those in which a state shall be party, the Supreme Court shall have original jurisdiction. In all the other cases before mentioned, the Supreme Court shall have appellate jurisdiction, both as to law and fact, with such exceptions, and under such regulations as the Congress shall make.

3.  The trial of all crimes, except in cases of impeachment, shall be by jury; and such trial shall be held in the state where the said crimes shall have been committed; but when not committed within any state, the trial shall be at such place or places as the Congress may by law have directed.

## SECTION 3

1.  Treason against the United States shall consist only in levying war against them, or in adhering to their enemies, giving them aid and comfort. No person shall be convicted of treason unless on the testimony of two witnesses to the same overt act, or on confession in open court.

2.  The Congress shall have power to declare the punishment of treason, but no attainder of treason shall work corruption of blood, or forfeiture except during the life of the person attained.

# Article IV: Interstate Relations

## SECTION 1

Full faith and credit shall be given in each state to the public acts, records and judicial proceedings of every other state. And the Congress may by general laws prescribe the manner in which such acts, records and proceedings shall be proved, and the effect thereof.

## SECTION 2

1.  The citizens of each state shall be entitled to all privileges and immunities of citizens in the several states.

2.  A person charged in any state with treason, felony, or other crime, who shall flee from justice, and be found in another state, shall on demand of the executive authority of the state from which he fled, be delivered up, to be removed to the state having jurisdiction of the crime.

3. *No person held to service or labor in one state, under the laws thereof, escaping into another, shall, in consequence of any law or regulation therein, be discharged from such service or labor but shall be delivered up on claim of the party to whom such service or labor may be due.*

## SECTION 3

1.  New states may be admitted by the Congress into this Union; but no new state shall be formed or erected within the jurisdiction of any other state; nor any state be formed by the junction of two or more states, or parts of states, without the consent of the legislatures of the states concerned as well as of the Congress.

2.  The Congress shall have power to dispose of and make all needful rules and regulations respecting the territory or other property belonging to the United States; and nothing in this Constitution shall be so construed as to prejudice any claims of the United States, or of any particular state.

## SECTION 4

The United States shall guarantee to every state in this Union a republican form of government, and shall protect each of them against invasion; and on application of the legislature, or of the executive (when the legislature cannot be convened), against domestic violence.

# Article V: Amending the Constitution

The Congress, whenever two-thirds of both houses shall deem it necessary, shall propose amendments to this Constitution, or, on the application of the legislatures of two-thirds of the several states, shall call a convention for proposing amendments, which, in either case, shall be valid to all intents and purposes, as part of this Constitution, when ratified by the legislatures of three-fourths of the several states, or by conventions in three-fourths thereof, as the one or the other mode of ratification may be proposed by the Congress; Provided that no amendment which may be made prior to the year 1808 shall in any manner affect the first and fourth clauses in the ninth section of the first article; and that no state, without its consent, shall be deprived of its equal suffrage in the Senate.

# Article VI: Constitutional and National Supremacy

1.  All debts contracted and engagements entered into, before the adoption of this Constitution, shall be as valid against the United States under this Constitution, as under the confederation.

2.  This Constitution, and the laws of the United States which shall be made in pursuance thereof; and all treaties made, or which shall be made, under the authority of the United States, shall be the supreme law of the land; and

the judges in every state shall be bound thereby, anything in the constitution or laws of any state to the contrary notwithstanding.

3. The senators and representatives before mentioned, and the members of the several state legislatures, and all executive and judicial officers, both of the United States and of the several states, shall be bound by oath or affirmation, to support this Constitution; but no religious test shall ever be required as a qualification to any office or public trust under the United States.

# Article VII: Ratifying the Constitution

The ratification of the conventions of nine states shall be sufficient for the establishment of this Constitution between the states so ratifying the same. Done in convention by the unanimous consent by the states present, the seventeenth day of September in the year of our Lord 1787 and of the independence of the United States of America the twelfth. In witness whereof we have hereunto subscribed our names,

George Washington, President and deputy from Virginia

## DELAWARE
George Read
Gunning Bedford Jr.
John Dickinson
Richard Bassett
Jacob Broom

## MARYLAND
James McHenry
Daniel of St. Thomas Jenifer
Daniel Carroll

## VIRGINIA
John Blair
James Madison Jr.

## NORTH CAROLINA
William Blount
Richard Dobbs Spaight
Hugh Williamson

## SOUTH CAROLINA
John Rutledge
Charles Cotesworth Pinckney
Charles Pinckney
Pierce Butler

## GEORGIA
William Few
Abraham Baldwin

## NEW HAMPSHIRE
John Langdon
Nicholas Gilman

## MASSACHUSETTS
Nathaniel Gorham
Rufus King

## CONNECTICUT
William Samuel Johnson
Roger Sherman

## NEW YORK
Alexander Hamilton

## NEW JERSEY
William Livingston
David Brearley
William Paterson
Jonathan Dayton

## PENNSYLVANIA
Benjamin Franklin
Thomas Mifflin
Robert Morris
George Clymer
Thomas FitzSimons
Jared Ingersoll
James Wilson
Gouverneur Morris

# Amendments to the Constitution

(Amendments I–X, known as the Bill of Rights, ratified December 15, 1791)

## Amendment I: Foundational Freedoms

Congress shall make no law respecting an establishment of religion, or prohibiting the free exercise thereof; or abridging the freedom of speech or of the press; or the right of the people peaceably to assemble, and to petition the government for a redress of grievances.

## Amendment II: The Right to Bear Arms

A well-regulated militia being necessary to the security of a free state, the right of the people to keep and bear arms shall not be infringed.

## Amendment III: No Quartering of Troops

No soldier shall, in time of peace, be quartered in any house without the consent of the owner, nor in time of war, but in a manner to be prescribed by law.

## Amendment IV: No Unreasonable Searches

The right of the people to be secure in their persons, houses, papers, and effects, against unreasonable searches and seizures, shall not be violated, and no warrants shall issue but upon probable cause, supported by oath or affirmation, and particularly describing the place to be searched, and the persons or things to be seized.

## Amendment V: Rights of the Accused

No person shall be held to answer for a capital or otherwise infamous crime, unless on a presentment or indictment of a grand jury, except in cases arising in the land or naval forces, or in the militia, when in actual service in time of war or public danger; nor shall any person be subject for the same offense to be twice put in jeopardy of life or limb; nor shall be compelled in any criminal case to be a witness against himself, nor be deprived of life, liberty, or property, without due process of law; nor shall private property be taken for public use without just compensation.

## Amendment VI: Rights of the Accused in Criminal Trials

In all criminal prosecutions, the accused shall enjoy the right to a speedy and public trial, by an impartial jury of the state and district wherein the crime shall have been committed, which district shall have been previously ascertained by law, and to be informed of the nature and cause of the accusation; to be confronted with the witnesses against him; to have compulsory process for obtaining witnesses in his favor, and to have the assistance of counsel for his defense.

## Amendment VII: Rights of Citizens in Civil Trials

In suits at common law, where the value in controversy shall exceed twenty dollars, the right of trial by jury shall be preserved, and no fact tried by a jury shall be otherwise re-examined in any court of the United States than according to the rules of the common law.

## Amendment VIII: Cruel, Unusual, and Unjust Punishments

Excessive bail shall not be required, nor excessive fines imposed, nor cruel and unusual punishments inflicted.

## Amendment IX: Unspecified Rights

The enumeration in the Constitution of certain rights shall not be construed to deny or disparage others retained by the people.

## Amendment X: Unlisted Rights Go to States or to the People

The powers not delegated to the United States by the Constitution, nor prohibited by it to the states, are reserved to the states respectively, or to the people.

## Amendment XI: Suing States

(Passed March 4, 1794; ratified February 7, 1795)

The judicial power of the United States shall not be construed to extend to any suit in law or equity, commenced or prosecuted against one of the United States by citizens of another state, or by citizens or subjects of any foreign state.

## Amendment XII: Separate Ballots for President and Vice President

(Passed December 9, 1803; ratified June 15, 1804)

The electors shall meet in their respective states and vote by ballot for president and vice president, one of whom, at least, shall not be an inhabitant of the same state with themselves; they shall name in their ballots the person voted for as president, and in distinct ballots the person voted for as vice president, and they shall make distinct lists of all persons voted for as president, and of all persons voted for as vice president, and of the number of votes for each, which lists they shall sign and certify, and transmit sealed to the seat of the government of the United States, directed to the president of the Senate; the president of the Senate shall, in the presence of the Senate and House of Representatives, open all the certificates and the votes shall then be counted; the person having the greatest number of votes for president, shall be the president, if such number be a majority of the whole number of electors appointed; and if no person have such majority, then from the persons having the highest numbers not exceeding three on the list of those voted for as president, the House of Representatives shall choose immediately, by ballot, the president. But in choosing the president, the votes shall be taken by states, the representation from each state having one vote; a quorum for this purpose shall consist of a member or members from two-thirds of the states, and a majority of all the states shall be necessary to a choice. And if the House of Representatives shall not choose a president whenever the right of choice shall devolve upon them, *before the fourth day of March next following,* then the vice president shall act as president, as in case of the death or other constitutional disability of the president. The person having the greatest number of votes as vice president shall be the vice president, if such number be a majority of the whole number of electors appointed, and if no person have a majority, then from the two highest numbers on the list, the Senate shall choose the vice president; a quorum for the purpose shall consist of two-thirds of the whole number of senators, and a majority of the whole number shall be necessary to a choice. But no person constitutionally ineligible to the office of president shall be eligible to that of vice president of the United States.

## Amendment XIII: Slavery

(Passed January 31, 1865; ratified December 6, 1865)

### SECTION 1

Neither slavery nor involuntary servitude, except as a punishment for crime whereof the party shall have been duly convicted, shall exist within the United States, or any place subject to their jurisdiction.

### SECTION 2

Congress shall have power to enforce this article by appropriate legislation.

## Amendment XIV: Citizenship

(Passed June 13, 1866; ratified July 9, 1868)

### SECTION 1

All persons born or naturalized in the United States, and subject to the jurisdiction thereof, are citizens of the United States and of the state wherein they reside. No state shall make or enforce any law which shall abridge the privileges or immunities of citizens of the United States; nor shall any state deprive any person of life, liberty, or property, without due process of law; nor deny to any person within its jurisdiction the equal protection of the laws.

### SECTION 2

Representatives shall be apportioned among the several states according to their respective numbers, counting the whole number of persons in each state, excluding Indians not taxed. But when the right to vote at any election for the choice of electors for president and vice president of the United States, representatives in Congress, the executive and judicial officers of a state, or the members of the legislature thereof, is denied to any of the *male inhabitants* of such state, *being of twenty-one years of age*, and citizens of the United States, or in any way abridged, except for participation in rebellion, or other crime, the basis of representation therein shall be reduced in the proportion which the number of such *male* citizens shall bear to the whole number of *male citizens twenty-one years of age* in such state.

### SECTION 3

No person shall be a senator or representative in Congress, or elector of president and vice president, or hold any office, civil or military, under the United States, or under any state, who having previously taken an oath, as a member of Congress, or as an officer of the United States, or as a member of any state legislature, or as an executive or judicial officer of any state, to support the Constitution of the United States, shall have engaged in insurrection or rebellion against the same, or given aid and comfort to the enemies thereof. But Congress may by a vote of two-thirds of each house remove such disability.

### SECTION 4

The validity of the public debt of the United States, authorized by law, including debts incurred for payment of pensions and bounties for services in suppressing insurrection or rebellion, shall not be questioned. But neither the United States nor any state shall assume or pay any debt or obligation incurred in aid of insurrection or rebellion against the United States, or any claim for the loss or emancipation of any slave; but all such debts, obligations, and claims shall be held illegal and void.

### SECTION 5

The Congress shall have the power to enforce, by appropriate legislation, the provisions of this article.

## Amendment XV: Black Voting Rights

(Passed February 26, 1869; ratified February 3, 1870)

### SECTION 1

The right of the citizens of the United States to vote shall not be denied or abridged by the United States or by any state on account of race, color, or previous condition of servitude.

### SECTION 2

The Congress shall have power to enforce this article by appropriate legislation.

## Amendment XVI: Income Tax

(Passed July 2, 1909; ratified February 3, 1913)

The Congress shall have power to lay and collect taxes on incomes, from whatever source derived, without apportionment among the several states, and without regard to any census or enumeration.

## Amendment XVII: Direct Election of Senators

(Passed May 13, 1912; ratified April 8, 1913)

The Senate of the United States shall be composed of two senators from each state, elected by the people thereof, for six years; and each senator shall have one vote. The electors in each state shall have the qualifications requisite for electors of the most numerous branch of the state legislatures.

When vacancies happen in the representation of any state in the Senate, the executive authority of such state shall issue writs of election to fill such vacancies: provided, that the legislature of any state may empower the executive thereof to make temporary appointments until the people fill the vacancies by election as the legislature may direct.

This amendment shall not be so construed as to affect the election or term of any senator chosen before it becomes valid as part of the Constitution.

## Amendment XVIII: Prohibition

(Passed December 18, 1917; ratified January 16, 1919; repealed by Amendment XXI.)

### SECTION 1

*After one year from the ratification of this article the manufacture, sale, or transportation of intoxicating liquors within, the importation thereof into, or the exportation thereof from the United States and all territory subject to the jurisdiction thereof for beverage purposes is hereby prohibited.*

### SECTION 2

*The Congress and the several states shall have concurrent power to enforce this article by appropriate legislation.*

### SECTION 3

*This article shall be inoperative unless it shall have been ratified as an amendment to the Constitution by the legislatures of the several states, as provided in the Constitution, within seven years from the date of the submission hereof to the states by the Congress.*

## Amendment XIX: Women's Suffrage

(Passed June 4, 1919; ratified August 18, 1920)

### SECTION 1

The right of the citizens of the United States to vote shall not be denied or abridged by the United States or by any state on account of sex.

### SECTION 2

Congress shall have power to enforce this article by appropriate legislation.

## Amendment XX: Lame Duck Amendment

(Passed March 2, 1932; ratified January 23, 1933)

### SECTION 1

The terms of the president and the vice president shall end at noon on the 20th day of January, and the terms of senators and representatives at noon on the 3rd day of January, of the years in which such terms would have ended if this article had not been ratified; and the terms of their successors shall then begin.

### SECTION 2

The Congress shall assemble at least once in every year, and such meeting shall begin at noon on the 3rd day of January, unless they shall by law appoint a different day.

### SECTION 3

If, at the time fixed for the beginning of the term of the president, the president-elect shall have died, the vice president-elect shall become president. If a president shall not have been chosen before the time fixed for the beginning of his term, or if the president-elect shall have failed to qualify, then the vice president-elect shall act as president until a president shall have qualified; and the Congress may by law provide for the case wherein neither a president-elect nor a vice president-elect shall have qualified, declaring who shall then act as president, or the manner in which one who is to act shall be selected, and such person shall act accordingly until a president or vice president shall have qualified.

### SECTION 4

The Congress may by law provide for the case of the death of any of the persons from whom the House of Representatives may choose a president whenever the right of choice shall have devolved upon them, and for the case of the death of any of the persons from whom the Senate may choose a vice president whenever the right of choice shall have devolved upon them.

### SECTION 5

Sections 1 and 2 shall take effect on the 15th day of October following the ratification of this article.

### SECTION 6

This article shall be inoperative unless it shall have been ratified as an amendment to the Constitution by the legislatures of three-fourths of the several states within seven years from the date of its submission.

## Amendment XXI: Repeal of Prohibition

(Passed February 20, 1933; ratified December 5, 1933)

### SECTION 1

The eighteenth article of amendment to the Constitution of the United States is hereby repealed.

### SECTION 2

The transportation or importation into any state, territory, or possession of the United States for delivery or use therein of intoxicating liquors, in violation of the laws thereof, is hereby prohibited.

### SECTION 3

This article shall be inoperative unless it shall have been ratified as an amendment to the Constitution by conventions in the several states, as provided in the Constitution, within seven years from the date of the submission thereof to the states by the Congress.

## Amendment XXII: Presidential Terms

(Passed March 21, 1947; ratified February 27, 1951)

### SECTION 1

No person shall be elected to the office of the president more than twice, and no person who has held the office of president, or acted as president, for more than two years of a term to which some other person who was elected president shall be elected to the office of the president more than once. But this article shall not apply to any person holding the office of president when this article was proposed by the Congress, and shall not prevent any person who may be holding the office of president, or acting as president, during the term within which this article becomes operative from holding the office of president, or acting as president during the remainder of such term.

## SECTION 2

This article shall be inoperative unless it shall have been ratified as an amendment to the Constitution by the legislatures of three-fourths of the several states within seven years from the date of its submission to the states by the Congress.

## Amendment XXIII: Voting for Washington, DC

(Passed June 16, 1960; ratified March 29, 1961)

### SECTION 1

The District constituting the seat of government of the United States shall appoint in such manner as the Congress may direct:

A number of electors of president and vice president equal to the whole number of senators and representatives in Congress to which the District would be entitled if it were a state, but in no event more than the least populous state; they shall be in addition to those appointed by the states, but they shall be considered, for the purposes of the election of president and vice president, to be electors appointed by a state; and they shall meet in the District and perform such duties as provided by the twelfth article of amendment.

### SECTION 2

The Congress shall have power to enforce this article by appropriate legislation.

## Amendment XXIV: No Poll Tax

(Passed August 27, 1962; ratified January 23, 1964)

### SECTION 1

The right of citizens of the United States to vote in any primary or other election for president or vice president, for electors for president or vice president, or for senator or representative in Congress, shall not be denied or abridged by the United States or any state by reason of failure to pay any poll tax or other tax.

### SECTION 2

The Congress shall have the power to enforce this article by appropriate legislation.

## Amendment XXV: Presidential Succession

(Passed July 6, 1965; ratified February 10, 1967)

### SECTION 1

In case of the removal of the president from office or of his death or resignation, the vice president shall become president.

### SECTION 2

Whenever there is a vacancy in the office of the vice president, the president shall nominate a vice president who shall take office upon confirmation by a majority vote of both houses of Congress.

### SECTION 3

Whenever the president transmits to the president pro tempore of the Senate and the Speaker of the House of Representatives his written declaration that he is unable to discharge the powers and duties of his office, and until he transmits to them a written declaration to the contrary, such powers and duties shall be discharged by the vice president as acting president.

### SECTION 4

Whenever the vice president and a majority of either the principal officers of the executive departments or of such other body as Congress may by law provide, transmit to the president pro tempore of the Senate and the Speaker of the House of Representatives their written declaration that the president is unable to discharge the powers and duties of his office, the vice president shall immediately assume the powers and duties of the office as acting president.

Thereafter, when the president transmits to the president pro tempore of the Senate and the Speaker of the House of Representatives his written declaration that no inability exists, he shall resume the powers and duties of his office unless the vice president and a majority of either the principal officers of the executive department or of such other body as Congress may by law provide, transmit within four days to the president pro tempore of the Senate and the Speaker of the House of Representatives their written declaration that the president is unable to discharge the powers and duties of his office. Thereupon Congress shall decide the issue, assembling within forty-eight hours for that purpose if not in session. If the Congress, within twenty-one days after receipt of the latter written declaration, or, if Congress is not in session, within twenty-one days after Congress is required to assemble, determines by two-thirds vote of both houses that the president is unable to discharge the powers and duties of his office, the vice president shall continue to discharge the same as acting president; otherwise, the president shall resume the powers and duties of his office.

## Amendment XXVI: Eighteen-Year-Old Vote

(Proposed March 23, 1971; ratified July 1, 1971)

### SECTION 1

The right of citizens of the United States, who are eighteen years of age or older, to vote shall not be denied or abridged by the United States or by any state on account of age.

### SECTION 2

The Congress shall have power to enforce this article by appropriate legislation.

## Amendment XXVII: Congressional Pay Raises

(Passed September 25, 1789; ratified May 7, 1992)

No law, varying the compensation for the services of the senators and representatives, shall take effect until an election of representatives shall have intervened.

# Appendix D. *States of the Union*

| Order of Admission | State | Year of Admission | Capital City |
|---|---|---|---|
| 1 | Delaware | 1787 | Dover |
| 2 | Pennsylvania | 1787 | Harrisburg |
| 3 | New Jersey | 1787 | Trenton |
| 4 | Georgia | 1788 | Atlanta |
| 5 | Connecticut | 1788 | Hartford |
| 6 | Massachusetts | 1788 | Boston |
| 7 | Maryland | 1788 | Annapolis |
| 8 | South Carolina | 1788 | Columbia |
| 9 | New Hampshire | 1788 | Concord |
| 10 | Virginia | 1788 | Richmond |
| 11 | New York | 1788 | Albany |
| 12 | North Carolina | 1789 | Raleigh |
| 13 | Rhode Island | 1790 | Providence |
| 14 | Vermont | 1791 | Montpelier |
| 15 | Kentucky | 1792 | Frankfort |
| 16 | Tennessee | 1796 | Nashville |
| 17 | Ohio | 1803 | Columbus |
| 18 | Louisiana | 1812 | Baton Rouge |
| 19 | Indiana | 1816 | Indianapolis |
| 20 | Mississippi | 1817 | Jackson |
| 21 | Illinois | 1818 | Springfield |
| 22 | Alabama | 1819 | Montgomery |
| 23 | Maine | 1820 | Augusta |
| 24 | Missouri | 1821 | Jefferson City |
| 25 | Arkansas | 1836 | Little Rock |
| 26 | Michigan | 1837 | Lansing |
| 27 | Florida | 1845 | Tallahassee |
| 28 | Texas | 1845 | Austin |
| 29 | Iowa | 1846 | Des Moines |
| 30 | Wisconsin | 1848 | Madison |
| 31 | California | 1850 | Sacramento |
| 32 | Minnesota | 1858 | St. Paul |
| 33 | Oregon | 1859 | Salem |
| 34 | Kansas | 1861 | Topeka |
| 35 | West Virginia | 1863 | Charleston |
| 36 | Nevada | 1864 | Carson City |
| 37 | Nebraska | 1867 | Lincoln |
| 38 | Colorado | 1876 | Denver |
| 39 | North Dakota | 1889 | Bismarck |
| 40 | South Dakota | 1889 | Pierre |
| 41 | Montana | 1889 | Helena |
| 42 | Washington | 1889 | Olympia |
| 43 | Idaho | 1890 | Boise |
| 44 | Wyoming | 1890 | Cheyenne |
| 45 | Utah | 1896 | Salt Lake City |
| 46 | Oklahoma | 1907 | Oklahoma City |
| 47 | New Mexico | 1912 | Santa Fe |
| 48 | Arizona | 1912 | Phoenix |
| 49 | Alaska | 1959 | Juneau |
| 50 | Hawaii | 1959 | Honolulu |

# Appendix E. *Presidents of the United States*

| | President | Term | Political Party | Home State | Vice President |
|---|---|---|---|---|---|
| 1 | George Washington | 1789–1797 | None | Virginia | John Adams |
| 2 | John Adams | 1797–1801 | Federalist | Massachusetts | Thomas Jefferson |
| 3 | Thomas Jefferson | 1801–1809 | Democratic-Republican | Virginia | Aaron Burr<br>George Clinton |
| 4 | James Madison | 1809–1817 | Democratic-Republican | Virginia | George Clinton<br>Elbridge Gerry |
| 5 | James Monroe | 1817–1825 | Democratic-Republican | Virginia | Daniel D. Tompkins |
| 6 | John Quincy Adams | 1825–1829 | Democratic-Republican | Massachusetts | John C. Calhoun |
| 7 | Andrew Jackson | 1829–1837 | Democrat | Tennessee | John C. Calhoun<br>Martin Van Buren |
| 8 | Martin Van Buren | 1837–1841 | Democrat | New York | Richard M. Johnson |
| 9 | William H. Harrison | 1841 | Whig | Ohio | John Tyler |
| 10 | John Tyler | 1841–1845 | Whig | Virginia | |
| 11 | James K. Polk | 1845–1849 | Democrat | Tennessee | George M. Dallas |
| 12 | Zachary Taylor | 1849–1850 | Whig | Louisiana | Millard Fillmore |
| 13 | Millard Fillmore | 1850–1853 | Whig | New York | |
| 14 | Franklin Pierce | 1853–1857 | Democrat | New Hampshire | William R. King |
| 15 | James Buchanan | 1857–1861 | Democrat | Pennsylvania | John C. Breckinridge |
| 16 | Abraham Lincoln | 1861–1865 | Republican | Illinois | Hannibal Hamlin<br>Andrew Johnson |
| 17 | Andrew Johnson | 1865–1869 | Republican | Tennessee | |
| 18 | Ulysses S. Grant | 1869–1877 | Republican | Illinois | Schuyler Colfax<br>Henry Wilson |
| 19 | Rutherford B. Hayes | 1877–1881 | Republican | Ohio | William A. Wheeler |
| 20 | James A. Garfield | 1881 | Republican | Ohio | Chester A. Arthur |
| 21 | Chester A. Arthur | 1881–1885 | Republican | New York | |
| 22 | Grover Cleveland | 1885–1889 | Democrat | New York | Thomas A. Hendricks |
| 23 | Benjamin Harrison | 1889–1893 | Republican | Indiana | Levi P. Morton |
| 24 | Grover Cleveland | 1893–1897 | Democrat | New York | Adlai E. Stevenson |
| 25 | William McKinley | 1897–1901 | Republican | Ohio | Garret A. Hobart<br>Theodore Roosevelt |
| 26 | Theodore Roosevelt | 1901–1909 | Republican | New York | Charles W. Fairbanks |
| 27 | William H. Taft | 1909–1913 | Republican | Ohio | James S. Sherman |
| 28 | Woodrow Wilson | 1913–1921 | Democrat | New Jersey | Thomas R. Marshall |
| 29 | Warren G. Harding | 1921–1923 | Republican | Ohio | Calvin Coolidge |
| 30 | Calvin Coolidge | 1923–1929 | Republican | Massachusetts | Charles G. Dawes |
| 31 | Herbert Hoover | 1929–1933 | Republican | California | Charles Curtis |
| 32 | Franklin D. Roosevelt | 1933–1945 | Democrat | New York | John Garner<br>John Garner<br>Henry A. Wallace<br>Harry S. Truman |
| 33 | Harry S. Truman | 1945–1953 | Democrat | Missouri | Alben W. Barkley |
| 34 | Dwight D. Eisenhower | 1953–1961 | Republican | Pennsylvania | Richard M. Nixon |
| 35 | John F. Kennedy | 1961–1963 | Democrat | Massachusetts | Lyndon B. Johnson |
| 36 | Lyndon B. Johnson | 1963–1969 | Democrat | Texas | Hubert H. Humphrey |
| 37 | Richard M. Nixon | 1969–1974 | Republican | California | Spiro T. Agnew<br>Gerald R. Ford |
| 38 | Gerald R. Ford | 1974–1977 | Republican | Michigan | Nelson A. Rockefeller |
| 39 | Jimmy Carter | 1977–1981 | Democrat | Georgia | Walter F. Mondale |
| 40 | Ronald Reagan | 1981–1989 | Republican | California | George H. W. Bush |
| 41 | George Bush | 1989–1993 | Republican | Texas | Dan Quayle |
| 42 | Bill Clinton | 1993–2001 | Democrat | Arkansas | Al Gore |
| 43 | George W. Bush | 2001–2009 | Republican | Texas | Richard "Dick" Cheney |
| 44 | Barack Obama | 2009–2017 | Democrat | Illinois | Joseph "Joe" Biden |
| 45 | Donald Trump | 2017–2021 | Republican | New York | Mike Pence |
| 46 | Joe Biden | 2021– | Democrat | Delaware | Kamala Harris |

# Glossary

## A

**abolition**  Reform movement which advocated the elimination of slavery

**Abraham Accords**  Peace agreements negotiated by Donald Trump between Israel and the United Arab Emirates (UAE), Bahrain, Sudan, and Morocco

**Adams-Onís Treaty**  Agreement in which Spain agreed to sell East Florida to the United States for $5 million and which established the boundary of Spanish territory west of the Mississippi River

**affirmative action**  A broad range of policies designed to make improvements for minority groups in jobs, college admissions, and other areas

**Affordable Care Act (ACA)**  Healthcare legislation, also known as Obamacare, which required all Americans to either obtain health insurance or pay a fine

**Agricultural Adjustment Act (AAA)**  New Deal legislation that established a new method of subsidizing farm products and aided debt-ridden farmers in danger of losing farms to foreclosure

**Alamo**  Abandoned Spanish mission in San Antonio where Texans were defeated by Santa Anna in 1836

**Albany Plan**  Proposal by Benjamin Franklin to unite the colonies under the king with a president and congress

**Alien and Sedition Acts**  Four laws passed by the Federalist-controlled Congress that were claimed to protect America from the threat of war but were used to weaken and silence the Democratic-Republican Party

**Allied Powers**  World War I alliance between Great Britain, France, Russia, Italy, and (later) the United States; World War II alliance between Great Britain, France, (later) Russia, and the United States

**al-Qaeda**  International terrorist organization led by Osama bin Laden; responsible for the attack on September 11, 2001; linked to several earlier terrorist attacks against the United States and its allies

**American Expeditionary Force (AEF)**  Name for the US troops that came to France beginning in 1917 during World War I

**American Federation of Labor**  Union formed in 1881 as a confederation of national trade unions for skilled laborers

**American Rescue Plan**  Government relief bill aimed at the economic crisis during the COVID-19 pandemic; passed during the Biden administration and provided $1.9 trillion in economic stimulus

**American System**  Plan proposed by Henry Clay which called for a new national bank, protective tariffs, and federal funds for internal improvements

**Americans with Disabilities Act**  Legislation passed during George H. W. Bush's administration, outlawing job discrimination based on certain disabilities and requiring local governments and businesses to improve and alter their accommodations for the disabled

**Anabaptists**  Groups such as the Amish and Mennonites who refused to serve in the military, vote, or hold office, and who stressed the importance of a holy, simple life

**Anaconda Plan**  Mocking name given to the Union's Civil War strategy devised by Winfield Scott to slowly squeeze the Confederacy through blockading southern ports and controlling the Mississippi River

**animism**  A Native American religious idea in which all things, living or nonliving, have souls

**Annapolis Convention**  Meeting held in September 1786 for states to discuss interstate trade; asked the Confederation Congress for a meeting of all the states to revise the Articles of Confederation

**Anti-Federalists**  Those who opposed the adoption of the Constitution

**appeasement**  Yielding to an aggressor's demands in order to preserve peace

**Appomattox Court House**  Site in Virginia of Robert E. Lee's surrender to Ulysses S. Grant on April 9, 1865, ending the Civil War

**armistice**  Agreement to stop fighting; signed to end World War I

**Articles of Confederation**  The first plan of government of the United States, in force from 1777 until ratification of the United States Constitution in 1789, containing a unicameral legislature, a weak national government, and strong state governments

**astrolabe**  Instrument which enabled sailors to determine a ship's latitude on the ocean

**Axis Powers**  Alliance between Italy, Germany, and Japan, the countries that formed the Rome-Berlin-Tokyo Axis and which fought together in World War II

## B

**baby boom**  Massive rise in the birth rate in the United States between 1945 and 1964

**Bacon's Rebellion**  Conflict in Virginia between frontier farmers and Native Americans that led to violence between Nathaniel Bacon and his followers and the government of Virginia

**balance of power** Preventing any one nation from gaining enough power to dominate other nations

**bank holiday** Temporary closing of all banks; declared by Franklin Roosevelt to calm the fears of the public about the banking situation during the Great Depression

**Baptists** Religious group that practices baptism by immersion for professing believers, practices congregational polity, and believes that only the regenerate should be church members

**Barbary States** The small Muslim countries in North Africa that demanded tribute payments from trade ships on the Mediterranean Sea

**Bataan Death March** Forced march of American and Filipino troops who surrendered to the Japanese in the Philippines in 1942 on which 10,000 prisoners died

**Battle of Antietam** Civil War battle fought in Maryland on September 17, 1862; bloodiest one-day battle in American history, with both sides fighting to a draw but the Confederate army withdrawing

**Battle of Atlanta** Civil War battle fought in Georgia on July 20–22, 1864; a Union victory; launching point for Sherman's March to the Sea

**Battle of Chancellorsville** Civil War battle fought in Virginia on May 2–6, 1863; a Confederate victory; battle in which Stonewall Jackson was wounded (from which he died eight days later)

**Battle of Chattanooga** Civil War battle fought in Tennessee on November 24–25, 1863; a Union victory

**Battle of Chickamauga** Civil War battle fought in northwest Georgia on September 19–20, 1863; a Confederate victory

**Battle of Cold Harbor** Civil War battle fought in Virginia on June 1–3, 1864; a Confederate victory with massive Union casualties

**Battle of Fallen Timbers** 1794 battle in which American forces under "Mad Anthony" Wayne defeated a group of Native Americans in present-day Ohio

**Battle of Fredericksburg** Civil War battle fought in Virginia on December 13, 1862; a Confederate victory

**Battle of Gettysburg** Civil War battle fought in Pennsylvania on July 1–3, 1863; a Union victory

**Battle of Iwo Jima** American World War II victory in the Pacific; began February 19, 1945; costliest battle in Marine Corps history

**Battle of Manila Bay** US naval battle in the Philippines during the Spanish-American War, resulting in the destruction of the Spanish fleet in the Pacific

**Battle of Midway** Victory won by the US Navy on June 4-7, 1942, in which four Japanese carriers were destroyed, turning the tide of the war as the Allies began to go on the offensive in the Pacific

**Battle of New Orleans** American victory, led by Andrew Jackson, over Britain in the War of 1812; fought on January 8, 1815, two weeks after the treaty ending the war was signed

**Battle of Okinawa** American assault beginning in April 1945; the bloodiest battle of the Pacific Theater; victory which gave the Allies a base 350 miles from the Japanese main island for bombing raids and a possible assault on Japan

**Battle of San Jacinto** Battle in 1836 in which the Texans under Sam Houston defeated the Mexicans and captured Santa Anna

**Battle of Shiloh** Civil War battle fought at Shiloh church near Corinth, Mississippi, on April 6–7, 1862; a Union victory

**Battle of the Bulge** German counterattack into Belgium in 1944 that created a fifty-mile-deep bulge into Allied lines

**Battle of the Little Bighorn** Also known as Custer's Last Stand (1876); failed attack by Colonel George Custer on the Sioux, resulting in all of Custer's force being killed in less than an hour

**Battle of Tippecanoe** 1811 clash between the forces of William Henry Harrison and Native Americans under the Prophet in the Indiana Territory

**Bay of Pigs** Site of a failed invasion of Cuba in 1961 which was led by Cuban exiles who intended to overthrow Fidel Castro

**Bear Flag Republic** Name of the Republic of California during its one-month period as an independent nation in 1846

**bear market** A stock market characterized by pessimism and declining stock prices

**Berlin airlift** Series of over 277,000 flights in 1948–49 to provide food and other essentials to West Berlin after the Soviets blockaded that part of the city

**Berlin Wall** Structure erected by Communist East Berlin around West Berlin to prevent movement between the two parts of the city

**bicameral** Having two houses in a legislature

**big stick diplomacy** Foreign policy of Theodore Roosevelt which relied on military strength to protect American interests

**Bill of Rights** Name for the first ten amendments to the Constitution, restricting the power of the national government and protecting individual rights

**black codes** State and local laws that severely limited the rights of black Americans

**Black Power** Groups within the civil rights movement calling for black Americans to take control of the social, political, and economic direction of the movement, some advocating black nationalism, separatism, and black pride, and some calling for more aggressive action, including violence

**Bleeding Kanas** Term describing the Kansas Territory during the violence between proslavery and antislavery forces

**blitzkrieg** "Lightning war"; swift assault strategy of Hitler during World War II

**blockade runners** Low, fast ships built by the Confederacy to get past Union blockades

**Bloody Sunday** March 7, 1965, the first day of a civil rights march from Selma to Montgomery, Alabama, when marchers were attacked by police with tear gas and beatings

**Bonus Army** Nickname for a large group of unemployed World War I veterans who gathered in Washington, DC, in 1932 to ask for early payment of the promised bonus

**bootlegging** Making and selling illegal liquor during Prohibition

**border states** Slave states that did not secede from the Union, including Missouri, Kentucky, Maryland, Delaware, and West Virginia

**Boston Tea Party** Protest in 1773 against the Tea Act in which colonists disguised as Mohawks dumped tea from British ships into Boston Harbor

**Boxer Rebellion** An uprising in China to remove foreigners and foreign influence from China, leading to the killing of many foreign missionaries, diplomats, businessmen, and converts to Christianity

***Brown v. Board of Education of Topeka*** Supreme Court decision in 1954 stating that separate schools for black and white students were inherently unequal and a violation of the equal protection clause of the Fourteenth Amendment

**bull market** A stock market characterized by optimism and rising stock prices

**Bunker Hill** Site of a major battle near Boston in June 1775 resulting in a costly British victory

***Bush v. Gore*** Supreme Court case involving the disputed votes in Florida for the presidential election in 2000; decision in favor of Bush, halting all recounts, and by default, making him the victor in Florida, and therefore the winner of the presidency

**busing** Court-ordered program to transport students to schools outside their neighborhoods until all schools reflected the overall racial makeup of the city or community as a whole

**buying on margin** A system where investors could purchase stock through a broker but pay only ten percent of the purchase price, with the broker financing the remaining amount with money borrowed from a bank or other sources

# C

**cabinet** A president's group of advisers

**California Gold Rush** The lure of wealth that drew several hundred thousand men after the discovery of gold in California

**California Trail** Most popular trail to California; trail that split off from the Oregon Trail

**Camp David Accords** Agreement mediated by President Carter in 1978 in which Israel agreed to return the Sinai Peninsula to Egypt and Egypt agreed to a guarantee of peace and recognized Israel's right to exist

**capitalism** An economic system in which a nation's businesses are privately owned and operated

**caravel** A small, light ship with two or three triangular sails

**carpetbaggers** Northerners who moved to the South during Reconstruction, named for their luggage material

**cash and carry** Policy that nations at war during World War II could purchase items from the United States on a cash basis and transport them on non-American ships

**caucus** A meeting of party leaders for the purpose of choosing a candidate for office

**Central Intelligence Agency (CIA)** Agency created to gather and analyze information about foreign countries, often through the use of spies

**Central Pacific Railroad** One of two railroads that build the transcontinental railroad; started in Sacramento, California, and built eastward

**Central Powers** World War I alliance between Germany, Austria-Hungary, Bulgaria, and Turkey

**charter colony** A colony governed by a trade company that received authorization from the king

**checks and balances** System that keeps each branch of government from exercising too much power by giving each branch the ability to limit the power of the other branches

**Chinese Exclusion Act** Law passed in 1882 prohibiting most Chinese workers from entering the United States

**Chisholm Trail** Cattle trail from Texas to Abilene, Kansas, used by cowboys

**Civilian Conservation Corps (CCC)** New Deal agency that put young, unmarried men to work in reforestation, building roads, developing parks, and soil conservation projects under the supervision of the army

**Civil Rights Act of 1957** The first civil rights legislation passed by Congress since Reconstruction; the law that created the Civil Rights Division of the Department of Justice, authorized the US Attorney General to prosecute individuals that attempted to deny another citizen's right to vote, created the US Commission on Civil Rights to investigate claims of voting rights violations, and allowed African Americans to serve on federal court juries

**Civil Rights Act of 1964** First civil rights legislation passed under President Johnson; the law that established fairer procedures for voter registration, forbade racial discrimination in public buildings, promoted the desegregation of public schools, authorized withholding federal funds from projects or institutions that discriminated against minorities, and created the Equal Employment Opportunity Commission (EEOC)

**civil rights movement** The struggle for African Americans to secure the exercise of their rights as citizens, particularly in the period after World War II

**Clayton Antitrust Act** Legislation that expanded the list of practices prohibited to corporations, exempted labor unions from antitrust legislation, and legalized strikes, picketing, and boycotts

**clipper ship** A type of sailing vessel with many sails whose hull "clipped" the waves, thus allowing increased speeds

**Coercive Acts** British acts of 1774 in response to the Boston Tea Party, closing Boston Harbor until the cost of the destroyed tea was repaid, revoking the Massachusetts colonial charter, dictating that British officials accused of committing crimes be tried in England, and enacting a new Quartering Act; called the "Intolerable Acts" by the colonists

**Cold War** The period of tension and intense competition from the end of World War II until the early 1990s between the United States and its allies and the Soviet Union and its allies

**Columbian Exchange** The flow of new goods between Europe and the Americas

**Commerce and Slave Trade Compromise** Agreement of the Constitutional Convention that the federal government could regulate trade but could not tax exports or interfere with the slave trade for at least twenty years

**Committee of Correspondence** Group established by the colonies to provide information to each other about British threats

**Committee on Public Information** Founded during World War I; government committee that led a propaganda crusade using artists to produce posters to recruit men and raise money for the war effort

**Committee to Re-Elect the President (CRP)** Committee formed to raise funds for Nixon's reelection campaign, but that also engaged in questionable and illegal activities, including the Watergate break-in

*Common Sense* Influential pamphlet written by Thomas Paine which made the case for American independence from Britain

**compass** An instrument that enabled sailors to know which direction they were heading

**Compromise of 1850** An attempt to resolve the issue of slavery by (1) admitting California as a free state, (2) abolishing the slave trade in the District of Columbia, (3) creating a new fugitive slave law, (4) protecting slavery in the District of Columbia, and (5) allowing popular sovereignty in the New Mexico and Utah territories

**Compromise of 1877** Agreement that Democrats would accept the election of Rutherford B. Hayes as president and accept the Reconstruction amendments and that Republicans would withdraw all remaining federal troops from the South, effectively ending Reconstruction

**Compromise Tariff of 1833** Compromise that lowered the rates from the Tariff of 1832 and resulted in South Carolina withdrawing its nullification of the Tariff of 1832 and accepting the compromise tariff, temporarily ending the threat of civil war

**Comstock Lode** Large deposit of gold and silver located in Nevada

**Concord** Town in Massachusetts that housed a large stockpile of colonial munitions

**Confederate States of America** Formation of the states that seceded from the Union in 1861

**confederation** A close alliance of sovereign states

**Confederation Congress** The unicameral legislature under the Articles of Confederation

**conscription** Also called a draft; a requirement by the government to serve in the military

**Constitutional Convention** Originally called the Philadelphia Convention; meeting of states in 1787 for the purpose of revising the Articles of Confederation but which instead formulated a new government governed by a constitution

**containment** US foreign policy stating that communism must be contained within its current boundaries and kept from expanding

**Continental Association** Formed by the First Continental Congress to enact and enforce a boycott of British goods

**Contract with America** Plan by Republicans in the House of Representatives to win the 1994 midterm elections; plan in which candidates pledged that if elected they would introduce ten popular bills during the first one hundred days in office

**convoy system** Huge shipments of troops and supplies protected by navy destroyers equipped with antisubmarine weapons

**Coronavirus Aid, Relief, and Economic Security (CARES) Act**  Government relief bill aimed at the economic crisis during the COVID-19 pandemic; passed during the Trump administration; provided $2.2 trillion in economic stimulus, including direct payments to individuals, loans to corporations and businesses, and funds for state and local governments

**corporations**  Businesses with a legal charter from a state to sell stocks to investors to raise capital

**Corps of Discovery**  The group of fifty men led by Meriwether Lewis and William Clark that explored the Louisiana Territory from 1804 to 1806

**corrupt bargain**  Idea claimed by Andrew Jackson and his supporters that a deal was made between John Quincy Adams and Henry Clay in which Clay would support Adams for president in the House of Representatives in the contested election of 1824 and Adams would name Clay secretary of state

**cotton diplomacy**  Strategy to pressure England to recognize the independence of the Confederacy by withholding cotton

**cotton gin**  A machine invented by Eli Whitney containing a series of metal teeth mounted on rollers that separated the cotton from the seeds fifty times faster than manual labor

**COVID-19**  A new illness caused by the SARS-COV-2 virus that started a global pandemic in 2020

**crop-lien**  System of credit where borrowers pledged future crops as collateral for a loan

**Cuban missile crisis**  Time of tension in response to the Soviet installation of nuclear missile sites in Cuba after the failed Bay of Pigs invasion; a period including a US blockade of Cuba and the USSR's agreement to remove the missiles in exchange for a US agreement to not invade Cuba and to remove missiles from Turkey

# D

**Dawes Act**  A law passed in 1887 designed to Americanize Native Americans and which parceled out Native American lands in allotments to individual Native Americans

**Dayton Accords**  Peace agreement signed between Serbian leaders and persecuted ethnic groups, especially Muslims; fashioned Bosnia into a confederation in which Serbs, Croats, and Bosnian Muslims shared power

**D-Day**  Allied invasion of Normandy, France, on June 6, 1944, which began Operation Overlord

**Declaration of Rights and Grievances**  Statement adopted by the First Continental Congress objecting to recent acts of Parliament, stating that the colonies must be self-governing in nearly every respect, and maintaining their allegiance to the king

**Declaratory Act**  1766 act which stated that Parliament had the right to pass any law that it desired regarding the colonies

**Defense of Marriage Act**  Law passed during the Clinton administration denying federal government recognition of any homosexual union as a marriage and securing federal benefits, such as health insurance, for spouses in traditional marriages only

**Deferred Action for Childhood Arrivals (DACA)**  Executive order granting undocumented aliens who arrived in the United States as children renewable two-year deferments from deportation; later expanded to include other illegal aliens; one of Barack Obama's executive orders regarding immigration enforcement

**de Lôme letter**  Private letter by Enrique Dupuy de Lôme, Spanish ambassador to the United States, that criticized President McKinley and which was stolen by Cuban rebels and printed in an American newspaper

**Democratic Party**  Portion of the former Democratic-Republican Party founded before the election of 1828 that supported Andrew Jackson and continues to the present day

**Democratic-Republican Party**  Political party of Thomas Jefferson and others who believed in a more limited national government and a strict interpretation of the Constitution

**Department of Homeland Security**  Newly formed agency created by President George W. Bush following the September 11, 2001 terrorist attack on the United States and which later became a cabinet-level department

**détente**  An easing of tensions between the United States and the Communist nations of China and the Soviet Union during the 1970s

***Dobbs v. Jackson Women's Health Organization***  Supreme Court decision that overturned the ruling in *Roe v. Wade*, determining that the Constitution did not protect a woman's right to an abortion, leaving states to decide on abortion laws

**dollar diplomacy**  Foreign policy of William Howard Taft that influenced foreign affairs through the investment of American dollars in foreign countries

**domino theory**  Idea that if one country in Southeast Asia fell to communism, then other nations would fall like a row of dominoes

**Doolittle Raid**  Secret attack on Tokyo and other cities on April 8, 1942, by American bombers launched from an aircraft carrier, causing a boost in American morale and a psychological shock to the Japanese

***Dred Scott v. Sandford***  Supreme Court decision which ruled that blacks were not citizens, that a slave's residence in a free state or territory did not make him free, and that Congress did not have the power to prohibit slavery in a territory

**Dust Bowl**  Nickname for the drought-ridden Great Plains affected by massive dust storms in the 1930s

# E

**Eighteenth Amendment**  Amendment that established Prohibition, banning the sale, manufacture, and transport of alcoholic beverages

**Ellis Island**  Port of entry in New York City that handled the largest number of European immigrants

**Emancipation Proclamation**  Declaration made by Abraham Lincoln on September 24, 1862, that all slaves in states that were in rebellion as of January 1, 1863, would be freed

**Embargo Act**  Act of Congress during President Jefferson's administration which banned all exports from the United States and all imports from Europe

**encomienda system**  Spanish system in which conquistadors were given land and the right to the labor and tribute of the native people, and in return they had the responsibility to care for, pay, protect, and Christianize the native people

**Environmental Protection Agency (EPA)**  Federal agency created in 1970 to oversee and coordinate environmental regulations

**Equal Rights Amendment (ERA)**  Controversial amendment passed by Congress in 1972 guaranteeing equal rights for women and which failed to gain the approval of enough states to be ratified

**Erie Canal**  Canal connecting Lake Erie to the Hudson River at Albany, New York

**Espionage and Sedition Acts**  Legislation that made it a criminal offense to criticize the war effort in any way

# F

**factory system**  System in which machines are housed in buildings and are owned by one or several people who purchase all machinery and resources and receive the profits, where workers do not need to be highly skilled, and where labor is divided with each worker responsible for one step of production

**Fair Deal**  Domestic government program under Truman intended to promote full employment, an increased minimum wage, subsidized medical insurance, and protection from racial or religious discrimination

**Fair Housing Act**  Another name for the Civil Rights Act of 1968 which prohibited discrimination based on race, religion, color, or national origin in the sale, rental, or financing of housing

**Farmers' Alliance**  Organization that worked for reforms to benefit farmers

**fascism**  Political and economic system that promoted extreme nationalism and placed great emphasis on militarism

**Federal Deposit Insurance Corporation (FDIC)**  Agency created under Franklin Roosevelt's administration to insure bank deposits against loss

**federalism**  The division of power between national and state levels of government

*Federalist Papers*  Series of eighty-five essays written by Alexander Hamilton, James Madison, and John Jay to persuade New York to support the Constitution

**Federalist Party**  Political party of John Adams and Alexander Hamilton that believed in a strong national government and a loose interpretation of the Constitution

**Federalists**  Those who favored the adoption of the Constitution

**Federal Reserve Act**  Law that established twelve regional Federal Reserve Banks supervised by a Federal Reserve Board which serve as "bankers' banks" that influence the nation's monetary policy and the amount of money in circulation by setting interest rates for loans between banks and exercising control over many banking operations

**Federal Trade Commission**  A regulatory board of five people authorized by the federal government to help define and halt unfair business practices

**Fifteenth Amendment**  Amendment that kept states from denying the right to vote to any citizen "on account of race, color, or previous condition of servitude"

**fireside chats**  Nickname for Franklin Roosevelt's radio addresses

**First Battle of Bull Run**  First major battle of the Civil War fought June 21, 1861; a Confederate victory

**First Continental Congress**  Meeting in 1774 in Philadelphia of representatives from all the colonies except Georgia which adopted a statement of objections to recent acts of Parliament

**flappers**  Young women of the 1920s who captured attention by wearing short haircuts, shorter skirts, and heavy makeup, and by drinking, smoking, and using slang

**Food Administration**  Government agency designed to address the need for an adequate food supply for the American forces and the Allies

**Force Bill**  Bill passed by Congress in response to the Nullification Crisis and allowing the president to use the military to enforce federal tariffs

**Fort Duquesne**  A French fort captured by the British during the French and Indian War and renamed Fort Pitt in honor of British Prime Minister William Pitt

**Fort Sumter**  Federal fort in Charleston Harbor, South Carolina, which was fired upon on March 4, 1861, by Confederate forces when Lincoln attempted to resupply it, which led to the outbreak of the Civil War

**Fort Ticonderoga** British fort in New York captured in 1775 by Ethan Allen's "Green Mountain Boys" and Benedict Arnold

**forty-niners** People who traveled to California in search of gold beginning in 1849

**Fourteen Points** Woodrow Wilson's peace proposal that included guidelines to help rebuild Europe and maintain peace following World War I

**Fourteenth Amendment** Granted citizenship to black Americans

**Frame of Government of Pennsylvania** Constitution of Pennsylvania that provided religious toleration and political liberty for the colony

**free silver** The unlimited production of silver coins, favored by populists including William Jennings Bryan

**Free Soil Party** Political party formed by Conscience Whigs, northern Democrats, and abolitionists before the election of 1848 which supported the Wilmot Proviso

**freedmen** Another name for freed slaves

**Freedmen's Bureau** Short-term agency whose primary purpose was to assist former slaves during Reconstruction

**Freedom Riders** Black and white people who traveled in interstate buses across the Deep South in 1961 to secure federal enforcement of desegregated interstate travel

**Freedom Summer** The coordinated effort during the summer of 1964 in which civil rights volunteers worked to register black Americans to vote in Mississippi and which met with violent opposition, including the murder of three civil rights workers by the Ku Klux Klan (KKK)

**freeholders** Adult white males who owned property and who had the right to vote for members of colonial legislatures

**French and Indian War** War from 1754–63 between Britain and its colonies and France and its Native American allies, known in Europe as the Seven Years' War (1756–63)

**Fugitive Slave Act of 1850** Part of the Compromise of 1850 that provided a new process for enforcing the fugitive slave clause that included federal commissioners, the use of US Marshals, and punishment of citizens who harbored fugitive slaves or obstructed their capture

**Fundamentalists** Term used beginning in the 1920s for those who defended the fundamental doctrines of Christianity against modernism

**Fundamental Orders of Connecticut** The first written constitution in America

## G

**Gadsden Purchase** Land on the southern border of Arizona and New Mexico that was purchased by the United States from Mexico in 1853 for $10 million

**Gaspee** British customs ship that ran aground in 1772 near Providence, Rhode Island, and was burned by colonists

**Gentlemen's Agreement** A verbal agreement used between Japan and the United States whereby Japan agreed to restrict emigration to the United States and the United States agreed to provide better treatment to Asian immigrants who were already in the country

**Gettysburg Address** Short speech given by Abraham Lincoln at the dedication of a cemetery for Union soldiers who died at the Battle of Gettysburg

**Gibbons v. Ogden** Supreme Court decision which ruled that where the Constitution entrusted Congress with a power, the states had no right to interfere with that power

**GI Bill** Legislation helping veterans with tuition grants, job training, and home loans

**Gilded Age** Period from the 1870s to about 1900; the term that described an era in which all appeared prosperous on the surface but beneath the surface lay challenges

**grandfather clause** A law that allowed those who could not pay the poll tax or pass a literacy test to vote if he or his father or grandfather was eligible to vote before 1867, a requirement that black citizens could not meet

**Grange** Social and political organization for farmers founded in 1867

**Great Awakening** Large religious revival in the American colonies from the 1720s to the 1740s

**Great Compromise** Also known as the Connecticut Compromise; proposal to the Constitutional Convention for a bicameral legislature with representation in the House of Representatives based on population and equal representation for each state in the Senate

**Great Depression** Severe economic downturn that occurred worldwide during the 1930s

**Great Migration** Movement of hundreds of thousands of African Americans between 1914 and 1930 for economic opportunity and to escape racial discrimination

**Great Northern Railroad** Transcontinental railroad built by James J. Hill without government funds

**Great Railroad Strike** Union strike in 1877 over cutting wages; strike that spread nationwide and became violent, requiring state militia and federal troops to restore order

**Great Recession** Period from the end of 2007 into 2009; the bursting of the housing "bubble" as more and more homes came back on the market, causing the price of houses to drastically decrease, investors to lose their profit, banks to declare bankruptcy, stores to close, and people to lose jobs

**Great Sioux War** The climax of the Indian wars in 1876 and 1877

**Great Society** President Lyndon Johnson's legislative program to end poverty and inequality

**Great Wagon Road** An old Iroquois trail that became the chief access to frontier settlements from Virginia to Georgia

**Great White Fleet** US naval fleet of white warships sent by Theodore Roosevelt on a world tour to impress Japan and other nations with America's strength

**Gulf of Tonkin Resolution** Act of Congress giving the president authority to take all necessary steps to repel any armed attack against US forces in Vietnam and to prevent further aggression

# H

**Half-Breeds** Term for Republicans during the Gilded Age who favored civil service reform

**Half-Way Covenant** Measure allowing New England church members who had not declared their personal faith in Christ to present their children for baptism

**Harlem Renaissance** Period in the 1920s when African American culture flourished in the Harlem neighborhood of New York City

**Harpers Ferry** Town in Virginia (now West Virginia) that was the site of a federal arsenal which was raided by abolitionist John Brown and his followers in an unsuccessful attempt to begin a slave rebellion

**Hartford Convention** Meeting of a group of New England Federalists who opposed the War of 1812 and proposed that the New England states secede from the United States

**Harvard College** The first college established in the American colonies, founded in 1636 in Cambridge, Massachusetts, to train ministers

**Haymarket Riot** Union rally in 1886 that resulted in violence and damaged the reputation of unions

**headright system** System that awarded fifty acres of land to any person who paid for another's passage to America

**Hiroshima** Site of first atomic bomb dropped on Japan, August 6, 1945

**historiography** The study of the writing of history

**holding companies** Companies which did not produce anything but which owned stock in companies that did produce goods

**Holocaust** Massacre of millions of people, especially Jews, but also political opponents, prisoners of war, Poles, the Roma, and the disabled, at the hands of the Nazis

**Homestead Act of 1862** Law giving 160 acres of land to an individual who paid a filing fee and promised to live on and improve the land

**Homestead Strike** Conflict in 1892 between Carnegie Steel workers who had been locked out by owners and security forces hired by the company

**Hoovervilles** Nickname for groups of shanties created by those who had lost homes during the Great Depression

**horizontal integration** Control of one aspect of production in an industry

**House of Burgesses** Lawmaking body in Virginia that was the first self-governing assembly of American colonists

**Hurricane Katrina** Category 3 storm in 2005 that hit the Gulf Coast of Louisiana, Mississippi, and Alabama, putting eighty percent of New Orleans under water; costliest hurricane in American history

# I

**Immigration Act of 1924** Act that included the Asian Exclusion Act and the National Origins Act, banning immigrants from Japan and reducing the quota of immigrants allowed to enter the United States

**impeachment** The process to bring charges against an elected or appointed official, such as the president

**imperialism** The process of building empires through more powerful nations gaining economic and political control over weaker nations which usually become colonies

**impressment** Act of seizing American sailors and forcing them to serve in the British navy

**indentured servant** A laborer who contracted to work for a specified period, usually between four and seven years, for the person who paid for their passage to America

**Indian Removal Act of 1830** Law passed by Congress which authorized the president to remove Native Americans from the states in which they resided to territory west of the Mississippi River

**Indian Reorganization Act** An act in 1934 that gave reservations limited self-government

**Industrial Revolution** Period of social and economic change in which production of goods by hand was replaced by machinery

**Inflation Reduction Act** Act passed during the Biden administration that attempted to control rising inflation rates due to economic effects of the pandemic and the American Rescue Plan

**Infrastructure Investment and Jobs Act** Act passed during the Biden administration that designated approximately $1 trillion for projects to improve roads, bridges, railways, and public transportation in cities and states and that also funded projects to improve drinking water and increase clean energy and internet access

**initiative** A process in which voters initiate legislation by collecting a certain number of signatures on a petition, after which proposed laws are sent to the state legislature or directly to the people to be accepted or rejected

**installment plans** Financing system that allows a person to pay for an item in small weekly or monthly payments

**interchangeable parts** Standardized, identical, machine-manufactured parts which made mass production and replacement of parts easier

**Interstate Commerce Act** First federal regulatory act of commerce, passed in 1887, creating the Interstate Commerce Commission and directing that railroad rates must be reasonable and just

**interstate highway system** National system of limited-access highways begun under Eisenhower which became main arteries of highway transportation to handle increased traffic and for national defense purposes

**Iran-Contra affair** Scandal during Reagan's administration involving money from the secret sale of weapons to Iran, some profits of which went to aid the Contras in Nicaragua although Congress had banned aid to the Contras

**Iranian hostage crisis** Incident in 1979 that developed during unrest in Iran over US support for the exiled Shah, when Iranian revolutionaries took more than fifty Americans hostage for 444 days until the day of Reagan's inauguration

**iron curtain** Term used to describe the division between Communist Eastern Europe and free Western Europe

**Islamic State of Iraq and Syria (ISIS)** Radical terrorist Muslim group that developed in the Middle East from the remains of al-Qaeda

**island hopping** The American strategy during World War II of bypassing and isolating heavily fortified islands and securing air bases on less-fortified islands to be used for launching air attacks and staging further invasions of islands progressively closer to Japan's main islands

**isolationism** The desire of a nation to stay out of foreign entanglements and wars

## J

**January 6 Capitol Riot** Protest of the 2020 election results in which hundreds of rioters stormed the US Capitol on January 6, 2021, and entered the building, disrupting the certification of the electoral vote in Congress

**Jay Treaty** Treaty negotiated by John Jay in which Britain agreed to abandon its forts in the Northwest Territory and pay reparations for seizures of American ships and in which the United States granted Britain preferred trading status and agreed to limitations on trade in the West Indies

**Jim Crow laws** Laws which required the forced segregation of the races in trains, restaurants, hotels, schools, and other public facilities

**joint-stock companies** Companies that raised large amounts of money to fund colonies by selling stock to investors in return for a share of any profits

**judicial review** The right of the Supreme Court to declare a law unconstitutional

**Judiciary Act of 1789** Act of the first Congress that established thirteen federal district courts, three circuit courts, and set the number of Supreme Court justices at six

## K

**kamikazes** Japanese pilots who deliberately tried to crash their planes into enemy ships during the closing months of World War II

**Kansas-Nebraska Act** Proposal in 1854 by Stephen A. Douglas to repeal the Missouri Compromise and allow popular sovereignty in the Kansas and Nebraska territories

**Kellogg-Briand Pact** Agreement signed by fifteen nations in 1928 in which nations pledged to abandon war as a means of settling disputes

**Kent State shooting** Tragedy in 1971 at Kent State University in Ohio where four college students were shot and killed by National Guard troops during a Vietnam War protest

**Kentucky Resolutions** Resolutions drafted by Thomas Jefferson which claimed that states had the right to declare federal laws they deemed unconstitutional to be null and void

**King Philip's War** Conflict from 1675 to 1678 between Wampanoag chief Metacomet (King Philip) and New England colonists

**Kitchen Cabinet** Informal group of unofficial advisers consulted by Andrew Jackson

**Knights of Labor** Union formed in 1869 for skilled and unskilled laborers from various occupations

**Know-Nothing Party** Another name for the American Party, a political party that wanted to reduce the influence of foreign-born voters and support only native-born Protestant candidates

**Korean War** Conflict from 1950 to 1953 between Communists and non-Communists over control of South Korea

**Ku Klux Klan (KKK)** Secret organization formed by some former Confederate soldiers in 1866 to place black people firmly under white control through violence and intimidation

## L

**labor unions** Organized groups of workers that were formed to obtain better working conditions and higher pay

**Land Ordinance of 1785** Law that provided for the distribution and settlement of the Northwest Territory and which divided the territory into townships and lots

**League of Nations** The last of Wilson's Fourteen Points; an organization of cooperating nations that would discuss and solve problems peacefully

**Lend-Lease Act** 1941 act that empowered the president to lend or lease, rather than sell, food and armaments to Allied nations

**Lexington** Town in Massachusetts where British troops on their way to Concord and colonial militia met on April 19, 1775, resulting in the first skirmish of the War for Independence

**Lincoln-Douglas debates** Series of seven debates between Abraham Lincoln and Stephen A. Douglas before the 1858 race for the US Senate seat from Illinois

**line of demarcation** Boundary created by Pope Alexander VI in 1493 giving Portugal rights to land east of the line and Spain rights to the land west of the line

**literacy test** A "reading" test that often deprived black people of their right to vote

**Little Rock Nine** The nine black students whose entrance to Central High School in Little Rock, Arkansas, in 1957 was blocked by angry parents opposed to integration and by the National Guard, requiring President Eisenhower to use US Army troops to escort the students into the school

**Lone Star Republic** Name for the Republic of Texas during the time between its independence from Mexico and its annexation into the United States

**long drive** Cattle drives from Texas to railroad lines in the Great Plains

**Louisiana Purchase** American purchase of the Louisiana Territory from France in 1803 for $15 million

**Loyalists** Colonists who continued to support the king, also called "Tories"

*Lusitania* British passenger ship that transported some American passengers and was sunk in 1915 as a result of Germany's unrestricted submarine warfare policy

# M

**Manhattan Project** Top secret American program during World War II to develop the first atomic bomb ahead of Germany

**Manifest Destiny** Belief that God had given the whole American continent to the United States to possess

*Marbury v. Madison* Supreme Court decision which established the principle of judicial review

**March on Washington for Jobs and Freedom** March of over 200,000 people in Washington, DC, in August 1963 to focus attention on a proposed civil rights bill and to call for federal legislation to end job discrimination; setting of Martin Luther King Jr.'s "I Have a Dream" speech

**March to the Sea** Union General William T. Sherman's march of destruction through Georgia from Atlanta to Savannah

**Marshall Plan** US program proposed by Secretary of State George Marshall providing billions of dollars in aid to rebuild European countries after World War II

**Maryland Toleration Act** Gave religious freedom to anyone who professed belief in the Trinity

**Mayflower Compact** An agreement that bound the Pilgrim settlers to submit to the colony's laws and leadership; the first document of self-government in America

*McCulloch v. Maryland* Supreme Court ruling that a state cannot tax the federal government or interfere with Congress's ability to enact legislation that is necessary and proper to carry out its delegated powers

**McKinley Tariff** Tariff passed in 1890 that imposed higher duties on manufactured and agricultural imports than any previous tariff

**Meat Inspection Act** Act that required the Department of Agriculture to oversee the preparation and packaging of meat and to inspect the health of animals before they were slaughtered

**Medicaid** Public healthcare program for low-income citizens of all ages

**Medicare** Health insurance program for those age 65 and older and those with disabilities

**mercantilism** An economic system that said a nation's wealth consisted of precious metals, especially gold, and that a country should increase its wealth by increasing its gold surplus

**Mexican Cession** Land ceded by Mexico to the United States after the Mexican War; included California, Utah, Nevada, and parts of New Mexico, Arizona, Colorado, and Wyoming

**Middle Passage** Sea voyage that brought slaves across the Atlantic to the Americas

**militarism** An increased emphasis on military might

**Missouri Compromise** Agreement proposed in 1820 by Henry Clay in which Maine would enter the union as a free state, Missouri would enter as a slave state, and slavery would be prohibited in the remainder of the Louisiana Territory north of 36°30′

**modernism** Liberal theology which attempted to adapt Christianity to modern ideas, saying that all claims to truth in theology must be made based on reason or experience alone

**monopoly** The control of an entire industry by one company

**Monroe Doctrine** Declaration by President Monroe that European nations could not intervene in the Western Hemisphere except where they already had colonies and that the United States would not meddle in European affairs

**Montgomery bus boycott** Boycott of city buses in Montgomery, Alabama, for more than a year, led by Dr. Martin Luther King Jr. and the Montgomery Improvement Association in response to the arrest of Rosa Parks for not giving up her seat on the bus

**moral diplomacy** Woodrow Wilson's foreign policy that promoted freedom and democratic ideas and help for other countries to improve economically

**Moravians** Reformed group from southern Germany that emphasized the importance of conversion, personal piety, the necessity of living a holy life, and missions

**Morill Land Grant Act** Law giving federal land to states for the purpose of establishing or supporting colleges that specialized in agricultural and mechanical education

**Mormons** Another name for the Church of Jesus Christ of Latter-Day Saints, founded by Joseph Smith; religious group that settled in Salt Lake City, Utah, under the leadership of Brigham Young

**Mormon Trail** The Mormons' route to the Great Salt Lake

**Mound Builders** Native Americans of the Eastern Woodlands and Southeast who constructed mounds to bury the dead

**muckrakers** Journalists who exposed abuse and corruption

**mudslinging** The spreading of negative information about opponents

**Mueller Investigation** Investigation led by FBI director Robert Mueller regarding allegations of collusion between Russia and the Trump campaign; report that concluded Russia had interfered in the 2016 presidential campaign and that several Trump associates had dealings with Russia but did not determine that the Trump campaign had conspired with the Russian government to interfere with the election

# N

**Nagasaki** Site of second atomic bomb dropped on Japan, August 9, 1945

**National Aeronautics and Space Administration (NASA)** Agency established to conduct America's space program

**National Association for the Advancement of Colored People (NAACP)** Organization founded in 1909 seeking equality for black Americans and focusing on fighting legal battles to achieve that objective

**nationalism** The feeling of loyalty or devotion toward one's country or cultural group

**National Recovery Administration (NRA)** New Deal agency which established over five hundred codes or regulations for businesses with the goals of increasing employment, maintaining wages, and reducing unwanted competition

**National Republican Party** Portion of the former Democratic-Republican Party that supported John Quincy Adams's nationalist agenda

**National Road** First federally funded road, stretching from Maryland to Illinois

**Navajo code talkers** Navajo Indians serving in the US Army during World War II who used their native language as code for the military

**Navigation and Trade Acts** Mercantile polices enacted by Parliament to restrict trade for the colonies in order to increase revenue for Britain

**Newburgh Conspiracy** Plan by a group of Revolutionary War army officers to force the Confederation Congress to grant back pay and pensions and possibly replace the government with a new government under a king or dictator

**New Deal** Name attached to Franklin Roosevelt's efforts to conquer the Great Depression

**New Jersey Plan** Proposal to the Constitutional Convention for a unicameral legislature with equal representation for all states which was favored by smaller states

**New Left** Radical groups that hoped to use resentment over the Vietnam War as a means of overthrowing established American institutions

**New Right** Group of conservatives that shared many beliefs of the traditionalists and was motivated by numerous social and moral issues

**New South** Movement promoted by some southern leaders to base the southern economy on manufacturing and industry, not just agriculture

**9/11 attack** Date of the terrorist attack on the United States in which Muslim extremists hijacked four planes, crashing into the World Trade Center towers, the Pentagon, and a field in Pennsylvania, killing over 2,700 people

**Nineteenth Amendment** Amendment that provided women the right to vote

**normalcy** Word used by Warren G. Harding to describe America's desire to return to life as it was before World War I

**North American Free Trade Agreement (NAFTA)** Free trade agreement designed to increase free trade between Mexico, Canada, and the United States

**North Atlantic Treaty Organization (NATO)** Military alliance of Western nations formed in 1949 in which members pledged to provide military support for any member that was attacked

**Northwest Ordinance of 1787** Law that required the Northwest Territory to be divided into at least three but no more than five states and provided steps for a territory to become a state

**Northwest Territory** All the lands west of the thirteen original colonies, north of the Ohio River, and east of the Mississippi River that passed from British to American control after the War for Independence

**nullify** To declare a law invalid because a state deemed it to be unconstitutional

**Nuremberg Trials** International court proceedings held in Nuremberg, Germany, to bring justice on those who committed war crimes and crimes against humanity during World War II

# O

*Obergefell v. Hodges* Supreme Court ruling that declared key sections of the Defense of Marriage Act (DOMA) to be unconstitutional and decreed that the 14th Amendment required all US state laws to recognize same-sex marriages

**Office of War Information** Agency created to inform Americans about World War II and to create propaganda to rally support for the war effort

**Okies** Nickname for thousands of Oklahoma farmers who moved to California to find work and escape from the Dust Bowl conditions

**Oklahoma City bombing** Bombing in 1995 of a federal office building in Oklahoma City by Timothy McVeigh, partly in reaction to the raid on the Branch Davidians two years before in Waco, Texas; deadliest act of domestic terrorism in American history to that point

**Old Deluder Satan Act** Law in Massachusetts that every village of fifty or more families hire a schoolmaster, and every town of one hundred or more families establish a grammar school

**Olive Branch Petition** Petition to settle matters peacefully, sent by the Second Continental Congress to King George III

**Open Door Policy** US policy proposing that nations with spheres of interest in China allow free trade to all nations

**Ordinance of 1784** Legislation, written by Thomas Jefferson, that created ten new states out of the Northwest Territory, banned slavery in the region, and gave land to settlers rather than selling it

**Ordinance of Nullification** Resolution passed by the South Carolina legislature nullifying the Tariffs of 1828 and 1832 and threatening secession if the federal government attempted to enforce the tariff

**Oregon Trail** Most important route for settlers and missionaries going west from the eastern part of the United States toward Oregon

**Organization of Petroleum Exporting Countries (OPEC)** Group of countries (mostly Arab) that produced much of the world's oil; proclaimed an embargo on oil exports to the United States in 1973 because of US support of Israel in the Yom Kippur War

# P

**Panama Canal Treaty** The 1977 treaty stating that the United States and Panama would jointly operate the canal until December 31, 1999, when Panama would take complete control of it

**Panic of 1873** A six-year-long economic depression that began in 1873

**Panic of 1819** A economic collapse that hurt southern and western farmers particularly hard

**Panic of 1837** A five-year economic recession during the presidency of Martin Van Buren

**Patriot Act** Congressional act making it easier to locate and imprison suspected terrorists and allowing the government to listen to phone conversations of people suspected of having terrorist connections, though some provisions were later deemed unconstitutional by the Supreme Court

**Patriots** Colonists who supported the cause of American independence from Britain

**Peace Corps** Program introduced by President Kennedy in 1961 to send skilled volunteers overseas to help underdeveloped nations

**Peace Democrats** Northern Democrats during the Civil War who wanted to preserve the Union through negotiation rather than through victory over the South; also called "Copperheads"

**Pearl Harbor** US naval and air base in Hawaii; attacked by the Japanese on December 7, 1941, resulting in a declaration of war by the United States

**Pendleton Act** Law passed in 1883 that attempted to end the spoils system and created the Civil Service Commission

**Pequot War** Conflict from 1636 to 1638 between Massachusetts Bay colonists and the Pequot tribe

**Persian Gulf War** A six-week intensive American-led military effort in 1991 that successfully ousted the invading country of Iraq (led by Saddam Hussein) from Kuwait

**pet banks** State banks in which federal revenues were deposited in Andrew Jackson's efforts to destroy the Second Bank of the United States

**petroglyphs** Rock drawings created by Native Americans of the Great Basin and Plateau

**Pickett's Charge** Unsuccessful Confederate attack on the Union lines at Gettysburg led by General George Pickett on July 3, 1863, in which half of his men were killed, wounded, or captured

**Pinckney Treaty** Treaty negotiated by Thomas Pinckney in which Spain agreed to open the port of New Orleans to American goods and which settled the boundary of Florida

**Plains Indians** Nations such as the Cheyenne, Comanche, and Sioux who lived in the Great Plains region

**Platt Amendment** 1901 law which prohibited Cuba from making alliances with other countries besides the United States, allowed American oversight of Cuba's finances, and authorized the United States to send troops to Cuba to keep order if necessary

*Plessy v. Ferguson* Supreme Court case in 1896 declaring "separate but equal" facilities for blacks and whites constitutional

**poll taxes** Special taxes required of voters, often preventing black citizens from voting

**Pony Express** Mail delivery system from Missouri to California using a relay of riders on horseback

**popular sovereignty** The idea that the ultimate source of governmental power lies in the people, this idea being applied in the nineteenth century to argue that the residents of the territories could decide the status of slavery in the territory

**populism** Appealing to the common people

**Populist Party** Also called the People's Party; political party formed in the 1890s to address the needs of farmers and laborers

**Proclamation of 1763** Prohibited colonists from settling beyond the Appalachian Mountains in order to reduce conflicts with Native Americans

**Proclamation of Neutrality** President Washington's proclamation that the United States would pursue a policy of friendliness toward Britain and France during their conflict

**Proclamation of Rebellion** King George III's declaration that parts of the American colonies were in "open and avowed rebellion"

**progressivism** A movement in the late nineteenth and early twentieth centuries that favored achieving political and social reform through education, wider political participation, and direct government action

**Prohibition** Period between 1920 and 1933 when alcoholic beverages were illegal

**Prohibitory Act** 1775 act that ordered that all trade with the American colonies be stopped and all ships involved in colonial trade be seized

**propaganda** Information that is spread to advance a cause or damage an opponent's cause

**proprietary colony** Colony in which the king gave control to one or more proprietors

**protective tariff** A high tax on imports designed to shield a nation's manufacturers from foreign competition

**Pullman Strike** Strike in 1894 by workers of the Pullman Palace Car Company over wage cuts that spread nationwide when the American Railway Union ordered all Pullman cars removed from trains, affecting mail delivery and resulting in federal troops being sent to break the strike, and federal courts issuing an injunction that forbade the union from further encouraging the strike

**Pure Food and Drug Act** Congressional act that outlawed the interstate sale of impure food and drugs and required honest labeling of such products

**Puritans** Group who wanted to purify the Anglican church from within

# Q

**Quakers** Members of the Society of Friends who taught that people possessed an "inner light" and who opposed participating in wars, taking oaths, or holding public office

**Quartering Act** 1765 act requiring colonists to pay for food and housing for British troops stationed in the colonies

**Quebec Act** 1774 act for British Canada that called for a governor appointed by the Crown and no elected legislative assembly, made Roman Catholicism the official religion of Quebec, and extended the boundaries of Quebec southward to the Ohio River

# R

**Radical Republicans** Influential minority in the Republican Party during Reconstruction who believed Lincoln's and Johnson's plans did not do enough to punish the South and transform southern attitudes

**ratification** The process of states giving their consent or approval (to the United States Constitution)

**Reagan Doctrine** One of the key aspects of Reagan's foreign policy pledging American support to insurgent groups battling Communist governments in the third world

**recall** A special election to decide whether to remove an elected official from office before his term is expired

**Reconstruction** Period from the end of the Civil War until 1877

**Reconstruction Act of 1867** Divided the South into military districts and required states to give black males the right to vote and hold office, create constitutional conventions that included blacks, submit their constitutions for Congress's approval, and ratify the Fourteenth Amendment

**Reconstruction Finance Corporation (RFC)** Act that gave $2 billion in loans to struggling banks, railroads, agricultural organizations, and other large businesses to help them maintain workers and create jobs

**Redeemers** White southern Democrats during Reconstruction who wanted to redeem (save) their state governments from "Black Republican" rule

**redlining** When banks charged higher interest rates or refused to offer mortgages for homes located in minority neighborhoods

**Red Scare** Time of increased public concern about communism in America

**referendum** Procedure allowing the people to vote directly on whether a law should be enacted

**Reform Darwinism** Idea which said that human progress comes through cooperation promoted by government action

**Religious Right** Important component of the New Right; various conservative Christian leaders and organizations that were concerned primarily with moral issues and encouraged Christians to be involved in politics

**reparations** Money a defeated country must pay for war damages

**republic** A government in which elected representatives govern the people

**Republican Party** Political party formed in 1854 that included abolitionists and Free Soil Party members

**reservationists** A group of senators, led by Republican Henry Cabot Lodge, who refused to ratify the Treaty of Versailles unless it was amended to address their reservations about US involvement in the League of Nations

**Respect for Marriage Act** Legislation passed during the Biden administration that reversed the Defense of Marriage Act and strengthened federal protection of same-sex and interracial marriages

**right of deposit** The freedom to stockpile goods at a port until ships transport them overseas

*Roe v. Wade* Supreme Court decision in 1973 that the Constitution contained a right to privacy and that restrictions on abortion early in pregnancy were unconstitutional

**Roosevelt Corollary** An addition to the Monroe Doctrine, stating that the United States had the right to act as the police to maintain economic and political stability in the Western Hemisphere

**royal colony** A colony controlled directly by the king who appointed a governor

# S

**San Juan Hill** Site outside Santiago, Cuba, where Colonel Leonard Wood and Lieutenant Colonel Theodore Roosevelt led the charge of the Rough Riders during the Spanish-American War

**Santa Fe Trail** First American route west of the Missouri River; primarily a trade route

**Saratoga** Site of a major American victory against the British in 1777 in New York which led to the French entering the War for Independence on America's side

**scalawags** White southerners who supported the Reconstruction governments; derisive term that means "scoundrel" or "worthless person"

**Scopes trial** Trial in Tennessee in 1925 involving the violation of a state law prohibiting the teaching of evolution in public schools

**Second Battle of Bull Run** Civil War battle fought on August 28, 1862; a Confederate victory

**Second Continental Congress** Delegates from the thirteen colonies that assembled in Philadelphia beginning in May 1775 which became the colonial government throughout the War for Independence; took control of the colonial army at Boston

**Second Great Awakening** Spiritual revival in the United States from 1795 to 1840

**Securities Exchange Commission (SEC)** Commission established under Franklin Roosevelt that regulates the stock market and prevents fraud in investments

**Selective Service Act** Congress's response to Wilson's call for war; a peacetime military draft to prepare America to enter World War I

**self-determination** Principle under which people would decide for themselves under what government or in which country they wished to live

**Seneca Falls Convention** 1848 meeting that discussed women's rights, including the right to vote

**separation of powers** The division of government into branches to ensure that no branch has too much power

**Separatists** Group that believed that Christians needed to separate from the Anglican church

**settlement houses** Homes established for reformers to settle in slum areas to address the needs of the urban poor

**Seventeenth Amendment** Provided for the direct election of US senators

**Seward's Folly** Nickname ridiculing the purchase of Alaska from Russia in 1867 negotiated by Secretary of State William Seward

**sharecropping** System where farmers worked small plots of a landowner's land; system in which a portion, or share, of the crop is paid to the landowner as rent

**Shays's Rebellion** Uprising led by Daniel Shays in Massachusetts to prevent farmers from losing their property to foreclosure by forcing some courts to close and attempting to seize a federal armory

**Sherman Antitrust Act** Law passed in 1890 declaring that trusts in restraint of trade were illegal; law used to break up, or dismantle, large companies

**silent majority** Term Nixon used to refer to the belief that most Americans were not violent radicals discontent with America but were quiet, hard-working people who wanted peace and order

**sit-ins** Nonviolent strategy in which protestors sat in a restaurant or business and refused to leave until they were served; strategy used in the civil rights movement to integrate lunch counters and other businesses

**Sixteenth Amendment** Amendment that established the federal income tax

**Smoot-Hawley Tariff** Tariff passed in June 1930 to protect American industries and agriculture from foreign competition; the highest tariff in United States history

**Social Darwinism** Philosophy that applied Darwin's theory of natural selection and survival of the fittest to society and business

**social gospel** Movement beginning in the Progressive Era that replaced an emphasis on regeneration of individuals with an emphasis on regeneration of society through social reform

**Social Security Act (SSA)** Act, passed as a New Deal measure, which provides unemployment insurance and a monthly pension for most retired individuals

**Sons of Liberty** Groups, such as the one in Boston led by Samuel Adams, that protested the Stamp Act

**Sooners** Settlers who illegally staked their claims before the allotted time during the Oklahoma Land Rush

**Southern Christian Leadership Conference (SCLC)** Organization formed after the Montgomery bus boycott to spread and organize the civil rights movement across the South; group that chose Dr. Martin Luther King Jr. to be its first president

**Spanish-American War** 1898 war between Spain and the United States fought in Cuba, Puerto Rico, and the Philippines

**Spanish Armada** Spanish naval fleet created by King Philip II to conquer Protestant England

**Specie Circular** Executive order by Andrew Jackson that all public land sales be done in specie (gold and silver) rather than paper money

**speculation** Buying or selling something that has an unusually high risk for the chance to gain an unusually large profit

**spoils system** Distribution of government jobs to friends and supporters

**Spot Resolution** Motion by Congressman Abraham Lincoln demanding that President Polk announce the exact spot where American forces were attacked by Mexico

**stagflation** An economic condition in which inflation and unemployment are both high; a stagnant economy coupled with inflation

**St. Augustine** The oldest permanent city settled by Europeans in the United States

**Stalwarts** Term for Republicans during the Gilded Age who favored high tariffs, hard money, and the spoils system

**Stamp Act** 1765 act that required colonists to purchase a special stamp for newspapers, printed sermons, playing cards, and other legal and commercial documents

**Stamp Act Congress** Meeting of nine colonies in 1765 that denounced the Stamp Act

**Strategic Arms Limitation Talks Agreement (SALT I)** 1972 agreement between the United States and the Soviet Union to limit the number of strategic nuclear missiles each nation had

**Student Nonviolent Coordinating Committee (SNCC)** Civil rights group organized in 1960 to organize student sit-ins and other forms of nonviolent protest

**Sugar Act** 1764 act that taxed goods imported to the colonies, such as sugar, molasses, and coffee

**supply-side economics** Also called Reaganomics or "trickle down" economics; economic policy of the Reagan administration based on tax cuts and dependent on a limited-government agenda: cutting taxes so that citizens will have incentive to earn, save, and invest; encouraging economic expansion by reducing government regulations on business; and providing corporate tax breaks

# T

**Taft-Hartley Act** 1947 anti-union measure that required a cooling off period before strikes in essential businesses, required union officials to swear they were not Communist, and permitted states to pass "right to work" laws banning the union shop

**Taliban** Muslim extremist group that controlled the government of Afghanistan and protected Osama bin Laden and al-Qaeda terrorists, was removed from power when the United States and allies invaded in 2001, and was returned to power when the United States withdrew in 2021

**Tammany Hall** Political organization that controlled most of New York's political affairs during the last half of the nineteenth century

**Tariff of 1832** Tariff that lowered the tariff rates from the Tariff of 1828 but was still nullified by South Carolina

**Tariff of Abominations** Southern name for the Tariff of 1828 which raised tariff rates

**Tea Act** 1773 act that reduced the tax on tea and granted a monopoly on the shipment and sale of tea in America to the British East India Company

**Teapot Dome scandal** Scandal during Harding's administration involving Secretary of the Interior Albert Fall accepting "loans" for leasing oil reserves and resulting in the first cabinet member to be imprisoned for misdeeds in office

**Teller Amendment** Resolution by Congress stating that the United States had no intention to control Cuba in the Spanish-American War but desired Cuba's independence

**Tennessee Valley Authority (TVA)** New Deal agency that built dams along the Tennessee River to provide navigation, flood control, and cheap electricity for Tennessee and portions of Alabama and Kentucky

**Ten Percent Plan** Lincoln's plan for Reconstruction in which the military governor was to reestablish a civilian government as soon as a number equal to ten percent of those who voted in the 1860 election took an oath of allegiance to the Union

**Tenure of Office Act** Act which made it illegal for the president to remove any appointee who received Senate approval without the Senate's consent; the act which Andrew Johnson violated, for which he was impeached, but which was later declared unconstitutional

**Tet Offensive** Multiple surprise attacks launched by Communist troops across South Vietnam on January 31, 1968, the Vietnamese New Year (Tet)

**Thirteenth Amendment** Amendment that abolished slavery

**Three-Fifths Compromise** Agreement of the Constitutional Convention that three-fifths of a state's slave population would be counted for purposes of representation and taxation

**Timbuktu** Center of Islamic learning and culture in the Mali Empire

***Titanic*** British passenger ship believed to be "unsinkable," but that sank after hitting an iceberg on its maiden voyage in 1912, killing about 1,500 people

**totem poles** Intricately carved logs erected by Native Americans of the Pacific Northwest to represent what was important to them

**Townshend Acts** Acts passed in 1767 that placed taxes on glass, paper, paint, and tea, and strengthened writs of assistance

**Trail of Tears** Forced marches of the Cherokee from Georgia to Indian Territory in which many Native Americans died

**transcendentalism** A form of romanticism; a religious movement which taught that man was essentially good and perfectible and which emphasized intuition and the senses over rationalism and logical reasoning; philosophy that inspired its followers to establish a utopian community at Brook Farm, Massachusetts

**Treaty of Fort Laramie (1868)** Agreement between the US government and Sioux chiefs that reduced Sioux lands established by previous treaties, created a new reservation that included the Black Hills, guaranteed a portion of land outside the reservation to be free from white settlement, and removed troops from the forts on that land

**Treaty of Ghent** Treaty ending the War of 1812

**Treaty of Guadalupe Hidalgo** Treaty ending the Mexican War in which the United States added the Mexican Cession and made the Rio Grande the southern border of Texas

**Treaty of Paris of 1763** Treaty that ended the French and Indian War in which France surrendered Canada and its claims east of the Mississippi River to Britain, Britain acquired Florida from Spain, and Spain gained the French lands west of the Mississippi River

**Treaty of Paris of 1783** Treaty that ended the War for Independence in which Britain recognized America's independence and awarded all land east of the Mississippi River except Florida to the United States

**Treaty of Paris of 1898** Treaty that ended the Spanish-American War in which Spain ceded Guam and Puerto Rico to the United States, Cuba became independent, and the United States purchased the Philippines for $20 million

**Treaty of Portsmouth** Treaty mediated by Theodore Roosevelt that ended the Russo-Japanese War, for which he was awarded a Nobel Peace Prize

**Treaty of Versailles** Peace treaty after World War I which placed the blame for the war on Germany and forced Germany to pay reparations

**trench warfare** Major tactic of World War I that used long ditches normally deep enough for a man to stand in, and that included frontline trenches, support trenches, and communication trenches

**Trenton** Site of a battle in which George Washington's troops quietly crossed the Delaware River and surprised and defeated a group of Hessian soldiers

**triangular trade** Trade between Europe, Africa, and North America

**Triple Alliance** Alliance of Germany, Austria-Hungary, and Italy

**Triple Entente** Alliance of Great Britain, France, and Russia

**Troubled Asset Relief Program** Bill passed under President George W. Bush's administration that provided $700 billion in government assistance to prevent US financial institutions from collapsing during the Great Recession

**Truman Doctrine** Giving money or other assistance to pro-Western, anti-Communist governments

**trust** Legal device by which a board of trustees is empowered to make decisions and control the operations of a whole group of companies

**Tuskegee Airmen** Highly-commended unit of the US Army Air Corps during World War II consisting of African American pilots and support personnel who were trained near Tuskegee Institute

**Twentieth Amendment** Amendment that moved presidential inaugurations from March 4 to January 20

**Twenty-First Amendment** Amendment that repealed the Eighteenth (Prohibition) Amendment

**Twenty-Fourth Amendment** Amendment that outlawed the use of poll taxes in federal elections

**Twenty-Second Amendment** Amendment that declared no one could be elected president more than two times

**Twenty-Seventh Amendment** Amendment that prohibits a Congressional pay raise from taking effect until after the next Congressional election

**Twenty-Sixth Amendment** Amendment that granted voting rights to citizens aged eighteen and older

**Twenty-Third Amendment** Amendment that granted electoral votes to Washington, DC, for presidential elections

# U

**U-boat** Another name for submarines; from *Unterseeboot*, the German word for a submarine

***Uncle Tom's Cabin*** Book published by Harriet Beecher Stowe in 1852 that depicted the plight of slave families and runaways

**Underground Railroad** Secret network of safe houses and people who "conducted" escaping slaves to the North and Canada

**Underwood Tariff Act of 1913** Congressional act which was the first genuine tariff reduction since the Civil War and which compensated for the loss of revenue by adopting the first federal income tax

**unicameral** Having only one house in a legislature

**Union Pacific Railroad** One of two railroads that built the transcontinental railroad; railroad that started in Omaha, Nebraska, and built westward

**Unitarianism** Religious movement which denied the Trinity and the deity of Christ

**United Nations** International organization formed after World War II as a body to further world peace

**United States-Mexico-Canada Agreement (USMCA)** Trade agreement passed during the Trump administration, replacing NAFTA in 2020

**USS *Maine*** US Navy battleship whose explosion in Havana Harbor, Cuba, in 1898 was blamed on Spain by yellow journalists

**utopia** An ideal society

# V

**V-E Day** Victory in Europe Day; May 7, 1945

**vertical integration** Control of every aspect of production in an industry

**Vicksburg** Mississippi town built on a high bluff overlooking the Mississippi River; last Confederate stronghold on the river; site of Union victory when the town surrendered July 4, 1863, after a months-long siege

**Viet Cong** Communists in South Vietnam who fought to overthrow the non-Communist government

**Vietnamization** President Nixon's plan for improving the South Vietnamese army's fighting ability through increased training and equipment and the gradual withdrawal of American combat forces from Vietnam

**Virginia Plan** Proposal to the Constitutional Convention for a bicameral legislature with representation based on state population, a strong executive, and a national judiciary; favored by larger states

**Virginia Resolutions** Resolutions drafted by James Madison which stated that the national government existed by consent of the states, that the states had the right to judge the constitutionality of laws, and that states had the right to interpose against unconstitutional laws

**Virginia Statute for Religious Freedom** 1786 law in Virginia which granted religious liberty, declared that the state had no official church and could not collect taxes to support churches, and removed religious tests for holding office

**V-J Day** Victory over Japan Day; September 2, 1945

**Volstead Act** Law that provided for the enforcement of Prohibition

**Voting Rights Act of 1965** Second civil rights legislation passed under President Johnson; law that outlawed literacy tests, allowed federal officials to be sent into states to oversee and ensure fairness in voter registration and elections, required changes to voting procedures in any areas where voter discrimination had previously occurred to obtain approval from a district court or the Attorney General, gave the Attorney General the power to challenge poll taxes used in state and local elections

# W

**Wade-Davis Bill** Radical Republican plan for Reconstruction, vetoed by Lincoln, that required military governors until fifty percent of adult white males took an oath of allegiance to the Union, demanded that states abolish slavery and any claims for the federal government to pay their war debts, and prohibited former Confederate leaders from voting or holding office

**Wagner Act** Also called the National Labor Relations Act; New Deal legislation that prohibited unfair labor practices such as employers firing or discriminating against employees who organized or joined a union; act that guaranteed workers the right to collective bargaining and established the National Labor Relations Board (NLRB)

**War Hawks** Group of western and southern members of the House of Representatives who wanted war against Britain

**War of 1812** War between the United States and Britain from 1812 to 1814

**war of attrition** War strategy meant to wear out the opponent and exhaust its resources and will to fight

**War Powers Act** 1973 Congressional act that limited the president's power to use American troops abroad without a declaration of war and required that the president notify Congress within forty-eight hours of committing US troops to military action and withdraw such troops within ninety days unless Congress approves continued use of those forces

**War Production Board** Organized the transition of American industries from civilian production to war production during World War II

**Warsaw Pact** Military alliance of the Soviet Union and its Eastern European satellites formed in response to NATO

**Washington Naval Conference** Meeting of nations in 1921 at which agreements were reached to limit the growth of naval power

**Watergate scandal** The 1972 break-in of the Democratic National Committee headquarters in the Watergate complex in Washington, DC, and the attempt to cover up the Nixon administration's role, which led to Nixon's resignation from the presidency in 1974

**weapons of mass destruction (WMDs)** Specially formulated weapons (such as chemical, biological, and nuclear) intended to harm or kill great numbers of people that Saddam Hussein was suspected of possessing after the end of the Persian Gulf War

**Welfare Reform Act of 1996** Legislation passed during the Clinton administration that rolled back federal guarantees for the poor for the first time since FDR's New Deal, required welfare recipients to go back to work within two years and set a lifetime maximum of five years for assistance, and gave blocks of federal funds to the states to address welfare reform

**Whig Party** Party formed before the election of 1836 that opposed Andrew Jackson and his concentration of power in the executive branch

**Whiskey Rebellion** Protest by Pennsylvania farmers over the excise tax on whiskey, which was put down by troops led by President Washington

**Wilderness Road** Road cut by Daniel Boone from Virginia through the Cumberland Gap to Kentucky

**Wilmot Proviso** Failed amendment by David Wilmot of Pennsylvania which would have prevented slavery in territory acquired from Mexico in the Mexican War

***Worcester v. Georgia*** 1832 Supreme Court decision, ignored by Andrew Jackson, which ruled that Georgia law was not valid in the Cherokee Nation

**Works Progress Administration (WPA)** New Deal program that created more than 8 million jobs to build and repair roads, construct public buildings and recreational areas, and that supported actors, directors, writers, and artists in art programs

**Wounded Knee Massacre** Tragic conclusion to the Indian Wars when the army tried to disarm and capture a band of Sioux resulting in the death of 25 soldiers and 150 Native American men, women, and children at Wounded Knee Creek, South Dakota

**writs of assistance** General search warrants given to customs agents to search for smuggled goods anywhere

# X

**XYZ Affair** Incident in which three French agents demanded a bribe and loans from the American delegation in order to open negotiations

# Y

**yellow journalism** Sensationalized news reporting aimed at attracting readers

**Yorktown** Site in Virginia of the last major battle of the War for Independence, in 1781, in which Charles Cornwallis surrendered his army

# Z

**Zimmerman telegram** German telegram, intercepted by British intelligence and forwarded to the United States, in which Germany promised Mexico part of the United States if Mexico would go to war with the United States, in the event that the United States decided to enter World War I

# Index

## A

AAA (Agricultural Adjustment Act), 479, 483

Abernathy, Ralph, 582, 587

abolition and abolitionist movement, 193–94, 229, 238, 240, 269

abortion, 621, 627, 642, 675, 683

Abraham Accords, 670

Adams, John
    presidency, 125, 126, 128, 129
    War for Independence and, 64, 65, 67, 73, 74, 92, 96
    in Washington administration, 115

Adams, John Quincy, 143, 144, 153–55, 156–57

Adams, Samuel, 62, 64, 67, 68

Adams-Onís Treaty (1819), 143

Addams, Jane, 400

Administration of Justice Act (1774), 66

affirmative action, 619, 675

Affordable Care Act (ACA), 662, 663, 666

Afghanistan, 615, 632, 650–51, 663, 670, 676

AFL (American Federation of Labor), 328, 400, 482

African Americans
    black codes, 286, 297
    constitutional amendments and, 289–90, 294, 302
    discrimination and segregation, 28990, 302, 392–94, 455–56, 483, 502 (see also civil rights movement)
    education access and rights, 289, 302, 578, 584–85, 619
    Freedmen's Bureau and, 288–89
    Great Migration, 450
    labor concerns, 400
    political leanings, 484
    religion and, 189, 227
    schools for, 391
    voting rights, 294, 297, 302, 392, 401, 575, 583, 589–90
    in World War I, 431, 432
    in World War II, 501

African slave trade, 13, 21–22, 102

Age of Exploration, 10–17

*Age of Reason* (Paine), 73

Agnew, Spiro, 606

Agricultural Adjustment Act (AAA), 479, 483

agricultural overproduction, 441, 466, 475, 479

agricultural technology, 186–87, 349

Aguinaldo, Emilio, 373, 376

AI (artificial intelligence), 680

AIDS (acquired immunodeficiency syndrome), 630

Aid to Families with Dependent Children (AFDC), 629

airplanes, 388, 419, 446, 473

Alabama, secession of, 243

Alamo, Battle of the (1836), 203

Alaska, state establishment, 368, 542

Albania, 527, 637

Albany Plan, 58

Alexander, James Waddel, 208

Alexander VI, Pope, 16

Algonquian Bible, 45

Alien and Sedition Acts (1798), 127, 131

Alito, Samuel Jr., 655

Allen, Ethan, 70, 79, 188

Allen, Richard, 189, 194

Alliance, Treaty of (1778), 122, 126

Alliance for Progress, 551

Allied Powers, 417, 495

al-Qaeda, 645, 651–52

amendments. *See under* Constitution

American Board of Commissioners for Foreign Missions (ABCFM), 191

American Civil Liberties Union (ACLU), 458

American Expeditionary Force (AEF), 430

American Federation of Labor (AFL), 328, 400, 482

American Indians. *See* Native Americans

American Party (Know-Nothing Party), 236

American Red Cross, 430

American Rescue Plan, 674

American Revolution. *See* War for Independence

Americans with Disabilities Act (1990), 640

American System, 145, 177

American Volunteer Group (AVG), 499

Amish, 48

Anabaptists, 48

Anaconda Plan, 257

Anderson, John, 628

Anderson, Robert, 245

André, John, 79

Anglican Church, 27, 29, 32, 48, 85

animism, 9

Annapolis Convention, 98

Anthony, Susan B., 401

Antietam, Battle of (1862), 261, 270

Anti-Federalists, 107–9

antiwar movement, 565

appeasement, 494

Appomattox Court House, 275

Arab Spring, 664

Arbery, Ahmaud, 669

Argentina, 144, 421

*Arizona*, USS, 500

Arkansas, secession of, 246

armistice, 432

Armour, Philip, 341

Armstrong, Louis, 451

Armstrong, Neil, 558

Arnold, Benedict, 70, 78, 79, 84

Arthur, Chester, 310–11

Articles of Confederation, 91, 92, 97, 98–100

artificial intelligence (AI), 680

Asbury, Francis, 189

Ashley, William H., 216

assimilation, 159, 160, 355–56, 454

Astor, Jacob, 216

astrolabes, 10

Atlanta, Battle of (1864), 272

atomic bombs, 517, 528, 541. *See also* nuclear weapons

Atomic Energy Commission, 523

Attlee, Clement, 512, 517

Attucks, Crispus, 64

Austin, Lloyd, 682

Austin, Moses, 201

Austin, Stephen, 201–2

Austria, 494

Austria-Hungary, 415–16, 417, 431

automobile industry, 388, 445

Axis Powers, 493

Aztec people, 7, 12

# B

Babcock, Orville, 294
baby boom, 538
Bacon's Rebellion (1676), 44
Bahrain, 670
Baker, Josephine, 450
balance of power (foreign policy), 382
Ballard, Robert, 389
bank holiday, 478
Banking Act (1933), 481
banks
    Great Depression and, 465, 466,
      477–78
    mortgage loans, 654
    national, 117, 131, 145, 147, 154,
      167–68, 409
    New Deal reforms and, 481
    redlining, 576
    savings and loan (S&L) crisis, 640
    state, 168–69, 171
    stockholding and, 321
Baptists, 47, 48, 109, 130, 230, 457
Barbary States, 131
Barrett, Amy Coney, 667
Barrow, Clyde, 472
Barton, Clara, 255
Bataan Death March, 513
Battle of Fallen Timbers (1794), 120
Battle of the Bulge (1944), 508
battles. *See specific locations, e.g.
    Bunker Hill, Battle of*
Bay of Pigs, 551
Bear Flag Republic, 210
bear market, 466
Beauregard, Pierre G. T., 245, 259
Bee, Bernard, 259
Beecher, Henry Ward, 196
Begin, Menachem, 614
Belgium, 416–17, 495, 508
Belknap, William, 294
Bell, Alexander Graham, 316
Bell, John, 242
Benz, Karl, 388
Berkeley, William, 44
Berlin airlift, 531
Berlin Wall, 552–53
Bernstein, Carl, 604, 605
Bible institutes and conferences, 396
bicameral legislature, 99
Biddle, Nicholas, 167
Biden, Hunter, 667, 676
Biden, Joe, 661, 667, 671, 673, 674–
    75, 682, 684
big stick diplomacy, 377

Bill of Rights, 116
Billy the Kid, 344
Bingham, Hiram, 370
bin Laden, Osama, 651–52, 663
Bird, Harry F., 578
Birney, James, 205
Bismarck, Otto von, 415
black Americans. *See* African
    Americans
black codes, 286, 289, 297
Blackfoot people, 8
Black Hawk, Sauk chief, 159
Black Lives Matter (BLM), 679
Black Panthers, 593
Black Power movement, 592–94
black pride, 593
Bladensburg, Battle of (1814), 139
Blaine, James, 312
Bland-Allison Act (1878), 362
Bleeding Kansas, 237
blitzkrieg, 495
blockade runners, 258
Bloody Sunday, 590
Bolívar, Simón, 144
Bolivia, 144
Bolshevik Revolution, 444
*Bonhomme Richard* (ship), 81
Bonus Army, 476
Boone, Daniel, 120, 177
Booth, John Wilkes, 278
bootlegging, 453
border states, 246, 269
border wall, 669
Bosnia, 644
Boston, Massachusetts
    early colonial, 29, 31, 38
    tensions over British rule, 62, 63,
      64, 65
    in War for Independence, 71
Boston Massacre (1768), 64
Boston Port Act (1774), 66
Boston Tea Party (1773), 65
Bow, Clara, 450
Bowie, Jim, 203
Boxer Rebellion (1900), 370, 381
Braddock, Edward, 58
Bradford, William, 28, 29
Brady Bill (1993), 642
Bragg, Braxton, 268
Brainerd, David, 45
Branch Davidians, 644
Brandywine Creek, Battle of (1777),
    78, 80
Brazil, 144, 421
Breckinridge, John C., 242

Bremer, Paul, 653
Breyer, Stephen, 642
Brezhnev, Leonid, 602, 615
Brisbane, William Henry, 194
Britain. *See also* War for
    Independence; World War I;
    World War II
    Civil War and, 258, 261, 264, 270
    colonization, 16–20, 21
    conflict with France, 44, 57–60,
      122, 132, 137
    imperialism, 366
    Industrial Revolution in, 183
    Monroe Doctrine and, 144
    Native American alliances, 120,
      136, 138, 139
    Persian Gulf War and, 638
    territorial conflict, 142, 172, 206,
      365
    Texas and, 205
    trade disputes, 61–65, 123, 132,
      137
    in War of 1812, 137–41
Brook Farm, 197
Brooks, Preston, 237
Brown, John, 238, 240–41
Brown, Joseph, 254
Brown, Linda, 578
Brown, Michael, 679
*Brown v. Board of Education of
    Topeka*, 557, 578–79
*Brown v. Board of Education II*, 578
Bryan, William Jennings, 362–64,
    377, 382, 398, 406, 420, 424, 458
Buchanan, James, 236, 243, 244
Bulgaria, 417, 431, 527, 637
bull market, 448
Bull Run, First Battle of (1861), 259
Bull Run, Second Battle of (1862),
    261
Bunau-Varilla, Philippe, 378
Bunker Hill, Battle of (1775), 70
Burgoyne, John, 78
Burnside, Ambrose, 262, 268
Burr, Aaron, 125, 128
Bush, George H. W., 628, 635–40, 641
Bush, George W., 646–47, 650–52,
    662
*Bush v. Gore*, 647
business models, 318–20
busing, 619
Butler, Andrew, 237
Butler, Elizur, 161
Butler, Pierce, 101
buying on margin, 448, 465

# C

cabinet (government), 115, 158

Cabot, John, 16

Calhoun, John C., 137, 143, 156, 157, 163–64, 165, 205, 208, 231, 232

California
Mexican War and, 206–7, 210, 212
state establishment, 232

California Gold Rush, 214, 335

California Trail, 217

Calley, William, 565

Calvert, Cecilius, 35

Calvin, John, 76

Cambodia, 560, 562, 569, 570

Camp David Accords, 614

Canada
British-controlled, 136, 138, 172, 206, 365
French colonization of, 14–15

canals, 178

capital, US, 116, 128, 139

capitalism, 321

Capone, Al, 453

Capra, Frank, 504

caravels, 10

CARES (Coronavirus Aid, Relief, and Economic Security) Act, 668

Caribbean
slavery in, 12, 21, 371
in Spanish-American War, 374
Spanish colonization of, 12, 371–72
US occupation of, 376, 420–21, 443

car industry, 388, 445

Carmichael, Stokely, 592, 593

Carnegie, Andrew, 318, 375, 391

Carpentier, Georges, 451

carpetbaggers, 292

Carranza, Venustiano, 421–22

Carson, Kit, 216, 218

Carter, Jimmy, 610–16, 619, 628

Carter, Rosalynn, 621

Cartier, Jacques, 14

Carver, George Washington, 391

cash and carry, 498

Cass, Lewis, 231

Castro, Fidel, 551–52

Castro, Raul, 664

Catholicism. *See* Roman Catholicism

cattle industry, 339–41

caucuses, 153

Cayuga people, 8

Cayuse people, 215, 218

CCC (Civilian Conservation Corps), 480

Central Intelligence Agency (CIA), 524, 543

Central Pacific Railroad, 335–37

Central Powers, 417

Chamberlain, Neville, 494

Chambers, Whittaker, 541

Champlain, Samuel de, 14

Chancellorsville, Battle of (1863), 262

Chaplin, Charlie, 450

Charbonneau, Toussaint, 133

Charles I, King of England, 35

Charles II, King of England, 35

charter colonies, 19, 27, 29, 43

Chattanooga, Battle of (1863), 268

checks and balances, 106

Chennault, Claire, 499

Cherokee people, 8, 58, 120, 160–62, 204, 346, 501

*Chesapeake,* USS, 132, 138

Cheyenne people, 8, 351, 352

Chiang Kai-shek, 533

Chicago, Illinois, 307, 314, 316, 318, 328, 330, 453

Chickamauga, Battle of (1863), 268

Chickasaw people, 8, 346

child labor, 185, 323, 326–27, 400

Chile, 144, 421

China
Boxer Rebellion (1900), 370, 381
Communist, 533–36, 561, 601–2, 637
dollar diplomacy and, 406
Japanese invasion of, 491
missions in, 370
trade with, 180, 380, 670
in World War II, 499

Chinese Exclusion Act (1882), 309

Chinese immigrants, 308, 309, 336

Chisholm Trail, 339

Chivington, John, 351

Choctaw people, 8, 346, 501

Christian and Missionary Alliance (C&MA), 370

Christian Science, 395

Churchill, Winston, 496, 499, 504, 505, 506, 509, 512, 529

Church of England (Anglican Church), 27, 29, 32, 48, 85

CIA (Central Intelligence Agency), 524, 543

Civilian Conservation Corps (CCC), 480

Civil Rights Act (1957), 583, 589

Civil Rights Act (1964), 588–89

civil rights movement
early efforts, 575–85
struggles, 591–96, 619
successes, 586–90

civil service reform, 311

Civil War (1861–65)
costs of, 276
eastern battles, 259–65
end of, 269–75
factors leading to, 244–46
preparations for, 251–55
strategies, 256–58
western battles, 266–68

Civil Works Administration (CWA), 480

Clark, George Rogers, 81, 120

Clark, William, 133–34

Clarke, George and Sarah, 395

Clay, Henry
political career, 145,146, 157, 166, 172, 177, 232
presidential campaigns, 153–54, 167, 168, 205
War of 1812 and, 137

Clayton Antitrust Act (1914), 410

Clean Air Act (1963), 617

Clean Air Act (1990), 640

Clean Water Act (1972), 617

Clemenceau, Georges, 433

*Clermont* (steamboat), 179

Cleveland, Grover, 312, 322, 330, 362, 369

climate change, 682

Clinton, Bill, 641–43, 644

Clinton, DeWitt, 178

Clinton, George, 108

Clinton, Hillary Rodham, 642, 663, 665

clipper ships, 180

coal industry, 317, 326, 405

Cody, William "Buffalo Bill," 345

Coercive ("Intolerable") Acts (1774), 66

Cold Harbor, Battle of (1864), 274

Cold War (1945–1991), 528, 533, 543, 549, 558, 560, 631, 636, 637,

*Cole,* USS, 645

Coleman, Bessie, 446

Colfax, Schuyler, 294

College of Philadelphia, 42

College of William & Mary, 42, 48

Colombia, 144, 378, 379

colonization

Dutch, 15
English, 16–20
French, 14–15
and slavery, 12, 13, 21–22
Spanish, 11–13, 16–17
Colt, Samuel, 184
Columbian Exchange, 13
Columbus, Christopher, 11–12
Comanche people, 218, 351, 501
comic strips, 471
Commerce and Slave Trade
  Compromise (1787), 102
Committee on Public Information,
  427
Committees of Correspondence, 64,
  67
Committee to Re-Elect the President
  (CRP), 604
*Common Sense* (Paine), 73
communism. *See also* Soviet Union
  and Cold War
    anticommunism, 541
    emergence of, 327, 444
    expansion of, 529–35, 543, 633
    fall of, 636–37
compasses, 10
Comprehensive Environmental
  Response, Compensation and
  Liability Act (1980), 617
Compromise of 1850, 232–33
Compromise of 1877, 299
Compromise Tariff of 1833, 166
Comstock Lode, 338
concentration camps, 509–11, 525
Concord, Massachusetts, 68–69
Confederate States of America, 243.
  *See also* Civil War
confederation, 91
Confederation Congress, 92
Congregationalists, 46, 49, 230
Congress
    authority of, 105–6, 117, 147
    Bill of Rights and, 116
    Confederation, 92
    Great Compromise and, 99–100
Congress of Industrial Organizations
  (CIO), 482
Conkling, Roscoe, 310
Connecticut, colonial, 30
Connelly, John, 554
conscription (military draft), 253,
  254, 427, 498, 563, 611
conservation (nature), 405, 406
Constitution

amendments to: First, 116, 127,
  130; Second, 116, 681; Third,
  116; Fourth, 116; Fifth, 116;
  Sixth, 116; Seventh, 116; Eighth,
  116; Ninth, 116; Tenth, 116,
  117, 225; Twelfth, 128, 154;
  Thirteenth, 284; Fourteenth,
  289–90; Fifteenth, 294, 302;
  Sixteenth, 402; Seventeenth,
  402; Eighteenth, 402, 452;
  Nineteenth, 402; Twentieth,
  477; Twenty-First, 453; Twenty-
  Second, 525; Twenty-Third,
  589; Twenty-Fourth, 589, 590;
  Twenty-Fifth, 555; Twenty-
  Sixth, 570; Twenty-Seventh, 640
Bill of Rights, 107, 108, 109, 116
Congressional authority and, 117,
  147
judicial review and, 129
principles, 102–6
ratification, 107–9
success, 11–12
Constitutional Convention (1787),
  98–101
Constitutional Union Party, 242
consumerism, 445–48, 537
containment policy, 530
Continental Association, 67
Contract with America, 642
convoy system, 429
Coolidge, Calvin, 443, 446, 448, 460
Cooper, Peter, 181
Coral Sea, Battle of the (1942), 514
Cornwallis, Charles, 82, 83, 84
Coronado, Francisco de, 13
Coronavirus Aid, Relief, and
  Economic Security (CARES) Act,
  668
corporations, 318
Corps of Discovery, 133–34
corrupt bargain, 154, 157
Cortés, Hernando, 12
cotton diplomacy, 258
cotton gin, 186
cotton industry, 186–87, 223, 226,
  391
Coughlin, Charles, 484
counterculture, 566
*Countess of Scarborough* (ship), 81
court system, organization of, 115.
  *See also* Supreme Court
COVID-19, 668, 671, 674
cowboys, 340
Cowpens, Battle of (1781), 83

Cox, James M., 459
Crane, Stephen, 371
Crawford, William, 153–54
Crazy Horse, Sioux leader, 352–54
Crédit Mobilier scandal, 294
Creek people, 8, 140, 155, 156, 346
Critical Race Theory (CRT), 679
Crockett, Davy, 203, 204
Cronkite, Walter, 616
Crook, George, 352, 353
crop-lien system, 300–301
Crosby, Bing, 470
CRP (Committee to Re-Elect the
  President), 604
Crusades, 10
Cuba
    Communist, 551–52, 633
    diplomatic restoration with US,
      664
    Spanish-American War and,
      371–72, 374
    as US protectorate, 376
Cuban missile crisis, 552
cultural diversity, 678
currency, 168, 169, 252, 361–62
Custer, George Armstrong, 352–53
Czechoslovakia, 434, 494, 637
Czolgosz, Leon, 377

# D

DACA (Deferred Action for
  Childhood Arrivals), 662, 669
Daladier, Édouard, 494
Darrow, Clarence, 458
Darwin, Charles, 313, 367, 452
Darwinism, Reform, 395
Darwinism, Social, 313, 318, 367
Daugherty, Harry, 459, 460
Davies, Samuel, 49
Davis, Benjamin, 501
Davis, Benjamin, Jr., 501
Davis, Jefferson, 243, 254, 267, 268,
  272, 275
Dawes, Charles, 444
Dawes, William, 68
Dawes Act (1887), 355
Dayton Accords, 644
D-Day (June 6, 1944), 506–7
Dean, James, 539
Debs, Eugene V., 330, 400, 408
Declaration of Independence, 74, 76
Declaration of Rights and Grievances,
  67
Declaratory Act (1766), 62

Deere, John, 186

Defense of Marriage Act (1996), 642, 663, 675

Deferred Action for Childhood Arrivals (DACA), 662, 669

deism, 188

Delaware, 33, 246

Delaware people, 120

de Lôme letter, 372

democracy, 105

Democratic Party, 156

Democratic-Republican Party, 118

Dempsey, Jack, 451

Department of Energy, 523

Department of Homeland Security, 652

Department of Housing and Urban Development (HUD), 557

Depression, Great, 465–67, 474–76. *See also* New Deal

détente, 601

Dewey, George, 373

Dewey, John, 390

Dewey, Thomas, 524, 525

Dias, Bartolomeu, 10

Díaz, Porfirio, 421

Dickinson, John, 91

Dillinger, John, 472

discrimination and segregation, racial, 28990, 302, 392–94, 455–56, 483, 502. *See also* civil rights movement

*District of Columbia v. Heller,* 681

diversity, cultural, 678

divorce rates, 539

Dix, Dorothea, 193

*Dobbs v. Jackson Women's Health Organization,* 621, 674, 683

Dole, Bob, 643

Dole, Sanford, 369

dollar diplomacy, 406

domestic terrorism, 644

Dominican Republic, 379, 421

domino theory, 561, 570

Donner Party, 217

Doolittle, Jimmy, 513

Doolittle Raid, 513

Douglas, Stephen A., 235, 239, 240, 242

Douglass, Frederick, 194, 208, 240, 269, 270, 301

draft (conscription), 253, 254, 427, 498, 563, 611

Drake, Sir Francis, 16–17

*Dred Scott v. Sandford,* 238

Drug Enforcement Administration, 630

Du Bois, W. E. B., 394

Dudley, Edward, 576

Dukakis, Michael, 634

Dust Bowl, 469

Dutch colonies, 15, 21, 32

Dwight, Timothy, 189

## E

Earhart, Amelia, 473

Earp, Wyatt, 345

Economic Opportunity Act (1964), 556

Economic Recovery Tax Act (1981), 629

economy and economic systems. *See also* banks; taxes and tariffs

American System, 145, 177

capitalism, 321

in colonies, 31, 33, 36–37

Columbian Exchange, 13

in Confederation government, 95

Congressional involvement in commerce, 102

consumerism, 445–48, 537

currency, 168, 169, 252, 361–62

depressions and recessions, 145, 154, 167, 169, 171, 296, 312, 465–67, 474–76, 656, 662

Hamilton's financial plan, 116–17

industrialization, 183–85, 315–17

inflation, 169, 609, 612, 674

mercantilism, 18, 61

Northern and Southern, 223–24

sharecropping, 300–301

supply-side economics, 629

triangular trade, 31

unemployment, 296, 441, 467, 469, 474–76, 480, 481, 485, 502, 612, 662, 668, 674

wartime, 428, 443, 503, 603

Ecuador, 144

ecumenical movement, 540

Eddy, Mary Baker, 395

Ederle, Gertrude, 451

Edison, Thomas, 316

education

affirmative action, 619, 675

African American access to, 289, 302, 578, 584–85, 619

colonial, 42

federal aid for, 557

for Native Americans, 45

No Child Left Behind, 654

progressive, 390–91

public schools, 192

Edwards, Jonathan, 44, 49

Egypt, 602, 614, 638, 664, 670

Einstein, Albert, 517

Eisenhower, Dwight D.

Korean War and, 535

NATO command, 532

presidency, 540, 542, 543, 544, 551, 561, 583, 584

in World War II, 505, 506, 508, 509, 512

elections. *See also* voting rights

of 1796, 125;

of 1800, 128, 130;

of 1824, 153–54;

of 1828, 157;

of 1832, 168;

of 1836, 170;

of 1844, 205;

of 1848, 231;

of 1856, 236;

of 1860, 242;

of 1864, 273;

of 1872, 296;

of 1876, 298–99;

of 1880, 310;

of 1884, 312;

of 1896, 362–64;

of 1900, 377;

of 1912, 407–8;

of 1916, 425;

of 1920, 459;

of 1928, 465;

of 1932, 477;

of 1936, 484;

of 1948, 524–25;

of 1952, 542;

of 1960, 549–50;

of 1964, 556;

of 1968, 568;

of 1972, 604;

of 1976, 610;

of 1980, 627–28;

of 1984, 630;

of 1988, 635;

of 1992, 641;

of 1996, 643;

of 2000, 646–47;

of 2004, 653;

of 2008, 661;

of 2012, 662;

of 2016, 665;

of 2020, 671

Electoral College system, 104, 154, 158
electricity, 446
Elementary and Secondary Education Act (1965), 557
Eliot, John, 45
Eliot, T. S. , 449
Elizabeth I, Queen of England, 16, 17
Ellington, Edward "Duke," 451
Ellis, Joseph, 98
Ellis Island, 308
Ellsberg, Daniel, 605
Ellsworth, Oliver, 100
El Salvador, 633
emancipation, 194, 269–70, 284
Emancipation Proclamation, 269–70
Embargo Act (1807), 132
Emergency Banking Act (1933), 478
Emergency Relief and Construction Act (1932), 474
Emerson, John, 238
Emerson, Ralph Waldo, 68, 188, 213
Employment Act (1946), 523
Empress of China (ship), 180
encomienda system, 12
energy crisis, 603, 612–13, 618
Enforcement Act (1870), 298
Engel v. Vitale, 557
England. See Britain
environmentalism, 617–18
Environmental Protection Agency (EPA), 617
Equal Employment Opportunity Commission (EEOC), 589
Equal Rights Amendment (ERA; 1972), 621, 627
Era of Good Feelings, 142
Erie Canal, 178
Espionage and Sedition Acts (1917, 1918), 429
Estonia, 434
eugenics, 392, 400
evangelicals, 540
Everett, Edward, 265
evolution, 458
evolutionary theory, 313, 318, 367
Ewell, Richard, 264
executive branch
    organization of, 105, 115
Exploration, Age of, 10–17

**F**

factory system, 183, 185
Fair Deal, 523

Fair Housing (Civil Rights) Act (1968), 596
Fall, Albert B., 459
Falwell, Jerry, 627
Family and Medical Leave Act (1993), 642
Farmers' Alliance, 349, 361
Farragut, David, 267
fascism, 492
Faubus, Orval, 584–85
Faulkner, William, 449
Federal Deposit Insurance Corporation (FDIC), 481
Federal Emergency Relief Administration (FERA), 480
federalism, 106
Federalist Papers, 108
Federalist Party, 118
Federalists, 107–9
Federal Republic of Germany (West Germany), 532
Federal Reserve Act (1913), 409
Federal Trade Commission (FTC), 410
Ferdinand, Francis (Franz), 416
Ferdinand II of Aragon, 11, 12
Ferraro, Geraldine, 630
Fetterman, William, 352
Fillmore, Millard, 180, 233, 234, 236
Finlay, Carlos, 376
Finney, Charles, 190
fireside chats, 478
First Continental Congress (1774), 67
Fisk, James, 325
Fitzgerald, F. Scott, 449
flappers, 450
Florida
    British control of, 60
    election of 2000 and, 646
    Native American conflict in, 160
    secession of, 243
    Spanish colonization of, 13, 85, 143
Floyd, George, 669
Floyd, "Pretty Boy," 472
Food Administration, 428
Forbes, Charles, 459
Force Bill (1833), 166
Ford, Gerald, 569, 606, 608–9, 610, 619
Ford, Henry, 388, 445, 498
Fordney-McCumber Tariff, 443
Fort Donelson, 266
Fort Duquesne, 57, 58, 59

Fort Henry, 266
Fort Laramie, Treaty of (1868), 352
Fort McHenry, 139
Fort Sumter, 244–45
Fort Ticonderoga, 70
forty-niners, 214
49th parallel, 206
Fourteen Points, 433
Fox people, 159
Frame of Government of Pennsylvania, 32
France. See also World War I; World War II
    Civil War and, 258, 261
    colonization, 14–15, 21, 560
    conflict with England, 44, 57–60, 122, 132, 137
    Monroe Doctrine and, 365
    Persian Gulf War and, 638
    revolution in, 121–23
    in War for Independence, 78, 80, 84, 92
    XYZ Affair and, 126
Franklin, Benjamin, 40, 42, 58, 65, 74, 81, 92, 107, 109, 182
Fredericksburg, Battle of (1862), 262
freedmen, 283
Freedmen's Bureau, 288–89, 297
Freedom Riders, 587
Freedom Summer, 589
freeholders, 43
Freeport Doctrine, 239
free silver, 362
Free Soil Party, 231
free speech, 429
Frelinghuysen, Theodore J., 49
Frémont, John C., 210, 216, 218, 236
French and Indian (Seven Years') War (1754–63), 57–60
French Huguenots, 35, 48
Freud, Sigmund, 452
Frick, Henry, 329
Friedan, Betty, 620
Fuchida, Mitsuo, 500
Fuchs, Klaus, 541
Fugitive Slave Act (1850), 233–34, 269
Fuller, Charles E., 540
Fulton, Robert, 179
Fundamentalists, 397, 457–58, 540
Fundamental Orders of Connecticut, 30

# G

Gadsden Purchase, 213
Gagarin, Yuri, 558
Gama, Vasco da, 10
Gandhi, Mahatma, 582
Garfield, James, 310–11
Garrison, William Lloyd, 193, 194, 228
Garvey, Marcus, 456
*Gaspee* (ship), 64
Gaulle, Charles de, 504
gay rights movement, 622. *See also* homosexuality
General Amnesty Act (1872), 297
Genêt, Edmond Charles Edouard, 123
Gentlemen's Agreement, 381
George III, King of England, 61, 63, 66, 73, 76
Georgia
    colonial, 36, 37, 48
    Native American conflict in, 161
    secession of, 243
    in War for Independence, 82
German Democratic Republic (East Germany), 532
German immigrants, 41, 48, 224, 236, 422
Germany. *See also* World War I; World War II
    Cold War era, 527, 531–32, 543, 552–53, 636
    Hitler's rise in, 493
    Nuremberg Trials and, 525
Geronimo, 354
Gerry, Elbridge, 107
Gettysburg, Battle of (1863), 264–65
Gettysburg Address, 265
Ghana Empire, 21
Ghent, Treaty of (1814), 141
*Gibbons v. Ogden,* 147
GI Bill, 523
*Gideon v. Wainwright,* 557
Gilded Age, 307
Ginsburg, Ruth Bader, 642, 667
Glenn, John, 558
Glidden, Joseph, 348
gold mining, 214, 338, 368
gold standard, 361, 362
Goldwater, Barry, 556
Gompers, Samuel, 460
Goodman, Benny, 470
Gorbachev, Mikhail, 631, 636, 637
Gore, Al, 646–47

Gorgas, William, 376, 378
Göring, Hermann, 525
Gorsuch, Neil, 667
Gould, Chester, 471
Gould, Jay, 325
government structure. *See also* elections; *specific branches*
    colonial, 43, 61, 63, 64
    Confederation, 91–92
    in Constitution, 99–100, 104–6, 115–16
Grady, Henry, 301
Graham, Billy, 540
grandfather clauses, 392
Grange (Patrons of Husbandry), 349
Grange, Red, 451
Grant, Ulysses S.
    in Civil War, 266–68, 271–72, 274–75
    in Mexican War, 209
    presidency, 293, 294, 296
Gray, Harold, 471
Great Awakening, 49–50. *See also* Second Great Awakening
Great Britain. *See* Britain
Great Compromise, 99–100
Great Depression, 465–67, 474–76. *See also* New Deal
Great Migration, 450
Great Northern Railroad, 317
Great Plains, 346–49
Great Railroad Strike, 329
Great Recession (2007–2009), 656, 662
Great Sioux War (1876–77), 352–54
Great Society, 556
Great Wagon Road, 41, 177
Great White Fleet, 382
Greece, 530
Greeley, Horace, 269, 296
greenbacks, 252, 361
Greene, Nathanael, 83
Greenglass, David, 541
*Greer,* USS, 499
Grenada, 633
Grimké, Sarah and Angelina, 194, 195
Guadalupe Hidalgo, Treaty of (1848), 212
Guiteau, Charles, 311
Gulf of Tonkin Resolution, 561
gun control, 681
gun production, 184
Gutenberg, Johannes, 11

# H

Haiti, 132, 379, 421, 644
Half-Breeds, 310
Half-Way Covenant, 46, 49
Hamer, Fannie Lou, 589
Hamilton, Alexander, 108, 115, 116–18, 122, 126, 128
Hancock, John, 68, 108
Harding, Warren G., 442, 443, 459
Harlan, John, 557
Harlem Renaissance, 450
Harpers Ferry, Virginia, 240–41
Harris, Kamala, 671, 674
Harrison, Benjamin, 312, 347
Harrison, William Henry, 136, 138, 170, 171
Hartford Convention, 142
Harvard College, 42, 188
Hastie, William, 576
Hauptmann, Bruno, 472
Hawaii, 369, 542
Hay, John, 378, 380–81
Hayes, Rutherford B., 298–99, 310, 329, 356
Haymarket Riot, 328
headright system, 34
Hearst, William Randolph, 371
Heinz, H. J., 324
Hemingway, Ernest, 449
Henry, Patrick, 49, 62, 63, 67, 68, 109
Henry the Navigator, Prince of Portugal, 10
Hepburn Act (1906), 405
Hickok, James Butler "Wild Bill," 345
Higher Education Act (1965), 557
Hill, James J., 317
*Hindenburg* (zeppelin), 473
Hirohito, Japanese emperor, 491, 517, 518, 526
Hiroshima, 517
Hiss, Alger, 541
historiography, 3
Hitler, Adolf, 434, 470, 493, 494–97, 506, 508, 510, 512
Hoar, George F., 375
Ho Chi Minh, 560–61
Hodge, Charles, 271
Holder, Eric, 663
holding companies, 320
Holly, Buddy, 539
Hollywood, movie industry, 450, 470, 504, 541
Holmes, Oliver Wendell, 429, 444
Holocaust, 509–11, 525

homelessness, 468

Homestead Act (1862), 346

Homestead Strike, 329

homosexuality, 622, 642, 662, 663, 684

Honduras, 379

Hong Kong, 670

Hood, John Bell, 272

Hooker, Joseph "Fighting Joe," 262, 264, 268

Hooker, Thomas, 30

Hoover, Herbert, 428, 453, 459, 465, 466–68, 474–77, 484

Hoover, J. Edgar, 472, 541

Hoovervilles, 468

horizontal integration, 319, 320

Horseshoe Bend, Battle of (1814), 140, 204

House of Burgesses, 20, 34

House of Representatives. *See also* Congress
  Great Compromise and, 99–100
  Three-Fifths Compromise and, 101

housing prices, 656

Houston, Sam, 203, 204, 205

Howard, Oliver O., 289, 355

Howe, Elias, 184

Howe, William, 77, 78

Hudson, Henry, 15, 32

Huerta, Victoriano, 421

Hughes, Charles Evans, 425, 443

Hughes, Langston, 450

Humphrey, Hubert H., 567, 568

Hungary, 527, 543, 636

*Hunley,* CSS, 256

Hurricane Katrina (2005), 655

Hussein, Saddam, 638, 639, 652–53

Hutchinson, Anne, 30

## I

identity politics, 594

immigrants and immigration, 41, 48, 224, 236, 308–9, 381, 454–55, 662, 669, 674–75, 680

Immigration Act (1924), 454

Immigration Act (1990), 640

impeachment, 292, 643, 667, 673

imperialism, 366–67, 375–76, 415, 491, 492

impressment, 123, 132, 137, 141

Incan civilization, 7

indentured servants, 22, 34, 39

Independence. *See* War for Independence

India, 582

Indian Removal Act (1830), 159

Indian Reorganization Act (1934), 356

Indian Territory, 346–47

Indian Wars, 351–52

indigenous Americans. *See* Native Americans

indigo cultivation, 37

industrialization, 183–85, 315–17

Industrial Revolution, 183–85

Industrial Workers of the World (IWW), 400

inflation, 169, 609, 612, 674

Inflation Reduction Act (2022), 674

Infrastructure Investment and Jobs Act (2021), 674

initiatives (voting), 399

insane asylums, 193

installment plans, 445

interchangeable parts (manufacturing), 184

Intermediate Nuclear Forces (INF) Treaty, 631

Interstate Commerce Act (1887), 322

Interstate Commerce Commission (ICC), 322, 405, 587

interstate highway system, 542

Inuit people, 8

Iran, 615–16, 634, 653, 664, 670

Iran-Contra affair, 634

Iranian hostage crisis, 615–16

Iraq, 634, 638–39, 652–53, 663, 664, 670

Irish immigrants, 35, 41, 48, 224, 236, 422

iron curtain, 529

Iroquois people, 8, 45, 57, 81

Isabella I of Castile, 11

ISIS (Islamic State of Iraq and Syria), 664, 676

Islam
  in Africa, 21
  radicalism and extremism, 632, 648–53, 663–64
  terrorism, 645, 648–52

Islamic State of Iraq and Syria (ISIS), 664, 676

island hopping, 514–15

isolationism, 442, 498

Israel, 602, 614, 670

Italian immigrants, 454

Italy

fascism in, 492
  in World War I, 415, 417, 433
  in World War II, 493, 496, 500, 504–6

Iwo Jima, Battle of (1945), 516

## J

Jackson, Andrew
  military career, 140, 143, 156
  Polk and, 205
  presidency, 158–59, 161, 165–70, 204
  presidential campaigns, 153–54, 156–57

Jackson, Helen Hunt, 355

Jackson, Jimmie Lee, 590

Jackson, Robert, 525

Jackson, Thomas J. "Stonewall," 213, 245, 259–62

James, Jesse and Frank, 344

James I, King of England, 19, 20, 34

Jamestown Colony, 19–20

January 6 Capitol Riot, 672–73

Japan
  imperialism, 380–382, 491, 500
  naval power, 442
  postwar reforms, 526
  territorial conflict, 381, 382
  trade with, 180, 380
  in World War II, 493, 500, 501, 509, 513–18, 525

Japanese immigrants, 381, 502

Jay, John, 92, 108, 115, 123

Jay Treaty (1794), 123

jazz music, 451

Jefferson, Thomas
  as Democratic-Republican, 117, 118, 125, 127
  French Revolution and, 121, 123
  presidency, 128, 130–31, 132
  territory proposals, 94
  War for Independence and, 67, 74
  in Washington administration, 115

Jehovah's Witnesses (Watch Tower Society), 395

Jews
  immigrants, 454–55
  in colonies, 32, 48
  Holocaust, 509–11, 525

Jim Crow laws, 392, 576

Johnson, Andrew, 273, 278, 284–85, 287–90, 292–93, 365

Johnson, James Weldon, 450

Johnson, Lyndon B.
  in Congress, 583
  in Kennedy administration, 549, 554, 589
  presidency, 556–57, 561, 563, 564, 565, 590, 596, 619
Johnston, Albert Sidney, 266
Johnston, Joseph E., 259, 260, 268, 272, 275
Joint Comprehensive Plan of Action (JCPOA), 664
joint-stock companies, 19
Joliet, Louis, 14
Jones, Bobby, 451
Jones, John Paul, 81
Jones, Paula, 643
Jordan, 670
Joseph, Nez Perce chief, 355
journalism, 371–72, 403–4
judicial branch, organization of, 105, 115, 129, 131. *See also* Supreme Court
judicial review, 129
Judiciary Act (1789), 115

**K**

Kagan, Elena, 662
kamikazes, 516
Kansas-Nebraska Act (1854), 235, 237, 240
Kavanaugh, Brett, 667
Kearny, Stephen, 210, 216
Kellogg-Briand Pact (1928), 443
Kelly, "Machine Gun," 472
Kennedy, Anthony, 630, 667
Kennedy, John F. (JFK)
  assassination of, 554, 555
  presidency, 549–52, 558, 561, 589, 619
Kennedy, Robert F., 567
Kent State shooting, 569
Kentucky, 120, 246
Kentucky Resolutions, 127
Kerry, John, 653, 682
Key, Francis Scott, 139
Khomeini, Ayatollah Ruhollah, 615
Khrushchev, Nikita, 543, 551
Kim Jong-un, 670
King, Martin Luther, Jr.
  assassination of, 567, 594–96
  civil rights leadership, 580–82, 587, 588, 590, 592, 593, 594
King Philip's War (1675–78), 44

Kings Mountain, Battle of (1780), 82
Kipling, Rudyard, 367
Kissinger, Henry, 601
Kitchen Cabinet, 158
Knights of Labor, 328
Know-Nothing Party (American Party), 236
Knox, Henry, 71, 115
Korean War (1950–53), 533–36
*Korematsu v. United States*, 502
Ku Klux Klan (KKK), 297–98, 455, 587, 589
Kuwait, 638–39

**L**

labor strikes, 328–30, 405, 482, 524
labor unions, 185, 327–30, 400, 405, 410, 482, 524
Lafayette, Marquis de, 80, 84
Lake Erie, Battle of (1813), 139
Landon, Alfred, 484
Land Ordinance of 1785, 94
land ownership
  in colonies, 18, 32, 34, 43
  in Confederation government, 94
  and voting rights, 30, 43, 154, 157
Lanphier, Jeremiah, 191
Laos, 560, 562, 570
La Salle, Robert de, 14
Latin America. *See also specific countries*
  communism in, 551–52, 633
  dollar diplomacy and, 406
  Monroe Doctrine and, 144
  Roosevelt Corollary and, 379
  slavery in, 12, 21, 371
Latvia, 434
lawmen and outlaws, 342–45
League of Nations, 433, 434–36
Lebanon, 632, 634
Lee, Richard Henry, 74
Lee, Robert E.
  Brown's raid and, 241
  in Civil War, 254, 260–64, 271, 274–75
  in Mexican War, 213
  secession and, 245
legislative branch, organization of, 105. *See also* Congress
Leif Ericson, 11
Leland, John, 109
Lenape people, 120
Lend-Lease Act (1941), 499
Lenin, Vladimir, 430

Lesseps, Ferdinand de, 378
Levitt, William, 538
Lewinsky, Monica, 643
Lewis, John (civil rights), 588
Lewis, John L. (labor), 482
Lewis, Meriwether, 133–34
Lexington, Massachusetts, 68–69
Leyte Gulf, Battle of (1945), 516
LGBTQ+ community, 684
Liberal Republicans, 296
Liberia, 194, 576
Libya, 632, 653, 664
Liliuokalani, Queen of Hawaii, 369
limited government, 105
Lincoln, Abraham
  assassination of, 278
  background, 240
  Lincoln-Douglas debates, 239
  presidency, 243–46, 253, 259–65, 268–70, 274, 284
  presidential campaigns, 242, 273
  Spot Resolution, 208
  Whig views, 225
Lincoln-Douglas debates, 239
Lindbergh, Charles A., 446, 472, 498
line of demarcation (Treaty of Tordesillas), 16
literacy tests, 392
Lithuania, 434
Little Bighorn, Battle of the (1876), 353
Little Richard, 539
Little Rock Nine, 584–85
Livingstone, Robert, 74, 132
Lloyd George, David, 433
Locke, Alain, 450
Locke, John, 72, 76
Lodge, Henry Cabot, 435
Lone Star Republic, 204
Long, Huey, 483
Long, Luz, 470
long drive, 339
Longstreet, James, 294
Louisiana, secession of, 243
Louisiana Purchase, 132, 143
Louis XVI, King of France, 121
Lowell, Francis Cabot, 183
Loyalists, 71–72
Ludendorff, Erich von, 430
*Lusitania* (ship), 423–24
Luther, Martin, 11
Luxembourg, 495, 508

# M

MacArthur, Douglas, 476, 500, 513, 514, 518, 526, 533–35
Machen, J. Gresham, 456
Machiavelli, 102
*Maddox*, USS, 561
Madero, Francisco, 421
Madison, Dolley, 139
Madison, James
    Constitution and, 99, 100, 102, 105, 108, 109, 116
    as Democratic-Republican, 118, 127, 129
    presidency, 130, 136, 137, 139, 145
magazines and newspapers, 371, 387, 403
Magellan, Ferdinand, 12
Mahan, Alfred Thayer, 366
Maine
    border disputes, 172
    state establishment, 146
*Maine*, USS, 372
majority conformity approach to race, 679
Malcolm X, 592, 593
Mali Empire, 21
Manhattan Project, 517
Manifest Destiny, 201
Manila Bay, Battle of (1898), 373
Mann, Horace, 192
Mansa Musa, 21
Mao Zedong, 533, 535, 602
Marbury, William, 129
*Marbury v. Madison*, 129
March on Washington for Jobs and Freedom, 588
March to the Sea, 272–73
Marco Polo, 10
Marion, Francis, 82
Marquette, Jacques, 14
marriage, legislation on, 642, 663, 684
Marsden, George, 594
Marshall, John, 104, 129, 147, 161
Marshall, Thurgood, 578, 596
Marshall Plan, 531
Martin, Luther, 101
Martin, Trayvon, 679
Marx, Karl, 327, 444, 452
Maryland
    Articles of Confederation and, 93
    border state, 246
    colonial, 35, 36, 48
Maryland Toleration Act (1649), 35
Mason, George, 101, 107, 109

Massachusetts
    colonial, 27–29, 30, 42, 44, 47
    Constitution ratification debate, 108
    education reform in, 192
    slavery and abolition in, 85
    tensions over British rule, 62, 63, 64, 65, 66
    in War for Independence, 68–71
Massachusetts Bay Colony, 29, 30, 44
Massachusetts Government Act (1774), 66
*Masterpiece Bakery v. Colorado Civil Rights Commission*, 663
materialism, 447, 537, 564
Mather, Increase, 47
Mayan people, 7
*Mayflower* (ship), 27
Mayflower Compact, 28
McAdam, John, 177
McAuley, Jerry, 395
McAuliffe, Anthony, 508
McCain, John, 661
McCarthy, Eugene, 567
McCarthy, Joseph, 541
McClellan, George B., 259–62, 273
McCormick, Cyrus, 186
McCoy, Joseph, 339
*McCulloch v. Maryland*, 147, 167
McDowell, Irvin, 259
McGovern, George, 604
McGready, James, 190
McGuffey, William, 192
McKinley, William, 312, 362, 363–64, 371–74, 376, 377
McKinley Tariff, 312, 362, 369
McVeigh, Timothy, 644
Meade, George, 264
Meat Inspection Act (1906), 404
meatpacking industry, 341, 404
Medicaid, 557
Medicare, 557, 674
Meek, Joe, 216, 218
Mellon, Andrew, 445, 459, 468
Mencken, H. L., 458
Mennonites, 48
mercantilism, 18, 61
Meredith, James, 586
*Merrimack*, USS, 256
Metacomet, Wampanoag chief, 44
Methodists, 48, 189, 191, 230, 540
Mexican Cession, 212
Mexican War (1846–48), 207–13
Mexico

border wall and, 669
independence from Spain, 144, 201
Monroe Doctrine and, 365
political unrest in, 421–22
Spanish colonization of, 12
Texan independence and, 201–4
World War I and, 425
Miami people, 120
Middle Passage, 22
Midway, Battle of (1942), 514
Midway Islands, 368
Miles, Nelson A., 356
militarism, 415, 564
militia, 69
Miller, William, 191
Mills, Samuel, 191
mining industry, 338–39, 368
Minui, Peter, 32
*Miranda v. Arizona*, 557
missionary activity
    foreign, 191, 367, 370
    in Hawaii, 369, 370
    Moravian, 48
    among Native Americans, 44–45, 160, 161, 214–15, 218, 356
Mississippi, secession of, 243
Mississippi Freedom Democratic Party (MFDP), 589
Missouri, 146, 246
Missouri Compromise, 146, 231, 235, 238
Mitchell, Margaret, 470
modernism, 395, 457
Mohawk people, 8
Mohegan people, 45
Mondale, Walter, 630
*Monitor*, USS, 256
monopolies, 322, 398. *See also* trusts
Monroe, James, 130, 132, 142, 143, 144, 194
Monroe Doctrine, 144, 365, 379, 633
Monrovia, Liberia, 194
Montcalm, Marquis de, 59
Montezuma, Aztec king, 12
Montgomery, Bernard "Monty," 505, 506, 508
Montgomery bus boycott, 580–81
Moody, Dwight L., 314, 370, 396, 397
Moon, Lottie, 370
moral diplomacy, 420
Moravians, 48, 72
Morgan, Daniel, 78
Morgan, J. P., 318, 321

Morgenthau, Henry, 485
Mormons, 215, 217, 218
Mormon Trail, 217
Morocco, 670
Morrill Land Grant Act (1862), 346
Morris, Gouverneur, 99
Morris, Robert, 95
Morse, Samuel F. B., 182
Mosby, John, 294
Mott, Lucretia, 195
Mound Builders, 8
Mountain Meadows Massacre (1857), 218
mountain men, 216, 218
movie industry, 450, 470, 504, 541
muckrakers, 403
mudslinging, 157
Mueller Investigation, 667
Muhammed, Elijah, 592, 593
Muslims. *See* Islam
Mussolini, Benito, 492, 494, 505, 506, 512
My Lai massacre, 565

# N

NAACP (National Association for the Advancement of Colored People), 394, 456, 575, 578
NAFTA (North American Free Trade Agreement), 644, 666
Nagasaki, 517
Napoleon Bonaparte, 126, 132, 137, 139, 144
Napoleon III, Emperor of France, 365, 415
NASA (National Aeronautics and Space Administration), 558
Nast, Thomas, 295
National Aeronautics and Space Administration (NASA), 558
National Energy Act (1978), 612
National Industrial Recovery Act (NIRA), 480, 483
nationalism, 415
National Labor Relations Board (NLRB), 482
National Recovery Administration (NRA), 480, 483
National Republican Party, 156
National Road, 177
National Security Act (1947), 524
National Union Party, 273
National Voter Registration Act (1993), 642
Nation of Islam, 592–93

Native Americans. *See also specific peoples*
   arrival in the Americas, 6
   assimilation of, 159, 160, 355–56
   civil rights protests, 620
   colonial relations, 15, 19, 20, 28, 29, 32, 44, 57, 60
   enslavement of, 12, 13
   forced removal of, 155, 159, 161–62
   land claims and conflict, 44, 94, 119–20, 136, 155, 159–60, 218, 338, 351–55
   land reservations and allotments, 346, 350, 351, 352, 355, 356
   major groups, 6–8
   missions to, 44–45, 160, 161, 214–15, 218, 356
   religion, 9, 136
   in War of 1812, 138, 139, 140
   in War for Independence, 81
   in World War II, 501
nativist movement, 454
NATO (North Atlantic Treaty Organization), 532
Naturalization Act (1798), 127, 131
Navajo code talkers, 501
naval history. *See* ships
Navigation and Trade Acts, 61
Nazi regime, 493. *See also* World War II
Nelson, "Baby Face," 472
Netherlands
   colonization, 15, 21, 32
   in World War II, 495, 508
   Separatists (Pilgrims) in, 27
Nettleton, Asahel, 189
Neutrality Act (1937), 498
Neutrality Act (1939), 498
Newburgh Conspiracy, 96
New Deal, 477
   legislation, 478–82
   responses to, 483–86
New Hampshire, colonial, 30
New Jersey
   colonial, 32
   in War for Independence, 77
New Jersey Plan, 99
New Left, 565
New Mexico, Mexican War and, 210, 212–213, 422
New Orleans, Battle of (1815), 140
New Right, 627
New South, 301

newspapers and magazines, 371, 387, 403
New York
   colonial, 32, 33
   Constitution ratification debate, 108, 109
   in War for Independence, 70, 77, 78
New York City
   colonial, 32, 33
   Harlem Renaissance, 450, 451
   political corruption in, 295
   World Trade Center, 645, 648
Nez Perce people, 7, 215, 218, 355
Ngo Dinh Diem, 560–61
Nicaragua, 378, 379, 406, 633, 634
Nimitz, Chester, 514, 515
9/11 attack, 648–51
Nixon, Richard
   in Congress, 541
   in Eisenhower administration, 542
   presidency, 565, 569, 601–3, 617, 619
   presidential campaigns, 549, 567, 568, 604
   resignation, 606–7, 608
   Watergate scandal, 604–5
No Child Left Behind (2002), 654
Noriega, Manuel, 635
normalcy, 442, 459
*Norris v. Alabama,* 575
North Africa, 505
North American Free Trade Agreement (NAFTA), 644, 666
North Atlantic Treaty Organization (NATO), 532
North Carolina
   colonial, 17, 35, 37
   secession of, 246
   in War for Independence, 83
North Korea, 533–35, 670
Northup, Solomon, 226
Northwest Ordinance of 1787, 94
Northwest Territory, 94, 119
Noyes, John Humphrey, 197
nuclear energy, 523, 613
nuclear weapons, 517, 528, 541, 543, 631
nullification, 164–66
nullify (declare void), 127
Nuremberg Trials, 525

# O

Obama, Barack, 661–64

Obamacare, 662
*Obergefell v. Hodges,* 663, 675
Occom, Samson, 45
O'Connor, Sandra Day, 630, 655
Office of Economic Opportunity (OEO), 556
Office of War Information (OWI), 504
Oglethorpe, James, 36, 48
Ohio, state establishment, 120
oil industry and supply, 319, 603, 612–13, 638
Okies, 469
Okinawa, Battle of (1945), 516
Oklahoma, state establishment, 347
Oklahoma City bombing, 644
Old Deluder Satan Act, 42
Olive Branch Petition, 73
Oneida Community, 197
Oneida people, 8
Onondaga people, 8
OPEC (Organization of Petroleum Exporting Countries), 603
Open Door Policy, 380–81
open-range ranching, 340, 341, 347
Operation Barbarossa, 497
Operation Desert Storm, 638
Oppenheimer, Robert, 517
Ordinance of Nullification, 165
Ordinance of 1784, 94
Oregon Territory, 142, 172, 206
Oregon Trail, 206, 216
Organization of Petroleum Exporting Countries (OPEC), 603
Orlando, Vittorio, 433
Osceola, Seminole chief, 160
Oswald, Lee Harvey, 554
outlaws and lawmen, 342–45
Owen, Robert, 196
Owens, Jesse, 470

## P

Pacific Garden Mission, 395, 397
Pacific Railway Act (1862), 335
Paine, Thomas, 73
Pakistan, 652, 653, 663
Palin, Sarah, 661
Palmer, A. Mitchell, 444
Panama, 144, 378–79, 635
Panama Canal, 378–79, 614
Panama Canal Treaty (1977), 614
Panic of 1819, 145, 154, 167
Panic of 1837, 169, 171
Panic of '73, 296, 349

Panic of '93, 312
paper money, 168, 169, 252, 361
Paris, Treaty of (1763), 60
Paris, Treaty of (1783), 85, 92, 96
Paris, Treaty of (1898), 374
Parker, Bonnie, 472
Parks, Rosa, 579, 583
patent system, 184
Paterson, William, 99
Patriot Act (2001), 652
Patriots, 71–72
Patton, George, 508
Peace Corps, 551
Peace Democrats, 261, 273
Pearl Harbor, 500
Pence, Mike, 665, 672
Pendleton Act (1883), 311
Penn, William, 32
Pennsylvania
    colonial, 32–33, 41, 47
    slavery and abolition in, 85
    in War for Independence, 78
Pentagon, Washington, DC, 648
Pentagon Papers, 565
Pequot War (1636-1638), 44
Perot, Ross, 641, 643
Perry, Matthew, 180
Perry, Oliver Hazard, 139
Pershing, John J. "Black Jack," 422, 430
Persian Gulf War (1991), 638–39, 652
Peru, 144
pet banks, 168
petroglyphs, 7
Pueblo people, 7
Philadelphia, Pennsylvania
    colonial, 33, 39
    in War for Independence, 78
philanthropy, 318, 324
Philip II, King of Spain, 16–17
Philippines
    imperialism and, 373–74, 376
    in World War II, 513, 515
Pickett, George, 264
Pickett's Charge, 264
Pierce, Franklin, 234
Pike, Zebulon, 135
Pilgrims, 27–28
Pinchot, Gifford, 406
Pinckney, Charles Cotesworth, 126, 128
Pinckney, Thomas, 123, 125
Pinckney Treaty (1795), 123
Pinkerton detectives, 342

Pitt, William, 59
Pittsburgh, Pennsylvania, 59, 318
Plains Indians, 351
plantations, 36–37, 223, 227
Platt Amendment, 376
Plattsburgh, Battle of (1814), 139
*Plessy v. Ferguson,* 392, 578
Plymouth Colony, 27–29, 44
Pocahontas, 19, 44
Poland, 434, 495, 527, 636
political freedom (liberty), 18, 32, 43, 50, 72, 74, 76, 85, 105, 109–10
Polk, James K., 172, 205–7, 208, 209, 211
poll taxes, 392, 589, 590
Pol Pot, 570
Ponce de León, Juan, 13
Pontiac, Ottawa chief, 60
Pony Express, 182
*Poor Richard's Almanack* (Franklin), 40, 81
Pope, John, 260–61
popular sovereignty, 104, 231, 235, 237, 238, 239
populism, 361
Populist Party, 361–62, 363
Portsmouth, Treaty of (1904), 381
Portugal, 10, 13, 16, 21, 144
Post, Wiley, 473
postal service, 182
Potsdam Conference (1945), 517
Pottawatomie Massacre, 238
Powderly, Terence, 328
Powers, Francis Gary, 544
Powhatan people, 19, 20
Prayer Meeting Revival, 191, 314
Presbyterians, 48, 230, 457
Prescott, Samuel, 68
Prescott, William, 70
presidents. *See* executive branch; *specific presidents*
Presley, Elvis, 539
Princeton, New Jersey, 77
Princeton Theological Seminary, 396
Princip, Gavrilo, 416
prison reform, 193, 400
Proclamation of Neutrality (1793), 122
Proclamation of Rebellion (1775), 73
Proclamation of 1763, 61
professions of faith, 46
Progressive Party, 407, 408
progressivism, 387
Prohibition, 452–53, 465

Prohibitory Act (1775), 73
propaganda, 422, 427
property ownership. *See* land
    ownership
proprietary colonies, 27, 35, 43
Prosser, Gabriel, 227
protective tariffs, 145, 163–66
Protestantism
    in colonies, 27, 35
    Reformation, 11
    and Spanish-English conflict,
        16–17
Public Works Administration (PWA),
    480, 483
Puerto Rico, 374, 376
Pulitzer, Joseph, 371
Pullman, George, 316
Pullman Strike, 330
Pure Food and Drug Act (1906), 404
Puritans, 27, 29, 30, 42, 46–47
Putin, Vladimir, 677
Putnam, Ann, 47

## Q

Qaddafi, Muammar al-, 632
al-Qaeda, 645, 651–52
Quakers (Society of Friends), 32, 42,
    47, 72, 193
Quartering Act (1765), 62
Quartering Act (1774, part of
    Coercive Acts), 66
Quebec, 14, 59, 66
Quebec Act (1774), 66

## R

race. *See also* civil rights movement;
    *specific groups*
    discrimination and segregation,
        392–94, 455–56, 483, 502
    racial unrest, 669, 679
Radical Republicans, 284, 287–90
radios, 446, 447, 470
railroads, 181, 235, 294, 316–17, 322,
    329, 330, 335–37, 405, 428
Rainey, Joseph, 291
Raleigh, Sir Walter, 17
ranchers and ranching, 339–41, 347
Randolph, A. Philip, 502, 588
Randolph, Edmund, 107, 109, 115
Rankin, Jeannette, 401
Rapp, George, 196
ratification, 107
Ray, James Earl, 595
Reagan, Nancy, 630

Reagan, Ronald, 610, 628–34
Reagan Doctrine, 631
reaping machines, 186
recall (voting), 399
Reclamation Act (1902), 405
Reconstruction, 283–85, 287, 289,
    294, 297, 299
Reconstruction Act (1867), 290, 294
Reconstruction Finance Corporation
    (RFC), 475
Red Cloud, Sioux chief, 352
Red Cross, 430, 502
Redeemers, 297
redlining, 576
Red Scare, 444
Reed, Walter, 376
referendums (voting), 399
Reformation, Protestant, 11
Reform Darwinism, 395
regulars (professional soldiers), 69
Rehnquist, William H., 630, 655
religion. *See also specific religions, de-
    nominations, and movements*
    in Cold War era, 540
    environmentalism and, 618
    government social programs and,
        654
    Jefferson and, 130
    Native American, 9, 136
    in progressive era, 395–97
    separation of church and state, 30,
        50, 85, 130, 549
    in slave culture, 227
    technology and, 185
    World War I and, 436
religious freedom, 18, 27, 32, 35, 47,
    72, 85, 94, 109, 116, 663
Religious Right, 627
Remington, Frederick, 371
Renaissance, 10
Reno, Janet, 644
reparations, 434
Republican Party, 236
republics, 104, 105
reservationists, 435
Respect for Marriage Act (2022), 675
*Reuben James,* USS, 499
Revels, Hiram, 291
Revenue Act (1932), 475
Revere, Paul, 68
revivals, 49, 189–90, 397
Revolutionary War. *See* War for
    Independence

RFC (Reconstruction Finance
    Corporation), 475
Rhode Island, colonial, 29–30, 47, 64
rice cultivation, 37
Richthofen, Manfred von, 419
Rickenbacker, Eddie, 432
Rickey, Branch, 577
right of deposit, 96
*Rights of Man* (Paine), 73
Riley, William Bell, 456
road improvements, 177
Roanoke Colony, 17
Roberts, John G., Jr., 655, 673
Robertson, Pat, 627
Robeson, Paul, 450
Robinson, Jackie, 577
rock and roll music, 539
Rockefeller, John D., 319, 391, 403,
    444
Rockefeller, Nelson, 608
Rockne, Knute, 451
*Roe v. Wade,* 621, 627, 675
Rogers, Will, 473
Rolfe, John, 19, 22, 34
Roman Catholicism
    Anglican church and, 27
    in colonies, 35, 48, 66
    Kennedy and, 549
    Protestant Reformation and, 11
    Spanish-English conflict and,
        16–17
Romania, 527, 637
Rommel, Erwin, 505, 506
Romney, Mitt, 662
Roosevelt, Eleanor, 478, 483
Roosevelt, Franklin Delano (FDR)
    presidency, New Deal, 477–81,
        483–85
    presidency, World War II, 498–
        500, 502–4, 506, 509, 513, 517
    presidential campaigns, 459, 477,
        484
Roosevelt, Theodore
    criticism of Taft, 406–7
    presidency, 377–79, 381–82, 394,
        402–5
    presidential campaigns, 407
    in Spanish-American War, 373,
        374
Roosevelt Corollary, 379
Rosecrans, William, 268
Rosenberg, Julius and Ethel, 541
Rosenwald, Julius, 391
*Roth v. United States,* 557

royal colonies, 20, 27, 30, 32, 34, 35, 43

Ruby, Jack, 554

Rural Electrification Act (REA), 480

Russell, Charles Taze, 395

Russia. *See also* Soviet Union
    revolution in, 430, 444
    territory and territorial conflict, 368, 381, 663, 677
    Trump election, 667
    in World War I, 415, 416, 417

Ruth, Babe, 451

Rutledge, John, 101

## S

Sacagawea, 133

Sacco, Nicola, 454

Sadat, Anwar, 614

Salem Witch Trials, 47

SALT I (Strategic Arms Limitation Talks Agreement), 602

SALT II (Strategic Arms Limitation Talks Agreement), 615

Salvation Army, 395

Samoa, 368

Samoset, Abenaki chief, 29

sanctuary cities, 669, 674–75

San Jacinto, Battle of (1836), 204

San Juan Hill, Battle of (1898), 374

Sankey, Ira, 314

San Martín, José de, 144

Santa Anna, Antonio López de, 202, 203, 204, 211, 212, 213

Santa Fe Trail, 216

Saratoga, Battle of (1777), 78, 79

Saudi Arabia, 638–39

Sauk people, 159

scalawags, 292

Scalia, Antonin, 662, 667

*Schenk v. United States*, 429

Schlafly, Phyllis, 621

schools. *See* education

Schrank, John F., 407

Schwarzkopf, Norman, 638

SCLC (Southern Christian Leadership Conference), 582

Scopes trial, 458

Scots-Irish immigrants, 35, 41, 48

Scott, Dred, 238

Scott, Winfield, 210, 211, 212, 213, 234, 257

SEC (Securities Exchange Commission), 481

secession, 164, 165, 243, 246

Second Continental Congress (1775–1781), 69, 73, 91

Second Great Awakening, 189–91, 214

secret ballots, 398

secular humanism, 390

Securities Act (1933), 481

Securities Exchange Commission (SEC), 481

segregation and discrimination, racial, 28990, 302, 392–94, 455–56, 483, 502. *See also* civil rights movement

Selective Service Act (1917), 427

self-determination, 415, 433, 434

Selma, Alabama, 590

Seminole people, 8, 143, 156, 160, 346

Seminole War (1835–42), 160

Senate, Great Compromise and, 99–100. *See also* Congress

Seneca Falls Convention, 195

Seneca people, 8

separation of church and state, 30, 50, 85, 130, 549

separation of powers, 105

Separatists, 27

September 11 attack, 648–51

Sequoyah, 160

*Serapis* (ship), 81

Serbia and Serbians, 415–16

settlement houses, 400

Seven Years' War (1754–63), 57–60

Seward, William H., 233, 365, 368

Seward's Folly, 368

Seymour, Horatio, 293

Shakers, 197

sharecropping, 300–301

Shawnee people, 120

Shays's Rebellion (1786), 97

Shenandoah Valley, 271

Shepard, Alan, 558

Sheridan, Philip, 271, 356

Sherman, Roger, 74, 100

Sherman, William Tecumseh, 268, 272–73, 275

Sherman Antitrust Act (1890), 322, 404, 410

Sherman Silver Purchase Act (1890), 362

Shiloh, Battle of (1862), 266–67

ships. *See also specific ships*
    Barbary States conflict, 131
    in Civil War, 256, 258
    Great White Fleet, 382
    shipbuilding industry, 31

shipping centers, 33

slave, 22

Spanish-English conflict, 16–17

technological advances, 10, 180

trade disputes and, 64, 65, 123, 132

treaties on naval power growth, 442

in War for Independence, 81

in War of 1812, 137, 138, 139

in World War I, 418, 423–24, 429

in World War II, 498, 499, 500

Shoshone people, 7, 133

Shuttlesworth, Fred, 582

silent majority, 601

silver coins, 361, 362

Simpson, A. B., 370, 396

Sinclair, Upton, 404

Sioux people, 8, 338, 351, 352–54

sit-ins, 586–87

Sitting Bull, Sioux leader, 352–54

Slater, Samuel, 183

slavery
    abolitionist movement, 193–94, 229, 238, 240, 269
    African slave trade, 13, 21–22, 102
    in colonies, 34, 37, 38, 39
    Compromise of 1850 and, 232–33
    cotton industry and, 187, 223, 226
    daily life, 226–27
    debates on, 101, 229–30
    emancipation and, 194, 269–70, 284
    Fugitive Slave Act and, 233–34, 269
    indentured servants, 22, 34, 39
    Mexican legislation on, 201, 202
    Mexican war and, 207–8
    Missouri Compromise and, 146, 231, 235, 238
    in Northwest territory land ordinances, 94
    popular sovereignty and, 231, 235, 237, 238
    revolts and resistance, 227, 240–41
    in Spanish colonies, 12, 13, 371
    Thirteenth Amendment and, 284
    Three-Fifths Compromise and, 101
    Underground Railroad, 228
    War of Independence and, 85

Slidell, John, 207

Smalls, Robert, 291

Smith, Al, 465

Smith, Jedediah, 216, 218

Smith, John, 20, 28
Smith, Joseph, 215
Smith, Margaret Bayard, 158
Smith, Oliver P., 536
Smoot-Hawley Tariff, 467
SNCC (Student Nonviolent Coordinating Committee), 587
social contract theory, 76
Social Darwinism, 313, 318, 367
social gospel movement, 396
social media, 680
Social Security Act (SSA), 482
Society of Friends (Quakers), 32, 42, 47, 72, 193
Somalia, 644
Songhai Empire, 21
Sons of Liberty, 62, 65
Sooners, 347
Soto, Hernando de, 13
Sotomayor, Sonia, 662
Souter, David, 662
South Carolina
    colonial, 35, 37
    secession of, 243
    states' rights concerns, 163–66
    in War for Independence, 82–83
Southeast Asia Treaty Organization (SEATO), 543
Southern Christian Leadership Conference (SCLC), 582
South Korea, 533–35
Soviet Union. See also Russia
    Cold War era, 527, 528–32, 533, 535, 543–44, 551–52, 558, 561, 602, 615, 631–32, 637
    in World War II, 494, 495, 497, 504, 506, 509, 512, 517
space race, 558
Spain
    colonization, 11–13, 16–17, 21, 60, 144, 201, 371
    Spanish-American War (1898), 371–74
    territorial conflict, 96, 123, 143
Spalding, Henry and Eliza, 214–15, 218
Spanish-American War (1898), 371–74
Spanish Armada, 17
Specie Circular, 169
speculation, 448, 465
spoils system, 158, 310
sports, 323, 387, 451, 470, 577
Spot Resolution, 208
Sputnik I, 558

Squanto, 29
SSA (Social Security Act), 482
stagflation, 609
Stalin, Joseph
    Cold War and, 527, 531, 535
    World War II and, 494, 495, 504, 506, 509, 512, 517
Stalwarts, 310
Stamp Act (1765), 62
Stamp Act Congress, 62
Stanton, Charles E., 430
Stanton, Edwin, 278, 292
Stanton, Elizabeth Cady, 195
Starr, Ellen Gates, 400
Starr, Kenneth, 643
state representation, 99–101
states' rights
    in Confederation government, 91, 92
    in Constitution, 116, 127, 225
    nullification and, 164–66
    Supreme Court cases on, 147, 161
St. Augustine (Spanish colonial city), 13
steamboats, 179
Steele, Christopher, 667
steel industry, 318
steel plow, 186
Steffens, Lincoln, 403
stem cell research, 654
Stephens, Alexander, 243, 287
Steuben, Friedrich von, 80
Stevens, John Paul, 662
Stevens, Thaddeus, 284
Stevenson, Adlai, 542
stockholding, 320–21
stock market, 448, 465–66
Stowe, Harriet Beecher, 234
Strategic Arms Limitation Talks Agreement (SALT I), 602
Strategic Arms Limitation Talks Agreement (SALT II), 615
Strategic Arms Reduction Talks (START), 631
Strategic Defense Initiative (SDI), 631
Strauss, Levi, 341
strikes, labor, 328–30, 405, 482, 524
Strong, Josiah, 367
Stuart, J.E.B., 261
Student Nonviolent Coordinating Committee (SNCC), 587
Student Volunteer Movement for Foreign Missions (SVMFM), 370
Stuyvesant, Peter, 32

submarines, 418, 423–24
suburbs, 445, 538
Sudan, 670
suffrage. See voting rights
Sugar Act (1764), 61
sugar industry, 369
Sumner, Charles, 231, 237, 273, 284
Sunday, William "Billy," 397, 401
Sunni Ali, Songhai king, 21
supply-side economics (Reaganomics), 629
Supreme Court. See also specific decisions
    authority of, 105–6
    Marshall as chief justice, 129, 147
    organization of, 115, 485
    presidential appointments, 115, 129, 485, 596, 630, 655, 662, 667
    Warren as chief justice, 557
Sussex (ship), 424
Sutter, John, 214
Swanson, Gloria, 450
Swift, Gustavus, 341
Syria, 602, 664

# T

Taft-Hartley Act (1947), 524
Taft, William Howard, 376, 406–7
Taiwan, 601–2, 670
Taliban, 651–52, 663, 670, 676
Talleyrand, Charles Maurice, 126
Tallmadge, James, 146
Tammany Hall, 295

Taney, Roger B., 168, 238, 246
Tarbell, Ida, 403
Tariff of Abominations, 163–64
Tariff of 1832, 165
Tarleton, Banastre, 83
TARP (Troubled Asset Relief Program), 662
taxes and tariffs
    colonial, 61–63, 65
    federal debt and, 95, 116, 131, 443, 629
    protective tariffs, 145, 163–66
    raising, 312, 475, 503, 603, 640, 670
    reducing, 311, 406, 409, 666
    as state right, 92
    supply-side economics and, 629
    war bonds, 429
Taylor, Maxwell, 507

Taylor, Zachary, 207, 210, 211, 213, 231, 232, 233
Tea Act (1773), 65
Teapot Dome scandal, 459
Tecumseh, Shawnee chief, 136, 139
telegraph, 182
telephone, 316
television industry, 539
Teller, Henry M., 355
Teller Amendment, 372
temperance movement, 196, 401
Temple, Shirley, 470
Tennent, Gilbert, 49
Tennessee
    secession of, 246
    state establishment, 120
Tennessee Valley Authority (TVA), 480
Ten Percent Plan, 284
Tenskwatawa (the Prophet), 136
Tenure of Office Act (1867), 292, 293
Terrell, Mary Church, 401
terrorism
    domestic, 644
    Islamic, 645, 648–52
Tet Offensive, 564
Texas
    annexation of, 172, 205
    independence from Mexico, 202–4
    Mexican War and, 207, 212
    secession of, 243
    settlement of, 201–2
textile industry, 183
Thames, Battle of the (1813), 139
Third Reich, 493. See also World War II
Thomas, George, 268
Thoreau, Henry David, 188
Three-Fifths Compromise, 101
Three Mile Island accident, 613
Thurmond, Strom, 524
Tiananmen Square, 637
Tibbets, Paul, 517
Tilden, Samuel J., 298–99
Tilden, William, 451
Till, Emmett, 583
Timbuktu, 21
Tippecanoe, Battle of (1811), 136
Titanic (ship), 389
tobacco cultivation, 34, 36, 37, 186
Tojo, Hideki, 491, 525
Tom Thumb (steam engine), 181
Toombs, Robert, 232
Tordesillas, Treaty of, 16

Tories, 71–72
total war, 271, 272–73
totem poles, 7
Townsend, Francis, 484
Townshend, Charles, 63
Townshend Acts (1767), 63, 65
Trail of Broken Treaties, 620
Trail of Tears, 162
transcendentalism, 188, 197
transcontinental railroad, 235, 294, 335–37
transgenderism, 684
transportation, advances in, 177–81, 388. See also specific modes of transportation
Travis, William, 203
treaties. See specific titles, e.g. Paris, Treaty of
trench warfare, 418
Trenton, New Jersey, 77
triangular trade, 31
Triple Alliance, 415
Triple Entente, 415
Tripoli, 131
Trist, Nicholas, 209
Troubled Asset Relief Program (TARP), 662
Truman, Harry
    presidency, Cold War era, 528, 530–31, 533, 535, 541
    presidency, postwar reforms, 523–24, 576
    presidency, World War II, 509, 512, 517
Truman Doctrine, 530
Trump, Donald, 665–67, 669–73, 676
trusts, 320, 322, 398, 404, 407, 410. See also monopolies
Truth, Sojourner, 194, 195
Tubman, Harriet, 228
Tunisia, 664
Turkey, 417, 431, 530, 552
Turner, Nat, 227
Tuscarora people, 8
Tuskegee Airmen, 501
Tuskegee Institute, 391
TVA (Tennessee Valley Authority), 480
Twain, Mark, 375
Tweed, William "Boss," 295
Tyler, John, 171–72, 205

U

U-boats, 418

Ukraine, 663, 667, 677
Uncle Tom's Cabin, (Stowe), 234
Underground Railroad, 228
Underwood Tariff Act (1913), 409
unemployment, 296, 441, 467, 469, 474–76, 480, 481, 485, 502, 612, 662, 668, 674
unicameral legislature, 92
Union, 243. See also Civil War
Union Pacific Railroad, 335–37
unions, labor, 185, 327–30, 400, 405, 410, 482, 524
Unitarianism, 188
United Arab Emirates (UAE), 670
United Kingdom. See Britain
United Nations (UN), 509, 526
United Service Organizations (USO), 502
United States-Mexico-Canada Agreement (USMCA), 666
Universal Negro Improvement Association (UNIA), 456
University of Pennsylvania, 42
urbanization, 185, 307, 323
USMCA (United States-Mexico-Canada Agreement), 666
USSR. See Soviet Union
Utah, state establishment, 215
Ute people, 7
utopia , 196

V

Valentino, Rudolph, 450
Valley Forge, 79–80
Van Buren, Martin, 153, 156, 158, 162, 170–71, 205, 231
Vanderbilt, Cornelius, 317
Vanzetti, Bartolomeo, 454
V-E Day, 512
Venezuela, 144
Vermont
    slavery and abolition in, 85
    state establishment, 120
Verrazano, Giovanni da, 14
Versailles, Treaty of (1919), 434–36, 494
vertical integration, 318, 320
Vespucci, Amerigo, 12
Vicksburg, Mississippi, siege of, 267
Viet Cong, 561, 562, 569
Vietnamization, 569
Vietnam War (1954–75), 560–66, 569–70, 592
Vikings, 11

Villa, Pancho, 421–22
Virginia
    colonial, 17, 19–20, 34–35, 36, 44,
        62
    Constitution ratification debate,
        108–9
    secession of, 245, 246
    in War for Independence, 84
*Virginia*, CSS, 256
Virginia Plan, 99
Virginia Resolutions, 127
Virginia Statute for Religious
    Freedom, 85
V-J Day, 518
Volstead Act, 452
Volunteers in Service to America
    (VISTA), 556
voting rights
    for African Americans, 293–94,
        297, 302, 392, 401, 575, 583,
        589–90
    age requirements, 570
    in colonies, 30, 43
    expansion of, 154, 157, 293–94,
        401–2, 570
    progressive reforms, 398–99
    for women, 195, 401–2
Voting Rights Act (1965), 590

# W

Waco siege, 644
Wade, Benjamin, 293
Wade-Davis Bill, 284
Wagner Act (1935), 482
Wallace, George, 568, 604
Wallace, Henry A., 524
Wampanoag people, 28, 44
war bonds, 429, 503
Ward, Lester Frank, 395
Warfield, Benjamin B., 396, 397
War Hawks, 137
War for Independence (1775–83)
    battles of, 70–71, 77–83
    beginning of, 68–69
    debating, 71–73
    Declaration of Independence, 74,
        76
    end of, 84–85, 92
    factors leading to, 61–67
    Treaty of Paris, 85, 92, 96
war of attrition, 258
War of 1812, 137–41, 145
War Powers Act (1973), 570
War Production Board (WPB), 503
Warren, Earl, 557, 578

Warsaw Pact, 532
Washington, Booker T., 391, 393
Washington, George
    in Constitutional Convention, 99,
        107
    First Continental Congress and,
        67
    in French and Indian War, 57, 58
    Newburgh Conspiracy and, 96
    presidency, 115, 118, 119, 120,
        122, 123, 124
    in "Quasi War," 126
    in War for Independence, 69, 71,
        77, 78, 79, 80, 84, 95
Washington, Treaty of (1871), 365
Washington Naval Conference
    (1921), 442
WASPs (Women Air Service Pilots),
    502
Watch Tower Society (Jehovah's
    Witnesses), 395
Watergate scandal, 604–5
Water Quality Act (1965), 557
Water Street Mission, 395
Watts riots, 591
WAVES (Women Accepted for
    Volunteer Emergency Service), 502
Wayne, "Mad Anthony," 120
weapons of mass destruction
    (WMDs), 652
Weaver, James B., 362
Weaver, Robert, 557
Webster-Ashburton Treaty (1842),
    172
Webster, Daniel, 94, 165, 170, 172,
    232
Webster, Noah, 192
Welfare Reform Act (1996), 642
Wells-Barnett, Ida B., 401
Wells, H. G., 470
Wesley, John and Charles, 48, 49, 189
Westinghouse, George, 316
Westmoreland, William, 564
West Virginia, 246
Weyler, Valeriano, 371
Wheelock, Eleazar, 45
Whig Party, 170
Whiskey Rebellion (1794), 119
Whiskey Ring, 294
White, Hugh, 170
White, John, 17
White, Lynn, 618
Whitefield, George, 49
Whitewater scandal, 643

Whitman, Marcus and Narcissa,
    214–15, 216, 218
Whitman, Walt, 188
Whitney, Eli, 184, 186
Wilderness Road, 177
Wilhelm II, Emperor of Germany,
    416
Wilkins, Roy, 594
Williams, Roger, 29–30, 44, 47
Willkie, Wendell, 498
Wills, Helen, 451
Wilmot, David, 208
Wilmot Proviso, 208, 231
Wilson, James, 101
Wilson, Woodrow, 408–10, 420–22,
    424–28, 433–36
Winthrop, John, 29
WMDs (weapons of mass destruc-
    tion), 652
Wolfe, James, 59
women
    in abolitionist movement, 194
    colonial political activity, 65
    labor concerns, 326, 400
    voting rights, 195, 401–2
    in workforce, 539
    in World War II, 502
Women's Army Corps (WAC), 502
women's rights, 195, 620–21
Women's Trade Union League, 400
Wood, Leonard, 374
Woodward, Bob, 604, 605
Worcester, Samuel, 161
*Worcester v. Georgia*, 161
Works Progress Administration
    (WPA), 481, 483
World Trade Center, New York City,
    645, 648
World War I (1914–18)
    aftermath of, 433–36, 441–44
    beginning of, 416–17
    end of, 430–32
    factors leading to, 415
    modern warfare and, 418–19
    US involvement, 427–30
    US neutrality, 420–26
World War II (1939–45)
    beginning of, 494–97
    end of, 509, 512, 518
    European theater, 504–8
    factors leading to, 491–94
    Holocaust, 509–11, 525
    Pacific theater, 513–17
    US involvement, 500–504
    US neutrality, 498–99

Wounded Knee Massacre, 354
WPA (Works Progress
    Administration), 481, 483
Wright, Orville and Wilber, 388
writs of assistance, 61
writs of habeas corpus, 246

# X

XYZ Affair, 126

# Y

Yale College, 42, 189
Yalta Conference (1945), 509, 527
yellow journalism, 371–72
Yeltsin, Boris, 637
Yemen, 664
YMCA (Young Men's Christian
    Association), 191, 395
York (slave), 133
York, Alvin C., 431, 432
*Yorktown,* USS, 514
Yorktown, Virginia, 84
Young, Brigham, 215, 218
Yousef, Ramzi, 645
Yugoslavia, 434, 527, 637, 644

# Z

Zelensky, Volodymyr, 677
Zhou Enlai, 602
Zimmermann telegram, 425–26

# Photo Credits

Photo; **123t** Culture Club/Contributor /Hulton Archive via Getty Images; **124** "Washington's Farewell Address, 1796" by Allyn Cox/flickr/Public Domain; **125i**, **139b** Everett Collection/Shutterstock.com; **125, 148b** Tom Freeman for the White House Historical Association; **126t** Archives du Ministere des Affaires Etrangeres, Paris, France © Archives Charmet/Bridgeman Images; **126b** Classic Collection 2/Alamy Stock Photo; **129** National Portrait Gallery, Smithsonian Institution; **130** deendesign /Shutterstock.com; **131** "Burning of the Frigate Philadelphia in the Harbor of Tripoli" by Edward Moran/Wikimedia Commons/Public Domain; **133t** Courtesy, American Philosophical Society; **133c** © 2009 JupiterImages Corporation/Stockxpert Image; **133b, 149t** Magite Historic /Alamy Stock Photo; **135** Ronda Kimbrow Photography/Moment via Getty Images; **137** "James Madison" by Gilbert Stuart /Wikimedia Commons/Public Domain; **136** Library of Congress/LC-DIG-pga-01891; **138** Gift of Edgar William and Bernice Chrysler Garbisch, 1962/Metropolitan Museum of Art; **139t, 149b** Tom Freeman 2004, copyright White House Historical Association; **140** Buyenlarge/Contributor via Archive Photos via Getty Images; **141** Gift of the Sulgrave Institution of the U.S. and Great Britain/Smithsonian American Art Museum; **142, 150** Bequest of Seth Low, 1916/Metropolitan Museum of Art; **151** "Lewis and Clark on the Lower Columbia" by Charles Marion Russell /Wikimedia Commons/Public Domain

**Chapter 6**

**152, 158b, 170t, 170b** Granger, NYC; **153l** Alpha Stock/Alamy Stock Photo; **153cl** "John Quincy Adams" by George Peter Alexander Healy/Wikimedia Commons/Public Domain; **153cr** "Henry Clay" by Matthew Harris Jouett /Wikimedia Commons/Public Domain; **153r** "Andrew Jackson" by Thomas Sully /Wikimedia Commons/Public Domain; **155, 173t** Mauro Toccaceli/Alamy Stock Photo; **156** PRISMA ARCHIVO/Alamy Stock Photo; **157, 158c, 166, 174t** North Wind Picture Archives/Alamy Stock Photo; **158t** Library of Congress/LC-DIG -ppmsca-50970; **159** "Battle of Bad Axe" by Henry Lewis/Wikimedia Commons /Public Domain; **160t** Newberry Library; **160b** Jackie Nix/Alamy Stock Photo; **162, 173b** Courtesy of the Oklahoma Historical Society.; **163t, 171b** Peter Newark American Pictures/Bridgeman Images; **163b** National Portrait Gallery, Smithsonian Institution; **164t** Georgios Kollidas/Alamy Stock Photo; **164b** Jeff Greenberg/Contributor /Universal Images Group via Getty Images; **165** Sean Pavone/Shutterstock.com; **167** © Philadelphia History Museum at the Atwater Kent/Courtesy of Historical Society of Pennsylvania Collection,/Bridgeman Images; **168** Collection of the New-York

Historical Society, USA © New York Historical Society/Bridgeman Images; **169** BJU Photo Services; **171** ("Am I Not a Woman & a Sister" token) YA/BOT /Alamy Stock Photo; **171** ($5 Gold Coin), **174i** "1839-C $5 Gold Coin"/Egwaltney /Wikimedia Commons/CC0; **171** (Hard Times Token Front), **171** (Hard Times Token Back) Division of Work and Industry, National Museum of American History, Smithsonian Institution; **171** (Silver Liberty Half Dollar), **174b** Mark_Kostich /Shutterstock.com; **172** incamerastock /Alamy Stock Photo

**Chapter 7**

**176** Everett Collection/Shutterstock.com; **179** Granger, NYC; **180** © Look and Learn /Bridgeman Images; **181** Vintage Images /Alamy Stock Photo; **182** North Wind Picture Archives/Alamy Stock Photo; **183** Dorling Kindersley ltd/Alamy Stock Photo; **184** "Colt Paterson"/Hmaag /Wikimedia Commons/Public Domain; **184bg** Glasshouse Images/Alamy Stock Photo; **185** "Ten Hour Day circular 1835"/National Archives and Records Administration/Wikimedia Commons /Public Domain; **186t** The Print Collector /Alamy Stock Photo; **186bl** Division of Work and Industry, National Museum of American History, Smithsonian Institution; **186br** Division of Home and Community Life, National Museum of American History, Smithsonian Institution; **189** Bill Cardoni; **190** Collection of the New -York Historical Society, USA © New York Historical Society/Bridgeman Images; **191** Library of Congress; **192t** Pictures Now /Alamy Stock Photo; **192b** Chronicle/Alamy Stock Photo; **193t** Everett Collection Inc /Alamy Stock Photo; **193b** "William Lloyd Garrison" by Nathaniel Jocelyn/Wikimedia Commons/Public Domain; **194t** Heritage Images/Contributor/Hulton Archive via Getty Images; **194c** Bettmann/Contributor /Bettmann via Getty Images; **194b** Library of Congress/gmd/g8882c.lm000002; **195** Jim West/Alamy Stock Photo; **196** "The Temperance Almanac for the Year of Our Lord 1834"/Digital Public Library of America/Wikimedia Commons/Public Domain; **196bg** Hansrad Collection/Alamy Stock Photo

**Chapter 8**

**200** North Wind Picture Archives/Alamy Stock Photo; **201, 215i** National Portrait Gallery, Smithsonian Institution; **202** DEA PICTURE LIBRARY/Contributor/ De Agostini via Getty Images; **203t** EndeavorMoorePhotography/Shutterstock .com; **203b** Superstock/Artist - Frederick Coffay Yohn/3LH-Fine Art; **204t** Maxim Studio/Shutterstock.com; **204b** "The Bayou Bend Collection, gift of Mr. and Mrs. R. E. Zimmerman"/The Museum of Fine Arts, Houston; **205, 219t** "POLK, James-President (BEP engraved portrait)"/The Bureau of Engraving and Printing/Wikimedia

Commons/Public Domain; **207** WDC Photos/Alamy Stock Photo; **209t** Collection of the New York Historical Society, USA © New York Historical Society/Bridgeman Images; **209b** "James K Polk - 11th President" by edwarddallas/Flickr/CC By 2.0; **210** P_Wei/E+ via Getty Images; **212i** "Winfield Scott" by Robert Walter Weir /Wikimedia Commons/Public Domain; **212, 219b** Heritage Image Partnership Ltd /Alamy Stock Photo; **214t, 220** Science History Images/Alamy Stock Photo; **214c** "How Marcus Whitman Saved Oregon scan p. 301"/Peteforsyth/Wikimedia Commons /Public Domain; **214b** MPI /Stringer/Archive Photos via Getty Images; **215** Leonid Andronov/Shutterstock.com; **216** © David H Wright. All rights reserved 2023/Bridgeman Images; **216-217bg** Butler Institute of American Art, Youngstown, OH, USA © Butler Institute of American Art /Gift of Joseph G. Butler III 1946 /Bridgeman Images; **218** Superstock/3LH -Fine Art

**Chapter 9**

**222, 234i, 244** Bettmann/Contributor /Bettmann via Getty Images; **223, 224, 224bg, 230, 232, 234t, 237i 237b, 240t, 240b, 249** North Wind Picture Archives /Alamy Stock Photo; **225** Library of Congress/LC-DIG-ppmsca-33122; **227t, 227c, 229, 230i** Granger, NYC; **227b** "Scourged back by McPherson & Oliver, 1863, retouched"/Mathew Benjamin Brady /Wikimedia Commons/Public Domain; **228** "Harriet Tubman c1868-69 (cropped)" /Benjamin F. Powelson/Wikimedia Commons/Public Domain; **231** "Free Soil Songs for the People" (1848), For Sale by Bela March/Public Domain; **234b** From The New York Public Library; **236t** Gift of Mrs. Constance Wharton Smith/RISD Museum; **236b** Everett Collection Inc /Alamy Stock Photo; **237t** MPI/Stringer /Archive Photos via Getty Images; **238t, 239t** National Portrait Gallery, Smithsonian Institution; **238c** "Oil on Canvas Portrait of Dred Scott (cropped)"/Missouri History Museum/Wikimedia Commons /Public Domain; **238b** Everett Collection /Shutterstock.com; **239b** Pictures Now /Alamy Stock Photo; **241** "The Last Moments of John Brown" by Thomas Hovenden/Wikimedia Commons /Public Domain; **243** The Color Archives /Alamy Stock Photo

**Chapter 10**

**250, 259b, 264** © Don Troiani. All Rights Reserved 2024/Bridgeman Images; **251, 252** (Textile Icon) Pavel K/Shutterstock.com; **251, 252** (Factory Icon) Cosmic_Design /Shutterstock.com; **252** (Warship) Battleship by Yair Cohen from Noun Project (CC By 3.0); **253t** Library Company of Philadelphia; **253c, 273t, 275, 277t** Granger, NYC; **253b** Library of Congress/LC-DIG-cwpb-04294;

Photo; **361** "US-\$1-LT-1862-Fr-16c" /National Numismatic Collection, National Museum of American History/Wikimedia Commons/CC-By SA 4.0; **362t** m.czosnek /iStock/Getty Images Plus via Getty Images; **362b** National Portrait Gallery, Smithsonian Institution; gift of Miss Marieli Benziger; **363t** Library of Congress/LC-DIG -bellcm-02244; **363bl, 367, 377t** Granger, NYC; **363br** RGB Ventures/SuperStock /Alamy Stock Photo; **365** Artepics/Alamy Stock Photo; **369t** Alpha Historica/Alamy Stock Photo; **369b** Aleditorial/Alamy Stock Photo; **370** Pictures from History /Bridgeman Images; **371t** Hulton Deutsch /Contributor/Corbis Historical via Getty Images; **371b** Library of Congress/LC-DIG -ppmsca-27675; **371b** Library of Congress /LC-DIG-ppmsca-27675; **372** Everett Collection/Shutterstock.com; **373, 385** Everett Collection Historical/Alamy Stock Photo; **374** "The Rough Riders" by Mort Kunstler/Wikimedia Commons/Public Domain; **375** Library of Congress/LC-DIG -ppmsca-25453; **377b** Library of Congress; **378** Solarisys/Shutterstock.com; **379** Library of Congress/LC-DIG-ds-05213; **380** Album /Alamy Stock Photo; **381l** © Look and Learn/Bridgeman Images; **381r** George Rinhart/Contributor/Corbis Historical via Getty Images; **382** Archive Farms Inc /Alamy Stock Photo

### Chapter 15

**386** Universal Art Archive/Alamy Stock Photo; **387r** INTERFOTO/Alamy Stock Photo; **387l** Heritage Image Partnership Ltd /Alamy Stock Photo; **387c** Retro AdArchives/Alamy Stock Photo; **388t, 395, 407** Bettmann/Contributor/Bettmann via Getty Images; **388b** Library of Congress/LC -DIG-ppprs-00626; **389t** Shawshots/Alamy Stock Photo; **389b** Everett Collection /Shutterstock.com; **390** JHU Sheridan Libraries/Gado/Contributor/Archive Photos via Getty Images; **391i** Library of Congress/LC-DIG-hec-16114; **391, 411t** Library of Congress/LC-DIG-ds-03647; **392** BE040876/Tullio Saba/flickr/Public Domain; **394t** National Portrait Gallery, Smithsonian Institution; **394b** agefotostock /Alamy Stock Photo; **396t** Library of Congress/Contributor/Corbis Historical via Getty Images; **396b** Alpha Historica /Alamy Stock Photo; **397** Billy Sunday by George Bellows/Boston Public Library /Public Domain; **399** "Political cartoon about Oregon direct democracy, 1912" /Peteforsyth/Wikimedia Commons/Public Domain; **400t** Science History Images /Alamy Stock Photo; **400b, 403** George Rinhart/Contributor/Corbis Historical via Getty Images; **401t** American Stock Archive/Archive Photos via Getty Images; **401b, 411b** Niday Picture Library/Alamy Stock Photo; **404t, 412** Library of Congress, LC-USZ62-55730; **404b** Historical /Contributor/Corbis Historical via Getty

Images; **405t** North Wind Picture Archives /Alamy Stock Photo; **405b** Brinley Clark /EyeEm via Getty Images; **406** Bill Waterson/Alamy Stock Photo; **408** Library of Congress/LC-DIG-hec-16841; **413** Chicago History Museum/Contributor /Archive Photos via Getty Images

### Chapter 16

**414** Private Collection/Peter Newark Military Pictures/Bridgeman Images; **415t** military tank by Marco Livolsi from Noun Project (CC BY 3.0); **415b** Globe by hans draiman from Noun Project (CC BY 3.0); **416t, 421t, 435** Bettmann/Contributor /Bettmann via Getty Images; **416i, 434i** Library of Congress; **416b** Library of Congress, LC-USZC4-13223; **417** Everett Collection/Shutterstock.com; **418t, 437t** Mirrorpix/Alamy Stock Photo; **418c** "Tanks passing dead Germans"/National Library of Scotland/Flickr/Public Domain; **418b** Library of Congress/ggbain 17781; **419t** Sabena Jane Blackbird/Alamy Stock Photo; **419b** Marc Tielemans/Alamy Stock Photo; **420** Granger, NYC; **421b** Library of Congress/ggbain 09255; **422, 437b** Hi-Story/Alamy Stock Photo; **423** "19150508 Lusitania Sunk By a Submarine - The New York Times"/RCraig09/ Wikimedia Commons/Public Domain; **424** Heritage Images/Contributor/Hulton Archive via Getty Images; **425** National Archives and Records Administration; **427l, 438t** Library of Congress/LC-USZC4-8890; **427r** Science History Images/Alamy Stock Photo; **428t** Universal History Archive /Contributor/Universal Images Group via Getty Images; **428b** swim ink 2 llc /Contributor/Corbis Historical via Getty Images; **429t** https://amcmuseum.org /collections/u-s-government-thrift-card /Air Mobility Command Museum; **429b** Historical Images Archive/Alamy Stock Photo; **430, 434, 438b** National Archives; **431t** Hulton Archive/Stringer/Hulton Archive viaGetty Images; **431c** National Archives (26431282); **431b** neftali /Shutterstock.com; **432t** PjrStudio/Alamy Stock Photo; **432b** Chronicle/Alamy Stock Photo; **433t** "Parisians Greet Wilson" /Woodrow Wilson Presidential Library Archives/Wikimedia Commons/Public Domain; **433b** Library of Congress, LC -DIG-ggbain-29038; **436** Stock Montage /Contributor/Archive Photos via Getty Images

### Chapter 17

**440** INTERFOTO/Alamy Stock Photo; **441r, 461t** Photo Courtesy Orange County Archives; **441l** Library of Congress /LC-DIG-ppmsca-39797; **442** Historic Collection/Alamy Stock Photo; **444, 454t** New York Daily News Archive/Contributor /New York Daily News via Getty Images; **445t, 454b, 456t** Granger, NYC; **445b** Library of Congress; **446t** Ewing Galloway /Alamy Stock Photo; **446b** Glasshouse Images/Alamy Stock Photo; **446bg** Everett

Collection/Alamy Stock Photo; **447t** American Stock Archive/Contributor /Archive Photos via Getty; **447c** fstop123 /iStock/Getty Images Plus via Getty Images; **447b, 461b** Retro AdArchives/Alamy Stock Photo; **449t** StudioB/Alamy Stock Photo; **449b** "Au Revoir (1920) fashion illustration in high resolution" by George Barbier. /Rawpixel Ltd/Flickr/CC By-SA 2.0; **452, 462t** Photo Researchers/Alamy Stock Photo; **453t** From Original Negative/Alamy Stock Photo; **453c** Science History Images /Alamy Stock Photo; **453b** Pictorial Press Ltd/Alamy Stock Photo; **455, 460, 462b** Everett Collection/Shutterstock.com; **456i** ASSOCIATED PRESS; **456b** "UNIA parade in Harlem, 1920" by James Van Der Zee /Wikimedia Commons/Public Domain; **457** Used with the Permission of the Archives of the Montgomery Library at Westminster Theological Seminary, Philadelphia, PA; **458** Bettmann/Contributor/Bettmann via Getty Images; **459t** Library of Congress/LC -DIG-hec-18296; **459b** Library of Congress /LC-DIG-ggbain-07698

### Chapter 18

**464** Fotosearch/Stringer/Archive Photos via Getty Images; **465t** ClassicStock /Alamy Stock Photo; **465b, 472b** John Frost Newspapers/Alamy Stock Photo; **466** GL Archive/Alamy Stock Photo; **467** Transcendental Graphics/Contributor /Archive Photos via Getty Images; **468t** Everett Collection/Bridgeman Images; **468b, 485** Granger, NYC; **469t** PhotoQuest /Contributor/Archive Photos via Getty Images; **469b** National Archives (195532); **470t** Harold M. Lambert/Contributor /Archive Photos via Getty Images; **470b** Historic Collection/Alamy Stock Photo; **471t** HAGLEY MUSEUM AND ARCHIVE /Science Source; **471b** Division of Culture and the Arts, National Museum of American History, Smithsonian Institution; **472t** New York Daily News Archive /Contributor/New York Daily News via Getty Images; **473** Library of Congress /LC-DIG-hec-40747; **474** Ethan Miller /Staff/Getty Images News via Getty Images; **476, 483** Everett Collection/Shutterstock .com; **477** National Archives (6037487) National Archives (6037487); **478l** From Original Negative/Alamy Stock Photo; **478r** Chronicle/Alamy Stock Photo; **479t** MPI /Stringer/Archive Photos via Getty Images; **479b** Library of Congress/Contributor /Corbis Historical via Getty Images; **480t** Everett Collection Historical/Alamy Stock Photo; **480c** National Archives (293521); **480b** "Norris"/Tennessee Valley Authority/flickr/CC-By SA 2.0; **481** New York Times Co./Contributor/Archive Photos via Getty Images; **482t** Mega Pixel /Shutterstock.com; **482b, 484t** Bettmann /Contributor/Bettmann via Getty Images; **484b** Everett Collection Inc/Alamy Stock Photo;

486 World History Archive/Alamy Stock Photo

**Chapter 19**

490 MGPhoto76/Alamy Stock Photo; 491 Fox Photos/Stringer/Hulton Royals Collection via Getty Images; 492 World History Archive/Alamy Stock Photo; 493 GK History Images/Alamy Stock Photo; 494t, 495b ullstein bild Dtl./Contributor /ullstein bild via Getty Images; 494b, 496t Shawshots/Alamy Stock Photo; 495t Sueddeutsche Zeitung Photo/Alamy Stock Photo; 496b, 503 CBW/Alamy Stock Photo; 497 Vintage_Space/Alamy Stock Photo; 498t, 503bg, 513t, 515 Bettmann /Contributor/Bettmann via Getty Images; 498b The New York Historical Society /Contributor/Archive Photos via Getty Images; 500i Ryan Tishken/Shutterstock .com; 500 National Archives (295975); 501t "Blue Star in window June 2012" by Djembayz/Wikimedia Commons /CC-BY SA 3.0; 501bl Afro Newspaper /Gado/Contributor/Archive Photos via Getty Images; 501br National Archives; 502t PhotoQuest/Contributor/Archive Photos via Getty Images; 502c Provided by BAC software; 502b Library of Congress /LC-USF34-073636-D; 504, 511b Galerie Bilderwelt/Contributor/Hulton Archive via Getty Images; 505 National Archives (208-PU-138LL(3)); 506 National Archives (26-G-2343); 508 Tony Vaccaro /Contributor/Archive Photos via Getty Images; 509t Universal History Archive /Contributor/Universal Images Group via Getty Images; 509b New York Daily News Archive/Contributor/New York Daily News via Getty Images; 509i "Presidential Portrait of Harry Truman" by Greta Kempton/Wikimedia Commons /Public Domain; 510t Universal History Archive/UIG/Bridgeman Images; 510c Niday Picture Library/Alamy Stock Photo; 510b Stefano Zaccaria/Shutterstock.com; 511c D. Kucharski K. Kucharska /Shutterstock.com; 511t Tango Images /Alamy Stock Photo; 512 SuperStock/3LH -B&W; 513b U.S. Army Air Force/420418 -O-ZZ999-001; 514 "Battle of Midway, June 1942"/National Museum of the U.S. Navy /Wikimedia Commons/Public Domain; 516t © Look and Learn/Bridgeman Images; 516c "Iwo Jima Another Wave Moves In" /USMC Archives/Wikimedia Commons /CC-By SA 2.0; 516b Pictorial Press Ltd /Alamy Stock Photo; 517 SuperStock/4X5 Collection/Devaney Collection; 518 National Archives (23658002); 518i John Frost Newspapers/Alamy Stock Photo

**Chapter 20**

522, 523, 525b, 527, 539b, 547 Bettmann /Contributor/Bettmann via Getty Images; 524 Glowimages/Glowimages via Getty Images; 525t National Archives; 526t, 545t American Photo Archive/Alamy Stock Photo; 526b, 537l Everett Collection

Historical/Alamy Stock Photo; 528 Historical/Contributor/Corbis Historical via Getty Images; 529 Popperfoto/Contributor /Popperfoto via Getty Images; 531, 545b Album/Alamy Stock Photo; 531bg Tony Vaccaro/Contributor/Archive Photos via Getty Images; 533 Jack Wilkes/The LIFE Picture Collection/Shutterstock.com; 534 U.S. Army/Handout/Archive Photos via Getty Images; 535t National Archives (306 -PS-51(6988)); 535b undefined undefined /iStock Editorial/Getty Images Plus via Getty Images; 536 "Chosin" by Corporal Peter McDonald, USMC/Wikimedia Commons/Public Domain; 537c Retro AdArchives/Alamy Stock Photo; 537r Silberkorn/iStock/Getty Images Plus via Getty Images; 538, 546 ClassicStock/Alamy Stock Photo; 539t Archive PL/Alamy Stock Photo; 540t j r Eyerman/The LIFE Picture Collection/Shutterstock.com; 540b BJU Photo Services; 541l Everett Collection Inc/Alamy Stock Photo; 541r New York Daily News Archive/Contributor/New York Daily News via Getty Images; 542t, 544 ASSOCIATED PRESS; 542b George Marks/Retrofile RF via Getty Images; 543t Underwood Archives, Inc/Alamy Stock Photo; 543b INTERFOTO/Alamy Stock Photo

**Chapter 21**

548 Wally McNamee/Contributor/Corbis Historical via Getty Images; 549t, 550, 552t, 554t, 557, 563, 567, 571t Bettmann /Contributor/Bettmann via Getty Images; 549b ASSOCIATED PRESS; 551t Paul Conklin/Contributor/Archive Photos via Getty Images; 551c New York Times Co. /Contributor/Archive Photos via Getty Images; 551b Photo 12/Alamy Stock Photo; 552c Pictorial Press Ltd/Alamy Stock Photo; 552b Ron Case/Stringer/Hulton Archive via Getty Images; 553 Hal Beral /Corbis via Getty Images; 554bl Shawshots /Alamy Stock Photo; 554br National Archives (194235); 555 United States Mint; 556t, 571b Historical/Contributor/Corbis Historical via Getty Images; 556b Internet Archive; 558–559 (stripes art reference) sensationaldesign/iStock/Getty Images Plus via Getty Images; 558–559 (stars art reference) Grace_Elaine/Shutterstock .com; 559 (swirls art reference) creamfeeder foundation/Shutterstock.om; 560, 565b CPA Media Pte Ltd/Alamy Stock Photo; 561 "Boeing B-52 dropping bombs"/U.S. Air Force/Wikimedia Commons/Public Domain; 562 Sovfoto/Contributor /Universal Images Group via Getty Images; 564 tim page/Contributor/Corbis Historical via Getty Images; 565t Wally McNamee /Contributor/Corbis Premium Historical via Getty Images; 566bg William L. Rukeyser /Contributor/Hulton Archive via Getty Images; 566 Barbara Alper/Contributor /Archive Photos via Getty Images; 568 Hudson Library & Historical Society; 569t

Howard Ruffner/Contributor/Archive Photos via Getty Images; 569c David Hume Kennerly/Contributor/Hulton Archive via Getty Images; 569b Terry Fincher /Stringer/Hulton Archive via Getty Images

**Chapter 22**

574 Everett Collection Inc/Alamy Stock Photo; 575 National Archives (111-SC -174129); 576, 577, 577bg, 579, 585, 586, 590, 592bg Bettmann/Contributor /Bettmann via Getty Images; 578t Carl Iwasaki/Contributor/The Chronical Collection via Getty Images; 578b, 594 Everett Collection Historical/Alamy Stock Photo; 579i Underwood Archives /Contributor/Archive Photos via Getty Images; 580 Dozier Mobley/Contributor /Hulton Archive via Getty Images; 581 Don Cravens/Contributor/The Chronical Collection via Getty Images; 583t, 583b, 584t, 587r ASSOCIATED PRESS; 584b Granger, NYC; 587l Archive Photos /Stringer/Archive Photos via Getty Images; 588t Hulton Archive/Staff/Hulton Archive via Getty Images; 588b Hulton Deutsch /Contributor/Corbis Premium Historical via Getty Images; 589 LBJ Library photo by Cecil Stoughton; 591t Glasshouse Images /Alamy Stock Photo; 591b SuperStock /Everett Collection; 592 Keystone Press /Alamy Stock Photo; 593 Retro AdArchives /Alamy Stock Photo; 595 CSU Archives /Everett Collection/Bridgeman Images; 596 "Black Panther demonstration"/CIR Online/Wikimedia Commons/CC-By 2.0; 599 Kenneth Guthrie/Contributor/Archive Photos via Getty Images

**Chapter 23**

600, 605r, 607, 620 Bettmann/Contributor /Bettmann via Getty Images; 601t Pictorial Press Ltd/Alamy Stock Photo; 601b Xinhua News Agency/Contributor/Xinhua News Agency via Getty Images; 602t World History Archive/Alamy Stock Photo; 602c Wally McNamee/Contributor/Corbis Historical via Getty Images; 602b Stan Meagher/Stringer/Hulton Archive via Getty Images; 603 Alexander Hafemann /Photodisc via Getty Images; 603bg ClassicStock/Alamy Stock Photo; 604 "2013 Watergate complex 02" by Farragutful /Wikimedia Commons/CC-By SA 3.0 Unported; 605l The Senate Historical Office; 606 PhotoQuest/Contributor /Archive Photos via Getty Images; 608 dpa picture alliance/Alamy Stock Photo; 608bg Bill Pierce/The LIFE Picture Collection /Shutterstock.com; 609 "A button from the 'Whip Inflation Now' initiative of the 1970's"/Gerald Ford Presidential Museum /Wikimedia Commons/Public Domain; 610t, 615b ZUMA Press, Inc./Alamy Stock Photo; 610b, 616t, 616b, 621r ASSOCIATED PRESS; 611 Ron Galella /Contributor/Ron Galella Collection via Getty Images; 611bg David Fenton /Contributor/Archive Photos via Getty Images; 613 Grant Heilman Photography